# COMPUTER GRAPHICS

Volume 25 • Number 4 • July 1991
A publication of ACM SIGGRAPH
Production Editor Richard J. Beach

SIGGRAPH '91 Conference Proceedings
28 July – 2 August 1991, Las Vegas, Nevada
Papers Chair Thomas W. Sederberg

Sponsored by the Association for Computing Machinery's
Special Interest Group on Computer Graphics

The Association for Computing
Machinery, Inc.
11 West 42nd Street
New York, NY 10036



Sample Citation Information:
...Proceedings of SIGGRAPH '91 (Las Vegas, Nevada, July 28-August 2, 1991). In *Computer Graphics*, *25*, 4 (July 1991) ACM SIGGRAPH, New York, 1991, pp. xx-yy.

## ORDERING INFORMATION

**Orders from nonmembers of ACM placed within the United States should be directed to:**

Addison-Wesley Publishing
Company
Order Department
Jacob way
Reading, MA 01867
Tel: 1-800-447-2226

Addison-Wesley will pay postage and handling on orders accompanied by check. Credit card orders may be placed by mail or by calling the Addison-Wesley Order Department at the number above. Follow-up inquiries should be directed to the Customer Service Department at the same number. Please include the Addison-Wesley ISBN number with your order: A-W ISBN 0 201-56291-X

**Orders from nonmembers of ACM placed from outside the United States should be addressed as noted below.**

**Latin America and Asia:**
Addison-Wesley Publishing Company Inc.
Reading, MA 01867, USA
Tel: 617-944-3700;
Cable: ADIWES READING;
Telex: 94-9416

**Canada:** Addison-Wesley Publishing (Canada) Ltd.
36 Prince Andrew Place
Don Mills, Ontario M3C2T8
Canada
Tel: 416-447-5101

**Australia and New Zealand:**
Addison-Wesley Publishing
Company
6 Byfield Street
North Ryde, N.S.W. 2113
Australia
Tel: 888-2733;
Cable: ADIWES SYDNEY;
Telex: AA71919

**United Kingdom, Republic of Ireland, Africa (excluding North Africa) and South Africa:**
Addison-Wesley Publishers Ltd.
Finchampstead Road
Workingham
Berkshire RG11 2NZ, England
Cable: ADIWES Workingham;
Telex: 846136

**Continental Europe, the Near East, Middle East, and North Africa:**
Addison-Wesley Publishing
Company
De Lairesstraat, 90
1071 P J Amsterdam
The Netherlands
Tel: 020 76 40-44
Cable: ADIWES AMSTERDAM
Telex: 844-14046

**Orders from ACM Members:**

A limited number of copies are available at the ACM member discount. Send order with payment to:

ACM Order Department
P.O. Box 64145
Baltimore, MD 21264

ACM will pay postage and handling on orders accompanied by check. Credit card orders only:
1-800-342-6626

Customer service, or credit card orders from Alaska, Maryland, and outside the United States:
301-528-4261

Credit card orders may also be placed by mail.

**Please include your ACM member number and the ACM Order number with your order.**

ACM Order Number: 428911
ACM ISBN: 0-89791-436-8
ISSN: 0097-8930

# Contents

## Technical Program, Thursday, 1 August 1991

## Technical Program, Friday, 2 August 1991

## Panel Sessions, Wednesday, 31 July 1991



## Panel Sessions, Thursday, 1 August 1991

## Panel Sessions, Friday, 2 August, 1991

# Preface

The 40 papers in these proceedings were selected from 207 submissions, representing 15 nations on five continents. Based on a conservative estimate that a typical SIGGRAPH submission involves six man months of work, these 207 submissions document at least one man century of creative effort, resulting in another SIGGRAPH proceedings of exceptionally high quality.

On January 9, 1991, the date that our local Federal Express delivery man set a personal volume record as the final 140 paper submissions arrived, Hank Christiansen, Elaine Cohen, Rich Riesenfeld, Dan Olsen, and myself met to distribute the papers to senior reviewers. During the subsequent six weeks, each paper would be read by at least two senior reviewers and by at least three additional reviewers. Most reviews were written with impressive care. In some cases the review was longer than the paper itself! This review process easily consumed three man years of volunteer effort.

On March 8 and 9, the papers selection meeting was held in Salt Lake City. These meetings are always stimulating experiences, characterized by vigorous discussion and a general spirit of goodwill. This year's committee was drawn from five nations — the United States, Canada, Japan, France, and Germany — and an even richer breadth of professional backgrounds. While the unpleasant task of rejecting a majority of submissions is inherent in the assignment, I am confident that the committee performed as fairly as is humanly possible.

We were pleased to receive, for the first time, two submissions from the Soviet Union. We look forward to increased SIGGRAPH involvement from Eastern Europe.

I express thanks to the committee members, who served at considerable personal sacrifice and with impressive collective wisdom. Thanks also to the 307 reviewers, whose willingness and even eagerness to help provide an ideal of professional citizenship.

Special thanks is due to Bruce Brereton, of Word Perfect Corporation, who served as my executive assistant. He is a genius at organizing data, and he energetically applied his talents to shaping thousands of data values into comprehensible form. We thank Evans & Sutherland for hosting our Friday paper selection meeting. Mike Bailey and Carol Byram, SIGGRAPH '91 co-chairs, deserve thanks for their unwavering support.

This is the final SIGGRAPH proceedings that will benefit from Rick Beach's skill as Editor-in-Chief, and I thank him for the hundreds of hours he has worked behind the scenes on this and four previous proceedings.

Thomas W. Sederberg
*SIGGRAPH '91 Technical Program Chair*

SIGGRAPH·91

Over 45 Sensational Curiosities Inside!!

The Veritable Culmination of All Automata!

The Supreme Limit of Sensational Novelty!

# The Greatest Show on Earth!

# Conference Committee

## CONFERENCE CO-CHAIRS

Michael Bailey
(San Diego Supercomputer Center)
Carol Byram
(Sony Computer Peripheral Products Company)

## CONFERENCE COMMITTEE CHAIRS

Molly Morgan-Kuhns, Conference Coordinator
Thomas W. Sederberg, *Papers*
(Brigham Young University)
Robert L. Judd, *Panels*
(Los Alamos National Laboratory)
Rich Ehlers, *Courses*
(Evans and Sutherland)
Sally Rosenthal, *Electronic Theatre*
(Digital Equipment Corporation)
Isaac Victor Kerlow, *Art and Design Show*
(Pratt Institute)
Norm Abelson, *Exhibits*
Steve Cunningham, *Educators' Program*
(California State University Stanislaus)
Garry Beirne, *Hypermedia*
(Alias Research Inc.)
Richard M. Mueller, *International Liaison*
(Dynamic Graphics, Inc.)
B.J. Anderson, *Local Arrangements*
(The Anderson Report)
Bob Pearson, *Marketing*
(Sun Microsystems, Inc.)
Mark Resch, *Materials*
(Computer Curriculum Corporation)
Richard J. Beach, *Proceedings Editor*
(Xerox PARC)
Larry Lytle, *Public Relations*
(Netwise, Inc.)
Jeff Yates, *Registration*
(Wavefront Technologies)
Eric Bosch, *Slide Sets*
(McMaster University)
Dave Nadeau, *Speaker Materials*
(San Diego Supercomputer Center)
John E. French, Jr., *Special Interest Groups*
(GeoQuest Systems, Inc.)
Vicki Putz, *Student Volunteer Program*
(Vicki Putz Design)
Brian Herzog, *Treasurer*
(Sun Microsystems, Inc.)
Steve E. Tice, *Virtual Reality*
(SimGraphics Engineering Corporation)
Ed Brabant, *Workshops*
(Megatek Corporation)
Smith, Bucklin & Associates, Inc., *Accounting*
Audio Visual Headquarters Corporation, *Audio Visual Support*
Smith, Bucklin & Associates, *Conference Management*
Robert T. Kenworthy, Inc., *Exhibition Management*
Quorum Incorporated, *Graphic Design*
Carlson Travel Network, *International Travel Agency*
Smith, Bucklin & Associates, Inc., *Public Relations*
Andrews-Bartlett Exposition Services, *Service Contractor*
ATI Travel Management, Inc., *Travel Agency*
Lois A. Blankstein, *ACM SIGGRAPH Program Director*
(Association for Computing Machinery)
Andrew C. Goodrich, *Vice Chair for Conference Planning*
(RasterOps)

## CONFERENCE PLANNING COMMITTEE

Andrew C. Goodrich (RasterOps)
Michael Bailey (San Diego Supercomputer Center)
Maxine Brown (University of Illinois at Chicago)
Carol Byram (Sony Computer Peripheral Products Company)
Branko J. Gerovac (Digital Equipment Corporation/MIT Media Lab)
Christopher F. Herot (Lotus Development Corporation)
Robert L. Judd (Los Alamos National Laboratory)
Mark Resch (Computer Curriculum Corporation)
Jacqueline M. Wollner (Convex Computer Corporation)

## PAPERS COMMITTEE

Thomas W. Sederberg, chair (Brigham Young University)
Alan H. Barr (California Institute of Technology)
Richard J. Beach (Xerox PARC)
Loren Carpenter (Pixar)
Edwin E. Catmull (Pixar)
Hank Christiansen (Brigham Young University)
Elaine Cohen (University of Utah)
Robert L. Cook (Light Source Computer Images, Inc.)
John C. Dill (Simon Fraser University)
Henry Fuchs (University of North Carolina at Chapel Hill)
Michel Gangnet (Digital Equipment Corporation)
Andrew S. Glassner (Xerox PARC)
Donald P. Greenberg (Cornell University)
Leo Guibas (Massachusetts Institute of Technology)
Pat Hanrahan (Princeton University)
Jeffrey Lane (Digital Equipment Corporation)
Eihachiro Nakamae (Hiroshima University)
Gregory M. Nielson (Arizona State University)
Dan Olsen (Brigham Young University)
Jim Rhyne (IBM Corporation)
Alyn Rockwood (Arizona State University)
Robert Sproull (Sun Microsystems, Inc.)
Wolfgang Strasser (University of Tübingen)
Turner Whitted (Numerical Design, Ltd.)
Jane Wilhelms (University of California at Santa Cruz)
Andrew Witkin (Carnegie Mellon University)

## PANELS COMMITTEE

Robert L. Judd, chair (Los Alamos National Laboratory)
Bruce Eric Brown (Oracle Corporation)
Chuck Hansen (Los Alamos National Laboratory)
Alyce Kaprow (The New Studio)
Mike Keeler (Kubota Pacific Computer, Inc.)
Bruce H. McCormick (The Texas A&M University System)
Peter Pathe (Stonehand, Inc.)
Dick Phillips (Los Alamos National Laboratory)
Vibeke Sorensen (California Institute of the Arts)

## COURSES COMMITTEE

Rich Ehlers, chair (Evans and Sutherland)
Mark Henderson (Arizona State University)

Mark Lee (Amoco Production Company)
Alan Norton (IBM T.J. Watson Research Center)
Nan Schaller (Rochester Institute of Technology)
Dino Schweitzer (U.S. Air Force Academy)
Deborah Sokolove (George Mason University)

## ART AND DESIGN SHOW COMMITTEE

Isaac Victor Kerlow, chair (Pratt Institute)

## FINE ARTS JURY

Timothy Binkley (The School of Visual Arts)
Eleanor Flomenhaft (Fine Arts Museum of Long Island)
Cynthia Goodman (Art Critic and Curator)
Judson Rosebush (Rosebush Visions Co.)

## DESIGN JURY

Kent Hunter (Frankfurt Gips Balkind)
David Peters (212 Associates)
Wendy Richmond (WGBH Design Lab)
Donald Rorke (The Knoll Group)

## EDUCATOR'S PROGRAM COMMITTEE

Steve Cunningham, chair (California State University Stanislaus)
Judith R. Brown (The University of Iowa)
Barbara Mones-Hattal (George Mason University)
Gregory M. Nielson (Arizona State University)
Ken O'Connell (University of Oregon)
Robert S. Wolff (Apple Computer, Inc.)

## ELECTRONIC THEATRE COMMITTEE

Sally Rosenthal, chair (Digital Equipment Corporation)
Loren Carpenter (Pixar)
Huguette Chesnais (Studio Base 2)
Johnie Hugh Horn (Big Research)
Ian McDowall (Fake Space Labs)
Timothy L. Parker (Interstitial Media Design)
Lucy Petrovich (Savannah School of Art and Design)
Kathy Tanaka (Independent)

## ELECTRONIC THEATRE JURY

Susan Amkraut (Stichting Computeranimate)
Loren Carpenter (Pixar)
Karl Sims (Thinking Machines)

## HYPERMEDIA JURY

Garry Beirne, chair (Alias Research Inc.)
Richard J. Beach (Xerox PARC)
Cathleen Britt (Xerox Corporation)
Bill Buxton (Xerox PARC/University of Toronto)
Hugh Dubberly (Apple Computer, Inc.)
Enrique Godreau III (Xerox PARC)

## SLIDE SETS JURY

Eric Bosch, chair (McMaster University)
Joe Cychosz (Purdue CADLAB University)
Rich Ehlers (Evans and Sutherland)
Robert L. Judd (Los Alamos National Laboratory)
Alan Paeth (Neural Ware, Inc.)
Thomas W. Sederberg (Brigham Young University)

## VIRTUAL REALITY JURY

Steve E. Tice, chair (SimGraphics Engineering Corporation)
Steven D. Arnold (LucasArts Entertainment Company)
William Bricken (University of Washington)
Peter Broadwell (Silicon Graphics Computer Systems)
Thomas A. Furness III (University of Washington)
Christopher T. Gentile (Abrams/Gentile Entertainment, Inc.)
Myron Krueger (Artificial Reality Corporation)
Brenda Laurel (Telepresence Research)
Michael Zyda (Naval Postgraduate School)

## WORKSHOPS COMMITTEE

Ed Brabant, chair (Megatek Corporation)
Mark Green (University of Alberta)
Holliday Horton (San Diego Supercomputer Center)
Mike Keeler (Kubota Pacific Computer, Inc.)
Rob Pike (AT&T Bell Laboratories)
Roger Spreen (Apple Computer, Inc.)

## TECHNICAL PROGRAM REVIEWERS

Debra Adams
John Airey
Kurt Akeley
John Amanatides
James Arvo
Larry Aupperle
Norman Badler
Chanderjit Bajaj
Michael Banks
David Baraff
Phil Barry
Brian A. Barsky
Daniel R. Baum
John Beatty
Walter Bender
Steve Benton
R. Daniel Bergeron
Larry Bergman
Clifford Beshers
Dharmajyoti Bhaumik
Eric Bier
John Bird
Gary Bishop
Teresa Bleser
James Blinn
Jules Bloomenthal
David Boal
Wolfgang Boehm
Christian Bouville
Eric Brisson
Wim Bronsvoort
Fred Brooks
Russ Brown
Armin Bruderlin
Beat Bruderlin
Thomas Calvert
Stu Card
Rikk Carey
Ken Carson
Rosemary Chang
Sheye-Ling Chang
Michael Chen
Norman Chin
Jin Chou
Richard Chuang
Danny Cohen
Michael F. Cohen
Sabine Coquillart
William Cowan
Roger Crawfis
Frank Crow
Roger Dannenberg
Tony DeRose
Jamal Deen
Michael Deering
Hubert Delany
Mark Dippe
David Dobkin
Bob Drebin
Tom Duff
Gershon Elber
Wu En-Hua
Bianca Falcidiono
Eliot Feibush
Steve Feiner
Mike Findler
Scott Fisher
Jim Flowers
James Foley
Tom Foley
A. Robin Forrest
David Forsey
Alain Fournier
Richard Franke
W.R. Franklin
Akira Fujimoto
Don Fussell
Steve Gabriel
Andre Gagalowicz
S. Kicha Ganapathy
Geoffrey Gardener
Severin Gaudet
John Gerth
Nader Gharachorloo
Djamchid Ghazanfarpour
Ron Goldman
Jeff Goldsmith
Howard Good
Henri Gouraud
Eric Grant
Mark Green
Ned Greene
R.L. Grimsdale
Georges Grinstein
John Gross
Eric Grosse
Satish Gupta
Paul Haeberli
Hans Hagen
Tom Hahn
Eric Haines
Roy Hall
Bernd Hamann
Diane Hanasford
Andreas Hartwia
Paul Heckbert
Jim Helman
John Hershberger
John Hobby
Larry Hodges
Eric Hoffert
Karl Heinz Hohne
Christoph Hornung
Scott Hudson
Peter Hughes
John Hughes
Erik Jansen
Tom Jensen
Robert B. Jerard
Devendra Kalra
James T. Kajiya
Kazufumi Kaneda
Michael Karasick
Peter Karow
Michael Kass
Arie Kaufman
Tim Kay
Gershom Kedem
Dave Kirk
R. Victor Klassen
Hyeongseol Ko
Doris Kochanek
Peter Kochevar
Craig Kolb
Larry Koved
Wolfgang Krueger
David Kurlander
David Lane

## TECHNICAL PROGRAM REVIEWERS (Continued)

Jaron Lanier
Michael Laszlo
Jim Lawson
Bruce Leak
Mark Leather
Mark Lee
Marc Levoy
John Lewis
Bruce J. Lindbloom
Andy Lippman
James S. Lipscomb
Bill Lorensen
Bruce Lucas
Dean Lucas
Tom Lyche
Jock Mackinlay
Nadia Magnenat-Thalmann
Abraham Mammen
Nelson Max
Mike McKenna
Victor Milenkovic
Gavin Miller
Yael Milo
Margaret Minsky
Don P. Mitchell
Joseph Mitchell
Steve Molnar
Chuck Mosher
Ken Musgrave
Mike Muss
Bruce Naylor
Greg Nelson
Robin A. Nichol
Basil Nicholas
Tomoyuki Nishita
Kevin Novins
Masataka Ohta
Karsten Optiz
Eben Ostby
Alex Pang
Michael Van De Panne
Randy Pausch
Darwyn Peachey
Alex Pentland
Ken Perlin
Jorg Peters
Chip Peterson
Cary Phillips
Flip Phillips
Richard L. Phillips
Les Piegl
Rob Pike
Steve Pitschke
Jon Pittman
Stephen M. Pizer
Wendy Plesniak
Daniel Pletinckx
Alex Pontland
Frits Post
Pierre Poulin
Dave Poulsen
Hartmut Prautzsch
Thierry Pudet
Claude Puech
Lyle Ramshaw
Ari Rappoport
Laurie Reuter
Craig Reynolds
Richard Riesenfeld
Jean-Jacques Risler
George Robertson
Phil Robertson
Warren Robinett
Dave Rogers
Jon Rokne
Jaroslaw Rossaignac
Larry Rosenblum
Holly E. Rushmeier
Bob Sabiston
David Salesin
Hanan Samet
Rick Sayre
Francis Schmitt
Kurt Schmucker
Bengt-Olaf Schneider
Peter Schroeder
Hans-Peter Seidel
Carlo Sequin
Chris Shaw
Mikio Shinya
Peter Shirley
Ken Shoemake
John Sibert
H.B. Siegel
Francois Sillion
Karl Sims
Philip Skolmoski
Alvy Ray Smith
John Snyder
Susan Spach
Dave Springer
John Stasko
Jorge Stolfi
Maureen Stone
Galyn Susman
Ivan E. Sutherland
Richard Szeliski
Brice Tebbs
Demetri Terzopoulos
Spencer Thomas
Godfriend Toussaint
Lloyd Treinish
Alan Tuchman
Martin Tuori
Greg Turk
Ken Turkowski
Craig Upson
Sam Uselton
George Vanacek
Mark VandeWettering
Felipe Vera
Richard Verburg
Anne Verroust
Don Vickers
Keith Voegele
John Wallace
Brian Wandell
Greg Ward
Gary Watkins
Steve Watson
Marcelli Wein
Richard Weinberg
Jeff Weinstein
Kevin Weiler
Chris Welman
Neil Weste
Lee Westover
Robert Wilhelmson
Lance Williams
Peter Williams
P.J. Willis
James Winget
Andrew Woo
Robert J. Woodham
Charles D. Woodward
William V. Wright
En-Hua Wu
Chris Van Wyk
Brian Wyvill
Brad Vander Zanden
David Zeltzer
Jianmin Zhao

## PROFESSIONAL SUPPORT

**ACM SIGGRAPH '91 Conference Coordinator**
Molly Morgan Kuhns

**ACM SIGGRAPH Senior Program Director**
Lois Blankstein
Donna Rosenberg, *ACM SIGGRAPH Coordinator*

**Administrative Assistants**
Bruce Breveton, *Papers*
Betty Guillen, *Panels*
Deedre Miller, *Courses*
Carolyn Cahill, *Art and Design Show*
Robin J. Hathaway, *Electronic Theatre*
Timothy L. Parker, *Electronic Theatre*
Mary Anne Loftus, *Hypermedia*
M.L. Gillies, *Virtual Reality*
Jan Chesshir, *Workshops*

**Audio/Visual Management**
*Audio Visual Headquarters Corporation*
Jim Bartolomucci
Rich Farnham
Doug Hunt

**Conference Accounting**
*Smith, Bucklin and Associates, Inc.*
Ruth Kerns
Shelley Johnson

**Conference Management**
*Smith, Bucklin and Associates, Inc.*
Jackie Groszek
Paul Jay
Peggy Rohs
Deidre Ross
Anne Lueck
Cynthia Stark

**Conference Travel Agency**
*Association Travel Management*
Laurie Shapiro

**Decorator/Drayage**
*Andrews-Bartlett and Associations, Inc.*
Bob Borsz
Betty Fuller
Ken Gallagher
Tom Gilmore
John Loveless
John Patronski

**Exhibition Management**
*Robert T. Kenworthy, Inc.*
Mary Christiana
Hank Cronan
Barbara Voss

**Graphic Design**
*Quorum, Inc.*
Doug Hesseltine
Tom Rieke

**International Travel Agency**
*Carlson Travel Network*
John George
Betsy Woodwyk

**Public Relations**
*Smith, Bucklin and Associates, Inc.*
Karen Baldwin
Leona Caffey
Sheila Hoffmeyer
Kathleen Nilles
Julie Ostrow

# Exhibitors

Abekas
ACM SIGGRAPH
Academic Press
Acrobat Graphics Systems
Addison-Wesley Publishing Company
Advanced Imaging Magazine
Advanced Micro Devices, Inc.
Advanced Technology Center
AGE
Alacron Inc.
Alias Research Inc.
Alias Research, Style Division
Alliant Computer Systems Corporation
American Institute of Physics
American Power Conversion
Ampex Corporation
Analog Devices, Inc.
Analogic Corporation, Computer Design & Applications Division
Androx Corporation
Apple Computer, Inc.
Asaca/Shibasoku Corporation of America
Association for Computing Machinery
AT&T Graphics Software Labs
ATI Technologies
Autodesk, Inc.
AXA Corporation
Aztek
BARCO, Inc.
Bit 3 Computer
Brooktree Corporation
CADalyst Magazine
Cahners Publishing Company
Canon U.S.A., Inc.
CELCO
Chase Technologies
C. Iteh Technology
Commodore Business Machines, Inc.
Computer Graphics World
Convex Computer Corporation
Covid, Inc.
CTX International, Inc.
Cyberware Laboratory
Cymbolic Sciences
Dassault Electronique
Diaquest, Inc.
Digital Arts
Digital Equipment Corporation
Digital F/X
Digital Micronics
Digital Review
Dimension Technologies, Inc.
Du Pont Imaging Systems
DYNAIR Electronics, Inc.
Dynamic Graphics, Inc.
Dynaware USA, Inc.
Eastman Kodak Company
ETAK
Eurographics
Evans and Sutherland
Everex Systems
Evolution Computing
Extron Electronics
F and S, Inc.
Folsom Research, Inc.
Fraunhofer Computer Graphics
Fresh Electronics Publishing
Global Information Group
Gretag Image Systems
Helios Systems
Herstal Automation Ltd.
Hewlett-Packard Company
Howtek, Inc.
Hyperspeed Technologies, Inc.
IBM Corporation
IEEE Computer Society
Ilford Photo Corporation
Imagina
IMSL, Inc.
Infotronic SpA
Intel Corporation
Intelligent Light, Inc.
Intelligent Resources
Intergraph Corporation
IRIS Graphics, Inc.
Ithaca Software
Jones & Bartlett Publications
JVC Professional Products Company
Kinesix
Kubota Pacific Computer, Inc.
Lasertek
LAZERUS
Levco Sales
LSI Logic
Lyon Lamb Video Animation Systems, Inc.
Macro Data, Inc.
Magni Systems, Inc.
Management Graphics, Inc.
Mars Microsystems Inc.
Matrox Electronic Systems Ltd.
Maximum Strategy Inc.
Meckler Publishing
Megatek Corporation
Meret Optical Communications, Inc.
Microfield Graphics, Inc.
Micrografx, Inc.
Midwest Litho Arts
Minc Incorporated
Minnesota Datametrics Corporation
Minolta Corporation
MIT Press
Mitsubishi Electronics
Mitsubishi Electronics America-PED
Mitsubishi International Corporation
ModaCAD
Montage Publishing, Inc.
Morgan Kaufmann Publishers, Inc.
Motorola Semiconductor Products Sector
Mupac Corporation
National Computer Graphics Association
NEC Technologies, Inc.

Newtek
Nissei Sangyo America, Ltd.
Numonics Corporation
Oce Graphics USA, Inc.
Octree Corporation
Omnicomp Graphics Corporation
Optibase
Oxberry
Panasonic Communications & Systems Company,
Office Automation Group
Panasonic Industrial Company
Paragon Imaging Inc.
Parallax Graphics, Inc.
P.E. Photron
Peritek Corporation
Philips Semiconductors-Signetics
Pixar
Pixelworks, Inc.
Polhemus Incorporated
Protech Marketing
Provato Technologies, Inc.
QMS, Inc.
Rainbow Technologies, Inc.
Ramtek Corporation
Rapid Technology
RasterOps Corporation
Ray Dream, Inc.
Raytheon Company Submarine Signal Division
Redlake Corporation
RFX Inc.
RGB Spectrum
Sampo Corporation of America
Scanning America
Ron Scott Inc.
Seiko Instruments USA, Inc.
SGS-Thomson Microelectronics Inc.
Sharp Electronics Corporation
Shima Seiki USA, Inc.
ShoGraphics, Inc.
SIGGRAPH '92
SIGGRAPH Education Committees
SIGGRAPH Local Groups
SIGGRAPH Video Review
Sigma Electronics Inc.
Silicon Graphics Computer Systems
Sixty Eight Thousand Inc.
SOFTIMAGE Inc.
Software Security, Inc.
Sony Corporation
Spatial Systems, Inc.
Springer-Verlag
Stardent Computer Inc.
StereoGraphics Corporation
Strata Inc.
Sun Microsystems, Inc.
Sun Expert Magazine
SunWorld
Symbolics, Inc.
TaraVisual Corporation
TEAC America, Inc.
Techexport, Inc.
Tech-Source Inc.
Tektronix, Inc.
Template Graphics Software
Texas Memory Systems, Inc.
Texnai Inc.
Thomson Digital Image (TDI)
Time Arts Inc.
Toshiba America Consumer Products
Trix Company
Truevision, Inc.
University of Lowell
Univision Technologies, Inc.
UNIXWorld Magazine
Vicom Systems, Inc.
Video Systems Magazine
Videomedia
Videotex Systems Inc.
Viewpoint Animation Engineering, Inc.
VisionBase, Inc.
Visionetics International
Visualization Technologies, VT Inc.
Vital Images, Inc.
VITec (Visual Information Technologies)
VPL Research
Wacom, Inc.
Wasatch Computer Technology
Wavefront Technologies, Inc.
WaveTracer, Inc.
John Wiley & Sons, Inc.
Winsted Corporation
Wolfram Research, Inc.
XRS, X-Ray Scanner Corporation
Yamashita Engineering Manufacture, Inc.
Yarc Systems, Inc.

## 1991 ACM SIGGRAPH Awards

# Steven A. Coons Award for Outstanding Creative Contributions to Computer Graphics

# Andries van Dam

The 1991 Steven A. Coons Award for Outstanding Creative Contributions is presented to Dr. Andries van Dam for his unwavering pursuit of excellence in the field of computer graphics, his contributions to computer graphics education.and related fields. He is a stimulator and a leader, as shown by his key role in founding SIGGRAPH.

Van Dam entered the computing field in 1960 via pattern recognition and focused his doctoral dissertation on digital processing of pictorial data, inspired by Ivan Sutherland's seminal Sketchpad film. From the beginning, dealing with pictures has been central to his interests in computing. As a consequence of his early work, he always had a keen interest in the synthesis of the two areas: computer graphics and image processing. This led to his role in the establishment of the *Journal of Computer Graphics and Image Processing,* of which he was an editor from 1971 to 1981.

As one of the founders of the Computer Science Department at Brown University, and, as the first and two-term chairman, van Dam has been influential in that department's eminence. He always emphasized that computing is most effective through the crossing of disciplines and sub-disciplines. Thus, he and his graphics group worked in distributed graphics on multi-processors and networked computers in the early 1970s, nearly two decades before this topic became fashionable in mainstream computing.

In addition, van Dam was also an early proponent of, and contributor to, hypertext and hypermedia. It was through his presentations in the 1960s that many professionals were exposed to these concepts, long before they were recognized by the computing community at large. Under his leadership, nearly 20 years of hypertext and hypermedia graphics research was conducted before the first ACM conference on this topic was held.

Professor van Dam played an important role in fashioning the professional status of computer graphics. Together with Sam Matsa of IBM, he presented the first ACM Professional Development Seminar in Computer Graphics, both in the United States and Europe. He and Matsa then founded the ACM Special Interest Committee in Computer Graphics, which evolved into SIGGRAPH.

In addition, van Dam was a prime mover in the 1976 launching of the SIGGRAPH CoreStandards group that published, through SIGGRAPH, key specification documents. This work led to the formation of the ANSI X3H3 Technical Committee on graphics standards. Van Dam revisited that arena a decade later when he observed that the resulting GKS and PHIGS standards did not adequately support modern graphics workstations. He then cajoled a group of interested participants into producing a draft of PHIGS+, leaving it again to the formal committees to create a formal PHIG+ standard.

Van Dam, with Brown University colleagues, introduced and established the concept of networks of graphics workstations for teaching and research, well before the term was coined in the computer graphics field.

Finally, this citation would be incomplete without mention of van Dam's literary achievements including, *Fundamentals of Computer Graphics*, co-authored with colleague James D. Foley in 1982, and the recent *Computer Graphics: Principles and Practice*, with J.D. Foley, S.K. Feiner, and J.F. Hughes.

SIGGRAPH has a tradition of recognizing individuals who have made major and long-term contributions to the field of computer graphics. This year's Coons award to Professor van Dam exemplifies that tradition. Professor van Dam is a tireless worker, an inspiration to students and a fine example to the industry as a whole. Andries van Dam has always had the right vision of what is important in computing, in computer graphics, and in related fields. Even as he was engaged in these and other technical activities, he found time to convince the computer graphics industry of needed improvements. He is truly one of the important people in our field — he has dedicated his talent, inspiration, and time to encourage everyone to excel.

### Previous award winners

1989 David C. Evans
1987 Donald P. Greenberg
1985 Pierre Bézier
1983 Ivan E. Sutherland

## 1991 ACM SIGGRAPH Awards

# Computer Graphics Achievement Award

# James T. Kajiya

The SIGGRAPH Computer Graphics Achievement Award is presented to Dr. James T. Kajiya for his development of the Rendering Equation. This work describes an integral equation that provides a theoretical description of surface rendering and shows how to make images by solving the equation with Monte Carlo methods.

Kajiya began his graphics career working for Evans and Sutherland Computer Corporation. In 1973, he served as project engineer for the E&S frame buffer, the first commercially available frame buffer using dynamic random access memories. Upon leaving E&S, he began his graduate studies at the University of Utah, where he received his PhD in computer science in 1979. His thesis research, by applying Lie Group representation theory to the modeling of the human visual system as a signal processing system, explained a wide range of phenomena in monochrome brightness perception and predicted several new visual illusions and phenomena.

Since 1979, Kajiya has been at the California Institute of Technology, first as an assistant professor, then as associate professor of computer science. He has published works on mathematical models for computer vision, high-level programming languages, computer architecture and mathematical logic for computer science.

Kajiya's recent work has focused on very high-quality computer graphics and is noted for its innovation and thorough mathematical approach. This work has included nonlinear anti-aliasing algorithms for the display of text on raster screens, invention of several new techniques for ray tracing primitives (such as swept volumes), parametric patches and fractal surfaces, the first paper on volume rendering via ray tracing, and, with Tim Kay, a hierarchical bounding box technique for accelerating ray tracing. In addition, he has made significant contributions in the introduction of anisotropic light reflection models for surfaces, the introduction of algebraic geometry in patch computations, a solution to the problem of rendering fuzzy surfaces, and most recently with his student John Snyder, a new technique for high-level design of subtle three-dimensional shapes called generative modeling.

SIGGRAPH is pleased to recognize Kajiya's continuing contribution by honoring him for his special contribution to the industry — the Rendering Equation. Like much of Kajiya's work, the Rendering Equation is a fundamental and seminal contribution to the field. It provides a framework for future research and a foundation upon which future algorithms can be developed.

### Previous award winners

1990 Richard Shoup and Alvy Ray Smith
1989 John Warnock
1988 Alan H. Barr
1987 Robert Cook
1986 Turner Whitted
1985 Loren Carpenter
1984 James H. Clark
1983 James F. Blinn

# *ANIMATION AERODYNAMICS*

JAKUB WEJCHERT and DAVID HAUMANN

European Visualization Centre
IBM Scientific Centre, Winchester
Hampshire SO23 9DR, England.

IBM Research
T. J. Watson Research Center
Yorktown Heights, New York 10598, USA.

## Abstract

Methods based on aerodynamics are developed to simulate and control the motion of objects in fluid flows. To simplify the physics for animation, the problem is broken down into two parts: a fluid flow regime and an object boundary regime. With this simplification one can approximate the realistic behaviour of objects moving in liquids or air. It also enables a simple way of designing and controlling animation sequences: from a set of flow primitives, an animator can design the spatial arrangement of flows, create flows around obstacles and direct flow timing. The approach is fast, simple, and is easily fitted into simulators that model objects governed by classical mechanics. The methods are applied to an animation that involves hundreds of flexible leaves being blown by wind currents.

**Keywords:** Animation, Simulation, Aerodynamics, Fluid Mechanics, Flow Primitives, Control, Motion Design, Wind, Leaves. **CR Categories** I.3.5, I.3.7, I.6.3, J.5.

## INTRODUCTION

Every year leaves fall from trees and gather on the autumn ground; winds blow and scatter them in currents, whirlpools and eddies. This charming motion is a consequence of aerodynamics: the description of fluid flow and its relation to the motion of solid objects.

**An Aerodynamic Model with Control:** We describe a fast aerodynamic way of *modelling* and *controlling* the motion of many flexible objects in fluid currents in 3D. Physics or engineering applications would require numerical solutions of fluid flow with immersed solid objects. Because animation has less stringent accuracy requirements, we can avoid computational expense by dividing the system into two parts: a linear flow regime and an object boundary regime. The first ranges over all space and the second is used in the close vicinity of objects. In the linear flow regime we use the analytic solutions of the equations *instead* of solving for the flow numerically. These solutions define a set of flow primitives which are given as fluid velocity fields. Solutions such as vortices, sinks and uniform flows, can be linearly mixed so as to create a complex flow scenario. The primitives enable the design and control of animation sequences. The second part of the model is the interaction between the flow and the objects. This is based upon simplified boundary effects, that describe the forces exerted on object surfaces. Once the forces acting on objects are known, object motion is governed by Newtonian mechanics.



**Relevant Models:** Particle based systems have mimicked the visual appearance of fire [12], waterfalls, falling snow [13], and viscous jets [7]. Although these models have produced stunning effects they can only account for particle-like objects. Simulations of elasticity [11, 5, 8], have displayed the flexibility of individual objects; related models could exhibit the flapping motion of flags in uniform wind fields [14, 5]. Animation models of liquids, such as ocean foam [4] and shallow water [6] have displayed the visual appearance of liquid surfaces, but are not useful for representing internal fluid currents. Usually, models of natural phenomena are too complex to be applied by an animator using traditional techniques; a number of researchers have addressed this. Pintado [10] describes an approach that allows the control of object motion in non-physical 2D fields. Other methods allow animations to be controlled by geometrical constraints or optimization [11, 2]. However, these techniques can be numerically intensive and become unwieldy for controlling collections of objects with many degrees of freedom. In summary, the above models do not explicitly address the simulation of many flexible objects in dynamic fluid flows, combined with a fast control method.

## LINEARIZED FLUID FLOW

The mechanics of a fluid can be described by the Navier Stokes equation [3, 9]. This can be simplified in the case of a fluid that is A) inviscid, B) irrotational ($\nabla \times \mathrm{v} = 0$) and C) incompresssible ($\nabla.\mathrm{v} = 0$). This is a reasonable model for air at normal speeds when it does not exhibit turbulence [1]. Here v, is the velocity field of the fluid, describing the magnitude and direction of the flow at every point. The simplified fluid satisfies the Laplace equation

$$\nabla.\mathrm{v} = \nabla.\nabla\phi = \nabla^2\phi = 0. \qquad (1)$$

The velocity field is given by the gradient of the scalar potential $\mathrm{v} = \nabla\phi$. Since (1) is a linear differential equation, if we find any two analytical solutions then their linear combination is also a solution; the application of boundary conditions then results in a *physical* solution. Typically, it is required that the flow should be A) uniform at infinity and B) have no normal component at obstacle boundaries [9].

Since solutions are analytic, we bypass the task of solving the fluid equations numerically and provide a fast and simple technique for creating flows for animation.

**Flow Primitives:** We call a velocity field that satisfies eq (1) and the boundary conditions, a *flow primitive*. Given a set of flow primitives, an animator can construct more complicated flows from these building blocks, in a manner similar to that used by Sims [13]. In fact, the primitives provide a physical basis for the "velocity operators" that he used to direct particle systems. Our simplest primitive is *uniform* flow: the velocity lines follow straight lines. Other solutions include source, sink and vortex flows. A *source* is a point from which fluid moves out in all directions; a *sink* is a point to which fluid flows uniformly in all directions and disappears; and fluid moves around a *vortex* in concentric circles (fig 1). Using cylindrical coordinates, the potential and the velocity field for a line of source at the origin, with strength a, is:

$$\phi = \frac{a}{2\pi} \ln r; \quad v_r = \frac{a}{2\pi r}; \quad v_\theta = 0; \quad v_z = 0. \qquad (2)$$

For a sink the constant a is set negative. A vortex at the origin with strength b is given by:

$$\phi = \frac{b}{2\pi}\theta; \quad v_r = 0; \quad v_\theta = \frac{b}{2\pi r}; \quad v_z = 0. \qquad (3)$$

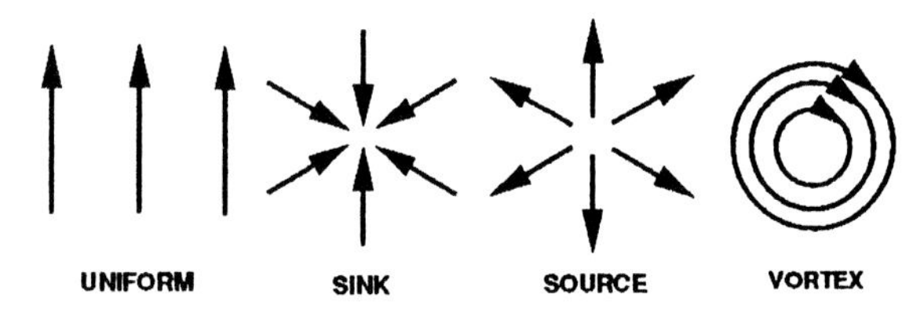


**Figure 1.** A schematic diagram of the flow primitives.

**Addition of Flows:** Because the system is linear (and because of a uniqueness theorem) if a flow satisfies eq (1) and has the required properties on object boundaries and at infinity, then it is the correct solution [1, 9]. Thus (as in aerodynamics) we can add the primitives to create more complicated flows:

$$\mathbf{V} = \mathbf{v}_{vort}(x,y,z) + \mathbf{v}_{sink}(x,y,z) + \mathbf{v}_{source}(x,y,z) + \ldots \qquad (4)$$

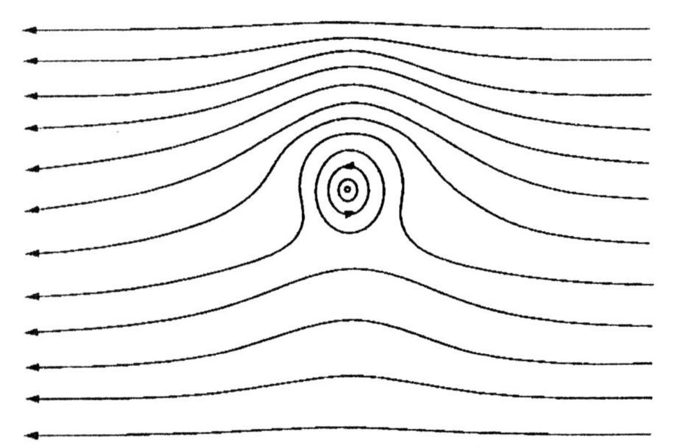

**Figure 2.** The addition of uniform and vortex flow.

Figure 2 shows the flowlines that result from the addition of a uniform flow with a vortex. The flow defines the whole temporal path of the fluid at the beginning, middle and end of the motion. Since the positions and strengths of the primitives can be chosen, the approach allows for a simple, physically-motivated way of designing the paths of objects. Once objects are placed in the fluid, their trajectories have already been determined by the user to a first approximation.

**Flow Obstacles:** We can also use flow primitives to design flows around large solid obstacles, and to bound the spatial extent of flows. Obstacles can be built out of primitives that are strong enough to cause a main flow to be directed from certain regions. Similar methods are used to study the flow around obstacles such as airfoils [1]. Figure 3 shows the effect of adding together a uniform flow with a point source. This can be taken to represent flow around a solid object. No fluid flows across the "stagnation" flow line shown in bold, so if a solid object with the geometry of the stagnation curve were placed in the fluid, there would be no flow across its surface. This approach is faster than normal collision detection algorithms and allows the smooth and natural motion of the objects as they interact with obstacles. The method was used to create the motion of leaves around obstacles such as slides or walls.

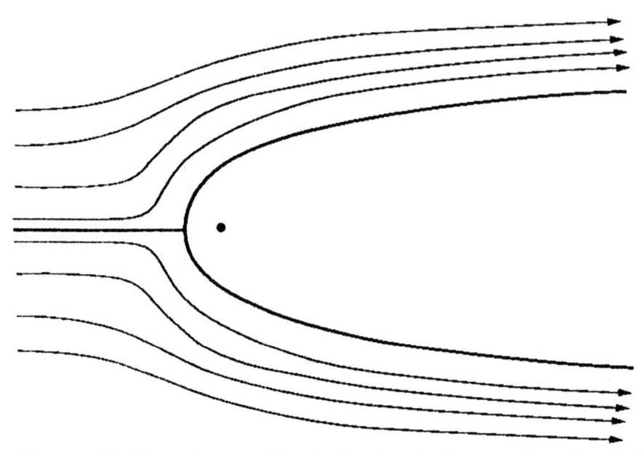

**Figure 3.** Creating solid obstacles to flow using the addition of primitives.

**Time-dependent Flows:** We can also model time-dependent flows with the condition that changes to the primitives are directed by forces that are external to the system (user specified). Although the time evolution of the forces may not be physically based, the resulting flow at each frame will be. Time-varying fields enable a user to change the flow lines, by directing the positions of the primitives with time. This gives a further degree of control, allowing obstacles to move and events to occur at specific times. Coupled with bounded fields, it enables the control of *collections* of objects to follow specified paths.

# OBJECT BOUNDARY REGIME

Dividing the system into two regimes, linear flow and boundary layer, simplifies our general problem. For the major part fluids are taken to behave as a linear inviscid system; however, in the vicinity of objects we must include boundary effects such as viscous drag and pressure. In this way forces exerted on the objects may be calculated.

**Particles in Flows:** A model for particles in flows can be based on the Stoke drag equation. This gives the force exerted on a spherical particle with radius a, moving with relative velocity $\mathbf{v}^r$ in a fluid with viscosity $\eta$ as:

$$\mathbf{F} = 6\pi a \eta \mathbf{v}^r. \qquad (5)$$

Given a mass particle with velocity $\mathbf{p}$, the relative velocity with respect to a fluid velocity field $\mathbf{v}$ is: $\mathbf{v}^r = \mathbf{v} - \mathbf{p}$. So from eq (5) we define the force on the particle as

$$\mathbf{F} = \alpha \mathbf{v}^r. \tag{6}$$

Here $\alpha$ represents a coupling strength between the flow and the particles. Particles not moving at the fluid velocity will experience adjustment forces until they do so. For $\alpha$ large, particles will be forced to track the flow closely, as they would in a viscous fluid ($\eta$ large). If $\alpha = 0$ then the fluid fields have no effect on the particles. The parameter $\alpha$ is similar to the 'field affinity' parameter used to direct particles along 2D spline fields by Pintado [10].

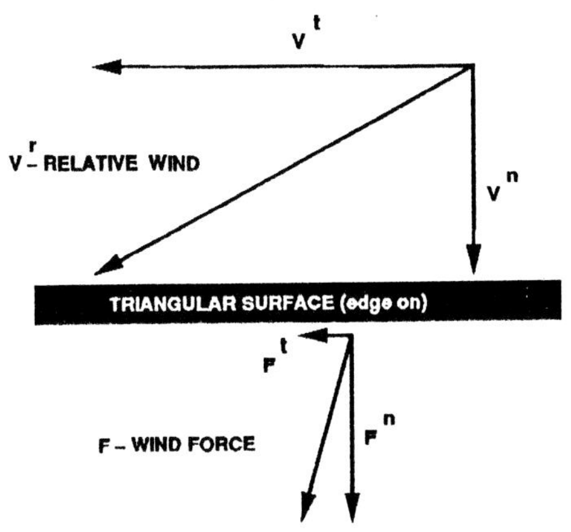


**Figure 4.** Side view of a triangular area in a fluid.

**Objects in Flows:** Unlike the case of particles, the forces acting on a surface depend on its area and orientation with respect to the flow. Surfaces defining an object are divided into triangular patches with a mass point at each vertex. The relative velocity of each particle is resolved into the normal and tangential components with respect to the triangular surface: $\mathbf{v}^r = \mathbf{v}^n + \mathbf{v}^t$ (see fig 4). The normal component of the force is due to pressure difference between the front and rear of the surface. It can be shown that the force of a uniform flow with speed $v$ and density $\rho$, that strikes a flat surface of area A, is given by:

$$F = \rho A v^2. \tag{7}$$

The tangential force component is due a fluid with viscosity moving across a surface. This is given by the viscous shear stress times the area.

$$F = A\eta \frac{dv}{dy}, \tag{8}$$

where y is measured perpendicularly from the object surface into the fluid. For a non-slip condition we have at $y = 0, v = 0$ and for $y \to \infty, v \to v^t$. Typically the velocity profile is parabolic, but in the vicinity of the surface we may take the velocity gradient to be linear: $F \sim A\eta v^t$. Therefore we write the normal and tangential forces as:

$$\begin{aligned} \mathbf{F}^n &= \alpha^n A v \mathbf{v}^n, \\ \mathbf{F}^t &= \alpha^t A \mathbf{v}^t. \end{aligned} \tag{9}$$

$\mathbf{F}^n$ is the force experienced by a surface facing into the fluid, while $\mathbf{F}^t$ is due to the viscous drag of fluid flowing across the surface. This may be interpreted as a generalization of eq (6): a set of physically based dynamic control equations, that determine the degree to which objects follow the fluid.

**Overall Approximations:** In our model we have chosen a balance between physical exactness, execution speed and control. For example, linearized air flow cannot exhibit turbulence - but if we used a non-linear system: a) mixing flow primitives would give non-physical solutions, b) it would be numerically intensive. Objects in wind exhibit complex motion mainly due to their geometry and the fluid-object interaction (little is due to the local turbulence of the fluid itself) so using a linear fluid is not unreasonable. It should also be understood that dividing the system into two parts results in the flows affecting the objects and not *vice versa.* This holds better for small objects, spaced relatively wide apart.

## APPLICATION

**Simulation:** We integrated the methods into a simulator developed by Norton [8], that models the flexibility and fracture of solids. Objects are constructed of masses and springs governed by Newtonian mechanics. The evolution of a collection of objects with time is carried out by integrating $F = ma$. F is the total force acting on a mass, made up of contributions from gravity, spring stretching *and* the external fluid forces:

$$\mathbf{F} = \mathbf{F}_{grav} + \mathbf{F}_{spring} + \mathbf{F}_{fluid} + \ldots \tag{10}$$

This determines the accelerations from which the extrapolated velocities and new positions can be calculated.

**Motion Design:** To design an animation of a collection of objects (leaves) being blown by wind, we: 1) Design leaf geometries and construct them out of masses and springs. 2) Design a set of wind fields that will define the motion paths of the objects during a sequence. 3) Simulate the motion and preview the results. 4) If needed, make changes to the wind velocities, fluid-object interaction, position of flow primitives, and the number of objects.

**Object Geometry:** Our first test leaves were point particles, whose motion in air was directed by eq (6). These were useful for seeing the overall motion of collections of leaves in air currents. To exhibit individual rotational motion, a leaf was built out of masses and springs using the geometry of six triangles. The leaf was duplicated with slight variations in geometry, mass distribution and stiffness. Even in a uniform flow objects glide and twirl in a realistic way because of the different forces experienced in the lateral and tangential directions due to eq (9).

**Figure 5.** Leaves being chased by a garbage bin.

**Adding Flow Primitives:** By combining field primitives (eq (4)), whole motion paths could be designed. In an animation sequence a garbage bin chases and then inhales leaves trying to escape. Uniform and vortex flows made leaves travel along the ground (fig 5) and then fly and twirl up into the air (fig 6). Finally, the leaves were funneled in by a cyclone consisting of vortex and sink primitives coincident with the bin mouth (fig 7).

**Flow Obstacles:** Mixing and positioning flow primitives, enabled us to build large flow obstacles around which leaves would travel. An animation sequence required leaves to be blown up a slide. To do this, a uniform field was used as the main driving flow and leaves then passed over an obstacle wedge made out of fields that prevented the flow lines from penetrating the slide geometry. This enabled the smooth motion of leaves blowing over the solid obstacle (fig 8).

**Figure 6.** Leaves escaping by flying in the air.

**Figure 7.** Leaves being sucked in by a garbage bin.

## CONCLUSION

We have described a model based on aerodynamics that can be used for object motion simulation and control. In the model we chose a balance between physical exactness, execution speed and animation control. Future extensions could include aerodynamic flight of birds or airplanes. In practice, the application of the methods are quite simple. We hope that the methods can be integrated and extended by others into their physically based simulation systems.

We wish to give credit to the members of the Animation Systems Group: Alan Norton, Bob Bacon, Paula Sweeney, Kavi Arya, Al Khorasani and Jane Jung; and to Mike Henderson for discussions on fluid mechanics. Thanks to the staff at Winchester for encouragement and support, and to Roz for proof reading.

**Figure 8.** Leaves being blow up and over a slide.

## REFERENCES

1. Anderson J (1985) "Fundamentals of Aerodynamics", McGraw-Hill Publishers.
2. Barzel R, Barr A (1988) "A Modeling System based on Dynamic Constraints", Computer Graphics (SIGGRAPH 88 Proceedings) 22 (4) 179.
3. Feynman R, Leighton R, Sands M (1965) "The Feynman Lectures on Physics", Addison Wesley.
4. Fournier A, Reeves W (1986) "A Simple Model of Ocean Waves", Computer Graphics (SIGGRAPH '86 Proceedings) 20 (4) 75.
5. Haumann D, Parent R (1988) "The Behavioral Test-Bed: Obtaining Complex Behavior from simple Rules" The Visual Computer 4 (6) 332.
6. Kass M, Miller G (1990) "Rapid, Stable Fluid Dynamics for Computer Graphics" Computer Graphics (SIGGRAPH 90 Proceedings) 24 (4) 49.
7. Miller G, Pearce A (1989) "Globular Dynamics: A Connected Particle System for Animating Viscous Fluids", Computers and Graphics, Vol 13, 305.
8. Norton A, Turk G, Bacon R (1990) "Animation and Fracture by Physical Modeling", To appear in "The Visual Computer".
9. Patterson A (1989) "A First Course in Fluid Dynamics" Cambridge University Press.
10. Pintado X, Fuime E (1989) "Grafields: Field-Directed Dynamic Splines for Interactive Motion Control" Computers and Graphics Vol 13, 77.
11. Platt J, Barr A (1988) "Constraint Methods for Flexible Models", Computer Graphics (SIGGRAPH 88 Proceedings) 22 (4) 279.
12. Reeves W (1983) "Particle Systems - A Technique for Modeling a Class of Fuzzy Objects" Computer Graphics (SIGGRAPH 83 Proceedings) 17 (3) 359.
13. Sims K (1990) "Particle Animation and Rendering Using Data Parallel Computation", Computer Graphics (SIGGRAPH 90 Proceedings) 24 (4) 405.
14. Terzopoulos D, Platt J, Barr A, Fleishcer K (1987) "Elastically Deformanble Models", Computer Graphics (SIGGRAPH 87 Proceedings) 21 (4) 205.

# Animated Free-Form Deformation: An Interactive Animation Technique

*Sabine Coquillart* and Pierre Jancène*

INRIA
78153 Le Chesnay, France

## Abstract

Current research efforts focus on providing interactive techniques that make 3D concepts easy to use and accessible to large numbers of people. In this paper, a new interactive technique for animating deformable objects is presented. The technique allows easy specification and control of a class of deformations that cannot be produced by existing techniques without considerable human intervention.

The methodology proposed relies on the Free-Form Deformation (FFD) technique. It makes use of a deformation tool that is animated like any other object.

This approach provides a representation of the deformations independent of the surface geometry, and can be easily integrated into traditional hierarchical animation systems.

**CR Categories and Subject Descriptors:** I.3.6 [Computer Graphics]: Methodology and Techniques - Interaction techniques; I.3.7 [Computer Graphics]: Three Dimensional Graphics and Realism - Animation.

## 1 Introduction

A great deal of work has been done towards the use of physical simulation as a means of animating deformable objects [1]. Considerably less attention has been given to interactively animating non physically-based models.

*Presently on sabbatical at Thomson Digital Images, Paris.



The predominant method in use today is *metamorphosis*. Metamorphosis is a method used to create intermediary shapes that make a smooth transition between two or more extreme or *key-shapes*. It is useful when every point of the animated model changes from one position to the next at the same time and speed. If this is not the case, metamorphosis may require a large number of key-positions, i.e. considerable human intervention, resulting in an animation that will be, nevertheless, only an approximation of the desired one.

In this paper, an alternative to the metamorphosis technique is described. It can be used to specify the motion of a local deformation such as an arbitrarily shaped bump whose shape may change over time or the motion of an object inside a global deformation whose shape may also change over time.

This technique, Animated Free-Form Deformation (AFFD), relies on the Free-Form Deformation (FFD) [4] technique together with the Extended Free-Form Deformation (EFFD) [3] extension. The Free-Form Deformation technique consists of embedding the geometric model, or the region of the model to be deformed, into a user-defined 3D lattice. The deformations of the 3D lattice are then automatically passed on to the model. The 3D lattice represents a piecewise parametric volume. AFFD is interactive, intuitive, and independent of the geometric model of the object to be deformed. Furthermore, it can be integrated into most traditional animation systems.

## 2 Animated Free-Form Deformations

This section concentrates on two types of animated deformations: the motion of a local deformation and the motion of a surface inside a global deformation. Until now, except in Chadwick et al. [2], FFD has mainly been exploited as a geometric modeling technique.

The animation technique described in this paper consists of taking advantage of the *deformation tool* paradigm. In FFD, the deformation tool is composed

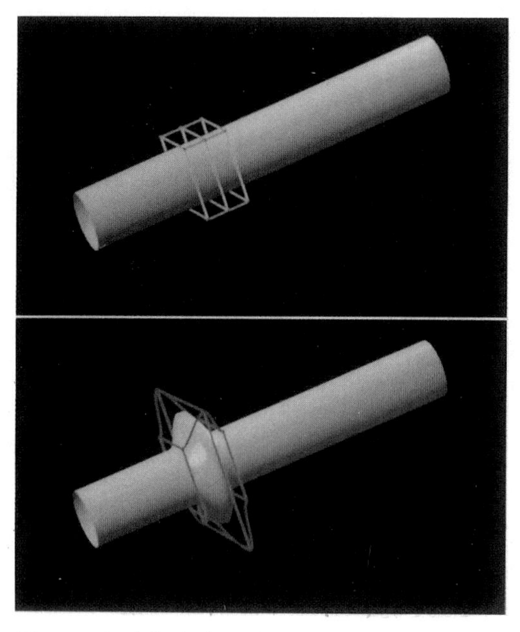

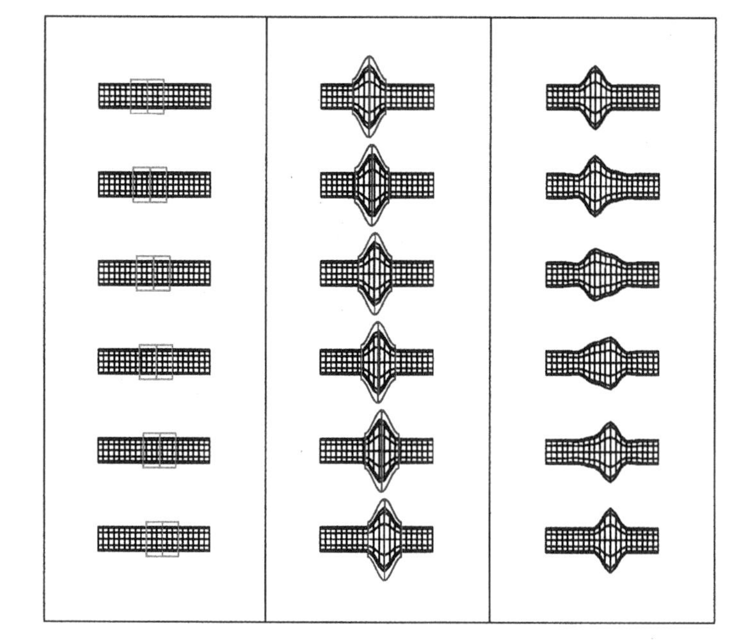

Figure 1: (a) Animating a swollen cylinder (b) undeformed (c) AFFD-deformed (d) metamorphic

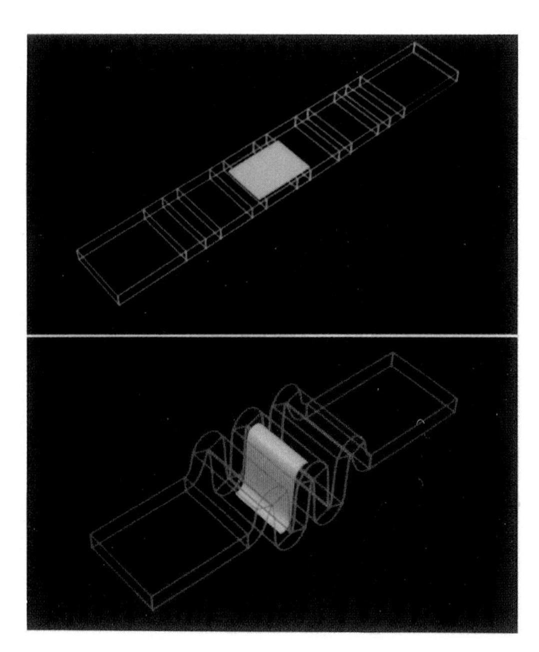

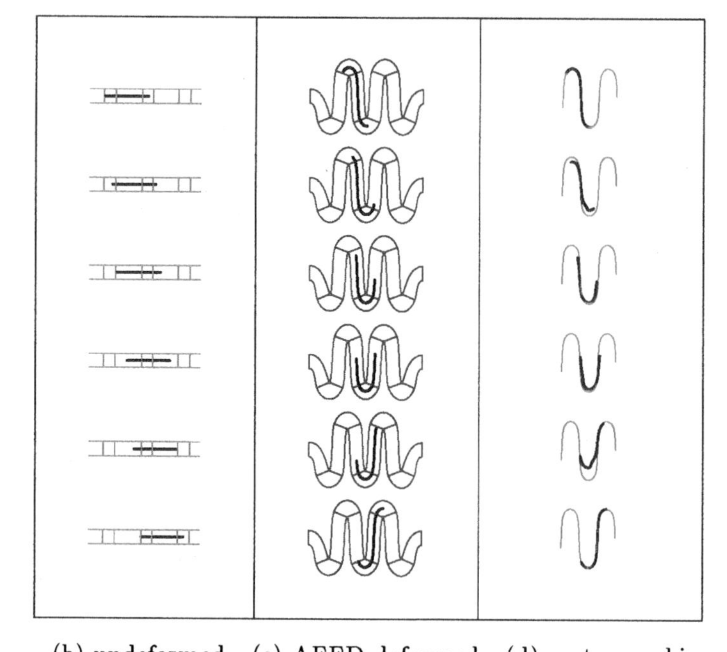

Figure 2: (a) Animating a paper sheet (b) undeformed (c) AFFD-deformed (d) metamorphic

of two 3D lattices: the initial and the final lattice. The initial lattice is a user defined lattice that is embedded in the region of the model to be deformed. The final lattice is a copy of the initial one that has been deformed by the user.

In order to deform an object, the deformation tool must be associated with this object, thus forming what we call an AFFD object. Differentiating the deformation tool from the object turns out to be a fruitful approach. It allows the definition of different motions for the deformation tool and the object. In this paragraph, the well-known key-frame animation technique is used to define the motion of each element. In its simplest form, the key-frame technique consists of specifying parameters such as the position, the orientation or the scaling factors of objects at some key-positions, and computing the inbetween values by interpolating the key-parameters.

This approach facilitates the control of the motion of a local deformation. Assuming that the object and the deformation tool have been designed, the motion of the deformation tool is interactively specified by using the

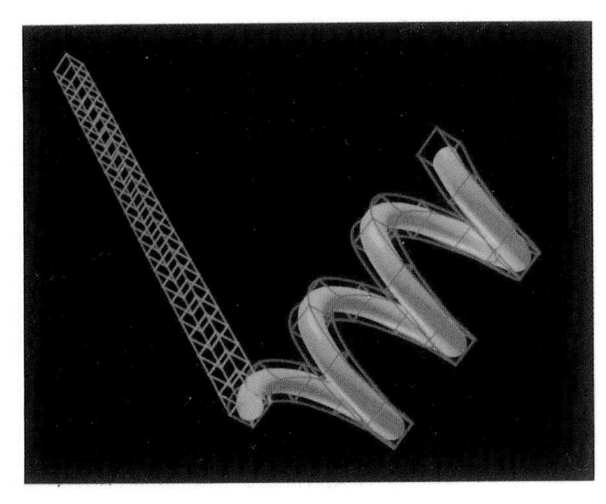

Figure 3: The spring lattices

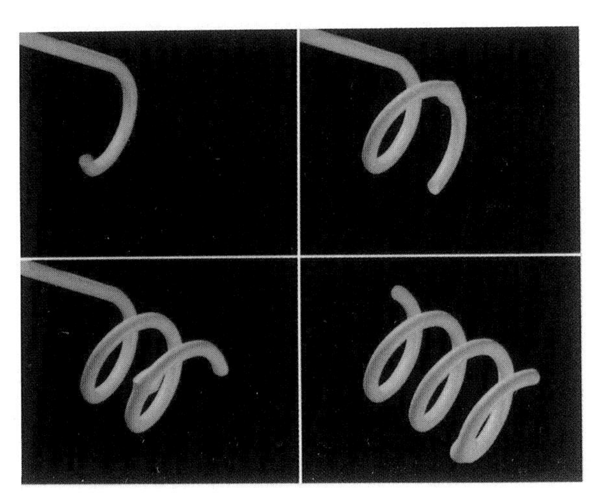

Figure 4: From a cylinder to a spring

key-frame technique.

This solution has been used to animate a swollen cylinder, i.e. a cylinder which contains a swelling made to move along it. First, the constant radius cylinder is designed. The deformation tool is described independently: the initial lattice of the deformation tool is a cube, i.e. a parallelepipedical lattice, while the final lattice is a copy of the initial one deformed as shown in Figure 1a (in every picture, the green objects represent initial lattices, and the red the final ones).

The animation of the swelling is specified by translating the deformation tool along the cylinder. For each frame, the position of the tool is computed according to the tool motion. Then, the surface is updated by applying the FFD transformation defined by the deformation tool. Thus, the shape of the deformed cylinder is always accurate. For each frame visualized, the initial lattice and the undeformed cylinder are represented in Figure 1b whereas the deformed lattice and the deformed cylinder are represented in Figure 1c. Only the side views are visualized.

Rather than animate the deformation tool, the object itself may be animated, allowing control of the motion of an object inside a global deformation. Let us consider the deformation of a soft surface following a given path, like a paper sheet inside a copier. Figures 2a, 2b, and 2c illustrate the AFFD technique applied to the sheet when it is made to move inside the initial lattice.

Both examples have been animated with metamorphosis using a C-spline interpolation function. In Figure 1d, the first and the last frames correspond to two successive key-positions of the cylinder. In Figure 2d, three key-positions have been used to describe the sheet movement: the first and the last correspond to the first and the last frames. The blue curve represents the curve the sheet should follow.

### 2.1 AFFD and Hierarchical Systems

The AFFD technique can easily be integrated into hierarchical animation systems. These systems allow the grouping of objects into clusters. A hierarchy of motion is created in which the position of an object is subordinated to the motion of its ancestors.

Integrating AFFD into such systems only consists of adding one new class of objects, the 3D lattices, and two new classes of clusters, the deformation tools and the AFFD objects. According to the previous section, a deformation tool is made of two 3D lattices, whereas an AFFD object is composed of an object and a deformation tool. A motion can be associated with each of these new classes.

Integrating AFFD into traditional hierarchical animation systems allows applying several deformations successively. The spring in Figures 3 and 4 demonstrates the use of several successive deformations. The original object is a long cylinder. It is first deformed by a deformation tool equivalent to the one used for the swollen cylinder. Then the result is deformed by a second deformation tool composed of the lattices shown in Figure 3. As the cylinder enters the initial lattice, it is smoothly transformed into a spring. Figure 4 presents 4 frames from an animation test. The change of the size of the swelling will be explained in the next paragraph.

### 2.2 Deforming Deformations

As we have seen, metamorphosis and AFFD are complementary. Metamorphosis can be integrated into hierarchical animation systems by adding one new cluster class: the *metamorphic object*, made of several objects, each of them representing one key-shape.

Metamorphosis and AFFD can be combined in different ways. The simplest method consists of applying a deformation tool to a metamorphic object. The metamorphosis technique may also be applied to the deformation tool. This approach allows the specification of new animated deformations in which the shape of the deformation changes over time.

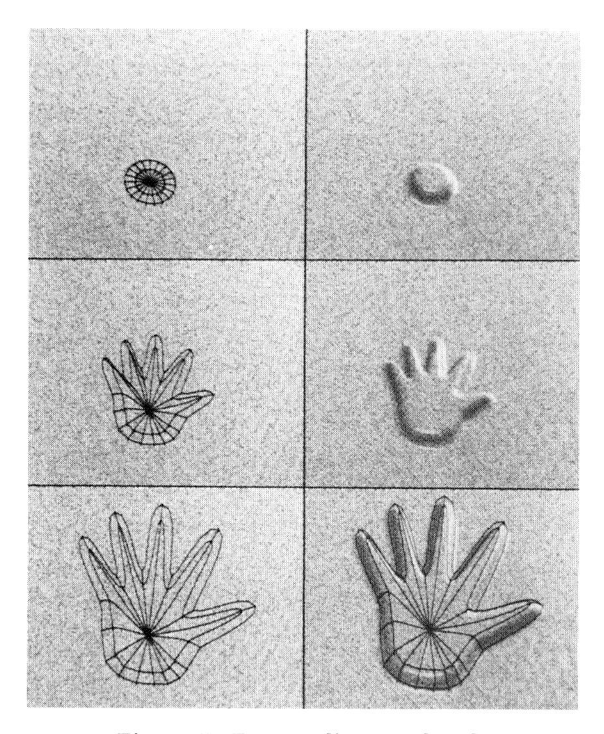

Figure 5: From a disc to a hand

Figure 5 illustrates this situation. The original object is a planar surface and a changing shape is sculpted into it. The first key-tool has a circular shape while the second has a hand-like shape (see first and last frames of Figure 5). The initial 3D lattice positioned on the original surface is shown on the left. The right column presents three frames from the resulting animation, the deformed lattice is shown on the last frame.

The change of the size of the swelling in the spring example is obtained by applying metamorphosis to the final lattice of the deformation tool. Note that this last alternative, the interpolation of the final lattice, was already used by Chadwick et al. in [2].

Other techniques may be used as well to change the shape of the deformation tool, in particular the AFFD technique.

## 3 Concluding Remarks

In addition to the ability to accurately control a new set of animated deformations, AFFD offers the following advantages:

- Since the deformation is independent of the object it is applied to, it can be reused to deform other objects.
- AFFD is less space consuming than metamorphosis because the geometric model does not have to be duplicated for each key-position. Furthermore, the surface can be adaptively subdivided for each frame according to the current deformation.
- Hierarchical animation systems can easily be modified to include the AFFD capability.
- The user gets better control of the animated deformation, whether by adjusting one of the 3D lattices or by modifying the motion.
- AFFD is very intuitive and fully interactive.

The examples presented are the result of a combination of the AFFD technique with the key-frame and metamorphosis techniques. Other animation techniques, such as dynamic motion, may be combined with AFFD as well.

In this paper, FFD is the foundation for the animation technique presented. It should be noted, however, that the ability to integrate different deformation techniques into motion control systems provides the framework for the developement of a set of new animation techniques. Furthermore, we believe that the deformation tool paradigm opens the door to other new and exciting uses of deformations.

AFFD is part of ACTION3D, a general interactive system developed jointly by SOGITEC and INRIA.

## Acknowledgements

We would like to thank D. Geman for his helpful comments on this paper. We are grateful to INRIA's audiovisual department for their assistance with color images and video demonstrations.

## References

[1] A. Barr. Dynamic Constraints. *Siggraph Course Notes*, 1986.

[2] J.E. Chadwick, D.R. Haumann, and R.E. Parent. Layered Construction for Deformable Animated Characters. In *SIGGRAPH'89*, volume 23, pages 243–252. ACM, July 1989.

[3] S. Coquillart. Extended Free-Form Deformation: A Sculpturing Tool for 3D Geometric Modeling. In *SIGGRAPH'90*, volume 24, pages 187–193. ACM, August 1990.

[4] T.W. Sederberg and S.R. Parry. Free-Form Deformation of Solid Geometric Models. In *SIGGRAPH'86*, volume 20, pages 151–160. ACM, August 1986.

# Motion Without Movement

William T. Freeman†, Edward H. Adelson†, and David J. Heeger§

†The Media Laboratory
Massachusetts Institute of Technology
Cambridge, MA 02139

§NASA-Ames Research Center 262-2
Moffet Field, CA 94035

## Abstract

We describe a technique for displaying patterns that appear to move continuously without changing their positions. The method uses a quadrature pair of oriented filters to vary the local phase, giving the sensation of motion. We have used this technique in various computer graphic and scientific visualization applications.

**CR Categories:** I.3.3 [Computer Graphics]: Picture/Image Generation; I.3.7 [Computer Graphics]: Graphics and Realism; I.4.9 [Image Processing]: Applications.

**Keywords:** Motion Display, Oriented Filters, Perception.

## 1 Introduction

Motion display is important in scientific visualization and computer graphic displays. One would often like to "paint" motion onto a scene, just as one can paint color or texture. Existing techniques for indicating motion have drawbacks. Superimposed arrows on a static image add clutter and give no sense of motion. If objects in the scene are set into actual motion in a film loop, then they must periodically snap back to their starting positions, giving a jerky display. Other techniques to display motion include the massively parallel simulation of particle systems [10], and pseudo-color techniques such as color table animation [9; 11].

## 2 Creating the motion illusion

We describe a method for assigning perceptual motion to objects that remain in fixed positions, by applying local filters and continuously varying their phase over time. The technique makes use of perceptual phenomena described by Shadlen *et al.* [8] and Anstis [1], where local phase changes are interpreted as global motions. Shadlen *et al.* produce the effect using patch-wise FFT's and Hilbert transforms. Our new technique is based on recently developed "steerable filters" [3; 4], which provide a convenient and flexible implementation of the illusion.

Consider two filters, identical except shifted in phase from each other by 90 degrees. The filters are called a quadrature pair, and are related by the Hilbert tranform [2]. Figure 1 shows such a pair of even and odd phase filters (chosen for orientation properties to be used later), (a) the second derivative of a Gaussian, $G_2$, and (b) its Hilbert transform, $H_2$. Filters of intermediate phases, shown in Fig. 1(c), may be constructed as weighted sums of the even and odd phase filters. Note in Fig. 1(c) that the filter ripples move rightward as the phase is shifted. This sequence of phase-shifted filters was computed using the following formula:

$$F(t) = \cos(\omega t)G_2 + \sin(\omega t)H_2 \tag{1}$$

where $F$ is the phase-shifted filter, $\omega$ is the rate of phase shift, and $t$ is time. When one views a phase-shifting stimulus, like the sequence of filters shown in Fig. 1(c), an interesting visual illusion occurs: it appears that the entire pattern (both the ripples and the modulation envelope) is moving.

This visual illusion of motion can be applied to any spatial pattern; an example is shown in Fig 2. Figs 2(a) and (b) show the results of convolving an image of Albert Einstein with a quadrature pair of filters (see [6] for background on image processing and convolution). Fig 2(c) shows the image sequence computed from combining (a) and (b) according to Eq. (1). When viewed as a temporal sequence, the result is a compelling illusion of continual (rightward) motion of a stationary image.

To display motion in different directions, we need to apply the filters at different orientations. For that, we use "steerable filters", which allow one to to synthesize a filter of arbitrary orientation from a linear combination of basis filters [3; 4]. Fig. 3 shows the basis sets for the $G_2$ and $H_2$ filters. One can span the space of all rotations of each filter with these basis sets. Introducing the notation $f^\theta$ to indicate rotation of the function $f$ through an angle $\theta$, we have, for the function $G_2$,

$$G_2^\theta(x,y) = k_1(\theta)G_{2a}(x,y) + k_2(\theta)G_{2b}(x,y)(\theta) + k_3(\theta)G_{2c}(x,y) \tag{2}$$

where $k_i(\theta)$ are the interpolation functions, and $G_{2a,2b,2c}(x,y)$ are the basis functions for $G_2^\theta(x,y)$. There is an analogous formula for $H_2^\theta(x,y)$ with four basis functions. (The number of basis filters required is related to the number of angular frequencies in the filter [3; 4]). Tables 1 – 4 give filter tap values and interpolation functions for computationally efficient x-y separable versions of the $G_2$ and $H_2$ steerable filters. The x-y separable basis filters are shown in Figure 6.

To cause an image, $I(x,y)$, to appear to move in a different direction, $\theta(x,y)$, at every point $(x, y)$ in the image, we use the even and odd phase images, $E(x,y)$ and $O(x,y)$:

$$E(x,y) = I(x,y) \otimes G_2^{\theta(x,y)} \tag{3}$$

$$O(x,y) = I(x,y) \otimes H_2^{\theta(x,y)} \tag{4}$$

$$D(x,y,t) = \cos(\omega t)E(x,y) + \sin(\omega t)O(x,y) \tag{5}$$

where $D(x,y,t)$ is the displayed image sequence, $\omega$ is the temporal frequency of the displayed motion, and $\otimes$ represents convolution. With steerable filters, this angularly adaptive filtering is simple to perform. The output at each pixel is simply a linear combination of

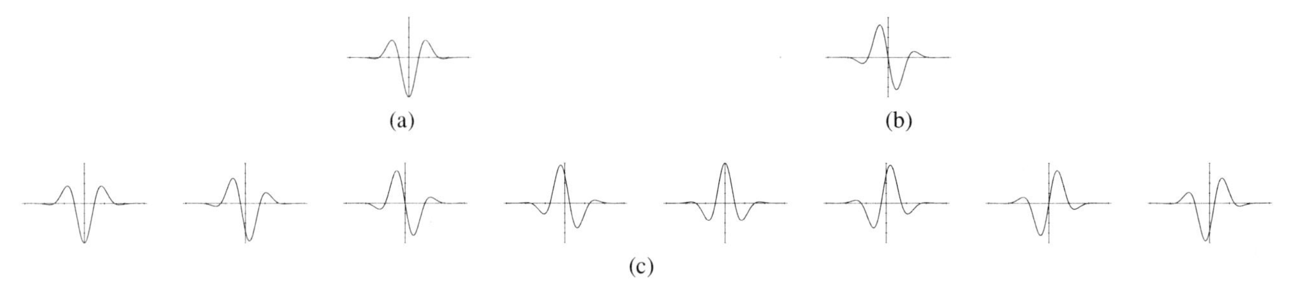

Figure 1: 1-d cross-sections of filters. (a) Even phase ($G_2$). (b) Odd phase ($H_2$). (c) Filters modulated in phase according to Eq. (1). Note the apparent rightward motion of the filter ripples.

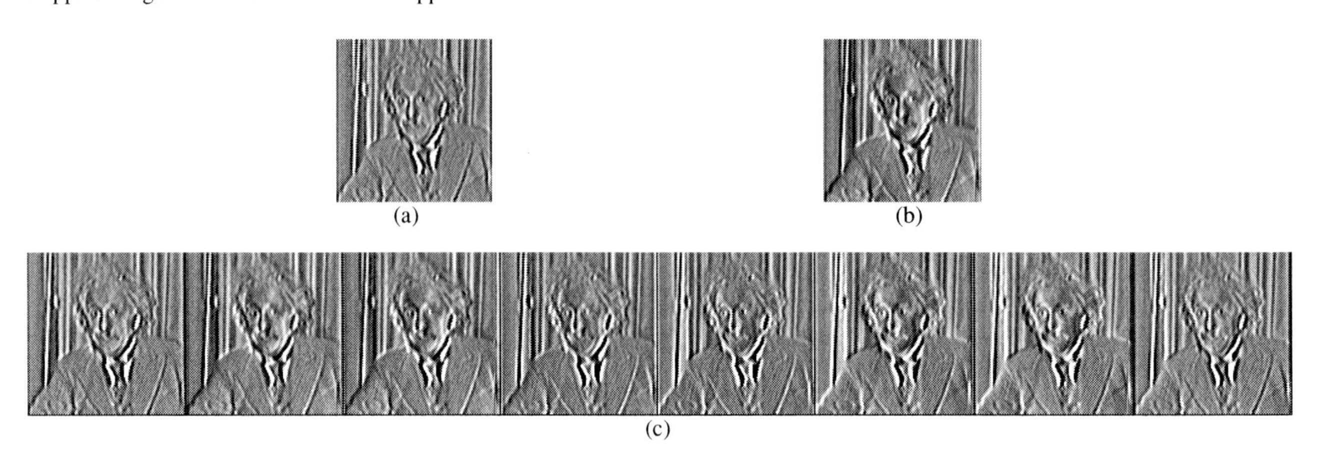

Figure 2: (a) and (b): $G_2$ and $H_2$ filters were applied to an image of Einstein. (c) Images modulated as in Eq. (1). When viewed as a temporal sequence, this generates the perception of rightward motion, yet image remains stationary.

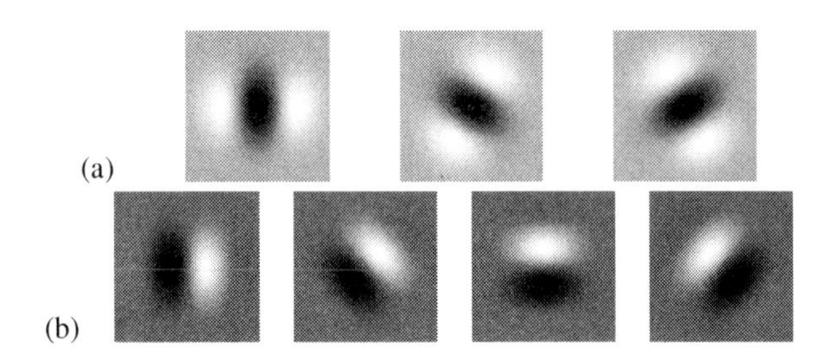

Figure 3: (a) $G_2$ and (b) $H_2$ quadrature pair steerable basis filters. The filter sets (a) and (b) span the space of all rotations of their respective filters.

the corresponding pixel values from several basis images. The basis images need to be calculated only once. Motion speed variations may be included by changing $\omega$ as a function of position (the speed is proportional to $\omega$).

A potential drawback of this technique is that the output images are bandpass filtered along the local direction of motion, and low-pass filtered in the perpendicular direction (reflecting the properties of the oriented filters). To improve the image quality, one can restore some of the frequency components perpendicular to $\theta(x, y)$ by adding $-I(x, y) \otimes G_2^{\theta(x,y)+\pi/2}$ to each frame of the processed sequence.

For color images, one can apply the technique to the luminance component of the image, and add in the stationary chrominance components. In the resulting sequence, both the luminance and the chrominance components are perceived to be moving. However, the color gamut is limited to pastelized colors, since there needs to be a positive bias to the luminance, to avoid negative light values.

## 3 Applications

Motion without movement adds a compelling motion cue, with a variety of applications in visualization and computer graphic display. This technique can be used to create a continuous display of instantaneous motion. Figure 4 (a) shows a single frame of a motion sequence of a man catching a teddy bear. From two consecutive frames of the video sequence, instantaneous motion vectors were derived, using the method of Lucas and Kanade [7]. These motion directions, Fig. 4 (b), were used for $\theta(x, y)$ in Eq. 5 to create the even and odd phase images, Fig. 4 (c) and (d). The resulting sequence, shown in Fig. 4 (e), is a continuous display that corresponds to the motion at one instant. The bear is constantly falling toward the man, who is forever reaching out to grab it.

Figure 5 shows single frames from several other applications of motion without movement. Fig. 5 (a) is a simulated air traffic controller's display, where the airplane velocities are shown by the motion illusion, yet the airplane icons maintain their positions. The sequence of Fig. 5 (b) displays instantaneous velocities in a physical simulation of several objects colliding. Fig. 5 (c) is from a computer art piece entitled "Nude Descending a Staircase" [5], a modern interpretation of Duchamp's painting.

In summary, we have described a flexible technique for indicating motion on graphics display screens. Objects or patterns appear to be continuously moving, yet stay at one position. This compelling motion illusion can be used to continuously display instantaneous motion. We have used this technique in various computer graphic and visualization applications.

## 4 Acknowledgement

This work was supported in part by a contract with Goldstar Co., Ltd., and by NSF grant IRI 871-939-4.

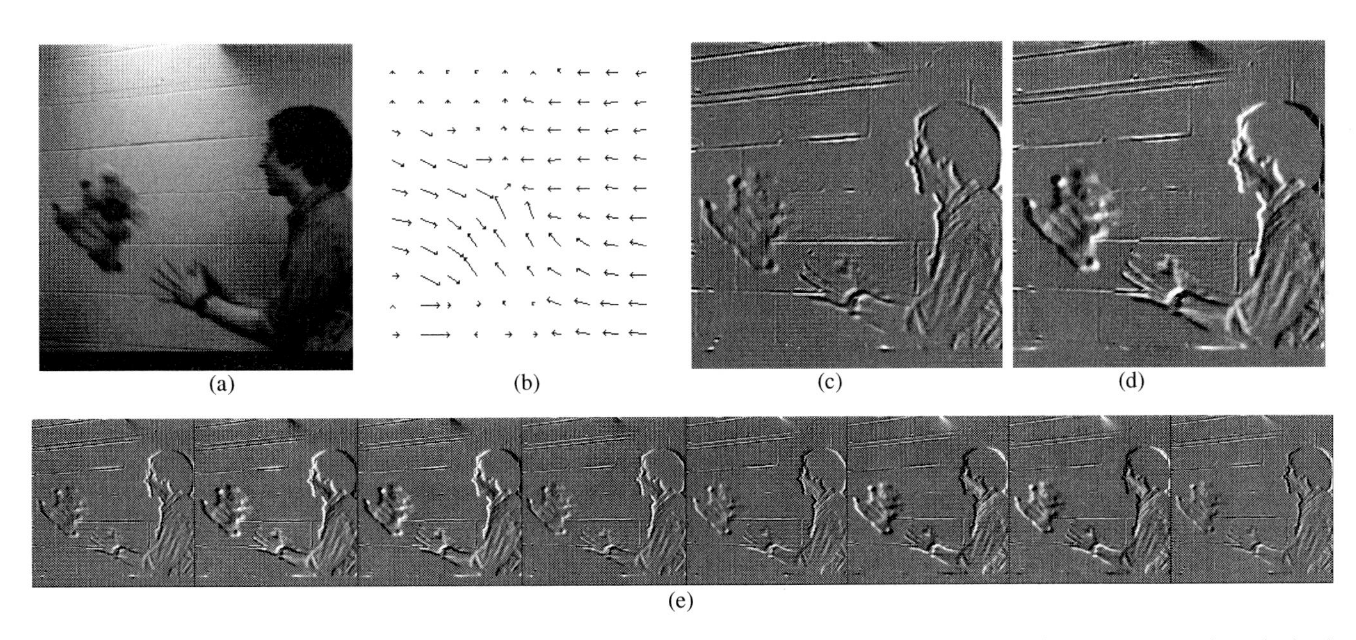

(a) (b) (c) (d)

(e)

Figure 4: Continuous display of instantaneous motion information. (a) single frame of video sequence. (b) instantaneous motion, obtained from (a) and the frame following it. Even (c) and odd (d) filtered images are combined using Eq. 5 to give the resulting image sequence (e).

## References


[1] S. Anstis. Luminance edges can kill motion. *Investigative Opthalmology and Visual Science Supplement*, page 426, 1989. (ARVO 1989).

[2] R. N. Bracewell. *The Fourier Transform and its Applications*. McGraw-Hill, 1978.

[3] W. T. Freeman and E. H. Adelson. Steerable filters for early vision, image analysis, and wavelet decomposition. In *Proc. 3rd Intl. Conf. Computer Vision*, Osaka, Japan, 1990. IEEE.

[4] W. T. Freeman and E. H. Adelson. The design and use of steerable filters for image analysis, enhancement, and multiscale representation. *IEEE Pat. Anal. Mach. Intell.*, 1991. Accepted for publication.

[5] D. J. Heeger, W. T. Freeman, and E. H. Adelson. Nude descending a staircase. In *Physics Art* at the California Museum of Science and Industry (Los Angeles, summer 1989), and in SIGGRAPH '90 Art Show (Dallas, August 1990).

[6] J. Lim. *Two-Dimensional Signal and Image Processing*. Prentice Hall, Englewood Cliffs, New Jersey, 1990.

[7] B. D. Lucas and T. Kanade. An iterative image registration technique with an application to stereo vision. In *Proc. Seventh IJCAI*, pages 674–679, Vancouver, 1981.

[8] M. Shadlen, T. Carney, and E. Switkes. Illusory rotation, expansion, and contraction from transitions in local symmetry. *Investigative Opthalmology and Visual Science Supplement*, page 300, 1987. (ARVO 1987).

[9] R. G. Shoup. Color table animation. In J. C. Beatty and K. S. Booth, editors, *Tutorial: Computer Graphics*, pages 214–219. IEEE Computer Society, Silver Spring, MD, 1982.

[10] K. Sims. Particle animation and rendering using data parallel computation. In *SIGGRAPH-90*, Dallas, 1990.

[11] A. R. Smith. Paint. In J. C. Beatty and K. S. Booth, editors, *Tutorial: Computer Graphics*, pages 501–515. IEEE Computer Society, Silver Spring, MD, 1982.


| | | |
|---|---|---|
| $G_{2a}$ | $=$ | $0.9213(2x^2-1)e^{-(x^2+y^2)}$ |
| $G_{2b}$ | $=$ | $1.843xye^{-(x^2+y^2)}$ |
| $G_{2c}$ | $=$ | $0.9213(2y^2-1)e^{-(x^2+y^2)}$ |
| $k_a(\theta)$ | $=$ | $\cos^2(\theta)$ |
| $k_b(\theta)$ | $=$ | $-2\cos(\theta)\sin(\theta)$ |
| $k_c(\theta)$ | $=$ | $\sin^2(\theta)$ |

Table 1: $X$-$Y$ separable basis set and interpolation functions for second derivative of Gaussian. To create a second derivative of a Gaussian rotated along to an angle $\theta$, use: $G_2^\theta = k_a(\theta)\,G_{2a} + k_b(\theta)\,G_{2b} + k_c(\theta)\,G_{2c}$.

| tap # | f1 | f2 | f3 |
|---|---|---|---|
| 0 | -0.9213 | 1.0 | 0.0 |
| 1 | -0.0601 | 0.6383 | 0.5806 |
| 2 | 0.3964 | 0.1660 | 0.3020 |
| 3 | 0.1148 | 0.0176 | 0.0480 |
| 4 | 0.0094 | 0.0008 | 0.0028 |

| $G_2$ basis filter | filter in $x$ | filter in $y$ |
|---|---|---|
| $G_{2a}$ | f1 | f2 |
| $G_{2b}$ | f3 | f3 |
| $G_{2c}$ | f2 | f1 |

Table 2: 9-tap filters for $x$-$y$ separable basis set for $G_2$. Filters f1 and f2 have even symmetry; f3 has odd symmetry. (The filter tap indices range from -4 to 4. For the even symmetric filters, tap[i] = tap[-i]; for the odd symmetric filter, tap[i] = -tap[-i]). These filters were taken from Table 1, with a sample spacing of 0.67. Use the $k(\theta)$ interpolation functions of Table 1.

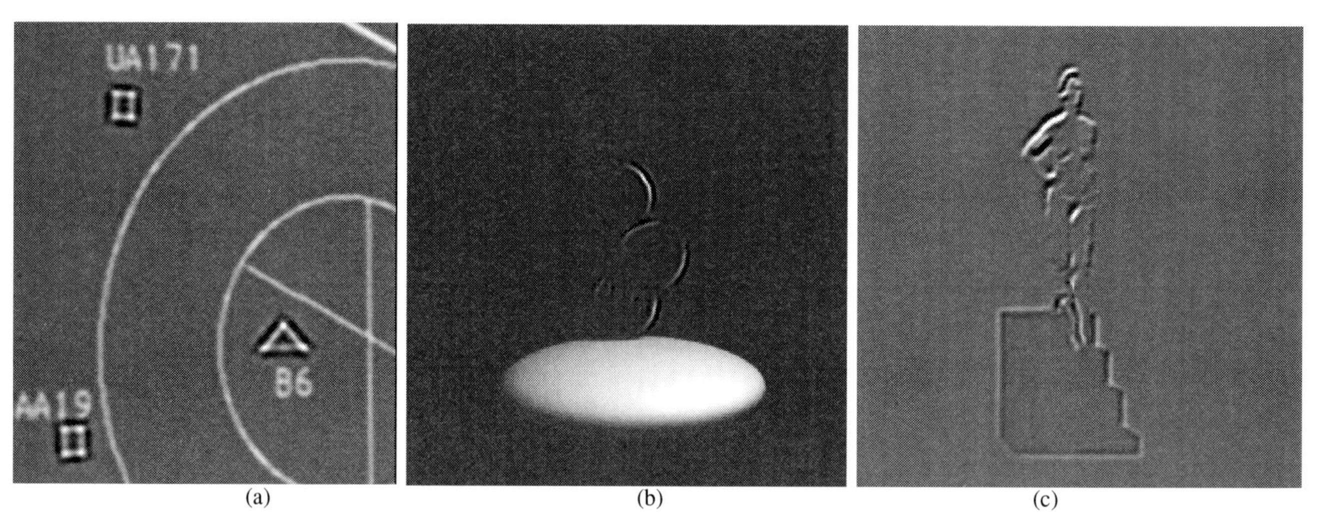


(a) (b) (c)

Figure 5: Single frames from several applications of motion without movement. (a) Air traffic controller display: the motion illusion is used to display airplane velocities, while maintaining the proper positions of the airplane symbols. (b) Display of instantaneous velocities of a physical simulation. (c) Computer art piece entitled "Nude Descending a Staircase"[5], after Duchamp.

| | | |
|---|---|---|
| $H_{2a}$ | $=$ | $0.9780(-2.254x + x^3)e^{-(x^2+y^2)}$ |
| $H_{2b}$ | $=$ | $0.9780(-.7515 + x^2)(y)e^{-(x^2+y^2)}$ |
| $H_{2c}$ | $=$ | $0.9780(-.7515 + y^2)(x)e^{-(x^2+y^2)}$ |
| $H_{2d}$ | $=$ | $0.9780(-2.254y + y^3)e^{-(x^2+y^2)}$ |
| $k_a(\theta)$ | $=$ | $\cos^3(\theta)$ |
| $k_b(\theta)$ | $=$ | $-3\cos^2(\theta)\sin(\theta)$ |
| $k_c(\theta)$ | $=$ | $3\cos(\theta)\sin^2(\theta)$ |
| $k_d(\theta)$ | $=$ | $-\sin^3(\theta)$ |

Table 3: $H_2$ basis set: $x$-$y$ separable basis set and interpolation functions for fit to Hilbert transform of second derivative of Gaussian. To synthesize a filter oriented along direction $\theta$, use: $H_2^\theta = k_a(\theta)H_{2a} + k_b(\theta)H_{2b} + k_c(\theta)H_{2c} + k_d(\theta)H_{2d}$.

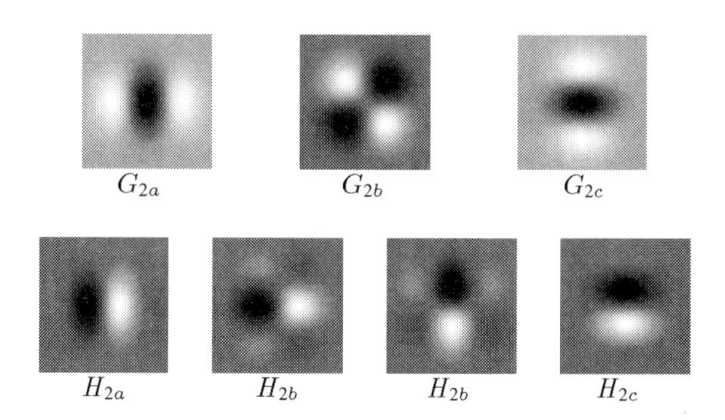


Figure 6: X-Y separable basis filters for $G_2$, listed in Tables 1 and 2, and $H_2$, listed in Tables 3 and 4.

| tap # | f1 | f2 | f3 | f4 |
|---|---|---|---|---|
| 0 | 0.0 | 1.0 | 0.0 | -0.7349 |
| 1 | -0.7551 | 0.6383 | 0.4277 | -0.1889 |
| 2 | -0.0998 | 0.1660 | 0.2225 | 0.1695 |
| 3 | 0.0618 | 0.0176 | 0.0354 | 0.0566 |
| 4 | 0.0098 | 0.0008 | 0.0020 | 0.0048 |

| $H_2$ basis filter | filter in $x$ | filter in $y$ |
|---|---|---|
| $H_{2a}$ | f1 | f2 |
| $H_{2b}$ | f4 | f3 |
| $H_{2c}$ | f3 | f4 |
| $H_{2d}$ | f2 | f1 |

Table 4: 9-tap filters for $x$-$y$ separable basis set for $H_2$. Filters for which tap 0 is 0.0 have odd symmetry about tap 0; the others have even symmetry. These filters were taken from Table 3, with a sample spacing of 0.67. Use the interpolation functions of Table 3.

# Coping with Friction for Non-penetrating Rigid Body Simulation

*David Baraff*

Program of Computer Graphics
Cornell University
Ithaca, NY 14853

**Abstract**

Algorithms and computational complexity measures for simulating the motion of contacting bodies with friction are presented. The bodies are restricted to be perfectly rigid bodies that contact at finitely many points. Contact forces between bodies must satisfy the Coulomb model of friction. A traditional principle of mechanics is that contact forces are impulsive if and only if non-impulsive contact forces are insufficient to maintain the non-penetration constraints between bodies. When friction is allowed, it is known that impulsive contact forces can be necessary even in the absence of collisions between bodies. This paper shows that computing contact forces according to this traditional principle is likely to require exponential time. An analysis of this result reveals that the principle for when impulses can occur is too restrictive, and a natural reformulation of the principle is proposed. Using the reformulated principle, an algorithm with expected polynomial time behavior for computing contact forces is presented.

Categories and Subject Descriptors: I.3.5 [**Computer Graphics**]: Computational Geometry and Object Modeling; I.3.7 [**Computer Graphics**]: Three-Dimensional Graphics and Realism

Additional Key Words and Phrases: dynamics, friction, simulation, *NP*-complete

## 1. Introduction

The synthesis of realistic motion is one of the goals of computer graphics. Recently, much attention has been given to physically based simulation methods, and in particular, rigid body simulation. To achieve realism, simulations must incorporate the effects of friction between contacting bodies. If the total number of contact points is small, for instance one to four, the effects of friction are easily computed. However, as the number of contact points grows, the problem becomes considerably more challenging. Simulation algorithms with exponential (in the number of contact points) running times are known[5] but are impractical for problems involving as few as 10 to 15 contact points. In order to make rigid body simulations with friction practical for computer graphics, efficient, polynomial time algorithms are needed.

This paper considers the problems of computing friction forces for configurations of perfectly rigid bodies with a finite number of contact points. For polyhedral bodies, only the vertices of the line segment and polygonal contact regions are considered as contact points. Unless otherwise stated, it is assumed that bodies are not colliding at any contact point. No restriction is placed on the allowable sliding motion between bodies at contact points. Forces at contact points are classified as either *normal* or *friction* forces. Normal forces prevent inter-penetration by acting perpendicularly to the contact surfaces. Friction forces act tangentially to the contact surfaces and oppose slipping motion. The friction force at a contact point is called *dynamic* friction if the two bodies are slipping at the contact point; otherwise, the friction force is called *static* friction. The contact forces (the normal and friction forces) must satisfy the Coulomb model of friction. The Coulomb model of friction is a well accepted empirical relationship between the normal and friction force at a contact point.



An important first step to coping with the problems of friction is understanding the simulation behavior specified by the Coulomb model of friction. We need to know both what kind of result the model specifies and the degree of difficulty in computing that result. When computing contact forces, a principle of rational mechanics called the *principle of constraints* [9] is usually accepted. The principle of constraints states that constraints should be satisfied by non-impulsive forces if possible; otherwise, impulsive forces should be used to satisfy constraints. (Impulsive forces, or impulses, have the units of mass times velocity and discontinuously change velocities; impulses most commonly arise when bodies collide. Non-impulsive forces, or just forces, have the units of mass times acceleration and cannot produce velocity discontinuities.) The first result of this paper is a proof that computing friction forces according to the principle of constraints is likely to require exponential time (section 5). Under the Coulomb friction model, even in the absence of collisions it is sometimes necessary to introduce impulses between contacting bodies to prevent inter-penetration. Adopting the principle of constraints requires that a particular behavior, non-impulsive contact forces, be searched for among possibly exponentially many other choices, whenever possible. In formal terms, we will prove that deciding if non-impulsive contact forces are sufficient to prevent inter-penetration is *NP*-complete. Essentially, this means that an efficient (that is, polynomial time) algorithm for computing contact forces is widely believed not to exist. (See Garey and Johnson[7] for a discussion on *P*, *NP*, *NP*-complete and *NP*-hard problems).

However, the preference for non-impulsive behavior is neither necessary nor justified. Using insights from the *NP*-completeness results of section 5, section 6 presents a physical model for contact that argues against the principle of constraints. We will use this model to reformulate the problem of computing contact forces. Using the reformulated problem, we present an efficient algorithmic simulation method for dealing with dynamic friction. The algorithm has an expected running time that is polynomial in the number of contact points of the configuration. This is the first efficient algorithm we know of for computing dynamic friction forces.

As a first step towards dealing with both static and dynamic friction, we present two preliminary approaches for computing static and dynamic friction forces (section 8). The first approach approximates both static and dynamic friction by using the general algorithm for dynamic friction. The second approach uses an iterative technique to compute static and dynamic friction forces; however, convergence is not guaranteed.

## 2. Definitions

For configurations without friction, a *valid* set of contact forces is a set of normal forces satisfying three conditions. First, the normal force at each contact point must be oriented to "push" the bodies apart. Second, the normal forces must be sufficient to prevent inter-penetration between bodies. Third, if two bodies are separating at a contact point, the normal force at the contact point must be zero. For configurations without friction, a valid set of contact forces exists for any configuration of bodies. Although a valid set of contact forces is not necessarily unique for frictionless configurations, all valid contact forces yield the same accelerations of the bodies in the configuration[4]. Contact forces for frictionless configurations with $n$ contact points can be found by formulating and solving a convex quadratic program (QP) of $n$ variables. Methods for formulating this QP for bodies composed of polyhedra and curved surfaces have been presented in [1,2,6,11]. Convex QP's with $n$ variables can be solved in time polynomial to $n$ and in practice are solved by algorithms whose worst case behavior is exponential but whose expected running time is polynomial[14].

Configurations with friction are more complicated. Contact forces with friction are valid if they satisfy both the previous three conditions for normal forces and the Coulomb friction model (sections 4 and 8). Valid contact forces for configurations with just dynamic friction (and no static friction) can be found, as in the frictionless case, by computing the solution to a QP. Unlike the frictionless case though, the QP associated with a configuration involving dynamic friction is not necessarily convex. The existence of a practical solution method for non-convex QP's is considered unlikely, because solving non-convex QP's is $NP$-hard.

Additionally, it is possible that the QP for a configuration with dynamic friction may not even have a solution. Although the Coulomb friction model is well accepted, it has been known for at least a century that configurations of rigid bodies with dynamic friction exist that have no valid set of contact forces. We call such a configuration *inconsistent*. Conversely, there are also configurations with dynamic friction where neither the set of valid contact forces nor the accelerations resulting from those contact forces are unique. Such a configuration is called *indeterminate*. (See sections 4.1 and 4.2).

## 3. Previous Work

Wang and Mason[16] present a detailed discussion on single contact point collisions involving friction; in particular, methods for computing the contact impulse resulting from the collision are described. (We will not consider the general problem of collisions involving friction in this paper). Mason and Wang[13] discuss inconsistent configurations and explain how to resolve the inconsistency by applying impulsive contact forces to the configuration. However, it is first necessary to identify configurations as inconsistent. As we will show, this turns out to be a difficult problem.

A paper by Lötstedt[11] discusses a simulation method that avoids inconsistency by modification of the friction law. Lötstedt's method changes the Coulomb model into a relation between normal forces from the *previous* time step and friction forces from the current time step. Lötstedt's method approximates both dynamic and static friction by solving a convex QP. It is not clear that Lötstedt's method can always be initialized so that it is numerically stable. It is also unclear how to perform such an initialization efficiently.

## 4. Contact Force Model

We begin by considering configurations with only dynamic friction. Static friction is not considered until section 8. This section introduces a special-case of a single contact point configuration (figure 1). This configuration, and minor variations of it, will be used several times throughout this paper.

In figure 1, body $A$ is a thin rod of length two with a symmetric mass distribution that contacts body $B$ at a single contact point. Body $B$ (the "base") is fixed.

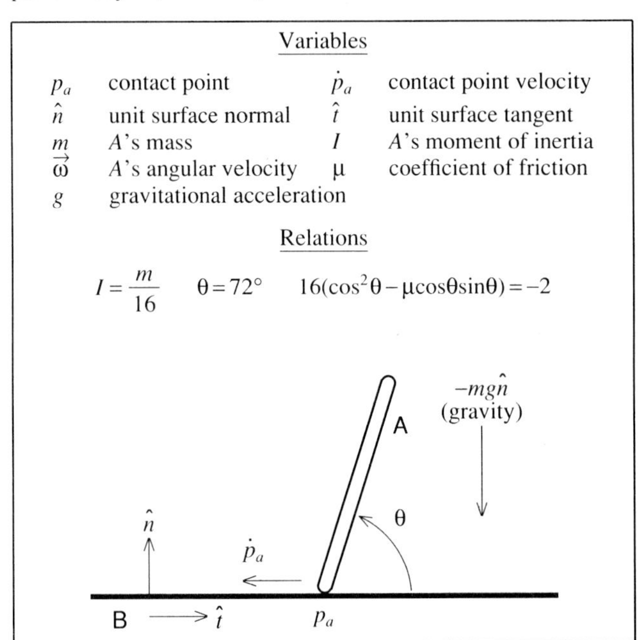


**Figure 1. A one contact point configuration with dynamic friction between a thin rod $A$ and a fixed base $B$.**

By choosing $A$'s angular velocity $\vec{\omega}$ and the magnitude $g$ of the gravity force $-mg\hat{n}$ acting on $A$, an indeterminate and an inconsistent configuration can be produced. This particular example can be found in a number of papers; for example, Lötstedt[10], Erdmann[5], or Mason and Wang[13].

For a given value of $\vec{\omega}$, the linear velocity of $A$ is chosen such that the point $p_a$ on $A$ has a non-zero velocity tangent to $B$, and zero velocity normal to $B$. The unit vector $\hat{n}$ is normal to the surface of $B$. The unit vector $\hat{t}$ is tangent to the surface of $B$, and is directed opposite to the motion of the point $p_a$; $\hat{n}$ and $\hat{t}$ are perpendicular. The particular values of $I$, $\theta$ and $\mu$ ($\mu \approx 3/4$) given in figure 1 are somewhat arbitrary; these values are chosen to simplify later computations.

The Coulomb model of friction states that since $p_a$ is sliding across $B$, a friction force in the direction $\hat{t}$ acts on $A$. (An equal and opposite friction force acts on $B$, but $B$ is fixed.) If the normal force acting on $A$ has magnitude $f$, then the Coulomb friction model states that the friction force has a magnitude of $\mu f$ (figure 2). The net contact force acting on $A$ is

$$f\hat{n} + \mu f\hat{t} = f(\hat{n} + \mu\hat{t}). \quad (1)$$

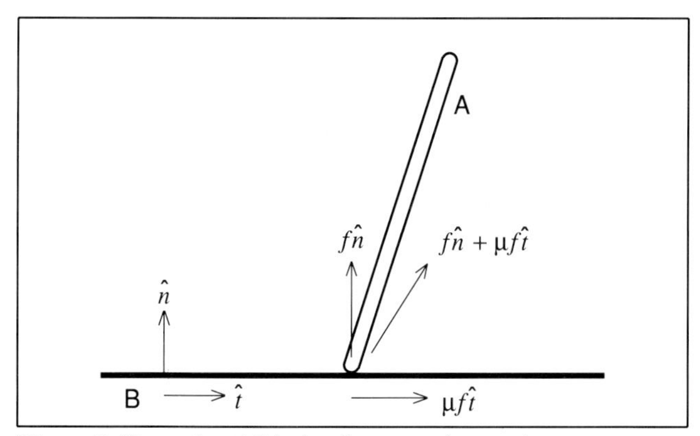


**Figure 2. Normal and friction forces acting on $A$.**

What effect do the contact and external force $-mg\hat{n}$ have on $A$? In appendix A, the component of acceleration of the point $p_a$, normal to $B$, is found to be

$$\hat{n}\cdot\ddot{p}_a = -\frac{f}{m} + (|\vec{\omega}|^2\sin\theta - g). \tag{2}$$

This configuration has the odd property that as the normal force magnitude $f$ is *increased*, the point $p_a$ is accelerated more strongly *towards* $B$! Geometrically, the *direction* of the net contact force $f(\hat{n}+\mu\hat{t})$ does not change as $f$ is increased. However, as $f$ is increased, the torque due to friction causes $p_a$ to angularly accelerate downward. The normal force $f\hat{n}$ also causes the center of mass of $A$, and thus $p_a$, to accelerate upwards, but not fast enough to overcome the downwards acceleration due to the torque. The net result is that increasing $f$ decreases the value of $\hat{n}\cdot\ddot{p}_a$. (See appendix A for details).

### 4.1 An Indeterminate Configuration

To produce an indeterminate configuration, let $\vec{\omega}$ and $g$ satisfy $|\vec{\omega}|^2\sin\theta - g = 1$. Then equation (2) becomes

$$\hat{n}\cdot\ddot{p}_a = -\frac{f}{m} + 1. \tag{3}$$

Recall that valid contact forces satisfy three conditions. The first condition, that the normal force "push" bodies apart is simply $f \geq 0$. The second condition, that contact forces prevent inter-penetration, requires the acceleration of $p_a$ in the $\hat{n}$ direction to be non-negative. This yields the constraint $\hat{n}\cdot\ddot{p}_a \geq 0$. The last condition is that if the bodies are separating, the normal force must be zero. Since the bodies are separating if and only if $\hat{n}\cdot\ddot{p}_a$ is strictly positive, this condition may be written as $f\hat{n}\cdot\ddot{p}_a = 0$. For $|\vec{\omega}|^2\sin\theta - g = 1$ and using equation (2), the above three conditions are

$$f \geq 0,\ -\frac{f}{m} + 1 \geq 0 \text{ and } f(-\frac{f}{m} + 1) = 0. \tag{4}$$

The valid contact forces are given by the solution of equation (4); $f = 0$ and $f = m$.

For the $f = 0$ solution, $\hat{n}\cdot\ddot{p}_a = 1$. In this solution, the centripetal acceleration of $\ddot{p}_a$ is stronger than the force of gravity pulling $A$ down; thus, $A$ merely continues its rotation and the point $p_a$ moves off of $B$ (figure 3a).

In the second solution, $f = m$ and $\hat{n}\cdot\ddot{p}_a = 0$. A normal force of $m\hat{n}$ and a friction force of $\mu m\hat{t}$ act on $A$. The torque generated by friction balances the centripetal acceleration of $p_a$; as a result, $A$ and $B$ do not break contact (figure 3b). Note that the *only* valid values of $f$ are $f = 0$ or $f = m$. Since the solutions produce different accelerations for $A$, the configuration is indeterminate.

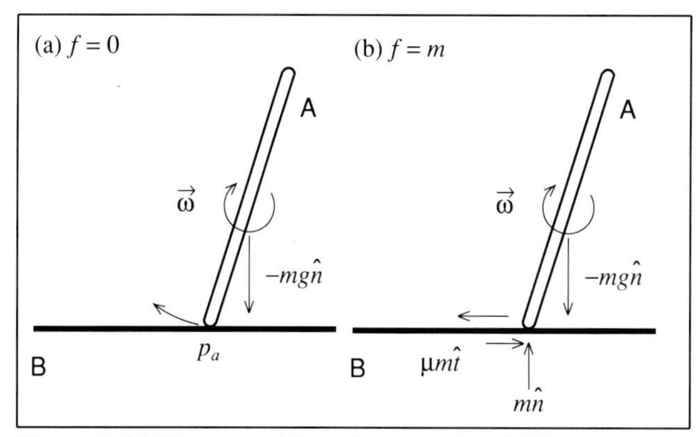


**Figure 3. (a) The contact force between $A$ and $B$ is zero. $p_a$ rotates to the left and up, breaking contact with $B$. (b) The normal and friction forces balance gravity and centripetal acceleration; $p_a$ moves horizontally and maintains contact with $B$.**

### 4.2 An Inconsistent Configuration

Now suppose that $|\vec{\omega}| = 0$ and $A$'s linear velocity $\vec{v}$ is opposite $\hat{t}$ (figure 4). Then the condition $\hat{n}\cdot\ddot{p}_a \geq 0$ is

$$\hat{n}\cdot\ddot{p}_a = -\frac{f}{m} - g \geq 0. \tag{5}$$

However, if $g > 0$ (figure 4a), then no positive value of $f$ can prevent $p_a$ from accelerating downwards and thus inter-penetrating; that is, equation (5) cannot be satisfied by any $f > 0$. This means that the configuration is inconsistent. The existence of such a configuration may seem counter-intuitive; however, we will have more to say on this phenomenon in section 6.1.

Note that the value of $g$ is crucial. If $g = 0$, so that no external force acts on $A$, then $f = 0$ becomes the (unique) valid contact force (figure 4b). Any positive value of $f$ for this configuration causes inter-penetration. Figure 4b corresponds to $p_a$ "skimming" horizontally over $B$, with neither a normal force nor a friction force exerted on $A$. If $g$ becomes even slightly positive however, the configuration is inconsistent. Note that the requirement that $B$ be fixed is not crucial. If $B$ is massive compared to $A$, then inconsistency occurs if an external force acts on $A$ to accelerate it towards $B$, or vice versa.

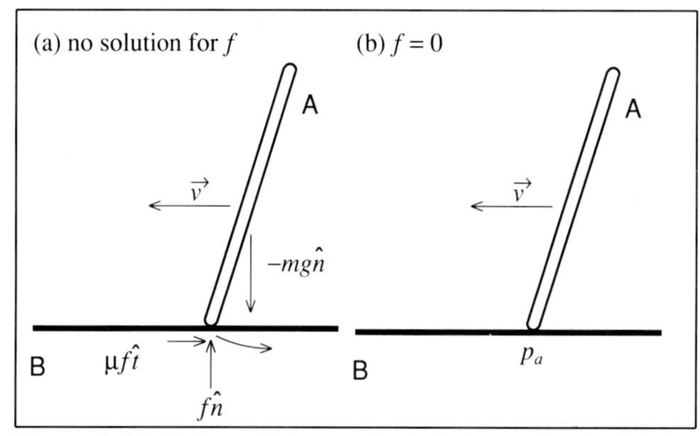


**Figure 4. (a) An inconsistent configuration. For any $f \geq 0$, $p_a$ is accelerated downwards into $B$. (b) The configuration has a unique solution of $f = 0$ when gravity is removed; $A$ skims along the surface of $B$.**

## 5. An *NP*-complete Class of Configurations

We define the *frictional consistency* problem as the problem of deciding if a given configuration is consistent. In this section, we prove that the frictional consistency problem is *NP*-complete. We begin by showing that the frictional consistency problem lies in *NP* and then show that the frictional consistency problem is *NP*-hard. Although the configurations constructed in this section seem contrived (and arguably are), the *NP*-hardness result has grave implications even when inconsistency is not a concern during simulation.

**Definition**. *An instance of the frictional consistency problem is a configuration* C *of bodies that contact at* n *distinct contact points. The physical properties of each body (mass, moment of inertia, linear and angular velocity, position and orientation, and external forces) are described by rational numbers. The specifics of a contact point (position, coefficient of friction, surface normal) are also described by rational numbers. The relative motion between bodies at contact points with friction is non-zero in the direction tangent to the contact surface and zero in the direction normal to the contact surface. The notation* $|C| = k$ *means that configuration* C *is describable in* k *bits. Clearly* $k > n$.

**Theorem 1**. *The frictional consistency problem lies in NP.*

**Proof**. Given an instance of $C$, a QP of size $n$ with the following two properties exists. (1) If $C$ is consistent, then an $n$-vector $\vec{x}$ that is a solution to the QP exists. The set of contact forces such that the magnitude of the normal force at the $i$th contact point is $x_i$ is a valid set of contact forces for the configuration $C$. (2) Otherwise, if $C$ is inconsistent, the QP has no solution. The specifics of constructing the QP can be found in [6]. The numerical quantities in the QP are computed from the rational entries of $C$ in a total of $O(n^3)$ arithmetical operations. The QP can therefore be constructed in time polynomial to $k$. Vavasis[15] has recently shown that quadratic programming lies in *NP*. It follows from this that deciding frictional consistency is also in *NP*. ∎

In order to show that deciding frictional consistency is *NP*-hard, we reduce the *NP*-complete problem "subset sum" to the frictional consistency problem.

**Definition**. *An instance of the subset sum problem is a pair* (A,S) *where* $A = \{a_1, \cdots, a_n\}$ *is a set of positive integers and* S *is a single positive integer. A subset sum instance* (A,S) *is* satisfiable *if there exists a subset* $A' \subset A$ *such that*

$$\sum_{a \in A'} a = S. \tag{6}$$

*Deciding if an instance of the subset sum problem is satisfiable is an NP*-complete *problem*[7].

To show that deciding frictional consistency is *NP*-hard we take an arbitrary instance $(A,S)$ of the subset sum problem and construct (in polynomial time) a configuration of bodies $C$. The configuration $C$ will have the property that $C$ is consistent if and only if $(A,S)$ is satisfiable.

**Theorem 2**. *Deciding frictional consistency is NP*-hard.

**Proof**. Consider the configuration of figure 5. Body $B$ of figure 5 is initially at rest and is positioned by four fixed triangular wedges that contact $B$ without friction. Body $B$ is therefore free to move horizontally, but can neither rotate nor move vertically. On either side of body $B$ are thin rods $E_1$ and $E_2$. $E_1$ and $E_2$ have no angular velocity and have a linear velocity as indicated. $E_1$ and $E_2$ contact $B$ in the same manner as the configuration of figure 4 (although the frames of reference for $E_1$ and $E_2$ are rotated by 90° with respect to figure 4). In figure 4, inconsistency occurred if external forces accelerated $A$ towards $B$ or vice versa. The same holds true for figure 5. If $B$ has an acceleration leftwards

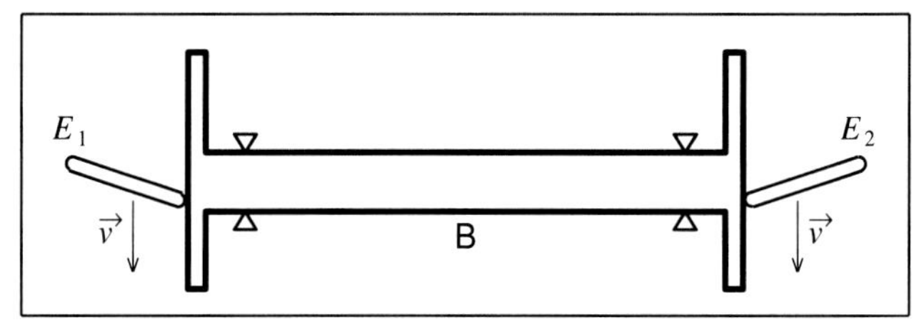


**Figure 5. $B$ is constrained by the fixed wedges and can only move horizontally. However, the configuration is consistent only if $B$ is not subject to a net horizontal force.**

(towards $E_1$), then inconsistency occurs. Likewise, if $B$ has an acceleration rightwards (towards $E_2$), then inconsistency also occurs. Thus, the configuration of figure 5 is consistent only if the net horizontal acceleration of $B$ is zero. In this case, the rods $E_1$ and $E_2$ skim along the surface of $B$ as in figure 4b.

Now consider figure 6, where a collection of thin rods $R_1, \cdots, R_n$ have been added. In addition, an external horizontal force with magnitude $\mu S$ acts on $B$, trying to accelerate $B$ to the right. Each rod $R_i$ has mass $m_i$. The configuration between each rod $R_i$ and $B$ is the same as the configuration of figure 3; thus each rod $R_i$ has angular velocity $\vec{\omega}$ and is subject to an external gravity force. Let $f_i$ be the magnitude of the normal force between $R_i$ and $B$. As in figure 3, the only valid solutions for $f_i$ are $f_i = 0$ and $f_i = m_i$. If $f_i = 0$, then no friction force acts between $R_i$ and $B$. Otherwise, $f_i = m_i$ and a friction force of magnitude $\mu m_i$ acts between $R_i$ and $B$. The friction force pushes $R_i$ to the right and $B$ to the left, with magnitude $\mu m_i$. The friction force on $B$ therefore acts to oppose the external force of magnitude $\mu S$.

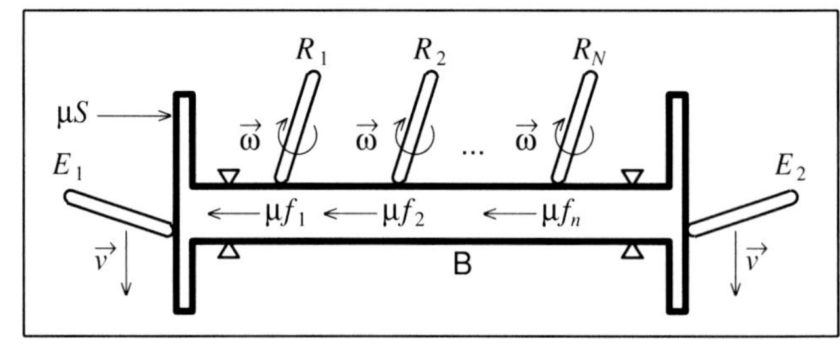


**Figure 6. The configuration is consistent if and only if the friction forces on $B$ sum to $\mu S$.**

In order for the configuration of figure 6 to be consistent, $B$ must have no net horizontal acceleration. This means that the friction forces exerted on $B$ from the $n$ rods must sum to $\mu S$, balancing the external force applied to $B$. Thus, the configuration is consistent if and only if

$$\sum_{i=1}^{n} \mu f_i = \mu S. \tag{7}$$

Since each $f_i$ is either 0 or $m_i$, the configuration is consistent if and only if some subset of $\{m_1, \cdots, m_n\}$ sums to $S$.

We can now perform the reduction from subset sum to show *NP*-hardness. Given any set $A = \{a_1, \cdots, a_n\}$ and any target sum $S$, construct the configuration of figure 6. Assign $m_i = a_i$ for $1 \le i \le n$, and let an external horizontal force of $\mu S$ act on $B$ as shown in figure 6. By the above discussion, the configuration is consistent if and only if there exists a subset of $\{m_1, \cdots, m_n\}$ that sums to $S$. But since $A = \{m_1, \cdots, m_n\}$, the configuration is consistent if and only if $(A,S)$ is satisfiable. We conclude that the problem of deciding frictional consistency is *NP*-hard. ∎

**Theorem 3.** *Deciding frictional consistency is $NP$-complete.*

**Proof.** The result follows immediately from Theorem 1 and Theorem 2. ∎

**Corollary 1.** *Computing contact forces (if they exist) for a configuration is $NP$-hard.*

**Proof.** Since deciding if a set of contact forces exists is an $NP$-complete problem, computing the contact forces (if they exist) is an $NP$-hard problem. ∎

### 5.1 Implications

At this point, it may seem that the above results, while possibly of some (marginal) theoretical interest, have no bearing on any practical problem. Certainly, the above configurations were carefully constructed to produce configurations whose consistency was difficult to determine. But how likely is it that a configuration this carefully constructed could occur during simulation? For that matter, suppose the occurrence of *any* inconsistent configuration is so unlikely that the possibility can be completely disregarded. (This may be a reasonable assumption. We have not encountered an inconsistent configuration during simulation when $\mu < 1$.) Can a polynomial time algorithm that computes contact forces only for consistent configurations be constructed? The answer to this is no, unless it turns out that $P$ and $NP$ are equivalent, and it is widely believed that they are not.

**Corollary 2.** *A polynomial time algorithm for computing valid contact forces for consistent configurations exists if and only if $P = NP$.*

**Proof.** Suppose that $P = NP$. Since quadratic programming lies in $NP$, $P = NP$ implies a polynomial time algorithm for finding the solution to a QP. Since valid contact forces for a consistent configuration of bodies can be found by solving an associated QP, valid contact forces are computable in polynomial time if $P = NP$.

Conversely, suppose that contact forces for consistent configurations can be computed in polynomial time. Then there exists a machine $M$ and a polynomial $p$ with the following behavior. Whenever $M$ is given a consistent configuration $C$ as input, $M$ outputs a valid set of contact forces within time $p(|C|)$. $M$'s behavior when $C$ is inconsistent is undefined. Given *any* configuration $C$, not necessarily consistent, $M$ can be used to decide consistency in polynomial time as follows.

Let $C$ be input to $M$ and run for $p(|C|)$ time. If $M$ fails to output within this time, then $C$ is inconsistent. Otherwise, $M$ has produced some output. Since deciding frictional consistency is in $NP$, the validity of $M$'s output can be decided in an additional amount of time that is also a polynomial function of $|C|$. If $M$'s output is a valid set of contact forces, then clearly $C$ is consistent. If $M$'s output is invalid, then $C$ must be inconsistent (else $M$ would have output a valid answer). In any event, the consistency of $C$ has been decided in polynomial time.

Since deciding consistency is $NP$-complete, we conclude that the existence of a polynomial time algorithm for computing contact forces on consistent configurations would imply that $P = NP$. ∎

Given the above conclusions, it is unlikely that an efficient algorithm for computing contact forces can be found. This depressing result can be viewed in several ways. First, the simulation of rigid bodies with friction can be considered an intractable problem, unless the number of contact points with friction in a configuration is small. Second, the general simulation problem can be rejected as being too difficult a problem, although we might hope to find some natural class of configurations with friction for which contact forces can be computed efficiently. Such a class would have to be sufficiently general to cover situations likely to be encountered in practice. Third, heuristic methods for computing contact forces can be considered. However, this is essentially the same as hoping to find a natural class of configurations with easily computed contact forces. Rather than adopt any of these viewpoints, the next section presents a physical model of inconsistency that leads to a natural reformulation of the problem of computing contact forces.

## 6. Physical Models

In this section, a physical model for both inconsistency and indeterminacy is presented. Certainly, other models are possible, and a different choice of model might lead to different conclusions and results. The model in this section was developed in order to understand the behavior of inconsistent and indeterminate configurations. After the model was developed, we found that the model leads to a natural refutation of the principle of constraints. By abandoning this principle, the problem of computing contact forces is naturally reformulated and a correspondingly efficient way of computing contact forces is found. The model in this section is *not* an *ad hoc* attempt at dealing with friction. We feel that the model is not unreasonably based on the physical properties of rigid bodies, and sensible in the context of simulating rigid bodies with friction. The model and subsequent reformulation of the problem is presented in this section. In the next section, a computational algorithm is presented for solving the reformulated problem.

The motivation of a physical model stems from the need to answer the following basic question: what should be the result of a simulation when inconsistency is encountered? For inconsistent configurations, such as figure 4a, the only resolution is the introduction of an impulsive contact force at $p_a$[9, 13]. Impulses, however, arise from collisions between bodies. Given the fact that $p_a$ has no velocity normal to $B$ (so that $A$ and $B$ do not appear to be colliding), why should an impulse be applied between $A$ and $B$? We answer this by presenting our physical model of inconsistency.

The physical model we present is based on questioning the rigid body assumption. In the physical world, there is of course no such thing as a perfectly rigid body. For near rigid bodies, contact forces arise as a result of small elastic deformations in the neighborhood of the contact area. Rather than geometrically model deformations, we shall (conceptually) allow bodies to inter-penetrate slightly, and consider a deformation in the contact surfaces proportional to the amount of inter-penetration. (We do not of course imagine that real bodies actually inter-penetrate). As the inter-penetration depth increases, a restoring normal force acts to oppose the inter-penetration. This is the so called "penalty method", a simulation method that models contact between bodies as spring and damper systems. The normal force between two bodies is zero when the amount of inter-penetration is zero, and increases monotonically as the inter-penetration increases. Typically, the normal force is modeled as a linear spring force $-Kd$, where $K$ is the spring constant and $d$ is the amount of inter-penetration. Although this is a very useful conceptual model, it is not well suited to simulation of very rigid bodies[1, 3]. We will use the penalty method to conceptually model inconsistency and indeterminacy, but we will *not* use the penalty method as a simulation technique.

### 6.1 A Model of Inconsistency

Figure 7 shows the behavior of the inconsistent configuration of 4a when the penalty method is applied. At time $t_0$, consider the tip of the rod, $p_a$, to be resting exactly on $B$, with zero inter-penetration. Since there is no inter-penetration, the normal force is zero. Even though $p_a$ is sliding along $B$, the friction

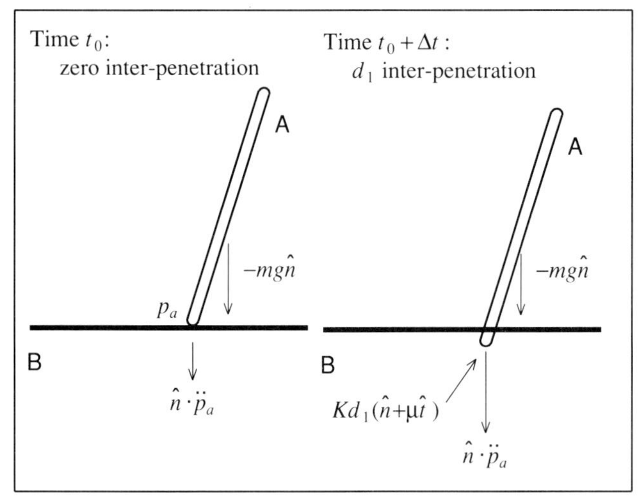


**Figure 7. At time $t_0$, only gravity acts on $A$. At time $t_0+\Delta t$, the inter-penetration distance is $d_1$ and both a penalty and a gravity force act on $A$, causing $p_a$'s downwards acceleration to increase.**

force is zero since the normal force is zero. Since the only force acting on $A$ is the external gravity force $-mg\hat{n}$, $p_a$ accelerates downwards. At time $t_0+\Delta t$, $p_a$ has inter-penetrated $B$ by an amount $d_1$, so a normal force $Kd_1\hat{n}$ acts on $A$. Since $p_a$ is still sliding, a friction force of $\mu K d_1 \hat{t}$ also acts on $A$. The net result, from equation (2), is that this causes $p_a$ to accelerate downwards even faster than before. As the penalty force continues to increase, it causes more inter-penetration between $A$ and $B$; a form of positive feedback. Accordingly, both the friction and the normal force increase, and the cycle continues. Since we are trying to model $A$ and $B$ as rigid bodies, the spring constant $K$ must be allowed to be arbitrarily large. (It is this feature that makes the penalty method ill-suited to rigid body simulation). The larger $K$ is, the faster inter-penetration increases and the faster the normal and friction forces build.

Recall that the friction force opposes the sliding motion of $A$ across $B$. By making $K$ arbitrarily large, the friction force brings $p_a$ to rest (horizontally) in an arbitrarily short time. Now, suppose $K$ is adjusted so that $p_a$ comes to rest within time $\Delta t$. Then the amount of inter-penetration is $O(\Delta t^2)$, since the vertical distance traveled by $p_a$ depends quadratically on the time for which it travels. In the limit as $K$ goes to infinity, the contact force on $A$ acts as an impulse and instantaneously brings $p_a$ to rest horizontally, without inter-penetration occurring. This impulse also causes $p_a$ to acquire a normal velocity towards $B$, bringing them into colliding contact. The (second) impulse resulting from this colliding contact can be computed according to [16].

Once $p_a$ is at rest horizontally, dynamic friction is replaced by static friction. The Coulomb friction model states that the magnitude $f_{static}$ of static friction satisfies $f_{static} \le \mu f$ whereas $f_{dynamic} = \mu f$ for dynamic friction. (Actually, $\mu$ is typically larger for static friction than dynamic friction, but this has no bearing on the model being developed.) Because static friction is less constrained than dynamic friction, once static friction occurs, a valid solution exists and the inconsistency is removed.

### 6.2 A Model of Indeterminacy

Consider the indeterminate configuration of figure 3, which has solutions $f=0$ and $f=m$. Using the penalty method, the indeterminacy can be removed by assuming some amount of initial inter-penetration between $A$ and $B$. If the initial inter-penetration between $A$ and $B$ is zero (figure 8) then no normal

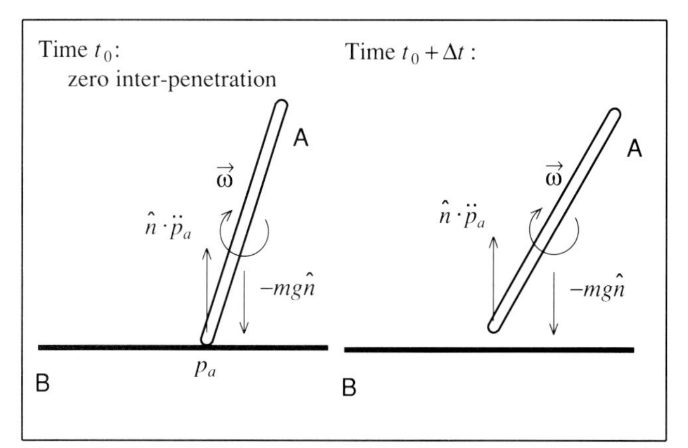


**Figure 8. The initial inter-penetration is zero and only gravity acts on $A$. The centripetal acceleration of $A$ pulls $p_a$ away from $B$ and contact is broken.**

force exists, and contact is immediately broken (due to the centripetal acceleration of $p_a$ away from $B$). The behavior is the same as in figure 3a. However, if the initial inter-penetration produces a normal force magnitude of $m$, then the normal and friction forces prevent $A$ from breaking contact with $B$. In figure 9, let the initial inter-penetration $d_1$ be $\frac{m}{K}$.

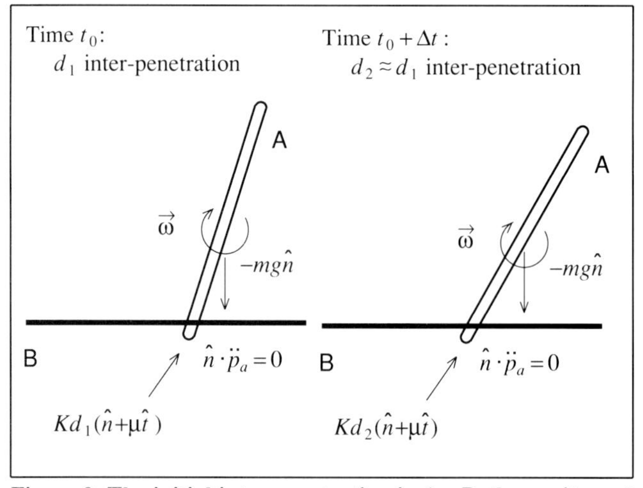


**Figure 9. The initial inter-penetration is $d_1$. Both gravity and a penalty force act on $A$. $A$ slides and falls without breaking contact with $B$.**

Then the normal force magnitude at time $t_0$ is $m$. Since $p_a$ is sliding on $B$, a friction force acts on $A$ as shown. As $A$ falls, maintaining contact with $B$, the inter-penetration varies smoothly, produce a varying normal force. At time $t_0+\Delta t$, $A$ still inter-penetrates $B$ by an amount $d_1 \approx d_2$, and the behavior of the configuration is that of figure 3b. Thus, the initial amount of inter-penetration determines which behavior occurs.

The simulation method of computing and applying contact forces and impulses to bodies does not model inter-penetration. Instead of determining behavior by initial choice of inter-penetration, we can consider an initial normal force between bodies at contact points, and use that to determine subsequent behavior. For the applications we are interested in, we generally have no basis for preferring one set of initial normal forces over another. The numerical routines used for solving the contact force equations arbitrarily determine the behavior simulated. This may or may not be sensible for other applications.

### 6.3 The Principle of Constraints

The principle of constraints, applied to configurations with friction, states the following: when computing forces for a configuration of bodies, impulsive forces should be used only if non-impulsive forces do not exist for the configuration. In other words, if a configuration is consistent, non-impulsive forces should be computed and applied to the configuration; otherwise impulsive forces must be introduced into the system. Initially, this seems like a sensible principle, but we know of no real justification for it. If the physical model presented in this section is adopted, then this principle must be abandoned (at least in the context of rigid body simulation).

Consider figure 10. Once again, the combination of gravity and the angular velocity of $R_1$ is the same as in figures 5 and 6. Similarly, a horizontal acceleration of $B$ results in inconsistency.

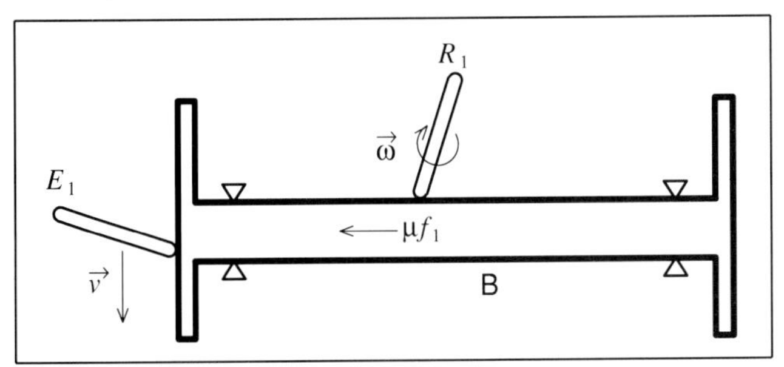


**Figure 10. $f_1$ must be either 0 or $m_1$ to be valid. However, $f_1 = m_1$ causes inconsistency. The only valid solution is $f_1 = 0$.**

If $E_1$ is ignored for the moment, then both $f_1 = 0$ and $f_1 = m_1$ are valid solutions for $f_1$. The only solution for the configuration as a whole though, is $f_1 = 0$; $f_1 = m_1$ pushes $B$ to the left, causing inconsistency. However, using the physical model of indeterminacy, the value $f_1$ assumes depends on the initial inter-penetration between $R_1$ and $B$. If we adopt the physical model presented, we must conclude the following: even though the configuration is consistent, there is no *a priori* reason to prefer impulse-free behavior to non-impulse-free behavior for this configuration. The inconsistency resulting from $f_1 = m_1$, and subsequent application of impulsive contact forces is *as acceptable a behavior* as the application of non-impulsive contact forces resulting from $f_1 = 0$. Even though the configuration in figure 10 has only one valid solution of contact forces, ($f_1 = 0$), it has two possible behaviors and is thus indeterminate.

### 6.4 Reformulating the Contact Force Problem

Up to now, we have viewed the problem of computing valid contact forces as: given a configuration, efficiently compute a valid set of contact forces, *if they exist*. This viewpoint is based on the principle of constraints; that is, impulsive forces should be applied if and only if the configuration is inconsistent. It is this absolute *insistence* on a non-impulsive solution, if it exists, that makes the problem of computing contact forces so difficult. However, now that we have abandoned the principle of constraints, a different viewpoint of the problem is possible.

We reformulate the problem of computing contact forces as: given a configuration, efficiently compute *either* a valid set of contact forces *or* a valid set of contact impulses. (Validity for contact impulses is defined in section 7). Under the physical model we have assumed, there is no intrinsic reason to prefer valid contact forces over valid contact impulses.

By computing a particular set of valid contact forces or impulses, a particular behavior is chosen for the configuration, and other possible behaviors ignored. This means that we do not bother to decide if a configuration is consistent or not. If a valid set of contact impulses are computed, it will not be known if the configuration was consistent and could have been solved with contact forces; however, this is unimportant. In the next section, an efficient method is presented for computing valid contact forces or impulses.

## 7. Computing Valid Contact Forces and Impulses

Before an efficient method for computing either contact forces or impulses can be considered, the definition of validity must be extended to cover contact impulses. We first define validity for contact impulses and then present a computational algorithm.

### 7.1 Valid Contact Impulses

In the penalty method interpretation of figure 7, an impulse occurred because no matter how strong the normal force became, it was insufficient to prevent inter-penetration. As a result, after the contact impulse was applied, the relative velocity of the bodies at the contact point was directed inwards. Since contact impulses may need to be applied to configurations involving more than one contact point, validity must be defined for a set of contact impulses. For example, in figure 10, if the $f_1 = m_1$ behavior is chosen, a contact impulse should occur between $E_1$ and $B$. However, there should be no contact impulse between $R_1$ and $B$. In order for our definition of validity to be useful, all inconsistent configurations should have a valid set of contact impulses. We show in section 7.2 that our definition of validity for contact impulses satisfies this requirement.

We call a set of contact impulses valid under the following two conditions. First, the contact impulses must convert at least one of the contact points with dynamic friction to static friction. Second, every contact point at which a contact impulse occurs must end up with a non-positive relative normal velocity; that is, after the contact impulses are applied, bodies should *not* be separating wherever contact impulses occurred. The justification for this is that the contact impulses occur only when the normal force grows without bound to oppose inter-penetration. Intuitively, valid contact impulses are the limiting result of increasing normal forces without bound under the penalty method. If bodies are separating at a contact point after contact impulses are applied, then the normal force at the contact point should not have grown without bound into a contact impulse. As in section 6.1, bodies will be colliding at some contact points after valid contact impulses are applied, and a secondary set of impulses will have to be applied. These impulses may be calculated according to [16].

### 7.2 Computing Contact Forces and Impulses with Lemke's Algorithm

How can either contact forces or impulses be computed efficiently, given that computing contact forces alone is hard? In section 3, it was stated that every configuration of $n$ contact points had an associated quadratic programming problem of $n$ variables. Let a set of valid normal force magnitudes (if it exists) be denoted by the unknown $n$-vector $\vec{f}$; the magnitude of the $i$th normal force is given by $f_i$. If $\vec{f}$ exists, it can be found by solving the QP

$$\underset{\vec{f}}{\text{minimize}}\ \vec{f}^{\,T}(A\vec{f}+\vec{b}) \text{ subject to } \begin{cases} \vec{f} \geq \vec{0} \\ A\vec{f}+\vec{b} \geq \vec{0} \end{cases} \tag{8}$$

where $A$ and $\vec{b}$ are determined by the configuration. $A$ is an $n \times n$ inverse mass matrix and $\vec{b}$ is an $n$-vector of known external and inertial accelerations. $A\vec{f}+\vec{b}$ represents the relative accelerations at contact points. (See [1, 2, 6, 11] for a discussion of the numerical properties of $A$ and methods for computing $A$). Every

$\vec{f}$ such that equation (8) attains zero is valid. If equation (8) cannot attain zero subject to the above restrictions, then the configuration has no valid solution and is inconsistent. Thus, a valid $\vec{f}$ is a solution to the equation

$$\vec{f}^T(A\vec{f} + \vec{b}) = 0, \ \vec{f} \geq 0 \text{ and } A\vec{f} + \vec{b} \geq \vec{0}. \tag{9}$$

Equation (9) is what is known as a *linear complementarity* (LCP) problem. Equation (9) is called a positive semidefinite (PSD) LCP if $A$ is PSD[14].

One of the first algorithms for solving linear complementarity problems was introduced by Lemke[12] and is known as Lemke's algorithm. Lemke's algorithm is a pivoting method, similar to the simplex method of linear programming and has similar numerical properties. The algorithm is exponential in the worst case, but has an expected running time polynomial in $n$[14]. Lemke's algorithm progresses, like the simplex method, by trying various descent directions. If an LCP is PSD and has no solution then Lemke's algorithm will at some point encounter an *unbounded ray*; a descent direction along which one can travel infinitely far without making any progress. Otherwise, if a PSD LCP has a solution, then no unbounded ray exists for that LCP, and Lemke's algorithm terminates by finding a solution to the LCP. The algorithm is viewed as a practical solution method to the problem of solving PSD LCP's.

However, for non-PSD LCP's, Lemke's algorithm is not guaranteed to terminate correctly (although it still takes only expected polynomial time to do so). For a non-PSD LCP, if there is no solution, Lemke's algorithm terminates by encountering an unbounded ray. Unfortunately, if there is a solution, the algorithm is not guaranteed to find it. For non-PSD LCP's with solutions, Lemke's algorithm terminates either by finding a solution or by encountering an unbounded ray.[1] As a result, Lemke's algorithm is not suitable for solving non-PSD LCP's.

However, when Lemke's algorithm terminates by encountering an unbounded ray, it has found an $n$-vector $\vec{z}$ with the property[14]

$$\vec{z} \geq \vec{0} \text{ and } \forall i \text{ such that } \vec{z}_i > 0, \ (A\vec{z})_i \leq 0 \tag{10}$$

where $(A\vec{z})_i$ is the $i$th component of the vector $A\vec{z}$. Why is this property of interest? Suppose that a set of contact impulses are applied to the configuration, with the magnitude of the normal impulse at the $i$th contact point denoted by $\vec{z}_i$. Then it can be shown[2, 6] that the relative velocity at the $i$th contact point after the impulse is $(A\vec{z})_i$. If the vector $\vec{z}$ satisfies equation (10) then every contact point subject to a non-zero contact impulse $\vec{z}_i > 0$ ends up with a non-positive relative normal velocity $(A\vec{z})_i \leq 0$. Thus, the vector $\vec{z}$ found by Lemke's algorithm gives rise to a valid set of contact impulses. To fully satisfy the definition of validity, $\vec{z}$ must be scaled upwards from zero until it causes a contact point with dynamic friction to be converted to static friction. After this, a real impact occurs, as described in section 6.1.

The behavior of Lemke's algorithm exactly matches our new view of the problem of computing contact forces. If the configuration has no valid contact impulse solutions, Lemke's algorithm cannot terminate with the special vector $\vec{z}$ and must therefore find a valid contact force solution. For inconsistent configurations, no valid contact force solution exists, so Lemke's algorithm must terminate with the vector $\vec{z}$, providing a contact impulse solution. For configurations with both a valid force and impulse solution, Lemke's algorithm will terminate by computing one or the other. Whenever Lemke's algorithm terminates by computing a contact impulse solution, it will still be unknown whether or not the configuration was consistent. For frictionless systems, the LCP is always PSD and has a solution, so frictionless configurations do not have valid impulse solutions. Thus, the reformulation of the problem does not add any new solutions to simulations of frictionless systems.

Although Lemke's algorithm runs, practically speaking, in polynomial time, this is not a proof that finding either valid contact forces or impulses is a polynomial time problem. From a practical standpoint, though, Lemke's algorithm provides an efficient algorithm for computing valid contact forces or impulses. The computational complexity of either solving an LCP or finding an unbounded ray is unknown.

[1]Encountering an unbounded ray when there is a solution is analogous to getting stuck at a non-global minimum in a non-convex minimization problem.

## 8. Approaches for Static Friction

We conclude with two approaches to dealing with static friction. We stress that these approaches are only a first step towards dealing with the problems of static friction. Both approaches have their drawbacks, and currently have only limited applicability. The two approaches appear to produce (approximately the same) reasonably realistic results for the configurations we have simulated.

Consider the $i$th contact point of a configuration, and let the normal force magnitude there be $f_i$. The coefficient of friction, $\mu$, is not indexed and may be different for each contact point. No distinction is made between the coefficient of static and dynamic friction, and both are assumed to be isotropic. In what follows, there is no difficulty in using a different value of $\mu$ depending on whether the friction force is static or dynamic. The next few computations take place in the tangent plane of the contact surface at each contact point; vectors are expressed in this plane as pairs $(x,y)$ where $(1,0)$ and $(0,1)$ are orthonormal. Let $(f_{x_i}, f_{y_i})$ be the friction force, and $(v_{x_i}, v_{y_i})$ and $(a_{x_i}, a_{y_i})$ the relative tangential velocity and acceleration between bodies at the $i$th contact point.[2] If $(v_{x_i}, v_{y_i})$ is non-zero, then dynamic friction occurs and and the friction force has magnitude $\mu f_i$ and is anti-parallel to the vector $(v_{x_i}, v_{y_i})$.

Static friction is more complex. For static friction,

$$|(f_{x_i}, f_{y_i})|^2 = f_{x_i}^2 + f_{y_i}^2 \leq (\mu f_i)^2. \tag{11}$$

The main difficulty in static friction is determining when a contact points makes a transition from sticking to sliding. When the static friction force is sufficient to prevent sliding, any direction of the friction force constraining $(a_{x_i}, a_{y_i})$ to be zero is valid. If the body begins to slide, then $(f_{x_i}, f_{y_i})$ must at least partially oppose the acceleration; that is,

$$(f_{x_i}, f_{y_i}) \cdot (a_{x_i}, a_{y_i}) \leq 0. \tag{12}$$

Also, if $(a_{x_i}, a_{y_i})$ is non-zero, then the friction force magnitude must attain its upper bound of $\mu f_i$. The law for static friction can be summarized as

$$f_{x_i}^2 + f_{y_i}^2 \leq (\mu f_i)^2, \ (f_{x_i}, f_{y_i}) \cdot (a_{x_i}, a_{y_i}) \leq 0 \text{ and}$$
$$((\mu f_i)^2 - (f_{x_i}^2 + f_{y_i}^2))(a_{x_i}^2 + a_{y_i}^2) = 0 \tag{13}$$

where the last condition forces either $(\mu f_i)^2 = f_{x_i}^2 + f_{y_i}^2$ or $a_{x_i}^2 + a_{y_i}^2 = 0$. Unfortunately, equation (13) is too complex to be

[2]Care must be taken here. The relative acceleration $(a_{x_i}, a_{y_i})$ is calculated by taking the first derivative of a velocity constraint, not the second derivative of a spatial constraint. See Goyal[8] for details.

formulated as part of a quadratic program. It also does not appear practical to solve with current non-linear programming techniques.

### 8.1 The Dynamic Friction Approximation

This approach for approximating static friction is extremely simple to implement. In order to determine whether static friction or dynamic friction should occur at a contact point, a simulator must have some threshold value $\varepsilon$. If $|(v_{x_i},v_{y_i})| \geq \varepsilon$, then dynamic friction occurs. Otherwise $|(v_{x_i},v_{y_i})| < \varepsilon$ and static friction occurs. Since dynamic friction is

$$(f_{x_i},f_{y_i}) = \mu f_i \frac{-(v_{x_i},v_{y_i})}{|(v_{x_i},v_{y_i})|} \tag{14}$$

we approximate static friction as

$$(f_{x_i},f_{y_i}) = \frac{|(v_{x_i},v_{y_i})|}{\varepsilon} \mu f_i \frac{-(v_{x_i},v_{y_i})}{|(v_{x_i},v_{y_i})|} = \frac{-(v_{x_i},v_{y_i})\mu f_i}{\varepsilon}. \tag{15}$$

Thus, we really use a dynamic friction force that varies in magnitude from zero to an upper limit of $\mu f_i$ as the relative contact speed varies from 0 to $\varepsilon$. This allows us to use the method of section 7.2 to compute both static and dynamic friction.

Since static friction occurs only when the relative tangential velocity is non-zero, bodies must acquire some small amount of "crawl" in order to maintain a static friction force. This approach is reminiscent of the penalty method, where bodies must acquire some degree of inter-penetration for a sufficient normal force to exist. However, in the penalty method, it is necessary to increase the spring constant $K$ without bound as the mass of bodies increases. Our approximation method does not suffer from this problem. If $\varepsilon$ is made small enough, the "crawling" behavior of bodies is not visible, no matter what masses or forces exist. If $\varepsilon$ is made excessively small, the differential equations of motion[1, 3] may become stiff; otherwise, the approach has a reasonable performance. The major advantage to this approach is that it is guaranteed to produce a result, using Lemke's algorithm as described in section 7.2. Thus, either a set of contact forces or impulses is computed. The major disadvantage to this approach is that it is an *ad hoc* approximation to the law of static friction.

### 8.2 Modeling Static Friction by Quadratic Programming

This approach is much more ambitious. We attempt to model static friction as a quadratic programming problem, which can be solved to find the contact forces. We approximate the static friction law as follows. Equation (11) is rewritten as

$$-\mu f_i \leq f_{x_i} \leq \mu f_i \text{ and } -\mu f_i \leq f_{y_i} \leq \mu f_i \,. \tag{16}$$

Unfortunately, this allows the static friction force magnitude to exceed $\mu f_i$ (by as much as a factor of $\frac{1}{2}\sqrt{2}$), unless the friction force happens to be aligned with a coordinate axis of the tangent plane. One possible solution is to iterate several times, trying to choose a coordinate system so either $f_{x_i}$ or $f_{y_i}$ is zero, for each contact point. For two-dimensional configurations however, the friction force is constrained to a line, not a plane, and is described by a single variable $f_{x_i}$. In this case, the constraint $-\mu f_i \leq f_{x_i} \leq \mu f_i$ is exact.

To satisfy equation (12), we add the conditions

$$\begin{aligned} &f_{x_i}\,\mathrm{sgn}(f_{x_i}) \geq 0 \text{ and } a_{x_i}\,\mathrm{sgn}(f_{x_i}) \leq 0 \\ &f_{y_i}\,\mathrm{sgn}(f_{y_i}) \geq 0 \text{ and } a_{y_i}\,\mathrm{sgn}(f_{y_i}) \leq 0 \end{aligned} \tag{17}$$

where $\mathrm{sgn}(x) = 1$ if $x \geq 0$ and $-1$ otherwise. These conditions ensure that $(f_{x_i},f_{y_i}) \cdot (a_{x_i},a_{y_i}) \leq 0$. The condition that static friction attains its upper bound when slipping begins is written

$$\begin{aligned} &(\mu f_i - f_{x_i}\,\mathrm{sgn}(f_{x_i}))(a_{x_i}\,\mathrm{sgn}(f_{x_i})) = 0 \\ &(\mu f_i - f_{y_i}\,\mathrm{sgn}(f_{y_i}))(a_{y_i}\,\mathrm{sgn}(f_{y_i})) = 0. \end{aligned} \tag{18}$$

Finally, we add the standard constraint on the normal forces that

$$f_i \geq 0,\ a_i \geq 0 \text{ and } f_i a_i = 0 \tag{19}$$

where $a_i$ is the relative normal acceleration of the $i$th contact point. If the signs of the $f_{x_i}$ and $f_{y_i}$ are known, then the above system of equations has unknown variables $f_i$, $f_{x_i}$, $f_{y_i}$ (for each contact point) which are used to express the $a_i$, $a_{x_i}$ and $a_{y_i}$ terms. The entire system can be solved by a quadratic program because the *sgn* functions become known. How can the signs of the $f_{x_i}$ and $f_{y_i}$ variables be determined?

Iterative methods for quadratic programming and linear complementarity exist that can be adopted to this problem[14]. These iterative techniques are very similar to the Gauss-Seidel or Jacobi iterative methods used to solve linear systems. Iterative methods for quadratic programming are modified in a straightforward fashion to solve the system of equations (16) thru (19), without initially knowing the signs of the $f_{x_i}$ and $f_{y_i}$. Unfortunately, convergence results are not available for the modified iterative methods. If the modified method fails to converge (or even before full convergence), the signs of $f_{x_i}$ and $f_{y_i}$ can be guessed by examining the unconverged solution. Quadratic programming is then used to solve equation (16) thru (19) as a quadratic program, given the estimate of the signs of the variables. If the estimate is correct, a solution is obtained for the friction forces.

However, the approach can break down at any number of places. If the method fails to converge, the estimates of the signs of the variables may not be correct. Even if the signs of the variables are correct, the form of the linear constraints in equation (16) do not allow us to use Lemke's algorithm for linear complementarity. Although we can apply standard quadratic programming methods, we know of no algorithm that will solve the quadratic program or indicate contact impulses, as Lemke's algorithm does. With regard to the entire issue of consistency and $NP$-hardness, this method for static friction is back to square one. It is possible that when the iterative step fails to converge, an analysis of the divergence of the iterates will indicate a valid set of contact impulses. At this time, however, we do not know how to perform such an analysis.

We have found however that the second approach, when it works, yields a very acceptable result. For large numbers of contact points ($n \approx 40$), the second approach sometimes breaks down, while the first approach does not. We have had reasonable success with the second approach for configurations with 40 contact points or less.

## 9. Conclusion

An efficient algorithm for dealing with configurations of bodies with only dynamic friction has been presented. Instead of attempting to force a behavior that avoids contact impulses, the algorithm allows either contact forces or contact impulses to occur. Two preliminary approaches for dealing with static friction are presented. The first approach is an approximation using the algorithm developed for simulating dynamic friction. The second approach is more exact but also more prone to failure than the first approach. Simulation of a complex configuration with static and dynamic friction is shown in figure 11.

## Acknowledgements

This research was funded by an AT&T Bell Laboratories PhD Fellowship and two NSF grants (#DCR8203979 and #ASC8715478). Simulations were performed on equipment generously donated by the Hewlett Packard Corporation and the Digital Equipment Corporation. I wish to thank both Bruce Donald and Andy Ruina for several stimulating conversations about *NP*-completeness results and frictional behavior.

### Appendix A: Acceleration due to Contact Force

We compute the normal acceleration of $p_a$, $\hat{n}\cdot\ddot{p}_a$, for the configuration of figure 2. Let $\vec{a}$ and $\vec{\alpha}$ denote the linear and angular acceleration of $A$, $\vec{\omega}$, the angular velocity of $A$, and $\vec{r}$, the displacement of $p_a$ from the center of mass of $A$. Vectors are treated as 3-space vectors: $\vec{a}$, $p_a$, $\ddot{p}_a$, $\hat{n}$ and $\vec{r}$ lie in the $xy$ plane while $\vec{\omega}$ and $\vec{\alpha}$ are parallel to the $z$ axis. From figure 1, $\vec{r} = (-\cos\theta, -\sin\theta, 0)$. $\ddot{p}_a$ may be expressed as the sum of three terms: the linear acceleration $\vec{a}$, the tangential acceleration $\vec{\alpha}\times\vec{r}$, and the centripetal acceleration $\vec{\omega}\times(\vec{\omega}\times\vec{r})$. The linear acceleration, $\vec{a}$, is

$$\vec{a} = \frac{f\hat{n} + \mu f\hat{t} + (-mg)\hat{n}}{m} = \frac{f\hat{n} + \mu f\hat{t}}{m} - g\hat{n}. \tag{20}$$

The torque on $A$ about its center of mass is $\vec{r}\times(f\hat{n} + \mu f\hat{t})$, which yields an angular acceleration of

$$\vec{\alpha} = \frac{\vec{r}\times(f\hat{n} + \mu f\hat{t})}{I}. \tag{21}$$

Then

$$\begin{aligned} \ddot{p}_a &= \vec{a} + \vec{\alpha}\times\vec{r} + \vec{\omega}\times(\vec{\omega}\times\vec{r}) \\ &= \frac{f\hat{n} + \mu f\hat{t}}{m} - g\hat{n} + \frac{\vec{r}\times(f\hat{n} + \mu f\hat{t})}{I}\times\vec{r} + \vec{\omega}\times(\vec{\omega}\times\vec{r}). \end{aligned} \tag{22}$$

Taking the dot product of equation (20) with $\hat{n}$,

$$\hat{n}\cdot\vec{a} = \frac{f\hat{n}\cdot\hat{n} + \mu f\hat{n}\cdot\hat{t}}{m} - g\hat{n}\cdot\hat{n} = \frac{f}{m} - g. \tag{23}$$

Taking the dot product of the tangential acceleration $\vec{\alpha}\times\vec{r}$ with $\hat{n}$ and using the geometry of figure 1, $\hat{n}\cdot\vec{\omega}\times(\vec{\omega}\times\vec{r}) = |\vec{\omega}|^2\sin\theta$ and

$$\begin{aligned} \hat{n}\cdot(\vec{\alpha}\times\vec{r}) &= \hat{n}\cdot\left(\frac{\vec{r}\times(f\hat{n} + \mu f\hat{t})}{I}\times\vec{r}\right) \\ &= \frac{f(\cos^2\theta - \mu\cos\theta\sin\theta)}{I}. \end{aligned} \tag{24}$$

Then, from the relations in figure 1,

$$\begin{aligned} \hat{n}\cdot\ddot{p}_a &= \frac{f}{m} - g + \frac{f(\cos^2\theta - \mu\cos\theta\sin\theta)}{I} + |\vec{\omega}|^2\sin\theta \\ &= \frac{f}{m}(1 + 16(\cos^2\theta - \mu\cos\theta\sin\theta)) + |\vec{\omega}|^2\sin\theta - g \qquad (25) \\ &= \frac{f}{m}(1 - 2) + |\vec{\omega}|^2\sin\theta - g = -\frac{f}{m} + (|\vec{\omega}|^2\sin\theta - g). \end{aligned}$$

### References

1. Baraff, D., ''Analytical methods for dynamic simulation of non-penetrating rigid bodies,'' *Computer Graphics (Proc. SIGGRAPH)*, vol. 23, pp. 223-232, 1989.
2. Baraff, D., ''Curved surfaces and coherence for non-penetrating rigid body simulation,'' *Computer Graphics (Proc. SIGGRAPH)*, vol. 24, pp. 19-28, 1990.
3. Barzel, R. and Barr, A.H., ''A modeling system based on dynamic constraints,'' *Computer Graphics (Proc. SIGGRAPH)*, vol. 22, pp. 179-188, 1988.
4. Cottle, R.W., ''On a problem in linear inequalities,'' *Journal of the London Mathematical Society*, vol. 43, pp. 378-384, 1968.
5. Erdmann, M.A., *On Motion Planning with Uncertainty*, M.S. Thesis, Massachusetts Institute of Technology, 1984.
6. Featherstone, R., *Robot Dynamics Algorithms*, Kluwer, Boston, 1987.
7. Garey, M.R. and Johnson, D.S., *Computers and Intractability*, Freeman, New York, 1979.
8. Goyal, S., ''Second order kinematic constraint between two bodies rolling, twisting and slipping against each other while maintaining point contact,'' *Technical Report TR 89-1043*, Department of Computer Science, Cornell University, 1989.
9. Kilmister, W. and Reeve, J.E., *Rational Mechanics*, Longman's, London, 1966.
10. Lötstedt, P., ''Coulomb friction in two-dimensional rigid body systems,'' *Zeitschrift für Angewandte Mathematik un Mechanik*, vol. 61, pp. 605-615, 1981.
11. Lötstedt, P., ''Numerical simulation of time-dependent contact friction problems in rigid body mechanics,'' *SIAM Journal of Scientific Statistical Computing*, vol. 5, no. 2, pp. 370-393, 1984.
12. Lemke, C.E., ''Bimatrix equilibrium points and mathematical programming,'' *Management Science*, vol. 11, pp. 681-689, 1965.
13. Mason, M.T. and Wang, Y., ''On the inconsistency of rigid-body frictional planar mechanics,'' *IEEE International Conference on Robotics and Automation*, 1988.
14. Murty, K.G., *Linear Complementarity, Linear and Nonlinear Programming*, Heldermann Verlag, Berlin, 1988.
15. Vavasis, S.A., ''Quadratic Programming is in NP,'' *Technical Report TR 90-1099*, Department of Computer Science, Cornell University, 1990.
16. Wang, Y. and Mason, M.T., ''Two dimensional rigid body collisions with friction,'' *Journal of Applied Mechanics*, (to appear).

**Figure 11. Simulation of a complex configuration.**

# Design and Simulation of Opera Lighting and Projection Effects

*Julie O'B. Dorsey*
*François X. Sillion*
*Donald P. Greenberg*

Program of Computer Graphics
Cornell University
Ithaca, New York 14853

## Abstract

A major problem challenging opera designers is the inability to coordinate lighting, projection systems, and set designs in the preliminary planning phase. New computer graphics techniques, which provide the set and lighting designer the opportunity to evaluate, test, and control opera designs prior to the construction of full scale systems are presented. These techniques—light source input, simulation of directional lighting, modeling of scenic projection systems, and full three-dimensional simulation—show the potential for the use of computer graphics in theater design.

The light source input component consists of a program for assigning light source attributes with a set of theater lighting icons. This module allows a designer to specify light source characteristics in a way familiar to the discipline and to make preliminary evaluations of the lighting conditions.

An extended progressive radiosity method is introduced to simulate the directional lighting characteristics which are specified by the input program.

A new projection approach is presented to simulate the optical effects of scenic projectors. In addition, a solution to the distortion problem produced by angular projections is described.

The above components are integrated to produce full three-dimensional simulations of the global illumination effects in an opera scene.

**CR Categories and Subject Descriptors:** I.3.0 [Computer Graphics]: General; I.3.7 [Computer Graphics]: Three Dimensional Graphics and Realism; J.2 [Computer Applications]: Performing Arts.
**General Terms:** Algorithms
**Additional Keywords and Phrases:** opera and stage design, angular projection, simulation, radiosity, directional light sources, texture mapping.

## 1 Introduction

Opera stage design is an extremely difficult task as, in addition to the standard architectural and aesthetic considerations, a number of additional issues are present, such as dynamic and intricate lighting and sets, projected background scenery, changing focus of attention, manipulation of implied perspective, multiple viewing points, motion of performers, and synchronization with music. Stage and lighting designers, as well as conductors, rarely have the opportunity to evaluate these effects together. Consequently, stage set and lighting designs are currently developed separately—being combined only in the last step of the process.

Presently, the only feasible method available for combining a limited stage and lighting design is the construction of small scale models. While this process does give some insight into the visual impact of the final production, it is a laborious, costly, incomplete, and time-consuming endeavor. Furthermore, because of their small scale, these models are so inadequate for the evaluation of complex lighting effects that they are not commonly used. Thus, in practice, the stage and lighting designers will often work in isolation from each other. The bulk of the lighting designer's task, then, occurs at the last minute—after the sets are assembled and in place on the stage.

The primary objective of this paper is to provide the stage and lighting designer the opportunity to *design and evaluate the lighting and projected scenery prior to the actual implementation.* In particular, techniques for light source descriptions and specification, the simulation of directional lighting, and the modeling of scenic projection systems have been developed. In addition, a solution for the distortion problem in angular projections is introduced. The procedures have been combined to provide full three-dimensional simulations so that the proposed design strategy can be evaluated from any viewer position. The variables are the positions of the stage sets, the locations, orientation, spatial emittance, and color of the lights, the number of lights which are illuminated, the background projection systems and scenery, all within the given theater geometry.

Three famous opera houses have been selected to demonstrate the system: the Metropolitan Opera at Lincoln Center in New York City, La Scala in Milan, Italy, and the Staatsoper in Vienna, Austria. Due to space limitations, only the Metropolitan Opera is illustrated.

## 2 Input for Lights

In general, light sources have well-defined finite geometries that greatly affect the distribution of the light emitted from the source. There are three types of abstract emissive geometries: point sources (zero dimensional), linear sources (one dimensional), and area sources (two dimensional) [23]. The light sources used in opera production can be treated as point sources, since the lights are very small and are located at a significant distance from the stage.

Perhaps the most important characteristic of a luminaire that must be included in a complete model of a light source is the luminous



©1991 ACM-0-89791-436-8/91/007/0041 $00.75

intensity distribution. In contrast to the assumption typically used in computer graphics, most of the lights used in opera production do not emit light of constant intensity in all directions.

A non-uniform intensity distribution must be specified, which describes the variations of the emitted intensity with direction. The lighting industry uses goniometric diagrams to represent these vector-valued functions for easy interpretation [3]. These diagrams represent a planar slice through the vector field and thus plot the relative intensity as a function of angular direction (Figure 1). For

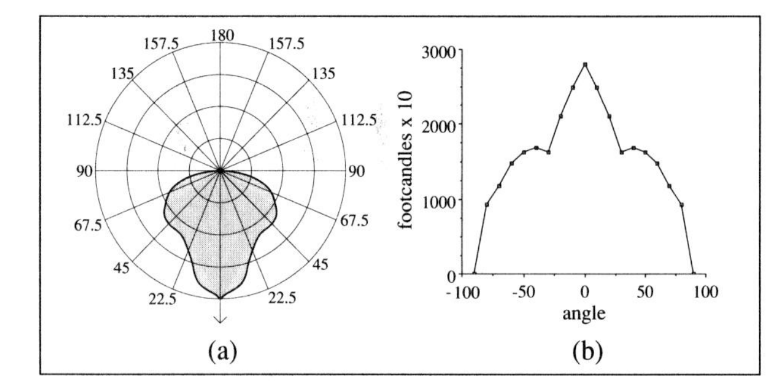


Figure 1: A sample emission distribution. (a) Polar goniometric diagram. (b) Corresponding cartesian diagram.

luminaires with concentrated beams, such as spotlights, cartesian coordinates are preferred because of the need for more precision than a polar curve allows.

### 2.1 Instruments and Lamps

In lighting design for opera, many different types of luminaires are used. Although there appear to be a large number of different instrument styles used, each style is a variation on five particular instruments: the ellipsoidal reflector spotlight; the Fresnel spotlight; the striplight; the ellipsoidal reflector floodlight; and the beam projector. The optical characteristics of each of these instruments (and variations thereof) have been modeled.

### 2.2 Assigning Light Source Attributes

An interactive graphical program has been developed to allow one to design a lighting scenario. While a final lighting layout is primarily a tool for communicating the designer's concept and intentions to the electricians, lighting crews, and board operators, who must "hang" the design and execute it in a performance, this program provides the means to develop ideas, experiment, move and change instruments and their attributes, and iteratively refine a design.

The input program allows for the complete specification of attributes for stage lighting. The user can specify the position of each instrument, its intensity pattern, color, projection pattern, and the area which it illuminates in addition to indicating its height above the floor and the angles of the beams of light. As the parameters associated with a light are adjusted, the lamp is instantly updated with the resulting beam and field angles as well as throw distance. This feature makes it possible to combine light sources and evaluate the design implications (e.g. if their beams overlap). Thus, while still in the modeling phase, one has a good idea of the overall lighting scheme. Once a preliminary design is specified, the user can simulate the illumination effects and, with a separate program, view the results to further refine the lighting design.

An attempt has been made to carefully design the graphical interface so the process of assigning attributes is similar to the way in which it is physically performed. A menu is available which contains a two dimensional graphical representation of the five major categories of lights used in opera production. Once a category has been selected, it is possible to choose from a variety of instrument types and manufacturers within that category.

Most of the luminaires used in theater production have a spot and flood focus intensity distribution associated with them. When a lamp has been selected, a two dimensional icon is drawn in one window, and the components of the lamp which move during the focusing of that particular instrument can be varied interactively, making it possible to focus the instrument to the desired setting (Figure 2). To specify the intensity distribution, one window shows either a cartesian or polar goniometric diagram of the current luminous intensity distribution or candle power distribution curve for the light source. This diagram is updated continuously as the instrument is focused. To scale the distribution, the maximum intensity which the lamp emits at the center of its beam is specified in units of candelas.

Each light source can have a unique pattern or slide. A library of patterns and slides to be used in projection has been compiled. The designer can select a pattern from the library and associate it with a given light source.

Color can be controlled by placing a transparent color filter between the light source and the receiving surface(s). Using the filter section of the input program, an interactive color tool allows the user to vary the characteristics of the filter used to color the light emitted by a lamp.

It is possible to position a lamp at any location relative to the stage environment. Most light sources are positioned on the light bridges, but occasionally they are placed on the front edge of the stage as footlights or on temporary ladder-like structures along the sides. To aid the user in positioning the lamps, one viewport displays the light source with three dimensional transparent cones attached to it (optionally displayed) in the model of the stage. These cones represent the beam and field angles as well as the throw distance of the instrument (see Appendix A). As the lights are positioned relative to the stage area, the cones allow the user to visualize the direction in which the light will be emitted as well as how much illumination a particular area will receive.

## 3 Simulation of Theater Lighting Conditions

Radiosity methods, derived from the field of radiative heat transfer, have been successfully applied to the area of realistic image synthesis [4, 5, 6, 9, 16, 24]. The radiosity method has the attractive characteristic of providing a view-independent solution. Hence, once the solution has been performed, a hardware renderer can be used to display the scene from changing viewpoints at interactive rates.

### 3.1 Modeling Directional Light Sources with Progressive Radiosity

The progressive radiosity method [4] can be extended to account for directional variations in a light source with non-uniform emission distributions (Figure 1). In this implementation, the form-factors are computed using the ray-traced form-factor approach proposed by Wallace et al.[24]. To account for the variation in light source directionality, the form factor from the light source to a vertex is computed as usual and then weighted by a directionality scaling factor, $s$. Each directional light source has a distribution associated with it which describes its normalized light source intensity versus angle. The value of $s$ is obtained from this distribution for each element vertex based on the direction $\theta_2$ (the angle between the direction vector of the light source and the direction of an element vertex).

In this way, the amount of light which is transferred from the light source to the environment is weighted according to the directional

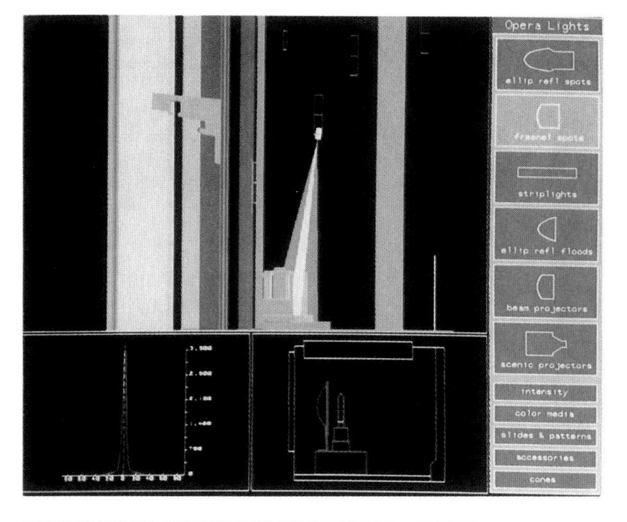


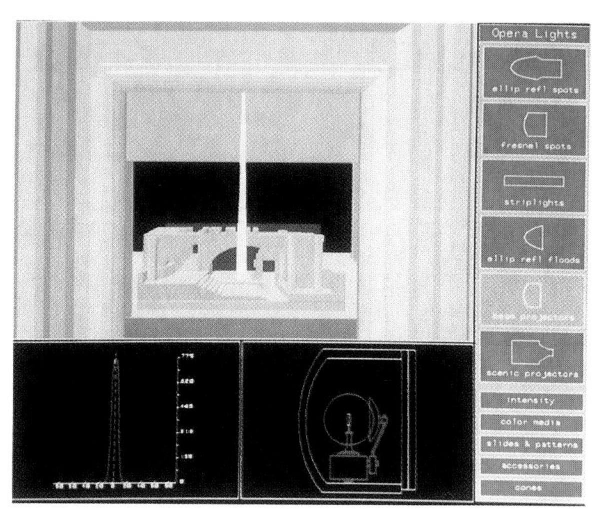


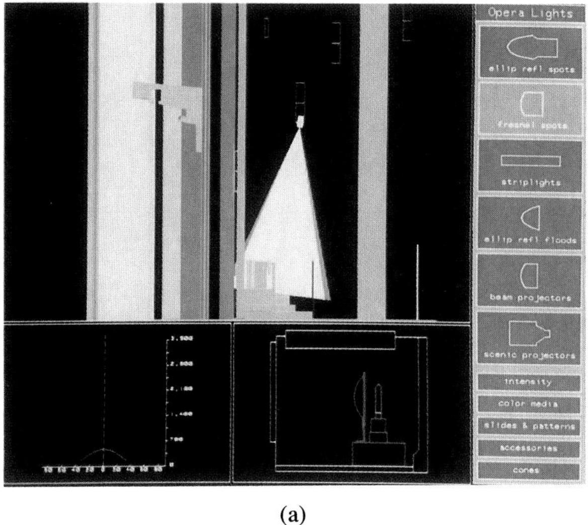


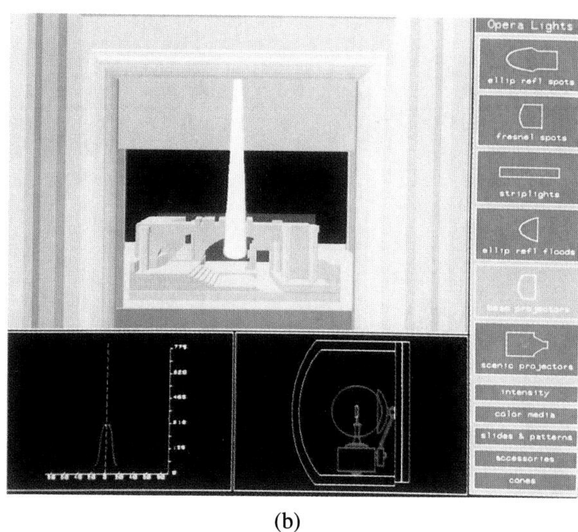


(a) (b)

Figure 2: Light Source Input and Attribute Assignment. (a) The Fresnel spotlight – spot and flood foci. (b) The beam projector – spot and flood foci.

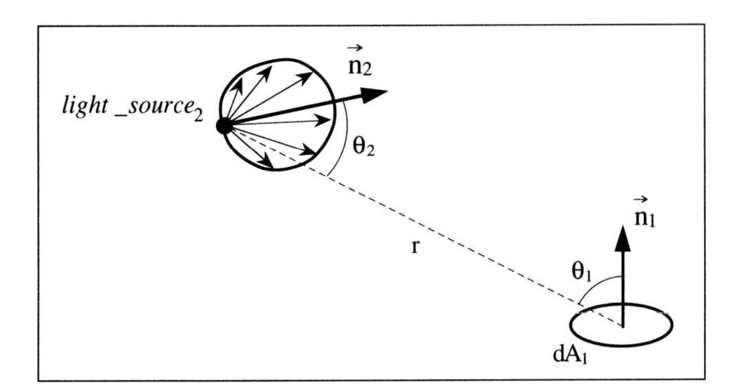


Figure 3: Modeling directional light sources with progressive radiosity.

distribution (Figure 3). The illumination received at vertex 1 from a spot light 2 can be represented by a weighted form-factor based on that light source's emission distribution:

$$dF_{light\_source_2-dA_1} = dA_1 \frac{\cos\theta_1 \cos\theta_2}{\pi r^2}\, s(\theta_2) \qquad (1)$$

For directional light sources, a single ray is traced from each vertex to the light for shadow testing. A single ray is sufficient because point sources are used. The amount of energy per unit area received at each vertex is then weighted as shown above. Figure 4 shows a radiosity rendering of several directional light sources.

In this method, the directional light sources initially shoot out their directional energy once, and calculations for any subsequent radiant energy exchange due to secondary reflections can be treated in the standard manner.

# 4 Projected Scenery

## 4.1 Overview

An effective method of creating a scenic background is to project a slide onto a neutral surface. Architectural features, general views, natural objects, cloud formations, and similar objects can be projected on to a backdrop. Projected scenery is fundamentally dif-

Figure 4: Radiosity rendering of directional light sources.

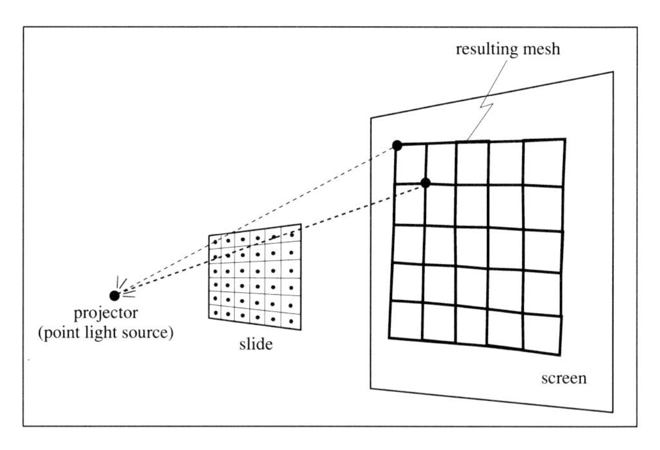


Figure 5: Radiosity Scenic Projection Technique. The backdrop is discretized according to the projected resolution of the slide. The initial radiosity at each element vertex is then based on the emission of the light source, the transmissivity of a point in the slide, and the color of the backdrop.

ferent from built or painted scenery in that it achieves its effects through the use of light. Because color in light is more brilliant than in paint, and has an unlimited value scale by comparison, its use in projection is far more dramatic and eye-catching. Additionally, it can give a greater illusion of size and depth in a setting [27]. In a sense, projection techniques create an imaginary space which extends the bounds of the real space defined by the set geometry. Furthermore, they permit not only rapid changes, but also gradual transitions from one setting to the next, such as from daylight, through sunset to night—all with the same background [11].

Typically, the picture to be projected is painted by hand or photographically produced. Slides for scenic projectors range in size from 5 to 10 inches square. Reduced to its simplest elements, the projection process consists of a light source, the object or slide, the projected image, and the projection surface [18]. There are two types of projection: *shadow projection* and *lens projection*. The term *lens projection* is used to define all projections obtained using one or more lenses; *shadow projection* is used to describe projections obtained without the use of lenses [26].

## 4.2 Simulation of Projected Scenery

The simulation of background scenery using slide projection techniques is common in opera production, but is new to the field of computer graphics. It is important to derive methods for projection simulation which will maintain the resolution and quality of the original slide, provide soft-focusing according to the optics of the projection system, allow arbitrary geometries for the receiving surfaces, mimic the correct dispersion and attenuation of light, and be computable in tractable amounts of time.

## 4.3 A Radiosity Projection Technique

This section describes an extension to the progressive radiosity algorithm which allows for the projection of scenery. The energy received at the surface of the backdrop from the projection is a function of the emission distribution of the light source, the transmissivity values of the slide, and the orientation and distance of element vertices on the backdrop relative to the projection system. The technique (Figure 5) can be expressed as follows:

1. A two-dimensional array, or "texture map," of values is obtained by scanning photographs or artistic renderings of actual images to be projected.

2. The backdrop/receiving surface is discretized into a series of element vertices, the locations of which are determined based on the intersection of casting a single ray from the projector through each point of the slide to the backdrop. The resolution of the slide varies according to the desired fuzziness or clarity of the projected image on the backdrop (typically a slide with a resolution between 50x50 and 100x100 = 2,500 to 10,000 element vertices is used).

3. The radiosity of each of these vertices is then based on the color/transmissivity of the relevant point in the slide, the backdrop color, and the emission of the light source in the direction of the element vertex.

The initial radiosity at a vertex on the screen due to the projection (source 2) only is expressed by this modified radiosity equation:

$$B_1 = \rho_1 E_2 \frac{\cos\theta_1 \cos\theta_2}{\pi r^2} s(\theta_2)\, t_q \qquad (2)$$

where,

$E_2$ = energy emitted by the point light source,
$t_q$ = transmissivity at a point $q$ in the slide.

It should be noted that the effect of a directional light source, $s(\theta_2)$ (projector) is also included in the above equation.

It is also possible, using computer graphics, to model the depth of focus of the projection system. One can "blur" the slide using a filter, sized according to the distance of the projector to the backdrop, so that the entire projection has the same out-of-focus effect. Figure 6 shows a sample projection which was generated using this method.

The radiosity projection technique closely simulates the real projection system in that it yields a view-independent solution with interpolation at the backdrop based on projection characteristics at the maximum stored resolution of the slide. In addition, the backdrop is subdivided according to the projection itself, rather than according to a separate and unrelated element meshing. Finally, the light attenuation of the projector is modeled precisely.

## 4.4 A General Solution for the Distortion Problem in Angular Projection

It is usual to place the projector(s) behind the proscenium, hidden from the view of the audience, and to project downward at an angle to the backdrop. Furthermore, it is common for the backdrop to

Figure 6: Radiosity Scenic Projection.

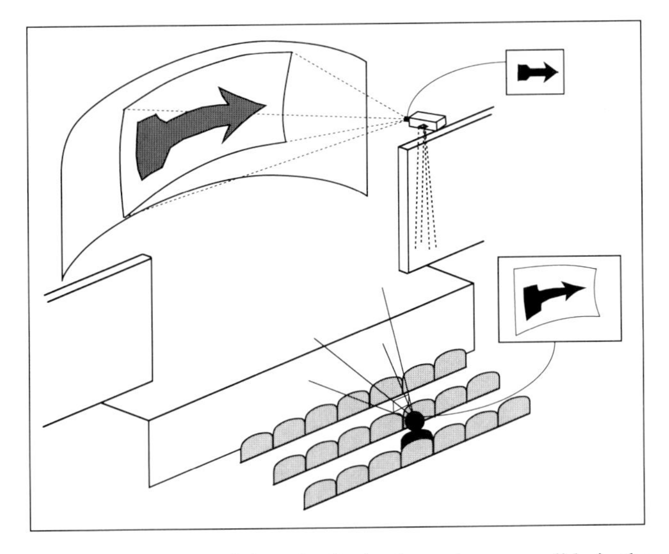

Figure 7: Uncorrected Angular Projection - A square slide in the projector will produce a distorted backdrop image for a viewer.

be non-planar and shaped in some way (e.g. a curved cyclorama). A slide in the projector will therefore produce a distorted backdrop image, which increases in size with the distance from the projector to the backdrop as shown in Figure 7. The problem then is how to predistort a slide such that, when projected and viewed from the position of an "ideal viewer," the backdrop image appears undistorted.

Currently, when a scene is to be projected, the lighting designer waits until the sets are built and in place. Then, a slide (known as a *raster*) of a regular grid of guide marks is projected from the position where the projector(s) will be located. Next, the resulting projected image (now a distorted grid) is photographed and examined from various viewer positions. Based on the distortion apparent in the projected grid at an ideal viewer location, a predistorted slide is produced using the distorted grid lines as guides. When the slide is projected, the viewer is presented with an undistorted scene. Generally, several iterations of this process are necessary to achieve the desired slide. This trial and error process is time-consuming, labor intensive, and restricted to a given set/projection geometry.

This process can be computer simulated using a digital image warping technique—providing a designer the opportunity to preview a projection and produce the distorted slide long before sets are built. The algorithm involves modeling the distortion which would result based on the geometry of a hypothetical projection schema and generating a pre-distorted slide to counteract the distortion.

Image warping is a growing branch of image processing that deals with the geometric transformation of digital images[28]. A geometric transformation is an operation that redefines the spatial relationship between points in an image. The basis of geometric transformations is the mapping of one coordinate system onto another. This mapping is defined by means of a spatial transformation—a mapping function that establishes a spatial correspondence between all points in the input and output images.

Geometric transformations were originally introduced to correct the distortions introduced by remote sensing methods [2, 10]. This process involved estimating the distortion model, usually by means of a set of reference points. The algorithm presented below differs from these previous techniques in three important respects. First, in this method, one begins with the undistorted image and models the distortion which is introduced. Second, the method is very general in that it does not rely on a particular sensor: it can be used to model any projection system and can account for a projection from any location. Third, this technique involves a two-step approach, because the new value at each point is not merely taken from the mapped coordinates (as is usually the case) but is instead derived from a second mapping (ideal/desired transformation).

#### 4.4.1 Definitions

In discussing the problem of an angular projection, it is useful to introduce definitions of the three pertinent coordinate systems. A point on the slide in the projector is referred to as $x_p y_p z_p$, a point in the projected image on the backdrop as $x_b y_b z_b$, and a point in the viewer's/spectator's space as $x_v y_v z_v$. The physical *slide* defines the continuous function of $(x_p y_p z_p)$ specifying a color at each position.

The ideal situation would be one in which the projection system would associate points in the projector (slide) and viewer space such that the viewer simply sees a window into the original picture. This operation would define an affine transformation $T$ such that,

$$(x_v y_v z_v) = (x_p y_p z_p)T \tag{3}$$

The color (intensity) at some point $x_v y_v z_v$ would then simply depend on the color of the slide at point $(x_p y_p z_p) = (x_v y_v z_v)T^{-1}$.

$$color(x_v y_v z_v) = F[original\_slide((x_v y_v z_v)T^{-1})] \tag{4}$$

where the function $F$ describes the effect of light attenuation and illumination (Its exact form does not need to be specified here).

However, in reality, a point on the slide $x_p y_p z_p$ will be first mapped to the backdrop by the projection, according to some projection transformation, $P$. The resulting point on the backdrop will in turn be transformed to the viewer's space by the usual perspective viewing transformation, $V$. Thus,

$$(x_b y_b z_b) = (x_p y_p z_p)P \tag{5}$$

and,

$$(x_v y_v z_v) = (x_b y_b z_b)V = (x_p y_p z_p)PV = (x_p y_p z_p)D \tag{6}$$

The transformation, $D = PV$, represents the combined mapping from the projection and viewing systems or the distortion, which is ultimately seen by the viewer. There is a parallel between the real distortion, $D$ and the ideal transformation, $T$.

The problem is to create a pre-distorted slide such that, after applying the physical transformation $D$ to this slide, the color at each point in the viewer space is the same as the color obtained by ideally transforming the original picture using the transformation $T$:

$$\forall(x_v y_v z_v) \quad F(original\_slide((x_v y_v z_v)T^{-1})) = F(distorted\_slide((x_v y_v z_v)D^{-1})) \qquad (7)$$

A simple way of guaranteeing this is to define the distorted slide as:

$$\forall(x_p y_p z_p) \quad distorted\_slide(x_p y_p z_p) = original\_slide((x_p y_p z_p)DT^{-1}) \qquad (8)$$

### 4.4.2 Producing a Pre-distorted Slide

An algorithm to produce a pre-distorted slide which simulates the actual process used by lighting engineers is presented below. By using Equation (8), the color at every point on the slide is computed. In order to evaluate this equation, a way to compute the distortion $D$ is needed. In general, $D$ is a complex non-linear transformation, and thus it is not practical to evaluate it analytically. The algorithm proposed computes $D$ exactly for a small number of points and uses a linear interpolation to approximate $D$ at all other points. A regular orthogonal grid (the resolution of which can be varied) can be used as a means to quantify the distortion function, $D$. Rays are sent out from the projector at regular intervals (based on the resolution of the grid and the beam angle of the projector) to the projection surface. By transforming the set of grid points from the projector coordinates, $x_p y_p z_p$ to the coordinates on the backdrop/projection surface $x_b y_b z_b$ the function $P$ is simulated. Next, the projected points are transformed into the viewer's coordinates, $x_v y_v z_v$, based on a camera specification which represents the view of an ideal spectator. This transformation represents the function $V$.

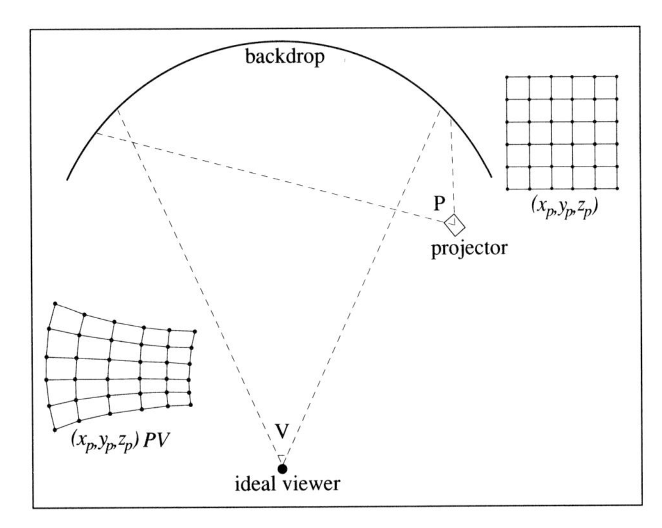


Figure 8: Modeling the distortion in a projection. A regular grid is projected from the projector to the backdrop and mapped to the viewer. The projection system $P$ maps a point from the projector to the screen. The observer's eye-system $V$ maps a point from the screen to the viewer.

The relationship between the original undistorted grid (the set of points $x_p y_p z_p$) and the resulting points as seen by the viewer $(x_v y_v z_v)$ represents the distortion, $D$, which was produced by the projection (Figure 8).

To compute the final slide, the following steps are taken:
First, the virtual, undistorted grid is overlayed onto the slide to be generated as shown in Figure 9. Next, for each point of the *slide*, $(x_p y_p z_p)$:

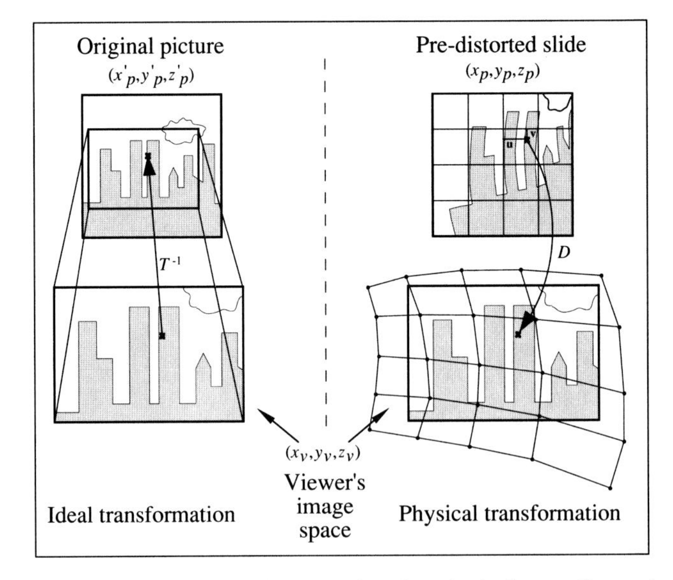


Figure 9: Process for finding the color of a point in the pre-distorted slide.

1. Find which grid cell of the undistorted grid the point is in,
2. Find the coordinates $(u, v)$ of the point within the undistorted grid cell (the local coordinates within the cell),
3. Compute the coordinates of the transformed point $(x_v y_v z_v)$ in the distorted grid. This computation is accomplished by bilinear interpolation (or a higher order interpolation if necessary) using the four transformed corners of the cell. (At this point the effect of $D$ has been evaluated),
4. Find the point $(x'_p y'_p z'_p)$ in the original image associated to $x_v y_v z_v$ by the ideal transformation $T^{-1}$. This is a standard windowing operation involving a simple affine transformation,
5. The color of the distorted slide at point $(x_p y_p z_p)$ is the color of the original slide at point $(x'_p y'_p z'_p)$.

The result of this procedure is the predistorted slide.

Figure 10 shows a projected image of a New York City skyline onto a curved backdrop along with an illustration of the corrected/pre-distorted slide which was generated using the above method.

## 5 Simulation Results

The geometric information in the opera hall is subdivided into two parts, the geometry of the permanent structure and the geometry and position of the stage sets.

#### Fixed Geometry - Definition of the Opera Hall

The geometry of the structure, such as the shell or roof over the stage, as well as the auditorium in general, is fixed. Since the focus of the simulation is only on the stage, a detailed model of the stage portion of the hall has been constructed along with an abstract overall building model. This detailed model includes the proscenium and stage with operable stage lifts as well as the light bridges/gantries where the lights are positioned. The model was

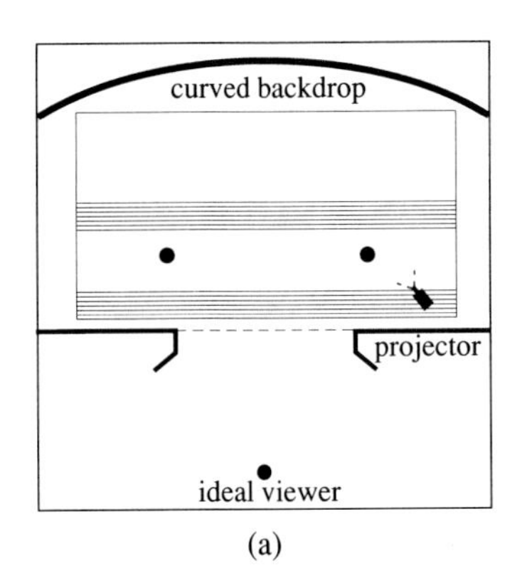


(a)

(b)

(c)

Figure 10: Radiosity scenic projection of a New York City skyline using a predistorted slide. The projection is from a height of 51.5 feet down at an angle to the curved backdrop. (a) Abstract plan of the environment showing the location of the projector, an ideal viewer, and the shape of the backdrop. (b) Final projected image on the backdrop. (c) Predistorted slide.

made to scale using precise dimensions from drawings and photographs received from the Metropolitan Opera House in New York City.

### Variable Geometry - Definition of the Stage Sets

Detailed models of the stage sets constitute the second part of the geometric definition. Most of the sets have been defined as extruded contours. Once a set has been modeled, it is possible to position it at any location on the stage and to view it from any position in the hall.

### Examples of Lit Opera Scenes

To demonstrate the usefulness of the techniques, three full simulations of real productions from the Metropolitan Opera have been generated and are shown in Figures 11, 12 and 13. Each of these examples shows the specialized lighting effects—projected scenery, angular projection solutions using pre-distorted slides, and stage lighting—combined with high quality view-independent simulations for practical use in opera design.

Figure 11 shows two views for Günther Schneider-Siemssen's design for the Palazzo on the Grand Canal in Venice from *Les Contes d'Hoffmann*. The left and right sides of the set are modeled and texture-mapped. The facades in the center background were projected from stage left at a height of 46.5 feet onto a curved backdrop using a pre-distorted slide. Striplights are used to provide an overall wash of light on the set. A series of floodlights were used to simulate moonlight on the facades to the right. A high intensity spotlight produces the effect of the lantern in the doorway.

Figures 12 and 13 show two distinct lighting schemes for Franco Zeffirelli's design of a Parisian garret from *La Bohème*. A prominent feature in these simulations is the sky, which was projected using two angular projections. The projectors are positioned on a lighting bridge at a height of 53 feet on the left and right sides of the stage. The slides were predistorted to account for the angular projections. A variety of stage lights are positioned on the bridges and used to illuminate the set.

## 6 Conclusions

A set of computer graphics techniques for the design and simulation of opera lighting effects has been presented. The light input, projection, and simulation components give the stage and lighting designer a unique opportunity to design, preview, and assess an opera design prior to the construction of full-scale systems. The results of this research clearly demonstrate that the use of computer graphics in theater design holds great promise, particularly since these techniques afford the opportunity for aesthetic evaluations to be made early in the design process and consequently allow many design professionals to work in unison in the preliminary design phase.

Future directions include the use of a higher order interpolation scheme for the projection distortion algorithm, anti-aliasing in the generation of a pre-distorted slide, and the control of the lighting as a function of time.

## 7 Acknowledgements

The authors are extremely grateful to the Hewlett Packard Corporation and the Digital Equipment Corporation for donating the equipment which was used for the simulations and displays. The authors also thank the National Science Foundation for long term support of the research at the Program of Computer Graphics. The Robert James Eidlitz Traveling Fellowship provided funding for a site visit to the Staatsoper, La Scala, and the Metropolitan Opera. Special thanks to Gil Wechsler and Wayne Chouinard at the Metropolitan Opera for providing documentation of real set and lighting designs and for their helpful discussions and input into this research. Mark Shepard modeled the *La Bohème* environment used in the simulations. Thanks to Kurk Dorsey, Hurf Sheldon, Ben Trumbore, Kevin Novins, Harold Zatz, Ellen French, and Fran Brown for their general assistance. All images were photographed by Emil Ghinger.

## References

[1] Baum, Daniel R., Holly E. Rushmeier, and James M. Winget. "Improving Radiosity Solutions Through the Use of Analytically Determined Form-Factors," Proceedings of SIGGRAPH'89 (Boston, Massachusetts, July 31 – August 4, 1989), in *Computer Graphics*, 23(3), July 1989, pages 325–334.

[2] Bernstein, Ralph. *Digital Image Processing of Earth Observation Sensor Data*, IBM J. Res. Develop., 1976.

[3] Cayless, M. A. and A. M. Marsden. *Lamps and Lighting*, Edward Arnold, London, 1983.

Figure 11: Two views of the Palazzo on the Grand Canal in Venice from *Les Contes d'Hoffmann*. The left and right sides of the set are modeled. The canal scenery in the center background was projected at an angle onto a curved backdrop using a predistorted slide. A series of floodlights are used to simulate a dim moonlight on the facades to the right. A high intensity spot is used to light the entrance to the left.

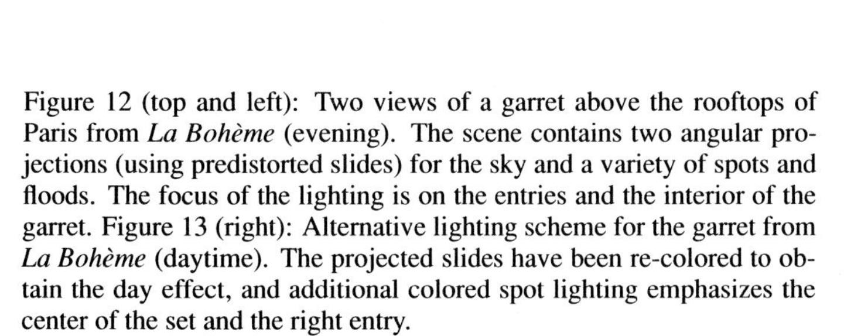

Figure 12 (top and left): Two views of a garret above the rooftops of Paris from *La Bohème* (evening). The scene contains two angular projections (using predistorted slides) for the sky and a variety of spots and floods. The focus of the lighting is on the entries and the interior of the garret. Figure 13 (right): Alternative lighting scheme for the garret from *La Bohème* (daytime). The projected slides have been re-colored to obtain the day effect, and additional colored spot lighting emphasizes the center of the set and the right entry.

[4] Cohen, Michael F., Shenchang Eric Chen, John R. Wallace, and Donald P. Greenberg. "A Progressive Refinement Approach to Fast Radiosity Image Generation," Proceedings of SIGGRAPH'88 (Atlanta, Georgia, August 1–5, 1988), in *Computer Graphics*, 22(4), August 1988, pages 75–84.

[5] Cohen, Michael F. and Donald P. Greenberg. "A Radiosity Solution for Complex Environments," Proceedings of SIGGRAPH'85 (San Francisco, California, July 22–26, 1985), in *Computer Graphics*, 19(3), July 1985, pages 31–40.

[6] Cohen, Michael F., Donald P. Greenberg, David S. Immel, and Philip J. Brock. "An Efficient Radiosity Approach for Realistic Image Synthesis," *IEEE Computer Graphics and Applications*, 6(3), March 1986, pages 26–35.

[7] Dorsey, Julie O'B. *Computer Graphics for the Design and Visualization of Opera Lighting Effects*, Master's thesis, Program of Computer Graphics, Cornell University, Ithaca, NY 14853, January 1990.

[8] Gilette, Michael J. *Designing With Light*, Mayfield Publishing Company, Palo Alto, 1978.

[9] Goral, Cindy M., Kenneth E. Torrance, Donald P. Greenberg, and Bennett Battaile. "Modeling the Interaction of Light Between Diffuse Surfaces," Proceedings of SIGGRAPH'84 (Minneapolis, Minnesota, July 23–27, 1984), in *Computer Graphics*, 18(3), July 1984, pages 213–222.

[10] Haralick, Robert M. "Automatic Remote Sensor Image Processing," *Topics in Applied Physics*, 11, 1976, pages 5–63.

[11] Hartmann, Rudolf. *Opera*, William Morrow and Company, New York, N.Y., 1977.

[12] Heckbert, Paul S. *Fundamentals of Texture Mapping and Image Warping*, Master's thesis, Department of EECS, UC Berkeley, Berkeley, CA 94720, June 1989.

[13] Kaufman, John E. *IES Lighting Handbook - Application Volume*, Illuminating Engineering Society of North America, New York, 1987.

[14] Max, Nelson L. "Computer Graphics Distortion for IMAX and OMNIMAX Projection," in Proceedings of Nicograph'83, 1983.

[15] Nishita, Tomoyuki, Yasuhiro Miyawaki, and Eihachiro Nakamae. "A Shading Model for Atmospheric Scattering Considering Luminous Intensity Distribution of Light Sources," Proceedings of SIGGRAPH'87 (Anaheim, California, July 27–31, 1987), in *Computer Graphics*, 21(4), July 1987, pages 303-310.

[16] Nishita, Tomoyuki and Eihachiro Nakamae. "Continuous Tone Representation of Three-Dimensional Objects Taking Account of Shadows and Interreflections," Proceedings of SIGGRAPH'85 (San Francisco, California, July 22–26, 1985), in *Computer Graphics*, 19(3), July 1985, pages 23–30.

[17] Nishita, Tomoyuki, Isao Okamura, and Eihachiro Nakamae. "Shading Models for Point and Linear Sources," *ACM Transactions on Graphics*, 4(2), April 1985, pages 124–146.

[18] Parker, W. Oren and Harvey K. Smith. *Scene Design and Stage Lighting*, Holt, Rinehart and Winston, Inc., New York, 1979.

[19] Pilbrow, Richard. *Stage Lighting*, Von Nostrand Reinhold Company, New York, 1979.

[20] Sellman, Hunton D. and Merrill Lessley. *Essentials of Stage Lighting*, Prentice-Hall, Inc, Englewood Cliffs, 1982.

[21] Siegel, Robert and John R. Howell. *Thermal Radiation Heat Transfer*, Hemisphere Publishing Corp., Washington DC., 1981.

[22] Sillion, François and Claude Puech. "A General Two-Pass Method Integrating Specular and Diffuse Reflection," Proceedings of SIGGRAPH'89 (Boston, Massachusetts, July 31 – August 4, 1989), in *Computer Graphics*, 23(3), July 1989, pages 335–344.

[23] Verbeck, Channing P. and Donald P. Greenberg. "A Comprehensive Light-Source Description for Computer Graphics," *IEEE Computer Graphics and Applications*, 4(7), July 1984, pages 66–75.

[24] Wallace, John R., Kells A. Elmquist, and Eric A. Haines. "A Ray Tracing Algorithm for Progressive Radiosity," Proceedings of SIGGRAPH'89 (Boston, Massachusetts, July 31 – August 4, 1989), in *Computer Graphics*, 23(3), July 1989, pages 315–324.

[25] Warn, David R. "Lighting Controls for Synthetic Images," Proceedings of SIGGRAPH'83 (Detroit, Michigan, July 25–29, 1983), in *Computer Graphics*, 17(3), July 1983, pages 13–21.

[26] Watson, Lee. *Lighting Design Handbook*, McGraw-Hill, New York, 1990.

[27] Wilfred, Thomas. *Projected Scenery - A Technical Manual*, The Drama Book Shop, New York, 1965.

[28] Wolberg, George. *Digital Image Warping*, IEEE Computer Society Press., Los Alamitos, CA, 1990.

## Appendix A — Beam and Field Angles

The beam angle is the central cone of light emitted from an instrument (Figure 14). The limit of the beam angle is usually defined as that point where the light diminishes to 50 percent of its intensity when compared with the center of the beam. The field angle is described as that point where the light diminishes to 10 percent of the output of the center of the beam.

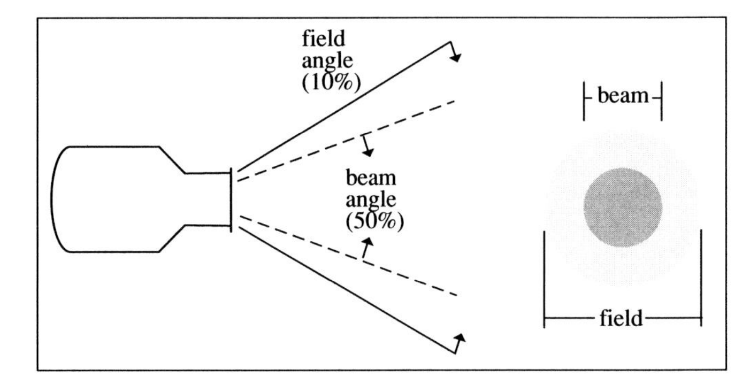


Figure 14: Relationship between the beam and field angles of a lighting instrument.

# Making Radiosity Usable: Automatic Preprocessing and Meshing Techniques for the Generation of Accurate Radiosity Solutions

**Daniel R. Baum, Stephen Mann†, Kevin P. Smith††, and James M. Winget**

Silicon Graphics Computer Systems
2011 N. Shoreline Blvd.
Mountain View, CA 94039-7311

†Department of Computer Science
University of Washington, Seattle, Wa. 98105

††Department of Computer Science
University of California, Berkeley, Ca. 94720

## ABSTRACT

Generating accurate radiosity solutions of real world environments is user-intensive and requires significant knowledge of the method. As a result, few end-users such as architects and designers use it. The output of most commercial modeling packages must be substantially "cleaned up" to satisfy the geometrical and topological criteria imposed by radiosity solution algorithms. Furthermore, the mesh used as the basis of the radiosity computation must meet several additional requirements for the solution to be accurate.

A set of geometrical and topological requirements is formalized that when satisfied yields an accurate radiosity solution. A series of algorithms is introduced that automatically processes raw model databases to meet these requirements. Thus, the end-user can concentrate on the design rather than on the details of the radiosity solution process. These algorithms are generally independent of the radiosity solution technique used, and thus apply to all mesh based radiosity methods.

**CR Categories and Subject Descriptors:** I.3.3 [Computer Graphics]: Picture/Image Generation; I.3.7 [Computer Graphics]: Three-Dimensional Graphics and Realism.
**General Terms:** Algorithms.
**Additional Key Words:** Radiosity, mesh-generation.

## 1. INTRODUCTION

Why is radiosity not more widely used today by its intended audience, the architect or designer? Aside from the computational expense of the method, the primary reason is that arriving at an accurate radiosity solution of a real world environment is a laborious process. The user must rework an input model by hand until it satisfies a set of technical criteria imposed by the radiosity solution algorithm in use. Most users are ill-equipped and disinclined to carry out this conversion.

To generate a solution, mesh based radiosity methods generally follow the pipeline outlined in Figure 1. First, the input model must be preprocessed. Output of popular CAD packages such as AutoCAD™ do not provide suitable input for radiosity algorithms without significant modification. *Environment preprocessing* includes cleaning the input geometry and topology as well as initial mesh generation. During the subsequent solution phase, the initial mesh may be adaptively refined. Achieving an accurate solution imposes several constraints on the input model and subsequent mesh. For example, the mesh must be sufficiently dense to capture high intensity gradients and shadow boundaries. Further, it must be topologically well-formed to avoid solution and display artifacts.

Until now, preprocessing a complex model required a person with expertise in the method. This person had to make many iterations through the solution process while interacting with the radiosity pipeline by either tweaking the model or manually adjusting the mesh. Even with user interaction, the solution might not have been accurate enough, resulting in a variety of visual anomalies.

Not surprisingly, the difficulties in generating accurate radiosity solutions are similar to those encountered in the finite element method (FEM). Although much research in FEM has concentrated on environment preprocessing and automatic mesh generation (for a review see [KELA87]), only recently has some attention been paid to similar problems for radiosity [BULL89] [CAMP90].

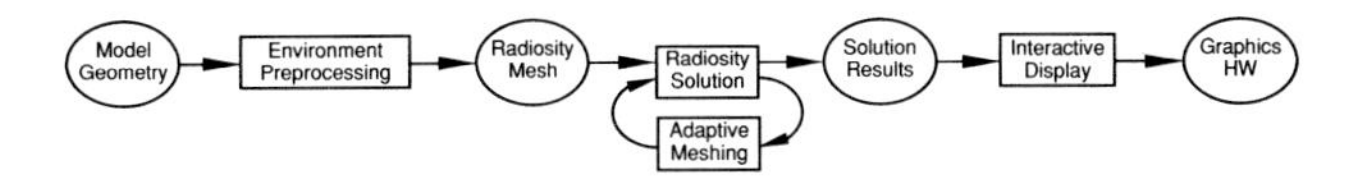


Figure 1. The Radiosity Pipeline.

The purpose of this paper is to introduce techniques that let the designer produce accurate radiosity rendered images of their model without knowledge of the radiosity method. More specifically, this paper introduces a series of algorithms that take databases from existing modeling packages as input. These new algorithms convert the input model database into a form that is geometrically and topologically suitable for radiosity solution algorithms. Additionally (and perhaps more importantly from the user's perspective), these algorithms accurately process complex input models automatically. Furthermore, since the concepts and techniques introduced in this paper are independent of the radiosity solution algorithm used, they are applicable to all mesh based radiosity methods.

The remainder of the paper is organized as follows. Section 2 specifies a number of geometrical and topological requirements that must be satisfied in the radiosity pipeline for

 ACM-0-89791-436-8/91/007/0051 $00.75

accurate radiosity solution generation. Section 3 introduces environment preprocessing algorithms that satisfy the requirements formalized in Section 2. In Section 4, a technique for adaptive mesh refinement within the solution phase is described. Finally, Section 5 presents results.

## 2. RADIOSITY PIPELINE REQUIREMENTS

Generating and displaying an accurate radiosity solution imposes many geometrical and topological requirements on the representations of data at various stages in the radiosity pipeline; the output at one stage in the pipeline must satisfy the input requirements of the next. For each stage there are two types of input requirements. The first, *internal*, is required by a particular stage of the pipeline to function. The second is *pass-through*, a requirement that must be met further downstream and has already been satisfied at an earlier stage. The output of a particular stage must satisfy such pass-through requirements, even if they are not internal requirements of that stage.

There is more than one way to impose requirements within the radiosity pipeline. For instance, one could design radiosity specific modeling software that would constrain the user to construct geometry in a fashion amenable to radiosity processing. This approach, however, would not function for existing modelers or existing databases. Other conceivable approaches may fall short when considering computational efficiency or numerical precision issues. The next three subsections outline a practical set of *radiosity pipeline requirements* that when imposed correct flaws in existing methods.

### 2.1 Model Geometry Requirements

In order to formalize the radiosity pipeline requirements, some terminology is first defined. An input model consists of *surfaces*, where a surface $S$ is a connected region with homogeneous material properties and continuous normals. Nonplanar surfaces are approximated with a set of planar faces. During mesh generation, surfaces are further discretized into collections of convex faces. These faces provide the underlying geometrical basis for the radiosity calculations. Radiosity *receiver nodes* are points in this discretization where radiosity values are computed and stored for subsequent interactive display. Receiver nodes frequently correspond to face vertices, facilitating the use of Gouraud interpolation for display. *Radiators* are those faces in the discretization that are used during the radiosity computation to radiate energy to the receiver nodes.

Because radiosity is a physically based global illumination technique, a physically based model is needed in order to obtain an accurate solution. Such a model is composed of solid objects. Thus, the first and foremost requirement imposed on the model geometry database is that it contain the information equivalent to that of a *solid model*. A true solid model representation allows the unambiguous classification of points into those lying inside of, outside of, or on an object's surface. Furthermore, for points on the object's surface, a solid model defines a unique outward pointing normal for each face.

Unfortunately, this solid modeling requirement is rarely met in practice and thus must be relaxed and supplemented to make automatic and accurate radiosity processing tractable. In particular, the single most common exception to the solid model database is the addition of *facades*: open single sided surfaces. In fact, many low-end commercial modelers used by architects encourage the user to construct facade objects.

More precisely, two types of facades occur: valid facades and invalid facades. A *valid facade* is one for which only the exterior surface radiates energy (i.e. no part of the interior surface is visible from anywhere in the viewing environment). An example of a valid facade is a box constructed without the bottom face, where the box is resting on a floor.

Radiosity solution algorithms cannot correctly determine illumination in environments containing valid facades unless they have a means to determine the outward pointing normal for each facade. Thus, even when valid facades are present in the model database, an additional requirement known as *normal consistency* must be imposed. If the sign of a face normal is not explicitly defined for a valid facade, it is assumed to be defined from the vertex ordering (e.g. all face vertexes occur in a counter-clockwise orientation the face).

An *invalid facade*, on the other hand, is one for which both sides are involved in the illumination computation. Consider what happens if the bottomless box is lifted off the floor. Energy radiated by the floor "passes through" the interior of the box. The interior of the box, because it is backfacing to the floor, becomes effectively invisible, leading to the computation of incorrect form-factors and subsequent solution inaccuracies.

Determination of a facade's validity is computationally demanding, thus complete identification of invalid facades is impractical prior to the solution phase. One option, which initially makes all facades double sided, fixes this particular problem but introduces several others. The most significant is a doubling of the problem complexity to unnecessarily model the "dark" interior of many objects. It also leads to substantially increased difficulties in numerical precision. In the current implementation the input model is limited to valid facades.

One additional complication introduced by facades is coplanar faces. *Overlapping coplanar faces* exist in a solid model when two objects are adjacent to one another (such as the bottom of a box sitting on a desktop). These coplanar faces cause no difficulties, as they are not visible. However, by allowing valid facades, a pair of coplanar faces might be visible, such as a facade sheet of paper on a desktop. Such overlapping coplanar face pairs cause difficulties for any rendering program as it is unclear which face should be seen and which should be occluded. For a radiosity program to function correctly, one of the coplanar faces must be removed.

### 2.2 Radiosity Mesh Requirements

The radiosity solution algorithm imposes its own input requirements on the radiosity mesh database. Fundamentally, obtaining an accurate radiosity solution involves both sampling and interpolation of an initially unknown function. The solution sampling is associated with radiator and receiver node density while interpolation is based on mesh topology.

Radiosity solutions are potentially discontinuous across surface boundaries due to the discontinuities in normals and material properties. Elsewhere, in regions without sharp shadow boundaries, the radiosity solution maintains a degree of continuity. It is important to continue to support the appropriate level of continuity in the solution as the surfaces are reduced to a collection of individual mesh faces. Thus, the first mesh requirement is the ability to perform continuous interpolation over individual surfaces after meshing.

Satisfaction of this requirement can be guaranteed through two associated meshing restrictions. First, the mesh must be composed of primitive faces: *triangles* or *convex quadrilaterals*. While arbitrary simple polygons could be used, restricting mesh faces to triangles and convex quadrilaterals substantially simplifies the associated local interpolation. In conjunction with this restriction is the further restriction that the meshing algorithm generate *no T-vertices* between adjacent faces within the same surface [Fig. 2]. The combination of these two mesh restrictions allows the use of finite element basis functions [HUGU87] to satisfy the desired level of continuity in the radiosity solution and in the subsequent display of the solution. In particular, these continuity requirements are useful in higher order finite element based radiosity solution techniques [HECK91]. Since the radiosity solution can be discontinuous across surface boundaries by definition, T-vertices are acceptable between surfaces.

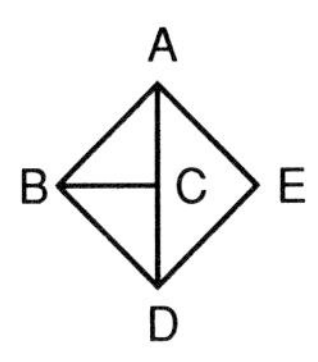


Figure 2. T-vertices. If the face on the right is defined by the vertices A,D,E, then there is a T-vertex at C.

The second requirement is that the faces be *well-shaped*. For triangles and convex quadrilaterals, the shape of a face can be characterized by its aspect ratio, $\rho$, where $\rho$ is defined as the ratio of the radius of the inscribed circle to the radius of the circumscribed circle of the face [FREY87]. The closer $\rho$ is to one, the better the shape of the face. Well-shaped faces are important to the radiosity solution phase for two reasons. First, approximations used during the solution phase are more accurate when based on well-shaped faces [BAUM89]. Second, these faces make the most efficient use of receiver nodes per unit area.

The third requirement is that the mesh have *sufficient radiator density*. If the radiators are too large, the solution will be inaccurate [BAUM89]. On the other hand, if the radiators are too small, the scene will be overly complex, and the solution time will be longer than necessary.

The fourth requirement is that the mesh have *sufficient receiver node density*. If the spacing between receiver nodes is inadequate, the radiosity solution will not accurately capture the true intensity gradients. On the other hand, if the node density is too high, intensity gradients will be over-determined at the expense of unnecessary computation. Some radiosity algorithms use adaptive refinement techniques to arrive at the appropriate node density [COHE85]. When using adaptive refinement, the initial mesh must have sufficient node density to allow automatic adaption criteria to be accurately evaluated. A second problem with insufficient node density is that it may make it impossible to meet the previously stated well-shaped face requirement [FREY87].

The fifth meshing requirement is that any *intersecting faces must be explicitly represented*. Failure to meet this requirement results in what is commonly referred to as light or shadow leakage. Consider the box in Color Plate 1. Although the box implicitly intersects the mesh of the ground, the ground contains no explicit contour representing the intersection. As a result, the box covers one of the receiver nodes associated with a face but not the entire face. When displaying the solution using Gouraud shading, a shadow incorrectly leaks out from beneath the box. If the box/ground intersection were explicitly represented, the box would completely cover the shadowed face, thus eliminating any leakage. Correctly removing these gradient discontinuities *a priori* avoids costly repeated adaptive subdivision to generate an approximate solution and is necessary for computing higher order radiosity solutions [HECK91].

Shadow leakage has been noted in both [BULL89] and [CAMP90]. Campbell approaches this problem by generating a mesh with the aid of shadow volumes. The mesh is constructed by projecting the shadow boundary created by a light source and occluding surface onto the occluded surface. The resulting mesh prevents shadow leakage and produces accurate shadow boundaries. However, such a mesh tends to exhibit poor aspect ratios and contains T-vertices. Additionally, because of the computational cost, the method does not appear to scale well to complex models.

### 2.3 Display Requirements

The display stage of the pipeline imposes its own requirements on the radiosity solution database. In particular, there can be no T-vertices in the solution database since it may cause cracks (sometimes referred to as pixel dropouts) to appear. Cracking occurs because the finite precision of the scan-conversion algorithms gives two different results along an edge where one side is split by an additional vertex [LATH90].

Although the radiosity mesh requirement implies that no T-vertices occur between faces of the same surface, there may be T-vertices between surfaces. Thus for display purposes, edges shared by more than one surface must be *ziplocked*. Ziplocking is a combined topological and geometric operation that fuses adjacent surfaces without affecting the interpolation of the solution within the individual surfaces. In Figure 2, ziplocking would convert the triangle A,D,E to the quadrilateral A,C,D,E.

Finally, well-shaped faces are also desirable in the display stage to avoid display artifacts sometimes induced when poorly shaped faces are Gouraud shaded [HALL90].

A summary of the radiosity pipeline requirements is given in Table 1.

| | | Environment Preprocessing | Radiosity Solution | Interactive Display |
|---|---|---|---|---|
| 1a. | solid model rep. + valid facades | » | R | |
| 1b. | normal consistency | R | R | |
| 2a. | no T-vertices | G | R | R |
| 2b. | no implicit intersections | G | R | |
| 2c. | no overlapping coplanar faces | G | R | R |
| 2d. | simple mesh faces | G | R | |
| 2e. | well-shaped faces | G | D | D |
| 2f. | sufficient radiator density | G | R | |
| 2g. | sufficient receiver density | G | R | |
| 3a. | ziplocking | G | » | R |

Table 1: Radiosity Pipeline Requirements.
»: Pass-through, **G**: Generated, **R**: Required, **D**: Desired

## 3. SATISFYING THE RADIOSITY PIPELINE REQUIREMENTS

This section introduces several algorithms which perform the environment preprocessing stage of the radiosity pipeline. The algorithms have been implemented as a series of geometry filters that when appropriately inserted into the radiosity pipeline yield substantially more accurate results. The expanded version of the environment preprocessing stage of the radiosity pipeline appears in Figure 3.

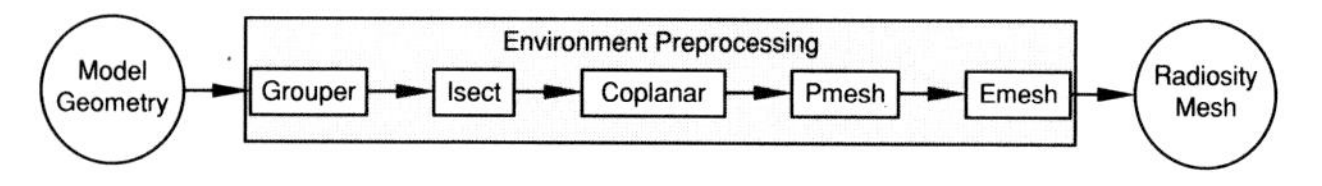


Figure 3: Expanded Environment Preprocessing Pipeline

Most of the requirements internal to the augmented environment preprocessing stage correspond to the radiosity pipeline requirements of Section 2. However, there is an additional requirement that the database contains *maximally connected planar faces*. That is, a planar region of homogeneous material must be represented as a single general face rather than a number of connected simpler faces.

To understand why this requirement is important, consider the green concave ground face with the hole in Color Plate 1. Many modelers will pre-tessellate concave faces (with or without holes) into a number of simpler canonical types such as convex quadrilaterals because they lack the ability to handle general faces. In doing this, the modeler imposes unnecessary constraints on meshing algorithms. Later independent meshing of the rectangles comprising the ground results in T-vertices along the shared edges. This in turn appears as shading discontinuities, or seams, during solution display [Color Plate 1]. Note that these same T-vertices also violate Requirement 3a, resulting in cracking. In [BULL89], Bullis notes the necessity for maximally connected planar faces although he does not provide an algorithm to process faces that fail to meet this requirement.

A summary of the expanded environment preprocessing requirements is given in Table 2.

| | Group | Isect | Copln | Pmesh | Emesh |
|---|---|---|---|---|---|
| 1a. solid model rep. + valid facades | » | » | » | » | » |
| 1b. normal consistency | R | » | R | » | » |
| 1c. max. connected planar faces | G | R | » | R | |
| 2a. no T-vertices | G | » | » | » | » |
| 2b. no implicit intersections | | G | R | » | » |
| 2c. no overlapping coplanar faces | | | G | » | » |
| 2d. simple mesh faces | | | | G | » |
| 2e. well-shaped faces | | | | G | » |
| 2f. sufficient radiator density | | | | G | » |
| 2g. sufficient receiver density | | | | | G |
| 3a. ziplocking | G | » | » | » | » |

Table 2: Environment Preprocessing Requirements
**»:** Pass-through, **G:** Generated, **R:** Required

### 3.1 Geometry Merging - The Grouper

The first filter, called the *Grouper*, is responsible for two tasks: generating surface connectivity information so that ziplocking can be performed at a later stage and forming maximally connected planar faces from adjacent coplanar faces. Note that T-vertices are removed as a result of forming maximally connected faces. As shown in Table 2, the Grouper requires an input model with consistent normals (1b) and has the pass-through requirement (1a).

To construct connectivity information, the Grouper first collapses sets of nearly coincident (where "nearly" is defined by a scene relative tolerance, *T*) vertices into one vertex. This is done by storing all model vertices into an octree. Each time another vertex is inserted, the algorithm checks if a vertex exists within *T* of the same position. If so, the new vertex is replaced by the existing one. Otherwise, the new vertex is inserted into the octree. Vertex merging is depicted in Figures 4a,b.

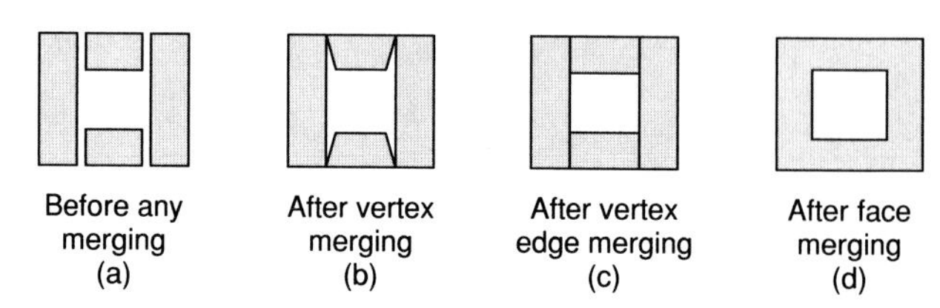


Figure 4. Steps performed by the Grouper.

Next, the Grouper iterates through all edges in the model and recursively searches the octree for any vertices that lie within *T* of that edge. These vertices are then inserted into the edge. At this point, the Grouper has created all of the connectivity information needed downstream in the pipeline [Fig. 4c].

The last step performed by the Grouper deals with the joining of coplanar faces that share edges. This is easily achieved by representing the model with a winged-edge data structure. Every edge in the data structure is examined, and if two coplanar faces of like material share that edge, then the two faces are merged [Fig. 4d].

### 3.2 Face Intersection - Isect

The next filter in the pipeline solves the shadow leakage problem by converting implicit face intersections into explicit face intersections. This is accomplished by identifying all pairs of intersecting faces and cutting them along their lines of intersection. The input to this filter is a set of maximally connected faces. Its output will be the same set of maximally connected faces split along their lines of intersection.

An existing program known as *Isect* performs these operations while paying particular attention to producing valid results in the presence of limited numerical precision. The Isect algorithms are detailed in [SEGA88][SEGA90].

### 3.3 Overlapping Coplanar Face Removal

There are two classes of coplanar faces that must be considered: when both faces are of the same material and when they are of different materials. The first case is trivial. Since Isect ensures that the faces have identical geometry, one of the faces is simply discarded. An example of the second case occurs when a piece of paper is placed on a desktop. The face from the desktop should be removed since the paper is supposed to be above the desktop. In general, however, it is impossible to determine which face is intended to be visible. A good heuristic is to remove the face that came from the larger surface.

### 3.4 Mesh Generation

The output of the Grouper/Isect/Coplanar has properties 1a-c and 2a-c from Table 2. However it fails to have the other properties in group 2: the faces may have any number of sides (though they will have at least three); they need not be convex (indeed, they may have holes); and there are no restrictions on their shapes or sizes. The purpose of the mesh generation software is to convert such a face set into a mesh that has the additional properties 2d-g.

The initial mesh generation strategy includes the substructuring concept developed by Cohen et al. [COHE85] which is based on a hierarchy of surfaces. Each surface is first subdivided into relatively large subsurfaces or *patches*. Each patch is then further subdivided into *elements*. During form-factor calculations, energy is radiated from patches and received by elements. Cohen introduced patch/element substructuring to increase solution detail without substantially increasing the size of the computation.

Patch/element substructuring serves an additional purpose in the augmented radiosity pipeline. In general, a radiosity mesh includes many more elements than patches. Furthermore, elements are frequently further subdivided during the radiosity solution phase if adaptive mesh refinement schemes are used [COHE85]. For these reasons, it is desirable that the element mesh generation algorithm and associated data structures be very efficient in both computation time and storage.

This leads to the following strategy for patch/element mesh generation. During patch generation much attention is paid ensuring that properties 2d-f are met. Given well-shaped triangular or convex quadrilateral patches, a very efficient algorithm can be designed to further subdivide these patches into well-shaped elements that achieve the necessary receiver node density (property 2g).

#### 3.4.1 Patch Meshing

Pmesh creates a patch mesh by first uniformly subdividing the face edges according to the desired patch edge length and the face geometry. A local rectangular grid is then placed on top of each face (note that other grids such as an equilateral triangular grid could be used as well). Any grid box that lies entirely within the interior of the face can be simply output as a rectangular patch. The remainder of the face is triangulated [Fig. 5].

A given radiator density imposes a maximum limit on the length of the patch edges, $l_{max}$. The edges of the faces are uniformly subdivided so as not to exceed this length: an edge of length $l$ is divided into ceiling($l/l_{max}$) subedges, each of length $l$/ceiling($l/l_{max}$). Since the radiator density is identical for all faces that share an edge, no T-vertices are created.

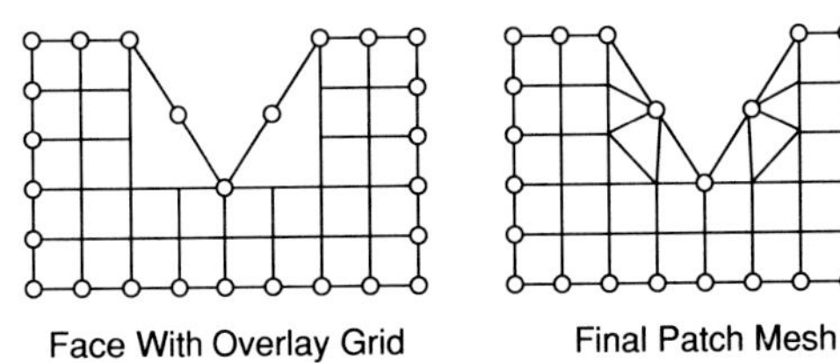


Figure 5. Subdivision created by Pmesh.

The grid edge length is a function of the desired patch edge length. One of the grid directions is aligned with the longest edge of the face. The grid edge length in this direction is the same as the subdivision size of this longest edge. The second grid direction is perpendicular to the first. The grid edge length in this direction is set to be $h$/ceiling($h/l_{max}$), where $h$ is the height of the face relative to its longest edge.

While most of the output patches produced by this method will be well-shaped, there are situations which may induce poorly shaped patches. One such situation is when one of the grid boxes that lies entirely inside the face has a corner near an edge of the face. This may result in a long skinny triangle. The problem is easily avoided by considering a grid box to be "outside" if one of its corners is near the edge of the face [Figs. 6a,b].

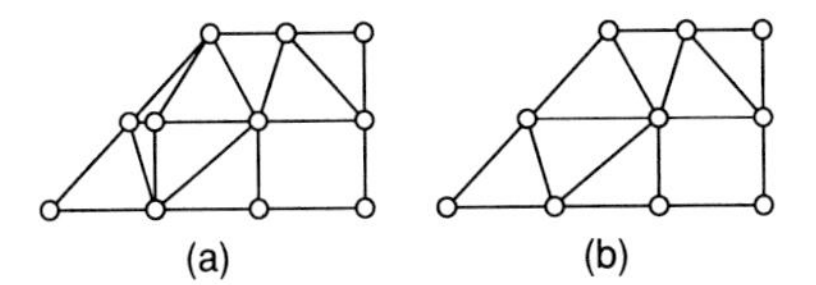


Figure 6. Invalidating grid boxes.

A second situation that results in poorly shaped patches occurs when the edge length of the input face is small compared to the length of the grid edges. One way to avoid this problem is to decrease the grid edge length so that it is more nearly equal to the minimum edge length of the face. However, this has the undesirable side effect of producing more output patches than needed by the radiosity solution program.

This problem is alleviated by using different radiator densities for different surfaces. Surfaces that have short edges can have a small grid edge length, while those without short edges can use a longer grid edge length. Thus, for each surface, the required radiator density will be based on an input minimum density and the minimum edge size of the faces in the surface.

Varying grid edge length on a surface by surface basis is only a partial solution since a single surface that has many faces might only have one edge that is short. In this case, all of the faces for that surface would use a small grid size, while a large size would suffice for most of them. Initial experience with non-adaptive Delaunay triangulation [SHAM85] failed to provide a better solution. What is needed is an adaptive method that creates smaller patches where needed and uses larger patches elsewhere, with a gradual change in size between the two regions. We are currently investigating methods to address this problem [CHEW89] [FREY87].

#### 3.4.2 Element Meshing Library

Since the receiving element density generally needs to be greater than the radiating patch density, an initial element mesh must be generated from the patch mesh. Once the radiosity computation has begun using the initial element mesh, the radiosity program may detect variations in intensity indicating that the element mesh node density needs to be further increased in certain areas. What is needed is an abstract data type for managing element mesh generation that allows the radiosity program to dynamically subdivide elements as needed.

An element meshing library was created that allows the radiosity program to create the initial element mesh and to refine the mesh as the radiosity solution progresses. The element mesh library guarantees that the mesh meets certain constraints, but leaves all decisions concerning when and where to mesh to the initial element mesher, *Emesh*, and the solution program.

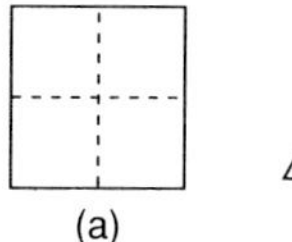
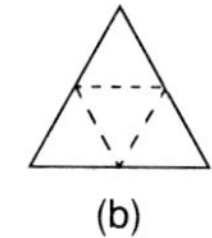
(a) (b)

Figure 7. 4-to-1 Subdivision

Mesh elements are refined by making four-to-one midpoint subdivisions [Figs. 7a,b]. Using this type of subdivision, if the input patch is well-shaped, the child elements also will be well-shaped. Certain constraints on the element mesh need to be maintained when subdividing, however. In particular, there should be a gradual change from regions of high node density to low node density. Thus, the element mesh should remain *balanced*. That is, two neighboring elements in the same surface should only have subdivision levels that differ by at most one [Fig. 8a]. A second constraint is that T-vertices not be introduced upon subdivision. None of the published radiosity methods that discuss mesh generation meet both these constraints [COHE85][BULL89] [CAMP89] [HANR90].

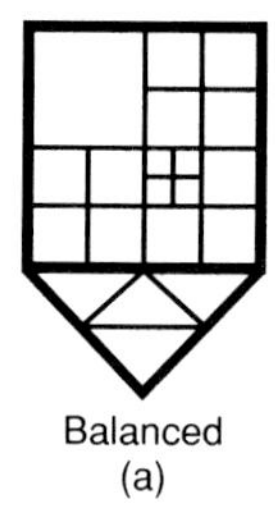

Figure 8. Balanced and Anchored Subdivisions

The operations to be performed on the data set include iterating over all of the vertices, iterating over all of the leaf elements, finding the neighbors of an element, and subdividing a set of elements. As previously mentioned, there will be large numbers of elements, necessitating a memory efficient data structure.

With all these considerations in mind, a new structure related to a quad tree was developed to store the elements. Since input patches can be triangular, the quadtree structure had to be extended to handle triangles, hence the name *tri-quad tree*. At the top level, there are a set of patches: the input faces. Each patch points to a tri-quad tree whose root is an element identical to the patch.

Before subdividing, it is assumed that the structure is balanced. A list of leaf elements is given to be subdivided. Subdividing these elements may unbalance the structure. The following pseudocode indicates how to rebalance the tree:

```
Subdivide(Element: E)
  Perform subdivision of E
  If (Level(E) - Level(Neighbor of E) > 1)
      Then Subdivide(Neighbor of E)
```

where Level(E) is the depth of the leaves of E relative to the root. This procedure is guaranteed to terminate since in each recursive call, the level of argument E is less than it was in the previous call.

The element mesh library is also designed so as not to create T-vertices. If an element is subdivided without subdividing its neighbors, T-vertices are created at these boundaries [Fig. 8a]. To eliminate these T-vertices, elements neighboring newly subdivided elements are *anchored*. That is, the neighbors are split to remove the T-vertices. To keep the adjustment local, the splits must only involve the T-vertices and the corner vertices of a neighboring element [Fig. 8b]. Disregarding symmetry, there are two such arrangements for triangles, and four for rectangles [Fig. 9]. If a new T-vertex is added to an anchored element, the element is unanchored and then reanchored using the new set of T-vertices. Rather than add a third anchor point to a triangle or a fourth one to a rectangle, the element is simply subdivided. Anchors are only necessary for leaf elements of the tri-quad tree, so if a leaf of an anchored element is to be subdivided, the anchored element is first unanchored and then subdivided.

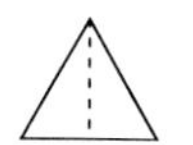

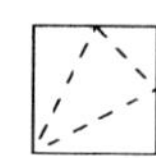
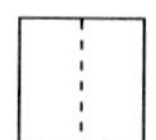
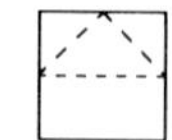

Figure 9. Six Types of Anchors

Balancing and anchoring have previously been applied to FEM mesh generation as a post process (for example, see [BAEH87]). The method presented here differs in that it balances and anchors dynamically. Such dynamic techniques are computationally beneficial for performing adaptive subdivision. Additionally, the tri-quad tree handles triangles and quadrilaterals simultaneously rather than just one or the other as in previous methods.

### 3.4.3 Initial Element Subdivision

The element meshing library provides the mechanism to form a suitable input mesh for the radiosity solution program, but it is up to the initial element mesher to determine the sufficient receiving element node density. It is important that the initial element node density be adequate to capture high intensity gradients such as shadow boundaries. If the initial element density is too low, subsequent adaptive mesh refinement schemes may not converge.

The algorithms for meeting the radiosity pipeline requirements are generally independent of the technique used during the radiosity solution phase. However, there are a few pertinent features of the solution algorithm used that simplify both the initial and adaptive mesh refinement strategies. A modified version of the progressive refinement algorithm presented in [BAUM89] is used. The primary difference is that all differential area-to-area form-factors are computed analytically and are computed from element vertices to the radiating patch rather than from points within the interior of the element. Element vertex visibility from the viewpoint of the radiating patch is computed directly using a proprietary algorithm embedded in the graphics hardware [AKEL88]. Adaptive refinement decisions are made using radiosity values at element vertices. Placing the radiosity receiver nodes at element vertices eliminates the need to interpolate radiosities from adjacent elements in order to arrive at vertex radiosities. Computing vertex radiosities directly is also advantageous when displaying the resultant solution using Gouraud interpolation [WALL89].

To ensure sufficient initial element node density, shadow boundaries must be identified *a priori*. The techniques of Campbell and Fussell analytically locate shadow boundaries and incorporate these boundaries into the initial element mesh [CAMP90]. For complex models, such an analytical approach is computationally infeasible. Thus, a numerical technique was developed to determine the necessary initial element node density. This entails detecting and further subdividing elements that are partially occluded from the light source. Since the radiosity program computes vertex visibilities directly, a candidate element for subdivision can be trivially identified if only some of its vertices are visible to the light source. The challenging case occurs when the vertices of a partially occluded element are either all visible to or all hidden from the light source.

Partially occluded elements whose vertices are all hidden from or all visible to the light source are detected by performing the following operations for each light source. First, all elements are rendered onto a hemi-cube using the standard hemi-cube algorithm [COHE85]. The hemi-cube item and Z buffers are then scanned for two adjacent hemi-cube pixels that are owned by different elements and that have significantly different Z values. In such a pair, the element owning the further pixel is marked as being partially occluded. A conservative heuristic is used to determine when the difference in Z values is large enough to warrant subdivision (note this occasionally results in unnecessary subdivision).

## 4. ADAPTIVE MESH REFINEMENT

Initial element subdivision concentrates on providing sufficient element node density for capturing shadow boundaries. However, intensity gradients resulting from indirect reflections are not known until the solution phase is invoked. Adaptive mesh refinement detects such gradients and further subdivides sections of the mesh to achieve the necessary receiver node density. Since the element meshing library is used, newly created mesh elements maintain properties 2d-f.

An element is subdivided if the intensity gradient across an edge is too high, and that edge is longer than a specified length. Since element subdivision adds new receiver nodes to the scene, the question remains as to what radiosity values should be assigned to these new nodes.

Consider the situation in Figure 11. Assume a substantial intensity gradient exists across the edge so that the refinement algorithm creates a new node W. To obtain the correct value for W, the effect of all previously shot radiators must be accounted for. For example, if 20 progressive refinement iterations had been performed before creating W, those 20 patches would have to be reshot at W.

Figure 11. What value should be assigned to W?

A less expensive method of estimating the radiosity value at W is to interpolate from the radiosities at U and V before the current radiating patch is shot. Only the current radiator is reshot at newly created element nodes (just W in this case) to accurately account for the energy contributed by the current radiating patch. If the intensity gradient along the edge UV is monotonic, the maximum error induced by this estimate is less than one half of the intensity difference.

At additional expense, the correct values for all nodes created by adaptive refinement are computed by restarting the solution phase after a specified number of iterations. The refined mesh is then used as the input for the next pass through the solution phase.

Sufficient radiator density is also achieved using the element meshing library. The determination of when to adaptively subdivide the radiator is made using the techniques from [BAUM89].

## 5. RESULTS

Each stage from the expanded environment preprocessing pipeline in Section 3 was implemented as a separate C program on a Silicon Graphics IRIS 4D/310 GTX superworkstation. The adaptive mesh refinement scheme was integrated into the radiosity solution program. By configuring these programs as a Unix™ pipeline, the user inputs the raw model geometry to the front of the pipeline and receives the accurate radiosity solution database as output.

The same raw input model that was used to generate the radiosity solution for Color Plate 1 was passed through the expanded environment preprocessing pipeline before being input to the solution program. The result is shown in Color Plate 2. Since the radiosity pipeline requirements were met, the resulting solution is free from the inaccuracies and visual artifacts present in the original solution. Specifically, note the absence of shadow leakage under the box, and lack of shading discontinuities and cracks on the ground. Furthermore, there is now sufficient receiver node density to capture shadow boundaries.

Clearly the lamp post model is trivial, and the radiosity pipeline requirements could have been met using human intervention during the modeling and meshing stages. However, user intervention is not practical for complex models, often making accurate radiosity solutions of complex models unobtainable.

To demonstrate the accuracy and robustness of the expanded pipeline, radiosity solutions for two complex models were generated. The first is a model of the residence of Dr. Fred Brooks of UNC Chapel Hill. The model was created using AutoCAD™ by UNC graduate students: Harry Marples, Michael Zaretsky, John Alspaugh, and Amitabh Varshney. The solution was performed on the entire house; the resulting mesh after adaptive refinement contains 420,026 elements. A view of the piano room is shown in Color Plate 3.

The second model was designed by Mark Mack Architects for a proposed theater near Candlestick Park in San Francisco. The theater model was built using GDS software by Charles Ehrlich from the Dept. of Architecture, UC Berkeley. At 1,061,543 elements, the Candlestick Theater is, to the authors' knowledge, the most complex radiosity solution yet computed. Two views of the theater are shown in Color Plates 4 and 5. The corresponding mesh is found in Color Plate 6. In Color Plate 4, note the shadows cast by the rungs of the catwalk onto the adjoining catwalk frame. Timings and statistics for both models are summarized in Table 3.

After testing the expanded radiosity pipeline on complex models, some areas for improvement and further research were identified. The numerical approach for detecting shadow boundaries is limited by the resolution of the hemi-cube. This problem can be rectified using the anti-aliasing techniques of [HAEB90]. Furthermore, since shadow boundaries are not necessarily aligned with the element mesh, a jagged shadow edge may result. Finally, although the implementation is reasonably fast, there is ample room for performance improvements. All stages of the pipeline are currently implemented sequentially, and there are several stages that could take advantage of parallel processing techniques.

| | Brooks' House | Candlestick Theater |
|---|---|---|
| # of input surfaces | 8,623 | 5,276 |
| # of patches | 68,186 | 78,094 |
| # of elements | 420,026 | 1,061,543 |
| Grouper time | 2:47 min | 2:50 min |
| Isect time | 2:23 min | 4:01 min |
| Pmesh time | 6:30 min | 25:53 min |
| Emesh time | 5 sec | 32 sec |
| Depth Buffer Subdivision | not used | 3:40 min/light |
| Solution time per iteration | 2:16 min | 7:12 min |
| Number of iterations | 2000 | 1600 |

Table 3. Program Timings and Statistics (all timings were done on a single processor IRIS 4D/310 GTX)

## 6. CONCLUSIONS

Producing an accurate radiosity solution for a complex model is difficult because the output of most modeling packages does not satisfy the geometrical and topological criteria imposed by radiosity solution algorithms. Generating an accurate solution has required a user to interact with the radiosity solution process by tweaking the model and adjusting the mesh.

A set of radiosity pipeline requirements have been specified that, when satisfied, yield accurate radiosity solutions. A series of "model cleaning" and mesh generation algorithms that automatically convert raw model databases to meet these pipeline requirements were then introduced, eliminating the need for user intervention. Since the algorithms are generally independent of the radiosity solution technique used, they apply to all mesh based radiosity methods.

Earlier work by the authors focused on improving the accuracy of radiosity solution techniques [BAUM89]. Combining accurate solution algorithms with the automatic preprocessing techniques presented here provide the foundation for a practical radiosity rendering system. It is hoped that this work will put the radiosity method into the hands of those who will benefit from it most: architects and designers.

## ACKNOWLEDGEMENTS

The authors thank Mark Segal for support on Isect and helpful comments on the paper.

## REFERENCES

[AKEL88] Akeley, Kurt and Tom Jermoluk, "High Performance Polygon Rendering," *Computer Graphics (SIGGRAPH '88 Proceedings)*, Vol 22. No. 4., August 1988. pp. 239-246.

[BAEH87] Baehann, Peggy L., Scott L. Wittchen, Mark S. Shepard, Kurt R. Grice, and Mark A. Yerry, "Robust, Geometrically Based, Automatic 2D Mesh Generation," *Int. Journal for Numerical Methods in Engineering*, Vol. 24, 1987, pp. 1043-1078.

[BAUM89] Baum, Daniel R., Holly E. Rushmeier, and James M. Winget, "Improving Radiosity Solutions Through The User of Analytically Determined Form-factors," *Computer Graphics (SIGGRAPH '89 Proceedings)*, Vol. 23. No. 3, July 1989, pp. 325-334.

[BULL89] Bullis, James M., "Models and Algorithms for Computing Realistic Images Containing Diffuse Reflections," Master's Thesis, U. of Minnesota, 1989.

[CAMP90] Campbell, A. T. III. and Donald S. Fussell, "Adaptive Mesh Generation," *Computer Graphics (SIGGRAPH '90 Proceedings)*, Vol 24. No. 4., August 1990. pp. 155-164.

[CHEW89] Chew, L. Paul, Guaranteed-Quality Triangular Meshes, Technical Report TR 89-983, April 1989, Department of Computer Science, Cornell University, Ithaca, New York.

[COHE85] Cohen, Michael F. "A Radiosity Method for the Realistic Image Synthesis of Complex Diffuse Environments," Master's Thesis, Cornell U., August 1985.

[FREY87] Frey, William H., "Selective Refinement: A New Strategy For Automatic Node Placement in Graded Triangular Meshes," *Int. Journal for Numerical Methods in Engineering*, Vol. 24, 1987, pp. 2183-2200.

[HAEB90] Haeberli, Paul and Kurt Akeley, "The Accumulation Buffer: Hardware Support for High-Quality Rendering," *Computer Graphics (SIGGRAPH '90 Proceedings)*, Vol. 24, No. 4, August, 1990.

[HALL90] Hall, Mark and Joe Warren, "Adaptive Polygonalization of Implicitly Defined Surfaces," *IEEE Computer Graphics & Applications*, Vol. 10, No. 6, Nov. 1990, pp. 33-42.

[HANR90] Hanrahan, Pat and David Salzman, "A Rapid Hierarchical Radiosity Algorithm for Unoccluded Environments," *Proc. of Eurographics Workshop on Photosimulation, Realism and Physics in Computer Graphics*, Rennes, France, June 1990, pp. 151-171.

[HECK91] Heckbert, Paul S. and James M. Winget, "Finite Element Methods for Global Illumination," tech memo, CS Division, EECS Dept., U.C. Berkeley, May 1991.

[HUGU87] Hugues, Thomas J. R., *The Finite Element Method*. Prentice-Hall, Englewood Cliffs, NJ, 1987.

[KELA87] Kela, Ajay, "Automatic Finite Element Mesh Generation And Self-Adaptive Incremental Analysis Through Geometric Modeling," Doctoral Dissertation, Univ. Of Rochester, January 1987.

[LATH90] Lathrop, Olin, David Kirk and Doug Voorhies, "Accurate Rendering by Subpixel Addressing," *IEEE Computer Graphics & Applications*, Vol. 10, No. 5, Sept. 1990, pp. 45-52.

[SEGA88] Segal, Mark and Carlo H. Sequin, "Partitioning Polyhedral Objects Into Non-intersecting Parts," *IEEE Computer Graphics & Applications*, Vol. 8, No. 1, Jan. 1988, pp. 53-67.

[SEGA90] Segal, Mark, "Using Tolerances to Guarantee Valid Polyhedral Modeling Results," *Computer Graphics (SIGGRAPH '90 Proceedings)*, Vol 24. No. 4., August 1990. pp. 105-114.

[SEUS53] Seuss, Dr. "The Sneetches," in *The Sneetches and Other Stories*, pp. 2-25, Random House, NY 1953.

[SHAM85] Shamos, Michael I. and Franco P. Preparata, editors, *Computational Geometry: an Introduction*, Springer-Verlag, 1985.

[WALL89] Wallace, John R., Kells A. Elmquist and Eric A. Haines, "A Ray Tracing Algorithm for Progressive Radiosity," *Computer Graphics* (*SIGGRAPH '89 Proceedings*), Vol. 23. No. 3, July 1989, pp. 315-324.

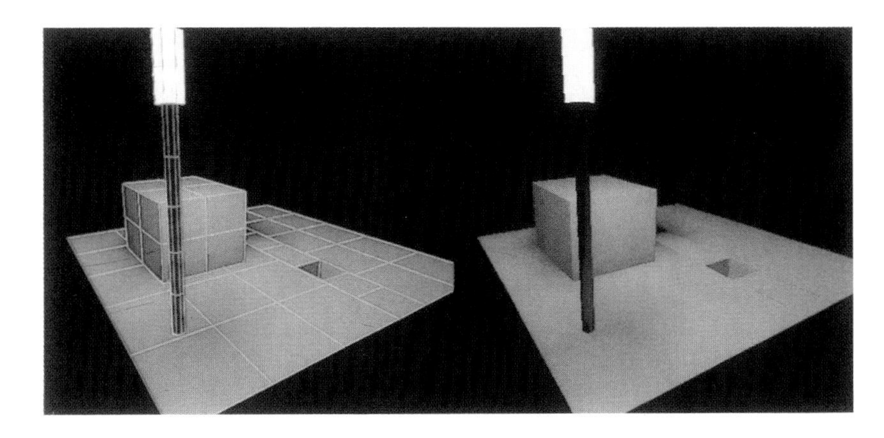

**Color Plate 1**

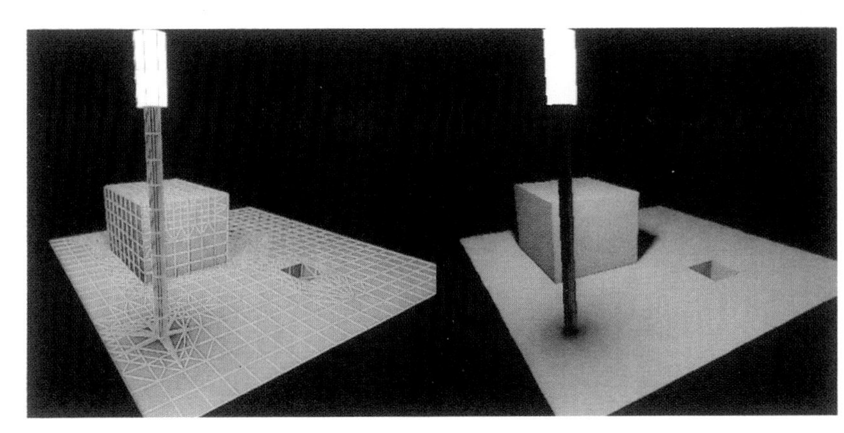

**Color Plate 2**

**Color Plate 3**

**Color Plate 4**

**Color Plate 5**

**Color Plate 6**

# Visibility Preprocessing For Interactive Walkthroughs

Seth J. Teller
Carlo H. Séquin
University of California at Berkeley‡

## Abstract

The number of polygons comprising interesting architectural models is many more than can be rendered at interactive frame rates. However, due to occlusion by opaque surfaces (e.g., walls), only a small fraction of a typical model is visible from most viewpoints.

We describe a method of visibility preprocessing that is efficient and effective for axis-aligned or *axial* architectural models. A model is subdivided into rectangular *cells* whose boundaries coincide with major opaque surfaces. Non-opaque *portals* are identified on cell boundaries, and used to form an *adjacency graph* connecting the cells of the subdivision. Next, the *cell-to-cell* visibility is computed for each cell of the subdivision, by linking pairs of cells between which unobstructed *sightlines* exist.

During an interactive *walkthrough* phase, an observer with a known position and *view cone* moves through the model. At each frame, the cell containing the observer is identified, and the contents of potentially visible cells are retrieved from storage. The set of potentially visible cells is further reduced by culling it against the observer's view cone, producing the *eye-to-cell visibility*. The contents of the remaining visible cells are then sent to a graphics pipeline for hidden-surface removal and rendering.

Tests on moderately complex 2-D and 3-D axial models reveal substantially reduced rendering loads.

**CR Categories and Subject Descriptors: [Computer Graphics]:** I.3.5 Computational Geometry and Object Modeling – *geometric algorithms, languages, and systems*; I.3.7 Three-Dimensional Graphics and Realism – *visible line/surface algorithms*.

**Additional Key Words and Phrases:** architectural simulation, linear programming, superset visibility.

‡Computer Science Department, Berkeley, CA 94720



## 1 Introduction

Interesting architectural models of furnished buildings may consist of several million polygons. This is many more than today's workstations can render in a fraction of a second, as is necessary for smooth interactive walkthroughs.

However, such scenes typically consist of large connected elements of opaque material (e.g., walls), so that from most vantage points only a small fraction of the model can be seen. The scene can be spatially subdivided into *cells*, and the model partitioned into sets of polygons attached to each cell. Approximate visibility information can then be computed offline, and associated with each cell for later use in an interactive rendering phase. This approximate information must contain a superset of the polygons visible from any viewpoint in the cell. If this "potentially visible set" or PVS [1] excluded some visible polygon for an observer position, the interactive rendering phase would exhibit flashing or holes there, detracting from the simulation's accuracy and realism.

### 1.1 Visibility Precomputation

Several researchers have proposed spatial subdivision techniques for rendering acceleration. We broadly refer to these methods as "visibility precomputations," since by performing work offline they reduce the effort involved in solving the hidden-surface problem. Much attention has focused on computing *exact* visibility (e.g., [5, 12, 16, 20, 22]); that is, computing an exact description of the visible elements of the scene data for every qualitatively distinct region of viewpoints. Such complete descriptions may be combinatorially complex and difficult to implement [16, 18], even for highly restricted viewpoint regions (e.g., viewpoints at infinity).

The binary space partition or BSP tree data structure [8] obviates the hidden-surface computation by producing a back-to-front ordering of polygons from any viewpoint. This technique has the drawback that, for an $n$-polygon scene, the splitting operations needed to construct the BSP tree may generate $O(n^2)$ new polygons [17]. Fixed-grid and octree spatial subdivisions [9, 11] accelerate ray-traced rendering by efficiently answering queries about rays propagating through ordered sets of parallelepipedal cells. To our knowledge, these ray-propagation techniques have not been used in interactive display systems.

Given the wide availability of fast polygon-rendering hardware [3, 14], it seems reasonable to search for simpler, faster algorithms which may *overestimate* the set of visible polygons, computing a *superset* of the true answer. Graphics hardware can then solve the

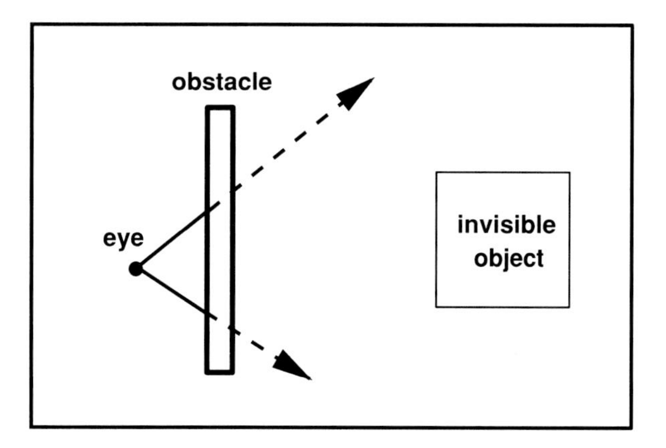


Figure 1: Cone-octree culling: the boxed object is reported visible.

hidden-surface problem for this polygon superset in screen-space. One approach involves intersecting a view cone with an octree-based spatial subdivision of the input [10]. This method has the undesirable property that it can report as visible an arbitrarily large part of the scene when, in fact, only a tiny portion can be seen (Figure 1). The algorithm may also have poor average case behavior for scenes with high depth complexity; i.e., many viewpoints for which a large number of overlapping polygons paint the same screen pixel.

Another overestimation method involves finding *portals*, or non-opaque regions, in otherwise opaque model elements, and treating these as lineal (in 2-D) or areal (in 3-D) light sources [1]. Opaque polygons in the model then cause *shadow volumes* [6] to arise with respect to the light sources; those parts of the model inside the shadow volumes can be marked invisible for any observer on the originating portal. This portal-polygon occlusion algorithm has not found use in practice due to implementation difficulties and high computational complexity [1, 2].

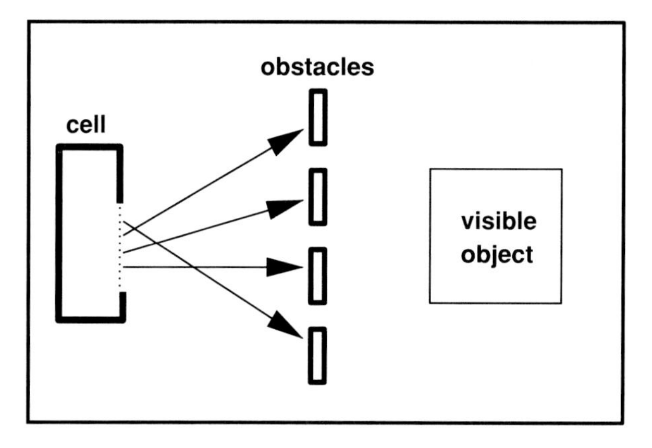


Figure 2: Ray casting: the boxed object is not reported visible.

A third approach estimates visibility using discrete sampling, after spatial subdivision. Conceptually, rays are cast outward from a stochastic, finite point set on the boundary of each spatial cell. Polygons hit by the rays are included in the PVS for that cell [1]. This approach can *underestimate* the cell's PVS by failing to report visible polygons (Figure 2). In practice, an extremely large number of rays must be cast to overcome this problem.

### 1.2 Overview

This paper describes a new approach to spatial subdivision and the visibility problem. The scene space is subdivided along its major opaque features; small, detailed scene elements are considered "non-occluding" and are ignored. After subdivision, a maximal set of *sightlines* is found from each cell to the rest of the subdivision. A novel aspect of our algorithm is that sightlines are not cast from discrete sample locations. Instead, *cell-to-cell visibility* is established if a sightline exists from any point in one cell to any point in another. As a consequence, the cells reached by sightlines provably contain a superset of the PVS for any given cell.

The data structure created during this gross visibility determination is stored with each cell, for use during an interactive walk-through phase. The cell-to-cell visibility can be further dynamically culled against the *view cone* of an observer, again producing a reliable superset of the visible scene data, the *eye-to-cell visibility*. The detailed data contained in each visible cell, along with associated normal, color, texture data etc., are passed to a hardware renderer for removal of hidden surfaces (including, crucially, those polygons invisible to the observer). The two-fold model pruning described admits a dramatic reduction in the complexity of the exact hidden-surface determination that must be performed by a real-time rendering system.

We describe the spatial subdivision along major structural elements in Section 2, and the cell-to-cell visibility computation in Section 3. Section 4 describes the additional culling possible when the position and viewing direction of the observer are known. Some quantitative experimental results are given in Section 5, based on an implementation for axial 2-D models. Section 6 describes work in progress toward a more general algorithm.

## 2 The Spatial Subdivision

### 2.1 Assumptions About Input

We make two simplifying assumptions. First, we restrict our attention to "faces" that are axial line segments in the plane; that is, line segments parallel to either the $x$- or $y$-axis. These admit a particularly simple subdivision technique, and are useful for visualization and expository purposes. Second, we assume that the coordinate data occur on a grid; this allows exact comparisons between positions, lengths, and areas. Relaxing either assumption would not affect the algorithms conceptually, but would of course increase the complexity of any robust implementation.

Throughout the paper we use example data suggestive of architectural floorplans, since realizing truly interactive architectural and environmental simulations is a primary goal of our research. However, we note that the methods we describe have a modular nature and can be used to accelerate a range of graphics computations, for example ray-tracing and radiosity methods, flight simulators, and object-space animation and shadowing algorithms.

### 2.2 Subdivision Requirements

We require that any spatial subdivision employed consist of *convex cells*, and support *point location*, *portal enumeration* on cell boundaries, and *neighbor finding*. We will demonstrate the algorithm's correctness for any such spatial subdivision. Its effectiveness, however, depends on the more subjective criterion that cell boundaries in the subdivision be "mostly opaque."

## 2.3 Subdivision Method

The input or *scene data* consists of $n$ axial faces. We perform the spatial subdivision using a BSP tree [8] whose splitting planes contain the major axial faces. For the special case of planar, axial data, the BSP tree becomes an instance of a $k$-D tree [4] with $k = 2$. Every node of a $k$-D tree is associated with a spatial cell bounded by $k$ half-open *extents* $[x_{0,min} \dots x_{0,max}), \dots, [x_{k-1,min} \dots x_{k-1,max})$. If a $k$-D node is not a leaf, it has a *split dimension* $s$ such that $0 \leq s < k$; a *split abscissa* $a$ such that $x_{s,min} < a < x_{s,max}$; and *low* and *high child* nodes with extents equivalent to that of the parent in every dimension except $k = s$, for which the extents are $[x_{s,min} \dots a)$ and $[a \dots x_{s,max})$, respectively. A balanced $k$-D tree supports logarithmic-time point location and linear-time neighbor queries.

The $k$-D tree root cell's extent is initialized to the bounding box of the input (Fig. 3-*a*). Each input face **F** is classified with respect to the root cell as:

- **disjoint** if **F** has no intersection with the cell;
- **spanning** if **F** partitions the cell interior into components that intersect only on their boundaries;
- **covering** if **F** lies on the cell boundary and intersects the boundary's relative interior;
- **incident** otherwise.

Spanning, covering, and incident faces, but not disjoint faces, are stored with each node. Clearly no face can be disjoint from the root cell. The disjoint class becomes relevant after subdivision, when a parent may contain faces disjoint from one or the other of its children.

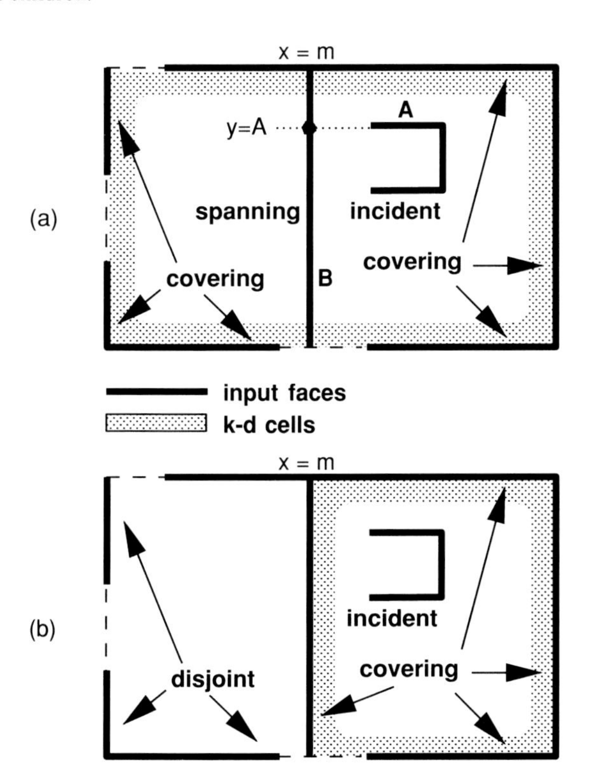


Figure 3: (a): A $k$-D tree root cell and input face classifications. (b): The right-hand cell and contents after the first split at $x = m$.

We say that face **A** *cleaves* face **B** if the line supporting **A** intersects **B** at a point in **B**'s relative interior (Fig. 3-*a*). We recursively subdivide the root node, repeatedly subjecting each leaf cell of the $k$-D tree to the following procedure:

- If the $k$-D cell has no incident faces (its interior is empty), do nothing;
- if any spanning faces exist, split on the median spanning face;
- otherwise, split on a sufficiently obscured minimum cleaving abscissa; i.e., along a face **A** cleaving a minimal set of faces orthogonal to **A**.

"Sufficiently obscured" means that the lengths of the faces at this abscissa sum to more than some threshold. If several abscissae are minimally cleaving, the candidate closest to that of the median face is chosen. Figure 4 depicts four minimally cleaving abscissae in $x$, marked as **0**; the median abscissa is marked as *.

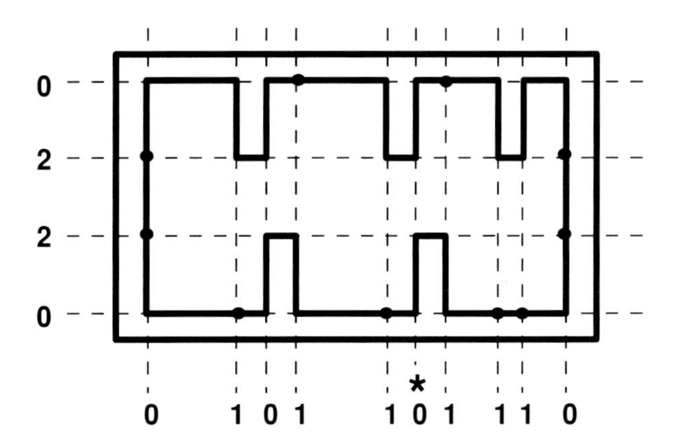


Figure 4: Cleaving abscissae (the split abscissa is marked *).

After each split, the contents of the parent node are reclassified as disjoint, spanning, covering, or incident with respect to each child, and all but the disjoint faces are stored with the child. Figure 3-*a* depicts a $k$-D tree root node; after this node is split at $x = m$, Figure 3-*b* shows the reclassification of the root's contents with respect to its high (i.e., right-hand) child.

This recursive subdivision continues until no suitable split abscissae are identified. We have found that these criteria, although somewhat naive, yield a tree whose cell structure reflects the "rooms" of the architectural models fairly well. Moreover, the splitting procedure can be applied quickly. At the cost of performing an initial $O(n \lg n)$ sort, the split dimension and abscissa can be determined in time $O(f)$ at each split, where $f$ is the number of faces stored with the node.

After subdivision terminates, the *portals* (i.e., non-opaque portions of shared boundaries) are enumerated and stored with each leaf cell, along with an identifier for the neighboring cell to which the portal leads (Figure 5). Enumerating the portals in this fashion amounts to constructing an *adjacency graph* over the subdivision leaf cells, in which two leaves (vertices) are adjacent (share an edge) if and only if there is a portal connecting them.

# 3 Cell-to-Cell Visibility

Once the spatial subdivision has been constructed, we compute *cell-to-cell visibility* information about the leaf cells by determining

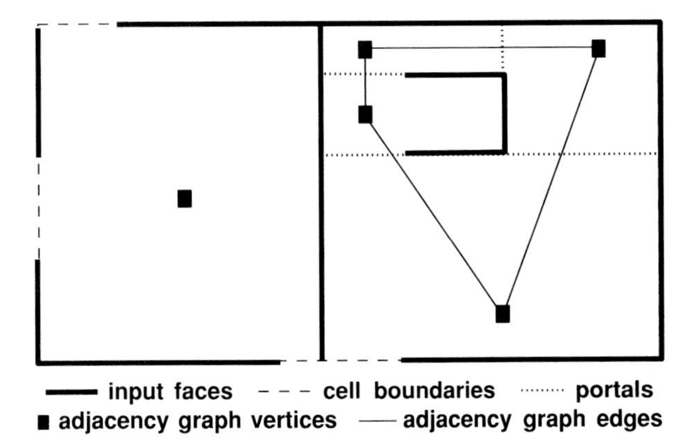


Figure 5: Subdivision, with portals and adjacency graph.

cells between which an unobstructed *sightline* exists. Clearly such a sightline must be disjoint from any opaque faces and thus must intersect, or *stab*, a portal in order to pass from one cell to the next. Sightlines connecting cells that are not immediate neighbors must traverse a *portal sequence*, each member of which lies on the boundary of an intervening cell. Observe that it is sufficient to consider sightlines originating and terminating on portals since, if there exists a sightline through two points in two cells' interiors, there must be a sightline intersecting a portal from each cell. The problem of finding sightlines between cell areas reduces to finding sightlines between line segments on cell boundaries.

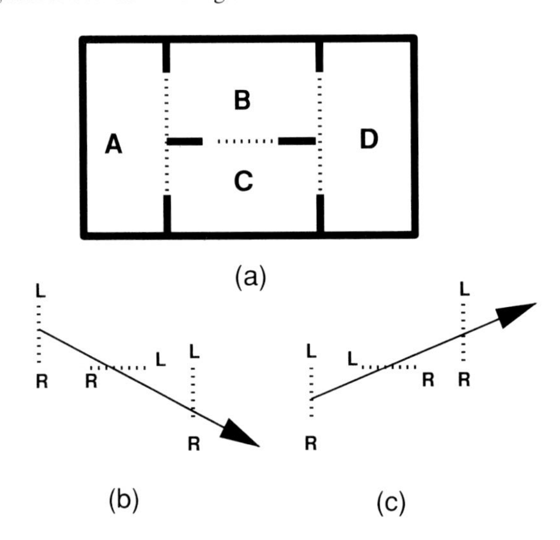


Figure 6: Oriented portal sequences, and separable sets **L** and **R**.

We say that a portal sequence *admits* a sightline if there exists a line that stabs every portal of the sequence. Figure 6 depicts four cells $A$, $B$, $C$, and $D$. There are four portal sequences originating at $A$ that admit sightlines: $[A/B,\ B/C,\ C/D]$, $[A/C,\ C/B,\ B/D]$, $[A/B,\ B/D]$, and $[A/C,\ C/D]$, where $P/Q$ denotes a portal from cell $P$ to cell $Q$. Thus $A$, $B$, $C$, and $D$ are mutually visible.

## 3.1 Generating Portal Sequences

To find sightlines, we must generate candidate portal sequences, and identify those sequences that admit sightlines. We find candidate portal sequences with a graph traversal on the cell adjacency graph. Two cells $P$ and $Q$ are *neighbors* if their shared boundary is not completely opaque. Each connected non-opaque region of this shared boundary is a portal from $P$ to $Q$. Given any starting cell $C$ for which we wish to compute visible cells, a recursive depth-first search (DFS) of $C$'s neighbors, rooted at $C$, produces candidate portal sequences. Searching proceeds incrementally; when a candidate portal sequence no longer admits a sightline (according to the criterion described below), the depth-first search on that portal sequence terminates. The cells reached by the DFS are stored in a *stab tree* (see below) as they are encountered.

## 3.2 Finding Sightlines Through Portal Sequences

The fact that portal sequences arise from directed paths in the subdivision adjacency graph allows us to *orient* each portal in the sequence and find sightlines easily. As the DFS encounters each portal, it places the portal endpoints in a set **L** or **R**, according to the portal's orientation (Figure 6). A sightline can stab this portal sequence *if and only if the point sets* **L** *and* **R** *are linearly separable*; that is, iff there exists a line $S$ such that

$$\begin{aligned} S \cdot L \geq 0, &\quad \forall\, L \in \mathbf{L} \\ S \cdot R \leq 0, &\quad \forall\, R \in \mathbf{R}. \end{aligned} \tag{1}$$

For a portal sequence of length $m$, this is a linear programming problem of $2m$ constraints. Both deterministic [15] and randomized [19] algorithms exist to solve this linear program (i.e., find a line stabbing the portal sequence) in linear time; that is, time $O(m)$. If no such stabbing line exists, the algorithms report this fact.

## 3.3 The Algorithm

Assume the existence of a routine *Stabbing_Line*($\mathbf{P}$) that, given a portal sequence $\mathbf{P}$, determines either a stabbing line for $\mathbf{P}$ or determines that no such stabbing line exists. All cells visible from a source cell $C$ can then be found with the recursive procedure:

```
Find_Visible_Cells (cell C, portal sequence P, visible cell set V)
    V = V ∪ C
    for each neighbor N of C
        for each portal p connecting C and N
            orient p from C to N
            P' = P concatenate p
            if Stabbing_Line (P') exists then
                Find_Visible_Cells (N, P', V)
```

Figure 7 depicts a spatial subdivision and the result of invoking *Find_Visible_Cells* (cell $I$, $\mathbf{P}$ = empty, $\mathcal{V} = \emptyset$). The invocation stack can be schematically represented as

*Find_Visible_Cells* ($I$, $\mathbf{P} = [\ ]$, $\mathcal{V} = \emptyset$)
  *Find_Visible_Cells* ($F$, $\mathbf{P} = [I/F]$, $\mathcal{V} = \{I\}$)
    *Find_Visible_Cells* ($B$, $\mathbf{P} = [I/F,\ F/B]$, $\mathcal{V} = \{I, F\}$)
    *Find_Visible_Cells* ($E$, $\mathbf{P} = [I/F,\ F/E]$, $\mathcal{V} = \{I, F, B\}$)
      *Find_Visible_Cells* ($C$, $\mathbf{P} = [I/F,\ F/E,\ E/C]$, $\mathcal{V} = \{I, F, B, E\}$)
  *Find_Visible_Cells* ($J$, $\mathbf{P} = [I/J]$, $\mathcal{V} = \{I, F, B, E, C\}$)
    *Find_Visible_Cells* ($H$, $\mathbf{P} = [I/J,\ J/H_1]$, $\mathcal{V} = \{I, F, B, E, C, J\}$)
    *Find_Visible_Cells* ($H$, $\mathbf{P} = [I/J,\ J/H_2]$, $\mathcal{V} = \{I, F, B, E, C, J, H\}$)

The last line shows that the cell-to-cell visibility $\mathcal{V}$ returned is $\{I, F, B, E, C, J, H\}$.

The recursive nature of *Find_Visible_Cells()* suggests an efficient data structure: the *stab tree* (Figure 8). Each node or vertex of the stab tree corresponds to a cell visible from the source cell (cell $I$ in Fig. 7). Each edge of the stab tree corresponds to a portal stabbed as part of a portal sequence originating on a boundary of

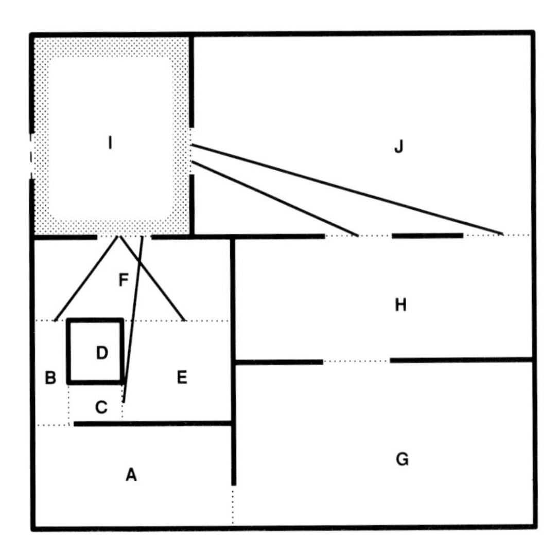


Figure 7: Finding sightlines from $I$.

the source cell. Note that the stab tree is isomorphic to the call graph of *Find_Visible_Cells()* above, and that leaf cells are included in the stab tree once for each distinct portal sequence reaching them. A stab tree is computed and stored with each leaf cell of the spatial subdivision; the cell-to-cell visibility is explicitly recoverable as the set of stab tree vertices.

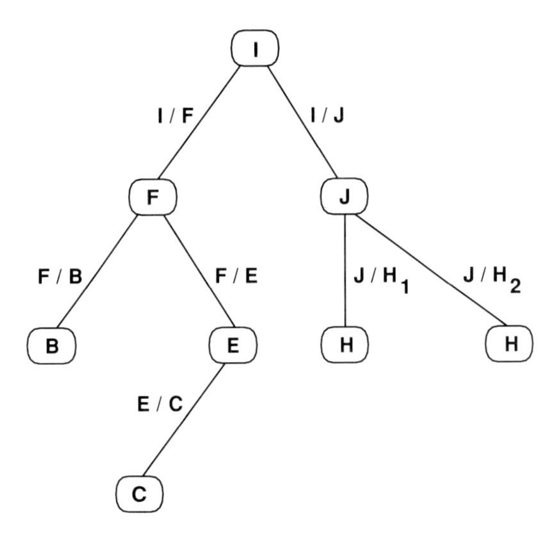


Figure 8: The stab tree rooted at $I$.

## 3.4 Algorithmic Complexity

Since linear programs are solvable in linear time, *Find_Visible_Cells* adds or rejects each candidate visible cell in time linear in the length of the portal sequence reaching that cell. Determining a useful upper bound on the total number of such sequences as a function of $|\mathcal{V}|$ seems challenging, as this quantity appears to depend on the spatial subdivision in a complicated way. However, for architectural models, we expect the length of most portal sequences to be a small constant, since most cells will not see more than a constant number of other cells. Were this not so, most of the model would be visible from most vantage points, and visibility preprocessing would be futile.

Our algorithm does not yet fully exploit the coherence and symmetry of the visibility relationship. Visibility is found one cell at a time, and the sightlines so generated are effectively useful only to the source cell. Later visibility computations on other cells do not "reuse" the already computed sightlines, but instead regenerate them from scratch. To see why reusing sightlines is not easily accomplished, consider a general cell with several portals. Many sightlines traverse this cell, each arriving with a different "history" or portal sequence. Upon encountering a cell, it may be more work for a sightline to check every prior-arriving sightline than it is for the new sightline to simply generate the (typically highly constrained) set of sightlines that can reach the cell's neighbors.

The algorithm as stated may require storage quadratic in the number of leaf cells (since, in the worst case, every leaf cell may see every other through many different portal sequences). In practice we expect the storage required to be linear in the number of leaf cells, with a constant close to the average portal sequence length. Nevertheless, we are seeking ways to combine all of the stab trees into a single, suitably annotated adjacency graph.

# 4 Eye-to-Cell Visibility

The cell-to-cell visibility is an upper bound on the view of an *unconstrained observer* in a particular cell; that is, one able to look simultaneously in all directions from all positions inside the cell. During an interactive walkthrough phase, however, the observer is at a known point and has vision limited to a *view cone* emanating from this point (in two dimensions, the cone can be defined by a view direction and field of view; in three dimensions, by the usual left, right, top, and bottom clip planes). We define the *eye-to-cell* visibility as the set of cells partially or completely visible to an observer with a specified view cone (Figure 9). Clearly the eye-to-cell visibility of any observer is a subset of the cell-to-cell visibility for the cell containing the observer.

## 4.1 Eye-to-Cell Culling Methods

Let $O$ be the cell containing the observer, $C$ the view cone, $\mathcal{S}$ the stab tree rooted at $O$, and $\mathcal{V}$ the set of cells visible from $O$ (i.e., $\{O, D, E, F, G, H\}$). We compute the observer's eye-to-cell visibility by *culling* $\mathcal{S}$ and $\mathcal{V}$ against $C$. We discuss several methods of performing this cull, in order of increasing effectiveness and computational complexity. All but the last method yield an overestimation of the eye-to-cell visibility; that is, they can fail to remove a cell from $\mathcal{V}$ for which no sightline exists in $C$. The last method computes exact eye-to-cell visibility.

**Disjoint cell.** The simplest cull removes from $\mathcal{V}$ those cells that are disjoint from $C$; for example, cells $E$ and $F$ in Figure 9-*a*. This can be done in $O(|\mathcal{V}|)$ time, but does not remove all invisible cells. Cell $G$ in Figure 9-*a* has a non-empty intersection with $C$, but is not visible; any sightline to it must traverse the cell $F$, which *is* disjoint from $C$. More generally, in the cell adjacency graph, the visible cells must form a single *connected component*, each cell of which has a non-empty intersection with $C$. This connected component must also, of course, contain the cell $O$.

**Connected component.** Thus, a more effective cull employs a depth-first search from $O$ in $\mathcal{S}$, subject to the constraint that every cell traversed must intersect the interior of $C$. This requires time $O(|\mathcal{S}|)$, and removes cell $G$ in Figure 9-*a*. However, it fails to remove $G$ in Figure 9-*b*, even though $G$ is invisible from the

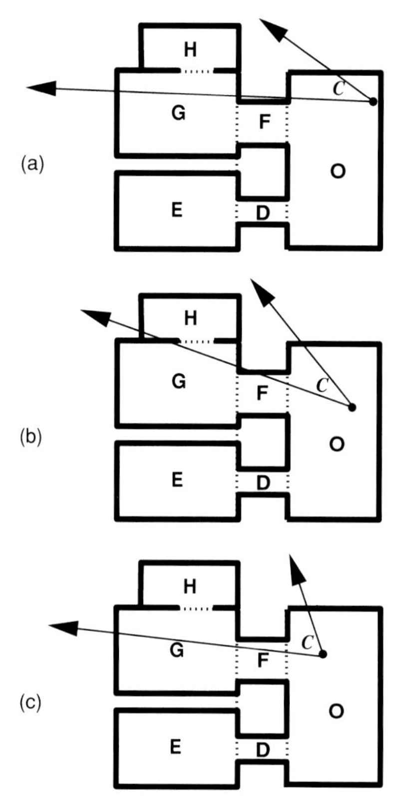


Figure 9: Culling $O$'s stab tree against a view cone $C$.

observer (because all sightlines in $C$ from the observer to $G$ must traverse some opaque input face).

**Incident portals.** The culling method can be refined further by searching only through cells reachable via *portals* that intersect $C$'s interior. Figure 9-*c* shows that this is still not sufficient to obtain an accurate list of visible cells; cell $H$ passes this test, but is not visible in $C$, since no sightline from the observer can stab the three portals necessary to reach $H$.

**Exact eye-to-cell.** The important observation is that for a cell to be visible, some portal sequence to that cell must admit a sightline that lies *inside* $C$ and *contains the view position.* Retaining the stab tree $\mathcal{S}$ permits an efficient implementation of this sufficient criterion, since $\mathcal{S}$ stores with $O$ every portal sequence originating at $O$. Suppose the portal sequence to some cell has length $m$. As before, this sequence implies $2m$ linear constraints on any stabbing line. To these we add three linear constraints: one demanding that the stabbing line contain the observer's view point, and two demanding that the stabbing *ray* lie inside the two halfspaces whose intersection defines $C$ (in two dimensions). The resulting linear program of $2m + 3$ constraints can be solved in time $O(m)$, i.e., $O(|\mathcal{V}|)$ for each portal sequence.

This final refinement of the culling algorithm computes exact eye-to-cell visibility. Figure 9-*c* shows that the cull removes $H$ from the observer's eye-to-cell visibility since the portal sequence [$O/F$, $F/G$, $G/H$] does not admit a sightline through the view point.

During the walkthrough phase, the visible area (volume, in 3-D) can readily be computed from the stored stab tree. The visible area in any cell is always the intersection of that (convex) cell with one or more (convex) wedges emanating from the observer's position (Figure 10). The stab tree depth-first search starts at the source cell, and propagates outward along the stab tree. Upon passing through a portal, the wedge is either suitably narrowed by the portal's extrema (e.g., portal $I/F$ in Figure 10), or completely eliminated if the wedge is disjoint from the portal (e.g., portal $F/B$ in Figure 10). In this case, the DFS branch terminates, descending no further into the stab tree.

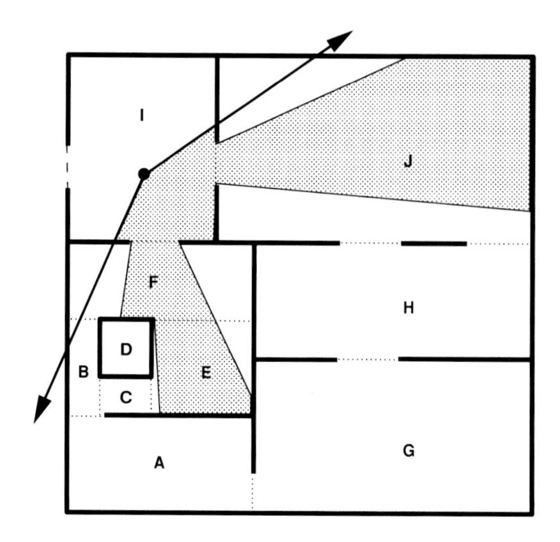


Figure 10: The view cone during the stab tree DFS.

### 4.2 Frame-to-Frame Coherence

In practice, there is considerable *frame-to-frame* coherence to be exploited in the eye-to-cell visibility computation. During smooth observer motion, the observer's view point will typically spend several frame-times in each cell it encounters. Thus, the stab tree for that cell can be cached in fast memory as long as the observer remains in the cell. Moreover, the cell adjacency graph allows substantial predictive power over the observer's motion. For instance, an observer exiting a known cell must emerge in a neighbor of that cell. An intelligent walkthrough program might prefetch all polygons visible to that cell *before* the observer's arrival, minimizing or eliminating the waiting times associated with typical high-latency mass-storage databases.

## 5 Experimental Results

We have implemented the algorithms described for 2-D axial environments, and all but the eye-to-cell computation for 3-D axial environments. The subdivision and visibility computation routines contain roughly five thousand lines of C language, embedded in an interactive visualization program written for a dual-processor, 50-MIP, 10-MFLOPS graphics superworkstation, the Silicon Graphics 320 GTX.

Our test model was a floorplan with 1000 axial faces (Figure 11-*a*). Subdividing the $k$-D tree to termination with the procedure of Section 2.3 required 15 CPU seconds, allocated 1 Mb of main memory, and produced about 700 leaf cells. Portal enumeration, creation of the cell adjacency graph, and the cell-to-cell visibility computation were then performed for every leaf cell. This required 30 CPU seconds and increased the memory usage to 2 Mb. Roughly 10,500 total stab tree vertices were allocated to store all of the 700 leaf cells' stab trees (Figure 11-*b*). Thus the average stab tree size was about 15.

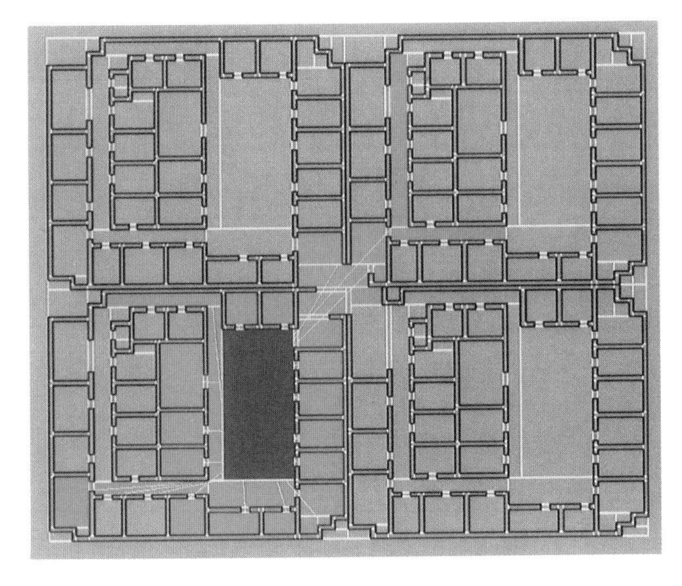

(a) A source cell (dark blue), its cell-to-cell visibility (light blue), and stabbing lines.

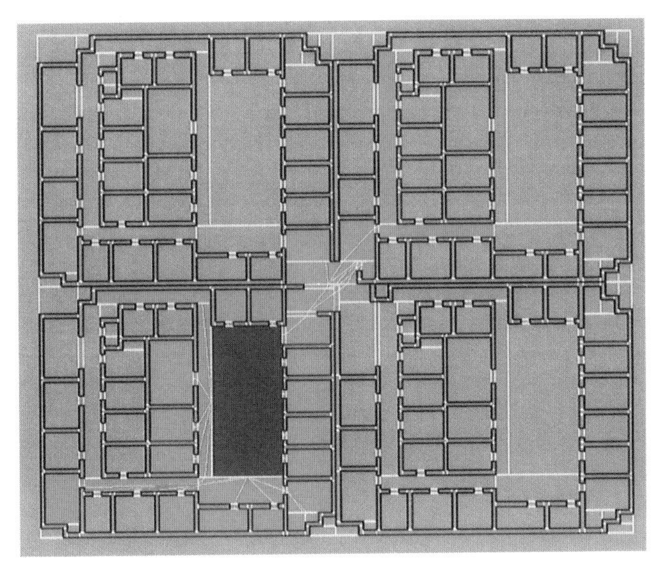

(b) The source cell (dark blue), cell-to-cell visibility (light blue), and stab tree.

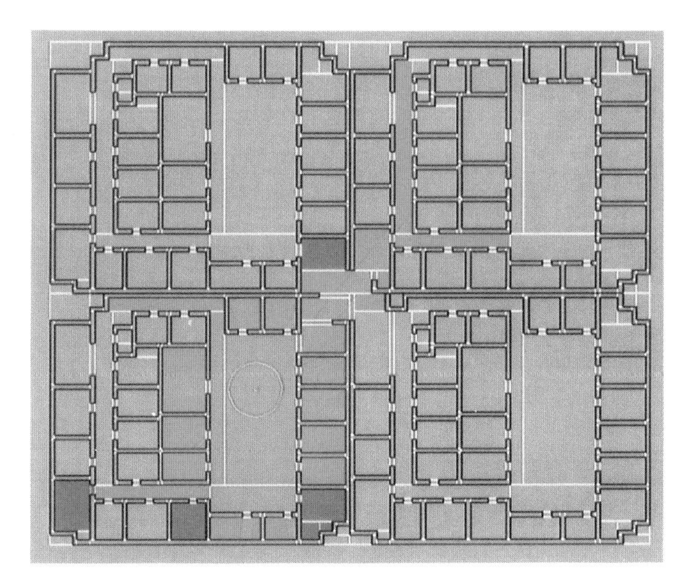

(c) An observer with a 360° view cone. The eye-to-cell visibility is shown in blue; the exact visible area is shown in blue-green. The green cells have been dynamically culled.

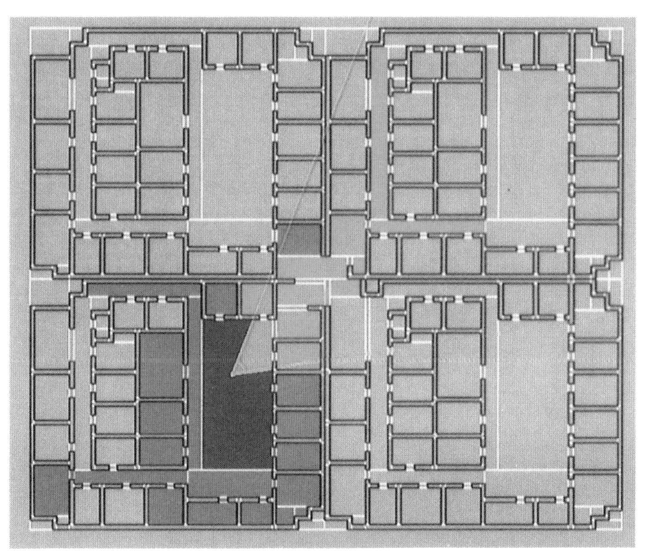

(d) The same observer, with a 60° view cone. The eye-to-cell visibility is shown in blue; the exact visible area is shown in blue-green. The green cells have been dynamically culled.

Figure 11: An axial model with roughly 1,000 faces (black), subdivided into about 700 spatial cells (white).

We empirically evaluated the efficacy of cell-to-cell visibility pruning and several eye-to-cell culling methods using the above floorplan. We performed 10,000 visibility queries at random locations within the model, with the view direction chosen randomly, and for both 360° and 60° view cones (Figures 11-*c* and 11-*d*). For every generated view cone, visibility was computed with each of the culling methods of Sections 3 and 4. The area of the potentially visible region was averaged over the random trials to produce the figures tabulated below. The quantities shown are generally sums of cell areas and are expressed as percentages of total model area. The last row displays the total area of the view cone's *intersection* with all cells reached by the stab tree DFS (e.g., the shaded areas in Figure 10).

| *culling method* | 360° view cone | | 60° view cone | |
|---|---|---|---|---|
| | *vis. area* | *reduction factor* | *vis. area* | *reduction factor* |
| none (cell-to-cell vis.) | 8.1% | 10x | 8.1% | 10x |
| disjoint cell | 8.1% | 10x | 3.1% | 30x |
| connected component | 8.1% | 10x | 2.4% | 40x |
| incident portals | 8.1% | 10x | 2.2% | 40x |
| exact eye-to-cell | 4.9% | 20x | 1.8% | 50x |
| exact visible area | 2.1% | 50x | 0.3% | 300x |

# 6 Extensions and Discussion

We briefly discuss extensions of the visibility computation algorithms to three-dimensional scenes.

## 6.1 Three-Dimensional Models

Here we assume that all faces are rectangles whose normals and edges are parallel to the $x$, $y$, or $z$ axis. Subdivision again proceeds with a $k$-D tree (and $k = 3$). The face classification and splitting criteria extend directly to three dimensions. Portals are no longer line segments, but are instead rectilinear non-convex regions formed by (rectangular) cell boundaries minus unions of covering faces.

There are at least two ways to accommodate these more general portals. First, given any set of non-convex portals, rectangular *large portals* may be created by computing the axial bounding box of the set. Replacing collections of portals (e.g., all portals through a boundary) with large portals can only increase the computed cell-to-cell visibility estimation, ensuring that it remains a superset of the true visibility.

A second alternative is to decompose each non-rectangular portal into rectangles. This approach should produce smaller potentially visible sets than the one above, since it does not overestimate portal sizes. However, this improved upper bound comes at the cost of increased combinatorial complexity, since many invocations of *Find_Visible_Cells* will be spawned in order to explore the more numerous portals.

In either event, sightlines are found by stabbing oriented rectangle sequences (Figure 12), in analogy to the two-dimensional case. To accomplish this, we have developed and implemented a novel algorithm that determines sightlines through rectangles [13]. Briefly, the algorithm operates in a dual space in which the problem reduces to performing a linear number of convex polygon-polygon intersections, each requiring logarithmic time [7]. The algorithm finds a stabbing line through $n$ oriented, axis-aligned rectangles, or determines that no such stabbing line exists, in $O(n \lg n)$ time.

Assuming a rectangular display for rendering, culling against a three-dimensional view pyramid is a direct extension of the planar

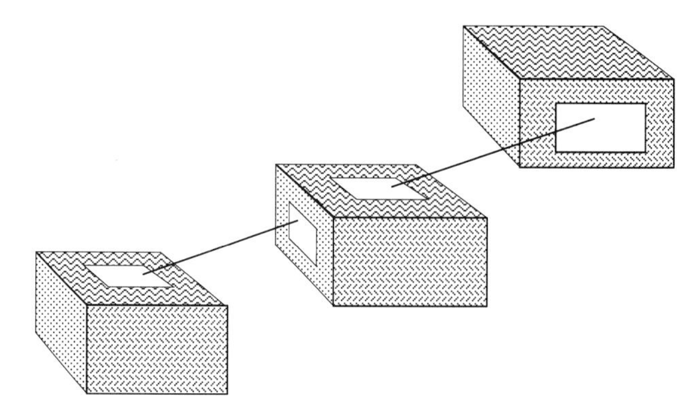

Figure 12: Stabbing a sequence of rectangular portals in 3-D.

culling methods described earlier. When the observer's position is known, each portal edge contributes a linear constraint on the eye-to-cell visibility. The view pyramid implies four additional linear constraints; one each for the left, right, top, and bottom clipping planes. Thus, computing eye-to-cell visibility in three dimensions again reduces to a linear-time linear programming problem.

Generalizing the visibility computations described here to non-axial scenes appears to pose problems both conceptual and technical in nature. First, suitable techniques must be found for decomposing large collections of general polygons into convex spatial subdivisions, generating an appropriate cell adjacency graph, and enumerating the portals of each subdivision cell. Second, efficient algorithms are needed for stabbing portal sequences comprised of general polygons in three dimensions. We have made some headway against the latter problem by developing a randomized $O(n^2)$ algorithm that stabs sequences of $n$ oriented convex polygons [21].

## 6.2 Discussion

The methods described here are particularly appropriate for input with somewhat restricted "true" visibility, such as that occurring in many architectural models. However, adversarially chosen input can produce unbalanced spatial subdivision trees under our naive criteria, slowing basic operations on the subdivision. Input with a large number of portals per cell boundary (for example, walls with tens or hundreds of windows) may confound the cell-to-cell visibility algorithm with a combinatorially explosive set of sightlines. Large portals ameliorate this problem, at the possible cost of decreasing the usefulness of the attained (overlarge) visibility estimates.

It may occur that subdivision on the scene's major structural elements alone does not sufficiently limit cell-to-cell visibility. In this instance, further refinement of the spatial subdivision might help (if it indeed reduces visibility) or hurt (if it leaves visibility unchanged but increases the combinatorial complexity of finding sightlines). Again, there is an ameliorating factor: when subdividing a leaf cell, its children can see only a subset of the cells seen by their parent, since no new exterior portals are introduced (and the childrens' freedom of vision is reduced). Thus each child's sightline search is heavily constrained by its parent's portal/visibility list. Moreover, the portals generated by the subdivision will generally restrict visibility during the walkthrough phase. We are studying the issue of how to subdivide spatial cells as a function of cell-to-cell visibility and cell data density.

## Conclusion

We have implemented and analyzed an efficient and effective visibility preprocessing and query algorithm for axial architectural models. The algorithm's effectiveness depends on a decomposition of the models into rectangular or parallelepipedal cells in which significant parts of most cell boundaries are opaque.

The cell-based visibility determination relies on an efficient search for sightlines connecting pairs of cells through non-opaque portals. In two dimensions, this search reduces to a linear programming problem. Finding sightlines through portals in three dimensions is somewhat harder. We show that, when relevant portal sequences are retained, determining viewpoint-based visibility in both two and three dimensions also reduces to a linear programming problem.

We present some empirical evidence of rendering speedups for axial two-dimensional environments. The visibility computation can be performed at reasonable preprocessing and storage costs and, for most viewpoints, dramatically reduces the number of polygons that must be processed by the renderer.

## Acknowledgments

Our special thanks go to Jim Winget, who has always held an active, supportive role in our research. We gratefully acknowledge the support of Silicon Graphics, Inc., and particularly thank Paul Haeberli for his help in preparing this material for submission and publication. Michael Hohmeyer contributed much valuable insight and an implementation of Raimund Seidel's randomized linear programming algorithm. Finally we thank Mark Segal, Efi Fogel, and the SIGGRAPH referees for their many helpful comments and suggestions.

## References

[1] John M. Airey. *Increasing Update Rates in the Building Walkthrough System with Automatic Model-Space Subdivision and Potentially Visible Set Calculations*. PhD thesis, UNC Chapel Hill, 1990.

[2] John M. Airey, John H. Rohlf, and Frederick P. Brooks Jr. Towards image realism with interactive update rates in complex virtual building environments. *ACM SIGGRAPH Special Issue on 1990 Symposium on Interactive 3D Graphics*, 24(2):41–50, 1990.

[3] Kurt Akeley. The Silicon Graphics 4D/240GTX superworkstation. *IEEE Computer Graphics and Applications*, 9(4):239–246, 1989.

[4] J.L. Bentley. Multidimensional binary search trees used for associative searching. *Communications of the ACM*, 18:509–517, 1975.

[5] B. Chazelle and L.J. Guibas. Visibility and intersection problems in plane geometry. In *Proc. $1^{st}$ ACM Symposium on Computational Geometry*, pages 135–146, 1985.

[6] Frank C. Crow. Shadow algorithms for computer graphics. *Computer Graphics (Proc. SIGGRAPH '77)*, 11(2):242–248, 1977.

[7] David P. Dobkin and Diane L. Souvaine. Detecting the intersection of convex objects in the plane. Technical Report No. 89-9, DIMACS, 1989.

[8] H. Fuchs, Z. Kedem, and B. Naylor. On visible surface generation by a priori tree structures. *Computer Graphics (Proc. SIGGRAPH '80)*, 14(3):124–133, July 1980.

[9] Akira Fujimoto and Kansei Iwata. Accelerated ray tracing. In *Computer Graphics: Visual Technology and Art (Proc. Computer Graphics Tokyo '85)*, pages 41–65, 1985.

[10] Benjamin Garlick, Daniel R. Baum, and James M. Winget. Interactive viewing of large geometric databases using multiprocessor graphics workstations. In *SIGGRAPH '90 Course Notes (Parallel Algorithms and Architectures for 3D Image Generation)*, August 1990.

[11] Andrew S. Glassner. Space subdivision for fast ray tracing. *IEEE Computer Graphics and Applications*, 4(10):15–22, October 1984.

[12] John E. Hershberger. *Efficient Algorithms for Shortest Path and Visibility Problems*. PhD thesis, Stanford University, June 1987.

[13] Michael E. Hohmeyer and Seth J. Teller. Stabbing isothetic rectangles and boxes in $O(n \lg n)$ time (in preparation).

[14] David Kirk and Douglas Voorhies. The rendering architecture of the DN10000VS. *Computer Graphics (Proc. SIGGRAPH '90)*, 24(4):299–307, August 1990.

[15] N. Megiddo. Linear-time algorithms for linear programming in $R^3$ and related problems. *SIAM Journal Computing*, 12:759–776, 1983.

[16] Joseph O' Rourke. *Art Gallery Theorems and Algorithms*. Oxford University Press, 1987.

[17] Michael S. Paterson and F. Frances Yao. Efficient binary space partitions for hidden-surface removal and solid modeling. *Discrete and Computational Geometry*, 5(5):485–503, 1990.

[18] W. H. Plantinga and C. R. Dyer. An algorithm for constructing the aspect graph. In *Proc. IEEE Symp. Foundations of Computer Science*, pages 123–131, 1986.

[19] Raimund Seidel. Linear programming and convex hulls made easy. In *Proc. $6^{th}$ ACM Symposium on Computational Geometry*, pages 211–215, 1990.

[20] Michael Ian Shamos and Franco P. Preparata. *Computational Geometry: an Introduction*. Springer-Verlag, 1985.

[21] Seth J. Teller and Michael E. Hohmeyer. Stabbing oriented convex polygons in randomized $O(n^2)$ time (in preparation).

[22] Gert Vegter. The visibility diagram: a data structure for visibility problems and motion planning. In *Proc. $2^{nd}$ Scandinavian Workshop on Algorithm Theory*, pages 97–110, 1990.

# Model-based Matching and Hinting of Fonts

Roger D. Hersch, Claude Betrisey

Swiss Federal Institute of Technology (EPFL)
CH-1015 Lausanne, Switzerland

## Abstract

In today's digital computers, phototypesetters and printers, typographic fonts are mainly given by their outline descriptions. Outline descriptions alone do not provide any information about character parts like stems, serifs, shoulders, and bowls. But, in order to produce the best looking characters at a given size on a specific printer, non-linear operations must be applied to parts of the character shape. At low-resolution, grid-fitting of character outlines is required for generating nice and regular raster characters. For this reason, grid-fitting rules called hints are added to the character description. Grid-fitting rules require as parameters certain characteristic points within the shape outlines. In order to be able to detect these characteristic points in any given input font, a topological model representing the essence of the shapes found in typographic latin typefaces is proposed. This model includes sufficient information for matching existing non-fancy outline fonts to the model description. For automatic hint generation, a table of applicable hints is added into the topological model description. After matching a given input shape to the model, hints which can be applied to the shape of the given font are taken and added to its outline description. Furthermore, a structural description of individual letter shape parts using characteristic model points can be added to the model. Such a description provides knowledge about typographic structure elements like stems, serifs and bowls.

**CR Categories and Subject Descriptors:** I.3.3 [Computer Graphics]: Picture/Image Generation; I.3.5 [Computer Graphics]: Computational Geometry and Object Modeling.

**Additional Key Words and Phrases:** Digital typography, outline fonts, topological model, shape matching, grid-fitting, automatic hinting.

## 1 Introduction

In the last century, hundreds of new font families have been created for metal type and photocomposition. Photocomposition equipment manufacturers and font trading companies now offer thousands of different fonts. Digital fonts are described by their outlines, mainly in the form of straight line and spline segments.

Character outline descriptions however are by no means adequate for creating and manipulating typographic shapes. They are only suitable for generating scalable fonts on high-resolution photocomposers. Outline characters should be considered only as the result of the font design process. During type design, type creators mainly consider important font features like stoke width relationships, curvature of rounded shapes, serif thickness and length, junctions between serifs and stems, alternation of white and black space, etc.. Previous work in digital typography has shown that typefaces can be assembled by using structural shape parts incorporating the basic font features [6] [13]. Computer-aided type design [9] starts with the study of structural letter parts like serifs, arms, shoulders, bowls, junctions and terminal endings (figure 1) and the generation of variants of representative characters (E, H, O, n, b, o, a, e, i). The remaining letters, numbers and signs of an alphabet can be partly synthesized into outline characters by assembling these structural letter parts. Previous attempts to develop computer tools for converting automatically structural descriptions into outline descriptions and vice-versa produced only limited results [1].

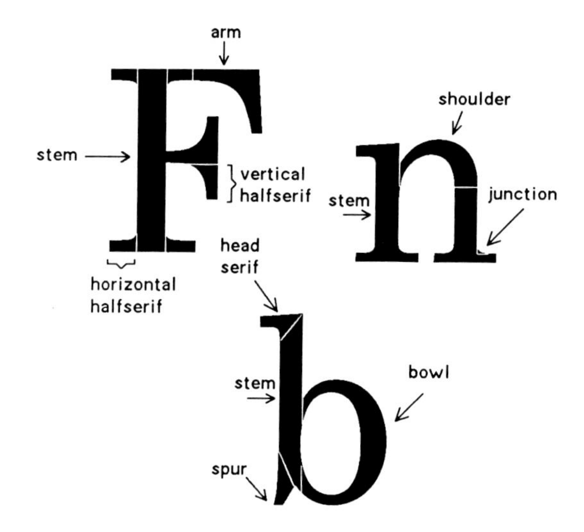


Figure 1: Structural letter parts [10]

Font outline descriptions are not sufficient for rendering outline fonts on middle and low-resolution devices like 300 dpi printers and 100 dpi displays. Recently, techniques have been developed for the grid-fitting of character outlines to a given rasterization grid [11] [2] [12]. These techniques require additional information in the form of rules specifying the kind of constraints to be applied on certain character parts. These rules, called *hints* or *grid constraints* refer to selected outline support points defining the width or thickness of particular character parts like staight stems, bowls, serifs and diagonals. The application of grid constraints adapts the original outline shape to the grid in order to maintain symmetry and regularity in the produced discrete shape. For a given font size, the rasterized characters will have equal stem width, identical serifs and nice discrete arcs.

Manually incorporating hints into outline font descriptions is tedious and labor intensive. Due to the large amount of available outline fonts, automated creation of hinted outline fonts is a necessity. For the application of basic hints on stems, bowls and shoulders, automatic hinting can be based on the recognition of horizontal and vertical bars and on the recognition of curvilinear shape extremas [3]. For the generation of more accurate hints like the control of serifs, of diagonal bars and the control of uniform weight at small sizes, there is a need for more elaborate hints, like those found in the *TrueType* language [2]. Such hints, which are tuned to the individual letter shapes, cannot be generated easily by a general purpose topological shape analyser. The model-based approach presented here enables advanced meta-hints to be associated with the model description of individual letter shapes. After having matched a given input font to the model, corresponding meta-hints are adapted to the features of the input font (sans-serif, italic) and reported into its outline description.

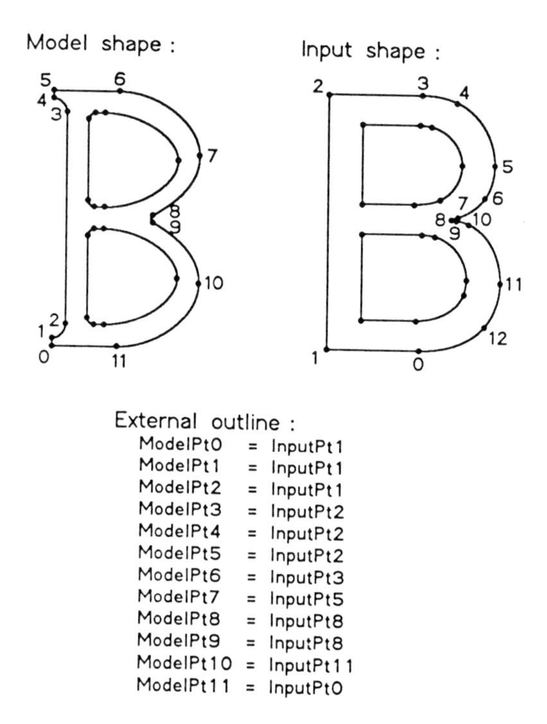


Figure 2: Association of input shape support points with characteristic model points

This paper proposes a topological font-independent model for the description of each letter shape. This model incorporates a loose outline description valid for all non-fancy instances of the corresponding letter shape. Model outlines are described by characteristic points and by their interconnecting outline segments. Characteristic points are essentially either local maximas or minimas or discontinuity points. They specify starting, intermediate and ending points of different shape parts (stems, serifs, shoulders, bowls, diagonals). Their location within the character shape is given by their relative position in the plane. Outline segments are specified by their relative length, their approximate orientation and the way they connect to neighbouring segments. Relevant knowledge can be associated with characteristic points and their interconnections. For example, structure elements like half-serifs can be defined by a series of characteristic points (starting point, intermediate points, ending point). Meta-descriptions of grid constraints referencing characteristic points can easily be incorporated into the topological model.

This paper addresses the problem of identifying characteristic points in given character shapes. In order to solve it, we propose to match the support points of existing real letter shapes to their corresponding characteristic points in the model (figure 2).

Automatic labelling of character parts becomes a shape and point matching problem. A given input character is matched with the correspondent model character, its glyphs and contours are matched to the model character's glyphs and contours. By using the topological rules associated with each characteristic point, candidate points in the input description are successively checked, kept or eliminated. A successful match leads to one point in the input character for each characteristic model point.

For the purpose of automated hint generation, points of a given input font are matched to characteristic points of the model font. Then, it becomes easy to adapt the constraint descriptions from the model font to the given input font and to replace the characteristic glyph, contour and point numbers by the corresponding input font glyph, contour and point numbers.

## 2 Topological modelling of letter shapes

The shape of latin characters has evolved over the last centuries but, with the exception of script and ornamental types, the topology of most character shapes has remained identical. In order to establish a topological model of latin characters, we have tried to define meaningful points on their outline (characteristic points). These points are generally either local extremas, or junction points between different contours parts. The topological model incorporates the topological essence of the shapes of the members of an alphabet. It should be valid for all its non-fancy instances, e.g. for the font families which can be found in type collections such as Berthold Types [4].

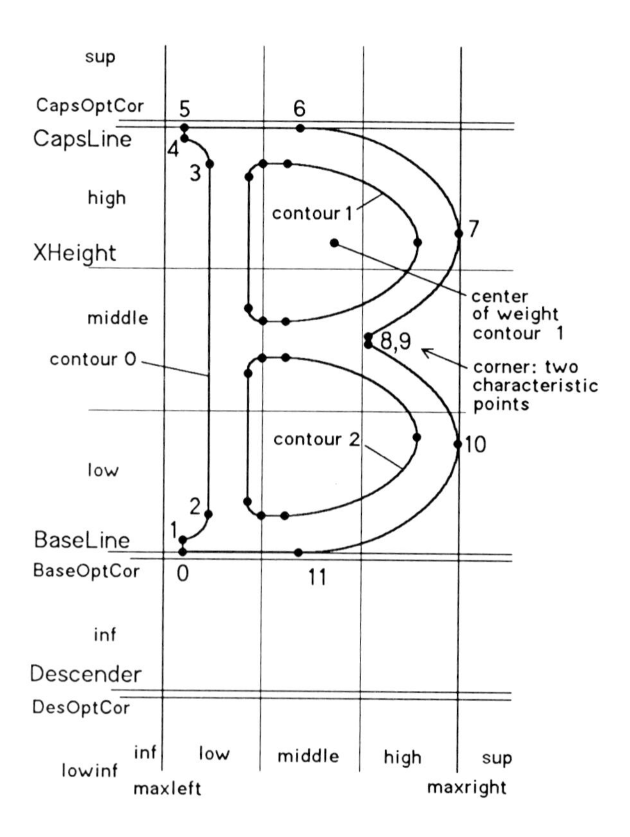


Figure 3: Loose representation of characteristic contour points of character "B"

Previous scientific approaches to topological modelling of letter shapes were established for the purpose of character recognition.

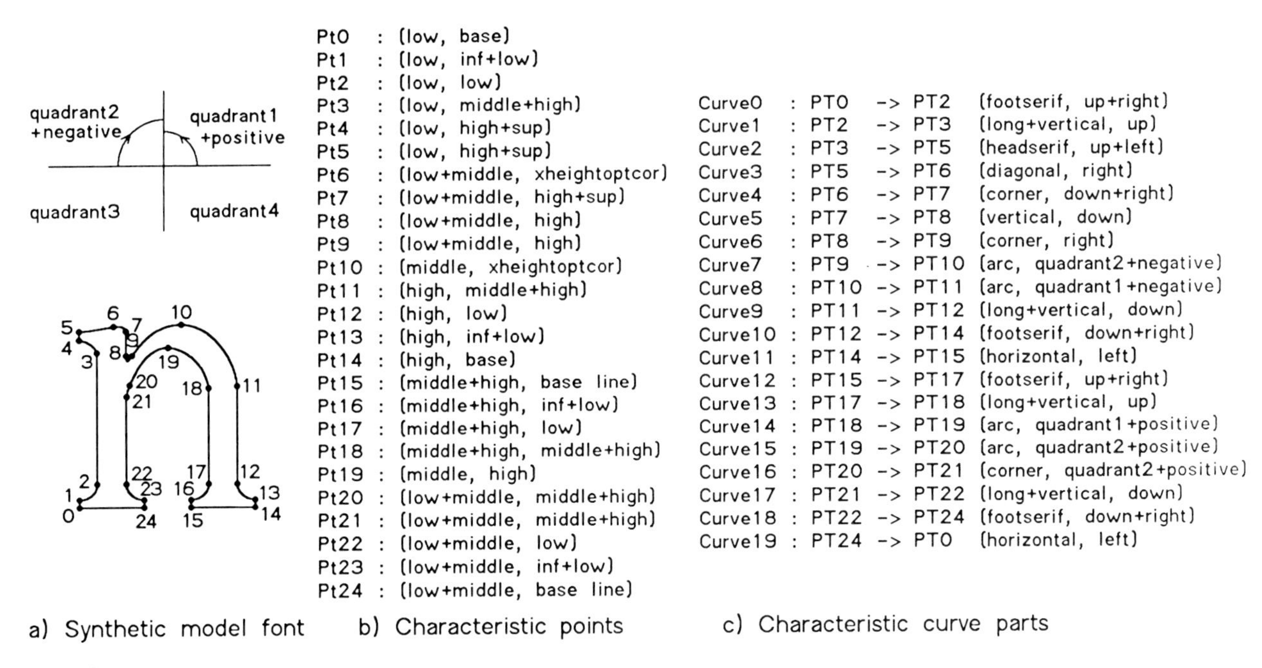


Figure 4: Shape model of character "n"

They used topological features with a high discrimination potential and goodness evaluation parameters to match an input shape with unknown ASCII code to the correct character shape in the set of ASCII letter shapes [7] [8] [15]. Since our task consists in matching a given input letter shape with a known ASCII code to its reference model, the matching problem is limited to matching the shape's glyphs (individual shapes of a character), contours and characteristic points. A successful match however requires that each characteristic model point be matched without contradictions to one input shape outline support point.

In order to match glyphs, contours and characteristic points, the topological model incorporates rough positional information, as well as information concerning the position of a characteristic point relative to its neighbouring points. Unprecise positional information can be given by partitioning the character space into a very coarse coordinate grid. In the present implementation, 5 horizontal and 6 vertical subspaces (low-inferior, inferior, low, middle, high, superior) are used. This grid definition matches nicely the geometry of latin shapes: lower-case letters fit in a space defined by three horizontal and two vertical subspaces, capitals fit in a three by three space and special characters like the "$" use the full vertical space (6 subspaces). Characters extending beyond their left and right reference lines like italics use all 5 horizontal subspaces. Shape locations are defined in an unprecise way by specifying their approximate location on this coarse grid (figure 3). Further uncertainty can be introduced by allowing given model points to belong to one of two neighbouring coarse grid locations.

Glyphs and contour parts, like the interior contours of character "B" are situated on the grid by considering the position of their bounding-box center. Contour parts are also characterized as being exterior or interior contours, depending on their orientation.

Shape locations are specified in a precise way if they lie on certain reference lines like baseline, x-height, capsline and their respective optical correction lines. Characteristic points also have topological attributes in relation to the contour they belong to. They can be either local or global extrema in x or in y direction.

Pairs of neighbouring characteristic points are also characterized by the outline segment joining them. An outline segment is either a straight or nearly straight segment or a curve segment. Straight line segments are short or long. They have either a vertical or a horizontal primary direction. Curved segments have positive or negative orientation. They lie within a given quadrant (figure 4).

Relative positional information about glyphs and contours is used to match subparts of an input character shape to its corresponding model subparts (figure 5).

Glyphs and contours cannot be matched if topological contradictions are found between the input shape and the model shape. For example, character shape "%" cannot be matched with model character "%". Therefore the same character may have a model description including several shape variants. At matching time, either the variant is known in advance (figure 6) or the program tries to match the input shape successively to all variants, until a match without contradictions is found.

## 3 Matching characteristic points

As explained in the introduction, characteristic points define the different shape parts completely. In order to start the matching process, a list of matching candidate points of a given input font will be associated to each characteristic point of the model font. The selected candidate points must have the same approximate location as their corresponding characteristic point.

This first association based on the approximate geometric location of model points and shape points will produce many candidates for each characteristic model point.

Subsequently, a hierarchical succession of matching criteria is used in order to eliminate unsuitable candidates from the candidate list until one candidate remains as a match for one characteristic point of the topological description. The matching process proceeds successively from specific strong features to more global uncertain features of model letter shapes. If one or several candidates match a criterion associated with a characteristic point, they are kept in the candidate list and all other candidates who do not match this criterion are eliminated. If no candidate matches a given criterion, no candidates are eliminated and the matching process proceeds with the next criterion.

Synthetic model font :

Input font :

contour 1

contour 2

contour 0

contour 2

contour 1

contour 0

center of bounding box contour 2

center of bounding box contour 0

center of bounding box contour 1

**Model contour positions :**
Contour 0 : (middle, middle)
Contour 1 : (middle, up)
Contour 2 : (middle, down)

**Model font contour sequence :**
hor. direction : (ModelCont0 = ModelCont1 = ModelCont2)
vert. direction : (ModelCont2 < ModelCont0 < ModelCont1)

**Input font contour sequence :**
hor. direction : (InputCont0 < InputCont2 < InputCont1)
vert. direction : (InputCont1 < InputCont0 < InputCont2)

**Contour matching list :**
ModelCont0 = InputCont0
ModelCont1 = InputCont2
ModelCont2 = InputCont1

Figure 5: Matching input contours of character "B" to correspondent model contours

Candidate acceptance is based on the following topological criteria:

*Criterion 1:*

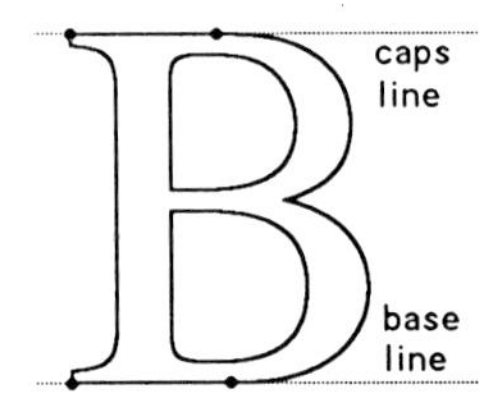


candidate point belongs to a reference line (base, x-height, capital lines)

*Criterion 2:*

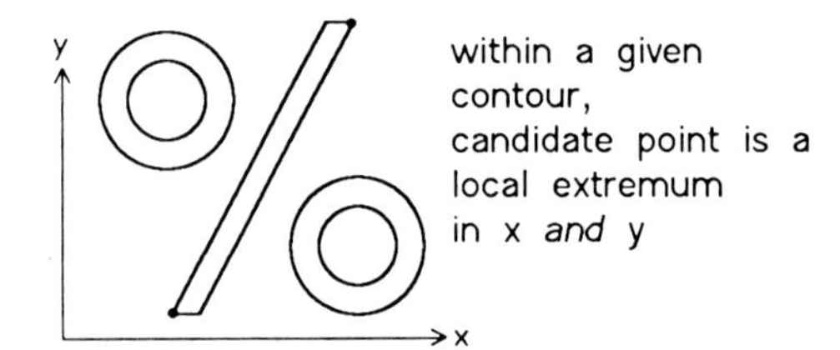

within a given contour, candidate point is a local extremum in x *and* y

*Criterion 3:*

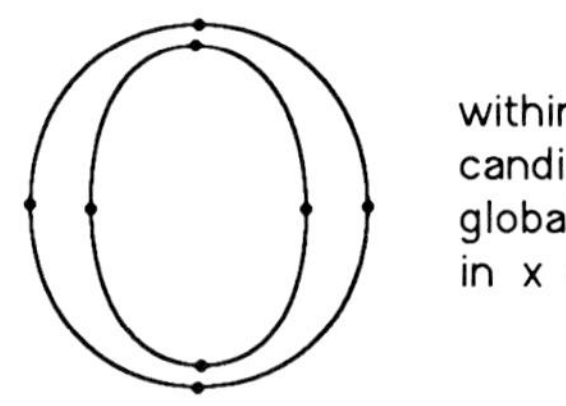

within a given contour, candidate point is a global extremum in x *or* y

*Criterion 4:*

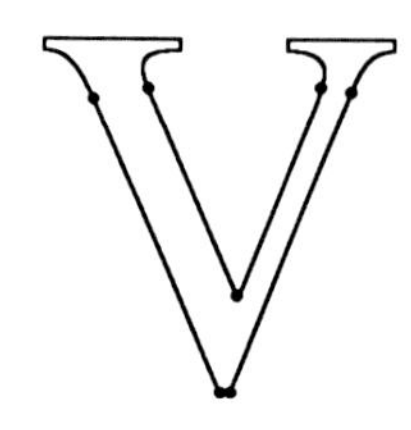

candidate point is a departure or an arrival point of a long straight line segment

*Criterion 5:*

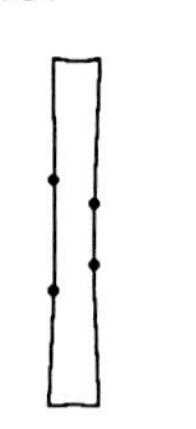

candidate point is not situated between straight line segments having similar slopes

*Criterion 6:*

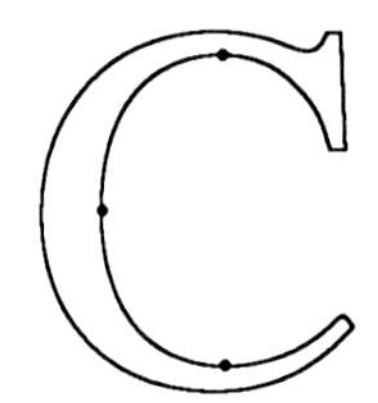

candidate point is a local extremum in the x or y direction

*Criterion 7:*

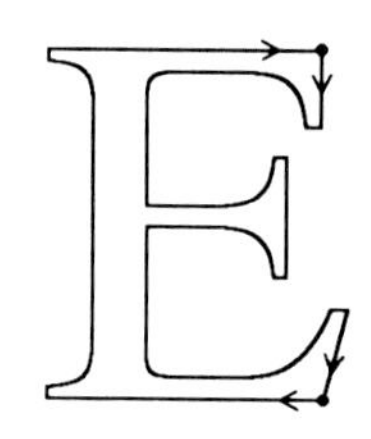

candidate point is both an arrival and a departure point of two oriented straight line segments with given directions

*Criterion 8:*

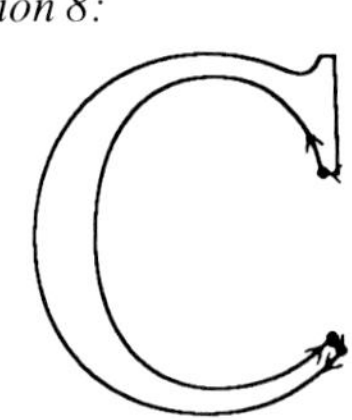

candidate point is both an arrival and a departure point of two oriented straight line or curve segments with given directions

| | a | g | i | j | s | t | w | J | S | W | 3 | 6 | 9 | % | & | $ |
|---|---|---|---|---|---|---|---|---|---|---|---|---|---|---|---|---|
| Variant 1 | a | g | i | j | s | t | w | J | S | W | 3 | 6 | 9 | % | & | $ |
| Variant 2 | a | g | i | j | s | t | w | J | S | W | 3 | 6 | 9 | % | & | $ |
| Variant 3 | | | | | | t | w | | | W | | | | | & | |

| | | | | | | | | | | | | | | | | |
|---|---|---|---|---|---|---|---|---|---|---|---|---|---|---|---|---|
| Times | a | g | i | j | s | t | w | J | S | W | 3 | 6 | 9 | % | & | $ |
| Helvetica | a | g | i | j | s | t | w | J | S | W | 3 | 6 | 9 | % | & | $ |
| Lucida | a | g | i | j | s | t | w | J | S | W | 3 | 6 | 9 | % | & | $ |
| Lucida Sans | a | g | i | j | s | t | w | J | S | W | 3 | 6 | 9 | % | & | $ |
| Courier | a | g | i | j | s | t | w | J | S | W | 3 | 6 | 9 | % | & | $ |
| Madeleine | a | g | i | j | s | t | w | J | S | W | 3 | 6 | 9 | % | & | $ |
| Avant Garde | a | g | i | j | s | t | w | J | S | W | 3 | 6 | 9 | % | & | $ |
| Haas Unica | a | g | i | j | s | t | w | J | S | W | 3 | 6 | 9 | % | & | $ |

Figure 6: Examples of fonts having different shape variants

*Criterion 9:*

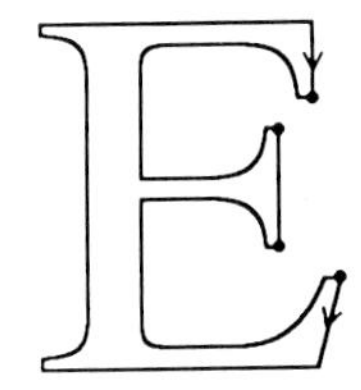

candidate point is an extremity point of an oriented straight line segment with given direction

*Criterion 10:*

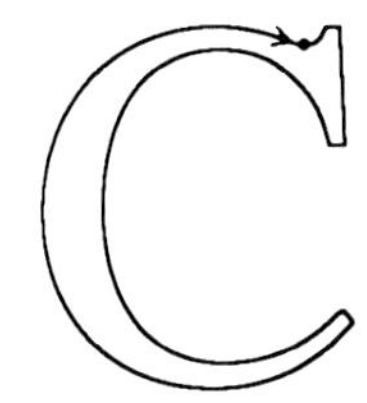

candidate point is an extremity point of an oriented straight line or curve segment with given direction

*Criterion 11:*

candidate point is an inflexion point

*Criterion 12:*

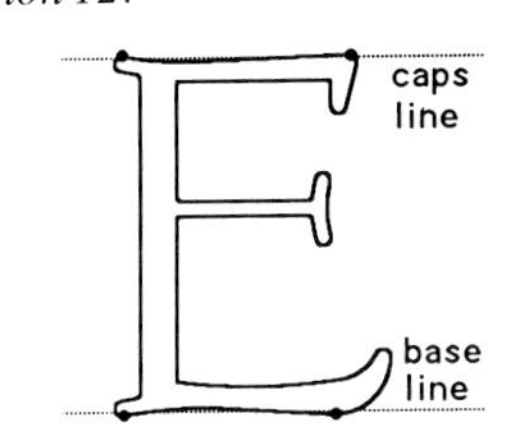


candidate point lies close to a reference line (baseline, descender line, x-height line, capital line)

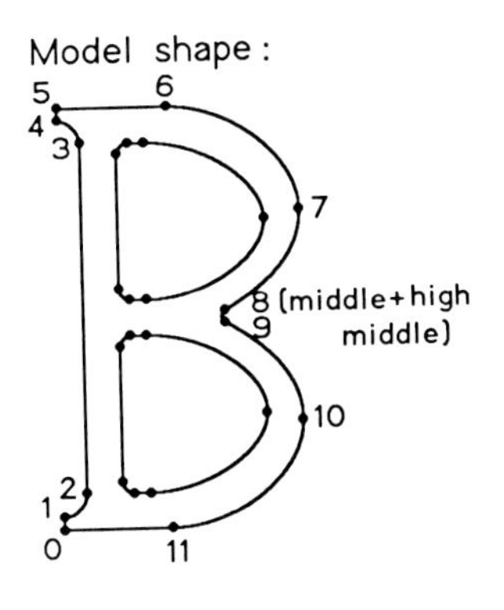


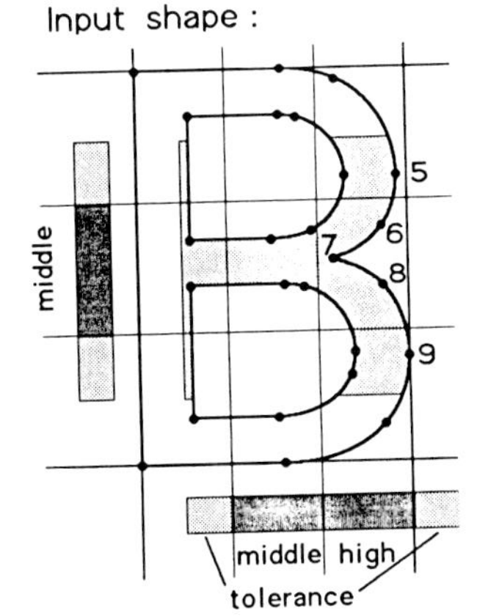


**Candidates for ModelPt8 on external contour:**

Criterion: geometric location :
(InputPt5, InputPt6, InputPt7, InputPt8, InputPt9)
Next applicable criterion :
Local extrema in x- or in y-direction,
==> Selection of InputPt7 (Xmin)

Figure 7: Matching the intersection point of two arcs in character "B"

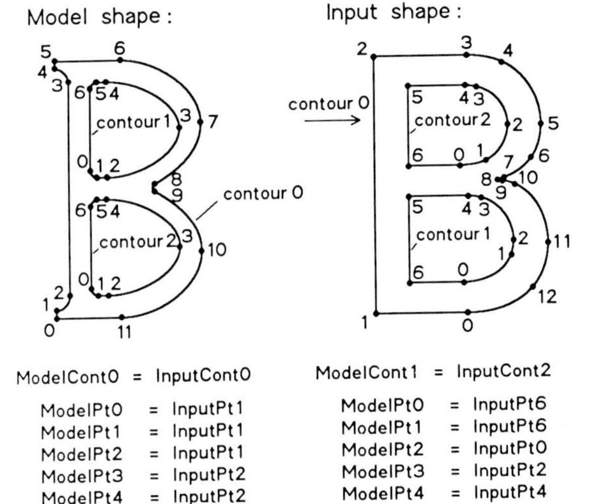


| ModelCont0 | = | InputCont0 |
|---|---|---|
| ModelPt0 | = | InputPt1 |
| ModelPt1 | = | InputPt1 |
| ModelPt2 | = | InputPt1 |
| ModelPt3 | = | InputPt2 |
| ModelPt4 | = | InputPt2 |
| ModelPt5 | = | InputPt2 |
| ModelPt6 | = | InputPt3 |
| ModelPt7 | = | InputPt5 |
| ModelPt8 | = | InputPt8 |
| ModelPt9 | = | InputPt8 |
| ModelPt10 | = | InputPt11 |
| ModelPt11 | = | InputPt0 |

| ModelCont1 | = | InputCont2 |
|---|---|---|
| ModelPt0 | = | InputPt6 |
| ModelPt1 | = | InputPt6 |
| ModelPt2 | = | InputPt0 |
| ModelPt3 | = | InputPt2 |
| ModelPt4 | = | InputPt4 |
| ModelPt5 | = | InputPt5 |
| ModelPt6 | = | InputPt5 |
| **ModelCont2** | = | **InputCont1** |
| ModelPt0 | = | InputPt6 |
| ModelPt1 | = | InputPt6 |
| ModelPt2 | = | InputPt0 |
| ModelPt3 | = | InputPt2 |
| ModelPt4 | = | InputPt4 |
| ModelPt5 | = | InputPt5 |
| ModelPt6 | = | InputPt5 |

Figure 8: Characteristic point table includes the correspondences between input shape points and model

The model description associates characteristic points with information about their approximate location and about their topological properties (local or global extrema, position on or close to a given reference line, direction of arrival and departure segments). The model also includes outline part descriptors (figure 9). These descriptors specify departure and arrival point numbers of given outline segments and their type (straight, curved of serif). Straight line segments are characterized by their primary direction (horizontal, vertical or diagonal) and orientation. Curve segments are characterized by their respective quadrant number and orientation. Outline segments can be short or long segments.

The previously enumerated criteria for the matching of characteristic points are hierarchical. Stronger and more specific features are tested first (location on reference lines, local extrema in x and y, global extrema in x or y). If applicable to a given model point, they result in rapid elimination of inappropriate candidate points.

Criteria (4) to (5) incorporate knowledge about incoming and outgoing outline segments. Again more specific criteria are tested first (criterion 4: extremity of a long straight line segment). Criterion (5) is used in order to remove candidate points, since model points do not lie between straight line segments having similar slopes. Criteria (7) to (10) use the directions of incoming and outgoing outline segments for the further discrimination of input points. Criteria (11) and (12) are two remaining criteria which provide additional information in order to find the best match between the few remaining candidate points.

After applying each criterion and eliminating unsuitable candidate points, the outline description of the remaining candidates is checked for coherence. Contradictions are detected and inappropriate candidate points are removed from the candidate point list.

Figures 7 and 10 illustrate the matching process for associating input points to corresponding model points.

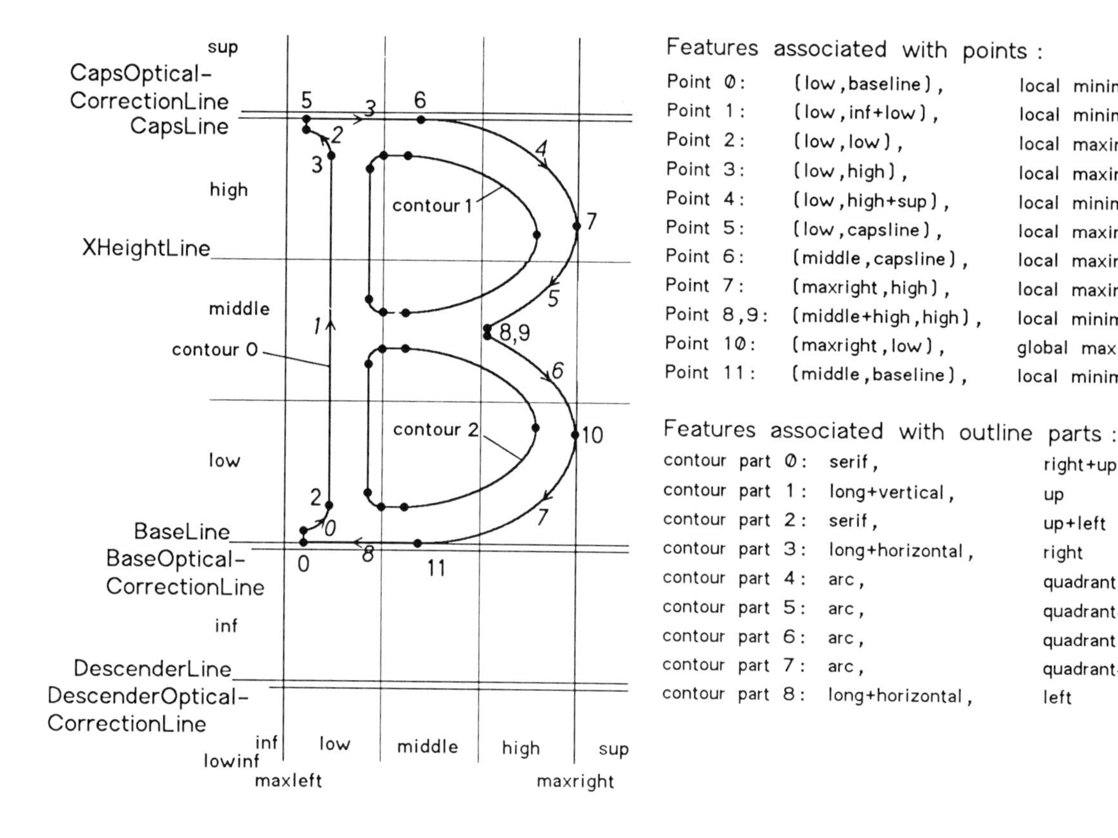
sup
CapsOptical-
CorrectionLine
CapsLine
high
XHeightLine
middle
contour 0
low
BaseLine
BaseOptical-
CorrectionLine
inf
DescenderLine
DescenderOptical-
CorrectionLine
inf
lowinf
low
middle
high
sup
maxleft
maxright
contour 1
contour 2
Features associated with points :
Point 0: (low,baseline), local minimum in y
Point 1: (low,inf+low), local minimum in x
Point 2: (low,low), local maximum in x
Point 3: (low,high), local maximum in x
Point 4: (low,high+sup), local minimum in x
Point 5: (low,capsline), local maximum in y
Point 6: (middle,capsline), local maximum in y
Point 7: (maxright,high), local maximum in x
Point 8,9: (middle+high,high), local minimum in x
Point 10: (maxright,low), global maximum in x
Point 11: (middle,baseline), local minimum in y
Features associated with outline parts :
contour part 0: serif, right+up
contour part 1: long+vertical, up
contour part 2: serif, up+left
contour part 3: long+horizontal, right
contour part 4: arc, quadrant1+negative
contour part 5: arc, quadrant4+negative
contour part 6: arc, quadrant1+negative
contour part 7: arc, quadrant4+negative
contour part 8: long+horizontal, left

Figure 9: Model description of character B

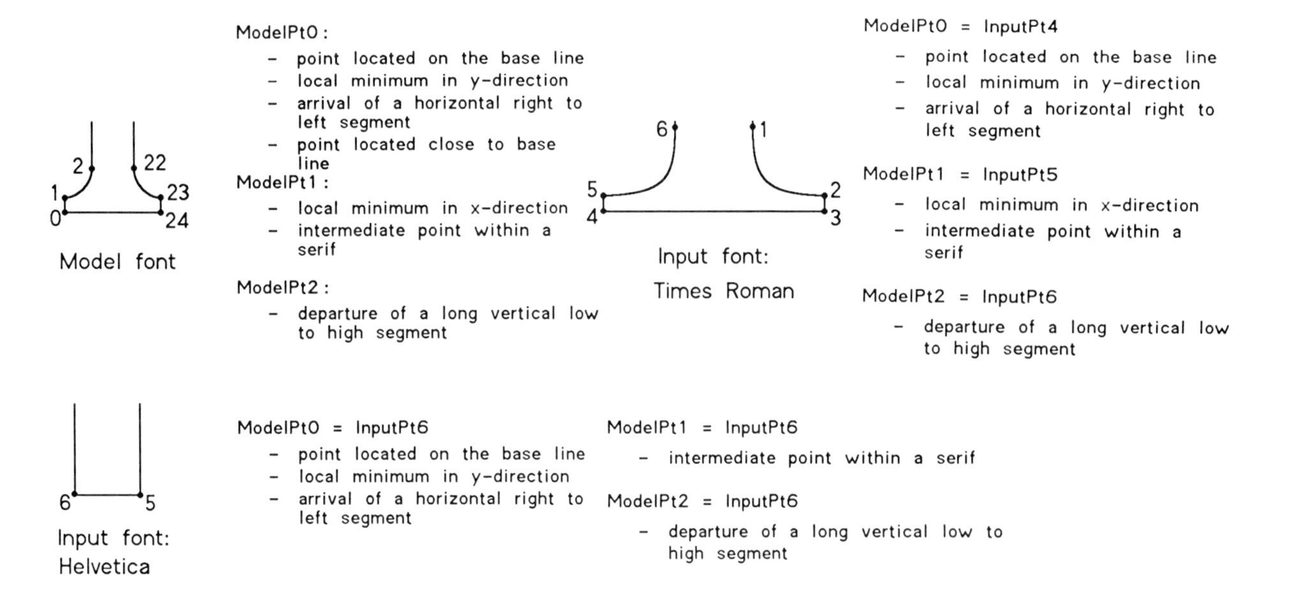
Model font
ModelPt0 :
- point located on the base line
- local minimum in y-direction
- arrival of a horizontal right to left segment
- point located close to base line
ModelPt1 :
- local minimum in x-direction
- intermediate point within a serif
ModelPt2 :
- departure of a long vertical low to high segment
Input font:
Times Roman
ModelPt0 = InputPt4
- point located on the base line
- local minimum in y-direction
- arrival of a horizontal right to left segment
ModelPt1 = InputPt5
- local minimum in x-direction
- intermediate point within a serif
ModelPt2 = InputPt6
- departure of a long vertical low to high segment
Input font:
Helvetica
ModelPt0 = InputPt6
- point located on the base line
- local minimum in y-direction
- arrival of a horizontal right to left segment
ModelPt1 = InputPt6
- intermediate point within a serif
ModelPt2 = InputPt6
- departure of a long vertical low to high segment

Figure 10: Matching serifs extremities

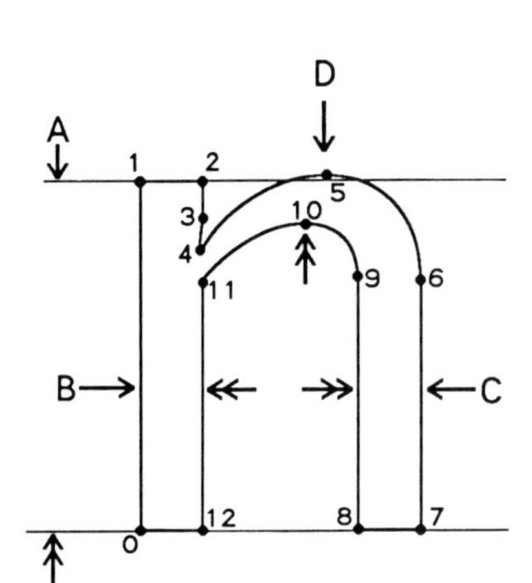


```
A: hint specification: vertical phase control of reference lines
   hint application: complete character
B: hint specification: horizontal phase control of vertical stem
                       stem width given by Pt0, Pt12
   hint application: complete character
C: hint specification: horizontal phase control of vertical stem
                       stem width given by Pt8, Pt7
   hint application:
     fixed displacement: Pt6 to Pt9
     proportional displacement: Pt4 to Pt6
       fixpoint: Pt4
       max. displacement point: Pt6
     proportional displacement: Pt9 to Pt11
       fixpoint: Pt11
       max. displacement point: Pt9
D: hint specification: vertical phase control of shoulder with
                       respect to reference lines
                       shoulder thickness given by Pt10, Pt5
   hint application:
     proportional displacement: Pt4 to Pt6
       fixpoint: Pt4, Pt6
       max. displacement point: Pt5
     proportional displacement: Pt9 to Pt11
       fixpoint: Pt9, Pt11
       max. displacement point: Pt10
```

Figure 11: Support points for the specification of grid constraints

The result of the matching process is fed back into the input shape outline description as a characteristic point table (figure 8). Each table entry specifies a given model point and its associated input point given by its glyph, contour and point number.

A model description has been established for all latin alphanumeric characters. Italic characters do not need a special model description: before matching, they are rectified by inverse slanting. After rectification, the normal matching process can be applied to them. The matching program has been tested on 70 different fonts, including italic fonts. Among these fonts, a full match has been obtained on 99% of all characters. For the remaining 1% of the characters, the program announces that no correct match has been found. Characters which could not be matched to the model belong to fonts having slightly rounded vertical, horizontal and diagonal strokes like Optima, Palatino or Zapf Book. Such characters require the implementation of additional processing steps for assimilating their long low-curvature outline parts to long vertical, horizontal or diagonal outline segments.

## 4 Automatic hinting

Hints are grid-fitting rules specifying which parts of outline characters should be adapted to the grid in order to obtain nice regular raster characters [11]. These grid-fitting rules mainly apply to character reference lines, stems, bowls and serifs. Grid-fitting rules for fitting stems and bowls require two outline support points specifying the stem or bowl width.

The evaluation of a given hint produces a subpixel displacement which must be applied to certain parts of the outline. The application part specifies the character parts on which the computed displacement is applied by giving their starting and ending outline support points (figure 11).

Similarly, special grid-fitting rules control the discrete appearance of serifs. They require outline support points for the control of serif length and serif thickness (figure 12).

Thanks to grid-fitting, the discrete size of serifs will decrease continuously and disappear at once when decreasing font size (figure 13).

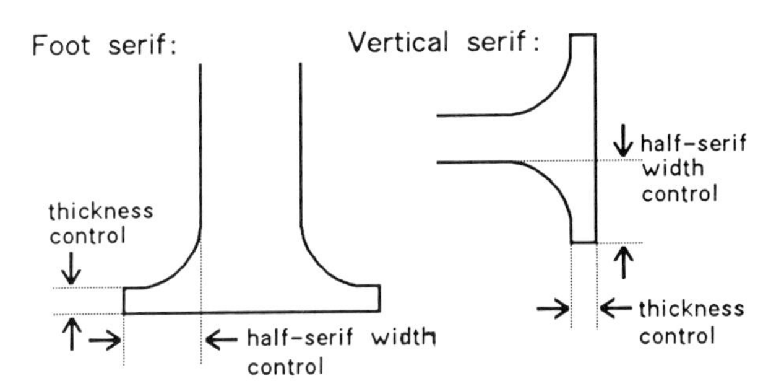


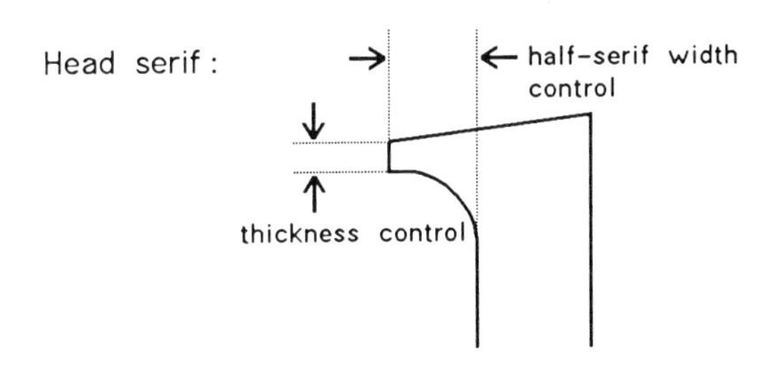


Figure 12: Serif control hints

Only those hints whose parameters are characteristic points of a given letter shape can be generated automatically. Their meta-description is inserted into the character model. When the correspondence between characteristic points of the model and points of the input shape has been found, applicable hints described in the model are copied into the input shape description and model point numbers are replaced by references to corresponding input shape point numbers.

Some input shapes only partially match model shapes. Matching sans-serif fonts with the model produces one input point for several characteristic points at serif locations (figure 10). Degenerated serifs are detected by the automatic hinting procedure. Hints whose parameters are two identical points are not copied into the input shape description.

As mentioned in the previous section, italic characters are matched to their model after applying inverse slanting. Meta-hints associated with the model are defined in a way which ensures that correct hints can be derived both for upright and italic typefaces. For the vertical phase control of horizontal bars, hint specifications remain essentially the same: the current displacement direction will follow the direction of the vertical stems (figure 14). Support points used for horizontal phase control of vertical or italized stems can be defined in such a way that hints for both cases derive from the same meta-hint description.

Italic serif shapes differ considerably from roman serifs. Such shape variations can be detected and meta-hints associated to such shapes need not be copied into the input typeface description (figure 15).

Figure 13: Serif appearence with decreasing font size

Using the same topological description and identical meta-hints for upright and italic typefaces, one achieves quite acceptable results (figure 16).

Characters including features not described by the model description are hinted manually. These hints are very special. Generally, they can be left out since their effect is rather limited. Such hints may be used for example for controlling the tail of character "Q" or the terminal drop of character "j". The number of special hints that may be added explicitely is smaller than 3%. The automatically generated hints already produce high quality character descriptions that can be rendered at any given screen or printer resolution.

## 5 Character structure elements

Most computer-aided font design systems incorporate either interactive or descriptive outline manipulation capabilities. Shape parts like shoulders, stems and serifs need to be specified and stored explicitely. These parts may then be reused for the synthesis of other similar letter shapes [14]. *Metafont* for example is a typographic synthesizing system based on a programming model that is used to superimpose parametrised character parts in order to generate the resulting letter shape. Parameters for defining and assembling character parts are specified explicitely using suitable expressions [13]. The complete shape is generated as a superimposition of each in-

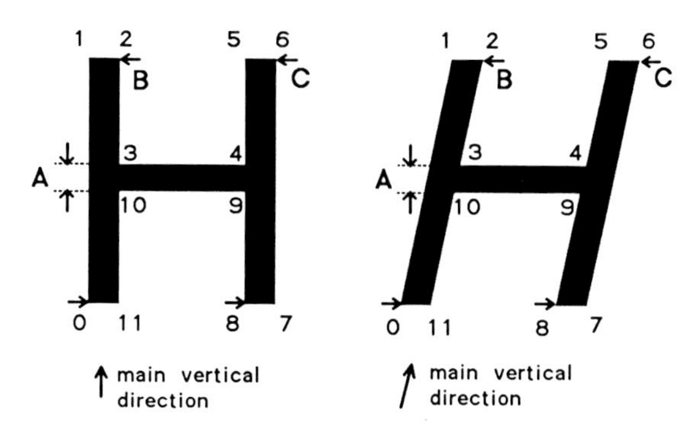


A: **hint specification:**
vertical phase control of horizontal bar
bar width given by Pt10, Pt3
**hint application:**
vertical displacement along main direction of horizontal bar: Pt3Pt4, Pt10Pt9

B: **hint specification:**
horizontal phase control of vertical stem;
stem support points given by Pt0, Pt2
**hint application:**
displacement of stem borders Pt0Pt1, Pt3Pt2, Pt10Pt11
if vertical stem: horizontal phase control only
if oblique stem: horizontal and diagonal phase control

Figure 14: Common hints for upright and italic characters

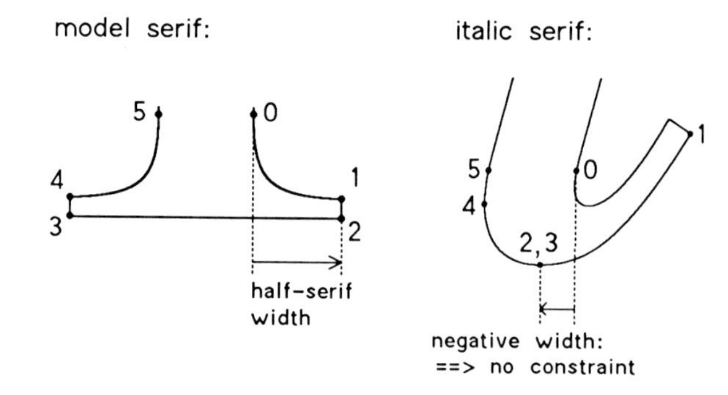


Figure 15: Detection of important shape variations in italic serifs

dividual shape. Metafont however provides no tools for extracting character parts from existing outline fonts. This section shows how our topological model is used in order to build higher level structure elements from outline descriptions for describing character parts like serifs and stems.

Serifs are specified directly by the topological model as outline parts having the *serif* attribute (see figure 4). In fact, each head serif is given by one and each foot or vertical serif is given by two half-serifs (see figure 12). Each half-serif is given by a starting point lying at the end of a long vertical or horizontal bar, by one intermediate point giving the serif's extension and by an end point lying on the continuation of the stroke base. A complete foot serif is given by its two component half-serifs. With such a description, a program can automatically extract the serifs of a given outline font. For uniformization purposes, new regularized serifs can be inserted in place of the original ones. Furthermore, vertical and horizontal stems and bowl pieces embedded in the character outline can be described by specifying corresponding stroke pieces (figure 17).

Description of stroke pieces may be useful for adjusting stroke thick-

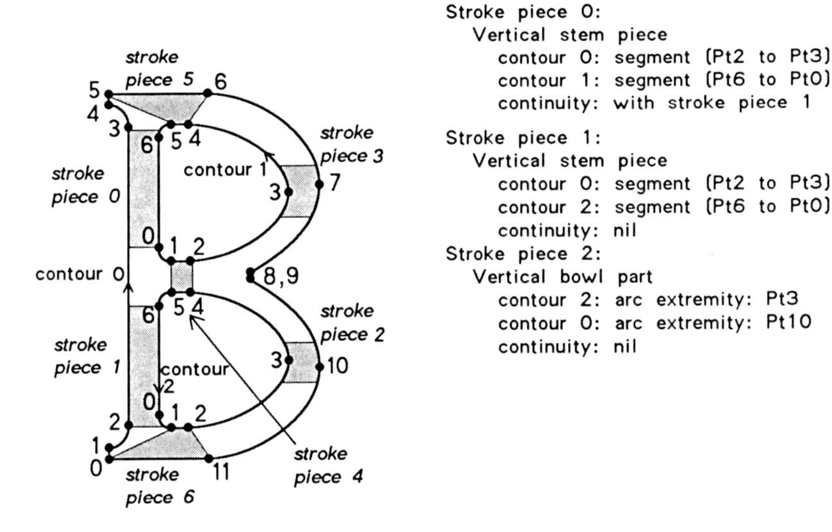


```
Stroke piece 0:
  Vertical stem piece
    contour 0: segment (Pt2 to Pt3)
    contour 1: segment (Pt6 to Pt0)
    continuity: with stroke piece 1

Stroke piece 1:
  Vertical stem piece
    contour 0: segment (Pt2 to Pt3)
    contour 2: segment (Pt6 to Pt0)
    continuity: nil
Stroke piece 2:
  Vertical bowl part
    contour 2: arc extremity: Pt3
    contour 0: arc extremity: Pt10
    continuity: nil

Stroke piece 3:
  Vertical bowl part
    contour 1: arc extremity: Pt3
    contour 0: arc extremity: Pt7
    continuity: nil

Stroke piece 4:
  Horizontal stroke piece
    contour 2: segment (Pt4 to Pt5)
    contour 1: segment (Pt1 to Pt2)
    continuity: nil

Stroke piece 5:
  Horizontal stroke piece on CapsLine
    contour 1: segment (Pt4 to Pt5)
    contour 0: segment (Pt5 to Pt6)
    continuity: nil

Stroke piece 6:
  Horizontal stroke piece on BaseLine
    contour 0: segment (Pt11 to Pt0)
    contour 2: segment (Pt1 to Pt2)
    continuity: nil
```

Figure 17: Description of stroke pieces embedded in the model character outline

ABCDEFGHIJKLMNOP
ABCDEFGHIJKLMNO
ABCDEFGHIJKLMN
ABCDEFGHIJKLM
ABCDEFGHIJKL
ABCDEFGHIJKL
ABCDEFGHIJK

Figure 16: Rasterization of automatically hinted italic outline characters

ness and position, which is important for producing more legible fonts at small sizes.

## 6 Conclusions

A topological model representing the essence of the shapes of typographic latin typefaces has been developed. This model provides sufficiently general information for it to be valid for all non-fancy typefaces, serif and sans-serif. It also provides sufficient topological information and relationships to match typefaces given by their outline description to the model shape.

The correspondence between characteristic model and input shape points is of great importance for further processing of character outline descriptions. Grid-fitting meta-hints can be taken automatically from the model, adapted and associated to any given input typeface. Furthermore, higher-order structures can be built upon characteristic points for describing structural character parts like serifs, stems, bowls and junctions. Mapping continuous outline descriptions into structural descriptions and vice-versa offers new opportunities for developing advanced computer-aided font design tools.

## Acknowledgements

The authors would like to thank Andre Gurtler from the School of Design, Basel, for his contribution to visual aspects of digital type. We would also like to thank Jakob Gonczarowski and Justin Bur for their critical review of our typographic font-independent topological model. This research was funded by the "Commission d'Encouragement de la Recherche Scientifique" of Switzerland.

## Bibliography

[1] D. Adams, "abcdefg: a better constraint driven environment for font generation", in Andre, Hersch (eds.), *Raster Imaging and Digital Typography,* Cambridge University Press, 1989, 54-70

[2] Apple Computer, *TrueType Spec – The TrueType Font Format Specification,* July 1990

[3] S. Andler, "Automatic Generation of Gridfitting Hints for Rasterization of Outline Fonts or Graphics", *EP90 – Proceedings of the International Conference on Electronic Publishing, Document Manipulation & Typography,* September 90, (R. Furuta, Ed.) Cambridge University Press, 221-234

[4] *Berthold Types,* H. Berthold AG, Berlin, 1988

[5] C. Betrisey, R.D. Hersch, "Flexible Application of Outline Grid Constraints", in Andre, Hersch (eds.), *Raster Imaging and Digital Typography,* Cambridge University Press, 1989, 242-250

[6] P. Coueignoux, "Character Generation by Computer", *Computer Graphics and Image Processing,* Vol. 16, 1981, pp 240-269.

[7] M. Eden, "Handwriting and pattern recognition", *IRE Trans. Inform. Theory,* Vol IT-8, 1962, pp 160-166.

[8] H.F. Feng, T. Pavlidis, "Decomposition of polygons into simpler components: Feature generation for syntactic pattern recognition", *IEEE Transactions on Computers,* Vol C-24, June 1975, pp 636-650.

[9] J. Flowers, "Digital type manufacture: an interactive approach", *IEEE Computer,* May 1984, pp. 40-48.

[10] P. Gaskell, "A Nomenclature for the Letterforms of Roman Type", *Visible Language,* Vol 10, No 1, 1976, 41-51.

[11] R.D. Hersch, "Character Generation under Grid Constraints", Proceedings SIGGRAPH'87, *ACM Computer Graphics*, Vol 21, No. 4, July 1987, 243-252

[12] P. Karow, *Digital Formats for Typefaces*, URW Verlag, Hamburg, 1987.

[13] D. Knuth, *Computer Modern Typefaces*, Addison-Wesley, 1986.

[14] R. Rubinstein, *Digital Typography, An Introduction to Type and Composition for Computer System Design*, Addison-Wesley, 1988.

[15] L.G. Shapiro, "A Structural Model of Shape", IEEE PAMI, Vol PAMI-2, No 2, March 1980, pp 111-126.

[16] W. Tracy, "Letters of Credit, a view of type design", Gordon Fraser, London, 1986, pp 52-55.

**Annex: Matching typographic letter shapes to their topological model**

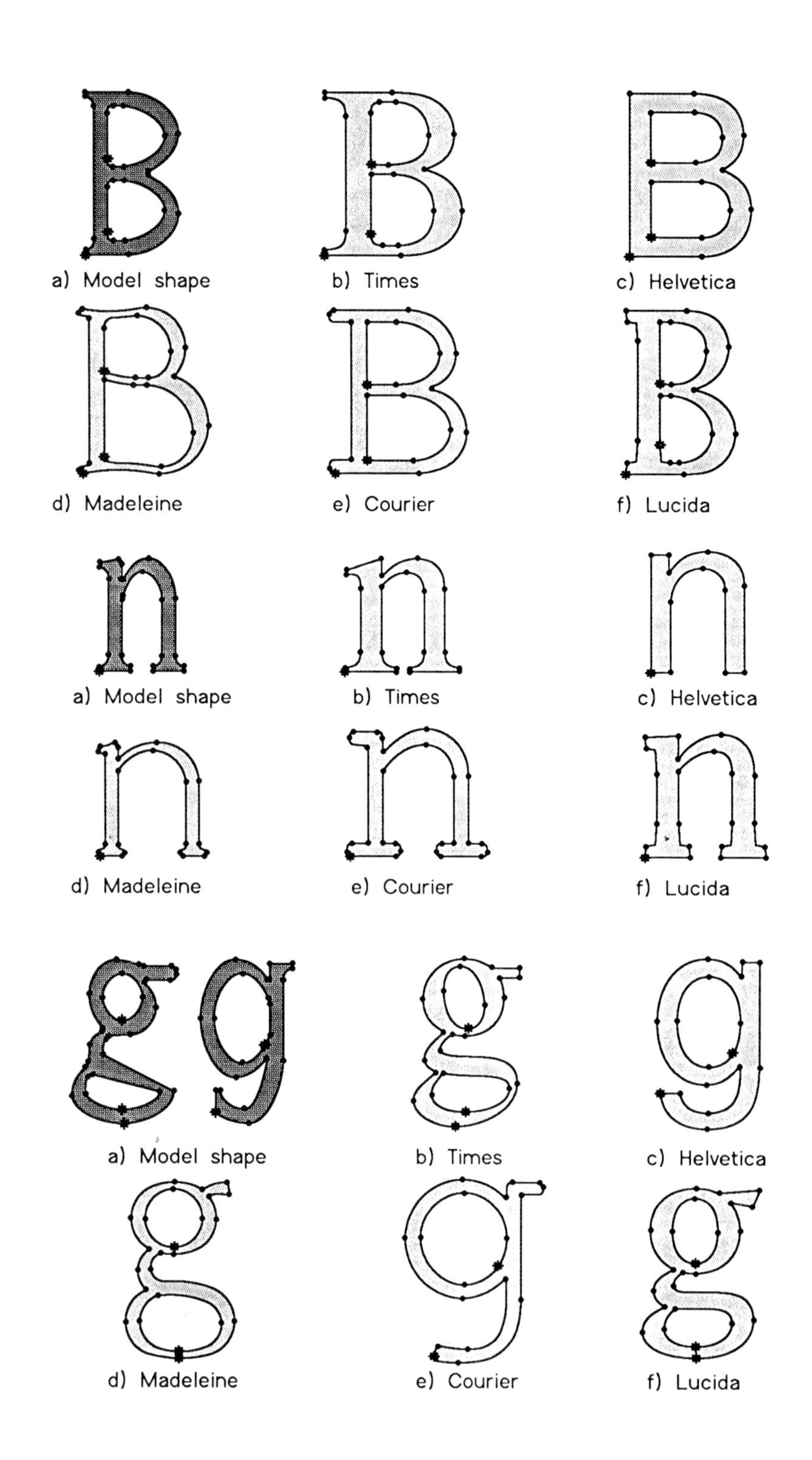

# Digital Halftoning with Space Filling Curves

**Luiz Velho***
**Jonas de Miranda Gomes**

IMPA – Instituto de Matemática Pura e Aplicada
Estrada Dona Castorina, 110
22460, Rio de Janeiro, Brazil

**ABSTRACT:** This paper introduces a new digital halftoning technique that uses space filling curves to generate aperiodic patterns of clustered dots. This method allows the parameterization of the size of pixel clusters, which can vary in one pixel steps. The algorithm unifies, in this way, the dispersed and clustered-dot dithering techniques.
**Keywords:** digital halftoning, quantization, dithering, space filling curves, bilevel display.

## 1. INTRODUCTION

The display of gray scale images on bilevel graphic devices requires a preprocessing step in order to adapt the data to the characteristics of the equipment. In particular, a process called *halftoning* creates the illusion of continuous-tone through the careful arrangement of the state of individual display cells. This process can be analog or digital, depending upon the underlying technology of the imaging system. The analog form of halftoning is well understood, and has been used in the printing industry for more than one century. *Digital halftoning*, also known as *spatial dithering*, is associated with the computer display of pictures, and has been object of intensive research.

### 1.1 MOTIVATION

The initial motivation for the development of dithering techniques was the popularity of graphic display devices, such as plasma panels, liquid crystal and CRT monitors. More recently, the availability of high resolution hardcopy devices such as laser printers and digital phototypesetters created a new motivation for the development of digital halftoning techniques.

The majority of existing dithering algorithms were designed for a class of graphic display devices that have a relatively low spatial resolution and allow precise control of individual pixels. These algorithms perform poorly on some hardcopy devices that do not have these properties and cannot properly reproduce isolated dots. An important class of devices of this type is the popular laser printer, based on electrophotographic technology.

The work presented in this paper addresses this problem. We propose an algorithm that is flexible enough to be used in a wide range of graphic devices.

### 1.2 OVERVIEW

The organization of the paper is as follows: In Section 2 we describe the architecture of an imaging system for bilevel displays; in Section 3 we give an introduction to digital halftoning; a brief review of space filling curves is provided in Section 4. The main aspects of the clustered-dot dithering method using space filling curves are described in Section 5. Implementation details of our method are provided in Section 6. Examples of images generated by the method and comparisons with other dithering methods are presented in Section 7. Concluding remarks and perspectives of future work are discussed in Section 8.

## 2. IMAGING SYSTEM FOR BILEVEL DISPLAYS

The imaging system must perform several preprocessing operations in order to generate the proper representation of a continuous-tone picture on a specific graphic display device. This process must also take into account the particular characteristics of the device to produce the best possible rendition of the picture.

The device's characteristics can be modeled as a mathematical function, defined on the space of images, called the *physical reconstruction function*. The *preprocessing operations* generally include: *tone scale adjustment, sharpening* and *halftoning*. This pipeline is illustrated in Figure 1 ([Ulichney 87]).

The *tone scale adjustment*, also known as *gamma correction*, is necessary because most devices have a non-linear intensity reconstruction function. This operation compensates, for example, the overlapping of contiguous dots, typical of some hardcopy devices. Detailed explanation on how to construct compensation tables for CRT monitors can be found in the literature (see for example [Catmull 79]). This procedure can be generalized for other types of graphic devices.

The *sharpening* is desirable because the dithering normally causes some reduction of the image spatial resolution. The quality of the final image can be greatly improved by an edge enhancement operation that emphasizes high frequencies bringing out the fine image details. Alternatively, the sharpening operation can be incor-

*Author's current address: University of Toronto.



©1991 ACM-0-89791-436-8/91/007/0081 $00.75

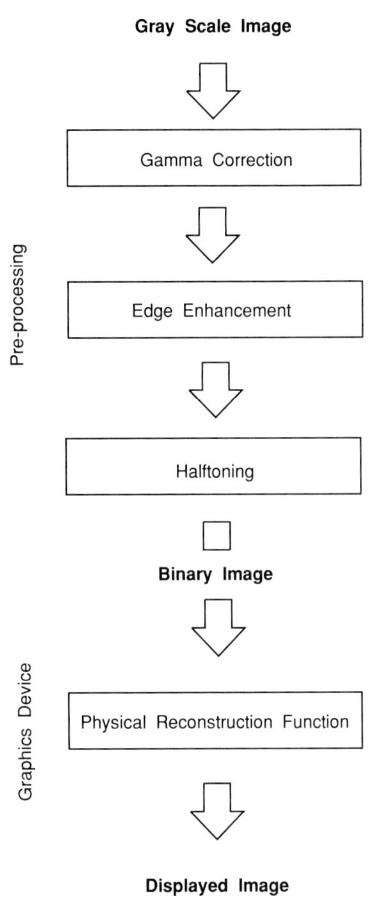


Figure 1 — Imaging pipeline for bilevel displays

porated into the halftoning process, as was observed by Jarvis [Jarvis et al 76].

## 3. HALFTONING

The existence of only two levels to be used in the display of continuous-tone images introduces visual artifacts, often manifested as false contours separating regions of different levels. Dithering alleviates this problem by properly controlling the distribution of bilevel intensities over the displayed image.

The dithering process is based on psychophysical characteristics of the human visual system. The eye integrates luminous stimuli over a solid angle of about 2 degrees [Wyszecki et al 82]. This means that we actually see the average intensities corresponding to small solid angles in our visual field. Dithering algorithms exploit this phenomenon, effectively redistributing the state of pixels in such a way that the average intensity in small areas of the dithered image is approximately the same of the original gray scale image.

Given a pixel $P$ of the image with intensity $I(P)$, it will be mapped into a pixel $P'$ of the dithered image whose intensity $I(P')$ is 0 or 1. The value of $I(P')$ is obtained by comparing the intensity $I(P)$ with a given intensity threshold $I_0$. The difference $I(P)–I(P')$ is the *quantization error* for the pixel $P$. In general, given a region of the image with $N$ pixels, $P_1, P_2, ..., P_N$, $N+1$ intensity levels can be represented by turning these pixels "on" and "off". The quantization error for this region is the difference

$$\sum_{j=1}^{N} I(P_j) - \sum_{j=1}^{N} I(P_j'),$$

between the sum of intensities of the gray scale image in the region and the sum of the intensities of the corresponding region in the dithered image.

Dithering algorithms distribute the error over small neighborhoods of the image in such a way that the average quantization error is as close to zero as possible. There are two main strategies to define the states of the pixels on the dithered image in order to achieve this goal. One of them perturbs the intensity threshold $I_0$ in a predefined way, so that the error is statistically neglectable; the other strategy perturbs the threshold for a pixel $P$ based on the quantization error in a neighborhood of $P$, obtaining an exact minimization of the error. In both cases, the perceived intensity of the dithered image at a given neighborhood will be close to that of the original image.

This technique implies in a trade-off between spatial and tonal resolution: as we spread the error over larger areas of the image, more tones can be represented at the cost of a poorer rendition of fine details. The gray levels are rendered as patterns of black and white pixels eliminating high frequency information. In this process contouring artifacts are transformed into patterning features.

### 3.1 DITHERING TECHNIQUES

Spatial dithering techniques can be classified according to the nature of patterns they generate and to the type of pixel configuration they produce. These two criteria capture the main features of the textures created to represent areas of uniform gray, one of the most important aspects of the halftoning process.

Textures can be rendered by *periodic* or *aperiodic* patterns. In general, periodic patterns are generated by deterministic processes based on regular sampling grids. Aperiodic patterns are generally associated with methods that can be modeled as stochastic processes.

The type of pixel configuration produced is determined by the spatial distribution of the "on" or "off" state of the image elements. *Dispersed-dot* methods depict a gray level by covering a small area with evenly distributed dots, while *clustered-dot* methods concentrate the dots in small groups.

### 3.2 PREVIOUS WORK

The most popular halftoning method is the ordered dither technique. It uses a deterministic perturbation to generate periodic patterns, and according to the distribution of perturbations it can produce dispersed or clustered dots. Other important methods are the error diffusion techniques. The well known algorithms in this category are the Floyd-Steinberg, and Knuth's dot-diffusion algorithm. They generate aperiodic patterns as the result of neighborhood operations. All published error diffusion algorithms fall into the dispersed-dot category.

The *ordered dither* algorithm determines a matrix of quantization thresholds that is replicated over the image. This is essentially a set of pseudo-random numbers uniformly distributed over the intensity range. The arrangement of thresholds is designed to avoid the introduction of low spatial frequency noise into the image. This algorithm is generally identified as a dispersed-dot technique [Limb 69], but if the intensity threshold levels are spatially concentrated it results in a clustered-dot dithering.

The *Floyd-Steinberg* algorithm [Floyd et al 75] computes the quantization error incurred in one image element and propagates it to the neighbors to the right and below. In this way, the local quantization error is distributed, minimizing globally the intensity difference between the original and quantized images.

The *dot diffusion* algorithm [Knuth 87] combines some characteristics of ordered dither and error diffusion techniques. Similarly to ordered dither it uses a matrix that is replicated over the entire image. This matrix gives the order by which the quantization error in one display cell will be distributed among its neighbors in the cell.

A comparison between dithering algorithms can be found in the survey [Jarvis et al 76]. A comprehensive study of dithering techniques with an analysis of the statistical properties can be found in [Ulichney 87].

We propose a digital halftoning method based on space filling curves, which uses the path of the curve to distribute the quantization error over the image. Witten and Neal [Witten et al 82] also described a dispersed-dot dithering algorithm that propagates the quantization error along a Peano curve.

Our technique parameterizes the dot aggregation factor allowing a precise control of the cluster size, which can vary in one pixel steps. This is the first algorithm that effectively unifies the dispersed and clustered-dot techniques. When the cluster size is one pixel it reduces to a dispersed-dot dithering using error diffusion. Therefore, Witten and Neal's algorithm is a particular case of our method.

As mentioned before, a large class of hardcopy devices cannot reproduce well configurations of sparse "on" and "off" pixels. For this reason, most page description languages employ clustered-dot ordered dithering, as the standard halftoning method [Adobe 85]. The method presented in this paper offers an alternative solution to the halftoning problem. It works very effectively in graphic displays as well as in hardcopy devices, and has potential applications in higher resolution printing.

## 4. SPACE FILLING CURVES

A continuous *plane curve* is a continuous map $c{:}I \to \mathbf{R}^2$ from the unit interval $I = [0,1]$ of the real line to the two-dimensional euclidean plane $\mathbf{R}^2 = \{(x, y)\ ;\ x, y \in \mathbf{R}\}$. The image $c(I)$ is called the *trace* of the curve $c$. A *space filling curve* is a continuous curve such that its trace covers the unit square $I^2 = [0,1] \times [0,1]$ of the plane. Therefore, for each point $P$ in the square $I^2$ there exists a real number $t$ in the interval $I$ such that $c(t) = P$. Intuitively, this means that the curve provides an ordered way to visit all points of the square as the parameter $t$ moves from 0 to 1.

Space filling curves were first discovered by the Italian mathematician Giuseppe Peano in 1890, and they constitute the first examples of the mathematical objects that Benoit Mandelbrot called fractal sets [Mandelbrot 77].

The mathematical construction of a space filling curve $c$ is done as a limiting process. We consider a sequence $c_n{:}I \to I^2$ of curves in the unit square, and we define $c$ as the limit

$$c = \lim_{n \to \infty} c_n$$

when this limit exists. The curves $c_n$ constitute approximations of $c$, and as we increase $n$ it visits a greater number of points in the unit square. It is possible to construct space filling curves for which each curve $c_n$ is simple, i.e. the map is 1–1. This means that it does not visit a point in the square more than once. In general it is possible to construct the sequence $c_1, c_2, \ldots, c_n, \ldots$ of approximating curves in a recursive way. In a certain sense a space filling curve defines a relationship between the area of subregions of the unit square $I^2$ and the length of subintervals of the unit interval $I$.

### 4.1 COMPUTATIONAL METHODS

Space filling curves can be properly specified by a formal geometric language. Sentences in this language are defined by a parallel graph grammar, and they are constructed by recursively applying a set of rewriting rules. Each sentence corresponds to a curve $c_n$ from the approximating sequence of the space filling curve. We will refer sometimes to this approximation itself as a space filling curve. A discussion about computational methods to generate space filling curves can be found in [Prusinkiewicz 90].

### 4.2 CLASSIC CURVES

The classic space filling curves are the *Peano curve*, the *Hilbert curve*, and the *Sierpinsky curve*. Figure 2(a)(b)(c) shows an approximation of these curves. All curves in the approximating sequence of these curves are simple.

### 4.3 IMAGE SCAN

When each curve $c_n$ in the approximating sequence of a space filling curve is simple, we obtain a method to visit, in a unique and ordered way, a subset of points of the square. The number of points visited increases as we increase the value of $n$. If we consider the square grid defined by the pixels of a raster image it is possible to address uniquely all pixels using a simple approximating curve $c_n$ of a space filling curve. Therefore, these curves constitute an effective method to scan a raster image. This idea has been exploited in the field of Digital Image Processing [Koo-Yan-Too 88], [Stevens et al 83].

The scan method described above has several advantages over the traditional scanline method for some class of image operations. The recursive nature of the construction of space filling curves allow a subdivision of the image into regions where each region is mapped to some subinterval of the unit interval $I$. This implies in a certain sense a reduction of the dimensionality of the problem, and simplifies immensely algorithms that deal with small regions of the image, as well as the computations involved.

The path followed by the space filling curve results in an image scan free of directional features presented by the traditional scanline raster pattern.

## 5. APERIODIC CLUSTERED-DOT DITHERING

The digital halftoning method using space filling curves exploits the properties of these mathematical objects to perform neighborhood operations essential to the spatial dithering process. This section presents the overall structure of the method and describes in detail its main aspects.

### 5.1 THE METHOD

The method consists of the following steps:

- Subdivision of the source image into small regions based on the trace of the space filling curve;
- Computation of the average intensities of each region;
- Determination of the dot patterns of the dithered image corresponding to each intensity;

Figure 2 — Approximations of: (a) Peano, (b) Hilbert, (c) Sierpinski space filling curves.

## 5.2 IMAGE SUBDIVISION

The method takes advantage of some properties of space filling curves that allow a subdivision of a raster image into regions with desirable characteristics. Let $c_n{:}I \rightarrow I^2$ be an approximation of a space filling curve $c$ that visits uniquely all pixels of the image. Let $I_1, I_2, ..., I_n$ be a subdivision of the unit interval $I$ into $n$ subintervals. By restricting the curve $c_n$ to each subinterval $I_j$ we obtain $n$ subregions $R_1, R_2, ..., R_n$ of the image. The size of each region $R_j$ varies proportionally with the length of the corresponding subinterval $I_j$. This gives an ordered way to visit all regions $R_j$, and also to visit all points in each of these regions. Besides this, the restriction $c_j{:}I_j \rightarrow R_j$ is by itself a space filling curve, that is a scaled version of the original curve $c$, because of the self-similarity properties of the space filling curves. This characteristic minimizes the grid effect often manifested in dithering methods that use standard methods of image scan.

## 5.3 DOT GENERATION

The dot generation strategy is a direct consequence of scanning the image with a space filling curve. The objective is to produce, for a given region, a configuration of clustered dots that will result in a perception equivalent to the intensity of the original image. This depends on the area of the region, the average intensity over the region, and the graphic device's physical reconstruction function.

As described above, the trace of the space filling curve determines a relationship between the area of the region and the length of the curve. Suppose that the average intensity of a region $R$ is $I$. Ideally, the desirable perceptual results would be obtained by partitioning $R=R_1 \cup R_2$ into two subregions $R_1$ of white pixels, and $R_2$ of black pixels, such that $R_1$ corresponds to a subinterval of length proportional to $I$ and $R_2$ corresponds to a subinterval of length proportional to $1-I$. In practice, this subdivision cannot be done exactly because there is a discretization process involved that is influenced by the physical characteristics of the output device.

The graphics output device is able to display only a discrete number of fixed size dots at a determined resolution. In general, the shape of the dot is not completely regular, and there is some overlapping between contiguous dots. This fact implies in a degree of non-linearity in the reconstruction function. As mentioned in Section 2, it is possible to account for the device's non-linear response by means of an independent preprocessing step.

The dot configuration produced by the space filling curve method results in an aggregate of pixels connected not only sequentially by the curve, but also in other directions because of the intertwined way the space filling curve traces the region. Consequently, the cluster of dots obtained is confined within the limits of a ball that has an area close to the area of the region. As a whole, the patterns generated by this type of dots are evenly distributed but not periodic.

In order to account for the fine details of the image, it is desirable that the dot configuration grows outwards from the point of highest intensity of the region. This can be accomplished by centering the white subregion with a proper translation of the corresponding subinterval.

Figure 3 illustrates clusters of dots corresponding to intensities 15/16 to 0 for the Hilbert curve, in a region of 4×4 pixels. In Figure 4 we used the method to render a black to white gradation using different sizes for the dot aggregation.

## 5.4 ERROR DIFFUSION

The discrete nature of the reproduction process, as we have seen, may result in quantization errors. This error can be propagated along the path of the space filling curve in order to minimize the total quantization error. This is similar to the dispersed-dot error diffusion dithering techniques, but works on display cells of more than one pixel.

## 6. IMPLEMENTATION

The halftoning method presented in this paper was developed under the VISGRAF project, as part of an image processing system in the Computer Graphics laboratory at IMPA.

The computing environment is integrated by a network of Sun workstations and the primary graphics hardcopy devices are 300 dpi Postscript laser printers.

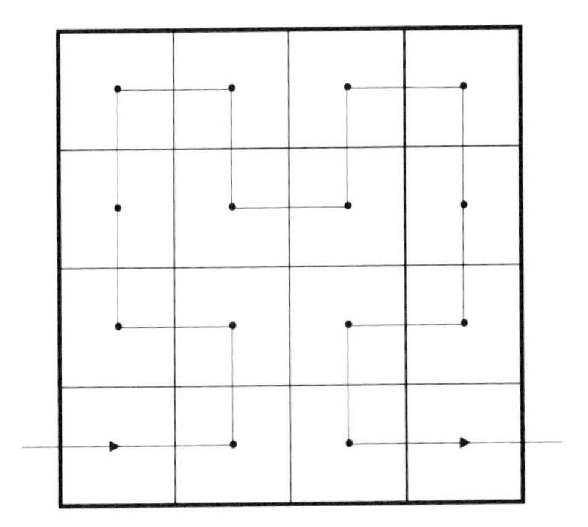

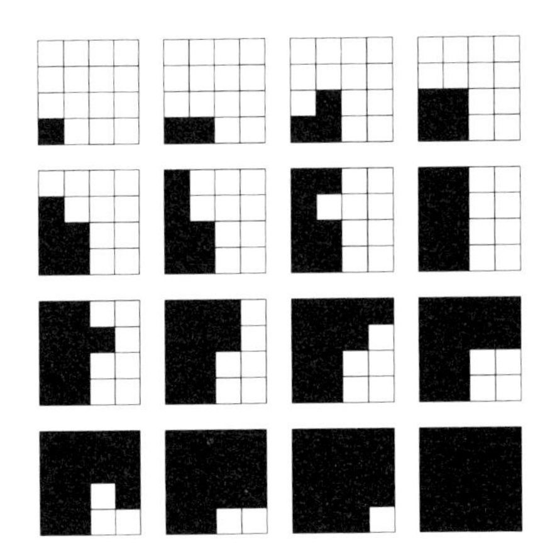

Figure 3 — Configuration of dots corresponding to intensity levels 15/16 to 0, for a cluster of 16 pixels using the Hilbert space filling curve.

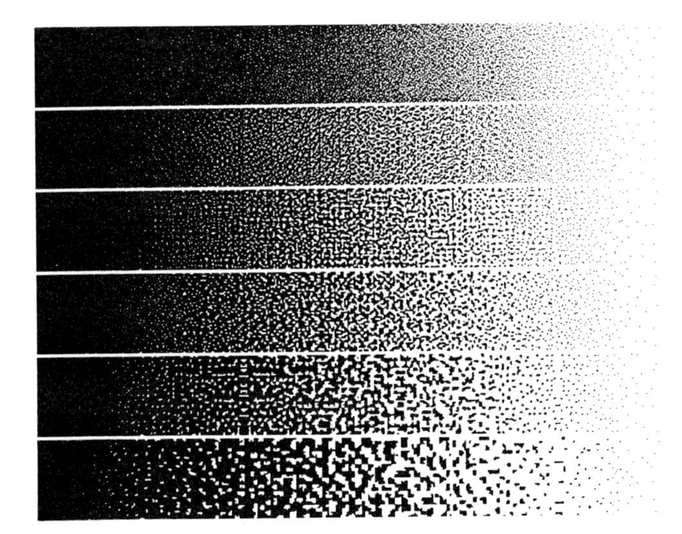

Figure 4 — Stripes with gradation dithered with the space filling curve algorithm (Hilbert curve) using different cluster sizes. From top to bottom, clusters of 2, 6, 12, 20, 32, 60 and 120 pixels.

The algorithm was implemented using the C language in the Unix operating system.

### 6.1 SCAN LIBRARY

The image scan pattern generation is implemented by a library of functions with a common interface. This simplifies the addition of new types of space filling curves to the dithering operation, and encourages experimentation.

The library's front-end consists of two functions. The first one selects the curve to be used for the image scan and, if necessary, executes initialization and setup procedures. The second function moves forward and backwards along the path incrementally returning the coordinates of image points to be visited. It should be called once for each element processed.

### 6.2 ALGORITHM

The pseudo-code below gives a description of the basic algorithm. $R$ is the maximum pixel intensity (255 for images with 8 bits of resolution), and $N$ is the cluster size in pixels.

```
Select image scan curve ;
Initialize intensity accumulator ;

While (image elements to be processed ) {
        Advance image pointer along the scan
        path to the end of interval ;

        Move backward N pixels, accumulating
        the intensity of the input image ;

        Move forward N pixels along the path,
        setting the output pixels :
        if ( accumulator = R ) then {
                decrement R from accumulator ;
                set output pixel "on" ;
        } else {
                set output pixel "off" ;
        }
}
```

Note that the algorithm implicitly accounts for the quantization error, propagating it along the path.

The processing structure of the algorithm allows the same buffer to be used for both input and output image.

### 7. RESULTS

Although the method works well in low resolution devices, the clustered-dot dithering using space filling curves is primarily intended for medium to high resolution bilevel devices that cannot accommodate isolated black or white pixels. For this reason, the tests of the method were performed using a 300 dpi laser printer as the graphics output device.

### 7.1 EXAMPLES

Two different images were chosen as representatives of the common types of pictures in graphics applications. The first image, Figure 5, was captured from a black and white photographic reproduction of a study for the mural painting, "Escola dos Jesuitas", by the Brazilian artist Candido Portinari. This drawing of an indian boy head was done using charcoal, red ocher and sepia on paper, and dates from 1938. The image was digitized using a 300 dpi, 8 bits gray scale scanner. The second image is a

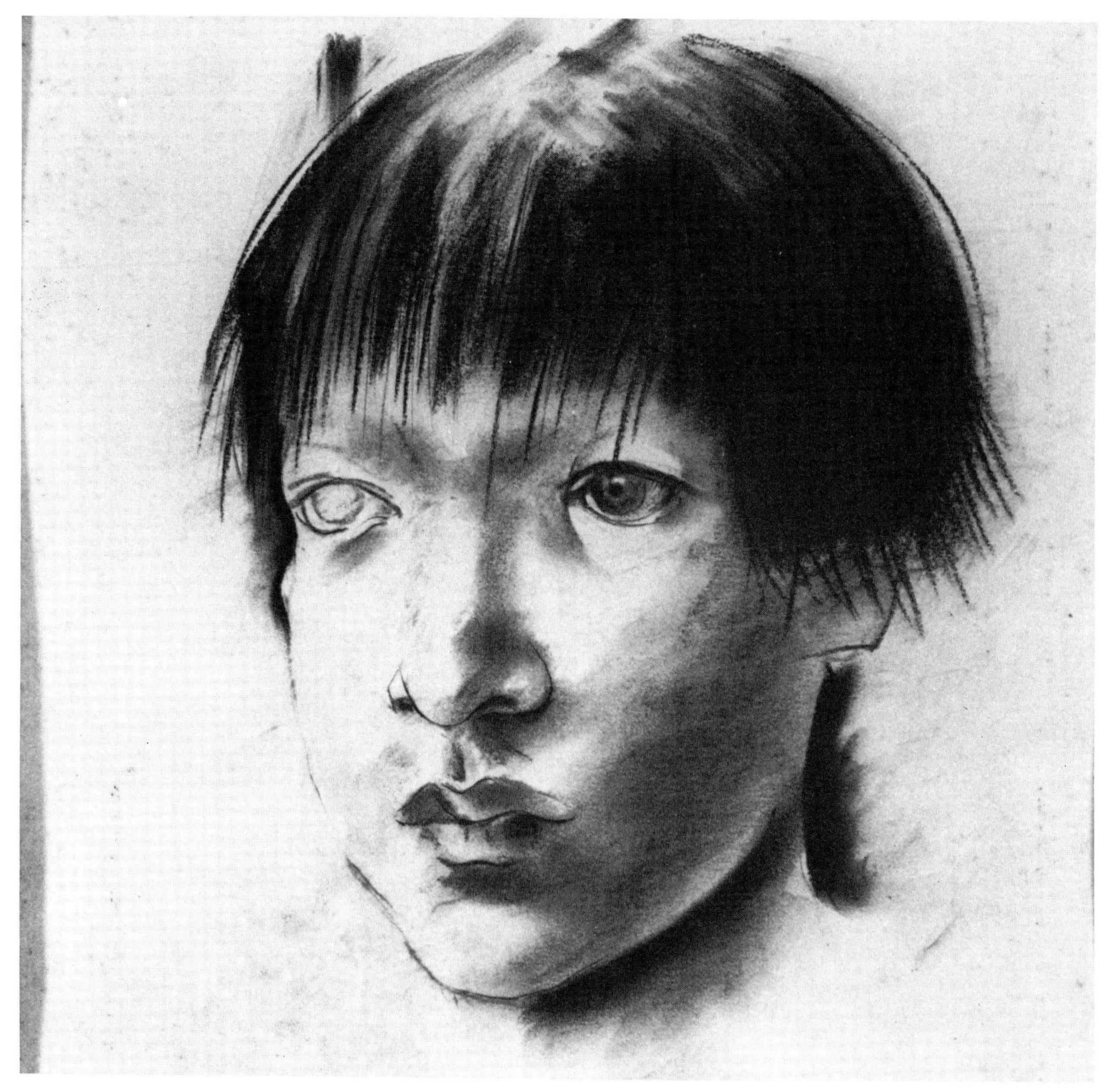

Figure 5 — Digitized test image: A drawing by the Brazilian artist Candido Portinari (1938).

computer generated image designed to include a wide range of features. It consists of a circular gradation inside a disc over a background with horizontal bands. Both images contain areas of smooth intensity variation as well as areas of high contrast and fine detail.

In the preprocessing step, only tone scale adjustment was performed prior to the halftoning operation. We decided not to do any edge enhancement in order to have a better feeling on how the algorithm handles fine details.

Figures 6 and 7 illustrate the clustered-dot dithering algorithm using Hilbert's space filling curve. The clustering size was of 11 pixels. Before dithering the two images were scaled down to 150 dpi. By increasing the viewing distance we can simulate the behaviour of the algorithm in higher resolution.

Figure 8 (A), (B) and (C) shows halftoned versions of the two images processed respectively by the space filling curve, the Floyd-Steinberg and the clustered-dot ordered dither algorithms. They were included to compare the results of the new method with both a standard error-diffusion technique and with the clustered-dot method used in most hardcopy devices. For the last comparison we used a 8×8 matrix in the clustered-dot ordered dither and a cluster size of 32 pixels in the space filling curve dither. These choices produce clusters of approximately the same size. Before dithering the two images were scaled down to 75 dpi.

### 7.2 ANALYSIS

The space filling curve dithering algorithm generates aperiodic patterns of evenly distributed dots without directional artifacts. It renders well the gray levels, and captures the fine details. These

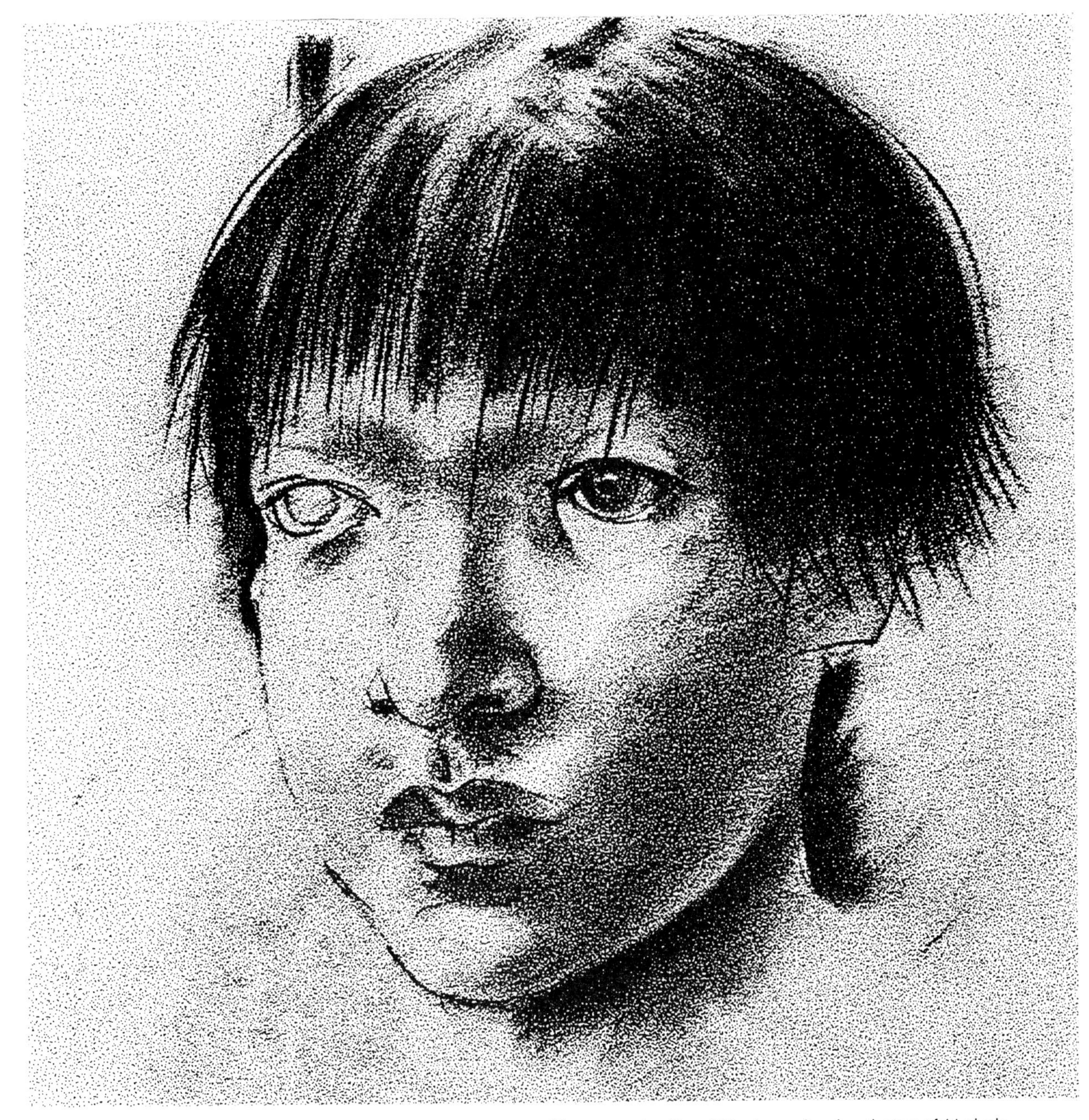

Figure 6 — Indian boy head at 150 dpi dithered with the space filling curve algorithm (Hilbert curve), using clusters of 11 pixels.

features are evident in both images, in particular in the face, eye and hair of the indian boy.

The Floyd-Steinberg algorithm, as was expected, did not produce satisfactory results on the laser printer. This is because the dispersed-dot method is not appropriate for this device. Groups of nearby individual small dots tend to be merged into a large blob. For this reason, the gray levels are not reproduced well, increasing the image contrast.

The clustered-dot ordered dither algorithm simulates the traditional analog halftoning screen. It reproduces very well the gray levels, but it blurs slightly the image. Depending on the cluster size contouring is more or less noticeable.

## 8. CONCLUSIONS

In this paper we introduced a new digital halftoning technique. The dithering method described is based on the trace of space filling curves to generate aperiodic patterns of clustered dots. To our knowledge this is the first algorithm that exploits random looking patterns of pixel agglomerates as a solution to the problem. Furthermore, the algorithm encompasses the dispersed dot error diffusion technique [Witten et al 82] as a particular case.

### 8.1 DISCUSSION

The space filling curve method has several advantages over previous ones. It generates patterns without the regular structure of the clustered-dot ordered dither. The patterns created are perceptually pleasant with similar characteristics to the photographic grain structure. The clustering factor can be easily parameterized,

Figure 7 — Computer generated picture at 150 dpi dithered with the space filling curve algorithm (Hilbert curve), using clusters of 11 pixels.

allowing the image rendition to match precisely the limits of the physical reconstruction function of the display device. The algorithm is computationally efficient requiring only 1 addition, 1 subtraction and 1 comparison per image element processed.

The main drawback of the algorithm is its high memory requirement, since it buffers the entire image because of its non-standard access pattern. This is probably not a serious restriction, except for very high resolution images. In this case, the problem can be addressed in two ways: the image can be subdivided in small blocks, and the algorithm is performed more or less independently in each one. This requires buffering of small strips of the image. Another solution is to store the image in a non-standard way such that its structure favors the access pattern. This is discussed by Blinn in the context of texture mapping [Blinn 90].

One inherent limitation of the method is that it is not truly bidimensional. For this reason, the error propagation is not totally uniform. This weakness is shared to some extent with all the published dithering techniques. The error diffusion can be cast as an equilibrium problem, which can be solved by relaxation techniques, such as simulated anealling [Kirkpatrick et al, 1982], [Fiume 89]. The computational effort required for an accurate solution is very expensive and has not yet been tried for this type of application.

### 8.2 FUTURE RESEARCH

Future work includes the extension of the method to process full color images, experiments with higher resolution graphics devices and the investigation of adaptive clustering techniques.

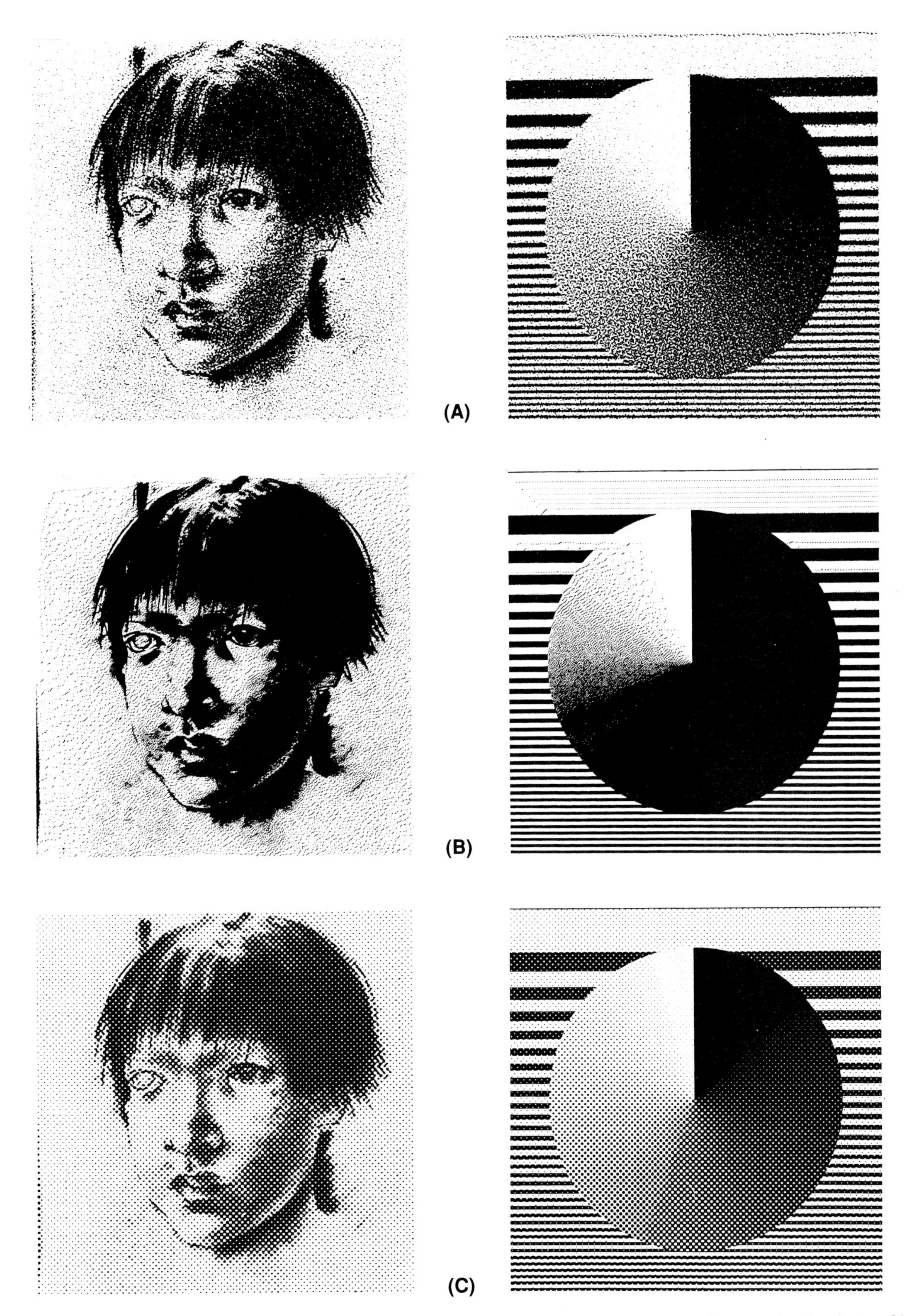


Figure 8 — The two test images at 75 dpi dithered with three different algorithms: (A) Space filling curve algorithm (Hilbert curve), using clusters of 32 pixels; (B) Floyd-Steinberg algorithm; (C) Clustered-dot ordered dither algorithm, using a matrix of order 8.

The method has also a potential to be used for illustration purposes. Other kinds of rendering effects can be obtained by a combination with image processing techniques. An example of this process, simulating pen-and-ink drawing, is shown in Figure 9.

## 9. ACKNOWLEDGEMENTS

The authors would like to thank João Candido Portinari, and Portinari Project's team for kindly providing the photographic reproduction of the study for the indian boy head. We also appreciate the helpful and encouraging comments provided by the reviewers.

## 10. REFERENCES

Adobe Systems, (1985): *Postscript Language Reference Manual.* Addison-Wesley, Reading Massachusetts.

Blinn, J. (1990): *The Truth About Texture Mapping.* IEEE Computer Graphics and Applications, March 1990, 78-83.

Catmull, E. (1979): *A Tutorial on Compensation Tables.* Proceedings SIGGRAPH '79, in Computer Graphics, Vol. 13, 1-7.

Fiume, E. and Ouellette, M. (1989): *On Distributed Probabilistic Algorithms for Computer Graphics.* Proceedings of Graphics Interface 89, 211-218.

Floyd, R. and Steinberg, L., (1975): *An Adaptive Algorithm for Spatial Gray Scale.* SID Symposium, 1975, 36-37.

Geist, R. and Reynolds, R. (1990): *Colored Noise Inversion in Digital Halftoning.* Proceedings of Graphics Interface 90, 31-38.

Jarvis, J., Judice, C. and Ninke, W., (1976): *A Survey of Techniques for The Display of Continuous Tone Pictures on Bilevel Displays.* Computer Graphics and Image Processing, n. 5, 13-40.

Kirkpatrick, S., C. D. Gelatt Jr., and M. P. Vecchi, (1982): *Optimization by Simulated Annealing*, IBM Research Report RC 9355.

Knuth, D., (1987): *Digital Halftones by Dot Diffusion.* ACM Transactions on Graphics, V. 6 N. 4, Oct 1987, 245-273

Koo-Yan-Too, H. C., (1988): *A Peano Scan Approach to Multivariate Data Clustering, with an Application.* Master Thesis, Dept. C. S., Univ. of Regina.

Limb, J. O., (1969): *Design of Dither Waveforms for Quantized Visual Signals.* Bell Systems Technical Journal, v. 48, n. 7, 2555-2582.

Mandelbrot, B., (1977): *The Fractal Geometry of Nature.* W. H. Freeman, New York

Prusinkiewicz P., and A. Lindenmayer (1990): *The Algorithmic Beauty of Plants.* Springer-Verlag, New York.

Sonnenberg, H., (1983): *Designing Scanners for Laser Printers.* Lasers & Applications, April 1983, 67-70.

Stevens, R. J., Lehar, F. A. and Perston, F. H. (1983): *Manipulation and Preservation of Multidimensional Image Data using the Peano Scan.* IEEE Trans. on Pattern Analysis and Machine Intelligence, 5, 520-526.

Ulichney, R., (1987): *Digital Halftoning.* MIT Press, Cambridge Massachusetts.

Witten, I. H., and Neal, M., (1982): *Using Peano Curves for Bilevel Display of Continuous Tone Images.* IEEE Computer Graphics and Applications, May 1982, 47-52.

Wyszecki, G. and Stiles, W. (1982): *Color Science: Concepts and Methods, Quantitative Data and Formulae.* Second edition. John Wiley & Sons.

Figure 9 — A pen-and-ink drawing effect obtained using image processing and the space filling curve dithering.

# Efficient Antialiased Rendering of 3-D Linear Fractals

John C. Hart  Thomas A. DeFanti
Electronic Visualization Laboratory
University of Illinois at Chicago

## Abstract

Object instancing is the efficient method of representing an hierarchical object with a directed graph instead of a tree. If this graph contains a cycle then the object it represents is a linear fractal. Linear fractals are difficult to render for three specific reasons: (1) ray-fractal intersection is not trivial, (2) surface normals are undefined and (3) the object aliases at all sampling resolutions.

Ray-fractal intersections are efficiently approximated to sub-pixel accuracy using procedural bounding volumes and a careful determination of the size of a pixel, giving the perception that the surface is infinitely detailed. Furthermore, a surface normal for these non-differentiable surfaces is defined and analyzed. Finally, the concept of antialiasing "covers" is adapted and used to solve the problem of sampling fractal surfaces.

An initial bounding volume estimation method is also described, allowing a linear fractal to be rendered given only its iterated function system. A parallel implementation of these methods is described and applications of these results to the rendering of other fractal models are given.

**CR Categories and Subject Descriptors:** I.3.5 [Computer Graphics]: Computational Geometry and Object Modeling — Hierarchical and geometric transformations. I.3.7 [Computer Graphics]: Three-Dimensional Graphics and Realism — Color, shading, shadowing and texture; visible surface algorithms.

**General Terms:** Algorithms, Theory.

**Additional Key Words and Phrases:** covers, fractal, object instancing, procedural modeling, ray tracing.

**Author's current address:** *EVL*, EECS Dept. M/C 154, *UIC*, Chicago, IL 60680-4348.
**E-mail:** hart@uicbert.eecs.uic.edu



## 1 Introduction

The use of bounding volumes has greatly increased the efficiency of ray tracing, particularly when they are organized hierarchically as a tree. By modeling objects canonically and using relative positioning at each node in the tree hierarchy, then subtrees denoting the same objects at different places in a scene are redundant. One subtree would suffice in this case but its root node would have more than one parent in the hierarchy. The tree is condensed into an acyclic directed graph, a process called "object instancing." This paper investigates and solves the problems that arise when this directed graph is allowed to be cyclic, representing a *linear fractal.*

### 1.1 History

Object instancing is an old technique, first used in Ivan Sutherland's "Sketchpad" [25]. It was first used for ray tracing in [20] as a method of reducing the size of object databases. In [20], the city of Pittsburgh (38,000 primitives) was rendered efficiently using little memory by storing only 600 actual primitives. Of particular interest was their treatment of bi-parametric surfaces. Using convex hull and subdivision properties, they were able to create a hierarchy of bounding boxes procedurally during ray intersection. At a fixed terminal level of the hierarchy, these bounding boxes were treated as "point" primitives.

Object instancing of fractal objects was first discussed in [10] where procedural "cheesecake extents" (extruded triangles) hierarchically bounded a fractal mountain. A later improvement used bounding ellipsoids [4]. One ray-traced fractal mountain mesh containing 262,144 primitives was shown in [10] and two fractal mountains appeared in [4] where the number of primitives was not listed.

Parallelepipeds were used as bounding volumes in [11]. They also maintained a heap of intersected bounding volumes rather than a list which improved the first-hit computation time complexity from $O(n)$ to $O(\log n)$. Using these tighter bounding volume hierarchies, a forest of trees (over 110,000 primitives)

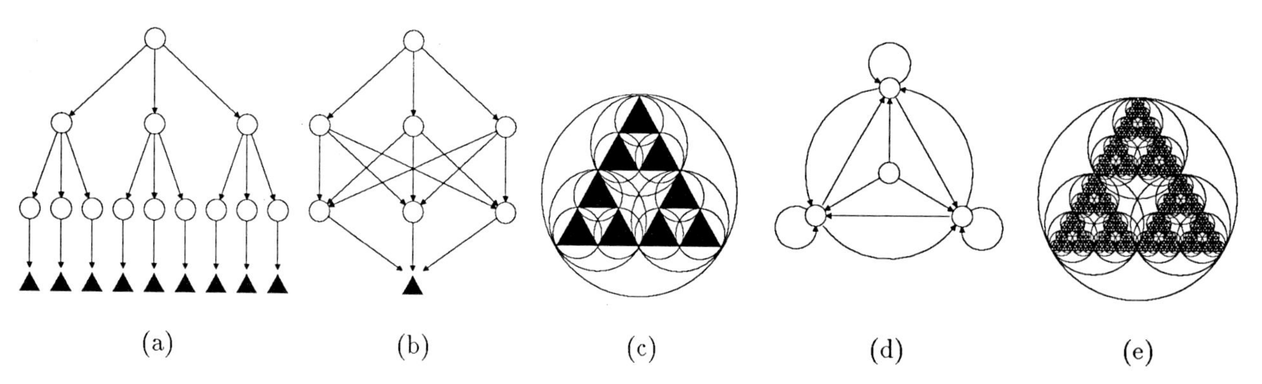


Figure 1: Hierarchical model topologies and corresponding images: (a) tree hierarchy; (b) object instancing hierarchy; (c) recursive object described by both tree (a) and acyclic digraph (b); (d) object instancing hierarchy with cycles; (e) linear fractal described by cyclic digraph (d).

surrounding a cement pond was rendered.

In [23], bounding boxes were used as well as both list and 3-D grid structures of objects. All this plus fast triangle and bounding box intersection routines enabled the authors to ray trace a carpet (125,000 primitives), a forest (2 billion primitives) and the still unsurpassed "field of grass" (over 400 billion primitives).

Most recently, object instancing was used in an animation of a multitude of robots cycling along a plane-filling fractal curve [14]. Also, some have modeled linear fractal shapes using tiny spheres [18, 7, 13] but their ray-tracing programs (Craig Kolb's "rayshade" and Don Mitchell's "FX"), though optimal for many other shapes, limited the renderable resolution of these linear fractal models.

### 1.2 Overview

When an object-instancing directed graph is allowed to cycle, the object it describes may be infinitely detailed, in other words, fractal. This causes three distinct problems when rendering such a model:

1. **Intersection of a ray with a fractal surface is not trivial.** There is no simple equation whose solution is the first intersection of a ray with the infinite geometry of a fractal surface.

2. **Surface normals are undefined.** A surface normal is orthogonal to the surface's derivative. The derivative of a fractal surface is undefined because its differentials do not converge as their span decreases.

3. **The object aliases at all sampling resolutions.** Fractal surfaces have infinite detail and thus require infinitely high sampling frequencies to avoid aliasing.

Problem 1 is solved in Sec. 3, where the ray-bounding volume intersections form a sequence through the bounding volume hierarchy that converges to the ray-fractal intersection. Ray-fractal intersections are approximated to a perceived infinite level of recursion by allowing objects to cycle until their projected image is smaller than a pixel. The "closeness criterion" from [3], also called "clarity" in [6], is rederived here in Sec. 3.1 and used to find the size of a pixel at a specific distance from the viewpoint. Furthermore, the use of bounding volumes for linear fractals is justified in Sec. 2.

Surface normals have been approximated for fractal surfaces using neighboring Z-buffer values [15] and gradients [6]. Problem 2 is solved in Sec. 4 by defining the fractal surface normal hierarchically as a weighted sum of surface normals across scale. Three weighting functions are described, illustrated and analyzed.

The concept of antialiasing "covers" is an object-space sampling method that uses single pixel thick bounding volumes [26]. This method is extended to arbitrary bounding volume hierarchies in Sec. 5 and solves Problem 3, antialiasing rendered fractal images using only one sample per pixel.

Another problem is the specification of an efficient initial bounding volume. Many times, fractal shapes are specified without any prior knowledge of what they will look like. An iterative method is derived in Sec. 3.3 that, given an iterated function system, produces a bounding sphere that contains the fractal shape it described. The result is a ray tracing method that renders a linear fractal described only by its IFS.

## 2 Linear Fractals

Linear fractals are shapes that can be constructed from finitely many smaller affine copies of themselves. The Cantor set and Sierpinski's gasket [12] are good introductory examples of linear fractal shapes. Other linear fractal models have been useful for texturing [5], image synthesis [2] and natural modeling [19].

## 2.1 Iterated Function Systems

A linear fractal can be specified by an iterated function system (IFS for short) consisting of a finite set of contractive affine maps (denoted $w_i(), i = 1 \ldots N$) [8]. An affine map $w : \mathbf{R}^3 \rightarrow \mathbf{R}^3$ can be specified by the popular homogeneous $4 \times 4$ matrix so long as its fourth column is $(0, 0, 0, 1)^T$.

This map is contractive if and only if there exists an $s \in [0, 1)$, called the *contractivity factor*, such that

$$|w(x) - w(y)| \leq s|x - y| \quad \forall x, y \in \mathbf{R}^3. \tag{1}$$

For example, if an affine map $w$ is a similtude[1] specified by a $4 \times 4$ homogeneous transformation matrix then the contractivity factor $s$ of $w$ is the cube-root of the determinant of its upper-left $3 \times 3$ submatrix. The contractivity factor s of an IFS, $\{w_i\}_{i=1}^N$, is given by

$$\mathrm{s} = \max_i s_i \tag{2}$$

where $s_i$ is the contractivity factor of map $w_i$.

The *Hutchinson operator*, $\mathbf{w}$, on a given set $A$ is defined as

$$\mathbf{w}(A) = \bigcup_{i=1}^{N} w_i(A). \tag{3}$$

Using it, we can define the set $\mathcal{A}$, called the *attractor* of the IFS, as the unique solution of

$$\mathcal{A} = \mathbf{w}(\mathcal{A}). \tag{4}$$

The attractor is so named because other sets will transform to it after repeated applications of the maps of an IFS. Specifically,

$$\mathcal{A} = \lim_{n \to \infty} \mathbf{w}^{\circ n}(A) \tag{5}$$

where $\mathbf{w}^{\circ n}$ is the $n$-fold composition of $\mathbf{w}$ and $A$ is any bounded non-empty set in $\mathbf{R}^3$.

## 2.2 The Inverse Problem

Currently, many researchers are trying to "solve the inverse problem," that is, to develop an automatic method for finding an IFS that will generate a given shape.

One step toward solving this problem is the Collage Theorem [1]. The Collage Theorem states that if a shape can be vaguely "tiled" out of smaller self-replicas, then it can be modeled approximately by an IFS. The maps of the IFS are just the transformations that take the whole to each of its smaller self-replicas. It provides the insight required to model a given shape as a linear fractal.

In 2-D, the solution to the inverse problem can be used to compress image data. In 3-D, it could compress volumetric data. Current methods for finding these transformations in $\mathbf{R}^2$ have had limited success [27, 9] and appear to be extendable to $\mathbf{R}^3$ as well. If such a volumetric compression algorithm is devised, the methods described in this paper would be able to directly visualize compressed volumetric data.

[1] A *similtude* is the composition of a rotation, a translation and a uniform scaling.

## 2.3 A Theorem Justifying Bounding Volumes

The Hausdorf metric $h$ measures the distance between two subsets $A$ and $B$ of a bounded set in $\mathbf{R}^3$ as[2]

$$h(A, B) = \max_{a \in A} \min_{b \in B} |a - b| + \max_{b \in B} \min_{a \in A} |a - b|. \tag{6}$$

It is basically the shortest distance of any point in $B$ to the point in $A$ farthest from $B$, plus the shortest distance of any point in $A$ to the points in $B$ farthest from $A$. It is commonly used as a measurement of how similar two shapes appear.

The following lemma is from [8] and was used in [1] to prove the Collage Theorem.

**Lemma:** *Let $A$ and $B$ be nonempty, bounded subsets of $\mathbf{R}^3$ and let $\mathbf{w}$ be the Hutchinson operator of an IFS $\{w_i\}_{i=1}^N$ with contractivity factor $\mathrm{s} \in [0, 1)$. Then*

$$h(\mathbf{w}(A), \mathbf{w}(B)) \leq \mathrm{s}h(A, B). \tag{7}$$

Its proof is from [1] and utilizes the definitions of contractivity and Hausdorf distance to produce a chain of inequalities.

**Proof:**

$$\begin{aligned} h(\mathbf{w}(A), \mathbf{w}(B)) &= \max_{a \in A, i} \min_{b \in B, j} |w_i(a) - w_j(b)| + \\ &\quad \max_{b \in B, i} \min_{a \in A, j} |w_i(b) - w_j(a)| \quad (8) \\ &\leq \max_{a \in A, i} \min_{b \in B} |w_i(a) - w_i(b)| + \\ &\quad \max_{b \in B, i} \min_{a \in A} |w_i(b) - w_i(a)| \quad (9) \\ &\leq \mathrm{s}h(A, B). \ \square \quad (10) \end{aligned}$$

The Lemma is used to prove the following theorem, actually just a simple corollary, which shows that the bounding volume hierarchy used by the ray intersection routine described in Sec. 3 is both valid (the union of bounding volumes contain the attractor at each level in the hierarchy) and efficient (the bounding volumes get tighter).

**Theorem:** *Let $\mathcal{A}$ be the attractor, and $\mathbf{w}$ be the Hutchinson operator, of an IFS $\{w_i\}_{i=1}^N$ with contractivity factor $s \in [0, 1)$. Let $B$ be a bounding volume of $\mathcal{A}$. Then*

$$\mathcal{A} \subset \mathbf{w}(B) \tag{11}$$

[2] In the original texts, the supremum and infinum are used. However, since the attractor and its bounding volumes are compact, and thus closed, it is permissible to use the more common maximum and minimum.

*and*

$$h(\mathcal{A}, \mathbf{w}(B)) \leq sh(\mathcal{A}, B). \quad (12)$$

*Hence, if $\mathcal{A}$ is bounded by $B$, it is bounded tighter by* $\mathbf{w}(B)$.

**Proof:** Validity, Eq. (11), is true since $\mathcal{A} \subset B$ implies $\mathbf{w}(\mathcal{A}) \subset \mathbf{w}(B)$ and Eq. (4) implies $\mathcal{A} \subset \mathbf{w}(\mathcal{A})$. Tightness, Eq. (12), is proven by substituting Eq. (4) into Eq. (7), resulting in

$$h(\mathbf{w}(\mathcal{A}), \mathbf{w}(B)) \leq sh(\mathcal{A}, B) \quad (13)$$

which is true by the Lemma. □

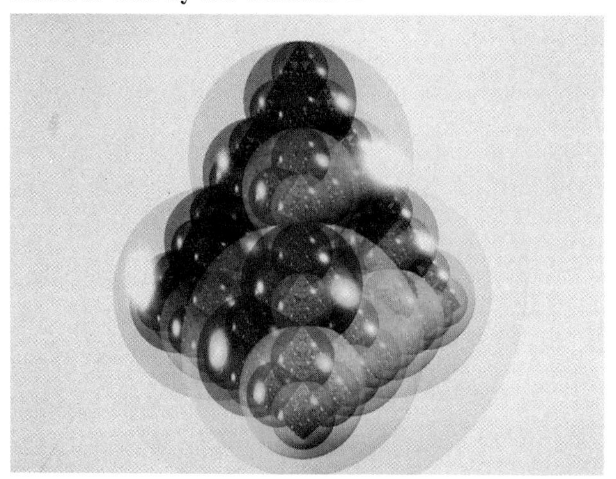

Figure 2: Bounding volume hierarchy for Sierpinski's Tetrahedron.

# 3 Ray Intersection

The ray-fractal intersection routine is based on the ray-patch intersection from [20]. A list is kept of bounding volumes that intersect the ray. This list is initialized with the root level bounding volumes that intersect the ray.

Until this list is empty, the bounding volume closest to the ray origin is removed. If this bounding volume is "smaller than a pixel," then it is treated as a primitive and its intersection with the ray is returned. Otherwise its children are constructed procedurally by applying each of the maps of the IFS to it; any that intersect the ray are added to the list. A snapshot of this method in action, intersecting a ray with Sierpinski's gasket, appears in Fig. 3.

As noted in [20], rather than applying the transformations to the bounding volumes, it is faster and often simpler to compose the inverse transformations and apply them to the ray.

The bounding volumes are treated as primitives when their diameters are smaller than a pixel's. Hence, the projected shape of a linear fractal at a fixed resolution is invariant, regardless of the shape and size of the initial bounding volume.

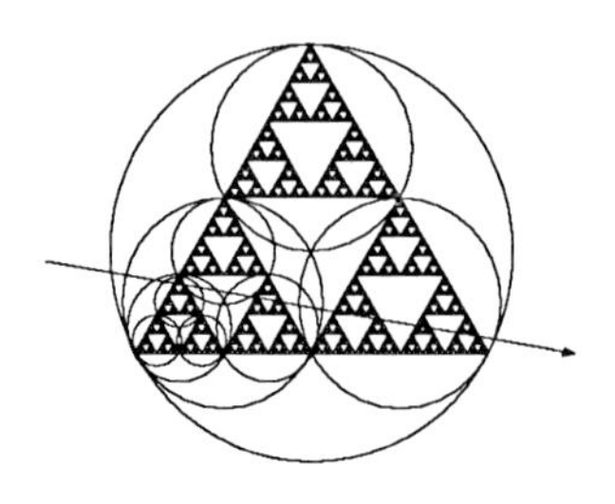

Figure 3: Procedural bounding volumes instanced during ray-fractal intersection.

## 3.1 The Size of a Pixel

The ray-fractal intersection algorithm needs to know the size of a pixel to determine if a bounding volume is to be treated as a primitive or not. Perspective distortion dictates that the diameter of an object's projection is proportional to its distance from the viewpoint. Hence, the size of a pixel is a linear function of the distance from the viewpoint to the ray-object intersection.

### 3.1.1 Eye Rays

The horizontal extent of a pixel projected a distance $t$ from the ray origin was originally approximated in [3] as

$$p(t) \approx \frac{2 \sin \frac{\theta}{2}}{N_h} t, \quad (14)$$

where $\theta$ is the field-of-view and $N_h$ is the horizontal resolution. The frame buffer is assumed one unit from the ray origin.

Eq. (14) is actually the minimum horizontal extent of any pixel from the middle scan-line. The horizontal size of a pixel from any scan line is bounded by

$$\frac{2 \tan \frac{\theta}{2}}{N_h \left( \frac{1}{\cos^2 \frac{\theta}{2}} + \frac{\tan^2 \frac{\theta}{2}}{A^2} \right)^{\frac{1}{2}}} t \leq p(t) \leq \frac{2 \tan \frac{\theta}{2}}{N_h} t \quad (15)$$

(illustrated in Fig. 4), where $A$ is the aspect ratio ($A = \frac{N_h}{N_v}$ if the pixels are square.) The exact size of a pixel at each pixel coordinate can be found but, except for large viewing screens or head-mounted displays where the field-of-view is quite large, it is usually much better to keep $p(t)$ constant (say, at the maximum) for fixed $t$.

### 3.1.2 Shadow Rays

If shadow rays are cast from the light source to the surfaces, then the size of a pixel can be used as a "closeness criterion" to determine if light rays reach the intersection point on the surface [3]. If the shadow rays are cast from the surface to the light source, then the ray's origin $R_o$ can be translated by $p$ in the ray's direction $R_d$ to avoid immediate self-intersection.

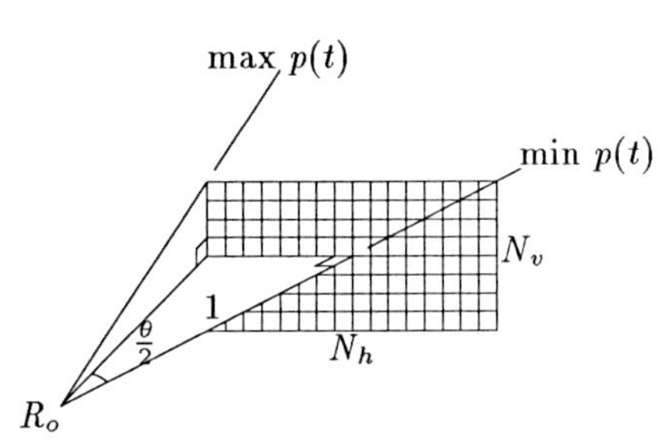


Figure 4: Pixel size geometry.

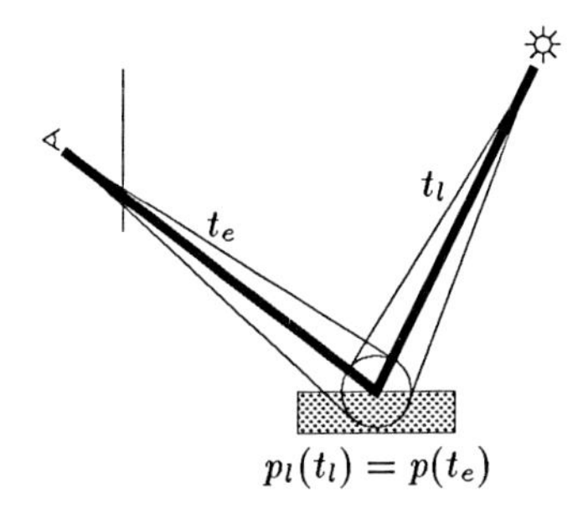


Figure 5: Light ray pixel size geometry.

Two particularly difficult situations can occur in the shadows of linear fractals. Both problems happen when the resolution of a shadow differs from the resolution of the surface it is cast upon.

The first case occurs when a linear fractal is illuminated from a distant light source, casting a shadow onto a surface near the linear fractal and the eye. If the light rays are cast from the light source, then the resolution of the shadows will be lower than the resolution of the surface. On the other hand, if the light rays are cast from the surface to the light source, then shadow's resolution will be greater than the surface's.

The second case happens when the shadow of a distant linear fractal near the light source is cast onto a surface inspected from a viewpoint somewhere between the surface and the fractal. In this case, if the rays are cast from the light source then the resolution of the linear fractal's shadow that will be higher than the resolution of the surface. Alternatively, if the rays are cast from the surface then the shadow's resolution is lower than the surface's.

Let $t_e$ and $t_l$ be the distance from the eye to the surface and the distance from the surface to the light, respectively. If the rays are cast from the light source to the surface then the size of a pixel $p_l(t)$ at distance $t$ from the light source, as shown in Fig. 5, is given by

$$p_l(t) = \frac{p(t_e)}{t_l}\, t. \tag{16}$$

If the rays are cast from the surface to the light source, then the size of a pixel at distance $t$ from the surface is

$$p_l(t) = \frac{p(t_e)}{t_l}\,(t_l - t). \tag{17}$$

### 3.1.3 Reflection and Refraction Rays

Planar reflection causes a new ray to be generated. The formula for the size of a pixel from this new ray origin almost always differs from the previous formula.

The reflected size of a pixel is computed using a new viewpoint $E_1$ found by reflecting the original viewpoint, denoted as $E_0$, across the plane $P = (a, b, c, d)$. Let $N = (a, b, c)^T$ be the unit normal vector of plane $P$ and let $\mathbf{x} = R_o + tR_d$ be the point that ray $R$ intersects plane $P$. The new viewpoint is then

$$E_1 = E_0 - 2|N \cdot (E_0 - \mathbf{x})|N, \tag{18}$$

and the reflected size of a pixel is given by

$$p_r(t) = \frac{p(t_e)}{|R_o - E_1|}\,(t + |R_o - E_1|), \tag{19}$$

where $R_o$ is the origin of the reflection ray and $p(t_e)$ is the size of a pixel at the previous ray-plane intersection point $R_o$. The size of a pixel through a refracting plane can be derived similarly.

Reflection and refraction from curved surfaces can change the size of a pixel dramatically. Convex reflection will increase the size of a pixel whereas concave reflection can increase and decrease the size of a pixel. A ray tracing microscope is alluded to in [3] which could be constructed out of refractive solids. Nonetheless, the size of a pixel in each of these cases is still a linear function. Even so, derivation of the new viewpoints for curved reflective or refractive surfaces is a difficult task and beyond the scope of this paper. See [22].

## 3.2 The Contractivity of an Affine Map

Cycles in a linear fractal instancing graph are terminated when the bounding volumes are smaller than a pixel. In order to find the diameter of a bounding volume, the contractivity of the affine map that instances the shape from its canonical form must be determined.

A simple method for determining the contractivity factor of an affine map is to accumulate the contractivity factors explicitly by storing an associated contractivity factor with each map. As maps are composed, the contractivities are multiplied. This method is accurate only when every scaling transformation is uniform in all three dimensions.

A better method determines the diameter of the ellipsoid resulting from the affine transformation of a unit sphere $\mathcal{S}$. Let $A$ be the linear part of affine map $w$, specified by its upper-left $3 \times 3$ submatrix. Since $A$ is a real, square and invertible, it can be factored

$$A = QS \tag{20}$$

where $Q$ is orthogonal (the rotation/inversion part) and S is positive definite (the scaling part), a process called *Polar Decomposition* [24]. Furthermore,

$$S^2 = A^T A, \tag{21}$$

hence $S^2$ is symmetric and its eigenvalues $\lambda_1, \lambda_2, \lambda_3$ can be found algorithmically using *Jacobi Transformations* [17]. Thus, the diameter of the ellipsoid is found as

$$w(\mathcal{S}) = \max_{i=1,2,3} \frac{2}{\sqrt{\lambda_i}}. \tag{22}$$

### 3.3 Initial Bounding Volume Determination

The initial bounding volume $B$ does not need to contain the images of itself under the affine maps of the IFS. That is, $\mathbf{w}(B) \not\subset B$. However it is necessary for $\mathcal{A} \subset B$. If not, then $\mathcal{A} - B$ will be chopped off along with all of its images, $\mathbf{w}(\mathcal{A} - B), \mathbf{w}^{\circ 2}(\mathcal{A} - B), \ldots$.

This can be useful but, in general, this kind of "fractal clipping" is not desired and a suitable initial bounding volume must be found. An iterative method that progressively refines an approximate bounding sphere given an IFS and an arbitrary initial sphere appears to work well.

Let $S$ be an approximate bounding sphere, (say, at the start, $S = \mathcal{S}$, the unit sphere at the origin). Then the next sphere in the sequence, $S^*$, is found as

$$S_o^* = \frac{1}{N} \sum_{i=1}^{N} w_i(S_o), \tag{23}$$

$$S_r^* = \max_{i=1\ldots N} \max_{a \in w_i(S)} |a - S_o^*|, \tag{24}$$

where $S_o$ and $S_r$ are the origin and radius of sphere $S$ and likewise for sphere $S^*$.

Equation (24) may be approximated using the upper bound[3]

$$\max_{a \in w_i(S)} |a - S_o^*| \leq |w_i(S_o) - S_o^*| + \frac{\mathrm{diam}(w_i(S))}{2}. \tag{25}$$

When $w_i$ is a similtude then $\mathrm{diam}(w_i(S)) = 2 s_i S_o$ and the upper bound is always achieved. If not, then $w_i(S)$ is an ellipsoid, and its diameter can be found using the eigenvalue technique described in Sec. 3.2.

## 4 Antialiased Surface Normal Formulation

Fractal surfaces are not differentiable since they have detail at every level of magnification. This means that surface normals are analytically undefined for fractal surfaces.

Fractal surface normals have been approximated several ways. If the surface is generated to a fixed resolution, then the surface normal of the primitive used to approximate the surface can be used, as in [10]. In [15], points were accumulated in a Z-buffer and neighboring Z-buffer values were used to approximate the surface normal. In [6], the gradient of a distance estimate function provided a good approximate surface normal.

Linear fractals, as rendered in this paper, are not generated to a set resolution, nor is a Z-buffer used. A distance estimate exists for linear fractals [7] but is not very efficient for these objects. Instead, the surface normal is approximated for linear fractal surfaces using the bounding volume information from ray intersection.

Consider a natural, almost linear, fractal shape: cauliflower. The surface of a cauliflower is made of an extremely large number of small buds but if the illumination from these buds was to be computed from point samples, the Nyquist limit would suggest that at least twice as many samples as buds be taken [21].

A more tractable solution is based on the fact that the cauliflower surface reflects light diffusely as a sphere since the small buds, albeit noisily, loosely approximate the surface of a sphere. The cauliflower reflects light more like several medium-sized spheres since the buds more closely approximate them. The illumination of many smaller spheres even more accurately represents the light reflected by these buds. This suggests that linear fractals should be shaded hierarchically.

This hierarchical shading is computed using the encountered surface normals. The resulting surface normal is the weighted sum of the surface normals at the intersections of the ray with the ancestry of bounding volumes that surround the ray-fractal intersection point[4].

### 4.1 Weighting Methods

Several weighting methods are described. Each encountered surface normal is accumulated in $N$ which is initialized with $(0,0,0)^T$ and will need to be normalized when used. Let $N_B(\mathbf{x})$ denote the surface normal of bounding volume $B$ at point $\mathbf{x}$.

The Constant weighting sums all encountered bounding volume surface normals equally so that the surface normal of the initial bounding volume contributes as much as the surface normal from a terminal bounding volume. The weights are shown in

[3] The diameter $\mathrm{diam}(A)$ of set $A$ is the maximum distance between any two points $a, b \in A$.

[4] One drawback to this formulation of the surface normal is that it is view dependent. Thus, changing the viewpoint may change the appearance of a surface. However, this property has not yet become conspicuous in renderings and animations thus far.

Fig. 6a and are accumulated as

$$N = N + N_B(R_o + tR_d). \tag{26}$$

This weighting is not uniform across scale; most of these normals are taken from the smaller bounding volumes. The Low-Pass surface normal weighting system that is more uniform across scale is shown in Fig. 6b and given by

$$N = N + \text{diam}(B)\ N_B(R_o + tR_d) \tag{27}$$

The High-Pass weighting function dampens the surface normals of larger bounding volumes and emphasizes the surface normals of the near terminal bounding volumes,

$$N = N + (\text{diam}(B_0) - \text{diam}(B))\ N_B(R_o + tR_d), \tag{28}$$

where $B_0$ is the initial bounding volume. These weights are illustrated in Fig. 6c.

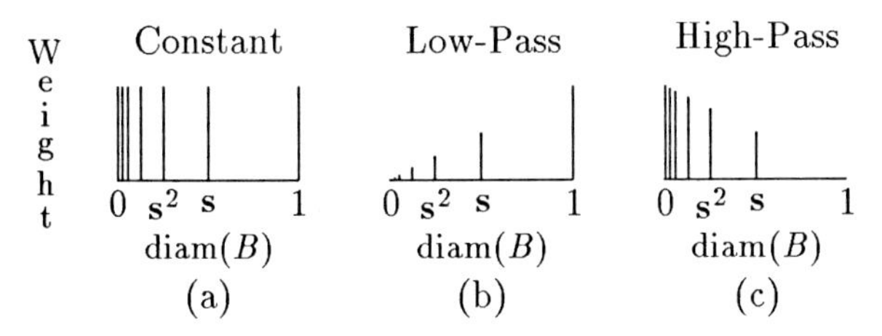


Figure 6: Surface normal weighting functions for Eqs. (26), (27) and (28), respectively.

## 4.2 Analysis

These surface normals can be checked by modeling an euclidean surface with an IFS. One such model is the Extruded Sierpinski's Gasket. This hybrid fractal shape looks like the standard planar Sierpinski's gasket when viewed down the axis of extrusion, but when viewed perpendicular to this axis, it reveals a planar surface.

Three extruded Sierpinski's gaskets appear in Fig. 7 corresponding to the weights from Eqs. (26), (27) and (28), respectively. The High-Pass surface normal definition produces moire patterns which are almost completely suppressed by the Constant surface normal. The Low-Pass surface normal does not reveal much detail, particularly from the fractal side of the middle extruded Sierpinski's gasket.

The analysis consists of comparing each of the three types of hierarchical normals of these planar surfaces with the normal of a similarly oriented euclidean surface. Let $N_c$ be the Constant fractal surface normal approximated by the weighting system in Eq. (26) and let $N_l$ be the Low-Pass normal, Eq. (27), and $N_h$ be the High-Pass normal, Eq. (28). Furthermore, let $N_p$ be the normal of a similarly oriented plane. The discrepancies between the fractal surface normals and the euclidean surface normal for 10,000 samples were measured by their dot product and plotted in Fig. 8.

Figure 7: Constant, Low-Pass and High-Pass surface normals on extruded Sierpinski's gaskets.

The Constant and High-Pass weightings produce very narrow distributions about the central value whereas the Low-Pass weighting is broader. Each distribution has mode 1; the most common fractal surface normal for this surface is its euclidean surface normal. Their standard distributions about the central value, 1, are .036, .084 and .031, respectively.

# 5 Antialiased Rasterization

Fractals have detail at every level of magnification. If point samples of this function are taken then infinite detail means that the result will be aliased regardless of the sampling frequency [21]. Rather than simply increasing the sampling frequency of the image, which would move these aliases to higher frequencies, an object-space sampling method is used.

One such object-space antialiasing method is the use of "covers" [26], which are very tight bounding volumes. These covers are precomputed to be within a pixel's width of the surface so that rays intersecting the cover but not the surface will blend the surface color with the rest of the colors encountered by the ray.

The cover of a linear fractal could be quite complex for small pixel sizes and would be quite difficult to precompute. Instead, as the ray progresses toward a linear fractal surface, the bounding volumes it encounters are considered possible covers.

A bounding volume is considered the cover of a point on a linear fractal surface if and only if (1) it intersects the ray, (2) its diameter is less than twice the size of a pixel, and (3) it contains no other bounding volumes that intersect the ray.

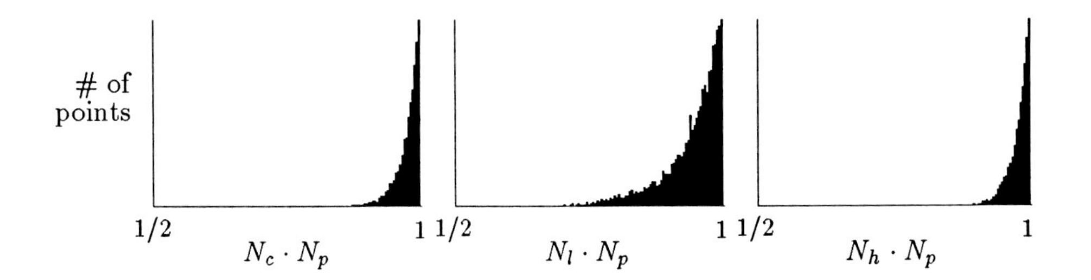


Figure 8: Distribution of surface normals for Eqs. (26), (27) and (28).

The diameter of the intersected cover is used to compute the transfer function that combines the color of the cover with the rest of the ray's encountered colors. Several transfer functions are available from the area of volume rendering; the simplest are the linear approximations used for image compositing [16].

If $\mathbf{c}$ and $\alpha$ are the current encountered ray color and opacity and $\mathbf{c}_B$ and $\alpha_B$ are the color and opacity of bounding volume $B$, then the linear transfer functions are

$$\mathbf{c} = \mathbf{c} + (1-\alpha)\alpha_B \mathbf{c}_B \quad (29)$$

$$\alpha = \alpha + (1-\alpha)\alpha_B \quad (30)$$

for source to surface ray traversal, and

$$\mathbf{c} = (1-\alpha_B)\mathbf{c} + \alpha_B \mathbf{c}_B \quad (31)$$

$$\alpha = \alpha + (1-\alpha)\alpha_B \quad (32)$$

for surface to source ray traversal (sometimes used for light rays).

A range of bounding volume diameters is needed. The upper limit, $\tau_{\max}$, is the scale at which bounding volumes take on non-zero opacity and should be set to $2p(t)$, twice the size of a pixel. The lower limit, $\tau_{\min}$, is the scale at which bounding volumes are completely opaque, thus no further subdivision is performed. This lower bound is recommended to be $\frac{1}{20}p(t)$ in [3], which appears to be about right.

A simple piecewise linear function of diameter produces the desired opacity values,

$$\alpha_B = \begin{cases} 1 & \text{if } \operatorname{diam}(B) < \tau_{\min}, \\ 1 - \frac{\operatorname{diam}(B) - \tau_{\min}}{\tau_{\max} - \tau_{\min}} & \text{if } \tau_{\min} \leq \operatorname{diam}(B) < \tau_{\max}, \\ 0 & \text{otherwise.} \end{cases} \quad (33)$$

This results in a smooth gradation from the object to its surroundings at its silhouette edges.

The bounding volume hierarchy may be visualized if $\tau_{\max} = \infty$ and a constant fractional opacity value is used independent of the diameter. This makes all of the bounding volumes uniformly translucent. An example of this appears in Fig. 2.

# 6 Conclusion

The result is a rendering algorithm that, given only an IFS, finds an initial bounding volumes, efficiently approximates ray-fractal intersections, computes well-behaved surface normals and produces an antialiased image of the IFS's linear fractal attractor.

The ray intersection method provides an arbitrarily precise ray-fractal intersection. The surface normal method is only an approximation based on appearance. Much work remains to rigorously define a fractal surface normal. Surface shading is simulated diffusely, but fractals, having detail smaller than the wavelengths of light, should exhibit spectral patterns when correctly shaded. The object-space "cover" dampens aliases on silhouette edges but the sampling of fractal shapes is an interesting problem that should be investigated further.

## 6.1 Results

Two images are produced here that demonstrate the varied shapes that an IFS can model. The first, Fig. 9, illustrates the fractal equivalents of the Five Platonic Solids. Each of these solids has infinite surface area and zero volume, a common characteristic of fractal shapes. Each IFS consists only of uniform scales and translations. They make good tutorial examples.

The second image, Fig. 10, shows some fractal models of nature. The fir trees are not meant to be accurate and the elm trees have no leaves, just tiny green branches. Nonetheless, this scene is perhaps one of the more complex in computer graphics.

## 6.2 Implementation

Currently, the ray tracing algorithm is implemented on an AT&T Pixel Machine 964dX, a 64 processor, 640 MFLOPS, MIMD parallel image computer. Each processor races[5] the others to finish an interleaved subset of the screen's 1280 × 1024 pixels.

Each of the Pixel Machine's 64 processors has only 36KB available for programs and non-image data. In

[5] No interprocessor communication or synchronization is used.

Figure 9: The Five Non-Platonic Non-Solids (from left to right: Menger's Sponge, Sierpinski's Icosahedron, Sierpinski's Tetrahedron, Von Koch's Snowflakahedron and Sierpinski's Octahedron)

order to use the bounding volume list, a main memory list of distance-from-ray-origin values was used while the associated bounding volume information was stored in the Pixel Machine's Z-buffer memory and was cached into main memory when needed.

The IFSs were also too consumptive for the 36KB program space so they were stored in the back frame buffer. Enough main memory was allocated to cache only one IFS at a time. This way, except when the bounding volumes of different linear fractals intersect, thrashing was minimized.

## 6.3 Applications to Other Fractal Models

**Recurrent a.k.a Hierarchical a.k.a Controlled a.k.a Markov Iterated Function Systems** These names all refer to the same enhancement of the standard IFS model: the restriction on the composition of IFS maps. For example, if map $w_1$ was just applied, then map $w_2$ may not be allowed. The rendering method can be easily extended to these enhanced IFS models by simply deleting the appropriate edges in the cyclic object-instancing di-graph.

**L-Systems** Most L-systems can be translated into the aforementioned IFS enhancement [19]. In 3-D, euclidean primitives are commonly integrated into the fractal model. This results in a terminal node[6] in the cyclic object-instancing di-graph.

[6]Only "in" edges, no "out" edges.

Figure 10: Fractal Forest. Every leaf, piece of bark, pine needle and blade of grass is accounted for in the model and those visible are rendered.

**Quaternion Julia Sets** The antialiasing "cover" can also be extended to antialias distance-estimate ray tracing [6]. The isovalue surface where the distance estimate is approximately the size of a pixel forms a single antialiasing cover. Rays that converge toward the surface but miss it can receive a portion of the surface's color depending on the minimum distance estimate encountered.

**Random Fractal Terrain** The pixel size, surface normal and antialiasing methods may be applied to the ray-tracing of random fractal terrain models [10, 4]. By determining the size of a pixel, the terrain would be procedurally generated only to the required resolution. The surface normals would be those of the encountered "cheesecake" or ellipsoid extents and these extents would also serve as "covers" at small scales.

**Everything Else** In fact, any object, when viewed from such a distance that it has sub-pixel detail, may be considered a fractal for rendering purposes. This occurs whenever the size of a bounding volume becomes less than twice the size of a pixel. In this case, the surface normal and antialiasing techniques can be used to render what might otherwise be a very noisy section of the image.

## 6.4 Acknowledgements

The authors would like to thank the Electronic Visualization Laboratory, particularly Dan Sandin, Maxine Brown, Bob Kenyon, Lou Kauffman, Irv Moy, Gary Lindahl, Sumit Das and Gordon Lescinsky, for their support of this project.

Steve Bourne and the software group at AT&T Pixel Machines deserve credit for supporting this research during the Summer of 1990. Alan Norton and his group at the IBM T. J. Watson Research Center should also be noted for their support during the very initial stages of this research at the end of the Summer of 1989 and for Alan's continuing involvement with this project.

Thanks also to Don Mitchell and his group at AT&T Bell Labs, Murray Hill, New Jersey, for their communication during the Summer of 1990.

## References

[1] Barnsley, M. F., Ervin, V., Hardin, D., and Lancaster, J. Solution of an inverse problem for fractals and other sets. *Proceedings of the National Academy of Science 83* (April 1986), 1975–1977.

[2] Barnsley, M. F., Jacquin, A., Mallassenet, F., Rueter, L., and Sloan, A. D. Harnessing chaos for image synthesis. *Computer Graphics 22*, 4 (1988), 131–140.

[3] Barr, A. H. Ray tracing deformed surfaces. *Computer Graphics 20*, 4 (1986), 287–296.

[4] Bouville, C. Bounding ellipsoids for ray-fractal intersection. *Computer Graphics 19*, 3 (1985), 45–51.

[5] Demko, S., Hodges, L., and Naylor, B. Construction of fractal objects with iterated function systems. *Computer Graphics 19*, 3 (1985), 271–278.

[6] Hart, J. C., Sandin, D. J., and Kauffman, L. H. Ray tracing deterministic 3-D fractals. *Computer Graphics 23*, 3 (1989), 289–296.

[7] Hepting, D., Prusinkiewicz, P., and Saupe, D. Rendering methods for iterated function systems. In *Proceedings of Fractals '90* (1990), IFIP.

[8] Hutchinson, J. Fractals and self-similarity. *Indiana University Mathematics Journal 30*, 5 (1981), 713–747.

[9] Jaquin, A. E. Image coding based on a fractal theory of iterated contractive image transformations. Preprint, 1990.

[10] Kajiya, J. T. New techniques for ray tracing procedurally defined objects. *ACM Transactions on Graphics 2*, 3 (1983), 161–181. Also appeared in *Computer Graphics 17*, 3 (1983), 91–102.

[11] Kay, T. L., and Kajiya, J. T. Ray tracing complex scenes. *Computer Graphics 20*, 4 (1986), 269–278.

[12] Mandelbrot, B. B. *The Fractal Geometry of Nature*, 2nd ed. Freeman, San Francisco, 1982.

[13] Mitchell, D. P., Summer 1990. personal communication.

[14] Mitchell, D. P., and Amanatides, J. Megacycles. *SIGGRAPH Video Review 51* (1989), #14.

[15] Norton, A. Generation and rendering of geometric fractals in 3-D. *Computer Graphics 16*, 3 (1982), 61–67.

[16] Porter, T., and Duff, T. Compositing digital images. *Computer Graphics 18*, 3 (1984), 253–259.

[17] Press, W. H., Flannery, B. P., Teukolsky, S. A., and Vetterling, W. T. *Numerical Recipes in C.* Cambridge University Press, 1988.

[18] Prusinkiewicz, P. About the cover: Exploring the beauty of plants. *IEEE Computer Graphics and Applications 10*, 2 (March 1990), 3–6.

[19] Prusinkiewicz, P., and Lindenmayer, A. *The Algorithmic Beauty of Plants.* Springer-Verlag, New York, 1990.

[20] Rubin, S. M., and Whitted, T. A 3-dimensional representation for fast rendering of complex scenes. *Computer Graphics 14*, 3 (1980), 110–116.

[21] Shannon, C. E. Communication in the presence of noise. *Proceedings of the Institute of Radio Engineers 37*, 1 (January 1949), 10–21.

[22] Shinya, M., Takahashi, T., and Naito, S. Principles and applications of pencil tracing. *Computer Graphics 21*, 4 (1987), 45–54.

[23] Snyder, J. M., and Barr, A. H. Ray tracing complex models containing surface tessellations. *Computer Graphics 21*, 4 (1987), 119–128.

[24] Strang, G. *Linear Algebra and its Applications*, 3rd ed. Harcourt Brace Jovanovich, 1988.

[25] Sutherland, I. E. Sketchpad: A man-machine graphical communication system. *Proceedings of the Spring Joint Computer Conference* (1963).

[26] Thomas, D., Netravali, A. N., and Fox, D. S. Antialiased ray tracing with covers. *Computer Graphics Forum 8*, 4 (December 1989), 325–336.

[27] Vrscay, E. R., and Roehrig, C. J. Iterated function systems and the inverse problem of fractal construction using moments. In *Computers and Mathematics* (New York, 1989), E. Kaltofen and S. M. Watt, Eds., Springer-Verlag, pp. 250–259.

# Trichromatic Approximation for Computer Graphics Illumination Models

Carlos F. Borges

Computer Graphics Research Laboratory
Division of Computer Science
University of California
Davis, California 95616

## Abstract

The complexity of computer graphics illumination models and the associated need to find ways of reducing evaluation time has led to the use of two methods for simplifying the spectral data needed for an exact solution. The first method, where spectral data is sampled at a number of discrete points, has been extensively investigated and bounds for the error are known. Unfortunately, the second method, where spectral data is replaced with tristimulus values (such as RGB values), is very little understood even though it is widely used. In this paper we examine the error incurred by the use of this method by investigating the problem of approximating the tristimulus coordinates of light reflected from a surface from those of the source and the surface. A variation on a well known and widely used approximation is presented. This variation uses the XYZ primaries which have unique properties that yield straightforward analytic bounds for the approximation error. This analysis is important because it gives a sound mathematical footing to the widely used method of trichromatic approximation. The error bounds will give some insights into the factors that affect accuracy and will indicate why this method often works quite well in practice.

**Keywords:** Illumination Models, Trichromatic Approximation, Tristimulus Coordinates, Spectral Power Density (SPD), Spectral Reflectance, Seminorm.

**CR Categories:** I.3.7 [Computer Graphics]: Three-Dimensional Graphics and Realism – Color, shading, shadowing, and texture.



## 1 Introduction

One of the most common procedures in computer graphics is that of evaluating an illumination model in order to determine the color of light emanating from some point on an object. This is a costly operation and is repeated many thousands of times in any rendering algorithm. Of course, any method for simplifying this task can yield a significant savings over the course of rendering an image and will be useful if it does not excessively degrade the fidelity of the final image.

One very common approach reduces the number of floating point operations by using simplified representations of the spectral data that characterizes the sources and surfaces in the scene. This is typically done in one of two ways. The first, and most intuitive method uses sampled representations of the SPD's and spectral reflectances that describe the sources and surfaces in the scene. These are used directly in the illumination model and yield a sampled representation of the SPD of light emanating from the surface which can be readily transformed into an appropriate coordinate system for rendering (e.g. RGB). This is the method of choice when high accuracy is a must; the error is clearly bounded only by the error of the quadrature method used to convert a point sampled SPD into tristimulus coordinates. Since the quadrature methods used are classical (Simpson's rule, etc.) the error is easily analyzed. A number of methods for implementing this approach have been examined and their performance has been found to be quite good (see [3,5,6,7]).

There is a second approach that is somewhat less intuitive. Here we replace the SPD's and spectral reflectances with tristimulus coordinates (e.g. RGB values).[1] This approach has several useful properties: only three numbers are required to represent an SPD or spectral reflectance (contrast this with the nine or more

[1] Of course, surfaces do not have tristimulus values. However, for pedagogical expedience it is common to call the tristimulus values of a given surface under spectrally white illumination of unit intensity the tristimulus values of the surface.

sample points usually required by the first method), additive color mixtures and specular reflections can be modelled exactly (by respectively adding or scaling the tristimulus coordinates), no spectral data is necessary (this can be hard to come by for certain objects). However, this approach has one substantial flaw, tristimulus coordinates do not contain enough information to correctly model non-specular reflection. For example, given the tristimulus coordinates of a colored light source and a colored matte surface it is not possible, using the Young-Helmholtz trichromatic theory, to determine the tristimulus coordinates of the surface when illuminated by the given light. Fortunately, it is possible to make an approximation by multiplying the tristimulus coordinates of the source with those of the surface. This is called a *trichromatic approximation* and is widely used. It has been pointed out that some of these methods "work relatively well for realistic scenes, but no one knows why" [2]. We will explore such an approximate method and give a full mathematical analysis of the error. This analysis will allow us to determine when the trichromatic approach is good enough and when we should fall back on a more stable sampling approach. We will also indicate why one might expect the trichromatic method to work well in a realistic scene.

First we note that the trichromatic approach is exact for additive mixtures and specular reflections; since these phenomena do not introduce any error, we will not discuss them any further. Instead, since it is a paradigm for the non-specular reflections that concern us, we will completely restrict our attention to approximating the color of a Lambertian surface under a single source of illumination.

## 2 Trichromatic Approximation for an Illuminated Lambertian Surface

We are interested in determining the color appearance of an illuminated Lambertian surface. In an ideal physical model light emanating from the surface has a spectral radiant power distribution that is proportional to $P_\lambda \rho(\lambda)$, the product of the spectral radiant power of the illuminant, $P_\lambda$, and the spectral reflectance of the surface, $\rho(\lambda)$. Following the Young-Helmholtz theory, the tristimulus coordinates of the reflected light, and hence the color appearance of the surface, can be found by evaluating the following definite integrals:

$$\begin{aligned} R &= \int_{\mathcal{V}} P_\lambda \rho(\lambda)\bar{\mathbf{r}}(\lambda)d\lambda \\ G &= \int_{\mathcal{V}} P_\lambda \rho(\lambda)\bar{\mathbf{g}}(\lambda)d\lambda \\ B &= \int_{\mathcal{V}} P_\lambda \rho(\lambda)\bar{\mathbf{b}}(\lambda)d\lambda \end{aligned} \quad (1)$$

where $\bar{\mathbf{r}}(\lambda), \bar{\mathbf{g}}(\lambda)$, and $\bar{\mathbf{b}}(\lambda)$ are the color matching functions, and $\mathcal{V}$ is the interval corresponding to the visible spectrum (see [8]).

This is a convenient physical model but requires that the spectral properties of both the source and surface be known in full since the RGB coordinates do not contain sufficient information to predict the outcome of such an interaction. The problem stems from the fact that metameric sources (lights with distinct spectral radiant power distributions but identical tristimulus values) do not always produce the same color when illuminating surfaces that are not spectrally white. Similarly, a pair of surfaces may have identical color appearance under spectrally white illumination, and hence the same tristimulus values, but dissimilar appearance under some other illuminant (this phenomenon is familiar to anyone who has had their hand stamped with an invisible design that only appears under UV illumination).

Let us consider an approximate method of a form that is very common in computer graphics and simply mimics the exact method used in the spectral domain. In particular, the tristimulus values of the illuminated surface are approximated by the product of the tristimulus values of the source and the surface. This approximation works quite well in practice. Indeed, Cowan and Ware [2] describe a similar method and note that it works "relatively well" in realistic scenes. Motivated by this, we shall consider a similar approximation but will use the XYZ primaries[2] instead of the RGB primaries. In particular:

$$\begin{aligned} X_{Reflected} &\approx X_{Source}X_{Surface} \\ Y_{Reflected} &\approx Y_{Source}Y_{Surface} \\ Z_{Reflected} &\approx Z_{Source}Z_{Surface} \end{aligned} \quad (2)$$

Note that the choice of system here is not at all arbitrary. The XYZ system is chosen because it has convenient properties that will simplify the derivation of bounds on the approximation error. They are:

1. All realizable stimuli (those that satisfy $P_\lambda \geq 0$ ) have non-negative tristimulus coordinates.

2. The tristimulus coordinates of an equal energy white ($P_\lambda \equiv 1.0$) are $X = Y = Z = 1.0$.

The first property implies that the XYZ matching functions are non-negative over the visible interval, that is $\bar{\mathbf{x}}(\lambda), \bar{\mathbf{y}}(\lambda), \bar{\mathbf{z}}(\lambda) \geq 0$ for all $\lambda \in \mathcal{V}$. The second property implies that:

$$\int_{\mathcal{V}} \bar{\mathbf{x}}(\lambda)d\lambda = \int_{\mathcal{V}} \bar{\mathbf{y}}(\lambda)d\lambda = \int_{\mathcal{V}} \bar{\mathbf{z}}(\lambda)d\lambda = 1.0 \quad (3)$$

Matching functions that satisfy equation 3 are called *normalized*.

[2]To be more precise, we will be using the matching functions for the *CIE 1931 Standard Colorimetric Observer*.

## 3 Error Analysis

To simplify the analysis that follows we consider the error associated with a single *generic* primary with a normalized non-negative matching function. Determining the behavior of the error for this primary is sufficient because the results can later be applied directly to the XYZ primaries since they also have normalized non-negative matching functions. Let the matching function of this generic primary be denoted $\bar{\mathrm{m}}(\lambda)$. The approximation error is given by:

$$\mathrm{Err}\,(f,g) = \int_{\mathcal{V}} fg\bar{\mathrm{m}}(\lambda)d\lambda - \int_{\mathcal{V}} f\bar{\mathrm{m}}(\lambda)d\lambda \int_{\mathcal{V}} g\bar{\mathrm{m}}(\lambda)d\lambda \tag{4}$$

where $f$ and $g$ represent a power distribution and a reflectance function (there is no reason to enforce any distinction between the two objects, both are simply functions). For mathematical expedience assume that $\bar{\mathrm{m}}(\lambda), f(\lambda)$, and $g(\lambda)$ are all elements of $C_{\mathcal{V}}$ the set of real-valued functions that are continuous on $\mathcal{V}$, this will ensure that all of the integrals exist and are bounded.

Given the problem in this form we can bound the error using techniques from functional analysis ([4] is an excellent reference for this material). First, it is not difficult to verify that $\mathrm{Err}(\cdot,\cdot)$ is an Hermitian form[3] that maps $C_{\mathcal{V}} \times C_{\mathcal{V}}$ to $\Re$. Second, notice that the error term is also positive semi-definite. To verify this consider:

$$\mathrm{Err}\,(f,f) = \int_{\mathcal{V}} f^2\bar{\mathrm{m}}(\lambda)d\lambda - \left\{\int_{\mathcal{V}} f\bar{\mathrm{m}}(\lambda)d\lambda\right\}^2 \tag{5}$$

Since $\bar{\mathrm{m}}(\lambda)$ is non-negative the Schwarz inequality implies that:

$$0 \leq \int_{\mathcal{V}} f^2\bar{\mathrm{m}}(\lambda)d\lambda - \left\{\int_{\mathcal{V}} f\bar{\mathrm{m}}(\lambda)d\lambda\right\}^2 \tag{6}$$

Hence the error functional is positive semi-definite.

Since the Schwarz inequality holds for *any* positive semi-definite Hermitian form ([4], p. 195) it holds for the error functional. In particular:

$$\{\mathrm{Err}\,(f,g)\}^2 \leq \mathrm{Err}\,(f,f)\,\mathrm{Err}\,(g,g) \tag{7}$$

This is a bound on the error of the approximation. Now, note that:

$$\|f\|^2_{\bar{\mathrm{m}}} = \int_{\mathcal{V}} f^2\bar{\mathrm{m}}(\lambda)d\lambda - \left\{\int_{\mathcal{V}} f\bar{\mathrm{m}}(\lambda)d\lambda\right\}^2 \tag{8}$$

is a seminorm on the space $C_{\mathcal{V}}$ ([4], p. 195). Hence, the error bound can be written:

$$|\mathrm{Err}\,(f,g)\,| \leq \|f\|_{\bar{\mathrm{m}}}\|g\|_{\bar{\mathrm{m}}} \tag{9}$$

and it is seen that the absolute error can be no worse than the product of the *seminorms* of the spectral reflectance and the SPD with respect to the matching function. This is useful because it makes it possible to determine, *a priori*, whether this method is an appropriate approximation for a given set of sources and surfaces (one could store the seminorms in a materials library along with other information about the various sources and surfaces). If the various spectral functions are sufficiently *small* with respect to this seminorm then it is reasonable to assume the method will work well.

We point out that this method (multiplying the tristimulus values) can be used with any tristimulus space. However, without normalized non-negative matching functions the error analysis is quite involved (it is omitted here but can be found in [1]).

Now, suppose that the source (or surface) is spectrally white, that is $f(\lambda) \equiv \alpha$ for some $\alpha \in \Re$. Equation 4 yields, after some manipulation:

$$\mathrm{Err}\,(\alpha,g) = \left[1 - \int_{\mathcal{V}} \bar{\mathrm{m}}(\lambda)d\lambda\right] \alpha \int_{\mathcal{V}} g(\lambda)\bar{\mathrm{m}}(\lambda)d\lambda \tag{10}$$

Since the matching function is normalized the error is zero and the approximation is exact when applied to spectrally white sources or surfaces. This will illustrate one of the reasons why this approximation works so well in realistic situations. Note that most common sources of illumination, like daylight and incandescent lights, are very nearly white. It is reasonable to represent a "nearly white" source with a spectral radiant power distribution of the following form:

$$P_\lambda = \epsilon(\lambda) + \alpha \tag{11}$$

where $\alpha$ is a constant, and $\epsilon(\lambda)$ is non-negative and small in comparison with $\alpha$. If $\rho(\lambda)$ is the spectral reflectance of the surface, then bilinearity and equation 10 yields:

$$\mathrm{Err}\,(\epsilon(\lambda)+\alpha,\rho) = \mathrm{Err}\,(\epsilon(\lambda),\rho) \tag{12}$$

the relative absolute error is given by:

$$\frac{|\mathrm{Err}\,(\epsilon(\lambda),\rho)\,|}{\int_{\mathcal{V}} [\alpha+\epsilon(\lambda)]\,\rho(\lambda)\bar{\mathrm{m}}(\lambda)d\lambda} \tag{13}$$

which, following equation 9 and the fact that $\epsilon(\lambda)$ and $\rho(\lambda)$ are non-negative, is certainly less than:

$$\frac{\|\epsilon(\lambda)\|_{\bar{\mathrm{m}}}\|\rho\|_{\bar{\mathrm{m}}}}{\alpha\int_{\mathcal{V}} \rho(\lambda)\bar{\mathrm{m}}(\lambda)d\lambda} \tag{14}$$

and will be small if $\epsilon(\lambda) \ll \alpha$ on the interval $\mathcal{V}$.

[3] If $X$ is a vector space over the real field $\Re$, and if $h : X \times X \rightarrow \Re$ is bilinear and symmetric then $h$ is called an Hermitian form.

## 4 An Example

We briefly demonstrate this method with two surfaces (one rose and one green) and a standard daylight energy source whose spectral distributions appear in figures 1 and 2. Only primary reflection is considered here, effects related to scene geometry are ignored ( e.g. Lambert's cosine law, the inverse square law, etc.). It is straightforward to compute the actual and approximate XYZ coordinates of the illuminated surfaces; these appear in table 1 along with the corresponding RGB coordinates for a 24-bit frame buffer. Note how close the approximate values are to the actual ones; the two are virtually indistinguishable on a standard display device.

| | Daylight-Rose | | Daylight-Green | |
|---|---|---|---|---|
| | Actual | Approx. | Actual | Approx. |
| X | 22.473 | 23.135 | 18.611 | 17.938 |
| Y | 11.241 | 11.799 | 36.161 | 35.481 |
| Z | 12.321 | 13.756 | 13.032 | 11.986 |
| R | 83 | 85 | 31 | 30 |
| G | 0 | 1 | 134 | 132 |
| B | 28 | 31 | 21 | 19 |

Table 1: Actual and approximate tristimulus values for the example in XYZ coordinates and in standard RGB coordinates for a 24-bit frame buffer.

Another brief calculation yields the error bounds and the observed approximation errors that appear in table 2. The error bounds indicate that the approximations will be accurate to within ±6% for the X and Y primaries, and ±15% for the Z primary. This is an excellent result considering how little information is used to make the approximations.

| | Daylight-Rose | | Daylight-Green | |
|---|---|---|---|---|
| | Error | Bound | Error | Bound |
| X | 0.6616 | 1.4708 | 0.6730 | 1.1423 |
| Y | 0.5581 | 0.6943 | 0.6806 | 0.8045 |
| Z | 1.4350 | 1.6839 | 1.0457 | 1.9322 |

Table 2: Observed errors and analytic error bounds of the trichromatic approximations from the example (XYZ coordinates).

## 5 Conclusions

We have presented a variation on a widely used approximation for computer graphics. This method is appealing because of its low computational costs and minimal storage requirements. We derived simple analytic bounds on the associated error using classical results from functional analysis and indicated why it might be expected to work relatively well in realistic scenes.

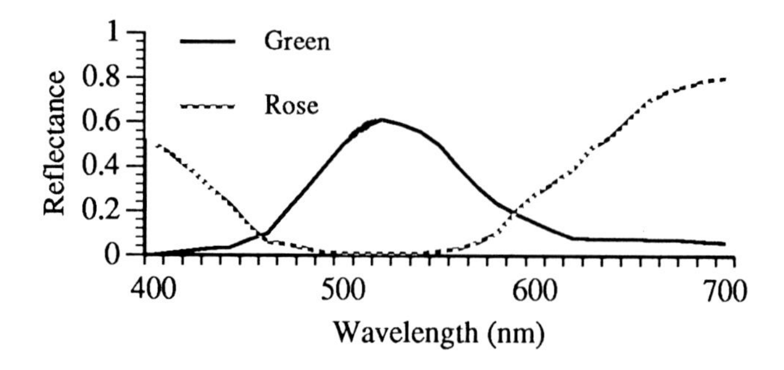


Figure 1: Reflectance functions of the two example surfaces.

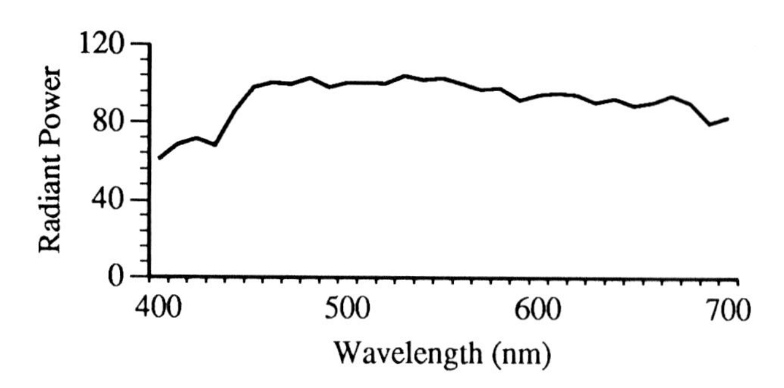


Figure 2: Spectral radiant power of daylight (CIE Standard Illuminant D55).

## References

[1] BORGES, C.F. *Numerical Methods for Illumination Models in Realistic Image Synthesis.* Ph.D. dissertation, University of California, Davis, 1990.

[2] COWAN, W., AND WARE, C. Tutorial on color perception. In *SIGGRAPH* (July 1983).

[3] HALL, R., AND GREENBERG, D. A testbed for realistic image synthesis. *IEEE CG&A* (November 1983), 10–20.

[4] KREYSZIG, E. *Introductory Functional Analysis with Applications.* John Wiley & Sons, 1978.

[5] MEYER, G. Wavelength selection for synthetic image generation. *Computer Vision, Graphics, and Image Processing* (January 1988), 57–79.

[6] MEYER, G., AND GREENBERG, D. Colorimetry and computer graphics. In *SIGGRAPH - State of the Art Tutorial on Color Spaces* (1984).

[7] WALLIS, R. Fast computation of tristimulus values by use of Gaussian quadrature. *J. Optical Soc. Am.* (January 1975), 91–94.

[8] WYSZECKI, G., AND STILES, W. *Color Science: Concepts and Methods, Quantitative Data and Formulae.* John Wiley and Sons, 1982.

# An Object-Oriented Framework for the Integration of Interactive Animation Techniques

Robert C. Zeleznik, D. Brookshire Conner,
Matthias M. Wloka, Daniel G. Aliaga, Nathan T. Huang, Philip M. Hubbard,
Brian Knep, Henry Kaufman, John F. Hughes and Andries van Dam

Department of Computer Science
Brown University
Providence, RI 02912

## ABSTRACT

We present an interactive modeling and animation system that facilitates the integration of a variety of simulation and animation paradigms. This system permits the modeling of diverse objects that change in shape, appearance, and behavior over time. Our system thus extends modeling tools to include animation controls. Changes can be effected by various methods of control, including scripted, gestural, and behavioral specification. The system is an extensible testbed that supports research in the interaction of disparate control methods embodied in controller objects. This paper discusses some of the issues involved in modeling such interactions and the mechanisms implemented to provide solutions to some of these issues.

The system's object-oriented architecture uses delegation hierarchies to let objects change all of their attributes dynamically. Objects include displayable objects, controllers, cameras, lights, renderers, and user interfaces. Techniques used to obtain interactive performance include the use of data-dependency networks, lazy evaluation, and extensive caching to exploit inter- and intra-frame coherency.

## CR Categories and Subject Descriptors

I.3.2 Graphics Systems; I.3.4 Graphics Utilities, Application Packages, Graphics Packages; I.3.7 Three-Dimensional Graphics and Realism, Animation; I.6.3 Simulation and Modeling Applications; D.3.3 Language Constructs

## Keywords

Real-time animation, object-oriented design, delegation, simulation, user interaction, electronic books, interactive illustrations.

## 1 Introduction

Over the last two decades, graphics research has concentrated on three main areas, loosely categorized as image synthesis, shape modeling, and behavioral modeling. While image synthesis (rendering) was stressed in the late 70s and early 80s, the emphasis has recently shifted to the modeling of various objects and phenomena — indeed, many researchers believe that graphics today *is* modeling. We wish to expand the definition of "modeling" to include the realms of simulation, animation, rendering, and user interaction.



Since the mid-60s, our research has focused on tools for creating electronic books, specifically hypermedia documents with interactive illustrations [21]. Such illustrations allow readers to interact not just with a canned "movie" but with a stored, parameterized model of a phenomenon they are trying to understand. Interactive illustrations require simulation and animation of the underlying model in an interactive, real-time environment.

Because we want to create interactive illustrations for a wide range of topics, our modeling tools must handle large (and extensible) sets of objects and operations on those objects that change any of their physical attributes over time. We need a rich collection of methods for controlling the time-varying structure and behavior of the objects, especially as they interact under various application-dependent systems of rules. In other words, we cannot use a single, "silver-bullet" modeling or animation technique.

The essence of animation control is the specification of time-varying properties. Traditional graphics packages (such as PHIGS+, Doré, and RenderMan), however, have no explicit notion of time. In these packages, time can be specified only implicitly, as the byproduct of a sequence of editing operations on the database or display-list representation. While today's animation systems do allow time to be explicitly specified, they generally permit only a subset of an object's properties to vary over time. They also tend to be restricted in the objects, properties and behaviors they support. Most limiting, they force the designer to conceptualize the animation process as a traditional pipeline of modeling, animation, and rendering phases. By contrast, we have concentrated on integrating modeling, animation, and rendering into a unified, coherent framework.

## 2 An Overview

Our system provides a general and extensible set of objects that may have geometric, algorithmic, or interactive (i.e., user-interface-controlled) properties. Geometric objects include quadrics, superquadrics, constructive solid geometry objects (CSGs) and other hierarchical collections of objects, spline patches, objects of revolution, prisms, generalized cylinders or ducts [9] (objects obtained by extruding a varying cross-section along a spline path), and implicit surfaces. Non-geometric objects include cameras, lights, and renderers. Behaviors such as gestural controls, spring constraints, finite-element techniques for cloth simulation [19], dynamics [13], inverse kinematics [4] [14], and constraint solvers [3] are also encapsulated as objects.

Objects can send and receive messages. These messages are persistent — a copy of each message is retained in the receiving object. They provide information on how an object should change itself over time. Objects can also inquire information from each other, information that depends on the nature and content of the messages a particular object has retained. Through messages, objects can be transformed (with scales, rotations, translations, shears, and reflections), deformed (with bends, twists, tapers, waves [2], and free-form deformations [16]), colored, shaded [17], texture-mapped, dynamically moved (with forces, torques, velocities, and accelerations), and volumetrically carved [8].

Messages are functions of time and, since objects retain them, they may be edited. An object's list of messages describes the object's time-varying structure and behavior. By editing this list, through inserting, deleting, adding, or modifying messages, that structure and behavior can be altered. Editing can be performed either by objects or by entities (e.g., a user) external to the set of objects comprising the model.

Our objects have several important characteristics. First, since they can have interactive properties, any object can have a graphical user interface as one of its attributes. Typically, an object supports a user interface for its own specialized information; for instance, a dynamics simulator may permit a user to specify its initial conditions with sliders. Other objects are primarily interactive, such as an object encapsulating a mouse which is queried by other objects for position information, or an object encapsulating a constraints editor.

Second, objects exploit communication, because they contain information that is often essential to other objects. A renderer needs information from other objects in order to make global lighting calculations. Constraint methods also require information from many objects to perform their calculations. Constructive solid geometry objects need information about the boundary representation of their component objects in order to compute their own boundary representations. A camera needs to know the position of another object in order to track it.

Finally, an object in our system is not part of a classical class-instance hierarchy, such as is found in the C++ and Smalltalk programming languages. The constantly changing nature of our models makes a static relationship such as class-instance too restrictive, since, for example, transforming a sphere into a torus would typically require a change in class. Instead, our system is a delegation system [18] [10]. In a class-instance system, objects have two sorts of associations: the association of an instance with its class and the association of a class with its super-class. A delegation system, on the other hand, has only one relation, that between an object and its prototype. An object, termed the *extension*, can be created from another object, its *prototype*; an object in a delegation system interprets a message by using one of its prototype's techniques. Changes to the prototype affect both objects, but changes to the extension affect only the extension. Although it has been suggested [5] [20] that delegation might provide a simpler and more elegant method of solving computer graphics problems, we are not aware of work prior to ours incorporating delegation into animation and modeling systems.

## 3 The System Architecture

### 3.1 Control points

At its simplest, a message is a name and a function of time. A message can be edited by changing the particular nature and form of its time-varying function, specified by the series of time-value pairs that we call *control points* (see Figure 1). Thus, editing a message can mean adding or removing control points, associating control points with new times, or changing the value in a control point.

The value in a control point may be scalars, vectors, or arbitrarily complex expressions. For example, a scaling transformation can be given as a single real number for a uniform scale or a list of three real numbers for a non-uniform scale. A control point specifying a CSG tree can be given as a list containing three items: an object name or a list (itself a CSG tree), an identifier specifying a CSG operation, and another object or list. Values can be functions of time: a translation can be given by a vector function of the position of another object in the scene. Function-based control points allow useful behaviors, such as objects following other objects or adjusting their colors to match those of other objects. Many systems support such tracking behavior as a special case for cameras, but our system allows any object to behave in this way.

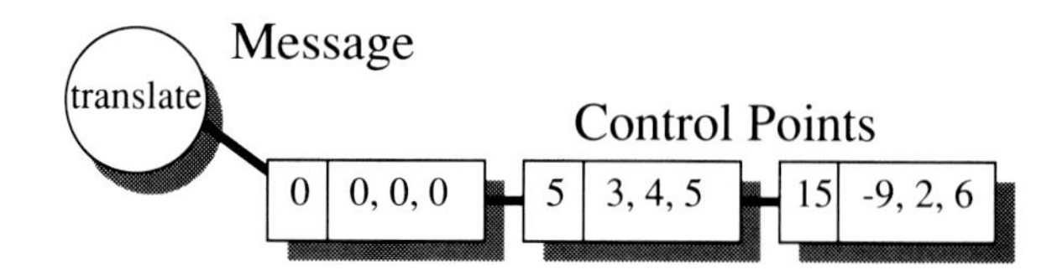


Figure 1: A message is a list of control points; a control point is a time and an associated value.

The CSG tree example above points out that the values of control points can be nested lists. Control-point values are very similar to Lisp s-expressions in this regard. They can contain atomic values, including numbers, strings, vectors, data structures, and object identifiers, or they can be lists of atomic values or other lists. Control point values are thus very flexible, permitting the use of mathematical expressions based on values in the scene. Figure 2 shows some sample control point values.

```
/*atomic values*/ 3.1416  "/u/john/paint.bi"
                  camera  sin(3.14 * 11.7)

/*a list of atoms*/ [1.0, 2.0, 3.0]
/*a list of lists*/ [[1,0,0],[2,[3.3,4.4]]]

/*functions*/
  /*obtain 2nd value of list*/
          select([1.0,sin(t),3.0],2)
  /*changinng position of an object*/
          robotHead.position
```

Figure 2: Examples of control point values (fragments of a scripting language used to describe objects and their messages).

Values at times not explicitly specified can be derived through an interpolation function, typically a weighted sum of control points. When interpolating a series of control points whose values are themselves functions of time, the system cannot just pass direct values to an interpolation method, but must first evaluate each control point at the target time. The series of evaluated values (not functions) thus produced can then be interpolated. As an example, consider a camera tracking two moving objects, smoothly shifting its focus from the first to the second. The value of a message over time can change dramatically, depending on the interpolation method used.

### 3.2 Messages

An important purpose of messages is to provide communication among objects. Objects such as a user interface or a physically based simulator apply and edit messages to other objects, thus modifying their appearance and behavior. An object can also affect another object by sending it a message containing a reference back to the sender (i.e., the message contains a control point that references another object). Whenever this message is interpreted, the sending object is called back and asked to provide the appropriate information. We use the term *controllers* for objects that modify messages on other objects, either by actively editing or passively being called back.

For example, large scientific visualization projects are often run in batch mode, separating a supercomputer analysis from an interactive visualization of the results. A simple controller could read in the results of such batch simulations, obtaining a list of positions (or whatever information is appropriate) and creating a list of messages from it. These messages could then be given to the appropriate objects, telling each how to behave in order to represent the scientific data [6]. Other more sophisticated controllers can apply and then edit a set of messages, adding new messages as they derive new results. Controllers will be discussed in more detail in Section 5.

Our system has a variety of messages to support its many kinds of objects. Highly specialized messages can provide information for an unusual object (for example, the parameters of an implicit equation or the tolerances of a constraint solver). More general changes, such as transformations, deformations, and dynamics (force or torque), provide a diverse class of changes applicable to more common objects.

### 3.3 Objects

Every object is represented by a retained list of all of the messages it has received. All objects are identical when first created, since no messages have yet been sent, i.e., a new object's list is empty. The message list is then modified in order to give the object interesting behaviors or appearances.

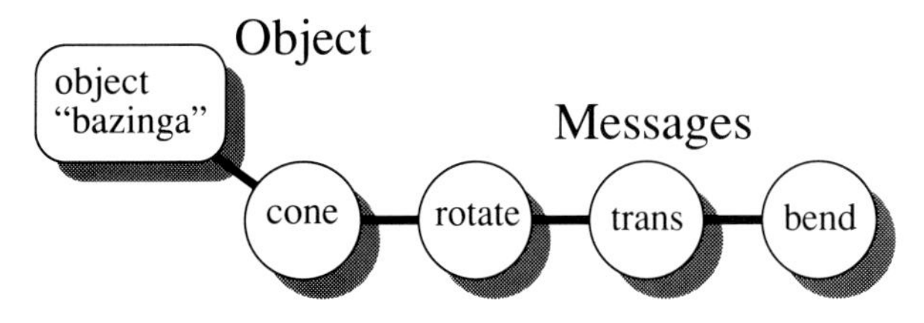


Figure 3: An object is a list of messages.

The interpretation of a message, i.e., its semantic meaning, is determined by the object that receives it. For example, a screen-aligned text object should not behave in the same way as a cube when it receives a message *rotate*; the rotation of the text should be projected onto the plane of the screen. Similarly, requests for information are handled in an object-specific manner: A sphere computes a ray intersection differently from a cube.

To handle variable semantics, an object has a set of methods (i.e., functions) to interpret messages that determine its behavior and appearance. Interpretation of a message can alter some or possibly all of the methods currently in use by an object, and thus can radically change its entire nature. This ability to change methods enables an object to adapt to different situations. For example, a deformed torus no longer performs ray intersections with itself by finding the roots of a quartic equation. Rather than requiring the torus's ray-intersection method to handle all eventualities, the procedure that interprets the deformation method changes its ray intersection method to a more suitable one, such as one that performs ray intersection with a set of polygons.

Many simple objects, such as spheres, cubes, and cylinders, have many methods in common. They handle most transformations identically and differ only in a few shape-specific methods, such as boundary representation, ray intersection, and computation of surface normals and parametric coordinates.

### 3.4 An example of making objects

A delegation system has straightforward mechanisms for object hierarchy [5] [10]. Recall that an object, the *extension*, can be made from another object, the *prototype*. In our system, an object can receive a message stating that it is to inherit all the messages of another object, thus becoming that object's extension. The extension implicitly inherits the prototype's behavior as well, since its methods are initially defined by the messages in the prototype. Since the prototype-extension relationship in our system is specified with a message, however, it can vary over time, a feature not normally present in a delegation system. For example, the history of automobiles can be modeled as a single object that uses a different model year car as its prototype for each year. This behavior is described very simply by a single time-varying message.

Objects can also be made from several objects. Consider a figure sitting in a chair, shown in figure 7. The chair is a CSG object, built from the parts of many different objects. The figure is made of several extruded duct objects, giving it a smooth, stylized appearance. A duct is itself a hierarchy of several objects, made from several spline path objects: one path describes the spine of the duct while the others describe the duct's cross-section along the length of that path. Paths are themselves composed of point objects used as the control points for the splines.

If the objects composing the CSG object change over time, the CSG object itself will also change. The CSG object asks its components for their boundary representations at a specified time, and the component objects return the boundary representations as functions of time, since the boundaries are specified by messages to the corresponding object. The composition of these functions in a CSG object is necessarily a function of time. Paths and ducts behave similarly: as the points specifying the hull of a path move, the hulls change shape, changing the spline path. As a path changes its orientation and shape, a duct made from this path also changes.

Suppose we want the figure to watch a fly a fly flitting about the scene. We can specify the motion of the fly with a path object, making the fly move along a spline path, and the fly can ask the path for the position of points further along and for tangent information at those points. Thus the fly can be oriented along the path, as if it were flying through the air. Likewise, the figure's eyes can ask the fly for its position and use that information to track it, and the points and paths comprising the figure's ducts can also ask the fly for its position and change their orientation accordingly.

## 4 Interpreting Messages

### 4.1 The Simple Case

An object computes the answer to an inquiry by interpreting each of its messages in sequence. As we said earlier, a message can change the methods used to interpret subsequent messages; therefore, the particular order of messages is important. The object's message list itself provides this ordering. This linear traversal is satisfactory until we begin using references to other objects and making multiple inquiries of an object. Under these circumstances, work will be repeated unnecessarily, and it becomes useful to exploit coherence, as discussed in Section 4.2.

Recall that some messages, like the deformations mentioned in Section 2, will, when interpreted, change the methods the object uses to interpret messages further along in the list. Note also that objects change their methods in different situations. For example, applying a deformation to a spline patch might not cause it to change its methods if the inaccuracy of applying the deformation to the control hull (and not the patch itself) is acceptable [7].

When objects depend on other objects, traversal becomes recursive. Consider the figure watching a fly discussed in Section 3.4. To determine the orientation of an eye, the position of the fly must be determined. When, in interpreting the messages of the eye, the message containing the reference to the fly (i.e., asking the fly for its position) is reached, a recursive traversal of the fly begins. The fly's position is determined by interpreting the fly's list of messages, and then interpretation of the eye's list continues.

The interpretation mechanism implicitly utilizes lazy evaluation: no calculations are performed until an object is actively asked for information. For example, time would be wasted in computing polygonal boundary representations of CSG objects if all inquiries concerned the tree hierarchy of the object. We use lazy evaluation and the caching scheme described next to simultaneously avoid unnecessary computation and exploit inter- and intra-frame coherency.

## 4.2 Caching

Messages can be used to store arbitrary information. Objects can send messages to themselves in order to cache useful but computationally expensive data. Since such data is a function of time and messages are also functions of time, messages are an appropriate mechanism for data caching.

The first time an inquiry is made, the object computes the value for the time of inquiry and the time interval over which that value holds. If a second inquiry is made within the valid interval, the object simply returns the previously computed value (see Figure 4). Note that some messages contain data relevant to the cache. If such a message is modified, the cache is marked as invalid (see Figure 5). Multiple edits to these messages simply flag the cache as invalid multiple times, a very cheap operation. Thus, several edits can be "batched" into one, and interactive updates become much faster, since the data is not recomputed until actually requested.

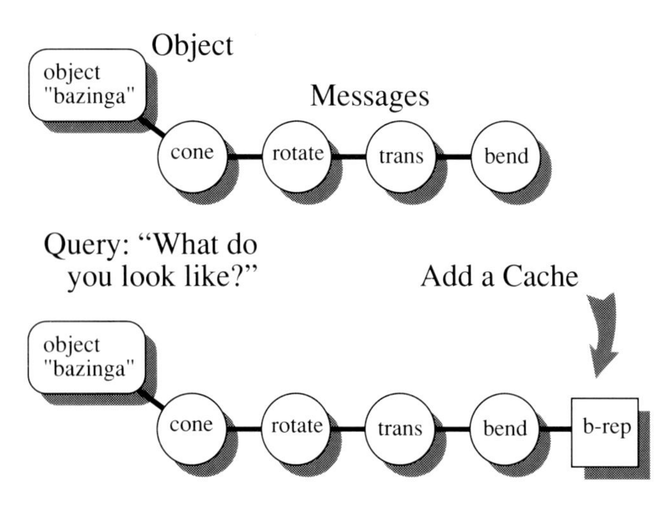


Figure 4: An inquiry adds a cache to the end of a list of messages. Here, the cache is of a boundary representation (b-rep) of the object.

Editing and subsequently invalidating a cache is a selective process: editing a translation invalidates only a cache of a transformation matrix, not a cache of a polygonal boundary representation. Objects understand how different messages affect each other. In particular, they know which messages invalidate which caches. Further, since each cache stores the interval over which it is valid, invalidation may merely change the size and shape of that interval (perhaps splitting it into multiple intervals) instead of completely invalidating it. If the edit changes the value of a message halfway through the time span of the cache's interval, the interval will be halved. More detailed manipulations of intervals are also supported, such as scaling and Boolean operations.

Profiling indicates that the improvement in performance with caching more than justifies its expense. By monitoring memory usage, we have seen that animations using extensive caching use approximately thirty percent more memory but achieve as much as a tenfold speedup. In these animations, the caching mechanism caches essentially *all* inquired data, for any time of inquiry, thereby minimizing the need to recalculate coherent data. Note that inter-frame coherency is automatically exploited, since caches are valid over intervals of time.

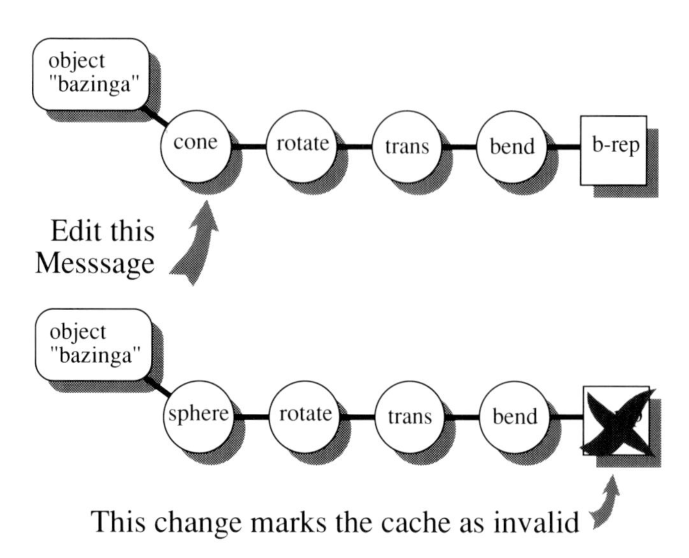


Figure 5: Editing a message before a cache can invalidate the cache.

## 4.3 Message list traversal with caching

To see how the system works with caching, let's consider a simple example: rendering all objects in a scene with a $z$-buffer. The renderer asks each object in the frame for its polygonal boundary representation. When inquired for the first time, each object computes its polygonal representation and caches it, marking it with the interval over which it is valid, and then gives the data to the renderer. The renderer then $z$-buffers the polygons, producing a frame. When the renderer asks an object for its polygons in the next frame, the object merely returns the previously computed boundary representation, if it is valid for the requested frame.

Caching helps expedite inquiry within a frame as well. If we ask the same object more than once for the same data, inquiries after the first will perform much faster by just returning the cache. Consider a car with four tires, each alike (up to a linear transformation). The tire could be an expensive-to-compute spline surface, yet this surface could be computed only once, not four times.

As another example, consider updating the figure in the fly animation of Section 3.4. Suppose one of the points used in a path is translated. This translation invalidates the point's CTM cache (current transformation matrix). Since caches are generated when an object is asked for information, the identity of the inquiring object (here, the path) is also stored in the cache. Thus, when the cache is invalidated, the path is informed and invalidates its own caches. These caches include references to the duct made from the path, so the duct's cache of its boundary representation is also marked as invalid. When the duct needs to provide its polygonal representation again, it will see its invalid cache and retraverse its list of messages, asking the path for the spline equations. The spline will notice its own invalid cache and recalculate the spline equations, asking the moved point for its new position.

## 5 Controllers

As mentioned in Section 2, behavior can be encapsulated in objects we call controllers. A controller affects other objects by sending them messages that refer back to the controller. Consider an inverse kinematics controller that must make an articulated arm reach for a goal (see Figure 8). Each joint is an object with a message that specifies its orientation through a reference to the inverse kinematics controller. This dependency allows the controller to indicate the amount of translation and rotation produced by any joint at any given time. Interactive techniques can be considered controllers as well, for example, when a user specifies the initial conditions of a simulation (see Figure 9). In this case, the simulated objects reference a user interface object.

The use of dependencies in this situation is similar to that described in Section 4.1. Thus, when the position of an object in the linkage is needed at a particular time $t$, the serial interpretation of the object's messages begins. Upon reaching the translation or rotation message referencing the controller, the object asks the controller for the correct value, and the controller then supplies the necessary translation or rotation for the given time $t$.

The messages sent to a controlled object by a controller are intentionally as abstract as possible. The responsibility of determining how these messages affect a controlled object is left to the object itself. Essentially, a controller determines *what* to do and a controlled object determines *how* to do it. Consider, for example, a rigid-body dynamics simulation involving collision detection and response. It would be possible to have one controller handle all aspects of the simulation, exerting control by sending only translation and rotation messages to the controlled objects. However, we use instead a collision-response controller that sends a "collision" message to each controlled object: the object itself interprets the details of the collision message in terms of velocity (for momentum transfers) or acceleration (for continuous contact).

This object-oriented approach to control has several advantages. First, it reduces the complexity of controller implementation. A controller need not keep track of how it is actually changing the specific attributes of a controlled object, and this controller thus can store less information than might be needed by another controller affecting the same object, reducing the need for communication between controllers. Second, our approach increases the efficiency of communication between controllers and objects. A single abstract message that directs changes to many attributes of an object requires less system overhead than many messages each of which concerns only a single attribute. Third, our approach allows different types of objects to respond differently to the same abstract command, so that a flexible object like cloth, for instance, can interpret a collision message differently from a rigid object.

## 6 Controller Interaction

Allowing heterogeneous controllers to coexist and communicate in the same environment has been a research goal in computer graphics for several years [1] [12]. Such interaction between controllers should allow many powerful behavioral control techniques to affect a common set of objects in a meaningful way. The ideal system should be flexible, extensible and efficient.

### 6.1 Problems with interaction

A number of difficult problems must be solved to achieve the goal of heterogenous controller interaction. The first involves identifying the aspects of interacting controllers that hinder successful cooperation.

Consider the situation depicted in Figure 6. The rod with endpoints $a$ and $b$ has length $l$. The distance between the two walls $A$ and $B$ is also $l$, so it should be possible to make the rod span the walls. Assume that we have a controller that can move $a$ to $A$ and a controller that can move $b$ to $B$, and assume also that we constrain the rod to remain rigid. The simplest way to make the rod span the walls is to invoke the two controllers independently so that each handles the task of moving one endpoint to the appropriate wall. This solution does not necessarily work, however. Each controller might, for instance, decide that the simplest way to move an endpoint to the wall is to translate the rigid rod. Neither controller will realize that the rod must be rotated to allow both endpoints to touch the walls, so spanning will not be achieved. This problem cannot be solved until the controllers consider both endpoints. Diagnosing

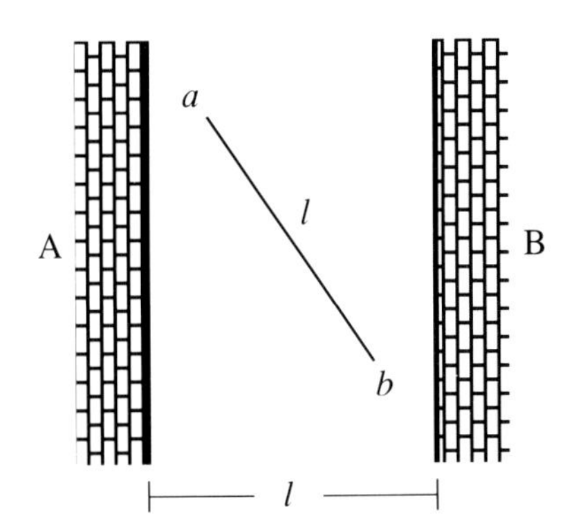


Figure 6: An example of incompatible controllers.

and correcting this lack of cooperation currently requires human intervention, and automation of the process does not seem feasible without severely restricting the possible controller types (e.g., to constraint solvers).

Another issue in controller interaction is data incompatibility. This arises, for example, when a kinematic controller and a dynamic controller both affect the same object. The dynamic controller works with velocity and acceleration data that the kinematic controller does not understand. When the kinematic controller changes the position of the object over time, however, the velocity of the object *appears* to change. If the dynamic controller is not made aware of this apparent change in velocity, its computations may produce visual inconsistencies.

Controllers that work iteratively present a third problem. The iterations of different controllers may proceed at different rates, and aliasing may result. This problem can appear when several controllers perform numerical integration with different time steps.

Our system provides several mechanisms that facilitate controller interaction, while trying to handle some of these problems. These mechanisms allow us to conduct further research into interaction policies.

### 6.2 Some solutions

Certain attributes of an object are dependent on its other attributes. The object's position, for instance, is related to its velocity and acceleration. Our system provides a mechanism to maintain the relationships among the attributes of an object. When a controller inquires an attribute of a controlled object, the system keeps that attribute consistent with any related attributes, even if those attributes have been changed by other controllers. Consider, for example, a controller that handles momentum transfers in response to collisions. This controller adds a collision-response message to each object it controls; the velocity resulting from the message is nonzero only if the object has just penetrated another object. If some other controller needs to know the position of an object whose momentum was changed, the controlled object will convert the change in momentum to a change in velocity; the collision-response controller need not be concerned with this issue.

Caching and its relation to controllers are especially important for attributes related by differential equations (parameterized by time). By caching the acceleration and velocity of an object at one instant in time, the system can use Euler's method [15] to obtain the velocity and position of that object at the next instant. We are currently investigating how to use the Runge-Kutta method of integration. This method is more effective overall than Euler's method, but because of our interobject dependencies, computing the necessary intermediate values may require global information; thus it cannot be implemented as easily in our system, which distributes

this global information and its interpretation among objects.

Caching is also useful for the numerical differentiation of attributes, helpful in solving the data incompatibility between kinematics and dynamics mentioned at the start of this section. A velocity corresponding to a kinematic change can be approximated by dividing the most recent displacement created by the kinematics controller by the elapsed time (in the animation's time units) from the previous displacement.

A variety of interesting controller interactions can be created simply by using the mechanisms for maintaining related attributes. When multiple controllers send messages to the same object, the relative ordering of the messages determines how the effects of the controllers combine to determine the object's overall behavior: messages earlier in the list affect the object first, because of the order of traversal. We call this type of interaction *strict priority ordering*. By allowing different orderings of the messages, the system can provide different effects, since messages are in general non-commutative (e.g., a translate followed by a rotate is not the same as a rotate followed by a translate).

A more general mechanism for controller interaction is supported by allowing multiple controllers to affect one or more objects indirectly through an intermediary controller. The multiple controllers are referenced by messages to the intermediary controller, not to the controlled object, and the controlled objects reference only the intermediary controller. The job of the intermediary controller is to combine the effects of the multiple controllers into a meaningful result and convey this result to the controlled objects. Such intermediary controllers can be used whenever strict priority ordering is not sufficient, e.g., when the behavior of an object should be the weighted average of the effects of two controllers. A toolbox of standard intermediary controllers that perform useful functions (such as the weighted average) could be added to the system.

## 7 An Example — 3D Pong

To see how this system works in practice, let's look at a sample interactive environment: a 3D pong game in which a sphere represents the ball, and two cylinders, appropriately scaled and translated, represent the paddles. We can play our game inside a court that is an object of revolution lying on its side, using scaled cylinders capping the ends of the revolve object for the back walls, the ones that the ball should not hit.

Two pairs of dial objects control the paddles, so that two users can manipulate the paddles next to the appropriate walls. A collision-detection object checks for intersections between the ball, the revolve object, the back walls, and the paddles. Finally, collision-response objects tell different objects what to do. One is responsible for collisions between the ball and anything except the back walls: when the ball hits the object of revolution, this object produces physically based collision-response messages. The ball then moves accordingly, while the revolve object uses a null interpretation of the response message and thus is unaffected by collisions. When the ball collides with a paddle, it uses the same collision-response interpretation as before, but the paddle would use its own, a different one, perhaps one that makes the paddle visually light up. A second collision-response object will be responsible for collisions between the ball and the back walls. When the ball hits one of the back walls, the ball will receive a different kind of collision response message, since it will not bounce back. The wall's collision response interpretation will add a point to the current score.

Many interesting features could be added to this game. For example, the walls of the court could change as the game progressed (possibly in response to collisions with the ball). The ball could move faster when hit by a faster paddle, despite the fact that the paddles are under kinematic control and have no intrinsic notion of velocity. Users could control their paddles in different ways, for example, using polar coordinates or Euclidean coordinates, simply by changing the messages between the dials and the paddles. Moving obstacles could be placed between the two players, perhaps obstacles that follow the ball, or follow a pre-scripted plan of motion. Since objects can be asked to display themselves at any time, instant replay of a game works automatically, allowing users to see what they just did, and change it. Finally, these features can be added interactively by the game players.

## 8 Summary

We have designed and implemented an interactive graphics system [11] with an unusually close integration of modeling and animation. All modeling is done through time-varying messages and thus all modeling tools can be used for animation. The system is object-oriented and provides a time-varying delegation hierarchy for maximum flexibility.

Behavioral control is supported by giving controllers the responsibility for calculating what controlled objects are to do, while letting each object interpret the abstract instructions according to its own methods. Multiple controllers can operate independently by instructing their objects in priority order. Alternatively, intermediary controllers can be written to integrate the behavior of control mechanisms. The system currently contains a large class of geometric primitives and a growing collection of user-interface objects and controllers.

A number of efficiency mechanisms contribute to interactive performance. In particular, lazy evaluation and caching exploit all inherent inter- and intra-frame coherence. By distributing the database, we expect to further improve the performance of the system. It should be possible for each object to evaluate its messages in parallel, but we will have to consider scheduling problems when objects depend on each other.

Our system is meant to go the next step beyond the scope of traditional graphics systems such as PHIGS+ or Doré. Such systems enforce a rigidly divided modeling/animation/rendering pipeline. We believe our system provides some indications of where the next generation of graphics systems software is headed: towards an environment with both time and behavior as first-class notions, and not just shape description and rendering.

## 9 Acknowledgements

We cannot begin to thank all the people that have made a system of this complexity possible. We would like to thank the many people who have commented on this paper, especially the reviewers. We would also like to thank Paul Strauss and Michael Natkin, architects of an earlier version of the system that provided much insight into the problem of a general animation system. In addition, the entire Brown Graphics Group, especially the artists, have provided much valuable criticism of the system's capabilities.

## References

[1] Phil Amburn, Eric Grant, and Turner Whitted. Managing geometric complexity with enhanced procedural models. In *Proceedings of the ACM SIGGRAPH, Computer Graphics*, volume 20(4), pages 189–195, August 1986.

[2] Alan H. Barr. Global and local deformations of solid primitives. In *Proceedings of the ACM SIGGRAPH, Computer Graphics*, volume 18(3), pages 21–30, July 1984.

[3] Ronen Barzel and Alan H. Barr. A modeling system based on dynamic constraints. In *Proceedings of the ACM SIGGRAPH, Computer Graphics*, volume 22(4), pages 179–188, August 1988.

[4] Lisa K. Borden. Articulated objects in BAGS. Master's thesis, Brown University, May 1990.

[5] A. H. Borning. Classes versus prototypes in object-oriented languages. In *IEEE/ACM Fall Joint Computer Conference*, pages 36–40, 1986.

[6] Ingfei Chen and David Busath. Animating a cellular transport mechanism. *Pixel Magazine*, 1(2), 1990.

[7] Gerald Farin. *Curves and Surfaces for Computer-Aided Geometric Design*. Academic Press, second edition, 1990.

[8] Tinsley A. Galyean. Sculpt: Interactive volumetric modeling. Master's thesis, Brown University, May 1990.

[9] Andrew Glassner, editor. *Graphics Gems*. Academic Press, 1990.

[10] Brent Halperin and Van Nguyen. A model for object-based inheritance. In Peter Wegner and Bruce Shriver, editors, *Research Directions in Object-Oriented Programming*. The MIT Press, 1987.

[11] Philip M. Hubbard, Matthias M. Wloka, Robert C. Zeleznik, Daniel G. Aliaga, and Nathan Huang. UGA: A unified graphics architecture. Technical Report CS-91-30, Brown University, 1991.

[12] Devendra Kalra. *A Unified Framework for Constraint-Based Modeling*. PhD thesis, California Institute of Technology, 1990.

[13] Matthew Moore and Jane Wilhelms. Collision detection and response for computer animation. In *Proceedings of the ACM SIGGRAPH, Computer Graphics*, volume 22(4), pages 289–298, August 1988.

[14] Cary B. Phillips, Jianmin Zhao, and Norman I. Badler. Interactive real-time articulated figure manipulation using multiple kinematic constraints. In *Proceedings of the Symposium on Interactive 3D Graphics*, pages 245–250, 1990.

[15] William H. Press, Brian P. Flannery, Saul A. Teukolsky, and William T. Vetterling. *Numerical Recipes in C*. Cambridge University Press, 1988.

[16] T. W. Sederberg and S. R. Parry. Free-form deformation of solid geometric models. In *Proceedings of the ACM SIGGRAPH, Computer Graphics*, volume 20(4), pages 151–160, August 1986.

[17] Paul S. Strauss. A realistic lighting model for computer animators. *IEEE Computer Graphics and Applications*, 10(6), November 1990.

[18] Peter Wegner. The object-oriented classification paradigm. In Peter Wegner and Bruce Shriver, editors, *Research Directions in Object-Oriented Programming*. The MIT Press, 1987.

[19] Jerry Weil. A simplified approach to animating cloth objects. Unpublished report written for Optomystic, 1988.

[20] Peter Wisskirchen. *Object-Oriented Graphics*. Springer-Verlag, 1990.

[21] N. Yankelovich, N. Meyrowitz, and Andries van Dam. Reading and writing the electronic book. *IEEE Computer*, 18(10), October 1985.

Figure 7: A figure assembled from several spline paths. One defines a path for extrusion. Others define the shape of the extrusion at various points along the path of extrusion. Because of the rich dependencies of our system, such an object will change as the paths used to make it change.

Figure 8: Inverse kinematics controllers (affecting the robots) interacting with a finite-element simulation (affecting the cloth) in a radiosity-rendered room. All are part of the same database, and work together. For example, note that the cloth is being dragged off of the table.

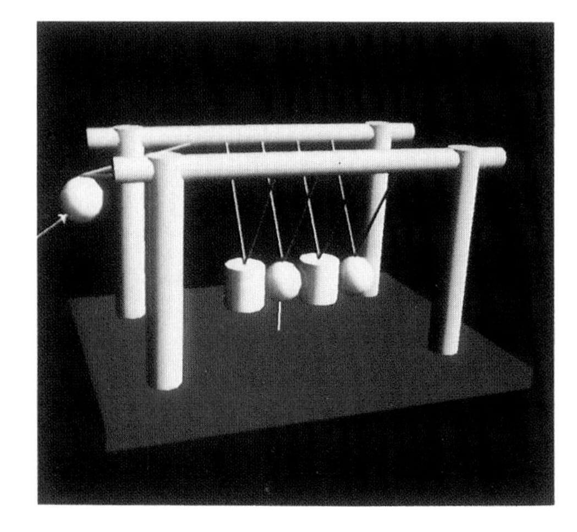
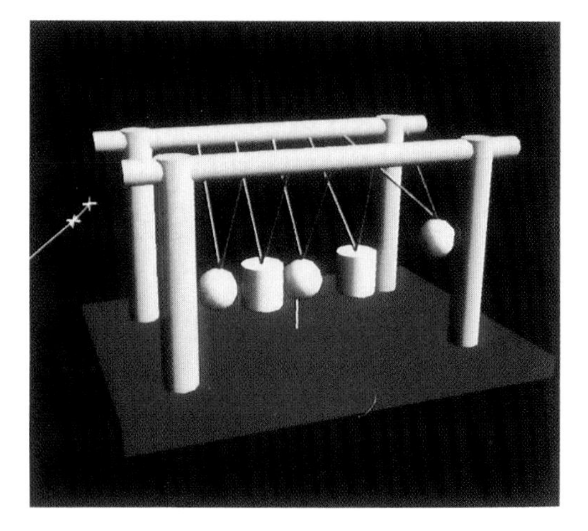

Figure 9: Newton's cradle, a physically simulated toy. The user can specify initial conditions, or interact with the simulation as it procedes.

# Inkwell: A 2½-D Animation System

*Peter C. Litwinowicz*

Advanced Technology Group
Apple Computer Inc.

## ABSTRACT

Inkwell, an experimental 2½-D keyframe animation system, is the subject of this paper. Inkwell provides an intuitive user interface for creating and animating polygons, ellipses and splines. These primitives may be outlined and filled with a variety of patterns to create animated diagrams, graphs and charts, and simple characters and cartoons. Inkwell also has a patch primitive that facilitates deformation and animation of textured regions. The system provides editing features that include shape and timing control as well as digital filtering of parameters. Finally, Inkwell has deformation primitives that enable an animator to warp geometry in an intuitive manner. Inkwell was used to produce *Pigment Promenade*, a computer animated short shown at SIGGRAPH 1990.

**CR Categories and Subject Descriptors:** I.3.6 [Computer Graphics]: Methodology and Techniques - Interaction Techniques.

**Additional Key Words and Phrases:** Animation, character animation, free form deformation.

## BACKGROUND

Interaction with pictures has been a focus of computer graphics since Sutherland's Sketchpad [Suth63]. It wasn't long before computer animation systems were created to choreograph drawings in motion. An early system, Genesys [Baeck69], enabled an animator to hand draw pictures, hierarchically arrange and transform them, and specify how to play them back. Another early system, described in [Burt71], performed actual metamorphoses between drawings, breaking up or combining lines if the number of primitives did not match between the two drawings. Tween, a commercial system developed at NYIT, provided for the animation of antialiased colored lines and filled regions [Catmull83].

Computer animation systems have become much more sophisticated since then. In most animation systems, when a parameter is set for a particular frame all other parameters need not be specified. Because of this, "keyframing" as such has taken on an entirely new meaning. Each parameter ("track") in the animation can have its own set of independent key frames [Gomez84].

Many techniques have been developed to give better control of parameters. These range from shape controls [Sturm85] to speed and acceleration controls [Stek85]. Parameter values may also be derived from video tracking or computed via computer simulations.

Scripting is an alternative to direct manipulation which may be a helpful supplement to direct manipulation for some applications [Reyn82]. Dynamic simulation of non-rigid 2D bodies in an interactive system (where the user specifies constraints and initial conditions) has been explored in [Witk90].

## INTRODUCTION

Creating a 2½-D animation system that is comprehensive and intuitive presents a real challenge. A "2½-D animation system" is defined here to be a system that maintains a drawing order for 2D objects causing the objects to appear to be layered on top of each other. We have borrowed many ideas from the systems referred to previously, added a few new ideas of our own and have tied them together with an intuitive user interface. Designing and building the user interface was the most difficult part of developing the system and will be the main focus of this paper.

In building Inkwell, we had three goals in mind. The first was to provide an animation system that is a natural extension of drawing and painting, and is as intuitive as possible. We believe that character animation is the most difficult challenge to a computer animation system so we adopted it as a benchmark: users had to be able to create believable personalities, feelings and expression through motion. Finally, we required that Inkwell provide a testbed for researching "clip motion," the flexible re-use of defined motion sequences.

In order to keep Inkwell intuitive, all of its capabilities may be exercised by direct manipulation. Inkwell allows animators to translate, rotate, scale and stretch 2D objects, either interactively or by entering precise values via the keyboard. Polylines, polygons and splines may be more generally deformed by simply moving their control points to change their shape. Objects may also be deformed using space warping operations. Objects can be hierarchically arranged into groups and then manipulated as a single object. Patch primitives may be rendered with color, translucency, and displacement maps. When displacement maps



 ACM-0-89791-436-8/91/007/0113 $00.75

**Figure 1.** This is Inkwell's drawing area. The top row of buttons are VCR-like controls that enable the animator to single step, rewind, fast forward and play the animation. The second row shows the current frame number, and the time span of current interest (the **Loop**, **LoopBack**, and **Rock** commands use the designated time span). A background picture is displayed and a number of splined "birds" are being animated. One of the birds is being edited at frame 0, and its control points are shown.

are applied, patches can be shaded as 3D objects. After keyframes have been specified, the various transformations are interpolated to create inbetweens. The animator can control the interpolation process with a variety of tools. At any time the animator can preview the animation with a set of VCR-like controls. Once the previewed motion is satisfactory, rendering occurs in a separate post-process. [Figure 1] depicts Inkwell's main drawing area.

The current implementation of Inkwell is an extension of Stanford's Idraw program, built upon Stanford's InterViews interaction toolkit [Lint87], which has been ported to Apple's Quickdraw library, the X Window System, and Silicon Graphics' Graphics Library. Hence, Inkwell runs on a Macintosh, or any machine running X, and takes full advantage of the hardware graphics pipeline on an SGI Iris.

### DRAWING INTERACTION

Drawing is a natural means of communication through pictures, and people without highly developed drawing skills can use computers to produce useful, communicative images and diagrams. Inkwell attempts to extend interactive drawing metaphors to govern time and motion.

Inkwell's drawing interaction is borrowed largely from AltoDraw, developed at Xerox Parc, and Claris' MacDraw [Mac84]. The animator is supplied a variety of tools that fit into two categories, creation and action tools. The creation tools allow the animator to make new objects, including polylines, polygons, and both open and closed B-splines. The borders of objects may have a variety of different line types and may be filled with a number of different patterns. Each object has specified colors for its pattern fill and border.

Inkwell has a large palette of action tools that allow the animator to manipulate objects. First, the animator selects an object to be manipulated. Many objects may be selected at the same time by depressing the shift key while picking. The animator may then translate, scale, stretch or rotate the selection(s). These transformations work about a center that may be set by the animator. The animator may change the shape of an object by moving some or all of its control points when the **reshape** tool has been chosen.

Objects may be grouped together by selecting them together and applying the **group** command. A group is an object that can be scaled, rotated, stretched and translated as a unit. A group may then be incorporated into larger groups. In MacDraw, once objects are grouped the individual objects can no longer be accessed. This is not acceptable in an animation program. The animator needs to be able to select and manipulate leaf nodes of the hierarchy, as well as the various groups and subgroups. This, of course, means that the way objects are selected must differ. First, if the cursor is actually touching a geometric primitive, it is picked, even if it is at a leaf node of a hierarchy. If the cursor does not touch a primitive, the smallest group whose bounding box encloses the cursor is chosen. If there is ambiguity, the object closest to the front is picked (the drawing order of objects, and thus their implicit front-to-back ordering, are initially determined by the order in which they are entered; editing commands are provided to change object priority). The animator can cycle through a series of objects over a given point by continuing to click the mouse. After selecting an object, the animator can optionally select its parent by invoking a **Go-Up-The-Hierarchy** command.

Inkwell, being an animation program, must allow for the editing of objects in time. Inkwell supports this by maintaining the notion of a current frame (and its associated time). When manipulating an object the animator is defining a key at the current frame for whatever parameter is being edited (translation, rotation, etc.). If the control button is depressed when an object is manipulated, the transformation specified is applied to the entire animation (all keys) of the selection. As an example, consider a user of the system who has animated a bird flying around a building. The animator then decides to move the building to the other side of the frame. Instead of having to redo every key for the bird so that it moves around the newly positioned building, all he needs to do is reposition one of the keys while holding the control button down, and the bird will then fly around the new position of the building. This obviates the need for creating another level of hierarchy for the bird, which should not be necessary simply to reposition the animated sequence. Creating another level of the hierarchy is often a very useful tactic as well, since this allows the user to transform the animation at any desired set of sparse keys. A simple walk cycle can be looped by copying keys, then adapted to a desired path for the character by transforming the "extra level" of the hierarchy. The character may be scaled, moved, and rotated at any set of frames (frames that may not have been "keys" in the original cycle), and the reinterpolated character will execute his walk along the desired path. By applying negative scales, the character can even "turn around" or "flip over," although an anorexic intermediate profile will result. This opens the door to significant adaptation and re-use of motion sequences, and suggests a very powerful form of animation based on modifying and blending libraries of motion.

Background pictures may be read into Inkwell. The animator may then create and interact with objects on top of the picture. This facilitates rotoscoping as well as texture map placement for patches (to be described subsequently). The animator also has at his disposal a computerized "light table." The animator can pick up to six frames (at times other than at the current frame) that will be faintly drawn ("ghosted") into the current frame. In this way the animator can determine how the shape and placement of the current frame relates to other frames.

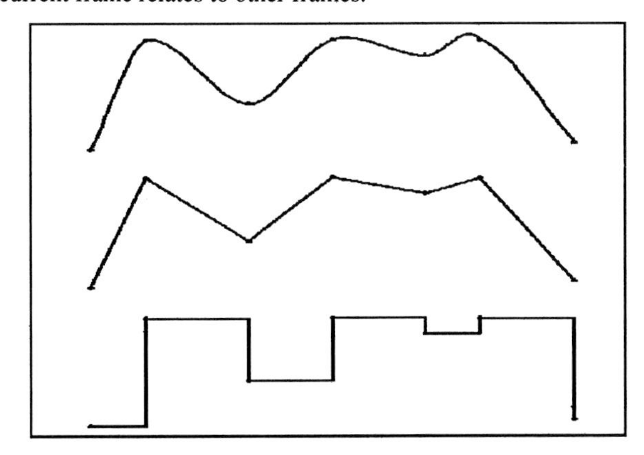

**Figure 2**. Three sets of identical keys with different types of interpolations.

### CONTROLLING PARAMETERS

#### Interpolation of Keys

A "key frame" is created automatically every time the animator changes a parameter, and every parameter is keyed separately. As the animator creates keys, they are, by default, inserted as knots into an interpolating cubic spline with local tension, bias and continuity control as described in [Koch84]. If desired, the animator can specify that the keys for a parameter should be linearly or stepwise interpolated [figure 2]. When selecting an object, its transformation parameter curves show up in a function editor window. The parameter curves may be edited directly here instead of manipulating objects in the main drawing area. The function editor allows simple editing, such as setting the tension, bias and continuity parameters for spline knots, deleting and moving spline knots, and cutting and pasting portions of curves.

### Filtering of parameters

The animator can create filters that smooth, overshoot, or add "wiggle" to a parameter [figure 3]. Filters essentially model the behavior of linear systems (the shock absorbers of a car, for example) at a high level of abstraction, with a direct visual representation of their effects. After specifying a particular filter, the animator can apply it to a parameter over a specified range of time. With the **filter** command the animator may smooth noisy data arising from hand input or some outside source such as video. The animator can also add dynamic effects that are easy to control, cheap to compute, and occur at exactly the times desired. In order to provide even greater visual control over filtering, the animator will be able to draw finite impulse responses directly in a future release of Inkwell.

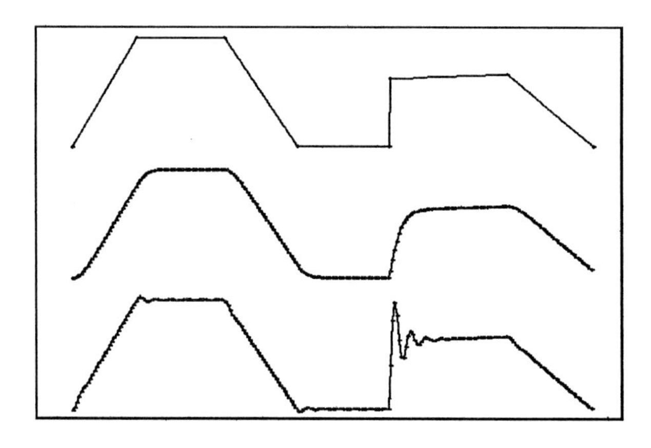

**Figure 3**. The top curve represents a parameter to be filtered. The lower two curves are the results after applying the filters shown in Figure 4.

In order to visualize the effects of a particular filter, a step function is displayed along with the step response to the filter [figure 4]. The filter may be modified by three sliders which control the gain, decay and amount of oscillation of the filter. Let k, r and θ be the variables for gain, decay and oscillation, respectively. We use a 3-tap infinite impulse response (IIR) filter, which has the following formula:

$$x'_i = a\,x_i + b\,x'_{i-1} + c\,x'_{i-2}$$

where x' variables represent values after the application of the filter [Oppen75]. We set a, b and c to be:

$$a = k \qquad b = 2\,r\cos(\theta) \qquad c = -r^2$$

where in practice we let $r \in [0,.95]$, $k \in [-3.0,3.0]$ and $\theta \in [0,\pi]$. The initial values for k, r and θ are 1.0, 0.0 and 0.0 respectively, giving the "identity" filter.

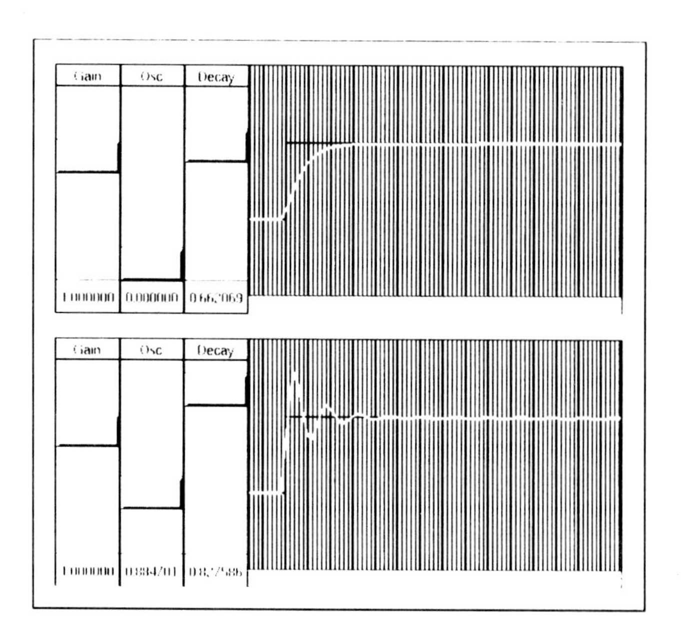


**Figure 4**. Two of many IIR filters that can be specified in Inkwell.

The gain at DC of this filter is:

$$1 / (1 - 2\,r\cos(\theta) + r^2)$$

It has been our experience that most users prefer that when k=1, they see a gain of 1.0 at DC. We therefore modify the first tap on the filter to have the formula:

$$a = k * (1 - 2\,r\cos(\theta) + r^2)$$

In this way, k is a direct control of the gain of the filter at DC.

This formal statement of the filter's specification is of no concern to animators. In practice, the filter parameters adjust the magnitude, wiggle, and lag of a filtered motion, and these effects are easily controlled with a little practice.

### Editing a Curve with Densely Spaced Knots

Conventional spline editing falls flat when a parameter has a key at every (or nearly every) frame. Densely spaced keys can occur from editing by hand, but more commonly occur after filtering a parameter or acquiring data from some other source, such as tracked video. When knots are densely spaced, editing one of these control points can introduce an undesired jump in the animation. To aid in smoothing the transition, Inkwell allows the animator to blend a key into its neighboring keys [figure 5]. A cosine window is used to blend in the change forward and backward in time, and can be scaled separately in each direction.

## WARPING GEOMETRY AND TEXTURE

### Coons Patches

This section discusses how the animator controls non-rigid body

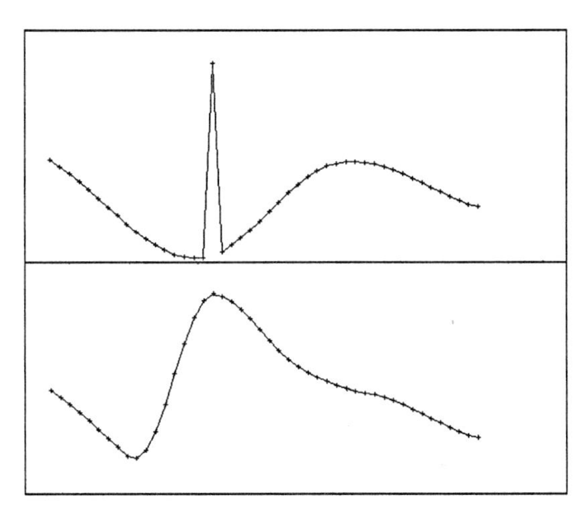

**Figure 5.** On the top a curve has been edited that has densely spaced knots. The lower curve shows the effects of blending this change into the eight previous and fifteen subsequent frames.

transformations. The animator is able to specify the shape of polylines, polygons, and splines at given times (as described above) and then have Inkwell calculate the inbetweens. In this way the animator can metamorphose an object from one shape to another. But there is a geometric primitive not yet discussed that allows the animator to deform textured regions as well. This is the Coons patch [Coons67][Forr72]. Coons patches are natural to use because they are specified solely by their boundaries, which may be hand-drawn curves as well as polylines or splines.

A space warping algorithm using linear "skeletons" is described in [Burt76]; a Coons-patch version should permit curved "bones." Other space-warping techniques using a 3D lattice of control points are described in [Sed86] and [Farin90]; these have their counterparts in "Coons volumes," which should extend the deformations naturally to 3D. In [Reeves81], an algorithm using Coons patches was described to warp shapes over time, where two sides of the Coons patch represented a curve's shape at two different times and the other two boundaries represented the path of the curve's endpoints over a specified span of time. All of these possibilities support our interest in Coons' parameterization for animation purposes. Thus far, we have only explored Coons

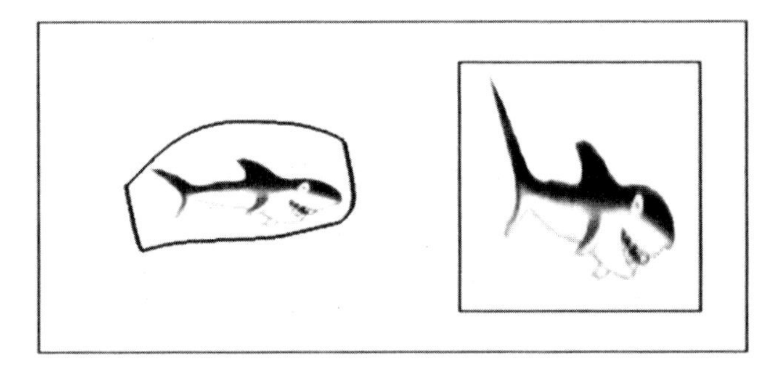

**Figure 6.** On the left, four boundaries for a Coons patch are drawn around a background picture containing a cartoon shark. On the right, the region of the background picture that is covered by the Coons patch has been inverse texture mapped to the unit square. It is this square texture that is used to texture map the patches in Figure 7.

patches as a means of animating textured shapes, with optional alpha mattes and displacement maps.

The animator first creates four splines or polylines that will enclose regions for animation. After selecting four of them, a **Make-Coons-Patch** command makes the four selected curves the boundaries for a bilinear Coons patch. If one or more of the objects selected is already part of a Coons patch, Inkwell adds the patch to a mesh of Coons patches where boundaries are shared.

Inkwell also facilitates the placement of texture maps for Coons patches. As described previously, a background picture may be loaded into the drawing area so that an animator may draw on top of it (or rotoscope from it). In [figure 6, left], the animator has drawn four boundaries of a Coons patch on top of the background image containing a shark. After creating a Coons patch, the animator may execute a command that acquires the portion of the picture under the Coons patch as its texture map. Inkwell performs inverse texture mapping to warp the portion of the picture underneath the Coons patch to the unit square [figure 6, right]. In subsequent frames, as the Coons patch metamorphosizes, the texture will also [figure 7].

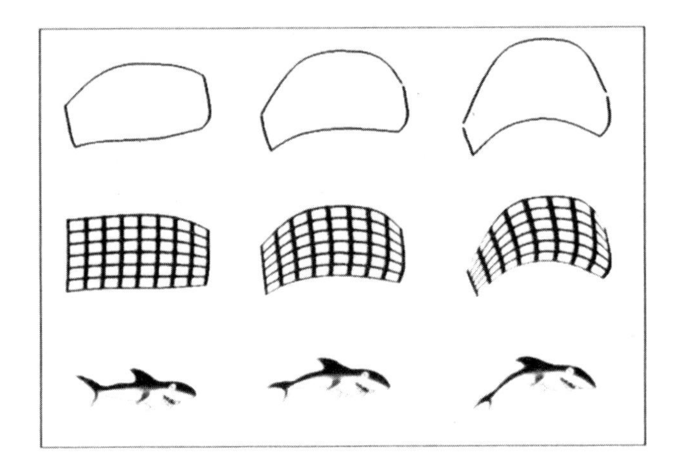

**Figure 7.** In the first row, boundaries for a Coons patch are shown at three different times. The second row shows the parameterizations for the patches. The third row shows the textured patches.

Displacement maps are read in as gray scale pictures, with white being nearest the viewer and black the farthest away. Once again, the animator may execute a command that acquires the portion of the picture under the Coons patch as its displacement map. In the rendering phase, the height of the object will be derived from the displacement map. In this way a 3D relief surface can be animated by manipulating its 2D outline.

Color texture, translucency and displacement maps may be changed over time. The values of the maps between keys are linearly interpolated (cross-dissolved). This offers another dimension of color and 3D shape control. Other types of transitions between textures such as wipes and pushes are planned for a future release of Inkwell.

In [figure 8] a more complex example is shown. In the top row, the animator has specified a walk cycle with ellipses. This is a typical instance of animation created using hierarchically transformed rigid geometric primitives. After refining the motion

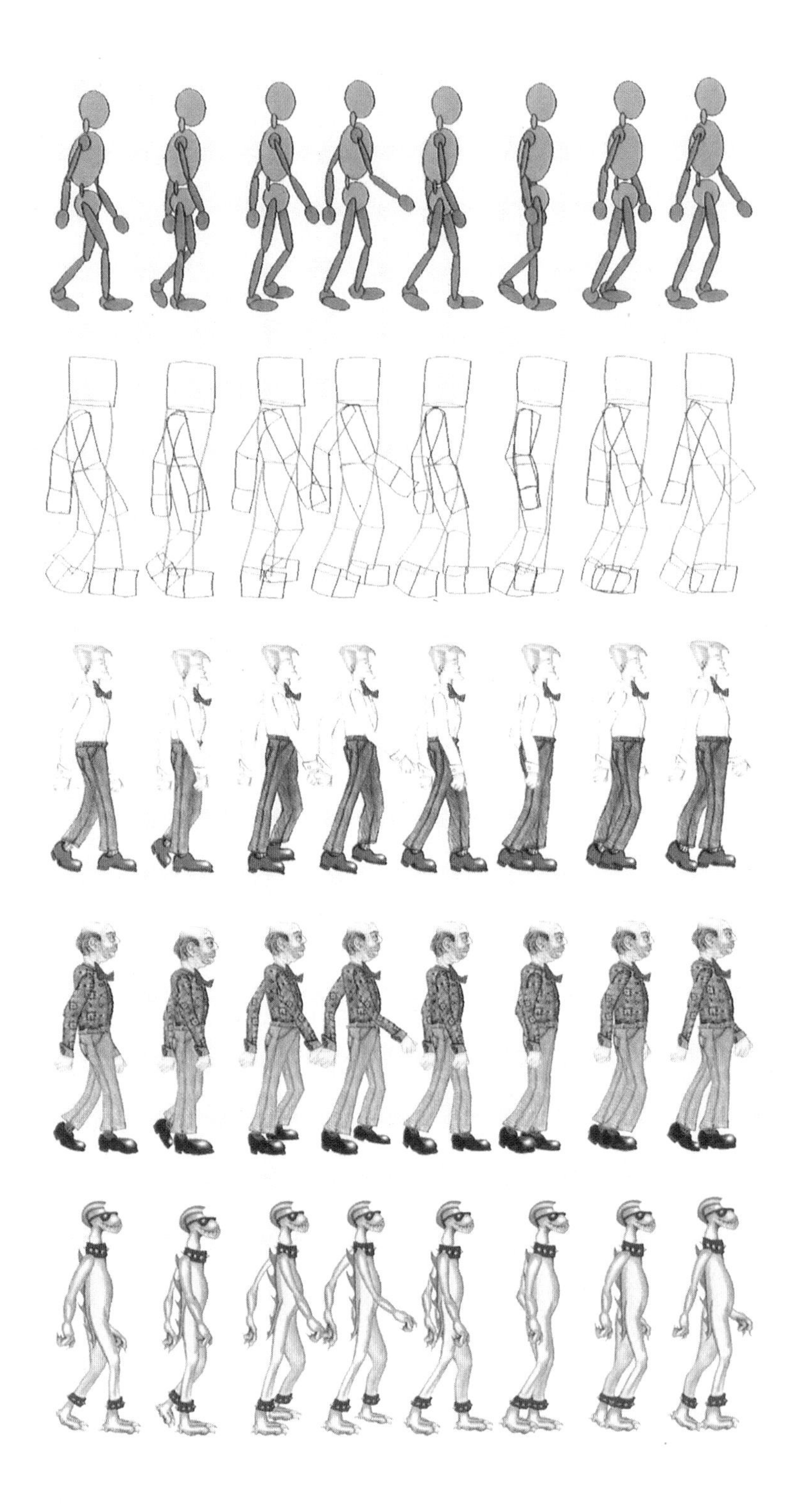

**Figure 8.** In the first row, a walk cycle has been animated with ellipses. In the second row, Coons patch boundaries have been animated by hand to follow the motion of the ellipses. The third, fourth, and fifth rows show these Coons patches textured with three different maps.

to get the timing desired, the animator then created and animated, by hand, Coons patches to follow the ellipses, as shown in the second row. The same Coons patches have been used to animate a number of different characters, as shown in the third, fourth and fifth rows. Now this patch animation can be applied to any texture maps, displacement maps, and mattes the user should desire. This sort of "rubber doll" animation of body parts mapped onto deformable regions is actually a throwback to very early digital-analog hybrid animation systems [Honey71]. Our strictly digital implementation provides a number of advantages (more general deformations, true 24-bit color, and better repeatability), but shares the basic flexibility of animating deformations that can subsequently be applied to different characters. This form of Coons patch animation is another powerful tool for the reuse of motion.

In future enhancements, Coons patches will also be used as deformation functions for geometric primitives as well as textures.

### Warping with Cosine Windows

Animations that contain a large number of primitives present the animator with many variables to orchestrate, including a set of transformations for each primitive and a potentially large number of control points for splines and polylines. It is often desirable to have higher levels of control. Currently, Inkwell provides a space warping operation that warps geometry using cosine (Hanning) basis window functions. The animator specifies a neutral position and extent for a warping window; as the warping window moves it pulls and pushes on the geometry around it. This is simply the 2D, spatial counterpart of blending changes in parameter values into the surrounding time-sequence, described earlier in "Editing a Curve with Densely Spaced Knots."

The space warping algorithm used in Inkwell requires a displacement vector and a radius of extent for each warping window. The animator first creates a warping window primitive (it is shown as a circle with a dot for the center). The original placement, or neutral position, of the window is one point used in determining the displacement vector. The second point used is the position of the window at the current frame. This window is scaled by the animator to the appropriate size and hence, extent. As the animator moves the warping window about, it will pull and push on the geometry near its neutral position towards the current position, with the geometry nearest the neutral position being pushed the most. (The neutral position can be changed if the original placement of the window is unsatisfactory).

To actually warp geometry, the animator selects the cosine window primitive along with the polylines and splines that are to be warped, and then executes the **Warp-Geometry** command. The lines and splines are warped depending on their proximity to the center of the neutral position of the warping window [fig 9].

The facial animation in *The Audition* was edited with Inkwell using this technique. The initial motion for the centers of the windows were tracked and mapped from a live performer and read into the program [Patt91]. The animator could then edit the positions of the warp windows to exaggerate or otherwise enhance the motion [figure 10]. Preview of the newly positioned warping functions and their effects can be seen in near real time.

### OUTPUT

Scenes may be rendered and sent to a video device for playback.

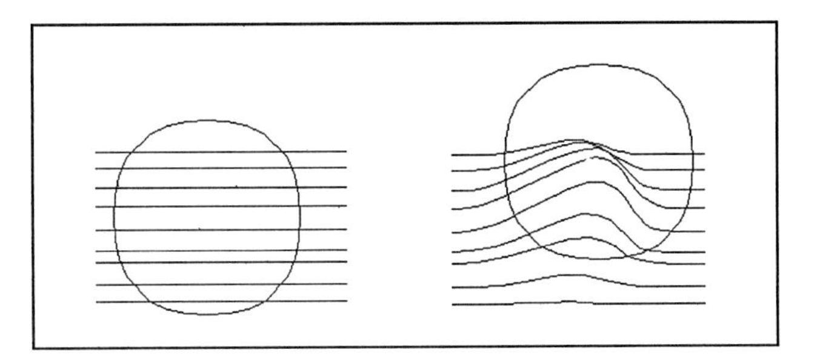

**Figure 9.** The neutral position of a warping window and geometric primitives to be warped are shown on the left. The warping window is then moved and the underlying geometry is warped as shown on the right. The arrow shows the displacement vector. This is the 2D counterpart of the cosine-window blending applied to edit a parameter curve in Figure 5.

But since the information is kept in a resolution independent format, Inkwell animations could also be sent to film or a laser printer for higher resolution output (and, in fact, short flip books have been printed).

### CONCLUSIONS, EXPERIENCE AND FUTURE DIRECTIONS

Inkwell has been used in-house to produce a variety of animations. *Pigment Promenade* was produced in two weeks (including soundtrack!) by two animators, without recourse to overtime or weekends. Using cosine warping windows and an overshooting IIR filter, an animation of a spider dropping onto its web, with bouncing, springy effects, was specified in one hour. A walk cycle, animated by Kim Tempest, required only a half day to specify with Inkwell, and has been used to animate three characters with minimal preparation and set-up time (1 hour each for the second and third characters).

In our introductory remarks, we stated three goals for Inkwell. The first was to achieve an easy and intuitive user interface for animation. The results are encouraging. One coworker's first animation consisted of a Mazda Miata zooming into the distance, accomplished in only three hours of work, after a couple of hours of instruction. We also stated that animation should be a natural extension of painting and drawing. Inkwell to date is not really a "drawing" program. Rather, Inkwell is more like a drafting program, forcing the user to input control points of splines and polylines. A drawing interface that allows curves to be input without placing control points is desirable, and should be easy to implement. The paradigm of moving each knot point in a spline or polyline to animate it is also somewhat restrictive. It would be nice to simply redraw the new shape, specifying which object becomes the newly drawn shape at the current frame.

Having a strictly prioritized drawing order can create problems when animating. To animate an arm it is sometimes desirable to detach the arm from the body and animate it as a separate Coons patch mesh. When doing this, it is impossible to have the top of the arm drawn behind the torso, while the hand is in front of the body. Currently, there are two solutions: 1) place the arm entirely in front of (or behind) the body or 2) break the arm into two pieces. Neither solution, in this case, is entirely satisfactory. It would be desirable to specify intermesh ordering of patches, but it

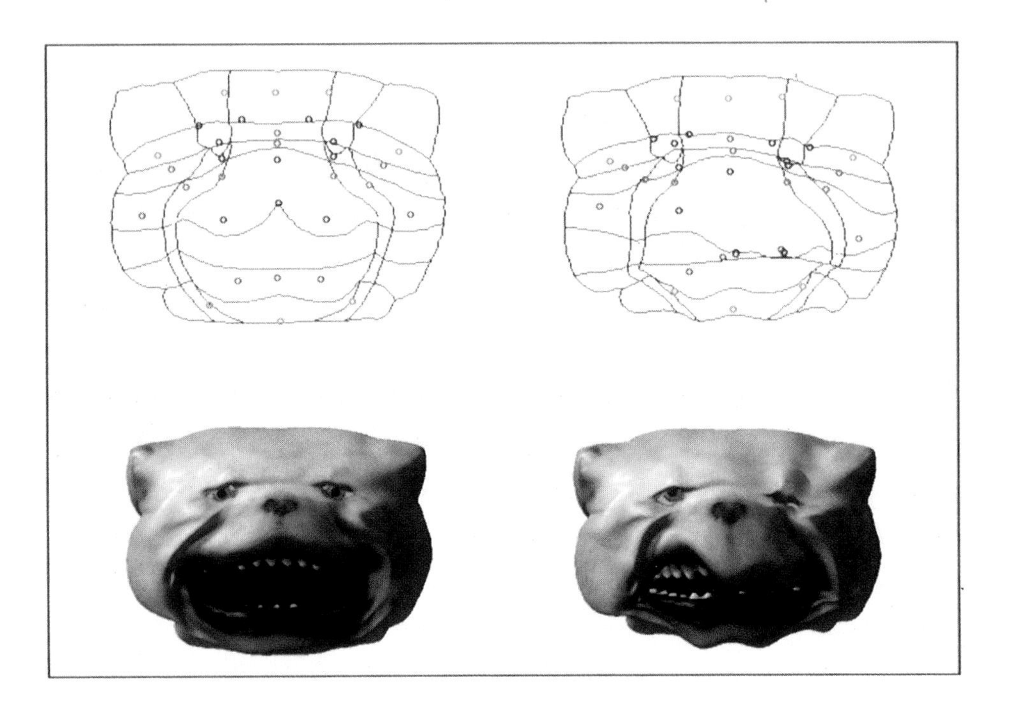

**Figure 10.** A more complicated example of animation with warping windows. The upper left picture shows the neutral position for a dog's face and the upper right picture shows the same face after warping (extents of warping windows not shown). The lower pictures show the faces rendered with color textures and displacement maps.

is unclear how to make such an interface intuitive. This will be a topic for further research.

Another problem getting in the way of "ease of use" is the abundance of data. How do we allow users to choose parameters to edit? How should we display the information? We currently display parameters graphically; other systems display information in a spreadsheet format. Sometimes, however, a less detailed view of the data and where it is located is more appropriate. For example, our users would like to see some representation of how "much" of an object is "keyed" at the current (or some other) frame. Determination of the metric could be as simple as dividing the number of parameters that are keys for an object at a given frame by the total number of parameters, giving rise to a scale from 0 to 1. This is just one example of the problem associated with data explosion.

The second major goal for Inkwell was the production of character animation. A contracting animator, Laurence Arcadias, was able to specify the motion for a 30 second animation of a hippo and a crocodile preparing to play tennis in just 3 weeks (this does not include drawing, scanning and painting time of the textures and associated mattes). We did find that there were limitations. Patches can only be attached to other patches by having whole boundaries shared. We found that animators really wanted to share subparts of patch boundaries too, and this will be included in a future release. Also, there were problems with ordering of patches as described previously.

The third stated goal was that Inkwell serve as a testbed for "clip motion." Inkwell already provides the capability to replace texture maps on patches. This ability alone allowed us to animate three characters walking in a very short amount of time. By varying the scale of the patches and manipulating a few of the Coons patch boundaries, we were able to give each character a slightly different walk, without having to specify each cycle from scratch. Inkwell has also allowed us to explore what "cut and paste" of parameter curves should mean, and how it should be accomplished. We plan to continue our research into other areas of reusability of motion as well, such as applying the motion of a dog to a cat. The length of the limbs and constraints on joint motion may be different, but we expect the mapping of motion from one character to another to be a fruitful field of inquiry.

We believe that the ideas presented here can easily extended into a 3D system. The user interface and controls would be very similar, if not exactly the same. We have been exploring $2^1/_2$-D animation to get a feel for what is involved in the animation process. At some point we plan to test our ideas in 3D also. Another planned extension is sound manipulation, allowing the timing of events to sound and vice-versa.

Inkwell will continue to be a launching pad for our research into animation algorithms and their user interface.

## ACKNOWLEDGEMENTS

The author would like to thank Ned Greene for his Coons patch and polygon mesh code, James Normile for his filtering expertise, and Robin Myers for printing support. Thanks to Libby Patterson, Kim Tempest and Laurence Arcadias for their abundance of ideas, patience, and ability to animate under stressful conditions that included hard deadlines and buggy code. Special thanks to Lance Williams for his ideas, motivation and inspiration. And of course, thanks to Susan Litwinowicz for empathy and support.

## REFERENCES

[Baeck69] Baecker, R. "Picture Driven Animation," *Interactive Computer Graphics*, edited by Herbert Freeman, IEEE Computer Society, 1980. Originally published in *Conference Proceedings, Spring Joint Computer Conference*, AFIPS, 1969.

[Burt71] Burtnyk, N. and M. Wein. "Computer-Generated Key-Frame Animation." *J. Society Motion Picture and Television Engineers.* Vol 80, Number 3, 1971, pp. 149-153.

[Burt76] Burtnyk, N. and M. Wein. "Interactive Skeleton Techniques for Enhancing Motion Dynamics in Key Frame Animation," *CACM*, Vol 19, Number 10, October 1976.

[Catmull83] Catmull,E. *Tween Users' Manual.* New York: CGL Inc., 1983.

[Coons67] Coons, S. *Surfaces for Computer-aided Design of Space Forms*, M.I.T MAC-TR-41, June 1967.

[Farin90] Farin, G. *Curves and Surfaces for Computer Aided Geometric Design, A Practical Guide.* Second Edition. Academic Press, Inc., 1990.

[Forr72] Forrest, A. "On Coons and Other Methods for the Representation of Curved Surfaces," *Computer Graphics and Image Processing*, 1, 1972, pp. 341-369.

[Gomez84] Gomez, J. "TWIXT: A 3D Animation System," *Computers and Graphics*, 9, Pergamon Press Ltd., 1985, pp. 291-298. Originally in *Proceedings of Eurographics '84.*

[Honey71] Honey, F. J., "Computer Animated Episodes by Single-Axis Rotations: CAESAR," *Proceedings of the 10th UAIDE*, 1971, pp. 3.210-3.226.

[Koch84] Kochanek, D. and R. Bartels. "Interpolating Splines with Local Tension, Continuity and Bias Control," *Computer Graphics*, Vol 18, Number 3, July 1984, pp. 33-41.

[Lint87] Linton, M., P. Calder and J. Vlissides. "The Design and Implementation of InterViews," *Proceedings of the USENIX C++ Workshop*, November 1987.

[Mac84] *MacDraw* (users' manual). Apple Computer, Product Number M1509.

[Oppen75] Oppenheim, A. and R. Schafer. *Digital Signal Processing*, Prentice-Hall, 1975.

[Patt91] Patterson, E., P. Litwinowicz, and N. Greene, "Facial Animation by Spatial Mapping." *Computer Animation 1991.*

[Reeves81] Reeves, W. "Inbetweening for Computer Animation Utilizing Moving Point Constraints," *Computer Graphics*, Vol 15, Number 3, August 1981, pp. 263-269.

[Reyn82] Reynolds, C. "Computer Animation with Scripts and Actors," *Computer Graphics*, Vol 16, Number 3, July 1982, pp. 157-166.

[Sed86] Sederberg, T. and S. Parry. "Free-Form Deformation of Solid Geometric Models," *Computer Graphics*, Vol 20, Number 4, August 1986, pp. 151-160.

[Stek85] Steketee, Scott N. and N. Badler. "Parametric Key Frame Interpolation Incorporating Kinetic and Phrasing Control," *Computer Graphics*, Vol 19, Number 3, July 1985, pp. 255-262.

[Sturm85] Sturman, D. "Interactive Keyframe Animation of 3D Articulated Models," Course notes, SIGGRAPH Course Number 10, *Computer Animation: 3D Motion Specification and Control*, July 1985, pp. 17-25.

[Suth63] Sutherland, I. "Sketchpad: A Man-Machine Graphical Communication System," MIT Lincoln Laboratory Technical Report, Number 296, January 1963.

[Witk90] Witkin, A. and W. Welch. "Fast Animation and Control of Nonrigid Structures," *Computer Graphics*, Vol 24, Number 4, August 1990, pp. 243-250.

## APPENDIX A Blending into Densely Spaced Knots

After an animator makes an adjustment to a curve, as shown in [figure 5, top], he can then blend this change into the previous and subsequent frames. Let the number of previous and subsequent frames be denoted by p and s respectively, and the current frame be denoted by c. Let the variables denoting the values of the curves before and after the blend be denoted by oldval and newval respectively. The following pseudo code will calculate the desired blend:

```
for i = p to c-1 step 1
        Note that the weighting factor
        ranges from 0 to 1 as i ranges
        from p-1 to c not from p to c.
        Therefore, we have the term
        (c-p+1) in the denominator, instead
        of (c-p)
    weight = (1+cos(π*(c-i)/(c-p+1))) / 2.0;
    newval[i] = oldval[i] * weight +
            oldval[c]*(1-weight);
for i = c+1 to s step 1
    weight = (1+cos(π*(s-i)/(s-c+1))) / 2.0;
    newval[i] = oldval[i] * weight +
            oldval[c]*(1-weight);
```

[Figure 5, bottom] shows the curve after blending an edit into the eight previous and fifteen subsequent frames.

## APPENDIX B Warping with Cosine Windows

The following pseudo code describes how warping is accomplished.

```
n = neutral position of a warping window
e = extent of the warping window
    note: this is a scalar
d = displacement vector
p = a point of a geometric primitive
     that is to be warped
p' = p after warping

if (length(p - n) > e)
        The point is not part of the
        affected region for the
        given cosine window,
         so no warping occurs
    p' = p
else {
      Modify the displacement
      by a scalar based on distance
      from the neutral position and then
      add it to the point to be warped.
  p'= p + d*((1+cos(π*length(p - n)/e))/ 2.0
  }
```

See [Patt91] for a discussion of how warping is handled when two or more warping windows overlap.

# Automated Generation of Intent-Based 3D Illustrations

Dorée Duncan Seligmann
Steven Feiner

Department of Computer Science
Columbia University
New York, New York 10027

## Abstract

This paper describes an automated intent-based approach to illustration. An *illustration* is a picture that is designed to fulfill a *communicative intent* such as showing the location of an object or showing how an object is manipulated. An illustration is generated by implementing a set of stylistic decisions, ranging from determining the way in which an individual object is lit, to deciding the general composition of the illustration. The design of an illustration is treated as a goal-driven process within a system of constraints. The goal is to achieve communicative intent; the constraints are the illustrative techniques an illustrator can apply.

We have developed IBIS (Intent-Based Illustration System), a system that puts these ideas into practice. IBIS designs illustrations using a generate-and-test approach, relying upon a rule–based system of methods and evaluators. Methods are rules that specify how to accomplish visual effects, while evaluators are rules that specify how to determine how well a visual effect is accomplished in an illustration. Examples of illustrations designed by IBIS are included.

**CR Categories and Subject Descriptors:** I.3.3[**Computer Graphics**]: Picture/Image Generation–display algorithms, viewing algorithms; I.3.4[**Computer Graphics**]: Graphics Utilities–Picture description languages; I.3.7[**Computer Graphics**]: Three-dimensional graphics and realism; I.2.1[**Artificial Intelligence**]: Applications and Expert Systems.

**Additional Keywords and Phrases:** illustrations, automated picture generation, knowledge-based graphics, non-photorealistic rendering.

## Introduction

The development over the last few centuries of printing and photographic technologies, and more recently of electronic mass media, has revolutionized communication by making the *exact same presentation* accessible to larger and larger groups of people. Nevertheless, communication involves both intent and interpretation. The same presentation, viewed by several people, may be interpreted to mean different things, while different presentations may be interpreted to mean the same thing. To further complicate matters, none of these interpretations may be the one intended by the presenter. With recent advances in computer technology, we may now embark upon a new phase of communication. By formalizing the intent of a communication, the language or medium to be used, the audience and context of the communication, and the way in which the language is used to achieve intent, we may create systems that generate presentations, each designed to satisfy the same communicative intent for a particular audience, thus making the *exact same meaning* accessible to many different people.

This paper describes the first steps in developing such a system for illustration. An *illustration* is a picture that has been designed to fulfill a communicative *intent*. For example, the intent of an illustration may be to show an object's material, size, or orientation. The intent might be more complex. It may, for example, be more important to show how to turn a dial, and less important to show where the dial is located.

Human illustrators plan and replan an illustration, considering at all times how the final illustration will look. An illustrator may try something on paper and then, after evaluating it, erase it and adopt another plan. Or, the illustrator may be so skilled that it is enough for her to simply imagine the consequences of a stylistic choice.

This characterization of illustration serves as the foundation for intent-based illustration. An *intent-based* illustration system designs illustrations to fulfill a high-level description of the communicative intent. The illustration process can be formalized as a goal-driven process: the goal is to achieve a specified communicative intent within a complex of stylistic choices. In order to use a generate-and-test approach, such a system must represent style in two ways. First, each stylistic choice represents a method for achieving a particular goal. For example, in order to highlight an object, it may be brightened or it may be colored in a special way. Second, each stylistic choice is associated with a set of criteria used to judge how well it has been accomplished.

This paper describes IBIS (Intent-Based Illustration System), concentrating on its rule base, architecture, and design process. It explains how IBIS both achieves and evaluates the highlighting, recognizability and visibility of objects using several examples.

# IBIS

## Overview

IBIS utilizes a generate-and-test approach to illustration design. Starting with a description of the communicative intent and a knowledge base representing the world to be depicted, IBIS begins to design an illustration. The communicative intent is specified using a language of *communicative goals*. For example, a communicative goal may be to show how an object has been moved or to show its color. For each communicative goal there exists at least one design rule in IBIS's rule base. A *design rule* specifies a prioritized set of style strategies. A *style strategy* specifies a visual effect, such as highlighting and is achieved by a set of style rules. A *style rule* determines some part of the traditional computer graphics specification of an image: a viewing specification, a lighting specification, the objects to be depicted, and rendering instructions. A style rule calls upon procedures that directly access and manipulate illustrations. Illustrators select style strategies by selecting design rules to accomplish communicative goals. Drafters select illustration methods by selecting style rules to accomplish style strategies.

The following subsections describe all the components of the system and their interaction.

## Input: Communicative Goals

IBIS currently supports communicative goals that have been designed to satisfy the needs imposed by COMET, a knowledge-based multi-media explanation generation system for which IBIS generates graphics [Elhadad et al. 89, Feiner and McKeown 90a, Feiner and McKeown 90b]. COMET designs explanations for equipment maintenance and repair that include pictures and text. Its current domain is the army radio shown in the figures in this paper. The communicative goals that IBIS can satisfy are:

- *location*: show the location of an object in a context (either explicitly specified or derived by the system)
- *relative location*: show the relative location of two or more objects in terms of a specified or derived context
- *property*: show one of the following physical properties of an object: material, color, size, shape
- *state*: show an object's state
- *change*: show the difference between a set of states

Both the goals *state* and *change* may be further qualified by concepts that refer to how the object is manipulated or has changed. For example, the state of a dial can be shown in terms of an agent turning it. IBIS currently supports three dozen concepts useful to our maintenance and repair domain, among them, *pushing*, *pulling*, *loosening*, *lifting*, *inserting* and *blinking*.

In response to a user request for information, COMET's *content planner* generates a description of the communicative intent for an explanation that is sent to COMET's *media-coordinator*. The media-coordinator annotates the intent specification to indicate which generators should communicate which information and passes the same intent specification to COMET's *media generators*. All generators work from the same annotated intent specification [Elhadad et al. 89]. IBIS translates the intent description into a prioritized list of *communicative goals*. This translation is more or less direct; concepts such as *location* and *turn* are identified in the intent specification. IBIS associates with each goal an indication of its importance, which in turn is used to calculate an acceptable degree of success when the goals are evaluated.

## Knowledge Base

IBIS has a knowledge base of the physical objects to be illustrated that includes not only geometric and material information, but also information about the object's features, physical properties, and abstract properties. Information about the features and abstract properties of physical objects is a superset of the information traditionally passed to a graphics system. It is, however, necessary to an intent-based system that designs its own pictures. For example, it may be important to represent how an object moves or its limits of articulation. IBIS currently utilizes a very simple model for object states. For example, the dials on the radio are represented as having discrete or continuous ranges with associated orientations; the latches have two states: snapped and unsnapped.

## Design Rules: Mapping Intent to Stylistic Choice

*Design rules* describe on a high level how illustrations should be put together. A design rule consists of a communicative goal and a set of style strategies. There are two types of design rules: design methods and design evaluators. *Design methods* specify how to accomplish communicative goals; *design evaluators* determine how well communicative goals have been accomplished. A design method specifies what *style strategies* must be achieved, in addition to how well each should be achieved in order to accomplish a communicative goal. A design evaluator determines how well a communicative goal is achieved based on the achievement ratings of a collection of *style strategies*. Each communicative goal formalized in IBIS's intent-specification language [Seligmann 91] must have one or more design rule to accomplish and evaluate it.

## Showing Location

Figure 1 lists two design rules for satisfying the communicative goal *location*. Figures 2 and 3 are illustrations that IBIS generated using design rules 1 and 2. In both illustrations, the location of the function dial is shown in context of the parent object, the radio. (How design rules are activated is described later.)

Design Rule 1 specifies that to show the location of an object (?object) in a specific context (?context-object), the following style strategies must be accomplished:

- The object must be *included* in the illustration. The achievement threshold "highest" indicates that this style strategy must be fully satisfied.
- The object must be recognizable.
- The context object must be included.
- The object must be visible.
- The object must be highlighted.
- The context object must also be recognizable, but with a lower threshold.
- The context object must also be visible, but with a lower threshold.

Design Rule 2 requires that a landmark object of the context object be visible and recognizable. A *landmark* is an object that serves as a key for identification, position, and/or location [Feiner 85]. IBIS uses a simplistic approach for identifying landmarks. It

**Design Rule #1:**

```
(method
(location ?object ?context-object highest)
=>
(include        ?object           highest)
(recognizable   ?object           high)
(include        ?context-object   highest)
(visible        ?object           high)
(highlight      ?object           high)
(recognizable   ?context-object   high)
(visible        ?context-object   medium-high))

(evaluator
(include        ?object           highest)
(recognizable   ?object           high)
(include        ?context-object   highest)
(visible        ?object           high)
(highlight      ?object           high)
(recognizable   ?context-object   high)
(visible        ?context-object   medium-high)
=>
(location ?object ?context-object highest))
```

**Design Rule #2**

```
(method
(location ?object ?context-object highest)
=>
(include        ?object           highest)
(recognizable   ?object           high)
(include        ?context-object   highest)
(visible        ?object           high)
(highlight      ?object           high)
?y <- (Landmark ?context-object)
(recognizable   ?y                high)
(visible        ?y                high))

(evaluator
(include        ?object           highest)
(recognizable   ?object           high)
(include        ?context-object   highest)
(visible        ?object           high)
(highlight      ?object           high)
?y <- (Landmark ?context-object)
(recognizable   ?y                high)
(visible        ?y                high)
=>
(location ?object ?context-object highest))
```

Figure 1. Two design rules for showing location

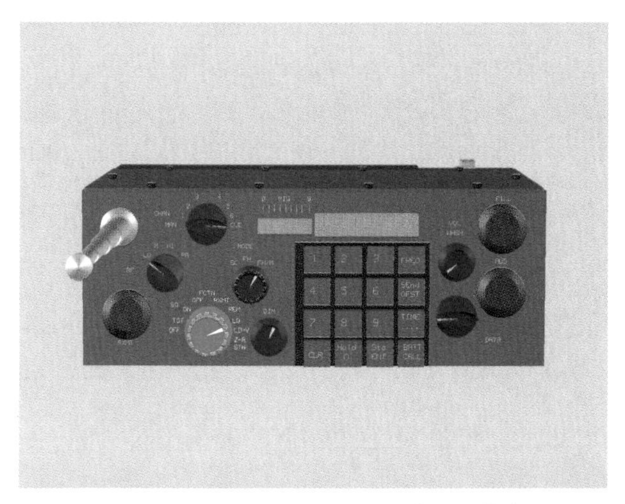

Figure 2. Showing location using Design Rule 1

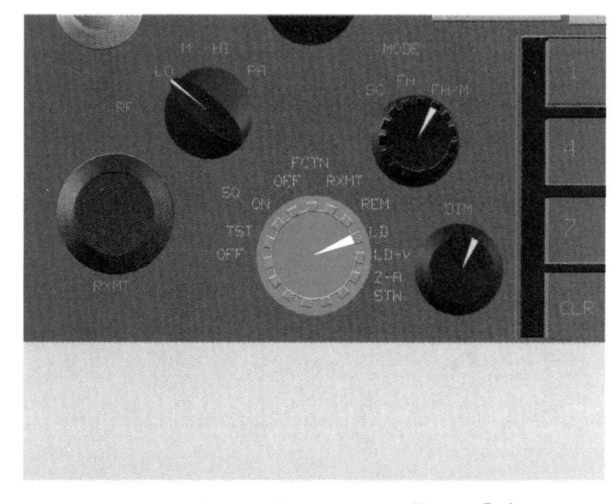


Figure 3. Showing location using Design Rule 2

considers any object with a unique property (such as shape, material, or color) to be a landmark.

## Style Rules: Mapping Stylistic Choice to Visual Effects

There are two types of *style rules*. *Style methods* accomplish visual effects specified by style strategies and *style evaluators* determine the success of style strategies in a given illustration. Style methods specify *illustration methods*, which are procedures to accomplish specific visual effects. Style evaluators match *illustration evaluators* which examine a representation of the planned illustration to determine how well a visual effect is accomplished. Illustration methods and illustration evaluators are the only components of IBIS that directly access the illustration.

## A Style Strategy: Highlighting

*Highlighting* is a style strategy that can be accomplished by applying one of several style rules. The purpose of highlighting an object is to emphasize it and draw attention to it. This can be accomplished by rendering it in a manner that distinguishes it from all the surrounding objects. Consider the following two style methods and two style evaluators.

**Style Methods: Highlight Object x**

1. Brighten x: Increase the intensity of the lights shone on x.
2. Subdue other objects: Decrease the intensity of the lights shone on other objects.

**Style Evaluators: Highlight Object x**

1. For every object with modified lighting: Evaluate the contrast between the object before and after the modification.
2. Evaluate the contrast between x and other objects.

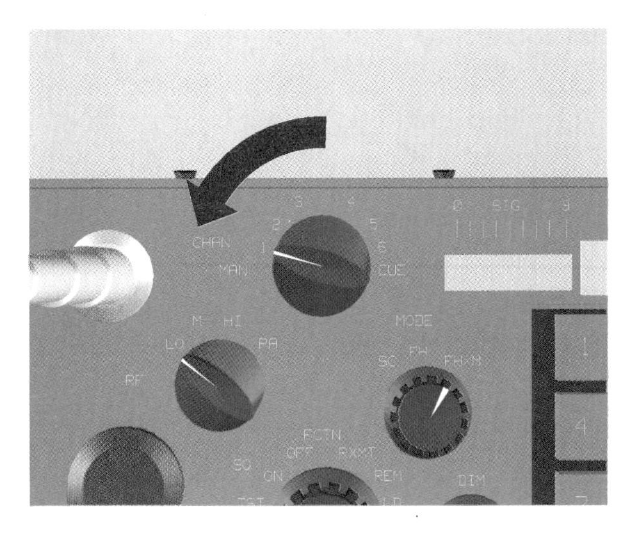


Figure 4. State of channel dial with no highlighting

Figure 5. Highlighting by Style Method 1: Brighten object

Figure 6. Highlighting by Style Method 2: Subdue other objects

Figure 7. Highlighting: Combine Style Methods 1 and 2

Let us examine how IBIS uses these rules to highlight an object. At this point, a design rule has already been activated that asserts that the channel dial should be shown in addition to the other parts of the radio. This design rule also specifies that the channel dial should be highlighted.

Figure 4 shows the illustration IBIS would generate if highlighting were not specified. (Figures 4–6, which show intermediate states of the illustration during the illustration design process, were generated by requesting that IBIS render its intermediate results. They would not normally be rendered during the illustration design process.) The style rules are prioritized so that Style Method 1 is tried first, which executes illustration methods whose results are shown in Figure 5. Both style evaluators return unsatisfactory ratings. Style Evaluator 1 fails because its illustration evaluators detect that the dial's markings are brightest white, so increasing their lighting does not change their appearance. Style Evaluator 2 fails because its illustration evaluators detect that the other objects also have markings that are white and therefore do not contrast sufficiently with the channel dial's markings. Therefore, IBIS backtracks and returns the illustration to the state shown in Figure 4.

IBIS next tries Style Method 2, resulting in Figure 6. Style Evaluator 1 is successful, since the other markings are now darkened. Style Evaluator 2, however, returns a poor rating since the contrast between the channel dial and other objects is insufficient. Once again, IBIS backtracks and returns the illustration to the state shown in Figure 4.

IBIS now tries both style methods in combination, as specified by its search control strategy, with the results shown in Figure 7. Both style evaluators now return success. Therefore, IBIS asserts that the channel dial has been successfully highlighted.

Style Method 2 attempts to mute the objects at varying percentages, stopping at a prescribed threshold. In Figure 6, the global lighting is dimmed by 40%, the maximum allowed. In

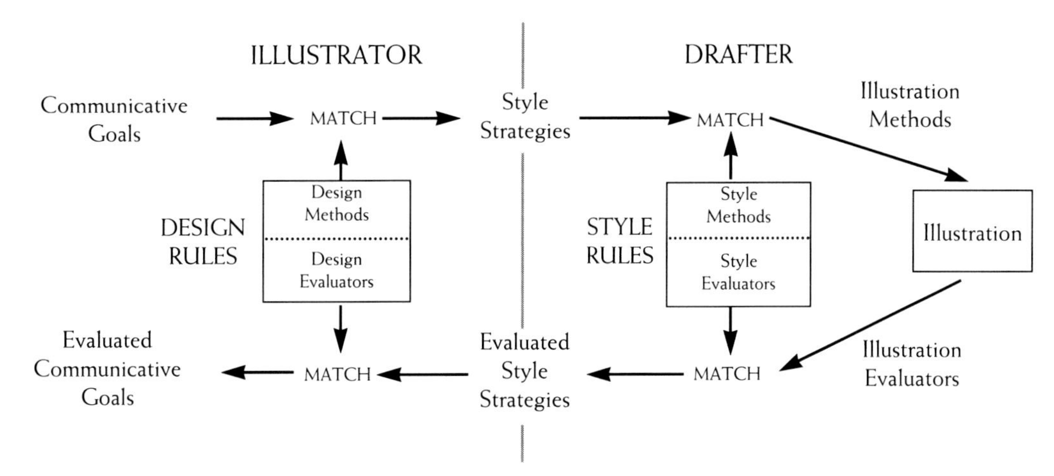


Figure 8. IBIS's illustration process

Figure 7, in which the global lighting is dimmed by 25%, IBIS decides that the brightened channel dial is sufficiently contrasted with other objects and that no additional muting is necessary.

# Architecture

## Illustrators

An IBIS illustration is designed by a component called an *illustrator*. An illustrator is assigned a set of communicative goals to fulfill. After trying the techniques at hand, an illustrator may detect that it cannot fulfill the complete set of communicative goals in just one illustration. For example, the communicative intent may be to show the opposite faces of the same object, or to show parts of an object in great detail, but also in context of a much larger object that must also be legible. No one view can satisfy these constraints. IBIS's rules allow it to create a *composite illustration*, which is defined as a set of related illustrations that in concert fulfill the communicative intent [Seligmann and Feiner 89]. Composite illustrations are made up of several sub-illustrations, each of which may be inside, overlapping, or next to others. The illustrator creates subordinate illustrators to which it contracts sets of communicative goals. One subordinate illustrator is responsible for the work already completed; the rest are assigned the remaining communicative goals. The original illustrator, which we call the *master illustrator*, is responsible for the work of the subordinates and the placement and sizing of their sub-illustrations. Although illustrations may have arbitrarily deep recursive hierarchies in theory, in practice the hierarchy is usually not very deep or broad.

While illustrators map communicative goals to style strategies with design methods and evaluate the success of communicative goals with design evaluators, they assign to *drafters* the task of accomplishing and evaluating style strategies.

## Drafters

Drafters do not know about communicative intent. They are the unheralded workers who translate the illustrators' plans into reality. Drafters are tied to the hardware they utilize. For example, it is the drafters who apply the procedures that examine the contents of the framebuffer. Drafters share a body of style rules. Each style rule specifies illustration methods or evaluators to call in order to achieve or evaluate visual effects. Drafters report back to the illustrators with the achievement rating of the various style strategies they implement. Once an illustration has been approved by the master illustrator, it is the drafters who render the illustration.

## Illustration Objects, Physical Objects, and their Relations

An illustration contains a set of *illustration objects*, each of which is created for that illustration. The drafter generates illustration objects when achieving style strategies. IBIS selects the objects to depict based on the communicative goals and design rules activated. Each illustration object usually depicts one or more corresponding physical objects in the knowledge base. Some illustration objects, however, may not correspond to any physical object, such as the arrow appearing in Figure 7. Such objects are called *meta-objects* [Feiner 85]. They are generated by the system to serve as visual annotations that illustrate those concepts that do not directly correspond to physical objects in the world being illustrated, such as the concept of turning in Figure 7.

An illustration includes a set of *object relations* that specifies the relationship between each illustration object and zero or more corresponding physical objects. Some physical objects have no corresponding illustration objects. These are the objects IBIS selects not to depict. In contrast, a physical object may correspond to several illustration objects. For example, two or more illustration objects can depict the same object in different states.

# Generate and Test Approach

Figure 8 summarizes IBIS's illustration design process. Communicative goals match with a design method in the illustrator's design rule base. The design method asserts a set of style strategies. Style strategies match with style methods in the drafter's style rule base. This, in turn, activates a set of illustration methods that access the illustration object directly. Corresponding style evaluators activate a set of illustration evaluators that also access the illustration. The illustration evaluators match with style evaluators to assert the success ratings for style strategies. The evaluated style strategies match with design evaluators and assert the success ratings for communicative goals.

All illustrators share a set of design rules. All drafters share a set of style rules. Each illustrator or drafter, however, can be specified with a different illustrative style. An *illustrative style* is represented by ordering the rules so that preferred methods are always attempted first. When a preferred method fails, the illustrative style is overridden. The illustrations IBIS generates can combine different illustrative styles. The illustrations shown in the figures were generated using the illustrative style *realistic*. The *realistic* illustrative style favors methods that do not alter physical properties of objects. For example, highlighting methods that use lighting are preferred to methods that change the color of an object.

Evaluation is based on a system of ratings and thresholds. *Thresholds* are assigned by the illustrators and are inherited by the drafters for each style strategy. A threshold represents a minimum degree of success required for a method to be considered acceptable. Evaluators can directly assert that either a style strategy or communicative goal has been achieved.

# Visibility and Recognizability

Style rules for evaluating and achieving highlighting were illustrated earlier. We now describe visibility and recognizability. First, we discuss the evaluators that the drafter uses to determine if objects are visible and recognizable in the current illustration. Then we discuss the methods the drafter uses to achieve visibility and recognizability.

## Evaluating Visibility

Every IBIS illustration depicts at least one object that must be visible. We call an object that must be visible an *unoccludable* object. IBIS stores its objects in a parts hierarchy. An unoccludable object may be any node in the hierarchy. An object is considered completely visible if it resides entirely within the view volume and no other objects obscure it. Thus, an object is partially visible if it is obscured by other objects or if it is not completely within the view volume.

We use several approaches to determine visibility quickly, described in [Feiner and Seligmann 90]. One approach uses z-buffer picking [Foley et al. 90] to detect occlusion. The hardware z-buffer is loaded with an unoccludable object and the remainder of the z-buffer in the unoccludable object's bounding box is set to the closest possible z-value. For each remaining object, the system will determine if any part of the object is visible relative to the z-buffer, which occurs only if the object (partially) obscures the unoccludable object. This returns a binary occluding/non-occluding status. Another approach using shadow volumes [Chin and Feiner 89] returns a partially occluding/completely-occluding classification.

## Evaluating Recognizability

An object is *recognizable* if its distinguishing features are shown. Some features depend upon the view; others depend on certain characteristics or attributes. We do not address the very difficult problem of determining or generating automatically *characteristic views* [Chakravarty 82, Kamada and Kawai 88] that ensure that an object's distinguishing characteristics are apparent. Instead each object is stored with an a priori characteristic view.

We represent a characteristic view as a union of volumes and a set of constraints. Each volume is specified by a ray originating from a point on the object. This volume represents a set of legal viewpoints that may be further restricted by the characteristic view's constraints. The constraints include a minimum screen size

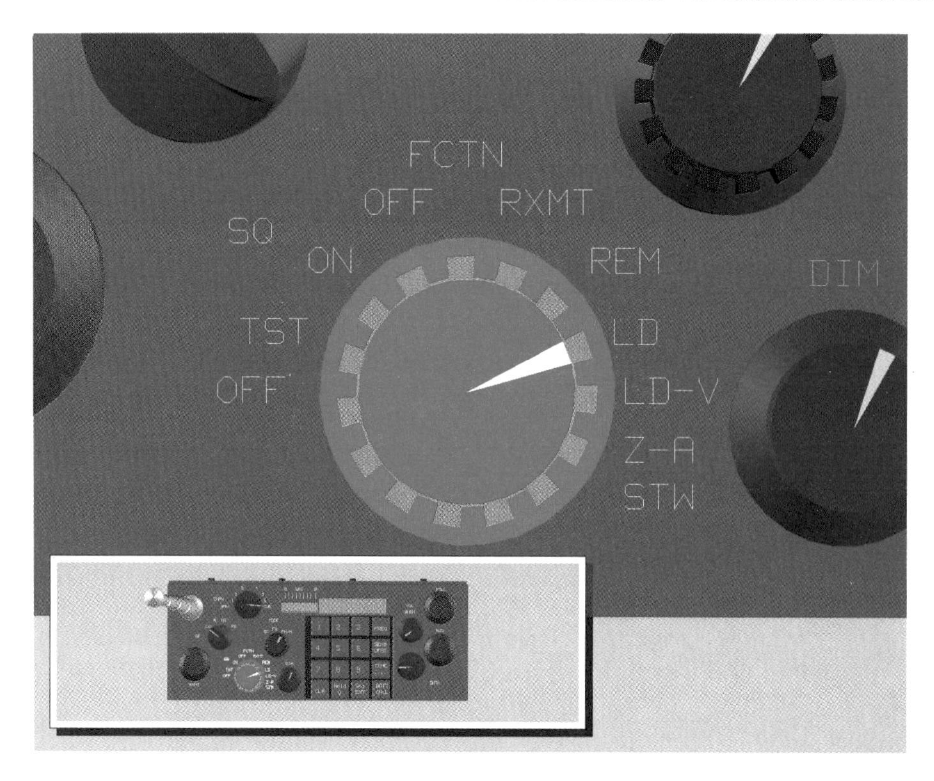


Figure 9. Automatically generated inset to show location during user navigation

the object must occupy and a list of properties that must be depicted.

## Style Methods for Visibility and Recognizability

The drafter maintains a set of possible view specifications for every object that must be recognizable. A view specification satisfies the recognizability goals associated with these objects if the viewpoint lies within the intersection of the characteristic views' volumes and if the additional constraints are satisfied.

The visibility of each unoccludable object is maintained, if possible, by selecting a view in which unoccludable objects are not obscured. IBIS has several different methods for realizing visibility constraints when an unoccludable object is obscured by another object (that is not itself unoccludable). The first and simplest method is to remove from an illustration an object that obscures an unoccludable object. An object can be made visible by removing from the illustration all the objects that obscure it. This solution is problematic. In some cases, it would be misleading to remove objects from the scene. In other cases, it would be ideal.

A variety of illustrative styles have been developed by technical illustrators to depict obscured objects more clearly without completely eliminating those that obscure them [Giesecke et al. 36, Thomas 68, Martin 89]. These techniques include cutaways, transparency, and ghosting. We have developed several approaches for efficiently applying simple versions of these techniques interactively using z-buffer–based graphics systems [Seligmann and Feiner 89, Feiner and McKeown 90a, Feiner and Seligmann 91].

## Interactive Illustrations

So far, we have treated IBIS's illustrations as static presentations. However, the same mechanisms that enable IBIS to design illustrations are utilized to maintain illustrations in their interactive state. An *interactive illustration* may be manipulated by a user. Currently, IBIS supports user-controlled view specification. In traditional user-controlled navigation, when the user specifies a new view, the same set of illustration objects is rendered from that view. In contrast, navigation in an illustrated 3D environment is more complex. The illustration is bound to the communicative goals with which it is specified. The illustration system's task is to satisfy continuously these communicative goals while the user changes the view specification. For example, consider an illustration in which the illustrator has determined that certain objects are unoccludable. As the user alters the view, these unoccludable objects may be obscured by other objects. The appearance of these otherwise occluding objects must be modified dynamically to maintain the unoccludable objects' visibility. (In [Feiner and Seligmann 91] we describe techniques for automatically maintaining visibility during an interactive session.)

Alternatively, different design rules may be activated to satisfy a communicative goal as the view specification changes. Consider an interactive session beginning with Figure 2, in which the communicative goal is to show the location of the function dial. Figure 2's view specification is generated by IBIS. As the user zooms in, using IBIS's interactive interface, Design Rule 1's evaluator is no longer satisfied: the context object is no longer completely recognizable and visible. However, Design Rule 2's evaluator is activated because the current view includes the keypad buttons, which are unique objects on the radio and considered landmarks of the radio. The communicative goal to show location is maintained and IBIS does not have to redesign the illustration. The user continues to zoom. Now, only the function dial is visible and recognizable. If design rules 1 and 2 are the only rules for showing location, then the communicative goal has been violated, since no design rule is satisfied. IBIS opts to generate a composite illustration, and designs and positions an inset illustration (using Design Rule 1), which pops up during the interactive session. The resulting illustration is shown in Figure 9.

# Composite Illustrations

Here we describe some of the top-level decisions IBIS made when designing the illustration shown in Figure 10. The illustration is intended to show the user how to snap the latches of the primary battery box, as well as to indicate, with lesser importance, where another battery (the holding battery) is located. The master illustrator is assigned the following communicative goals:

(state latch1 snapped highest)
(state latch2 snapped highest)
(state latch3 snapped highest)
(state latch4 snapped highest)
(location holding-battery radio medium-low)

These communicative goals activate the following design rules that specify the following style strategies.

For each latch:
(include latch highest)
(context latch medium)
(recognizable latch high)
(visible latch high)
(highlight latch high)
(change latch snapped highest)
(meta-object latch snapped highest)

For the battery:
(include holding-battery highest)
(visible holding-battery medium-low)
(recognizable holding-battery low)
(context holding-battery medium-low)
(highlight holding-battery medium-low)

The illustrator's drafter tries to satisfy the highest priority style strategies first and begins by generating illustration objects for the latches, holding battery, and the rest of the radio. The recognizability constraints are set up for each object. The drafter fails when trying to make the fourth latch recognizable. Since all goal cannot be satisfied, IBIS decides that a composite illustration is needed. The master illustrator contracts two subordinate illustrators to handle the following communicative goals:

Illustrator One:
(state latch1 snapped highest)
(state latch2 snapped highest)
(state latch3 snapped highest)
(location holding-battery radio medium-low)

Illustrator Two:
(state latch4 snapped highest)

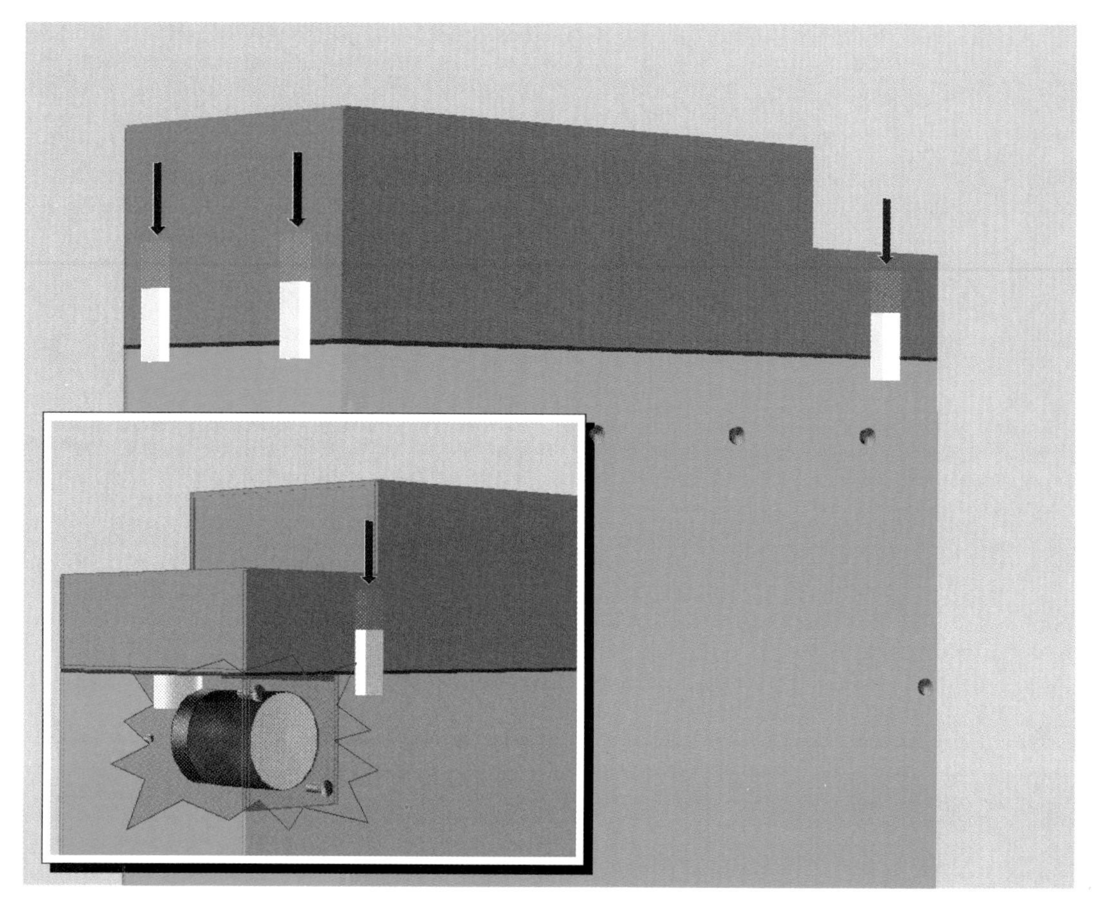

Figure 10. Showing snapping of latches and location of holding battery with a cutaway view

The latches are highlighted by increasing the intensity of their lighting. The drafter for Illustrator One reports failure for showing the battery—an unoccludable latch obscures it. Because the visibility goal for the holding battery is of low priority, the view specification that currently satisfies the high-priority recognizability and visibility goals associated with the latches is not altered. The master illustrator therefore assigns the holding battery's location goal to Illustrator Two:

Illustrator One:
(state latch1 snapped highest)
(state latch2 snapped highest)
(state latch3 snapped highest)

Illustrator Two:
(state latch4 snapped highest)
(location holding-battery radio medium-low)

Illustrator Two's drafter determines that the holding battery's recognizability and visibility goals can be achieved using the current view specification. The drafter then specifies a cutaway view for the holding battery. In the rule base for this illustration, a style method specifies that occluding objects be drawn using a wireframe style, and that the cutaway itself be semi-transparent. The concept of *snapping* is shown in the following way. The style rule specifies how to shape, position and orient an arrow meta-object based on the geometric information of the latch in the two states as well as the final view specification. The arrow begins at the previous state and points to the next state. The communicative goal to show the change of state is activated by a design rule that handles state and snapping. It activates a style strategy to show the object in both states. A style method specifies that a "ghost image" [Martin 89] be used to show the previous state of each latch. Illustration objects representing each latch in its previous state are generated. These ghost objects inherit the material and lighting from the illustration objects that are related to the same physical object, but their material is set to be partially transparent. The following constraints are added for each arrow and ghost object:

(visible ?object high)
(recognizable ?object high)

The master illustrator is notified that both illustrators have achieved the communicative goals they have been assigned. The master illustrator must now size and position the two illustrations. An inset style is selected for the illustration generated by Illustrator Two. The illustration must be sized so that the constraints are not violated (such as recognizability) and it must be positioned so that it does not obscure the unoccludable objects in Illustrator One's illustration. The resulting illustration is shown in Figure 10.

## Related Work

Several researchers have addressed the problem of automatic picture generation. Simmons's CLOWNS [Simmons 75] generates simple line drawings of a 2D clown. Neiman's GAK [Neiman 82] generates animated pictures for a CAD system help facility. Both these systems, however, rely on predesigned vector objects. Friedell [Friedell 84] has generated synthesized 3D graphic environments using evaluators and backtracking, but this work emphasized modeling environments, rather than designing pictures. Feiner's APEX [Feiner 85] system designs pictures that depict actions performed in a 3D world, but without backtracking, self-evaluation, style combination, or visibility checks. Mackinlay's APT system [Mackinlay 86] designs 2D presentation graphics for quantitative data using a system of evaluation and backtracking, which enables the system to combine styles. Strothotte's chemistry explanation system [Strothotte 89] generates pictorial explanations automatically, but relies on handmade bitmapped images.

Other researchers have addressed rendering problems related to the illustration of objects. Kamada and Kawai [Kamada and Kawai 87] have developed techniques for generating line drawings that show the internal structure of complex objects. Saito and Takahashi [Saito and Takahashi 90] and Dooley and Cohen [Dooley and Cohen 90a, Dooley and Cohen 90b] have also developed non real–time techniques using transparency, cross-hatching, and different line styles to generate high-quality images that convey shape and construction.

The work described here differs from previous work in a number of ways emphasized in this paper. Our approach to automated illustration of 3D worlds is intent-based and depends upon a system of methods and evaluators that enables multi-level backtracking based on evaluations of a partially generated illustration. Illustration objects are generated based on both the representation of the physical object as well as the communicative intent. IBIS's evaluation process attempts to approximate the relationship between the visual appearance of an object in the real world (limited by the models used) and its appearance in the illustration. Finally, IBIS introduces an approach for generating composite illustrations, as well as semantically bound interactive illustrations.

## Implementation

IBIS is written in C++ and the CLIPS production system language [Culbert 88]. It runs under UNIX on an HP 9000 375 TurboSRX workstation, which provides hardware support for realtime 3D shaded graphics. Drafters currently use the HP Starbase 3D graphics package, while the user interface is written in X.

The radio featured in the illustrations consists of over 8000 polygons rendered at 1280 x 1024 resolution. IBIS took .8 seconds to design Figure 7 and 7 seconds for IBIS to design Figure 10. It takes approximately .3 seconds to render either illustration.

## Summary and Future Work

IBIS demonstrates an automated intent-based approach to illustration. Illustrations are designed by first considering a specified communicative intent and the world depicted. IBIS treats illustration as a goal-driven process using a generate–and–test approach and relies upon a rule base to make stylistic and design choices. These rules are represented as both methods for accomplishing visual effects and evaluators for determining how well visual effects have been accomplished in an illustration. Any choice may negatively affect the success of others; IBIS backtracks to find alternative solutions.

Our current efforts concentrate on the development of a visual language for 3D worlds [Seligmann 91] that will incorporate formalisms for communicative intent, style, design, viewer model, and session model. Communicative intent will be extended to include goals to represent the *purpose* of the communication, such as warnings and reminders. Style rules are being arranged into a hierarchy of constraints, ranging from those that identify conformant classes of illustration elements (e.g. colors and lines) to those that identify unaesthetic choices. We are also developing meta-rules to select methods based on the overall problem (rather than searching for the first adequate solution). For example, while IBIS currently generates composite illustrations only as a last resort, a meta-rule could allow them to be created as a regular design option. Finally, IBIS is being enhanced to allow for user control on all levels of specification, including the choice of design rules and style strategies.

## Acknowledgments

This work is supported in part by the Defense Advanced Research Projects Agency under Contract N00039-84-C-0165 and the Hewlett-Packard Company under its AI University Grants Program. Esther Woo, John Edmark, Garry Johnson and Alan Waxman implemented portions of the system. Norman Chin developed the efficient procedures that we use to manipulate shadow volumes. Michael Elhadad is a a fellow comrade in arms in the COMET project. Conversations with Tom Ellman, J.R. Ensor, Allen Ginsberg, Jacques Robin, Frank Smadja have been more than helpful. Much appreciation is due to Suzanne Oboler and Cynthia King for their critical reading of this paper. Many thanks to David Kurlander and Rick Beach for help with the color separations.

## References

Chakravarty, I., and Freeman, H. Characteristic Views as a Basis for Three-Dimensional Object Recognition. In *Proc. Society for Photo-Optical Instrumentation Engineers Conf. on Robot Vision*, Bellingham, WA, SPIE, vol. 336, 1982. 37–54.

Chin, N. and Feiner S. Near Real-Time Shadow Generation using BSP Trees. In *Proc. ACM SIGGRAPH 89* (*Computer Graphics*, 23(3), July 1989), Boston, MA, July 31–August 4, 1989, 99–106.

Culbert, C. *CLIPS Reference Manual*. NASA/Johnson Space Center, TX, 1988.

Dooley, D. and Cohen, M. Automatic Illustration of 3D Geometric Models: Lines. In *Proc. 1990 Symp. on Interactive 3D Graphics* (*Computer Graphics* 24(2), March 1990), Snowbird, UT, March 25–28, 1990, 77–82.

Dooley, D. and Cohen, M. Automatic Illustration of 3D Geometric Models: Surfaces. In *Proc. Visualization '90*, San Francisco, CA, October 23–26, 1990, 307–314.

Elhadad, M., Seligmann, D.D., Feiner, S., and McKeown, K. A Common Intention Description Language for Interactive Multi-

Media Systems. *IJCAI-89 Workshop on Intelligent Interfaces,* Detroit, MI, August 22, 1989, 46–52.

Feiner, Steven K. APEX: An Experiment in the Automated Creation of Pictoral Explanations. *IEEE Computer Graphics and Applications 5(11)*, November 1985, 29–38.

Feiner, S. and McKeown, K. Generating Coordinated Multimedia Explanations. In *Proc. CAIA90 (6th IEEE Conf. on Artificial Intelligence Applications)*, Santa Barbara, CA, March 5–9, 1900, 290–296.

Feiner, S. and McKeown, K. Coordinating text and graphics in explanation generation. In *Proc. AAAI-90*, Boston, MA, July 29–August 3,1990. 442–449.

Feiner, S. and Seligmann, D.D. Dynamic 3D Illustrations with Visibility Constraints. In *Proc. Computer Graphics International 91*, Cambridge, MA, June 24–28, 1991.

Foley, J., van Dam, A., Feiner, S., and Hughes, J. *Computer Graphics: Principles and Practice 2nd Edition*. Addison-Wesley, Reading, MA, 1990.

Friedell, M. Automatic Synthesis of Graphical Object Descriptions. *Computer Graphics 18(3)*, July 1984, 53–62.

Giesecke, F., Mitchell, A., and Spencer, H. *Technical Drawing*. New York, The Macmillan Co., 1936.

Kamada, T. and Kawai, S. An Enhanced Treatment of Hidden Lines. *ACM Trans. on Graphics* 6(4), October, 1987, 308–323.

Kamada, T. and Kawai, S. A Simple Method for Computing General Position in Displaying Three-Dimensional Objects. *Computer Vision, Graphics and Image Processing 41(1)*, January, 1988, 43–56.

Mackinlay, J. Automating the Design of Graphical Presentations of Relational Information. *ACM Trans. on Graphics 5(2)*, April 1986, 110–141.

Martin, J. *High Tech Illustration*. Cincinnati, OH, North Light Books, 1989.

Neiman, D. Graphical Animation from Knowledge. In *Proc. AAAI '82*, Pittsburgh, PA, August 18–20, 1982, 373–376.

Saito, T. and Takahashi, T. Comprehensible Rendering of 3-D Shapes. In *Proc. ACM SIGGRAPH '90 (Computer Graphics, 24(4)*, August 1990). Dallas, TX, August 6-10, 1990, 197–206.

Seligmann, D. D. Intent-Based Illustration: A Visual Language for 3D Worlds. Thesis Proposal. Department of Computer Science, Columbia University. New York, January 1991.

Seligmann, D. D., and Feiner, S. Specifying Composite Illustrations with Communicative Goals. In *Proc. UIST '89*. Williamsburg, VA, November 13–15, 1989, 1–9.

Simmons, R. F. The Clowns Microworld. In *Proc. TINLAP '75*, 17–19.

Strothotte, T. Pictures in Advice-Giving Dialog Systems: From Knowledge Representation to the User Interface. In *Proc. Graphics Interface '89*, London Ontario, June 19–23, 1989, 94–99.

Thomas, T.A. *Technical Illustration, 2nd. Edition*. McGraw-Hill, New York, NY. 1968.

# A New Simple and Efficient Antialiasing with Subpixel Masks

Andreas Schilling
Universität Tübingen
Bundesrepublik Deutschland *

## Abstract

Antialiasing of edges is often performed with the help of subpixel masks that indicate which parts of the pixel are covered by the object that has to be drawn. For this purpose, subpixel masks have to be generated during the scan conversion of an image. This paper introduces a new algorithm for creating subpixel masks that avoids some problems of traditional algorithms, like aliasing of high frequencies or blinking of small moving objects. The new algorithm can be implemented by lookup tables that make use of the inherent symmetry of the algorithm. The results are compared with conventional supersampling[1]. A hardware implementation is described.

**CR Categories and Subject Descriptors:** I.3.1 [**Computer Graphics**]: Hardware Architecture - *raster display devices*; I.3.3 [**Computer Graphics**]: Picture/Image generation - *display algorithms*

**Additional Key Words and Phrases:** antialiasing, exact area subpixel algorithm.

## 1 Introduction

The use of a subpixel mask for antialiasing purposes is very common [6, 7, 3, 9, 1]. It has several advantages compared with other antialiasing techniques. First, it preserves spatial information that is lost, when other methods are used. This information is very important if more than two objects contribute to a pixel. Second, it can be determined quite easily. At the end of the rendering process, the final brightness of the pixel can be calculated easily by adding up the contributions from the subpixels.

However, the subpixel mask is usually computed in a way that introduces avoidable errors. In the following section, the artifacts that occur when using supersampling are shown. Analyzing these artifacts leads to a simple algorithm, the Exact Area Subpixel Algorithm, that can avoid the described disadvantages by combining the benefits of the subpixel mask with the calculation of the exact pixel coverage.

## 2 The Problem

The easiest and therefore most common way to determine the subpixel mask is by sampling at the subpixel centers. The subpixel is on, if the subpixel center is inside the polygon, otherwise it is off (Of course, the results of this calculation can be precomputed and stored in a lookup table).

The problems with that method are obvious. Consider for example the following case (Fig. 1). The pixels consist of $4 \times 4$ subpixels. An object with a horizontal lower edge is moving slowly downward across the pixel. Nothing happens, until the edge reaches the topmost line of subpixel centers. As soon as the subpixel centers are reached, all the four upper subpixels are switched on at the same time. As a result, the brightness of the pixel is increased in four big steps instead of the 16 steps, which we would like to obtain with 16 subpixels. This is shown in Fig. 2 a), where the number of subpixels that are set is plotted as a function of the exact area, covered by the polygon.

The same applies for diagonal lines. In Fig. 2 b) we see the result for edges with a slope of $45^0$. Fig. 2 c) represents the ideal function that we would like to obtain. This function is achieved with the algorithm introduced in the next section.

If the objects are very small (smaller than a subpixel), the effect of the errors of the conventional approach is

*Wilhelm-Schickard-Institut für Informatik, Graphisch-Interaktive Systeme, Auf der Morgenstelle 10/C9, 7400 Tübingen, E-mail: andreas@gris.informatik.uni-tuebingen.de.

[1]The experiences, described here were gained in a research project, partly supported by the Commission of the European Communities through the ESPRIT II-Project SPIRIT, Project No. 2484.



©1991 ACM-0-89791-436-8/91/007/0133 $00.75

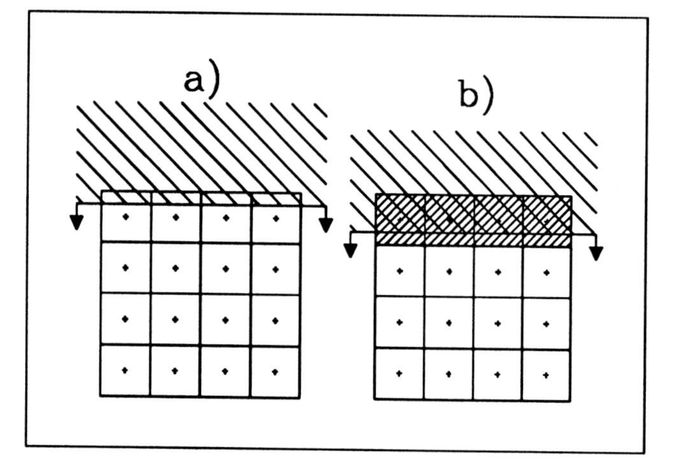


Figure 1: Problems with oversampling: horizontal edge moving downward over a pixel, consisting of 4 × 4 subpixels. The first line of subpixels is switched on simultaneously.

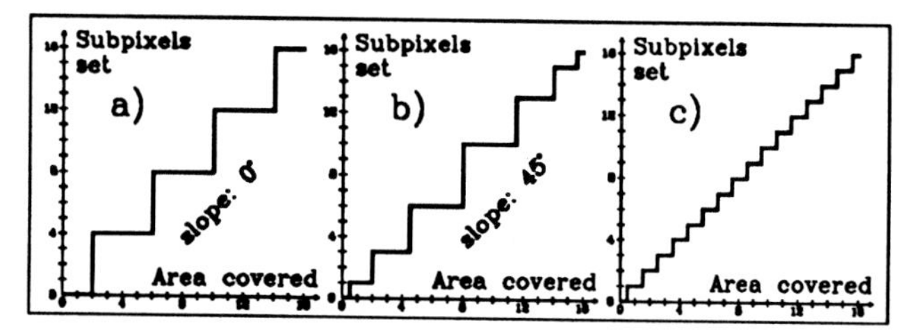


Figure 2: Number of set subpixels vs. area covered. a) Result of supersampling with a horizontal or vertical line, b) Supersampling with a diagonal line, c) Ideal function.

especially bothersome. The whole object appears and disappears again as it moves across the screen. A thin line or the end of a skinny triangle appears as a dashed line (Fig. 3).

A way to minimize aliases, generated by regular supersampling, is the use of stochastic sampling [5, 1, 4]. Although the most annoying artifact (alias effect) is replaced by an artifact (noise) that is more tolerable, other objectionable effects, like the blinking of small moving objects or holes in thin lines etc. are not dealt with correctly.

# 3 Exact Area Subpixel Algorithm

Our new approach, therefore does not sample at the subpixel centers. Instead, the exact portion of the pixel area is calculated. But in contrast to other approaches that also calculate this area, but then have to store it as an extra value for later processing [3], we convert the area into a subpixel count that represents the area portion best. In the following, the algorithm is explained for 4 × 4 subpixels, later on, a generalization for $n \times n$

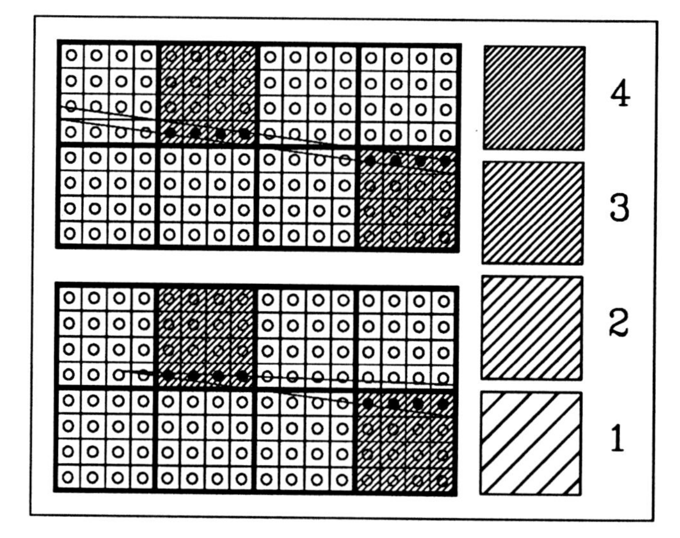


Figure 3: Problems with oversampling (thin line and sharp triangle). Each pixel consists of 4 × 4 subpixels. Subpixels that are set are indicated by filled circles. The density of the hatching indicates the final pixel brightness.

subpixels is presented. Let us look again at the horizontal edge, mentioned above. With the new approach, we get a coverage of one subpixel, when the line is 1/16 of the pixel width under the upper pixel edge (in fact we get one subpixel between a coverage of 1/32 and 3/32 of the pixel area). If the line has reached 2/16, we get a coverage of 2 subpixels instead of 0 or 4 with the old method.

Now, the only problem that remains to be solved is to find the right locations for those subpixels. A simple observation can help us. If we look at an edge of a certain slope that moves slowly over a pixel, we see that the subpixels are touched in a certain order. We would get the same sequence, if we observed the order, in which the subpixel centers are covered, or the order in which the subpixels are covered totally (e.g. Fig. 4 c) or d)). Normally it starts with a subpixel at one corner. The next in the row will be the neighbors of the first one and so on until the opposite corner is reached. Now we can show, that there is only a certain number of different orders that are possible. In Fig. 4 we see, that all edges that have a slope between that of $E_1$ and $E_2$ cover the subpixels in the same order. The total number of possible sequences is only 32 for a subpixel mask of $4 \times 4$ subpixels. Now we can assign one of these sequences to each slope. At the borders, where two sequences would be possible, we choose one and make sure that an edge of the opposite orientation gets the opposite sequence. Such we can ensure that two adjacent objects that cover the whole pixel cause all subpixels to be set in any case. In Fig. 4 a) the numbering scheme for the subpixels is shown. Fig. 4 b) shows the different sequences that are possible for edges between $0^0$ and $45^0$. As examples,

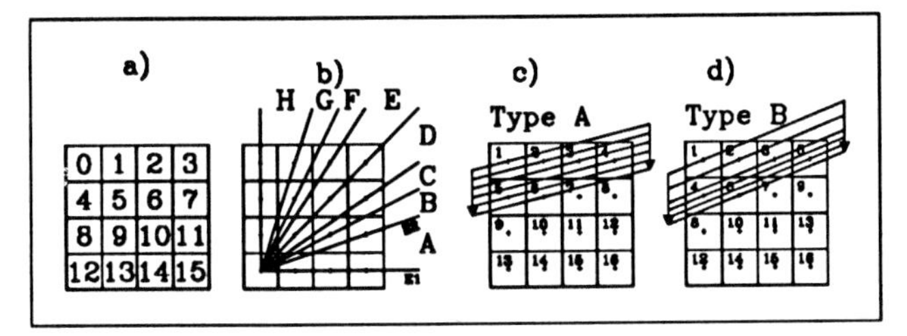


Figure 4: Numbering scheme and possible sequences for subpixel coverage. (See Section 3 for explanation)

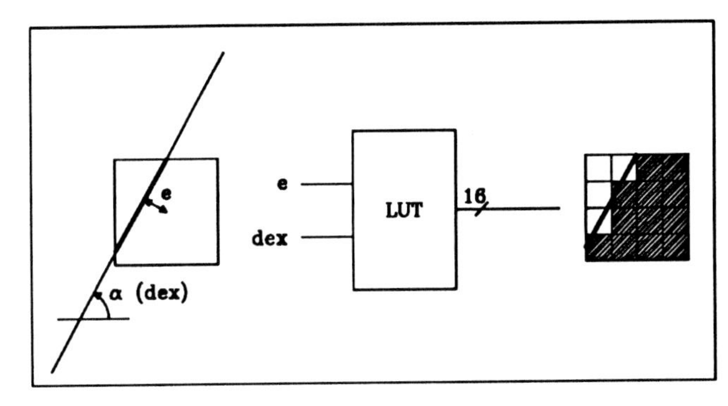


Figure 5: Lookup table for the subpixel mask.

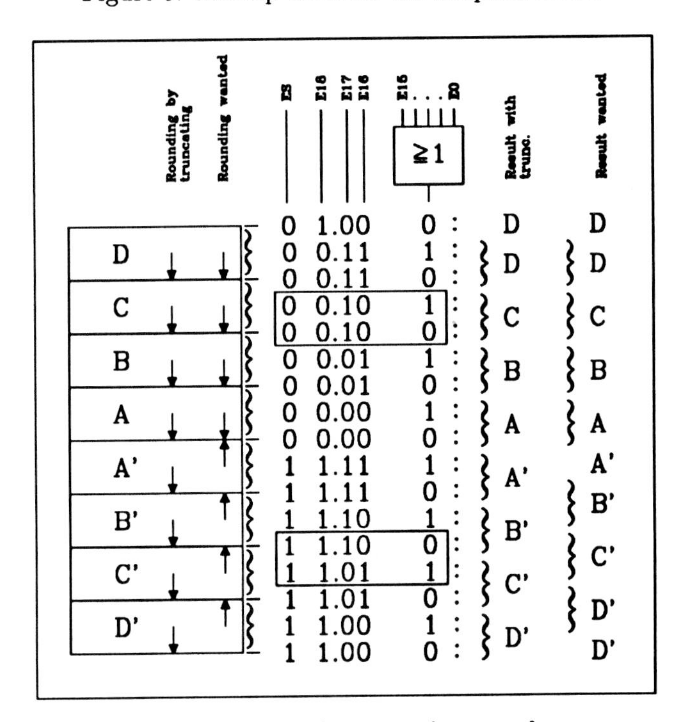


Figure 6: Problems with truncating numbers represented in the two's complement.

lines of type A and B are drawn in Fig. 4 c) and d) resp. The figures show how the subpixel centers are touched by the edges in different sequences.

## 4 Exact Area Subpixel Algorithm for $n \times n$ subpixels

In the following, we have to make use of an arbitrary representation of the polygons. The representation with edge functions, chosen for this paper is explained in Appendix A. For the $n \times n$ subpixel mask, the approach is the same as in the $4 \times 4$ case. First we calculate the number of subpixels we want to set ($n_{os}$) with the general formula[2]:

$$n_{os} = \begin{cases} floor\,(A * n^2 + 0.5) & : \quad 0 \leq slope < 180^\circ \\ ceil\,(A * n^2 - 0.5) & : \quad 180^\circ \leq slope \end{cases}$$

$A$ denotes the area of the pixel that is covered by the half plane defined by the polygon edge. (The two cases have to be distinguished in order to ensure that two adjacent polygons always complement each other, i.e. that we don't get a total coverage of more than $n \times n$ subpixels.)

The next step is a sort of the subpixels $s_1 \ldots s_{n \times n}$. They are sorted in a way that the most covered one is the first, the least covered one the last in the list (falling edge function). If there exist groups of subpixels with equal coverage (equal edge function), the subpixels of these groups are sorted using a function that results from the original edge function through a rotation by $+90^\circ$.

Now we take the first $n_{os}$ subpixels from the list and set them to 1, all others to 0.

In a final step, the resulting subpixel masks for all edges of the (convex) polygon are ANDed together.

## 5 Hardware Implementation

Several problems had to be solved in order to implement the coverage unit in hardware. The function of the unit is simple. We can think of it as a single lookup table like the one shown in Fig. 5. Input parameters are the distance or error term $e$ and the x-increment of the edge function $de_x$, which serves as a measure for the slope of the edge . In addition to that we need only the sign of the y-increment $de_y$.

The first question was the required precision of the input parameters. Under the condition that the result of the quantization error has to be smaller than one subpixel we get required resolutions for the distance or error term $e$ of 5 bits and for the slope measure $de_x$ of 4 bits. The condition for the slope measure with regard to the sequence leads to the same resolution of 5 bits for $de_x$. In order to cover all directions, the signs of $de_x$ and $de_y$ have to be considered also. As a result, we get a total of 11 input bits which correspond to a lookup table size of 2k $\times$ 16 bits.

But if we look into the details, we still have to increase the size. The reason for this is that our input

[2] *floor(x)* means the largest integer not greater than $x$, *ceil(x)* means the smallest integer not less than $x$.

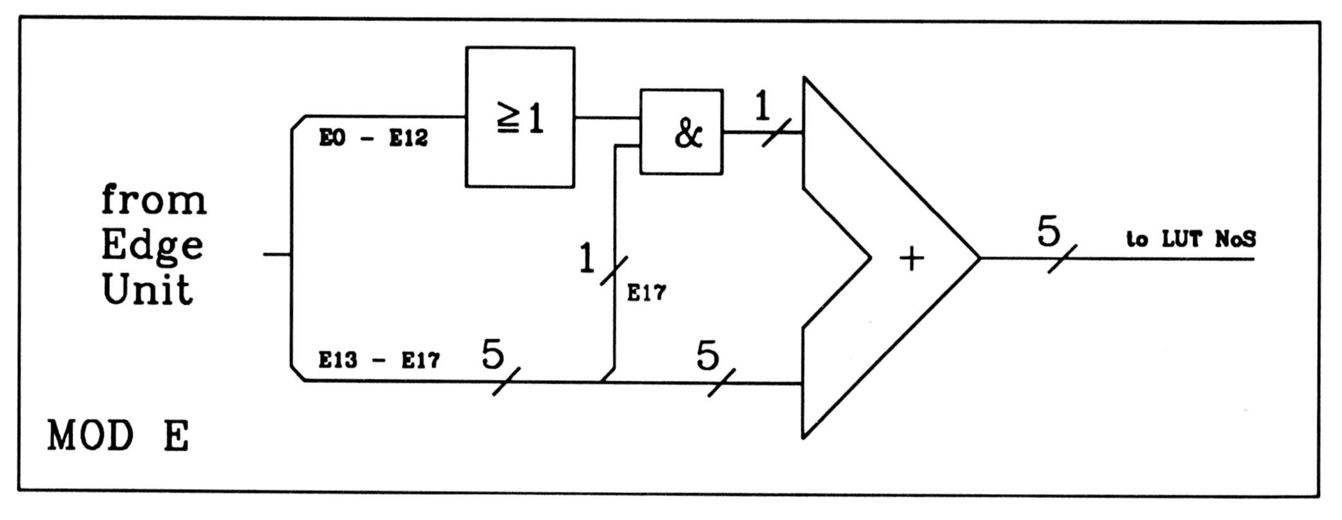


Figure 7: Modification unit for distance e.

parameters are coded in the two's complement form, meaning, that if we only truncate the numbers to the required bit count, we always round down to the next smaller number (Fig. 6; the bits are numbered E0 (LSB) to E18 (MSB), ES is the sign bit). However, we want the two adjacent polygons to complement each other exactly. This means that the sum of subpixels for a given error term and slope adds up to 16 subpixels, if the error terms add up to 0 ($e_1 = -e_2$). But with the property of the two's complement, that truncation always rounds down, this cannot be fulfilled. An example can clarify this. If we truncate as shown in Fig. 6, we want to obtain the same result for an input of 0/0.100 and 0/0.101. Now consider the negative value for both of these numbers: for 0/0.100 we get 1/1.100, for 0/0.101 1/1.011. If we truncate these negative numbers, we do not get the same result anymore: 1/1.10 and 1/1.01 are not equal. This simple example shows that one more input bit for the lookup table is required for each input parameter. This bit has to indicate whether a value was changed by truncation or if we already had a flat number. This bit can be generated by ORing all truncated (lower) bits together. A single stage lookup table would thus have a size of 8k by 16 bits.

## 5.1 Multi Stage Implementation

The size of the lookup table can be reduced by a factor of more than 8, if it is implemented in several stages. The easiest approach, then, is to replicate the logical structure of the algorithm into the hardware structure. Thus the unit consists of three subunits, which perform the following functions: 1. Determination of the subpixel count, 2. Determination of the angle index (sequence), 3. Determination of the final subpixel mask. A more explicit examination leads to a three stage design (Fig. 8). In the first stage, the input data coming from the three units that calculate the edge functions (EU1 – EU3) is modified in order to eliminate the problems with the two's complement. The blocks are labelled MOD E and MOD DEX. The stage MOD E is used to modify the error term $e$, in the stage MOD DEX the slope parameter including the sign bits is modified. The need to modify the sign bits comes out of similar observations to those about the two's complement. This modification is performed with a PLA that is also used to determine one bit of the angle index. A schematic of the unit MOD E (Fig. 7) shows how the modification is performed, however the adder was replaced by a PLA with the same function in the final design. The second stage consists of the lookup table for the subpixel count and the lookup table for the remaining two bits of the angle index. In the third stage, those two parameters are used to lookup the final subpixel mask. Three special cases are also handled in this stage:

1. The edge unit is disabled – all 16 subpixel bits are set to 1 (Line DE).

2. The error term is greater or equal to 0.5 – all 16 subpixel bits are set to 1 (Line E_GE_0P5).

3. The error term is smaller than -0.5 – all 16 subpixel bits are set to 0 (Line E_LT_M0P5).

The whole coverage unit consists of three of the described multi-stage lookup tables (one for each edge).The final subpixel mask is the result of ANDing together on a bit-by-bit basis the three outputs for each edge. Fig. 9 shows the result for the slim line and the sharp triangle of Fig. 3. In Figures 10 – 12, simulation results for the exact area subpixel algorithm compared with supersampling and no antialiasing at all are shown.

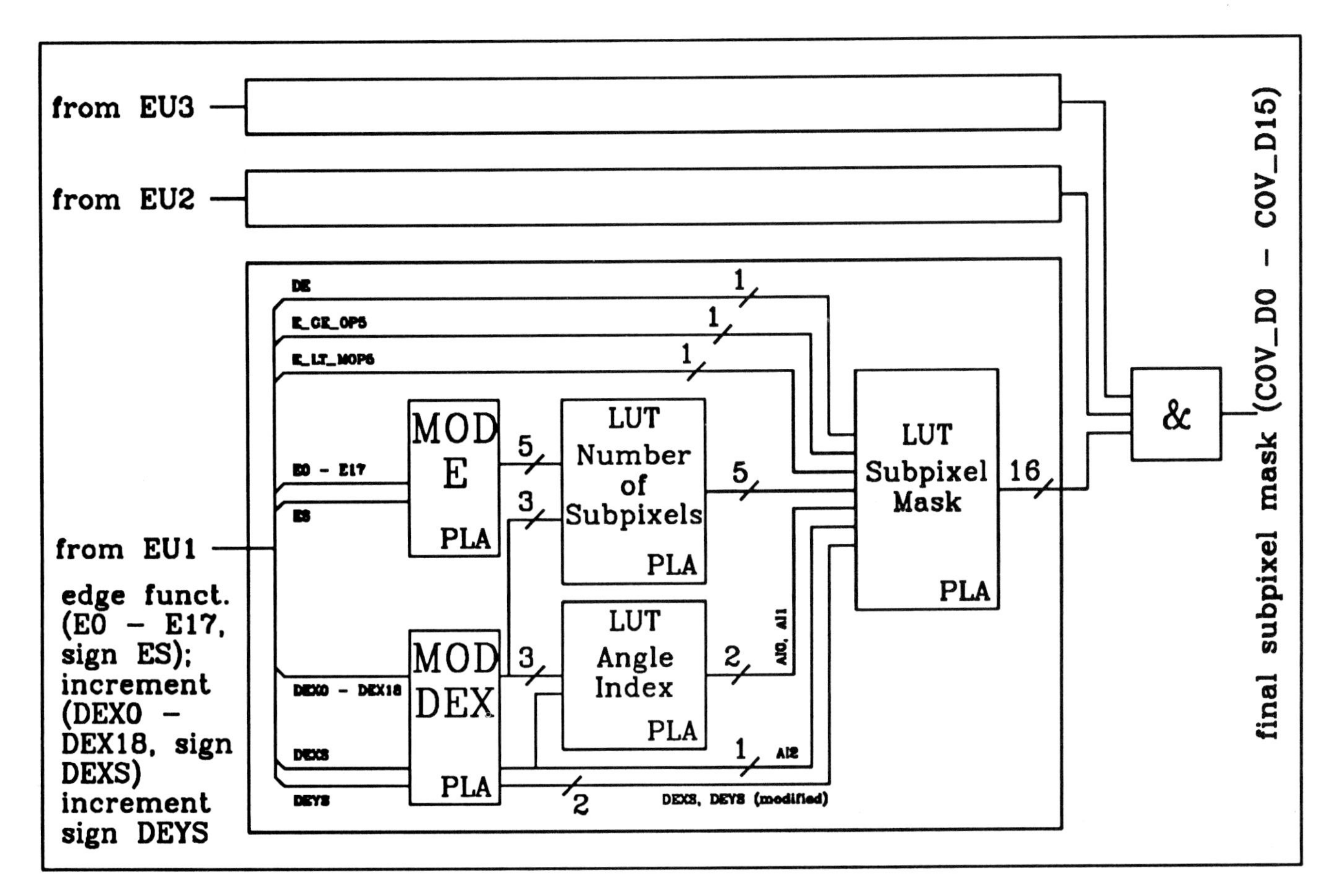


Figure 8: Coverage Unit.

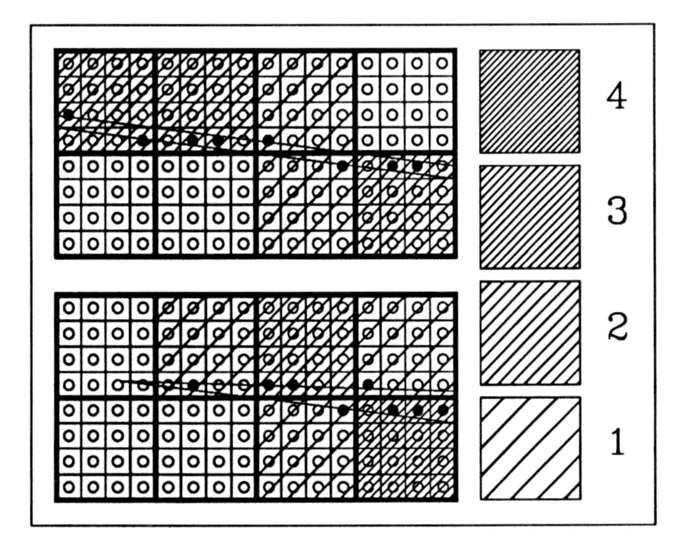


Figure 9: Thin line and sharp triangle treated correctly. The density of the hatching indicates the final pixel brightness.

# 6 Conclusion

An algorithm for antialiasing and its realization in hardware has been presented that obtains better results than other methods with comparable simplicity, e.g. regular supersampling (see Figures 10 – 12). Existing systems that already use subpixel mask lookup, can be modified to apply this algorithm simply by changing the contents of the lookup tables at nearly no costs.

# 7 Acknowledgement

I thank Paul Munsch of Caption for the idea with the "square distance" representation. Claudia Romanova provided me with *a lot of* useful information and literature on the topic of antialiasing. I also appreciate the guidance of Wolfgang Straßer and the cooperation with my colleagues at the Graphics Department of the University of Tübingen.

# A Appendix

## A.1 Representation of polygon edges

Polygons can be represented by edge functions, that are negative on one, and positive on the other side of the

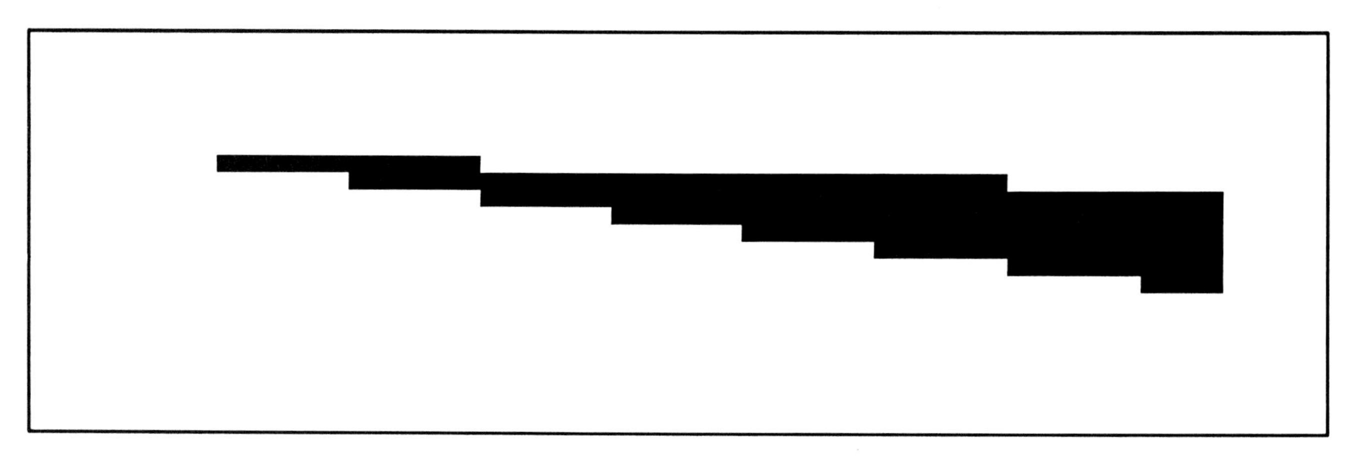

Figure 10: Sharp triangle of Figures. 9 and 3 without antialiasing.

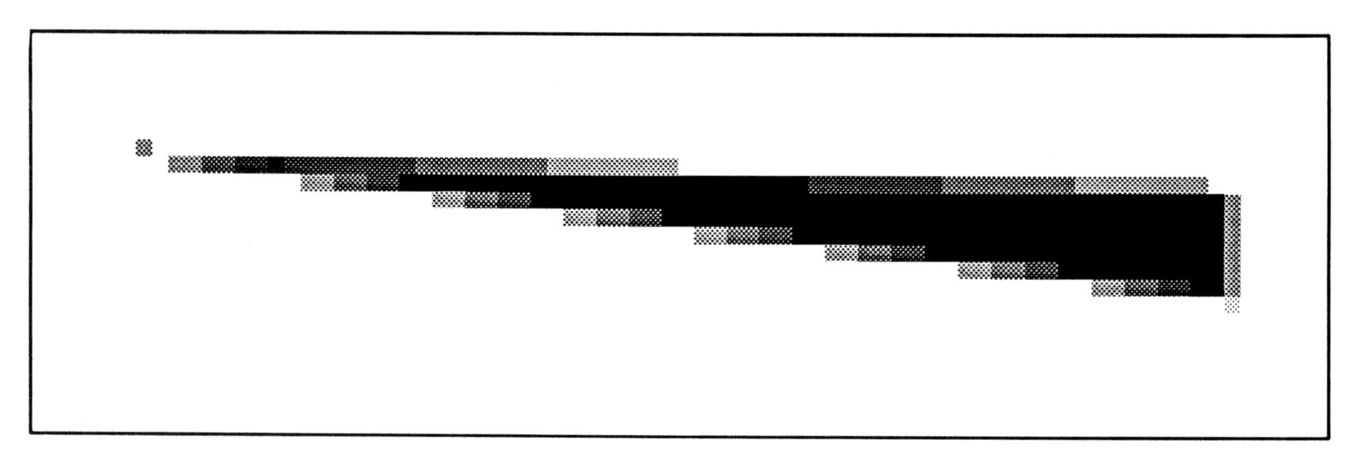

Figure 11: Sharp triangle of Figures. 9 and 3. Problems with conventional supersampling.

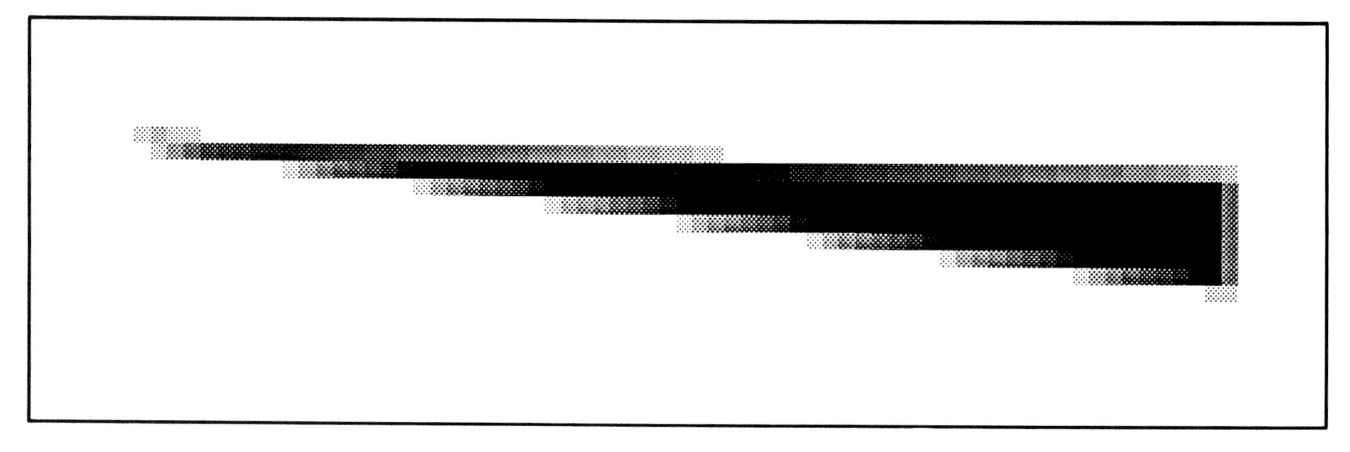

Figure 12: Sharp triangle of Figures. 9 and 3. Correct treatment with Exact Area Subpixel Algorithm.

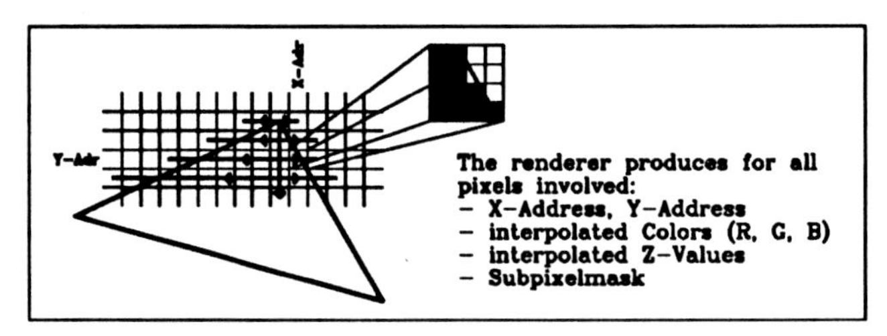


Figure 13: Rendering machine, functionality.

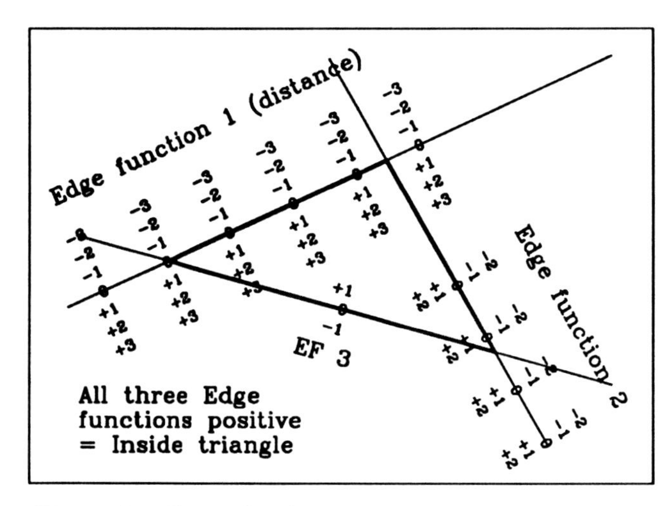


Figure 14: Example of Edge Functions for Rendering.

edge. This representation is used in rendering hardware like PROOF [12], Pixel Planes [8] or in software algorithms like the one described by Pineda [11]. In Fig. 13, the rendering with the Pineda algorithm is illustrated and the desired results of the rendering process are shown.

The process of rendering consists of deciding wether or not pixels belong to a given polygon. For a rendering algorithms like the above mentioned, we need an edge function that behaves like the ones shown in Fig. 14. It is positive on one side and negative on the other side of the edge. With three units that can calculate such edge functions, we can now decide whether a certain point lies inside the triangle or outside. If all three edge functions are positive, the point is inside, otherwise it is outside.

### A.1.1 How can we get such a function?

The easiest way is to choose a linear function

$$E(x,y) = (x - X)de_x + (y - Y)de_y$$

with the condition:

$$de_x \Delta X + de_y \Delta Y = 0$$

If we use

$$de_x = \Delta Y$$

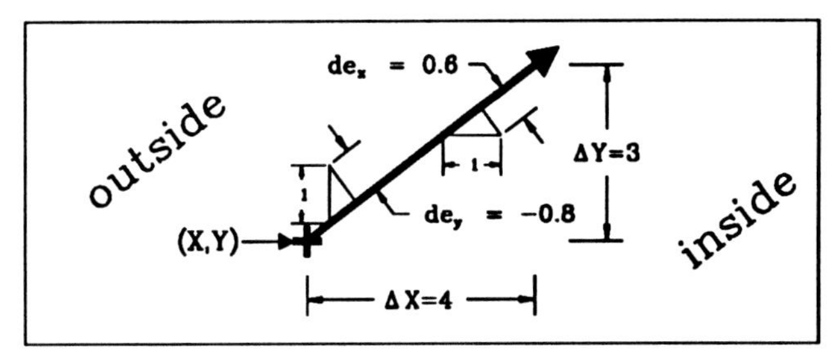


Figure 15: X and Y Increments of the Edge Function.

as x increment and

$$de_y = -\Delta X$$

as increment in y direction, we get the formula suggested by Pineda with the advantage that the calculation is very simple. Now the edge units can be built of only adders, without multipliers, as we only have to add the increments proceeding from one pixel to its neighbor.

We can scale the above formula by an arbitrary factor. So if we need the euclidean distance, we can normalize the increments $de_x$ and $de_y$ by dividing the values by the euclidean length of the vector ($L_2$ norm). We then get the following increments:

$$de_x = \frac{\Delta Y}{\sqrt{\Delta X^2 + \Delta Y^2}}$$

and

$$de_y = -\frac{\Delta X}{\sqrt{\Delta X^2 + \Delta Y^2}}$$

and we can still use the same edge units, because the distance is a linear function in x and y (see example edge in Fig. 15).

### A.1.2 Why do we need this distance?

Until now, we used only the sign of the edge function for the decision if we are in or out. So the value of the distance is of no interest. But if we want to calculate subpixel information for later antialiasing (which is in fact the scope of this paper), we need exact data about the edge. In this case, the normalization is essential [7]. The distance, together with the slope information is enough to look up the subpixel mask, i.e. the information, which part of the pixel is covered (see Fig. 13). One little detail has to be noticed. We now have to consider not only pixels with their center inside the polygon (positive edge function), but also pixels that are covered less than half (edge function between 0 and –0.something). We cannot give a fixed distance, because it is different for edges with different slopes ($1/\sqrt{2}$ for edges with a slope of 45°, 1/2 for vertical or horizontal edges). So if we take all pixels not more than $1/\sqrt{2}$ away from the edge into consideration, we will get too

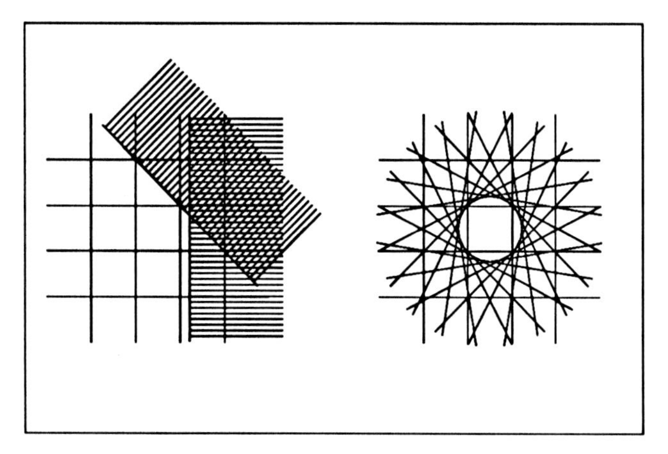

Figure 16: "Circular" Distance.

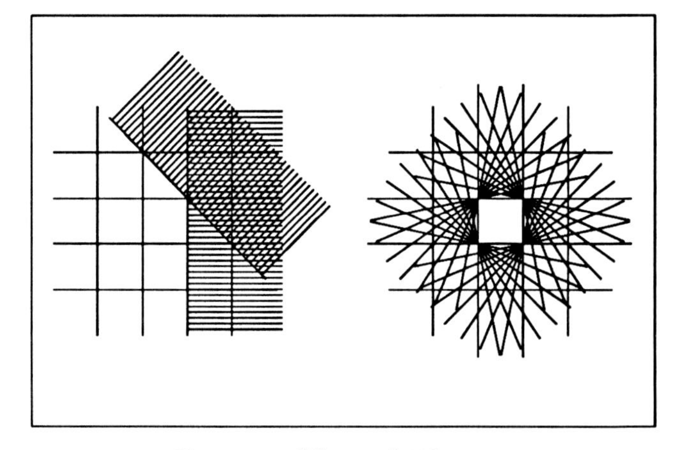

Figure 17: "Square" Distance.

many pixels, but that is better than losing pixels that we wanted to get. Fig. 16 shows, that all edges that have a given distance from the pixel center form a circle.

Now there is a formula for the increments that solves several problems at one time[3]. If we look at the most demanding part of the increment calculation above, we see the square root in that formula. Now the simplest solution is to omit the root and take the sum of the absolute values of $\Delta X$ and $\Delta Y$ instead. Speaking in mathematical terms, we divide by the $L_1$ norm or Manhattan distance instead of the $L_2$norm. The new increments are:

$$de_x = \frac{\Delta Y}{|\Delta X| + |\Delta Y|}$$

and

$$de_y = -\frac{\Delta X}{|\Delta X| + |\Delta Y|}$$

The result is a change in the distance function. It is not independent of the angle anymore, which was the case for the euclidean distance. But if we do not want to do a more complex filtering (like e.g. a convolution with sinc(dist)), than we need something like a rectangular box filter. A circular filter never would result in a homogeneous coverage of the screen. So this formula which is easier to calculate is not an approximation for something else, we originally wanted to get, it gives in fact a more desired result. Fig. 17 shows, that all edges that have a given distance from the pixel center form a square.

For the calculation of the subpixel mask, the "square" distance is as useful as the euclidean distance, because all information about the edge is contained in the distance and the increments (for the slope of the edge).

[3]I got this formula from Paul Munsch, who developed several distance formulas, to be used as an approximation for the euclidean distance, among them an "octagonal distance" and the "square distance", described here.



# References


[1] Abram, G., Westover, L., and Whitted, T. Efficient alias-free rendering using bit-masks and look-up tables. *Computer Graphics 19*, 3 (July 1985), 53–59.

[2] Blinn, J. F. What we need around here is more aliasing. *IEEE Computer Graphics & Applications* (Jan. 1989), 75–79.

[3] Carpenter, L. The a-buffer, an antialiased hidden surface method. *Computer Graphics 18*, 3 (July 1984), 103–108.

[4] Cook, R. L. Stochastic sampling in computer graphics. *ACM Transactions on Graphics 5*, 1 (January 1986), 51–72.

[5] Dippé, M. A. Z., and Wold, E. H. Antialiasing through stochastic sampling. *Computer Graphics 19*, 3 (July 1985), 69–78.

[6] Fiume, E., Fournier, A., and Rudolph, L. A parallel scan conversion algorithm with antialiasing for a general-purpose ultracomputer. *Computer Graphics 17*, 3 (July 1983), 141–150.

[7] Fuchs, H., Goldfeather, J., Hultquist, J. P., Spach, S., Austin, J. D., Brooks, F. P., Eyles, J. G., and Poulton, J. Fast spheres, shadows, textures, transparencies, and image enhancements in pixel-planes. *Computer Graphics 19*, 3 (July 1985), 111–120.

[8] Fuchs, H., Poulton, J., Eyles, J., Greer, T., Goldfeather, J., Ellsworth, D., Molnar, S., Turk, G., Tebbs, B., and Israel, L. Pixel-planes 5: A heterogeneous multiprocessor graphics system using processor-enhanced memories. *Computer Graphics 23*, 3 (July 1989), 79–88.

[9] HOFFERT, E. M., AND BISHOP, G. Exact and efficient area sampling techniques for spatial antialiasing. Technical Memorandum, AT & T Bell Laboratories, December 1985.

[10] MUNSCH, P. Private communication. On the occasion of a meeting in Rennes, France, Dec. 1989.

[11] PINEDA, J. A parallel algorithm for polygon rasterization. *Computer Graphics 22*, 4 (Aug. 1988), 17–20.

[12] SCHNEIDER, B.-O. *Eine objektorientierte Architektur für Hochleistungs-Display-Prozessoren.* PhD thesis, Eberhard-Karls-Universität Tübingen, 1990.

# An Efficient Antialiasing Technique

Xiaolin Wu
Department of Computer Science
University of Western Ontario
London, Ontario, Canada N6A 5B7

**Abstract**– An intuitive concept of antialiasing is developed into very efficient antialiased line and circle generators that require even less amount of integer arithmetic than Bresenham's line and circle algorithms. Unlike its predecessors, the new antialiasing technique is derived in spatial domain (raster plane) under a subjectively meaningful error measure to preserve the dynamics of curve and object boundaries. A formal analysis of the new antialiasing technique in frequency domain is also conducted. It is shown that our antialiasing technique computes the same antialiased images as Fujimoto-Iwata's algorithm but at a fraction of the latter's computational cost. The simplicities of the new antialiased line and circle generators also mean their easy hardware implementations.

CR Category: I.3.3 [**Computer Graphics**]: Picture/Image Generation - *display algorithms*.

**Key Words**: Antialiasing, curve digitization, digital geometry, convolution.

## 1 Introduction

Curve-rendering on raster devices, a fundamental operation in computer graphics, is essentially a process of quantizing (digitizing) continuous two-dimensional visual signals at the sampling rate of device resolution. This sampling rate is usually significantly lower than twice the maximum frequency of object boundaries and curve edges, [1] resulting in loss of information as explained by the Shannon sampling theorem. This information loss is the reason for the existence of visually unpleasant "aliasing" (staircasing effect) on digitized object boundaries and curves. There are two ways to attack the problem: increasing the sampling rate and removing high frequency components of the image. The first approach calls for increasing the resolution of the raster device. But the size of frame buffer and consequently the rendering costs increase quadratically in the resolution. Even at a resolution of 1024 × 1024, objectionable staircasing effects still exist. High-resolution alone is not an economic solution to the problem. The second approach of filtering high frequency components of the image was adopted by many researchers [1, 4, 5, 6, 7, 8] to combat aliasing. These techniques utilize grayscales to increase the effective spatial resolution. The disadvantages of the second approach are high computational cost involved in low-pass filtering operations, and fuzzy object edges.

Proposed in this paper is a new concept of antialiasing that leads to efficient smooth curve rendering algorithms. Our antialiasing research is done in both spatial and frequency domains. The new algorithms achieve exactly the same antialiasing effects as Fujimoto-Iwata's algorithm for line segments but at a fraction of the latter's cost. A new antialiased line generator is designed for smooth line generation that requires only half as much integer arithmetic as Bresenham's line algorithm [2]. And the antialiased line generation can be easily implemented by hardware. Smooth circles can also be generated by the new technique

[1] For physical displays a curve should be modeled as a narrow 2-dimensional image rather than a 1-dimensional mathematical entity of no area.



©1991 ACM-0-89791-436-8/91/007/0143 $00.75

at a lower cost than Bresenham's circle algorithm [3]. The paper is organized as follows. In the next section a dynamic error measure for the quality of digitized curves is introduced, and the correspondence between the measure and the image quality is demonstrated. Then based on this error measure the new antialiasing concept is introduced in section 3. The rationale for the new antialiasing algorithm is also established using convolution theorem, hence it is in principle congruent to the current antialiasing algorithms. In section 4 we prove the equivalence between our algorithm and Fujimoto-Iwata's algorithm. In sections 5 and 6 the high efficiency of the new antialiasing technique is demonstrated by the development of fast antialiased line and circle generators. Section 7 deals with the generalization of the new antialiasing technique to general curves and to antialiased object boundaries blent in colorful background.

## 2 Dynamic Error in Curve Digitization

Previously image aliasing was investigated in the frequency domain. In this section we study image aliasing in the spatial domain (raster plane). Some of our previous results in digital geometry [10, 12] are used to study the quality of digitized curves. Let $y = f(x)$ be a differentiable curve to be digitized in the raster plane, and partition the curve into segments where either $0 \leq |f'(x)| \leq 1$ or $1 < |f'(x)| < \infty$, called x-dominant and y-dominant segments, respectively. Now consider an x-dominant curve segment without loss of generality (the discussion on $y$-dominant curve segments is the same through symmetry). Then the digitization of this curve segment is defined to be an ordered point set $\{(i, Y_i) : 1 \leq i \leq N\}$. This definition means that the curve segment is sampled in unit raster steps along the x axis, and the sample value $f(i)$ is quantized to $Y_i$. Due to the finite precision of the raster plane $Y_i$ must be an integer, resulting in the commonly used quantization scheme

$$Y_i = \left\lfloor f(i) + \frac{1}{2} \right\rfloor \tag{1}$$

to minimize the $y$ distance between the sampled value $f(i)$ and its image point in the raster plane. But how meaningful in terms of human perception is this simple criterion Eq(1)? Let us consider the geometry of Fig.1 where the three pixels indicated by solid dots are chosen

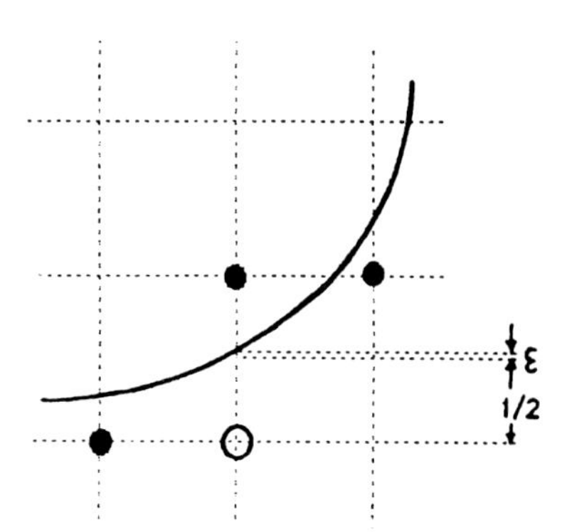


Figure 1: Dynamic error in curve digitization.

by Eq(1) as the discrete image of the continuous curve. If, however, the pixel labeled by o replaces the one just above it, then the so-called dynamic error defined by

$$E_{i,j} = f(j) - f(i) - [Y_j - Y_i] \tag{2}$$

is minimized. The above dynamic error relates to the first-order difference and hence characterizes the digitization error in curve dynamics. Visually, the new pixel configuration obtained by pulling the pixel in the middle column down by one raster unit presents a better approximation to the original curve. This improvement results because the pixel pattern of the solid dots distorts the dynamic context of the original curve segment. Namely, the convex curve $f(x)$ is mapped to a concave pixel pattern. By moving the middle pixel down by a raster unit, the convexity is preserved, resulting in a more pleasant rendering. Human eyes are more sensitive to the dynamic context of a curve than to its absolute spatial position. It is difficult for viewers to detect a translation of an object if the amount of shift is relatively small compared with the size of background, but easy to catch a slight distortion of the dynamic context of the object as a disturbing image alias. This observation suggests that the error measure Eq(2) is subjectively more meaningful than Eq(1), and antialiasing should aim for minimizing the loss of dynamic information of original curves due to digitization. Given an x-dominant curve segment $f(x)$ and its digitization $\{(i, Y_i) : 1 \leq i \leq N\}$, an $N \times N$ matrix of dynamic errors $\{E_{i,j}\}$, $1 \leq i, j \leq N$, is defined (see [12] for more detailed discussions on the dynamic error matrix $\mathbf{E}$). Our goal is to minimize $\| \mathbf{E} \|$, the norm of the error matrix. For binary raster displays minimizing $\| \mathbf{E} \|$ is a very difficult optimization problem [12]. Fortunately, for grayscale devices we can have a simple solution to the problem.

# 3 Two-Point Anti-Aliasing Scheme

The dynamic error is caused by rounding $f(i)$ to an integer $Y_i$. The dynamic error matrix $\mathbf{E}$ becames a zero matrix, i.e., $\| \mathbf{E} \| = 0$, if $Y_i$ were chosen to be $f(i)$. We would like to have an addressable pixel centered at the coordinates $(i, f(i))$. Let $I[i,j]$ be the intensity of the pixel $(i,j)$ and $I_0$ be the intended intensity for the curve. Then the imaginary pixel $(i, f(i))$ may be visually simulated by setting

$$\begin{cases} I[i, \lfloor f(i) \rfloor] = I_0(\lceil f(i) \rceil - f(i)) \\ I[i, \lceil f(i) \rceil] = I_0(f(i) - \lfloor f(i) \rfloor) \end{cases} \quad (3)$$

If we consider the pixel $(i,j)$ as a unit square centered at $(i,j)$ containing light energy $I[i,j]$, then point $\mathbf{p}_\mu = (i, f(i))$ is the center of gravity of the two lit points $\mathbf{p}_0 = (i, \lfloor f(i) \rfloor)$ and $\mathbf{p}_1 = (i, \lceil f(i) \rceil)$, because

$$I_0 \mathbf{p}_\mu = I[i, \lfloor f(i) \rfloor] \mathbf{p}_0 + I[i, \lceil f(i) \rceil] \mathbf{p}_1. \quad (4)$$

Therefore, the overall effect of Eq(3) is a lit area of energy $I_0$ focused at the real point $\mathbf{p}_\mu = (i, f(i))$ which is a perceived pixel exactly on the original curve $f(x)$. The ordered set $\{(i, f(i)) : 1 \le i \le N\}$ of those perceived pixels renders a perceived curve. Clearly the dynamic error $\| \mathbf{E} \|$ for this perceived curve is zero, eliminating the loss of dynamic information. The practical significance of Eq(3) is its simplicity which leads very fast anti-aliasing algorithms as we will see later. Eq(3) is a two-point antialiasing scheme. We plot all pixels in the two-pixel wide band that bounds the true curve $y = f(x)$ with their intensities inversely proportional to the distances between these pixels to the curve. The closer is a pixel to the line, the brighter it is, then the overall visual effect of this band will be the illumination area of the lit curve at its real position after our eyes integrate the contributions of all pixels in the band.

In addition to being intuitively appealing the antialiasing scheme Eq(3) can also relates to removing high frequency components of sharp intensity jumps at the image edges. In order to apply a filter to the image we no longer treat $y = f(x)$ as a mathematical curve of no width; instead we model the curve by a two-dimensional grayscale signal $g(x,y)$ with interior intensity $I_0$ and exterior intensity 0. The curve $y = f(x)$ is the center line of the two-dimensional signal $g(x,y)$. The image intensity $I(i,j)$ after applying a low-pass filter to $g(x,y)$ is given by

$$I[i,j] = \int\int \delta(u,v) g(i-u, j-v) du dv. \quad (5)$$

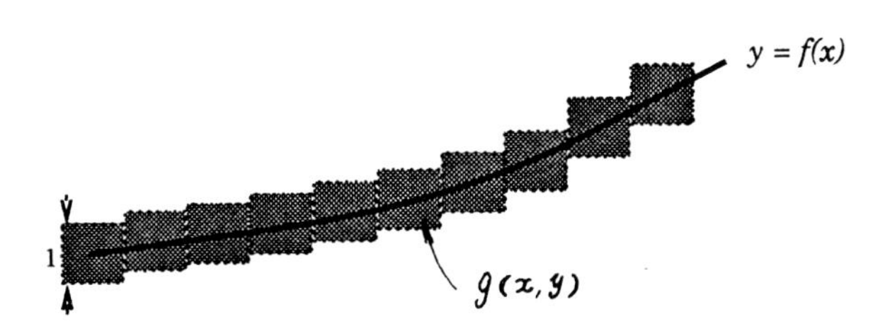


Figure 2: The two-dimensional signal $g(x,y)$ modeling the physical image of the curve $y = f(x)$ before filtering.

The convolution kernel $\delta(u,v)$ is determined by the intensity density of a pixel in its neighborhood. It is easy to verify that if we choose the box filter

$$\delta(u,v) = \begin{cases} 1 & |u| \le \frac{1}{2}, |v| \le \frac{1}{2} \\ 0 & \text{otherwise} \end{cases} \quad (6)$$

and model the curve $y = f(x)$ in raster plane by the two-dimensional signal

$$g(x,y) = \begin{cases} I_0 & |y - f(\lfloor x + \frac{1}{2} \rfloor)| \le \frac{1}{2} \\ 0 & \text{otherwise} \end{cases} \quad (7)$$

then the solution of the convolution Eq(5) is the simple expression of Eq(3). The signal $g(x,y)$ is a chain of two-dimensional unit square impulses as depicted by Fig. 2. The above analysis reveals that the two-point anti-aliasing scheme Eq(3) is a two-step process. First the image of the curve $y = f(x)$ is modeled by the two dimensional impulse signal signal $g(x,y)$ of Eq(7), then the impulse signal is put through the box filters $\delta(u,v)$ centered at individual pixels. The additive responses of these atomic filters yields the antialiased digital curve.

Admittedly the above anti-aliasing model is far from ideal. The box filter does not reflect the fact that the intensity density of a pixel has Gaussian-like rather than uniform shape. Moreover, the curve $y = f(x)$ is modeled by a stripe image $g(x,y)$ whose edge is not smooth. But aliasing is primarily caused by sharp intensity changes (high frequency components at the intensity transition from $g(x,y) = 0$ to $g(x,y) = I_0$). The low-pass filtering aims at smoothing the steep intensity jump not at smoothing the geometric shape of the input signal. The tendency of $g(x,y)$ to preserve the dynamic information of $y = f(x)$ is far more important than its geometric smoothness in our principle of antialiasing.

The staircase appearance of the $g(x, y)$ will be eventually subdued since the low-pass filter will blur the input image $g(x, y)$ anyway.

For comparison Fig.3 gives three groups of lines with various orientations done by Bresenham's, Gupta-Sproull's and the two-point antialiasing scheme Eq(3). Gupta-Sproull's antialiased line algorithm [7], generally regarded as a better performed one, uses a cone-shaped low-pass filter as an approximation of Gaussian filter to suppress the jaggies. The algorithm understandably is quite computationally demanding. The photos show that the line images produced by the new technique are not inferior in quality to those produced by Gupta-Sproull's algorithm in quality. Note that Gupta-Sproull's algorithm is a three-point antialiasing scheme in the sense that in each column three pixels are usually set to different intensities. Consequently, the lines generated by this algorithm look fuzzier than those done by the two-point scheme.

Our real motive for developing the model Eq(7) is to convert the convolution integration of Eq(5) to the simple intensity interpolation between two adjacent pixels in Eq(3), gaining computational efficiency of antialiasing as we will see in sections 5 and 6.

## 4 Equivalence to Fujimoto-Iwata's Algorithm

Interestingly, we can prove the equivalence between the simple formula Eq(3) and the seemingly more complicated antialiasing operation by Fujimoto and Iwata [6]. Indeed, after some intricate derivation, Fujimoto and Iwata arrived at

$$\begin{aligned} I[i, \lfloor f(i) \rfloor] &= I(d - 2d_1)/d \\ I[i, \lceil f(i) \rceil] &= I(d - 2d_2)/d, \end{aligned} \qquad (8)$$

where, as marked in Fig. 4, $d = 2\cos\alpha$, $d_1$ and $d_2$ are the distances from the pixels $(i, \lfloor f(i) \rfloor)$ and $(i, \lceil f(i) \rceil)$ to the true line. Eq(8) is the formula for antialiased lines using the smallest Fourier window. It is apparent from the figure that

$$\begin{aligned} d_1 &= (f(i) - \lfloor f(i) \rfloor)\cos\alpha \\ d_2 &= (\lceil f(i) \rceil - f(i))\cos\alpha. \end{aligned} \qquad (9)$$

Plugging $d_1$ and $d_2$ into Eq(8) we can simplify Eq(8) to Eq(3).

The above simplification gives Fujimoto-Iwata's antialiasing algorithm a more intuitive interpretation of

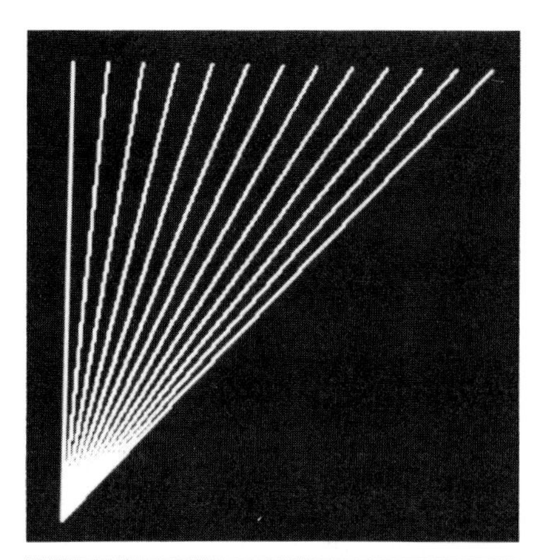

Figure 3: Lines generated by Bresenham's (above), Gupta-Sproull's (middle) and the two-point antialiasing (bottom) algorithms.

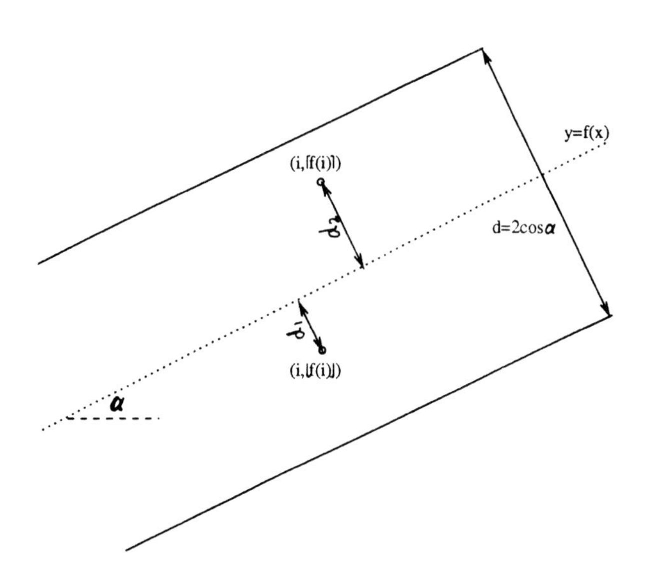


Figure 4: The geometry of Fujimoto-Iwata's antialiasing algorithm.

Eq(3), another analytical basis formed by Eqs(5)-(7), and more importantly, a simpler and more efficient implementation.

# 5 Fast Anti-Aliased Line Generator

In this section we convert the simple antialiasing scheme Eq(3) to a fast antialiased line generator. Without loss of generality only lines in the first octant are considered. Other cases follow trivially through symmetry. Let $(x0, y0)$, $(x1, y1)$, $x2 > x1$, $y2 > y1$, be the two points in the raster plane defining a line. We translate the point $(x0, y0)$ to the origin, so the equation of the line becomes $y = kx$, $0 \leq k = \frac{y1-y0}{x1-x0} \leq 1$. Then Eq(3) can be rewritten for $f(x) = kx$ as

$$\begin{aligned} I(x, \lceil kx \rceil) &= I_0(kx - \lfloor kx \rfloor) \\ I(x, \lfloor kx \rfloor) &= I_0 - I(x, \lceil kx \rceil). \end{aligned} \tag{10}$$

where $(x, \lfloor kx \rfloor)$ and $(x, \lceil kx \rceil)$ are the two adjacent pixels in the $x$ column that are immediately below and above the true line. Clearly, the total intensity in a column is the constant $I$, so the even brightness of the band can be achieved.

To implement the antialiasing scheme Eq(10), we need to determine for a given $x$ the pixel positions $(x, \lfloor kx \rfloor)$ and $(x, \lceil kx \rceil)$ (they coincide if $kx$ is an integer) and their intensities $I(x, \lfloor kx \rfloor)$ and $I(x, \lceil kx \rceil)$. These four values can be determined by an elegant incremental algorithm operating on a single integer $D$ represented by a machine word of $n$ bits. The integer increment involved is $d = \lfloor k2^n + 0.5 \rfloor$. As the initialization, we set $D = 0$, $I(x0, y0) = I$. Then we march $x$ from $x0$ to $x1$ and increment $D$ by $d$ at unit step. The operation $D \leftarrow D + d$ is a module $2^n$ addition with the overflow recorded. Whenever $D$ overflows the two-point high pixel band pixel moves diagonally; otherwise it moves horizontally. This is essentially a classical DDA method. The only difference is in that both the $x$ and $y$ increments, namely, $\Delta x = 1$ and $\Delta y = d$, are integer rather than real values. For the following analysis we may consider $D$ as a fixed point number with the decimal point before its most significant bit, or conceptually perceive the proposed integer arithmetic as fixed point arithmetic. Thus the error between the real DDA increment and our integer DDA increment is

$$e = k - d2^{-n}. \tag{11}$$

Clearly, $|e| < 2^{-n}$, and this error will be shown to be negligible.

All gray-scale raster devices have $2^m$, for some $m > 1$, discrete intensity levels from 0 (absolutely black) to $2^m - 1$ (absolute white). Thus the intensity interpolation between the two vertically adjacent pixels of Eq(10) becomes a bi-partition of the integer $I$, the maximum intensity. The intensity of the upper pixel for the line is

$$\begin{aligned} I(x, \lceil kx \rceil) &= I_0(kx - \lfloor kx \rfloor) \\ &= (2^m - 1)(D2^{-n} + ex) \\ &= D2^{m-n} + (2^m - 1)ex - D2^{-n}. \end{aligned} \tag{12}$$

Since the intensity $I(x, \lceil kx \rceil)$ must be an integer, we approximate it by the first term of Eq(12), $D2^{m-n}$, assuming $n > m$. This approximation gains great computational efficiency while the error incurred (the last two terms of Eq(12) has no or little impact on image quality as we will analyze later.

The approximated $I(x, \lceil kx \rceil) \approx D2^{m-n}$ is simply presented by the $m$ most significant bits of $D$. Moreover, it is evident that the intensity of the lower pixel $I(x, \lfloor kx \rfloor) = I_0 - I(x, \lceil kx \rceil) = \overline{I(x, \lceil kx \rceil)}$, where $\overline{I(x, \lceil kx \rceil)}$ is the integer obtained by the bitwise-inverse operation on $I(x, \lceil kx \rceil)$. This is because the bit pattern for the integer $2^m - 1 - D2^{m-n}$ is the inverse of that for $D2^{m-n}$ due to the fact $I_0 = 2^m - 1$. Now we can see that the integer $D$ controls both pixel positions

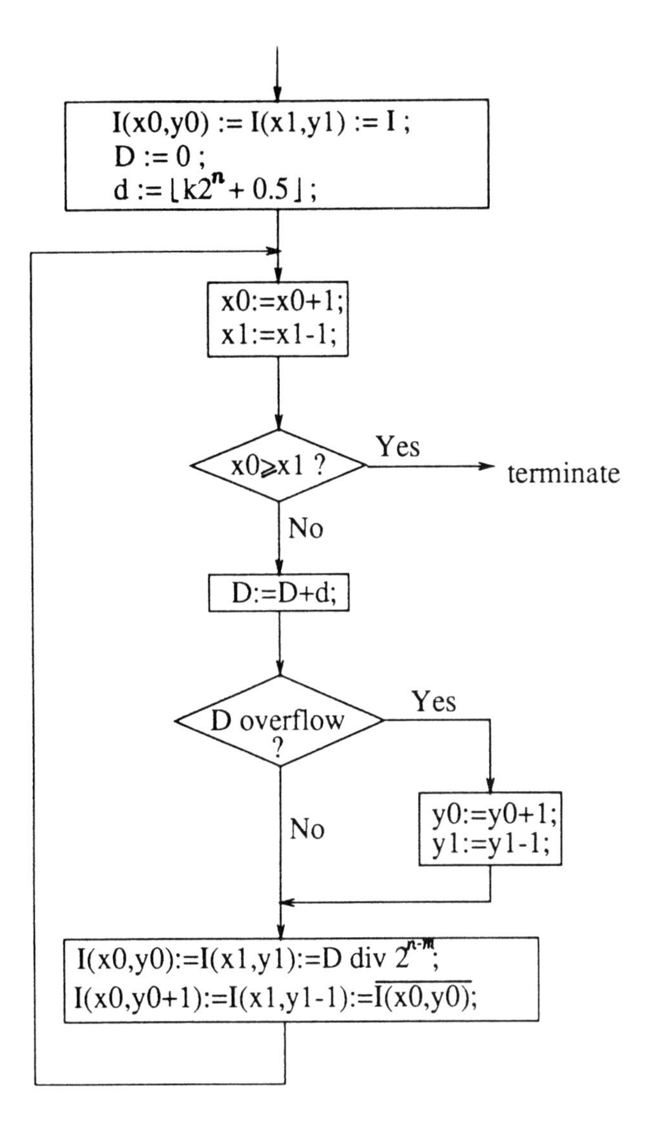


Figure 5: The antialiased line generator ($0 \leq k \leq 1$).

and intensities, and the inner loop of the algorithm only requires an integer addition to $D$.

Furthermore, since the line segment has mirror symmetry with respect to its center, we can plot it from the two ends toward the center using the same logic [13], saving half of the computations. The new algorithm for lines with $0 \leq k \leq 1$ is described by the flowchart in Fig. 5.

Unlike all its predecessors, the above antialiased line generator requires only integer addition and bit manipulations. While producing smooth lines, the new algorithm requires only half as many operations as Bresenham's algorithm because it propagates two pixels per iteration while using the same amount of computations per iteration. The numbers of different operations for

| | Bresenham | New |
|---|---|---|
| Addition | $N$ | $N/2$ |
| Sign Test | $N$ | $N/2$ |
| Comparison | $N$ | $N/2$ |
| Buffer Writing | $N$ | $< 2N$ |

Table 1: The number of different operations required by Bresenham's algorithm and the new antialiased line algorithm.

plotting a line of length $N$ required by Bresenham's algorithm and the new antialiased line algorithm are tabulated in Table 1.

The new algorithm requires twice as many buffer writes as Bresenham's algorithm, but still its buffer access, a bottleneck in rendering, is a minimum (tie with Fujimoto and Iwata's algorithm with the smallest Fourier window) among all current antialiased line generators.

An attractive feature of the new antialiased line generator is that it simultaneously meets two usually mutually exclusive criteria: good image quality and high computational efficiency. At the same time the logic of the new line algorithm remains simple and its hardware implementation is straightforward. An integer adder for $D$ is all we need with its overflow controlling the pixel positioning and its original and inverse values being the required intensities. Historically, we used a very crude fifty-fifty intensity split scheme as a trick to speed up curve scan-conversion [9, 11] under a guise of antialiasing. The above work drew a satisfactory conclusion to our attempt to unify antialiasing and scan-conversion.

The new algorithm is not complete without an error bound for the approximation it employs. The error in approximating $I(x, \lceil kx \rceil)$ by $D2^{m-n}$ is determined by the magnitude of $x$ and the difference $n - m$. Let $L$ be the line length. If $2^{t-1} < L \leq 2^t$, $t > 0$, then the truncation error can be bounded by

$$\begin{aligned} \left| I_0(kx - \lfloor kx \rfloor) - D2^{m-n} \right| &< (2^m - 1)2^{-n}2^{t-1} + D2^{-n} \\ &< 2^{t-n-1}(2^m - 1) + 1. \quad (13) \end{aligned}$$

In the above inequality we used the facts that $D < 2^n$, $|e| < 2^{-n}$, and $x \leq L/2$ due to symmetric generation of the antialiased line. For $L < 2^{n-m+1}$ the error in $I(x, \lceil kx \rceil)$ has a magnitude less than 2. In our experiments, a 10% relative error in distributing $I$ between two adjacent pixels does not lead to noticeable degradation in image quality. It was also observed that 32 different gray scales are sufficient to eliminate the most of aliasing. For a 1024 × 1024 display, the maximum $L < 2^{11}$ ($t = 11$). Suppose that 32 gray scales ($m = 5$) is used for antialiasing. Then we need $n \geq 15$ to bound the error in $I(x, \lceil kx \rceil)$ by 2, or the relative error by 0.063. This only requires $D$ to be a two-bytes integer.

Our recent research revealed that the proposed antialiased line algorithm is particularly suitable to be incorporated into a logic-enhanced frame buffer to solve the bottleneck of frame buffer access [14]. An intelligent frame buffer architecture in the form of wavefront array processors was designed to scan-convert lines right inside the frame buffer. This design achieves extremely high rendering throughput with very low frame buffer bandwidth requirement.

# 6 Fast Anti-Aliased Circle Generator

Due to the 8-way symmetry of the circle, it suffices to consider the circle $x^2 + y^2 = r^2$ in the first octant. For the circle equation, the two-point antialiasing scheme Eq(3) becomes

$$\begin{aligned} I\left(\left\lfloor\sqrt{r^2-j^2}\right\rfloor, j\right) &= I\left(\left\lceil\sqrt{r^2-j^2}\right\rceil - \sqrt{r^2-j^2}\right) \\ I\left(\left\lceil\sqrt{r^2-j^2}\right\rceil, j\right) &= I - I\left(\left\lfloor\sqrt{r^2-j^2}\right\rfloor, j\right), \\ 1 \leq j \leq \frac{r}{\sqrt{2}}. \end{aligned} \quad (14)$$

Now we derive the algorithm to compute Eq(14) as $j$ marches in the $y$ axis from 0 to $\frac{r}{\sqrt{2}}$ in scan-converting the first octant circular arc. The first issue is to determine when the integer-valued function $\left\lceil\sqrt{r^2-j^2}\right\rceil$ decreases by 1 as $j$ increases. We need the critical values $t$ such that $\left\lceil\sqrt{r^2-(t-1)^2}\right\rceil - \left\lceil\sqrt{r^2-t^2}\right\rceil = 1$ to move the pixel band being plotted to the left by one step. This computation can be simplified by the following lemma.

**LEMMA 1**
*The relation* $\left\lceil\sqrt{r^2-(t-1)^2}\right\rceil - \left\lceil\sqrt{r^2-t^2}\right\rceil = 1$ *holds if and only if* $\left\lceil\sqrt{r^2-(t-1)^2}\right\rceil - \sqrt{r^2-(t-1)^2} > \left\lceil\sqrt{r^2-t^2}\right\rceil - \sqrt{r^2-t^2}$.

**Proof**. Since $\sqrt{r^2-j^2}$ is monotonically decreasing in $j$, $\left\lceil\sqrt{r^2-(t-1)^2}\right\rceil - \sqrt{r^2-(t-1)^2} > \left\lceil\sqrt{r^2-t^2}\right\rceil - \sqrt{r^2-t^2}$ implies $\left\lceil\sqrt{r^2-(t-1)^2}\right\rceil - \left\lceil\sqrt{r^2-t^2}\right\rceil > 0$. But in the first octant we have

$$\sqrt{r^2-(t-1)^2} - \sqrt{r^2-t^2} \leq 1 \quad (15)$$

prohibiting $\left\lceil\sqrt{r^2-(t-1)^2}\right\rceil - \left\lceil\sqrt{r^2-t^2}\right\rceil > 1$, hence $\left\lceil\sqrt{r^2-(t-1)^2}\right\rceil - \left\lceil\sqrt{r^2-t^2}\right\rceil = 1$.

The only-if part can be proven by contradiction. Assume that $\left\lceil\sqrt{r^2-(t-1)^2}\right\rceil - \left\lceil\sqrt{r^2-t^2}\right\rceil = 1$ but $\left\lceil\sqrt{r^2-(t-1)^2}\right\rceil - \sqrt{r^2-(t-1)^2} \leq \left\lceil\sqrt{r^2-t^2}\right\rceil - \sqrt{r^2-t^2}$. This requires $\sqrt{r^2-(t-1)^2} - \sqrt{r^2-t^2} > 1$, an impossibility in the first octant. □

For given $r$ the values $\left\lceil\sqrt{r^2-j^2}\right\rceil - \sqrt{r^2-j^2}$, $1 \leq j \leq \frac{r}{\sqrt{2}}$, serve dual purposes: determining the pixel positions as suggested by the above lemma and determining the pixel intensities as in Eq(14). Let the intensity range for the display be from 0 to $2^m - 1$ and define the integer variable

$$D(r,j) = \left\lfloor (2^m-1)\left(\left\lceil\sqrt{r^2-j^2}\right\rceil - \sqrt{r^2-j^2}\right) + 0.5\right\rfloor \quad (16)$$

Then it follows from Eq(14) that

$$\begin{aligned} I\left(\left\lfloor\sqrt{r^2-j^2}\right\rfloor, j\right) &= D(r,j) \\ I\left(\left\lceil\sqrt{r^2-j^2}\right\rceil, j\right) &= \overline{D(r,j)}, \quad 1 \leq j \leq \frac{r}{\sqrt{2}}, \end{aligned} \quad (17)$$

where $\overline{D(r,j)}$ is the integer value obtained through bitwise-inverse operation on $D(r,j)$ since

$$I\left(\left\lceil\sqrt{r^2-j^2}\right\rceil, j\right) + I\left(\left\lfloor\sqrt{r^2-j^2}\right\rfloor, j\right) = I = 2^m - 1 \quad (18)$$

and since the intensity values are integers. By Eq(16) every decrement of the function $\left\lceil\sqrt{r^2-j^2}\right\rceil - \sqrt{r^2-j^2}$ as $j$ increases is reflected by a decrement of $D(r,j)$, thus $D(r,j)$ can be used to control the scan-conversion of the circle. The new antialiased circle algorithm based on precomputed $D(r,j)$ is extremely simple and fast. The algorithm for the first octant is described by the flowchart in Fig. 6.

The inner loop of the antialiased circle algorithm requires even fewer operations than Bresenham's circle algorithm. Of course, the gains in image quality and scan-conversion speed are obtained by using the $D(r,j)$ table. If $R_{max}$ is the maximum radius handled by the circle generator, then the table size will be $\frac{\sqrt{2}}{4}R_{max}$. It is my opinion that the rapidly decreasing memory cost makes the above simple idea a viable solution to real-time antialiased circle generation. For instance, for a 64K bytes ROM the above algorithm can display antialiased circular arcs of radius up to 430. Without the

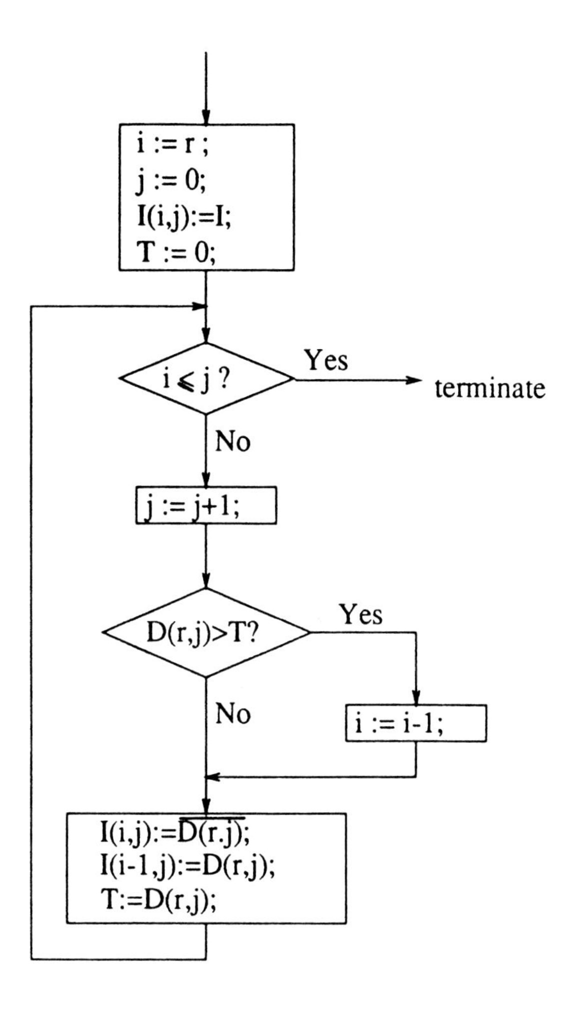


Figure 6: Antialiased circle generator (1st octant).

precomputed table $D(r, j)$ the antialiased circle algorithm can be implemented by computing the function $D(r, j)$.

The performance of the new antialiased circle algorithm is demonstrated by Fig. 7.

# 7 Other Antialiasing Issues

We demonstrated that the new antialiasing technique is particularly efficient for generating antialiased lines and circles since Eq(3) can be incorporated into the classical incremental curve scan-conversion framework. But it is not restricted to those two graphics primitives. The intensity interpolation of Eq(3) applies to any curves or object edges. We should not partition a general curve into line segments and then antialias line

Figure 7: Circles by Bresenham's (above) and the new antialiasing algorithms (below).

segments as suggested by some authors before. Instead an antialiased curve can be computed by directly scan-converting the curve, i.e., for increasing raster ordinate $i$, computing $f(i)$ and then interpolate the intended curve intensity $I_0$ between the two pixels $(i, \lfloor f(i) \rfloor)$ and $(i, \lceil f(i) \rceil)$. The main cost is to compute the real value $f(i)$, but it is required by scan-conversion anyway. So antialiasing will not be a computational burden for general curves.

Although our algorithms were presented for antialiasing curves, their extension to object boundaries is straightforward. We simply partition the object boundaries into x-dominant and y-dominant curve segments, and scan-convert them. It is easy to determine which side of such a curve segment is exterior. We use Eq(3) to interpolate the object color on two adjacent pixels at the two sides of the continuous boundary curve, and then blend the outer pixel value with the background color. Let $I_0$ and $I_b$ be the intensities (colors) for object and its background, and $d < 1$ be the distance between the outer pixel and the true object boundary, then the blending formula for the boundary pixel is

$$I = dI_0 + (1 - d)I_b. \qquad (19)$$

Note that unlike the blending formula by Fujimoto and Iwata [6] no division is required here. Furthermore, for antialiasing polygon edges in uniform background, we can solve Eq(19) incrementally with only integer additions and binary shifts much like our antialiased line algorithm. We will not pursue this efficiency issue any further due to the space limitation. The performance of the new technique on antialiased object edges in colorful background is shown by Fig. 8, where a filled circle with antialiasing in a complex background is compared with the one without. The antialiased filled circle appears smooth and sharp. Note that the results of Fig. 8 were obtained on an 8-bit color device, so color quantization was necessarily performed. On a 24-bit color device with more subtle shades available the antialiased disk looked even better.

Our antialiasing technique has the same subpixel addressability as Fujimoto-Iwata's method due to their equivalence.

Figure 8: Filled circles embedded in colorful background without antialiasing (above) and with antialiasing (below).

# 8 Conclusion

Unlike all previous antialiasing research, our two-point antialiasing scheme was derived in spatial domain under a subjectively meaningful error measure to preserve dynamic information of the original curves or object edges. The behaviour of this antialiasing scheme in frequency domain was also analyzed. It was shown that the new antialiasing technique can generate smooth line segments and circular arcs at even higher speeds than those of Bresenham's line and circle algorithms. The hardware or assembly-language realization of our new antialiasing algorithms is straightforward. These features have practical significance when antialiasing is performed on small economical graphics devices or in time-constrained applications.

### Acknowledgment

The author gratefully acknowledges the financial support of the Canadian Government through NSERC grant OGP0041926 and thanks SIGGRAPH reviewers for their polishing of his original manuscript.

## References

[1] A. C. Barkans, "High speed high quality antialiased vector generation," *Computer Graphics*, vol. 24, no. 4, p. 319-326, Aug. 1990.

[2] J. E. Bresenham, "Algorithm for computer control of digital plotter," *IBM Syst. J.*, vol. 4, no. 1, 1965, p. 25-30.

[3] J. E. Bresenham, "A linear algorithm for incremental digital display of circular arcs", *Comm. ACM*, vol. 20, no. 2, 1977, p. 750-752.

[4] F. Crow, "The aliasing problem in computer-generated shaded images," *Comm. ACM*, vol. 20, no. 11, Nov. 1977.

[5] D. Field, "Algorithms for drawing anti-aliased circles and ellipses," *Computer Vision, Graphics, and Image Proc.*, vol. 33, p. 1-15, 1986.

[6] A. Fujimoto and K. Iwata, "Jay-free images on raster displays," *IEEE CG&A*, vol. 3, no. 9, p. 26-34, Dec. 1983.

[7] S. Gupta and R. F. Sproull, "Filtering edges for gray-scale displays," *Computer Graphics*, vol. 15, no. 3, p. 1-5, Aug. 1981.

[8] M. Pitteway and D. Watkinson, "Bresenham's algorithm with gray scale," *Comm. ACM*, vol 23, no. 11, November 1980.

[9] X. Wu and J. Rokne, "Double-step incremental generation of lines and circles", *Computer Vision, Graphics, Image Proc.*, vol. 37, 1987, p. 331-344.

[10] X. Wu and J. Rokne, "On properties of discretized convex curves," *IEEE Trans. Pattern Analysis and Machine Intelligence*, vol. 11, p. 217-223, Feb. 1989.

[11] X. Wu and J. Rokne, "Double-step generation of ellipses", *IEEE CG&A*, vol. 9, no. 3. p. 56-69, May 1989.

[12] X. Wu and J. Rokne, "Dynamic error measure for curve scan-conversion," *Proc. Graphics/Interface'89*, London, Ontario, p. 183-190, June 1989.

[13] J. Rokne, B. Wyvill and X. Wu, "Fast line scan-conversion," *ACM Trans. on Graphics*, vol. 9, no. 4, p. 377-388, Oct. 1990.

[14] X. Wu, "A frame buffer architecture for parallel vector generation," *Proc. Graphics/Interface'91*, Calgary, June 1991.

# Unbiased Sampling Techniques for Image Synthesis

David Kirk
California Institute of Technology
Computer Graphics 350-74
Pasadena, CA 91125

James Arvo
Program of Computer Graphics
Cornell University
Ithaca, NY 14853

## Abstract

We examine a class of adaptive sampling techniques employed in image synthesis and show that those commonly used for efficient anti-aliasing are statistically biased. This bias is dependent upon the image function being sampled as well as the strategy for determining the number of samples to use. It is most prominent in areas of high contrast and is attributable to early stages of sampling systematically favoring one extreme or the other. If the expected outcome of the entire adaptive sampling algorithm is considered, we find that the bias of the early decisions is still present in the final estimator. We propose an alternative strategy for performing adaptive sampling that is unbiased but potentially more costly. We conclude that it may not always be practical to mitigate this source of bias, but as a source of error it should be considered when high accuracy and image fidelity are a central concern.

**CR Categories and Subject Descriptors:** I.3.7—[Computer Graphics]: Three-Dimensional Graphics and Realism; I.3.3—[Computer Graphics]: Picture/Image Generation;
**General Terms:** Algorithms, Graphics
**Additional Key Words and Phrases:** Adaptive Sampling, Anti-aliasing, Monte Carlo, Statistical Bias.

## 1 Introduction

Many of the sampling techniques employed in computer graphics are adaptive in the sense that they attempt to concentrate effort in areas where complexity is high. In particular, adaptive anti-aliasing schemes choose to sample at a higher rate where the scene is interesting, such as near edges. Many such schemes have been devised, both deterministic [11, 4] and stochastic [6, 2, 9, 7, 8]. The latter category has received the most attention and essentially consists of multi-stage Monte Carlo integration techniques. Common to all of these is the notion of using a small number of samples to detect regions where additional sampling is required to achieve a reliable answer, that is, one with an acceptably low level of noise.



©1991 ACM-0-89791-436-8/91/007/0153 $00.75

While all of these methods have been reasonably successful in achieving this goal, it is important to understand the statistical effects of such a strategy. To do this we must examine multi-stage sampling plans *in toto* and characterize their statistical behavior. In particular, we wish to determine whether they in fact attain the correct answer on average.

Every stochastic anti-aliasing algorithm can be viewed as defining a random variable at each pixel to estimate the quantity of interest. This quantity is typically the unknown image function integrated with a filter kernel such as a gaussian or a box-filter. The purpose of adaptive sampling is to reduce the variance of these random variables, or *estimators*, with minimal increase in computation. If the expected value of an estimator is the solution we are seeking, it is said to be *unbiased*. If the estimator has a bias that can be made arbitrarily small, perhaps by increasing the number of initial samples sufficiently, then it is said to be *consistent* [3].

By analyzing the behavior of a prototypical multi-stage sampling algorithm operating on a simple class of test cases, we will show that most adaptive sampling plans fall into the category of consistent but biased estimators. Although the bias is typically small, this is a source of error that should be taken into consideration when high accuracy is required.

## 2 Common Sources of Bias

Sources of statistical bias can be found in many seemingly innocuous operations in image synthesis. For example, pixel values are frequently truncated or otherwise transformed so as to fall within the gamut of color monitors. Removing out-of-gamut colors can shift the distribution mean. At a very low level, the pseudo-random number generators at the heart of Monte Carlo approaches often have a built-in bias. At higher levels, the practice of *importance sampling* [5, 10] reduces variance by sampling more frequently where the result is large, which requires precise renormalization if the original expected value is to be maintained. Another example is the practice of truncating excessively deep ray trees in ray tracing. This can cause a systematic bias by eliminating a large number of small contributions [1].

In general, whenever we depart from naive Monte Carlo in an attempt to improve statistical efficiency, care must be taken to avoid introducing unnecessary bias. This is also true in screen space, for example, when anti-

```
EstimateMean(X, n, ε)
  begin
    Draw a set of n identically distributed random
    samples from X.

    S_n ← {X_1, X_2, ..., X_n};

    if Variation(S_n) ≤ ε then begin
      This is the "easy" case: use the sample
      mean as an estimate of the true mean.
      ξ ← mean(S_n);
      end
    else begin
      This is the "hard" case: invoke a costly
      oracle to compute the true mean.
      ξ ← TrueMean(X);
      end

    return ξ;
  end
```

Figure 1: A hypothetical adaptive sampling algorithm similar in spirit to most existing algorithms. This is biased for most inputs.

aliasing at the pixel level. As we show in the following section, adaptive anti-aliasing algorithms can introduce a systematic bias dependent upon the image function. This bias is greatest in areas of high contrast and is caused by early stages of sampling systematically favoring one extreme or the other. In Section 4 we propose a modified approach that is unbiased.

## 3 Bias From Adaptive Sampling

In this section, we examine the statistical behavior of common adaptive anti-aliasing algorithms. We begin by formulating a hypothetical sampling algorithm that retains the salient features of most multi-level sampling plans yet is simple enough to allow convenient analysis. The basic strategy is to use samples sparingly except where more work is deemed necessary. The decision to invoke a more costly method as a second stage is based upon a statistic we will call "variation," a function of the first-stage, or *pilot*, sample. This could be the sample variance, the "contrast", or a function of the sample size and variance as in [6] and [9]. An idealized algorithm using this strategy is shown in Figure 1, where $X$ is the "population" whose mean we wish to estimate. For anti-aliasing, $X$ will be the set of image values with probabilities influenced by the filter kernel.

Although the meaning of variation differs among the various approaches, a universal feature is that it goes to zero as the maximum deviation within the sample goes to zero. Thus, any such algorithm would be satisfied with only the first-stage sample when all values are identical.

If the variation is greater than some $\epsilon$, then we will classify the population as "hard" to sample, and invoke a more expensive second-stage sampling technique. For simplicity we will assume here that the second-stage "oracle" computes the exact mean; in reality, this action would be simulated through a large number of samples. Because this ideal can be approximated to any given precision, our conclusions carry over to real algorithms, although the actual amount of bias will differ.

To demonstrate that the strategy in Figure 1 can be problematic we need only examine its behavior on a simple class of inputs. In particular, we will assume that $X$ consists of a finite number of distinct values, $I_1, I_2, \ldots, I_k$, with corresponding probabilities $\omega_1, \omega_2, \ldots, \omega_k$. This situation occurs, for example, when applying a box filter to a pixel area consisting of $k$ constant-intensity regions; the $I$'s would represent the intensities within the pixel and the $\omega$'s would represent their fractional coverages. The actual mean is then

$$I = \sum_{i=1}^{k} I_i \omega_i. \tag{1}$$

With this characterization of $X$ we can easily compute the expected value of the random variable $\xi$ returned by the algorithm in Figure 1. Using conditional expectations based on a classification of "easy" or "hard", indicating that the variation of $S_n$ is below or above the threshold $\epsilon$, respectively, we have

$$\begin{aligned} \mathrm{E}[\xi] &= \mathrm{E}[\xi \mid \mathrm{easy}] \times \mathrm{Prob}[\mathrm{easy}] \\ &+ \mathrm{E}[\xi \mid \mathrm{hard}] \times \mathrm{Prob}[\mathrm{hard}] \end{aligned} \tag{2}$$

The oracle guarantees that $\mathrm{E}[\xi \mid \mathrm{hard}] = I$, the true mean. To analyze the conditional expectations we observe that any sample, $S_n$, can be characterized as a $k$-tuple, $(n_1, n_2, \ldots, n_k)$, where $n_j$ is the number of samples assuming the value $I_j$. Then $n_1 + \cdots + n_k = n$ and the probability of a $k$-tuple is given by the multinomial distribution [3]:

$$\mathrm{Prob}[n_1, n_2, \ldots, n_k] = \frac{\omega_1^{n_1} \omega_2^{n_2} \cdots \omega_k^{n_k}}{n_1! n_2! \cdots n_k!} n!. \tag{3}$$

Using this fact, we can compute $\mathrm{E}[\xi]$ for any input of the form described above. We simply step the algorithm through all distinct $k$-tuples and sum the resulting values of $\xi$ weighted by the corresponding probabilities. However, if we assume $\epsilon$ to be sufficiently small that $S_n$ will be classified as "easy" only when all $n$ samples are of the same value, then Equation 2 reduces to a very simple expression. In this case we have

$$\mathrm{Prob}[\mathrm{easy}] = \omega_1^n + \omega_2^n + \cdots + \omega_k^n \tag{4}$$

and the expected value of $\xi$, given that the initial sample was found to be "easy", is

$$\mathrm{E}[\xi \mid \mathrm{easy}] = \frac{\omega_1^n I_1 + \cdots + \omega_k^n I_k}{\omega_1^n + \cdots + \omega_k^n}. \tag{5}$$

Substituting these into Equation 2 and observing that $\mathrm{Prob}[\mathrm{hard}] = 1 - \mathrm{Prob}[\mathrm{easy}]$ we arrive at the expression

$$\mathrm{E}[\xi] = I + \sum_{i=1}^{k} \omega_i^n (I_i - I). \tag{6}$$

Because $I$ is the true mean, the summation on the right of Equation 6 is the amount of bias. This will be nonzero for all but a small class of inputs. The bias diminishes as the number of initial samples increases, indicating that the estimator is consistent. In Section 5 we present experimental data obtained from Equation 6.

## 4 An Unbiased Adaptive Sampling Plan

The hidden flaw in the algorithm above is that the first-stage samples deemed "easy" are not completely random, and therefore may not fairly represent the entire population. That is, the test for accepting a first-stage sample is usually correlated in some way with the mean of the sample.

There is a straightforward modification of the above sampling plan to avoid this bias. First select a small subset of the area $X$, call it $R$, and draw a sample of size $n$ from this subset. We may examine this sample to determine the number of samples to draw from the rest of the region, $X - R$, but in any case we use the initial sample mean to estimate the mean of $R$. Because we do not alter the estimate of $R$, no bias is introduced there. Also, because the second stage is simply a choice among two or more unbiased estimators for a disjoint region, it also remains unbiased. It follows that a weighted sum of the these sample means, weighted proportionately by area, results in an unbiased estimate over the entire region. This approach is outlined in Figure 2.

As with any multi-stage scheme, the goal is to estimate the population variance by means of a first-stage sample. To the extent that the region $R$ is representative of the entire region, drawing the pilot sample from it will serve this purpose. This suggests that $R$ should be "scattered" throughout $X$.

As a special case of this strategy, note what happens if we allow the area of region $R$ to shrink to zero. The result is a strategy whereby the pilot sample is used solely to select the sample size for the second stage – not for estimating the mean. This clearly avoids any possibility of a correlation between the estimator of the mean and the variation of the pilot sample.

These examples suggest a simple rule that will avoid introducing bias in multi-stage sampling schemes: decide how a sample is going to be used *before* it is drawn – not based on the actual values drawn. Observing this rule prevents us from modifying estimates in any way that may be correlated with the result.

This technique can be applied in a hierarchical fashion and stratified, similar to [6]. After the first decision has been made based on the pilot sample, we can make additional decisions later, provided that we either discard the samples used to influence the strategy, or decide ahead of time that they will be used to estimate the mean over the subregion from which they were drawn.

The main disadvantage of using a technique such as this is that it is difficult to avoid either wasting samples or producing a high-variance result that cannot be remedied. The former occurs if $R$ is chosen to be so small that the pilot sample contributes very little to the final estimate. The latter occurs if $R$ is large and the pilot sample fails to provide a sufficiently reliable estimate of its mean. We are then left with a poor estimate. Improving it with further sampling will, in most cases, alter the distribution of the "easy" cases and introduce bias.

UnbiasedEstimateMean($X$, $R$, $p$, $n_1$, $n_2$, $\epsilon$)
**begin**

*Draw a set of p identically distributed random samples from* $R \subset X$.

$S_p \leftarrow \{X_1, X_2, \ldots, X_p\} \subset R$;

**if** Variation($S_p$) $\leq \epsilon$ **then** $n \leftarrow n_1$
**else** $n \leftarrow n_2$;

*Draw a set of n identically distributed random samples from the rest of* $X$.

$S_n \leftarrow \{X_1, X_2, \ldots, X_n\} \subset X - R$

*Compute* $\xi$ *based on the unbiased estimates of the two disjoint components.*

$\xi \leftarrow \overline{S_p} \times |R| + \overline{S_n} \times |X - R|$;

**return** $\xi$;
**end**

Figure 2: An unbiased adaptive sampling algorithm. It is assumed that $R \subset X$ and $n_1 < n_2$.

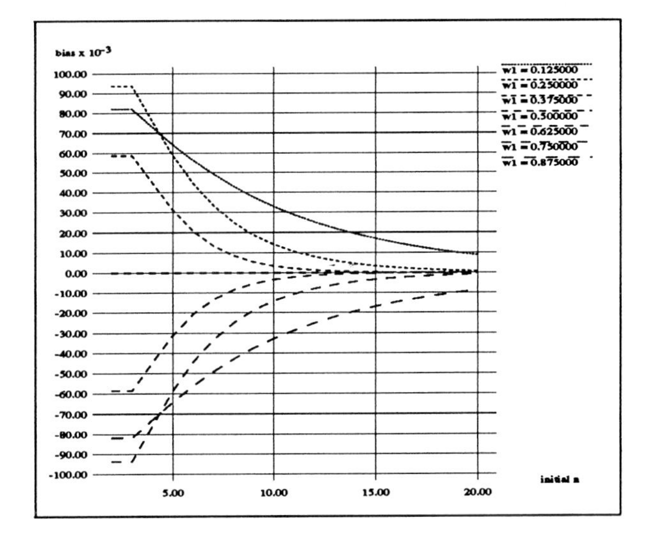


Figure 3: Absolute Bias as a function of initial sample size $n$ for a collection of fractional areas.

## 5 Results

To study the extent of the biasing problem we have computed the exact bias introduced by the algorighm in Figure 1 for a range of initial sample sizes and a variety of two-intensity pixels. In this case Equation 6 provides the actual bias. Both Figures Fig. 3 and Fig. 4 show curves for $\omega_1$ ranging from 0.125 to 0.875. For each of these curves, $\omega_2 = 1 - \omega_1$, $I_1 = 0$, and $I_2 = 1$. Note that while the absolute bias is symmetric about zero, the percent bias increases as the actual mean decreases.

While these figures are informative, it is difficult to see how this really affects an image. Fig. 5a (upper left)

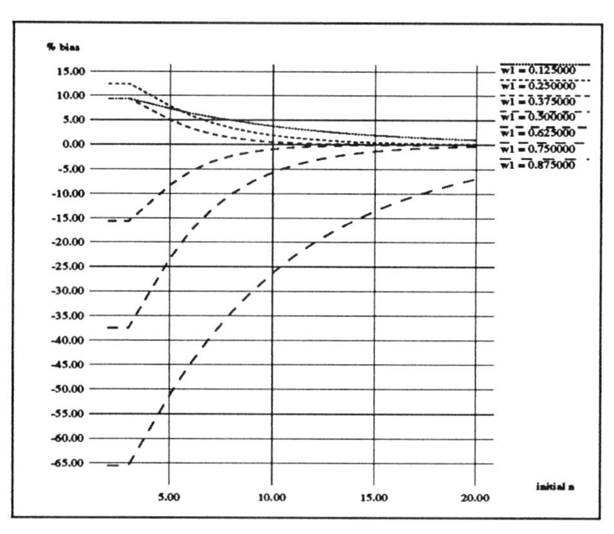


Figure 4: Percent Bias as a function of initial sample size $n$ for a collection of fractional areas.

Figure 5: a) Unbiased image, b) Unbiased image (hi-res), c) Biased image, d) Biased image (hi-res)

shows a black / white edge, and a thin white polygon on a black background, at 32x32 resolution. Fig. 5b (upper right) is a hi-res version of Fig. 5a. Fig. 5a & b were computed using the expected value of the unbiased algorithm from Figure 2. Fig. 5c & d were computed using the expected value of the biased algorithm described in Figure 1. Therefore, these images illustrate the *tendencies* of these algorithms, not actual results. Pixels in all figures were integrated using a box filter.

Note that in Fig. 5c & d, the familiar "roping" in the antialiased edges is worse than in Fig. 5a & b. This is because the small partial coverages in each pixel are underestimated in the biased approach. Likewise, the large partial coverages are overestimated. In this case, the bias accentuates problems with antialiasing of edges.

## 6 Conclusions

We have shown that common adaptive anti-aliasing algorithms can be statistically biased, and have proposed an alternative algorithm that is unbiased.

It may not always be worthwhile to remove this source of bias. The error is typically small, especially when the initial sample is large. Our alternative sampling plan, while unbiased, possesses other drawbacks in terms of additional cost and parameter selection. For each application the cost must be weighed against the benefit of improved accuracy.

The analysis presented here has identified a subtle deficiency hidden within most anti-aliasing approaches which should be addressed in future schemes.

## Acknowledgements

Much of this research was performed while the authors were employed at Apollo Computer and Hewlett-Packard. The authors also wish to thank the anonymous reviewers for their thoughtful and detailed comments.

## References

[1] Arvo, James, and David Kirk, "Particle Transport and Image Synthesis," *Computer Graphics*, 24(4), August 1990, pp. 63-66.

[2] Dippe, Mark A. Z., and Erling Henry Wold, "Antialiasing through Stochastic Sampling," *Computer Graphics*, 19(3), July 1985, pp. 69-78.

[3] Freund, John E., and Ronald E. Walpole, *Mathematical Statistics*, 4th edition, Prentice Hall, New Jersey, 1987.

[4] Glassner, Andrew S., "An Overview of Ray Tracing," in *An Introduction to Ray Tracing*, A. S. Glassner, ed., Academic Press, New York, 1989.

[5] Kajiya, J. T., "The Rendering Equation," *Computer Graphics*, 20(4), August 1986, pp. 143-150.

[6] Lee, Mark E., Richard A. Redner, and Samuel P. Uselton, "Statistically Optimized Sampling for Distributed Ray Tracing," *Computer Graphics*, 19(3), July 1985, pp. 61-68.

[7] Mitchell, Don P., "Generating Antialiased Images at Low Sampling Densities," *Computer Graphics*, 21(4), July 1987, pp. 65-69.

[8] Painter, James, and Kenneth Sloan, "Antialiased Ray Tracing by Adaptive Progressive Refinement," *Computer Graphics*, 23(3), July 1989, pp. 281-288.

[9] Purgathofer, W., "A Statistical Method for Adaptive Stochastic Sampling," in *Proceedings of Eurographics 86*, ed. A.A.G. Requicha, Elsevier, North-Holland, 1986, pp. 145-152.

[10] Rubinstein, R. Y., *Simulation and the Monte Carlo Method*, J. Wiley, New York, 1981.

[11] Whitted, Turner, "An Improved Illumination Model for Shaded Display," *Communications of the ACM*, 32(6), June 1980, pp. 343-349.

# Spectrally Optimal Sampling for Distribution Ray Tracing

*Don P. Mitchell*

AT&T Bell Laboratories
Murray Hill, NJ 07974

## Abstract

Nonuniform sampling of images is a useful technique in computer graphics, because a properly designed pattern of samples can make aliasing take the form of high-frequency random noise. In this paper, the technique of nonuniform sampling is extended from two dimensions to include the extra parameter dimensions of distribution ray tracing. A condition for optimality is suggested, and algorithms for approximating optimal sampling are developed. The technique is demonstrated at low sampling densities, so the characteristics of aliasing noise are clearly visible. At supersampling rates, this technique should move noise into frequencies above the passband of the pixel-reconstruction filter.

CR Categories and Subject Descriptions: I.3.3 [ **Computer Graphics** ]: Picture/Image Generation; I.3.7 [ **Computer Graphics** ]: Three-Dimensional Graphics and Realism

General Terms: Algorithms

Additional Keywords and Phrases: Antialiasing, Distribution Ray Tracing, Nonuniform Sampling, Noise Perception

## 1. Introduction

In 1979, Whitted demonstrated that ray tracing could be used to simulate a number of realistic shading effects [Whitted80]. Unfortunately, ray tracing has a special difficulty with aliasing, a problem sometimes encountered when sampling signals. To focus on this issue, Whitted's algorithm can be cast into the form of a two-dimensional sampling problem. At each point $(x,y)$ on the image plane, a brightness sample is defined by calculating the radiance of a ray from the viewpoint through that point. Assuming the image-plane coordinates range between zero and one, the image brightness is defined by the mapping:

$$f:\ [0,1]^2 \rightarrow \textbf{radiance} \qquad (1)$$

Any synthetic image might be described as (1), but the details of ray tracing have special implications: the values of $f$ can only be evaluated at a point, and it is virtually impossible to symbolically intergrate or low-pass filter the function. In other words, the signal can be sampled but generally cannot be prefiltered to avoid aliasing. An interesting approach to this problem is *nonuniform sampling* which an yield aliasing in the form of high-frequency random noise [Dippé85, Cook86, Mitchell87].



An elegant extension of Whitted's algorithm is *distribution ray tracing* (previously "distributed ray tracing"), introduced by Cook, Porter and Carpenter [Cook84]. Their algorithm simulates motion blur, shadow penumbras from finite-area light sources, depth-of-field effects, and glossy reflections from partially polished surfaces. This is achieved by sampling in an additional set of parameter dimensions. For example, an object in motion will have a position in the scene parameterized by the time $t$, and motion blurred pixels can be calculated by averaging over many different samples of $t$. Depth-of-field effects are associated with a finite aperture on the camera and are simulated by deflecting rays through different points on the lens, parameterized by two more variables $a,b$. Glossy reflection results from varying the direction of a surface normal, as if the surface were made up of randomly distributed microscopic facets parameterized by an orientation $\theta,\phi$.

With these extra parameters, distribution ray tracing defines a multidimensional brightness function $f'(x,\,y;\,t,\,u,\,\cdots)$. A sample of this function is evaluated by performing a Whitted-style ray tracing operation. However, first moving objects would be transformed to their location at time $t$, a point light source is defined by $(u,v)$ representing a sample of the area light, the primary ray from the camera is deflected through a focal point from a position $(a,b)$ on the lens, etc. Once the scene is prepared for a given set of parameter values, a ray-tracing calculation can be done. Assuming $x$, $y$, and $D-2$ parameters range from zero to one, we have the brightness mapping:

$$f':\ [0,1]^D \rightarrow \textbf{radiance} \qquad (2)$$

The two-dimensional image is an integration over the parameters

$$f(x,y) = \int_0^1\int_0^1 \cdots \int_0^1 f'(x,\,y;\,t,\,u,\,\cdots)\,dt\,du\,\cdots \qquad (3)$$

Additional integration or convolution (with a filter) may be done in $x$ and $y$ to define a bandlimited image function $i(x,y)$ suitable for alias-free digitization. The integration in (3) cannot be evaluated analytically, but the process of distribution ray tracing estimates $f(x,y)$ by averaging many samples per pixel. This process can be viewed as a *Monte Carlo integration,* or as a classical *statistical sampling problem* of estimating the mean value of $f$ in a region of the image plane, or it can be viewed as a sampling problem in the *signal processing* sense. These viewpoints are not independent, and all of them can be found with varying degrees of emphasis in discussions of distribution ray tracing [Cook84, Lee85, Cook86, Kajiya86, Shirley90].

The question investigated in this paper is how to extend the techniques of nonuniform sampling, used in Whitted-style ray tracing, to the multiple dimensions of distribution ray tracing. This is not simply the problem of generating a D-dimensional image from samples of $f'$, which might be a obvious extension of the two-dimensional methods. We are still interested in the characteristics of noise in a two-dimensional image, and we expect the parameter dimensions $t, u, v, \cdots$ to play a qualitatively different role than the image coordinates $x$, $y$.

## 2. Incomplete Block Sampling Designs

An important problem in distribution ray tracing is how to choose samples effectively to produce the highest quality image with the fewest rays. We might simply choose samples randomly with a uniform distribution in $[0,1]^D$. In *sequential sampling*, random samples are made until we are statistically confident that the average value has a low variance [Lee85, Kajiya86]. This procedure is usually improved by *stratified sampling*, where the interval $[0,1]$ is divided into $N$ levels, dropping a random sample into each subinterval. This spreads the samples out more evenly and often results in a lower variance of the average.

In the two-dimensional antialiasing problem of Whitted-style ray tracing, each pixel area $[0,1]^2$ can be divided into $N \times N$ subsquares for stratified sampling. This is more or less the same as jittered sampling, a common approach to the antialiasing problem [Dippé85, Cook86, Kajiya86, Painter89]. However, this is not a practical approach to sampling the parameter space of distribution ray tracing because of the high number of dimensions. Stratification of all $D$ dimensions would result in $N^D$ blocks to be sampled. This could easily be tens of thousands of samples per pixel, many more than would be reasonable or necessary. In practice, stratification has been applied to distribution ray tracing, but with *incomplete block sampling designs* that do not fully populate the $N^D$ blocks.

Cook created incomplete block designs by subdividing the pixel area into an $N \times N$ mesh of subsquares. The time dimension was divided into $N^2$ levels, and pairs of "area-like" parameters like $(u,v)$ and $(a,b)$ were subdividing into $N \times N$ meshes. $N^2$ samples are then made which projected onto each subsquare of the pixel once, each level of time once, each subsquare of the $(u,v)$ dimension once, etc. Thus only $N^2$ of the possible $N^D$ blocks are occupied by a sample. Little has been said about how these associations between blocks should be chosen, but it is clear that linear correlation between parameter values should be avoided [Cook86]. Linear correlation would mean a tendency for samples to fall on hyperplanes in $[0,1]^D$ which could cause aliasing. The visual consequences of parameter correlation are objectionable and conspicuous.

Shirley describes another incomplete block design called "N-rook" sampling, where $N$ out of $N^D$ blocks are populated [Shirley90]. Let $\pi_1, \pi_2, .. \pi_{D-1}$ be permutations of the sequence $(0,1, \cdots, N-1)$. Then we choose one sample in each subinterval of each parameter dimension. The $n^{th}$ sample is placed in level $n$ of the $x$ dimension, in level $\pi_1(n)$ of the $y$ dimension, level $\pi_2(n)$ of the $t$ dimension, etc. Once again, little is known about what are good or bad choices for the permutations, except to avoid linear correlation. An example in two dimensions is shown below:

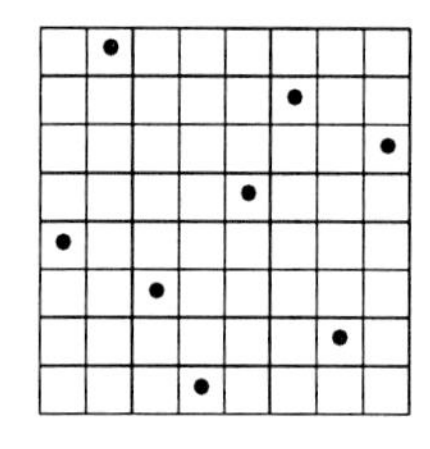

Figure 1. An 8-Rook Sampling Design in Two Dimensions

There seems to remain an important piece of unfinished business. We do not really know very much about what constitutes a good sampling design versus a bad one. Avoiding linear correlation is known to be important. Explicit in the two incomplete block designs described above is the property that the sampling pattern is "good" when projected onto certain lower-dimensional planes or axes. For example, the N-rook patterns are fully populated stratified designs when projected onto any coordinate axis.

Linear correlation could be avoided by randomly choosing sampling designs of either Cook's style or Shirley's. Moreover, sequential sampling (i.e., sampling until statistical confidence is achieved) is probably capable of giving satisfactory image quality [Lee85], whether the sampling design is good or not. The danger is that many more samples might be computed than are necessary.

## 3. Nonuniform Sampling in Two Dimensions

Before tackling the problem of sampling in $D$ dimensions, it will be useful to review the two-dimensional problem of sampling in the $(x,y)$ dimensions. This is the problem in Whitted-style ray tracing. Typically, the image is "supersampled" at a high rate (by casting rays), and then filtered and resampled to a lower rate to produce the pixels of a digital image. The filter may be an average over the pixel area, or it may be a more sophisticated low-pass filter. The process of sampling is represented mathematically by multiplication of the image signal with delta-function pulses, as diagramed below:

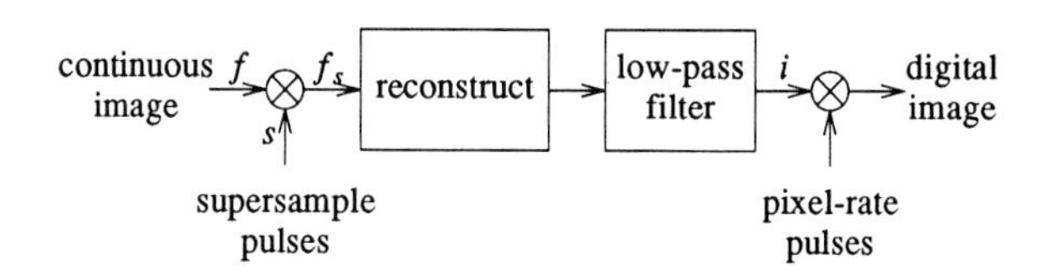


Figure 2. Conversion of Ray-Casting Samples into Pixels

The reconstruction filter interpolates samples to recreate a continuous image. The low-pass filter makes sure that image is bandlimited so aliasing will not result when it is resampled at the pixel rate. These two filters are traditionally combined into one, but when supersampling is nonuniform, it is often the case that reconstruction and low-pass filtering are distinctly separate stages [Mitchell87, Painter89].

If the supersampling pattern is nonuniform, and its spectrum has certain characteristics, the sampling error (or aliasing) will take the form of random noise at high frequencies. This is desirable for two reasons. If noise is concentrated in the high frequencies, more of it will be attenuated by the low-pass filter pictured in Figure 2. Secondly, randomness and high frequency both help to make the noise less perceptible to a human observer.

This can be understood by looking at the sampling process in the frequency domain. Let $f(x,y)$ represent the continuous image, $s(x,y)$ represents the sampling pattern (delta functions), and let $r(x,y)$ be the combined reconstruction/low-pass filter. $F$, $S$, and $R$ will represent the corresponding spectra. In the spatial domain, the sampling and filtering process is expressed by:

$$i(x,y) = r(x,y) * [f(x,y) \cdot s(x,y)] \qquad (4)$$

And in the frequency domain:

$$I(\omega_x, \omega_y) = R(\omega_x, \omega_y) \cdot [F(\omega_x, \omega_y) * S(\omega_x, \omega_y)] \qquad (5)$$

where $\cdot$ and $*$ represent multiplication and convolution respectively.

The reconstruction filter is described above as a linear low-pass filter, which is ideal for uniform samples but can give a distorted reconstruction of nonuniform samples. Nonuniform reconstruction for images is not perfectly understood; but in practice, nonlinear or space-varying filters (which are not representable by a convolution) give better results [Dippé85, Mitchell87, Marvasti87]. The result is still some type of low-pass filter (i.e., a "smooth" surface interpolating the sample spikes). When the reconstruction and low-pass stages (in Figure 2) are implemented separately, the low-pass stage could be a linear filter [Painter89]. If the supersampling rate is much higher than the pixel rate, the linear low-pass stage should dominate the behavior of the system. We will model the reconstruction as a linear low-pass filter for the purposes of qualitative analysis.

The spectrum of the sampling pattern $S$ will be a delta-function spike at the origin (the DC component) and some pattern of noise surrounding it. The convolution $F*S$ (shown in Figure 3) of a image spectrum with the nonuniform-sampling spectrum gives a copy of the true image spectrum (the symmetric shape at the center of the figure) and a halo of noise energy (represented by the scattered dots). The low-pass filter $R$ (represented by the dotted box) attenuates energy outside its bounds.

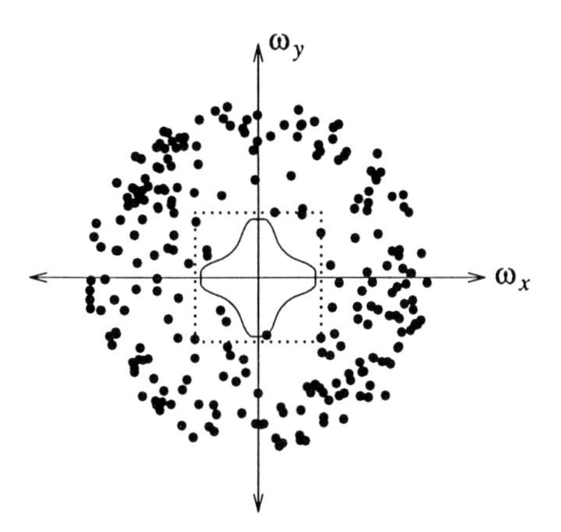


Figure 3. Spectrum of Nonuniformly Sampled Image

If the spectrum of the sampling pattern has energy concentrated in high frequencies, then the halo of noise will be pushed farther out from the origin, and more of it will be outside of the pass band of the filter. The best known patterns having this high-frequency characteristic are the *Poisson-Disk* stochastic point processes. These patterns are random, but include a constraint that no two points can be closer than some minimum distance (as if each point was surrounded by a hard disk) [Ripley77]. The spectral consequences of this sampling pattern were first investigated by Yellott, who found this arrangement in the photoreceptors of monkey retinas [Yellott83].

More commonly used are patterns based on *jitter* processes. These are formed by randomly perturbing the points in a periodic uniform lattice. Jitter sampling contains more low-frequency energy in its spectrum than Poisson-disk patterns, and images produced with it have a more grainy appearance at low sampling rates [Mitchell87]. However, jitter sampling is easy to generate, and straightforward adaptive-sampling schemes exist for generating jitter samples at variable density [Dippé85, Cook86, Kajiya86, Painter89]. Some of these methods could also be described as stratified sampling.

### 4. Sequential Poisson-Disk Sampling

Poisson-disk samples are typically generated by a "dart-throwing" algorithm which is computationally expensive and which makes it difficult to control the final density of samples (one initially choses the hard-disk diameter, not the desired sample density) [Dippé85, Mitchell87].

With the following new algorithm, it is possible to generate good high-frequency sampling patterns with sequentially increasing density. Begin by choosing the first sample at random in a region. To add the $(n+1)^{th}$ sample, generate $mn$ uniformly distributed random candidate points (where $m$ is a constant parameter). For each of these random points, compute the distance to the closest of the $n$ points already in the pattern. Then chose the candidate point with the largest closest-point distance, and add it to the pattern. By scaling up the number of random candidate points, in proportion to $n$, we maintain a constant ratio $m$ of candidates to pattern points in the process. Thus we expect the statistics of the pattern (the autocorrelation, etc) to also scale and remain similar as the sample density increases. The high-frequency quality of the pattern increases with $m$.

This is an $O(n^2)$ algorithm, but it is an improvement over the poorly defined termination of the dart-throwing algorithm (which runs until it cannot add new samples). The speed was improved dramatically by using grid methods for the nearest-neighbor calculation. This point process is not strictly hard-disk, because it is possible (although unlikely) for samples to lie very close together. However, the resulting patterns are excellent if $m$ is not too small. The following figure shows some snapshots from this process, using $m = 10$:

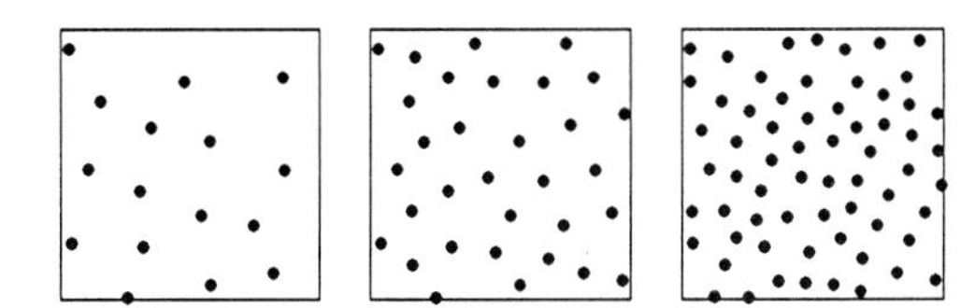

Figure 4. Sequential Generation of High-Frequency Samples

It is sometimes useful to perform this algorithm with wrap-around boundary conditions, so the pattern can be replicated periodically over the plane (with much longer period than the pixel rate, of course). The algorithm can be extended to higher dimensions, and it could also be used to generate isotropic high-frequency sampling patterns on the surface of a sphere. That may be useful because area light sources and glossy reflections require *sampling solid angles.* The alternative of stratified sampling of latitude and longitude is not isotropic because strata near the pole are very different in shape than equatorial strata. The concept of choosing the best samples from random candidates will be used again in the algorithms applied to distribution ray tracing.

By "hard disk" we usually mean a circular region of avoidance around each sample. By using an ellipse or other shape, the spectrum of the pattern can be made anisotropic in some fashion. The human visual sensitivity extends higher into vertical and horizontal frequencies than it does into diagonal frequencies, so a Poisson-diamond pattern might be better than Poisson-disk. Bouatouch *et al* support this idea in their experiments with uniform quincunx sampling [Bouatouch91]. This is an issue that could be studied further.

### 5. Motion Blur and Spatiotemporal Sampling

If two-dimensional sampling can push noise into high frequencies, can the same effect be obtained while sampling the extra parameters of distribution ray tracing? Let us begin by considering motion blur effects, where a single extra parameter $t$ is added. This is not an obvious three-dimensional generalization of the problem of the previous section. $f'(x,y;\,t)$ is sampled in *three dimensions,* but we are still concerned with the resulting sampling noise in the *two-dimensional* image $i(x,y)$.

To derive the spectrum of $i(x,y)$, let $f_s(x,y,t) = f'(x,y;\,t)\cdot s(x,y,t)$ be the sampled multiparameter image function, where $s(x,y,t)$ is a distribution of delta functions in space/time. The sampled image function is low-pass filtered spatially with $r(x,y)$, and integrated over an exposure-time interval for motion blur:

$$i(x,y) = r(x,y) * \int_0^1 f_s(x,y,t)\,dt \tag{6}$$

The spectrum is a little easier to derive if we replace the integration over a time interval with the equivalent operations of convolution with a box function in $t$ followed by sampling one slice through $t$. Then using the Convolution Theorem, we find the spectrum of $i(x,y)$ to be:†

$$I(\omega_x,\omega_y) = R(\omega_x,\omega_y) \int_{-\infty}^{\infty} Sinc(\omega_t/2\pi)\cdot F_s(\omega_x,\omega_y,\omega_t)\,d\omega_t \quad (7)$$

The important difference between the expression for the static-image spectrum (5) and the spectrum of the motion-blurred image (7) is the integration over $\omega_t$. This means the three-dimensional spectrum (at least, the portion passed by the $R$ and $Sinc$ filters) will be projected onto the spatial $(\omega_x,\omega_y)$ plane. Ideally, we would like the noisy part of this spectrum to be pushed out of a cylindrical region around the $\omega_t$ axis, so its projection will contain only the highest possible spatial noise frequencies.

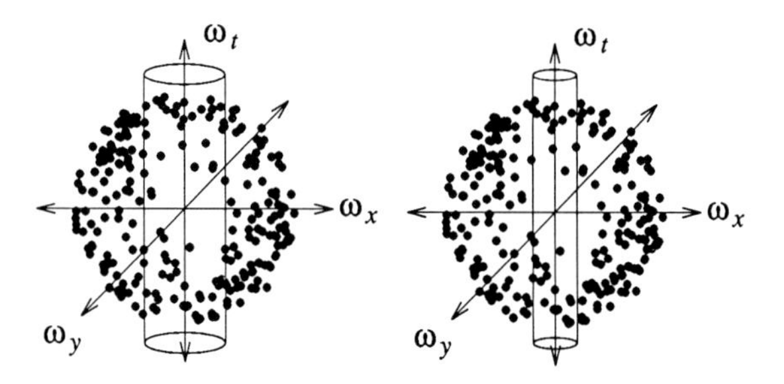


Figure 5. Cylinders of Medium and Low Spatial Frequencies

This suggests that the best general sampling pattern will be one with little power in the low-spatial-frequency region around the $\omega_t$ axis. Figure 5 depicts the spectrum of the sampling pattern with cylindrical regions around the $\omega_t$ axis enclosing spatial frequencies below some bandlimit. The wide cylinder on the left contains frequencies up to some medium value, and the cylinder on the right represents a lower bandlimit. We would like these cylinders to be as vacant of power as possible. In fact, the practical requirement is to have the power within each cylinder be concentrated at the highest possible frequencies. It is also important to give the highest priority to removing the lowest spatial frequencies, so we require the power in the right-hand cylinder to be concentrated at higher temporal frequencies than in the left-hand cylinder.

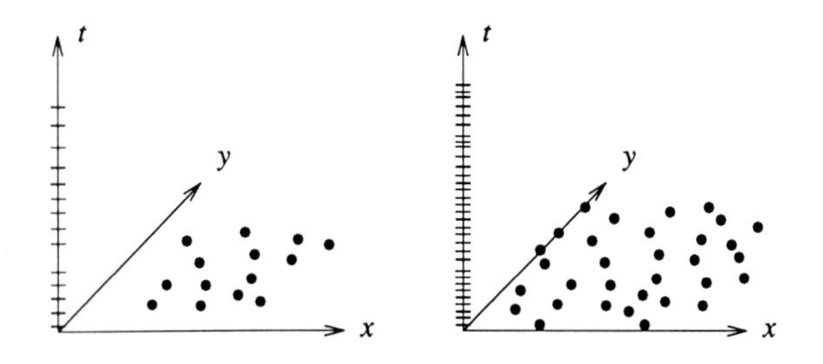


Figure 6. Marginal Distributions of Samples in Space and Time

These conditions in the frequency domain imply some conditions on the arrangement of samples in space and time. The two graphs in Figure 6 illustrate situations corresponding to the spectra in Figure 5. They show the projection of samples onto the spatial plane (dots) and onto the time axis (tick marks). We are not yet certain where these samples should be in space/time, but we will be able to give conditions on their projections into space and time.

If there is no movement in a region of the image, then only the spatial projection of the pattern is important, so we could begin by constraining it to form an optimal distribution, like Poisson-disk.

We are interested in the power contained within cylinders of spatial frequencies, in Figure 5, and in the temporal-frequency distribution of that power. Imagine that we have convolved the spectrum with a cylinder and sampled the result on the $\omega_t$ axis (this is equivalent to averaging over spatial frequencies inside the cylinders). That operation corresponds approximately to selecting the samples within a cylindrical region of space, and considering their time distribution. The narrower cylinder of frequencies in Figure 5 corresponds to a wider region of space in Figure 6. The temporal distribution of samples, shown in Figure 6, represent one-dimensional patterns of the highest possible frequency (such as Poisson-rod distributions).

Therefore, the desired property of space/time sampling patterns is that in any cylindrical region of space, the distribution of samples in time will be a high-frequency pattern. An interesting consequence of this is that samples which are adjacent in space should differ greatly in time or other parameter coordinates. This is quite different from the most obvious three-dimensional analog of Poisson-disk sampling. A Poisson-sphere point distribution would not necessarily have this property of high-frequency time distribution.

### 6. A Scanning Sample-Generation Algorithm

A simple scanning algorithm is one possible way to generate sampling patterns which approximate the conditions described in the previous section. Begin by stratifying the $x$ and $y$ dimensions into a mesh of subsquares, assuming that one jittered sample is contained in each. The goal is to assign each sample a value of the parameter $t$. This is done in scanning order, from left to right, and top to bottom.

| S | S | S | S | S |
|---|---|---|---|---|
| S | P | P | P | S |
| S | P | • | | |

Figure 7. Neighborhood of the Next Unprocessed Subsquare

Figure 7 illustrates the situation at some point in the scanning process. We wish to choose a parameter value for the subsquare containing the dot. In the $5 \times 5$ region surrounding the dot, some subsquares above and behind (indicated by "P" or "S") have already been assigned $t$ values. Call these the P-cells and S-cells (meaning primary and secondary).

We would like the new $t$ value to fit into a high-frequency Poisson-rod distribution, as shown in Figure 6. In a manner reminiscent of the sequential Poisson-disk algorithm of section 4, we generate a set of primary candidate $t$ values with uniform random distribution in $[0,1]$. For example, let us say we generate 100 primary candidates. The candidates are sorted by their maximum closest distance to the $t$ values of the P-cells. Distance is defined with wrap-around boundary conditions, so the pattern can used periodically from frame to frame.. From the sorted list, we might pick (for example) the 10 with largest max-min distance. Any one of these 10 values should be a good choice to complete a coarse Poisson-rod distribution as suggested on the left of Figure 6.

The set of 10 values selected above are now considered as secondary candidates. For each secondary candidate, compute the maximum

† This actually corresponds to the integration of time from $-\frac{1}{2}$ to $\frac{1}{2}$. A phase-shift factor could be added to reflect integration from 0 to 1.

$sinc(x) = sin(\pi x)/\pi x$.

closest distance to the $t$ values of the S-cells, and pick the one with the largest max-min distance. This should be a good choice to complete the denser distribution as suggested on the right of Figure 6. We are trying to meet two constraints, picking 100 primary candidates and evaluating how well they match the situation on the left of Figure 6, then selecting 10 secondary candidates to match the conditions on the right.

## 7. Experiments with Scan-Generated Sampling Patterns

Figures 8 and 9 demonstrate the use of this sampling pattern on a ray-traced scene containing spinning wheels. Figure 8 was made by choosing $t$ values with a uniform random distribution. Figure 9 uses the spectrally optimized $t$ values generated by the scanning algorithm. In fact, a $32 \times 32$ pattern of samples was generated and replicated periodically on the plane. Both image were generated with just *one sample per pixel* so the sampling noise can be seen clearly. Essentially, we are looking at the raw supersamples $f_s$, which would be passed into the filter stages of Figure 2 in order to make an antialiased digital image.

Figures 10a and 10b show the corresponding noise spectra (with lighter shades indicating higher power). These were obtained by subtracting Figures 8 and 9 from a reference image (generated with 100 rays per pixel), to create an error image. The discrete Fourier transform of the error images show a typical "white noise" spectrum in Figure 10a, corresponding to the random sampling. However, Figure 10b shows a considerable concentration of power in the higher frequencies.

Even though the mean square error of Figures 8 and 9 are about the same, the frequency distribution of power has a large impact on subjective appearance. A series of randomly-sampled images like Figure 8 were generated using from 1 to 9 samples per pixel, and several expert observers were asked to select the best comparison with Figure 9. Figure 9 was obviously better looking that 1 sample per pixel and obviously worse than 9. The consensus was that three or four random time samples per pixel were required to match the subjective quality of Figure 9.

Figures 11 and 12 show a similar comparison of the technique applied to depth-of-field effects. Figure 11 was generated with uniformly random values of $(a,b)$, the parameters controlling the deflection of primary rays through the camera aperture. Figure 12 used parameter values generated by the scanning algorithm. The only difference from scanning generation of $t$ values is the use of a two-dimensional Euclidean distance for the max-min distance selections. Once again, both figures were generated with one ray per pixel. Figure 11 shows the clumpy pattern of sampling error characteristic of white noise, and Figure 12 shows the finer structure of high-frequency noise.

A critical observer may notice, from the point-spread, that the simulated camera has a square lens. There is no special problem in simulating a round lens, which should have been done if this were not a simple experimental ray tracer.

Figures 13 and 14 demonstrate another two-parameter experiment, using parameter values to perturb the normal vector of a surface and simulate glossy reflection. Figure 13 uses random perturbations and Figure 14 uses scan-generated parameters.

These images provide evidence that the condition for optimal parameter sampling is correct. The scanning sample-generation algorithm should not be thought of as a definitive way to generate optimal samples, however. It is an *ad hoc* way to generate a pattern with approximates the conditions defined in section 5, but only in a $5 \times 5$ region, and probably not with perfect isotropy. There is a great deal of opportunity for experiment and improvement.

## 8. N-Parameter Sampling

Suppose an image of the spinning-wheels picture (seen in Figures 8 and 9) is generated with motion blur and also an area light source, creating shadows with penumbras. Using an optimized pattern of $t$ parameters ensures that the spinning spokes of the wheels are well sampled as in Figure 9. Using an optimized pattern of $(u,v)$ parameters ensures that the penumbra around the rim of the wheels has good high-frequency sampling noise. However, in regions where both distribution ray-tracing effects are combined—in a moving penumbra—the sampling noise has a coarser white-noise appearance.

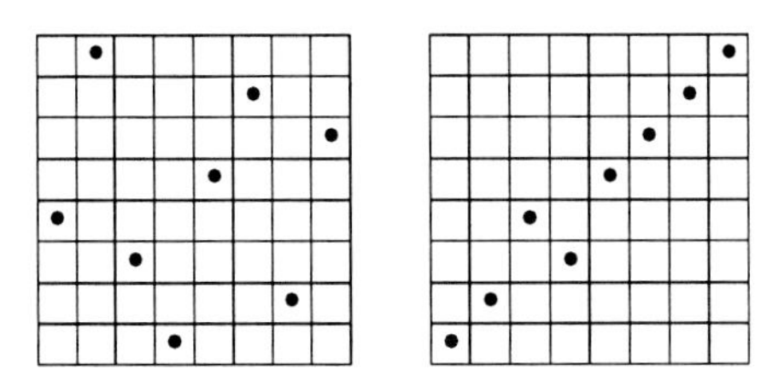

Figure 15. 8-Rook Sampling Patterns

It is not sufficient to optimize the $t$ and $(u,v)$ distributions of samples alone. The joint distribution of $(t,u,v)$ matters. Figure 15 demonstrates this concept. Here, two patterns both have the same projected ("marginal") distributions in $u$ and $v$ (in this case, uniform periodic). However, the overall joint distributions of the two patterns are very different. Suppose a signal was sampled with the pattern on the right. If the signal contains only variations in the $u$ or only in the $v$ dimensions, it may be sampled well enough. But if the image contains variation along the diagonal perpendicular to the row of samples, severe aliasing might occur. In distribution ray tracing, a similar situation can occur, and aliasing caused by poor joint distribution of the parameter samples can be projected onto the image.

It is also not sufficient to just optimize the joint distribution of $(t,u,v)$ without considering the marginal distributions of $t$ and $(u,v)$. The scanning algorithm was used to generate samples in $(t,u,v)$ with Poisson-sphere joint distributions, and this resulted in relatively poor image quality. The region of moving penumbra was much improved, however.

The best image quality in the moving-penumbra test was achieved by generating sampling patterns in which both the joint distribution and the marginal distributions are spectrally optimized. Figure 16 shows the spinning wheels image, using a sampling pattern which combines a joint distribution of $(t,u,v)$ which is Poisson-sphere, and a marginal distribution of $t$ which is Poisson-rod. This suggests that as the parameter space becomes higher in dimension, sampling patterns must be found which meet the conditions of Figure 6 in a combination of marginal and joint distributions. This combination of conditions was met by extending the scanning algorithm to select a series of primary, secondary, and tertiary candidates.

## 9. Adaptive Sampling

No matter how optimal a supersampling pattern may be, we cannot ignore the computational efficiency of adaptive sampling. It is often the case (except in the most complex scenes) that many portions of an image can be sampled at relatively low density. A simple solution might be to use a few discrete levels of sampling density. The two-level sampling algorithm described by the author in [Mitchell87] was very easily adapted to use a five-dimensional $(x,y,t,u,v)$ periodic pattern of 1024 samples.

In that scheme, an image is sampled at a low base rate. It is a good idea to make this base rate selectable by the user, and typically one or a few samples per pixel area are sufficient. The results of the base-rate sampling are then used to estimate local bandwidth and identify regions that require sampling at a higher rate.

Variable sampling rates can be achieved by simply scaling the stored pattern. If the pattern is optimal in the sense discussed above, it will only be necessary to scale the pattern in $x,y$. As the sampling rate per pixel area increases, the rate per parameter dimension should also increase and the distribution should remain spectrally optimal, as indicated in Figure 6.

## 10. Conclusions

Optimal nonuniform sampling is a familiar approach to the aliasing problem in Whitted's ray-tracing algorithm. This paper takes a first step in extending this technique to the multidimensional algorithm of distribution ray tracing. This is nontrivial for two reasons. First, a simple extension of the stratified/jitter sampling techniques to higher dimensions requires a number of samples exponential in the dimension. Secondly, this is not simply the problem of generating a $D$-dimensional image, which would be an obvious extension of the two-dimensional theory.

An analysis of the sampling problem in distribution ray tracing suggests a criteria for sampling patterns that can force aliasing noise into higher frequencies. Samples contained in any circular region in space (on the $x,y$ image plane) should have parameter values which form a pattern of the highest possible frequency. It appears that in addition to requiring the overall joint distribution of parameter values to be high-frequency (e.g., a Poisson-hypersphere distribution), it is important to insure that certain marginal distributions are of the highest frequency (e.g., time values being Poisson-rod, $(u,v)$ parameters being Poisson-disk, etc.). This problem could be studied further.

A scanning sample-generation algorithm is proposed, which gives sampling patterns which locally approximate the optimal. This was good enough to demonstrate the correctness of the optimality condition in a number of test images. Further work could be done on better sample-generation algorithms, perhaps using exhaustive Monte Carlo search.

Much more difficult sampling problems arise in the current most advanced rendering algorithms. These problems are made explicit in several recent works [Kajiya86, Heckbert90, Shirley90].

## 11. Acknowledgements

I would like to thank John Amanatides, Pat Hanrahan, Paul Heckbert, Peter Shirley, and the SIGGRAPH reviewers for their helpful comments on this work and discussions of sampling issues.

## 12. References

[Bouatouch91] Bouatouch, K., Bouville, C., Tellier, P. Low sampling densities using a psychovisual approach. *Eurographics '91*, to appear.

[Cook84] Cook, R. L., Porter, T., Carpenter, L. Distributed ray tracing. *Computer Graphics*, 18, 3 (July 1984), 137-145.

[Cook86] Cook, R. L. Stochastic sampling in computer graphics. *ACM Trans. Graphics*, 5, 1 (January 1986), 51-72.

[Dippé85] Dippé, M. A. Z. and Wold, E. H. Antialiasing through stochastic sampling. *Computer Graphics*, 19, 3 (July 1985), 69-78.

[Heckbert90] Heckbert, P. S. Adaptive radiosity textures for bidirectional ray tracing. *Computer Graphics*. 24, 4 (August 1990), 145-154.

[Kajiya86] Kajiya, J. T. The rendering equation. *Computer Graphics*, 20, 4 (July 1986), 143-150.

[Lee85] Lee, M., Redner, R. A., Uselton, S. P. Statistically optimized sampling for distributed ray tracing. *Computer Graphics*, 19, 3 (July 1985), 61-67.

[Marvasti87] Marvasti, F. A. *A Unified Approach to Zero-Crossings and Nonuniform Sampling*, Nonuniform Press (1987).

[Mitchell87] Mitchell, D. P. Generating antialiased images at low sampling densities. *Computer Graphics*, 21, 4 (July 1987), 65-72.

[Painter89] Painter, J., and Sloan, K. Antialiased ray tracing by adaptive progressive refinement. *Computer Graphics*, 23, 3 (July 1989), 281-288.

[Ripley77] Ripley, B. D. Modeling spatial patterns. *J. Roy. Statist. Soc. B*, 39, (1977), 172-212.

[Shirley90] Shirley, P. Physically based lighting calculations for computer graphics. PhD Thesis, University of Illinois, (1990).

[Whitted80] Whitted, T. An improved illumination model for shaded display. *Comm. ACM*, 23, 6 (June 1980), 343-349.

[Yellott83] Yellott, J. I. Jr. Spectral consequences of photoreceptor sampling in the rhesus retina. *Science*, 221, (1983), 382-385.

FIGURE 8

FIGURE 9

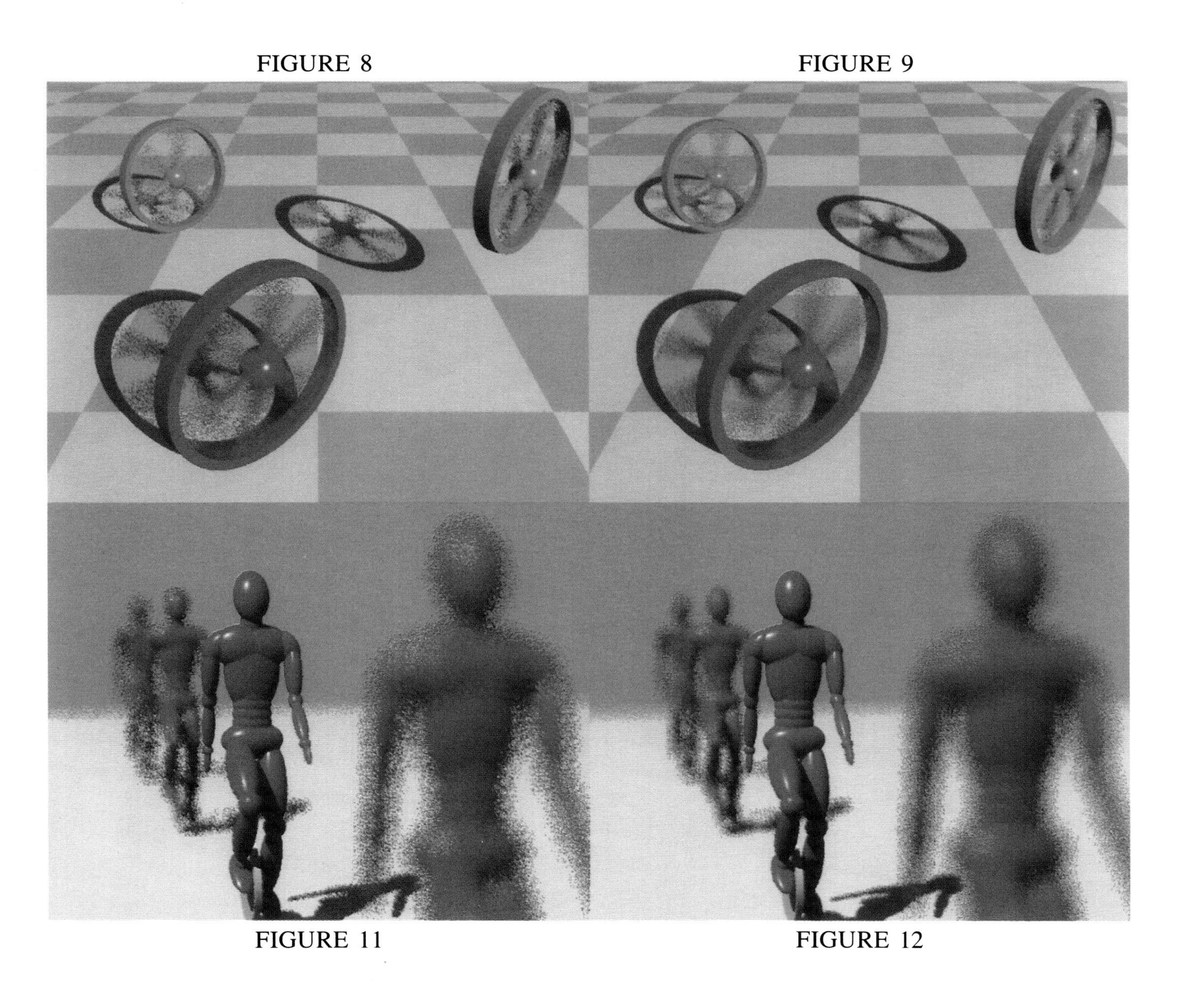

FIGURE 11

FIGURE 12

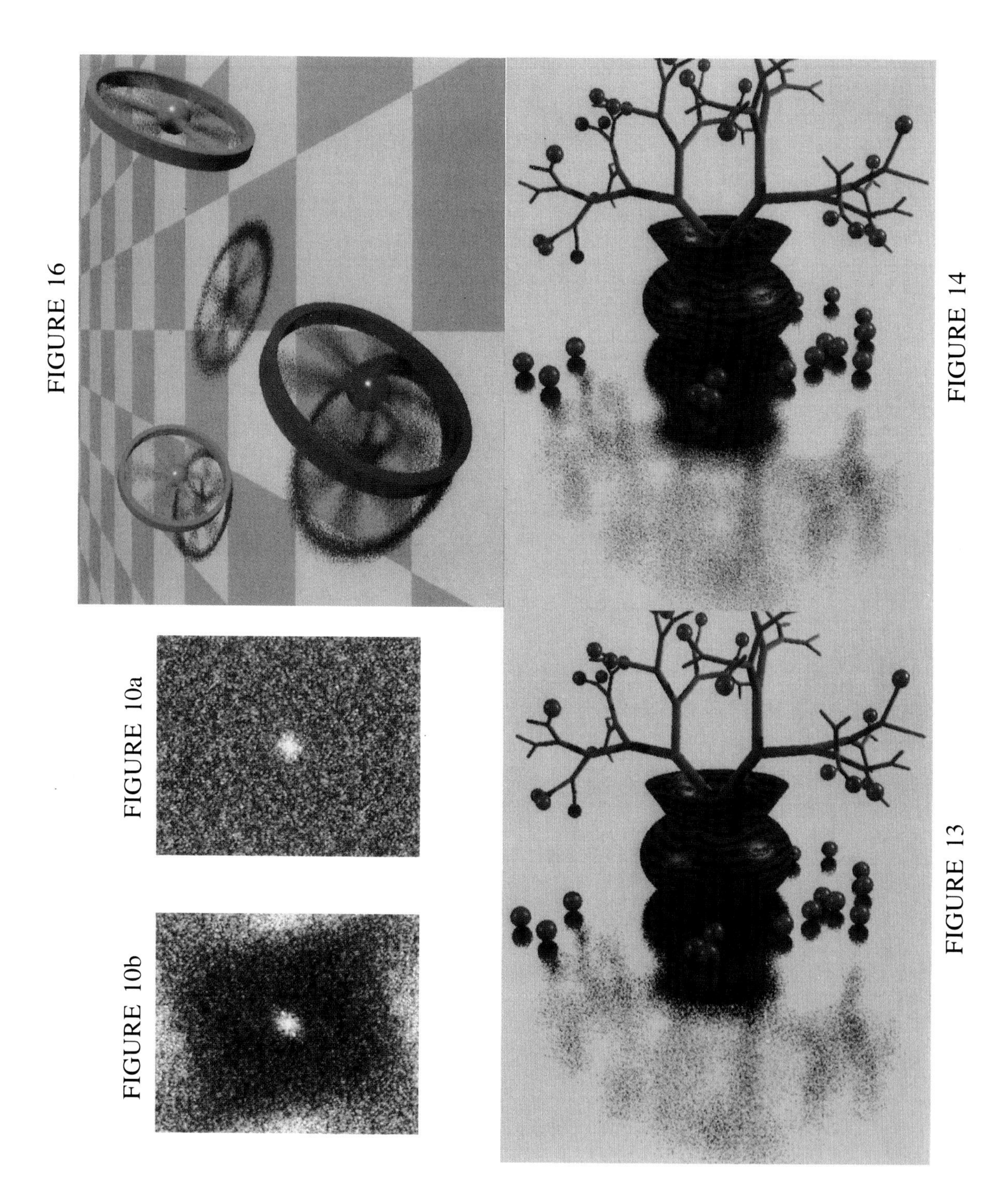

FIGURE 16

FIGURE 10a

FIGURE 10b

FIGURE 14

FIGURE 13

# A Progressive Multi-Pass Method for Global Illumination

Shenchang Eric Chen, Holly E. Rushmeier†, Gavin Miller, Douglass Turner

Advanced Technology Group
Apple Computer Inc.

†The George Woodruff School of Mechanical Engineering
Georgia Institute of Technology

## ABSTRACT

A new progressive global illumination method is presented which produces approximate images quickly, and then continues to systematically produce more accurate images. The method combines the existing methods of progressive refinement radiosity, Monte Carlo path tracing and light ray tracing. The method does not place any limitation on surface properties such as ideal Lambertian or mirror-like. To increase efficiency and accuracy, the new concepts of light source reclassification, caustics reconstruction, Monte Carlo path tracing with a radiosity preprocess and an interruptible radiosity solution are introduced. The method presents the user with most useful information about the scene as early as possible by reorganizing the method into a radiosity pass, a high frequency refinement pass and a low frequency refinement pass. The implementation of the method is demonstrated, and sample images are presented.

**CR Categories and Subject Descriptors:** I.3.3 [Computer Graphics]: Picture/Image Generation - Display Algorithms. I.3.7 [Computer Graphics]: Three-Dimensional Graphics and Realism
**General Terms:** Algorithms
**Additional Key Words and Phrases:** Radiosity, Ray Tracing, Monte Carlo, Caustics, Global Illumination, Progressive Refinement.

## INTRODUCTION

Generating realistic images of complex scenes is still far from a real time process. To handle this problem, Bergman et. al. [1] introduced the concept of "adaptive refinement" for generating high quality images. An adaptive refinement method has two fundamental properties: the image continues to improve indefinitely with time, and the most useful information is produced earliest in the rendering process. In this paper we present a global illumination method for generating physically accurate images which follows the adaptive refinement paradigm.

In Bergman's adaptive refinement method, only simple shading models are presented. The global illumination effects, such as shadowing and inter-reflection between surfaces, are ignored. In addition, the refinement process leaps from one shading model to another. The transition between refinement steps is not smooth. Cohen et. al. [2] subsequently extended the concept to develop a "progressive refinement" radiosity method that allows the user to view the images as the radiosity solution evolves. The new method uses a more sophisticated global illumination model and generates images that progress smoothly and gracefully to the final image. The idea of progressive refinement is readily applied to ray tracing methods as well. Painter, Sloan [3] and Ward [4] have presented ray tracing methods that evolve by casting increasing numbers of rays to increasing numbers of pixels.

Both pure radiosity and pure ray tracing solutions to the global illumination problem have disadvantages. Radiosity methods require careful, detailed meshing to correctly capture shadows, which may have very high spatial frequency [5], [6]. Radiosity methods also require an excessive computation time and storage to directly solve for non-diffuse reflections [7]. While radiosity methods have been developed with the capability of capturing caustic effects (e.g., [8]), meshing methods to guarantee the capture of these effects do not exist. Ray tracing methods can be formulated to produce physically accurate solutions (i.e., [9], [10]). However, such methods require huge numbers of rays to be cast per pixel to avoid perceptible noise in the image. While caustic effects can be captured with eye ray tracing, using "backward ray tracing" (i.e., light ray tracing) and "caustic maps" ([11], [12]) is generally more effective.

Because of the relative advantages and disadvantages of radiosity and ray tracing, many hybrid or "multi-pass" methods have been developed. The first such multi-pass method was the radiosity method developed by Nishita and Nakamae [13], in which different techniques were used for direct and indirect illumination. Wallace et. al. [14] and Sillion and Peuch [15] developed hybrid methods in which an extended radiosity method was followed by a ray tracing pass to solve for view dependent directional reflections. Shirley [16] developed the most extensive multi-pass method to date. In Shirley's method, radiosity is used for indirect illumination, Monte Carlo ray tracing is used for direct illumination, and light ray tracing is used for caustics.

While multi-pass methods such as Shirley's can produce excellent and physically accurate images, they may still produce noticeable artifacts. The surface discretization from the radiosity pass is still used in the final image. If the environment has strong indirect illumination, the quality of the final image will be strongly dependent on the meshing of the visible surfaces. Diffuse surfaces are still assumed to be ideal Lambertian in the final image. There is no mechanism for rendering surfaces which are neither strongly



©1991 ACM-0-89791-436-8/91/007/0165 $00.75

directional nor ideal Lambertian.

Another drawback of all the previous multi-pass methods is that they do not provide intermediate feedback to the user. Since global illumination rendering is generally a very lengthy process, intermediate feedback is very important in detecting mistakes early on . In the case of Shirley's method, the user must wait for many higher order diffuse interreflections which produce little new information about the scene in the progressive radiosity phase before sharp shadows, textures and surface bumps can be obtained in the Monte Carlo ray tracing phase. The ray tracing phase then progresses in the order of pixels. No complete image is available for fast feedback until every pixel is finished.

We present an extended, reorganized version of the multi-pass concept which is designed to overcome these disadvantages. The method consists of a series of passes which continuously provide user feedback. The rendering process begins with a progressive refinement radiosity pass with extended form factors computed by ray tracing for non-diffuse surfaces. This pass provides a good approximation to the overall illumination. A high frequency refinement pass follows to perform a Monte Carlo path tracing from the eye and the lights to create shadows and caustics. Unlike earlier methods, the path tracing is only directed at surfaces that are considered "bright" enough to create high frequency details. A caustics reconstruction technique is introduced to compute a caustic map for each surface. A low frequency refinement pass continues to refine the image using Monte Carlo path tracing for accurate low frequency illumination effects such as color bleeding. The low frequency refinement makes use of the results from the radiosity pass for high order reflections. Therefore, it should be faster than pure path tracing. Since the pass is performed pixel by pixel, the radiosity meshing artifacts are invisible in the final image.

In the new method, the user does not need to wait for the first pass to finish before the next pass begins. The radiosity pass can be interrupted to compute the high frequency details. All the three passes potentially can be run in parallel.

We begin with a description of the multi-pass method in the next section. We then describe how the method is organized into a progressive refinement solution, followed by a description of implementation and results. Conclusions and future directions are presented at the end.

## EXTENDED MULTI-PASS METHOD

A solution for global illumination must account for all of the energy which can pass from sources of light to the eye. In the following sections, we present two ways of examining how our method solves the global illumination problem. Firstly, we examine how all possible light paths between the sources and the eye are accounted for. Secondly, we examine how all the terms in the rendering equations [9] are accounted for. We then present a detailed discussion of two new features of our method–light source reclassification and caustics reconstructions. Finally, we contrast the new extended method with existing multi-pass methods.

### Accounting for All Light Paths

We use three techniques to find all the significant light paths:

1. Progressive Refinement Radiosity (PRR), with ray tracing for extended form factors.
2. Light Ray Tracing (LRT), which traces rays from light sources for caustic map generation.
3. Monte Carlo Path Tracing (MCPT), with distributed ray tracing [17] being a subset of MCPT.

We divide all possible light paths into four classes. Let *s* be a reflection or transmission off of a "specular-like" surface (i.e. highly directional but not necessarily a perfect mirror), and *d* be a reflection or transmission off of a "diffuse-like" surface (i.e. weakly direction but not necessarily Lambertian). Using s and d to denote reflection/transmission events, the four path classes are shown in Fig. 1.

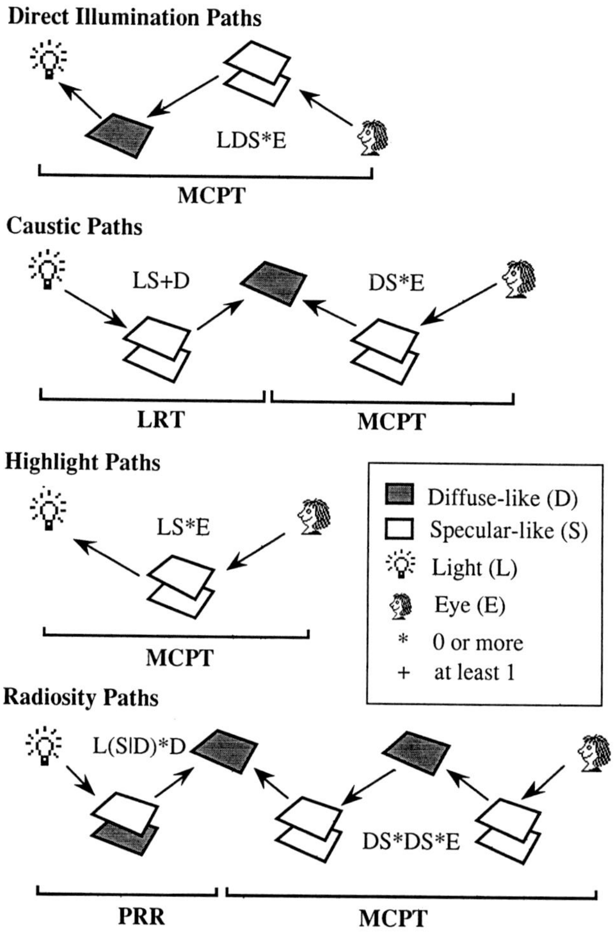

**Direct Illumination Paths**

LDS*E

**MCPT**

**Caustic Paths**

LS+D DS*E

**LRT** **MCPT**

**Highlight Paths**

LS*E

**MCPT**

**Radiosity Paths**

L(S|D)*D DS*DS*E

**PRR** **MCPT**

Diffuse-like (D)
Specular-like (S)
Light (L)
Eye (E)
* 0 or more
\+ at least 1

*Fig. 1. Four classes of light paths are shown both pictorially and with Heckbert's style of notations[18]. The paths are followed with three techniques–PRR, LRT and MCPT. Arrows indicate the direction in which the path is followed.*

Direct illumination paths refer to paths from sources to the eye via one *d* followed by zero or more *s*'s. These paths are followed using MCPT. As soon as a ray traced from the eye hits a *d*, another ray is cast at a light source. The direction of this second ray is chosen using a probability density function (*pdf*) based on the area distribution of energy/time on the light sources. An example of these paths is the shadowing effects created by light sources.

Caustic paths contain one or more *s*'s, a single *d*, and zero or more *s*'s before the eye. These paths are followed using LRT and the results are deposited on the caustic maps attached to diffuse surfaces. The caustic maps are created from the intersections of the caustic paths with the diffuse surfaces using a reconstruction method that will be described in “Caustic Reconstruction”.

Highlight paths consist of zero or more *s*'s and are traced by MCPT. Highlight paths account for the direct rendering of light sources, the rendering of light sources through specular-like transmitters, and the production of specular-like highlights in opaque surfaces.

Radiosity paths contain at least two *d*'s. Radiosity paths are followed using a combination of PRR and MCPT. Paths from the eye up to the second *d* are followed using MCPT. Paths which continue on through any number of *s* and *d* until reaching the source are followed using PRR. Radiosity paths produce the classic radiosity effects such as color bleeding.

These four paths encompass paths with any combination of *s* and *d* between the source and the eye. This can be shown with the number of *d*'s contained in the paths. Any path that has at least two *d*'s is a radiosity path. Paths with one *d* is either a caustic path or a direct illumination path. Paths contain zero *d* belong to the highlight path.

### Solving the Rendering Equation

In this section we describe how the strategies outlined above produce a solution to the rendering equation. The quantity of light which we compute at each step in the solution is the radiance, I, the light energy per unit time, projected area and solid angle (also called the intensity). The reflectance of each surface is given by its bidirectional reflectance, $\rho_{bd}(\theta_i,\phi_i;\theta_r,\phi_r)$, which is the radiance reflected in a direction *r* as the result of incident energy per unit time area and solid angle from a direction *i*.

As outline in the previous section, our method combines PRR, LRT and MCPT. MCPT involves using Monte Carlo methods to estimate integrals of various forms. The methods for estimating integrals are well established. To simplify the discussion in this section, many of the details of the Monte Carlo estimates will be omitted. These details can be found elsewhere, such as in [19].

For a particular view, an image is formed by finding an approximate solution to the following rendering equation for each pixel:

$$I_{pixel} = \int_{pixel\_area} I_o(p,\theta_r,\phi_r) f(x_s,y_s)\,dx_s\,dy_s \qquad \text{(eq. 1)}$$

where $I_{pixel}$ is the pixel radiance, $I_o(p,\theta_r,\phi_r)$ is the radiance leaving a point "p" in the scene visible through screen location (xs,ys) in direction $(\theta_r,\phi_r)$ to the eye, and f(xs,ys) is a filtering function for anti-aliasing. $I_o$ is a function of wavelength, and RGB values must be determined for $I_{pixel}$. To simplify discussion, we omit explicit wavelength dependencies and the transformations which convert a discrete wavelength sampling $I_o$ to RGB values for $I_{pixel}$.

Pixel radiance is computed by averaging the results of many trial estimates of $I_{pixel}$. Each trial begins by tracing a ray from the eye through the pixel using a pdf based on f(xs,ys). $I_o(p,\theta_r,\phi_r)$ must be found for the surface which the ray hits. The radiance leaving a surface as the sum of the emitted and reflected radiance:

$$I_o(p,\theta_r,\phi_r) = \underbrace{I_e(p,\theta_r,\phi_r)}_{\text{emitted}} + \underbrace{I_r(p,\theta_r,\phi_r)}_{\text{reflected}} \qquad \text{(eq. 2)}$$

In general, there is a transmitted radiance as well. However, since it is treated exactly analogously to the reflected component, we will omit transmission for now.

$I_e(p,\theta_r,\phi_r)$ must be specified, and $I_r(p,\theta_r,\phi_r)$ is given by:

$$I_r(p,\theta_r,\phi_r) = \int_\Omega \rho_{bd}(\theta_i,\phi_i;\theta_r,\phi_r) I_i(\theta_i,\phi_i)\cos\theta_i\,d\omega_i \qquad \text{(eq. 4)}$$

where $I_i(\theta_i,\phi_i)$ is the radiance incident from a direction i, $\theta_i$ is the angle between the surface normal and the direction i, $d\omega_i$ is a differential solid angle, and the integral is over the incident hemisphere.

Formally, we can rewrite $\rho_{bd}(\theta_i,\phi_i;\theta_r,\phi_r)$ in terms of a diffuse-like component $\rho_l(\theta_i,\phi_i;\theta_r,\phi_r)$, which has a weak dependence on direction, and a specular-like component $\rho_h(\theta_i,\phi_i;\theta_r,\phi_r)$, which has a strong dependence on direction:

$$\rho_{bd}(\theta_i,\phi_i;\theta_r,\phi_r) = \rho_l(\theta_i,\phi_i;\theta_r,\phi_r) + \rho_h(\theta_i,\phi_i;\theta_r,\phi_r) \qquad \text{(eq. 5)}$$

We use $\rho_l$ and $\rho_h$ rather than $\rho_d$ and $\rho_s$ to avoid confusion with idealized Lambertian $(\rho_{bd} = \rho_d/\pi)$ and mirror-like $(\rho_{bd} = \rho_s/\cos\theta\, d\omega)$ reflectances. Lambertian and mirror-like reflectances may be included in $\rho_l$ and $\rho_h$, but this decomposition does not require assuming these idealized reflectances.

We can express $I_r(p,\theta_r,\phi_r)$ as the sum of $I_h(p,\theta_r,\phi_r)$ and $I_l(p,\theta_r,\phi_r)$, where:

$$I_h(p,\theta_r,\phi_r) = \int_\Omega \rho_h(\theta_i,\phi_i;\theta_r,\phi_r) I_i(\theta_i,\phi_i)\cos\theta_i\,d\omega_i \qquad \text{(eq. 6)}$$

$$I_l(p,\theta_r,\phi_r) = \int_\Omega \rho_l(\theta_i,\phi_i;\theta_r,\phi_r) I_i(\theta_i,\phi_i)\cos\theta_i\,d\omega_i \qquad \text{(eq. 7)}$$

$I_h$ is the radiance reflected from the specular-like component and $I_l$ is the radiance reflected from the diffuse-like component. $I_h$ is evaluated by MCPT. A direction is chosen using a pdf based on the reflectance, and the surface visible in that direction is found by ray casting. This process is performed recursively until a light source or a diffuse-like surface is encountered. The integral for $I_h$ is then approximated using $I_l$ of the last surface.

$I_l$ is evaluated by decomposing it into four parts:

$$I_l = I_{l,s} + I_{l,c} + I_{l,h} + I_{l,l} \qquad \text{(eq. 8)}$$

where $I_{l,s}$ is light directly from light sources, $I_{l,c}$ is light from light sources via a series of specular-like reflections, $I_{l,h}$ is light from non-light sources via a a series of specular-like reflections, and $I_{l,l}$ is light from other diffuse-like surfaces. These four parts are expressed in the following equation:

$$I_{l,\beta}(p,\theta_r,\phi_r) = \int_\Omega \rho_l(\theta_i,\phi_i;\theta_r,\phi_r) I_{i,\beta}(\theta_i,\phi_i)\cos\theta_i\,d\omega_i \qquad \text{(eq. 9)}$$

where $\beta = s,c,h,l$

All of the values on the right hand side for $I_{l,s}$ are known. The integral for $I_{l,s}$ is reexpressed as a sum of area integrals over each source g:

$$I_{l,s} = \sum_g \int_{A_g} \rho_l(\theta_i,\phi_i;\theta_r,\phi_r) I_g(\theta_g,\phi_g)\cos\theta_i\cos\theta_g V\,dA_g / r^2 \qquad \text{(eq. 10)}$$

where $A_g$ is the area of light source g, $\theta_g$ is the angle between the normal to surface $dA_g$ and the direction to p (i.e. the point where radiance is being evaluated) and r is the distance from $dA_g$ to p. The integral over a source is estimated by casting a ray at a random point on the source. The term V is one if the light is visible in the direction, and is zero otherwise. The integral is then approximated using the value of the integrand in that direction.

$I_{l,c}$ is found by LRT and is stored in a caustic map. When a ray from the eye hits a diffuse-like surface, the value of $I_{l,c}$ is computed from the map and then added to the radiance for that ray.

$I_{l,h}$ is evaluated recursively just as $I_h$ is, with the exception that paths leading to the light source via a series of specular-like reflections are excluded to prevent double counting the caustic paths.

$I_{l,l}$ is evaluated as an integral in which the whole right hand side is known, by using the values of $I_l$ calculated from the PRR solution to approximate the values of $I_{i,l}$. A ray is cast into a random direction in the incident hemisphere to determine the direction for evaluating the integrand. To avoid double counting the direct illumination paths, surfaces which are treated as light sources are not included in this integral.

The techniques described above are used to calculate trial values for each pixel. Let $\rho_{l,ave}$ and $\rho_{h,ave}$ be average reflectances. In an individual trial $I_r$ is estimated using Russian Roulette [20] by rewriting $I_r$ in the equivalent form:

$$I_r = \rho_{l,ave}(I_l / \rho_{l,ave}) + \rho_{h,ave}(I_h / \rho_{h,ave}) + (1 - \rho_{l,ave} - \rho_{h,ave})0 \quad \text{(eq. 11)}$$

Based on a choice of a uniformly distributed random number, $I_r$ is estimated as either $I_l / \rho_{l,ave}$, $I_h / \rho_{h,ave}$ or zero. $I_h$ is estimated by recursion. $I_l$ is estimated by finding a trial value of $I_{l,s}$, adding $I_{l,c}$ and using Russian Roulette again to either estimate $I_{l,l}$ or $I_{l,h}$. The number of trials required depends on the value of the sample standard deviation of the estimated $I_{pixel}$ compared to a user selected level of accuracy (i.e., [21], [22]).

### Light Source Reclassification

Like many other global illumination methods, much more work is done in our method to estimate the radiances from light sources than from other surfaces. This is justified by the substantially greater radiosity of lights. Usually all self-emitting surfaces are defined as sources. In many environments, however, some non-emitting surfaces reflect enough energy to warrant treatment as light sources. Conversely, some self-emitters are very dim, and special treatment of these is not necessary. Goral et. al. [23] have treated surfaces directly illuminated by point lights as emitters. However, their motivation is to handle point lights rather than to capture strong indirect illumination.

Light source classification is performed after the PRR pass. A surface is classified as a light source if its radiosity, computed in the PRR pass, is considered large enough. Some self-emitters may not be considered as light sources and will be treated like the other reflecting surfaces.

### Caustics Reconstruction

The caustic maps are constructed in the following steps:

First, the caustic map resolutions are determined for each surface either from a particular view or from the area of the surface if view independent solutions are desired. To compute view dependent resolutions, the scene is ray traced from the eye. The smallest ray-surface intersection kernel required for each surface by this pass determines the resolution of the caustic map required for that surface. This approach creates uniform maps instead of hierarchical ones like [18]. This is convenient when using MIP maps [24] or summed area tables [25] for caustic map anti-aliasing in the final pass. The algorithm will be conservative in that it will create more detailed caustic maps than required for objects which occupy both the foreground and the background. However, it will always provide adequate resolution for the near-by parts of a surface.

Second, for each light in turn, rays are fired off towards the specular surfaces. This may be achieved either by Monte Carlo sampling over a hemisphere, or by using one or more hemi-cubes [5] for item-buffer preprocessing [26]. Each ray is generated such that it carries the same amount of energy. The rays are reflected or refracted when they hit specular-like surfaces and stop when they encounter diffuse-like surfaces. All the decisions of treating a surface as specular-like or diffuse-like are made using Russian Roulette discussed previously. The result of this pass is that each diffuse-like surface has a list of ray-surface intersections for caustic rays.

Third, for each surface, the list of intersections is used to reconstruct a smooth caustic map. In the method proposed by Arvo [11], each ray deposits energy over four pixels with a bilinear ramp of the intensity. This is equivalent to depositing a square convolution kernel one pixel wide into the caustic map. The energy of a ray will be deposited into a rectangle which is $d_u$ wide and $d_v$ high in the parameter space where $d_u$ is $1 / n_u$ and $d_v$ is $1 / n_v$, and $n_u$ and $n_v$ are the resolutions of the caustic map in the u and v directions respectively. Since the caustic map is scaled by the tangent vector magnitudes when it is transformed to the world space during rendering, it is necessary to scale the intensity of the kernel in the caustic map (b) so that it will correspond to the ray energy (E) in the world space. For the sake of simplicity we assume that the tangent vectors are constant over the extent of the kernel.

A kernel with intensity b in the parameter space will correspond to an energy E in the world space according to the following equation.

$$b = E \Big/ \left(d_u d_v |p_u \times p_v|\right) \quad \text{(eq. 12)}$$

where $p_u$ is the u-tangent vector for the surface at the ray-surface intersection and $p_v$ is the v- tangent vector.

Equation (eq. 12) is used to find b, which is deposited onto the final reconstructed caustic map.

For regions of the caustic map in which there are less than about four overlapping kernels per caustic map pixel, the resultant image will be very noisy (i.e., some pixels may not be hit by any ray at all). One method to diminish the noise is to use a larger convolution kernel for light deposition. This is called the fixed kernel method for the reconstruction of pdf's [27]. It has the disadvantage that it is hard to set the kernel size in a way which filters out the noise in sparse regions of the map and keeps high frequency detail in dense regions. Because of this limitation, adaptive kernel size methods should be used in which the size of the deposition kernel depends on the local density. This becomes a chicken and egg problem, in that the kernel size depends on the density, which in turn is the very thing we are trying to compute.

In this paper, a "nearest neighbors" method is used [27]. This involves expanding each convolution kernel until it covers n neighbors. A preprocessing step, for the sake of computational efficiency, is used to produce an "accumulation" image, at the reconstruction resolution, in which one pixel wide convolution kernels are deposited for each ray (i.e., these kernels all have the amplitude of one). Then, around each ray-intersection, a rectangular region is expanded until it covers n neighbors, with n being computed by integrating the image over the rectangle. The ratio of the width to height of the rectangular region is set to the ratio of the corresponding tangent vector magnitudes. This means that the rectangle in the parameter space maps to an approximately square region in the world space. The dimensions of the rectangular region are then used to scale an elliptical-conical kernel which is deposited onto the final caustic map. The kernel amplitude is first set to normalize the filter and then multiplied by the intensity computed using eq. 12 to take into account the effects of the tangent vector magnitudes. This algorithm is illustrated in Fig. 2.

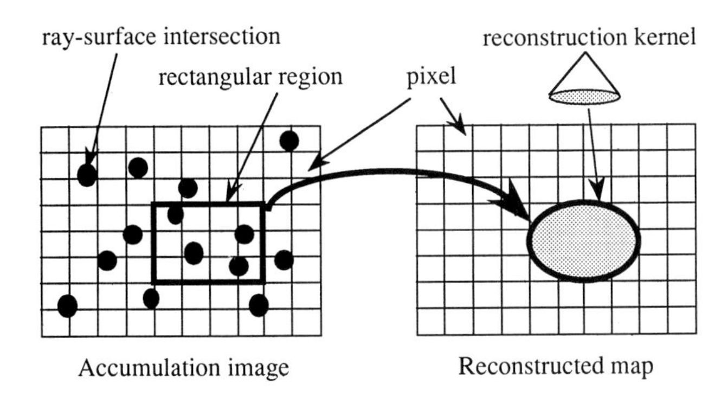


*Fig. 2. Caustic map reconstruction*

The integral of the accumulation image over the rectangular region may either be evaluated by direct summation or it could be computed using a summed-area table [25]. This would allow a binary search to be made on the rectangle size and would speed up the reconstruction process when ray intersections are very sparse. However, the subsequent large convolution kernels would still need to be deposited into the reconstructed map. When there are half the number of ray-surface intersections, the convolution kernels have twice the area. The computation time for the reconstruction depends linearly on the number of caustic map pixels, and is relatively insensitive to the number of ray-surface intersections.

Finally, the results are read out from the caustic maps during the Monte Carlo path tracing step as described previously.

### Comparison to Previous Formulations

Previous global illumination methods can be described in the terms used in "Solving the Rendering Equation." In Wallace's method[14], $I_r$ is decomposed into $I_l$ and $I_h$, and $\rho_l$ is Lambertian. $I_l$ is given by the radiosity solution and $I_h$ by distributed ray tracing. In Shirley's method[16], $I_l$ is decomposed into $I_{l,s}$ , $I_{l,c}$ and $I_{l,l+h}$. $I_{l,s}$ is evaluated as in our method (except that only self-emitters are sources). $I_{l,c}$ is calculated by interpolating a caustic map, rather than by reconstruction. $I_{l,l+h}$ is taken directly from the radiosity solution. Our reclassification of light sources allows improved shadows and caustics cast by indirect sources. The reconstruction produces a better representation of caustics. Finding $I_{l,l+h}$ by Monte Carlo integration, rather than using the PRR solution directly has two advantages. First, in the final rendering, the true bidirectional reflectance can be used. Second, the surface discretization used in the radiosity solution never appears in the final image, reducing the work required in meshing.

Kajiya's pure MCPT approach is accurate but inefficient. Several researchers(e.g.[18]) have discussed the advantages of using LRT for caustics. Our major improvements are the caustic reconstruction and the use of PRR for higher order interreflections. Using the PRR solution has two advantages. The length of each individual trial is reduced, since paths end at diffuse-like surfaces. Also, the variance in the trials is reduced, reducing the number of trials for a particular level of accuracy. This variance reduction results from the value of $I_{i,l}$ being known, rather than being a high variance quantity which itself must be evaluated by recursion. Ward [10] used a similar strategy to reduce path length and variance by using "cached" radiance values for higher order interreflections.

## PROGRESSIVE REFINEMENT

The method described in the previous section is not organized to present the user with the most important information at the earliest time possible. In this section we present a reorganization of the extended multi-pass method into a true progressive refinement method. The key ideas in this reorganization are an interruptible PRR, a high frequency refinement and a low frequency refinement pass.

First of all, the information to be presented must be prioritized. We have chosen the following ordering:

Overall global illumination of the environment:
- Approximate direct illumination
- Approximate diffuse-like interreflections
- Approximate specular-like reflections
- Approximate caustics

High spatial frequency variations in illumination:
- Sharp shadows
- Textures and surface bumps
- Specular-like reflections
- Caustics

Low spatial frequency variations in illumination:
- Accurate diffuse-like reflections

The user is presented with the overall global illumination using the first steps in a PRR solution. High spatial frequency variations are then presented by computing direct illumination, caustic and highlight paths. The low spatial frequency variations are calculated by computing the radiosity path.

### Interruptible PRR

The first several iterations of a PRR solution provide a large quantity of useful information per unit time. However, as the method goes on, the rate at which images improve decreases dramatically. Each additional "shot" produces little visible effect on the solution. However, the solution must run for many more iterations to produce an accurate, converged solution. In our method an interrupted PRR solution is used to produce more detailed images, with the results of the completed PRR solution added in later.

An interrupted PRR solution can be used because of the linearity of the rendering equation. Let $I_{int}$ be the interrupted PRR solution and $I_{final}$ be the final PRR solution. Roughly, the process can be thought of as using the values of $I_{int}$ as the radiosity values for the extended multi-pass method in one image, and the values of $(I_{final} - I_{int})$ in a second image, and then summing the results.

### High Frequency Refinement

After the the PRR solution has been interrupted by the user, and a view chosen, high frequency refinement begins. Initially all surfaces are displayed with the values $I_{int}$. To approximate specular reflections quickly, a pass is made in which specular-like surfaces are ray traced from the eye (with the initial assumption that they are mirror-like). In this pass the interrupted PRR solution can also be modified using texture maps.

Next, the direct illumination, highlights and caustics resulting from each light source are calculated. To make the transition in the solution smooth, these effects are added into the image source by source. Three types of radiance values are calculated for each pixel – $I_{approx}$, $I_{true}$ and $I_{disp}$. $I_{approx}$ is the value for the pixel found from PRR. $I_{true}$ is the value which has been accurately calculated for the pixel by MCPT. $I_{disp}$ is the value displayed, and is the sum of $I_{approx}$ and $I_{true}$. In the pass for each source g, the portion of $I_{approx}$ for each diffuse-like surface due to direct illumination and caustics from g is subtracted out, and value of $I_{true}$ is increased by using the caustic map for g and by following direct illumination paths from g. In estimating direct illumination, the bump maps and texture maps for that surface can be used. For each specular-like surface, the values of $I_{approx}$ and $I_{true}$ are replaced using the values of $I_{approx}$ and $I_{true}$ for the diffuse-like surfaces visible through the surface. The true value of $\rho_h$ is used for the surface to find the visible diffuse-like surface (i.e., Note that the diffuse-like surface may be visible through a chain of specular-like reflections.) Treating specular-like surfaces in this way insures that diffuse-like surfaces will be treated in the same way when seen through a specular-like surface as when seen directly.

Let $I_e$ be the emission, $I_{prr}$ be the radiosity result maintained for each surface, and let the initial value of $I_{prr}$ be $I_{int}$. The following is simplified pseudo-code for adding in the effect of each source g:

```
HighFrequencyPass(g) {
  Shoot out "negative" light from g to remove the effects of
  direct illumination and caustics of g from all Iprr's;
  Build caustic maps by shooting out caustic rays from g;
  For each pixel p {
     converged = false;
     trial = 0;
     sum_approx = 0;
     sum_true = 0;
     While not converged {
        trial++;
        shoot ray at p using f(p) as weighting function to find
        surface_hit;
        GetRadiance(g, surface_hit , trial_Iapprox, trial_Itrue);
        sum_approx += trial_Iapprox;
        sum_true += trial_Itrue;
        new_Iapprox = sum_approx/trial;
        new_Itrue = sum_true/trial;
        trial_Idisp = Itrue(p) + new_Iapprox + new_Itrue;
        If ((standard_deviation( new_Itrue)/trial_Idisp)
           < accuracy) {
           converged = true;
           Itrue(p) += new_Itrue;
           Idisp(p) = trial_Idisp;
        }
     }
  }
}
```

```
GetRadiance(g, surface_hit,trial_Iapprox, trial_Itrue) {
  If Il chosen by Russian Roulette {
     trial_Iapprox = Iprr(surface_hit) ;
     trial_Itrue = estimate of Il,s† obtained by shooting at
     source g;
     trial_Itrue += estimate of Il,c† from caustic map of
     surface_hit;
  } Else If Ih chosen {
     Shoot ray in direction given by pdf based on ρh;
     GetRadiance(next_surface_hit , trial_I'approx,
     trial_I'true);
     trial_Itrue = trial_I'true†;
     trial_Iapprox = trial_I'approx†;
  }
}
```

For ease of explanation several details have been omitted from the pseudo-code. For example, more variables need to be saved to check the convergence of the value of radiance for each pixel. The convergence check does not need to be made after each trial, but after a group of trials. The number of trials in a group is determined on the fly, based on the initial estimates of the variance of the trials. The accuracy used in the convergence check must be smaller than the overall accuracy required for each pixel, because the errors from several passes will be summed. However, the effect of the higher accuracy requirement is mitigated by considering the sample standard deviation as a fraction of the total radiance for the pixel, not as the fraction of the current value of Itrue being estimated.

The quantities marked with a † need to be weighted to account for the Russian Roulette selection and multiplied by the surface reflectance. As noted by Arvo and Kirk, trees of rays, rather than strict paths may result in lower variances. Null results for rays directly to the eye increase the variance, so null selection in Russian Roulette is only used for higher order interreflections.

At the end of the high frequency refinement, the radiance of all direct illumination, caustic, and highlight paths have been accurately estimated. The user can either resume the interrupted PRR solution or can move on to the low frequency refinement pass.

### Low Frequency Refinement

In the final pass, more accurate values for $I_{approx}$ are found by evaluating radiosity paths by MCPT with results from PRR. The value of $I_{prr}$ for all light sources is set to $I_{final}$ - $I_{int}$, since the direct and caustic contributions of $I_{int}$ from these sources on other surfaces have already been calculated. The value of $I_{prr}$ for all other surfaces is set to $I_{final}$ since the effects of interreflections from these surfaces are now going to be estimated by integration over the hemisphere.

As in high frequency refinement, trials are made pixel by pixel until $I_{true}$ converges. Pseudo-code for calculating radiance in the low frequency refinement is given by:

```
/* hit_d indicates if a diffuse surface has been hit along the
  path. Initially, hit_d is false */
GetLRadiance(surface_hit, trial_Itrue, hit_d) {
  If Il chosen by Russian Roulette {
     If hit_d is false { /* hit the first d */
        Shoot ray out into hemisphere above surface_hit to find
        next_surface_hit;
        hit_d=true;
        GetLRadiance(next_surface_hit , trial_I'true, hit_d);
```

```
            trial_Itrue = trial_I'true†;
        } Else { /* hit the second d */
            trial_Itrue = Iprr(surface_hit);
        }
    } Else If Ih chosen {
        Shoot ray in direction given by a pdf based on ρh to find
        next_surface_hit;
        GetLRadiance(next_surface_hit , trial_I'true);
        trial_Itrue = trial_I'true†;
    }
}
```

When solving pixel by pixel, the change in image quality per unit time is extremely slow. By storing extra data per pixel for convergence checks, the refinement can proceed by doing passes of one trial (or some small set of trials) per unconverged pixel, and displaying the intermediate results.

## IMPLEMENTATION AND RESULTS

The multi-pass method has been implemented on a rendering testbed developed at Apple. A test scene was constructed to demonstrate the ideas presented in the paper. The scene contains a diffuse area light and two spotlights illuminating a diffuse room with a planar mirror, a mirrored-surface sphere, a glass sphere, a diffuse box and stick sculptures. The scene is designed to test illumination effects such as sharp shadows, soft shadows, color bleeding, caustics, specular reflection and refraction.

Fig. 3 shows a series of images generated in the progressive refinement process. Fig. 3a was generated at the end of the radiosity pass. The scene was tessellated to 114 patches and 4358 elements with patches and elements defined as in [28]. The radiosity pass was implemented with the hemi-cube algorithm [29]. The extended form-factors due to the specular reflection and refraction were computed with ray tracing. This image provides a good overall approximation but is lacking in high frequency details, such as sharp shadows and caustics. Since the radiosity pass is view independent, the user can inspect the scene from various views before continuing the refinement. Fig. 3b was generated at the end of the high frequency refinement pass, where the direct illumination from the two spot lights and the overhead area light was replaced with a more accurate, view dependent Monte Carlo solution. Notice the improved shadows and caustics on the floor. In this particular example, the high frequency details are created mostly by the lights and the radiosity pass provides a good approximation to the low frequency component. Therefore, this pass effectively renders the image close to its final form as shown in Fig. 3c. In Fig. 3c, the low frequency component is replaced by the Monte Carlo solution. Artifacts, such as the extraneous dark blob next to the stick's shadow on the left wall, from the radiosity meshing are therefore eliminated.

The Monte Carlo path tracing sent from 16 to 256 paths per pixel per light, based on the variance of each pixel. The number of paths per pixel per light is 25 on average in the high frequency pass and 250 per pixel in the low frequency pass. The image resolution is 540 by 300. Item buffer preprocessing was used to speed up the tracing of initial rays from the eye[26].

The timing data in Fig. 3 are based on computing the images on a Silicon Graphics' Iris 4D GTX. Since the actual computation time is machine and implementation dependent, the relative timing for each pass is a better indicator of the cost of the solution.

*Fig. 3(a) At the end of the radiosity pass (12 minutes)*

*Fig. 3(b) At the end of the high frequency pass (4.5 hours)*

*Fig. 3(c) At the end of the low frequency pass (21 hours)*

*Fig. 3. Images generated in the progressive refinement process. Notice the caustics on the floor created by the spot light pointing at the mirror in Fig. 3b and Fig. 3c.*

Fig. 4 shows the difference between the images in Fig. 3 with color coding. The main difference between Fig. 3a, the radiosity image, and Fig. 3b, the high frequency refined image, is in the high frequency details. The difference between Fig. 3b and Fig. 3c is not very significant in this example.

*Fig. 4(a): Fig. 3b - Fig. 3a*

*Fig. 4(b): Fig. 3c - Fig. 3b*

*Fig. 4. Differences of images in Fig. 3. Color coding is used to show the difference. Grey means no difference. Red means the first image's intensity is above the second one and conversely for blue.*

The images in Fig. 3 are actually composed of partial images that show different illumination components. Fig. 3a is composed of Fig. 5a, the direct illumination from the light sources, and Fig. 5b, the interreflections between all the other surfaces. These two images were computed by recording the results of radiosity shootings from the light sources and non-light sources separately. Fig. 5a shows high frequency details that are not adequately represented with the coarse radiosity meshing. Fig. 5b is a better representation since the interreflection is very low frequency. However, some noticeable artifacts are still present. Fig. 5c is the direct illumination from the light sources computed by Monte Carlo path tracing. Fig. 5d shows the caustics computed by light ray tracing. Fig. 5b, Fig. 5c, Fig. 5d altogether compose the image in Fig. 3b, the results after the high frequency refinement. Fig. 5e shows the interreflections from non-light sources computed in the low frequency refinement pass. This image is more accurate than Fig. 5b but took significantly longer to compute. Fig. 5c, Fig. 5d and Fig. 5e altogether compose the image in Fig. 3c, the results after the low frequency refinement pass.

Fig. 6 shows the caustic maps before the reconstruction. The reconstructed results are shown in Fig. 5d. In this example, each light source sent out up to 262144 rays randomly based on the light's distribution function. The resolutions used for the caustic maps range from 4 to 128 pixels per side.

*Fig. 5(a) Direct illumination and caustics computed by PRR.*

*Fig. 5(b) Interreflections computed by PRR.*

*Fig. 5(c) Direct illumination computed by MCPT.*

*Fig. 5(d) Caustics computed by LRT.*

*Fig. 5(e) Interreflections computed by MCPT.*

*Fig. 5. Partial images which demonstrate different illumination components. These images compose the images in Fig. 3. Fig. 3a=Fig. 5a+Fig. 5b. Fig. 3b=Fig. 5b+Fig. 5c+Fig. 5d. Fig. 3c=Fig. 5c+Fig. 5d+Fig. 5e.*

*Fig. 6. Caustic maps before reconstruction. The light spots on the surfaces show the caustic maps with bilinear interpolation of ray-surface intersections. The reconstructed results using a variable sized kernel is shown in Fig. 5d*[1].

Fig. 7 shows the same test scene computed with our method by omitting the high frequency refinement pass. Therefore, no ray was sent specifically to the directions of bright emitters or reflectors. This image was computed with 256 paths per pixel. The high level of noise indicates that high frequency sources should be treated separately from the low frequency ones.

Our method is also effective in creating shadows created by secondary light sources, such as a very bright diffuse reflectors. Fig. 8 shows a room in which the only lighting is from the spot light pointing at the diffuse wall. The rest of the room is lit by reflection from the wall, which acts as a secondary light source. The pole in the center casts a soft shadow on the floor because of this illumination. The shadow is well defined because in our method the bright wall surface is treated as a light source.

## CONCLUSIONS AND FUTURE WORK

We have presented a new multi-pass progressive refinement method for global illumination. The method combines high efficiency and accuracy with practicality.

*Fig. 7. Noisy image created by skipping the high frequency refinement pass. 256 paths were shot per pixel in the low frequency refinement pass.*

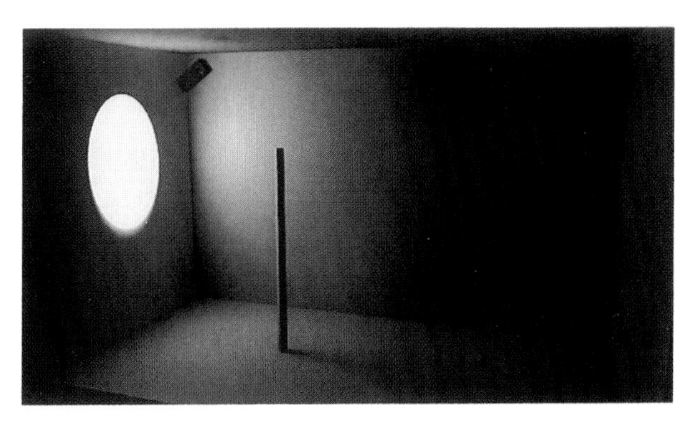

*Fig. 8. Soft shadows created by indirect lighting. The shadow is well defined because the wall lit by the spot light is treated as a light source in the high frequency refinement pass. No low frequency refinement pass was performed on this image. The image took 2 hours to compute.*

Efficiency and accuracy are obtained by using light source reclassification, caustics reconstruction and Monte Carlo integration with a radiosity preprocess. Light source reclassification allows the efficient approximation of the effect of strong indirect light sources. Caustics reconstruction provides a more accurate representation of caustic effects than simple interpolation. Monte Carlo integration with a radiosity preprocess eliminates radiosity discretization from the final image, while avoiding the high cost of pure path tracing.

The method has been made practical by reorganizing the solution into an interruptible progressive radiosity solution followed by high and low frequency refinement passes. Unlike previous radiosity methods, the user does not have to wait for multiple high order interreflections before seeing important high spatial frequency features such as sharp shadows and caustics. Unlike previous ray tracing methods, intermediate images show individual objects clearly, with a minimal level of noise.

Further areas of research include acceleration of the the method, improvements for handling a wide range geometric detail, and developing strategies for parallel implementation. The high frequency pass may be significantly accelerated with a preprocess to identify the number of objects each light can see. Different sampling strategies can be used to reduce the variance in the Monte Carlo integration. Radiosity methods are slow when a scene contains many small objects (e.g. plants with leaves, Venetian blinds, piles of rubber bands and paper clips). The trade-off between the illumination estimate provided by the initial radiosity

1. The gamma of Fig. 5d and Fig. 6 was increased for printing.

solution and the high spatial frequency variations caused by rendering large numbers of small objects needs to be examined. Parallel processing of the radiosity, high and low frequency refinement passes is straightforward. The potential of distributing the computation to a larger number of processors needs to be investigated.

## ACKNOWLEDGEMENTS

We greatly appreciate Apple Computer for providing an exciting environment in which this research was conducted. The algorithm was implemented in a rendering testbed developed by Ken Turkowski, Douglass Turner and Shenchang Eric Chen. We would like to thank reviewers for their helpful suggestions, especially the 13-page hand-written comments from one of them. The second author would like to acknowledge the support in part by a grant from the National Science Foundation, ECS-8909251, "Progressive Refinement Algorithms for Radiant Transfer." Thanks also go to Robin Myers for his help in printing the color images.

## REFERENCES

[1] Larry Bergman, Henry Fuchs, Eric Grant, Susan Spach, "Image Rendering by Adaptive Refinement," Computer Graphics (SIGGRAPH '86 Proceedings), V 20, N 4, Aug. 1986, 29-38.

[2] Michael Cohen, Shenchang Eric Chen, John R. Wallace, Donald P. Greenberg, "A Progressive Refinement Approach to Fast Radiosity Image Generation," Computer Graphics (SIGGRAPH '88 Proceedings), V 22, N 4, Aug. 1988, 75-84.

[3] James Painter and Kenneth Sloan, "Antialiased Ray Tracing by Adaptive Progressive Refinement," Computer Graphics (SIGGRAPH '89 Proceedings, V 23, N 3, July 1989, 281-288.

[4] Gregory J. Ward, "RADIANCE: A Tool for Computing Luminance and Synthetic Images," to appear in Lighting Design and Applications.

[5] Michael Cohen, Donald P. Greenberg "The Hemi-cube: A Radiosity Solution for Complex Environments," Computer Graphics (SIGGRAPH '85 Proceedings) V 19, N 3, July 1985, 31-40.

[6] A.T. Campbell,III, Donald S. Fussell, "Adaptive Mesh Generation for Global Diffuse Illumination," Computer Graphics (SIGGRAPH '90 Proceedings) V 24, N 4, August 1990, 155-164.

[7] David S. Immel, Michael F. Cohen, Donald P. Greenberg, "A Radiosity Method for Non-Diffuse Environments," Computer Graphics (SIGGRAPH '86 Proceedings), V 20, N 4, Aug. 1986, 133-142.

[8] Thomas J.V. Malley, *A Shading Method for Computer Generated Images*, Master's Thesis, University of Utah, June 1988.

[9] James T. Kajiya, "The Rendering Equation," Computer Graphics (SIGGRAPH '86 Proceedings), V 20, N 4, Aug. 1986, 143-150.

[10] Gregory J. Ward, Francis M. Rubinstein, Robert D. Clear, "A Ray Tracing Solution for Diffuse Interreflection," Computer Graphics (SIGGRAPH '88 Proceedings)," V 22, N 4, Aug. 1988, 85-92.

[11] James Arvo,"Backward Ray Tracing," SIGGRAPH '86 Developments in Ray Tracing seminar notes V 12, Aug. 1986.

[12] Mark Watt, "Light-Water Interaction using Backward Beam Tracing," Computer Graphics (SIGGRAPH '90 Proceedings), V 24, N 4, August 1990, 377-385.

[13] Tomoyuki Nishita, Eihachiro Nakamae, "Continuous Tone Representation of Three-Dimensional Objects Taking Account of Shadows and Interreflection," Computer Graphics (SIGGRAPH '85 Proceedings), V 19, N 3, July 1985, 23-30.

[14] John R. Wallace, Michael F. Cohen, Donald P. Greenberg, "A Two-Pass Solution to the Rendering Equation: A Synthesis of Ray Tracing and Radiosity Methods," Computer Graphics, (SIGGRAPH '87 Proceedings), V 21, N 4, July 1987, 311-320.

[15] Francois Sillion, Claude Puech, "A General Two-Pass Method Integrating Specular and Diffuse Reflection," Computer Graphics (SIGGRAPH '89 Proceedings), V 23, N 3, July 1989, 335-344.

[16] Peter Shirley, "A Ray Tracing Method for Illumination Calculation in Diffuse-Specular Scenes," Proceedings of Graphics Interface '90, May 1990, 205-212.

[17] Robert L. Cook, Thomas Porter and Loren Carpenter, "Distributed Ray Tracing," Computer Graphics (SIGGRAPH '84 Proceedings), V 18, N 3, July 1984, 137-144.

[18] Paul Heckbert, "Adaptive Radiosity Textures for Bidirectional Ray Tracing," Computer Graphics (SIGGRAPH '90 Proceedings), V 24, N 4, August 1990, 145-154.

[19] Holly Rushmeier, *Realistic Image Synthesis for Scenes with Radiatively Participating Media*, Doctoral Thesis, Cornell University, May 1988.

[20] James Arvo, David Kirk, "Particle Transport and Image Synthesis," Computer Graphics (SIGGRAPH '90 Proceedings) V 24, N 4, August 1990, 63-66.

[21] Werner Purgatohofer, "A Statistical Method for Adaptive Stochastic Sampling," Computers and Graphics, V 11, N 2, 157-162, 1987.

[22] Mark E. Lee, Richard A. Redner, Samuel P. Uselton, "Statistically Optimized Sampling for Distributed Ray Tracing," Computer Graphics (SIGGRAPH '85 Proceedings), V 19, N 3, July 1985, 61-68.

[23] Cindy M. Goral, Kenneth E. Torrance, Donald P.Greenberg and Bennett Battaile, "Modeling the Interaction of Light Between Diffuse Surfaces," Computer Graphics (SIGGRAPH '84 Proceedings), V 18, N 3, July 1984, 213-222.

[24] Lance Williams, "Pyramidal Parametrics," Computer Graphics (SIGGRAPH '83 Proceedings), V 17, N 3, July 1983, 1-9.

[25] Frank Crow, "Summed-Area Tables for Texture Mapping", Computer Graphics (SIGGRAPH '84 Proceedings), V 18, N 3, July 1984, 207-212.

[26] H. Weghorst, Gary Hooper, and Donald. P. Greenberg, "Improved Computational Methods for Ray Tracing," ACM Transactions on Graphics, V 3, N 1, January 1984, 52-69.

[27] B. W. Silverman, *Density Estimation for Statistics and Data Analysis*, Chapman and Hall, ISBN 0 412 24620 1, 1986.

[28] Michael Cohen, Donald P. Greenberg, Dave S. Immel, Philip J. Brock, "An Efficient Radiosity Approach for Realistic Image Synthesis," IEEE Computer Graphics and Applications, V 6, N 3, March 1986, 26-35.

[29] Michael Cohen, Donald P. Greenberg "The Hemi-cube: A Radiosity Solution for Complex Environments," Computer Graphics (SIGGRAPH '85 Proceedings) V 19, N 3, July 1985, 31-40.

# A Comprehensive Physical Model for Light Reflection

*Xiao D. He*
*Kenneth E. Torrance*
*François X. Sillion*
*Donald P. Greenberg*

Program of Computer Graphics
Cornell University
Ithaca, NY 14853

## Abstract

A new general reflectance model for computer graphics is presented. The model is based on physical optics and describes specular, directional diffuse, and uniform diffuse reflection by a surface. The reflected light pattern depends on wavelength, incidence angle, two surface roughness parameters, and surface refractive index. The formulation is self consistent in terms of polarization, surface roughness, masking/shadowing, and energy. The model applies to a wide range of materials and surface finishes and provides a smooth transition from diffuse-like to specular reflection as the wavelength and incidence angle are increased or the surface roughness is decreased. The model is analytic and suitable for Computer Graphics applications. Predicted reflectance distributions compare favorably with experiment. The model is applied to metallic, nonmetallic, and plastic materials, with smooth and rough surfaces.

**CR Categories and Subject Descriptors:** I.3.7—[**Computer Graphics**]: Three-Dimensional Graphics and Realism; I.3.3—[**Computer Graphics**]: Picture/Image Generation; J.2—[**Physical Sciences and Engineering**]: Physics.

**Additional Key Words and Phrases:** reflectance model, specular and diffuse reflection, comparison with experiment.

## 1 Introduction

Photorealistic image generation is an active research area in Computer Graphics. Ray-tracing and Radiosity have been developed to obtain realistic images for specular and diffuse environments, respectively. However, applications of these methods to general environments have been hindered by the lack of a broadly-applicable local light reflection model. To obtain a true global illumination solution of a general environment, a physically based reflection model of general applicability is needed.

A comprehensive light reflection model is presented in this paper. The model compares favorably with experiment and describes specular, directional diffuse, uniform diffuse and combined types of reflection behavior. The model is analytic and provides a smooth transition from specular to diffuse-like behavior as a function of wavelength, incidence angle and surface roughness.

As illustrated in Figure 1, we classify the reflection process from

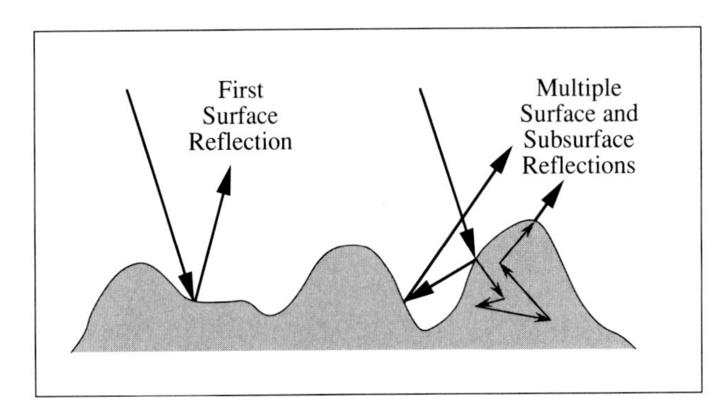


Figure 1: Reflection processes at a surface.

an arbitrary surface as consisting of first-surface reflections and multiple surface and/or subsurface reflections. The first-surface reflection process is described by physical optics and is strongly directional. As the surface becomes smooth this part evolves toward specular or mirror-like behavior. As the surface becomes rough, a diffuse-like behavior due to diffraction and interference effects becomes more important and, at larger roughnesses, it controls the directional distribution of the first-surface reflected light. The model partitions energy into specular and diffuse-like components according to the roughness of the surface. The multiple surface and subsurface reflections sketched in Figure 1 are geometrically complex, but may be expected to be less strongly directional than the first-surface reflected light. Hence, they are approximated as uniform diffuse. Our model leads to analytic expressions suitable for the full range of surface roughnesses and thus is useful for implementation in computer graphics.

The present model builds on, and extends, existing models from optics [3] [5]. It allows for polarization and masking/shadowing effects. The model extends the geometric optics model of Cook [8] to the physical optics region, and correctly includes specular reflection as the surface roughness is decreased. The model is physically based in contrast to empirical approaches [13].

The following sections provide a conceptual introduction, the model, a comparison with physical experiments, and example implementations. The mathematical derivation of the model appears in Appendix A. For unpolarized incident light, the reflectance model is summarized in Appendix B.



©1991 ACM-0-89791-436-8/91/007/0175 $00.75

| | | |
|---|---|---|
| $A$ | = | projected area of the surface (Figure 5) |
| $BRDF$ | = | bidirectional reflectance distribution function |
| $C(r)$ | = | correlation coefficient, equation (48) |
| $c$ | = | complex coefficient of polarization state |
| $D$ | = | distribution function, equation (78) |
| $E_s, \vec{E}_s$ | = | scalar and vector electric fields |
| $F$ | = | Fresnel reflection coefficient, equation (44) |
| $\|F\|^2$ | = | Fresnel reflectivity |
| $\bar{F}$ | = | Fresnel matrix, equation (44) |
| $G$ | = | geometrical factor, equation (76) |
| $G'$ | = | Green's function, equation (2) |
| $g$ | = | surface roughness function, equation (9) |
| $I$ | = | intensity |
| $\bar{I}$ | = | unit tensor |
| $i$ | = | unit imaginary number, i.e., $i = \sqrt{-1}$ |
| $k$ | = | wave number, i.e., $k = 2\pi/\lambda$ |
| $\vec{k}$ | = | wave vector |
| $\hat{k}$ | = | unit vector in wave direction |
| $L$ | = | length |
| $L_x, L_y$ | = | length dimensions of the surface |
| $m$ | = | summation index |
| $\bar{n}$ | = | refractive index |
| $\hat{n}$ | = | local surface normal, unit vector |
| $\hat{n}_b$ | = | bisecting unit vector, equation (51) |
| $\mathbf{p}$ | = | incident polarization state vector, equation (34) |
| $p(z)$ | = | Gaussian distribution function, equation (3) |
| $R$ | = | distance from origin to field point |
| $\vec{R}$ | = | positional vector to field point |
| $\vec{r}$ | = | positional vector of a surface point |
| $S$ | = | shadowing function, equation (23) |
| $\hat{s}, \hat{p}$ | = | $s$ and $p$ polarization unit vectors |
| $\bar{T}$ | = | transformation matrix, equation (39) |
| $\vec{v}$ | = | wave vector change, equation (20) |
| $v_{xy}$ | = | $\sqrt{v_x^2 + v_y^2}$ |
| $\hat{x}, \hat{y}, \hat{z}$ | = | unit vectors in Cartesian coordinates |
| $z$ | = | surface height |
| $\Gamma$ | = | area of bounding surface, Figure 2 |
| $\Delta$ | = | delta function |
| $\vec{\eta}$ | = | horizontal distance vector, equation (28) |
| $\theta, \phi$ | = | polar and azimuthal angles (Figure 5) |
| $\lambda$ | = | wavelength |
| $\xi(x, y)$ | = | Gaussian distributed random function |
| $\rho_{bd}$ | = | bidirectional reflectivity, equation (4) |
| $\rho_{dh}$ | = | directional-hemispherical reflectivity |
| $\rho_{hd}$ | = | hemispherical-directional reflectivity |
| $\sigma^2$ | = | apparent variance of $z = \xi(x, y)$ |
| $\sigma_0^2$ | = | variance of $z = \xi(x, y)$ |
| $\tau$ | = | autocorrelation length, equation (48) |
| $\omega$ | = | solid angle |
| | | **Subscripts** |
| $a$ | = | ambient |
| $b$ | = | bisecting |
| $bd$ | = | bidirectional |
| $dd$ | = | directional-diffuse |
| $i$ | = | incident |
| $p$ | = | $p$ polarization |
| $r$ | = | reflected |
| $s$ | = | $s$ polarization |
| $sp$ | = | specular |
| $ud$ | = | uniform-diffuse |
| $x, y, z$ | = | Cartesian coordinates |
| $1, 2$ | = | surface points |
| | | **Superscripts** |
| $n$ | = | local plane |
| $*$ | = | complex conjugate |

Table 1: Nomenclature

## 2 Theory of light reflection

This section introduces the principal techniques often used to analyze the reflection of an electromagnetic wave by a general surface [3] [5]. The improved model presented later in this paper uses all of these techniques.

### 2.1 Kirchhoff theory

Consider the geometry sketched in Figure 2. According to classical electromagnetic theory, the scalar electromagnetic field $E(\vec{R})$ at an arbitrary point in space can be expressed as a function of the scalar field $E_s$ and its normal derivative $\partial E_s/\partial n$ on any enclosing surface $\Gamma$. The governing equation is [5]

$$E(\vec{R}) = \frac{1}{4\pi}\int_{\Gamma}\left(E_s(\vec{r})\frac{\partial G'(\vec{R},\vec{r})}{\partial n} - G'(\vec{R},\vec{r})\frac{\partial E_s(\vec{r})}{\partial n}\right)d\Gamma \quad (1)$$

where $G'$ is the free space Green's function given by [12]

$$G'(\vec{R},\vec{r}) = \frac{e^{ik|\vec{R}-\vec{r}|}}{|\vec{R}-\vec{r}|} \quad (2)$$

Equation (1) is an integral representation of the wave equation and is known as the Kirchhoff integral of scalar diffraction theory.

For a single reflecting surface, the domain of integration $\Gamma$ reduces to the area of the reflecting surface. This has allowed a class of surface reflection models, known as "physical or wave optics" models, to be derived [5]. "Physical optics" uses a complete physical or wave description of the reflection process, thus allowing for diffraction and interference effects. Wave effects must be included if a reflection model is to describe both specular and diffuse-like reflection from a surface.

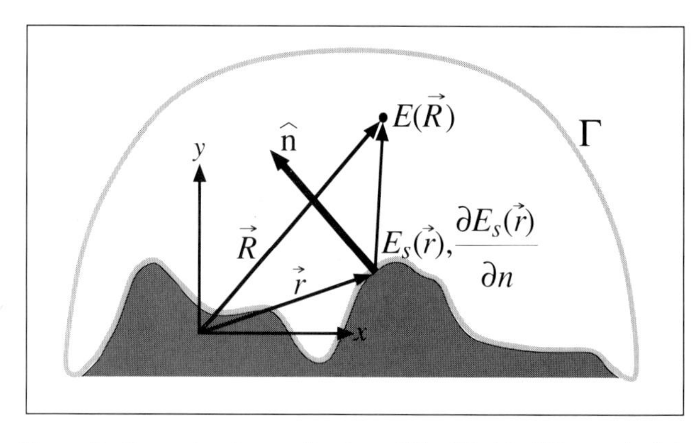


Figure 2: Geometry for application of the Kirchhoff integral. $\hat{n}$ is the local surface normal.

### 2.2 Tangent plane approximation

For reflection processes, the Kirchhoff formulation reduces the general problem of computing the field everywhere in space to the simpler one of determining the field on the reflecting surface. However, even this is a complex task, and the so-called "tangent plane approximation" is often used. This is done by setting the value of the field at a given point on the surface to be the value that would exist if the surface were replaced by its local tangent plane. This is sketched in Figure 3 where $E_i$ and $E_s$ are the incident and scattered fields, respectively, and $F(\theta)$ is the local Fresnel (electric field) reflection coefficient. The approximation is valid when the local radius of curvature of the surface is large compared to the wavelength. The reflected field depends on the Fresnel reflection coefficients for horizontal and vertical polarizations, as well as on the local slope and position of the reflecting point.

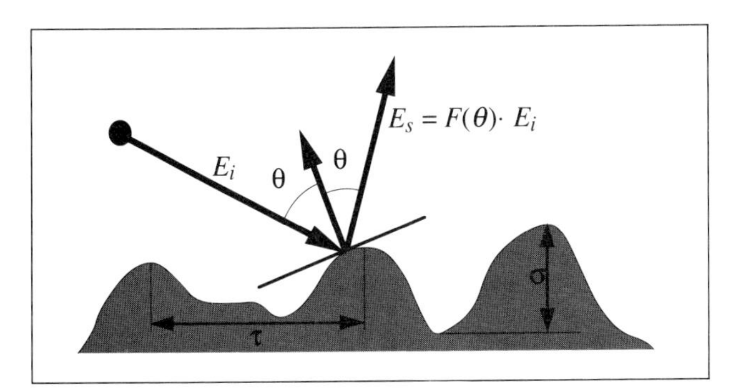


Figure 3: Tangent plane approximation for a reflecting surface. The statistical parameters $\sigma$ and $\tau$ for the surface are indicated schematically.

### 2.3 Statistical surfaces

The complete geometrical specification of a reflecting surface is rarely known, but information at length scales comparable to the radiation wavelength is required when the Kirchhoff theory is used. However, small scale variations of the electromagnetic field on the surface are averaged out when viewed from a distance. This averaging over points on a surface is statistically equivalent to averaging over an entire class of surfaces with the same statistical description. Interesting quantities, such as the reflected intensity in a given direction, can then be obtained by a weighted average of the Kirchhoff integral.

Frequently, the height distribution on a surface (Figure 3) is assumed to be Gaussian and spatially isotropic. Under such conditions, the probability that a surface point falls in the height range $z$ to $z + dz$ is given by $p(z)dz$, with a probability distribution

$$p(z) = \frac{1}{\sqrt{2\pi}\sigma_0} e^{-(z^2/2\sigma_0^2)} \quad (3)$$

A mean value of $z = 0$ is assumed and $\sigma_0$ is the *rms roughness* of the surface. To fully specify an isotropic surface a horizontal length measure is also needed. One such measure is the *autocorrelation length* $\tau$ (defined in equation (48)), which is a measure of the spacing between surface peaks. The rms slope of the surface is proportional to $\sigma_0/\tau$.

### 2.4 Shadowing and masking

The effect of self-shadowing and self-masking by a rough surface (Figure 4) was introduced in computer graphics by Blinn [6] and Cook [8]. This effect manifests itself at large angles of incidence or reflection, where parts of the surface are shadowed and/or masked by other parts, reducing the amount of reflection. Beckmann [4] argued that to first order, the effect of shadowing/masking can be obtained by using a multiplicative factor which accounts for the fraction of the surface that is visible both to the source and the receiver. Such a concept was used by both Blinn and Cook in their geometrical optics approaches, but the V-groove shadowing/masking factor they used [20] is first-derivative discontinuous. Many other shadowing/masking factors have appeared in the literature. Of these, the one due to Smith [16] is continuous in all derivatives and has been found to agree with statistical numerical simulations of a Gaussian rough surface [7].

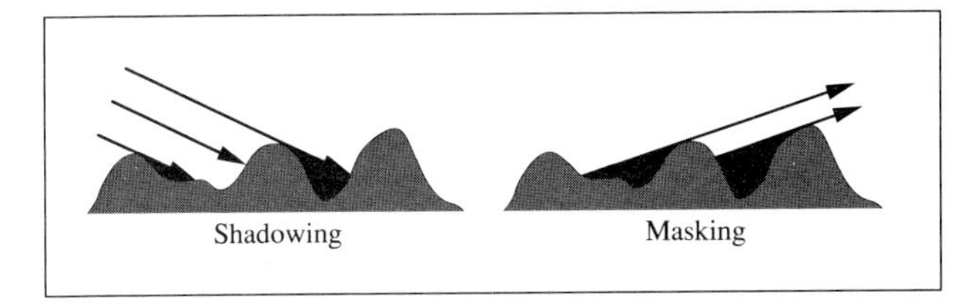


Figure 4: Shadowing and masking.

### 2.5 Discussion

An early comprehensive model of light reflection from a rough surface, using physical optics, was introduced by Beckmann [5]. Beckmann applied the scalar form of the Kirchhoff theory, used the tangent plane approximation, and performed a statistical average over the distribution of heights to get the reflected intensity. The Beckmann distribution function was used by Blinn and Cook for their computer graphics applications.

Stogryn applied a more general, vector form of the Kirchhoff theory, thus taking polarization effects and the correct dependency of the Fresnel reflectivity into account [18]. Furthermore, he used a more complete statistical averaging scheme that averages over both height and slope. However, shadowing/masking was not considered, and the derivation of the reflected intensity was limited to special cases of incident polarization. A more general model, which accounts for polarization, Fresnel, and shadowing/masking effects, has been described by Bahar [1] [2]. However, it is difficult to implement because it relies on the solution of a set of coupled integro-differential equations.

Finally, it should be noted that these models were very rarely compared with experimental results.

## 3 An improved model

This section presents an improved light reflection model of broad applicability. Section 3.1 summarizes the techniques and key assumptions; Section 3.2 presents the improved model. Details of the mathematical derivation appear in Appendix A and a full set of equations for unpolarized incident light in Appendix B.

### 3.1 Techniques and key assumptions

To develop a general reflection model which avoids many of the limitations of previous models, the overall formulation of Beckmann was used, but with the following improvements:

- The vector form of the Kirchhoff diffraction theory is used. This allows, for the first time, a complete treatment of polarization and directional Fresnel effects to be included. Such effects are required for a comprehensive formulation. The model permits abitrary incident polarization states (e.g., plane, circular, unpolarized, partially polarized, etc.) and includes effects like depolarization and cross-polarization.

- The surface averaging scheme of Stogryn [18] is employed with its improved representation of the effects of surface height and slope. Averaging of the Kirchhoff integral is over a four-fold joint probability function (i.e., height, slope, and two spatial points).

- The scheme of Stogryn [18] is extended to average only over the *illuminated* (unshadowed/unmasked) parts of the surface. This requires a modified probability function with an *effective roughness*, $\sigma$, given by equation (53). When roughness valleys are shadowed/masked (Figure 4), the effective surface roughness can be significantly smaller than the rms roughness, $\sigma_0$, especially at grazing angles of incidence or reflection. For the first time, the concept of an effective roughness, which depends on the angles of illumination and reflection, is applied.

- The geometrical shadowing/masking factor of Smith [16] is introduced as a multiplicative factor. The function has appropriate smoothness and symmetry.

With the above, the model leads to a fairly-complex integral formulation. Simplifications result by making the local tangent-plane approximation and assuming gentle roughness slopes. These assumptions should be realistic for many surfaces over a wide range of radiation wavelengths. Significantly, the assumptions lead to an analytical form for the light reflection model.

### 3.2 The improved light-reflection model

The light reflection model is presented in terms of the bidirectional reflectivity $\rho_{bd}$, also called the bidirectional reflectance distribution function (BRDF). The coordinates are shown in Figure 5, together with the propagation unit vectors $(\hat{k}_i, \hat{k}_r)$ and the polarization unit vectors $(\hat{s}, \hat{p})$ for the polarization components perpendicular $(\hat{s})$ and parallel $(\hat{p})$ to the incident and reflecting planes (i.e., the $(\hat{k}, \hat{z})$ planes). The total BRDF is defined as the ratio of the total reflected

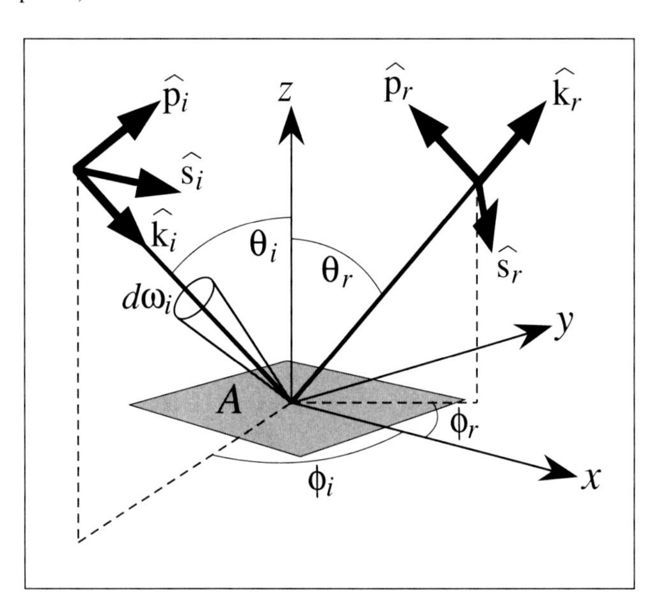


Figure 5: Coordinates of illumination and reflection.

intensity (i.e., the sum of reflected $s$ and $p$ intensities) in the direction $(\theta_r, \phi_r)$ to the energy incident per unit time and per unit area onto the surface from the direction $(\theta_i, \phi_i)$ [14]. The incident energy flux may be expressed in terms of the incident intensity $I_i$ and the incident solid angle $d\omega_i$:

$$\rho_{bd}(\theta_r, \phi_r, \theta_i, \phi_i) = \frac{dI_r(\theta_r, \phi_r; \theta_i, \phi_i)}{I_i(\theta_i, \phi_i)\cos\theta_i d\omega_i} \quad (4)$$

The BRDF may also be defined for each polarization component of the reflected intensity (see Appendix A). Equation (4) gives the frequently-used total BRDF.

We propose a bidirectional reflectivity consisting of three components:

$$\rho_{bd} = \rho_{bd,sp} + \rho_{bd,dd} + \rho_{bd,ud} \quad (5)$$

The additional subscripts correspond to specular $(sp)$, directional-diffuse $(dd)$, and uniform-diffuse $(ud)$ reflection. The first two components in (5) result from the first-surface reflection process (see Figure 1) and are respectively due to specular reflection by the mean surface and diffraction scattering by the surface roughness. The third component, taken as uniform diffuse, is attributed to multiple surface and/or subsurface reflections.

An example of a light intensity distribution corresponding to equation (5) is shown in Figure 6. A general reflecting surface is

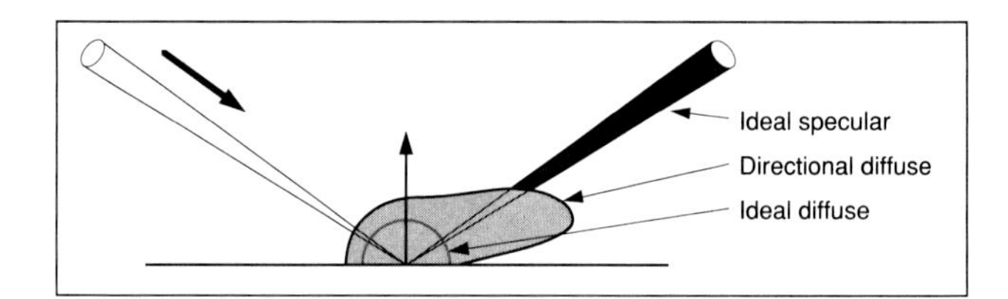


Figure 6: Example of a light intensity distribution.

assumed, with some specular reflection, some diffraction scattering due to roughness, and some multiple or subsurface scattering. The specularly-reflected part is contained within the specular cone of reflection. The diffraction-scattered part shows a directional distribution which is far from ideal diffuse. The last part is uniform diffuse (Lambertian).

An analytic form for the first two terms in (5) is derived in Appendix A. With the local-tangent-plane and gentle-slope assumptions for the first-surface reflection process, and for arbitrary incident polarization, we have:

$$\rho_{bd,sp} = \frac{\rho_s}{\cos\theta_i d\omega_i} \cdot \Delta = \frac{|F|^2 \cdot e^{-g} \cdot S}{\cos\theta_i d\omega_i} \cdot \Delta \quad (6)$$

$$\rho_{bd,dd} = \frac{\mathcal{F}(\hat{n}_b, \hat{n}_b, \mathbf{p}) \cdot S}{\cos\theta_i \cdot \cos\theta_r} \cdot \frac{\tau^2}{16\pi} \cdot \sum_{m=1}^{\infty} \frac{g^m e^{-g}}{m! \cdot m} \cdot \exp(-\frac{v_{xy}^2 \tau^2}{4m}) \quad (7)$$

$$\rho_{bd,ud} = a(\lambda) \quad (8)$$

where $\rho_s$ is the specular reflectivity of the surface, $\Delta$ is a delta function which is unity in the specular cone of reflection and zero otherwise, $|F|^2$ is the Fresnel reflectivity which depends on the index of refraction $(\bar{n}(\lambda))$ of the surface material [14, p.100], $g$ is a function of the effective surface roughness given by

$$g = [\left(2\pi\sigma/\lambda\right)(\cos\theta_i + \cos\theta_r)]^2, \quad (9)$$

$S$ is the shadowing function (see equation (23)), $\mathcal{F}$ is a function involving the Fresnel reflection coefficients (see equations (68) and

(59), (60)), **p** is the polarization state vector of the incident light (see equation (34)), $v_{xy}$ is a function which depends on the illumination and reflection angles (see equation (20)), and $a(\lambda)$ is a parameter to be discussed later.

For convenience and for the special case of incident unpolarized light, the governing equations are gathered together and presented in Appendix B. The directional-diffuse term in this appendix (equation (71)) uses nomenclature to permit comparison with the geometric optics model of Cook-Torrance [8].

The physical basis of the three reflection components in (5) is discussed in the following subsections. Before proceeding, we note that the dependence of the specular component on $d\omega_i$ drops out if equation (5) is converted to an intensity basis by multiplying by $I_i \cos\theta_i d\omega_i$. From (6), the specular term becomes $\rho_s I_i \Delta$, which is the well known form used in Ray-tracing. The specular intensity is then independent of $d\omega_i$, but the directional-diffuse and uniform-diffuse intensities are proportional to $d\omega_i$.

### 3.2.1 Specular contribution: $\rho_{bd,sp}$

The specular term accounts for mirror-like reflection from the *mean* plane of the reflecting surface. The term is proportional to the Fresnel or mirror reflectivity, $|F|^2$. For rough surfaces, the specular term is reduced by the roughness and shadowing factors $e^{-g}$ and $S$, respectively.

For a smooth surface, as the wavelength of the incident light becomes large relative to the projected surface roughness, i.e., $\lambda \gg \sigma\cos\theta_i$, the specular term is not attenuated since $g \rightarrow 0$ and $S \rightarrow 1$. Also in this limit, the specular component dominates the first-surface reflection process, since the contribution from equation (7) diminishes as $g \rightarrow 0$. For smooth surfaces, equation (6) reduces to

$$|F|^2 / \cos\theta_i d\omega_i, \tag{10}$$

which is the usual form of the bidirectional reflectivity for a specular surface.

### 3.2.2 Directional diffuse contribution: $\rho_{bd,dd}$

When the wavelength of the incident light is comparable to or smaller than the projected size of surface roughness elements (i.e., $\lambda \sim \sigma\cos\theta_i$), the first-surface reflection process introduces diffraction and interference effects. The reflected field is spread out to the hemisphere above the reflecting surface. We call this *directional diffuse*, to indicate that the field is diffused to the hemisphere but may have a directional, nonuniform character.

The reflected light pattern given by equation (7) depends on surface statistics through the effective roughness $\sigma$ and the autocorrelation length $\tau$. For smooth surfaces, as $\sigma/\lambda$ or $g$ approach zero, the bidirectional reflectivity given by equation (7) diminishes to zero. For rough surfaces, with $\sigma/\lambda$ or $g$ large, equation (7) describes the directional distribution of the first-surface reflected light. The reflected pattern can be complex with maximal values in the specular direction for slightly rough surfaces, at off-specular angles for intermediate roughnesses, or at grazing reflection angles for very rough surfaces.

### 3.2.3 Uniform diffuse contribution: $\rho_{bd,ud}$

The light reflected by multiple surface reflections or by subsurface reflections is generally more difficult to describe analytically than light reflected by the first-surface reflection process. This contribution is small for metallic (opaque) surfaces with shallow roughness slopes. However, the contribution can be important for surfaces with large slopes, or for nonmetals if significant radiation crosses the first surface and is reflected by subsurface scattering centers (e.g., paints, ceramics, plastics).

Estimates of the multiple-reflection process within surface V-grooves, based on geometrical optics, have been carried out [10] [17]. Also, estimates of the subsurface scattering are available [14]. The analytical results often suggest that the reflected field due to these two processes may be approximated as nearly directionally uniform. Therefore, the multiply-reflected and/or subsurface scattered light is approximated as *uniform-diffuse* (i.e., Lambertian), and we denote it by $a(\lambda)$.

The coefficient $a(\lambda)$ can be estimated theoretically if the V-groove geometry is applicable, or if the subsurface scattering parameters are known. Alternatively, $a(\lambda)$ can be estimated experimentally if equation (5) is integrated over the reflecting hemisphere, and the results are compared with measured values of the directional-hemispherical reflectivity, $\rho_{dh}$. This reflectivity is equal to the hemispherical-directional reflectivity $\rho_{hd}$ (for the case of uniform incident intensity [14]), and which can be easily measured using an integrating sphere reflectometer. For the present paper, in the absence of additional surface or subsurface scattering parameters, or experimental measurements, we will treat $a(\lambda)$ as a constrained, but otherwise free, parameter. The constraint is based on energy conservation and gives an upper bound for $a(\lambda)$.

## 3.3 Discussion

The theoretical model described by equation (5) allows specular, directional-diffuse, and uniform-diffuse reflection behavior as sketched in Figure 6. The governing equations in general form are given in equations (5) to (8) and Appendix A, or for unpolarized incident light in Appendix B. The actual reflection patterns depend on wavelength, incidence angle, surface roughness and subsurface parameters, and index of refraction. The model provides a unified approach for a wide range of materials and surface finishes, and is in a form suitable for use in computer graphics.

# 4 Comparison with experiments

In this section we compare the reflection model with experimental measurements. Appropriate comparison experiments appear only infrequently in the literature, since well-characterized surfaces as well as good wavelength and directional resolution are required. The measurements selected for comparison consist of BRDF's for roughened aluminum [19], roughened magnesium oxide ceramic [19], sandpaper [9], and smooth plastic [11]. The comparisons cover a wide range of materials (metallic, nonmetallic) and reflection behavior (specular, directional diffuse, uniform diffuse).

Polar comparisons are presented in Figures 7 to 10. Results are shown in the plane of incidence; the polar angle is $\theta_r$ and the curve parameter is the angle of incidence $\theta_i$. Theoretical predictions are shown with solid lines and experimental measurements with dashed lines. The polar radius is the BRDF normalized with respect to the specular reflecting ray direction, i.e.,

$$\frac{\rho_{bd}(\theta_i, 0; \theta_r, \phi_r)}{\rho_{bd}(\theta_i, 0; \theta_i, 0)} \tag{11}$$

Results for an aluminum surface (very pure; measured roughness: $\sigma_0 = 0.28\mu m$) are shown in Figures 7 and 8, respectively, for wavelengths of $\lambda = 2.0\mu m$ and $0.5\mu m$. These figures illustrate the effects of wavelength and incidence angle. The autocorrelation length and measured hemispherical reflectances were not reported. Therefore, values of $\tau = 1.77\mu m$ and $a(\lambda) = 0$ were selected as best fits at both wavelengths. Several points can be noted.

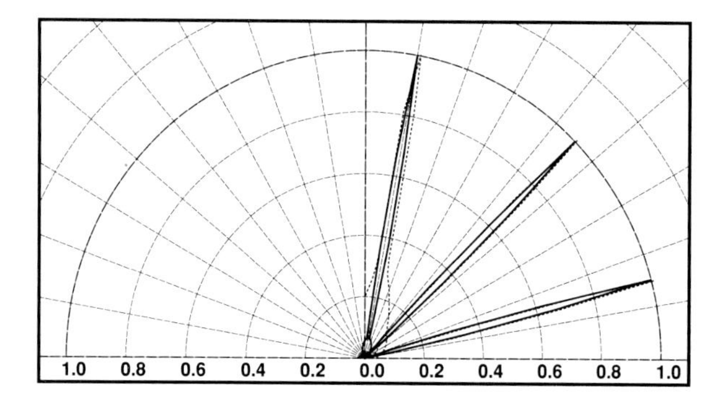


Figure 7: Normalized BRDF's of roughened aluminum as obtained from theory (solid lines) and experiment (dashed lines) for incidence angles of $\theta_i$ = 10°, 45°, and 75°. $\lambda$ = 2.0$\mu m$. This is the same surface as in Figure 8. The surface shows strong specular reflection at this wavelength.

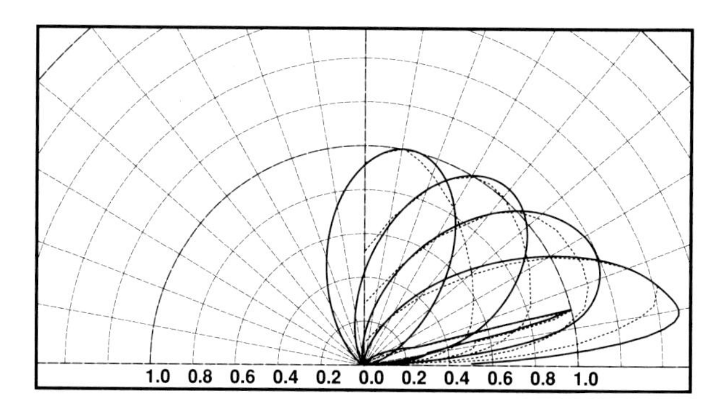


Figure 8: Normalized BRDF's of roughened aluminum as obtained from theory (solid lines) and experiment (dashed lines) for incidence angles of $\theta_i$ = 10°, 30°, 45°, 60°, and 75°. $\lambda$ = 0.5$\mu m$. This is the same surface as in Figure 7. The surface shows strong directional diffuse and emerging specular reflection at this wavelength.

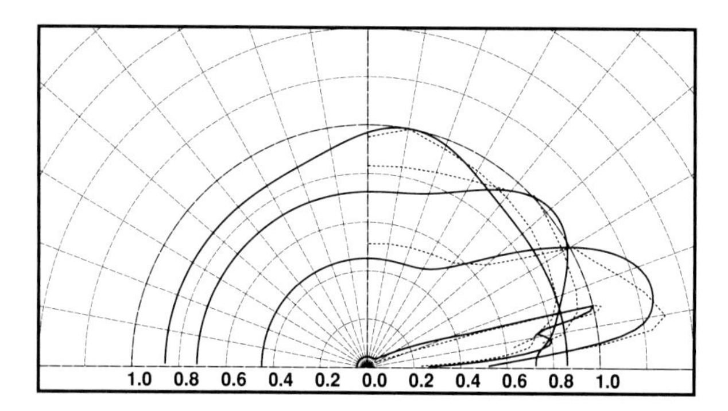


Figure 9: Normalized BRDF's of roughened magnesium oxide ceramic as obtained from theory (solid lines) and experiment (dashed lines) for incidence angles of $\theta_i$ = 10°, 45°, 60°, and 75°. $\lambda$ = 0.5$\mu m$. The surface shows strong uniform diffuse and emerging specular reflection.

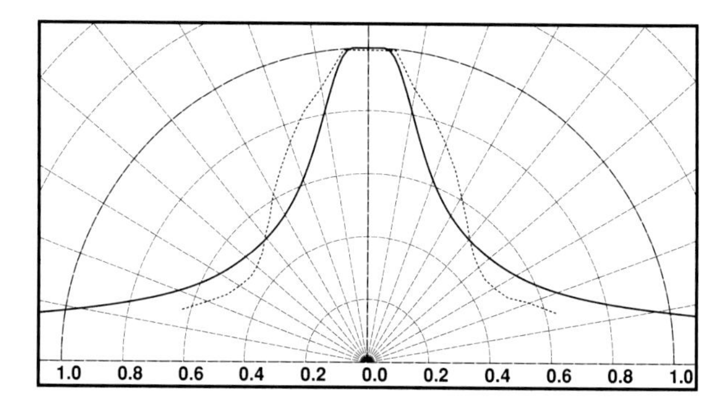


Figure 10: Normalized BRDF's of sandpaper as obtained from theory (solid lines) and experiment (dashed lines) for normal incidence, $\theta_i$ = 0°. $\lambda$ = 0.5$\mu m$. The surface shows a large reflectance at grazing reflection angles.

When $\sigma_0$ is small compared to $\lambda$, as in Figure 7, strong specular reflection occurs. The angular width of the measured specular peak is determined by the solid angles of incident and received light in the experiments ($d\omega_i = d\omega_r = \pi/1024$). To allow comparisons, the theoretical peaks have been averaged over the same solid angles. For incidence at $\theta_i$ = 10°, the reflected pattern displays both specular and directional diffuse components. In Figure 8, when the roughness is more comparable to the wavelength, a strong directional diffuse pattern appears, and for $\theta_i$ = 10°, 30°, 45°, and 60°, the reflected intensity is maximal at larger-than-specular angles. For $\theta_i$ = 75°, a specular peak emerges as the surface appears somewhat smoother to the incident radiation.

A comparison with a magnesium oxide ceramic (very pure; measured roughness: $\sigma_0$ = 1.90$\mu m$, but model best fit $\sigma_0$ = 1.45$\mu m$) at $\lambda$ = 0.5$\mu m$ is displayed in Figure 9. This surface shows nearly uniform diffuse behavior at $\theta_i$ = 10° and an emerging specular peak for larger values of $\theta_i$. The model employed best-fit parameters of $\tau$ = 13.2$\mu m$ and $a(\lambda)$ = 0.9, the latter expressing the relatively stronger role of subsurface scattering as compared to the aluminum surface. Significantly, the experimental and theoretical trends in Figures 7 to 9 for both the metal and the nonmetal are in qualitative accord. Importantly, both materials display an emerging specular peak as the angle of incidence is increased, and, for the metal, as the wavelength is increased. Further, the metal shows a strong directional diffuse pattern, and the nonmetal a strong uniform diffuse pattern, both of which are in accord with the model.

A dramatically different reflection pattern is displayed in Figure 10, corresponding to 220 grit sandpaper at $\theta_i$ = 0° and $\lambda$ = 0.55$\mu m$. Parameters used for the comparison are $\sigma_0/\tau$ = 4.4 and $a(\lambda)$ = 0. For very rough surfaces, only the ratio $\sigma_0/\tau$ is required, not $\sigma_0$ and $\tau$ separately [5]. Although the large ratio of $\sigma_0/\tau$ challenges the gentle slope assumption of the model, the agreement between experiment and theory is striking as both display large reflected intensities at grazing angles of reflection.

A comparison of experiment and theory in terms of absolute BRDF's is shown in semilog form in Figure 11 for a smooth blue plastic at $\lambda$ = 0.46$\mu m$. The shape of the specular spikes is determined by the geometry of the incident and receiving optical systems. The distributions for four incidence angles reveal a linear combination of specular and uniform diffuse behavior. This is consistent with the model (equations (5) to (8)). For a smooth surface with $\sigma_0$ = 0, the directional-diffuse term drops out and the specular term reduces to equation (10). The directional-hemispherical reflectivity at $\theta_i$ = 0° and $\lambda$ = 0.46$\mu m$ was measured ($\rho_{dh}$ = 0.195) and yields the value $a(\lambda)$ = 0.15 used for the uniform diffuse term in the model. The agreement between experiment and theory in Figure 11 in terms of shape and absolute magnitude is encouraging.

In conclusion, the experimentally-measured directional distributions in Figures 7 to 11 show a wide range of behavior and complexity. The present model describes the major features of the dis-

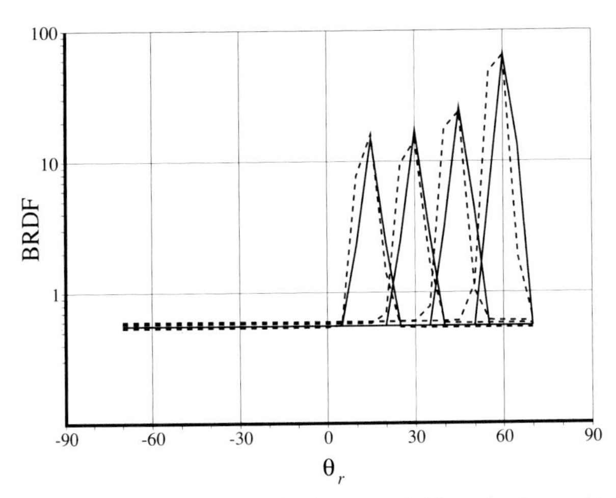


Figure 11: Absolute BRDF's for smooth blue plastic as obtained from theory (solid lines) and experiment (dashed lines) for incidence angles of $\theta_i$ = 15°, 30°, 45°, and 60°. $\lambda = 0.46\mu m$. This surface shows a typical smooth plastic reflection pattern with combined specular and uniform diffuse behavior.

tributions.

## 5 Example scenes

The reflection model described by equations (5) to (8) can be incorporated in ray-tracing or extended radiosity [15] methods. We have employed ray tracing. A single reflected ray is used together with ambient and point source illumination. The reflected intensity is given by

$$I_r(\lambda) = \sum_{i=1}^{N_l} \{|F(\theta_i)|^2 \cdot e^{-g_i} \cdot S \cdot \Delta + [(\rho_{bd,dd})_i + a(\lambda)] \cdot \cos\theta_i \cdot d\omega_i\} \cdot I_i(\lambda) + \rho_{hd}(\lambda) \cdot I_a(\lambda) \quad (12)$$

where $N_l$ is the number of light sources, subscript $i$ denotes the $i$th light source, the terms inside the braces respectively correspond to the three terms in equation (5), $\rho_{hd}(\lambda)$ is the hemispherical-directional reflectivity of the surface (taken as a function of $\lambda$ only, and found from experiment or by integrating (5) over the incident hemisphere), and $I_a$ is the uniform ambient illumination. The directional-diffuse term is included only for light sources. To include a directional-diffuse term from the environment, a distributed ray-tracer or an extended radiosity method [15] must be employed.

Figure 12 displays six aluminum cylinders in front of a brick wall. Each cylinder is rendered in isolation. Cylinders (a) to (f) are in order of increasing surface roughness. Other parameters are $\tau = 3.0\mu m$ for cylinders (a) to (e) and $\tau = 16.0\mu m$ for cylinder (f), and $a(\lambda) = 0$. Note that the sharp specular image in the top faces of the cylinders diminishes, but is not blurred, with increasing surface roughness, and the image of the light source on the front vertical face spreads out. These are characteristics, respectively, of the specular and directional diffuse terms in the reflection model that are derived from physical optics. Note also that the apparent roughness of a given cylinder varies with viewing angle. The top and lateral edges can appear specular or nearly specular at grazing angles, even when the vertical face on the front side appears to be rough. A slight color shift is also apparent for a given rough surface (i.e., as $\lambda$ in $\sigma_0/\lambda$ varies). For visible light, this is most apparent in the blue shift on the front faces of the cylinders. The enhanced red shift of the specular images is not so apparent. Clearly, the specular and directional diffuse terms of the model vary with wavelength, incidence angle, and roughness, and are responsible for the realism of the cylinders in Figure 12.

The aluminum cylinders (a) to (c) in Figure 13 illustrate limiting cases of each of the three terms in the reflection model. Cylinder (a) in Figure 13 is the same as cylinder (f) in Figure 12. Cylinder (b) is a smooth cylinder described by the specular term, in which the reflectance is a function of incidence angle according to the Fresnel reflectivity. Specular images are apparent on the top and lateral edges. (To emphasize the specular images, we have set the ambient illumination term to zero in rendering cylinder (b).) Cylinder (a) represents the directional diffuse term in the limit of $\sigma_0/\lambda \to \infty$ with $\sigma_0/\tau$ fixed at 0.16 (i.e., a limiting form for very rough surfaces). Cylinder (c) is ideal diffuse and is described by the uniform diffuse term. Note the striking differences between the three cylinders.

Figure 14 illustrates a scene consisting of a rough aluminum cylinder ($\sigma_0 = 0.18\mu m, \tau = 3.0\mu m, a(\lambda) = 0$), a rough copper sphere ($\sigma_0 = 0.13\mu m, \tau = 1.2\mu m, a(\lambda) = 0$), and a smooth plastic cube ($\sigma_0 = 0, \tau = 2.0\mu m, a(\lambda = 0.55\mu m) = 0.28$), all resting on a rough plastic table ($\sigma_0 = 0.20\mu m, \tau = 2.0\mu m, a(\lambda = 0.55\mu m) = 0.28$). The cube and table have the same Fresnel reflectivity.

Several effects can be noted in Figure 14. On the faces of the cube, the specular image varies with reflection angle, an effect caused solely by the Fresnel reflectivity $|F|^2$ in equation (6). The specular images on the table top also vary with reflection angle (and disappear), but this is caused mainly by roughness effects (i.e., $e^{-g}$) in equation (6). The cylinder in Figure 14 corresponds to cylinder (a) in Figure 12 and displays some of the specular and directional diffuse characteristics of that image.

Figure 14 gives a hint of the comprehensiveness of the light reflection model derived in this paper. Several materials of different roughnesses appear. A given surface can display specular or diffuse-like behavior depending on reflection angles and surface properties. Specular images appear or disappear based on correct physical principles. The high level of realism in Figure 14 is due to a physically-correct treatment of specular, directional diffuse, and uniform diffuse effects by the reflection model.

## 6 Conclusions

1. The general reflection model given by equations (5) to (8), in a single formulation, describes specular, directional diffuse, and uniform diffuse behavior. For unpolarized incident light, the model reduces to the form given in Appendix B. All of the parameters of the model are physically based.

2. The model compares favorably with experimental measurements of reflected radiation for metals, nonmetals, and plastics, with smooth and rough surfaces.

3. The model accurately predicts the emergence of specular reflection with increasing wavelength or angle of incidence, or decreasing surface roughness.

4. The model predicts a directional-diffuse pattern which can have maximal values at specular, off-specular, or grazing angles, depending on surface roughness.

5. The model is in analytical form and can improve the realism of synthetic images.

6. The model can be employed for ray-tracing or extended radiosity [15] methods.

(a) $\sigma_0 = 0.18$ (b) $\sigma_0 = 0.28$ (c) $\sigma_0 = 0.38$ (d) $\sigma_0 = 0.48$ (e) $\sigma_0 = 0.58$ (f) $\sigma_0 = 2.50$

Figure 12: Aluminum cylinders with different surface roughnesses. $\sigma_0$ is in $\mu m$. $\tau = 3.0\mu m$ for cylinders (a) to (e) and $\tau = 16.0\mu m$ for cylinder (f). Note that the specular and directional-diffuse reflection characteristics vary with reflection angle and roughness.

7. The model highlights the need for tabulated databases of parameterized bidirectional reflectivities. The parameters include two surface roughness parameters $(\sigma_0, \tau)$, the index of refraction (as a function of wavelength), and the constrained parameter $a(\lambda)$. The latter can be inferred from measured hemispherical reflectivities.

In conclusion, the reflection model is comprehensive, physically-based, and provides an accurate transition from specular to diffuse-like reflection. Further, the model is computable and thus useful for graphics applications.

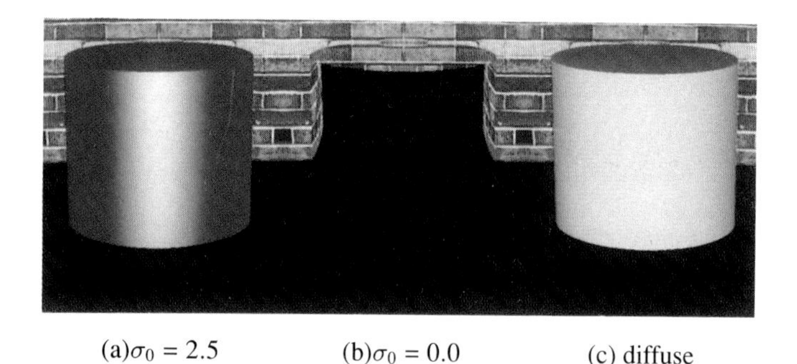

(a)$\sigma_0 = 2.5$ (b)$\sigma_0 = 0.0$ (c) diffuse

Figure 13: Aluminum cylinders in extreme limiting cases. Each cylinder corresponds to one of the three terms in the reflection model. $\sigma_0$ is in $\mu m$. (a) Directional diffuse reflection; (b) Ideal specular reflection; (c) Uniform diffuse (Lambertian) reflection.

Figure 14: A general scene with metallic and plastic objects in the foreground, with smooth and rough surfaces. The specular images in the smooth plastic box vary with incidence angle due to the Fresnel effect. In the table top, the decay of the specular images with reflection angle is due to roughness. In the rough metallic surfaces, the glossy highlights result from directional diffuse reflection.

## Acknowledgments

We acknowledge the support of the National Science Foundation under a grant entitled "Interactive Input and Display Techniques" (CCR8617880) and the Hewlett-Packard Corporation and the Digital Equipment Corporation for generous donations of equipment. The authors are indebted to many individuals, including Kevin Koestner and Lisa Maynes for early work on a reflection model, to Xiaofen Feng and Professor John Schott of the Rochester Institute of Technology for providing access to their laboratory and to unpublished data, to Stephen Westin for preparing some of the diagrams, to Ted Himlan, Michael Monks, and Jim Arvo for helpful discussions, and to Emil Ghinger for photographing the raster images. We thank the reviewers for their extensive and constructive comments which have helped to clarify a difficult paper.

## References

[1] Bahar, E. and S. Chakrabarti. "Full wave theory applied to computer-aided graphics for 3-D objects," *IEEE Computer Graphics and Applications*, 7(7), 1987, pages 46–60.

[2] Bahar, Ezekiel. "Review of the full wave solutions for rough surface scattering and depolarization," *Journal of Geophysical Research*, May 1987, pages 5209–5227.

[3] Bass, F.G. and I.M. Fuks. *Wave Scattering from Statistically Rough Surfaces*, Pergamon Press, 1979.

[4] Beckmann, Petr. "Shadowing of Random Rough Surfaces," *IEEE Transactions on Antennas and Propagation*, May 1965, pages 384–388.

[5] Beckmann, Petr and André Spizzichino. *The Scattering of Electromagnetic Waves from Rough Surfaces*, Pergamon Press, 1963.

[6] Blinn, James F. "Models of Light Reflection for Computer Synthesized Pictures," *Computer Graphics*, 11, 1977, pages 192–198. (Proceedings SIGGRAPH '77.)

[7] Brockelman, R. A. and T. Hagfors. "Note on the Effect of Shadowing on the Backscattering of Waves from a Random Rough Surfaces," *IEEE Transactions on Antennas and Propagation*, AP-14(5), September 1966, pages 621–629.

[8] Cook, Robert L. and Kenneth E. Torrance. "A Reflectance Model for Computer Graphics," *ACM Transactions on Graphics*, 1, 1982, pages 7–24.

[9] Feng, Xiaofen. *Comparison of methods for generation of absolute reflectance factors for BRDF studies*, Master's thesis, Rochester Institute of Technology, 1990.

[10] Hering, R.G. and T.F. Smith. "Apparent radiation properties of a rough surface," *Application to Thermal Design of Spacecraft*, 23, 1970, pages 337–361.

[11] Himlan, Theodore H., Michael C. Monks, Stephan H. Westin, Donald P. Greenberg, and Kenneth E. Torrance. "Physical measurement Techniques for Improving and Evaluating Computer Graphic Simulations.," 1991. (To be published.)

[12] Jackson, John D. *Classical Electrodynamics*, John Wiley & Son Inc., 1975.

[13] Phong, Bui Tuong. "Illumination for Computer Generated Pictures," *Communications of the ACM*, 18(6), June 1975, pages 311–317.

[14] Siegel, Robert and John R. Howell. *Thermal Radiation Heat Transfer*, McGraw-Hill book Company, 2nd edition, 1981.

[15] Sillion, François, James Arvo, Stephen Westin, and Donald P. Greenberg. "A Global Illumination Solution for General Reflectance Distributions," *Computer Graphics*, 25(4), August 1991. (Proceedings SIGGRAPH '91 in Las Vegas.)

[16] Smith, Bruce G. "Geometrical Shadowing of a Random Rough Surface," *IEEE Transactions on Antennas and Propagation*, AP-15(5), September 1967, pages 668–671.

[17] Smith, T.F. and K.E. Nichols. "Effects of polarization on bidirectional reflectance of a one-dimensional randomly rough surface," *Spacecraft Radiative Transfer and Temperature Control*, 83, 1981, pages 3–21.

[18] Stogryn, Alex. "Electromagnetic Scattering From Rough, Finitely Conducting Surfaces," *Radio Science*, 2(4), 1967, pages 415–428.

[19] Torrance, K.E. and E.M. Sparrow. "Off-Specular Peaks in the Directional Distribution of Reflected Thermal Radiation," *Journal of Heat Transfer – Transactions of the ASME*, May 1966, pages 223–230.

[20] Torrance, K.E. and E.M. Sparrow. "Theory for Off-Specular Reflection from Roughened Surfaces," *Journal of the Optical Society of America*, 57(9), September 1967, pages 1105–1114.

# A Appendix: Derivations

## A.1 Reflected intensities

The reflected intensities for the $s$ and $p$ components of polarizations are given by [14][18]

$$dI_r(\theta_r, \phi_r; \theta_i, \phi_i)_s = \frac{R^2}{A \cdot \cos\theta_r} < |\hat{s}_r \cdot \vec{E}_r(\vec{R})|^2 >$$
$$dI_r(\theta_r, \phi_r; \theta_i, \phi_i)_p = \frac{R^2}{A \cdot \cos\theta_r} < |\hat{p}_r \cdot \vec{E}_r(\vec{R})|^2 > \quad (13)$$

where the coordinates are as shown in Figure 5, $\vec{E}_r(\vec{R})$ is the reflected field in vector form, $R$ is the distance from the origin to an arbitrary point in space, $A$ is the area of the reflecting surface projected on the x-y plane, and $\hat{s_r}, \hat{p_r}$ are unit polarization vectors, given by

$$\hat{s}_r = \frac{\hat{k}_r \times \hat{z}}{|\hat{k}_r \times \hat{z}|}$$
$$\hat{p}_r = \hat{s}_r \times \hat{k}_r \quad (14)$$

which are normal and parallel, respectively, to the plane formed by the viewing direction and the mean surface normal. The symbol $<>$ denotes an average over the joint probability distribution function of the random rough surface characterized by

$$z = \xi(x, y). \quad (15)$$

The reflected field can be expressed in terms of the scattered field on the surface by using the vector form of the Kirchhoff diffraction theory [12]:

$$\vec{E}_r(\vec{R}) = \frac{e^{ikR}}{4\pi R}\left(\bar{I} - \hat{k}_r\hat{k}_r\right) \cdot \int_\Gamma e^{-i\vec{k}_r\cdot\vec{r}} \left\{-i\vec{k}_r \times (\vec{E}_s \times \hat{n}) - (\nabla \times \vec{E}_s) \times \hat{n}\right\} d\Gamma \quad (16)$$

where $\vec{k}_i, \vec{k}_r$ are wave vectors in the incident and reflection directions, $|k| = 2\pi/\lambda$ is the wave number, $\vec{r}$ is the position vector for a point on the surface, and the tensor $\bar{I} - \hat{k}_r\hat{k}_r = \hat{s}_r\hat{s}_r + \hat{p}_r\hat{p}_r$ is introduced to to make the reflected field transverse.

Substituting (16) into (13), we have

$$dI_s = \frac{1}{A\cos\theta_r(4\pi)^2} \cdot < | \int_\Gamma e^{-i\vec{k}_r\cdot\vec{r}} \cdot \left\{ik\hat{p}_r \cdot (\vec{E}_s \times \hat{n}) + \hat{s}_r \cdot [(\nabla \times \vec{E}_s) \times \hat{n}]\right\} d\Gamma|^2 >$$
$$dI_p = \frac{1}{A\cos\theta_r(4\pi)^2} \cdot < | \int_\Gamma e^{-i\vec{k}_r\cdot\vec{r}} \cdot \left\{ik\hat{s}_r \cdot (\vec{E}_s \times \hat{n}) - \hat{p}_r \cdot [(\nabla \times \vec{E}_s) \times \hat{n}]\right\} d\Gamma|^2 > \quad (17)$$

To evaluate the right side of (17), the surface element $d\Gamma$ is expressed in terms of the planar surface area $dA = dx \cdot dy$ by

$$d\Gamma = dA/(\hat{n} \cdot \hat{z}) \quad (18)$$

Further, the squares of the absolute values of the integrals in (17) can be expanded in terms of double surface integrals. We find

$$< | \int_\Gamma e^{-i\vec{k}_r\cdot\vec{r}}\{\}d\Gamma|^2 >=$$

$$< \int_A dA_1 \int_A dA_2 e^{-i\vec{v}\cdot(\vec{r}_1-\vec{r}_2)} \cdot \left(e^{-i\vec{k}_i\cdot\vec{r}_1}\{\}_1\right)\left(e^{-i\vec{k}_i\cdot\vec{r}_2}\{\}_2\right)^* /(\hat{n}_1\cdot\hat{z})(\hat{n}_2\cdot\hat{z}) > \tag{19}$$

where $v$ is the wave vector change

$$\vec{v} = k(\hat{k}_r - \hat{k}_i), \tag{20}$$

$*$ denotes a complex conjugate, $\{\}$ refers to the terms in braces in (17), and the subscripts refer to points on area elements $dA_1$ and $dA_2$.

The $<>$ in (19) commutes with the surface integral and a term of the form

$$< e^{-i\vec{v}\cdot\hat{z}(\xi_1-\xi_2)}\{\}_1\{\}_2^*/(\hat{n}_1\cdot\hat{z})(\hat{n}_2\cdot\hat{z}) > \tag{21}$$

results. Since the surface is assumed to be isotropic and stationary, (21) is a function only of $x_1 - x_2$ and $y_1 - y_2$. Thus, by making the change of variables

$$\begin{aligned} x' &= x_1 - x_2 \qquad & x'' &= x_2 \\ y' &= y_1 - y_2 \qquad & y'' &= y_2 \end{aligned} \tag{22}$$

the integrals over $x''$ and $y''$ may be carried out separately to give a factor $S \cdot A$, where $S$ is the fraction of the surface that is both illuminated and viewed and represents the shadowing function given by [16]:

$$S = S_i(\theta_i) \cdot S_r(\theta_r) \tag{23}$$

where

$$\begin{aligned} S_i(\theta_i) &= (1 - \frac{1}{2}\mathrm{erfc}(\frac{\tau \cot\theta_i}{2\sigma_0}))/(\Lambda(\cot\theta_i)+1) \\ S_r(\theta_r) &= (1 - \frac{1}{2}\mathrm{erfc}(\frac{\tau \cot\theta_r}{2\sigma_0}))/(\Lambda(\cot\theta_r)+1) \end{aligned} \tag{24}$$

and

$$\Lambda(\cot\theta) = \frac{1}{2}\left(\frac{2}{\pi^{1/2}} \cdot \frac{\sigma_0}{\tau\cot\theta} - \mathrm{erfc}(\frac{\tau\cot\theta}{2\sigma_0})\right) \tag{25}$$

Hence, the reflected intensities in (17) are

$$dI_s = \frac{S}{\cos\theta_r(4\pi)^2}\int_{-\infty}^{+\infty}\int_{-\infty}^{+\infty} dx'dy'\, e^{-i\vec{v}\cdot\vec{\eta}}B_s \tag{26}$$

$$dI_p = \frac{S}{\cos\theta_r(4\pi)^2}\int_{-\infty}^{+\infty}\int_{-\infty}^{+\infty} dx'dy'\, e^{-i\vec{v}\cdot\vec{\eta}}B_p \tag{27}$$

where

$$\vec{\eta} = x'\hat{x} + y'\hat{y} \tag{28}$$

and

$$\begin{aligned} B_s &= < e^{-i\vec{v}\cdot\hat{z}(\xi_1-\xi_2)}\mathcal{F}(\hat{n}_1,\hat{n}_2)_s > \\ B_p &= < e^{-i\vec{v}\cdot\hat{z}(\xi_1-\xi_2)}\mathcal{F}(\hat{n}_1,\hat{n}_2)_p > \end{aligned} \tag{29}$$

where

$$\begin{aligned} \mathcal{F}(\hat{n}_1,\hat{n}_2)_s &= e^{-i\vec{k}_i\cdot(\vec{r}_1-\vec{r}_2)}/(\hat{n}_1\cdot\hat{z})(\hat{n}_2\cdot\hat{z}) \\ &\cdot \left(\{ik\hat{p}_r\cdot(\vec{E}_s\times\hat{n}) + \hat{s}_r\cdot[(\nabla\times\vec{E}_s)\times\hat{n}]\}\right)_1 \\ &\cdot \left(\{ik\hat{p}_r\cdot(\vec{E}_s\times\hat{n}) + \hat{s}_r\cdot[(\nabla\times\vec{E}_s)\times\hat{n}]\}\right)_2^* \end{aligned} \tag{30}$$

$$\begin{aligned} \mathcal{F}(\hat{n}_1,\hat{n}_2)_p &= e^{-i\vec{k}_i\cdot(\vec{r}_1-\vec{r}_2)}/(\hat{n}_1\cdot\hat{z})(\hat{n}_2\cdot\hat{z}) \\ &\cdot \left(\{ik\hat{s}_r\cdot(\vec{E}_s\times\hat{n}) - \hat{p}_r\cdot[(\nabla\times\vec{E}_s)\times\hat{n}]\}\right)_1 \\ &\cdot \left(\{ik\hat{s}_r\cdot(\vec{E}_s\times\hat{n}) - \hat{p}_r\cdot[(\nabla\times\vec{E}_s)\times\hat{n}]\}\right)_2^* \end{aligned} \tag{31}$$

The functions $B_s$ and $B_p$ in (29) depend only on $x'$ and $y'$. Notice that $dI_s$ and $dI_p$ are the $s$ and $p$ polarized reflected intensities, respectively. The total reflected intensity, as used in equation (4), is given by

$$dI_r = dI_s + dI_p \tag{32}$$

### A.2 Tangent plane approximation

The reflected intensities in (26) and (27) are expressed in terms of the scattered field $\vec{E}_s$ on the surface. In turn, $\vec{E}_s$ depends on the incident field, and may be related to the incident field by using the local tangent plane approximation.

For the case of a unidirectional incident field, we have

$$\begin{aligned} \vec{E}_i &= E_0 e^{i\vec{k}_i\cdot\vec{r}}\mathbf{p} \qquad (33) \\ \mathbf{p} &= c_s\hat{s}_i + c_p\hat{p}_i \qquad (34) \end{aligned}$$

where $E_0$ is the wave amplitude, **p** is the polarization state vector of the incident radiation, $c_s, c_p$ are called the polarization coefficients[1], and $\hat{s}_i$ , $\hat{p}_i$ are unit polarization vectors with respect to the plane of incidence $(\hat{k}_i, \hat{z})$. The unit vectors are given by

$$\begin{aligned} \hat{s}_i &= \frac{\hat{k}_i\times\hat{z}}{|\hat{k}_i\times\hat{z}|} \\ \hat{p}_i &= \hat{s}_i\times\hat{k}_i \end{aligned} \tag{35}$$

Equation (33) can be written in the more compact matrix form

$$\vec{E}_i = E_0 e^{i\vec{k}_i\cdot\vec{r}}\left(c_s, c_p\right)\cdot\begin{pmatrix}\hat{s}_i \\ \hat{p}_i\end{pmatrix} \tag{36}$$

$\hat{s}_i, \hat{p}_i$ decompose into incident local polarization unit vectors $\hat{s}_i^n$, $\hat{p}_i^n$ with respect to the local incident plane $(\hat{k}_i, \hat{n})$, given by

$$\begin{aligned} \hat{s}_i^n &= \frac{\hat{k}_i\times\hat{n}}{|\hat{k}_i\times\hat{n}|} \\ \hat{p}_i^n &= \hat{s}_i^n\times\hat{k}_i \end{aligned} \tag{37}$$

Therefore,

$$\begin{pmatrix}\hat{s}_i \\ \hat{p}_i\end{pmatrix} = T_{in}\cdot\begin{pmatrix}\hat{s}_i^n \\ \hat{p}_i^n\end{pmatrix} \tag{38}$$

where $T_{in}$ is the transformation matrix from incident coordinates to local coordinates

$$\bar{T}_{in} = \begin{pmatrix}\hat{s}_i\cdot\hat{s}_i^n & \hat{s}_i\cdot\hat{p}_i^n \\ \hat{p}_i\cdot\hat{s}_i^n & \hat{p}_i\cdot\hat{p}_i^n\end{pmatrix} \tag{39}$$

Substituting (38) into (36), we have the incident field in terms of $\hat{s}_i^n, \hat{p}_i^n$ as

$$\vec{E}_i = E_0 e^{i\vec{k}_i\cdot\vec{r}}\left(c_s, c_p\right)\cdot\bar{T}_{in}\begin{pmatrix}\hat{s}_i^n \\ \hat{p}_i^n\end{pmatrix} \tag{40}$$

Reflections of the $\hat{s}_i^n, \hat{p}_i^n$ fields are found from the local Fresnel reflection coefficients for each component of polarization, i.e.,

$$\begin{aligned} \hat{s}_i^n &\longrightarrow F_s\cdot\hat{s}_r^n \\ \hat{p}_i^n &\longrightarrow F_p\cdot\hat{p}_r^n \end{aligned} \tag{41}$$

[1]For example: for $s$ polarization, $c_s = 1.0$, $c_p = 0$; for $p$ polarization, $c_s = 0$, $c_p = 1$.

where $F_s$ and $F_p$ are the Fresnel reflection coefficients for $s$ and $p$ polarizations, respectively [14, p.100]. The unit vectors $\hat{s}_r^n, \hat{p}_r^n$ are the local polarization unit vectors for reflection from the tangent plane:

$$\begin{aligned} \hat{s}_r^n &= \frac{\hat{k}_r \times \hat{n}}{|\hat{k}_r \times \hat{n}|} \\ \hat{p}_r^n &= \hat{s}_r^n \times \hat{k}_r \end{aligned} \tag{42}$$

where $\hat{k}_r$ is the unit vector in the specular direction from the tangent plane, given by

$$\hat{k}_r = \hat{k}_i - 2(\hat{k}_i \cdot \hat{n})\hat{n} \tag{43}$$

Using the Fresnel matrix

$$\bar{F} = \begin{pmatrix} F_s & 0 \\ 0 & F_p \end{pmatrix} \tag{44}$$

we have in more compact form

$$\begin{pmatrix} \hat{s}_i^n \\ \hat{p}_i^n \end{pmatrix} \longrightarrow \bar{F} \begin{pmatrix} \hat{s}_r^n \\ \hat{p}_r^n \end{pmatrix} \tag{45}$$

From equations (40) and (45), the scattered field on the surface can be expressed as a linear combination of the Fresnel reflection coefficients

$$\begin{aligned} \vec{E}_s &= E_0 e^{i\vec{k}_i \cdot \vec{r}} \left(c_s, c_p\right) \cdot \begin{pmatrix} \hat{s}_i \cdot \hat{s}_i^n & \hat{s}_i \cdot \hat{p}_i^n \\ \hat{p}_i \cdot \hat{s}_i^n & \hat{p}_i \cdot \hat{p}_i^n \end{pmatrix} \cdot \\ & \begin{pmatrix} F_s & 0 \\ 0 & F_p \end{pmatrix} \cdot \begin{pmatrix} \hat{s}_r^n \\ \hat{p}_r^n \end{pmatrix} \end{aligned} \tag{46}$$

The scattered field is a function of the incident polarization state, the local surface normal $\hat{n}$, the Fresnel reflection coefficients $F_s$ and $F_p$ of the surface, and the incident and reflection directions $\hat{k}_i, \hat{k}_r$.

### A.3 Representation of the surface

Specification of the surface topography is required to carry out the surface integrals and surface averages appearing in equations (26), (27) and (29). Without losing generality, we assume the surface to be Gaussian distributed [5], i.e., we assume the surface height in (15) to be a stationary normally distributed random process whose mean value is zero. In addition we assume the surface to be directionally isotropic. An appropriate two-point joint probability function is given by

$$P(z_1, z_2) = \frac{exp\left[-(z_1^2 + z_2^2 - 2C(r)z_1 z_2)/2\sigma_0^2(1 - C(r)^2)\right]}{2\pi\sigma_0^2\sqrt{1 - C(r)^2}} \tag{47}$$

where $r^2 = (x_1 - x_2)^2 + (y_1 - y_2)^2$, $\sigma_0^2$ is the variance of $z_1 = \xi(x_1, y_1)$ and $z_2 = \xi(x_2, y_2)$, and $C(r)$ is the correlation coefficient, which is assumed to be [5]

$$C(r) = e^{-\frac{r^2}{\tau^2}} \tag{48}$$

where $\tau$ is the autocorrelation length.

The parameters $\sigma_0$ and $\tau$ are the only two surface parameters required for the surface integrations.

### A.4 Analytic evaluation of the integrals

Substituting (46) into (29) to (31), $B_s$ and $B_p$ are expressed in terms of known quantities and depend on the surface only through the normals $n_1$ and $n_2$ at two surface points. Further, the integrals in equations (26) and (27) can be written as:

$$\int_{-\infty}^{+\infty}\int_{-\infty}^{+\infty} e^{-i\vec{v}\cdot\vec{\eta}} < e^{-i\vec{v}\cdot\hat{z}(\xi_1 - \xi_2)}\mathcal{F}(n_1, n_2, \mathbf{p}) > dxdy \tag{49}$$

Stogryn [18] has shown that an integral and average of the form in (49) can be approximatly evaluated under either of the following two conditions:

- the surface is very rough (i.e., $(v_z\sigma)^2 \gg 1$)
- the surface has gentle slopes (i.e. $(\frac{\sigma}{\tau}) \ll 1$)

As a result, (49) reduces to

$$\mathcal{F}(\hat{n}_b, \hat{n}_b, \mathbf{p}) \cdot \int_{-\infty}^{+\infty}\int_{-\infty}^{+\infty} e^{-i\vec{v}\cdot\vec{\eta}} < e^{-i\vec{v}\cdot\hat{z}(\xi_1 - \xi_2)} > dxdy \tag{50}$$

where $\mathcal{F}$ is evaluated at $\hat{n}_b$, which is the unit vector bisecting $\hat{k}_i$ and $\hat{k}_r$, given by

$$\hat{n}_b = \frac{\hat{k}_r - \hat{k}_i}{|\hat{k}_r - \hat{k}_i|} \tag{51}$$

Furthermore, the $<>$ in (50) can be shown to be [5]:

$$< e^{-i\vec{v}\cdot\hat{z}(\xi_1 - \xi_2)} >= e^{-(v_z\sigma)^2[1 - C(\eta)]} \tag{52}$$

where $C(\eta)$ is given by (48).

Note that $\sigma$ in (52) is the effective surface roughness, not $\sigma_0$. This is because the surface averaging is carried over illuminated and visible parts only. $\sigma$ is given by [4]:

$$\sigma = \frac{\sigma_0}{\sqrt{1 + \frac{z_0^2}{\sigma_0^2}}} \tag{53}$$

where $z_0$ depends on $\theta_i$, and $\theta_r$ and is the root of the following equation

$$\sqrt{\frac{\pi}{2}}z = \sigma_0 K \cdot \exp(-\frac{z^2}{2\sigma_0^2}) \tag{54}$$

and

$$\begin{aligned} K &= K_i + K_r \\ K_i &= \frac{1}{4}\tan\theta_i \cdot erfc(\frac{\tau}{2\sigma_0}\cot\theta_i) \\ K_r &= \frac{1}{4}\tan\theta_r \cdot erfc(\frac{\tau}{2\sigma_0}\cot\theta_r) \end{aligned} \tag{55}$$

The double integral in (50) can be evaluated analytically [5]:

$$\begin{aligned} N &= \int_{-\infty}^{+\infty}\int_{-\infty}^{+\infty} e^{-i\vec{v}\cdot\vec{\eta}} < e^{-i\vec{v}\cdot\hat{z}(\xi_1 - \xi_2)} > dxdy \\ &= e^{-g} \cdot A \cdot sinc^2(v_x L_x) sinc^2(v_y L_y) + \\ & \pi\tau^2 \sum_{m=1}^{\infty} \frac{g^m e^{-g}}{m! \cdot m} \cdot \exp(-v_{xy}^2\tau^2/4m) \end{aligned} \tag{56}$$

where $L_x, L_y$ are the dimensions of the reflecting surface. Since we are only interested in cases when $L_x, L_y \gg \lambda$, the first term is nonzero only in the specular direction and zero otherwise. For the case of unidirectional incidence with solid angle $d\omega_i$ and $L_x, L_y \gg \lambda$, the averaged form of the first term in (56) is

$$A \cdot sinc^2(v_x L_x) sinc^2(v_y L_y) \rightarrow (2\pi\lambda)^2 \cdot \Delta/(d\omega_i \cdot \cos\theta_r) \quad (57)$$

Hence, (56) becomes

$$N = e^{-g} \cdot (2\pi\lambda)^2 \cdot \Delta/(d\omega_i \cdot \cos\theta_r) + \pi\tau^2 \sum_{m=1}^{\infty} \frac{g^m e^{-g}}{m! \cdot m} \cdot \exp(-v_{xy}^2 \tau^2/4m) \quad (58)$$

Next, $\mathcal{F}_s$ and $\mathcal{F}_p$ in (30) and (31) are evaluated. First, $\hat{n}_1, \hat{n}_2$ are replaced by $\hat{n}_b$ defined in (51). Then they are substituted into (30) and (31). After lengthy vector manipulations, we find

$$\mathcal{F}(\hat{n}_b, \hat{n}_b, \mathbf{p})_s = \delta \cdot |c_s M_{ss} + c_p M_{sp}|^2 \quad (59)$$

$$\mathcal{F}(\hat{n}_b, \hat{n}_b, \mathbf{p})_p = \delta \cdot |c_s M_{ps} + c_p M_{pp}|^2 \quad (60)$$

where

$$M_{ss} = \left(F_s(\hat{p}_i \cdot \hat{k}_r)(\hat{p}_r \cdot \hat{k}_i) + F_p(\hat{s}_i \cdot \hat{k}_r)(\hat{s}_r \cdot \hat{k}_i)\right) \quad (61)$$

$$M_{sp} = -\left(F_s(\hat{s}_i \cdot \hat{k}_r)(\hat{p}_r \cdot \hat{k}_i) - F_p(\hat{p}_i \cdot \hat{k}_r)(\hat{s}_r \cdot \hat{k}_i)\right) \quad (62)$$

$$M_{pp} = \left(F_s(\hat{s}_i \cdot \hat{k}_r)(\hat{s}_r \cdot \hat{k}_i) + F_p(\hat{p}_i \cdot \hat{k}_r)(\hat{p}_r \cdot \hat{k}_i)\right) \quad (63)$$

$$M_{ps} = \left(F_s(\hat{p}_i \cdot \hat{k}_r)(\hat{s}_r \cdot \hat{k}_i) - F_p(\hat{s}_i \cdot \hat{k}_r)(\hat{p}_r \cdot \hat{k}_i)\right) \quad (64)$$

$$\delta = \left(\frac{2\pi}{\lambda}\right)^2 \cdot \frac{|\hat{k}_r - \hat{k}_i|^4}{|\hat{k}_r \times \hat{k}_i|^4 \left(\hat{z} \cdot (\hat{k}_r - \hat{k}_i)\right)^2} \quad (65)$$

The Fresnel reflection coefficients $F_s$ and $F_p$ in (61) to (64) are evaluated at the bisecting angle given by $\cos^{-1}(|\hat{k}_r - \hat{k}_i|/2)$.

Using (59)-(65) and (58) in (26) and (27), we find an analytical expression for the reflected intensity

$$dI_s = \frac{|E_0|^2}{\cos\theta_r (4\pi)^2} \mathcal{F}(\hat{n}_b, \hat{n}_b, \mathbf{p})_s \cdot N$$

$$dI_p = \frac{|E_0|^2}{\cos\theta_r (4\pi)^2} \mathcal{F}(\hat{n}_b, \hat{n}_b, \mathbf{p})_p \cdot N \quad (66)$$

where the square of the absolute value of the incident field amplitude, $|E_0|^2$, is related to the incident intensity $I_i$ by

$$|E_0|^2 = I_i d\omega_i \quad (67)$$

Note that the right side of (66) has the correct dimensions of intensity since $N$ has dimension $[L^2]$ whereas the $\mathcal{F}$'s have dimension $[L^{-2}]$.

Finally, substituting (67) into (66) and using (4) and (32), we get exactly the first two terms in (5), given that

$$\mathcal{F}(\hat{k}_i, \hat{k}_r, \mathbf{p}) = \mathcal{F}(\hat{n}_b, \hat{n}_b, \mathbf{p})_s + \mathcal{F}(\hat{n}_b, \hat{n}_b, \mathbf{p})_p \quad (68)$$

since the BRDF defined in (4) is the total BRDF, which is the sum of the BRDF's for the reflected $s$ and $p$ components.

# B Appendix: Governing equations of the reflectance model for unpolarized incident light

Equations (5) to (8) together with the defining equations for all the symbols in (5) to (8) completely define the general BRDF for arbitrarily-polarized incident light. In most applications, however, we are only interested in the BRDF for unpolarized incident light. The expressions for the BRDF are greatly simplified for this special but useful case. For convenience, the BRDF equations for unpolarized incident light are presented in this appendix. The reader should refer to Figure 5 and the nomenclature list in Table 1 for the angular coordinates and other physical parameters that appear in the reflectance model:

$$\rho_{bd} = \rho_{bd}(\lambda, \sigma_0, \tau, \bar{n}(\lambda), a(\lambda)) = \rho_{bd,sp} + \rho_{bd,dd} + \rho_{bd,ud} \quad (69)$$

$$\rho_{bd,sp} = \frac{\rho_s}{\cos\theta_i d\omega_i} \cdot \Delta \quad (70)$$

$$\rho_{bd,dd} = \frac{|F|^2}{\pi} \cdot \frac{G \cdot S \cdot D}{\cos\theta_i \cos\theta_r} \quad (71)$$

$$\rho_{bd,ud} = a(\lambda) \quad (72)$$

$$\rho_s = |F|^2 \cdot e^{-g} \cdot S \quad (73)$$

$$\Delta = \begin{cases} 1 & \text{if in specular cone} \\ 0 & \text{otherwise} \end{cases} \quad (74)$$

$$|F|^2 = \frac{1}{2}(F_s^2 + F_p^2) = f(\theta_i, \theta_r, \bar{n}(\lambda)) \quad (75)$$

$$G = \left(\frac{\vec{v} \cdot \vec{v}}{v_z}\right)^2 \cdot \frac{1}{|\hat{k}_r \times \hat{k}_i|^4} \cdot [(\hat{s}_r \cdot \hat{k}_i)^2 + (\hat{p}_r \cdot \hat{k}_i)^2] \cdot [(\hat{s}_i \cdot \hat{k}_r)^2 + (\hat{p}_i \cdot \hat{k}_r)^2] \quad (76)$$

$$S = S(\theta_i, \theta_r, \sigma_0/\tau) \quad (77)$$

$$D = \frac{\pi^2 \tau^2}{4\lambda^2} \cdot \sum_{m=1}^{\infty} \frac{g^m e^{-g}}{m! \cdot m} \cdot \exp(-v_{xy}^2 \tau^2/4m) \quad (78)$$

$$g = [(2\pi\sigma/\lambda)(\cos\theta_i + \cos\theta_r)]^2 \quad (79)$$

$$\sigma = \sigma_0 \cdot [1 + (\frac{z_0}{\sigma_0})^2]^{-1/2} \quad (80)$$

$$\sqrt{\frac{\pi}{2}} z_0 = \frac{\sigma_0}{4}(K_i + K_r) \cdot \exp(-\frac{z_0^2}{2\sigma_0^2}) \quad (81)$$

$$K_i = \tan\theta_i \cdot erfc(\frac{\tau}{2\sigma_0} \cot\theta_i) \quad (82)$$

$$K_r = \tan\theta_r \cdot erfc(\frac{\tau}{2\sigma_0} \cot\theta_r) \quad (83)$$

$$\vec{v} = \hat{k}_r - \hat{k}_i, \qquad v_{xy} = \sqrt{v_x^2 + v_y^2} \quad (84)$$

$$\hat{s}_i = \frac{\hat{k}_i \times \hat{n}}{|\hat{k}_i \times \hat{n}|}, \qquad \hat{p}_i = \hat{s}_i \times \hat{k}_i \quad (85)$$

$$\hat{s}_r = \frac{\hat{k}_r \times \hat{n}}{|\hat{k}_r \times \hat{n}|}, \qquad \hat{p}_r = \hat{s}_r \times \hat{k}_r \quad (86)$$

where $\bar{n}$ is the index of refraction, $\rho_s$ is the specular reflectivity, $\Delta$ is a delta function, $|F|^2$ is the Fresnel reflectivity for unpolarized light [14, p.100] evaluated at the bisecting angle given by $\cos^{-1}(|\hat{k}_r - \hat{k}_i|/2)$, $G$ is a geometrical factor, $S$ is the shadowing/masking factor given in equation (23), and $D$ is a distribution function for the directional diffuse reflection term.

# A Global Illumination Solution for General Reflectance Distributions

*François X. Sillion*
*James R. Arvo*
*Stephen H. Westin*
*Donald P. Greenberg*

Program of Computer Graphics
Cornell University
Ithaca, NY 14853

## Abstract

A general light transfer simulation algorithm for environments composed of materials with arbitrary reflectance functions is presented. This algorithm removes the previous practical restriction to ideal specular and/or ideal diffuse environments, and supports complex physically based reflectance distributions. This is accomplished by extending previous two-pass ray-casting radiosity approaches to handle non-uniform intensity distributions, and resolving all possible energy transfers between sample points. An implementation is described based on a spherical harmonic decomposition for encoding both bidirectional reflectance distribution functions for materials, and directional intensity distributions for illuminated surfaces. The method compares favorably with experimental measurements.

**CR Categories and Subject Descriptors:** I.3.7 [**Computer Graphics**]: Three-Dimensional Graphics and Realism; I.3.3 [**Computer Graphics**]: Picture/Image Generation.
**Additional Keywords and Phrases :** global illumination, BRDF, specular reflection, directional-diffuse, progressive radiosity, spherical harmonics.

## 1 Introduction

The simulation of global illumination is one of the major requirements for realistic image synthesis. Global illumination effects produced by multiple surface reflections are significant in all but the simplest environments. For instance, indirect lighting and *color bleeding*, or the transfer of color by reflection, can be observed in almost all indoor scenes. This paper presents a completely general algorithm designed to solve the global illumination problem for arbitrarily complex reflectance models.

Solution techniques for the simulation of complex light transfer mechanisms, where every point in the environment can potentially act as an illuminator for all other points, have thus far been quite limited. Two major paths have been explored. Light can be followed as it leaves the light sources and is propagated and reflected throughout the environment. For example, this approach is used by progressive refinement radiosity algorithms, and can be characterized as *view-independent* shading [3]. Conversely, standard ray tracing [20] and its derivatives usually start from the eye and follow light paths in the reverse direction. It is therefore strongly *view-dependent*.

These approaches work well for certain types of reflective behaviors, such as ideal diffuse (radiosity), ideal specular (ray tracing), or combinations of these [18, 17, 9]. The actual reflectance distributions of most surfaces are far more complicated, exhibiting some directionality which must be taken into account for accurate simulation.

The approach presented here extends the progressive radiosity method to include arbitrary reflectance distributions. While previous algorithms incorporating general reflectances have relied upon a discrete set of directions [11, 1, 13], no such restriction is introduced here. This is accomplished by using continuous functions to encode the directional dependence of intensity distributions.

In the next section we discuss the applicability of *view-independent* and *view-dependent* approaches to the case of general reflectance distributions and introduce a classification of reflectance types into *ideal diffuse*, *ideal specular* and *directional diffuse* components. The third section is devoted to the presentation of a complete algorithm to solve the general problem. Two specific issues are then detailed : treatment of ideal specular reflection in Section 4, and storage of directional diffuse contributions in Section 5.

## 2 Algorithmic choices for a general solution

The goal of this research is to develop a method for the simulation of global illumination that is general enough to provide accurate solutions for scenes incorporating any reflectance distribution. The problems encountered in devising a completely general algorithm are reviewed below, together with some of their design implications.

### 2.1 General reflectance distributions

The reflective properties of a surface are generally described by means of a *bidirectional reflectance distribution function* (BRDF), which is defined as the ratio of the reflected radiance in a given outgoing direction to the incoming energy flux (per unit area) in another direction. A similar quantity is defined for transmission. For the sake of clarity, we will refer only to reflection in this paper, although the algorithm is equally applicable to transmission. The two well-understood limiting cases are *ideal diffuse* and *ideal specular* reflection.

- An ideal diffuse reflector has a constant BRDF, that is, the scattered intensity is the same in all directions. Diffuse reflection can thus be fully described by a single scalar value.

- An ideal specular reflector has a Dirac delta function as its BRDF, where the only direction in which there is non-zero scattering is the mirrored direction. The relevant quantity to describe specular reflection is the ratio of the outgoing intensity in the specular direction to the incoming intensity, or *specular reflectance*.

Most materials have BRDFs that are not this simple, exhibiting a more elaborate directionality. Recent work on light reflection models has shown that different physical processes contribute to different parts of a BRDF [8], and the term *directional diffuse* has been introduced to describe the general BRDF excluding its ideal specular component. (Figure 1).

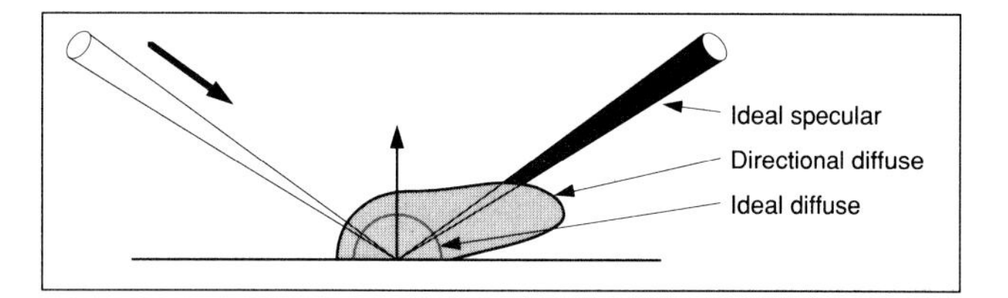


Figure 1: Different components of a general BRDF.

The directional diffuse component of a BRDF is a function of many variables, including surface finish (roughness), wavelength, and the electrical properties of the material. This produces a great variety of behaviors, all of which must be correctly simulated. The algorithm presented below is capable of incorporating both arbitrary directional diffuse and ideal specular reflection into a global solution.

## 2.2 View-independence vs. view-dependence

*View-independent* methods in general require the storage of illumination information on the surfaces, both for the purpose of the illumination computation and for use by a final *view-dependent* display algorithm. In the case of diffuse surfaces, storing a single radiosity value per wavelength channel at each sample point is sufficient, resulting in reasonable storage demands. In the same spirit, Immel *et al.* stored the directional information regarding the reflected intensity at each point, using a discrete set of directions [11]. If, however, the distribution of emitted or reflected light is sharply directional, as is the case with specular surfaces, storage becomes unmanageable if accuracy is to be maintained.

On the *view-dependent* side, distribution ray tracing [5] uses brute force, firing many reflection rays to simulate complex BRDFs, while path tracing [12] follows many paths through the scene to obtain a statistically reliable estimate. Here again, the property that made standard ray tracing [20] computationally tractable disappears (namely the restriction to ideal specular reflection that limits the number of rays), as rays must be fired towards all potential illuminators.

The method presented below combines elements of both strategies into a two-pass algorithm. The first pass computes a view-independent solution for the directional diffuse distribution of light, including the effect of intermediate specular reflections, and the second pass supplies the view-dependent ideal specular effects. This partitioning of reflectance behaviors resembles earlier two-pass approaches, but now accounts for all possible transport chains and incorporates arbitrary reflectance distributions, not only the extreme cases of ideal diffuse and ideal specular.

In the following discussion we use the vocabulary of radiosity-style algorithms for two reasons. One reason is the energy consistency of the radiosity method: a physical consideration necessary to obtain accurate simulations. The second reason is the appeal of the progressive refinement paradigm [3], where useful intermediate results can be obtained early in the computation.

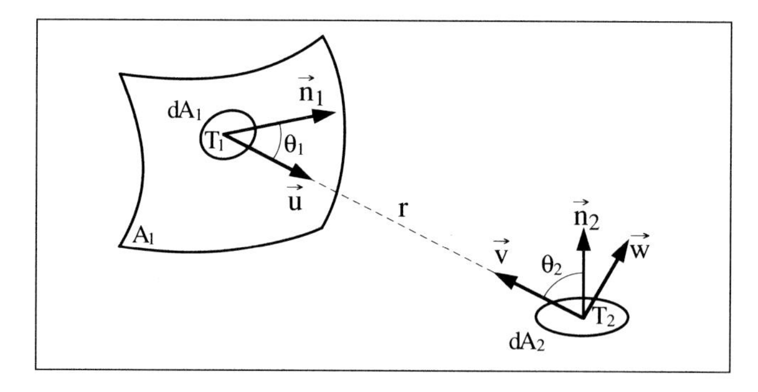


Figure 2: Energy transfer between a patch and a differential area

The notion of radiosity is extended to include the directional diffuse part of the light reflected at a given point. Because it does not include specularly reflected light, this *intensity distribution* is fairly smooth and thus can be stored at reasonable cost (See section 5). The ideal specular distribution of light is sharply discontinuous and is too costly to store on the surfaces; it is properly computed "on the fly" to resolve *specular to directional diffuse* transfers.

By using ray-casting, which has proven to be an effective sampling method to evaluate light transfers, all sample points in the environment are considered [19]. Furthermore, the use of ray casting imposes no restriction on the geometry of the environment and allows every illuminator to be sampled adaptively.

The algorithm proceeds by successive steps similar to progressive radiosity "shots", but directional intensity distributions are continuously maintained on the surfaces instead of scalar radiosity values. The ideal specular contributions to the energy transfers are propagated immediately so they need never be stored.

## 2.3 Energy transfers for non-diffuse surfaces

Traditional radiosity methods assume an ideal diffuse behavior on all the surfaces, and express the transfers between surfaces by means of a *form factor* [7]. For the general case the amount of light reflected from a point can be expressed as follows.

Let us denote by $I(T_1, \vec{u})$ the *intensity* (or *radiance*, expressed in Watts per unit solid angle per unit projected area) leaving a surface at point $T_1$, in the direction of the unit vector $\vec{u}$ (Figure 2). The energy $d^2E$ emitted by a differential surface area $dA_1$ around $T_1$ in the direction $\vec{u}$ and falling on a differential surface $dA_2$ around point $T_2$ is given by :

$$d^2E = I(T_1, \vec{u}) \underbrace{(dA_1 \cos\theta_1)}_{\text{projected area}} \underbrace{\left(\frac{dA_2 \cos\theta_2}{r^2}\right)}_{\text{solid angle as seen from } T_1} \quad (1)$$

$$= I(T_1, \vec{u}) \frac{\cos\theta_1 \, \cos\theta_2}{r^2} dA_2 \, dA_1 \quad (2)$$

This energy is scattered by the surface at $T_2$ in all directions. By definition of the BRDF $\rho_2$ at $T_2$, the intensity leaving $T_2$ in the direction $\vec{w}$, due to the incident light from $dA_1$, is given by :

$$dI(T_2, \vec{w}) = \rho_2(\vec{v}, \vec{w}) \frac{d^2E}{dA_2} \quad (3)$$

where $\vec{v} = -\vec{u}$ is the unit vector pointing from $T_2$ to $T_1$.

To evaluate the total intensity leaving $T_2$ in direction $\vec{w}$, due to the reflection of light originating from a finite area $A_1$, Equation (2) must be integrated across $A_1$ giving :

$$I(T_2, \vec{w}) = \int_{A_1} I(T_1, \vec{u}) \frac{\cos\theta_1 \cos\theta_2}{r^2} \rho_2(\vec{v}, \vec{w}) dA_1 \quad (4)$$

Equation (4) represents the effect of the light emitted by a particular surface on the light that is scattered around a point on another surface. It describes the elementary *shooting* operation of the radiosity method. The traditional radiosity method simplifies Equation (4) in two ways : first, the BRDF $\rho$ is assumed to be diffuse, which makes it a constant independent of both $\vec{v}$ and $\vec{w}$, and can thus be moved out of the integral. The diffuse assumption also makes $I(T_1, \vec{u})$ independent of $\vec{u}$. Second, the radiosity $\pi I(T_1)$ is assumed to be constant across the surface of the patch. The intensity term can thus be moved out of the integral, which then becomes purely geometric and is called the *differential form factor*.

If more general BRDFs are considered for the surface at $T_2$, however, the entire integrand must be considered. The next section explains how a form factor computation algorithm is adapted for that purpose.

# 3 General solution for arbitrary reflectances

A detailed description of the algorithm is presented below. The first pass, or solution pass, is very similar to progressive radiosity, and the implementation is a straightforward modification of an existing radiosity program. The second pass employs a simple ray tracer to retrieve the directional intensity information stored on the surfaces.

A central assumption of the method is that a directional intensity distribution $I(\vec{u})$ can be stored and accessed at each vertex of the environment. We discuss this topic further in section 5, where an efficient storage scheme is presented.

The method is explained here in terms of a meshed environment, composed of patches and elements [4], but it could be applied to radiosity textures [9] as well, if directional distributions are stored in the texture. The second (view-dependent) pass is described first, as it is a straightforward application of ray tracing.

## 3.1 Second pass

Once the view-independent solution has been computed in the first pass, a simple ray tracing pass is used to supply the view-dependent portion and create the final image. When rays encounter surfaces with a *directional diffuse* component, the intensity leaving a surface is retrieved from the directional distributions computed and stored in the first pass. The intensity contributed by *ideal specular* reflection is obtained by recursively following reflected rays as in conventional ray tracing. Note that a *specular reflectance function* is used to attenuate the reflected rays instead of a simple "specular coefficient". This allows a precise treatment of specular reflection, where roughness effects as well as Fresnel reflection are properly accounted for [8].

## 3.2 First pass

The first phase of the computation is an extension of progressive radiosity, but directional distributions are used throughout the algorithm in place of diffuse radiosities. The basic *shooting* operation now uses the directional intensity distribution emitted by the shooting patch to update the directional intensity distributions of the receiving vertices according to Equation (4).

This equation can be rewritten as a function of the intensity distributions rather than scalar values. If $\rho_2(\vec{v}, \cdot)$ denotes the BRDF for an incoming direction $\vec{v}$ as a function of the outgoing direction, and $I(T, \cdot)$ denotes the intensity distribution at point $T$, then the effect of shooting from $T_1$ to $T_2$ is

$$I(T_2, \cdot) = \int_{A_1} I(T_1, \vec{u}) \frac{\cos\theta_1 \cos\theta_2}{r^2} \rho_2(\vec{v}, \cdot) dA_1 \quad (5)$$

The algorithm presented below follows Equation (5) and decomposes the integral into a discrete sum. This is similar to the form factor computation algorithm of Wallace *et al.*[19], but modified to sum complete directional intensity distributions.

### Approximation of the integral

To obtain the reflected intensity distribution given by (5), we follow the computation of the *area-to-differential-area* form factor used in [19].

Patch $A_1$ is broken into a number of smaller pieces according to any given sampling scheme, and a contribution (a scalar *delta-form-factor* in the diffuse radiosity case, a directional distribution in our case) is computed for each piece. A variety of sampling strategies is available, and this formulation is independent of the particular scheme chosen. For $N$ samples, the total integral is expressed as :

$$I(T_2, \cdot) = \sum_{i=1}^{N} \delta I_i(T_2, \cdot) \quad (6)$$

Given sample $i$, with area $\delta A_i$ centered at $T_i$, the associated contribution to the integral in (4) could be crudely approximated by assuming the integrand constant, yielding :

$$\delta I_i(T_2, \cdot) = I(T_i, \vec{u}_i) \frac{\cos\theta_{1_i} \cos\theta_{2_i}}{r_i^2} \rho_2(\vec{v}_i, \cdot) \delta A_i \quad (7)$$

To avoid possible singularities when $T_1$ and $T_2$ are close together, we treat piece $i$ as a finite area, and use the approximation of a disk-shaped area as in [19]. This amounts to assuming that the emitted intensity does not vary significantly over the area of the piece, which is a common assumption of the radiosity formulation. The contribution of piece $i$ is then :

$$\delta I_i(T_2, \cdot) = I(T_i, \vec{u}_i) \cos\theta_{1_i} \cos\theta_{2_i} \frac{\pi \delta A_i}{\delta A_i + \pi r_i^2} \rho_2(\vec{v}_i, \cdot) \quad (8)$$

Introducing the incident energy flux (Watts per unit area) incident on point $T_2$ from piece $i$

$$\delta \Phi_i = I(\vec{u}_i) \frac{\cos\theta_{1_i} \cos\theta_{2_i} \pi \delta A_i}{\delta A_i + \pi r_i^2} = I(\vec{u}_i) \delta F_i \quad (9)$$

Equation (5) can be conveniently rewritten as :

$$I(T_2, \cdot) = \sum_{i=1}^{N} \delta \Phi_i \rho_2(\vec{v}_i, \cdot) \quad (10)$$

It is apparent from equation (10) that $I$ is simply a weighted sum of the BRDF at $T_2$ over a set of incident directions. Each energy flux term, $\delta \Phi_i$, is the product of the intensity leaving a sample point on the shooting patch in the direction of the receiving vertex and the *delta-form-factor* for that sample point.

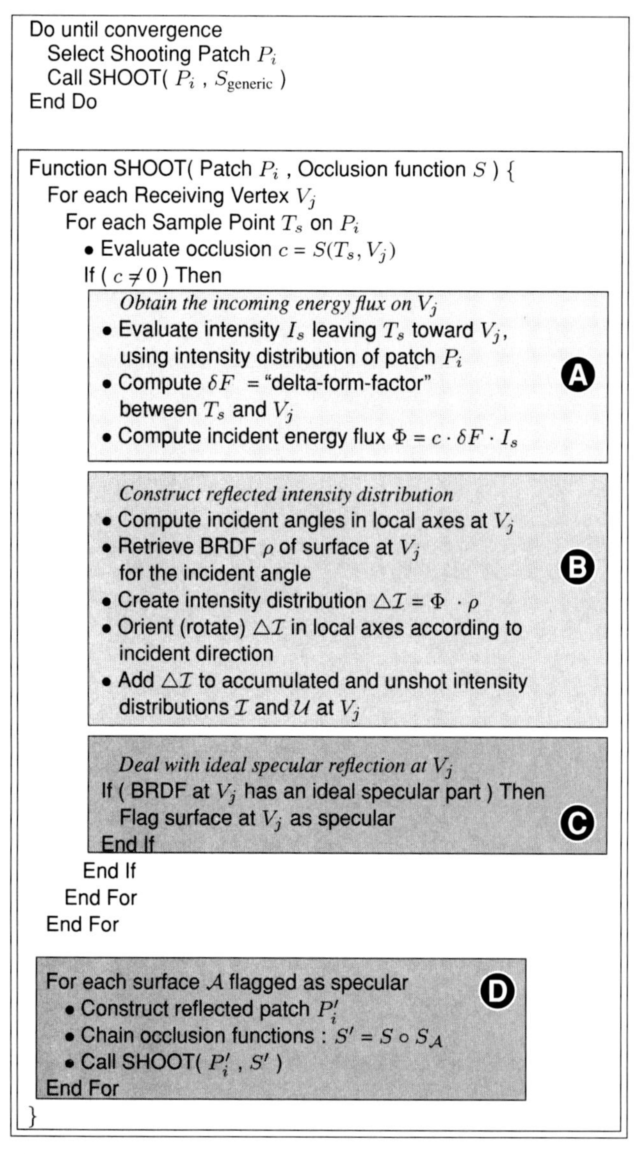


Figure 3: Algorithm for first pass. Step D is explained in section 4

## Discussion of the algorithm

The *shooting* operation that propagates the accumulated energy of a patch into the environment is presented as a pseudocode subroutine (called SHOOT) in Figure 3. Given a shooting patch $P_i$ and a receiving sample point (vertex $V_j$), the following operations are needed to update the directional intensity distribution of the vertex :

Sample points are selected on the shooting patch according to a sampling algorithm. Our implementation uses an adaptive sampling technique where the number and location of the sample points depend on the results obtained from previous samples [19]. For each sample point, a contribution is added to the reflected intensity distribution of the vertex.

The first task of the algorithm is to compute the incident energy flux on the vertex, which is used to weight the BRDF as in equation (10). This involves a visibility determination accomplished by the *occlusion function* $S$. In the simple cases where no ideal specular reflection is present, this function simply returns 0 or 1 to encode occlusion between the sample point and the vertex The more complex cases are explained in Section 4. If the two points

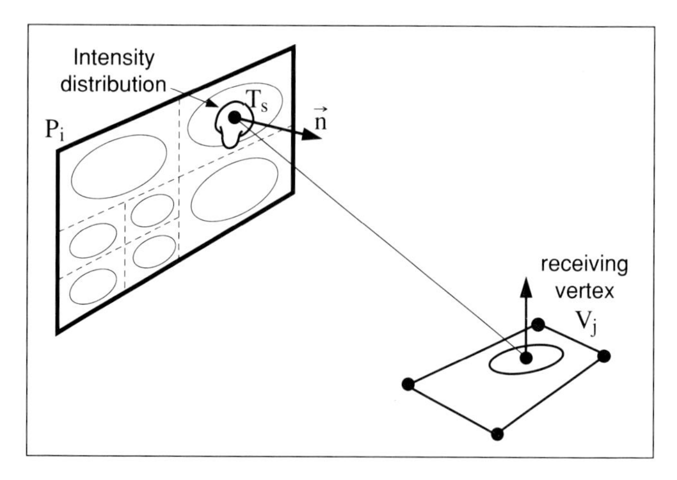


Figure 4: Computation of the energy flux.

can "see" each other, the intensity leaving the shooting patch is obtained from the stored directional distribution of the patch, and a *delta-form-factor* $\delta F$ (geometric attenuation term) is computed (Figure 3-A). The desired energy flux is the product of the intensity, the *delta-form-factor* and the attenuation given by the occlusion function (Figure 4).

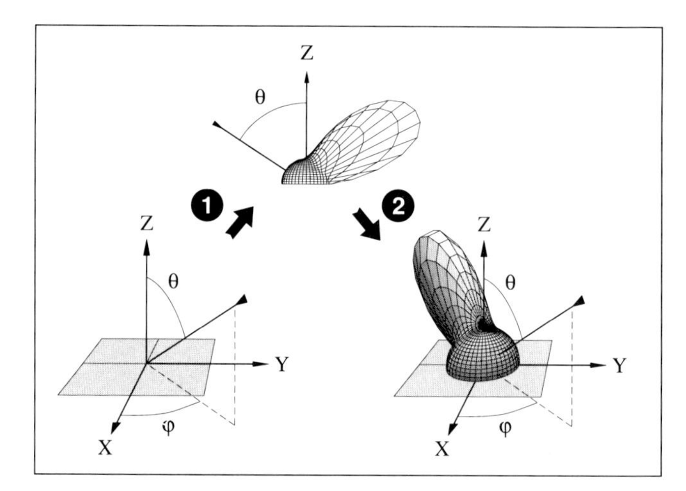


Figure 5: Orientation of the BRDF. (1) : obtaining the BRDF according to $\theta$. (2) : rotating the BRDF according to $\phi$.

The second step is to compute the contribution of the current sample point to the intensity distribution (Figure 3-B). We start by obtaining a directional distribution representing $\rho_2(\vec{v_i}, \cdot)$, that is, the BRDF for the given incident direction. This is retrieved by means of the storage method described in section 5. The BRDF is then *scaled* by the energy flux value $\delta\Phi_i$, which results in the distribution of reflected intensity $\triangle\mathcal{I}$ due to the current sample point. If an isotropic BRDF is used, the directional distribution depends only on the incident elevation angle $\theta$, and is obtained in a canonical coordinate system : it must be *rotated* to be properly aligned with the incident azimuth angle $\phi$ in the local coordinate system of the receiver (Figure 5). Finally this contribution is added to the *unshot* intensity distribution and the *accumulated* intensity distribution, much as in traditional progressive radiosity (Figure 6).

Previous work has shown that a complete treatment of light transfers requires exchanges incorporating different modes of reflection. Our shooting operation also includes a complete treatment of *ideal specular* reflection, so that the effect of specular reflection on the

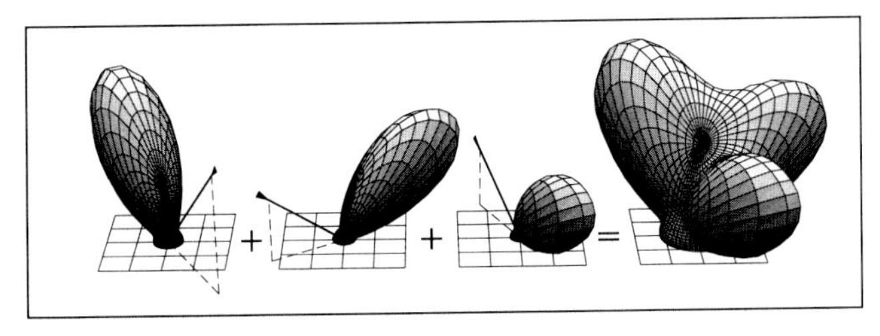

Figure 6: Addition of directional distributions.

intensity distributions is completely evaluated, but no "specular intensity" is stored (see section 2). Section 4 explains this part of the algorithm in more detail.

## 4 Ideal specular transfers

As explained in Section 2, specularly reflected light is not stored in the directional distributions on the specular reflector. Instead it is immediately propagated to other surfaces where part of it will be stored in a directional distribution, and part may again be specularly reflected to other surfaces.

Our implementation is an adaptation of the "image method" [16] to the ray-traced form factor idea : if the specular surfaces are planar, one can simply reflect the shooting patch across the surface, and shoot light from this "virtual patch" to all receiving vertices (Figure 7). Note that the direction for each shot is chosen deterministically based on the position of a vertex; this is not a Monte Carlo sampling technique.

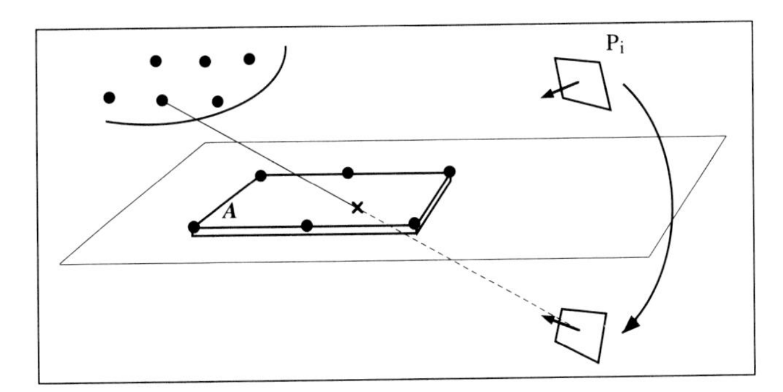


Figure 7: Reflecting the shooting patch on a specular surface. Original vertices from the environment mesh are shown as dots.

This method has several important benefits :

- In contrast to the original "image method", where the entire environment had to be reflected into a virtual environment, only the shooting patch need be reflected.
- The evaluation of one specular reflection on a given specular surface can be implemented as a normal shooting step with a slightly modified occlusion testing routine. Furthermore, since we are shooting directly to vertices, it is possible to restrict the expensive occlusion testing operation to the portions of the environment that can potentially receive reflected light, using a technique similar to a *shadow volume* [14].

  This allows us to retain benefits of the normal ray-casting method, such as adaptive meshing based on the results of a shot, and various sampling stategies for the shooting patch.
- Multiple specular reflections can be implemented by recursively creating virtual patches. It should be noted that since the shooting patch is the only one that need be reflected, there is no explosion of the complexity of the scene.

The current implementation is limited to planar specular surfaces. If more complex geometries are needed for the specular surfaces, it is no longer simple to construct a modified patch from which to shoot. Instead, specular rays can be fired from each receiving vertex lying on a specular surface, in a manner similar to [17]. However, the distribution of specular rays then depends on the mesh of vertices on the specular surface, with no guarantee that all vertices in the environment will receive their share of the specularly reflected light. A major benefit of the ray-casting approach to radiosity is then lost. Furthermore, rays must be properly weighted, taking surface curvature into account, to ensure a physically correct energy transfer.

### 4.1 Algorithm

The pseudo-code algorithm in Figure 3 contains two parts involving specular reflection (note that the treatment of specular reflection within the first pass occurs entirely within the shooting operation).

In the general loop that considers all receiving vertices in turn, specular surfaces are flagged whenever one of their vertices receives some energy from the shooting patch (Figure 3-C). Entire surfaces (planar patches) are flagged regardless of their subdivision into patches or elements, or their number of vertices.

Once all the vertices have had their directional intensity distributions updated with respect to the shooting patch, the specular reflectors are then considered in turn (Figure 3-D). For each specular surface, a new patch is created and the occlusion testing function is modified in preparation for a recursive call to the shooting procedure SHOOT.

The new patch is obtained by reflecting the original shooting patch and its attached coordinate system across the specular surface $\mathcal{A}$. The new, virtual patch possesses the same intensity distributions as the original shooting patch except that they are reflected by virtue of the reflected coordinate system.

A shot from the virtual patch $P_i'$ affects only those vertices in the environments that can "see" the original shooting patch in the specular surface. This is easily accomplished by sampling the virtual patch as a normal shooting patch, but using a modified occlusion testing routine between the receiving vertex and the sample point. Figure 8 depicts the extended occlusion test.

An occlusion function (called $S_{\mathcal{A}}$ in Figure 3, and described as pseudo-code in Figure 9) is first called : this function first looks for an intersection between the specular surface $\mathcal{A}$ and the ray linking the receiving vertex $V_j$ and a sample point on the virtual patch $T_S$. If no intersection is found, there can be no light reflected in that direction, and the function returns. Next, if an intersection point $\tau_S$ was found, a normal occlusion test is performed between $V_j$ and $\tau_S$. If the two points are visible to one another, the *specular reflectance* of the specular surface is computed for the appropriate reflection angle at $\tau_S$.

If $S_{\mathcal{A}}$ returns a non-zero value, the only remaining operation consists in determining the occlusion between $\tau_S$ and a sample point on the original shooting patch, that is, the reflected image of $T_S$ (Figure 8). This is accomplished by calling whatever occlusion function was in use at the current level of recursion : if we are dealing with a first specular reflection, the generic occlusion testing routine $S_{\text{generic}}$ is used. At deeper levels of recursion, a composite function obtained by previous chaining operations is used.

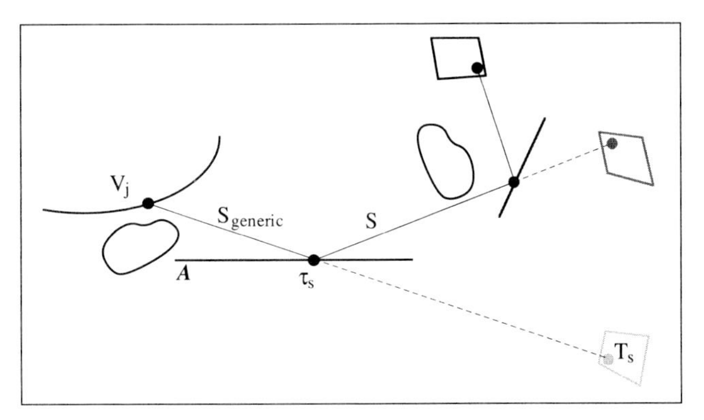


Figure 8: Chaining the occlusion functions. Once occlusion between $V_j$ and $\tau_S$ is resolved, the composite occlusion test is performed between $\tau_S$ and the sample point on the original patch, possibly involving several specular reflections.

The entire operation can be described as chaining together the current occlusion testing function with the occlusion routine for the current specular surface. Note that once point $\tau_S$ has been found on the specular surface, the order in which the two occlusion tests are carried out is arbitrary. However, since the occlusion test between $\tau_S$ and $V_j$ is generally a simpler test, it is performed first.

```
Function S_A ( T_S , V_j ) {
    • Find intersection τ_S between V_j T_S and A
    If ( No Intersection is Found ) Then
        • Return 0
    End If
    • Evaluate occlusion c = S_generic(τ_S, V_j)
    If ( c ≠ 0 ) Then
        • Compute specular reflectance ρ^s_A
        • Return c · ρ^s_A
    Else
        • Return 0
    End If
}
```

Figure 9: Occlusion testing for a virtual patch

# 5 Storing Intensity Distributions

The main departure of the current algorithm from previous progressive radiosity methods is that unshot and accumulated intensities now take the form of distribution functions at each vertex instead of scalar values. Because the number of vertices required for an accurate simulation can be quite large, it is crucial that the representation of these functions be economical in terms of storage. Moreover, the representation must allow for efficient "shooting" steps, which are performed many thousands of times in the course of a single simulation.

To fit within the framework of progressive radiosity, intensity distributions must also be computed incrementally by summing the directional distributions resulting from impinging shots. After accumulating contributions shot from $n$ sample points on other patches, the intensity distribution at vertex $k$ on an isotropic surface is given by the following equation.

$$I_k(\theta, \phi) = \sum_{i=1}^{n} \Phi_i \, \rho_k(\theta_i^{\text{in}}, \theta, \phi + \Delta\phi_i) \tag{11}$$

Here $\Phi_i$, $\theta_i^{\text{in}}$, and $\Delta\phi_i$ are the energy flux, angle of incidence, and azimuthal angle of the $i$'th contribution respectively. Here we have expressed the BRDF parameters as angles with respect to a fixed local coordinate system at vertex $k$ (Figure 5). The vertical axis of this coordinate system corresponds to the surface normal at that vertex though the other axes are arbitrary.

We can interpret Equation (11) as a sequence of four operations applied to the underlying BRDF, $\rho_k$, for each contribution arriving at vertex $k$: retrieving the directional distribution for a given angle of incidence, scaling and rotating this distribution, and finally adding it to the accumulated and unshot distributions stored at the vertex. These steps are shown in Figure 3-B.

From these operations it is clear that the shape of each intensity distribution depends solely on the BRDF associated with the vertex and not on the distributions from which the energy was shot. While this constrains the class of distributions that can arise at any given vertex, the distributions resulting from many contributions may nonetheless be quite irregular if the BRDF has a directional component (Figure 6).

We therefore require a representation that is general enough to account for this variation while also accomodating the steps in Figure 3-B. High-order continuity is also a requirement, since a discrete description, such as the *global cube* [11], can result in severe aliasing problems. Furthermore, derivative discontinuities in the intensity distributions can cause artifacts such as Mach-banding on the illuminated surfaces, even if a perfectly accurate transfer of light is computed.

In the following sections we describe an approach based on spherical harmonics which meets these requirements. Using this mechanism we can compactly and accurately represent arbitrary BRDFs and their associated intensity distributions and efficiently perform all of the operations required for shooting and incremental creation. It is therefore a nearly ideal mechanism for storing the intensity distributions for this global illumination algorithm.

## 5.1 Approximation using Spherical Harmonics

Spherical harmonics form an orthogonal basis for the space of functions defined over the unit sphere [6]. This infinite collection of basis functions is typically denoted by $Y_{l,m}(\theta, \phi)$ where $0 \le l < \infty$ and $-l \le m \le l$. In direct analogy with Fourier series in one dimension, any square-integrable function, $f(\theta, \phi)$, can be represented by an infinite series of the form

$$f(\theta, \phi) = \sum_{l=0}^{\infty} \sum_{m=-l}^{l} C_{l,m} \, Y_{l,m}(\theta, \phi) \tag{12}$$

where the coefficients are given by

$$C_{l,m} = \int_0^{2\pi} \int_0^{\pi} f(\theta, \phi) \, Y_{l,m}(\theta, \phi) \, \sin(\theta) \, d\theta \, d\phi. \tag{13}$$

The practical value of this is that a finite number of terms can be used to approximate relatively smooth functions defined on the sphere. This allows us to store intensity distributions as a vector of $N$ coefficients, where $N$ depends upon the characteristics of the underlying BRDF and the desired accuracy of the approximation. A diffuse, smoothly varying BRDF will typically require fewer coefficients than a very directional one.

To construct such a representation for the intensity distributions we begin by approximating the BRDFs in terms of spherical harmonics. In previous work, Cabral *et al.* have used a similar approximation for the purpose of simulating diffuse and glossy reflections of the environment [2]. In the present work the dependence of the BRDF on the angle of incidence is accounted for by representing each spherical harmonic coefficient as a function of $\theta^{\text{in}}$. That is, for every BRDF we construct a collection of scalar functions, $B_{l,m}(\cdot)$, such that

$$\rho(\theta^{\text{in}}, \theta, \phi) \cos\theta \approx \sum_{l=0}^{N} \sum_{m=-l}^{l} B_{l,m}(\theta^{\text{in}})\, Y_{l,m}(\theta, \phi). \tag{14}$$

In this way we can model the behavior of a BRDF over the entire range of incident angles. In our implementation the $B_{l,m}$ functions are stored as one-dimensional cubic splines; one for each spherical harmonic in the BRDF approximation. The $\cos\theta$ factor is included at this stage because it reduces evaluation time and tends to reduce ringing in the approximation. Figure 10 shows several of these curves for slightly rough aluminum. Additional details on this approximation can be found in Appendix A.

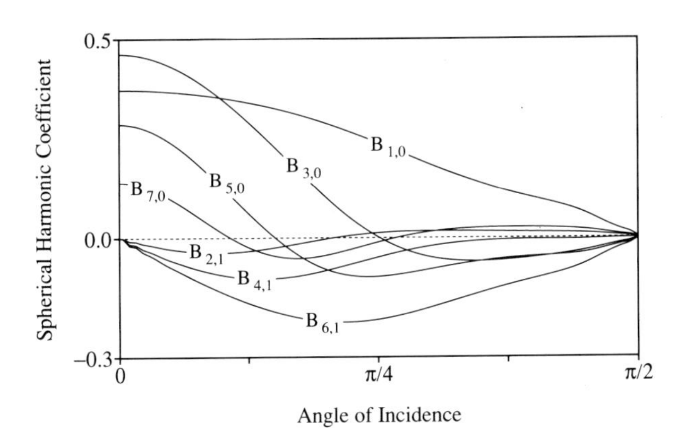


Figure 10: Seven spherical harmonic coefficients for the BRDF of slightly rough aluminum plotted as functions of the incident angle.

## 5.2 Operations on Spherical Harmonic Coefficients

Given a BRDF approximation of the form in equation (14) we can construct a corresponding intensity distribution using Equation (11). For every intensity contribution we first evaluate the BRDF at the given angle of incidence, $\theta^{\text{in}}$, by computing the spherical harmonic coefficients of the resulting directional distribution. This consists of evaluating an interpolating spline, $B_{l,m}(\cdot)$, for each coefficient.

Next, we scale the distribution by multiplying each of these coefficients by the energy flux. The third step, rotating the distribution about the vertical axis, is made simple by the following property of spherical harmonics (shown in real form).

$$\begin{bmatrix} Y_{l,m}(\theta, \phi + \alpha) \\ Y_{l,-m}(\theta, \phi + \alpha) \end{bmatrix} = \begin{bmatrix} \cos(m\alpha) & -\sin(m\alpha) \\ \sin(m\alpha) & \cos(m\alpha) \end{bmatrix} \begin{bmatrix} Y_{l,m}(\theta, \phi) \\ Y_{l,-m}(\theta, \phi) \end{bmatrix}$$

This property follows immediately from the definition of spherical harmonics given in Appendix A. Rotation about this axis is particularly straightforward, and the usual symmetry of the BRDFs with respect to the incident plane simplifies it even further. Because negatively subscripted spherical harmonics are odd functions with respect to $\phi$, we are guaranteed that all such coefficients will vanish in the BRDF approximation. These coefficients reappear in the intensity distributions, however, because the symmetry is destroyed when the BRDFs undergo arbitrary rotations. This can be seen in step 3 of figure 11.

**Initialize:** $C^k_{l,m} \leftarrow 0$

For Each Contribution $(\Phi, \theta^{\text{in}}, \Delta\phi)$ arriving at Vertex $k$

For Each index pair, $(l, m)$, used in the approximation of $\rho_k$

1. **Interpolate:** $A_{l,m} \leftarrow B^k_{l,m}(\theta^{\text{in}})$
2. **Scale:** $A'_{l,m} \leftarrow \Phi\, A_{l,m}$
3. **Rotate:** $\begin{bmatrix} A''_{l,m} \\ A''_{l,-m} \end{bmatrix} \leftarrow A'_{l,m} \begin{bmatrix} \cos(m\,\Delta\phi) \\ \sin(m\,\Delta\phi) \end{bmatrix}$
4. **Add:** $\begin{bmatrix} C^k_{l,m} \\ C^k_{l,-m} \end{bmatrix} \leftarrow \begin{bmatrix} C^k_{l,m} \\ C^k_{l,-m} \end{bmatrix} + \begin{bmatrix} A''_{l,m} \\ A''_{l,-m} \end{bmatrix}$

End For

End For

Figure 11: Creating an intensity distribution. When $m = 0$, steps 2 through 4 reduce to $C^k_{l,0} \leftarrow C^k_{l,0} + \Phi A_{l,0}$.

As the fourth and final step we add the resulting distribution to the current total by adding the corresponding coefficients. Thus, we have rephrased each of the steps in Figure 3-B in terms of operations on spherical harmonic coefficients. The actual steps are shown in Figure 11 where the $C^k_{l,m}$ denote coefficients of an intensity distribution at vertex $k$.

It is apparent from these operations that summing scaled and rotated instances of a single representation introduces no additional coefficients once the symmetry has been broken. Therefore, *the storage required for a given intensity distribution does not grow as intensity is accumulated.* Furthermore, the intensity distributions retain the full accuracy of the original BRDF approximations.

To perform the shooting step we must evaluate an intensity distribution in directions toward all vertices to which intensity is to be shot. This requires evaluating the $Y_{l,m}$ functions associated with the coefficients of the intensity distribution in each of these directions. These evaluations can be performed efficiently using the recurrence relations shown in Appendix A.

# 6 Results

Solutions have been computed for several test environments to demonstrate the feasibility of the simulation for arbitrary reflectance distributions. The resulting pictures exhibit all the expected visual effects produced by directional diffuse as well as ideal specular energy transfers.

Figure 12 shows a side by side comparison of a simulated environment with a scanned physical environment. The scanned picture was obtained by scanning through three colored filters, where each channel is spectrally integrated over a large range of wavelengths. Thus, the comparison with a simulation computed with three well-defined monochromatic channels can only be qualitative (for example the general color tone is noticably different). However, important features such as the structure of the shadow on the left, or the illumination of the ceiling via specular reflection from the top of the tall box, appear to be very similar. A related research project is un-

Figure 13: First-surface mirror

Figure 14: Smooth Aluminum box #1

Figure 15: Smooth Aluminum box #2

Figure 16: Rough Aluminum

In figure 13, the tall box is covered with perfectly smooth aluminum, making it a first surface mirror. In figure 14 the surface has been roughened slightly. Note that ideal specular effects are still very strong, both in the reflected image on the box, and in the upper left corner of the environment, where light is reflected by the top of the tall box. The directional nature of the diffused light can also be seen on the front face of the tall box. In figure 15, the box is made somewhat rougher, and more of the light is being reflected in a directional diffuse manner. Note that the specular reflection is stronger on the left face of the box than it is on the front face because of the different incident angles for rays reaching the eye. This is a result of the model used to predict the specular reflectance [8] and is observed on real materials. Figure 16 shows an aluminum box that is rougher still, and the ideal specular component of the reflectance has almost disappeared. Note that there is still a concentration of light in the upper left corner of the scene, because light reflected by the top face of the box has a definite directional character. Figures 17 and 18 show the results of the algorithm run on more complex scenes. In figure 17 the aluminum bowl and cupboard doors are directional diffuse reflectors, and in figure 18 the telephone, the drawer handles and the blackboard frame are made of different varieties of aluminum.

Figure 17: Kitchen with directional diffuse cupboards and mixing bowl. Note the highlights on the cupboards.

Figure 18: Desk with aluminum phone and drawer handles. Note the caustics on the back wall.

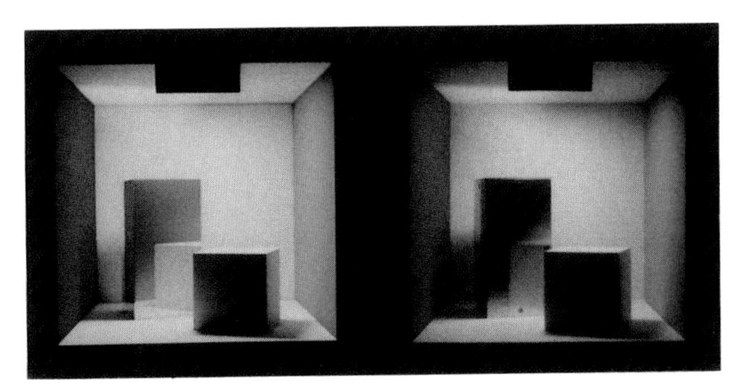

Figure 12: Comparison of a simulation with a scanned image.

der way to develop precise radiometric measurement procedures so that accurate quantitative comparisons can be made [10].

Figures 13 to 16 show simulations of a simple environment with varying surface properties. The tall box is made of aluminum with increasing roughness throughout the sequence. Figures 17 and 18 demonstrate the method applied to complex scenes (consisting of 34400 and 30200 elements, respectively). The last two pictures required an average time of 5 minutes per radiosity shot, on an Apollo DN 10000 computer with 64 Megabytes of main memory.

In all these simulations, between 80 and 133 coefficients were used to approximate the BRDFs, resulting in intensity distributions of 148 to 254 coefficients. The number of coefficients in the latter increases due to loss of symmetry as described in section 5.2. The number of coefficients was determined for each material in order to achieve a given precision in the approximation of the BRDF over the entire range of incidence angles. Ideal diffuse surfaces require only one coefficient, and in general the more directional the BRDF, the more coefficients are required to account for the higher frequencies in the shape.

In all cases the intensity distributions have been stored using fewer than 1K bytes at each vertex, while the error in the approximation was kept to a few percent. For any fixed number of coefficients, however, the approximation will generally begin to degrade as the BRDF becomes increasingly directional. Fortunately, according to physical optics, this will be somewhat compensated by the fact that the ideal specular component, which is handled separately, begins to dominate in this case [8]. Therefore, even for nearly-perfect mirrors, we can maintain a reasonable accuracy in terms of energy balance without increasing storage.

# 7 Conclusions and future directions

An algorithm for the simulation of global illumination with arbitrary reflectance behaviors was presented. A general treatment of *ideal specular to directional diffuse* transfers was introduced, allowing all chains of reflection to be effectively simulated. An efficient method using spherical harmonics to store the directional diffuse intensity distributions has been demonstrated, which permits a given accuracy to be maintained with a fixed amount of storage per vertex throughout the simulation.

Other features could be added easily to the system. An extension to anisotropic reflectance models would require an extra level of interpolation to obtain the BRDF, since it would depend on both incident angles (elevation and azimuth). This can be accomplished by using a two-dimensional spline surface instead of the current one-dimensional spline function for the spherical harmonics coefficients.

Polarization effects that are predicted by general reflectance models [8] could also be incorporated into the system very naturally, by using the complex formulation of spherical harmonics.

This method suffers from several limitations inherited from the progressive radiosity method. For example, the intensity distribution is assumed to be uniform across a patch at shooting time, even though more detailed information might already be available from the subdivision of the patch into elements. Better sampling strategies are also needed. However, we believe that the formulation of the global illumination problem in terms of directional distributions attached to the surfaces, combined with a physically consistent treatment of ideal specular reflection, allows a truly general solution to be computed for arbitrary reflectance distributions.

# 8 Acknowledgements

The authors are extremely grateful to the Hewlett Packard Corporation and the Digital Equipment Corporation for donating the equipment used in this work. This research was conducted under a National Science Foundation grant (#CCR-8617880) entitled "Interactive Input and Display Techniques". Stephen Westin was supported by a fellowship from Ford Motor Company. The authors wish to thank Roy Hall for reviewing this paper, and Ben Trumbore and Mark Reichert for their help in getting the software to run. Particular thanks go to all members of "Team Reality"; Professor Ken Torrance, Xiao-Dong He, Michael Monks, and Ted Himlan, for helping to keep a very large project running. The kitchen and office models were designed by Suzanne Smits, and Harold Zatz helped format the manuscript. The images were photographed by Emil Ghinger.

# References

[1] Buckalew, Chris and Donald Fussell. "Illumination Networks: Fast Realistic Rendering with General Reflectance Functions," *Computer Graphics*, 23(3), July 1989, pages 89–98. (Proceedings SIGGRAPH '89 in Boston.)

[2] Cabral, Brian, Nelson L. Max, and Rebecca Springmayer. "Bidirectional Reflection Functions from Surface Bump Maps," *Computer Graphics*, 21(4), July 1987, pages 273–281. (Proceedings SIGGRAPH '87 in Anaheim.)

[3] Cohen, Michael F., Shenchang Eric Chen, John R. Wallace, and Donald P. Greenberg. "A Progressive Refinement Approach to Fast Radiosity Image Generation," *Computer Graphics*, 22(4), August 1988, pages 75–84. (Proceedings SIGGRAPH '88 in Atlanta.)

[4] Cohen, Michael F., Donald P. Greenberg, David S. Immel, and Philip J. Brock. "An Efficient Radiosity Approach for Realistic Image Synthesis," *IEEE Computer Graphics and Applications*, 6(3), March 1986, pages 25–35.

[5] Cook, Robert L., Thomas Porter, and Loren Carpenter. "Distributed Ray Tracing," *Computer Graphics*, 18, July 1984, pages 137–147. (Proceedings SIGGRAPH '84 in Minneapolis.)

[6] Courant, R. and D. Hilbert. *Methods of Mathematical Physics*, Interscience Publishers, Inc., New York, 1953.

[7] Goral, Cindy M., Kenneth E. Torrance, Donald P. Greenberg, and Bennett Battaile. "Modeling the Interaction of Light Between Diffuse Surfaces," *Computer Graphics*, 18(3), July 1984, pages 213–222. (Proceedings SIGGRAPH '84 in Minneapolis.)

[8] He, XiaoDong, Kenneth E. Torrance, François Sillion, and Donald P. Greenberg. "A comprehensive Physical Model for Light Reflection," *Computer Graphics*, 25(4), August 1991. (Proceedings SIGGRAPH '91 in Las Vegas.)

[9] Heckbert, Paul S. "Adaptive Radiosity Textures for Bidirectional Ray Tracing," *Computer Graphics*, 24(4), August 1990, pages 145–154. (Proceedings SIGGRAPH '90 in Dallas.)

[10] Himlan, Theodore H., Michael C. Monks, Stephen H. Westin, Donald P. Greenberg, and Kenneth E. Torrance. "Physical Measurement Techniques for Improving and Evaluating Computer Graphic Simulations," January 1991. (Submitted for publication.)

[11] Immel, David S., Michael F. Cohen, and Donald P. Greenberg. "A Radiosity Method for Non-Diffuse Environments," *Computer Graphics*, 20(4), August 1986, pages 133–142. (Proceedings SIGGRAPH '86 in Dallas.)

[12] Kajiya, James T. "The Rendering Equation," *Computer Graphics*, 20(4), August 1986, pages 143–150. (Proceedings SIGGRAPH '86 in Dallas.)

[13] Le Saec, Bertrand and Christophe Schlick. "A Progressive Ray-Tracing based Radiosity with General Reflectance Functions," June 1990. (Proceedings of the Eurographics Workshop on Photosimulation, Realism and Physics in Computer Graphics (Rennes, France).)

[14] Nishita, T. and E. Nakamae. "Continuous Tone Representation of Three-dimesional Objects Taking Account of Shadows and Interreflection," *Computer Graphics*, 19(3), July 1985, pages 23–30. (Proceedings SIGGRAPH '85 in San Francisco.)

[15] Press, William H., Brian P. Flannery, and Saul A. Teukolsky. *Numerical Recipes*, Cambridge University Press, New York, 1986.

[16] Rushmeier, Holly E. and Kenneth E. Torrance. "Extending the Radiosity Method to Include Specularly Reflecting and Translucent Materials," *ACM Transactions on Graphics*, 9(1), January 1990, pages 1–27.

[17] Sillion, François and Claude Puech. "A General Two-Pass Method Integrating Specular and Diffuse Reflection," *Computer Graphics*, 23(4), August 1989. (Proceedings SIGGRAPH '89 in Boston.)

[18] Wallace, John R., Michael F. Cohen, and Donald P. Greenberg. "A Two-Pass Solution to the Rendering Equation : a Synthesis of Ray-Tracing and Radiosity methods," *Computer Graphics*, 21(4), July 1987, pages 311–320. (Proceedings SIGGRAPH '87 in Anaheim.)

[19] Wallace, John R., Kells A. Elmquist, and Eric A. Haines. "A Ray Tracing Algorithm for Progressive Radiosity," *Computer Graphics*, 23(3), July 1989, pages 315–324. (Proceedings SIGGRAPH '89 in Boston.)

[20] Whitted, Turner. "An Improved Illumination Model for Shaded Display," *Communications of the ACM*, 23, 1980, pages 343–349.

# Appendix A: More on spherical harmonics

In real form, the normalized spherical harmonics are defined by

$$Y_{l,m}(\theta,\phi) = \begin{cases} N_{l,m}\, P_{l,m}(\cos\theta)\cos(m\phi) & \text{if } m > 0 \\ N_{l,0}\, P_{l,0}(\cos\theta)/\sqrt{2} & \text{if } m = 0 \\ N_{l,m}\, P_{l,|m|}(\cos\theta)\sin(|m|\phi) & \text{if } m < 0 \end{cases} \tag{15}$$

where the normalizing constants, $N_{l,m}$, are given by

$$N_{l,m} = \sqrt{\frac{2l+1}{2\pi}\frac{(l-|m|)!}{(l+|m|)!}} \tag{16}$$

and the $P_{l,m}(x)$ factors are *associated Legendre polynomials*. The latter can be evaluated with the recurrence relations

$$\begin{aligned} P_{m,m}(x) &= (1-2m)\sqrt{1-x^2}P_{m-1,m-1}(x) \\ P_{m+1,m}(x) &= x(2m+1)P_{m,m}(x) \\ P_{l,m}(x) &= x\left(\tfrac{2l-1}{l-m}\right)P_{l-1,m}(x) - \left(\tfrac{l+m-1}{l-m}\right)P_{l-2,m}(x) \end{aligned}$$

beginning with $P_{0,0}(x) = 1$ [15]. Applying these in conjunction with recurrence relations for generating $\sin(\phi)$, $\sin(2\phi), \ldots, \sin(m\phi)$ and $\cos(\phi), \cos(2\phi), \ldots, \cos(m\phi)$, it is possible to evaluate spherical harmonic expansions using approximately 10 floating point operations per coefficient and no trigonometric function evaluations whatsoever.

Evaluation of the spherical harmonic functions is required for two purposes: shooting from an intensity distribution and creating the initial BRDF approximations. The former is a straightforward application of Equation 12 while the latter is more complicated and is performed once per distinct BRDF. To approximate an isotropic BRDF for all incident angles, we first compute

$$b^j_{l,m} = \int_0^{\pi}\int_0^{\pi} \rho(\theta^{\text{in}}_j,\theta,\phi)\,Y_{l,m}(\theta,\phi)\,\sin(\theta)\,d\theta\,d\phi \tag{17}$$

for $j = 0, 1, \ldots q$ where $0 = \theta^{\text{in}}_0 \le \theta^{\text{in}}_1 \le \cdots \le \theta^{\text{in}}_q = \pi/2$. Then the functions $B_{l,m}$ can be approximated by cubic interpolating splines through the the points $(\theta^{\text{in}}_0, b^0_{l,m})$, $(\theta^{\text{in}}_1, b^1_{l,m}), \ldots, (\theta^{\text{in}}_q, b^q_{l,m})$. For each distinct BRDF, $\rho$, we select $q$ as well as a specific set of spherical harmonic coefficients to achieve the desired accuracy of approximation over all incident angles. The value of $q$ affects the accuracy of the interpolation but does not otherwise influence the intensity distributions. In contrast, the number of coefficients used in the BRDF approximation directly determines the sorage required for the intensity distributions. It is therefore important to keep this number reasonably small.

If the BRDF that we wish to approximate is only defined on the upper hemisphere, as with an opaque material, we extend the function to the lower hemisphere before computing the approximation. We do this in such a way that the complete BRDF satisfies

$$\rho(\theta^{\text{in}},\theta,\phi) = -\rho(\theta^{\text{in}},\pi-\theta,\phi). \tag{18}$$

This introduces a vertical symmetry which has the advantage of eliminating all spherical harmonics for which $l + m$ is even. It also maintains $C^1$ continuitiy between the upper and lower hemispheres when the function is zero at the equator, a condition that is guaranteed if the $\cos\theta$ factor is included as described in section 5.1.

# A Rapid Hierarchical Radiosity Algorithm

Pat Hanrahan
Department of Computer Science
Princeton University
Princeton, NJ 08540

David Salzman
68 Francis Avenue
Cambridge, MA 02138

Larry Aupperle
Department of Computer Science
Princeton University
Princeton, NJ 08540

## Abstract

This paper presents a rapid hierarchical radiosity algorithm for illuminating scenes containing large polygonal patches. The algorithm constructs a hierarchical representation of the form factor matrix by adaptively subdividing patches into subpatches according to a user-supplied error bound. The algorithm guarantees that all form factors are calculated to the same precision, removing many common image artifacts due to inaccurate form factors. More importantly, the algorithm decomposes the form factor matrix into at most $O(n)$ blocks (where $n$ is the number of elements). Previous radiosity algorithms represented the element-to-element transport interactions with $n^2$ form factors. Visibility algorithms are given that work well with this approach. Standard techniques for shooting and gathering can be used with the hierarchical representation to solve for equilibrium radiosities, but we also discuss using a brightness-weighted error criteria, in conjunction with multigridding, to even more rapidly progressively refine the image.

**CR Categories and Subject Descriptors:** I.3.7 [Computer Graphics]: Three-Dimensional Graphics and Realism.
**Key Words:** radiosity, ray-tracing, global illumination, n-body problem.

## 1 Introduction

Developing a correct treatment of the physics of bidirectional reflectance and of light transport is an important focus of modern research in image synthesis. Although efficient solutions to the fully general case are not known, these physically-based models have produced some of the most realistic computer-generated images to date. The most successful approach has been *radiosity*, which, by making the simplifying assumption that all the surfaces are diffuse reflectors, allows for straightforward computation of the equilibrium distribution of light for complex scene geometries.

This paper presents efficient computational techniques for solving the transport equations that arise for radiosity in complex scenes. Our algorithm draws from recent insights into fast numerical algorithms for solving the N-body problem (Appel 1985; Barnes and Hut 1986; Greengard 1988). Computational efficiency is achieved by carefully analyzing the error in performing form factor integrals. Without careful error analysis, pictures may contain artifacts where the form factors have large error. More importantly, many form factor computations are done at much higher precision than is necessary. Careful error analysis, in combination with a multi-resolution representation, can be used to reduce significantly the number of interactions that are considered.



Previously we analyzed the form factor calculation between two unoccluded polygonal patches, discretized into $n$ finer polygonal elements (Hanrahan and Salzman, 1990). We showed that the form factor matrix can always be approximated to within some preset numerical tolerance with at most $O(n)$ terms, and often many fewer. This paper extends our previous radiosity algorithm to handle scenes with many polygons, where occlusion plays an important role. Occlusion, although costly to detect, reduces the number of interactions even further. The form factor matrix is therefore sparser, allowing faster solution for equilibrium radiosities. The technique used for determining visibility is based on ray tracing, but two important optimizing heuristics are introduced. One takes advantage of visibility coherence between different levels of detail; the other is based on the observation that most interactions between patches are either totally visible or totally invisible with respect to each other. Finally, we show how to use multigridding in combination with a brightness-weighted error estimate. This leads to a faster progressive radiosity algorithm.

## 2 Review of Previous Work

### 2.1 Radiosity

Radiosity algorithms assume the environment has been discretized into small elements which have constant brightness. In this paper, we use the term "element" to describe the smallest piece of a surface subdivision, and the term "patch" for any larger pieces, including the original polygon, formed by combining elements or other patches, Enforcing an energy balance at every element yields a system of equations of the form:

$$B_i = E_i + \rho_i \sum_{j}^{n} F_{ij} B_j$$

where $B_i$ is the radiosity, $E_i$ is the emissivity, $\rho_i$ is the diffuse reflectance, $F_{ij}$ is the form factor (the percentage of light leaving element $i$ that arrives at element $j$), and $n$ is the number of elements in the scene. Similar equations exist for all elements, yielding a linear system of equations.

$$\begin{pmatrix} 1 & -\rho_1 F_{1,2} & \dots & -\rho_1 F_{1,n} \\ -\rho_2 F_{2,1} & 1 & \dots & -\rho_2 F_{2,n} \\ \vdots & \vdots & \ddots & \vdots \\ -\rho_n F_{n,1} & -\rho_n F_{n,2} & \dots & 1 \end{pmatrix} \begin{pmatrix} B_1 \\ B_2 \\ \vdots \\ B_n \end{pmatrix} = \begin{pmatrix} E_1 \\ E_2 \\ \vdots \\ E_n \end{pmatrix}$$

This system of equations can be efficiently solved using iterative algorithms such as the Gauss-Seidel method. Physically, the Gauss-Seidel method is equivalent to successively *gathering* incoming light. An alternative iteration scheme is to reverse this process by successively *shooting* light from patches in order of their brightness (Cohen et al. 1988). This has the advantage that the solution converges more quickly, and if the scene is drawn during the iteration, successive images gradually improve as the computation proceeds (Bergman et al. 1986).

The most expensive part of the calculation is computing the form factors. Assuming two infinitesimal elements, the differential form factor between them is given by

$$F_{ij} = \frac{\cos\theta_i \cos\theta_j}{\pi r_{ij}^2} dA_j.$$

The angle $\theta_i$ (or $\theta_j$) relates the normal vector of element $i$ (or $j$) to the vector joining the two elements. The form factor from an infinitesimal area to a finite area is the integral

$$F_{ij} = \int_{A_j} \frac{\cos\theta_i \cos\theta_j}{\pi r_{ij}^2} dA_j,$$

and the form factor between two finite areas is the double integral

$$F_{ij} = \frac{1}{A_i} \int_{A_i} \int_{A_j} \frac{\cos\theta_i \cos\theta_j}{\pi r_{ij}^2} dA_i dA_j.$$

These form factor formulae do not take into account occlusion. To do this requires that differential form factors be accumulated only if the two infinitesimal elements are mutually visible. The first practical approach to integrating visibility into form factor computations was the *hemi-cube* algorithm (Cohen and Greenberg 1985). The hemi-cube algorithm is simple and fast, and can be accelerated using current workstation graphics hardware. Algorithms based on ray tracing also have been proposed for form factor calculation (Malley 1988; Ward et al. 1988; Wallace et al. 1989; Sillion and Puech, 1989)

There are two major sources of error when computing form factor integrals. First, the integral is evaluated by sampling the patches in some way; since the results of uniform sampling process are subject to aliasing, early methods had noticeable aliasing errors. However, more recent methods (Wallace et al 1989) have overcome sampling errors by incorporating stochastic sampling into a ray tracer (Cook, 1986). Second, the form factor between two surface samples can be approximated by the differential form factor only if the distance separating the two samples is large compared to their size. This condition frequently occurs along edges and in corners where polygons meet. To avoid this problem, Baum et al. (1989) switch to an analytically calculated form factor in these situations. Another approach, used by Wallace et al. (1989), is to supersample adaptively the integral.

The form factor matrix is $n$ by $n$, where $n$ is the number of elements. This $n^2$ growth causes time and memory problems for complex scenes, The first method to reduce the computational costs was motivated by the method of *substructuring* used in finite element calculations. The polygons comprising the scene are discretized at two levels (Cohen et al. 1986). One level contains the patches into which input polygons are broken, and the other level contains the elements into which each patch is broken. Normally, the number of patches and elements are determined *a-priori*, but the number of elements can also be determined by recursive subdivision based on radiosity gradients Cohen et al.(1986). Other attempts to utilize adaptive subdivision are described in Campbell & Fussel (1990) and Heckbert (1990).

## 2.2 N-Body Problem

The hierarchical subdivision algorithm proposed in this paper is inspired by methods recently developed for solving the N-body problem. In the N-body problem, each of the $n$ particles exerts a force on all the other $n-1$ particles, implying $n(n-1)/2$ pairwise interactions. The fast algorithms compute all the forces on a particle in less than quadratic time, building on two key ideas:

1) Numerical calculations are subject to error, and therefore, the force acting on a particle need only be calculated to within the given precision.

2) The force due to a cluster of particles at some distant point can be approximated, within the given precision, with a single term—cutting down on the total number of interactions.

Appel was the first to develop a hierarchical algorithm for solving the N-body problem, by approximating the forces between particles in two clusters with a single force, when the separation between the clusters significantly exceeded their sizes. A top-down traversal of a hierarchical k-*d* tree representing the clusters yielded an $O(n \log n)$ algorithm (Appel 1985). More recently, Esselink analyzed Appel's algorithm and showed that time needed to calculate the forces takes only $O(n)$ time (Esselink 1989), and that the observed $O(n \log n)$ running time is a consequence of the preprocessing time required to build the hierarchical data structures. Barnes & Hut developed a similar algorithm based on octrees (Barnes & Hut 1986). Greengard and Rokhlin devised the first $O(n)$ algorithm, using a $p$-term multipole expansion for the potential due to any cluster, along with algorithms for splitting, merging, and translating the resulting multipole expansions (Greengard 1988). The algorithm proposed in this paper is most closely related to Appel's and Barnes & Hut's algorithms; it should be mentioned that these two algorithms are very easy implement, and only take a few hundred lines of code.

The radiosity problem shares many similarities with the N-body problem which suggest that these ideas can be used to increase its efficiency. In both the N-body and the radiosity problem, there are $n(n-1)/2$ pairs of interactions. Moreover, just as gravitational or electromagnetic forces fall off as $1/r^2$, the magnitude of the form factor between two patches also falls off as $1/r^2$. Finally, according to Newton's Third Law, gravitational forces are equal and opposite, and, according to the reciprocity principle, form factors between two polygons are related.

One major difference between the two problems is the manner in which the hierarchical data structures are formed. The N-body algorithms begin with $n$ particles and cluster them into larger and larger groups. Our radiosity algorithm, however, begins with a few large polygons and subdivides them into smaller and smaller patches. Subdividing based on the error of a potential interaction provides an automatic method for discretizing the scene within the given error bounds. The specifics of our subdivision algorithm is discussed in Section 3. The separate problem of building clusters out of individual patches is not dealt with in this paper.

Another difference is that the N-body algorithms take advantage of linear superposition; the principle of superposition states that the potential due to a cluster of particles is the sum of the potentials of the individual particles. This principle does not always apply to the radiosity problem, because of occlusion: intervening opaque surfaces can block the transport of light between two other surfaces, which makes the system non-linear. Occlusion thereby introduces an additional cost to the radiosity problem. This is discussed in Section 4.

Finally, the N-body problem is based on a differential equation, whereas the radiosity problem is based on an integral equation. The integral equation arising from the radiosity problem can, however, be solved efficiently using iterative matrix techniques. Fortunately, the hierarchy of interactions produced by our subdivision is equivalent to a block structured matrix, and the iteration can be efficiently computed. This is discussed in Section 5.

## 3 Form Factor Matrix Approximation

This section describes a recursive refinement procedure which simultaneously decomposes a polygon into a hierarchy of patches and elements, and builds a hierarchical representation of the form factor matrix by recording interactions at different levels of detail. We begin by describing the procedure and its results, and then proceed to analyze the error in the resulting form factors, and the number of interactions that need to be considered. This section is quite similar to Hanrahan and Salzman (1990).

Consider the procedure **Refine**:

```
Refine(Patch *p, Patch *q, float Feps, float Aeps)
{
    float Fpq, Fqp;

    Fpq = FormFactorEstimate( p, q );
    Fqp = FormFactorEstimate( q, p );

    if( Fpq < Feps && Fqp < Feps )
        Link( p, q );
    else {
        if( Fpq > Fqp ) {
            if( Subdiv( q, Aeps ) ) {
                Refine( p, q->ne, Feps, Aeps );
                Refine( p, q->nw, Feps, Aeps );
                Refine( p, q->se, Feps, Aeps );
                Refine( p, q->sw, Feps, Aeps );
            }
            else
                Link( p, q );
        }
        else {
            if( Subdiv( p, Aeps ) ) {
                Refine( q, p->ne, Feps, Aeps );
                Refine( q, p->nw, Feps, Aeps );
                Refine( q, p->se, Feps, Aeps );
                Refine( q, p->sw, Feps, Aeps );
            }
            else
                Link( p, q );
        }
    }
}
```

**Refine** first estimates the form factor between two patches, and then either subdivides the patches and refines further, or terminates the recursion and records an interaction between the two patches. If the form factor estimate is less than $F_\epsilon$ (**Feps** in the program), then the true form factor (not taking into consideration occlusion) can be approximated accurately by the estimate (see below), and the patches are allowed to interact at this level of detail. (The procedure **Link** records the interaction between the two patches.) However, if either of the form factor estimates is larger than $F_\epsilon$, then the form factor estimate is not accurate, and so the patch with the larger form factor is subdivided, and **Refine** is called recursively with the smaller subpatches.

**Subdiv** subdivides a patch into subpatches. In our implementation, a patch is a planar quadrilateral, and it is subdivided equally into four new quadrilaterals by splitting it at its center. The subdivision hierarchy is stored in a quadtree; the pointers to the four children are stored in the fields **nw**, **ne**, **sw**, and **se**. (This data structure is similar to adaptive radiosity textures proposed in Heckbert (1990), although information is stored at all levels of the hierarchy, not just at the leaf nodes, and each level also stores a list of its interactions.) **Subdiv** returns *false* if the patch cannot be split; this condition occurs if the area of the patch is smaller than some absolute predetermined area $A_\epsilon$, and is necessary to prevent infinite recursion in corners and along edges. If subdivision is not possible, we force the two patches to interact. Note that a patch may be refined against many patches, and so the actual subdivision of a patch may have

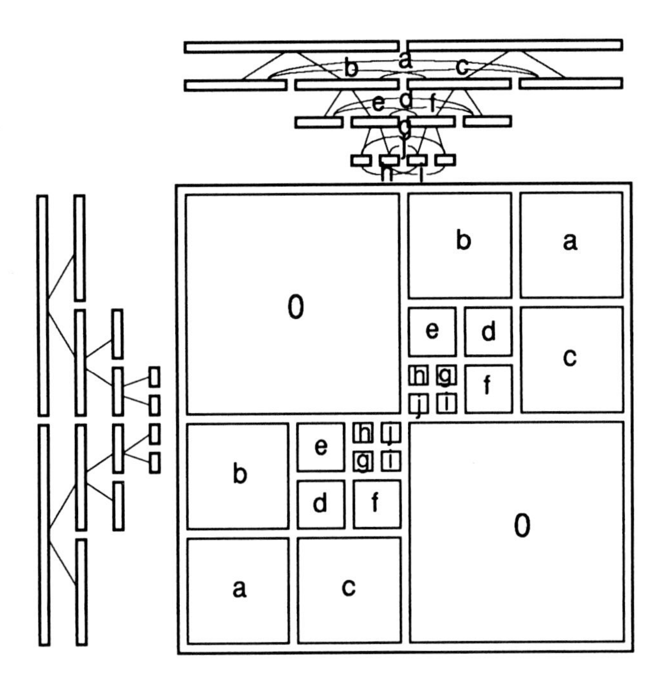


Figure 1: The block form factor matrix for a particular binary tree example. Each labelled block corresponds to a labelled arc connecting nodes in the hierarchical subdivision. Although the blocks are all square in this example, that is not the case in general.

been performed previously. When this occurs **Subdiv** need do no other work and simply returns *true*.

The procedure **FormFactorEstimate** returns an upper bound on the form factor from the first patch to the second patch, assuming the first patch has infinitesimal size and the second patch has finite size. The form factor can be estimated by either calculating the solid angle subtended by a disk with cross sectional area equal to the surface area of the patch (Wallace et al. 1989), or by circumscribing a sphere around the patch and estimating the solid angle subtended by the sphere.

An example of a tree that might be produced by **Refine** and its associated form factor matrix is shown in Figure 1. For simplicity, the figure illustrates the interactions between two hypothetical 1D patches; in this case the hierarchy can be represented with a binary rather than quaternary tree. The two binary trees representing the induced subdivision, and are drawn side by side along the edges of the form factor matrix. Since in this example each binary tree represents a polygon, no interactions are shown with itself. The leaves of the tree are the elements in the discretization. The combination of all the leaf nodes completely cover the input patch. Interactions between patches at different levels are represented by labelled blocks in the form factor matrix, and by labelled arcs between nodes in the trees. Notice that the size of the block in the form factor matrix depends on the level in the tree the patches interact at. The higher the level, the bigger the block.

The first point in the analysis is the relationship between the termination criteria and the accuracy of the computed form factors. Obviously, the termination criteria causes the form factor corresponding to each interaction to have approximately the same magnitude, because, if an estimated form factor were larger, the patches would be subdivided, otherwise, they are allowed to interact. More importantly, the termination criteria also places an upper bound on the error associated with the form factor integral between the two interacting patches. This can be verified by examining

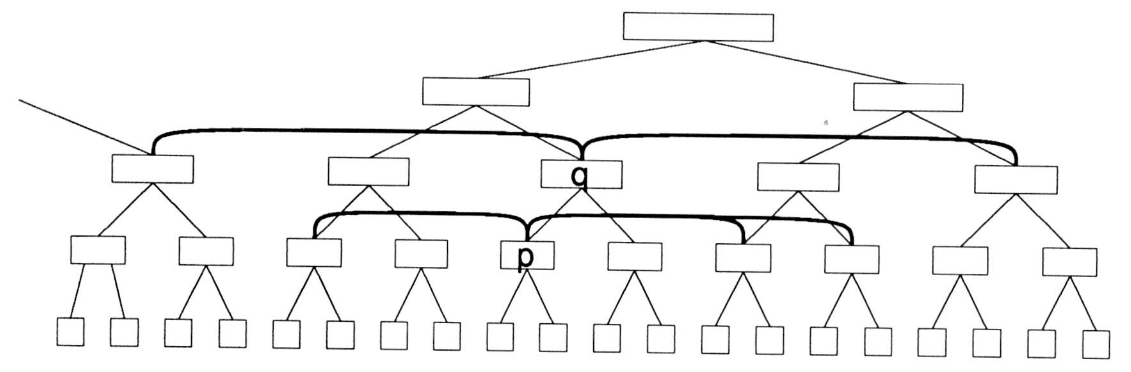


Figure 2: Interactions of the node **p** with neighboring nodes in a one-dimensional subdivision.

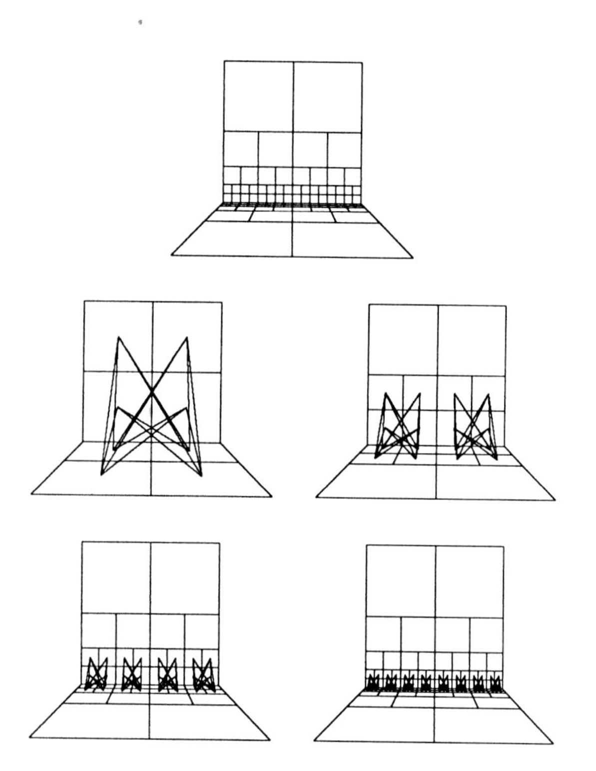

Figure 3: Interactions between a pair of perpendicular polygons.

the form factor from a point to a disk of radius $r$.

$$F_{\text{disk}} \approx \frac{r^2}{R^2 + r^2} = \left(\frac{r}{R}\right)^2 \left(1 - \left(\frac{r}{R}\right)^2 + \left(\frac{r}{R}\right)^4 + \cdots\right) \tag{11}$$

where $R$ is the distance from the point to the center of the disk. Thus, the error due to the finiteness of the geometry is given by terms involving powers of $(r/R)$. Because $F$ goes as $(r/R)^2$, when $F$ is small (implying that the size of the patch is small compared to the distance separating the patches), the differential form factor is also a good estimate of the true form factor. A more rigorous proof of this result can be obtained by forming the Taylor expansion of the form factor integral. In the N-body problem, this expansion is the multipole expansion. However, one need not ever calculate the expansion explicitly to use this algorithm.

The second point in the analysis is that the resulting form factor matrix has fewer than $n^2$ blocks. To a certain extent this is obvious, because every time an interaction occurs at some higher level of detail, the number of interactions is reduced, but we wish to count the interactions more precisely. For simplicity, again consider the 1D problem of $n$ equally spaced patches along a line. Later we will consider what happens if the patches are 2D and non-uniformly distributed. Let us construct a binary tree above the patches by merging adjacent contiguous patches recursively. This is shown in Figure 2. The error criterion says that two patches can interact directly only if $(r/R)^2 < F_\epsilon$. In other words, two patches of size $r$ can interact only if the distance $R$ between them is greater than $r/\sqrt{F_\epsilon}$. For concreteness, let us fix $F_\epsilon$ so that this criterion is equivalent to saying that two patches at the same level in the binary tree can interact only if at least one other patch at that level is between them: Otherwise, they would subtend too large a solid angle and would subdivide, pushing the interaction down a level in the tree. Now consider the interactions of a patch $p$ in the interior of the tree. At any level in the tree, the rule forbids the patch $p$ from interacting with its immediate neighbors. These immediate neighbor interactions, therefore, must be handled by $p$'s children. In the same way, $p$ is only responsible for handling the interactions from its parent $q$'s immediate neighbors. Therefore, $p$ need only interact with the children of $q$'s immediate neighbors. Figure 2 shows the node $p$ and its parent $q$. The above considerations imply that $p$ need only make three connections to nodes at its level. This argument applies to all levels of the tree (except the top and the bottom, but these levels result in fewer interactions), and therefore each node in the tree connects to a constant number of other nodes. Thus, the total number of interactions is proportional to the number of nodes in the tree, which is $O(n)$. A similar analysis has been derived independently by (Esselink 1989).

Figure 3 shows the quadtree subdivision and the interactions at each level in the hierarchy computed by `Refine` between a pair of perpendicular polygons. This figure shows that each interior patch has a constant number of interactions with other patches regardless of the level in the tree.

Figure 4 plots the actual number of interactions versus the number of potential interactions at a fixed uniform level of discretization. The number of interactions for perpendicular polygons goes, surprisingly, as $O(\sqrt{n})$. The subdivision induced between two perpendicular polygons is comparable to a binary tree turned on its side with its leaf nodes along the common edge, and the total number of nodes in such a sideways binary tree will be $O(\sqrt{n})$. The worst case for `Refine` is two parallel polygons whose size is much larger than the distance separating them. In this case, there will be $O(n)$ interactions. As the polygons move further apart, or are tilted relative to each other as in the case of perpendicular polygons, the number of interactions is reduced. Finally, as the two polygons move still farther apart, eventually only a

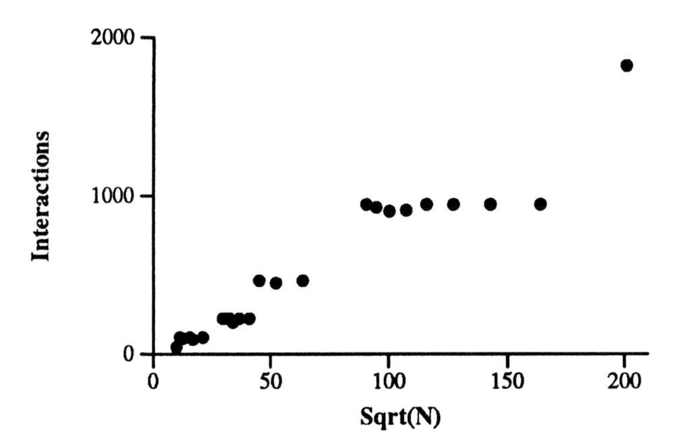


Figure 4: Number of interactions vs. number of elements for a pair of perpendicular polygons.

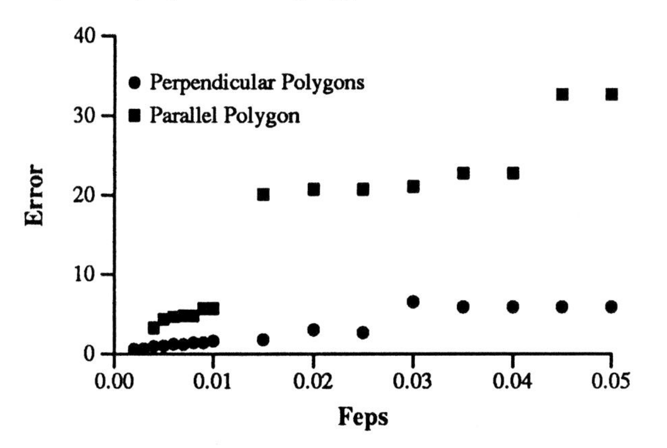


Figure 5: Measured relative percentage error vs. $F_\epsilon$.

single interaction is required.

To verify the accuracy of the form factors generated by our method, we compared the computed form factors with the analytical form factors which are available for the parallel and perpendicular geometries (see, for example, (Siegel and Howell 1981)). To compute the form factor between two finite areas, `Refine` can be modified to return the sum of the form factors of a patch's children or, if the patch is a leaf, the product of the patch's area and the differential form factor to the other patch. Figure 5 shows the measured relative error between the computed and the analytical form factors as a function of $F_\epsilon$. As expected, the actual error in the form factor is proportional to the $F_\epsilon$ given to `Refine`, as predicted by the theory. Note that the plateaus in these figures are due to the discrete nature of the subdivision.

In summary, our hierarchical refinement method estimates the form factor matrix between two unoccluded patches to within a fixed error tolerance automatically. In the process it reorganizes the form factor matrix into $O(n)$ or fewer blocks; the estimated form factor associated with each block has the same value and error as other blocks.

## 4 Visibility

The pairwise method for computing form factors described in the previous section is accurate as long as each patch is completely visible with respect to the other patch. Unfortunately, occlusion exists in all realistic environments, and so this idealization is not very useful in practice. In this section we modify the algorithm to take into consideration visibility.

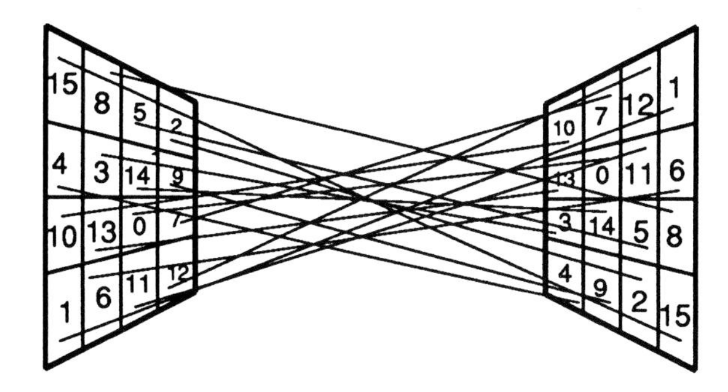


Figure 6: Jittered rays fired between two polygons to determine the percentage visibility.

Intervening occluding surfaces can only decrease light transport between two patches, thus, the true form factor in the presence of occlusion is never greater than the form factor estimate described above. The effect of occlusion can be modeled by multiplying the estimated form factor by a visibility correction factor which estimates the percentage each patch sees of the other.

$$F = V_e F_e$$

where $F_e$ is the estimated form factor without considering occlusion, and $V_e$ is the estimated visibility. If $V_e = 1$ then the two patches are totally visible; if $V_e = 0$ then they are completely occluded; and otherwise they are partially visible. Thus, assuming no visibility error, the level of detail for the interaction between two patches need never be finer than that computed by the procedure `Refine`.

Recall that all the form factor estimates computed by `Refine` have approximately the same error. This fact has two important consequences. First, since the form factor is not precise, the calculation of $V_e$ need only be estimated to the same precision. Ideally, the visibility module should take into account the precision required; in reality, current visibility modules probably compute visibility much more accurately than is necessary. Second, since all the visibility estimates should have approximately the same error, it is reasonable to perform the same amount of work per estimate. This means that the total number of visibility tests required is proportional to the number of interactions. The total amount of work performed is:

$$T(n) = F(n)V(n)$$

where $F(n)$ is the number of computed form factors and $V(n)$ is the cost of performing the visibility test for a given number of elements. As has been shown, $F(n)$ varies at most linearly with $n$, so many fewer visibility tests need be done than with conventional radiosity algorithms.

In our current implementation, we perform two types of visibility tests. The first visibility test determines whether two polygons face each other, face away from each other, or if the support plane of one polygon splits the other. This test considers only the two polygons and not the environment, and therefore can be done in constant time. The second visibility test checks how much of each polygon is visible from the other polygon given the global environment. The test fires a fixed number of rays between the two patches, and computes the percentage of rays not blocked by intervening surfaces. The same number of rays are fired per interaction, because all the visibility estimates should have the same error. Each patch is subdivided into a 2D grid (typically 4x4), and the cells in the grid are assigned numbers from a magic square (Cook 1986). Each ray is really a line segment formed by joining jittered points within corresponding cells with the same number as shown in Figure 6. A naive ray intersection test takes $O(n)$ time. In order to accelerate the visibility test, we use a modified version of the BSP-tree algorithm,

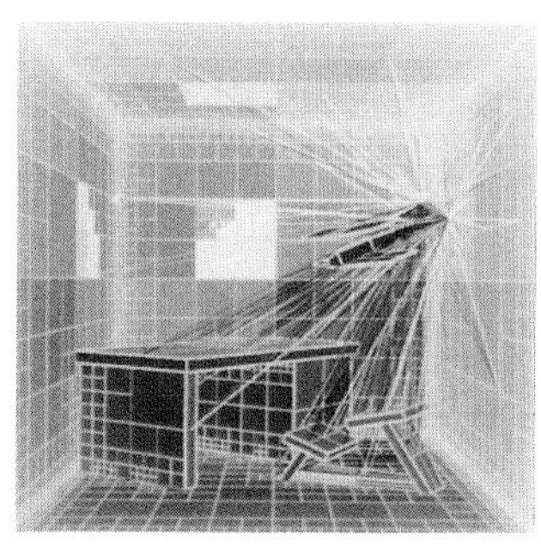
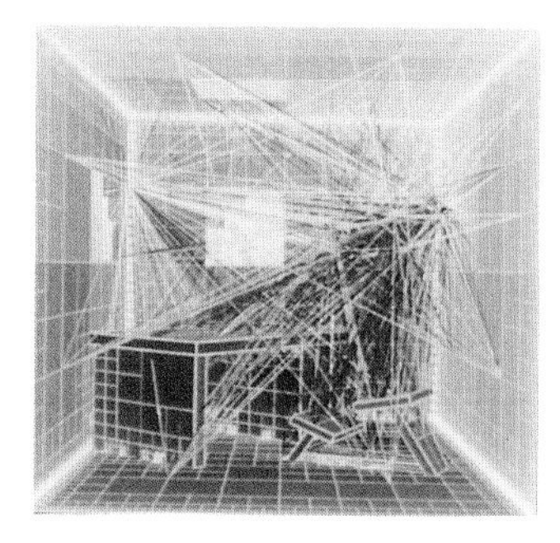
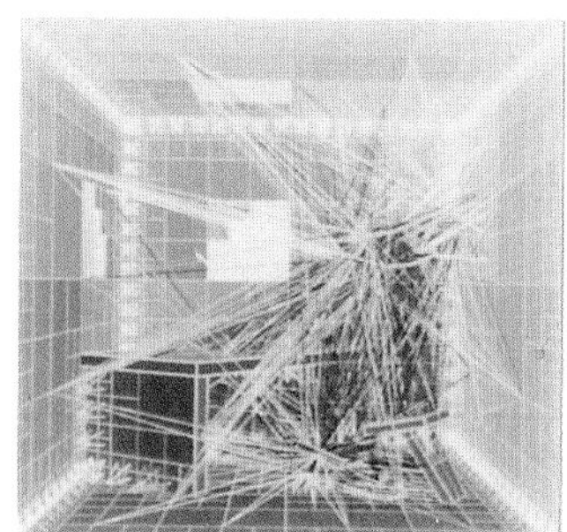
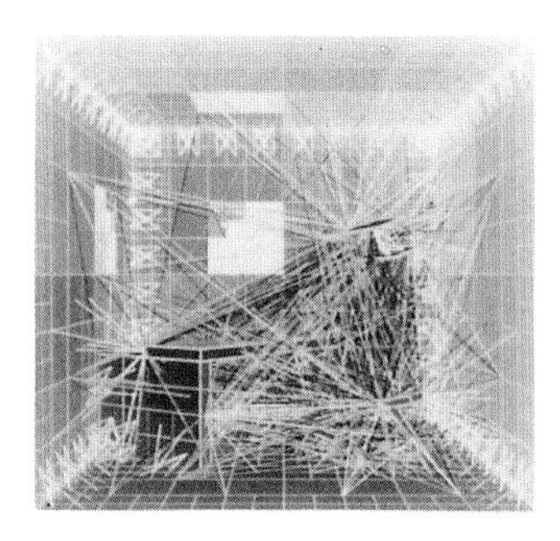

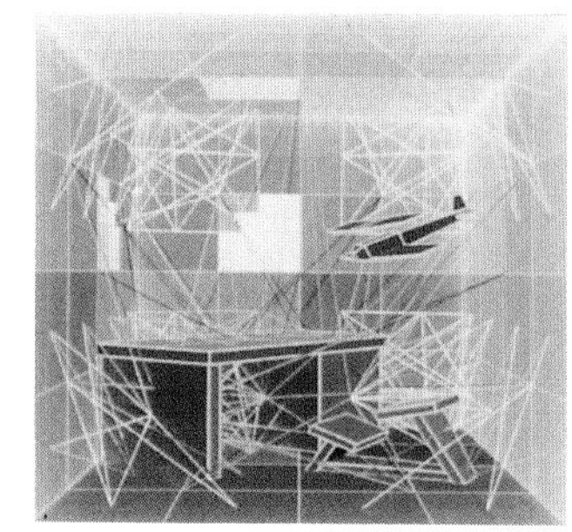

Figure 7: Hierarchical subdivision, interactions, and visibility. This sequence shows the hierarchical subdivision of each polygon, from the smallest elements in the upper left image, up the hierarchy to the largest subpatches shown in the image at lower right. Line segments link interacting patches, shown at the hierarchical level of the smaller patch. Segment color indicates visibility: white – completely visible, green – partially visible, pink – cut by supporting plane, and dark blue – relatively invisible. Note that there are many more visible and invisible links than partial.

described in Thibault & Naylor (1987), which in principle reduces the intersection cost to $O(\log n)$. This ray intersection module recalls shadow testing, because it returns only whether the ray is blocked or not, and not the closest intersection along the ray direction.

Figure 7 shows a simple scene. Induced subdivision is indicated for each polygon, and interactions between subpatches are illustrated as links. The series shows all links, ordered by increasing height, within the hierarchy, of the linked subpatches. Note that large patches interact with other large patches that are far away, whereas smaller patches interact with similarly sized patches at closer distances. This hierarchy is most clearly shown in the corners and along the edges of the room.

A tentative list of interactions was computed by refining patches relative to each other irrespective of visibility. Each interaction was then tested for visibility and the form factor adjusted. In the figure, links between interacting patches that are completely visible relative to each other are colored white. Green links interacting patches that are partially visible with respect to each other, pink links those for which one patch's supporting plane splits the other, and dark blue links those patches whose interactions are found to be completely occluded (invisible).

Table 1 shows some basic statistics for this scene. Note that the total number of interactions is only 15526, compared with over $10^9$, assuming all elements interacted directly. The total time to compute this picture was approximately one minute (all times quoted in this paper are on a SiliconGraphics 210 GTX).

The interactions in scenes such as those shown in Figure 7 exhibit a great deal of *visibility coherence*. Fringes of partial and splitting links tend to surround larger areas of complete visibility or occlusion (see also Figure 8, below). Partial visibility corresponds to penumbral areas generated along the silhouettes of an object, which occur less often than the interior or exterior of an object, although pathological exceptions may be easily constructed. In the scene shown in Figure 7, (see Table 1), we find that 52.6% of the interactions are totally visible, 28.8% are totally invisible, and only 18.5% are partially visible.

The recursive refinement procedure can exploit visibility coherence in a natural fashion to prune out unnecessary refinement and visibility calculation. If, in the course of subdivision, two subpatches become totally invisible relative to each other, then the refinement between them can be immediately terminated, significantly reducing the number of calls to `Refine`. If two patches become totally visible, there is no need for further visibility tests between them, although further refinement may still need to occur. Finally, if two patches are partially visible with respect to each other, further refinement would require additional visibility computation. However, as patches are subdivided, their visibility will tend to fall into the visible or invisible category, only those on the fringes remaining partial. Employing these optimizations on the scenes shown in Figure 7 cuts in half the number of rays fired in visibility tests, reducing running time by fifty percent as well.

The nature of visibility coherence, and the refinement procedure's use of this coherence, should be reflected in the visibility test. Total visibility or invisibility are the most common visibility interactions, and result in immediate pruning of computation, thus the visibility test should quickly detect these cases. Jim Blinn calls this principle *triage* (Blinn 1990). A partial visibility result simply indicates that further visibility computation is necessary lower in the hierarchy. An precise estimate of percentage visibility is not required until refinement is terminated and the patches are to be linked. Thus, for the purposes of refinement, the visibility test need only detect partial visibility situations, not completely analyze them. Furthermore, it is acceptable to

| | | |
|---|---|---|
| Polygons | 98 | |
| Potential elements | 44773 | |
| Potential interactions | 1002288378 | |
| **Without visibility coherence** | | |
| Patches | 7286 | |
| Elements | 5489 | |
| Interactions | 15526 | |
| Totally-invisible | 4477 | 28.8% |
| Totally-visible | 8171 | 52.6% |
| Partially-visible | 2878 | 18.5% |
| **Tests** | | |
| Refinement tests | 19117 | |
| Visibility tests | 11123 | |
| Ray tests | 177968 | |
| **With visibility coherence** | | |
| Patches | 7350 | |
| Elements | 5537 | |
| Interactions | 15598 | |
| Totally-invisible interactions | 4495 | 28.8% |
| Totally-visible interactions | 8249 | 52.9% |
| Partially-visible interactions | 2854 | 18.3% |
| **Tests** | | |
| Refinement tests | 19213 | |
| Totally-invisible refines | 3600 | 18.7% |
| Pre-Totally-invisible refines | 0 | 0.0% |
| Totally-visible refines | 10487 | 54.6% |
| Pre-Totally-visible refines | 9700 | 50.5% |
| Partially-visible refines | 5126 | 26.7% |
| Partial visibility tests | 9513 | |
| Ray tests | 20527 | |
| Visibility tests | 4296 | |
| Ray tests | 68736 | |

Table 1. Statistics for Figure 7.

return a partial visibility result if the visibility situation is complex, as additional subdivision will tend to reduce the complexity of the visibility calculation. This is very similar to Warnock's visible surface algorithm (Warnock 1969).

The methods used to detect visibility are likely to be more accurate when patches are totally visible or totally invisible. When two patches are partially visible, we assume there is more likely to be an error in visibility and increase the error in the form factor estimate. This causes increased subdivision in regions of partial visibility; the cost of this is minor because they occur so infrequently, however, the benefits are great because these often arise at shadow boundaries where there are sharp intensity gradients.

## 5 Solution Techniques

Once the form factors have been determined, the next step is to solve for the radiosities. The most efficient way to do this is to invert the matrix iteratively. Each iteration involves multiplying a matrix times a vector, which normally takes $O(n^2)$ operations. However, because the form factor matrix is represented with $O(n)$ blocks, each matrix multiplication can be done in linear time. In this section we give program fragments that implement the technique of gathering and briefly explain how to implement shooting. These techniques are quite similar to the unoccluded case, and we refer the reader to Hanrahan and Salzman (1990) for more details.

### 5.1 Shooting and Gathering

The classic Jacobi iteration (which differs from the Gauss-Seidel in that the brightnesses are not updated in-place) can be implemented using the following simple recursive procedure.

```
Gather( Patch *p )
{
    Patch *q;
    float Fpq;

    if( p ) {
        p->Bg = 0.0;
        ForAllElements( q, p->interactions ) {
            Fpq = FormFactor( p, q );
            p->Bg += Fpq * p->Cd * q->B;
        }
        Gather( p->sw );
        Gather( p->se );
        Gather( p->nw );
        Gather( p->ne );
    }
}
```

The average brightness of each patch is stored in `B` and its diffuse color is stored in `Cd`. The brightness gathered is stored in `Bg`, and is computed by receiving energy from all the patches `q` stored on the list of interactions of `p` (`p->interactions`).

The total amount of energy received by an element is the sum of the energy received by it directly, plus the sum of all the energy received by its parent subpatches. To update the energies for the next iteration, all the energy gathered is *pushed* down to the leaf nodes, and then *pulled* upward towards the root polygon. During this upward pass, the radiosity of interior subpatches are set equal to the area weighted average of its children's radiosities. Both these operations can be done in a single depth-first traversal of the quadtree, which takes time proportional to the number of nodes in the hierarchy.

The radiosity equation can be solved by shooting instead of gathering. All patches in the hierarchy are sorted into a priority queue based on their brightness. A patch at a time is taken off the queue, and its energy shot to the patches that interact with it. This version of shooting, however, has a much smaller granularity then the classic method of shooting used in progressive refinement. This is because in our algorithm each patch shoots light to a constant number of other patches, whereas in the previous algorithms a patch shoots light to the entire scene.

### 5.2 Multigridding and $BF$ Refinement

An interesting variation of shooting or gathering refines the hierarchy as the iteration proceeds. This is similar to the idea of multigridding, where a finite difference equation is solved first at a coarse resolution, and then at successively finer resolutions. The advantage of multigridding is that the coarse solution involves a low resolution iteration that can be performed cheaply. This coarse solution provides a better starting point for the costlier iterations at the finer resolutions, resulting in fewer expensive iterations before convergence. Multigridding allows for an even more progressive radiosity algorithm: Shooting is performed in the early stages at coarse resolutions to get a rough idea of the image, and then at successively finer and finer resolutions as the calculation proceeds.

Multigridding is easily incorporated into the algorithm by successively refining the mesh with smaller and smaller $F_\epsilon$'s. The procedure `Refine` is extended to delete the link indicating a previous interaction at a given level of detail, if subdivision is required. `Refine` is then called between iterations to increase the resolution of the grid.

A final improvement to the algorithm bases the refinement of two patches on $BF$; that is, on the total amount of energy potentially transported between the patches. The procedure `Refine` is extended to use this test for subdivision rather than $F$ alone. This causes refinement of the mesh to be put off until energy is actually available to be transported,

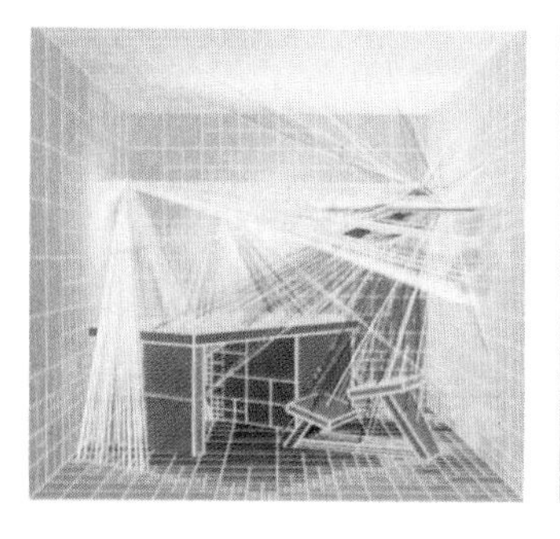

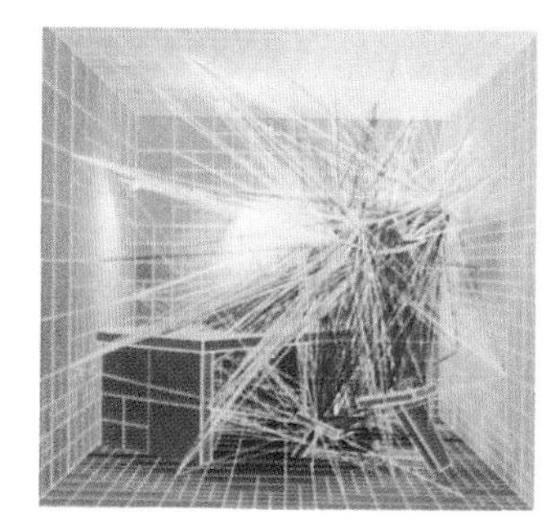
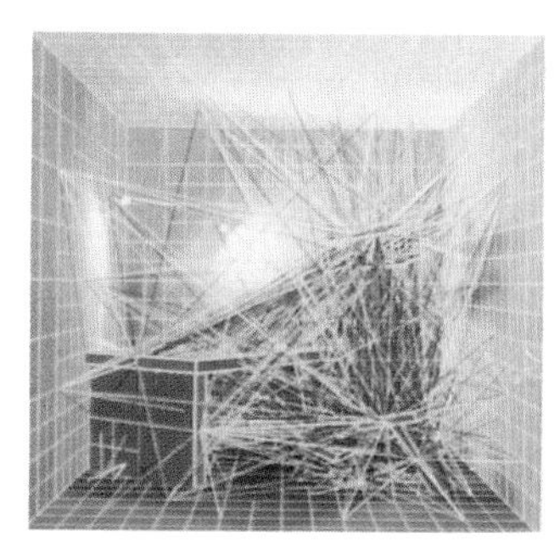

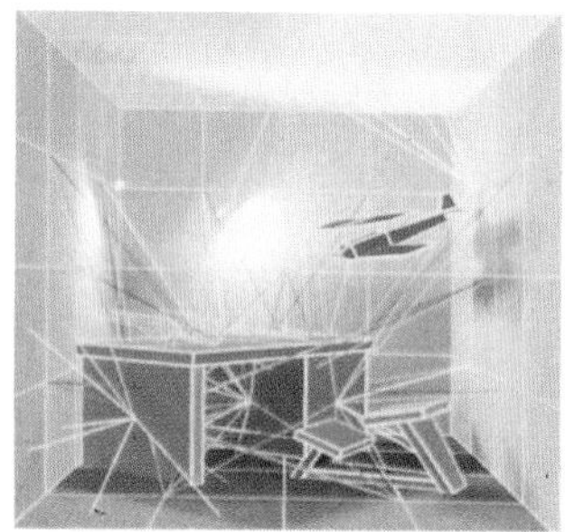
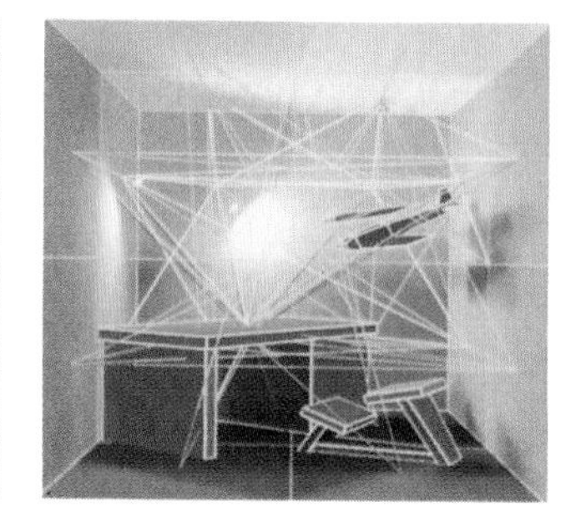
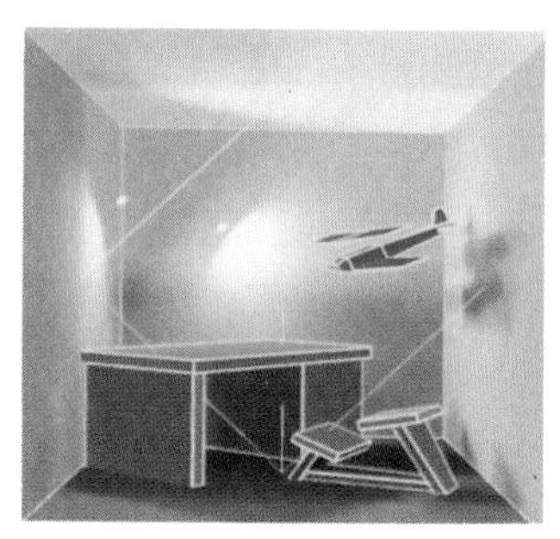

Figure 8: $BF$ refinement. Refinement is based on total energy transport between patches. Thus there are many interactions with the light sources, and a reduced number of interactions in areas exhibiting less energy transport, such as corners. White – total visibility, green – partial visibility, pink – cut by supporting plane, and dark blue – total occlusion.

thus saving even more work on early iterations. This works particularly well in corners which normally contain a large number of interactions because of their proximity, but tend to be dark because light must reflect off several surfaces to reach the inner recesses.

With $BF$ refinement and multigridding, shooting has no advantage over gathering. Since all interactions carry approximately the same amount of energy, there is no advantage to sorting them based on brightness.

Figure 8 shows the subdivision and interactions based on a $BF$ error criteria for the same scene as shown in Figure 7. As in the previous figure, the series shows all links, ordered by increasing height in the hierarchy. To accentuate the effect, we have made the two lamps small and very bright. Note that this causes many more interactions with the lights than between other parts of the room; all the interactions at the finest level of detail in the corners are eliminated because they are inconsequential compared to the light interactions.

Another effect clearly shown in this figure is the increased subdivision along shadow boundaries. This is exhibited in the first image of the series in the subdivision of the right wall behind the biplane, and on the floor in the neighborhood of the desk. The second and third images in the series illustrate the corresponding links; note the spray of interactions ranging in from white (visible) to green (partial) to dark blue (occluded).

Table 2 gives basic statistics for the scene in Figure 8. The number of interactions is approximately 10,000, which is less than the number in Figure 7, even though the number of potential interactions in this scene is sixteen times greater.

Figure 9 shows a series of iterations using multigridding coupled with $BF$ refinement. At the bottom are the induced subdivisions, and above the resulting images. The first image shows the initial mesh, the next two images show the mesh after iterations in which the error has been decreased, and the final iteration improves the final image, but does not

| | | |
|---|---|---|
| Polygons | 98 | |
| Potential elements | 175964 | |
| Potential interactions | 15481576666 | |
| Patches | 5674 | |
| Elements | 4280 | |
| Interactions | 11800 | |
| Totally-invisible | 4605 | 39.0% |
| Totally-visible | 4519 | 38.3% |
| Partially-visible | 2676 | 22.7% |
| Tests | | |
| Refinement tests | 14149 | |
| Totally-invisible refines | 3901 | 27.6% |
| Pre-Totally-invisible refines | 0 | 0.0% |
| Totally-visible refines | 5414 | 38.3% |
| Pre-Totally-visible refines | 4128 | 29.2% |
| Partially-visible refines | 4834 | 34.2% |
| Partial visibility tests | 10021 | |
| Ray tests | 53187 | |
| Visibility tests | 3545 | |
| Ray tests | 56720 | |

Table 2. Statistics for Figure 8.

involve decreasing the error in the mesh. Note the gradual refinement of the ceiling and right wall, as they are illuminated by the lamps and light reflected from the desktop. In the last image, enough light has been transported into the neighborhood of the near end of the desk to induce its subdivision. Table 3 gives the error bound for each iteration, as well as the number of patches, elements and interactions. Note that the last iteration in which error bound was not changed does not involve refining, and hence takes much less time than the other iterations.

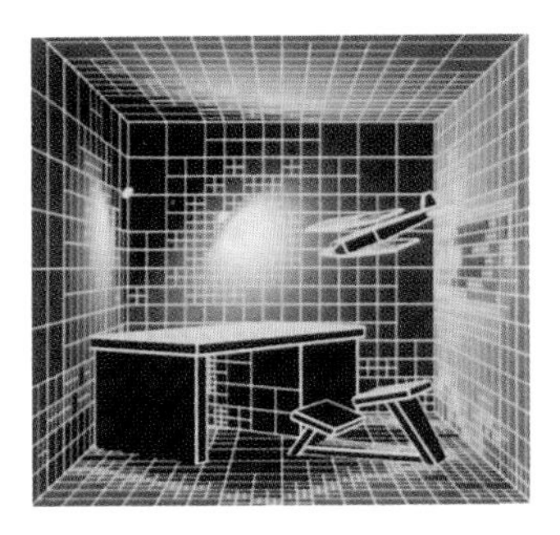 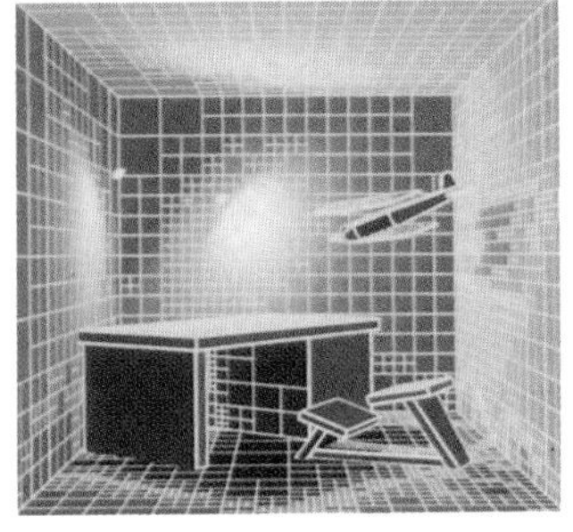 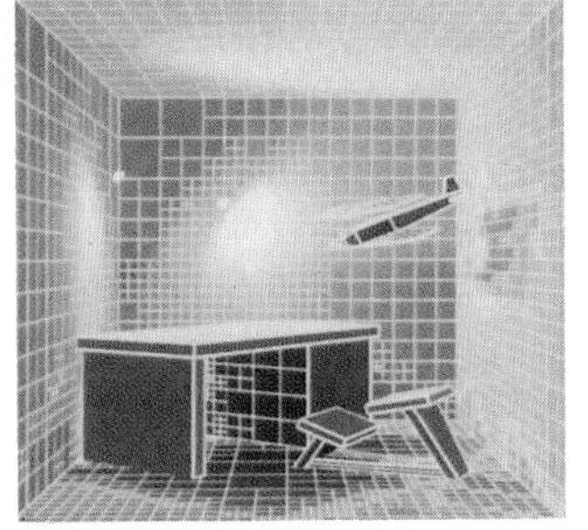 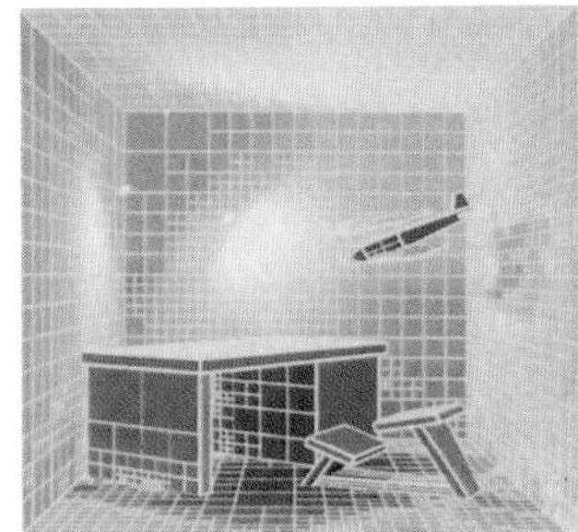

Figure 9: Multigridding and $BF$ refinement.

| Patches | Elements | Interactions | Error | Time(s) |
|---|---|---|---|---|
| 5674 | 4280 | 11800 | 1.000 | 45 |
| 7646 | 5759 | 16216 | 0.707 | 34 |
| 10462 | 7871 | 24091 | 0.500 | 62 |
| 10714 | 8060 | 24886 | 0.500 | 10 |

Table 3. Statistics for Figure 9.

## 6 Results

Figure 10 shows an example image created by the algorithm. At the maximum level of detail, it contains potentially 52841 elements, of which 12635 patches are actually created by refinement. Using classical radiosity, this would require 1.4 billion interactions, whereas the algorithm requires only 20150. This image was produced in three minutes and fifty-seven seconds.

## 7 Summary and Discussion

The radiosity algorithm proposed in this paper drastically reduces the number of interactions that need to be considered while maintaining the precision of the form factors that are calculated. This reduction in the number of form factors allows much higher-quality imagery to be generated within a given amount of time or memory. Successively refining the environment using a brightness-weighted error criteria leads to a algorithm where the granularity of each step in the progression is much smaller than in the standard progressive refinement algorithm. This allows for more control and faster updates in interactive situations.

The algorithm proposed works best for environments with relatively few large polygons with high brightness gradients that require the polygon to be broken into many elements. This is very common in architectural environments, but there are situations where this assumption is not valid. The general principles outlined in this paper are still valid in these situations, but the methods for producing the hierarchy and estimating visibility would be quite different. Useful

Figure 10:

applications for such algorithms are for rendering volumes and participating media.

One of the emerging themes of realistic image synthesis is that the geometric aspects of the problem are becoming subservient to the optical aspects. The optical portion involves numerically solving an integral equation; the geometric portion involves primarily determining visibility between the finite elements used to discretize the equation. Unfortunately, most visibility algorithms developed in computer graphics were not developed with these numerical calculations in mind. What are needed are fast algorithms that compute visibility to within a given precision. Ideally, the less the precision, the faster the algorithm. Visibility algorithms also need to be developed that consider patch-to-patch interactions and not just point-to-patch interactions, as are almost exclusively the case. Finally, what are needed to take advantage of the coherence found in typical environments are fast algorithms for detecting whether patches are totally visible or totally invisible with respect to each other.

## 8 Acknowledgements

The authors wish to thank Andrew Appel, Dan Baum, David Laur, Toby Orloff, Jeffrey Posdamer, and James Winget for helpful comments. Brian Danella and S.V. Krishnan provided assistance with modeling and rendering.

## 9 References

Appel, A.A. (1985) An efficient program for many-body simulation. *SIAM J. Sci. Stat. Computing* 6(1), 85-103.

Barnes, J., Hut, P. (1986) A hierarchical $O(NlogN)$ force-calculation algorithm. *Nature* 324, 446-449.

Baum, D.R., Rushmeier, H.E., Winget, J.M. (1989) Improving radiosity solutions through the use of analytically determined form factors. *Computer Graphics* 23(3), 325-334.

Bergman, L., Fuchs, H., Grant, E., Spach, S. (1986) Image rendering by adaptive refinement. *Computer Graphics* 20(4), 29-38.

Blinn, J. (1990) Triage Tables. *IEEE Computer Graphics and Applications*, 10(1) 70-75.

Campbell, A.T., Fussel, D.S. (1990) Adaptive mesh generation for global diffuse illumination. *Computer Graphics* 24(4), 155-164.

Cohen, M.F., Greenberg, D.P. (1985) The hemi-cube: A radiosity approach for complex environments. *Computer Graphics* 19(3), 31-40.

Cohen, M.F., Greenberg, D.P., Immel, D.S., Brock, P.J. (1986) An efficient radiosity approach for realistic image synthesis. *IEEE Computer Graphics and Applications* 6(2), 26-30.

Cohen, M.F., Chen, S.E., Wallace, J.R., Greenberg, D.P. (1988) A progressive refinement approach to fast radiosity image generation. *Computer Graphics* 22(4), 75-84.

Cook, R.L. (1986) Stochastic sampling in computer graphics. *ACM Transactions on Graphics* 5(1), 51-72.

Esselink, E. (1989) About the order of Appel's algorithm. Computing Science Note KE5-1, Department of Computer Science, University of Groningen.

Greengard, L. (1988) *The rapid evaluation of potential fields in particle systems.* MIT Press, Cambridge, MA.

Hanrahan, P., Salzman, D.B. (1990) A rapid hierarchical radiosity algorithm for unoccluded environments. Published in K. Bouatouch, Photosimulation, Realism and Physics in Computer Graphics. Springer-Verlag (1991), Reprinted as Princeton University CS-TR-281-90.

Heckbert, P.S. (1990) Adaptive radiosity textures for bidirectional ray tracing. *Computer Graphics* 24(4), 145-154.

Malley, T.J.V. (1988) A shading method for computer generated images. Master's Thesis, The University of Utah

Siegel, R., Howell, J.R. (1981) *Thermal radiation heat transfer.* Hemisphere Publishing Co., Washington, DC

Sillion, F., Puech, C. (1989) A general two-pass method for integrating specular and diffuse reflection. *Computer Graphics* 23(3), 335-344.

Thibault, W., Naylor, B. (1987) Set operations on polyhedra using binary space partitioning trees. *Computer Graphics* 21(4), 153-162.

Wallace, J.R., Elmquist, K.A., Haines, E.A. (1989) A ray tracing algorithm for progressive radiosity. *Computer Graphics* 23(3), 315-324.

Ward, G.J., Rubinstein, F.M., Clear, R.D. (1988) A ray tracing solution for diffuse environments. *Computer Graphics* 22(3), 85-92.

Warnock, J. (1969) A hidden-surface algorithm for computer-generated half-tone pictures. Technical Report TR 4-15, NTIS AD-753 671, Computer Science Department, University of Utah.

# NC Machining with G-buffer Method

Takafumi Saito
Tokiichiro Takahashi

NTT Human Interface Laboratories
Nippon Telegraph and Telephone Corporation
1-2356, Take, Yokosuka-shi
Kanagawa 238-03, JAPAN

## Abstract

The G-buffer method is applied to NC machining. A total NC system is created that consists of all essential functions, such as tool path generation, path verification, and feed rate control. Moreover, any combination of object surface and tool shape is acceptable. By utilizing G-buffers created from a parallel projection, the required NC functions are realized as image processing operations. This ensures that the NC software is independent from surface description. Conventional rendering software can be used to make the G-buffers. Any surface can be milled if it can be rendered by parallel projection. Tool shape changes can be easily handled by changing the image processing filters. 3D examples of geometric surfaces, mesh data, and volume data are milled with this method, and the results show that the method is very effective.

**CR Categories and Subject Descriptors:** I.3.3 [Computer Graphics]: Picture/Image Generation; I.4.9 [Image Processing]: Applications; J.6 [Computer-Aided Engineering]: Computer-Aided Manufacturing.

**Additional Key Words and Phrases:** NC machine, tool path, G-buffer method, interference avoidance, simulation.



## 1 Introduction

While the thrust of modern computer graphics is the visualization of the real world, people must use actual 3D objects to survive. One interface between conceptual and actual objects is that created by CAD/CAM systems coupled to numerically controlled (NC) milling machines. Unfortunately, this interface is not as efficient or productive as it should be. The problem lies in the large number of factors that must be considered when machining a complex object.

CAD/CAM systems were initially used to produce relatively simple objects whose profiles could be described as combination of geometric primitives. The production of more complex objects demands the creation of highly sophisticated tool paths. This is due to the following factors.

1. *Shape accuracy:*
   Over cutting must be prevented and the degree of under-cutting accurately evaluated. This requires the interference[1] between tool and required surface to be constantly monitored.
2. *Tool load:*
   Cutting rate must not exceed the limits of tool, milling machine, or workpiece.
3. *Tool movements:*
   Unplanned collisions between workpiece and tool or tool holder must be prevented.
4. *Machining time:*
   Tool selection, tool path, and feed rate should be optimized.
5. *Variations in tool types and surface shapes:*
   The tool path must accommodate the available tools and all possible workpiece shapes.

[1] In this paper, the words *interference* and *collision* are used as the following meanings.

**interference:** Relation between tool and required surface. It is a measure of over-cutting.

**collision:** Contact of workpiece and upper part (without milling edge) of a tool. It damages the tool and/or the workpiece.

A number of sophisticated methods have been developed to address one or more of these factors, and some have turned into commercial systems. Each method can be characterized as one of two types: tool path generation, or machining simulation/verification. In path generation, the main purpose is to obtain an adequate tool path that produces an accurate shape. The tool path can be obtained from the offset surface, *i.e.* the trace of the limit position of the tool center, and a lot of research has been performed to calculate an accurate offset surface [1,2]. Kishinami *et al.* have proposed a flexible algorithm called the Inverse Offset Method [3] which uses the rasterization technique. In simulation and verification, the tool path is verified for each factor listed above. Many systems have been developed for this purpose, and one of the major differences among them is the shape representation for interference calculation. Wang *et al.* [4,5], Hook [6], and Atherton *et al.* [7] all used a projection from a view point and applied a variation of the z-buffer algorithm. Thus, their methods are termed 'view based methods'. Kawashima *et al.* [8] implemented such a method by using an oct-tree data structure. Chappel [9] and Jerard *et al.* [10,11,12] represented the shape with 'direction vectors' from discrete points distributed on the object's surfaces.

Unfortunately, in conventional CAD/CAM systems, these two activities, tool path generation and simulation/verification, are usually independent of each other and based on different methodologies. This has two disadvantages. First, the entire software package is huge and excessively complicated. This is because different programs are required for each activity in order to accommodate various shapes and tool types. Second, it is difficult to generate tool paths by using simulation results. This function is necessary because, for example, adequacy of a tool path for fine cutting depends on the result of rough cutting.

To build a total NC program on one methodology, we extend the G-buffer[2] method [13] to 3 axis NC machining. A G-buffer (Geometric Buffer) is a 2 dimensional array, like an image. Each G-buffer contains one geometric property for all pixels such as depth, surface normal, etc.. By manipulating G-buffers, various kinds of rendering techniques can be realized with image processing operations. Moreover, G-buffers generated from a parallel projection can also easily realize the many functions required for a total NC system by employing image processing operations. For example, it is easy to generate tool paths based on collision as well as interference. Many kinds of scanning operations are also available by referring to G-buffers. Tool paths can be simulated and evaluated with a series of image processing sequences. The optimum tool path and feed rate can be chosen from the evaluation results.

Some functions of the proposed method are identical or similar to previously proposed functions. The offset surface generation algorithm is equivalent to Kishinami's Inverse Offset Method [3]. The simulation and verification methods can be regarded as simplifications of the conventional view based methods. However, these functions are very synergistic when implemented in a total G-buffer machining system.

げ～ :-)

[2] The pronunciation of 'G' is [ge:] as in the German alphabet [13]

One of the notable advantages of the proposed method is that all parts of the NC software are independent of surface description. In order to make the G-buffers, conventional rendering software can be used. This means that any surface can be milled if it can be rendered by parallel projection. Various tool shapes can be employed by simply changing the image processing filters. Dedicated graphics or image processing hardware, such as graphics workstations, can effectively perform all required computations.

## 2 G-buffers for NC Machining

### 2.1 Concept of G-buffer Method

The G-buffer method [13] was originally developed for comprehensible rendering, and has the two following features:

- The geometric properties for each pixel of the visible object are preserved in G-buffers;
- Various rendering techniques are realized with image processing operations.

By using G-buffers as the intermediate result, geometric procedures (such as scan conversion and hidden surface removal) and other procedures (such as shading, texture mapping, and enhancement) are completely separated. Therefore, they can be performed independently and efficiently.

### 2.2 G-buffer Set Required for NC

The concept of the G-buffer method can be effectively extended to 3 axis NC machining. By preparing a G-buffer set from a parallel projection, it is possible to realize many kinds of NC software procedures as image processing operations. For NC machining, the following geometric properties are the typical contents of a set of G-buffers.

- **Z**: world coordinate $z$ (depth)
- **nx**: normal vector $x$
- **ny**: normal vector $y$
- **nz**: normal vector $z$
- **id**: object/patch identifier
- **ou**: patch coordinate $u$
- **ov**: patch coordinate $v$

Only **Z** in this list is indispensable; the use of the other G-buffers depends on the procedures required for machining or verification. Figure 1 shows a shaded image and a **Z**-image of the famous Utah teapot.

In this paper, all G-buffers and derived 2-dimensional arrays are called *images*. Images whose names begin with an upper case character contain absolute or relative height data. The unit height is equal to the pixel interval.

# 3 Image Processing for NC Functions

## 3.1 Basic Tool Path Generation

Once G-buffers of a required object are generated, an offset surface between the object and a tool can be obtained from the **Z**-image with the following operation. Let $\mathbf{L_I}$ be the height field of offset surface, and $h(d)$ be the height of the tool-end at the distance $d$ from the tool axis, where $h(0) = 0$. When the tool-end touches the required surface at $(x_t, y_t)$, the height of the tool center must satisfy the following relation (Fig.2):

$$\mathbf{L_I}(x,y) = \mathbf{Z}(x_t, y_t) - h(\sqrt{(x-x_t)^2 + (y-y_t)^2}). \quad (1)$$

Therefore, $\mathbf{L_I}$-image is obtained as follows:

$$\mathbf{L_I}(x,y) = \max_{i,j} (\mathbf{Z}(x+i, y+j) - H(i,j)) \quad (2)$$
$$(i^2 + j^2 < r^2),$$

where $H$ is the height field of the tool-end shape, *i.e.*

$$H(i,j) = h(\sqrt{i^2 + j^2}), \quad (3)$$

and $r$ is the radius of the tool. Equation 2 is equivalent to the Inverse Offset Method [3].

Figure 3 shows two examples of tool shapes; (a) is a flat endmill and (b) is a ball endmill. In some cases, especially for rough cutting, some amount of under-cutting is required everywhere. For this requirement, the virtual endmill profile (a) is used. Figure 4 shows the offset surfaces when the tools shown in Fig.3 are used to produce the teapot shown in Fig.1. Here, higher intensity (white region) means larger $z$ values. In this example, the image size is $400 \times 200$ pixels, and the pixel interval is $0.2mm$ (*i.e.* the simulation size is $80mm \times 40mm$).

Basic tool paths are obtained by scanning $\mathbf{L_I}$. In this stage, various kinds of tool paths are possible by referring to the G-buffers. The following paths are typical examples:

- *x- or y-scanning:*
  simply scanning on the $x$ or $y$ axis using an appropriate interval;
- *contour tracking:*
  tracking a constant $z$ value in the $\mathbf{L_I}$-image;
- *u- or v-scanning:*
  tracking a constant $u$ or $v$ value in the **ou**- or **ov**-image.

The tool scanning strategy can be chosen independently for each surface of the object if the **id**-image is referred to.

(a) shaded image

(b) depth image (**Z**)

**Fig.1** Shaded and depth images of the Utah Teapot.

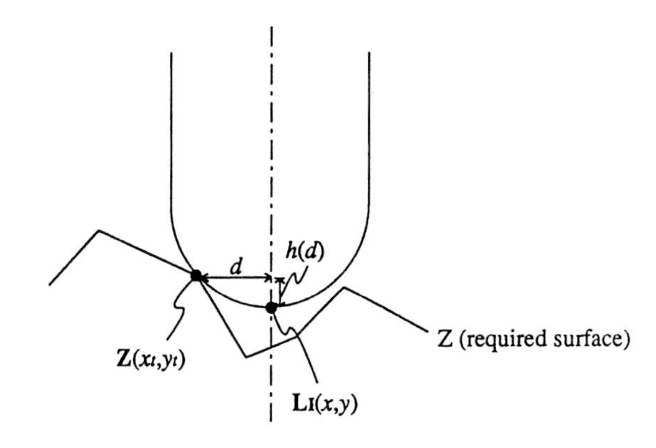


**Fig.2** Obtaining an offset surface.

(a) flat endmill ($R = 6mm$) with under-cutting ($1mm$)

(b) ball endmill ($\phi = 1.5mm$)

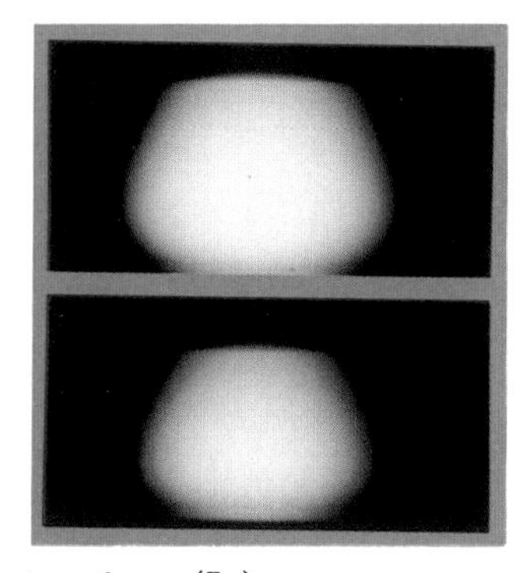

**Fig.4** Offset surfaces ($\mathbf{L_I}$).

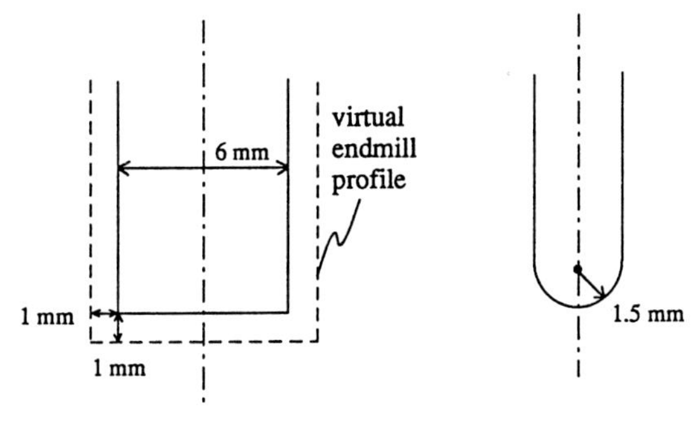


**Fig.3** Example tool shapes.

### 3.2 Tool Path Verification and Evaluation

#### 3.2.1 Accuracy of a Final Shape

This section introduces a verification and evaluation method for over- and under-cutting. For this purpose, the generated tool path has to be converted to a height field and preserved in a **P**-image, where each $\mathbf{P}(x, y)$ contains the height of the tool path when the tool goes through the pixel. If the tool passes the pixel more than once, the minimum height is preserved. If the tool does not pass, the maximum z-value is stored. The shape of the milling result **F** is calculated as follows:

$$\mathbf{F}(x,y) = \min_{i,j} (\mathbf{R}(x,y),\ \mathbf{P}(x+i, y+j) + H(i,j)) \quad (i^2 + j^2 < r^2), \tag{4}$$

where **R** is the shape of the workpiece before milling, which is either the initial shape of the workpiece or the previous milling result **F**. The relations among **Z**-, $\mathbf{L_I}$-, **R**-, **P**-, and **F**-images are shown in Fig.5.

By comparing **F** with **Z**, the over/under-cutting amount **D** is obtained for each pixel:

$$\mathbf{D}(x,y) = \mathbf{F}(x,y) - \mathbf{Z}(x,y), \tag{5}$$

where a negative $\mathbf{D}(x,y)$ value indicates over-cutting. Note that this verification is possible for tool paths generated by *any* method. If they are generated by the method given in section 3.1, it is obvious that there is no over-cutting.

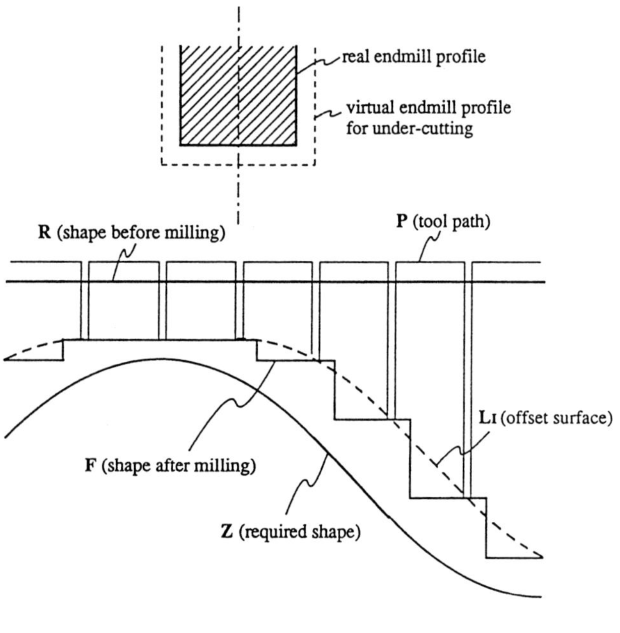

real endmill profile
virtual endmill profile for under-cutting
R (shape before milling)
P (tool path)
LI (offset surface)
F (shape after milling)
Z (required shape)

**Fig.5** Tool path generation and verification.

An example of rough cutting process is described. The scanning direction of the tool is perpendicular to this paper.

Example images from the teapot data are shown in Figs.6–8. Figure 6 is the tool path images (**P**). The path interval for rough cutting is $3mm$, while that for fine cutting is the same as the pixel interval ($0.2mm$). The cutting simulation results (**F**-images) are presented in Fig.7. These results can be evaluated by calculating the under-cutting amount (**D**-images) shown in Fig.8.

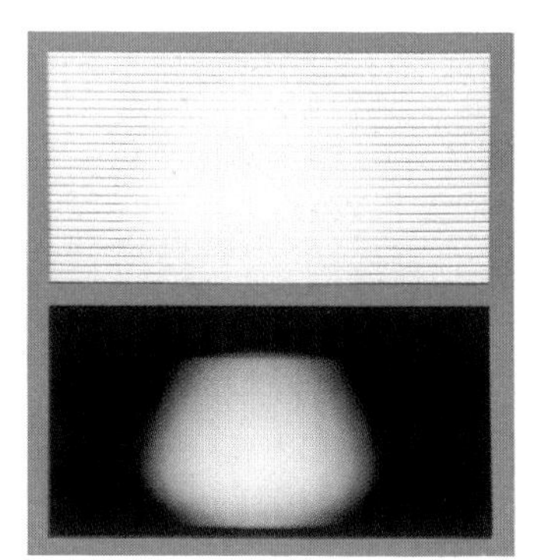

(a) rough cutting with the flat endmill

(b) fine cutting with the ball endmill

**Fig.6** Path images (**P**).

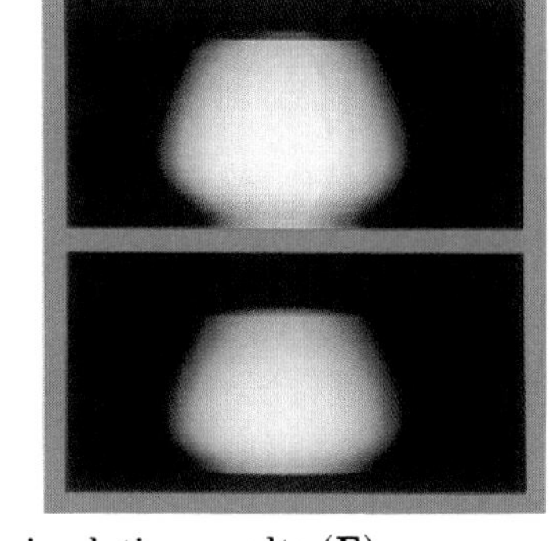

(a) rough cutting with the flat endmill

(b) fine cutting with the ball endmill

**Fig.7** Cutting simulation results (**F**).

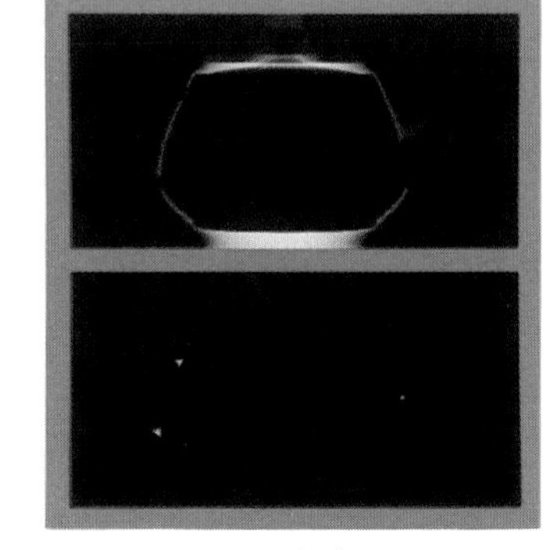

(a) rough cutting with the flat endmill (max: $17.47mm$)

(b) fine cutting with the ball endmill (max: $2.99mm$)

**Fig.8** Under-cutting amount (**D**).

### 3.2.2 Tool Load

A tool can be overloaded and damaged in either of the following situations.

- The machine attempts to mill off an excessive amount of material.
- Milling direction is illegal.
  One example is to try to make a vertical hole with a flat endmill.

These situations can be detected by simulating the milling operations step by step using the **R**-image. In this section, a method of evaluating milling volume is introduced as an example. To begin with, the tool path is divided into small steps so that each step consists of only one pixel movement or vertical tool setting. Let the location of the tool at the $s$-th step be $(x_s, y_s, z_s)$, and the intermediate resulting shape at that time be $\mathbf{F}_s$. Then, $\mathbf{F}_s$ and the cutting volume $c_s$ are obtained as follows:

$$\mathbf{F}_s(x,y) = \begin{cases} \mathbf{F}_{s-1}(x,y) \\ \qquad \left(\text{if } (x-x_s)^2 + (y-y_s)^2 \geq r^2\right) \\ \min\left(\mathbf{F}_{s-1}(x,y),\ z_s + H(x-x_s, y-y_s)\right) \\ \qquad \left(\text{if } (x-x_s)^2 + (y-y_s)^2 < r^2\right), \end{cases} \tag{6}$$

$$c_s = \sum_{x,y} \left(\mathbf{F}_{s-1}(x,y) - \mathbf{F}_s(x,y)\right). \tag{7}$$

Note that the initial shape $\mathbf{F}_0$ is **R**, and the final shape is **F**.

(a) offset surface for interference avoidance ($\mathbf{L}_\mathrm{I}$)

(b) offset surface for collision avoidance ($\mathbf{L}_\mathrm{C}$)

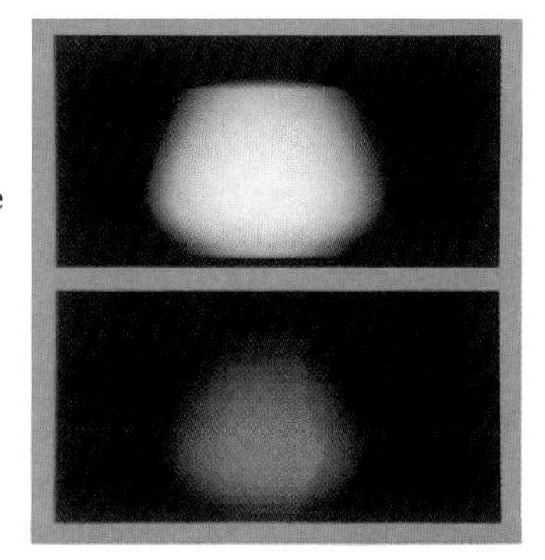

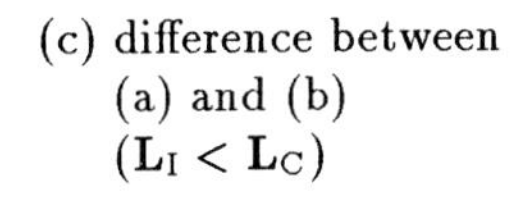

(c) difference between (a) and (b) ($\mathbf{L}_\mathrm{I} < \mathbf{L}_\mathrm{C}$)

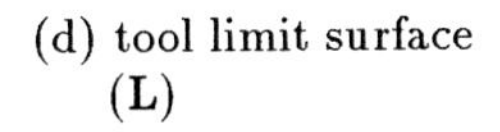

(d) tool limit surface (**L**)

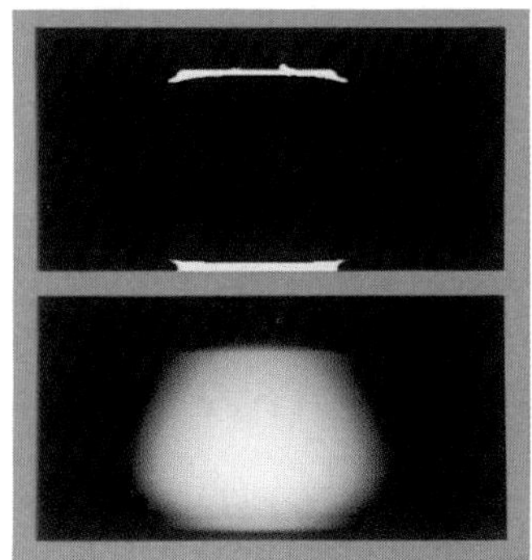

**Fig.10** Tool path generation with collision avoidance.

## 3.3 Advanced Tool Path Generation

### 3.3.1 Collision Avoidance

Collision avoidance between the workpiece and tool or tool holder is important in path generation. In Fig.9, for example, the length of the milling edge, $h_1$, restricts the maximum depth of lateral side milling. The depth of the tool must be limited to a safe $z$ value during each scanning path. In this case, deep regions must be scanned many times while steadily increasing the depth. This method is effective for the initial rough cutting process since the shape of the workpiece is flat. However, it is inefficient for later cutting processes, and efficient tool paths for such cases must take the constraints of the tool or tool holder into account.

This problem is simply solved with image processing operations. Let $H_C$ be a height field of the upper part of the tool (without milling edge), and let $\mathbf{L}_\mathrm{C}$ be the offset surface between **R** and $H_C$, *i.e.*

$$\mathbf{L}_\mathrm{C}(x,y) = \max_{i,j}\left(\mathbf{R}(x+i, y+j) - H_C(i,j)\right) \tag{8}$$
$$(i^2 + j^2 < r^2).$$

$\mathbf{L}_\mathrm{C}$ is the limit surface to avoid tool collision. The tool can move above both offset surfaces $\mathbf{L}_\mathrm{I}$ and $\mathbf{L}_\mathrm{C}$ (Fig.9). Therefore, the tool limit surface **L** is defined as follows:

$$\mathbf{L}(x,y) = \max\left(\mathbf{L}_\mathrm{I}(x,y), \mathbf{L}_\mathrm{C}(x,y)\right). \tag{9}$$

After milling along surface **L**, **R** is changed and deeper milling may be possible in the next stage. This can also be simulated easily.

Figure 10 shows an example using the teapot. For fine cutting after rough cutting, $\mathbf{L}_\mathrm{I}$- and $\mathbf{L}_\mathrm{C}$-images are calculated. If the tool path is generated from just the $\mathbf{L}_\mathrm{I}$-image, collision occurs in the white region displayed in (c).

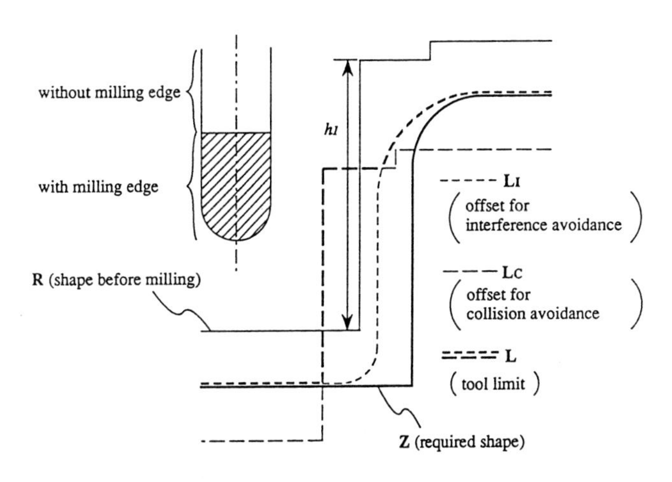


**Fig.9** Tool path with collision avoidance.

### 3.3.2 Final Cutting for Concave Regions

To minimize under-cutting in concave regions, the tool appropriate for the concave shape must be selected. In this case, the tool path should trace only the essential points. This is also possible with image processing techniques.

An example is presented in Fig.11, where the tool path for a flat endmill is generated in order to mill the concave corners of the teapot after fine cutting. First, the offset surface $\mathbf{L}_\mathrm{I}$ (a) and its Laplacian (second order differential) image (b) are calculated. A positive value in the Laplacian image means that the offset surface is concave at that point. Next, static cutting volume $\mathbf{c}$ (c) is calculated as follows:

$$\mathbf{c}(x,y) = \sum_{i,j} \max(\mathbf{R}(x+i, y+j) - (\mathbf{L}_\mathrm{I}(x,y) + H(i,j)),\ 0) \quad (10)$$
$$(i^2 + j^2 < r^2).$$

If this volume is large at a pixel, then it is effective to pass the tool over the pixel. By tracing the peak values in the c-image (c) only when the Laplacian value (b) is positive, the tool path (d) can be obtained. The effect of the tool path is shown in the simulation results (e) and (f).

### 3.4 Feed Rate Control

In order to minimize machining time, the maximum feed rate should be selected within the load limit of the tool or material. By using the load evaluation discussed in Section 3.2.2, the optimum feed rate can be selected. Let $c_{max}$ be the maximum cutting volume per unit time, and let $v_{max}$ be the maximum feed rate. Then, the feed rate is obtained as follows:

$$v = \min\left(\frac{c_{max} l}{c_s},\ v_{max}\right) \quad (11)$$

where

$$l = \sqrt{(x_s - x_{s-1})^2 + (y_s - y_{s-1})^2 + (z_s - z_{s-1})^2}. \quad (12)$$

(a) offset surface of flat endmill ($\mathbf{L}_\mathrm{I}$) ($R = 3mm$)

(b) Laplacian of (a) (concave region)

(c) static milling volume ($\mathbf{c}$) (white is $> 1.0$)

(d) tool path for corner cutting

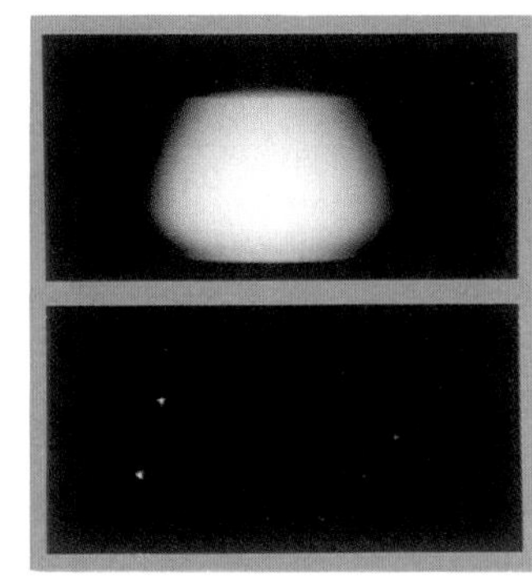

(e) simulation result ($\mathbf{F}$)

(f) under-cutting amount ($\mathbf{D}$) (max: $2.94mm$)

**Fig.11** Tool path generation for corner cutting.

## 4 Examples

Some examples of NC machining results are shown in this section. A low-cost personal NC machine (Roland DG, CAMM-3) connected to a workstation (Sun-4) was used. Figure 12 shows the NC machine.

### 4.1 Machining Geometric Surfaces

The most important usage of NC machines is to produce accurate 3D shapes from geometrically defined objects. Here, the teapot was machined by using the G-buffer method. The process followed these steps.

1. *Rough cutting with flat endmill* ($\phi = 6mm$, $x$-scanning).
   The path interval was $3mm$. $1mm$ under-cutting was specified. A maximum of four scans was needed, and the tool depth was increased by $5mm$ for each scan. The simulation results are shown in Figs.4,6–8 (a), and the machining result is shown in Fig.13 (a).
2. *Fine cutting with ball endmill* ($R = 1.5mm$, $x$-scanning).
   The path interval was $0.2mm$, the same as the pixel interval. A maximum of two scans was needed to ensure collision avoidance. The simulation results are shown in Figs.4,6–8 (b) and Fig.10, while the machining result is given in Fig.13 (b).
3. *Fine cutting with ball endmill* ($R = 1.5mm$, $y$-scanning).
   Since step 2 resulted in rippled surfaces where the gradient along the $y$ direction was large, $y$-scans were generated from the same $\mathbf{L}_I$-image. The machining result is shown in Fig.13 (c).
4. *Corner cutting with flat endmill* ($\phi = 3mm$).
   The simulation results are shown in Fig.11, and the machining result is given in Fig.13 (d).

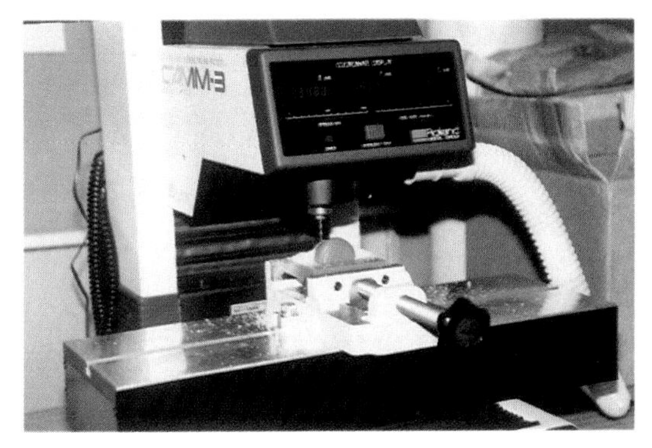

**Fig.12** The NC Milling Machine.

(a) result of rough cutting

(b) result of fine cutting (only $x$-scanning)

(c) result of fine cutting ($x$- and $y$-scanning)

(d) result of corner cutting

**Fig.13** Process of machining the teapot.

### 4.2 Machining Meshed or Volume Data

In addition to geometric surfaces, 3D shapes defined by meshed or volume data can be easily created with the G-buffer method. Thus, it is a powerful tool for visualization. Two examples are shown in this section.

The first one is a topographical map. The G-buffer method is useful to draw maps with various enhancements, however, it is also possible to produce 3D maps with G-buffer machining. Fig.14 (a) is a regular topographical map of the region around the NTT Yokosuka R&D Center. Fig.14 (b) shows a 3D map of the same region. Both were made with the G-buffer method from the same height data.

The next example is a medical application. Figure 15 (a) shows a depth image of a human brain. The original data consists of 256×256×30 voxels from MRI. Figure 15 (b) is a 3D model of the brain. Although reentrant machining was impossible, the shape of the brain's upper surface can be recognized much more easily than is possible with 2D images.

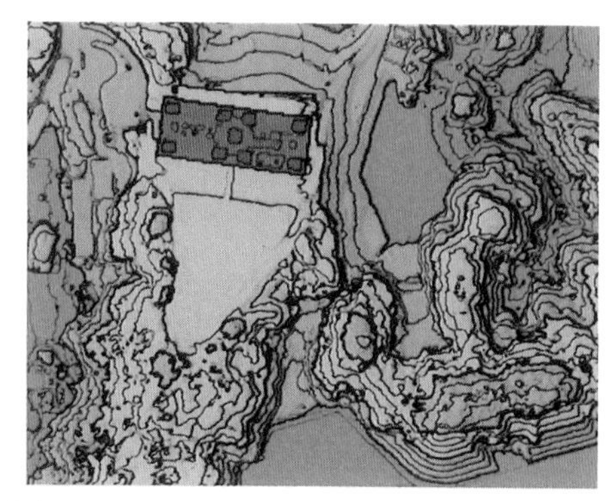

(a) enhanced 2D map by G-buffer rendering

(b) 3D map by G-buffer machining

**Fig.14** Topographical map.

## 5 Discussion

### 5.1 Advantages of the G-buffer Machining

One of the notable advantages of the proposed method is its simplicity. Actually, our experimental NC machining system consists of about 20 small independent software modules. Most of them perform simple image processing operations, and all the functions described in section 3 are realized by combining them. Another program is required to generate the G-buffers. However, conventional rendering programs, such as z-buffer, ray-tracing, or volume rendering routines, can be used without major changes.

For NC machining, people have been required to possess some skill in manufacturing technology, and most computer graphics people could not produce actual 3D objects by themselves. The G-buffer method, however, can make NC technology accessible to these people. Researchers and artists who render 3D shapes with computer graphics can easily obtain models of the objects with G-buffer machining.

Another advantage of G-buffer machining is its good combination of path generation and simulation. In conventional systems, the main purpose of simulation and verification is the error detection of tool paths. In G-buffer machining, on the other hand, the simulation result is effectively used in the path generation for the next cutting phase. Collision avoidance and corner cutting described in section 3.3 are good examples.

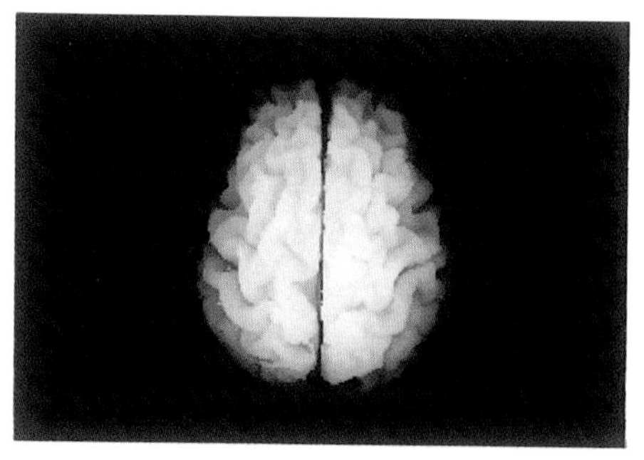

(a) depth image

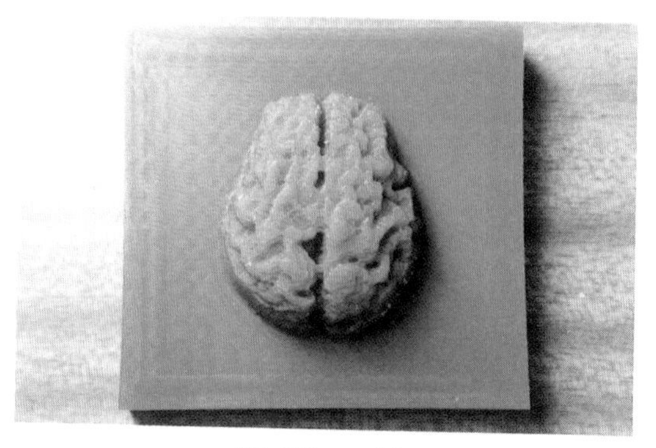

(b) 3D model

**Fig.15** Human brain.
Data courtesy of Dr. Jin Tamai of Nippon Medical School.

### 5.2 Sampling Error

Sampling error is one disadvantage of G-buffer machining. Since height fields are calculated only at the center of each pixel, sampling errors occur at less than the pixel interval in horizontal directions. Over-cutting can be prevented by using tool shapes with 1 pixel under-cutting, however, *aliasing artifacts* in large gradient regions cannot be avoided.

Some anti-aliasing techniques in computer graphics can reduce sampling errors. Subpixel sampling is a powerful yet simple approach, but it requires a large amount of memory and computing power. According to Kishinami *et al.* [3], they succeeded in reducing the required memory capacity by employing the quad-tree data structure for path generation in their Inverse Offset Method. However, the quad-tree data structure makes the image processing operations for the NC functions so complicated that one of the most significant advantages of G-buffer machining, its simplicity, may be lost.

The tolerance of the machining result depends on the user's purpose. If the machined object is only to verify or evaluate the designed or given shape, then G-buffer machining is acceptable. On the other hand, if the object is the final product, much more investigation about sampling error is required.

### 5.3 Computation Cost

The proposed method incurs high computation cost when processing large objects with high precision. Table 1 shows the computation time to machine the examples in section 4. This table presents the total time of path generation, simulation, and evaluation for each cutting phase. Although the values are reasonable for these examples, they become large for large objects. If the operations are simply implemented, the required memory space is $O(S_xS_y)$ and the computation cost is $O(S_xS_yH_r{}^2)$, where $S_xS_y$ is the G-buffer size in pixels and $H_r$ is the tool radius in pixels.

However, the problem of memory size will become less important in the near future since memory space of commercial computers is still increasing. Computation time can be reduced by using dedicated image processing hardware. Most operations are simple and iterative, so that vector processors or massively parallel processors can effectively accelerate the calculation speed. There is also some possibility to reduce the computation cost with efficient algorithms, especially for flat endmills.

## 6 Conclusion

We applied the G-buffer method to NC machining. By preparing G-buffers from a parallel projection, the various functions required for a NC system were realized with image processing operations. This allows any surface description and any tool shape to be used. Conventional hardware and software for computer graphics and image processing can be employed with this method. This makes NC system development much easier. Experimental results show that our method can be effectively used in an actual machining process. The method should be a great tool, not only for CAD/CAM, but also for scientific visualization.


### Acknowledgements

We would like to thank Dr. Rikuo Takano and Dr. Masashi Okudaira for their continuous support. We also wish to thank Hiroki Kobayashi for coding the programs of the experimental system. We are very grateful to Dr. Jin Tamai of Nippon Medical School for providing us the original MRI image data of Fig.15, and the colleagues in our section for helpful discussions.


**Table 1** Required memory space and computation time for G-buffer machining.

Sun-4/370 was used for this experiment. Computation time for G-buffer generation is not included.
Tool types are indicated as follows.
$F6$: $\phi = 6mm$ flat endmill;
$F3$: $\phi = 3mm$ flat endmill;
$F1$: $\phi = 1mm$ flat endmill;
$B3$: $R = 1.5mm$ ball endmill.

| Shape | Fig.13 (Teapot) | Fig.14 (Map) | Fig.15 (Brain) |
|---|---|---|---|
| G-buffer Size (pixels) | 400 × 200 | 301 × 301 | 200 × 200 |
| Pixel Size | 0.20 mm | 0.20 mm | 0.30 mm |
| Required Memory Space | 1.14 MB | 1.26 MB | 0.56 MB |
| Rough Cutting | 1007 sec ($F6$) | 1140 sec ($F6$) | 224 sec ($F6$) |
| Fine Cutting | 378 sec ($B3:1st$) 181 sec ($B3:2nd$) 7 sec ($B3:y$) | 207 sec ($B3$) | 112 sec ($B3:1st$) 54 sec ($B3:2nd$) 188 sec ($F1:1st$) 94 sec ($F1:2nd$) |
| Corner Cutting | 257 sec ($F3$) | | |

## References

[1] Zhang, D., and Bowyer, A., "CSG Set-Theoretic Solid Modeling and NC Machining of Blend Surfaces", *Proc. 2nd Annual ACM Conf. Computational Geometry*, pp. 236–245, 1986.

[2] Sakuta, T., Kawai, M., and Amano, Y., "Development of an NC Machining System for Stamping Dies of Offset Surface Method", *Proc. Autofact '87*, pp. 2-13 – 2-27 (1987).

[3] Kishinami, T., Kondo, T., and Saito, K., "Inverse Offset Method for Cutter Path Generation", *Proc. 6th Int'l Conf. Production Engineering*, pp. 807–812, 1987.

[4] Wang, W. P., and Wang, K. K., "Real-Time Verification of Multiaxis NC Programs with Raster Graphics", *Proc. IEEE Int'l Conf. Robotics and Automation*, pp. 166–171, 1986.

[5] Wang, W. P., and Wang, K. K., "Geometric Modeling for Swept Volume of Moving Solids", *IEEE Computer Graphics and Applications*, Vol. 6, No. 12, pp. 8–17 (1986).

[6] Hook, T. V., "Real-Time Shaded NC Milling Display", *Computer Graphics*, Vol. 20, No. 4, (*Proc. SIGGRAPH '86*), pp. 15–20 (1986).

[7] Atherton, P., Earl, C., and Fred, C., "A Graphical Simulation System for Dynamic Five-Axis NC Verification", *Proc. Autofact '87*, pp. 2-1 – 2-12 (1987).

[8] Kawashima, Y., Itoh, K., Nonaka, S., and Ejiri, K., "A Flexible, Quantitative Method for NC Machining Verification Using a Space Division Based Solid Model", *New Advances in Computer Graphics* (*Proc. CG International '89*), pp. 421–437 (1989).

[9] Chappel, I. T., "The Use of Vectors to Simulate Material Removal by Numerically Controlled Milling", *Computer Aided Design*, Vol. 15, No. 3, pp. 156–158 (1983).

[10] Drysdale, R. L., and Jerard, R. B., "Discrete Simulation of NC Machining", *Proc. 3rd Annual ACM Conf. Computational Geometry*, pp. 126–135, 1987.

[11] Jerard, R. B., Drysdale, R. L., Hauck, K., Schaudt, B., and Magewick, J., "Methods for Detecting Errors in Numerical Controlled Machining of Sculptured Surfaces", *IEEE Computer Graphics and Applications*, Vol. 9, No. 1, pp. 26–39 (1989).

[12] Jerard, R. B., Hussaini, S. Z., Drysdale, R. L., and Schaudt, B., "Approximate Methods for Simulation and Verification of Numerical Controlled Machining Programs", *Visual Computer*, Vol. 5, No. 6, pp. 329–348 (1989).

[13] Saito, T., and Takahashi, T., "Comprehensible Rendering of 3-D Shapes", *Computer Graphics*, Vol. 24, No. 4, (*Proc. SIGGRAPH '90*), pp. 197–206 (1990).

# Geometrically Deformed Models: A Method for Extracting Closed Geometric Models from Volume Data

James V. Miller David E. Breen William E. Lorensen†
Robert M. O'Bara Michael J. Wozny

Rensselaer Design Research Center
Rensselaer Polytechnic Institute

†General Electric Company
Corporate Research and Development

## ABSTRACT

We propose a new approach to the problem of generating a simple topologically-closed geometric model from a point-sampled volume data set. We call such a model a Geometrically Deformed Model or GDM. A GDM is created by placing a 'seed' model in the volume data set. The model is then deformed by a relaxation process that minimizes a set of constraints that provides a measure of how well the model fits the features in the data. Constraints are associated with each vertex in the model that control local deformation, interaction between the model and the data set, and the shape and topology of the model. Once generated, a GDM can be used for visualization, shape recognition, geometric measurements, or subjected to a series of geometric operations. This technique is of special importance because of the advent of nondestructive sensing equipment (CT, MRI) that generates point samples of true three-dimensional objects.

**CR Categories:** I.3.3 **[Computer Graphics]:** Picture/Image Generation — *display algorithms — viewing algorithms*; I.3.5 **[Computer Graphics]:** — Computational Geometry and Object Modelling — *curve, surface, solid, and object representations*;

**Additional Keywords and Phrases:** Deformable Models, Geometric Modelling, Volume Visualization, Volume Modelling, Constraint Minimization

## 1 INTRODUCTION

The development of remote sensing and scanning technology permits the nondestructive examination of an object's internal structure. This ability has proven to be essential in numerous engineering and medical fields. It allows for the inspection of mechanical parts without destroying the product and the examination of internal organs without operating on the patient. The technology generates a discrete three-dimensional scalar field where each value is a measure of some physical property, for example density. Since this data is produced via point sampling, it inherits all the properties and problems of sampled data. These include sampling artifacts, spatial aliasing, and noise. The scalar field can be composed of a series of two-dimensional slices, that when stacked, form the three-dimensional volume. Traditionally, each 2D slice was viewed separately, requiring a specialist to deduce the true 3D structure represented in the data. There are two alternative methods of displaying and analyzing the raw scalar field. One treats the volume data in its original form, as in both morphology and volume rendering [1, 2, 3]. The other transforms the data into something that is more readily displayed, such as a surface [4, 5, 6, 7, 8].

However, a more powerful approach generates geometric models of the scanned objects using the volume data as a measure of the object configuration [9, 10, 11]. This differs from the second method in that it approximates rather than interpolates the data. The major motivation behind this approach is that a geometric model provides the greatest number of options for analyzing and visualizing the original object. Once created, such a model can be used for inspection, visualization, or subjected to a series of geometric measurements and operations. Generating a model has the effect of removing the "noise" from scanned data making object identification easier. Defects in an object will result in a model that is malformed, thus emphasizing the defect. A geometric measurement, such as volume, may be easily performed on a geometric model. CSG operations may be applied to both the model and other geometry in order to convey further information about the extents and interrelationships of the structures.

In this paper, we present a methodology for extracting a topologically closed geometric model from a volume data set. The technique, called Geometrically Deformed Models (GDM's), starts with a simple model that is already topologically closed, and deforms the model based on a set of constraints, so that the model grows (or shrinks) to fit the object within the volume while maintaining its closed and locally simple (non-self-intersecting) nature. The initial model is a non-self-intersecting polyhedron that is either embedded in the object or surrounds the object in the volume data representation. A function is associated with every vertex of the polyhedron that associates costs with local deformation, adherence to properties of simple polyhedra, and the relationship between noise and feature. By minimizing these constraints, one achieves an effect similar to inflating a balloon within a container or collapsing a piece of shrink wrap around an object.

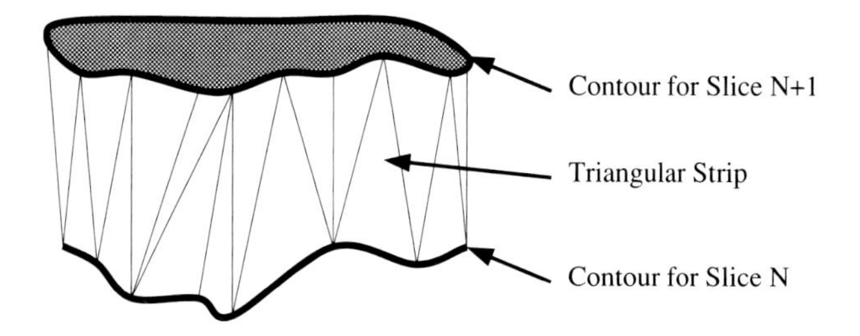


Figure 1 A surface can be created by stitching together the 2D contours extracted from adjacent slices in a volume data set.

## 2 PREVIOUS WORK

Previous techniques for extracting three-dimensional geometries from volume data fall into three categories: contour stitching, surface construction, and deformable models. Fuchs, Kedem and Uselton developed a means of stitching a series of two-dimensional contours together by fitting a triangular strip between adjacent contours [6] (Figure 1). Lin, Chen and Chen connected two-dimensional contours using spline theory, quadratic variation-based surface interpolation, and dynamic elastic contour interpolation [5]. In either method, every contour that composes the object needs to be identified for every slice in the data set. Plus the complexity of the algorithms increases when adjacent slices have a different number of contours, referred to as the branching problem. GDM's have neither of these complications because they treat the data set as a complete volume as opposed to a series of slices. This allows the branching problem to be handled implictly by treating concavities in the direction normal to the slice plane (branches) in the same manner as any other concavity in the data set. The problem of identifying all the contours that compose the object is removed because a GDM naturally probes through the entire object following all of its branches.

Herman, Frieder, and Artzy tracked the surface of an object using the voxel data as a graph [4]. A voxel containing the surface of the object is identified and the algorithm traverses the neighboring voxels generating a topology that is guaranteed to be closed. This work does not suffer from the branching problem discussed with contour stitching because the algorithm follows the surface as it travels through the volume. Lorensen and Cline developed marching cubes [7] to simply extract a list of polygons from volume data with no connectivity information. In their algorithm, a cube is bounded by eight pixels located on two adjacent slices. Each vertex is coded as either inside or outside the object relative to the surface defining threshold. Based on the configuration of vertices that lie inside and outside the object; the cube is triangulated, each triangle indicating a portion of the surface. Marching cubes was extended into dividing cubes [8] by Cline et al. Dividing cubes resamples the voxels to the desired display resolution in order to generate points with normals instead of triangles. Marching and Dividing cubes do not suffer from the branching problem because they extract the entire surface located in the volume. The problem with this group of surface construction algorithms is that they are restricted to generating models where each element in the model is at most the size of a voxel, hence they cannot approximate the data. Also, these algorithms are not applicable to the task of generating a closed model of an object that is not necessarily closed, for instance the interior of an opened wine bottle. In this case, they will either extract a model with little resemblance to the desired object, or they will extract multiple objects. GDM's on the other hand can produce models of varying resolution. This provides a data reduction and aides in the GDM's ability to "bridge" over the holes in the boundary of an object.

Kass, Witkin, and Terzopolous have developed snakes [9] which model the contours of an image by minimizing the energy associated with a spline. The energy of a snake configuration is based upon the image and its first and second derivative, the curvature of the edge components in the image, and the first and second derivative of the spline. Terzopoulus, Witkin, and Kass extended the concept of snakes into symmetry-seeking models [10], that derive a three-dimensional shape from a two-dimensional image by modelling an axisymmetric elastic skin spread over a flexible spine. These approaches provide a compact representation of an object or feature and should be tolerant of noise, but they are currently limited to 2D data and at most 2.5D models (for symmetry-seeking models). Snakes and symmetry–seeking models can take advantage of *a priori* information about the configuration and orientation of the object being modelled, but they do not provide a multi-resolution approach to probing the data. Finally, since the internal energy of the spline is a global operation, it would appear to be difficult to parallelize the algorithm. GDM's are very similar to snakes except they can probe volume data, thus generating 3D models; they can probe the data with a low resolution model then substitute a higher resolution model; and a GDM is controlled through local geometric operations on a discrete model, hence it is easily parallelized.

In another deformable matching technique, Bajcsy and Kovačič used a multiresolution approach to elastically deform a known brain atlas to match a scanned brain[12]. This approach decreases the resolution of the data set then deforms the brain atlas so the outer edge and ventricles matches the data. The resolution is then increased and the deformation process repeated. This approach motivated GDM's to operate on the slice data as a true volume and to vary the resolution of the model during its deformation. The drawback to deforming an atlas to fit an object is that an atlas is required for every object to be modelled.

The proposed solution of deforming a model to fit an object is based upon Witkin et al.'s [13] work on energy constraints and Breen's work on goal-oriented motion for computer animation [14], and reflects a simpler approach to the problems presented by Kass et al. [9], Terzopoulos et al. [15, 10], and Bajcsy et al. [12]. These other approaches model the elastic nature of a curve or surface to control the model's deformation. Such models are based on the differential equations of elastic materials. GDM's, on the other hand, do not try to model an elastic substance; in contrast they model a simpler discrete deforming structure influenced by local geometric constraints.

## 3 CONSTRAINT MODELLING AND MINIMIZATION

GDM's may be envisioned as a semi-permeable balloon located inside the scanned object. The balloon expands until its surface reaches the boundary of the scanned object. The balloon is actually a collection of discrete polygons. The volume data is sampled only at the vertices of these polygons. Permeability is achieved because elements of noise and insignificant features pass through the faces of the polyhedron, thus allowing the vertices of the polygonal mesh to miss or work around these elements. By placing a cost function at each vertex in the mesh, the relevant characteristics of the balloon can be modelled. By minimizing these cost functions, the balloon is expanded while maintaining its topology.

### 3.1 CONSTRAINT MODELLING

GDM's are created using a top down algorithm specification. First the behavior and characteristics of the model are defined. Then constraints are selected to achieve the desired behavior. Finally, functions are developed that model the constraints. Three orthogonal behaviors must be specified. The first is a mechanism for generating gross deformations. In the balloon analogy, this mechanism expands the balloon. Second, a mechanism is needed that will interact with the data set and identify voxels possibly containing the object boundary. This function restricts the balloon from expanding through the boundary of the object being modelled. Finally, since all operations are performed locally and the boundary of the object may be incomplete, the third function maintains the local topology of the model. This keeps the balloon from intersecting itself locally.

Each of these behaviors can be modelled by a term in a local cost function associated with each vertex in the model (cost functions are also referred to as potential functions). As each cost function is minimized, the model deforms while searching for the boundary of the object and maintaining its topology ([11] provides cost functions suitable for a 2D GDM). At each time step, every model point has the opportunity to move to a position of lower potential. Each constraint function, therefore, must produce a lower cost as the model moves towards satisfying that constraint. The cost for the current position of the vertex is a linear combination of the individual cost functions, which allows for one term to dominate the deformation. Each cost term must therefore have the ability to assert itself and dominate the overall cost function when its constraint is being violated, as well as seem insignificant when its constraint is being satisfied.

The cost function associated with the current location of a model point is the weighted sum

$$C_i(x, y, z) = a_0 D(x, y, z) + a_1 I(x, y, z) + a_2 T_i \quad (1)$$

where:

$C_i(x, y, z)$ is the cost associated with this position of the current model point,
$D(x, y, z)$ is the potential field that drives the model point towards the boundary,
$I(x, y, z)$ is the image term that identifies feature events,
$T_i$ is a measure of how the local configuration of polygonal faces satisfies the topology of the model,
$a_0, a_1, a_2$ are the individual weighting coefficients that allow the magnitudes of the various parameters to be scaled,
$C_i(x, y, z), D(x, y, z), I(x, y, z), T_i, a_0, a_1, a_2 \geq 0$.

#### 3.1.1 DEFORMATION POTENTIAL — $D(x, y, z)$

The deformation potential defines a scalar field where each position in space is assigned a value based on a frame of reference. In this case, a frame of reference can be any configuration of image or model parameters. The frame of reference may be a point inside the feature to be modelled, or it may be a set of vertex points in their previous configuration. The deformation potential must monotonically decrease (or increase) from the frame of reference and will repel (or attract) the current model point away from (or towards) its frame of reference.

**Normal Tracking:** Simple concave models can be created using a localized deformation potential. Each vertex is attracted to a point located in the direction of the polyhedron surface normal at that vertex. During each deformation cycle, each vertex moves in the general direction of the local surface normal. As a concavity is encountered, the topology and image event constraints influence the deformation. The surface normal rotates around the concavity, allowing the model to continue its deformation inside of the region that was previously hidden from view (Figure 2).

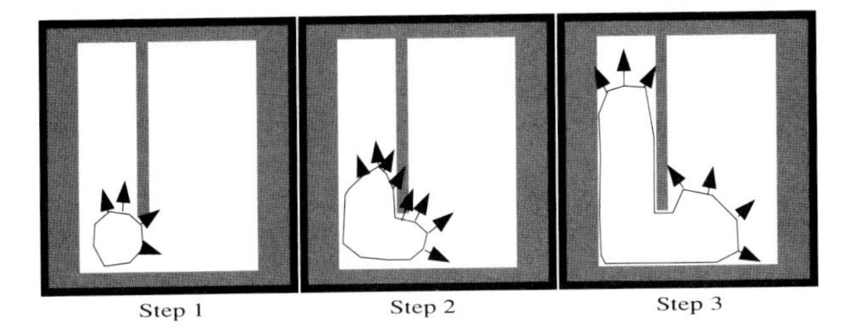


Figure 2 Surface normals directing a model to bend around a concavity.

#### 3.1.2 IMAGE EVENTS — $I(x, y, z)$

This class of constraint counterbalances the deformation potential. It is used to restrict, direct, and oppose the general progression of the deformation. Basically this constraint informs the vertex that it may be in contact with a voxel containing the original object (feature voxel). This constraint need not be able to distinguish noise and object since at the resolution of 1 voxel the two are indistinguishable, but must be able to identify the transition from a region of the data set that could be a feature to a region of the data set that is definitely not a feature. The important aspect of this constraint is that it introduces a local minimum at boundary events. Operations that identify boundary events include digital gradients [16], the Canny operator [17], and morphological operations [2]. Although any of these operators would suffice, GDM's can operate with a much simpler event detector.

A shifted threshold operator

$$I(x, y, z) = \begin{cases} 0 & Image(x, y, z) < T \\ Image(x, y, z) - T & Image(x, y, z) \geq T \end{cases} \quad (2)$$

where:

$Image(x, y, z)$ is the grey-level intensity of the voxel at (x,y,z),
$T$ is a threshold value that identifies the object;

is shown in Figure 3. Recall that the image event detector identifies the transitions from regions that are definitely not-object to regions of the image that could be object. The threshold, $T$, categorizes each voxel as either not-object or possibly object. Here a voxel that is not part of the object returns a value of zero, while a voxel that is part of the object returns the amount it exceeds the object identifying threshold. The image event operator in conjunction with the minimization process and the trilinear interpolation of voxel values allows for the true object edge to be located. When a model point steps over the edge of an object, $I(x, y, z)$ returns a value that should increase the overall cost of the system. The minimization process is forced, therefore, to either move the vertex by a smaller amount or to not move the vertex at all. Hence the vertex will approach the edge without crossing over it (unless its neighbors pull it over the edge).

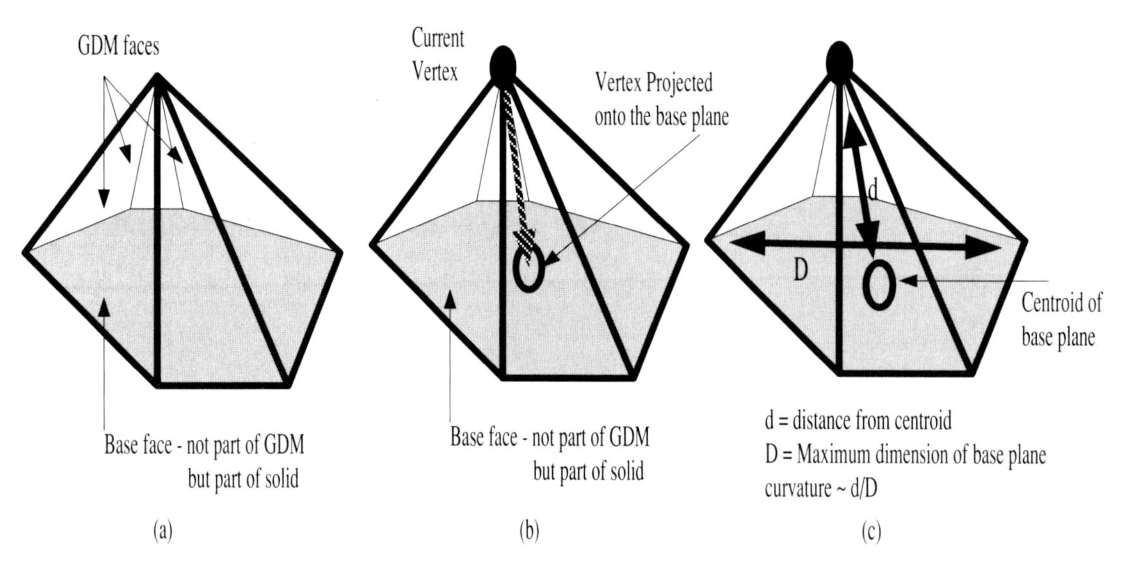


Figure 4 (a) A local solid model can be cut out of a GDM, by assuming that adjacent neighbors are connected in a fashion that will close the local solid model. (b) A vertex is contained by its base if the projection of the vertex onto the base is a point interior to the base. (c) The ratio of the distance between a model point and the centroid of its neighbors to the maximum dimension of the base plane gives an estimate of the curvature.

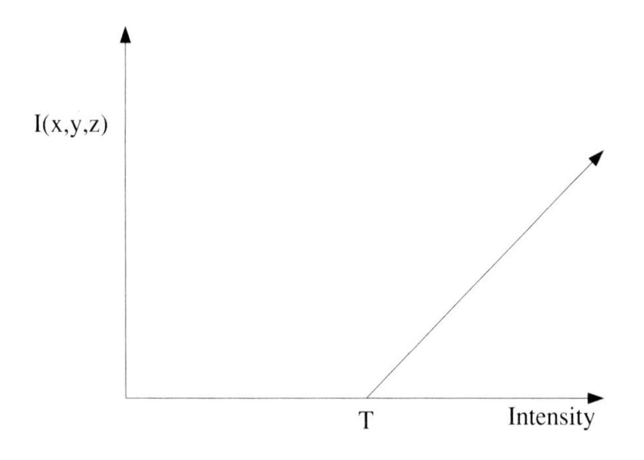


Figure 3 The image event detector used for GDM's is a simple shifted threshold $(X - T)^+$. Here the cost function returns zero if the voxel value is below the edge threshold, otherwise it returns a value that indicates how much the voxel value exceeds the edge threshold.

### 3.1.3 MAINTAINING TOPOLOGY — $T_i$

The final constraint maintains the topological integrity of the model and controls the spatial frequency of the model. The first two constraints cause the model to deform until all the vertices reach the boundary of the object. These two constraints are not sufficient to extract a geometric model from real data. For instance, the boundary of the object may be incomplete, consisting of gaps and holes. This may allow the vertices of the model to leak out of the object and travel without restriction towards the boundary of the data set. Alternatively, the data set may have elements of noise that could cause the image event detector to incorrectly categorize the noise as the boundary of the object. These two situations, coupled with the expansion or lack of expansion of the remainder of the model, may result in a geometric model that has little resemblance to the original object.

It is therefore necessary to have the geometry of the model influence a portion of the deformation. Since a topologically simple geometric model is desired, a constraint is added to the system that will maintain the locally simple nature of the initial model. The topological constraint is also referred to as a maintenance constraint. This term also controls the spatial frequency of the model by keeping vertices from leaking out of the holes in the boundary of object, as well as preventing vertices from being caught on an element of noise. These two behaviors are essentially duals. In the case of a vertex leaking out of a hole, there is a single vertex that is continuing its deformation while its neighbors have reached the boundary of the object. In the case of noise confrontation, a single vertex believes that it has found the boundary of the object while its neighbors continue their deformation. In either case, the faces associated with this vertex will become much larger than the faces in the immediate vicinity.

It is desirable for a vertex not to stray far from its neighbors or have its neighbors stray far from it. It is also desirable that the topology be maintained. Therefore, a vertex should be contained by its neighbors. A solid can be formed by the current model point and its neighbors. Imagine that the current model point and its neighbors are cut out of the GDM. By connecting the adjacent neighbors, a solid is created. (Figure 4(a)). Any face of this solid that contains the current model point is also a face of the GDM. Any face strictly composed of the current model point's neighbors is not a face in the GDM, but will be referred to as the "base" in the new solid. For a planar "base", the current model point is contained by its neighbors if, when it is projected onto the base plane, the projected point is in the interior of the polygon defined by the base (Figure 4(b)). If the "base" is not planar, this concept can still be applied to a polygon that is a planar approximation to the base.

**Curvature Estimation:** Keeping a model point contained by its neighbors while keeping the model point from straying too far from its neighbors suggests that the local curvature of the model should be constrained. The ratio of the distance from the current model point to the centroid of its neighbors and the maximum distance between the neighbors of the current model point gives an indication of the curvature (Figure 4(c)). This ratio defines the topological constraint

$$T_i = \frac{\left\| (x, y, z) - \frac{1}{n} \sum_{1}^{n} (x_j, y_j, z_j) \right\|}{\max_{j,k} \left( \| (x_j, y_j, z_j) - (x_k, y_k, z_k) \| \right)} \quad (3)$$

where:

$(x, y, z)$ is the current model point,
$n$ is the number of neighbors to the current model point,
$(x_j, y_j, z_j), (x_k, y_k, z_k)$ are the neighbors of the current model point, $1 \leq j, k \leq n$.

This function directs the vertex towards the centroid of the base, which in turn, attempts to make all the faces incident to the current model point coplanar. Since all the vertices are simultaneously trying to move onto the plane of their neighbors, the entire model defaults to being spherical (in the absence of the other constraints). Dividing the distance to the centroid by the maximum base point separation maintains scale invariance.

### 3.2 OPTIMIZATION METHOD

The cost function minimization technique utilizes an adaptive algorithm to move a vertex of the model in the direction of steepest descent along the cost surface. This direction is opposite to the gradient of the cost function $C_i$, and is estimated by numerically approximating the differentials $\left(\frac{\partial C_i}{\partial x}, \frac{\partial C_i}{\partial y}, \frac{\partial C_i}{\partial z}\right)$. The amount that a point moves is adjusted based upon the current configuration of the cost space. The stepsize can be reduced three times if movement by the current stepsize results in an increase in the cost function. If a step cannot be completed that will reduce the cost of the vertex point, then the vertex point is not moved. For the purposes of geometrically deformed models, the stepsizes are maintained in the range of [1/4, 1] voxels. This allows for rapid changes in the dimensions of the model when it is in a void, as well as fine adjustments in the model when it encounters an element of noise or the boundary of the cavity.

This technique will find local minima. No global minimization techniques such as simulated annealing [18] are performed; so global minima are not always found; however, a gradient descent has proven sufficient for the data sets tested. The algorithm actually exploits the fact that only local minima are found, by defining its cost functions to introduce local minima whenever a critical point is crossed. A critical point occurs whenever a maintenance constraint ($T_i$) is violated or when a possible feature voxel is encountered.

## 4 3D MODELS

The initial model chosen for 3D GDM's is an icosahedron. An icosahedron is a 20 sided approximation to a sphere. The methodology does not require an icosahedron for its initial model; it was simply chosen for the property that when resampled, forming a geodesic, the connectivity remains relatively uniform. Triangular faces ensure that the faces of the model are planar and allow the model the greatest degree of flexibility when fitting the scanned object. Each vertex in an icosahedron is connected to five other vertices. If the entire icosahedron is resampled, then each new vertex is six connected while the original vertices remain five connected. All vertices added through subsequent global resamplings of the geodesic result in new vertices that are six connected while maintaining the 12 original vertices as five-connected. Figure 5 illustrates how the triangular faces in an icosahedron can be resampled to form the faces of a geodesic [19]. Bisection of each edge produces three vertices that are connected to form four faces from the original face.

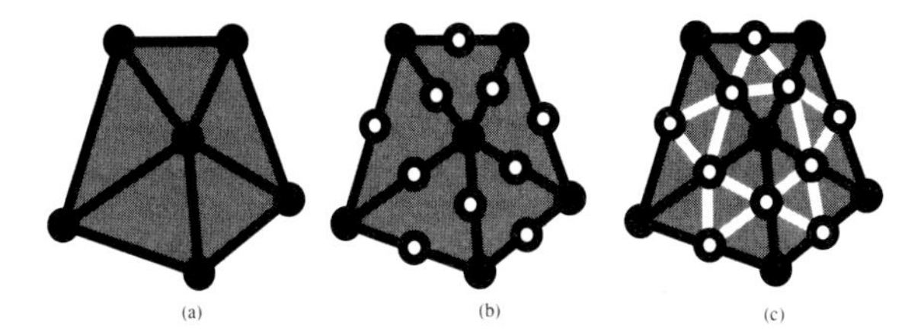


Figure 5 An icosahedron's triangular face is divided into four faces by connecting the midpoints of each edge. The connectivity of the new vertices is six while the connectivity of the original vertices remains five.

A global resampling of a GDM follows the same steps as a global resampling of a geodesic. It is irrelevant that the faces of the GDM may not be as regular as the faces of a geodesic. Any triangular face can be divided into four faces by connecting the midpoints of the edges. A global resampling of a GDM refines the entire model on command. This allows a low resolution model to probe the data initially, while a higher resolution GDM can be substituted in order to capture finer detail. Using an initial low resolution GDM greatly reduces the computation time in extracting models. Note that the number of vertices increases with the number of edges (each edge is subdivided to form a new vertex). The number of vertices in the globally resampled model is roughly four times the number of vertices in the original model.

Although a global resampling of a GDM refines the model, the increase in the number of model points limits its appeal. After each refinement, the amount of work to deform the model increases by a factor of four. Thus a global resampling must be used judiciously. Alternatively the resampling may be localized, increasing the complexity of the model only in those regions where it is necessary.

A local resampling can be performed in two operations. The first operation identifies the regions of the model that need to be resampled. The second step subdivides the associated faces while maintaining the topological database and keeping all faces triangular. The simplest way to identify the regions of the model that need to be resampled is based upon the desired level of detail. The level of detail in the extracted model is essentially the number of voxels approximated by a single face. Thus in order to maintain the level of detail, subdivide the faces that exceed the threshold set by the level of detail. Identifying these faces can be accomplished by a simple area calculation. Miller [20] discusses the details of face resampling.

## 5 CREATING GDM'S

Before a GDM can probe a data set, several parameters and facets of the algorithm must be specified: the object ($\mathrm{Object}$) and not-object ($\overline{\mathrm{Object}}$) classification, the deformation mode (grow, shrink), and the GDM parameters $(a_0, a_1, a_2, T_i)$. Fortunately this process benefits from the high degree of duality inherent to a GDM. Figure 6 and Table 1 summarize the duality between both

| Duals | | | |
|---|---|---|---|
| Mode | Image Event | Mode | Image Event |
| shrink | $\overline{\text{Object}} \rightarrow \text{Object}$ | grow | $\text{Object} \rightarrow \overline{\text{Object}}$ |
| shrink | $\text{Object} \rightarrow \overline{\text{Object}}$ | grow | $\overline{\text{Object}} \rightarrow \text{Object}$ |

Table 1 Duality relationships

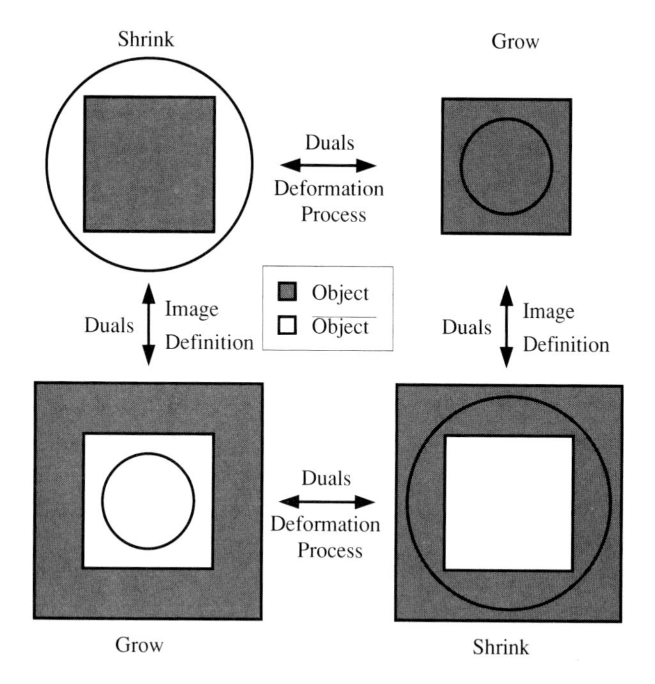


Figure 6 Duality relationships - the rows indicate duals formed by changing the deformation mode while the columns indicate duals formed by changing the object definition.

the deformation mode and object classification. Growing a GDM with one classification of Objectand $\overline{\text{Object}}$ results in the same model as shrinking a GDM with the roles of Object and $\overline{\text{Object}}$ reversed. The two models differ only in deformation time.

Due to the resampling process embedded in the GDM topological database, it is possible for a vertex to be added to the model on the wrong side of the $\text{Object} \rightarrow \overline{\text{Object}}$ boundary. Recall that the minimization technique does not allow a vertex to move to a position of higher potential. Therefore all of the model points will approach the boundary of the object from the same side. A model point that tries to move to the opposite side of the boundary will have its image event detector active and thus will have a higher potential. But the resampling algorithm may place new vertices on the opposite side of this boundary. Therefore, in order to move these model points to the other side of the boundary and hence increase the accuracy and quality of the model, the surface normal used in the deformation potential is defined to point in the opposite direction. This locally flips the deformation mode (i.e. from growing to shrinking). The effect is that a model point will migrate towards the true boundary of the object regardless of whether the model point is located in Object or $\overline{\text{Object}}$.

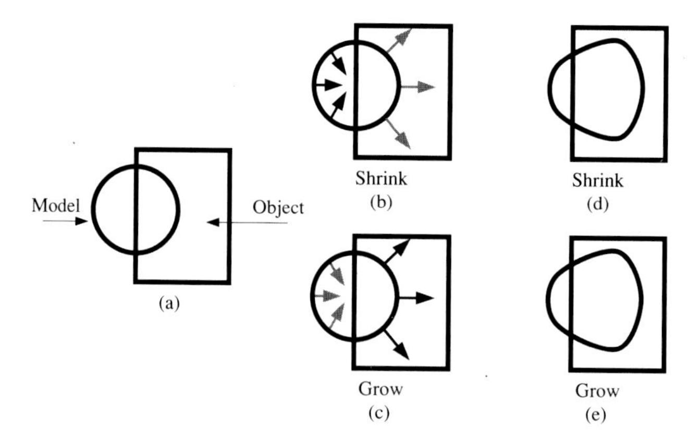


Figure 7 A GDM intersects the boundary of the Object $\rightarrow\overline{\text{Object}}$. The two deformation modes are equivalent in this case because the normals locally flip (dotted arrows indicate a change in the deformation sense).

A beneficial side effect of a GDM locally reversing the sense of deformation is related to the placement of the initial model. As long as the initial model intersects the $\text{Object} \rightarrow \overline{\text{Object}}$ boundary (i.e. some of the model points are inside object, the remainder are inside not-object), the model tends to seek out the true boundary of the object regardless of the deformation mode. This is a direct consequence of the duality and locality of deformation modes. Note that the model extracted from growing will differ from the model extracted by shrinking only by the dimensions of the boundary. Figure 7(a) shows a model intersecting an $\text{Object} \rightarrow \overline{\text{Object}}$ boundary. The deformation direction is shown for shrinking (Figure 7(b)) and growing (Figure 7(c)) a model. The solid deformation arrows indicate the deformation direction agrees with the primary deformation mode while the dotted deformation arrows indicate that the deformation mode has locally flipped sense. Figures 7(d) and (e) show the models at a later time step. Note that the two models approach the same boundary but they approach the boundary from different sides.

The duality and locality of deformation modes works in favor of a GDM if the GDM intersects both object and not-object and if the GDM does not intersect multiple objects. If a GDM does not intersect both regions of the data, then the deformation mode must agree with the placement of the initial model (in object or not-object). If the deformation mode is indeed correct, the GDM process extracts a geometric model of the boundary of the object. Otherwise, the GDM either collapses upon itself or extends out to infinity. Note that from the duality and locality of deformation modes, either case is feasible with either deformation mode.

Our experiments show that the GDM parameter values $(a_0, a_1, a_2)$ are relatively data independent. This is due to $a_0, a_1, a_2$ governing the GDM process, not the sampled data. Table 2 summarizes the suggested parameter values. Note that the object classifying threshold, $T$, is data dependent.

## 6 RESULTS

The 3D GDM figures all present a GDM expanding within an object. The figures contain four frames. The first frame shows the initial model (upper-left). The second frame (upper-right) shows the model after several iterations. The third frame (lower-left) presents the GDM after an initial convergence to the shape of the

| 3D Parameters | | |
|---|---|---|
| Deformation Gain | $a_0$ | 1 |
| Image Event Gain | $a_1$ | 1 |
| Topological Gain | $a_2$ | 5 |
| Resampling Threshold | face area | 10 |

Table 2 3D Suggested Parameters

object. The final frame (lower-right) presents the final model. The final model was created by performing a global resampling on the GDM after the initial convergence to the shape of the object. The GDM was then allowed to converge to the shape of the object a second time.

### 6.1 CUBE

The first 3D example is an artificially generated cube with one of its corners removed (Figure 8). The voxels inside the cube were assigned one intensity while the voxels outside the cube were assigned a different intensity (creating a 64x64x64 volume). The initial model consisted of 20 triangles and the resampling algorithm added roughly 1000 triangles. A global resampling was then performed to increase the model quality. The final model contains 4080 triangles. The marching cubes model consists of 11528 triangles. Therefore, a substantial data reduction was achieved (1000 triangles vs. 11528 triangles) before the final global resampling was applied (1000 face model is in the lower-left of Figure 8). A moderate data reduction is achieved if a final global resampling is applied to the model after the initial convergence (4080 triangles vs 11528 triangles). The lower-right frame of Figure 8 shows the 4080 triangle GDM. The entire deformation required 50 iterations (approximately 15 minutes on an HP9000 835).

### 6.2 TURBINE BLADE

The next 3D GDM example is a cooling chamber of a turbine blade. The source of the data is 96 industrial CT slices (256 by 256). The data is very clean, and the resulting GDM is shown in Figure 9. This model consists of 6560 faces and required 100 deformation cycles (approximately 30 minutes on an HP9000 835). The marching cubes model for this object is composed of 19000 triangles.

### 6.3 TOOTH

The final 3D GDM is a model of the nerve in a tooth (Figure 10). The tooth was scanned using industrial CT (161 slices at 256 by 256 pixels). The initial model was placed in one of the roots of the nerve. This GDM illustrates that highly concave models can be created. The final model has remarkable detail and is composed of only 7392 faces while the marching cubes model for this object is composed of 20944 triangles.. This model required 200 deformation cycles (approximately 1.25 hours on an HP9000 835).

### 6.4 VERTEX GENERATION

Figure 11 shows a GDM where each vertex is assigned a scalar value based upon the generation (deformation cycle) of its creation. The red vertices were created early in the deformation,

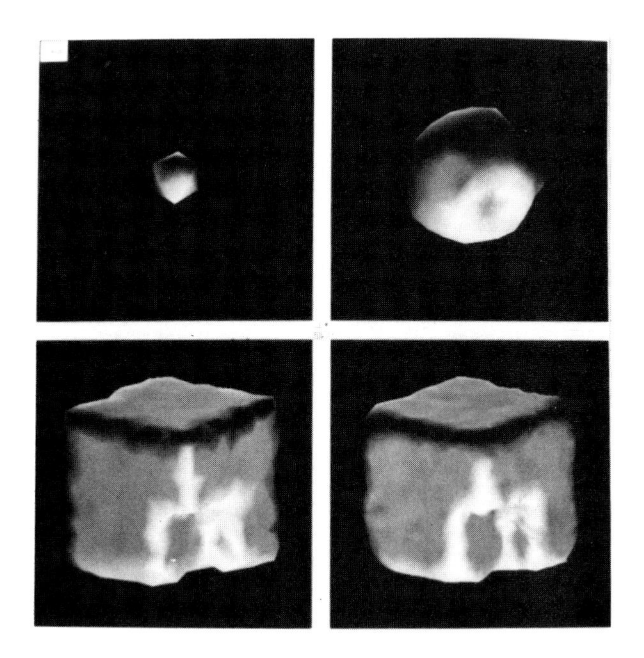

Figure 8 A 3D GDM expanding within a cube with a corner missing. The final model is composed of 4080 faces. Note that the corners and edges of the cube are rounded. The topology constraint lowered the spatial bandwidth of the model below the spatial bandwidth of the original data.

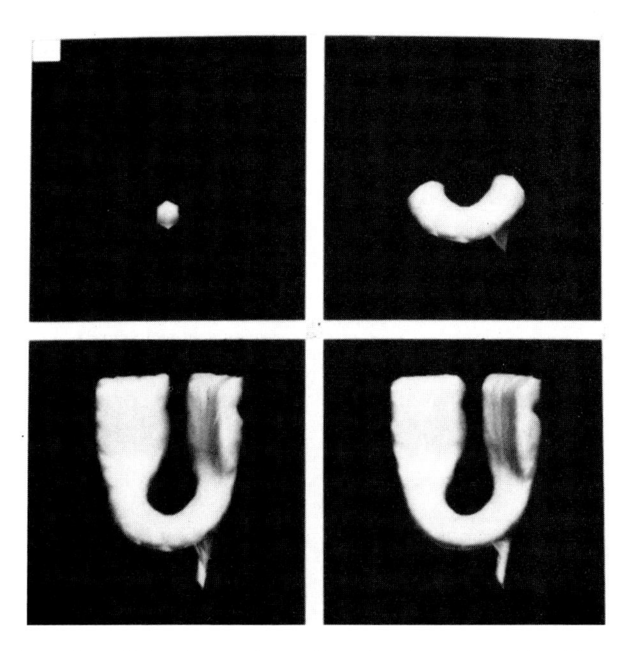

Figure 9 A 3D GDM of the cooling chamber in a turbine blade. The normal tracking deformation potential allows for the concave model to be extracted.

hence they are the oldest vertices. The yellow and green vertices were added later in the deformation process, hence they are progressively younger. Finally the blue vertices were added to the model as it approached its final orientation, hence they are the youngest of all. This illustrates how the vertices are added only in

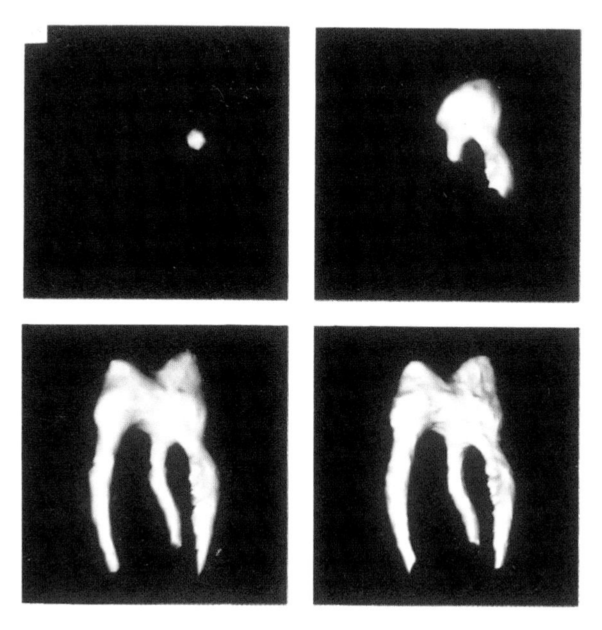

Figure 10 The nerve in a tooth is modelled through a highly concave GDM.

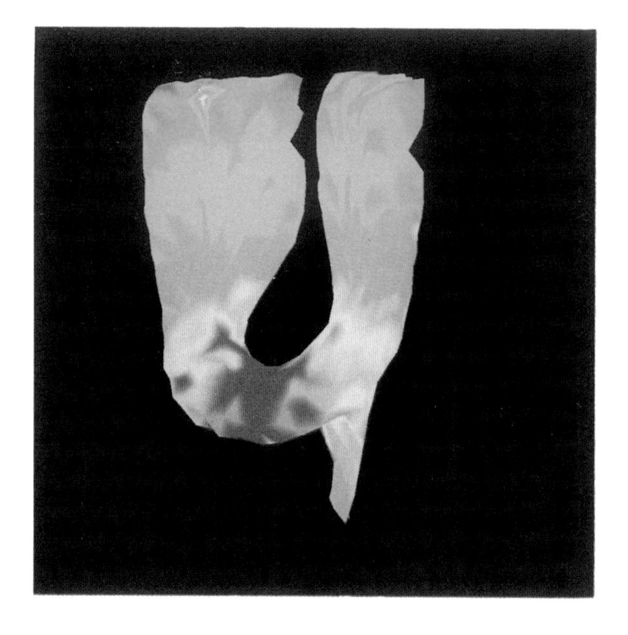

Figure 11 The GDM has its vertices colored based upon the generation which the vertex was created. This illustrates that model points are only added in the regions of the model still expanding.

the regions of the model that are still deforming. This emphasizes the importance of the proper selection of the initial location for the GDM. The GDM should be placed such that the model can deform across the maximum number of fronts. This figure also illustrates the locality of the resampling algorithm. Since vertices are only added in the region still deforming, the colored model has a series of "bands".

## 7 DISCUSSION

A GDM's performance can be measured by the quality of the final model and the amount of time required to generate the model. Several factors influence both of these measures. These include *a priori* information, the weights associated with the GDM constraints, global crossings, locality of measures, and precision.

*A priori* information about an object's geometry can be presented to a GDM in the form of its initial configuration. This information can influence the initial size and shape of the model. Our experiments show that the initial shape of the model does not affect the quality of the final GDM model. A simple convex model such as an icosahedron can be deformed to fit a topologically simple object with the same level of success as a more complicated initial model. The initial size of the model also has little effect on the quality of the final GDM. Both the size and shape of the model, however, may influence the time required to extract the final model. The closer the initial model is to the size and shape of the final model, the less time that is required to extract the GDM since the vertices of the GDM have less distance to travel in order to find the boundary of the object.

The parameters presented in Table 2 are for the most part data independent; however, a GDM's performance is greatly affected by their values. The weights were devised to compensate for any scale invariance in the constraint functions and to scale each constraint function to the same order of magnitude. If these weights are altered, one constraint function may dominate the deformation and result in a malformed GDM.

Since GDM's are currently ruled by local constraints, there is a possibility that the model will self-intersect. The GDM has no means of knowing that the model has self-intersected globally and will continue to deform. This can result in a model that continuously intersects itself. The probability for self-intersection can be minimized by presenting GDM's only with topologically simple objects to model. Unfortunately, even using topologically simple objects, self-intersection is possible. There exist topologically simple data sets that cause a GDM to fold into itself. Objects with components of high spatial frequency can cause such an occurrence.

GDM's are governed by local geometric operations. The size of the neighborhood used to calculate the geometric measures influences the GDM process. If the neighborhood is too large, the measure is not really local. If it is too small, the measure may not be accurate. The surface normal defines the deformation potential's influence on the deformation direction. Ideally, the surface normal can be calculated as the shared normal of all the incoming faces to that vertex; however, through experimentation it has been found that the GDM process is more stable when a larger neighborhood of faces is used to calculate the surface normal (a GDM is stable if global crossings do not occur). For instance, using the incoming faces and the faces adjacent to them provides the GDM with added stability; however, if this neighborhood is made too large, then the surface normal in not accurate and the added stability of a large neighborhood is lost.

The presentation thus far has hinted that a lack of precision may be the cause of a number of GDM idiosyncracies. The sensitivity of weights, global crossings in simple objects, and the surface normal stability are a function of precision. After all, the geometric measures are composed of a series of floating point operations. Each operation reduces the numerical precision. This can easily explain the global crossings in a simple object. An edge of a concavity can be smaller than the faces in the GDM. If new vertices are added in this region, imprecision may place them on different sides of the edge or perhaps within the other faces of the model. The surface normal can also be affected by a lack of precision. If the faces in the model are rather small, small errors in arithmetic can produce a large errors in the surface normal. Therefore the larger neighborhood is essentially performing a low pass filter on the surface normals in order to compensate for precision problems. Precision also limits the choice of initial models. For example, a 640 point geodesic approximation to a sphere of radius 1 created a very nonuniform model until the size of the model increased to a sphere of reasonable radius.

## 8 FUTURE WORK

The framework for GDM's is complete; however, there are a few ideas and concepts that could not be completely investigated. These concepts are secondary in nature, in that they are not essential to the theory or operation of a GDM, but they may improve performance or create additional applications. The current implementation of GDM's was established so that various ideas and geometrical relationships could be tested with relative ease. As such, the implementation is far from optimal. An alternative data structure that stores semi-permanent relations (information that is constant through a deformation iteration) could reduce the deformation time by an order of magnitude.

Future research efforts should concentrate on two basic areas: model quality and alternative data sets. Model quality may be improved by an alternative resampling algorithm and by preventing global crossings (model self-intersection). GDM's should also be extended to automatically handle data sets with multiple objects and to handle higher dimensional spaces, for instance time varying volumes.

## 9 CONCLUSION

A GDM extracts a closed topologically simple (non-self-intersecting) geometric model of an object located in a discrete or continuous data set. An initially closed model is embedded in the data set and deformed to fit the object through the minimization of a set of constraints. These constraints are local operations that quantify the deformation, the properties of simple polyhedra, and the relationship between object and not-object. The final model remains closed, because the initial model is closed and the constraints used to deform the model maintain the closed and locally simple nature.

The major benefit of GDM's is that they aggregate sampled data by placing geometrical relationships on the model, as opposed to interpreting and analyzing the sampled data directly. This allows the model to interact favorably with artifacts of noise that either remove portions of the boundary or insert false boundaries. GDM's are highly adaptive allowing for a generic initial convex model to be transformed into a highly concave object. Alternative initial models can be used that reduce the deformation time. GDM's explicitly handle the branching problem, multiple contours in one slice of a volume data set mapping into one contour in an adjacent slice, by treating a collection of 2D slices as a true 3D data set. Therefore, concavities in the direction normal to the slice plane are treated with the same mechanism as any other concavity in the data set. GDM's can use a local resampling algorithm to minimize the amount of work required to deform a model and to increase the model's quality. The level of detail can be set by the user, so quick estimates of an object can be generated and later refined for higher quality. GDM's provide a considerable data reduction in comparison to traditional techniques.

A GDM can be used for visualization, object recognition, geometric measurements, or subjected to a series of geometric operations. Applications abound in such fields as medicine, where GDM's could be used to generate models of internal organs; engineering, where GDM's could be used to model scanned mechanical parts or their faults; and science, where GDM's could be used to model higher dimensional spaces not accessible using traditional algorithms.

The computation to extract a model is proportional to the size and complexity of the object, not the size of the original data. GDM's are controlled through local geometric operations rather than the physical modelling of an elastic or plastic structure, hence the computations are much simpler. Finally, the dual GDM problem may be simpler to solve, resulting in a model of the same quality as the primal problem but with a much shorter deformation time.

## 10 ACKNOWLEDGMENTS

We would like to thank Prof. W. Randolph Franklin for his suggestions on the geodesic data structure and Dr. Donald House for his comments on this manuscript. This research was partially funded by General Electric Corporate Research and Development through the Rensselaer Design Research Center's Industrial Associates Program. The research was conducted at both GE CR&D and the RDRC.

## REFERENCES

[1] J. Serra. *Image Analysis and Mathematical Morphology Volume 1*. Academic Press, 1982.

[2] S.R. Sternberg. Grayscale morphology. *Computer Vision, Graphics, and Image Processing*, (35):333–355, 1986.

[3] R.A Drebin, L. Carpenter, and P. Hanrahan. Volume rendering. *Computer Graphics*, 22(4):65–74, 1988.

[4] E. Artzy, G. Frieder, and G. Herman. The theory, design, implementation, and evaluation of a three-dimensional surface detection algorithm. *Computer Graphics and Image Processing*, 15:1–24, 1980.

[5] W.C. Lin, S.Y. Chen, and C.T. Chen. A new surface interpolation technique for reconstructing 3d objects from serial cross-sections. *Computer Vision, Graphics, and Image Processing*, 48:124–143, 1989.

[6] H. Fuchs, Kedem Z.M., and Uselton S.P. Optimal surface reconstruction from planar contours. *Comm. ACM*, 20(10):693–702, 1977.

[7] W.E. Lorensen and H.E. Cline. Marching cubes: A high resolution 3d surface construction algorithm. *Computer Graphics*, 21(4):163–169, 1987.

[8] H.E. Cline, W.E. Lorensen, S. Ludke, Crawford C.R., and B.C. Teeter. Two algorithms for the three-dimensional reconstruction of tomograms. *Medical Physics*, 15(3):320–327, 1988.

[9] M. Kass, A. Witkin, and D. Terzopoulos. Snakes: Active contour models. *International Journal of Computer Vision*, pages 321–331, 1988.

[10] D. Terzopoulus, A. Witkin, and M. Kass. Symmetry-seeking models and 3d object reconstruction. *International Journal of Computer Vision*, 1(3):211–221, October 1987.

[11] J.V. Miller, D.E. Breen, and M.J. Wozny. Extracting geometric models through constraint minimization. *Visualization '90 Proceedings*, pages 74–82, 1990.

[12] R. Bajcsy and S. Kovačič. Multiresolution elastic matching. *Computer Vision, Graphics and Image Processing*, (46):1–21, 1989.

[13] A. Witkin, K. Fleischer, and A. Barr. Energy constraints on parameterized models. *Computer Graphics*, 21(4):225–232, July 1987.

[14] D.E. Breen. Choreographing goal-oriented motion using cost functions. *State–of–the–Art in Computer Animation (Computer Animation '89 Conference Proceedings)*, pages 141–151. eds N. Magnenat-Thalmann and D. Thalmann (Springer-Verlag, Tokyo, June 1989).

[15] D. Terzopoulos and K. Fleischer. Deformable models. *The Visual Computer*, 4:306–311, 1988.

[16] R.C. Gonzalez and P. Wintz. *Digital Image Processing*. Addison-Wesley, 1987.

[17] J.F. Canny. Finding edges and lines in images. Masters thesis, Massachusetts Institute of Technology, Cambridge, Massachusetts, June 1983.

[18] S. Kirkpatrick, C.D. Gelatt, and M.P. Vecchi. Optimization by simulated annealing. *Science*, 220(4598):671–680, 1983.

[19] M.J. Wennington. *Spherical Models*. Cambridge Univerity Press.

[20] J.V. Miller. On gdm's: Geometrically deformed models for the extraction of closed shapes from volume data. Masters thesis, Rensselaer Polytechnic Institute, Troy, New York, December 1990.

# Volumetric Shape Description of Range Data using "Blobby Model"

Shigeru Muraki

Electrotechnical Laboratory
Tsukuba, Ibaraki, 305 Japan

## Abstract

Recently in the field of computer vision, there have been many attempts to obtain a symbolic shape description of an object by fitting simple primitives to the range data of the object. In this paper, we introduce the "*Blobby Model*" for automatically generating a shape description from range data. This model can express a 3D surface as an isosurface of a scalar field which is produced by a number of field generating primitives. The fields from many primitives are blended with each other and can form a very complicated shape. To determine the number and distribution of primitives required to adequately represent a complex 3D surface, an energy function is minimized which measures the shape difference between the range data and the "*Blobby Model*". We start with a single primitive and introduce more primitives by splitting each primitive into two further primitives so as to reduce the energy value. In this manner, the shape of the 3D object is slowly recovered as the isosurface produced by many primitives. We have successfully applied this method to human face range data and typical results are shown. The method herein does not require any prior range segmentation.

**Keywords**: blobby model, generalized algebraic surface, implicit surface, volumetric shape description, range data analysis, energy minimization, ray tracing.



## 1 Introduction

In the field of computer vision, one of the most important problems is to obtain scene information from 2D images. The typical method is stereo matching which obtains the depth information from the disparity of the images of two cameras placed parallel. The recovered information from this method is often called a "$2\frac{1}{2}D$ *model*"[1], because it consists of depth data which is measured from a single direction and so it does not form a full 3D description of the object. There have been many attempts to fit 3D volumetric shape description models, such as superquadrics[2] to range data[3~8]. However, the shape primitive of these models is usually very simple and so one must combine many primitives in order to adequately express the shape of a complicated object. Then one needs to divide the range data into segments so each segment can be approximated by a single primitive. However, this *segmentation problem* is also a serious problem in the field of computer vision. Further, the connections between primitives are not smooth and it is difficult to express soft objects with smooth changing shapes. Hence, a 3D shape description model is needed that can express a smooth object with a small number of primitives which preferably avoids the segmentation problems.

In the field of computer graphics, modeling and rendering of 3D objects are both important problems. Regular shapes such as machine parts can be simply described. However, a large amount of numerical data is necessary to describe a smooth and soft object such as a human body. At present, designers obtain such descriptions by tedious manual methods. Recently, a new modeling method, which is called "*Blobby Model*"[9], has been used to describe smooth objects. This method expresses a surface of an object as an isosurface of a scalar field which is generated from field generating primitives. Since the shapes of the primitives are blended with each other, it is possible to express the surface of a complicated object with a small number of primitives. However, because of the fusion of the primitives, it is very difficult to design "*Blobby Models*" manually and so an automatic method of obtaining "*Blobby Models*" of 3D objects is desired.

In this paper we present a method for automatically generating a "*Blobby Model*" of a complex 3D object, given a set of range data. The $2\frac{1}{2}D$ *model* obtained by a computer vision technique can be precisely described with a set of blended shape primitives. If the number of primitives is small, then this method also becomes an efficient $2\frac{1}{2}D$ or 3D data compression method. Since the "*Blobby Model*" obtained by this method changes its form from a simple shape to a complicated shape as the number of primitives is increased, we don't need to segment the range data in advance. Further, the history of the changes of the shape show the hierarchical structure of the object and this may be used to further analyze the structure of the object. By adding different kinds of primitives, such as superquadrics, this method can be used as a general modeling tool for computer graphics. In the following section, the "*Blobby Model*" concept is explained and then our method for automatically fitting the model to a set of range data is presented in section 3. Experimental results for human face range data are shown in section 4.

## 2 Blobby Model

Blinn(1982) developed a generalized algebraic modeling method which is now called the "*Blobby Model*". This model can express a 3D object in terms of the isosurface of a scalar field which is generated from many field generating primitives[9]. The field value at any point $(x, y, z)$ created by a primitive $P_i$ at a point $(x_i, y_i, z_i)$, is expressed as follows.

$$V_i(x, y, z) = b_i exp\{-a_i f_i(x, y, z)\} \quad (1)$$

The function $f_i(x, y, z)$ defines the shape of the scalar field. For example, in the case of a spherically symmetric field, $f_i(x, y, z)$ is the square of the distance between $(x, y, z)$ and $(x_i, y_i, z_i)$

$$f_i(x, y, z) = (x - x_i)^2 + (y - y_i)^2 + (z - z_i)^2, \quad (2)$$

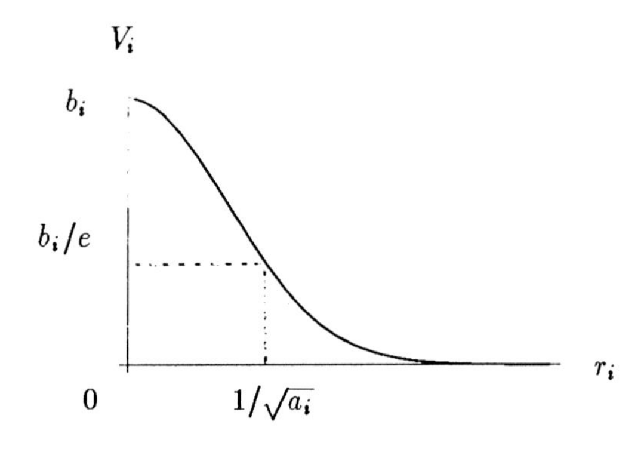


Figure 1: The decay of field value $V_i(x, y, z)$ according to the distance $r_i$ from the point $(x_i, y_i, z_i)$. Eq.(2) was used for the function $f_i(x, y, z)$ of Eq.(1).

and in the case of a superquadric[2] shaped field, it is written as

$$f_i(x, y, z) = \{(x - x_i)^{2/\nu_i} + (y - y_i)^{2/\nu_i}\}^{\nu_i/\mu_i} + (z - z_i)^{2/\mu_i}, \quad (3)$$

where $\mu_i$ and $\nu_i$ are the parameters related to the shape of the superquadrics. If Eq.(2) is used, the field value $V_i$ decays exponentially with the distance from $(x_i, y_i, z_i)$ as shown in Fig.1. Parameter $a_i(> 0)$ affects the degree of the decay and $b_i$ affects the strength of the field. If several primitives are used at once, then the scalar field from each primitive is summed and the resulting isosurface can show a very complicated shape. From Eq.(1) the field which is produced from $N$ primitives for any point $(x, y, z)$ is expressed as follows.

$$V(x, y, z) = \sum_{i=1}^{N} b_i exp\{-a_i f_i(x, y, z)\} \quad (4)$$

Consequently, the isosurface of value $T(> 0)$ is expressed as an implicit function:

$$V(x, y, z) = T. \quad (5)$$

If an attribute value is defined, such as the color component $C_i$, for each primitive, we can calculate the value for a point $(x, y, z)$ as follows:

$$C(x, y, z) = \frac{1}{V(x, y, z)} \sum_{i=1}^{N} C_i V_i(x, y, z). \quad (6)$$

If there is only one primitive, the primitive makes an isosurface of the function $f_i(x, y, z)$. Fig.2(a) shows

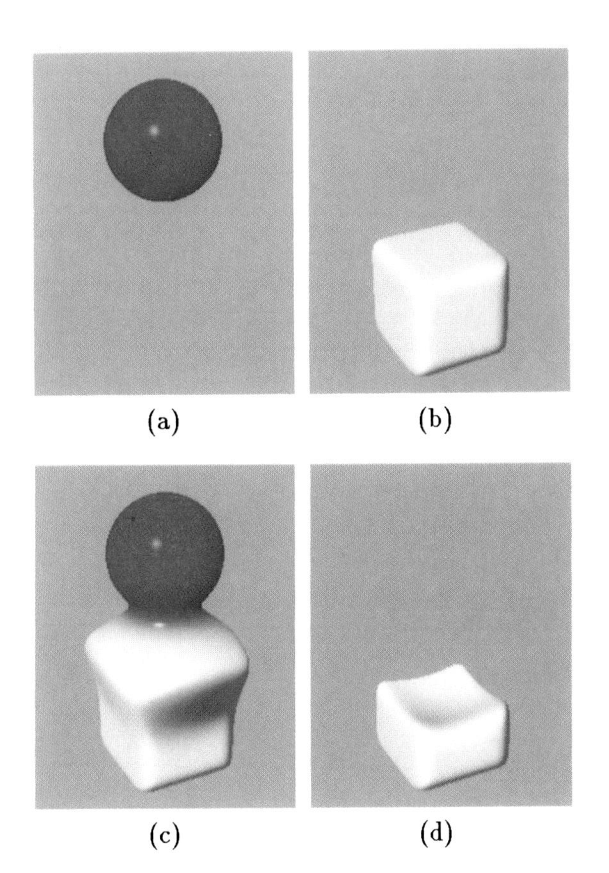

Figure 2: The features of "*Blobby Model*". The parameters for (a) are $a_i = 1.0$ and $b_i = 2.718$. The parameters for (b) are $\mu_i = \nu_i = 0.2$, $a_i = 0.001$ and $b_i = 1.001$.

the isosurface of a spherical field of Eq.(2) and Fig.2(b) shows the isosurface of a superquadric shaped field of Eq.(3). If there are more than two primitives, each primitive is blended and makes a different shape. Fig.2 (c) shows the blended shape of Fig.2(a) and (b). Another interesting feature of the "*Blobby Model*" is the effect of primitives which have a negative $b_i$ value. Since we have assumed that $T$ is positive, we never directly see this kind of primitive. However, such a primitive will form a concavity in any neighboring primitive. Fig.2(d) shows the blended isosurface of Fig.2(a) and (b) when the sign of $b_i$ of the primitive of Fig.2(b) was changed to a negative value. By changing $a_i$s and $b_i$s of Eq.(4), we can control the blending condition of the primitives.

Besides Blinn's "*Blobby Model*", there are similar methods such as "*Metaball*"[10] and "*Soft object*"[11]. These methods change the field function according to the distance from the primitive so that the effect of the field of the primitive is finite. Although this character makes it possible to neglect the effect of the outlying primitives, it creates a problem of necessitating a change in the energy function, which is defined in the next section, according to the distance from the primitives. In this paper, we only consider Blinn's "*Blobby Model*" and we use $f_i$ as defined in Eq.(2) in order to simplify the numerical calculations.

# 3 Fitting of "Blobby Model" to Range Data

## 3.1 Formulation of the Optimization Problem

Let us assume that the surface coordinates of $M$ points on the object are measured. If this object is approximated by an isosurface of a field value $T$, the potential value $V$ of a range data point $(x_j, y_j, z_j)$ should be close to $T$. Then the function

$$E_{value} = \sum_{j=1}^{M} \{V(x_j, y_j, z_j) - T\}^2 \qquad (7)$$

should be minimized. In other words, the most suitable set of primitives to approximate the range data is obtained by solving the minimization problem of Eq.(7). However, the "*Blobby Model*" has distinctions of both an inside and an outside surface and so the problem arises as to which side should be fitted to the range data. To avoid this problem, we consider the direction of the surface normals of the range data and the model. For the unit surface normal $\mathbf{n}_j$ of a range data point $j$, the normal vector which is calculated from the depth value of the neighboring pixels in the range data array can be used, as shown in Fig.3. The direction of the normal vector $\mathbf{N}(x, y, z)$ of the "*Blobby Model*" is defined so that it coincides with the negative direction of the gradient of the scalar field, which is represented as:

$$\mathbf{N}(x, y, z) = -\nabla V(x, y, z), \qquad (8)$$

where $\nabla$ is the vector operator,

$$\nabla = (\partial/\partial x, \partial/\partial y, \partial/\partial z). \qquad (9)$$

Therefore, the most suitable correction of primitives must minimize not only Eq.(7) but also the following function.

$$E_{normal} = \sum_{j=1}^{M} \left| \mathbf{n}_j - \frac{\mathbf{N}(x_j, y_j, z_j)}{|\mathbf{N}(x_j, y_j, z_j)|} \right|^2 \qquad (10)$$

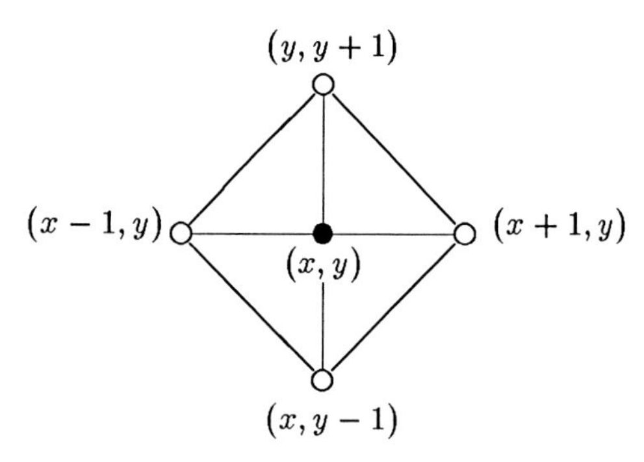


Figure 3: The surface normal vector of each pixel $(x, y)$ is calculated by averaging the normal vectors of the 4 triangles that consist of the pixel and its 4 neighbors.

However, if the range data forms a flat surface, the primitive which is placed infinitely far from the surface and has values $a_i = 0$ and $b_i = T$ exactly satisfies both Eq.(7) and (10). But the computed surface is not limited only to the vicinity of the range data points. Further, the constraints of Eq.(7) and (10) are defined only at range data points, and consequently there is no constraint on the shape forming primitive in the area where there is no range data. Therefore, there is a possibility that the primitive which fits to the range data makes strange shapes away from the vicinity of the range data points. To avoid these problems, a new constraint is added which minimizes the influence of the field of each primitive. From Eq.(1) and (2), the integration of the field of a primitive over 3D space can be expressed as,

$$\int_{-\infty}^{\infty}\int_{-\infty}^{\infty}\int_{-\infty}^{\infty} V_i(x,y,z)dxdydz = \left(\frac{\pi}{a_i}\right)^{\frac{3}{2}} b_i. \quad (11)$$

Considering the case where $b_i$ has a negative value, the new constraint is defined as follows:

$$E_{shrink} = \left(\sum_{i=1}^{N} {a_i}^{-\frac{3}{2}} |b_i|\right)^2. \quad (12)$$

This constraint has a shrinking effect on the primitives. Consequently, the desired arrangement of primitives can be obtained by minimizing the following energy function, which is the summation of Eq.(7),(10) and (12).

$$E = \frac{1}{M}(E_{value} + \alpha E_{normal}) + \beta E_{shrink} \quad (13)$$

Here $\alpha$ and $\beta$ are weighting parameters which control the strength of the surface normal constraint and the shrink constraint. By changing these values, we can change the behavior of the fitting to be suitable for the range data.

### 3.2 Procedure for "Blobby Model" Fitting

A set of $N$ primitives which minimizes Eq.(13) must be found. Since each primitive has five parameters, we must solve the minimization problem of Eq.(13) for $5N$ unknowns. The minimization of Eq.(13) is a nonlinear problem and cannot be solved by an analytical technique. A numerical method such as the Newton method could be used, but it would be extremely difficult to find all of the $5N$ unknowns simultaneously when $N$ is a large number. Our approach is to make an initial fit between a primitive and the range data, and then divide the primitive into two primitives so as to increase the goodness of fit. Continuing this division for all primitives, the detailed surface of the object can be expressed by the isosurface, which is generated by the primitives.

A 5D vector is used to express the parameters of a primitive $P_i$ as follows:

$$P_i = (x_i, y_i, z_i, a_i, b_i). \quad (14)$$

For the initial primitive $P_0$, the center of the mass of the range data is used for $(x_0, y_0, z_0)$, the reciprocal of the variance of the range data is used for $a_0$, and $b_0$ is set at the value $eT(e \simeq 2.718)$. The minimization problem of Eq.(13) is solved using these initial values and then the five parameters of $P_0$ are determined. A primitive list is created and the primitive $P_0$ is added to the list. Our method is based on the selection of a primitive $P_i$ from this list and its division into two new primitives. At this stage $P_0$ is the only primitive in the list and so $P_0$ is used as $P_i$. Then $P_i$ is deleted from the primitive list and two new primitives $P_i'$ and $P_i''$ are appended to the list instead. The initial parameter values of $P_i'$ and $P_i''$ are calculated as,

$$P_i' = P_i'' = (x_i, y_i, z_i, a_i, b_i/2). \quad (15)$$

We then solve the minimization problem of Eq.(13) for the 10 parameters of $P_i'$ and $P_i''$ and determine the parameter values. Now there are two primitives in the primitive list. After this the procedure that selects a primitive $P_i$ from the primitive list is repeated and then it is divided into two primitives while holding fixed the parameters of the other primitives in the list. Since the potential field of each primitive is blended,

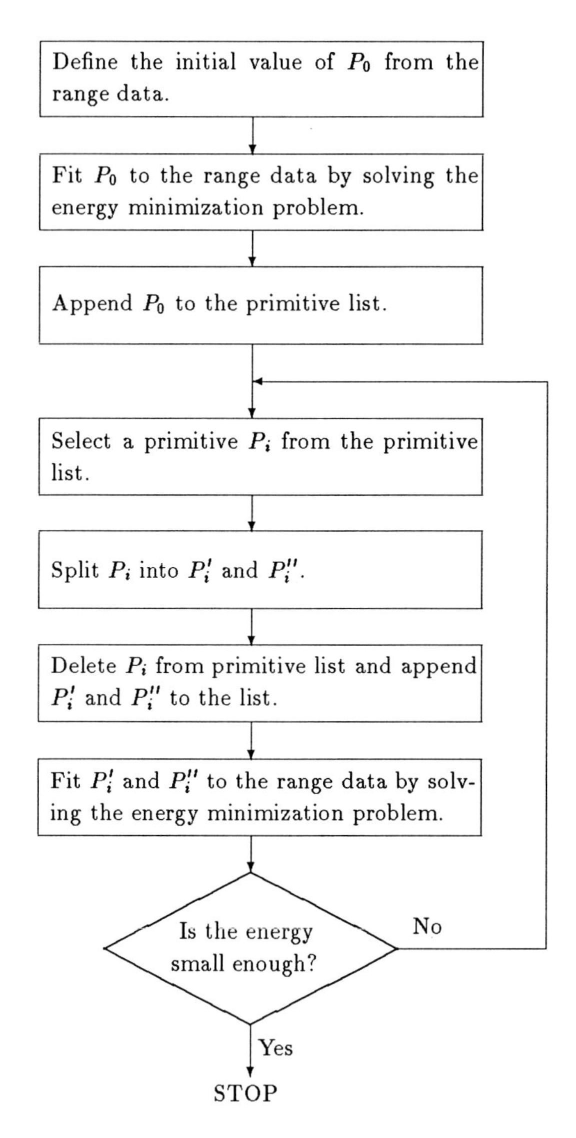


Figure 4: The flow chart of the "*Blobby Model*" fitting procedure.

the selection order of the primitives strongly influences the result of the minimization of Eq.(13). So it is best to choose the effective division in order to obtain a "*Blobby Model*" which preferably approximates the range data with a small number of primitives. To find this effective division, one must examine all of the primitives in the primitive list and determine how much the energy value is reduced by the division of the primitive, and then adopt the division which reduces the energy value the most. However this selection method consumes so much time, so other methods should be used when $N$ becomes a large number. In any case, by continuing this "selection and division" sequence until the energy value becomes sufficiently small, the "*Blobby Model*" gradually comes to approximate the range data as the number of primitives is increased. Fig.4 shows the flowchart of this procedure.

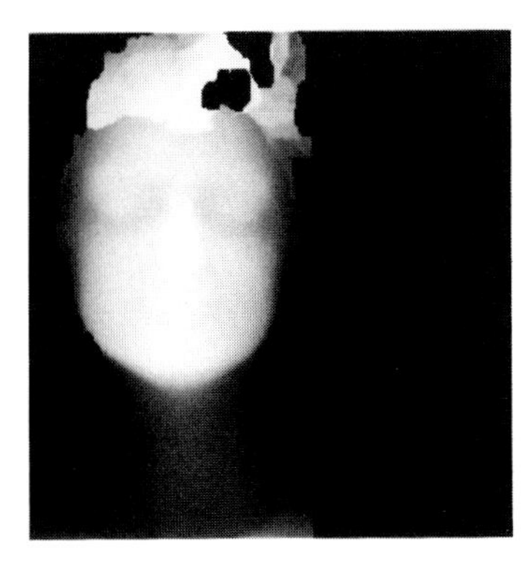

Figure 5: A range image of a human face distributed by NRCC (Face 5).

# 4 Experimental Results

## 4.1 Application to Human Face Range Image

We have applied our method to real range data. Fig.5 shows a human face range image (Face 5) distributed by the National Research Council Canada (NRCC) [12]. This image has 256×256 pixels. The depth values are expressed by the intensity of the pixels. The surface normal vector of each pixel is calculated by using the value of neighboring pixels as shown in Fig.3. In order to reduce the amount of calculation, the range image of Fig.5 is blurred by a Gaussian filter of $\sigma = 2$ and one value for every 3×3 pixels is used and 2893 points are obtained with a depth value and a unit normal vector. Then we calculate the parameters of the initial primitive and start the dividing sequence according to Fig.4. To solve the minimization problem of Eq.(13), an approximate solution is determined by using the downhill simplex method[13], which is used as the initial value of the quasi-Newton method[13]. The downhill simplex method is used initially to obtain a reasonable estimate of the unknowns. However, this method is slow. Consequently, the quasi-Newton method is then used, which is much faster, but it does need to have a reasonable estimate of the unknowns. The parameters we used were $\alpha = 1.0$, $\beta = 0.01$ and $T = 1$. Fig.6 shows the change of the "*Blobby Model*"

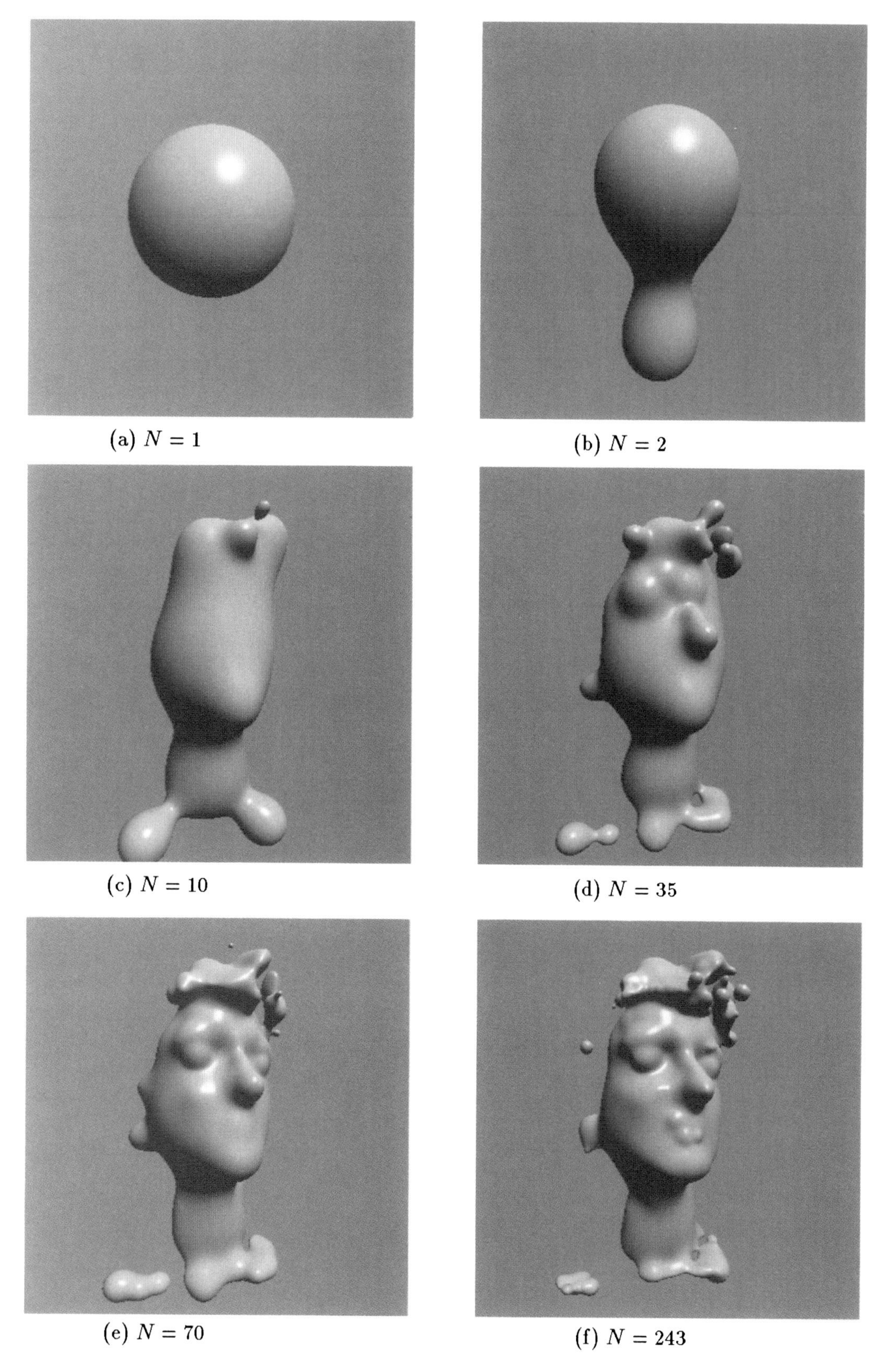

(a) $N = 1$

(b) $N = 2$

(c) $N = 10$

(d) $N = 35$

(e) $N = 70$

(f) $N = 243$

Figure 6: The transformation of "*Blobby Model*" with the number of primitives $N$ for NRCC range data (Face 5).

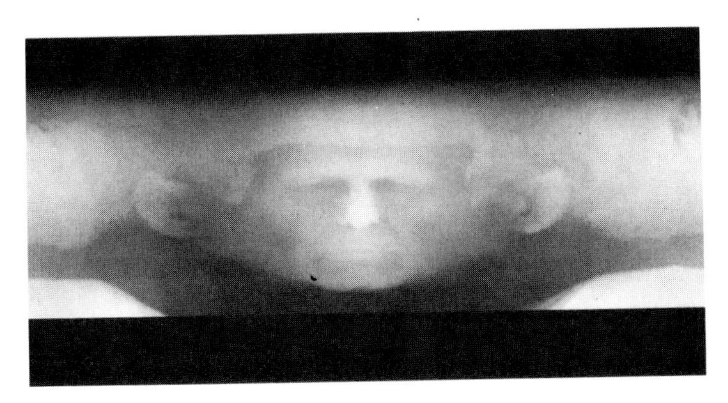

Figure 7: A panoramic range image of an actor's face.

with the number of primitives by using a ray tracing technique[14]. It is clearly seen that the detailed features of the face become more apparent as the number of primitives increases. By the image of Fig.6(e), the selection method of a primitive described in section 3.2 was used, however this method was too slow to continue, so we changed the selection method as to choose a primitive merely successively from the primitive list until we obtained Fig.6(f).

### 4.2 Application to Panoramic Human Face Range Image

Since the range image of Fig.5 has been taken from a single direction, it does not have any information from behind the head. Hence, from the effect of the shrinking constraint of Eq.(12), the resultant "*Blobby Model*" only represents the facial surface as shown in Fig.6. To obtain the whole shape of a 3D object, one must use multiple range images taken from many directions. Fig.7 is a panoramic range image of a movie actor which has been taken by a special range finder (Cyberware 4020/PS 3-D Digitizer). This image has 512×256 pixels. After we blurred this image by the same Gaussian filter as described in section 4.1, we used one value for every 4×4 pixels from the face area of Fig.7 and obtained 5334 points with a depth value and a normal vector. Fig.8 is the resultant "*Blobby Model*" from this data. In comparison to Fig.6, one can see that the entire shape of the head is correctly reconstructed. The parameters used were $\alpha = 0.1$, $\beta = 0.1$ and $T = 1$. As in Fig.6, we also changed the selection method of a primitive between Fig.8(e) and Fig.8(f).

## 5 Conclusions

We have proposed a method to obtain a volumetric shape description of range data by a "*Blobby Model*" and have successfully applied this method to human face range data. Sufficiently fine features of the faces were restored by using several hundreds of primitives. The history of the primitive division shows a quad tree structure and can be used for hierarchical analysis of an object. For example, one can use a color to represent a branch of the tree and see how the primitives in the branch work. Fig.9(a) shows a "*Blobby Model*" obtained in the experiment of section 4.1. This model consist of 11 primitives and we used red color for the primitive which formed the nose area of the face. Fig.9(b) is a "*Blobby Model*" which consists of 243 primitives. We used a red color for the 13 primitives generated by the division of the initial red primitive of Fig.9(a). Since the primitives are stored in a list structure, this kind of procedure is very simple. Fig.9(c) is the isosurface when these red primitives are removed from Fig.9(b). These pictures show that we can deal with the object structure *by parts* by using the list structure of the primitives of the "*Blobby Model*". In future work, we are going to apply this method to object recognition problems. We also intend to experiment using superquadrics as the primitive.

This method is computationally expensive. For the data of Fig.6(f), it took a few days on a UNIX workstation (Stardent TITAN3000 2CPU). To deal with larger range data sets, further improvement of the algorithm is necessary. The range data we used was obtained by using special devices. To apply this method to the problems of computer vision, one needs to use depth values obtained by stereo matching.

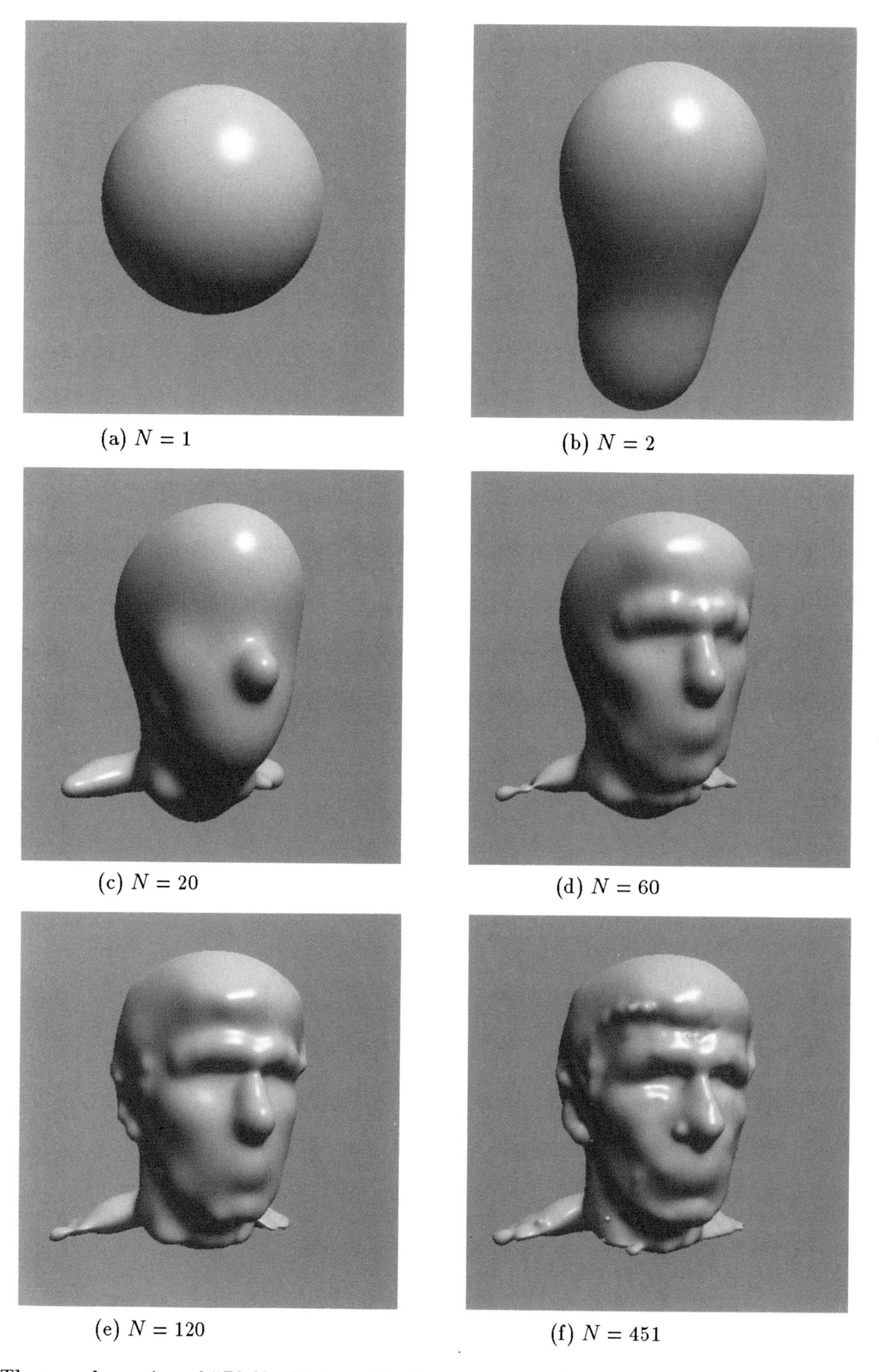

(a) $N = 1$ (b) $N = 2$

(c) $N = 20$ (d) $N = 60$

(e) $N = 120$ (f) $N = 451$

Figure 8: The transformation of "*Blobby Model*" with the number of primitives $N$ for Cyberware 4020/PS image.

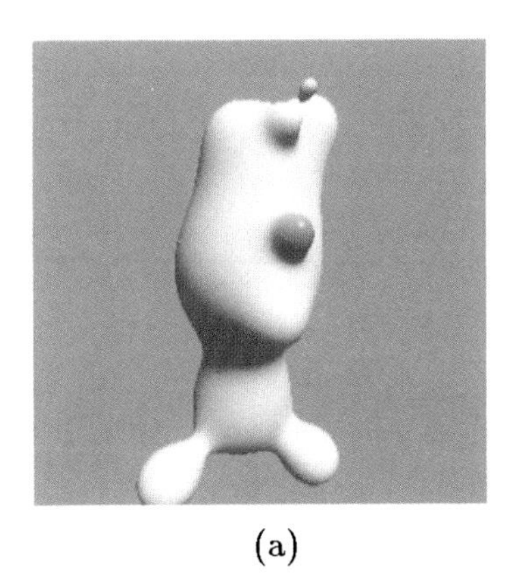

(a)

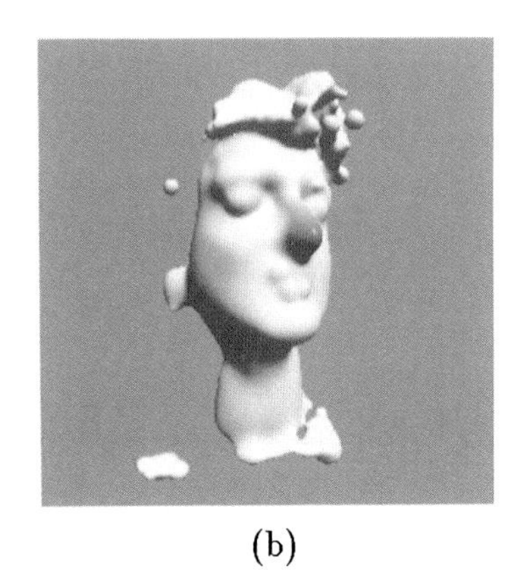

(b)

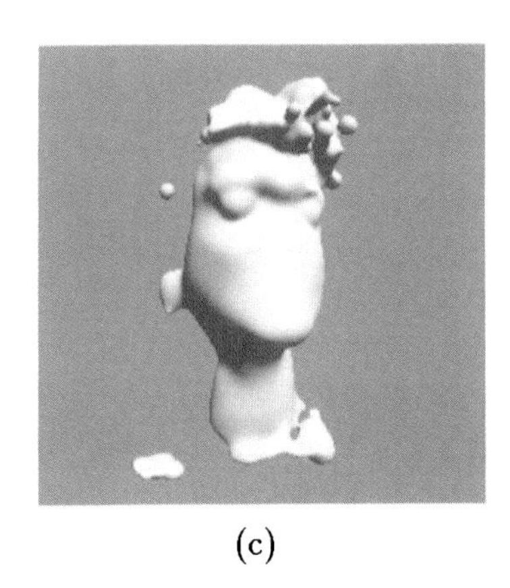

(c)

Figure 9: The structure analysis of a "*Blobby Model*".

## Acknowledgements

The author thanks Dr. Naokazu Yokoya for helpful discussions about optimization techniques. Special thanks are due to Gaile Gordon of Harvard University and Cyberware Laboratory in making arrangements to use their data. I also thank Richard Baldwin of the Polytechnic of East London and Lisa Bond of Tsukuba University for kindly reading the draft of this paper.

## References

[ 1] Marr, D.: "Vision", Freeman, San Francisco, 1982.

[ 2] Barr, A.H.: "Superquadrics and Angle-Preserving Transformations", *IEEE Computer Graphics and Applications*, Vol.1, No.1, pp.11-23, 1981.

[ 3] Kaneta, M., Yokoya, N. and Yamamoto, K.: "Recovery of Superquadric Primitives from Range images by Simulated Annealing",*SIG Notes of the Information Processing Society of Japan*, SIGCV 65-6, 1990. (in Japanese).

[ 4] Pentland, A.P.: "Recognition by Parts", *SRI International Technical Note*, No.406, 1986.

[ 5] Boult, T.E. and Gross, A.D.: "Recovery of Superquadrics from Depth Information", *Proc. of Workshop on Spatial Reasoning and Multi-Sensor Fusion*, pp.128-137, 1987.

[ 6] Horikosi, T. and Kasahara, H.: "A 3D Indexing Method for an Image Database", *Technical Report of the Institute of Electronics, Information and Communication Engineers of Japan*, IE88-111, pp.33-40, 1988. (in Japanese).

[ 7] Solina, F. and Bajcsy, R.: "Recovery of Parametric Models from Range Images: The Case for Superquadrics with Global Deformations", *IEEE Trans. PAMI*, Vol.12, No.2, pp.131-147, 1990.

[ 8] Ferrie, F.P., Lagarde,J. and Whaite, P.: "Recovery of Volumetric Object Descriptions From Laser Rangefinder Images", *Proc. of ECCV 90*, pp.387-396, 1990.

[ 9] Blinn, J.F.: "A Generalization of Algebraic Surface Drawing", *ACM Trans. on Graphics*, Vol.1, No.3, pp.235-256, 1982.

[10] Nishimura, H., Hirai, M., Kawai, T., Kawata, T., Shirakawa, I. and Omura, K."Object Modeling by Distribution Function and a Method of Image Generation", *Trans. IEICE Japan*, Vol.J68-D, No.4, pp.718-725, 1985. (in Japanese).

[11] Wyvill, G., McPheeters, C. and Wyvill, B.:"Data Structure for Soft Objects", *The Visual Computer*, Vol.2, pp.227-234, 1986.

[12] Rioux, M. and Cournoyer, L.: "The NRCC Three-dimensional Image Data Files", *Thec. Report, CNRC* 29077, National Research Council Canada, Ottawa, Canada, 1988.

[13] Press, W.H., Flannery, B.P., Teukolsky, S.A. and Vetterling, W.T.: "Numerical Recipes in C", *Cambridge*, 1988.

[14] Kalra, D. and Barr, A.H.: "Guaranteed Ray Intersections with Implicit Surfaces", *Computer Graphics (SIGGRAPH '89 Proceedings)*, Vol.23, No.3, pp. 297-306, 1989.

# Piecewise Surface Flattening for Non-Distorted Texture Mapping

Chakib Bennis * Jean-Marc Vézien Gérard Iglésias †

INRIA
BP. 105, 78153 Le Chesnay cedex France

**Abstract**

This paper introduces new techniques for interactive piecewise flattening of parametric 3-D surfaces, leading to a non-distorted, hence realistic, texture mapping. Cuts are allowed on the mapped texture and we make a compromise between discontinuities and distortions. These techniques are based on results from differential geometry, more precisely on the notion of "**geodesic curvature**": isoparametric curves of the surface are mapped, in a constructive way, onto curves in the texture plane with preservation of geodesic curvature at each point. As an application, we give a concrete example which is a first step towards an efficient and robust CAD tool for shoe modeling.

**CR Categories and Subject Descriptors:** I.33 [Computer Graphics]: Picture/Image Generation; I.4.3 [Image Processing]: Enhancement-Geometric Correction, Texture.
**Additional Keywords and Phrases:** Non Distorted Texture Mapping, Piecewise Surface Flattening, Differential Geometry, Geodesic Curvature.

## 1 Introduction

Texture mapping techniques are widely used to reproduce textural information available in a planar image onto a 3-D surface. This is made possible by making a correspondence between a planar image and a 3-D surface, in order to give each sample point of the output screen reached by the projected 3-D surface an intensity value computed from a point or a set of points of the 2-D image sample. This correspondence is called the "mapping function".

Catmull [8] first introduced a recursive subdivision algorithm to map a 2-D rectangular image onto a 3-D bicubic patch. This method has been refined and enhanced by several authors [9, 6]. These techniques are equivalent to warping the planar rectangle until it takes the shape of the bicubic patch. Unfortunately, these techniques do not preserve distances or angles, resulting in spatial distortions of texture patterns, which can sometimes change the visual appearance of the texture on the surface. Other authors have proposed solutions to reduce these distortions. Bier et al. [5] proposed a 2-part mapping which consists in decomposing the mapping in two steps: the texture pattern is first embedded in a 3-D intermediate surface and then projected onto the target surface in a way that depends only on the geometry of the target object. The distortion is reduced by heuristically choosing the appropriate intermediate surface and the projection method. Unfortunately this is not always easy to do. Fiume et al. [13] have proposed a "polygonal conformal mapping" to map a polygon (e.g., a square) onto an arbitrary convex polygon with preservation of angles. This technique gives good results on polygons for some applications. However, the technique does not preserve distances, thus creating distortions. Moreover, it is not easily extendable to free form surfaces. In [17], Ma et al. used an optimization technique to minimize distortions for general surfaces. The mapping is performed on a grid of sample points of the 3-D surface. Starting from an arbitrary initial mapping, the algorithm converges to the optimal mapping by minimizing a global metric taking into account distances between each point and its direct neighbours on the 3-D grid. A similar technique was proposed at the same time by Schwartz et al. [11] for general surface flattening. Since most surfaces are not developable (i.e. unfolded without deformations or cuts, think of a sphere), distortions still remain. Moreover, optimization techniques offer no control on the distribution of the remaining distortions.

A non-distorted mapping of a planar texture onto a 3-D surface is equivalent to a non-warped flattening of the surface. As it is well known, fully spreading out a non-developable surface would induce distortions. The basic idea of this work is to permit discontinuities on the mapped texture and to make a compromise between cuts and distortions. The cuts here play the role of seam lines (such as on a cloth). The surface is first piecewise flattened (with different maps in the plane), then texture is computed on the surface using the flattened parts. This could have many applications in different fields, varying from graphics concerning non-distorted texture mapping, to cartography and manufacturing (cloth modeling) for piecewise flattening. The example emphasised here is a first step towards an efficient and robust CAD tool for shoe modeling.

This paper introduces new techniques for interactive piecewise flattening of parametric 3-D surfaces, leading to a non-distorted texture mapping. The flattening of a region grows around an isoparametric curve selected by hand. A distortion metric is introduced to control and stop the growth when the accumulated distortion exceeds a previously determined threshold. The flattening methods are based on results from differential geometry ([7] [12]), more precisely on the notion of "**geodesic curvature**": isoparametric curves of the surface are mapped in a constructive way onto curves in the texture plane, with preservation of geodesic curvature at each point.

The next section gives the outlines of the global texture mapping approach. This section also reviews our previous work [3] on revolution surface flattening. In section 3, concepts from differential geometry (geodesic curvature) are introduced and utilized to straightforwardly extend the previous work to more general surfaces. A more robust technique (based on a relaxation procedure)

*Current address: Institut Français du Pétrole 1 et 4 avenue du Bois-Préau 92506 Rueil-Malmaison.

†Current address: Sociéte Stratégies, 41-43 rue de Villeneuve -Silic 429- 94583 Rungis France.



©1991 ACM-0-89791-436-8/91/007/0237 $00.75

is proposed in section 4. All these techniques are compared on well known examples: a cone and a hemisphere. Section 5 presents an application to shoe modeling. The paper concludes with a discussion of the limitations of the proposed techniques and with some suggestions for future developments.

# 2 General considerations and previous work

The surfaces considered here are given by a piecewise parametric representation:

$$\begin{cases} X &= x(u,v) \\ Y &= y(u,v) \\ Z &= z(u,v) \end{cases}$$

We require the surfaces to be $C^2$ (to have continuous second order derivatives at each point), especially on the joining curves (the reason for this constraint is explained later). Moreover, the two families of isoparametric lines must be nowhere tangent to each other (i.e. a normal and a tangent plane exist at every point).
The surface is first regularly sampled into a grid of 3-D points, along the isoparametrics (in parameters space). Moreover, the sampling must be refined enough to approximate the arc length between two successive sample points along an isoparametric by their euclidian distance. In the following, sample curves along $u$ and $v$ directions are respectively denoted $C_{.j}$ ($v = v_j$) and $C_{i.}$ ($u = u_i$). We note the points of the 3-D grid $M_{ij}$, and their correspondents in the flattening plane[1] $P_{ij}$. The euclidian distance between two points $M_1$ and $M_2$ is loosely denoted $d(M_1, M_2)$ or $||M_2 - M_1||$.

## 2.1 Outlines of the general approach

The texture mapping algorithm can be divided into two main steps:

I) An initial chord curve (a portion of an isoparametric) is first selected on the grid and the surface is unfolded around this curve until a preliminarily fixed distortion threshold is reached. The same process is repeated on the unprocessed region of the grid until all the surface, or an interesting part of it, is covered.

II) The processed regions of the grid are then triangulated, and a locally affine interpolation, affine in each triangle, is used to texture them.

Step I) constitutes the piecewise flattening part of the algorithm. More precisely, for each presented flattening technique, an appropriate distortion metric is defined. The initial curve is chosen by hand depending on where the texture is desired to be the less distorted. This curve divides the surface into two sub-regions, e.g. "left" and "right". Let the curve be $C_{i_0.}$, where $v_{j_1} < v < v_{j_2}\}$. Unfolding the surface around this curve is done in three steps:

1. Develop the initial curve: find for each sample point $M_{i_0j}$ of this curve a corresponding point $P_{i_0j}$ in the flattening plane (e.g., a texture plane).
2. develop the surface on the left side of the initial curve: fix a left side threshold, then develop successively curves $\{C_{i.},\ i < i_0, v_{j_1} < v < v_{j_2}\}$ (parallel to the initial one) until the provided distortion exceeds the left side threshold, or the current curve belongs to an already developed region.
3. Develop the surface on the right side of the initial curve using a right side threshold (the same as the leftside development but developed curves are $\{C_{i.},\ i > i_0, v_{j_1} < v < v_{j_2}\}$)

Step II) constitutes the texturing part: the triangulation of a processed region is obtained by splitting each quad $\{M_{i-1j-1}, M_{i-1j}, M_{ij-1}, M_{ij}\}$, of four neighbouring sample points, into two triangles $\{M_{i-1j-1}, M_{ij-1}, M_{i-1j}\}$ and $\{M_{i-1j}, M_{ij-1}, M_{ij}\}$. This gives rise to two triangles in the texture plane, $\{P_{i-1j-1}, P_{ij-1}, P_{i-1j}\}$ and $\{P_{i-1j}, P_{ij-1}, P_{ij}\}$, where the $P_{kl}$ are the corresponding points of the $M_{kl}$ and have already been obtained with the flattening process. The 3-D triangular faces are projected onto the output screen. A triangle-to-triangle affine interpolation from the texture plane to the output screen is used to compute the texture value at each pixel of the output screen. A Z-buffer is used for hidden surface parts elimination and a prefiltered summed table [10] is used for antialiasing. The locally affine approximation of the mapping function is well explained in [4], and compared with the approximation proposed by Oka. and al. in [18] (see [4] for more details). Local affine approximations to a mapping are also discussed in [14].
From now on we will emphasize the geometrical aspect of the non distorted piecewise flattening.

[1] For the texture mapping application the flattening plane is considered to be the texture space.

## 2.2 Previous work

In [3] we have proposed a piecewise flattening technique for surfaces of revolution. The outline of the algorithm is:

1. Map an initial meridian $C_{i_0.}$ of the surface onto a straight line $D_{i_0.}$ in the plane with distance preservation between sample points. *One has only to fix a correspondence for a starting point and a direction for the straight line. Obtaining the other correspondences is immediate.*
2. Extend the development step by step around $C_{i_0.}$ (at each step a meridian $C_{i.}$ is reached) while mapping parallels onto straight lines orthogonal to $D_{i_0.}$ with distance preservation between sample points, until the distortion threshold is reached. (see Figure 1).

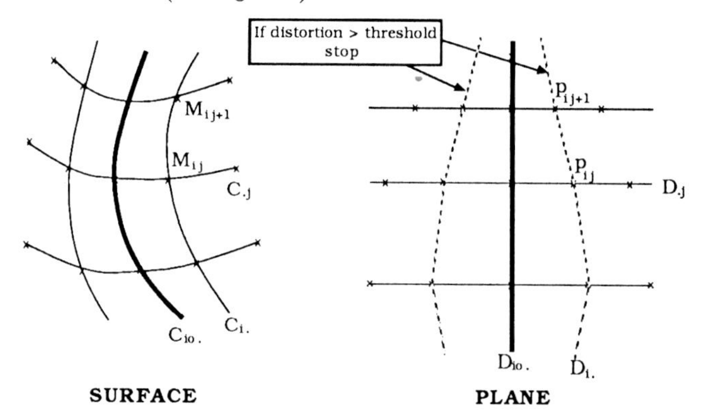


Figure 1: Previous flattening of surfaces of revolution.

This method preserves distances on the initial meridian $C_{i_0.}$ and on parallels $C_{.j}$ but not on the other meridians $C_{i.}$ (unless the surface is a cylinder). Moreover, we preserve the cross angles between $C_{i_0.}$ and $C_{.j}$. Distance distortion on meridians and cross angle distortion (between the two families of curves) increase as one gets far from the first meridian. All distortions are concentrated on meridians $C_{i.}$, $i \neq i_0$, so we choose as a distortion metric for each successive curve $C_{i.}$, the mean of the errors induced on its chord segments:

$$Cr(C_{i.}) = \frac{1}{N-1} \sum_{j=0}^{N-1} \frac{|\, d(M_{ij}, M_{ij+1}) - d(P_{ij}, P_{ij+1}) \,|}{d(M_{ij}, M_{ij+1})} \quad (1)$$

Here, $N$ is the number of sample points of $C_{i.}$, and $P_{kl}$ are the corresponding texture points of 3-D points $M_{kl}$. Note that here, due to revolution symmetry, one has only one threshold for both leftside and rightside development.
Figure 2 shows the development of a cone and a hemisphere with this technique. We have developed them entirely, onto only one piece, to emphasize the nature of distortions. Note that there are fewer distortions than with Catmull's technique ([8]) where both surfaces would be mapped onto a rectangle. Moreover, we find

for the hemisphere the well known Sanson's projection (pseudo-cylindric projection) used in cartography.
Although the cone is a developable surface, the algorithm of [3] does not give its proper development. However, this technique gives satisfying results if we develop the surface into sufficiently small pieces, because the meridians of a surface of revolution are geodesics (they have at any point a zero curvature with respect to the surface) so they are equivalent to straight lines in the plane. One possible enhancement and extension of the algorithm of [3]

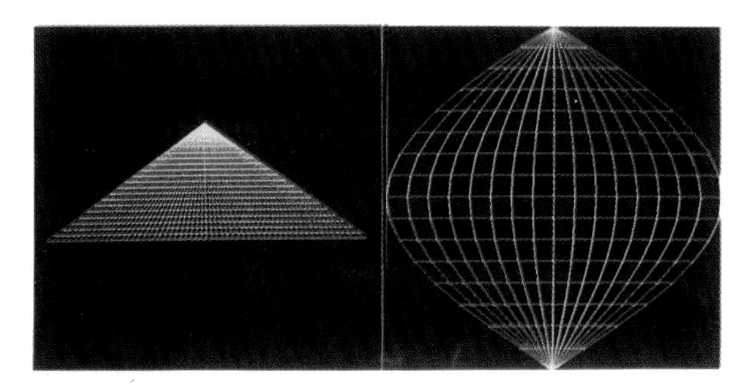

Figure 2: Cone and hemisphere flattening.

to more general surfaces (see Figure 3) consists in computing the geodesic $G_1$ joining two extremal points of an initial curve and mapping it onto a straight line $D_1$ in the plane (with distance preservation). Then, for any other point $M_{ij}$, compute the shortest geodesic $G$ starting from $G_1$ and joining $M_{ij}$. Let $M$ be the intersection point of $G$ and $G_1$. The planar correspondent $P$ of $M$ is obtained by preserving the distance between $M$ and $M_2$ ($d(M, M_2)$=$d(P, P_2)$). $P_{ij}$ is then given by drawing a straight line $D$ orthogonal to $D_1$ and by preserving the distance between $M$ and $M_{ij}$ ($d(M, M_{ij})$= $d(P, P_{ij})$).

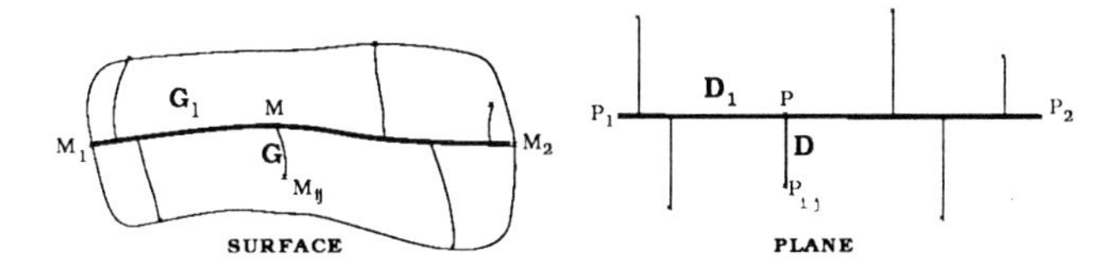


Figure 3: A possible extension using geodesics.

Geodesics on a 3D surface are very attractive because they behave much like straight lines on the plane. Unfortunately, although this class of curves has long been studied in differential geometry [7] and are now well known, their characterization is rather local. Given a curve drawn on a 3-D surface one can determine whether or not it is a geodesic at a given point. The entire curve is then a geodesic if it is geodesic at each point. But what we need here is the inverse problem: find a curve on a surface which is a geodesic between two given surface points. This problem is very difficult because we have to make a global numerical computation using local properties.
Numerical approximations of computation of geodesics proposed up to now [16, 1] are very slow. In addition, they do not always give good results.
In the next section we give an almost equivalent extension avoiding geodesic computation.

# 3 Geodesic curvature preservation flattening

Instead of mapping onto the plane unknown (and difficult to compute) curves of the surfaces such as geodesics, we use already available isoparametric curves and take into account their topological properties in the mapping process. The main idea of the proposed technique is to map isoparametric curves of the surface onto curves of the plane, with geodesic curvature preservation at sample points and with arc length (i.e. chord length) preservation.
We will first recall some results from the differential geometry of curves in order to define the notion of geodesic curvature, then outline the new general flattening algorithm, and finally give a numerical and constructive algorithm for mapping curves of a surface onto curves of a plane with geodesic curvature and arc length preservation.

## 3.1 Local properties of curves and surface curves: short review

The results in differential geometry that we use may be found in [7] and [12], both excellent references.
Let $C$ be a curve in $R^3$ given by arc length parametrization:

$$X(s) = \begin{bmatrix} x(s) \\ y(s) \\ z(s) \end{bmatrix}, s \in [0, a] \subset R,$$

where the Cartesian coordinates $x(s), y(s)$ and $z(s)$ of each point $X$ of $C$, are differentiable functions of arc length $s$ (the length of $C$ from $X(0)$ to $X(s)$).
To study the local behavior of a curve, a fundamental concept in differential geometry is to use a local frame and to express its local change in its own coordinate system. The Frenet local frame $(X, \mathbf{t}, \mathbf{m}, \mathbf{b})$ is a good candidate for this purpose (see Figure 4). The origin of the frame is point $X$ around which one would like to study the local behavior of the curve. Axes $(\mathbf{t}, \mathbf{m}, \mathbf{b})$ are given by the formulas:

- $\mathbf{t} = X' = \frac{dX}{ds}$
- $\mathbf{m} = \frac{X''}{\|X''\|}$
- $\mathbf{b} = \mathbf{t} \wedge \mathbf{m}$,

where primes denote derivatives with respect to arc length and $\wedge$ denotes the cross product. $\mathbf{t}(s)$ is the *tangent* vector, $\mathbf{m}(s)$ is called *main normal vector* and $\mathbf{b}(s)$ is called *binormal* vector at $s$. The plane $O(s)$ generated by $\mathbf{t}(s)$ and $\mathbf{m}(s)$ is called the *osculating* plane at $s$; it is the plane which contains the curve around $X(s)$. One can easily show that variation of the Frenet frame can be

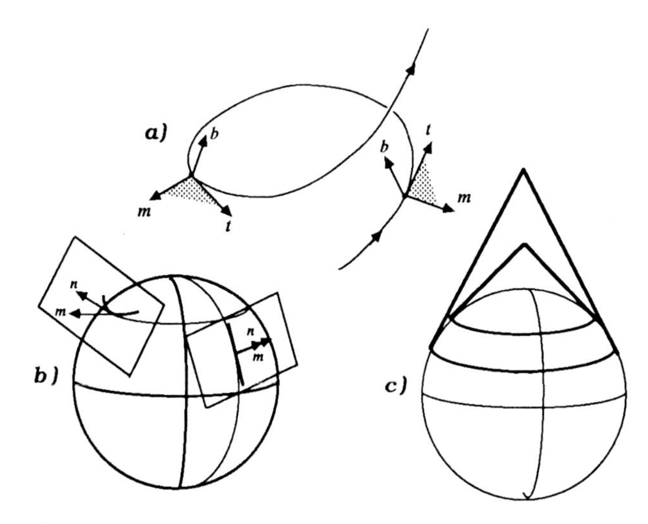


Figure 4: a): Frenet frame variation along a curve, b): Local behavior of a sphere circle, c): cones parallel to a sphere along circles.

expressed through the following formulas:

$$\begin{cases} \mathbf{t}' &= k\mathbf{m} \\ \mathbf{m}' &= -k\mathbf{t} - \tau\mathbf{b} \\ \mathbf{b}' &= \tau\mathbf{m} \end{cases}$$

The variables $|k(s)|=||\mathbf{t}'(s)||$ and $|\tau(s)|=||\mathbf{b}'||$ are called respectively *main curvature* and *torsion* at $s$. Curvature and torsion have an intuitive geometric meaning: let $d\alpha(s)$ and $d\theta(s)$ be respectively the angle between $\mathbf{t}(s)$ and $\mathbf{t}(s+ds)$ and the angle between $\mathbf{b}(s)$ and $\mathbf{b}(s+ds)$, at "consecutive" points $X(s)$ and $X(s+ds)$. Then:

$$|k| = ||\frac{d\alpha}{ds}||, \ |\tau| = ||\frac{d\theta}{ds}||.$$

In other words $k$ and $\tau$ are the angular velocities of the tangent and the osculating plane, respectively, as the frame is moved along the curve with $s$ playing the role of "time".
Moreover, these two variables are independent of parametrization. When $k$ is zero everywhere the curve is a straight line, and when $\tau$ is zero everywhere the curve is planar.
Now, consider a surface $S$ given by a parametric function from $R^2$ to $R^3$:

$$X(u,v) = \begin{bmatrix} x(u,v) \\ y(u,v) \\ z(u,v) \end{bmatrix}, (u,v) \in [a,b] \times [a,b] \subset R^2,$$

where the Cartesian coordinates $x, y, z$ of a surface point are differentiable functions of $u$ and $v$. Let us suppose in addition, that the isoparametric lines are nowhere tangent to each other:

$$N(u,v) = X_u \wedge X_v \neq 0 \ \forall u,v \in [a,b]$$

where $X_u$ an $X_v$ are first derivatives vectors according to $u$ parameter and $v$ parameter respectively.
The vector $\mathbf{n}=\frac{N}{||N||}$ is called the *normal vector* to $S$ at point $X(u,v)$.
The plane $\mathbf{Tp}$ spanned by the set of points $Y$ such that:

$$(X - Y).\mathbf{n} = 0,$$

(where dot denotes the scalar product of vectors) is called the *tangent plane* to surface $S$ at point $X$.
Let $C_S$ be a curve belonging to surface $S$ and given by arc length parametric function $X(s)$. Recall that the curvature is defined by the acceleration $\mathbf{t}'=k\mathbf{m}$ of $C_S$. This vector can be expressed with two components where the one, $\mathbf{t}'_g$, is tangent to the surface and the other, $\mathbf{t}'_n$, is normal to the surface:

$$\begin{aligned} \mathbf{t}' &= \mathbf{t}'_g + \mathbf{t}'_n \\ \mathbf{t}'_n &= (\mathbf{t}'.\mathbf{n})\mathbf{n} \end{aligned}$$

Seen from a view-point linked to the surface, the acceleration $\mathbf{t}'$ is reduced to tangential component $\mathbf{t}'_g$.
**Definition** : The *geodesic curvature* $k_g$ of a curve $C_S$ belonging to a surface $S$, at a point $X$, is the norm of tangential acceleration[2] of $C_S$ at $X$ according to arc length parameter:

$$|k_g| = ||\mathbf{t}'_g||.$$

$k_g$ corresponds to the curvature of $C_S$ seen from a view-point attached to the surface $S$. It is different from main curvature $k$ ($k_g$ could be null while $k$ is not null).
$C_S$ is said to be *geodesic at a point* $X$ if and only if $k_g$ is nil at $X$ and $C_S$ is called a geodesic if it is geodesic at every point. One necessary and sufficient condition for $C_S$ to be geodesic at point $X$ is that the main normal vector $\mathbf{m}$ of curve $C_S$ at $X$ is parallel to the normal vector $\mathbf{n}$ to surface $S$ at $X$.
At any point $X$ the local projection of a curve $C_S$ on the tangent plane along the normal vector to the surface $S$ provides a straight line if $C_S$ is a geodesic, and non-zero curvature (at $X$) on the planar curve otherwise. Figure 4 shows the behavior of circles of a sphere: a circle is a geodesic if and only if it is a great circle.
**Lemma:** The *Geodesic curvature $k_g$ of a curve $C_S$ belonging to a surface $S$ at a point $X$ is equal to curvature at $X$ of the planar curve $C_{T_p}$ obtained by locally projecting $C_S$ onto the tangent plane ($\mathbf{Tp}$) along the normal vector to surface $S$ at point $X$.*
As for main curvature, intuitively geodesic curvature $k_g(s)$, at a point $X(s)$, is the angular velocity of tangents to the **resulting projected** curve $C_{T_p}(s)$ according to arc length $s$.
This Lemma leads us to an efficient and constructive numerical way of mapping a chord line of a surface onto a chord line in a plane with preservation of chord length and geodesic curvature. This is the basis of the new flattening algorithm described below.

[2]That is the reason why we require a surface to be $C^2$.

## 3.2 Outline of the new general algorithm

The new algorithm runs as follows (see Figure 5):

1. Map the initial selected curve $C_{i_0.}$ of the surface (for instance $\{u = u_{i_0}, \ j_1 \leq j \leq j_2\}$) onto a curve in the plane with geodesic curvature preservation at sample points and with arc length preservation (*distance preservation between any pair of successive sample points*).
2. Extend step by step the development on the left side of $C_{i_0.}$. At each step one reaches a curve $C_{i.}$, $(i < i_0)$ while mapping transversal curves $C_{.j}$ $(\{v = v_j, \ j_1 \leq j \leq j_2\})$ onto curves in the plane with geodesic curvature and arc length preservation. At the same time, one requires preservation of the cross angle between the initial curve $C_{i_0.}$ and each transversal curve $C_{.j}$. The process is stopped when the left side distortion threshold is reached, or curve $C_{i.}$ belongs to an already flattened region.
3. Extend the development on the right side of $C_{i_0.}$ according to the right side threshold (same process as the left side one).

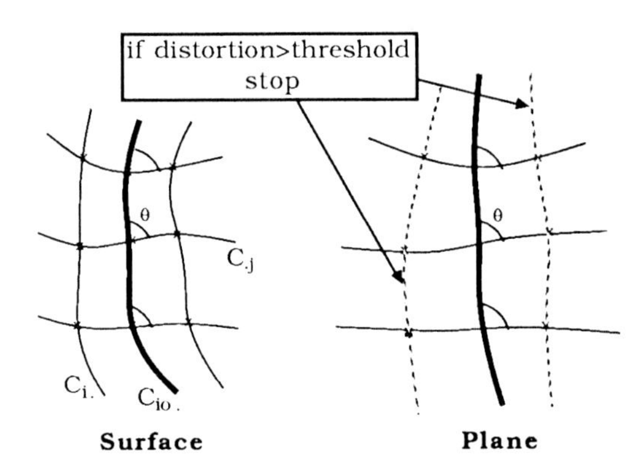


Figure 5: Geodesic curvature preservation flattening.

Notice that here again distances are preserved along the initial curve $C_{i_0.}$ and in the transversal ones $C_{.j}$. All distortions are concentrated on curves $C_{i.}$ parallel to $C_{i_0.}$. So, the distortion metric for a specific curve $C_{i.}$ is the same as for the previous technique (formula (1)).

## 3.3 Mapping a 3D surface curve onto a planar curve with arc length and geodesic curvature preservation

Let us recall that the surface is sampled and that surface curves are given by chord lines, arc length between two consecutive points being approximated with euclidian distance. Suppose the curve $C$ that we want to map onto the plane contains $n+1$ sample points $M_i$, $i = 0..n$. Let us denote by $\mathbf{n_i}$ and $\mathbf{Tp_i}$, respectively, the normal vector and the tangent plane to the surface at point $M_i$. The curve flattening algorithm can then be described as follows:

i) Map the first curve segment $M_0M_1$ onto a segment $P_0P_1$ in the plane (let us call this plane $Oxy$) such that $d(M_0, M_1) = d(P_0, P_1)$. It is sufficient to fix an initial point $P_0$ and a direction in the plane.

ii) For each $j$, $2 \leq j \leq n$, $P_j$ is iteratively computed in the plane as follows (see Figure 6):

   1. Project $M_j$ and $M_{j-2}$ onto the tangent plane to the surface at $M_{j-1}$. This provides two points in $\mathbf{Tp}_{j-1}$, called $\tilde{M}_j$ and $\tilde{M}_{j-2}$ and given by the formulas:

$$\tilde{M}_j = M_j + ((M_{j-1} - M_j).\mathbf{n}_{j-1})\mathbf{n}_{j-1}.$$

$$\tilde{M}_{j-2} = M_{j-2} + ((M_{j-1} - M_{j-2}).\mathbf{n}_{j-1})\mathbf{n}_{j-1}.$$

2. Use a dilation in $\mathbf{Tp}_{j-1}$ to transform $\tilde{M}_j$ into a point $M'_j$ such that $d(M_{j-1}, M_j) = d(M_{j-1}, M'_j)$.

$$M'_j = M_{j-1} + \frac{\|M_j - M_{j-1}\|}{\|\tilde{M}_j - M_{j-1}\|}(\tilde{M}_j - M_{j-1})$$

3. As $P_{j-2}$ and $P_{j-1}$ are already computed, the desired point $P_j$ is the point of $Oxy$ that preserves simultaneously the angle $\theta_{j-1}$ between $\tilde{M}_{j-2}M_{j-1}$ and $M_{j-1}M'_j$, and the distance $d(M_{j-1}, M'_j)$.

$$(P_{j-2}\widehat{P_{j-1}}P_j) = (\tilde{M}_{j-2}\widehat{M_{j-1}}M'_j)$$

$$d(P_{j-1}, P_j) = d(M_{j-1}, M'_j)$$

The way we obtain $p_j$ is to first compute coordinates

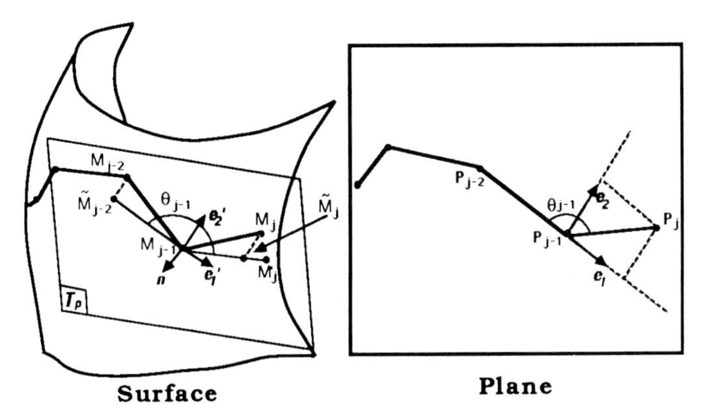


Figure 6: Mapping a curve of a surface onto a planar curve: step *ii*).

$(x'_1, x'_2)$ of $M'_j$ according to the local orthogonal frame $(M_{j-1}, e'_1, e'_2)$ in $\mathbf{Tp}_{j-1}$ where axes $e'_1$ and $e'_2$ and the coordinates are given by the formulas:

$$\begin{cases} e'_1 = \frac{M_{j-1} - \tilde{M}_{j-2}}{\|M_{j-1} - \tilde{M}_{j-2}\|} \\ e'_2 = \mathbf{n}_{j-1} \wedge e'_1 \\ x'_1 = (M'_j - M_{j-1}).e'_1 \\ x'_2 = (M'_j - M_{j-1}).e'_2 \end{cases}$$

$P_j$ is the point of $Oxy$ having the same coordinates according to the orthogonal and positive frame $(P_{j-1}, e_1, e_2)$ given by:

$$\begin{cases} e_1 = \frac{P_{j-1} - P_{j-2}}{\|P_{j-1} - P_{j-2}\|} = a\vec{i} + b\vec{j} \\ e_2 = -b\vec{i} + a\vec{j} \\ P_j = P_{j-1} + (x'_1 e_1 + x'_2 e_2) \end{cases}$$

where $(O, \vec{i}, \vec{j})$ is the canonical coordinate system of $Oxy$.

Step *ii*) of this algorithm will be used in other circumstances, in what follows . It can be thought of as an operator $\mathcal{P}$. Given three neighbouring surface points $(M_1, M_2, M_3)$ and two corresponding points $(P_1, P_2)$ of $(M_1, M_2)$ in the flattening plane $Oxy$, $\mathcal{P}$ computes point $P_3$ in $Oxy$, that preserves the distance $d(M_2, M_3)$ and the projection of the angle $\theta_2 = (M_1\widehat{M_2}M_3)$ in $\mathbf{Tp}_{M_2}$. We will call this operator the *angle preserver* and we will write:

$$P_3 = \mathcal{P}_{\theta_2}(M_3)$$

**Theorem**: *The above curve flattening algorithm preserves geodesic curvature and arc lengths within the chord line approximation.*

As we initially have $d(P_0, P_1) = d(M_0, M_1)$ and by construction of $P_j$, $j$, $2 \leq j \leq n$, we have $d(P_{j-1}, P_j) = d(M_{j-1}, M_j)$, so arc lengths are preserved.

As the sampling is sufficiently refined, the tangents to a curve can be approximated with chord segments. So, at step *ii*), $\theta_{j-1}$ can be considered as the angle variation between two "consecutive" tangent vectors to the locally projected curve, into $\mathbf{Tp}_{j-1}$. We preserve $\theta_{j-1}$ and chord lengths. We then preserve locally the angular velocity of tangents to the curve projection into $\mathbf{Tp}_{j-1}$. **(Q.E.D)**.

Notice that the computation of $P_j$ involves geodesic curvature preservation at $M_{j-1}$.

### 3.4 Preserving the cross angles between the initial curve and a transversal curve

In fact, the preserved angles are the cross angles between the local projection of the two curves onto the tangent plane at their intersecting point (see Figure 7). Suppose that the initial curve

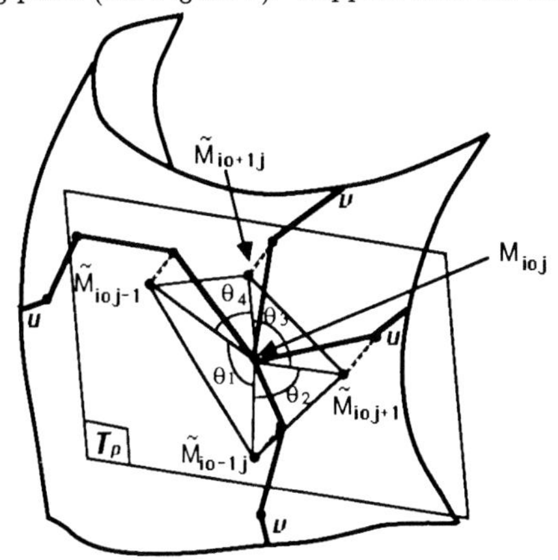


Figure 7: Cross angle preservation.

$C_{i_0.}$ and a transversal curve $C_{.j}$ meet at the point $M_{i_0j}$. Let us denote by $M_{i_0j-1}$, $M_{i_0j+1}$ and by $M_{i_0-1j}$, $M_{i_0+1j}$, respectively, the neighbours of $M_{i_0j}$ along the $u$ and $v$ direction. When we project these four neighbours onto $\mathbf{Tp}_{i_0j}$, we obtain a quadrilateral $(\tilde{M}_{i_0j-1}, \tilde{M}_{i_0-1j}, \tilde{M}_{i_0j+1}, \tilde{M}_{i_0+1j})$. Four angles must then be preserved:

$$\theta_1 = (\tilde{M}_{i_0j-1}\widehat{M_{i_0j}}\tilde{M}_{i_0-1j}) \quad \theta_2 = (\tilde{M}_{i_0-1j}\widehat{M_{i_0j}}\tilde{M}_{i_0j+1})$$

$$\theta_3 = (\tilde{M}_{i_0j+1}\widehat{M_{i_0j}}\tilde{M}_{i_0+1j}) \quad \theta_4 = (\tilde{M}_{i_0+1j}\widehat{M_{i_0j}}\tilde{M}_{i_0j-1})$$

As the initial curve $C_{i_0.}$ is already mapped, the points $P_{i_0j-1}, P_{i_0j}, P_{i_0j+1}$ are available in the flattening plane. In addition, we have $(P_{i_0j-1}\widehat{P_{i_0j}}P_{i_0j+1}) = (\tilde{M}_{i_0j-1}\widehat{M_{i_0j}}\tilde{M}_{i_0j+1})$ (geodesic curvature preservation at $M_{i_0j}$, on $C_{i_0.}$). We then only have to preserve $\theta_1$ and $\theta_4$, respectively, when we initialize the mapping of $C_{.j}$ on the left side of $C_{i_0.}$ (when we compute $P_{i_0-1j}$) and on the right side of $C_{i_0.}$ (when we compute $P_{i_0+1j}$). This implies the preservation of all the other angles. $P_{i_0-1j}$ and $P_{i_0+1j}$ are then given by the angle preserver operators:

$$P_{i_0-1j} = \mathcal{P}_{\theta_1}(M_{i_0-1j}), \quad P_{i_0+1j} = \mathcal{P}_{\theta_4}(M_{i_0+1j})$$

Moreover, this preserves the angle $(\tilde{M}_{i_0-1j}\widehat{M_{i_0j}}\tilde{M}_{i_0+1j})$, hence, geodesic curvature at $M_{i_0j}$ on $C_{.j}$.

### 3.5 Flattening of the cone and the hemisphere

Figure 8-a and 8-b show the flattenings of the cone with this technique. In 8-a, the cone is spread out around a generatrix. In 8-b a circle is used as initial curve. Both give the same result, which is the proper development of the cone (an angular sector of a disc). In Figure 9, we show the mapping of a checkerboard pattern onto the cone according to three different techniques: With Catmull's technique, in 9-a and 9-b, squares are compressed along circles as one gets close to the tip. The advantage of this technique is that

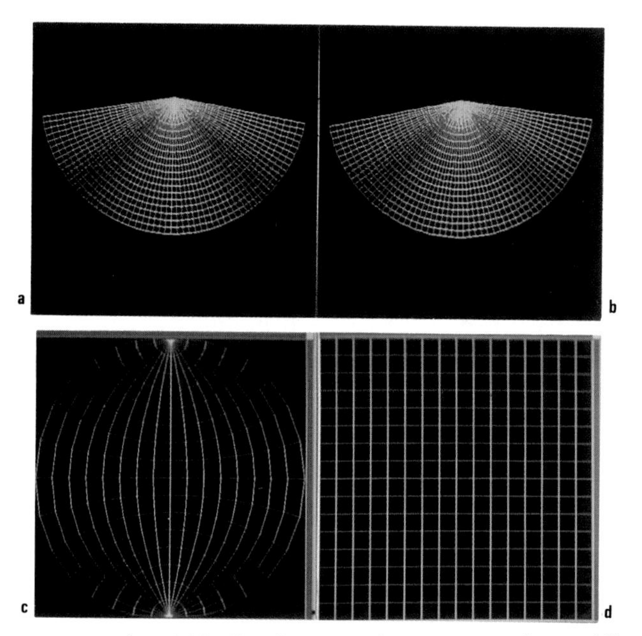

Figure 8: a) and b): Development of a cone around a meridian and a parallel respectively. c) and d) Development of a hemisphere around a meridian and the equator respectively.

one can manage to avoid the line of discontinuities with repeated patterns.
The second mapping (9-c and 9-d) is based on the flattening technique described in section 2.2 (previous work). One can see that distortions are not very noticeable beside the initial generatrix (9-c). Squares are more and more stretched along meridians (the inverse of flattening distortions impression) and angles more distorted, beside the cutting line (9-d).
The mapping based on geodesic curvature flattening (9-e and 9-f) provides no distortions but the texture contains a line of discontinuities (9-f). Thus it is topologically faithful.
The cone contains 1281 points. Its flattening takes about 0.05s with the algorithm of section 2.2 and 0.5s with the geodesic curvature preservation algorithm on a GOULD 9000. Mapping texture from the flattened cone has taken about 25s.
The full development of the hemisphere around the central meridian is shown in Figure 8-c. The initial meridian and the equator are mapped onto straight lines, because both are geodesic curves. The parallel circles are mapped onto circles, because along each parallel circle there exists a cone tangent to the sphere: as along the circle the tangent planes are the same according to the sphere or to the cone, at each point geodesic curvature is the same according to the two surfaces. So, flattening of a parallel circle of the sphere gives the same result as if it were considered as belonging to the cone, hence a circle. One can notice that with the latter flattening technique, angles are less distorted than with the technique of section 2.2 (Figure 2). The same flattening is obtained with Bonne's projection (or pseudo-cylindric projection), also used in cartography. In [2] it is shown that, starting from different initial curves, geodesic curvature preservation flattening provides other types of projections used in cartography. For instance, when the initial curve is not a great circle, the development provides a cone (a conic projection). The hemisphere has about 300 points. Its flattening takes about 0.008s with the technique described in section 2.2 and has taken about 0.2s with the geodesic curvature preservation algorithm.
The major disadvantage of this technique is due to preservation of geodesic curvature in only one direction during the development process. This concentrates all the distortions on the curves parallel to the initial one. This also makes the technique strongly dependent on the initial curve. Figure 8-d shows the development of

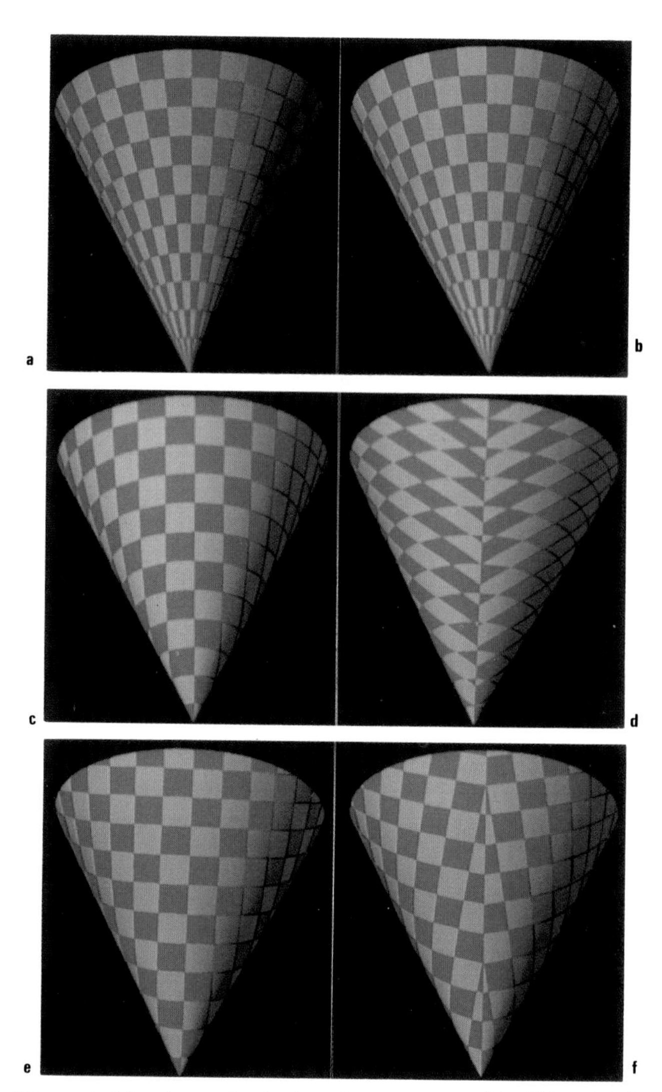

Figure 9: Mapping a checkerboard onto a cone with different techniques.

the hemisphere around the equator. One obtains a rectangle: the equator is a geodesic, and is mapped onto a straight line. All the meridians being geodesics, they are also mapped onto straight lines orthogonal to the first one and having the same length. However this technique remains suitable for all developable surfaces (or developable parts of a surface). It also gives good results on almost developable surfaces.
In the next section, we present a technique that takes into account geodesic curvature in both directions and then reduce the drawbacks encountered with non-developable surfaces.

# 4 Incorporating geodesic curvature in both directions: Relaxation technique

The technique described in this section consists of distributing distortions in both directions. This is done in two steps:

1. One first develops the surface around an initial curve, taking into account at each point the geodesic curvature in both directions $u$ and $v$ and the projected cross angles. As will be explained later, this development induces a gradient of distortions on the flattened region. This gradient enables one to measure the distortions and stop the development propaga-

tion when necessary.

2. A relaxation procedure is then used to reduce and better distribute the distortions in the flattened region.

   For simplicity, in the following, the projected angle (in the tangent plane) between two intersecting curves is loosely called the angle.

## 4.1 Development technique

The new development algorithm is almost the same as the algorithm of the previous section. One first maps the initial curve $C_{i_0}.$ onto the plane with geodesic curvature and arc length preservation. The development of the region is then propagated step by step to the curves parallel to $C_{i_0}.$, on the left side of $C_{i_0}.$, then on the right side of $C_{i_0}.$. The new feature introduced here is the way in which the points of the parallel curves are mapped onto the flattening plane.

As illustrated in Figure 10, let $M_{ij} = C_{i.} \cap C_{.j}$ be the point being processed. $P_{ij}$ is obtained by preserving at each neighbour $M_{kl} \in \{M_{i-1j}, M_{ij+1}, M_{i+1j}, M_{ij-1}\}$ already processed, the three angles $(\theta^1{}_{kl}, \theta^2{}_{kl}, \theta^3{}_{kl})$. $\theta^1{}_{kl}$ and $\theta^2{}_{kl}$ are cross angles (facing $M_{ij}$) between the curves that intersect at $M_{kl}$. Preserving $\theta^3{}_{kl}$ is equivalent to preserving the geodesic curvature at $M_{kl}$ on the curve containing $M_{ij}$ and $M_{kl}$. One can not always preserve all three angles. For instance, in Figure 10 the point $M_{i+1j-1}$ has not yet been processed, so one cannot preserve $\theta^2{}_{ij-1}$. Each angle

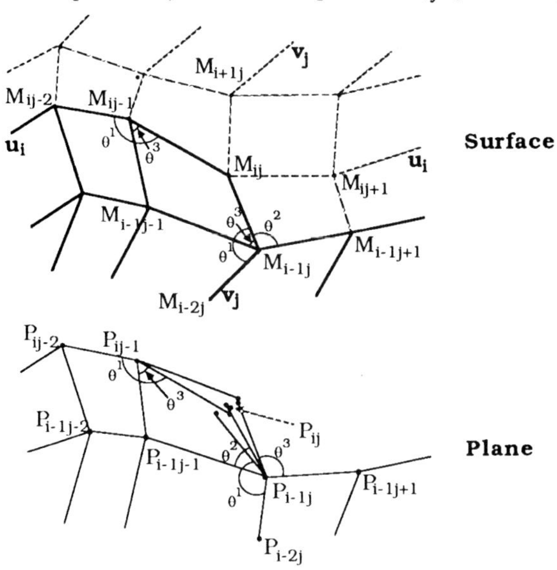


Figure 10: Preserving angles at processed neighbours (development step).

preservation provides a different point in the flattening plane. This point is obtained using the angle preserver:

$$P_{ij}^{r,kl} = \mathcal{P}_{\theta^r{}_{kl}}(M_{ij}),\ r = 1,2,3;\ kl \in \{i-1j, ij+1, i+1j, ij-1\}$$

The point $P_{ij}$ corresponding to $M_{ij}$ in the flattening plane is then the centroid of the points[3] $P_{ij}^{r,kl}$.

The choice of the centroid induces slight errors on the angles and distances. The accumulation of these errors provides a gradient of distortions in the scanning direction. So, for a better distribution of the distortions the curve being processed is not scanned from one extremal point to the other extremal point. Instead, the curve is scanned from the central point to the extremal points.

With this technique distortions are present on both $C_{i.}$, $C_{.j}$ curves. The distortions increase in diagonal directions as one gets far from the central point of the initial curve. Let $v_{j_1} \leq v \leq v_{j_2}$ on the initial curve $C_{i_0}.$. The distortion metric for a specific curve $C_{i.}$ is then:

$$C(C_{i.}) = \frac{1}{2I+J}\Big(\sum_{k=j_1}^{k=j_2-1} \frac{||d(M_{ik},M_{ik+1}) - d(P_{ik},P_{ik+1})||}{d(M_{ik},M_{ik+1})} + \sum_{k=i_0}^{k=i-1} \frac{||d(M_{kj_1},M_{k+1j_1}) - d(P_{kj_1},P_{k+1j_1})||}{d(M_{kj_1},M_{k+1j_1})} + \sum_{k=i_0}^{k=i-1} \frac{||d(M_{kj_2},M_{k+1j_2}) - d(P_{kj_2},P_{k+1j_2})||}{d(M_{kj_2},M_{k+1j_2})}\Big)$$

Here one has $I = i - i_0$ and $J = j_2 - j_1$.

## 4.2 Relaxation procedure

In the above development, when mapping a point onto the flattening plane, one does not take into account all the neighbouring points (see figure 11). The reason is that some neighbours have not been processed yet. In addition, for a given neighbour one can not always preserve all the angles. The relaxation procedure consists

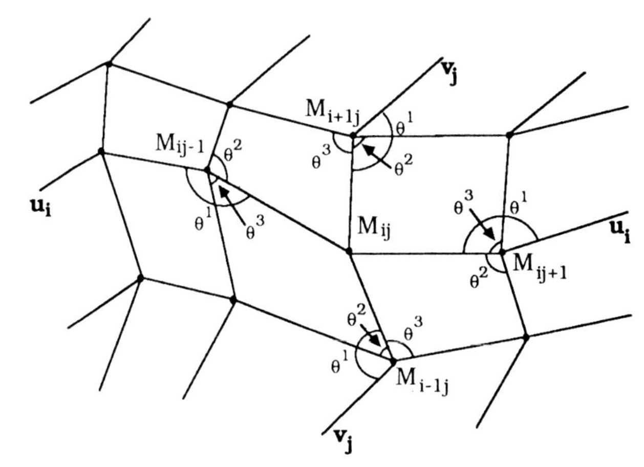


Figure 11: Preserving three angles at four neighbours (relaxation step).

of recomputing points of the obtained flat piece several times until the change becomes insignificant. At each iteration one uses the results of the previous iteration. The location of a point $P_{ij}^n$ at iteration $n$ is then:

$$P_{ij}^n = \frac{1}{12}\sum_{r=1}^{3}(\mathcal{P}^{n-1}_{\theta^r{}_{i-1j}} + \mathcal{P}^{n-1}_{\theta^r{}_{i+1j}} + \mathcal{P}^{n-1}_{\theta^r{}_{ij-1}} + \mathcal{P}^{n-1}_{\theta^r{}_{ij+1}})(M_{ij}).$$

$P_{ij}^n$ is thus the centroid of the twelve points obtained by preserving the three angles of each neighbour. The angle preserver $\mathcal{P}^{n-1}$ uses the flattening points of iteration $n-1$.

Let $P_1, P_2, \cdots, P_n$ be a cluster of $n$ points within a plane and let $P$ be a point in this plane. One calls the "dispersion" of the cluster around $P$ the value:

$$Dsp(P) = \frac{1}{n}\sum_{k=1}^{n} ||P - P_k||^2.$$

$Dsp(P)$ is minimum for the centroid $P_m$ of the cluster of points. $Dsp(P_m)$ is then called the dispersion of the cluster of points. For our purposes, the quality of the flattening at a given point $P_{ij}$ can be measured by the dispersion $Dsp(P_{ij})$ of the twelve points given by the twelve angle preservers. The smaller $Dsp(P_{ij})$ is, the better is the flattening at $P_{ij}$. Thus taking the centroid of the twelve points at each iteration is better for distributing and reducing the distortions.

[3] When the surface is developable the preservation of each angle gives the same point in the flattening plane.

The quality of the whole flattening can be measured by the mean dispersion:

$$Dsp = \frac{1}{N}\sum_{ij} Dsp(P_{ij}).$$

Here $N$ is the number of points within the flattened piece. Thus, the relaxation procedure stops when the dispersion $Dsp^n$ at iteration $n$ has not changed significantly, i.e. when $\frac{|Dsp^n - Dsp^{n-1}|}{Dsp^n}$ becomes less then some fixed variation threshold (about $10^{-3}$).
The relaxation algorithm can thus be simply described as follows:

$Dsp^{n-1} = Greatnumber$

$Dsp^n = Smallnumber$

While $\frac{|Dsp^n - Dsp^{n-1}|}{Dsp^n} > threshold$

For each i,j indexing the region points

$P^n_{ij} = \frac{1}{12}\sum_{r=1}^{3}(\mathcal{P}^{n-1}_{\theta^r i-1j} + \mathcal{P}^{n-1}_{\theta^r i+1j} + \mathcal{P}^{n-1}_{\theta^r ij-1} + \mathcal{P}^{n-1}_{\theta^r ij+1})\,(M_{ij})$

$Dsp^{n-1} \leftarrow Dsp^n$

$Dsp^n = \frac{1}{N}\sum_{ij} Dsp(P^n_{ij})$

endFor
endWhile.

### 4.3 Flattening of the sphere

Figures 12-a and 12-b show the flattening of the hemisphere around the central meridian before (12-a) and after (12-b) the relaxation process. With the relaxation technique, it is clear that distortions are better distributed and angles more preserved than previously (i.e., with the geodesic curvature flattening preservation in only one direction).
Figures 12-c and 12-d show the flattening of the hemisphere around the equator before (12-c) and after (12-d) the relaxation process. One can notice that after the relaxation, the flattening is almost the same as when the initial curve is a meridian. Starting from

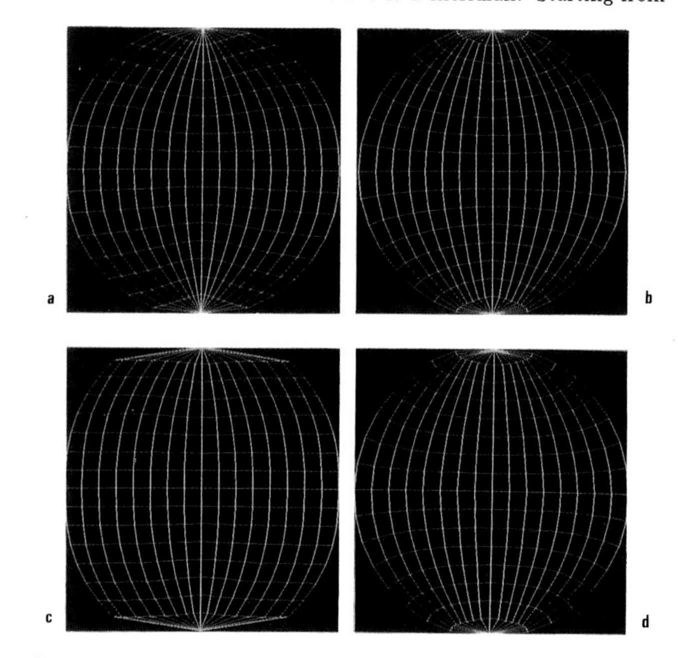

Figure 12: Development of a hemisphere - a: around a meridian before and after relaxation b: around the equator before and after relaxation.

the development around the meridian the relaxation has taken 6 iterations and 3 seconds. Starting from the development around the equator the relaxation has taken about 16 iterations and 15s.
Figure 13 highlights the compromise between discontinuities and distortions. A digitized photograph (in Figures 13-a and 13-b) and an artificial material (in Figures 13-c and 13-d) are mapped onto the sphere. Catmull's technique is used in the pictures on the left: patterns are strongly deformed beside the pole, but there are no discontinuities. In the pictures on the right the mapping is based on the relaxation procedure. The sphere is segmented into four equal pieces, a meridian being chosen for each piece. Distortions are hardly noticeable, but seam lines are evident in the mapped photograph. In the mapped material, seam lines are not quite visible but one can guess where they are because of the sudden changes of orientation.

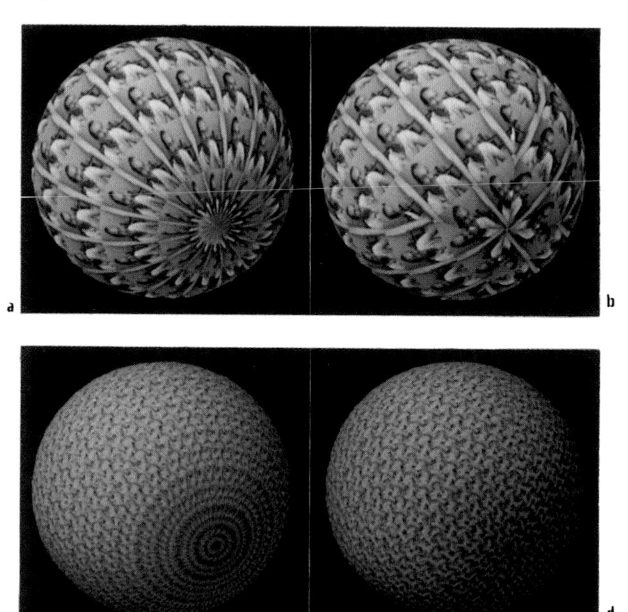

Figure 13: Comparison on the sphere of Catmull's mapping and the mapping based on the piecewise relaxation.

## 5 Application: shoe modeling

One of the possible applications of our mapping and texturing techniques is computer-aided shoe design. Shoemakers naturally use geodesics to cut patterns, by drawing lines on a shape of the shoe: these lines become the edges of the flattened 3-D patterns constituting the different pieces of the resulting shoe.
To determine the pattern of a region (see picture of Figure 14-a), the shoemaker sticks a paper strip on a median curve of the region to flatten. He then cuts the sheet from this line in fine "fish bones"; each of them is folded back on the shoe form, determining a geodesic on the surface. Finally, the trace of the region border is marked on each bone, giving the edge of the flattened zone. One notes that the choice of the geodesics is here completely empirical, and therefore difficult to automate. Our method enables one to overcome this difficulty.
Figure 14-b shows a wire frame of a shoe shape. A real wooden shoe pattern has first been sampled by a laser sensor along successive slices. Each slice has been approximated by a *spline* curve. A spline surface (of NURBS type) has then been generated by transverse interpolation between splines. The parametric surface has then been sampled along isoparametrics. The parametric surface modeling algorithm is explained in detail in [15].
In Figure 14-b, the shoe model is being mapped: the pink zone is already flattened, while the yellow side is currently treated: the starting curve for development is drawn in green. The sole (in white) is not treated yet.

As described above, we use isoparametrics as cut lines: starting from a given curve, we develop the shoe surface until a deformation threshold is reached. As the whole surface is not developable, we can play on the width of the pieces by varying the distortion threshold.
The shoe form is cut into three pieces (which flattenings are shown in Figures 14-c, 14-d and 14-e): the sole, the interior and the exterior sides. The sole, as relatively flat, is flattened with the simple geodesic curvature flattening. The relaxation process has been applied to both sides.
Figures 14-f and 14-g show, from different viewpoints, the entirely textured shoe shape, obtained by mapping on it successively a digitized natural leather and an artificial weaving.
Figures 14-h and 14-i show the modeling of a sandal and its flattened pieces. Small pieces have been obtained with the geodesic curvature preservation algorithm. The big piece has needed the relaxation algorithm. Finally, one can see the sandal textured with the leather and the artificial material in Figures 14-j and 14-k.
Each of the shoe models has taken less than 3s computation time for flattening the pieces. The affine interpolation for texture mapping has taken between 15 and 20s.
From a practical point of a view, an efficient CAD tool should enable one to draw "manually" the region edge curves on the 3-D surface. Our techniques could then be used for the flattening of each region, by developing the parametric pattern containing the selected region, projecting the edges on the 2-D mapping, and finally cutting the plane along these borders. In this case, the choice of the initial development curve could even be automatic: the user needs only to know the distortion rate induced on each piece of the shoe. This will be pursued in future work. The algorithm of drawing curves on 3-D surfaces is described in [15].

## 6 Conclusion

We have presented in this paper new and efficient algorithms for non-distorted texture mapping. Unlike more conventional approaches based on global minimization of distortions, our techniques enable a controlled unfolding around an initial curve by choosing a distortion metric on isoparametrics of the surface. Moreover, distortions are lessened by introducing discontinuities on the unfolded surface. Possible applications (among others) could be umbrella and underwear designing, and, more generally, manufacturing.
The new algorithms are easy to implement, although they are based on uncommon concepts (from differential geometry); nevertheless, they present several aspects for further study. First, a human intervention for the choice of the initial curve and the distortion threshold is necessary. Also, our techniques can only be used on surfaces given explicitely by their parametric equations, thus reducing their scope. The generalization to polygonal surfaces would then be desirable. Another disadvantage is that seam lines (cuts) are located on isoparametric curves, and thus depend on the parametrization chosen. On most natural objects covered with planar texture (clothes and walls for example), seam lines are located on lines of main curvature, giving a harmonious look to the mapping. It could then be useful to parametrize the surface again along the main directions ([1]) before flattening it. This is not always true, though, and in certain cases (shoe modeling for example) aesthetics are important. This is a very subjective notion; drawing edge curves by hand on the surface becomes necessary in such cases.
Another interesting problem consists of how to reduce as much as possible the number of cut pieces . A preliminary idea would be to extend a previously mapped piece, by choosing its borders as being the initial curves of the flattening algorithms described in this paper. Another solution consists of finding a strategy to merge different pieces previously obtained. This is still an open problem. The last point that could be explored is the texture orientation: how can one locate and orient the several flattened pieces in the texture plane, in order to obtain a good appearance at seam lines. A possible solution would consist of minimizing a global metric of positions and orientations on the common borders of the unfolded parts.

## Acknowledgements

The authors are very grateful to Dr. D. Geman, Dr. J. Ralston and Dr. P. Sander for revising the paper; to Dr. M. Gangnet and Dr. F. Schmitt for their valuable comments; to L. Doghman, F. Ledru and L. Vinet for their precious help; and to Dr. A. Gagalowicz for his support.

### References

[1] J.M. Beck, R.T. Farouki, and J.K. Hinds. Surface analysis methods. *IEE CGA*, pages 18–37, December 1986.

[2] C. Bennis. Synthèse de textures hiérarchiques planes - développement de surfaces 3d pour un placage de textures minimisant les distorsions. *Thèse de Doctorat en Science, Université de Paris XI, centre d'Orsay*, Décembre 1990.

[3] C. Bennis and A. Gagalowicz. Hierarchical texture synthesis on 3-d surfaces. *EUROGRAPHICS' 89*, pages 257–268, September 1989.

[4] C. Bennis and A. Gagalowicz. Mapping de textures sur une approximation triangulaire des surfaces. *PIXIM' 89*, pages 139–152, 1989.

[5] E. Bier and K. Sloan. Two-part texture mapping. *IEEE Computer Graphics and Applications*, pages 40–53, September 1986.

[6] J.F. Blinn and M.E. Newell. Texture and reflection in computer generated images. *Communications of the ACM, 19, 10*, pages 542–547, October 1976.

[7] M.F. Do Carmo. Differential geometry of curves and surfaces. *Prentice-Hall, Englewood Cliffs, Inc.*, 1976.

[8] E. Catmull. A subdivision algorithm for computer display of curved surfaces. *Ph.D. Dissertation. Dept. of Computer Sciences, University of Utah*, December 1974.

[9] E. Catmull and A.R. Smith. 3-d transformation of images in scanline order. *Computer Graphics*, 14(3), July 1980.

[10] F.C. Crow. Summed-area tables for texture mapping. *SIGGRAPH 84, Proc. of Computer Graphics*, pages 207–212, July 1984.

[11] E.L. Schwartz et al. Computational neuroscience: Applications of computer graphics and image processing to 2d and 3d modelling of functional architechture of visual cortex. *CGA, Vol. 8, No. 4*, pages 13–23, July 1988.

[12] G. Farin. Curves and surfaces for aided geometric design. *Academic Press, San Diego, Inc.*, 1988.

[13] E. Fiume, A. Fournier, and V. Canale. Conformal texture mapping. *EUROGRAPHICS' 87*, pages 53–64, 1987.

[14] P. Heckbert. Fundamentals of texture mapping and image warping. *UCB/CSD 89/516, Computer Science Dept, Univ. of California, Berkeley.*

[15] G. Iglesias and S. Coquillart. Curve design on surfaces. *In preparation.*

[16] S.D. Ma and A. Gagalowicz. Determination of local coordinate systems for texture synthesis in 3-d surface. *EUROGRAPHICS'85*, September 1985.

[17] S.D. Ma and H. Lin. Optimal texture mapping. *EUROGRAPHICS'88*, pages 421–428, September 1988.

[18] M. Oka, K. Tsutsui, A. Ohba, Y. Kurauchi, and T. Tago. Real-time manipulation of texture-mapped surfaces. *SIGGRAPH 87, Proc. of Computer Graphics*, 21(4):181–188, 1987.

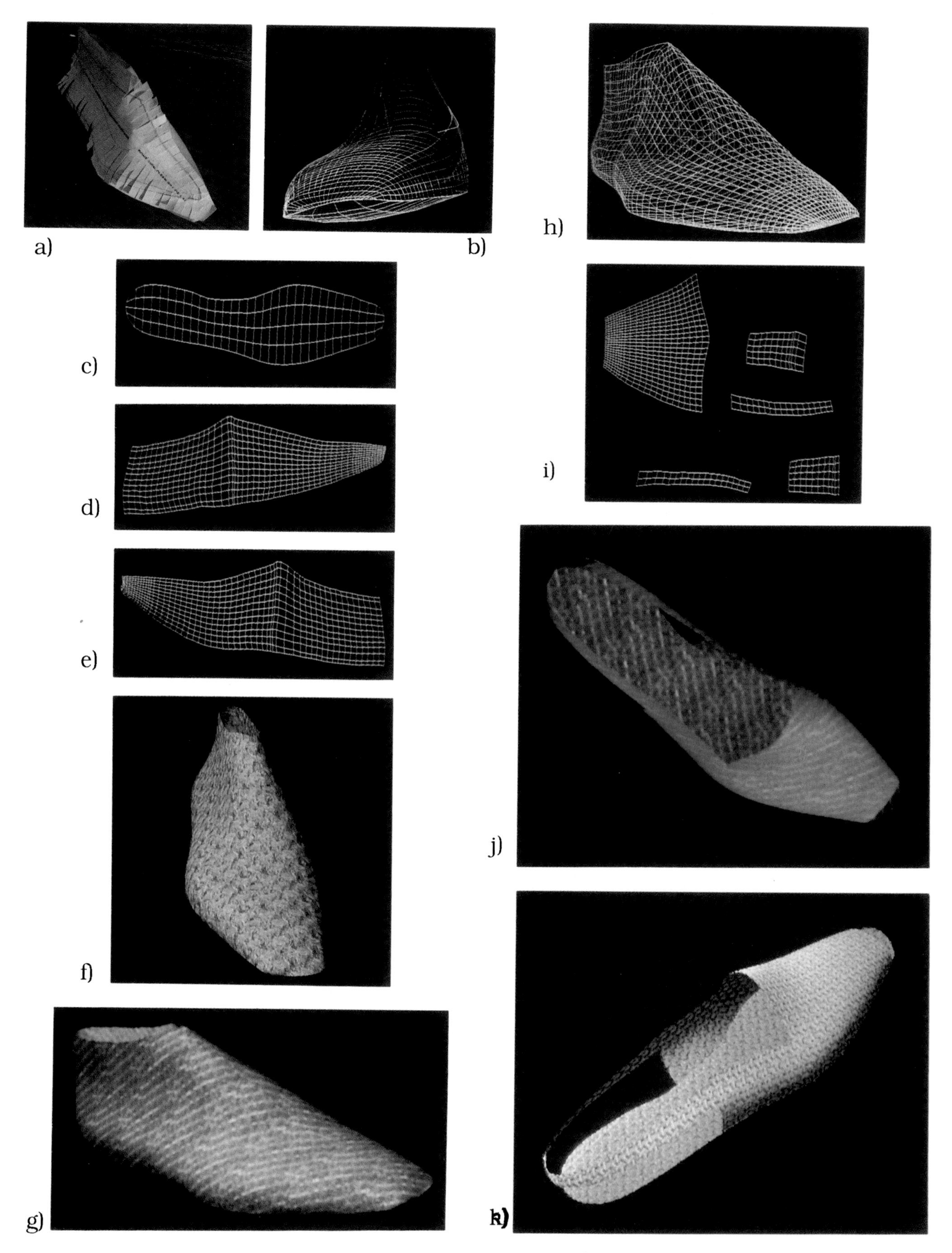


Figure 14: Modelling and Texturing of the shoe.

# Generalized Implicit Functions For Computer Graphics

Stan Sclaroff and Alex Pentland

Vision and Modeling Group
The Media Laboratory
Massachusetts Institute of Technology
Cambridge, MA 02139

## Abstract

We describe a method of generalizing implicit functions by use of modal deformations and displacement maps. Modal deformations, also known as free vibration modes, are used to describe the overall shape of a solid, while displacement maps provide local and fine surface detail by offsetting the surface of the solid along its surface normals. The advantage of this approach to geometric description is that collision detection and dynamic simulation become simple and inexpensive even for complex shapes. In addition, we outline an efficient method for fitting such models to three dimensional point data.

**CR Categories:** I.3.5 [Computer Graphics]: Computational Geometry and Object Modeling; I.3.7 [Computer Graphics]: Graphics and Realism.

**Additional Keywords:** Collision Detection, Implicit Surfaces, Simulation, Dynamics, Deformations, Solid Modeling, Computer Modeling.

## 1 Introduction

In many graphics applications, and especially in physical simulations, the ability to efficiently detect and characterize collisions and intersections is essential. Unfortunately, the polygon and spline representations normally employed in computer graphics are ill suited to this task. When using a polygon representation, for instance, the computational complexity of collision detection is $O(nm)$ operations, where $n$ is the number of polygons and $m$ is the number of points to be considered after pruning via bounding box considerations [8]. As a consequence, collision detection is one of the most costly operations in many graphics applications [6], despite significant efforts to optimize algorithms for collision and intersection detection [1; 8].

In contrast, one can perform collision detection relatively efficiently when employing an implicit function representation (*e.g.*, spheres, swept solids, deformable superquadrics [3]) by making use of their inside-outside function. In each case, the computational complexity of this type of collision checking is only $O(m)$ rather than $O(nm)$ [9]. A more subtle but perhaps equally important advantage of this approach is that the collision surface may often be characterized analytically [7; 12], allowing more accurate simulation of multibody collisions.



Unfortunately, implicit function representations have not been sufficiently expressive for general use. The contribution of this paper will be to show how implicit function representations may be generalized to allow fast collision detection for more general shapes, and to outline an efficient technique for fitting these generalized implicit functions to three dimensional point data.

## 2 Generalized Implicit Functions

An implicit function representation defines a surface as a level set of a function $f$, most commonly the set of points for which $f(\mathbf{x}) = 0$. For instance, the inside-outside function we use for superquadric ellipsoids, before rotation, translation or deformation, is:

$$f(\mathbf{x}) = \left[ \left(x^{2/\epsilon_2} + y^{2/\epsilon_2}\right)^{\epsilon_2/\epsilon_1} + z^{2/\epsilon_1} \right]^{\epsilon_1/2} - 1. \quad (1)$$

In practice we have found this better behaved than the standard superquadric inside-outside function, as it is more similar to the a normal $\mathbf{L}_2$ distance metric.

A solid defined in this way can be easily positioned and oriented, by transforming the implicit function:

$$\hat{\mathbf{x}} = \mathbf{M}\mathbf{x} + \mathbf{b} \quad (2)$$

where $\mathbf{M}$ is a rotation matrix, and $\mathbf{b}$ is a translation vector. Similarly, the implicit function's positioned and oriented inside-outside function becomes:

$$f(\mathbf{x}) = f(\mathbf{M}^{-1}(\hat{\mathbf{x}} - \mathbf{b})). \quad (3)$$

To detect a collision between a point $\mathbf{x} = (x, y, z)$ and the volume bounded by this surface, one simply substitutes the coordinates of $\mathbf{x}$ into the function $f$. If the result is negative, then the point is inside the surface and a collision has occurred. Generalizations of this basic operation may be used to find line-surface intersections or surface-surface intersections [12].

### 2.1 Deformations

As in Barr [2; 3], this basic set of functions can be generalized further by defining an appropriate set of global deformations $\mathcal{D}$ with parameters $\mathbf{u}$. For particular values of $\mathbf{u}$ the new deformed surface is defined using a deformation matrix $\mathcal{D}_{\mathbf{u}}$:

$$\hat{\mathbf{x}} = \mathbf{M}\mathcal{D}_{\mathbf{u}}\mathbf{x} + \mathbf{b} \quad (4)$$

where $\hat{\mathbf{x}}$ is the position vector after rotation, deformation, and translation. Similarly, the inside-outside function becomes

$$f(\mathbf{x}) = f(\mathcal{D}_{\mathbf{u}}^{-1}\mathbf{M}^{-1}(\hat{\mathbf{x}} - \mathbf{b})). \quad (5)$$

This inside-outside function is valid as long as the inverse deformation $\mathcal{D}_{\mathbf{u}}^{-1}$ exists. Thus by selecting a set of deformations that can be easily inverted, we can greatly expand the class of shapes that can be described using an implicit function representation.

Figure 1: Two frames from a physically-based animation in which seashell-like shapes drop through water and come to rest.

In the ThingWorld modeling system [11] deformations are described by a 3 x 3 deformation matrix $\mathcal{D}_{\mathbf{u}}$, referred to as the *modal deformation matrix*, whose entries are polynomials which mimic the free vibration modes found in real objects. As a consequence, the linear superposition of these deformation polynomials allows accurate description of the dynamic, non-rigid behavior of real objects.

For many computer graphics applications, it is sufficient to pick the following polynomials to be the entries of $\mathcal{D}_{\mathbf{u}}$:

$$\begin{aligned}
d_{00} &= u_6 + yu_{12} + zu_{15} - (u_{13} + u_{16})\mathrm{sgn}(x) - u_{14} - u_{17}, \\
d_{01} &= u_{11} + 2y(u_{13} + \mathrm{sgn}(x)u_{14}), \\
d_{02} &= u_{10} + 2z(u_{16} + \mathrm{sgn}(x)u_{17}), \\
d_{10} &= u_{11} + 2x(u_{19} + \mathrm{sgn}(y)u_{20}), \\
d_{11} &= u_7 + xu_{18} + zu_{21} - (u_{19} + u_{22})\mathrm{sgn}(y) - u_{20} - u_{23}, \\
d_{12} &= u_9 + 2z(u_{22} + \mathrm{sgn}(y)u_{23}), \\
d_{20} &= u_{10} + 2x(u_{25} + \mathrm{sgn}(z)u_{26}), \\
d_{21} &= u_9 + 2y(u_{28} + \mathrm{sgn}(z)u_{29}), \\
d_{22} &= u_8 + xu_{24} + yu_{27} - (u_{25} + u_{28})\mathrm{sgn}(z) - u_{26} - u_{29}.
\end{aligned}$$

The parameters $u_i$ are the amplitudes of the various free vibration modes, and have simple, intuitive meanings. The lowest frequency modes are the rigid-body modes of translation ($u_0$ through $u_2$) and rotation ($u_3$ through $u_5$) which specify the values of $\mathbf{b}$ and $\mathbf{M}$. The next-lowest frequency modes are smooth, whole-body deformations that leave the center of mass and rotation fixed: $u_6$ through $u_8$ control the x, y, and z radii, $u_9$ through $u_{11}$ are shears about the x, y, and z axes, and $u_{12+3j}$ through $u_{12+3j+2}$ are tapering, bending, and pinching around the $j^{th}$ pairwise combination of the x, y, and z axes. Note that because the rigid body modes are calculated in the object's coordinate system, they must be rotated to global coordinates before being integrated with the remainder of any dynamic simulation.

## 2.2 Displacement Maps

The class of implicit functions can be generalized still further by defining the surface as the set of points for which $f(\mathbf{x}) = d$ for some displacement function $d(\eta, \omega)$, where $\eta$, $\omega$ are the point's coordinates in the surface's two-dimensional parametric space. We define $\tilde{\mathbf{x}}(\eta, \omega)$ to be the displaced surface point before rotation, deformation or translation:

$$\tilde{\mathbf{x}} = \mathbf{x} + d\mathbf{n} \tag{6}$$

This will have the effect of displacing the surface along the surface normal in the original undeformed space before applying the deformation $\mathcal{D}_{\mathbf{u}}$.

In the ThingWorld system displacement maps are stored as two-dimensional floating point image arrays. In our examples, the displacement map function $d(\eta, \omega)$ is defined by bilinear interpolation between point samples. If a smoother interpolation is desired, standard spline or pyramid-based multiresolution methods [4] can be employed.

Given a point $\mathbf{x}(\eta, \omega)$ and normal $\mathbf{n}(\eta, \omega)$ on the undeformed implicit surface, deformation transform $\mathcal{D}_{\mathbf{u}}$, and scalar displacement map function $d(\eta, \omega)$, we define $\bar{\mathbf{x}}$ to be the position vector including deformations and displacement map:

$$\bar{\mathbf{x}} = \mathbf{M}\mathcal{D}_{\mathbf{u}}\tilde{\mathbf{x}} + \mathbf{b} = \mathbf{M}\mathcal{D}_{\mathbf{u}}(\mathbf{x} + d\mathbf{n}) + \mathbf{b} \tag{7}$$

We also need to define $\bar{\mathbf{n}}$ to be the normal vector including deformations and displacement. To find $\bar{\mathbf{n}}$, it is first necessary to find $\tilde{\mathbf{n}}$, the surface normal for the displaced surface before deformation, and then apply deformations to get $\bar{\mathbf{n}}$. The normal $\tilde{\mathbf{n}}(\eta, \omega)$ is derived by taking the cross product of the partial derivatives for the undeformed displaced surface function, $\tilde{\mathbf{x}}(\eta, \omega)$:

$$\frac{\partial \tilde{\mathbf{x}}}{\partial \eta} = \frac{\partial \mathbf{x}}{\partial \eta} + d\frac{\partial \mathbf{n}}{\partial \eta} + \mathbf{n}\frac{\partial d}{\partial \eta}$$

and

$$\frac{\partial \tilde{\mathbf{x}}}{\partial \omega} = \frac{\partial \mathbf{x}}{\partial \omega} + d\frac{\partial \mathbf{n}}{\partial \omega} + \mathbf{n}\frac{\partial d}{\partial \omega}. \tag{8}$$

In our current implementation, the partials are calculated by finite differences.

The inside-outside function associated with Equation 7 is then:

$$f(\mathbf{x}) = f(\mathcal{D}_{\mathbf{u}}^{-1}\mathbf{M}^{-1}(\bar{\mathbf{x}} - \mathbf{b}) - d\mathbf{n}). \tag{9}$$

It is difficult to evaluate a displacement mapped and deformed inside-outside function because we cannot know $d$ or $\mathbf{n}$ in Equation 9 before we know $\mathbf{x}$, and *vice versa*. We therefore need a parametric projection function $P(\tilde{\mathbf{x}}) = (\eta, \omega)$, which can project an undeformed, displacement-mapped $\tilde{\mathbf{x}}$ point back onto the original, undisplaced implicit surface. These parameters can then be used to determine $\mathbf{n}$, $\mathbf{x}$, and $d$. The projection should be *normal projection* since the displacement map displaces surface points along the surface normal.

For example, the projection function $P(\tilde{\mathbf{x}}) = (\eta, \omega)$ for superquadric ellipsoids is computed as follows. We first find $\omega$ by observing:

$$\frac{\tilde{y}}{\tilde{x}} = \frac{\cos^{\epsilon_1}\eta \sin^{\epsilon_2}\omega}{\cos^{\epsilon_1}\eta \cos^{\epsilon_2}\omega} = \tan^{\epsilon_2}\omega \qquad (10)$$

where $(\tilde{x}, \tilde{y}, \tilde{z})^T = \tilde{\mathbf{x}}$ is the undeformed, displaced surface point. From Equation 10, we see that $\omega = \text{atan}^{1/\epsilon_2}(\tilde{y}/\tilde{x})$. The remaining parameter, $\eta$, is determined by either $\eta = \text{atan}^{1/\epsilon_1}((\tilde{z}\cos^{\epsilon_2}\omega)/\tilde{x})$ or $\eta = \text{atan}^{1/\epsilon_1}((\tilde{z}\sin^{\epsilon_2}\omega)/\tilde{y})$ depending on whether $\tilde{x}$ or $\tilde{y}$ is larger.

### 2.3 An Example

Figure 1 shows two frames from a physically-based animation in which three seashell-like shapes drop through a viscous medium (*e.g.*, seawater), hit the sea bottom, bump into each other, and then come to rest. The simulations were conducted using the technique of modal dynamics as implemented in the ThingWorld system [11].

The seashell shapes were modeled as superquadric ellipsoids with displacement maps. Each displacement map consisted of a 100 x 100 uniformly spaced grid generated by combinations of sines and cosines. The shells were polygonalized for display and simulation purposes — approximately 2300 polygons for the spike seashell, and 576 polygons for the other seashells. Bounding boxes were also computed for the objects. During the simulation, if these bounding boxes crossed, then polygon vertices were plugged into the offending objects' inside/outside functions to test for collisions.

Execution time for the three active objects was 0.05 seconds per time step during the initial frames of the animation (before any contact), and 0.081 seconds per time step during the final few frames, when the three seashells were colliding with the seabed (which is not planar), and the shells were colliding with each other. Subtracting the pre-contact time from the execution time during contact, we find it took approximately 0.031 seconds per time step for contact detection and calculation of the non-rigid dynamics. Contact detection, physical simulation, and geometric updates were computed on a Sun 4/330, with a TAAC board performing rendering.

## 3 Fitting 3-D Point Data

It is useful to be able to fit a generalized implicit function representation to three-dimensional point data, so that objects in the world can be sampled and brought into our computer where they can participate in simulations. To fit point data with a generalized implicit function requires determining both the deformation parameters $\mathbf{u} = (u_1 ... u_m)^T$ used in $\mathcal{D}_\mathbf{u}$, and a displacement map.

Let us assume that we are given $n$ three-dimensional sensor measurements $\bar{\mathbf{X}}$ (in the global coordinate system) that originate from the surface of a single object:

$$\bar{\mathbf{X}} = [\bar{x}_1, \bar{y}_1, \bar{z}_1, \cdots \bar{x}_n, \bar{y}_n, \bar{z}_n]^T \qquad (11)$$

We need to determine a mapping between $\mathbf{X}$, points on the undeformed surface, and $\bar{\mathbf{X}}$, the sensor measurements that specify the points' target positions after displacement and deformation. To determine this mapping, we first define an ellipsoidal coordinate system by examination of the data's center of mass and central moments of inertia. For a detailed description of this initialization step, see [10]. This ellipsoid will serve as our initial guess of the undeformed implicit surface.

The sensor measurements are then projected onto this ellipsoid by using the projection function, $P(\mathbf{x})$. This projection implicitly defines a correspondence between the undeformed surface points and their desired positions after deformation. When the number of data points is large it is more efficient to project the data onto a predetermined grid of undeformed surface points. Each data point's position is distributed among nearby surface points using a Gaussian weighting [13].

### 3.1 Recovering Deformation Modes

Once point correspondences have been established, we can proceed with fitting. The task will be to deform the original undeformed points, $\mathbf{X}$, to their desired positions, $\bar{\mathbf{X}}$. At the end of this process, we will have recovered the deformed implicit function which best fits the data points.

To begin with, the effect of each of the $m$ deformation parameters $u_i$ in $\mathcal{D}_\mathbf{u}$ on the position of the undeformed points, $\mathbf{X}$ is calculated, to obtain a m x 3n matrix $\mathbf{\Phi}$ whose $i^{th}$ column $\phi_{i*}$ is:

$$\phi_{i*} = (\frac{\partial x_1}{\partial u_i}, \frac{\partial y_1}{\partial u_i}, \frac{\partial z_1}{\partial u_i}, \cdots \frac{\partial x_n}{\partial u_i}, \frac{\partial y_n}{\partial u_i}, \frac{\partial z_n}{\partial u_i})^T \qquad (12)$$

The matrix $\mathbf{\Phi}$ can be computed by finite differences — *i.e.*, analytically, or by applying a small amount of each deformation $u_i$ and measuring the resulting change in the coordinates of each point. In the ThingWorld modeling system the deformations used are the object's free vibration modes, so that the columns of $\mathbf{\Phi}$ define a coordinate transformation that diagonalizes the object's finite element equations. This allows the object's rigid and non-rigid dynamics to be simulated very inexpensively, as described in reference [11].

The matrix $\mathbf{\Phi}$ is the Jacobian of $\mathcal{D}_\mathbf{u}$ at each point in $\mathbf{X}$, and so may be used in a modified Newton-Raphson iteration to obtain the minimum RMS error estimate of deformation parameters $\mathbf{u}$ as follows:

$$\mathbf{u}^{k+1} = \mathbf{\Phi}^{-1}\left(\bar{\mathbf{X}} - \mathbf{X}^k\right) + \mathbf{u}^k \qquad (13)$$

where $\mathbf{X}^k$ is the projection of the data points on the surface defined by the deformations $\mathbf{u}^k$ at iteration $k$, and $\mathbf{u}^0 = \mathbf{0}$, $\mathbf{X}^0 = \mathbf{X}$. We have found that a single iteration is often sufficient to obtain a satisfactory estimate of the deformation parameters $\mathbf{u}$. Because $\mathbf{\Phi}$ is usually not square, use of the pseudoinverse $\mathbf{\Phi}^{-1} = (\mathbf{\Phi}\mathbf{\Phi}^T)^{-1}\mathbf{\Phi}^T$ is required; as $(\mathbf{\Phi}\mathbf{\Phi}^T)$ is only an m x m matrix, this calculation is inexpensive.

### 3.2 Computing a Displacement Map

If there are more degrees of freedom in the data points than in the deformation parameters, the deformed model will not generally pass through the data points exactly (*i.e.*, $f(\mathcal{D}_\mathbf{u}^{-1}\mathbf{M}^{-1}(\bar{\mathbf{x}} - \mathbf{b})) \neq 0$). A more accurate approximation to the data points can be obtained by incorporating these residual differences into a displacement map. This is done by solving for the displacement map value $d(\eta, \omega)$ that yields $\bar{\mathbf{x}} = \mathbf{M}\mathcal{D}_\mathbf{u}(\mathbf{x} + d\mathbf{n}) + \mathbf{b}$ for some point $\mathbf{x}$ on the undeformed implicit surface. The final result is a generalized implicit function representation that normally provides an exact fit to the set of initial data points, and provides a smoothly interpolated surface between those points — except in certain degenerate cases, such as when Nyquist criteria are not statisfied.

To compute the displacement map each data point $\bar{\mathbf{x}}$ is subjected to the inverse deformation $\mathcal{D}_\mathbf{u}^{-1}$ to obtain $\tilde{\mathbf{x}}$, the point in the undeformed space. Next, we project $\tilde{\mathbf{x}}$ along the surface normal using $P(\tilde{\mathbf{x}})$ to obtain its two-dimensional parametric space coordinate $(\eta, \omega)$. Finally, we compute the undeformed point's normal distance to the undeformed implicit surface by substituting it's coordinates into the surface's inside-outside function:

$$d(\eta, \omega) = f(\tilde{\mathbf{x}}). \qquad (14)$$

In the ThingWorld system displacement maps are represented by a regularly spaced grid in the surface's parametric space. Thus as each point is projected and its displacement determined, the result is spread to nearest grid points by Gaussian weighted averaging. This interpolation method works well when data points are fairly dense, however when there are only a few data points more sophisticated interpolation methods must be used [5].

Figure 2: Two frames from a physically-based animation in which a head deforms in response to getting bonked.

### 3.3 Example: Modeling a Head

Figure 2 shows two frames from a physically-based animation in which a jello-like head is struck with a wooden mallet. The head shape was recovered by converting 360° laser range data of a human head that was scanned by Cyberware at SIGGRAPH '90.

The model for the head was recovered with the method described above. It took about 5 seconds on a Sun 4/330 to recover the deformations and displacement map from 2500 data points. A color map had to be computed at higher resolution — about 10,000 data points were used. The color map was computed by projecting the color points onto the surface using $P(\mathbf{x})$ and gaussian interpolation for smoothing.

For the simulation, the head was sampled with 7200 polygons. The other objects had about 600 polygons each. Execution time for the three active objects averaged 0.13 seconds per time step during the collision, with approximately 0.05 seconds per time step attributable to contact detection and calculation of the non-rigid dynamics. The greater execution times for this example are primarily due to the large amount of detail in the head model.

## 4 Conclusion

Pentland and Williams [11] presented a method for combining implicit function representations with modal dynamics to obtain near-real-time non-rigid dynamic simulations. This paper extends this method by developing a generalized implicit function representation that is sufficiently powerful to describe many of the objects commonly used in computer graphics. The representation can therefore be used to reduce the cost of contact detection and physical simulation in most computer graphics applications. Even degenerate contact geometries, such as vertex-edge intersections, can be handled by techniques such as described in [3; 7; 12].

Finally, we have presented an efficient method for converting from surface point position data to our generalized implicit function representation. This allows automatic calculation of an implicit function representation from either physical measurements (*e.g.*, from laser rangefinders, or Polhemus measurements) or from vertex position data (*e.g.*, from polygon vertices, or samples from spline surfaces). For a more detailed description of our fitting method, initial model placement, and applications, see [10].

## Acknowledgments

We would like to thank the ThingWorld programming posse: Irfan Essa, Thad Starner, Brad Horowitz, and Martin Friedmann.

## References

[1] D. Baraff. Curved Surfaces and Coherence for Non-penetrating Rigid Body Simulation. *Computer Graphics*, 24(4):19–28, 1990.

[2] A. Barr. Global and Local Deformations of Solid Primitives. *Computer Graphics*, 18(3):21–30, 1984.

[3] A. Barr. Superquadrics and Angle-Preserving Transforms. *IEEE Computer Graphics and Applications*, 1(1):11–23, 1981.

[4] P. J. Burt and E. H. Adelson. A Multiresolution Spline With Application to Image Mosaics. *ACM Transactions on Graphics*, 2(4):217–236, 1983.

[5] T. Foley, D. Lane, and G. Nielson. Interpolation of Scattered Data on Closed Surfaces. *Computer Aided Geometric Design*, 7:303–312, 1990.

[6] J. K. Hahn. Realistic Animation of Rigid Bodies. *Computer Graphics*, 22(4):299–308, 1988.

[7] D. Kalra and A. H. Barr. Guaranteed Ray Intersections with Implicit Surfaces. *Computer Graphics*, 23(3):297–306, 1989.

[8] M. Moore and J. Wilhelms. Collision Detection and Response for Computer Animation. *Computer Graphics*, 22(4):289–298, 1988.

[9] A. Pentland. Computational Complexity Versus Virtual Worlds. *Computer Graphics*, 24(2):185–192, 1990.

[10] A. Pentland and S. Sclaroff. Closed-Form Solutions for Physically-Based Shape Modeling and Recognition. *IEEE Trans. on Pattern Analysis and Machine Intelligence*, 13, to appear in July 1991. Special Issue on Physically-Based Modeling.

[11] A. Pentland and J. Williams. Good Vibrations : Modal Dynamics for Graphics and Animation. *Computer Graphics*, 23(4):215–222, 1989.

[12] B. von Herzen, A. Barr, and H. Zatz. Geometric Collisions for Time-Dependent Parametric Surfaces. *Computer Graphics*, 24(4):39–48, 1990.

[13] L. Williams. Performance-Driven Facial Animation. *Computer Graphics*, 24(4):235–242, 1990.

# Convolution Surfaces

**Jules Bloomenthal**
**Ken Shoemake**

Xerox Palo Alto Research Center
Palo Alto, California 94304

**Abstract**

Smoothly blended articulated models are often difficult to construct using current techniques. Our solution in this paper is to extend the surfaces introduced by Blinn [Blinn 1982] by using three-dimensional convolution with skeletons composed of polygons or curves. The resulting convolution surfaces permit fluid topology changes, seamless part joins, and efficient implementation.

**CR Categories and Subject Descriptors**: I.3.5 **[Computer Graphics]**: Computational Geometry and Object Modeling - curve, surface, solid, and object representations.

**Additional Keywords and Phrases**: Implicit Surface, Parametric Surface, Convolution, Solid Modeling, Blends.

## INTRODUCTION

Animators seek models that flex and transform, but which are easy to position and mold. Designers often create these lively shapes by skillfully combining primitives, such as parametric surfaces (including polygons), or implicit surfaces and solids.

A parametric surface is given by a spatial position function: $\mathbf{p}(u,v) = [x(u,v),\ y(u,v),\ z(u,v)]$. In practice, the functions are splines defined by pieces of polynomials, or ratios of polynomials [Farin 1990], and are shaped by a sparse set of control points with an intuitive geometric relation to the surface. A single B-spline surface is naturally smooth, despite its piecewise construction. It is difficult, however, to create a smooth union of surfaces automatically.

An implicit surface is the zero-set of an implicit function $f(\mathbf{p}) = f(x, y, z)$. Including points for which $f(\mathbf{p})$ is positive gives a solid. In practice the most common functions used are polynomials, especially quadratics. The resulting algebraic surfaces can represent any rational polynomial parametric surface, as shown by classical algebraic geometry theory [Sederberg 1983]. The reverse is not true, however, suggesting that algebraic surfaces are more powerful than parametric surfaces. Unfortunately, quadrics are limited in shape, higher degree surface methods are in their infancy [Sederberg 1985] [Bajaj 1990], and blending surface construction [Warren 1989] seems difficult to automate.

Although algebraic surfaces show promise, in this paper we explore the advantages of implicit surfaces based on *skeletons*. Like control points for a spline surface, a simple lower dimensional object, the skeleton, resembles and controls the shape of a more complicated object. Vision research suggests that stick figure skeletons are natural abstractions for shapes [Nevatia 1982].



In particular, we extend the approach of Blinn [Blinn 1982], Wyvill et al. [Wyvill 1986], and Nishimura et al. [Nishimura 1985], who used implicit functions defined by the summation of point potentials. The points generate spherical iso-surfaces which blend smoothly into each other when brought together; hence a point may be considered a skeleton which is fleshed out to form a body. Points, however, are not entirely satisfactory skeletons; for example, points that approximate a flat surface must be closely packed to avoid bumps.

After briefly considering an alternative generalization, we propose the use of *convolution surfaces*, and show they are a natural, powerful re-interpretation and generalization of potential surfaces. Colburn has used implicit surfaces based on convolution to round a solid model [Colburn 1990]; we use convolution with piecewise planar skeletons to generate models. Convolution surfaces incorporate the smooth blending power and easy manipulability of potential surfaces while expanding the skeletons from points to lines, polygons, planar curves and regions, and in principle, any geometric primitive. We exploit properties of convolution in general, and Gaussian convolutions in particular, to compute our surfaces efficiently.

## POTENTIAL SURFACES

Blinn stepped beyond algebraic surfaces for molecular modeling by generating an exponentially decreasing field from the center of each atom and rendering the iso-potential surfaces [Blinn 1982]. That is, from a set S of atom centers an implicit function is defined at any point $\mathbf{p}$ in space as

$$f(S, \mathbf{p}) = \sum_{s \in S} \exp\left(\frac{-\| \mathbf{s}-\mathbf{p} \|^2}{2}\right).$$

The surface is given by those points $\mathbf{p}$ satisfying $f(S,\mathbf{p}) - c = 0$, where c is the iso-potential value.

Others have preferred pieces of polynomials for the field functions [Wyvill 1986], [Nishimura 1985]. Essential features of any such function are that it decrease monotonically, and drop to a negligible value beyond a moderate radius. (Although Blinn observed that the decay need not be spherically symmetric, this possibility seems to have been largely neglected.) Thus a single point generates a spherical shell, and well-separated points generate separate spheres. As two points are brought together, their shells reach out and merge smoothly. When the points are coincident, a single larger sphere results.

Because the non-negative regions of these implicit functions define solid volumes, CSG set operations are also possible. Simple arithmetic operations on the function values suffice [Ricci 1973]; for example, $\max(f(S_1, \mathbf{p}), f(S_2, \mathbf{p}))$ gives the union of the two volumes generated by $S_1$ and $S_2$. Negating the implicit function is also of interest, allowing us to subtract volumes.

 ACM-0-89791-436-8/91/007/0251 $00.75 

One advantage of potential surfaces is that they blend smoothly. Another is that they are simple to edit; to alter the surface one merely moves, adds, or deletes points. Unfortunately, flat surfaces can only be approximated.

## DISTANCE SURFACES

Point skeletons can be generalized to polygonal skeletons in at least two ways: by computing the potential from only the nearest point of the polygon, or by summing the potentials from all the points. The second possibility gives convolution surfaces; the first gives distance surfaces—or offset solids in the sense of Requicha [Requicha 1983]. Distance surfaces are iso-surfaces of $\mu(S, \mathbf{p})$, the function value at a point $\mathbf{p}$ defined by

$$\mu(S, \mathbf{p}) = \min_{s \in S} \| \mathbf{s}-\mathbf{p} \|.$$

When S is a spline curve or planar polygon, $\mu$ can be computed without explicitly calculating the distance to each point $\mathbf{s}$ of the curve or polygon [Bloomenthal 1989]. For a polygon, projecting $\mathbf{p}$ onto the plane of S reduces the problem to one in two dimensions. If the projection lies inside S, use the distance to the plane; otherwise, use the distance to the nearest point on an edge.

As defined, $\mu$ is not suitable for blending; however we can use it to replace the distance calculation in Blinn's exponential, giving one generalization of potential surfaces, $f(S, \mathbf{p}) = \exp(\mu^2(S, \mathbf{p})/2)$. Because this is a composition of monotonic functions, one of which is decreasing, it can be written as

$$f(S, \mathbf{p}) = \max_{s \in S} \exp\left(\frac{-\| \mathbf{s}-\mathbf{p} \|^2}{2}\right).$$

This function gives the union of the volumes generated by all the individual points of the collective skeleton, S. When the skeletons are not convex, the resulting distance surfaces can show creases, or curvature discontinuity, as seen in Figure 1; these are often undesirable.

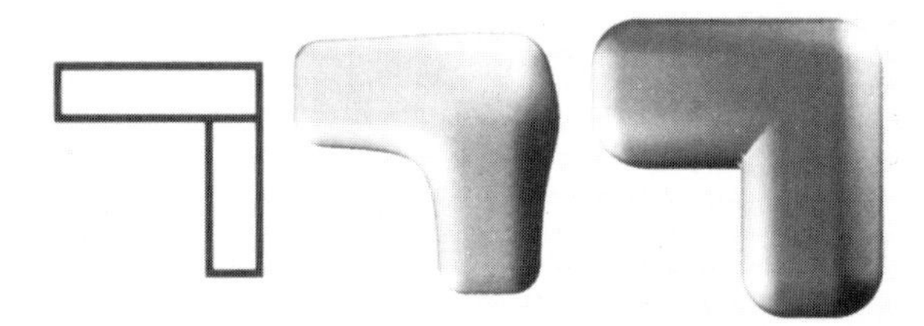

**Figure 1: Distance surfaces—skeletons, sum, union**

The blending of primitives within a solid modeling system has received considerable study, as shown by the survey of methods in [Woodwark 1986], and the more recent [Rockwood 1989], [Sederberg 1987], and [Warren 1989]. As Warren [Warren 1989] has shown, for algebraic surfaces blends have a well-defined form involving a weighted sum of products of the defining polynomials. The simplest approach for blending distance surfaces is to sum the values from each of the skeletons. This eliminates creases but also creates bulges. For polygonal skeletons, especially, it is awkward to achieve blends without bulges. One bulge prevention method for algebraic surfaces is proposed in [Middleditch 1985]; it is expensive and complex, however, especially for more than two primitives. Furthermore, our surfaces are not algebraic.

## CONVOLUTION SURFACES

We propose to have the best of both worlds: the spline and polygon generators of distance surfaces plus the well-behaved blends of potential surfaces. Although potential functions based on $\mu$ reduce to Blinn potentials when applied to a skeleton consisting of a single point, they behave differently for extended skeletons like polygons. One particular difference is instructive: the surface from a skeleton broken into pieces is not the same as that of the unbroken skeleton. For example, two halves of a line segment produce a surface which bulges at the joint. This is because each skeleton generates a surface which is a union, using max, while the blending uses summation. If the skeleton is broken down into infinitesimal pieces, i.e., individual points, the union becomes irrelevant, and the result is a pure summation,

$$f(S, \mathbf{p}) = \sum_{s \in S} \exp\left(\frac{-\| \mathbf{s}-\mathbf{p} \|^2}{2}\right).$$

or more properly, an integration,

$$f(S, \mathbf{p}) = \int_S \exp\left(\frac{-\| \mathbf{s}-\mathbf{p} \|^2}{2}\right) ds.$$

This new f is, in fact, the convolution of a spatially extended skeleton, not just a point, with a three-dimensional Gaussian filter kernel [Dudgeon 1984]. Formally, let $S(\mathbf{p})$ be the characteristic function for the skeleton (meaning $S(\mathbf{p}) = 1$ if $\mathbf{p}$ is a point of the skeleton, otherwise 0), and let

$$h(\mathbf{p}) = \exp\left(\frac{-\|\mathbf{p}\|^2}{2}\right).$$

(For the sake of brevity, we omit a more rigorous development involving Dirac delta functions.) Then, using ★ to represent convolution, we have

$$f(\mathbf{p}) = (h \star S)(\mathbf{p}) = \int_S \exp\left(\frac{-\| \mathbf{s}-\mathbf{p} \|^2}{2}\right) ds.$$

Convolution is usually considered part of the signal processing theory used to discuss and deal with aliasing in rendering [Foley 1990]; it is not commonly thought of for modeling shapes. Yet uniform B-spline curves and surfaces can be defined as the convolution of the B-spline basis functions with the control points [Farin 1990, p. 147], and robot path planning is simplified by convolving the room obstacle geometry with the robot's shape (the robot can then be treated as a point [Lengyel 1990]). Colburn has used an implicit surface based on convolution of a solid model with a Gaussian kernel as a way to round the corners of the solid [Colburn 1988, 1990].

Since we base our kernel on the potential function, when the skeletons are points convolution exactly reproduces the potential surface. For isolated convex skeletons such as triangles, rectangles, or line segments, convolution surfaces have almost the same shape as distance surfaces. Now, however, concave skeletons will also be smooth, and adjacent surfaces will blend seamlessly. Indeed, the superposition property of convolution guarantees that two abutting polygons will yield the same surface as a single more complex polygon which is their union:

$$h \star (S_1 + S_2) = (h \star S_1) + (h \star S_2).$$

This is shown diagrammatically in Figure 2.

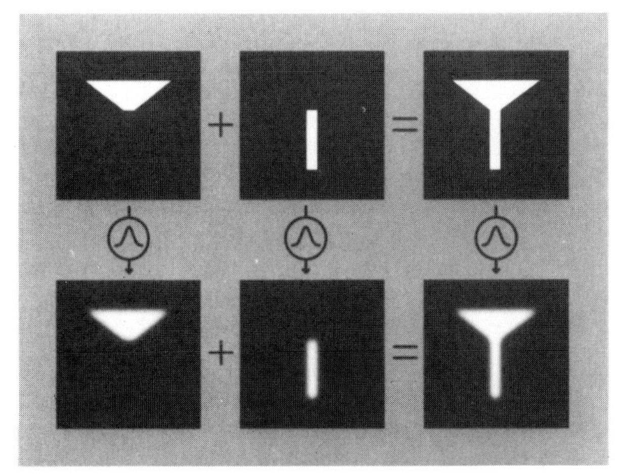


**Figure 2: Superposition**

To construct a smooth, complex surface from simple skeletons, we need only sum their convolutions. Figure 3 illustrates results for the animation of two adjacent rectangular skeletons, with the upper one rotating; the primitives merge smoothly into a single shape. In contrast, the sum of algebraic surfaces is completely unsatisfactory, since the complexity of the surface is limited by the degree, which summing does not increase. For example, the sum of any number of quadric surfaces, say spheres, is a single quadric surface!

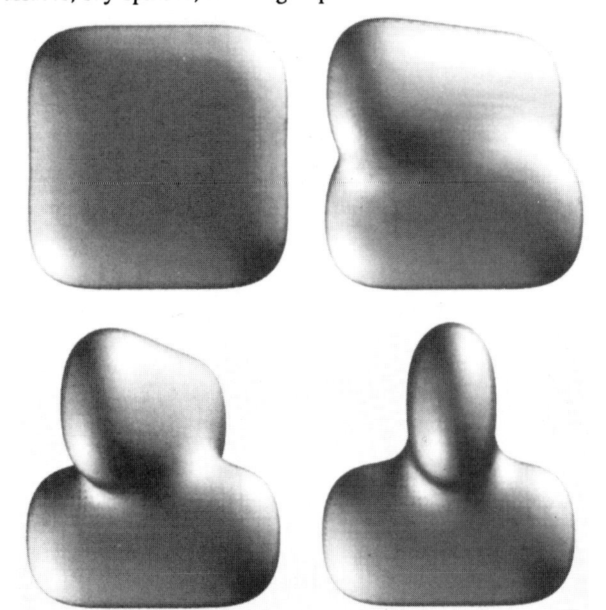

**Figure 3: Model articulations.**

## IMPLEMENTATION

One motivation for using distance surfaces is that they are reasonable to compute; it is not immediately clear that the same is true for convolution surfaces. In some sense, however, convolution is less complicated than minimizing distance, and is more efficient to compute.

Because of the superposition property, we are free to partition a skeleton. Still, it is impossible to evaluate the convolution, even for a polygon, by explicitly summing the influence of each point. A Gaussian filter, however, has the special property of being separable; it can be factored into a product of lower-dimensional Gaussians. We can, for example, separate the z component:

$$h(p) = \exp\left(\frac{-\|p\|^2}{2}\right) = \exp\left(\frac{-(x^2+y^2+z^2)}{2}\right)$$
$$= \exp\left(\frac{-(x^2+y^2)}{2}\right)\exp\left(\frac{-z^2}{2}\right).$$

Thus to convolve with a polygon lying in the x-y plane, we can first perform a planar convolution, then convolve in z. Because polygons have infinitesimal depth, the z convolution is trivial. The planar convolution requires more work, but is again separable into x and y. We have reduced the spatial convolution of a polygon to

$$f(S, \mathbf{p}) = \exp\left(\frac{-\| z_S - z_\mathbf{p} \|^2}{2}\right)$$
$$\int_{S_y}\exp\left(\frac{-\| y-y_\mathbf{p} \|^2}{2}\right)\int_{S_x}\exp\left(\frac{-\| x-x_\mathbf{p} \|^2}{2}\right) dx\, dy.$$

For a skeleton such as a line segment, the y integral collapses like z; a point requires no integration. A Gaussian is also spherically symmetric—it looks the same in all directions—so this same kind of three axis separation can be used no matter how the skeleton is oriented in space.

This suggests a convenient approach for planar skeletons. Scan convert each polygon into its own digital image, filter the image in two directions by a Gaussian, then multiply a Gaussian function of the distance from **p** to the plane of the image by the intensity at the point onto which it projects. Figure 4 illustrates the process. The images cache planar convolution results, and can be computed efficiently if convolution is performed during scan conversion.

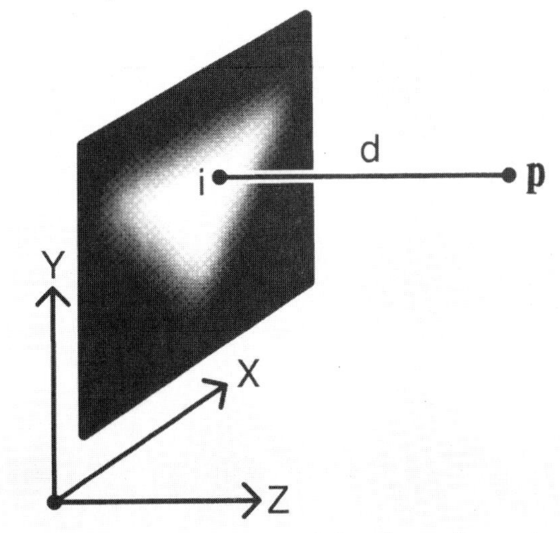


**Figure 4: Computing value of the three-dimensional convolution at a point in space.**

In practice, we approximate a Gaussian with a cubic spline, to simplify computation and to limit kernel width. Artifacts of the scan conversion can be avoided by choice of a suitable resolution. A Gaussian kernel approximates an ideal low-pass filter, removing high frequency details of the skeletons. Hence the effective bandwidth of the Gaussian can be used to determine the sampling frequency needed to preserve accuracy in the sampled images, and can guide the choice of spatial sampling frequency for polygonization [Bloomenthal 1988], [Hall 1990], [Dobkin 1990]. A standard Gaussian passes less than 1% of the energy in frequencies higher than half a unit, so in this case four samples per unit should suffice. Colburn discusses analogous resolution requirements for his octrees.

Although Colburn quotes compute times of days, we polygonize a surface in minutes. Colburn, however, is solving a different problem: he wants to make minimal changes to an existing solid. The solid is diced into tiny cubes before convolving; and while he uses separability, he cannot cache planar convolutions as we do. His method requires significant operator input to define patches through which to trace rays.

Our planar approach can be especially fast for animation; when a skeletal piece is used in many frames without change in shape, the planar images can be reused. Convolution surfaces are cheap in other situations as well. For a potential surface, evaluating the implicit function at a point requires calculating the distance to each nearby point, mapping each distance through a Gaussian, and summing. For a convolution surface, a swarm of co-planar points can be replaced by a single planar image, which requires only one distance calculation, one Gaussian evaluation, and interrogation of the image. The sum over points has been replaced by a planar convolution that is factored out of the inner evaluation loop and need only be calculated within a kernel width of the polygon perimeter.

Any point, line, or planar skeleton can be handled, and more general skeletons can be diced into polygons or polylines using standard techniques; the bandwidth of the Gaussian filters provides a least upper bound on the size of the pieces. As an example of the versatility of our method, Figure 5 is a convolution surface whose skeleton is a five-sided S-patch [Loop 1989].

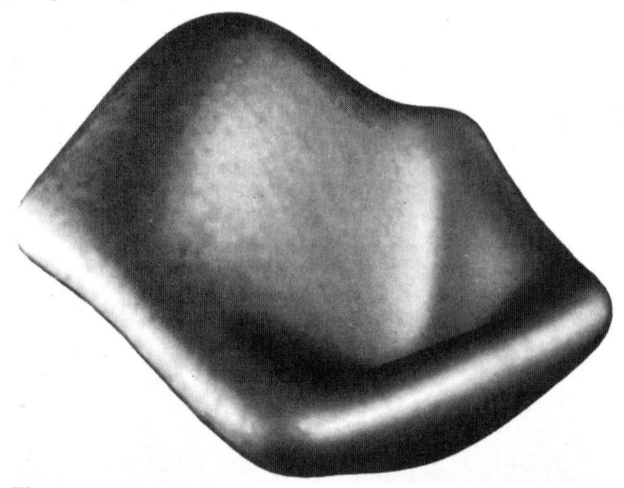

**Figure 5: Convolution surface from S-patch skeleton.**

## VARIATIONS

The shape of a convolution surface can be varied in (at least) five ways: by changing the iso-value, changing the shape of the skeleton, changing the skeleton "weight," changing the convolution kernel, and by spatial deformation. These can be illustrated with the two-dimensional potential function depicted as a height field in Figure 6. The usual CSG operations are still possible, so components of a model need not blend together. As noted previously, unions and intersections can be obtained by applying max and min to the component functions.

**Figure 6: Convolution variations.**

The iso-value defining the surface (or curves, in this two-dimensional example) is represented by a horizontal plane that intersects the mounds in a contour. Raising and lowering the plane, which is equivalent to adding a constant to the potential field, causes the plane to intersect different contours. Contours could also be determined as the intersection of some curved surface with the mounds; but again, the same effect can be had by changing the potential field.

Changes in the shape of the skeleton correspond to moving the mounds. This is the most basic design variation.

It is not necessary for $S(\mathbf{p})$ to be restricted to 0 or 1. When S is a set of points, each point can be given its own weight, and its influence will be scaled accordingly. In the illustration, this corresponds to the differences in height of the mounds. Negative weights correspond to pits rather than mounds, and offer a way to avoid unwanted blending, such as between the fingers of a hand. Decreasing the skeleton weight along a line, for example, gives a tapered shape, like a carrot. Incorporating a weight function, $w(\mathbf{s})$, in our defining function yields

$$f(S, \mathbf{p}) = \int_S w(\mathbf{s}) \exp\left(\frac{-\|\mathbf{s}-\mathbf{p}\|^2}{2}\right) ds.$$

If the kernel is to remain a Gaussian, the only aspect of its shape that can change is its width. It is not necessary to convolve all parts of a skeleton with the same width Gaussian; narrow widths can be used where more detail is desired, while still blending well. This difference is illustrated by the low mounds in the figure. We speculate that Gaussians with broader widths can be used to provide models with less detail for small or distant objects.

Deformations [Barr 1984] [Sederberg 1986] can be applied to any form of surface, but convolution surfaces allow new possibilities. For example, the skeleton offers a convenient reference frame for a spatially variant function, such as a stretch perpendicular to the skeleton, breaking the symmetry of the Gaussian. The general quadric kernels Blinn used for his "Blobby Man" can also be considered deformations [Blinn 1982]. Note that deforming the skeleton produces a different effect than deforming the surface. Figure 7 illustrates a surface in which the convolution is twisted; the arm muscles in Figure 8 are stretched.

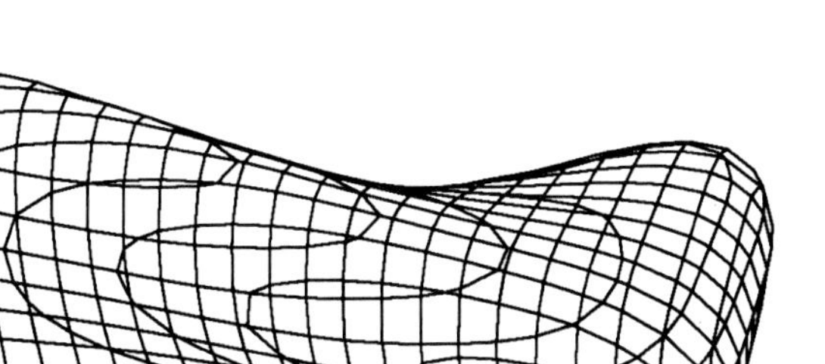

Figure 7: A twisted convolution.

## SUMMARY

The use of convolution surfaces based on skeletons suggests numerous applications in design and animation. We have used them to embed organic forms, such as muscles, within other organic forms, such as an arm. A procedurally generated example is shown in Figure 8. The arm was procedurally generated according to joint angles and muscle size; a corresponding parametric shape would be difficult to generate procedurally. Figure 9 depicts a mosaic of convolved planar images.

Convolution surfaces offer a number of advantages, such as:

- The shape of the skeleton suggests the shape of the surface.
- The surfaces are smooth even if the skeletons are not.
- The topology of the surface can vary fluidly with changes in the skeleton.
- The kernel width limits the influence of skeletons, providing local control and allowing surface bounds estimation.
- The blends are well behaved.
- The implementation is simple and efficient.

One disadvantage is the loss of an analytic representation for the resulting surface.

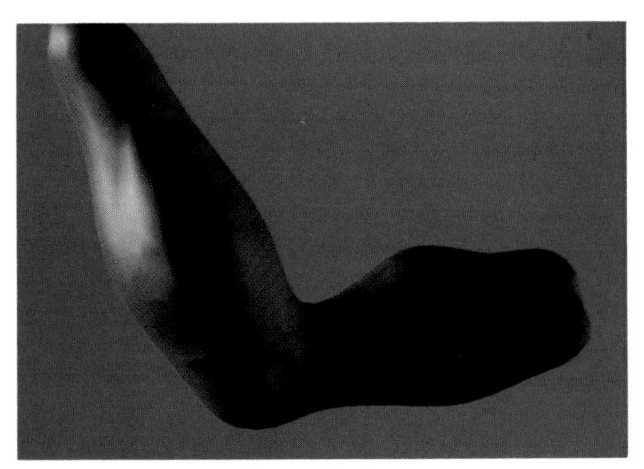

Figure 8: Arm.

## ACKNOWLEDGEMENTS

We are grateful to Paul Heckbert, Pat Hanrahan, and Michael Plass for technical advice; we especially thank Paul for a critical reading. We also thank Mark Bloomenthal, Kim Brook, Liz Chase, Richard Manuck, George Robertson, and Brian Tramontana for their help.

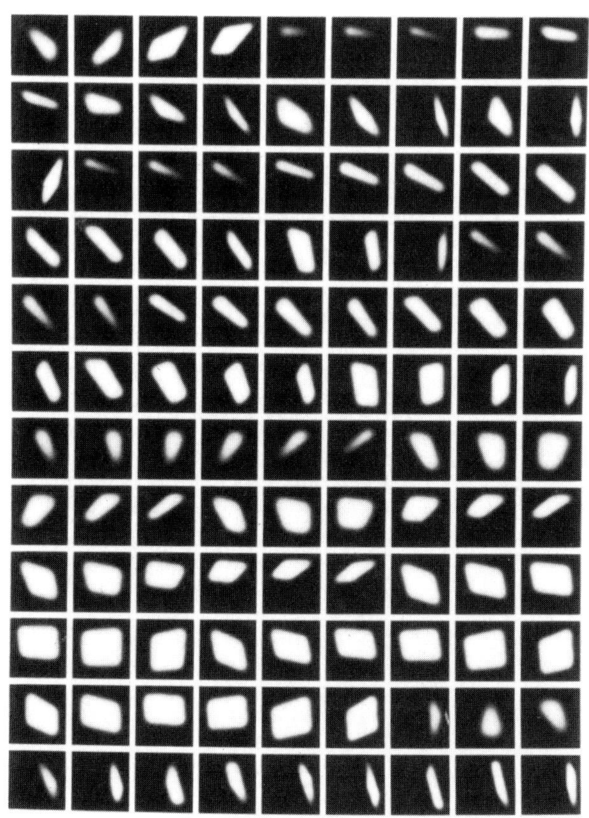

Figure 10: Convolution mosaic.

## REFERENCES

Bajaj, C., and Ihm, I. *Algebraic Surface Design with Hermite Interpolation.* Technical Report CSD-TR-939, Computer Sciences Dept., Purdue University, January 1990.

Barr, A. "Global and Local Deformations of Solid Primitives." Proceedings of SIGGRAPH'84 (Minneapolis, Minnesota, July 23–27, 1984). In *Computer Graphics* **18** (3), (July 1984), 21–30.

Blinn, J.F. "A Generalization of Algebraic Surface Drawing." *ACM Transactions on Graphics* **1** (3) (July 1982), 235–256.

Bloomenthal, J. "Polygonization of Implicit Surfaces." *Computer Aided Geometric Design* **5** (1988), 341–355.

Bloomenthal, J. "Techniques for Implicit Modeling." Xerox PARC Technical Report P89-00106. 1989.

Colburn, S. "Method for Global Blending of Computer Modeled Solid Objects using a Convolution Integral." United States Patent No. 4,791,583, December 1988.

Colburn, S. "Solid Modeling with Global Blending for Machining Dies and Patterns." SAE Technical Paper Series #900878, Society of Automotive Engineers, Inc., 1990.

DeRose, T.D. *Geometric Continuity: a Parametrization-Independent Measure of Continuity for Computer-Aided Geometric Design.* Ph.D. dissertation, Computer Science division, University of California, Berkeley, California, August 1985.

Dobkin, D., Levy, S., Thurston, W., and Wilks, A. "Contour Tracing by Piecewise Linear Approximations." *ACM Transactions on Graphics*, **9** (4), (October 1990), 389–423.

Dudgeon, D. and Mersereau, R. *Multidimensional Digital Signal Processing.* Prentice Hall, 1984.

Duff, T. "Polygon Scan Conversion by Exact Convolution." *Proceedings of the International Conference on Raster Imaging and Digital Typography* (Lausanne, Switzerland, October, 1989), 154–168.

Farin, G. *Curves and Surfaces for Computer Aided Geometric Design, 2nd Edition.* Academic Press, 1990.

Foley, J., van Dam, A., Feiner, S., and Hughes, J. *Computer Graphics: Principles and Practice, 2nd Edition.* Addison-Wesley, 1990.

Hall, M., and Warren, J. "Adaptive Polygonalization of Implicitly Defined Surfaces." *IEEE Computer Graphics and Applications* **10** (6), (November 1990), 33–42.

Hoffman, C. and Hopcroft, J. *The Potential Method for Blending Surfaces and Corners.* Technical Report TR 85-674 Computer Science Dept., Cornell University, 1985.

Lengyel, J., Reichert, M., Donald, B.R., and Greenberg, D.P. "Real-Time Robot Motion Planning Using Rasterizing Computer Graphics Hardware." Proceedings of SIGGRAPH'90 (Dallas, Texas, August 6–10, 1990). In *Computer Graphics* **24** (4), (August 1990), 327–335.

Loop, C., and DeRose, T. "A Multisided Generalization of Bezier Surfaces." *ACM Transactions on Graphics* **8** (3), (July 1989), 204–234.

Middleditch, A.E. and Sears, K.H. "Blend Surfaces for Set Theoretic Volume Modeling Systems." Proceedings of SIGGRAPH'85 (San Francisco, California, July 22–26, 1985). In *Computer Graphics* **19** (3), (July 1985), 161–170.

Nevatia, R. *Machine Perception.* Prentice-Hall, 1982.

Nishimura, H., Hirai, A., Kawai, T., Kawata, T., Shirakawa, I., and Omura, K. "Object modeling by distribution function and a method of image generation." Journal of papers given at the Electronics Communications Conference 1985, J68-D(4), 1985 (In Japanese).

Requicha, A.A.G. "Toward a Theory of Geometric Tolerancing." *International Journal of Robotics Research* **2** (4) (Winter 1983), 45–49.

Ricci, A. "A Constructive Geometry for Computer Graphics." *The Computer Journal* **16** (2), (May 1973), 157–160.

Rockwood, A.P. "The Displacement Method for Implicit Blending Surfaces in Solid Models." *ACM Transactions on Graphics* **8** (4), (October 1989), 279–297.

Rossignac, J.R. and Requicha, A.A.G. "Constant-Radius Blending in Solid Modeling." *Computers in Mechanical Engineering* (July 1984), 65–73.

Sederberg, T. *Implicit and Parametric Curves and Surfaces for Computer Aided Geometric Design.* Ph.D. dissertation, Mechanical Engineering, Purdue University, 1983.

Sederberg, T. "Piecewise Algebraic Surface Patches." *Computer Aided Geometric Design*, **2**, (1985), 53–59.

Sederberg, T., and Parry, S. "Free-Form Deformations of Solid Geometric Models." Proceedings of SIGGRAPH'86 (Dallas, Texas, August 18–22, 1986). In *Computer Graphics* **20** (4) (August 1986), 151–160.

Sederberg, T. "Algebraic Geometry for Surface and Solid Modeling." *Geometric Modeling: Algorithms and Trends*, G. Farin, ed., SIAM Press, 1987.

Warren, J. "Blending Algebraic Surfaces." *ACM Transactions on Graphics* **8** (4) (October 1989), 263–278.

Woodwark, J.R. "Blends in Geometric Modelling." *The Mathematics of Surfaces II*, ed. R. Martin, 255–297.

Wyvill, G., McPheeters, C., and Wyvill, B. "Data Structure for Soft Objects." *Visual Computer* **2** (4), (August 1986), 227–234.

# Deformable Curve and Surface Finite-Elements for Free-Form Shape Design

George Celniker[a] and Dave Gossard[b]

[a] Schlumberger Laboratory for Computer Science, P.O. Box 200015, Austin, Texas 78720

[b]Massachusetts Institute of Technology, Department of Mechanical Engineering
Computer Aided Design Laboratory, 77 Massachusetts Ave., Cambridge, Ma. 02139

## ABSTRACT

The finite element method is applied to generate primitives that build continuous deformable shapes designed to support a new free-form modeling paradigm. The primitives autonomously deform to minimize an energy functional subject to user controlled geometric constraints and loads. The approach requires less user input than conventional free-form modeling approaches because the shape can be parameterized independently of the number of degrees of freedom needed to describe the shape.

Both a curve and a surface finite element are developed. The properties of these geometric primitives have been engineered to support an interactive three phase approach for defining very fair free-form shapes as found in automobiles, ship hulls and car bodies. The shape's character lines or folds and edges are defined with deformable curve segments. These character lines are then "skinned" with a deformable surface. The final shape is sculpted interactively by applying loads to the surface to control the surface shape between character lines. Shapes created with this technique enjoy the advantage that they are already meshed for further finite element analysis.

### Categories and Subject Descriptors

I.3.5 [Computer Graphics]: Computational Geometry and Object Modeling; I.3.7 [Computer Graphics]: Three-dimensional Graphics and Realism; I.6.3 [Simulation and Modeling]: Applications; J.6 [Computer-Aided Engineering]: Computer-Aided Design (CAD);

### Additional Key Words and Phrases

Finite Elements, Deformable Modeling, Computer Aided Geometric Design, Dynamics, Interactive Sculpting

## 1 INTRODUCTION

The objective of this work is to develop an improved computer-based free-form design methodology capable of interactively defining fair shapes with a minimal amount of user input. The central idea is that shapes can be sculpted with "energy-based" deformable computer models that mimic real surface behavior to achieve this objective.



Physical deformable media are commonly used for sculpting because their naturally properties can simplify creating controlled shapes. For example long slender beams resist bending and so deform in gracefully smooth curves. Such beams are used for the lofting of ship hulls. Physical shapes are difficult to describe and so are difficult to use for a variety of downstream applications such as manufacturing, analysis, and visualization. As a result, an extensive literature has developed to support computer-based design of free-form shapes (see [5]). The problem has been that these approaches lack the ease of use of sculpting in a deformable medium. The challenge is to recreate this sculpting effect in a computer where the shape is defined exactly and is available for other applications.

Computer-based deformable shape modeling is the combination of parametrically described geometry and an energy minimization algorithm. The energy minimization algorithm automatically adjusts a shape to minimize its energy as measured by an energy functional subject to user controlled geometric constraints and loads. This automatic adjustment mimics the behavior of physical media and so can be exploited.

Figure 1 shows the three step paradigm proposed for the design of free-form shapes. First the object's essence is defined as a set of three dimensional character lines. A character line is added wherever the object's surface tangent is discontinuous such as at edges and along creases. The object is then skinned so that over every face there is a deformable surface. Finally, the object's shape is completed by interactively sculpting the surfaces with forces and loads. Once completed the object's shape can be modified by changing the character lines or by continued sculpting of the surfaces. This is the ShapeWright paradigm.

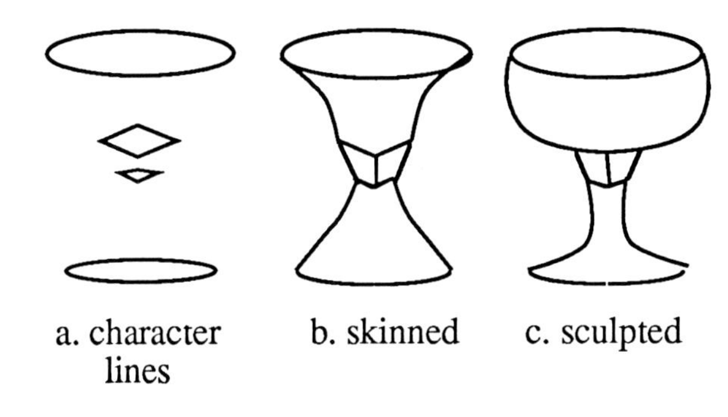


Figure 1) The ShapeWright design paradigm

©1991 ACM-0-89791-436-8/91/007/0257 $00.75

The deformable curve and surface primitives presented in this paper have the following interesting properties.

1.) Continuous Curve and Surface representations
2.) $C^1$ enforced shape with solutions that tend to $C^3$ in the presence of continuous loads and geometric constraints
3.) Explicitly enforced geometric constraints
  a) enforced point locations
  b) enforced point tangent and normal directions
  c) enforced curve shapes within and on edges of a surface
  d) enforced normal direction along an edge or internal curve within a surface
4.) Arbitrarily shaped and topologically arbitrarily meshed parametric domains

Geometric constraints can be freely mixed with sculpting. All geometric constraints are satisfied while sculpting and additional constraints can be added or modified at any time.

Interactive control is generated by parameterizing the shape with sculpting loads and geometric constraints. The user can create a mix of sculpting loads and geometric constraints to define shape modeling effects. Each load and constraint is a separate entity. Any load or constraint parameter can be assigned to a slider bar to be used to sculpt shape as an interactive, dynamic search of a parameter space. The size of this parameter space is independent of the number of degrees of freedom (dofs) needed to describe the free-form surface. This strategy encourages the user to work at a high level, thinking in terms such as bigger, smaller, fatter, thinner, etc.

## 2 PREVIOUS WORK

Terzopoulos, Witkin, Kass et. al.[7,19] introduced the use of deformable models for extracting shapes from video images and for simplifying the generation of realistic animations. To extract shape from video images, the video intensity array is converted into a force field that operates on the deformable model. In this manner deformable models are able to automatically extract features of the video image.

Schweikert [17] introduced energy-based shape formulations to the Computer Aided Geometric Design field with his splines in tension made for improved interpolating. Nielson [12] noted that solving Schweikert's differential problem for shape was equivalent to finding the shape that minimizes an equivalent energy functional and developed a piecewise polynomial interpolant that approximated the minimum while interpolating the constraints. Since then energy-based or minimization algorithms have subsequently been used by a variety of researchers to incrementally improve the fairness of a shape by tuning the parameters of a shape model after setting them interactively [4,6,8,9,10,11,13,16].

Previous deformable based shape modeling systems used finite difference techniques [1,2]. Consequently continuous shapes were approximated as sets of distinct points yielding a shape representation inappropriate for manufacturing applications.

This work presents a method to model shape with deformable models using continuous representations.

## 3 DEFORMABLE MODELING

### 3.a) Deformable Models

A deformable model's shape is calculated indirectly by finding a minimum to an energy functional or by solving a set of differential equations. It is this indirection that enables the geometry to act autonomously. The deformable models used in this work have functionals of the general form

$$E_{deformation} = \int_\sigma (\alpha \text{ stretch} + \beta \text{ bending})\, d\sigma \qquad 1$$

The energy stored in a shape is the sum of an $\alpha$ weighted stretching term and a $\beta$ weighted bending term. By finding the shape which minimizes the above functional subject to geometric constraints and user loads we build a shape which naturally attempts to resist stretching and bending. The curve and surface energy functionals presented in this paper are

$$E_{curve} = \int_{curve} (\alpha(u)\, w_u^2 + \beta(u) w_{uu}^2 - 2\, \mathbf{f}\, \mathbf{w})\, du \qquad 2$$

and

$$E_{surface} = \int_\sigma \left[ \begin{pmatrix} (\alpha_{11} w_u^2 + 2\alpha_{12} w_u w_v + \alpha_{22} w_v^2) \\ + (\beta_{11} w_{uu}^2 + 2\beta_{12} w_{uv}^2 + \beta_{22} w_{vv}^2) \end{pmatrix} - 2\, \mathbf{f}\, \mathbf{w} \right] du dv \qquad 3$$

where $\mathbf{w}$ is a contiguous set of points in 3-space.

$\mathbf{w} = \mathbf{w}(u) = [x(u),y(u),z(u)]$ for a curve
$\mathbf{w} = \mathbf{w}(u,v) = [x(u,v),y(u,v),z(u,v)]$ for a surface

The range on the parametric variables u and v may vary for each shape but are limited to the real number set.

$w_u$ is shorthand for $\partial w / \partial u$ while

$w_{vv}$ is shorthand for $\partial^2 w / \partial v^2$

$\mathbf{f} = \mathbf{f}(\mathbf{w},t)$ denotes the applied sculpting forces which are changed over time t by the user.

The term $2\mathbf{f}\mathbf{w}$ represents the amount of work added to the system due to deformations caused by the application of external sculpting loads.

A result of the calculus of variations shows that the one shape $\mathbf{w}$ which minimizes a functional of the form used here will also satisfy a related set of differential equations known as the Euler equations. The Euler equations for the curve are

$$\frac{d^2(\beta w_{uu})}{du^2} - \frac{d(\alpha w_u)}{du} = \mathbf{f} \qquad 4$$

and for the surface are

$$\left( \frac{\partial^2(\beta_{11} w_{uu})}{\partial u^2} + \frac{\partial^2(\beta_{12} w_{uv})}{\partial u \partial v} + \frac{\partial^2(\beta_{22} w_{vv})}{\partial v^2} \right) - \left( \frac{\partial(\alpha_{11} w_u + \alpha_{12} w_v)}{\partial u} + \frac{\partial(\alpha_{12} w_u + \alpha_{22} w_v)}{\partial v} \right) = \mathbf{f} \qquad 5$$

Note that the above single vector equations represents three independent scalar equations in x, y and z. The effect of the sculpting forces $\mathbf{f}$ are best seen in the Euler equations. They balance the internal forces due to stretching and bending. In some sense the shape is made to deform until the resulting internal forces exactly balance the applied external forces. For a discussion of the generation of the Euler equations and the relationship between the integral and differential forms of the problem see Strang's text on applied mathematics [18].

The curve and surface behavior is best described by the terms of the defining energy functional. These shapes resist stretching and bending. The curve tends to minimize its length and the surface tends to minimize it area. These properties were selected to help avoid folding while shrinking a shape. The resistance to bending tends to distribute local bending over large regions. The effect of this property is to produce very smooth shapes. The combination of these properties builds well behaved geometric primitives suitable for shape design.

The curve scalar $\alpha$ and $\beta$ values become 2nd order tensors in the surface equation described as 2x2 matrices. Nonisotropic material behavior can be generated by varying the different values of these matrices.

Adding dynamic terms to the Euler equations introduces time dependent behavior into the system. Time dependence allows a user to select between different local minimum solutions and adds realism to the interface to further enhance the system's ability to mimic physical behavior.

$$\frac{\partial}{\partial t}\left(\rho\frac{\partial \mathbf{w}}{\partial t}\right)+\mu\frac{\partial \mathbf{w}}{\partial t}+\mathrm{L}\mathbf{w}=\mathbf{f}(\mathbf{w},t) \qquad 6$$

where $\rho$ is a mass density
$\mu$ is a viscous damping term needed for stability and
Lw is short for the left hand side of equations 4 or 5

This scheme depends on finding a method for solving for shape which is interactive and supports a continuous shape representation. For this problem there are two main numerical schemes for generating approximate solutions to the actual shape **w**. These are the finite difference method and the finite element method. Finite difference solutions begin by approximating the continuous solution **w** as a set of discrete points in space. The disadvantage of the approach is that the final solution is always stated as a set of points in space. The original continuity of the solution has been lost.

### 3.b) Solving for Deformable Shape

The solution scheme for finding **w** presented here is based on Ritz's finite element method and results in continuous deformable geometric curve and surface primitives, or finite elements, appropriate for interactive geometric modeling.

The Ritz solution method for solving the ShapeWright deformable model problem starts with the variational statement of the problem: find the shape **w** to minimize the energy functional in equations 2 and 3. The first step is to approximate the actual solution **w** by $\mathbf{w}^h$ a weighted sum of continuous shape functions.

$$\mathbf{w}(u,v) \approx \mathbf{w}^h(u,v) = \sum_i \mathbf{x}_i\, \varphi_i(u,v) \qquad 7$$

The shape functions $\varphi_i$ are fixed in advance and the weights $\mathbf{x}_i$ are the unknowns. This step discretizes the problem since there are always a finite number of $\mathbf{x}_i$ values.

The next step is to select a class of allowed sculpting functions **f**. All functions of finite energy will be used such that

$$\int_a \mathbf{f}(a)^2\, da < \infty \qquad 8$$

This set of functions includes the important point load as well as all continuous functions. Having selected the class of functions allowed for the sculpting loads we can determine what class of functions need to be considered for the shape functions $\varphi_i$ of the solution. Inspecting the Euler equations 4 and 5 we might want to consider all functions that have finite energy in their 4th derivatives. As it turns out, the finite element theory shows that this is too stringent a requirement. Since the Ritz method uses only the variational statement of the problem, we need only to consider functions that have finite energy in their 2nd order derivatives. This is the set of $C^1$ functions.

This is an important attribute of the Ritz theory. Although the approximate solution $\mathbf{w}^h$ is attempting to generate a solution with finite energy in its fourth order derivatives it can be generated from functions that have finite energy in the 2nd order term. As more $\varphi_i$ functions are used, the approximation $\mathbf{w}^h$ will converge to the actual solution **w**. This property has significant implications for shape smoothness. Although the $\varphi_i$ shapes need only guarantee $C^1$ continuity, the final shape $\mathbf{w}^h$ will tend to be $C^3$ continuous.

Placing the approximation for shape into the original minimum principle yields the matrix minimum principle

$$\min\,(\mathbf{X}^T \mathbf{K}_\sigma \mathbf{X} - \mathbf{F}_\sigma^T \mathbf{X}) \qquad 9$$

where the unknowns and the shape functions are ordered into vectors as

$$\mathbf{X}^T = [\mathbf{x}_1\ \mathbf{x}_2 \cdots\ \mathbf{x}_n] \quad \text{and} \quad \Phi = [\varphi_1\ \varphi_2 \cdots\ \varphi_n] \qquad 10$$

and $\mathbf{K}_\sigma$ and $\mathbf{F}_\sigma$ define the stiffness matrix and forcing vector. These terms are given by

$$\mathbf{K}_\sigma = \int_\sigma \Phi_b^T\, \bar{\beta}\, \Phi_b + \Phi_s^T\, \bar{\alpha}\, \Phi_s\, du dv \qquad \mathbf{F}_\sigma = \int_\sigma \Phi^T\, \mathbf{f}\, du dv \qquad 11$$

where $\Phi_b = \begin{bmatrix} \Phi_{uu} \\ \Phi_{vv} \\ 2\Phi_{uv} \end{bmatrix} \qquad \Phi_s = \begin{bmatrix} \Phi_u \\ \Phi_v \end{bmatrix}$

$$\bar{\alpha} = \begin{bmatrix} \alpha_{11} & \alpha_{12} \\ \alpha_{12} & \alpha_{22} \end{bmatrix} \quad \bar{\beta} = \begin{bmatrix} \beta_{11} & & \\ & \beta_{22} & \\ & & \beta_{12} \end{bmatrix}$$

Finding the minimum of equation 9 is equivalent to solving the matrix problem

$$K_\sigma X = F_\sigma \quad (12)$$

The Ritz method becomes the finite element method when the shape functions are constrained to be zero everywhere except in the neighborhood of some node in the surface. The principle advantage of using local support shape functions is the ease of matching complicated boundary conditions. These boundary conditions include the previously cited requirements that the curves and surfaces must be able to interpolate sets of points and maintain specified tangent conditions.

The time dependent Euler equation 6 can be rewritten using the finite element stiffness matrix as

$$\frac{\partial}{\partial t}\left(\rho\frac{\partial w}{\partial t}\right) + \mu\frac{\partial w}{\partial t} + K_\sigma X = F_\sigma(w,t) \quad (13)$$

These equations are integrated through time by approximating the temporal partials with finite differences which results in a matrix equation relating the shape at time $t+\Delta t$ to the shape and sculpting loads at time t (see [2]). Once the unknowns in **X** are found the final shape can be generated by using the original parametric representation for shape given in equation 7.

The matrix $K_\sigma$ is guaranteed to be symmetric and positive definite due to the form of the selected energy functionals. The finite element constraint on the shape functions will make $K_\sigma$ sparse and usually banded. These properties reduce the cost of solving equation 12 and help to support interactivity.

Both the finite difference and the finite element solutions for shape **w** result in an approximation found by solving a set of algebraic equations. The difference between the two methods is the semantics of the unknown variables. In finite differences the unknowns are a discrete set of points in space. In finite elements the unknowns are a discrete set of weights used to sum continuous functions to generate a continuous description of shape appropriate for the ShapeWright modeling scheme.

### 3.c) Enforcing Geometric Constraints

A geometric modeling package needs a general means to enforce geometric constraints. A restricted class of geometric constraints, which includes quite a useful number of situations, can be achieved by operating on the problems explicit dofs. When the system dofs are chosen with care this scheme can implement quite general constraints. In this application this approach will be used to support all the geometric constraints listed in the introduction. For the matrix problem

$$AX = G \quad (14)$$

Where A = The system Matrix
X = A column vector of the dofs
G = A column forcing vector

any set of linear functions of the problem's dofs is expressed as

$$X = DY + D_0. \quad (15)$$

Where Y = A vector of unknowns generally smaller than **X**
**D** = A matrix, generally non-square,
$D_0$ = A column vector.

Constraints using equations of this form can be automatically enforced by substituting the constraint equations in the system matrix equation and premultiplying by $D^T$ to yield the new set of system matrix equations

$$[D^TAD]\, Y = D^TG - D^TAD_0 \quad (16)$$

The matrix $D^TAD$ retains the symmetry, positive definiteness and usually the bandedness of the original **A** matrix. In practice, the most common constraint is to fix one of the displacement locations at a known location. Generating the $D^TAD$ matrix for this case becomes very simple. It is just **A** with one row and one column deleted. For most simple constraints the **A** matrix can be modified without multiplying.

## 4 DEFORMABLE SURFACE ELEMENT

A deformable surface is made of a set of connected triangular elements. Triangular elements were chosen so that a large range of topological shapes could be modeled. In these transformations corners in the shape of the parametric region are mapped to corners in the deformed 3-space object. If a surface is to be modeled with 5 corners then the parametric region will need to be a pentagon. Using a triangular finite element in the parametric domain allows any polygonal parametric region to be modeled.

### 4.a) Barycentric Coordinates in 2 Dimensions

Barycentric coordinates in 2 dimensions are a natural choice for defining shape functions over a triangular domain. Functions written in Barycentric coordinates can be mapped to any shaped triangle simply by changing the vertex locations of the mapping triangle. Barycentric coordinates are defined by the mapping shown in Figure 2.

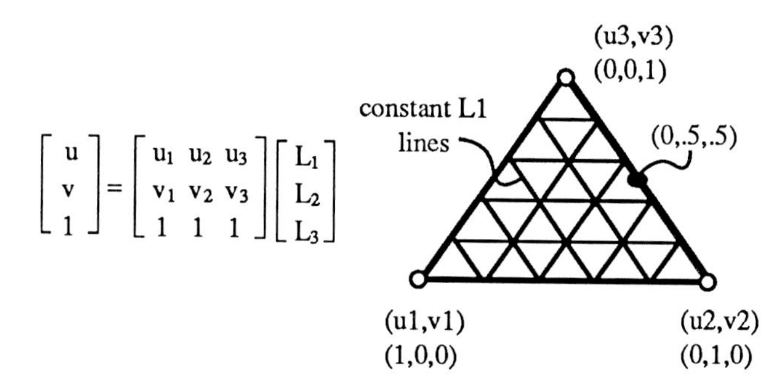


Figure 2) Barycentric coordinates in 2 dimensions

A point location in the uv plane is given as [u,v] in Cartesian coordinates and $[L_1, L_2, L_3]$ in Barycentric coordinates. The locations $[u_1,v_1]$, $[u_2,v_2]$, and $[u_3,v_3]$ define the vertex locations of the mapping triangle.

The Barycentric mapping can always be inverted as long as the three mapping vertices are not co-linear. This relationship is

$$\begin{bmatrix} L_1 \\ L_2 \\ L_3 \end{bmatrix} = \frac{1}{2\Delta} \begin{bmatrix} a_1 & b_1 & c_1 \\ a_2 & b_2 & c_2 \\ a_3 & b_3 & c_3 \end{bmatrix} \begin{bmatrix} 1 \\ u \\ v \end{bmatrix} \quad \text{and } L \equiv \begin{bmatrix} a_1 & b_1 & c_1 \\ a_2 & b_2 & c_2 \\ a_3 & b_3 & c_3 \end{bmatrix} \quad (17)$$

where $\Delta$ = area of the mapping triangle

Cartesian partial derivatives of Barycentric functions can be found by using the chain rule as

$$\begin{bmatrix} \frac{\partial}{\partial u} \\ \frac{\partial}{\partial v} \end{bmatrix} = J_1^{-1} \nabla_L \qquad 18$$

where $J_1^{-1} = \frac{1}{2\Delta}\begin{bmatrix} b_1 & b_2 & b_3 \\ c_1 & c_2 & c_3 \end{bmatrix}$ and $\nabla_L = \begin{bmatrix} \frac{\partial}{\partial L_1} \\ \frac{\partial}{\partial L_2} \\ \frac{\partial}{\partial L_3} \end{bmatrix}$

and

$$\begin{bmatrix} \frac{\partial^2}{\partial u^2} \\ \frac{\partial^2}{\partial v^2} \\ \frac{2\partial^2}{\partial u \partial v} \end{bmatrix} = \frac{J_2^{-1}}{2\Delta^2} \nabla_L^2 \qquad 19$$

where

$$J_2^{-1T} = \begin{bmatrix} b_1b_1 & c_1c_1 & 2b_1c_1 \\ 2b_1b_2 & 2c_1c_2 & 2\begin{pmatrix} b_1c_2 \\ + \\ b_2c_1 \end{pmatrix} \\ b_2b_2 & c_2c_2 & 2b_2c_2 \\ 2b_2b_3 & 2c_2c_3 & 2\begin{pmatrix} b_2c_3 \\ + \\ b_3c_2 \end{pmatrix} \\ b_3b_3 & c_3c_3 & 2b_3c_3 \\ 2b_3b_1 & 2c_3c_1 & 2\begin{pmatrix} b_3c_1 \\ + \\ b_1c_3 \end{pmatrix} \end{bmatrix} \text{ and } \nabla_L^2 = \begin{bmatrix} \frac{\partial^2}{\partial L_1 \partial L_1} \\ \frac{\partial^2}{\partial L_1 \partial L_2} \\ \frac{\partial^2}{\partial L_2 \partial L_2} \\ \frac{\partial^2}{\partial L_2 \partial L_3} \\ \frac{\partial^2}{\partial L_3 \partial L_3} \\ \frac{\partial^2}{\partial L_3 \partial L_1} \end{bmatrix}$$

The partial derivatives in a direction parallel or normal to one of the mapping triangle edges can be found by rotating the Cartesian first order derivatives as

$$\begin{bmatrix} \frac{\partial}{\partial t_{ij}} \\ \frac{\partial}{\partial n_{ij}} \end{bmatrix} = \begin{bmatrix} \cos(\gamma_{ij}) & \sin(\gamma_{ij}) \\ -\sin(\gamma_{ij}) & \cos(\gamma_{ij}) \end{bmatrix} \begin{bmatrix} \frac{\partial}{\partial u} \\ \frac{\partial}{\partial v} \end{bmatrix} \qquad 20$$

Where $J_{\gamma ij} \equiv \begin{bmatrix} \cos(\gamma_{ij}) & \sin(\gamma_{ij}) \\ -\sin(\gamma_{ij}) & \cos(\gamma_{ij}) \end{bmatrix}$

The normal and tangent direction partials can be related directly to $\nabla_L$ by the transformation matrix $T_{tn} \equiv J_{\gamma ij} J_1^{-1}$. The terms of the $T_{tn}$ matrix are constant depending only on the L matrix. Figure 3 defines the edge angle $\gamma$ and shows how the edge normal is defined so that there is always a common definition of the normal direction for an edge shared by two elements.

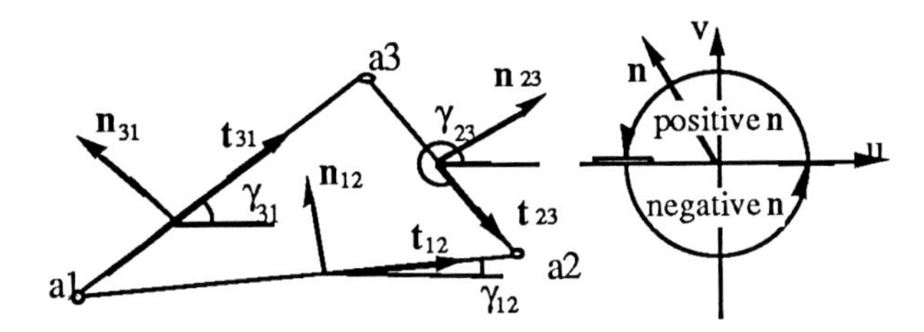


Figure 3) Barycentric triangle edge tangents and normals

### 4.b) Triangular Shape Functions

The triangle shape functions are built in two steps. First the weights of each function are selected to be a physical triangle dof. Each of these dofs will have three values, e.g. the location of a triangle vertex has an [x,y,z] location. The second step is to generate shape functions which set the physical dofs independently. This is accomplished by defining functions which have a value of 1 for one of the dofs and a value of 0 for the rest. One function is needed for each selected triangle dof.

We start with a 9 dof triangle and later expand to 12 dofs. The dofs selected include the position and the tangent vectors in the u and v directions at each triangle vertex as shown in Figure 4.

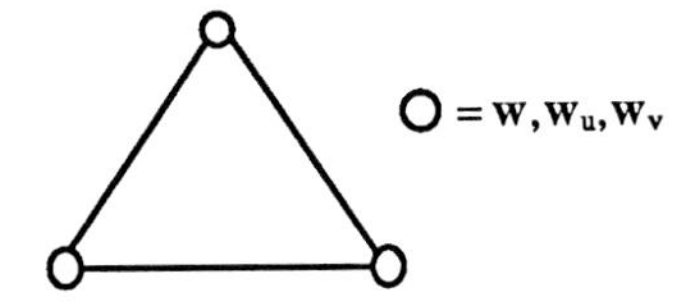


Figure 4) 3 node, 9 dof triangular element

The shape functions for the 9 dof triangle as published in Zienkiewicz's text on the Finite Element Method [20] are

$$w^h = N^9 a^e \qquad 21$$

where $N^9 = N^9(L_1, L_2, L_3, L) = [N_1^9 \, N_2^9 \, N_3^9]$

$$N_1^{9T} = \begin{bmatrix} L_1 + L_1^2L_2 + L_1^2L_3 - L_1L_2^2 - L_1L_3^2 \\ c_3(L_1^2L_2 + .5L_1L_2L_3) - c_2(L_1^2L_3 + .5L_1L_2L_3) \\ -b_3(L_1^2L_2 + .5L_1L_2L_3) + b_2(L_1^2L_3 + .5L_1L_2L_3) \end{bmatrix}$$

$$= \begin{bmatrix} \varphi_1 \\ \varphi_2 \\ \varphi_3 \end{bmatrix} = \begin{bmatrix} f_1 \\ c_3 f_{12} - c_2 f_{13} \\ -b_3 f_{12} + b_2 f_{13} \end{bmatrix}$$

and the $f_i$, $f_{ij}$, and $e_{ij}$ are defined in figure 5

The triangle's symmetry in Barycentric coordinates can be used to generate the shape functions for the 2nd and 3rd nodes in terms of the first. To generate $N_2^9$ use the above equations but add a 1 to each index so that 1 => 2 and 2 => 3 and 3 => 1. The $N_3^9$. functions are made by adding another 1 to each index.

These functions independently set the triangle's 9 dofs as required. However they do not guarantee $C^1$ continuity between adjacent triangular elements. To see this consider that to be $C^1$ across an edge boundary both triangles must generate the same

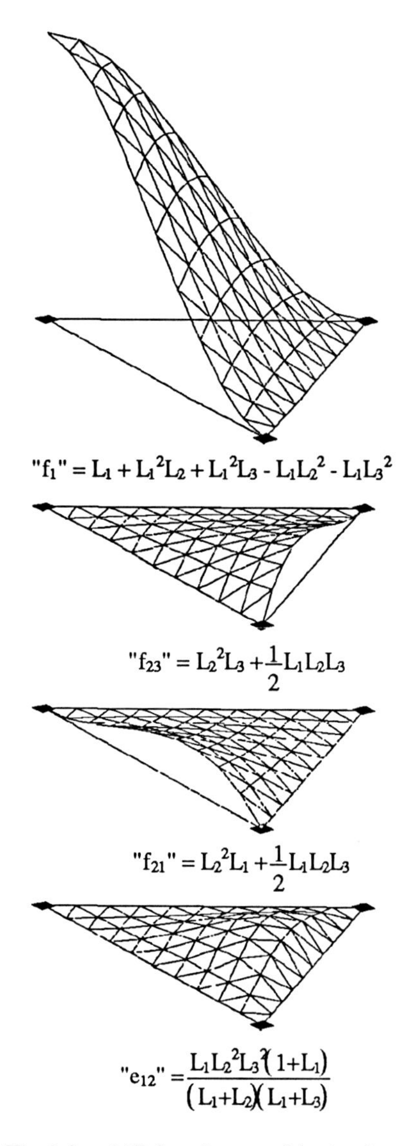


Figure 5) The 'e' and 'f' functions used in the shape functions

edge shape and the same partial of shape in the direction of the edge normal. These shape functions vary cubically along each triangle edge. Their first partial in the edge normal direction varies parabolically. It takes 7 dofs to set the shape and the edge normal direction along an edge. The 9 dof triangle has only 6 dofs on an edge and can not set the shape and the normal direction based only on the dof values located on that edge. These shape functions can be made $C^1$ continuous by adding a 7th dof on each edge to make the 12 dof triangle in Figure 6.

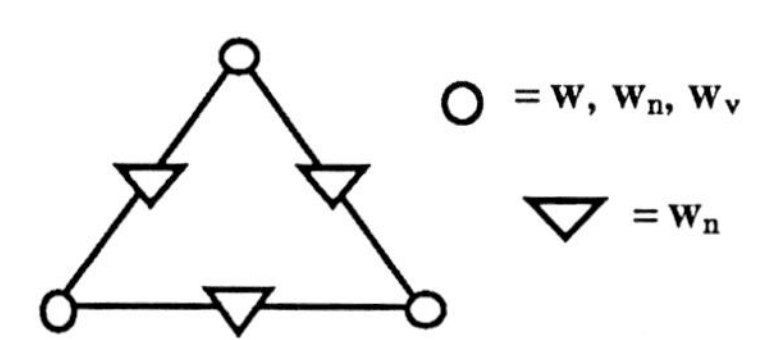


Figure 6) Triangular element with 12 dofs

The 'e' function introduced by Zienkiewicz [20] and shown in Figure 5 has the properties that its shape value along all three edges is zero and that the only non-zero shape edge derivative is in the normal direction of one of the three edges. Along that edge, the normal derivative varies parabolically with a maximum of 1/4 at the edge's center. The 12 dof shape functions can be generated by adding the appropriately weighted 'e' functions to set the mid-side normal derivatives to equal the values of the mid-side nodal dofs.

$$w^h = \left[N^9 \mid 0\ 0\ 0\right] + 4[e_{12}\, e_{23}\, e_{31}]\left[\begin{array}{c|ccc} & 1 & 0 & 0 \\ -Z & 0 & 1 & 0 \\ & 0 & 0 & 1 \end{array}\right]\left[\begin{array}{c} a^e \\ \hline w_{n12} \\ w_{n23} \\ w_{n31} \end{array}\right]$$

$$\text{where } \mathbf{Z}\, \mathbf{a}^e \equiv \begin{bmatrix} w^h_{n12}(.5,.5,0) \\ w^h_{n23}(0,.5,.5) \\ w^h_{n31}(.5,0,.5) \end{bmatrix}$$

The new set of shape functions can be written as

$$w^h = N^{12}\ \widehat{a^e} \quad \text{defining} \tag{22}$$

$$\widehat{a^e}^T \equiv [\, w_1\ w_{u1}\ w_{v1}\ w_2\ w_{u2}\ w_{v2}\ w_3\ w_{u3}\ w_{v3}\ w_{n12}\ w_{n23}\ w_{n31}]$$

This builds a set of shape functions that has the required 7 dofs per edge needed to support $C^1$ continuity between adjoining elements. The triangle shape varies cubically and the normal derivative varies parabolically along each edge.

## 4.c) Triangular Deformable Surface Element Forcing and Stiffness Matrices

Once the dofs $\widehat{a^e}$ and the associated shape functions $N^{12}$ for the triangular element and the minimum principle have been selected the actual generation of the element stiffness and forcing matrices is just an exercise in algebra and calculus.

The energy contributed by each element can be calculated as

$$E^h_{element_i} = \int_{\sigma_i} \widehat{a^e}^T \left(N_b^{12T}\, \bar{\beta}\, N_b^{12} + N_s^{12T}\, \bar{\alpha}\, N_s^{12}\right) \widehat{a^e}\, dudv \tag{23}$$

And taking the element dofs $\widehat{a^e}$ out of the integral since they are constant over the integral domain and rewriting yields

$$E_i = \widehat{a^e}^T K_{\sigma i}\, \widehat{a^e} - 2F_{\sigma i}\, \widehat{a^e} \tag{24}$$

with

$$K_{\sigma i} = \int_{\sigma_i} N_{L2}^{12T} J_2^{-T}\, \bar{\beta}\, J_2^{-1} N_{L2}^{12} + N_{L1}^{12T} J_1^{-T}\, \bar{\alpha}\, J_1^{-1} N_{L1}^{12}\, dudv$$

$$F_{\sigma i} = \int_{\sigma_i} f^T N^{12}\, dudv$$

$$N_{L2}^{12} \equiv \nabla_L^{\,2}(N^{12}) \quad N_{L1}^{12} \equiv \nabla_L(N^{12})$$

The stiffness and forcing matrix integrals are evaluated approximately with Gaussian quadrature because the rational 'e' functions are too complicated to bother evaluating them analytically. These stiffness matrices are built at run time and whenever the triangle's [u,v] node values change. The applied sculpting loads can vary at each iteration of the solution and so the forcing vector must be recalculated at each iteration.

The terms of each element stiffness matrix are combined into a a single system stiffness matrix. The final system stiffness matrix size will be nxn where n is the number of dofs for the entire surface. For details on using Gaussian quadrature and for building the system matrix see Zienkiewicz's text [20].

## 5 DEFORMABLE CURVE ELEMENT

In this section the finite element method is applied to the curve equations to develop a deformable curve primitive. The resulting curve is piecewise cubic and $C^1$ continuous. The curves were made $C^1$ piecewise cubic so that they could easily interface with the surface primitive during a skinning step. Each segment of a deformable character line will map to one edge of a deformable surface primitive.

### 5.a) Cubic Shape Functions

The developed finite element curve is shown in Figure 7. It has 4 dofs distributed between two nodes located at the ends of the curve segment. The dofs at each node correspond to its position and tangent.

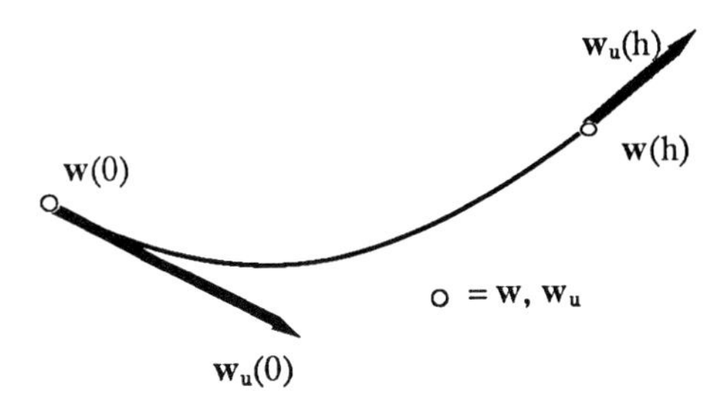


Figure 7) 4 dof curve element

The curve's shape is the weighted sum of a set of Hermite polynomials as

$$w^h(u) = \sum_{i=0}^{3} x_i \varphi_i \qquad 25$$

The Hermite polynomials and their associated geometric weights are listed below in Figure 8.

| i | $x_i$ | $\varphi_i$ |
|---|---|---|
| 0 | $w(0)$ | $1 - 3(u/h)^2 + 2(u/h)^3$ |
| 1 | $w_u(0)$ | $h(u/h - 2(u/h)^2 + (u/h)^3)$ |
| 2 | $w(h)$ | $3(u/h)^2 - 2(u/h)^3$ |
| 3 | $w_u(h)$ | $h(-(u/h)^2 + (u/h)^3)$ |

where $0 \le u \le h$ = length of element

Figure 8) Hermite polynomials

Hermite polynomials are not commonly found in CAGD tools. They are notably unstable when the nodal positions and tangents are set directly. These stability problems are avoided when energy minimization is used to control the curve's dofs.

The Hermite polynomials were selected as the shape functions because they explicitly represent the geometric terms that will be constrained. This simplifies the implementation, increases the understanding of the system, and uses the previously described constraint approach in its simplest form. The selection of the shape basis functions is a question of preference and convenience. If desired, any piecewise cubic parametric representation could serve as acceptable shape functions for the curve element.

### 5.b) The Curve Stiffness and Forcing Matrices

The stiffness and curve matrices are made by substituting the approximate shape $\mathbf{w}^h$ into the energy minimum principle of equation 2. The approximate curve equation becomes

$$E_{curve} = \int_C \hat{a}_e^T\left(\Phi_{uu}^T \,\beta\, \Phi_{uu} + \Phi_u^T \,\alpha\, \Phi_u\right)\hat{a}_e - 2\, f^T \Phi \hat{a}_e \, du \qquad 26$$

where $\Phi^T = [\varphi_0 \; \varphi_1 \; \varphi_2 \; \varphi_3]$ and $\hat{a}_e^T = [w_1 \; w_{1u} \; w_2 \; w_{2u}]$

The stiffness matrix is found by evaluating this integral as

$$K_{curve} = \alpha K_s + \beta K_b \qquad 27$$

$$\text{where } K_b = \frac{1}{h^3}\begin{bmatrix} 12 & 6h & -12 & 6h \\ 6h & 4h^2 & -6h & 2h^2 \\ -12 & -6h & 12 & -6h \\ 6h & 2h^2 & -6h & 4h^2 \end{bmatrix}$$

$$K_s = \frac{1}{30h}\begin{bmatrix} 36 & 3h & -36 & 3h \\ 3h & 4h^2 & -3h & -h^2 \\ -36 & -3h & 36 & -3h \\ 3h & -h^2 & -3h & 4h^2 \end{bmatrix}$$

Calculating the element forcing vector exactly for every supported forcing function requires a unique evaluation of equation 11. To simplify the implementation, all forcing functions are approximated by a linear interpolation between the actual force nodal values. The force integral becomes

$$F_c = \int_0^h \left(f_0 + \frac{u}{h}(f_1 - f_0)\right)\Phi \, du \qquad 28$$

where $f_0$ = applied force on node$_0$ and

$f_1$ = applied force on node$_1$

Taking this integral for cubic Hermite polynomials yields

$$F_c = \frac{h}{60}\begin{bmatrix} 21 & 9 \\ 3h & 2h \\ 9 & 21 \\ -2h & -3h \end{bmatrix}\begin{bmatrix} f_0 \\ f_1 \end{bmatrix} \qquad 29$$

The element stiffness and forcing matrices are functions of the parametric element length h. Each element in a curve can be of a different length so that small elements can be used in regions of complicated geometry and large elements used for simple geometry to save on the size of the model.

## 6 RESULTS

Continuous deformable curves and surfaces were implemented on a Silicon Graphics work station under the 4Sight window manager and using the GL graphics library. The graphical primitives can be shaped interactively by applying point, slope, and edge geometric constraints and user defined loads and by modifying the alpha and beta values.

A deformable surface's fairness was evaluated qualitatively by viewing light shaded images annotated with contour lines made by intersecting a family of parallel planes with the object. This graphical report was adopted because other surface curvature reports tended to obscure the shape of the object. Using the light shaded models with contour lines greatly enhanced the perception of shape and deformation.

Figure 9 shows two sequences of shapes made by varying a single load parameter on a 5 triangle deformable surface. The surface's parametric shape is a pentagon so that the 3 space object has five distinct corners. The surface has 28 3-space dofs that are specified by 84 scalar quantities. The initial shape of each sequence is made by constraining the 5 corner vertices to be fixed in space leaving the rest of the dofs free to move to minimize the energy functional of the total surface. The first sequence renders 3 of the 5 elements to help visualize the internal shape of the object and shows the shape responding to an increase in its resistance to bending along the spine of the bird like object. As the $\beta_{11}$ term increases the bird to flattens. The second sequence shows all 5 elements of the shape responding to an increasing pressure applied to the bottom of the entire surface. Both cases illustrate how a single load parameter can be used to modify the global shape.

Figure 10 shows a car door shape built as an exercise in controlled geometry building. The door was made by fixing the outer edge shapes with constraints and using a pressure to generate a nicely convex surface. The rib in the door panel was made in two additional steps. First the edges on either side of the rib were constrained in advance to isolate the rib deformation from the rest of the door shape. Then the edge running along the center of the rib was constrained so that its shape would be fixed but the surface normal along the edge could vary. Once the appropriate constraints were in place the rib was made by moving the constrained central edge a fixed distance normal to the surface. The depth of the hinge was modified by the user while the algorithm modified the model's free dofs to build nice blending surfaces.

The final image in Figure 10 shows the results of a finite element linear stress analysis simulating someone leaning on the door with a point load. One exciting potential for this free-form design approach is the possibility for automating the transition from shape models to analytic models. Because the shape is defined as the result of a finite element analysis the computer based representation of shape is appropriate for further finite element analysis. The analytic model of Figure 10's central image was made by refining the grid of the original shape and adding material properties and mechanical boundary conditions. The equations for the stress analysis were compiled and solved using the same code as the deformable shape models but using a different subroutine for generating the element stiffness matrix. Extending the original program for this analysis was done by MIT post doctorate Hiroshi Sakurai in one week.

The deformable curves were applied to fairing hand drawn 3 dimensional curves. Andy Roberts and Dave Stoops created the 3-Draw program at the MIT CADlab [15]. The 3-Draw program captures a sequence of discrete point locations while a user draws 3 dimensional curves in space using a magnetic detector made by the Polhemus Company. This package has been optimized to assist a user in drawing complicated geometric wire frame models. Figure 11 shows the results of fairing a curve. The first curve is shown as originally captured in 3-Draw where the noise in the shape was deliberately exaggerated. The first application of fairing is automatic and applied to the whole curve. This step tends to eliminate high frequency noise from the overall shape. The second phase of fairing allows the user to artfully smooth out larger scale disturbances in the curve.

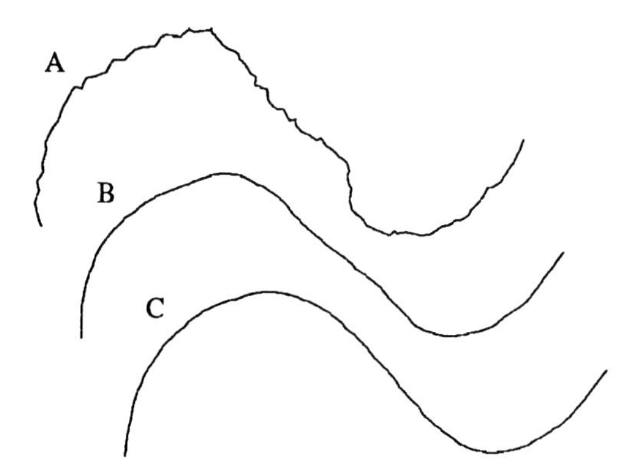


Figure 11) Fairing a curve. A: curve as input B: Curve after initial smoothing C: Curve after final smoothing

The ShapeWright modeling paradigm was tested in an earlier program based on a finite difference implementation of the deformable surface Euler equations. The objective of the exercise was to sculpt an object defined by skinning the surface of a set of character lines. Figure 12 shows the results of this exercise, a goblet. The initial goblet was made by constraining a surface to interpolate two circles centered on the z axis. The hyperbolic surface shape was due to the effect of the $\alpha$ weighted energy minimization terms which tend to minimize the area of the surface. The character line set of the goblet was augmented by adding two squares to the middle of the shape. The surface, no longer axis symmetric, automatically defined the complicated blending shapes needed to transition from a circle to a square. The final goblet shape was made by sculpting. Pressures were applied internally to the goblet bowl until an acceptable looking shape was generated. While sculpting the user modified the the magnitude of the pressure and the minimization algorithm automatically updated the dofs of the model. This exercise was run in less than a minute. It took 4 commands to specify the character lines and another 3 to parameterize the pressure load so that it acts on the upper surface of the goblet. There were a total of 204 3-space dofs in this model.

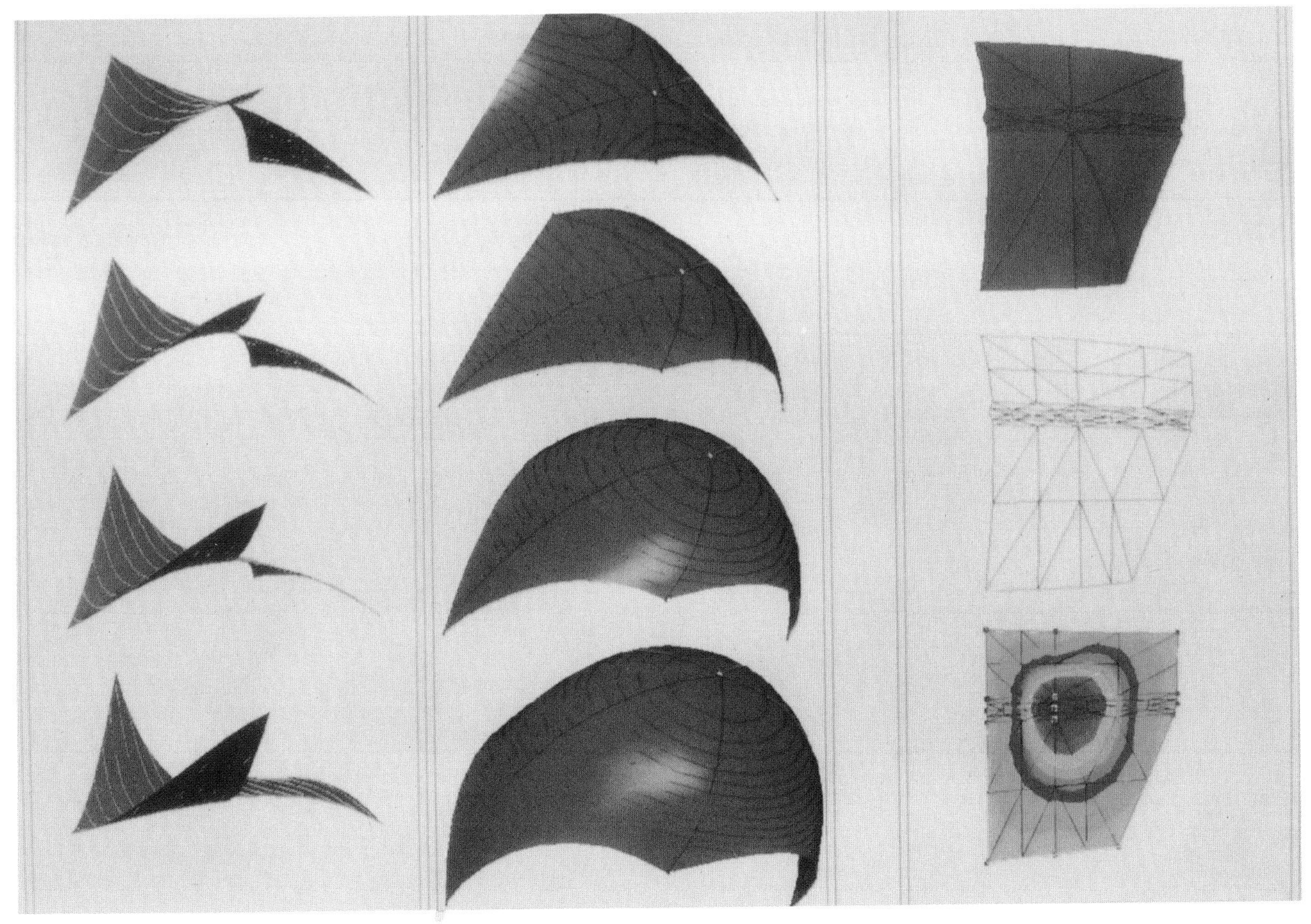

Figure 9) 1 parameter variations on shape constrained to interpolate 5 points.
A: Increasing bending resistance in the main axis direction.
B: Increasing internal pressure.

Figure 10) Car door with blended rib
A: Shape Model.
B: Finite Element stress model.
C: Constant stress contour results

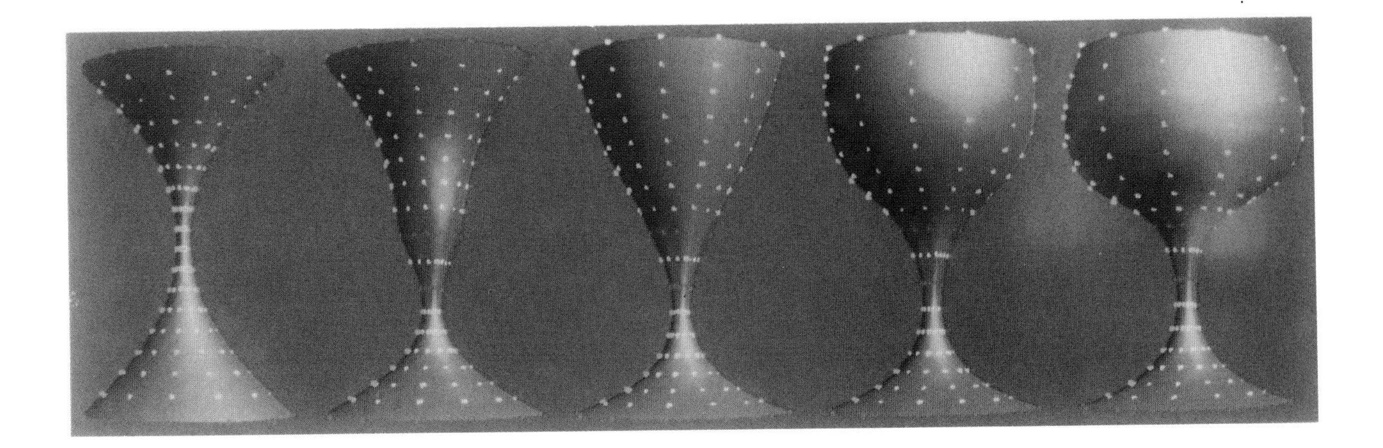

Figure 12) Generating a Goblet with the ShapeWright paradigm. A: 2 circle lines centered on the z axis are skinned to form a starting shape. B: Additional square character lines are added to enrich the shape. C: The goblet bowl is sculpted with an internal pressure. D: increasing pressure. E: even more pressure.

## 7 CONCLUSIONS AND FUTURE WORK

The ShapeWright deformable surface modeling paradigm works well for the interactive definition of objects with free-form surfaces. Complicated free-form shapes were defined with very few commands. The shapes were parameterized with the use of loads so that the design of shape was accomplished as a search in a small user built parameter space independent of the number of dofs in the surface.

Solving the deformable model equations using the Ritz finite element method supports continuous shape models suitable for aesthetic design with representations that can support applications like manufacturing and analysis. The range of topological structures that could be modeled was greatly extended by using triangular finite elements instead of square ones. An additional benefit of using the finite element solution scheme was that these models could be exploited to directly generate finite element models for applications like stress-strain analysis.

The curve and surface geometric shape primitives were designed to work together to support the ShapeWright paradigm for modeling objects with free-form surfaces. The deformable curve's shape was made piece-wise cubic so that it would easily fit with the edge of a deformable surface which varies cubically. The curves were made to be used to define the character lines of an object and the surfaces were made to skin and sculpt the final form of that object. What remains as future work is to combine these primitives into a single geometric package. The remaining technical issues for this task include automating the skinning of a set of character lines and the generation of a reasonable finite element grid appropriate for subsequent sculpting.

## ACKNOWLEDGMENTS

The authors gratefully acknowledge the financial support provided for this work by Schlumberger and the Ford Motor Company.

## REFERENCES

1. Bloor, M.I.G. and Wilson, M.J., "Blend Design as a Boundary-Value Problem", Theory and Practice of Geometric Modeling, Wolfgang Staber and Hans-Peter Seidel (Eds.), 1989

2. Celniker G., Gossard D., "Energy-Based Models for Free-Form Surface Shape Design", ASME Design Automation Conference, Montreal Canada, Sep. 1989

3. Celniker G., ShapeWright: Finite Element Based Free-Form Shape Design, M.I.T. Ph.D., Dept. of Mechanical Engineering, September, 1990

4. Farin, Gerald and Sapidis, Nickolas, "Shape Representation of Sculpted Objects: the Fairness of Curves and Surfaces", Proceeding of Sea Grant Conference, MIT, October, 1988

5. Farin, Gerald, Curves and Surfaces for Computer Aided Geometric Design, Academic Press Inc., Harcourt Brace Jovanovich Publishers, Boston, 1988

6. Hagen, H., and Schulze, G., "Automatic Smoothing with Geometric Surface Patches", Computer Aided Geometric Design, Vol. 4, pp. 231-236, 1987

7. Kass, Michael and Witkin, Andrew, and Terzopoulos, Demetri, "Snakes: Active Contour Models", International Journal of Computer Vision, 1988

8. Kallay, Michael and Ravani B. , "Optimal twist vectors as a tool for interpolation a Network of curves with a minimal energy surface", CAGD, 1990

9. Kjellander, J.A., "Smoothing of bicubic parametric surfaces", Computer-Aided Design, Vol. 15, pp. 288-293, 1983

10. Kjellander, J.A.P., "Smoothing of cubic parametric splines", Computer-Aided Design, vol 15, No. 3, May, 1983

11. Lott, N.J. and Pullin, D.I., "Methods for fairing B-Spline surfaces", Computer-Aided Design, vol. 20, no. 10, December, 1988

12. Nielson, G.M., "Some piecewise polynomial alternatives to splines in tension", in Barnhill, RE and Riesenfeld, RF (eds) Computer Aided Geometric Design, Academic Press, 1974

13. Nowacki, H. and Reese, D., "Design and fairing of ship surfaces", in Barnhill R.E. and Boehm, W. (eds), Surfaces in CAGD, North-Holland, Amsterdam, pp 121-134, 1983

14. Pramila, A., "Ship Hull Surface design using finite elements", Int. Shipbuild. Prog. Vol. 25 No. 284, pp. 97-107, 1978

15. Sacks, E., and Stoops, D. and Roberts, A., "3-Draw: A Three Dimensional Computer Aided Design Tool", proceedings IEEE international conference of systems, man, and cybernetics, pp 1194-1196, November 1989

16. Sapidis, N. and Farin, G., "Automatic fairing algorithm for B-spline curves", Computer-Aided Design, Vol. 22, No. 2 pp. 121-129, March 1990

17. Schweikert, D.G., "An interpolation curve using a spline in tension", Journal of Math and Phys. No 45, pp. 312-317, 1966

18. Strang, Gilbert, Introduction to Applied Mathematics, Wellesley-Cambridge Press, Massachusetts, 1986

19. Terzopoulos, Demetri and Platt, John and Barr, Alan and Fleischer, Kurt, "Elastic Deformable Models", ACM, Computer Graphics, vol. 21, no. 4, July, 1987

20. Zienkiewicz, The Finite Element Method, third edition, McGraw-Hill Book Co., U.K., 1967

# Sculpting: An Interactive Volumetric Modeling Technique*

Tinsley A. Galyean
The Media Laboratory
Massachusetts Institute of Technology
Cambridge, MA 02139

John F. Hughes
Department of Computer Science
Box 1910
Brown University
Providence, RI 02906

## ABSTRACT

We present a new interactive modeling technique based on the notion of sculpting a solid material. A sculpting tool is controlled by a 3D input device and the material is represented by voxel data; the tool acts by modifying the values in the voxel array, much as a "paint" program's "paintbrush" modifies bitmap values. The voxel data is converted to a polygonal surface using a "marching-cubes" algorithm; since the modifications to the voxel data are local, we accelerate this computation by an incremental algorithm and accelerate the display by using a special data structure for determining which polygons must be redrawn in a particular screen region. We provide a variety of tools: one that cuts away material, one that adds material, a "sandpaper" tool, a "heat gun," etc. The technique provides an intuitive direct interaction, as if the user were working with clay or wax. The models created are free-form and may have complex topology; however, they are not precise, so the technique is appropriate for modeling a boulder or a tooth but not for modeling a crankshaft.

**CR Categories:** I.3.5 [Computer Graphics]: Computational Geometry and Object Modeling; Curve, surface, solid, and object representations; I.3.3 [Computer Graphics]: Picture/Image Generation; Display algorithms; I.3.6 [Computer Graphics]: Methodologies and Techniques; Interaction techniques.

**Additional Keywords:** Sculpting, volumetric data, 3D interaction, antialiasing, free-form modeling.

## 1 INTRODUCTION

We present a new modeling technique for computer graphics based on the notion of sculpting a solid material with a tool. This technique is derived from traditional 2D paint systems, from Blinn's blobby objects [1], and from the soft objects of Wyvill et al. [17]. The term "sculpting" has been used by others: Naylor [9] uses it to describe a polyhedral CSG system that is capable of interactive performance when implemented on a Pixel Machine; Coquillart [3] uses it to describe her interface to free-form deformations [12], that edit the geometry of an object but not its topology; Pentland et al. [10] use it to describe the altering of shapes by modal forces. In related work, Williams 3D paint system [15] lets the user edit the $z$-depths of points on an object that is a union of two topological disks, using color as a proxy for height. Bloomenthal et al. [2] describe an object by forming a geometric skeleton, associating a potential function with it, and drawing isosurfaces of the potential function; editing the skeleton then modifies the surface. We prefer to avoid the fixed structure of these last four systems and the potential proliferation of polygons of the first, and aim instead for a system that gives the user control of both the geometry and topology of an object and at the same time provides an extremely intuitive interface. Our sculpting may appear similar to work of Van Hook on milling machines [6], but his system only removes material from an object (i.e., no additive tools are allowed), and retains an *image* of the object but not the structure of the object itself. The resulting object cannot be viewed from any direction other than the one in which it was constructed.

Our fundamental notion is to describe the shape of a piece of clay by its *characteristic function*, whose value is 1.0 at any point in space where there is clay and 0.0 elsewhere.[1] Modifying the shape of the clay is therefore equivalent to modifying this function. The same idea applies in a traditional 2D paint system: we think of the canvas as the cartesian plane and assign values to the pixels of the canvas; certain values indicate the presence of ink and others indicate its absence. Painting is done in such systems by moving a brush across the canvas, and data associated with the brush edits the data in the pixmap; for example, moving the tip of a pen across the canvas changes the values of all pixels underneath it to the current color. Our system modifies the values of volumetric data by moving a 3D tool through space, in exact analogy to the brush. Our standard tool is the opposite of the pen in a paint system, however, in that we start with a block of material and remove it bit-by-bit, and hence we refer to the process as *sculpting*. Just as traditional paint systems offer many ways to apply and remove paint, we provide several different tools with which to edit the volumetric data, including ones that add material, smooth a surface, or melt away material as a heat gun melts styrofoam. Many users are familiar with paint programs, and therefore readily accept this variety of tools.

The models created by our technique are free-form and often lack fine detail, but they can have complex topology. They are *not* precise geometric models of the sort traditionally generated by CAD systems. However the technique opens the door to modeling that would otherwise be difficult; it is also well-suited to a free-form design process, in which the user starts with no particular goal, and just plays with the material in an intuitive fashion.

While the underlying idea of our technique is simple and attractive, making it work in practice is not trivial. Paint systems have the advantage that they work by modifying the data in a framebuffer or an offscreen copy of the screen canvas; this memory is typically easy to read and write, and the image can be transferred to the screen

*This work was supported in part by grants from IBM, NCR, and Sun Microsystems.

[1]We represent volumetric functions by giving their values at the vertices of a rectangular lattice in 3-space, and call this *voxel data*, or a *voxmap* for short.

extremely quickly with most current hardware. This is partly because we always look at a 2D painting from the same point of view. By contrast, we may wish to view volumetric data from any angle. Also, since we actually want to see the *boundary* between the material and the empty space, this boundary must be computed by some thresholding algorithm. The computation of an isosurface from the volumetric data is $O(n^3)$, using the marching-cubes algorithm [7], for an $n \times n \times n$ data array. Clearly, for interactivity, we must improve the algorithm. Fortunately, sculpting the data modifies it only *locally*, so one need not recompute an entire isosurface. Of course, the isosurface for such data may contain many polygons, and even if we recompute only the local data and replace some polygons with others, we must find a way to redisplay only the local area or the process becomes polygon bound. Even with only local updates, over 50% of the time is spent rendering polygons on an HP835 Turbo SRX.

Simply sampling the characteristic function of a solid will lead to aliasing. We avoid this by using a low-pass filtered version of the characteristic function. This means that certain samples may be neither 1.0 nor 0.0, but rather some intermediate value, indicating transition from material to empty space. To avoid the introduction of aliases, the values written by the tool must also be band-limited, as discussed in Section 3.1.

Before giving a detailed explanation of the technique and the associated algorithms, we make two important remarks:

1. The success of the program is greatly enhanced by the use of 3D interaction devices. We use the Polhemus Isotrack device, and have begun to experiment with the Ascension 'Bird' and a 3D force-feedback joystick with good results [8].

2. User response indicates that this method of modeling has substantial initial appeal and is extremely easy to learn. Although we have not performed any perceptual studies on the system, we have found that many users of the system say one of two things: "Can I come back and use this again later?" or, from the more experienced users, "This is what I *thought* that 3D modeling would be like when I first started learning about computers."

The remainder of this paper describes the modeling technique at two levels: the user's view of the system and the internal implementation. We include throughout ideas for future work. While the system is a full-fledged modeling system, we view it as comparable to early painting programs like MacPaint; the future work is what will make it more like the painting programs of today.

## 2 THE USER'S VIEW

In calling our modeling technique "sculpting," we hope to connote a very free-form interaction; a sculptor can carve away bits of material, stick on new pieces of clay, change the topology of a sculpture, etc. (A sculptor using physical clay can also squeeze or flex the clay; our system does not yet provide this functionality.)

To present this free-form modeling technique, we provide the user with a cubical "lump of clay" (called the *object*) and a small *tool*. The tool, displayed as a sphere or cube, is directly controlled by a 3D interaction device such as the Polhemus Isotrack. In a separate window, the user has a traditional user interface, consisting of menus for file management and buttons for selecting how the tool should act on the object and for resetting the system. Interaction with this part of the interface is done with a mouse and keyboard. A typical session begins with the default (a cube of clay) or with the selection of a previous sculpture, and continues as the user holds the Polhemus device and sculpts away material. When the user wishes to change the effect of the tool, she uses the mouse to select a new tool type (see Figure 1).

### 2.1 Types of Tools

The tool, in its simplest form, is analogous to the eraser provided in many paint programs: wherever the tool moves, it cuts away the object. In 3D terms, the tool acts like a milling head or a router, but unlike these, the tool leaves no chips. We call this a *routing tool* or *subtractive tool.*

The analogy between the subtractive tool and a paint program's eraser is of considerable value. Most users are familiar with 2D paint programs, and are used to the notion that the mouse can have different effects. This makes it simple to give the user a variety of sculpting tools and to invent new types of tools. Here are the tools we have implemented:

*Additive Tool* or *Toothpaste Tube*. This tool leaves a trail of material wherever it moves, much like a tube of toothpaste that is squeezed as it is moved.

*Heat Gun*. This tool "melts away" material much as a heat gun melts styrofoam. If held in one place for a while, it removes all the material, like the routing tool; if moved quickly past a region, it melts the material there slightly.

*Sandpaper*. This "smoothing" tool alters the object by wearing away the ridges and filling the valleys. (This is analogous to the low-pass filter brushes available in some sophisticated 2D paint systems.)

Other possible tools include a filleting tool, to smooth the joins between adjacent surfaces, and geometric construction tools, which would allow the user to create a cylindrical tube between two points, or create a torus with a certain center and radii, much the way that painting programs allow one to draw straight lines and circles. We also envision adding tools for deforming the object as a clay model, squeezing or bending it, as described in [13].

We have also implemented a primitive color tool, which assigns a chosen RGB color triple to each vertex of the data array that lies within the current tool region. We currently apply a low-pass filter to these assigned color values to create a smoother appearance. There is much more work to be done in this area.

### 2.2 Interaction

#### 2.2.1 Low and high resolution modes

To make a good sculpture the user must be allowed to view it from different perspectives and work on the back as well as the front. Furthermore, it is often desirable to rough out the coarse shape of a sculpture first, and work on finer detail afterwards. Making this coarse sculpting efficient requires a larger tool for the initial shaping. Thus we provide both low-resolution (*low-res*) and high-resolution (*hi-res*) modes. In low-res mode, we provide full control of the view and all tool functions, but with coarse tools. In hi-res mode, view control is unavailable, but much greater resolution is provided.

In low-res mode, the object is displayed by applying the marching cubes algorithm to a subsample of the data that represents the object. In hi-res mode we use a $30 \times 30 \times 30$ voxel array; in low-res mode the array is $10 \times 10 \times 10$. The visual effect is that the low-res view of an object is very coarse and shows only its general form. Of course, subsampling is not ideal because of the aliasing implicit in the process: small details may disappear completely. The correct approach is to filter the large voxel array into the smaller array; we will do this in the future, but have not found it to be a significant problem in the current implementation.

In low-res mode, the $10 \times 10 \times 10$ array *might* give rise to an object with as many as 5000 polygons (five polygons from each cube in the array). This would be extremely unusual, and 500 polygons is more likely. On the HP835 Turbo SRX, 5000 polygons can be displayed with a refresh rate of 7 per second, allowing the user to rotate the view of the low-res representation of the object in real time.

The conversion from low-res to hi-res mode requires a substantial computation, since the full marching-cubes algorithm must be

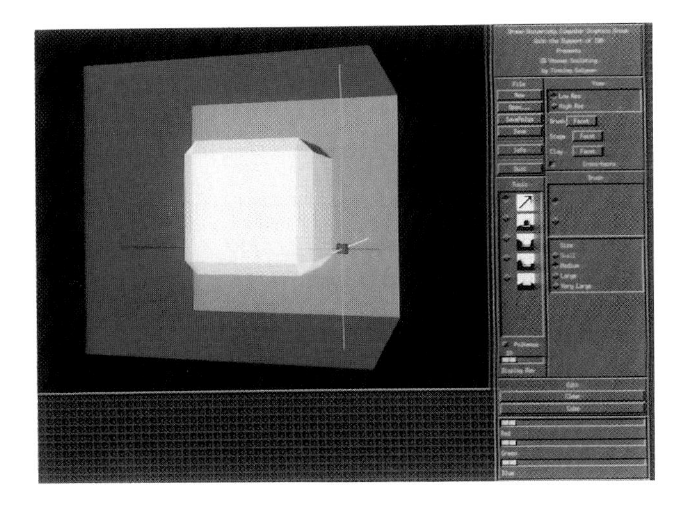

Figure 1: The interface to the system

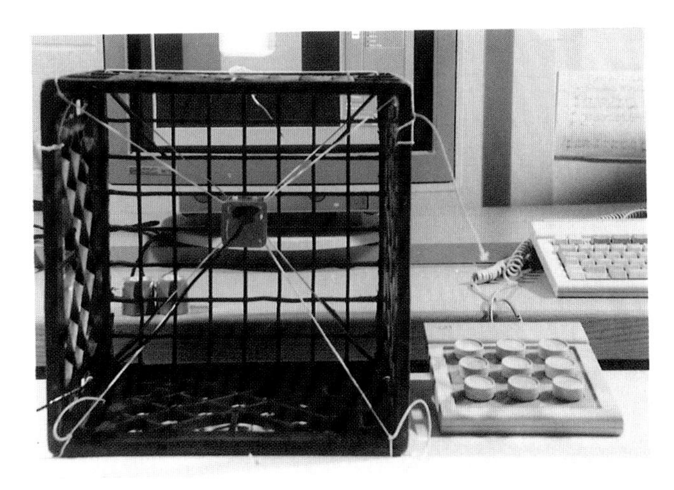

Figure 2: The poor man's force feedback unit

executed and the hashgrid data structure (see Section 3.3) must be recreated; furthermore, all the polygons created in the hi-res model (perhaps several hundred thousand) must be displayed. This conversion causes a slight delay; we are attempting to reduce this, but have not yet found a method to do so. The length of this delay is the prime determinant of the high-res data array size of $30 \times 30 \times 30$.

### 2.2.2 3D control of the tool

We use the Polhemus Isotrack device to control the position of the sculpting tool. This device provides a constant stream of samples indicating the $xyz$-position of a pen-shaped pointer; it also provides data describing the orientation of the pointer, which we do not currently use.

There are two problems with using the Polhemus. The data stream is somewhat noisy (this seems not to be as significant a problem with the Ascension 'Bird'), and the natural mapping of the physical space of the Polhemus pointer to the screen space representation of the tool makes the pointer an absolute device instead of a relative one. We have addressed these as follows:

To smooth the Polhemus data, we use a limited predictive tracking process: we use previous samples to predict (by linear interpolation) where we expect the tool to be at the next sample time. We then average the actual sample with the predicted value, assigning a weight of 7 to the actual sample and a weight of 1 to the predicted value. To prevent overshoot, we limit the distance of the predicted position from the previous position; if the predicted position is more than a certain distance from the previous position, the difference vector is truncated. This provides a compromise between the lag of a moving average and the overshoot of predictive tracking.

Using a simple linear transformation to map the coordinates provided by the Polhemus to the modeling coordinates is adequate but not particularly satisfactory. Our initial mapping made the region in front of the monitor (about a $2' \times 2' \times 2'$ cube) correspond to the region occupied by the object (the *sculpting space*). This gives good large-scale control, but sculpting fine details is difficult because of the noise in the Polhemus. We therefore introduce a relative mode, that lets the user move the Polhemus much as one moves a cursor a long distance by repeatedly lifting and replacing a mouse on a mouse pad. (Instead of "lifting," the user presses a button.) The $2'$ cube is then mapped to a small portion of the sculpting space, giving fine control.

Controlling the tool position is not easy. Even though the Polhemus pointer is held in a well-defined region, it is often difficult to correlate the position of the pointer in space with the position of the tool on the screen. To assist in this, we draw a box around the object being sculpted and do front-face culling on the box, so that no matter what the orientation of the sculpture, three walls behind it form a "stage." We then show the tool position by drawing three crosshairs; the intersections of the crosshairs with the stage walls help the user determine the tool's position.

We have also begun to experiment with a force-feedback joystick to help the user position the tool. The joystick generates a small force as the tool approaches the surface, allowing us to "feel" that we are close to it. Using the joystick also helps relieve the user from holding up the Polhemus pointer. We have also implemented a "poor man's force-feedback Polhemus," which alleviates this problem by providing a certain resistance to motion (although there is no real feedback involved) (see Figure 2). The device consists of a Polhemus suspended in a cube by eight elastic cords attached to the corners of the cube.

## 2.3 Sample Sculptures

Figure 3-Figure 9 show the kinds of sculptures possible with this system; Figure 8 was made using a dial box as input device instead of the Polhemus, which accounts for the orthogonal appearance of the object.

## 2.4 The Object as a Voxmap

As we have said, the *object* is described by a data array, which we call a *voxmap* in analogy with the 2D notions of bitmaps and pixmaps. (Recall that we think of the values in the array as giving values at the vertices of the lattice, not the centers of cubes in the lattice.) Because the object's characteristic function is discontinuous at its boundary, it has an infinite frequency spectrum, and hence sampling it yields aliases. We therefore store the values of the *low-pass-filtered* (or *band-limited*) characteristic function of the object, which may be between 0 and 1. They are analogous to the grey pixels drawn near a sloping line to reduce the jaggies [4].[2]

We use the values in the voxmap to determine the values of the band-limited characteristic function at intermediate points. To do this precisely, we would have to apply a perfect reconstruction filter; instead, we simply interpolate the values linearly, which amounts to reconstructing with a triangle filter.

[2]We actually use 8-bit integers to represent the function: 0 and 255 correspond to 0.0 and 1.0, respectively.

Figure 3: Low-res model of a tree: 1138 polygons

Figure 4: Hi-res model of a tree: 17216 polygons

Figure 5: The thinker: only 2118 polygons!

Figure 6: Teapot, chiseled from stone: 9244 polygons

Figure 7: Teapot, after application of sanding tool: 8374 polygons

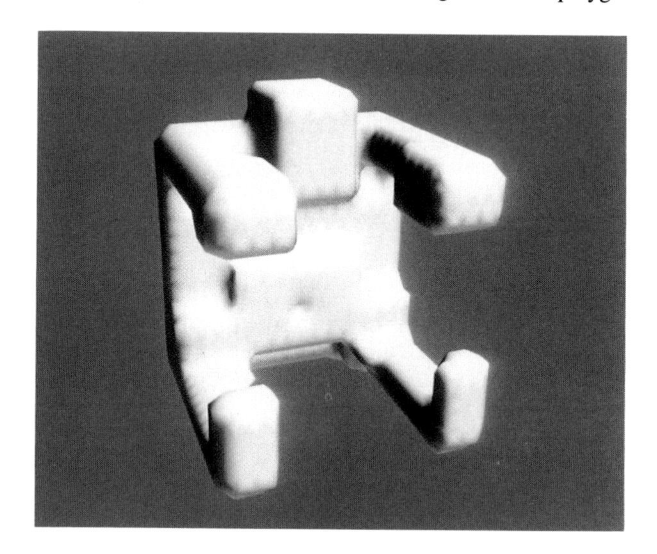

Figure 8: Sculpture made with dial box control

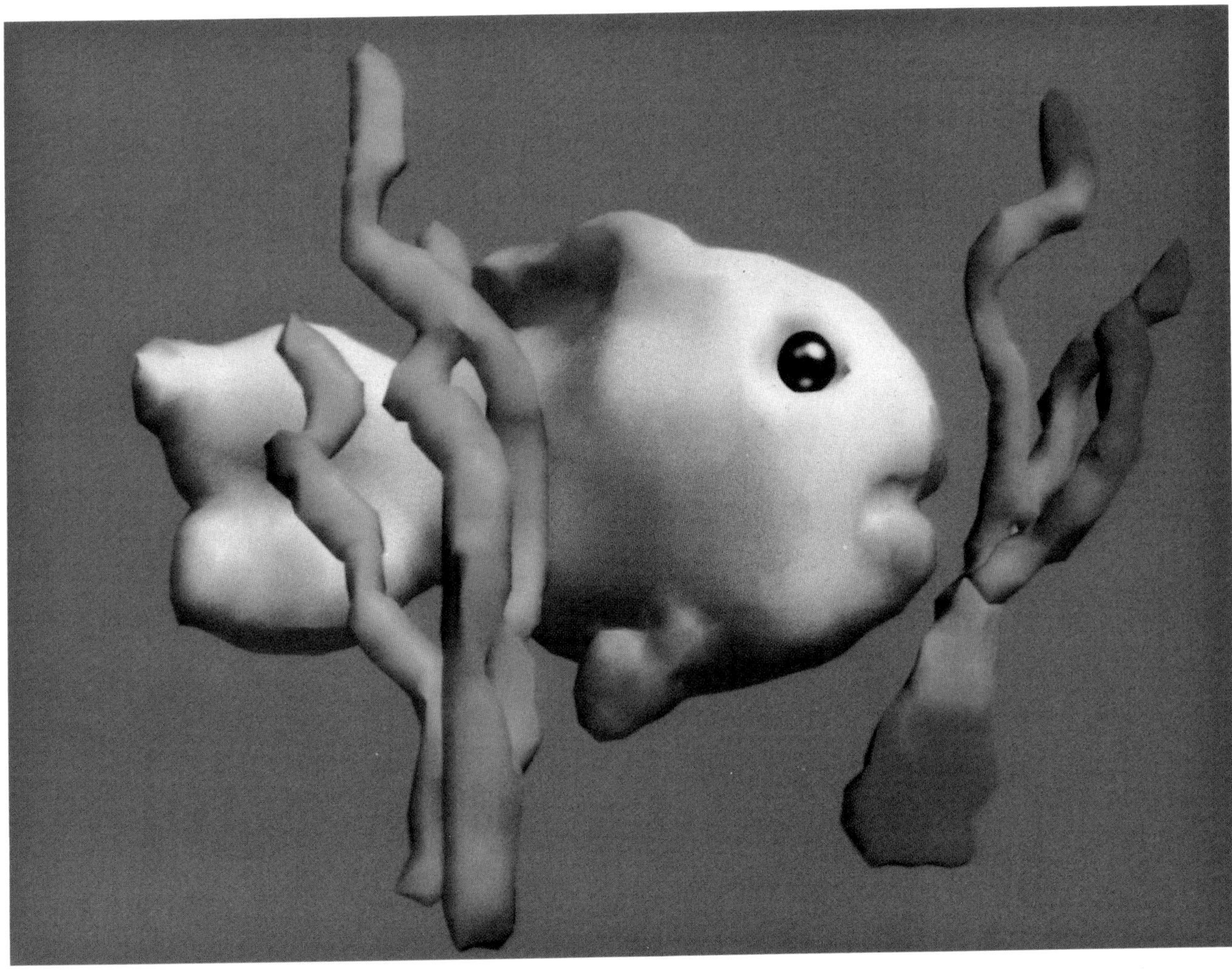

Figure 9: A fish smoothed out using sandpaper: 5066 polygons. The eye (a specular black sphere) was added after the sculpture was completed.

We make an initial image of the object described by the voxmap using a slight modification of the standard "marching-cubes" algorithm: Following the work in [16], we generate all the intersections of the isosurface with the edge of each cube, and if there are more than three we find the center of mass of these points, and then join each point to this center. (An improved algorithm, like the one in [16], might help performance somewhat, particularly as the models become more complex.) Our space is composed of an array of cubes; the voxmap gives the value of the band-limited characteristic function at the corners of the cubes. For each such cube, we use the values at the corners to estimate the intersection of the isosurface at level 0.5 with the cube's edges. These vertices are then connected to fill in a collection of polygons that approximate the intersection of the isosurface at level 0.5 with the interior of the cube (see Figure 10).

We use the gradient technique of [7] to estimate the normal to the isosurface at each polygon vertex, thus allowing smooth shading computations.

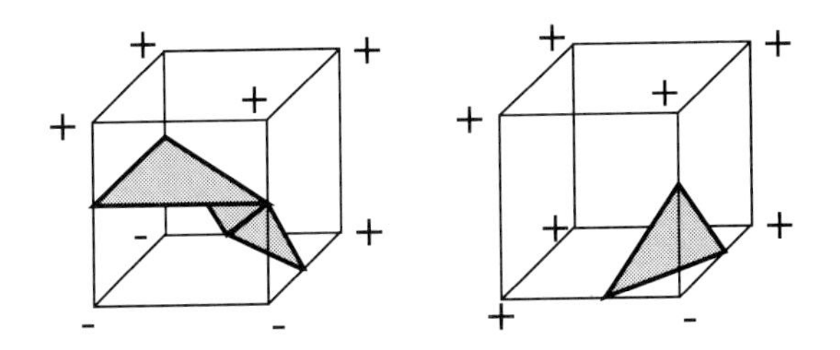

Figure 10: Determining an isosurface within a cube in the lattice. The vertices marked "+" values above the threshold, those marked "–" have values below.

## 3 IMPLEMENTATION DETAILS

### 3.1 The Tool as a Voxmap

The sculpting tool is also represented by a voxmap. One might suppose that the subtractive tool, for example, would be represented

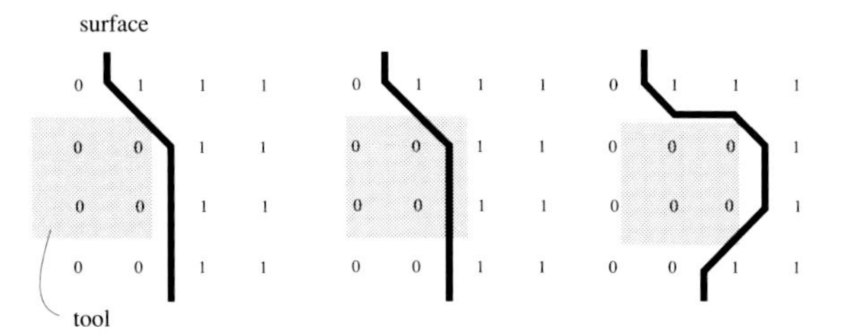


Figure 11: With a 0/1 tool, the surface of the object jumps as the tool approaches. This figure shows the analogous behavior in 2D: the gray square is the tool and the solid black line is the isocurve.

by a voxmap filled with 0s, and that the act of cutting away material would consist of copying data values from the tool voxmap to the object voxmap. This is, however, only approximately correct. Values in the tool voxmap *are* combined with those in the object map; the combination rules are described in Section 3.2.1. But the actual values in the tool voxmap are not as simple as they might seem.

If values of 0 are copied directly from the tool voxmap to the object voxmap, the results are jumpy. As the tool moves towards the object, nothing happens for a while; then, when it is sufficiently close, the object voxmap values change all at once, and the surface of the object moves rapidly. This is a consequence of the low sampling rate used to represent the characteristic function of the object (see Figure 11 for the analogous behavior in a 2D system).

We compensate for this with two tricks based on the notion of antialiased brushes [14]. First, we create a voxmap for the tool that is sampled at a higher rate than is the object (four times as many samples in each direction). The tool voxmap, for a spherical subtractive tool, is filled with 0s on the inside of a sphere, and 1s elsewhere, i.e., with the characteristic function of the sphere. We then remove most of the high-frequency components of this voxmap by filtering it twice with a $2 \times 2 \times 2$ box filter [5].[3] Second, we apply the tool to the object voxmap by determining its sub-voxel location and then selecting particular values from the tool voxmap to combine with the object voxel values. The details are presented in the following section.

## 3.2 Tool-Object Interaction

The central loop of the program is essentially

1. Poll repeatedly until the tool has an effect.[4]
2. Modify values in the object voxmap.
3. Recompute isosurface.
4. Redisplay isosurface and tool.
5. Return to step 1.

We will describe these steps in order: step 2 in the following subsection, and steps 3 and 4 in Section 3.3.

### 3.2.1 Applying the tool to the object voxmap

Points in the voxmap are identified by three indices, so that a typical voxel value is referenced as $v[i][j][k]$, where each of $i$, $j$, and $k$ is an integer between 0 and 29. We can think of *any* point in the object region as having $ijk$-coordinates: a point whose coordinates are $(i, j, k) = (1.5, 2, 2)$ is on the line segment between the points represented by the voxels $v[1][2][2]$ and $v[2][2][2]$. We compute the $ijk$-coordinates of the tool's location, and then round

[3] Our choice of this filter size and number of iterations was determined by experimentation.

[4] For most tools, this means "until the tool has moved." The melting tool, however, has an effect at every instant.

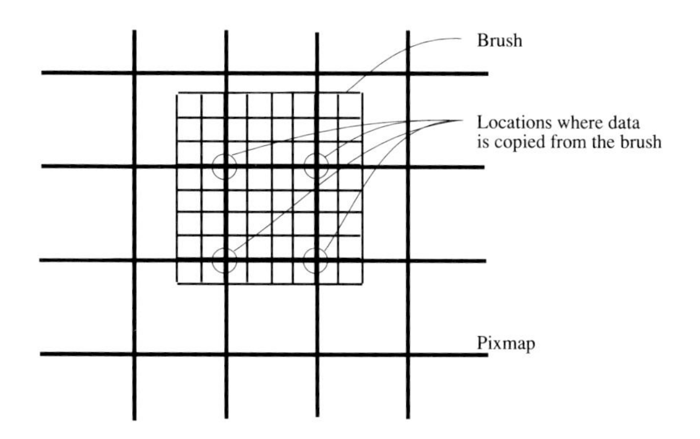


Figure 12: The 2D paintbrush location is determined to a finer resolution than that of the canvas. Values that correspond to pixel centers are actually used in applying the brush to the canvas.

each coordinate to the nearest 1/4. We then imagine the tool's voxmap as superimposed on the object voxmap at that position; 1/64th of the tool's voxel locations correspond exactly to the object voxel locations, and it is this subsample of the tool's voxmap that is combined with the object voxmap. Figure 12 shows the analogous situation in 2D.

How are object voxel values and tool voxel values combined? We use the *min* operator on each voxel:

$$\text{OBJECT} \leftarrow \min(\text{OBJECT}, \text{TOOL});$$

this prevents the 1s in the tool's voxmap from depositing material in empty space.

The additive tool is created by filtering a sphere full of 1s (with 0s outside), and applied by using the *max* operator. Two other tools use this tool data as well. The "heat gun" is applied by the rule

$$\text{OBJECT} \leftarrow \max(0, \text{OBJECT} - \text{TOOL}),$$

and the "building tool," which gradually pastes new material on in the same way that the heat gun removes it, is applied by the rule

$$\text{OBJECT} \leftarrow \min(1, \text{OBJECT} + \text{TOOL}).$$

The "sandpaper" tool is anomalous, in that it has no associated data. It is applied as follows: each voxmap value within the tool's extent is replaced by a weighted average of its current value and those of its six adjacent voxels. The central voxel is given a weight between 4 and 24, and the adjacent voxels are given weight 1. The user then adjusts the rate of "sanding" by varying the weight of the central voxel.

The tool voxel data and the object voxel data arrays must both have the same axes in this model. We would like to add other tools in the future, and allow the tool orientation to be controlled by the orientation of the Polhemus pointer; however, this requires resampling the tool voxel data to get a rotated sample, and at present this is not feasible at a reasonable refresh rate.

## 3.3 Regenerating the Isosurface

When the tool voxmap is applied to the object voxmap, the object data is modified only in a small region. Thus we need not recompute the entire level 0.5 isosurface — only certain polygons change, namely those that arose from cubes the values of whose vertices have been modified. Since we know exactly which vertices these are, we can readily compute the new polygons to be displayed. We call this the *incremental marching-cubes algorithm.*

To redisplay the isosurface, we wish to display the newly computed polygons and remove the polygons formerly associated with the modified regions. The removal of these defunct polygons might

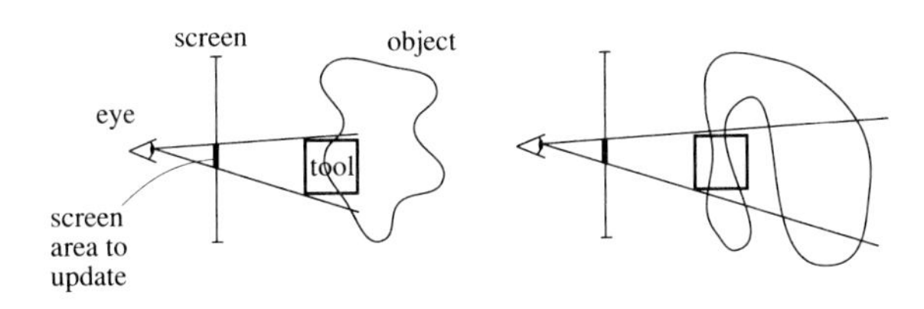


Figure 13: When the square tool cuts away material, polygons that were formerly obscured may be revealed, as shown in the right hand case.

expose certain other polygons. These obscured polygons are no longer in the $z$-buffer, having been overwritten by the now-defunct polygons, so we must redisplay the formerly obscured polygons too (see Figure 13 for a 2D slice of this situation). To facilitate this, we use a data structure we call a *hashgrid*.

The hashgrid makes it easy to determine which cubes in the object voxel array contribute polygons to a specific screen region. We divide the screen into a grid of squares, which we call *cells*, and associate a bucket (implemented as a linked list) to each. Whenever a cube that contributes polygons has a screen projection overlapping a cell, that cube is added to the cell's bucket. Once this array of cells, the hashgrid, has been computed, it is easy to determine which cubes' polygons must be redrawn to update a region of the screen.

To make the hashgrid efficient, we make two requirements: (1) a hashgrid cell must be at least as large as the projection of any cube to the screen; (2) a hashgrid cell must be at least as large as the largest screen extent of the projection of the tool from any point in the sculpting space. Since our tools are always at least as large as a single cube, it suffices to satisfy the second condition.

We compute the bounding rectangle of this maximum-size tool projection analytically. This is possible because the tool is constrained to lie in the sculpting space and the camera's field of view is fixed. We also compute the bounding rectangle for the projection of the entire sculpting-space cube. The larger dimension of the first rectangle is what we choose for the size of each cell edge in the hashgrid; the larger dimension of the second rectangle, divided by this cell edge length, determines the size of the array of cells.

We initialize the hashgrid during the marching-cubes algorithm. Each cube in the voxmap is examined to see whether it contributes polygons to the object; if so, it is flagged (the *contribution flag* of the cube is set), we determine which cells the cube's projection overlaps, and add the cube to the bucket for each such cell.

To determine which cells a cube hits, we project the eight vertices of the cube, and note which cells these projected vertices lie in (because of the first requirement on the size of grid cells, the projected vertices can lie in at most four different cells). Then, if the projected vertices lie in exactly three cells, we add a fourth cell to the list, as shown in Figure 14, which indicates why we must do this: it is possible for the screen extent of a cube's projection to intersect a cell in which no projected vertex lies. This *L-shape anomaly* will arise again when we discuss the effect of tool motion.

The obvious way to project the vertices of a cube to the screen is to take the coordinates of each vertex, multiply them by the current (4 x 4) transformation matrix, and then project to screen space via the perspective projection transformation. Both of these operations are linear functions, except for the homogeneous division in the perspective transformation. We use this linearity as follows: We project the corners of the entire object voxmap to homogeneous coordinates (just before the perspective divide), and use the resulting coordinates to infer the locations of each small cube's corners in this space via linear interpolation. We then perform the homogeneous division; this interpolated computation of the projected vertices reduces the per-cube computation of associated hashgrid cells from 128 multiplies, 96 additions, and 16 divisions (the cost of the two

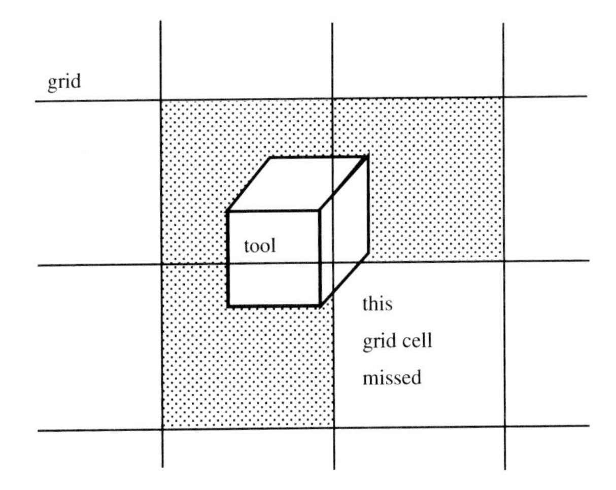


Figure 14: A projected cube may intersect four grid cells even though the projected vertices lie in only three cells. Because of this, we always add the cube to the bucket of the fourth cell.

matrix multiplies and the perspective divide of the naive approach) to just 9 multiplies, 30 additions, and 16 divisions.

To update the hashgrid when the tool is moved, each cube in the voxmap whose vertices have been modified by the tool is examined. If the cube's contribution flag is not set but the cube now contributes polygons, the flag is set and the cube is added to the hashgrid data structure. If the cube's contribution flag is set but the cube no longer contributes polygons, the flag is cleared and the cube is removed from the hashgrid.

The display is updated by determining which cells in the hashgrid might have been affected by the tool. By the second condition on hashgrid cell size, the screen projection of the tool intersects at most four cells. As before, in the event of an L-shape anomaly, the fourth cell is added to the list of affected cells. This cell list is merged with the list of cells associated with the previous tool position (these two lists often overlap, especially when the tool is being moved slowly). The screen area and $z$-buffer area associated with these cells are cleared. Then, for each cube in the bucket of each grid cell on the list, the polygons are regenerated and drawn. (We regenerate the polygons to save the prohibitively large space required to store them).

When we alter our view of the object, the hashgrid must be recomputed. Rather than recompute it from scratch, we use the old hashgrid to compute the new one. By examining only those cubes that appear in some bucket in the old hashgrid, we avoid performing marching-cubes computations on those parts of the object voxmap that will not contribute polygons. The process for creating the new hashgrid is therefore: (1) for each cell of the old hashgrid, look at the cubes in its bucket; (2) for each such cube, check a flag (the *already-processed* flag); if it is not set, set it, perform the marching-cubes algorithm on that cube, and insert the cube into the new hashgrid; (3) once the whole old hashgrid has been processed, clear the already-processed flags on all cubes. Using the already-processed flag is necessary because a single cube is likely to be in the buckets of more than one hashgrid cell (but no more than four).

## 4 FUTURE WORK

We have many plans for future work in extending this modeling paradigm. We are in the process of improving the color editing in the system, and look forward to adding patterning or even solid textures like those described in [11]. We would like to develop a voxmap with so many cubes that the screen projection of a typical cube is about the size of a screen pixel. This actually simplifies some of the algorithms (polygon rendering in the display device is no longer needed, for example); unfortunately, the memory requirements are still prohibitive. We are eager to experiment further with force feedback, as we feel that this will provide an extremely intuitive user interface. We want to add tools that have orientation, so that we can use the full range of data from the Polhemus device. We want to add various high-level operations on the sculpture such as scaling, translation, cutting, copying, and pasting regions of the sculpture, reflecting and rotating portions of the sculpture; in general, we would like to make available as many as possible of the other operations available in traditional paint programs. We would like to add hierarchy to the system, so that in regions where more detail is needed, we could locally increase the resolution of the voxel lattice. Finally, we want to gain experience with a wide selection of users so that we know better how to make sculpting a natural inclusion in the standard repertoire of modeling techniques. This should include further study of the user interface and its ease of use; our current experience involves no rigorous perceptual studies, and we feel that these may considerably enhance the interface.

## 5 ACKNOWLEDGMENTS

Much of this work was done by the first author as his Master's project under the direction of the second author. We appreciate the support of the Brown Computer Graphics Group, in particular Bob Zeleznik and Dan Robbins, and of the MIT Media Lab, especially the Computer Graphics and Animation Group. The first author thanks Sheri Galyean for her support and encouragement.

## References

[1] J.F. Blinn. A generalization of algebraic surface drawing. *ACM TOG*, 1(3):235–256, 1982.

[2] J. Bloomenthal and B. Wyvill. Interactive techniques for implicit modeling. *Computer Graphics*, 24(2):109–116, March 1990.

[3] S. Coquillart. Extended free-form deformation: A sculpting tool for 3d geometric modeling. *Computer Graphics*, 24(4):187–196, August 1990.

[4] J. Foley, A. van Dam, S. Feiner, and J. Hughes. *Computer Graphics: Principles and Practice*. Addison-Wesley, second edition, 1990.

[5] P.S. Heckbert. Filtering by repeated integration. *Computer Graphics*, 20(4):315–321, August 1986.

[6] T. Van Hook. Real-time shaded nc milling display. *Computer Graphics*, 20(4):15–20, August 1986.

[7] W.E. Lorenson and H.E. Cline. Marching cubes: A high resolution 3d surface construction algorithm. *Computer Graphics*, 21(4):163–169, July 1987.

[8] M. Minsky, M. Ouh-young, O. Steele, and F. Brooks. Feeling and seeing: Issues in force display. *Computer Graphics*, 24(2):235–243, March 1990.

[9] B. F. Naylor. Sculpt: An interactive solid modeling tool. In *Proceedings of Graphics Interface '90*, pages 138–148, May 1990.

[10] A. Pentland, I. Essa, M. Friendmann, B. Horowitz, and S. Sclaroff. The thingworld modeling system: Virtual sculpting by modal forces. *Computer Graphics*, 24(2):143–146, March 1990.

[11] K. Perlin. An image synthesizer. *Computer Graphics*, 19(3):287–296, July 1985.

[12] T.W. Sederberg and S.R. Parry. Free-form deformation of solid geometric models. *Computer Graphics*, 20(4):151–160, August 1986.

[13] D. Terzopoulos and K. Fleischer. Modeling inelastic deformation: Viscoelasticity, plasticity, fracture. *Computer Graphics*, 22(4):269–278, August 1988.

[14] T. Whitted. Anti-aliased line drawing using brush extrusion. *Computer Graphics*, 17(3):151–156, July 1983.

[15] L. Williams. 3d paint. *Computer Graphics*, 24(2):225–233, March 1990.

[16] B. Wyvill and D. Jevans. Table driven polygonization. In *SIGGRAPH '90 Course Notes, Modeling and Animation with Implicit Surfaces*, pages 7/1–7/6, August 1990.

[17] B. Wyvill, C. McPheeters, and G. Wyvill. Data structure for soft objects. *The Visual Computer*, 2(4), 1986.

# A Coherent Projection Approach for Direct Volume Rendering

Jane Wilhelms and Allen Van Gelder
Computer and Information Sciences
University of California, Santa Cruz 95064

## Abstract

Direct volume rendering offers the opportunity to visualize all of a three-dimensional sample volume in one image. However, processing such images can be very expensive and good quality high-resolution images are far from interactive. Projection approaches to direct volume rendering process the volume region by region as opposed to ray-casting methods that process it ray by ray. Projection approaches have generated interest because they use coherence to provide greater speed than ray casting and generate the image in a layered, informative fashion. This paper discusses two topics: First, it introduces a projection approach for directly rendering rectilinear, parallel-projected sample volumes that takes advantage of coherence across cells and the identical shape of their projection. Second, it considers the repercussions of various methods of integration in depth and interpolation across the scan plane. Some of these methods take advantage of Gouraud-shading hardware, with advantages in speed but potential disadvantages in image quality.

## 1 Introduction

The two main approaches for rendering three-dimensional scalar sample volumes are extraction of isosurfaces [LC87] and direct volume rendering [DCH88, Lev88, Sab88, UK88, Wes90, MHC90, ST90]. While extraction of isosurfaces produces clearcut delineation of features, the binary decision made about the location of surfaces means that only a limited amount of the total information contained in the volume can be presented in one image. Direct volume rendering can use semi-transparency to visualize much more of the volume contents, and all cells become capable of contributing to the image. The use of independent transfer functions to map the volume's original scalar values to color and opacity makes it possible to combine continuous variations with feature extraction in a very flexible fashion.

Because the amount of information presented in one directly rendered image and its sometimes blurry appearance can make it difficult to fully understand, the ability to view the volume interactively from various positions is of considerable importance. Unfortunately, direct volume rendering is very expensive and most animations depend upon precalculated images which are replayed as film loops. Techniques that do provide fast rendering tend to do so at the expense of image quality.

This paper presents an approach to direct volume rendering using projection of individual volume cells [DCH88, UK88, Wes90]. Processing is cell by cell, not pixel by pixel as in the alternative ray-casting approach [Lev88, Sab88, UK88]. Projection seems in many ways preferable to ray casting. It can take advantage of coherence when a cell projects onto many neighboring pixels. It can avoid some of the aliasing inherent in point-sampling approaches. It can process the image plane by plane, so that if the total rendering time is considerable, the viewer can gain useful information during the rendering process by watching the image being created. This is particularly useful if the image is drawn back to front, because regions of the image that might be obscured later are all visible at some point during rendering. It has been suggested that projection is more amenable to parallel processing [UK88].

The coherent projection approach presented here takes advantage of the regularity of rectilinear volumes in two ways. First, the projection of each cell is an exact but translated geometrical copy of every other cell, so an analysis of the geometry of a single cell can be used to hasten processing of every other cell. This assumes parallel projection, though perspective projection is possible if cells are individually projected at some extra cost. Second, a cell projects as one to seven polygons. The intensity and opacity values of the pixels involved can be found by interpolating (in one of several ways) between their vertices.



©1991 ACM-0-89791-436-8/91/007/0275 $00.75

Several methods are presented for calculating cumulative intensity and opacity by integration in depth and interpolation across the scan plane. They are investigated in terms of their speed and image quality.

## 2 Coherent Projection Algorithm

A *cell* refers to the rectilinear region bounded by eight neighboring sample points, the *cell corners*. Cells are modeled as containing a semi-transparent material that both emits light and occludes it in amounts dependent upon the scalar data values of the cell corners and their mapping to intensity (red, green, and blue) and opacity values using transfer functions. The coherent projection method depends upon three observations concerning the parallel projection of rectilinear cells. (For simplicity, cells are assumed to be identical in size. The algorithm also works for hierarchical volumes where cells are uniformly scaled versions of each other [WC+90].)

1. The projection of each of these cells is geometrically a translated copy of the projection of any one cell.
2. From any eyepoint, a generic cell can be simplified into at most seven subcells with the same front and back face.
3. The projection of these subcells is either a triangular or a quadrilateral *projected polygon.*

The first step of coherent projection is to determine an appropriate template for the particular shape and orientation of the cells making up the volume (Section 2.1). The volume is then traversed, relying on the template for geometry, but taking into account the unique data values of each cell (Section 2.2). For each cell, intensity and opacity values for the subcell vertices are determined (Section 2.3), and then intensity and opacity values of the pixels that the subcells project onto are determined using interpolation (Section 2.4). These pixels are composited with the accumulating image in the frame buffer (Section 2.5).

### 2.1 Determining the Generic Cell Type

Depending upon orientation, one, two, or three faces will form the front of the rectilinear cell (Figure 1). If the projection of the cell is divided into regions having the same front and back face, up to seven *subcells* result from each cell. (Use of coherence in regions with the same front and back cell faces has also been investigated elsewhere [UK88, MHC90, ST90].) Subcells are polyhedra whose front and back faces project to the same screen location and form *projected polygons.* Thus, each projected polygon vertex can be thought of as a *vertex pair,*consisting of a front vertex and a back vertex which may have no distance between them along silhouette edges. Some subcell vertices are original cell corners. Others are *intersection points* that must be calculated. The distance from front to back between the vertex pairs is the same for all pairs with a non-zero distance, and can be precalculated.

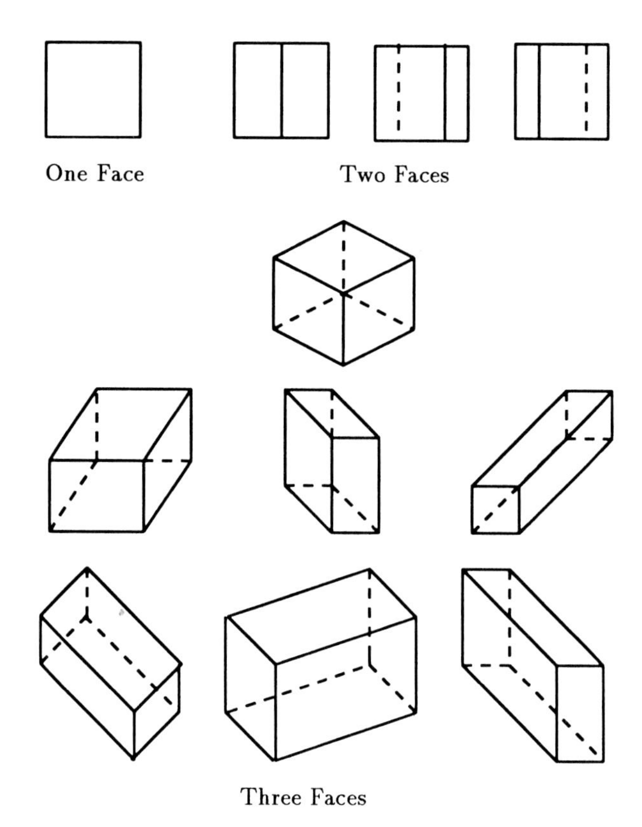


Figure 1: Cell Projections

When only one face is visible (see Figure 1), there is only one projected quadrilateral polygon, and its vertices are projections of original cell corners.

When two faces are visible (e.g., front and left), two or three quadrilateral projected polygons face the front. Two corners of the original cell are nearest the front, and two are farthest away. If the two farthest vertices project exactly onto the two nearest, no new intersection points are needed and two projected polygons result. Otherwise, a face is split and four new intersection points located on cell edges must be found. In this case three projected polygons result.

If three faces are visible, six or seven polygons are needed to represent the cell. There are seven possible subcases, determined by the location of the farthest cell corner relative to the nearest. If the farthest cell corner projects onto a face (three cases), four new edge intersections and two new face intersections must be calculated. If the farthest cell corner projects onto a line (three cases), only two new edge intersections are needed. If the farthest cell corner projects onto the nearest, no new intersections are needed.

In this implementation, a table was generated to specify each of these cases, assuming they represent front, front-left, and front-left-bottom faces. All other cases are mapped to these. The table describes which edges and faces contain intersections, which cell corners and intersection points form vertex pairs, and which front vertices form polygons. Once a generic cell type is determined the table is used to find appropriate properties from one particular generic cell. These values are stored and reused for all other cells.

## 2.2 Traversal of the Volume

The algorithm works either by traversing the volume back to front, or front to back. There are advantages to both traversals. Back-to-front traversal avoids the need for an opacity buffer to store accumulated opacity values. Furthermore, this traversal shows each layer of the image in front of the last, so all cells at some time appear in front. If the traversal is front to back, an opacity buffer is needed. A potential advantage of front-to-back rendering is that rendering can be bypassed for the new cells that lie behind fully opaque cells. This requires a suitable saving strategy, which is being investigated.

Because of the regularity of the volume, an appropriate traversal order can be determined from its orientation. (The transformation matrix can provide this.) More than one traversal order is possible. For example, if only the front face is visible, the traversal can be $XYZ$, $YXZ$, $-XYZ$, etc. The current implementation traverses the volume in the order that accesses the data most efficiently: if $X$ varies fastest, an $XYZ$ traversal is used when possible. This means that sometimes the slice whose projection covers the smallest area is projected, making the image less understandable as it is developing. A more visually appealing alternative would be to project the slice with the largest projected area first.

## 2.3 Integration in Depth

Each cell is assumed to consist of a semi-transparent material which emits its own light, transmits some light coming from behind, and occludes some light both from behind and from within the cell. Such a model is related to previous work in computer graphics for modeling semi-transparent media [Bli82, KH84, Max86, Sab88]. Luminosity and occlusion are represented as intensity and opacity.

To create the image, the scalar values from the original data are converted to intensity and opacity values using transfer functions stored in red, green, blue, and opacity tables. Estimated data values for edge intersections are found by linear interpolation between adjacent corner vertices, and for face intersections by bilinear interpolation of face vertices; these values are then used for mapping.

The cumulative intensity and opacity contribution of the medium between the front and back cell face must be determined. This process will be referred to as *integration in depth*, and involves solving (approximately) a linear differential equation. The discussion that follows is general and is applicable to any method that seeks the intensity and opacity contribution along the line of sight through the volume, such as ray casting approaches that trace between entry and exit points of cells [UK88]. Three approaches are described, providing a trade-off between image quality and speed. For coherent projection, one of these methods is used to find intensity and opacity at projected polygon vertices.

### 2.3.1 Some Definitions

The intensity and opacity contribution of a cell at each pixel (or along each line of sight ray) should take into account the emission and occlusion properties of the material being modeled. We define *material opacity* as the fraction of light entering from behind that would be occluded *if that material were present for a depth distance of 1.* For example, if the material opacity value is 0.5, 50% of any light coming from behind the material would be removed if the material were present for a depth of one unit distance. Our implementation treats the value returned by the opacity transfer function as the material opacity (in the range 0 to 1) and converts it into the differential opacity (in the range 0 to $\infty$) as described below. (It would also be reasonable to specify that the transfer function return the differential opacity directly, but then there is some awkwardness about representing $\infty$.)

The *differential opacity* of a material, denoted by $\Omega$, is defined as the rate at which light is occluded as it travels through the material. That is, in an infinitesimal distance $dz$, a fraction $\Omega(z)dz$ of light is occluded, and $(1 - \Omega(z)dz)$ of the light is transmitted. From these definitions it follows (see Equation 7) that a differential opacity $\Omega$ acting over a unit distance gives a material opacity

$$O = 1 - e^{-\Omega} \tag{1}$$

Inverting this function,

$$\Omega = \log\left(\frac{1}{1-O}\right) \tag{2}$$

The color transfer functions return *material intensity*, which is defined as the amount of light emitted by the material if present for a depth distance of 1. However, the material intensity value is the same as the differential intensity value.

The intensity and opacity contributed by the material between the front and the back of a cell along the line of sight are called *cumulative intensity* and *cumulative opacity*. These quantities are defined as solutions of differential equations; they are found and used in compositing.

### 2.3.2 Integration Methods

Throughout this discussion we use *integration* somewhat liberally to mean (exact or approximate) solution of a differential equation. Three approaches have been implemented. In all cases the underlying differential equations are the same, as described next.

Let $z$ represent distance through the cell from the back vertex. Let $\Omega(z)$ be differential opacity and let $E_c(z)$ be the differential intensity of light of color $c$ (which, as mentioned before, is the same as material intensity). Let $T(z)$ denote the fraction of light entering the cell that is transmitted through distance $z$ (needed for compositing). Let $I_c(z)$ denote the intensity of light of color $c$ that is emitted within the cell and reaches $z$. Then:

$$\frac{dT}{dz} = -\Omega(z)T(z) \quad (3)$$

$$\frac{dI_c}{dz} = -\Omega(z)I_c(z) + E_c(z) \quad (4)$$

The boundary conditions are that $T(0) = 1$ and $I_c(0) = 0$. Letting $d$ be the back-to-front distance between vertices, the cumulative intensity of color $c$ is $I_c(d)$ and the cumulative opacity is $O_{cum} = (1 - T(d))$.

Assuming $\Omega(z)$ has a closed form integral (it is normally a simple interpolation function of some kind), Equation 3 has the standard closed form solution,

$$T(z) = e^{-\int_0^z \Omega(u)du} \quad (5)$$

The solution of Equation 4 can also be expressed as an integral:

$$I_c(z) = T(z)\int_0^z \left(\frac{E_c(v)}{T(v)}\right) dv \quad (6)$$

However, this integral has a closed form expression only in special cases. For example, if there is a constant $\mu_c$ such that $E_c(z) = \mu_c\Omega(z)$, then the substitution $U_c(z) = I_c(z) - \mu_c$ in Equation 4 gives a differential equation for $U_c$ that is the same as Equation 3 (except for the boundary condition), and $I(z)$ is "as solvable as" as $T(z)$; this method is employed by Max *et al.* [MHC90]. The conditions $E_c(z) = \mu_c\Omega(z)$ effectively restrict the mapping from scalar values to a single transfer function plus different multipliers $\mu_c$ for different colors. It is not employed here because we wished to permit the specification of independent transfer functions for all four quantities.

For the rest of the discussion, we shall drop the subscript $c$ on intensities $E$ and $I$, with the understanding that intensity calculations are done independently for each color.

An important case that has closed form solutions is used in several of the methods, sometimes as an approximation: that is when $\Omega(z)$ and $E(z)$ are constant within the cell. Then we have

$$T(z) = e^{-\Omega z} \quad (7)$$

$$I(z) = \frac{E}{\Omega}\left(1 - e^{-\Omega z}\right) \quad (8)$$

Substituting $d$ for $z$ gives the cumulative values, $O_{cum} = (1 - T(d))$ and $I_{cum} = I(d)$.

**1. Average C*D Integration:** A simple way to determine cumulative intensity and opacity is to average the front and back intensity and differential opacity values, and to approximate $(1 - e^{-\Omega d})$ by $\min(1, \Omega d)$ in Equations 7 and 8. This gives

$$O_{cum} = \min(1, \Omega_{ave}d) \quad (9)$$

$$I_{cum} = \left(\frac{E_{ave}}{\Omega_{ave}}\right) O_{cum} \quad (10)$$

The name "C*D" is based on the fact that in the common case that $O_{cum} < 1$, the cumulative intensity becomes "color times distance".

This is not always a desirable choice: for example, the intensity and opacity calculated for a ray through a homogeneous volume (constant data values throughout) will generally not be the same if the volume is treated as one large cell compared to the same volume treated as many small cells composited together (see Section 3.1). However, this approach is fast, as no transcendental functions are used, and for large volumes may be visually indistinguishable from more expensive methods (see Section 3.4). This method tends to overestimate intensity and opacity.

**2. Exponential Homogeneous Integration:** A more complex and yet computationally acceptable method is to assume the region between the front and back of the cell is *homogeneous.* The front and back material intensity and opacity are averaged to provide the average material intensity $E_{ave}$ and average material opacity $O_{ave}$. Then $O_{ave}$ is converted to $\Omega_{ave}$ by Equation 2, and the closed form solutions in Equations 7 and 8 are used with $E_{ave}$ for $E$ and $\Omega_{ave}$ for $\Omega$. Related exponential methods have been used by other visualization researchers [MHC90, ST90, Sab88]. The distance $d$ between front and back vertices can be scaled by a user-defined factor for flexibility.

**3. Exponential Linear Integration:** Here the material intensity and opacity are assumed to vary *linearly* (but independently) between front and back cell faces. A closed form solution does not exist in general, and numerical solution is used. The user defines a number of divisions between the front and back faces, and linear interpolation is used to estimate the material intensity and opacity values at those points. Then exponential homogeneous integration is applied to each of the subregions, and these are composited as described in Section 2.5. As mentioned before, Max *et al.* [MHC90] require that intensity is some constant multiple of opacity, and use the faster analytical solution based on Equation 5 and the discussion following it.

## 2.4 Interpolating to Pixel Values

Once the intensity and opacity of the polygon vertices have been determined, it is necessary to find the values of the pixels that lie between them and are projected onto. These pixels are located by the usual process of polygon scan conversion, either in hardware or software. A major motivation of this method is that this job can be relegated to hardware. The cumulative intensity and opacity associated with the pixels projected onto are found by one of the three methods described below. These will be referred to as *interpolation* methods, though, more correctly, they are a choice of which integration to apply to each pixel. Again, there is a tradeoff of cost and accuracy. Three approaches have been implemented:

**1. Gouraud Shading Interpolation:** This is an extension of the common Gouraud shading model [Gou71] which first linearly interpolates cumulative color and opacity along edges from scanline to scanline, and, within each scanline, linearly interpolates between the values for edge pairs. Shirley and Tuchman [ST90] recently published a method using Gouraud-shaded tetrahedrons for volume rendering.

The assumption of a linear variation between vertices is not completely in keeping with the basic model of a semi-transparent gas. However, the method often works quite well in practice (see Section 3). Many graphics workstations have hardware-assisted Gouraud shading and this step can done efficiently and in parallel with the rest of the volume renderer. It is essential, however, that the Gouraud shader interpolates in the opacity channel, as well as red, green, and blue. The limited precision of interpolation in hardware can also cause aliasing, so a software version which works in floating point has also been implemented.

**2. Exponential Homogeneous Interpolation:** This uses exponential homogeneous integration to calculate the cumulative intensity and opacity at each pixel. First, the average material intensity and opacity are found for each projected polygon vertex. Then, polygon scan conversion is used to linearly interpolate across the projected polygon face and find the average material intensity and opacity at each pixel.[1] Finally, exponential homogeneous integration is used between front and back faces to find the cumulative intensity and opacity at each pixel.

**3. Exponential Linear Interpolation:** This approach uses exponential linear integration at each pixel projected onto. In this case, the material intensity and opacity values of the front and back face polygons are linearly interpolated separately, again using scan conversion to find these values at each pixel. Then exponential linear integration is applied at each pixel. This is most closely related to the work of Max et al.[MHC90], but permits separate independent transfer functions for different colors and opacity.

### 2.5 Compositing

Compositing is used at each pixel to combine the effects of cells that project there [PD84]. For back-to-front traversal

$$C_{acc} = (1 - O_{new})C_{acc} + C_{new} \tag{11}$$

$$O_{acc} = (1 - O_{new})O_{acc} + O_{new} \tag{12}$$

[1] This facilitates comparison of methods. More consistent here and in the next method would be to interpolate on data, then apply the transfer functions.

| | Exponential | | Average C*D | |
|---|---|---|---|---|
| | Intensity | Opacity | Intensity | Opacity |
| 1 Cell | 91.97 | 0.500 | 127.50 | 0.693 |
| 2 Cells | 91.97 | 0.500 | 105.41 | 0.573 |
| 5 Cells | 91.97 | 0.500 | 96.72 | 0.526 |
| 10 Cells | 91.97 | 0.500 | 94.26 | 0.512 |
| 50 Cells | 91.97 | 0.500 | 92.42 | 0.502 |
| 100 Cells | 91.97 | 0.500 | 92.19 | 0.501 |
| 10000 Cells | 91.97 | 0.500 | 91.97 | 0.500 |

Table 1: Combining Compositing and Integration

where $C_{new}$ and $O_{new}$ are the color and opacity values of the newly calculated cell at a particular pixel, and $C_{acc}$ and $O_{acc}$ are the accumulated color and opacity values of the pixel projected onto before and after projection. However, it is not necessary to calculate $O_{acc}$ or store it.

For front-to-back traversal,

$$C_{acc} = (1 - O_{acc})C_{new} + C_{acc} \tag{13}$$

$$O_{acc} = (1 - O_{acc})O_{new} + O_{acc} \tag{14}$$

and $O_{acc}$ must be stored.

## 3 Experimental Results

Coherent projection methods have been explored on a number of data sets. This section will explore: 1) integration approaches; 2) interpolation approaches; 3) compositing; and 4) cost and quality of final images.

### 3.1 Results Concerning Integration in Depth

Three issues to consider in choosing an integration method are: behavior within a single cell; behavior when compositing many cells; and time costs. After some illustrative examples are used to explore these issues, values are compared for two real data volumes.

**Behavior within a Single Cell:** Consider integration of one front-back vertex pair. Generally, cumulative intensity and cumulative opacity are higher using average C*D integration, compared to the "exponential" integration methods. The exponential homogeneous approach averages out differences between front and back faces, while the exponential linear approach interpolates. Consider three cases with the same cell depth:

| | Front Vertex | | Back Vertex | |
|---|---|---|---|---|
| | opacity | intensity | opacity | intensity |
| (A) | 0.4 | 100 | 0.4 | 100 |
| (B) | 0.8 | 200 | 0.0 | 0 |
| (C) | 0.0 | 200 | 0.8 | 0 |

Exponential homogeneous integration will find the same cumulative intensity and opacity for all three because of averaging. Exponential linear integration will not. In fact, as the number of subdivisions increases, cell B will become increasingly dark, because the high opacity at the front will occlude both light from behind and light being emitted within the cell itself. (In cases where opacity is very high, even cells with high material intensity values will become very dark. This is a rather undesirable though not unrealistic property of high opacity regions in this approach.)

If, instead of material opacity, the *differential* opacity were linearly interpolated through the cell in the exponential linear integration method, then cases A and B would give identical results because intensity is a linear multiple of opacity and the opacities have the same integrals, so the discussion following Equation 6 applies. Case C, however, would still differ.

**Compositing Between Cells Combined with Integration within Cells:** Compositing brings out an inadequacy of Gouraud interpolation methods. Inter-cell compositing is itself an exponential process, comparable to the exponential integration methods described above. Table 1 shows the problem with a simple example: a constant value region with intensity 127.5, material opacity 0.5, and distance 1. (Compositing was done in floating point.) Using exponential integration methods, the same intensity and opacity result from treating the region as one cell or many cells, as should occur in reality. This is not the case when average C*D integration is used.

If a hierarchy or progressive refinement is used, the resultant image will vary in intensity depending upon the number of subdivisions. Intensity variations can also occur when viewing the volume at an angle, because the line of sight rays through pixels pass through different numbers and depths of cells.

**Time Costs:** The exponential integration methods are clearly more expensive. Considering only the subroutines involved in integration in depth, the average C*D method was from 25% to 50% faster than exponential homogeneous integration, and this latter was about three times as fast as exponential linear integration with five subdivisions. The relative costs of these routines in the whole program depend upon volume size and orientations. On tested volumes (40x32x32 and 256x256x51 resolution), exponential homogeneous integration routines took from 35% to 60% of the total running time.

**Integration on Two Larger Volumes:** The effect of the three approaches on two real data sets was examined. One was a 256x256x50 section of an MR brain data set.[2]

The transfer functions for this were a mostly linear ramp with increased red and opacity in the middle ranges. (See Figure 5). The other volume was the pressure scalar field from a computational fluid dynamics simulation of air flow around a blunt fin.[3] The original curvilinear-gridded data was resampled to a regular grid with dimensions 115x100x51 [WC+90]. Transfer functions mapped high pressure regions to red and medium pressure regions to blue. (See Figure 2 for a smaller 40x32x32 version of this volume.)

The cumulative intensity and opacity values found by the three integration methods for each front/back vertex pair were compared. In summary, comparing mean values and standard deviations, differences were at most 2%. Occasionally, C*D integration differed by 8%.

### 3.2 Interpolation Between Projected Vertices

Next, methods for finding cumulative intensity and opacity at pixels were explored (see Section 2.3). When Gouraud interpolation was used, all of the three integration methods were used to find cumulative intensity and opacity at the subcell vertices. When exponential interpolation methods were used, both subcell vertices and interpolated pixels used the same method.

**Interpolation within One Cell:** When viewing a single cell, all methods appear visually reasonable, though Gouraud-interpolated cells are somewhat darker around the borders when viewed with more than one face visible. This is because the cumulative intensity and opacity at some silhouette vertices is zero, due to the distance between front and back subcells vertices being zero. For example, as we move horizontally across a cell of constant opacity $\Omega$, say from $x = 0$ at a silhouette vertex of cell-depth 0 to an interior vertex at $x = a$, where the cell-depth is $d$, intensity should increase according to the nonlinear function $(1-e^{-\Omega x d/a})/\Omega$. However, linear interpolation yields only the smaller function $\frac{x}{a}\left(1 - e^{-\Omega d}\right)/\Omega$. "Exponential" interpolation methods use the correct nonlinear function for pixel calculations and do not have this problem.

It is possible to somewhat alleviate linear interpolation artifacts and still use hardware Gouraud interpolation through the use of blend functions and multiple blendings. We have implemented a "three-pass" method inspired by a suggestion of Pat Hanrahan and Peter Shirley. It requires back-to-front traversal. The essential step is to compute a "half-way" opacity such that $(1-O_{half})^2 = (1-O_{cum})$. Blending the back twice with this $O_{half}$ causes the hardware (effectively) to multiply two linear interpolations yielding a net quadratic interpolation that more closely approximates the desired exponential function. In the third pass the hardware blends the intensity of the new cell into the background. Additional details are omitted for lack of

[2]MR data was from a Siemens Magneton and provided courtesy of Siemens Medical Systems, Inc., Iselin, MJ. Data edited by Dr. Julian Rosenman, North Carolina Memorial Hospital. Data is from UNC 1989 Volume Visualization Workshop dataset.

[3]CFD data courtesy of NAS/NASA Ames Research Center.

| Subcells | 1 | | 2 | | 10 | | 50 | | 100 | |
|---|---|---|---|---|---|---|---|---|---|---|
| | Int. | Opac. | Int. | Opac. | Int. | Opac. | Int. | Opac. | Int. | Opac. |
| Double Real | 92 | 128 | 92 | 128 | 92 | 128 | 92 | 128 | 92 | 128 |
| Float Real | 92 | 128 | 92 | 128 | 92 | 128 | 92 | 128 | 92 | 128 |
| 16-bit Integer | 92 | 128 | 92 | 128 | 92 | 127 | 92 | 127 | 90 | 127 |
| 8-bit Integer | 92 | 128 | 92 | 127 | 87 | 124 | 83 | 122 | 1 | 101 |
| Iris 4D-50GT | 92 | 128 | 91 | 127 | 87 | 119 | 34 | 32 | 1 | 1 |

Table 2: Comparison of Compositing Using Integer or Real Arithmetic (Intensity and Opacity)

space. This method is inaccurate when $\Omega d << 1$ due to limited hardware precision, but may be useful when the scene consists of a few large cells, as shown in Figure 3.B.

**Interpolation with Layers of Cells:** Problems with Gouraud interpolation methods become more obvious when layers of cells are composited. The inaccurate interaction of integration and compositing described in Section 3.1 will occur when linear methods are used, because the integration method simulated at each pixel is inaccurate. However, this problem is not very obvious unless the volume consists of a few large cells. Figure 3 illustrates this effect on a 4x4x4 constant value volume rendered using four methods: the upper left image used exponential homogeneous integration at subcell vertices and hardware Gouraud interpolation; the upper right used the same methods but with the multiple blending mentioned above; the lower left used average C*D integration at subcells vertices and hardware Gouraud interpolation; and the lower right used exponential homogeneous integration and interpolation. It is possible to see some artifacts between cells in all images except the lower right.

**Precision Problems with Hardware Shading:** A much greater problem may occur when using hardware Gouraud shading as opposed to software Gouraud shading, because if the individual cells of the volume are *very dim*, precision and truncation errors become a major consideration. Figure 4 shows the problems due to hardware interpolation that show up when many layers are composited together. These images show a 20x20x20 scalar field with material opacity values decreasing radially from the center. Left images use exponential homogeneous integration at subcell vertices and right images uses average C*D integration at subcell vertices. Upper images use hardware Gouraud shading and lower images use software Gouraud shading. All images use hardware compositing, so the compositing behavior itself is not the problem here. Rather the accumulation of tiny (one bit) errors from each dim cell layer (average cumulative intensity was 7 and average opacity 0.1) when many layers are composited together produce this result. Further, the blocky nature of the pictures is also seen on a single layer of cells when the monitor brightness is enhanced. These problems become much less noticeable if cells are bright, because truncation is less significant.

### 3.3 Compositing

A related problem can occur due to hardware compositing that uses only eight bits for the opacity channel. To explore this, a single cell of homogeneous material intensity and opacity (both 128 from a maximum of 255) was used. As described in Section 2.3, using exponential methods, integration in depth through this cell should provide the same intensity and opacity whether it is treated as one or many cells. This is the case using floating point arithmetic. Compositing in software on a Sun 4 provides the results in Table 2 for double- and single-precision floating point, eight-bit integer, and sixteen-bit integer arithmetic. The cell depth is 1 and the cell is divided into 1, 2, 10, 50, and 100 subcells. The final row shows results gained from compositing on an Iris 4D-50GT and reading the frame buffer.

Of course, most graphics systems are designed to render fairly bright objects and composite a few layers. This was what they were designed for, and they are very good at it. However, some of us insist on trying to extend their uses in new directions, and encounter the problems described above. For us, it would certainly be desirable that the machines use more bits per pixel for interpolation and compositing.

### 3.4 Timings and Image Quality

In this section the various approaches are compared in terms of the images produced and time taken on few data sets (See Table 3). The machine used for timings and still images was a Silicon Graphics Iris 4D50-GT, and images for timings were drawn into a 500x500 pixel window.

As a brief comment, coherent projection takes advantage of the identical parallel projection of all cells. If perspective projection were used, each cell would have to be independently projected. This would approximately double the cost of rendering when using hardware Gouraud interpolation.

Considering subcell vertex integration methods, average C*D integration was only slightly less expensive than exponential homogeneous integration considering the overall time

| Integration Method / Interpolation Method | Pixel Coverage | Ave. C*D Hrd.Gour. | Exp.Homog. Hrd.Gour. | Exp.Homog. Sft.Gour. | Exp.Homog. Exp.Homog. | Exp.Lin.(5) Exp.Lin.(5) |
|---|---|---|---|---|---|---|
| Sphere 20x20x20 | | | | | | |
| Front | 13x13 | 3 | 4 | 48 | 103 | 359 |
| 2xZoom | 25x25 | 3 | 4 | 155 | 373 | 1395 |
| Rot. 30,30,30 | | 5 | 6 | 96 | 193 | 623 |
| Blunt Fin 40x32x32 | | | | | | |
| Front | 7x8 | 16 | 21 | 62 | 90 | - |
| 2xZoom | 13x16 | 16 | 21 | 138 | 274 | - |
| Rot. 30,30,30 | | 27 | 32 | 132 | 177 | - |
| SOD 97x97x116 | | | | | | |
| Front | 3x3 | 495 | 542 | 1095 | - | - |
| 2xZoom | 5x5 | 516 | 545 | 1771 | - | - |
| Rot. 30,30,30 | | 830 | 833 | 2161 | - | - |

Table 3: Timings on Projection Methods (seconds)

of image creation. This is particularly true on large volumes with small dim cells, where the integration approximates by multiplying color times distance. Exponential linear integration did incur a large time cost and provided minimal differences in image quality compared to exponential homogeneous integration on most volumes viewed anyway.

Considering methods of determining pixel values, software Gouraud interpolation was considerably more expensive than hardware Gouraud interpolation, though how much is dependent upon the cell size. The extra cost of software interpolation decreases with cell size. Also, when cells cover only a few pixels, artifacts due to hardware interpolation also become less significant. But then, advantages of any type of coherent projection disappear when cells are only a pixel or a few pixels in area. A considerable advantage of hardware interpolation is seen when volumes are zoomed. Hardware interpolation is little affected by cell size, while software methods become far more expensive. Applying either of the exponential integration methods at each pixel was prohibitively expensive for medium to large volumes. When a few large cells are visible, however, these methods do produce better images.

The figures show some illustrative images done using exponential homogeneous integration at polygon vertices and hardware Gouraud interpolation. Figure 2 is a 40x32x32 resampled volume based on a CFD simulation of the blunt fin. Figure 5 shows two views of the MR Brain data set. Both volumes were cited in Section 3.1. Figure 6 shows part (zoomed) of the SOD enzyme volume (resolution 97x97x116).[4] Figure 7 is an image of a sampled function, which shows the present implementation's rudimentary isosurface extraction (green) and gradient shading (red and blue) abilities.

[4]Electron density map of active site of superoxide dismutase [SOD] enzyme as determined by X-ray crystallography, Duncan McRee, Scripps Clinic, La Jolla, California. Data is from UNC 1989 Volume Visualization Workshop datset.

## 4 Future Directions

There are several improvements that can be implemented. Exponential linear integration is important only when a large variation exists between front and back vertex values. To avoid the expense of the calculation when unnecessary, the system could compare values and choose between the two exponential methods based on their variation.

The advantages of projection disappear when cells are very small. When this occurs, it would be intelligent to automatically reduce the calculations on each cell, perhaps treating each as one projected polygon with values that are an average of corner vertices.

When imaging front to back, it would be useful to stop rendering cells that project to already opaque regions. The implementation for this is preliminary.

Most images shown here assume the only light is that emitted by the volume. Better gradient shading and isosurface extraction should be implemented. Preliminary tests suggest this should be feasible.

It has become obvious in exploring volume rendering on real data sets that speed is only a small part of the problem. The laborious process of finding an appropriate mapping from data values to color and opacity deserves much future attention. The ability to shade according to gradients and isolate surfaces would also improve the program's usefulness.

## 5 Conclusions

Coherent projection offers rapid imaging, good quality images, and the ability to watch the whole image appear in layers as it is rendered. It is most advantageous when cells cover a number of pixels, as with medium-sized volumes or large volumes zoomed.

The images produced by the various methods explored are generally close as long as cells are the same size. Indeed, particularly when cells are fairly small, it is remarkable how little difference even the inexpensive simple average method makes in the final image. The choice of integration and interpolation should be based on the tradeoffs of quality versus speed. For initial exploration and manipulation of a volume, the cheapest possible method might be desirable. When a desired view is found, more accurate renderings using exponential methods and software interpolation can be used.

In considering the varied approaches to direct volume rendering and the cost involved, it is worth keeping in mind the level of abstraction with which we are often dealing. The model of a semi-luminous material is itself generally an abstraction with no reality: what is the luminosity of a pressure field? The transfer functions are completely under user control: how transparent is bone? The underlying function is often not known: is a linear variation at all accurate? The method that conveys desired information to the viewer without grossly ignoring or adding volume contents and works quickly enough to encourage its use will be most desirable.

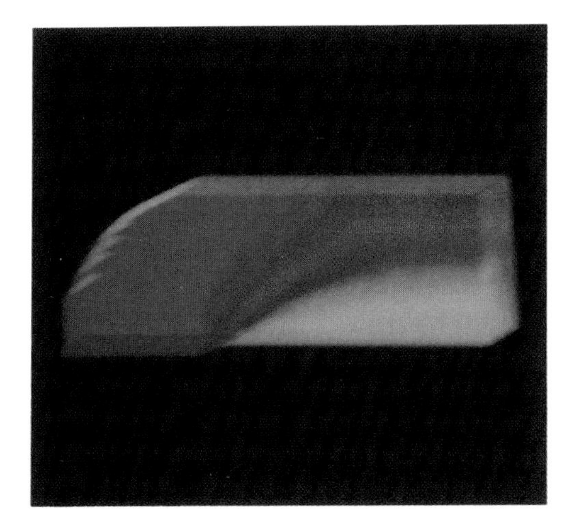

Figure 2: A 40x32x32 Blunt Fin

## Acknowledgements

Particular thanks go to Pat Hanrahan, Nelson Max, Marc Levoy, and Peter Shirley for useful discussions, to the careful reviewers whose suggestions have hopefully clarified the paper, and to Sam Uselton for his initial user-interface. Funds for the support of this study have been allocated by the NASA-Ames Research Center, Moffett Field, California, under Interchange No. NCA2-430.

## References

[Bli82] Jim F. Blinn. Light reflection functions for simulation for clouds and dusty surfaces. *Computer Graphics*, 16(3), July 1982.

[DCH88] Robert A. Drebin, Loren Carpenter, and Pat Hanrahan. Volume rendering. *Computer Graphics*, 22(4):65–74, July 1988.

[Gou71] H. Gouraud. Continuous shading of curved surfaces. *IEEE Transactions on Computer*, 20(6):623–628, 1971.

[KH84] James T. Kajiya and B. P. Von Herzen. Ray tracing volume densities. *Computer Graphics*, 18(4):165–174, July 1984.

[Lev88] Marc Levoy. Display of surfaces from volume data. *IEEE Computer Graphics and Applications*, 8(3):29–37, March 1988.

[LC87] William E. Lorensen and Harvey E. Cline. Marching cubes: A high resolution 3D surface construction algorithm. *Computer Graphics*, 21(4):163–169, July 1987.

[Max86] Nelson Max. Light diffusion through clouds and haze. *Computer Vision, Graphics, and Image Processing*, 33:280–292, 1986.

[MHC90] Nelson Max, Pat Hanrahan, and Roger Crawfis. Area and volume coherence for efficient visualization of 3d scalar functions. *Computer Graphics*, 24(5):27–33, December 1990.

[PD84] Thomas Porter and Tom Duff. Compositing digital images. *Computer Graphics*, 18(3):253–260, July 1984.

[Sab88] Paolo Sabella. A rendering algorithm for visualizing 3D scalar fields. *Computer Graphics*, 22(4):51–58, July 1988.

[ST90] Peter Shirley and Allan Tuchman. A polygonal approximation to direct scalar volume rendering. *Computer Graphics*, 24(5):63–70, December 1990.

[UK88] Craig Upson and Michael Keeler. The v-buffer: Visible volume rendering. *Computer Graphics*, 22(4):59–64, July 1988.

[Wes90] Lee Westover. Footprint evaluation for volume rendering. *Computer Graphics*, 24(4):367–76, August 1990.

[WC+90] Jane Wilhelms, Judy Challinger, , Naim Alper, Shankar Ramamoorthy, and Arsi Vaziri. Direct volume rendering of curvilinear volumes. *Computer Graphics*, 24(5), December 1990.

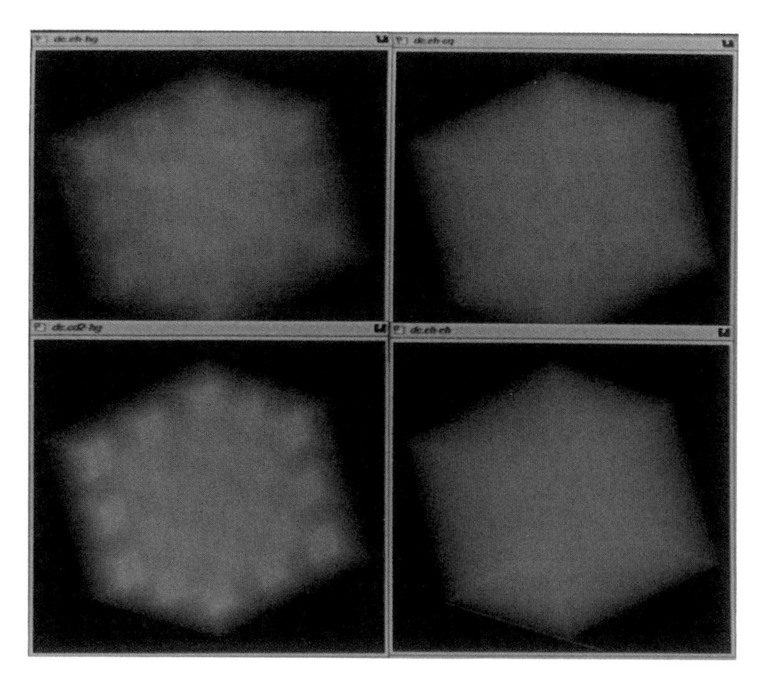

Figure 3: A 4x4x4 Constant Value Volume
(Integration at Vertex/Interpolation at Pixel)
A. Exp.Hom./Hard.Gour. B. With Multiple Blends
C. C*D/Hard.Gour. D. Exp.Hom./Exp.Hom.

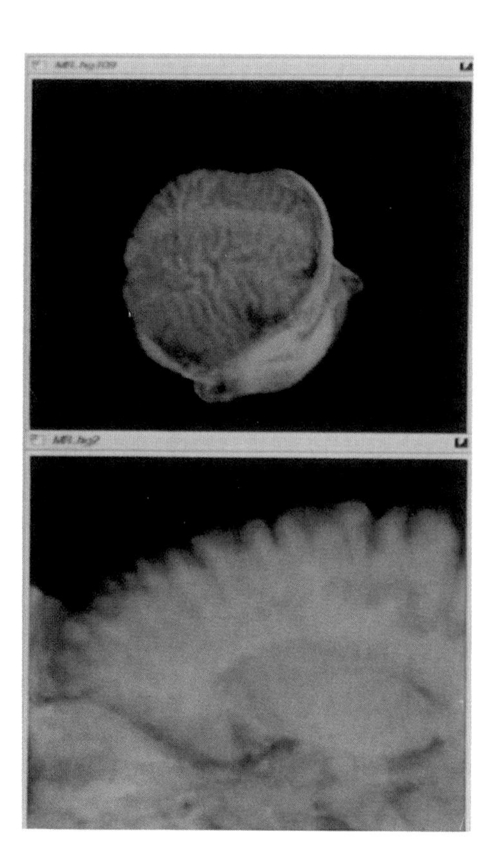

Figure 5: MR Brain

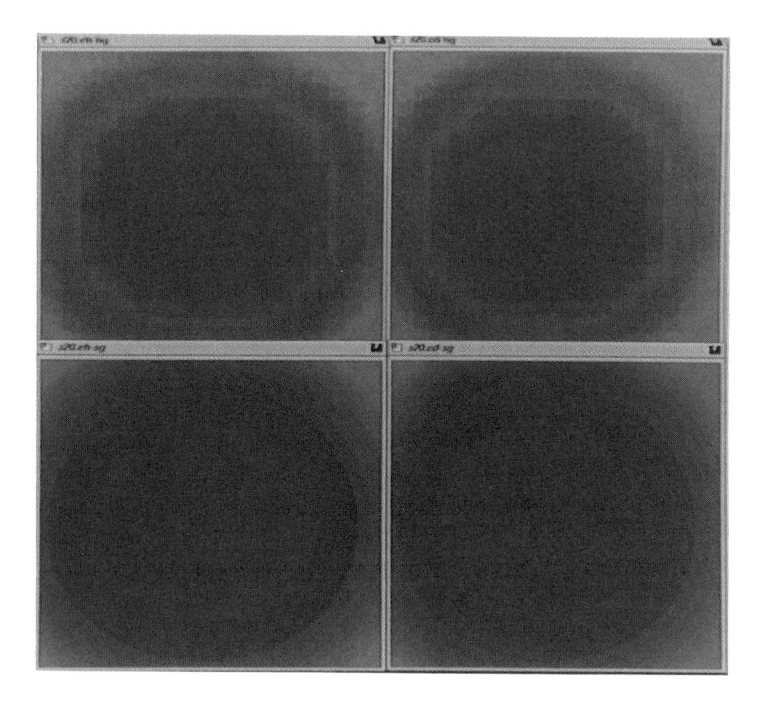

Figure 4: A 20x20x20 Radially Decreasing Volume
(Integration at Vertex/Interpolation at Pixel)
A. Exp.Hom./Hard.Gour. B. C*D/Hard.Gour.
C. Exp.Hom./Soft.Gour. D. C*D/Soft.Gour.

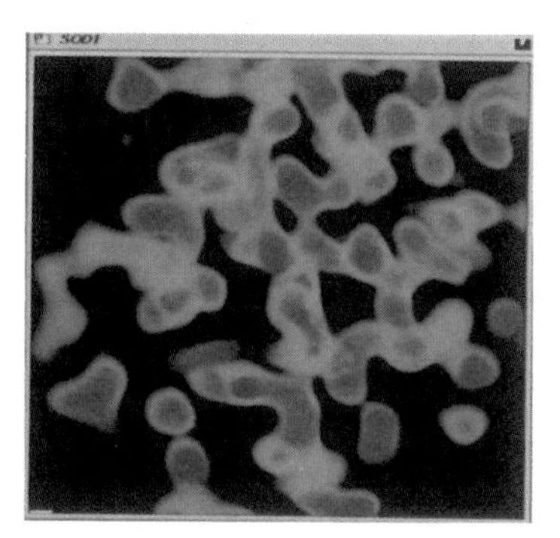

Figure 6: SOD Enzyme

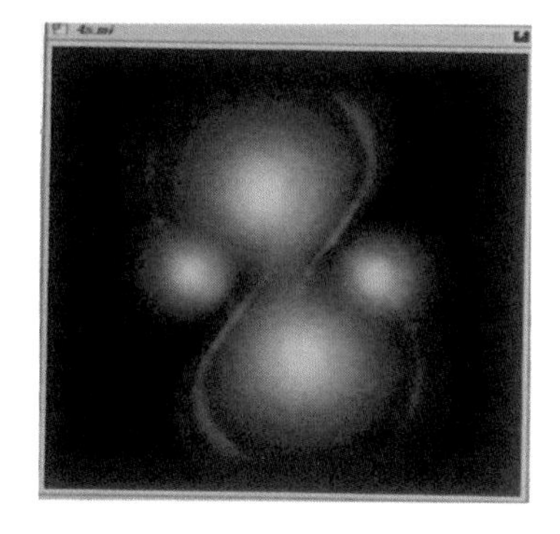

Figure 7: Abstract

# Hierarchical Splatting: A Progressive Refinement Algorithm for Volume Rendering

David Laur and Pat Hanrahan

Princeton University
Princeton, NJ 08544, USA

## Abstract

This paper presents a progressive refinement algorithm for volume rendering which uses a pyramidal volume representation. Besides storing average values, the pyramid stores estimated error, so an octtree can be fit to the pyramid given a user-supplied precision. This octtree is then drawn using a set of splats, or footprints, each scaled to match the size of the projection of a cell. The splats themselves are approximated with RGBA Gouraud-shaded polygons, so that they can be drawn efficiently on modern graphics workstations. The result is a real-time rendering algorithm suitable for interactive applications.

**CR Categories and Subject Descriptors:** I.3.7 [Computer Graphics]: Three-Dimensional Graphics and Realism.

**Key Words:** volume rendering, coherence, progressive refinement, interactive techniques.

## 1 Introduction

Volume visualization is a collection of techniques for visualizing 3D functions. The earliest methods extracted conventional computer graphics primitives such as surfaces, curves, or points, and then displayed them. More recent methods render the volume directly, without this intermediate conversion. This involves forming an RGBA (color and opacity) volume, and projecting it from the desired point of view. RGBA volumes can represent both interiors and the surfaces representing the boundaries between different regions. If just surfaces are shown, the pictures look quite similar to those generated by first extracting surfaces and then rendering them. However, if interiors are also shown, they appear as clouds with varying density and color. A big advantage of volume rendering is that this interior information is not thrown away; a disadvantage is that cloudy interiors are hard to interpret.

This paper presents an algorithm for rendering opacity projections at interactive rates on a typical high performance graphics workstation. Motion is very helpful in understanding opacity projections. For example, the output of commercial medical imaging systems generate film loops and not just static imagery. Furthermore, the amount of information gained from a motion study is much greater if the motion is under interactive control, for then the user can vary the motion to highlight what they are currently focusing on.



© 1991 ACM-0-89791-436-8/91/007/0285 $00.75

Our algorithm is based on two key ideas: *coherence* and *progressive refinement*. Recent research has shown how to take advantage of coherence when performing opacity projections of large cells filled with cloudy material [9; 8; 6; 11]. The most relevant to the work reported here are those methods that approximate the projection with a collection of Gouraud-shaded RGBA polygons [8; 11]. Progressive refinement involves simplifying either the model or the rendering algorithm, or both, until pictures can be produced at interactive rates, and then computing successively better images when free time is available, for example, when the user pauses to examine an interesting image [1].

This paper proposes a *splatting algorithm* [3; 10] that works on a pyramidal representation of the volume. Splatting works by first sorting cells from back to front and then compositing the projection of each cell, called its *footprint*, into an accumulating projection image. Our algorithm builds a set of footprints at different sizes—one for each level in the pyramid. The time to draw a splat is constant, or at worst proportional to its area, so substantial time is saved by drawing a single large splat instead of a volume of smaller splats. More interestingly, the algorithm does not just draw a reduced resolution version of the volume, but determines the number of the splats by fitting a collection of cells at different resolutions in the pyramid to the original data based on a user-supplied *error criteria*. Progressive refinement proceeds by gradually reducing the error associated with the fit,

## 2 Reconstruction and Projection

The ideal volume rendering algorithm performs the following three steps: (i) reconstructs the continuous function from the discrete samples, (ii) transforms the continuous function for viewing, and (iii) evaluates the opacity integral along each line-of-sight. Splatting algorithms approximate this procedure. The reconstruction function is transformed according to the current viewing transformation, and then is projected using the opacity integral to form a 2D footprint. There is only one footprint per view per volume if the data is uniformly sampled and the viewing transformation is a parallel projection. To generate the complete image, the footprints are composited on top of each other in back to front order[1]. Splatting algorithms are not equivalent to the idealized rendering process outlined above, because reconstruction and projection cannot be reordered, if the reconstruction functions from different samples overlap, which is necessary to

[1] Actually Westover's algorithm reconstructs all the samples from a planar slice into a slice image, and then composites the slice image onto the accumulating final image.

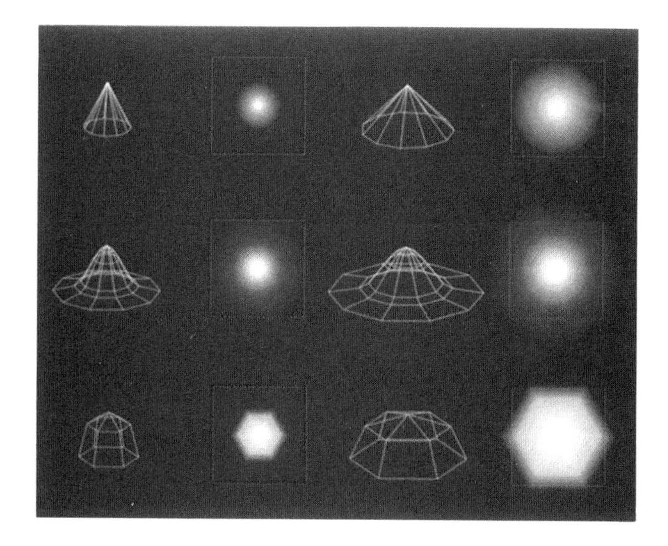

Figure 1: Different splat shapes and their footprints.

generate a smooth continuous image.

Current splatting algorithms simplify this procedure even further. Westover approximates the footprint with a 2D elliptical Gaussian [10]. This is an approximation because the reconstruction function and scattering model are never specified. More recently, methods have been developed for rendering the opacity projections of polyhedral cells using RGBA polygons. Wilhelms breaks the projection of a cubical cell into topologically uniform regions, and then computes the opacity at the vertices according to various projection formula [11]. A similar approach can be applied to tetrahedra, which have the advantage that there are only two topologically distinct cases to consider [8].

We have built a flexible system based on approximating footprints with a collection of Gouraud-shaded polygons. These polygons can be used to build a piecewise linear approximation to any footprint function. A generalized "Gaussian" splat is defined by (1) the number of angular subdivisions, (2) the number of radial subdivisions, and (3) the opacity of the splat at a given radial distance. Some typical splats are shown in Figure 1.

The advantage of outputting Gouraud-shaded polygons is that workstations have been optimized to draw them for surface rendering applications. Recent workstations have added the ability to interpolate $\alpha$ along with color, and to provide hardware assist for compositing [7]. Also, since the graphics hardware is handling the transformation and scan conversion, both orthographic and perspective projections are possible. Furthermore, if the polygon is point sampled correctly and if the vertices have subpixel position, then the center of the splat can also be positioned accurately. Our algorithm approximates the volume at multiple resolutions, and hence, we need to draw different sized splats. This is easily done by simply scaling the polygons, and hence, the amount of data describing a splat is independent of splat size. Therefore, the overhead involved in transferring the splat to the graphics engine is independent of size. The cost of rendering a splat, however, does involve an area dependent term, because the time needed for scan conversion and compositing depend on the actual number of pixels output.

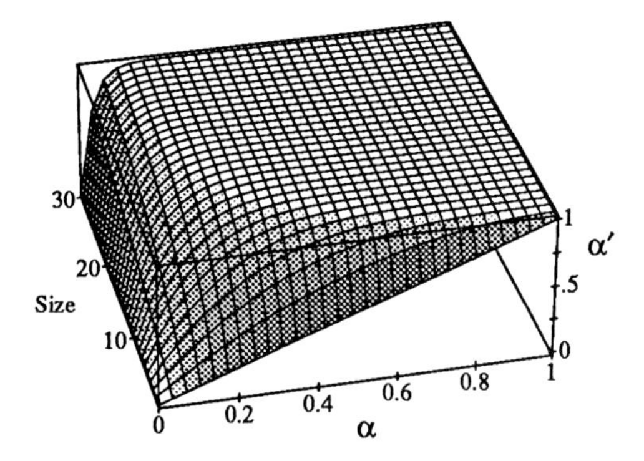


Figure 2: Plot of opacity correction

There is one major complication when rendering different sized splats, and that is that doubling the size of the splat more than doubles its opacity. This is an important effect that we would like to capture qualitatively. To approximate this effect, we compute the transparency of a single double-sized Gaussian splat that is equivalent to compositing two smaller unit-sized splats directly on top of each other.

$$(1-\alpha_2)e^{-x^2/\sigma_2^2} = ((1-\alpha_1)e^{-x^2/\sigma_1^2})^2$$

where $\alpha_1$ and $\sigma_1$ are the opacities and standard deviations, respectively, of the smaller unit splat, and $\alpha_2$ and $\sigma_2$ are the corresponding derived quantities for the double-sized splat. The effective opacity and sigma for the larger splat are

$$(1-\alpha_2) = (1-\alpha_1)^2$$

and

$$\sigma_2^2 = \sigma_1^2/2$$

Thus, when a splat is doubled in size, a new opacity can be computed using this formula. Figure 2 plots this *opacity correction* as a function of opacity and resolution. As can be seen, this is a large effect. Note also that the shape of the footprint also changes with scale. Regions close to the center are less transparent than regions far from the center, causing the splat to appear narrower and more concentrated. However, this effect is countered by the fact that not only are splats composited in depth, but they also cover the image in x-y; this causes the two smaller splats to actually be larger than the double-size splat. For this reason, we simply scale splats and ignore any shape changes.

Figure 3 shows a set of splats at different resolutions with and without opacity correction. Figure 4 shows the projection of a constant-valued volume with different sized splats, with and without the opacity correction. Ideally, changing the resolution should have no effect. Although our approximation does not work perfectly, it is much better than using no correction, as can be seen by the examples.

## 3 Hierarchical Traversal

To take advantage of the ability to draw different sized splats efficiently, we build a multiresolution representation of the original volume. In this paper, we use the word "pyramid" to indicate a complete resolution set, and the word "oct-tree" to indicate some subset of the pyramid that completely spans the volume. Pyramids and oct-trees have been used

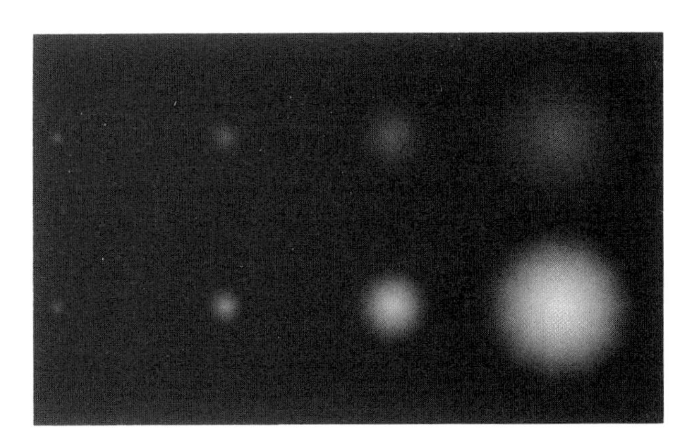

Figure 3: Footprint of a single splat vs. power-of-two resolution. The upper row shows the uncorrected opacity projection, and hence, as the splats increase in size they become more transparent. The lower row shows the corrected opacity projection.

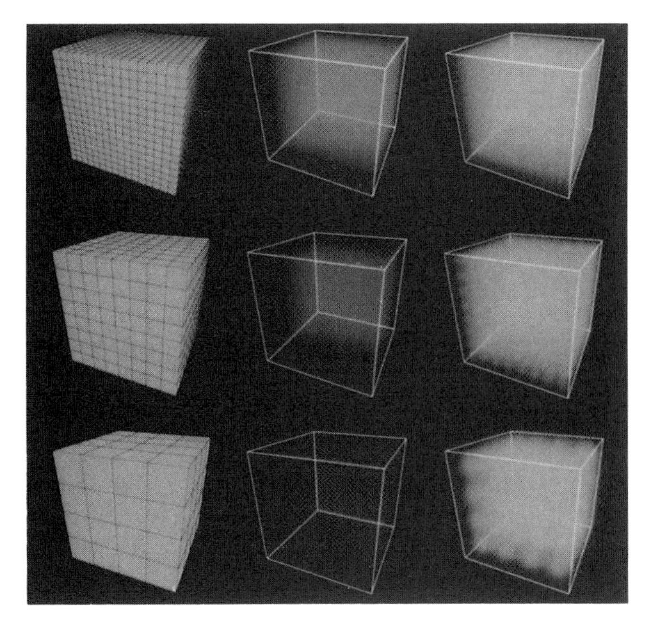

Figure 4: Projection of a constant-valued volume with different sized splats. The left column shows the resolution, the middle column shows the uncorrected opacity projection, and the right column the corrected opacity projection.

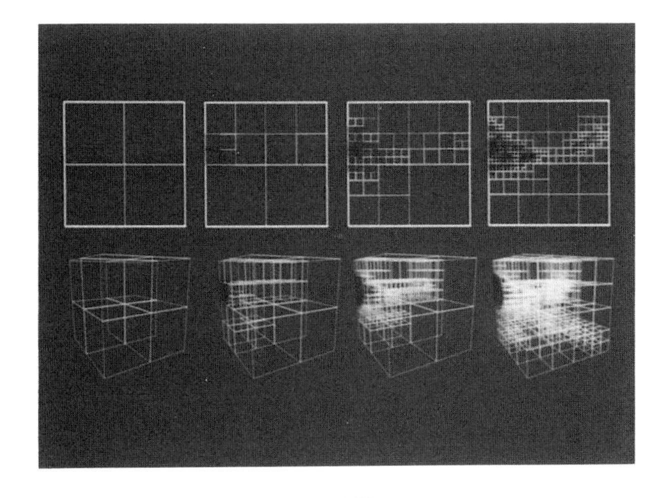

Figure 5: Oct-trees with different error contours

previously for volume rendering. Levoy [4] used a binary pyramid to indicate the presence of non-transparent material to accelerate ray tracing. Levoy [5] also used a pyramid of averaged values, commonly called a *mip-map* [13]. for gaze-directed rendering. Others have used *min-max* or range pyramids to allow efficient iso-surface extraction [14; 2; 12].

The regular structure of pyramids and oct-trees allows them to be traversed in front-to-back or back-to-front order just as easily as uniformly sampled voxel arrays. Note that the order in which the children are traversed is the same everywhere for a parallel projection, but may change for a perspective projection.

In the pyramid that we build, each node contains several pieces of information. As with a mip-map, every node contains the average RGBA value of all its children. These values are used for drawing the splats. Since the RGBA assignments depend on the current scalar to RGBA mapping, the mip-map needs to be recomputed every time the transfer function changes. Also since the RGBA assignment depends on shading, only view-independent shading formula are handled efficiently by this approach.

Every node in the pyramid also contains a variable indicating the average error associated with that node. This error term measures the average cost of approximating this region of space with a constant function equal to the node's average value, rather than with the original set of voxel values contained in the region. The root mean square error due to this approximation is

$$e_j^l = \sqrt{\frac{\sum s_i^2}{n_j^l} - \left(\frac{\sum s_i}{n_j^l}\right)^2}$$

where $e_j^l$ is the error associated with node $j$ at level $l$, $n_j^l$ is the number of voxels comprising that region, and $s_i$ is the value of voxel $i$. This error measure can be computed efficiently using a single traversal of the pyramid.

To approximate the volume most efficiently, we would like the error per unit volume to be uniformly distributed throughout the volume. Moreover, we would like to use the lowest resolution in the pyramid that falls within the allowable error. Since the error in the approximation is data dependent, different regions in the volume will in general need different levels of detail. We can think of this process as fitting an oct-tree to a pyramid. This fit can be performed with a single traversal of the pyramid. At each level in the pyramid, the desired error per unit volume is compared to the average error for the given node, if the average error is less than the desired error, the traversal is terminated at this level, otherwise it proceeds downward.

Several oct-trees, with decreasing total error, are shown in Figure 5. Note the desired effect, where the data changes rapidly it is approximated with many small nodes, and where it changes slowly, it is approximated with fewer large nodes. Furthermore, the number of nodes varies with error; the lower the error the more nodes. Thus, this error representation is ideal for automatically adjusting the number of nodes in the volume representation, as required for progressive refinement.

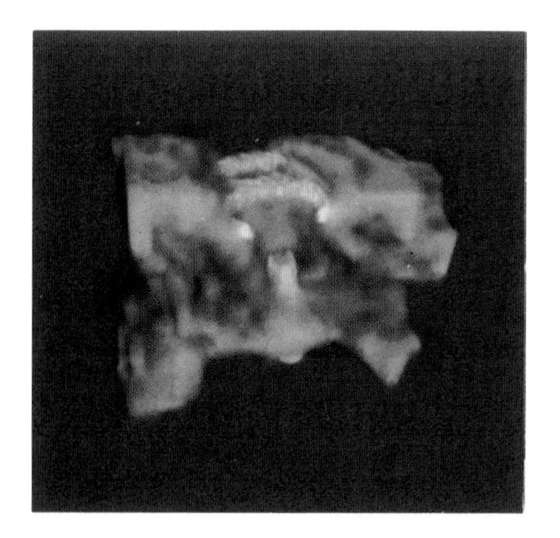
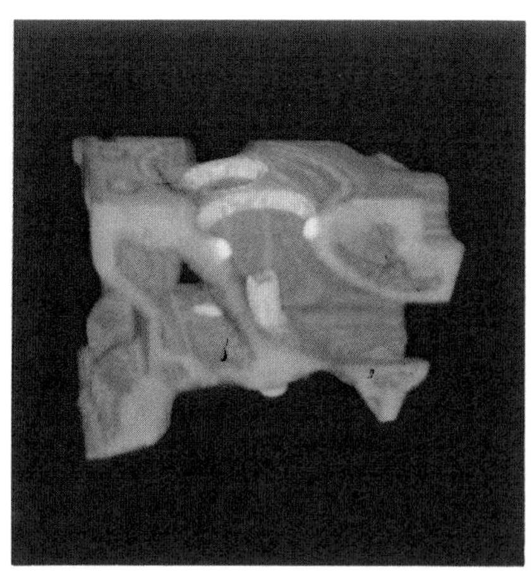
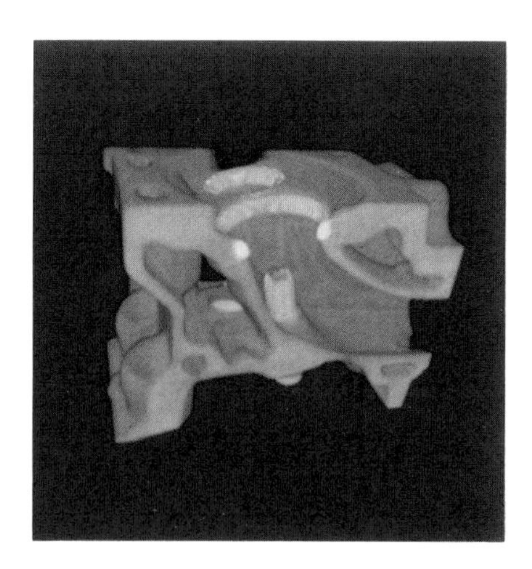

Figure 6: Engine block (256x256x110).

## 4 Results

Figure 6 shows an industrial CT-scan of an engine block drawn at three different resolutions. The resolutions were chosen by the following three criteria: (i) What can be drawn 5 times a second—this is what the image looks like during motion, (ii) what can be drawn in 5 seconds—this is what the image looks like after motion has stopped and the image has been refined for a reasonable amount of time, and (iii) what the resulting image looks like at full resolution.

Several conclusions can be drawn. First, the highest resolution pictures do not look as good as the very best previous volume rendering techniques. The approximations introduced to achieve interactive rates, unfortunately, still sacrifices quality for speed. Second, although the lowest resolution image looks crude when viewed as a still, it is surprisingly effective when viewed in motion.

## 5 Discussion

Previous approaches to using multi-resolution volume representations were based on the discrete concept of pruning away regions which didn't contribute to the final answer. A desirable property of the algorithm described in this paper is that the pruning is function of both opacity and accuracy. Opacity indicates presence, and if no material is present, cells are pruned just as in the previous work. However, the error indicates the accuracy of the approximation, and low error in a large region indicates that it is homogeneous, and homogeneous regions can be drawn efficiently using large splats. We expect that these ideas also can be used to accelerate high-quality ray tracing-based volume rendering algorithms. We also think this multi-resolution approximation scheme has many other applications in computer graphics.

## Acknowledgments

This research was supported by an equipment grant from Silicon Graphics.

## References

[1] Larry Bergman, Henry Fuchs, Eric Grant, and Susan Spach. Image rendering by adaptive refinement. *Computer Graphics (SIGGRAPH '86 Proceedings)*, 20(4):29–38, August 1986.

[2] Jules Bloomenthal. Polygonization of implicit surfaces. *Computer Aided Geometric Design*, 5(4):341–355, November 1988.

[3] Harvey E. Cline, William E. Lorensen, Sigwalt Ludke, Carl R. Crawford, and Bruce C. Teeter. Two algorithms for the reconstruction of surfaces from tomograms. *Medical Physics*, 15(3):320–327, June, 1988.

[4] Marc Levoy. Efficient ray tracing of volume data. *ACM Transactions on Graphics*, 9(3):245–261, July 1990.

[5] Marc Levoy and Ross Whitaker. Gaze-directed volume rendering. *Computer Graphics (Symposium on Interactive 3D Graphics)*, 24(2):217–223, March 1990.

[6] Nelson Max, Pat Hanrahan, and Roger Crawfis. Area and volume coherence for efficient visualization of 3d scalar functions. *Computer Graphics (San Diego Workshop on Volume Visualizaton)*, 24(5):27–33, November 1990.

[7] Thomas Porter and Tom Duff. Compositing digital images. *Computer Graphics (SIGGRAPH '84 Proceedings)*, 18(3):253–260, July 1984.

[8] Peter Shirley and Allan Tuchman. A polygonal approximation to direct scalar volume rendering. *Computer Graphics (San Diego Workshop on Volume Visualizaton)*, 24(5):63–70, November 1990.

[9] Craig Upson and Michael Keeler. V-buffer: Visible volume rendering. *Computer Graphics (Proceedings of SIGGRAPH '88)*, 22(4):59–64, August 1988.

[10] Lee Westover. Footprint evaluation for volume rendering. *Computer Graphics*, 24(4):367–376, August 1990.

[11] Jane Wilhelms. A coherent projection approach to direct volume rendering. *Computer Graphics (SIGGRAPH '91 Proceedings)*, July 1991.

[12] Jane Wilhelms and Allan Van Gelder. Octrees for faster isosurface generation. *Computer Graphics (San Diego Workshop on Volume Visualizaton)*, 24(5):57–62, November 1990.

[13] Lance Williams. Pyramidal parametrics. *Computer Graphics (SIGGRAPH '83 Proceedings)*, 17(3):1–11, July 1983.

[14] Brian Wyvill, Craig McPheeters, and Geoff Wyvill. Data structure for soft objects. *The Visual Computer*, 2(4):227–234, 1986.

# Generating Textures on Arbitrary Surfaces Using Reaction-Diffusion

Greg Turk
University of North Carolina at Chapel Hill

## Abstract

This paper describes a biologically motivated method of texture synthesis called *reaction-diffusion* and demonstrates how these textures can be generated in a manner that directly matches the geometry of a given surface. Reaction-diffusion is a process in which two or more chemicals diffuse at unequal rates over a surface and react with one another to form stable patterns such as spots and stripes. Biologists and mathematicians have explored the patterns made by several reaction-diffusion systems. We extend the range of textures that have previously been generated by using a cascade of multiple reaction-diffusion systems in which one system lays down an initial pattern and then one or more later systems refine the pattern. Examples of patterns generated by such a cascade process include the clusters of spots on leopards known as rosettes and the web-like patterns found on giraffes. In addition, this paper introduces a method by which reaction-diffusion textures are created to match the geometry of an arbitrary polyhedral surface. This is accomplished by creating a mesh over a given surface and then simulating the reaction-diffusion process directly on this mesh. This avoids the often difficult task of assigning texture coordinates to a complex surface. A mesh is generated by evenly distributing points over the model using relaxation and then determining which points are adjacent by constructing their Voronoi regions. Textures are rendered directly from the mesh by using a weighted sum of mesh values to compute surface color at a given position. Such textures can also be used as bump maps.

**CR Categories and Subject Descriptors:** I.3.3 [Computer Graphics]: Picture/Image Generation; I.3.5 [Computer Graphics]: Three-Dimensional Graphics and Realism - Color, shading, shadowing and texture; J.3 [Life and Medical Sciences]: Biology.

**Additional Keywords and Phrases:** Reaction-diffusion, biological models, texture mapping.



## Introduction

Texture mapping was introduced in [Catmull 74] as a method of adding to the visual richness of a computer generated image without adding geometry. There are three fundamental issues that must be addressed to render textures. First, a texture must be acquired. Possibilities include creating a texture procedurally, painting a texture, or digitally scanning a texture from a photograph. Next, we need to define a mapping from the texture space to the space of the model to be textured. Defining this mapping should not require a great deal of a user's time. This mapping should not noticeably distort the texture. Finally, we require a method of sampling the texture during rendering so that the final image contains no artifacts due to aliasing or resulting from the underlying texture representation [Heckbert 89]. These three issues are often interrelated, and this is true of the techniques in this paper.

This paper explores a procedural method for texture synthesis and also introduces a new method for fitting a texture to a surface. Either of these techniques can be used separately, but the examples given here shows the strength of using them together to produce natural textures on complex models. After a discussion of previous texturing methods, the majority of the paper is divided into two parts, one for each of these topics.

The first part of this paper describes a chemical mechanism for pattern formation know as *reaction-diffusion*. This mechanism, first described in [Turing 52], shows how two or more chemicals that diffuse across a surface and react with one another can form stable patterns. A number of researchers have shown how simple patterns of spots and stripes can be created by reaction-diffusion systems [Bard 81; Murray 81; Meinhardt 82]. We begin by introducing the basics of how a reaction-diffusion system can form simple patterns. We then introduce new results that show how more complex patterns can be generated by having an initial pattern set down by one chemical system and further refined by later chemical systems. This widens the range of patterns that can be generated by reaction-diffusion to include such patterns as the rosettes found on leopards and the multiple-width stripes found on some fish and snakes. These patterns could be generated on a square grid and then mapped onto an object's surface using traditional techniques, but there are advantages to synthesizing the pattern directly on the surface to be textured in a manner that will be described next.

The second part of this paper presents a method of generating a mesh over the surface of a polyhedral model that can be used for texture synthesis. The approach uses relaxation to evenly distribute points across the model's surface and then divides the surface into cells centered at these points. We can simulate reaction-diffusion systems directly on this mesh to create textures. Because there is no mapping from texture space to the object, there is no need to assign texture coordinates to polygons and there is no distortion of the textures. At no time is the texture stored in some regular $m \times n$ grid, as are most textures. It is likely that other texture generation methods in addition to reaction-diffusion could also make use of such a mesh. Images of surfaces that have been textured using a mesh do not show aliasing artifacts or visual indication of the underlying mesh structure. These textures can also be used for bump mapping, a technique introduced in [Blinn 78] to give the appearance of a rough or wrinkled surface. The three steps involved in texturing a model as in Figures 4, 5 and 6 are: (1) generate a mesh that fits the polyhedral model, (2) simulate a reaction-diffusion system on the mesh (solve a partial differential equation) and (3) use the final values from the simulation to specify surface color while rendering the polygons of the model.

**Artificial Texture Synthesis**

A great strength of procedurally generating textures is that each new method can be used in conjunction with already existing functions. Several methods have been demonstrated that use composition of various functions to generate textures. Gardner introduced the idea of summing a small number of sine waves of different periods, phases and amplitudes to create a texture [Gardner 85]. Pure sine waves generate fairly bland textures, so Gardner uses the values of the low period waves to alter the shape of the higher period waves. This method gives textures that are evocative of patterns found in nature such as those of clouds and trees. Perlin uses band-limited noise as the basic function from which to construct textures [Perlin 85]. He has shown that a wide variety of textures (stucco, wrinkles, marble, fire) can be created by manipulating such a noise function in various ways. [Lewis 89] describes several methods for generating isotropic noise functions to be used for texture synthesis. A stunning example of using physical simulation for texture creation is the dynamic cloud patterns of Jupiter in the movie 2010 [Yaeger and Upson 86].

Recent work on texture synthesis using reaction-diffusion is described in [Witkin and Kass 91]. They show the importance of anisotropy by introducing a rich set of new patterns that are generated by anisotropic reaction-diffusion. In addition, they demonstrate how reaction-diffusion systems can be simulated rapidly using fast approximations to Gaussian convolution.

A texture can be created by painting an image, and the kinds of textures that may be created this way are limitless. An unusual variant of this is to paint an "image" in the frequency domain and then take the inverse transform to create the final texture [Lewis 84]. Lewis demonstrates how textures such as canvas and wood grain can be created by this method. An extension to digital painting, described in [Hanrahan and Haeberli 90], shows how use of a hardware z-buffer can allow a user to paint interactively onto the image of a three-dimensional surface.

**Mapping Textures onto Surfaces**

Once a texture has been created, a method is needed to map it onto the surface to be textured. This is commonly cast into the problem of assigning texture coordinates $(u,v)$ from a rectangle to the vertices of the polygons in a model. Mapping texture coordinates onto a complex surface is not easy, and several methods have been proposed to accomplish this. A common approach is to define a mapping from the rectangle to the natural coordinate system of the target object's surface. For example, latitude and longitude can be used to define a mapping onto a sphere, and parametric coordinates can be used when mapping a texture onto a cubic patch [Catmull 74]. In some cases an object might be covered by multiple patches, and in these instances care must be taken to make the edges of the patches match. A successful example of this is found in the bark texture for a model of a maple tree in [Bloomenthal 85].

Another approach to texture mapping is to project the texture onto the surface of the object. One example of this is to orient the texture square in $\mathbf{R}^3$ (Euclidean three-space) and perform a projection from this square onto the surface [Peachey 85]. Related to this is a two-step texture mapping method given by [Bier and Sloan 86]. The first step maps the texture onto a simple intermediate surface in $\mathbf{R}^3$, such as a box or cylinder. The second step projects the texture from this surface onto the target object. A different method of texture mapping is to make use of the polygonal nature of many graphical models. In this approach, taken by [Samek 86], the surface of a polyhedral object is unfolded onto the plane one or more times and the average of the unfolded positions of each vertex is used to determine texture placement. A user can adjust the mapping by specifying where to begin the unfolding of the polyhedral object.

Each of the above methods has been used with success for some models and textures. There are pitfalls to these methods, however. Each of the methods can cause a texture to be distorted because there is often no natural map from the texture space to the surface of the object. This is a fundamental problem that comes from defining the texture pattern over a geometry that is different than that of the object to be textured. Some of these techniques also require a good deal of user intervention. One solution to these problems for some images is the use of solid textures. A *solid texture* is a color function defined over a portion of $\mathbf{R}^3$, and such a texture is easily mapped onto the surfaces of objects [Peachey 85; Perlin 85]. A point $(x,y,z)$ on the surface of an object is colored by the value of the solid texture function at this point in space. This method is well suited for simulating objects that are formed from a solid piece of material such as a block of wood or a slab of marble. Solid texturing is a successful technique because the texture function matches the geometry of the material being simulated, namely the geometry of $\mathbf{R}^3$. No assignment of texture coordinates is necessary.

Quite a different approach to matching texture to surface geometry is given in [Ma and Gagalowicz 85]. They describe several methods for creating a local coordinate system at each point on the surface of a given model. Statistical properties of a texture are then used to synthesize texture on the surface so that it is oriented to the local coordinate system.

**Part One: Reaction-Diffusion**

This section describes a class of patterns that are formed by reaction-diffusion systems. These patterns are an addition to the texture synthesist's toolbox, a collection of tools that include such procedural methods as Perlin's noise function and Gardner's sum-of-sine waves. The reaction-diffusion patterns can either be used alone or they can be used as an initial pattern that can be built on using other procedures. This section begins by discussing reaction-diffusion as it relates to developmental biology and then gives specific examples of patterns that can be generated using reaction-diffusion.

A central issue in developmental biology is how the cells of an embryo arrange themselves into particular patterns. For example, how is it that the cells in the embryo of a worm become organized into segments? Undoubtedly there are many organizing mechanisms working together throughout the development of an animal. One possible mechanism, first described by Turing, is that two or more chemicals can diffuse through an embryo and react with each other until a stable pattern of chemical concentrations is reached [Turing 52]. These chemical pre-patterns can then act as a trigger for cells of different types to develop in different positions in the embryo. Such chemical systems are known as *reaction-diffusion* systems, and the hypothetical chemical agents are called *morphogens*. Since the introduction of these ideas, several mathematical models of such systems have been studied to see what patterns can be formed and to see how these matched actual animal patterns such as coat spotting

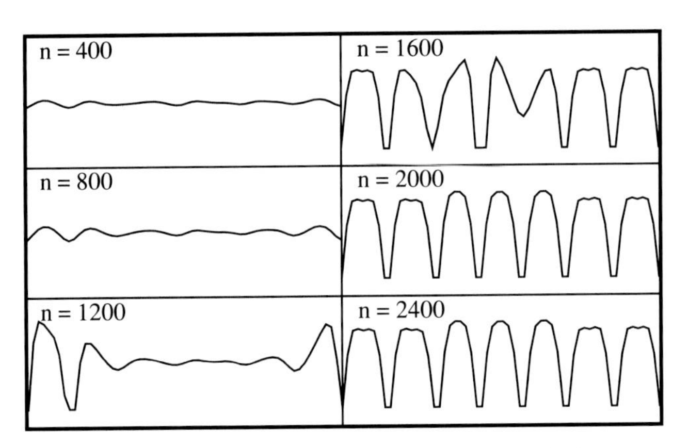


**Figure 1:** One-dimensional example of reaction-diffusion. Chemical concentration is shown in intervals of 400 time steps.

and stripes on mammals [Bard 81; Murray 81]. Only recently has an actual reaction-diffusion system been observed in the laboratory [Lengyel and Epstein 91]. So far no direct evidence has been found to show that reaction-diffusion is the operating mechanism in the development of any particular embryo pattern. This should not be taken as a refutation of the model, however, because the field of developmental biology is still young and very few mechanisms have been verified to be the agents of pattern formation in embryo development.

The basic form of a simple reaction-diffusion system is to have two chemicals (call them $a$ and $b$) that diffuse through the embryo at different rates and that react with each other to either build up or break down $a$ and $b$. These systems can be explored in any dimension. For example, we might use a one-dimensional system to look at segment formation in worms, or we could look at reaction-diffusion on a surface for spot-pattern formation. Here are the equations showing the general form of a two-chemical reaction-diffusion system:

$$\frac{\partial a}{\partial t} = F(a,b) + D_a \nabla^2 a$$

$$\frac{\partial b}{\partial t} = G(a,b) + D_b \nabla^2 b$$

The first equation says that the change of the concentration of $a$ at a given time depends on the sum of a function $F$ of the local concentrations of $a$ and $b$ and the diffusion of $a$ from places nearby. The constant $D_a$ says how fast $a$ is diffusing, and the Laplacian $\nabla^2 a$ is a measure of how high the concentration of $a$ is at one location with respect to the concentration of $a$ nearby. If nearby places have a higher concentration of $a$, then $\nabla^2 a$ will be positive and $a$ diffuses toward this position. If nearby places have lower concentrations, then $\nabla^2 a$ will be negative and $a$ will diffuse away from this position.

The key to pattern formation based on reaction-diffusion is that an initial small amount of variation in the chemical concentrations can cause the system to be unstable initially and to be driven to a stable state in which the concentrations of $a$ and $b$ vary across the surface. A set of equations that Turing proposed for generating patterns in one dimension provides a specific example of reaction-diffusion:

$$\Delta a_i = s\,(16 - a_i b_i) + D_a (a_{i+1} + a_{i-1} - 2a_i)$$
$$\Delta b_i = s\,(a_i b_i - b_i - \beta_i) + D_b (b_{i+1} + b_{i-1} - 2b_i)$$

These equations are given for a discrete model, where each $a_i$ is one "cell" in a line of cells and where the neighbors of this cell are $a_{i-1}$ and $a_{i+1}$. The values for $\beta_i$ are the sources of slight irregularities in chemical concentration across the line of cells. Figure 1 illustrates the progress of the chemical concentration of $b$ across a line of 60 cells as its concentration varies over time. Initially the values of $a_i$ and $b_i$ were set to 4 for all cells along the line. The values of $\beta_i$ were clustered around 12, with the values varying randomly by $\pm 0.05$. The diffusion constants were set to $D_a = .25$ and $D_b = .0625$, which means that $a$ diffuses more rapidly than $b$, and $s = 0.03125$. Notice how after about 2000 iterations the concentration of $b$ has settled down into a pattern of peaks and valleys. The simulation results look different in detail to this when a different random seed is used for $\beta_i$, but such simulations have the same characteristic peaks and valleys with roughly the same scale to these features.

**Reaction-Diffusion on a Grid**

The reaction-diffusion system given above can also be simulated on a two-dimensional field of cells. The most common form for such a simulation is to have each cell be a square in a regular grid, and have a cell diffuse to each of its four neighbors on the grid. The discrete form of the equations is:

$$\Delta a_{i,j} = s\,(16 - a_{i,j} b_{i,j}) + D_a (a_{i+1,j} + a_{i-1,j} + a_{i,j+1} + a_{i,j-1} - 4a_{i,j})$$
$$\Delta b_{i,j} = s\,(a_{i,j} b_{i,j} - b_{i,j} - \beta_{i,j}) + D_b (b_{i+1,j} + b_{i-1,j} + b_{i,j+1} + b_{i,j-1} - 4b_{i,j})$$

In this form, the value of $\nabla^2 a$ at a cell is found by summing each of the four neighboring values of $a$ and subtracting four times the value of $a$ at the cell. Each of the neighboring values for $a$ are given the same weight in this computation because the length of the shared edge between any two cells is always the same on a square grid. This will not be the case when we perform a similar computation on a less regular grid, where different neighbors will be weighted differently when calculating $\nabla^2 a$.

Figure 2 (upper left) shows the result of a simulation of these equations on a $64 \times 64$ grid of cells. Notice that the valleys of concentration in $b$ take the form of spots in two dimensions. It is the nature of this system to have high concentrations for $a$ in these spot regions where $b$ is low. Sometimes chemical $a$ is called an *inhibitor* because high values for $a$ in a spot region prevent other spots from forming nearby. In two-chemical reaction-diffusion systems the inhibitor is always the chemical that diffuses more rapidly.

We can create spots of different sizes by changing the value of the constant $s$ for this system. Small values for $s$ ($s = 0.05$ in Figure 2, upper left) cause the reaction part of the system to proceed more slowly relative to the diffusion and this creates larger spots. Larger values for $s$ produce smaller spots ($s = 0.2$ in Figure 2, upper right). The spot patterns at the top of Figure 2 were generated with $\beta_{i,j} = 12 \pm 0.1$. If the random variation of $\beta_{i,j}$ is increased to $12 \pm 3$, the spots become more irregular in shape (Figure 3, upper left). The patterns that can be generated by this reaction-diffusion system were extensively studied in [Bard and Lauder 74] and [Bard 81].

Reaction-diffusion need not be restricted to two-chemical systems. For the generation of striped patterns, Meinhardt has proposed a system involving five chemicals that react with one another [Meinhardt 82]. See the appendix of this paper for details of Meinhardts's system. The result of simulating such a system on a two-dimensional grid can be seen in Figure 3 (lower left). Notice that the system generates random stripes that tend to fork and sometimes form islands of one color or the other. This pattern is like random stripes found on some tropical fish and is also similar to the pattern of right eye and left eye regions of the ocular dominance columns found in mammals [Hubel and Wiesel 79].

**Figure 2:** Reaction-diffusion on a square grid. Large spots, small spots, cheetah and leopard patterns.

**Figure 3:** Irregular spots, reticulation, random stripes and mixed large-and-small stripes.

**Complex Patterns**

This section shows how we can generate more complex patterns using reaction-diffusion by allowing one chemical system to set down an initial pattern and then having this pattern refined by simulating a second system. One model of embryogenesis of the fruit fly shows how several reaction-diffusion systems might lay down increasingly refined stripes to give a final pattern that matches the segmentation pattern in the embryo [Hunding 90]. Bard has suggested that such a *cascade process* might be responsible for some of the less regular coat patterns of some mammals [Bard 81], but he gives no details about how two chemical systems might interact. The patterns shown in this section are new results that are inspired by Bard's idea of cascade processes.

The upper portion of Figure 2 shows how we can change the spot size of a pattern by changing the size parameter $s$ of Turing's reaction-diffusion system from 0.05 to 0.2. The lower left portion of Figure 2 demonstrates that these two systems can be combined to create the large-and-small spot pattern found on cheetahs. We can make this pattern by running the large spot simulation, "freezing" part of this pattern, and then running the small spot simulation in the unfrozen portion of the computation mesh. Specifically, once the large spots are made (using $s = 0.05$) we set a boolean flag *frozen* to TRUE for each cell that has a concentration for chemical $b$ between 0 and 4. These marked cells are precisely those that form the dark spots in the upper left of Figure 2. Then we run the spot forming mechanism again using $s = 0.2$ to form the smaller spots. During this second phase all of the cells marked as frozen retain their old values for the concentrations of $a$ and $b$. These marked cells must still participate in the calculation of the values of the Laplacian for $a$ and $b$ for neighboring cells. This allows the inhibitory nature of chemical $a$ to prevent the smaller spots from forming too near the larger spots. This final image is more natural than the image we would get if we simply superimposed the top two images of Figure 2.

We can create the leopard spot pattern of Figure 2 (lower right) in much the same way as we created the cheetah spots. We lay down the overall plan for this pattern by creating the large spots as in the upper left of Figure 2 ($s = 0.05$). Now, in addition to marking as frozen those cells that form the large spots, we also change the values of chemicals $a$ and $b$ to be 4 at these marked cells. When we run the second system to form smaller spots ($s = 0.2$) the small spots tend to form in the areas adjacent to the large spots. The smaller spots can form near the large spots because the inhibitor $a$ is not high at the marked cells. This texture can also be seen on the horse model in Figure 4.

In a manner analogous to the large-and-small spots of Figure 2 (lower left) we can create a pattern with small stripes running between larger stripes. The stripe pattern of Figure 3 (lower right) is such a pattern and is modelled after the stripes found on fish such as the lionfish. We can make the large stripes that set the overall structure of the pattern by running Meinhardt's stripe-formation system with diffusion rates of $D_g = 0.1$ and $D_s = 0.06$ (see Appendix). Then we mark those cells in the white stripe regions as frozen and run a second stripe-forming system with $D_g = 0.008$ and $D_s = 0.06$. The slower diffusion of chemicals $g_1$ and $g_2$ (a smaller value for $D_g$) causes thinner stripes to form between the larger stripes.

We can use both the spot and stripe formation systems together to form the web-like pattern called *reticulation* that is found on giraffes. Figure 3 (upper right) shows the result of first creating slightly irregular spots as in Figure 3 (upper left) and then using the stripe-formation system to make stripes between the spots. Once again we mark as frozen those cells that comprise the spots. We also set the concentrations of the five chemicals at the frozen cells to the values found in the white regions of the patterns made by the stripe-formation system. This causes black stripes to form between the marked cells when the stripe-formation system is run as the second step in the cascade process. Figure 5 is an example of how such a texture looks on a polyhedral model.

**Regular Stripe Patterns**

The chemical system that produces random stripes like those in Figure 3 (lower left) can also be used to produce more regular stripe patterns. The random stripes are a result of the slight random perturbations in the "substrate" for the chemical system. If these random perturbations are removed so the system starts with a completely homogeneous substrate, then no stripes will form anywhere. Regular stripes will form on a mesh that is homogeneous everywhere except at a few "stripe initiator" cells, and the stripes will radiate from these special cells. One way to create an initiator cell is to slightly raise or lower the substrate value at that cell. Another way is to mark the cell as frozen and set the value of one of the chemicals to be higher or lower than at other cells. The pseudo-zebra in Figure 6 was created in this manner. Its stripes were initiated by choosing several cells on the head and one cell on each of the hooves, marking these cells as frozen and setting the initial value of chemical $g_1$ at these cells to be slightly higher than at other cells.

### Varying Parameters Across a Surface

On many animals the size of the spots or stripes varies across the coat. For example, the stripes on a zebra are more broad on the hind quarters than the stripes on the neck and legs. Bard has suggested that, after the striped pattern is set, the rate of tissue growth may vary at different locations on the embryo [Bard 77]. This effect can be approximated by varying the diffusion rates of the chemicals across the computation mesh. The pseudo-zebra of Figure 6 has wider stripes near the hind quarters than elsewhere on the model. This was accomplished by allowing the chemicals to diffuse more rapidly at the places where wider stripes were desired.

### Part Two: Mesh Generation and Rendering

This section describes how to generate a mesh over a polyhedral model that can be used for texture synthesis and that will lend itself to high-quality image generation. The strength of this technique is that no explicit mapping from texture space to an object's surface is required. There is no texture distortion. There is no need for a user to manually assign texture coordinates to the vertices of polygons. Portions of this section will describe how such a mesh can be used to simulate a reaction-diffusion system for an arbitrary polyhedral model. This mesh will serve as a replacement to the regular square grids used to generate Figures 2 and 3. We will create textures by simulating a reaction-diffusion system directly on the mesh. It is likely that these meshes can also be used for other forms of texture synthesis. Such a mesh can be used for texture generation wherever a texture creation method only requires the passing of information between neighboring texture elements (mesh cells).

There are a wide variety of sources for polyhedral models in computer graphics. Models generated by special-effects houses are often digitized by hand from a scale model. Models taken from CAD might be created by conversion from constructive solid geometry to a polygonal boundary representation. Some models are generated procedurally, such as fractals used to create mountain ranges and trees. Often these methods will give us few guarantees about the shapes of the polygons, the density of vertices across the surface or the range of sizes of the polygons. Sometimes such models will contain very skinny polygons or vertices where dozens of polygons meet. For these reasons it is unwise to use the original polygons as the mesh to be used for creating textures. Instead, a new mesh needs to be generated that closely matches the original model but that has properties that make it suitable for texture synthesis. This mesh-generation method must be robust in order to handle the wide variety of polyhedral models used in computer graphics.

Mesh generation is a common problem in finite-element analysis, and a wide variety of methods have been proposed to create meshes [Ho-Le 88]. Automatic mesh generation is a difficult problem in general, but the requirements of texture synthesis will serve to simplify the problem. We only require that the model be divided up into relatively evenly-spaced regions. The mesh-generation technique described below divides a polyhedral surface into cells that abut one another and fully tile the polyhedral model. The actual description of a cell consists of a position in $\mathbf{R}^3$, a list of adjacent cells and a list of scalar values that tell how much diffusion occurs between this cell and each of its neighbors. No explicit geometric

**Figure 4:** Leopard-Horse

**Figure 5:** Giraffe

**Figure 6:** Pseudo-Zebra

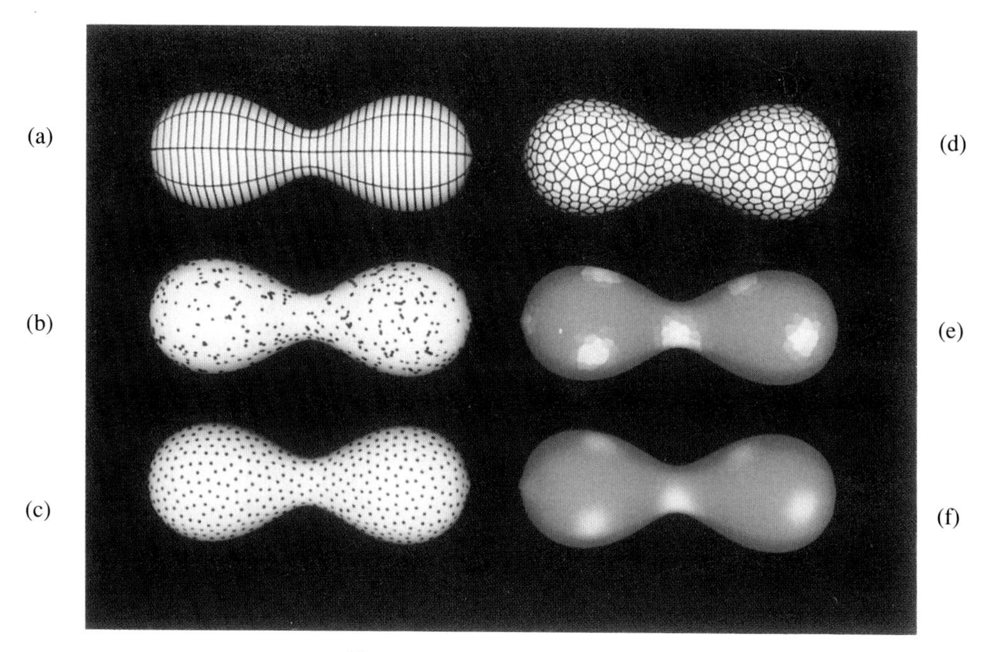


**Figure 7:** Mesh construction.

representation of the boundaries of these cells is necessary. Given a value for cell density, the mesh-generation method first randomly distributes the appropriate number of points on the surface of the polyhedral model. A relaxation procedure then moves these points across the surface until they are fairly evenly spaced from one another. At this stage, each point gives an $(x,y,z)$ position that is a part of the description of a single cell. The region surrounding each point is examined to determine which pairs of cells will diffuse to one another, and the result of this step gives the adjacency information and the diffusion coefficients that complete the cell's description. The only user-supplied parameter for this mesh-generation method is the desired density of cells in the mesh.

### Relaxation of Random Points

The first step in mesh generation is to distribute $n$ points randomly on the model's surface. In order to distribute points randomly over a polyhedral model, care must be taken so that the probability of having a point deposited at any one location is the same everywhere on the surface. To place a random point on the model we need to make an area-weighted choice of the polygon on which a point should be placed. This can be accomplished using a binary search through a list of partial sums of the polygon areas in the model. Now a random point on this polygon can be chosen [Turk 90].

Once the proper number of points has been randomly placed across the surface, we need to move the points around until they are somewhat regularly spaced. This is accomplished using relaxation. Intuitively, the method has each point push around other points on the surface by repelling neighboring points. The method requires choosing a repulsive force and a repulsive radius for the points. We use a repulsive force that falls off linearly with distance. Two points that are greater than the repulsive radius $r$ from one another do not affect each other. The relaxation method also requires a method for moving a point that is being pushed across the surface, especially if the point is pushed off its original polygon. Here is an outline of the relaxation process:

```
loop k times
   for each point P on surface
      determine nearby points to P
      map these nearby points onto the plane
        containing the polygon of P
      compute and store the repulsive forces that the
        mapped points exert on P
   for each point P on surface
      compute the new position of P based on the
        repulsive forces
```

Each iteration moves the points into a more even distribution across the polyhedron. Figure 7b shows an initially random distribution of 1000 points over a polyhedral model, and Figure 7c gives the positions of the same points with $k = 40$ iterations of the relaxation procedure. The underlying polygons of the model are outlined in Figure 7a.

The repulsive radius of the points should be chosen based on the average density of the points across the whole surface. The meshes used in this paper were created using a radius of repulsion given by:

$$r = 2\sqrt{a / n}$$

$a$ = area of surface
$n$ = number of points on surface

The above value for $r$ gives a fixed average number of neighboring points to any point, independent of the number of points on the surface and independent of surface geometry. This is important because uniform spatial subdivision can then be used to find neighboring points quickly.

To compute how nearby points repel a given point $P$ on polygon $A$, these other points are mapped onto the plane containing polygon $A$. Points that already lie on polygon $A$ remain where they are. Points on polygons that share an edge with $A$ are rotated about the common edge until they lie within the given plane. Points on more remote polygons are first rotated about the nearest edge of $A$ and then projected onto the plane. We use this method for mapping nearby points onto the plane because of its simplicity. A different method, at the cost of execution speed and algorithm complexity, would be to search for a geodesic path between $P$ and a given nearby point and then to unfold along this path.

Making the points repel one another becomes straightforward once we can map nearby points onto a given point's plane. For each point $P$ on the surface we need to determine a vector $S$ that is the sum of all repelling forces from nearby points. The new position for the point $P$ on polygon $A$ will be $P' = P + kS$, where $k$ is some small scaling value. In many cases the new point $P'$ will lie on $A$. If $P'$ is not on $A$, it will often not even lie on the surface of the polyhedron. In this case, we determine which edge of $A$ that $P'$ was "pushed" across and also find which polygon (call it $B$) that shares this edge with $A$. The point $P'$ can be rotated about the common edge between $A$ and $B$ so that it lies in the plane of $B$. This new point may not lie on the polygon $B$, but we can repeat the procedure to move the point onto the plane of a polygon adjacent to $B$. Each step of this process brings the point nearer to lying on a polygon and eventually this process will terminate. Most polygons of a model should have another polygon sharing each edge, but some polygons may have no neighbor across one or more edges. If a point is "pushed" across such an edge, the point should be moved back onto the nearest position still on the polygon.

**Mesh Cells from Voronoi Regions**

The positions of these points become the locations of the mesh cells once relaxation has evened out the distribution of points on the surface. Now regions need to be formed around each point to determine adjacency of cells and to give the diffusion coefficients between adjacent cells. In keeping with many finite-element mesh-generation techniques, we choose to use the Voronoi regions of the points to form the regions surrounding the points. A description of Voronoi regions can be found in a book on computational geometry, e.g., [Melhorn 84]. Given a set of points $S$ in a plane, the Voronoi region of a particular point $P$ is that region on the plane where $P$ is the closest point of all points in $S$. For points on a plane, the Voronoi regions will always be bounded by line segments positioned halfway between pairs of points. When we simulate a diffusing system on such a set of cells, we will use the lengths of the edges separating pairs of cells to determine how much of a given chemical can move between the two cells. Figure 7d shows the Voronoi regions for the set of points shown in Figure 7c.

Finding the exact Voronoi regions of the points on a polyhedral surface is not simple since one of these regions might be parts of several different polygons. Instead of solving this exactly, a planar variation of the exact Voronoi region for a point is used to determine the lengths of edges between cells. Using the same procedure as before, all points near a given point $P$ are mapped onto the plane of the polygon $A$ containing $P$. Then the planar Voronoi region of $P$ is constructed and the lengths of the line segments that form the region are calculated. It is the lengths of these segments that are used as the diffusion coefficients between pairs of cells. In general, computing the Voronoi regions for $n$ points in a plane has a computational complexity of $O(n \log n)$ [Melhorn 84]. However, the relaxation process distributes points evenly over the surface of the object so that all points that contribute to the Voronoi region of a point can be found by looking only at those points within a small fixed distance from that point. In practice we have found that we need only consider those points within $2r$ of a given point to construct a Voronoi region, where $r$ is the radius of repulsion used in the relaxation process. Because uniform spatial subdivision can be used to find these points in a constant amount of time, constructing the Voronoi regions is of $O(n)$ complexity in this case.

The above construction of the Voronoi regions assumes that the diffusion over a surface is isotropic (has no preferred direction). The striking textures in [Witkin and Kass 91] show that simulation of anisotropy can add to the richness of patterns generated with reaction-diffusion. Given a vector field over a polyhedral surface, we can simulate anisotropic diffusion on the surface if we take into account the anisotropy during the construction of the Voronoi regions. This is done by contracting the positions of nearby points in the direction of anisotropy after projecting neighboring points onto a given point's plane. Then the Voronoi region around the point is constructed based on these new positions of nearby points. The contraction affects the lengths of the line segments separating the cells, and thus affects the diffusion coefficients between cells. This contraction will also affect which cells are neighbors. Figure 8 shows that anisotropic diffusion creates spots that are stretched when Turing's system is simulated on the surface of a model.

**Reaction-Diffusion on a Mesh**

We can create any of the reaction-diffusion patterns described earlier on the surface of any polyhedral model by simulating the appropriate chemical system directly on a mesh for the model. The square cells of a regular grid are now replaced by the Voronoi regions that comprise the cells of the mesh. Simulation proceeds exactly as before except that calculation of the Laplacian terms now takes into account that the segments that form the boundaries of the cells are not all the same length. These boundary lengths are the diffusion coefficients, and the collection of coefficients at each cell should be normalized so they sum to one. $\nabla^2 a$ is computed at a particular cell by multiplying each diffusion coefficient of the cell by the value of $a$ at the corresponding neighboring cell, summing these values for all neighboring cells, and subtracting the value of $a$ at the given cell. This value should then be multiplied by four to match the feature sizes generated on the regular square grid. When the simulation is complete, we have a concentration for each participating chemical at each cell in the mesh. The next section tells how these concentrations are rendered as textures.

**Rendering**

Once the simulation on a mesh is finished, we require a method for displaying the resulting chemical concentrations as a texture. First, we need a smooth way of interpolating the chemical concentrations across the surface. The chemical value can then be used as input to a function that maps chemical concentration to color. We have chosen to let the chemical concentration at a location be a weighted sum of the concentrations at mesh points that fall within a given radius of the location. If the chemical concentration at a nearby mesh cell $Q$ is $v(Q)$, the value $v'(P)$ of an arbitrary point $P$ on the surface is:

$$v'(P) = \frac{\sum_{Q \text{ near } P} v(Q)\, w(|P - Q| / s)}{\sum_{Q \text{ near } P} w(|P - Q| / s)}$$

The weighting function $w$ can be any function that monotonically decreases in the range zero to one. The function used for the images in this paper is:

$$w(d) = 2d^3 - 3d^2 + 1 \qquad \text{if } 0 \le d \le 1$$
$$w(d) = 0 \qquad \text{if } d > 1$$

This function falls smoothly from the value 1 down to 0 in the range [0,1], and its first derivative is zero at 0 and at 1 [Perlin and Hoffert 89]. Any similar function that falls off smoothly could be used for

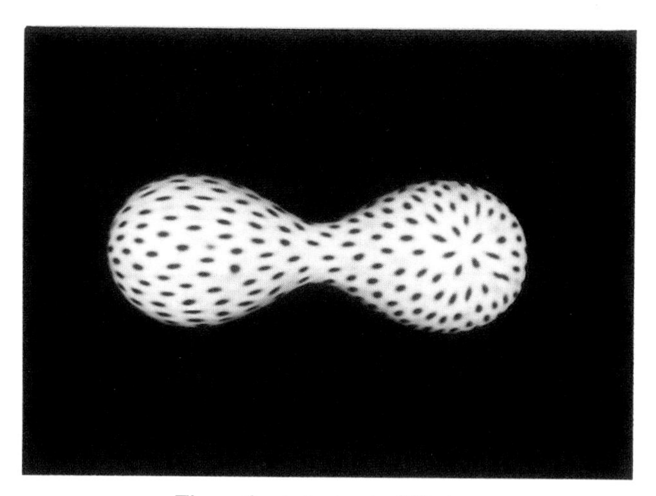

**Figure 8:** Anisotropic diffusion

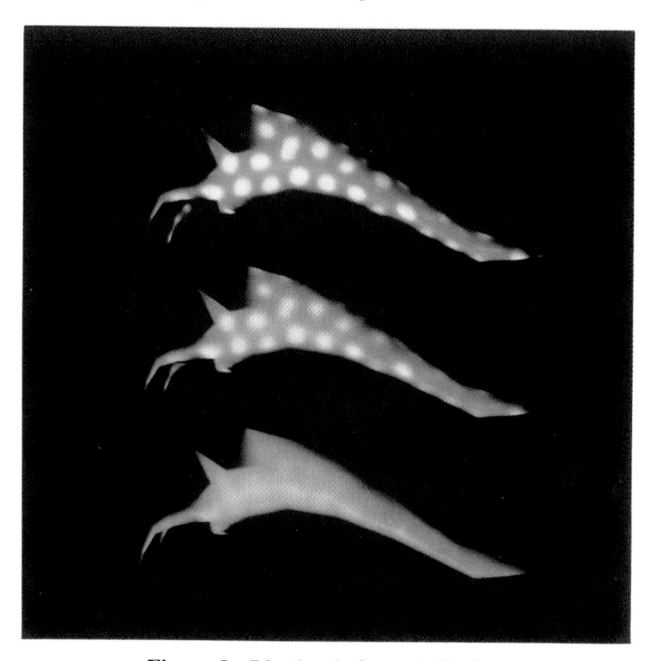

**Figure 9:** Blur levels for anti-aliasing

**Figure 10:** Bump mapping

the weighting function. The images in this paper have been made using a value of $s = 2r$, where $r$ is the repulsive radius from the relaxation method. Much smaller values for $s$ make the individual mesh points noticeable, and values much larger than this will blur together the values of more nearby mesh points. Uniform spatial subdivision makes finding nearby mesh points a fast operation because only those mesh points within a distance $s$ contribute to a point's value. Figure 7e shows the individual cell values from a pattern generated by reaction-diffusion, where the chemical concentrations have been mapped to a color gradation from blue to white. Figure 7f shows the surface colors given by the weighted average for $v'(P)$ described above.

The method described above gives smooth changes of chemical concentration across the surface of the model, and rendered images do not show evidence of the underlying mesh used to create the texture. Aliasing of the texture can occur, however, when a textured object is scaled down small enough that the texture features, say stripes, are about the same width as the pixels of the image. Super-sampling of the texture is one possible way to lessen this problem, but computing the texture value many times to find the color at one pixel is costly. A better approach is to extend the notion of levels of increasingly blurred textures [Williams 83] to those textures defined by the simulation mesh.

The blurred versions of the texture are generated using the simulation mesh, and each mesh point has associated with it an RGB (red, green, blue) color triple for each blur level. Level 0 is an unblurred version of the texture and is created by evaluating the concentration-to-color function at the mesh points for each concentration value and storing the color as an RGB triple at each mesh point. Blur levels 1 and higher are created by allowing these initial color values to diffuse across the surface. When the values of a two-dimensional gray-scale image are allowed to diffuse across the image, the result is the same as convolving the original image with a Gaussian filter. Larger amounts of blurring (wider Gaussian filters) are obtained by diffusing for longer periods of time. Similarly, allowing the RGB values at the mesh points to diffuse across the mesh results in increasingly blurred versions of the texture given on the mesh. The relationship between diffusion for a time $t$ and convolution with a Gaussian kernel of standard deviation $\sigma$ is $t = \sigma^2 / 2$ [Koenderink 84]. The blur levels of Figure 9 were generated so that each level's Gaussian kernel has a standard deviation twice that of the preceding blur level.

The texture color at a point is given by a weighted average between the colors from two blur levels. The choice of blur levels and the weighting between the levels at a pixel is derived from an approximation to the amount of textured surface that is covered by the pixel. This estimate of surface area can be computed from the distance to the surface and the angle the surface normal makes with the direction to the eye. The natural unit of length for this area is $r$, the repulsion radius for mesh building. The proper blur level at a pixel is the base two logarithm of the square root of $a$, where $a$ is the area of the surface covered by the pixel in square units of $r$. We have produced short animated sequences using this anti-aliasing technique and they show no aliasing of the textures.

Bump mapping is a technique used to make a surface appear rough or wrinkled without explicitly altering the surface geometry [Blinn 78]. The rough appearance is created from a gray-scale texture by adding a perturbation vector to the surface normal and then evaluating the lighting model based on this new surface normal. Perlin showed that the gradient of a scalar-valued function in $\mathbf{R}^3$ can be used as a perturbation vector to produce convincing surface roughness [Perlin 85]. We can use the gradient of the values $v'(P)$ of a reaction-diffusion simulation to give a perturbation vector at a given point $P$:

$d = r / 100$
$gx = (v'(P) - v'(P + [d,0,0])) / d$
$gy = (v'(P) - v'(P + [0,d,0])) / d$
$gz = (v'(P) - v'(P + [0,0,d])) / d$
perturbation vector = $[k * gx, k * gy, k * gz]$

The above method for computing the gradient of $v'$ evaluates the function at $P$ and at three nearby points in each of the $x$, $y$ and $z$ directions. The value $d$ is taken to be a small fraction of the repulsive radius $r$ to make sure we stay close enough to $P$ that we get an accurate estimate for the gradient. The gradient can also be computed directly from the definition of $v'$ by calculating exactly the partial derivatives in $x$, $y$ and $z$. The scalar parameter $k$ is used to scale the bump features, and changing $k$'s sign causes bumps to become indentations and vice versa. Figure 10 shows bumps created in this manner based the results of a reaction-diffusion system.

**Implementation and Performance**

Creating a texture using reaction-diffusion for a given model can be a CPU-intensive task. Each of the textures in Figures 4, 5 and 6 took several hours to generate on a DEC 3100 workstation. These meshes contained 64,000 points. Perhaps there is some consolation in the thought that nature requires the same order of magnitude in time to lay down such a pattern in an embryo. Such texture synthesis times would seem to prohibit much experimenting with reaction-diffusion textures. It is fortunate that a given reaction-diffusion system with a particular set of parameters produces the same texture features on small square grids as the features from a simulation on much larger meshes. The patterns in this paper were first simulated on a $64 \times 64$ grid of cells where the simulations required less than a minute to finish. These simulations were run on a Maspar MP-I, which is a SIMD computer with 4096 processing elements connected in a two-dimensional grid. A workstation such as a DEC 3100 can perform similar simulations on a $32 \times 32$ grid in about two minutes, which is fast enough to explore new textures. Once a texture is generated by reaction-diffusion, the time to render the model with a texture is reasonably fast. The image in Figure 4 required 70 seconds to render at $512 \times 512$ resolution without anti-aliasing on a DEC 3100. The same horse without texture takes 16 seconds to render.

**Future Work**

The cascade processes that formed the textures in this paper are just a few of the patterns that can be generated by reaction-diffusion. More exploration should be made on how one chemical system can leave a pattern for later systems. For example, one chemical system could affect the random substrate of a second system. What patterns can be formed if one system causes different rates of diffusion in different locations in a second system?

Other methods of pattern creation could be performed on the meshes used for texture synthesis. Examples that might be adapted from cellular automata [Toffoli and Margolus 87] include two-dimensional annealing, diffusion-limited aggregation and the Belousov-Zhabotinskii reaction.

**Acknowledgments**

I would like to thank those people who have offered ideas and encouragement for this work. These people include David Banks, Henry Fuchs, Albert Harris, Steve Molnar, Brice Tebbs, and Turner Whitted. Thanks also for the suggestions provided by the anonymous reviewers. Linda Houseman helped clean up my writing and David Ellsworth provided valuable photographic assistance. Thanks to Rhythm & Hues for the horse, Steve Speer for the giraffe and Apple Computer's Vivarium Program for the sea-slug.

This work was supported by a Graduate Fellowship from IBM and by the Pixel-Planes project. Pixel-Planes is supported by the National Science Foundation (MIP-9000894) and the Defense Advanced Research Projects Agency, Information Science and Technology Office (Order No. 7510).

**Appendix: Meinhardt's Stripe-Formation System**

The stripes of Figure 3 (lower images) and Figure 6 were created with a five-chemical reaction-diffusion system given in [Meinhardt 82]. The equations of Meinhardt's system are as follows:

$$\frac{\partial g_1}{\partial t} = \frac{c s_2 g_1^2}{r} - \alpha g_1 + D_g \frac{\partial^2 g_1}{\partial x^2} + \rho_0$$

$$\frac{\partial g_2}{\partial t} = \frac{c s_1 g_2^2}{r} - \alpha g_2 + D_g \frac{\partial^2 g_2}{\partial x^2} + \rho_0$$

$$\frac{\partial r}{\partial t} = c s_2 g_1^2 + c s_1 g_2^2 - \beta r$$

$$\frac{\partial s_1}{\partial t} = \gamma (g_1 - s_1) + D_s \frac{\partial^2 s_1}{\partial x^2} + \rho_1$$

$$\frac{\partial s_2}{\partial t} = \gamma (g_2 - s_2) + D_s \frac{\partial^2 s_2}{\partial x^2} + \rho_1$$

In this system, the chemicals $g_1$ and $g_2$ indicate the presence of one or the other stripe color (white or black, for instance). The concentration of $r$ is used to make sure that only one of $g_1$ and $g_2$ are present at any one location. Chemicals $s_1$ and $s_2$ assure that the regions of $g_1$ and $g_2$ are limited in width. A program written in FORTRAN to simulate this system can be found in [Meinhardt 82].

**References**

[Bard 77] Bard, Jonathan, "A Unity Underlying the Different Zebra Striping Patterns," *Journal of Zoology*, Vol. 183, No. 4, pp. 527–539 (December 1977).

[Bard 81] Bard, Jonathan B. L., "A Model for Generating Aspects of Zebra and Other Mammalian Coat Patterns," *Journal of Theoretical Biology*, Vol. 93, No. 2, pp. 363–385 (November 1981).

[Bard and Lauder 74] Bard, Jonathan and Ian Lauder, "How Well Does Turing's Theory of Morphogenesis Work?," *Journal of Theoretical Biology*, Vol. 45, No. 2, pp. 501–531 (June 1974).

[Bier and Sloan 86] Bier, Eric A. and Kenneth R. Sloan, Jr., "Two-Part Texture Mapping," *IEEE Computer Graphics and Applications*, Vol. 6, No. 9, pp. 40–53 (September 1986).

[Blinn 78] Blinn, James F., "Simulation of Wrinkled Surfaces," *Computer Graphics*, Vol. 12, No. 3 (SIGGRAPH '78), pp. 286–292 (August 1978).

[Bloomenthal 85] Bloomenthal, Jules, "Modeling the Mighty Maple," *Computer Graphics*, Vol. 19, No. 3 (SIGGRAPH '85), pp. 305–311 (July 1985).

[Catmull 74] Catmull, Edwin E., "A Subdivision Algorithm for Computer Display of Curved Surfaces," Ph.D. Thesis, Department of Computer Science, University of Utah (December 1974).

[Gardner 85] Gardner, Geoffrey Y., "Visual Simulation of Clouds," *Computer Graphics*, Vol. 19, No. 3 (SIGGRAPH '85), pp. 297–303 (July 1985).

[Hanrahan and Haeberli 90] Hanrahan, Pat and Paul Haeberli, "Direct WYSIWYG Painting and Texturing on 3D Shapes," *Computer Graphics*, Vol. 24, No. 4 (SIGGRAPH '90), pp. 215–223 (August 1990).

[Heckbert 89] Heckbert, Paul S., "Fundamentals of Texture Mapping and Image Warping," M.S. Thesis, Department of Electrical Engineering and Computer Science, University of California at Berkeley (June 1989).

[Ho-Le 88] Ho-Le, K., "Finite Element Mesh Generation Methods: A Review and Classification," *Computer Aided Design*, Vol. 20, No. 1, pp. 27–38 (January/February 1988).

[Hubel and Wiesel 79] Hubel, David H. and Torsten N. Wiesel, "Brain Mechanisms of Vision," *Scientific American*, Vol. 241, No. 3, pp. 150–162 (September 1979).

[Hunding 90] Hunding, Axel, Stuart A. Kauffman, and Brian C. Goodwin, "*Drosophila* Segmentation: Supercomputer Simulation of Prepattern Hierarchy," *Journal of Theoretical Biology*, Vol. 145, pp. 369–384 (1990).

[Koenderink 84] Koenderink, Jan J., "The Structure of Images," *Biological Cybernetics*, Vol. 50, No. 5, pp. 363–370 (August 1984).

[Lengyel and Epstein 91] Lengyel, István and Irving R. Epstein, "Modeling of Turing Structures in the Chlorite–Iodide–Malonic Acid–Starch Reaction System," *Science*, Vol. 251, No. 4994, pp. 650–652 (February 8, 1991).

[Lewis 84] Lewis, John-Peter, "Texture Synthesis for Digital Painting," *Computer Graphics*, Vol. 18, No. 3 (SIGGRAPH '84), pp. 245–252 (July 1984).

[Lewis 89] Lewis, J. P., "Algorithms for Solid Noise Synthesis," *Computer Graphics*, Vol. 23, No. 3 (SIGGRAPH '89), pp. 263–270 (July 1989).

[Ma and Gagalowicz 85] Ma, Song De and Andre Gagalowicz, "Determination of Local Coordinate Systems for Texture Synthesis on 3-D Surfaces," *Eurographics '85*, edited by C. E. Vandoni.

[Meinhardt 82] Meinhardt, Hans, *Models of Biological Pattern Formation*, Academic Press, London, 1982.

[Melhorn 84] Melhorn, Kurt, *Multi-dimensional Searching and Computational Geometry*, Springer-Verlag, 1984.

[Murray 81] Murray, J. D., "On Pattern Formation Mechanisms for Lepidopteran Wing Patterns and Mammalian Coat Markings," *Philosophical Transactions of the Royal Society B*, Vol. 295, pp. 473–496.

[Peachey 85] Peachey, Darwyn R., "Solid Texturing of Complex Surfaces," *Computer Graphics*, Vol. 19, No. 3 (SIGGRAPH '85), pp. 279–286 (July 1985).

[Perlin 85] Perlin, Ken, "An Image Synthesizer," *Computer Graphics*, Vol. 19, No. 3 (SIGGRAPH '85), pp. 287–296 (July 1985).

[Perlin and Hoffert 89] Perlin, Ken and Eric M. Hoffert, "Hypertexture," *Computer Graphics*, Vol. 23, No. 3 (SIGGRAPH '89), pp. 253–262 (July 1989).

[Samek 86] Samek, Marcel, Cheryl Slean and Hank Weghorst, "Texture Mapping and Distortion in Digital Graphics," *The Visual Computer*, Vol. 2, No. 5, pp. 313–320 (September 1986).

[Toffoli and Margolus 87] Toffoli, Tommaso and Norman Margolus, *Cellular Automata Machines*, MIT Press, 1987.

[Turing 52] Turing, Alan, "The Chemical Basis of Morphogenesis," *Philosophical Transactions of the Royal Society B*, Vol. 237, pp. 37–72 (August 14, 1952).

[Turk 90] Turk, Greg, "Generating Random Points in Triangles," in *Graphics Gems*, edited by Andrew Glassner, Academic Press, 1990.

[Williams 83] Williams, Lance, "Pyramidal Parametrics," *Computer Graphics*, Vol. 17, No. 3 (SIGGRAPH '83), pp. 1–11 (July 1983).

[Witkin and Kass 91] Witkin, Andrew and Michael Kass, "Reaction-Diffusion Textures," *Computer Graphics*, Vol. 25 (SIGGRAPH '91).

[Yeager and Upson] Yeager, Larry and Craig Upson, "Combining Physical and Visual Simulation — Creation of the Planet Jupiter for the Film 2010," *Computer Graphics*, Vol. 20, No. 4 (SIGGRAPH '86), pp. 85–93 (August 1986).

# Reaction-Diffusion Textures

Andrew Witkin* and Michael Kass†

**Keywords**—Texture Synthesis; Natural Phenomena; Simulation.

## Abstract

We present a method for texture synthesis based on the simulation of a process of local nonlinear interaction, called reaction-diffusion, which has been proposed as a model of biological pattern formation. We extend traditional reaction-diffusion systems by allowing anisotropic and spatially non-uniform diffusion, as well as multiple competing directions of diffusion. We adapt reaction-diffusion systems to the needs of computer graphics by presenting a method to synthesize patterns which compensate for the effects of non-uniform surface parameterization. Finally, we develop efficient algorithms for simulating reaction-diffusion systems and display a collection of resulting textures using standard texture- and displacement-mapping techniques.

## 1 Introduction

Texture mapping techniques have become so highly developed and so widely used that textureless images tend to appear barren, unrealistic, and boring. To date, though, techniques for *synthesizing* natural textures have advanced far less than texture rendering methods. A few noise-based textures, such as marble and fractal bumps, have become standard (see, e.g.,[12, 18, 17]), and specialized methods for synthesizing stone walls are presented in [13]. In [7], a statistical method is presented for encoding and reproducing natural textures, while [3] describes the use of fractal methods for statistical texture encoding. Even so, scanned real-world images still provide a principal source of realistic texture maps.

In this paper, we investigate a class of patterns that arise from local, nonlinear interactions of excitation and inhibition. Our starting point is a chemical mechanism that was first proposed by Alan Turing [23] to account for pattern formation in biological morphogenesis. The basis for Turing's idea is the notion that cell properties, such as pigment production, are fixed during the development of the embryo in a way that depends on the concentrations of one or more chemical messengers which he dubbed *morphogens*. He postulated that patterning is governed primarily by two concurrently operating processes: *diffusion* of morphogens through the tissue and chemical *reactions* that produce and destroy morphogens at a rate that depends, among other things, on their concentrations. Such mechanisms are called *reaction-diffusion* (RD) systems.

Reaction-diffusion systems give rise to nonlinear partial differential equations, in which the time derivative of morphogen concentration at each point in the medium is given as a function of the current concentration and of derivatives of concentration with respect to position. The nonlinear model largely defies analysis; its behavior must be understood through numerical simulation. In [23], Turing extensively analyzed a linear approximation to the nonlinear equation, but lacked the computing tools to attack the nonlinear model numerically.

Since Turing's initial proposal, mechanisms of this kind have been invoked to account for several biological patterns, including spotted and striped coats of cats, zebras and giraffes [1, 15, 2, 25, 24], the markings on certain butterfly wings [14], and the arrangement of ocular dominance columns in mammalian cerebral cortex [22]. Reaction-diffusion equations have also arisen in such diverse fields as image processing [19], population dynamics[6] and epidemiology[11]. In [9] we considered

*School Of Computer Science, Carnegie Mellon University, Pittsburgh PA 15213. aw@cs.cmu.edu
†Advanced Technnology Group, Apple Computer, Cupertino, CA 95014. kass@apple.com



©1991 ACM-0-89791-436-8/91/007/0299 $00.75

Figure 1: Glass. Reaction-diffusion patterns are used to control opacity, displacement, and shading parameters of some glassware.

reaction-diffusion systems as a model for fingerprints.

Here we will address three main questions: (1) How can we extend the range of patterns we can create with reaction-diffusion systems? (2) How can we adapt reaction-diffusion systems to the needs of computer graphics? (3) How can we simulate the reaction-diffusion process efficiently? Our answers to these questions lead to the following specific contributions:

We generalize the basic RD model by introducing anisotropic and space-varying diffusion. The addition of anisotropy allows the creation of zebra stripes, and also, surprisingly, of sand ripples. Allowing diffusion rates and directions to vary over space creates more complex patterns, including the swirling patterns typical of fingerprints.

We consider new reaction function models, including functions that allow multiple competing orientations at each point. The addition of multiple competing directions gives rise to a host of new patterns, including some exhibiting a striking woven or lattice-like appearance.

We investigate new patterns that can be created by using non-standard initial conditions or reaction-diffusion parameters that change during the simulation. These include, for example, convincing giraffe markings.

We show how RD textures can avoid some standard difficulties of parametric texture mapping. First, by adjusting diffusion rates and directions, it is possible to grow textures that incorporate correction for parametric distortion, appearing uniform when applied to the surface. Second, texture patches can be seamlessly joined through the use of shared boundary conditions. Similarly, cyclic boundary conditions may be used to join a patch to itself, or to create seamless periodic textures.

We derive two fast but simple algorithms for the solution of the partial differential equations governing reaction-diffusion systems. The first makes use of the fact that the Green's function of the diffusion equation is a Gaussian and computes the effects of diffusion with efficient Gaussian convolution techniques. The second is a multigrid technique which simulates the equations rapidly on a coarse grid and then refines its results on a series of finer and finer grids.

## 2 Basic Reaction-Diffusion Dynamics

Our RD model incorporates three processes—diffusion, dissipation, and reaction. Diffusion governs the transport of morphogens from points of higher concentration to points of lower concentration. Dissipation involves the breakdown of morphogens, causing concentrations, in the absence of other influences, to decay exponentially toward zero. Reaction governs the rate of morphogen production. The effects of these three processes sum to provide the time derivative of concentration.

Since we are interested in generating surface textures, we assume throughout that diffusion occurs through a two-dimensional medium, although analogous results can be derived for arbitrary dimensions. The concentration of each of the morphogens is a function of position and of time. We denote the concentration function for a particular morphogen by $C(x, y)$. The reaction-diffusion equation governing the morphogen is then given by

$$\dot{C} = a^2 \nabla^2 C - bC + R, \tag{1}$$

where $\dot{C}$ is the time derivative of $C$, $\nabla^2 C$ is the *Laplacian* of $C$, defined by

$$\nabla^2 C = \frac{\partial^2 C}{\partial x^2} + \frac{\partial^2 C}{\partial y^2}, \tag{2}$$

$a$ is the rate constant for diffusion, and $b$ is the rate constant for dissipation. The function $R$ is the reaction function governing $C$, which can depend on all the other concentrations. The three terms on the right hand side of equation 1 represent diffusion, dissipation, and reaction, respectively.

In practice, we represent the concentration functions as two-dimensional arrays of discrete samples. To evaluate $\dot{C}$ we approximate the space derivative $\nabla^2 C$ by a *finite difference*. The second finite difference in the $x$ direction is

$$\frac{\partial^2 C}{\partial x^2} \approx \frac{C_{i+1,j} + C_{i-1,j} - 2C_{i,j}}{h^2},$$

where the $i$'s and $j$'s are array subscripts, and $h$ is the distance between adjacent samples. Taking the corresponding second difference in the $y$ direction, and summing, gives

$$\nabla^2 C_{i,j} \approx \frac{C_{i+1,j} + C_{i-1,j} + C_{i,j+1} + C_{i,j-1} - 4C_{i,j}}{h^2}. \tag{3}$$

The discrete Laplacian can also be expressed as the convolution of the concentration array with the $3 \times 3$ mask

$$L = \frac{1}{h^2}\left[\begin{array}{ccc} 0 & 1 & 0 \\ 1 & -4 & 1 \\ 0 & 1 & 0 \end{array}\right].$$

The values in the mask simply represent the coefficients in equation 3. The convolution form offers the advantage that any additional terms that are linear functions of $C_{i,j}$ and its neighbors may be readily combined to form a single $3 \times 3$ mask. Multiplying the Laplacian by $a^2$, and including the term $-bC_{i,j}$ gives the mask

$$M = \frac{1}{h^2}\left[\begin{array}{ccc} 0 & a^2 & 0 \\ a^2 & -4 - h^2 b & a^2 \\ 0 & a^2 & 0 \end{array}\right], \tag{4}$$

in terms of which equation 1 becomes

$$\dot{C} = M * C + R,$$

using "$*$" to denote discrete convolution.

To compute $C$ using 1, we must integrate $\dot{C}$ through time. The simplest integration formula, known as *Euler's method*, is

$$C_{t+\Delta t} = \Delta t(M * C_t + R_t), \tag{5}$$

which takes a timestep of size $\Delta t$.

## 3 Anisotropic Diffusion

The simple model of equation 1 assumes that diffusion occurs at a uniform rate in all directions and at all positions. In relaxing this restriction, we make it possible to produce a far wider range of patterns, including oriented patterns typical of zebra stripes or sand dunes.

Recall that the isotropic diffusion term of equation 1 is $\dot{C}_d = a^2(\partial^2 C/\partial x^2 + \partial^2 C/\partial y^2)$. To make $C$ diffuse at different rates in $x$ and $y$, we replace $a^2$ by independent rate constants for $x$ and $y$, so that $\dot{C}_d = a_1^2 \partial^2 C/\partial x^2 + a_2^2 \partial^2 C/\partial y^2$. By varying $a_1$ and $a_2$, the RD pattern can be stretched or compressed, but only along the two coordinate axes.

To handle the general case, we introduce the *Hessian* matrix, defined by

$$H_{ij} = \frac{\partial^2 C}{\partial r_i \partial r_j},$$

where the vector $\mathbf{r} = [x, y]$. In terms of the Hessian, the isotropic diffusion term is $a^2\,\mathrm{Tr}\,(H)$, where $\mathrm{Tr}\,(H)$, the *trace* of the Hessian, is the the sum of its diagonal elements. For the special case of anisotropic diffusion with axis-aligned principal directions, we can define the matrix

$$D = \left[\begin{array}{cc} a_1 & 0 \\ 0 & a_2 \end{array}\right],$$

in terms of which $\dot{C}_d = \mathrm{Tr}\,(D^T H D)$. We model diffusion with arbitrary principal directions by rotating the matrix $D$ to bring the $x$ and $y$ axes onto the desired principal directions, giving the diffusion term $\dot{C}_d = \mathrm{Tr}\,(D^T Q^T H Q D)$, where $Q$ is the rotation matrix.

Rather than working with this compound matrix directly, it is convenient to define the single *diffusion matrix*

$$A = Q^T D^T D Q,$$

in terms of which the diffusion is $\dot{C}_d = \sum_i \sum_j A_{ij} H_{ij}$. The diffusion matrix is given by

$$A = \left[\begin{array}{cc} a_1^2 \cos^2\theta + a_2^2 \sin^2\theta & (a_2^2 - a_1^2)\cos\theta\sin\theta \\ (a_2^2 - a_1^2)\cos\theta\sin\theta & a_2^2\cos^2\theta + a_1^2\sin^2\theta \end{array}\right] \tag{6}$$

where $a_1$ is the diffusion rate in the principal direction $[\cos\theta, \sin\theta]$ and $a_2$ is the diffusion rate in the principal direction $[-\sin\theta, \cos\theta]$.

When the Hessian is expressed in terms of finite differences, the quantity $\sum_i \sum_j A_{ij} H_{ij} - bC$, representing diffusion and dissipation, can be expressed as the convolution of $C$ with a $3 \times 3$ mask which is a generalization of the isotropic mask given in equation 4. That mask is

$$M = \frac{1}{2h^2}\left[\begin{array}{ccc} -a_{12} & 2a_{22} & a_{12} \\ 2a_{11} & -4(a_{11} + a_{22}) - 2h^2 b & 2a_{11} \\ a_{12} & 2a_{22} & -a_{12} \end{array}\right], \tag{7}$$

where $a_{11}$, $a_{12}$ and $a_{22}$ are the three distinct elements of the symmetric matrix $A$.

The Euler update formula for anisotropic diffusion still has the form

$$C_{t+\Delta t} = \Delta t(M * C_t + R_t),$$

but now the mask $M$ is the one given in equation 7.

### 3.1 Space-varying diffusion

A diffusion matrix that is constant over position can only produce patterns whose direction and degree of elongation are constant as well. A further important generalization of the model is obtained by allowing the matrix $A$ to vary with position. This is done by means of a *diffusion map*, an array that specifies the three distinct elements of $A$ at each position. In practice, the diffusion map can be much coarser than the concentration map, with bilinear interpolation sufficing to obtain intermediate samples. Usually, the diffusion map is most naturally specified indirectly, by giving $[\theta, a_1, a_2]$, or often just $\theta$, as a function of position. Direction fields may in turn be created in a variety of ways—for example by interactive specification [20], by analyzing natural images [9], or through analytic forms.

# 4 Mapping onto surfaces

A well-known difficulty with parametric texture mapping is that textures undergo distortion in the mapping from parameter space to the surface. Although solid texture methods [18, 17] are not subject to this problem, they are not well suited to modeling textures that actually grow on surfaces, rather than in space. Generally, it is not possible to correct parametric distortion by inverse warping a texture after the fact. However, in this section, we show how RD textures may be *grown* in a way that incorporates the inverse warp by transforming the diffusion matrix. Like trick pictures that are meant to be viewed in curved mirrors, the resulting patterns appear grossly distorted when viewed in parameter space, but map correctly onto the surface.

The correction we will describe is based on a simplifying assumption that the parametric surface function is locally linear. Under this approximation, we correct fully for parametric stretch and shear, but not for distortion due to the second derivative of the parametric function. In our experience to date, this approximation has not produced visible artifacts. A related approach to the creation of inverse-warped statistical textures is describe in [7]. In a different approach, Turk [24] computes reaction diffusion textures directly on the vertices and edges of a polygonal mesh.

Previously, we described anisotropic diffusion in terms of $[\theta, a_1, a_2]$ where $\theta$ is the angle between the first principal direction and one of the texture coordinate axes, and $a_1$ and $a_2$ are the rates in the principal directions. We wish to use essentially the same description for diffusion on a surface, except that $\theta$ is to be interpreted as the angle on the tangent plane of the surface between one of the principal diffusion directions and an arbitrary reference direction, which could conveniently be chosen to be one of the two parametric directions. Of course $a_1$ and $a_2$ should describe the desired principal diffusion rates on the surface, not in parameter space.

If the parametric surface function is $\mathbf{x}(\mathbf{u})$, then the *Jacobian* matrix, $J = \partial\mathbf{x}/\partial\mathbf{u}$, serves as a basis for the surface's tangent plane at $\mathbf{x}$, i.e. $\delta\mathbf{x} = J\delta\mathbf{u}$ is a tangent vector. First-order distortion arises because $J$ generally is not orthonormal, so lengths and angles are not preserved. We remove the distortion by performing a change of variables from $\mathbf{u}$ to $\mathbf{v}(\mathbf{u})$ such that $\partial\mathbf{x}/\partial\mathbf{v}$ is an orthonormal basis. To apply the correction, we then post-multiply the diffusion matrix $A$ by the inverse of the matrix $\partial\mathbf{v}/\partial\mathbf{u}$, and pre-multiply by the inverse transpose.

To orthonormalize $J$, we must find a $2 \times 2$ matrix $V$ such that

$$V^T J^T J V = V^T M V = I,$$

where $M = J^T J$ is the *metric tensor* of the surface, and $I$ is the identity matrix. Then $JV$ is by definition orthonormal. Orthonormal bases are only unique down to a rotation, so we must also pick an arbitrary reference direction on the surface with respect to which $\theta$ will be measured. Letting $\alpha = [1, 0]$ and $\beta = [0, 1]$, we choose $J\alpha$ as the reference direction, giving the additional condition on $V$ that $\beta^T V \alpha = 0$, which simply means $v_{21} = 0$. This leaves a quadratic system to solve for the remaining components of $V$. Solving and inverting the matrix gives, in terms of the components of $M$,

$$\tilde{V} = \frac{1}{\sqrt{m_{11}}} \begin{bmatrix} m_{11} & m_{12} \\ 0 & \sqrt{m_{11}m_{22} - m_{12}^2} \end{bmatrix}. \quad (8)$$

In summary, given the desired $\theta$ relative to the $[1, 0]$ parameter direction on the surface and the principal rates $a_1$ and $a_2$, the corrected diffusion matrix $\hat{A}$ can be computed in the following steps:

- Compute the uncorrected diffusion matrix $A$, in terms of $[\theta, a_1, a_2]$, according to equation 6.
- Compute the surface Jacobian $J = \partial x/\partial u$.
- Compute the metric tensor $M = J^T J$.
- Evaluate $\tilde{V}$ according to equation 8.
- Obtain the corrected diffusion matrix by evaluating $\hat{A} = \tilde{V}^T A \tilde{V}$.

The $3 \times 3$ convolution mask is then computed, and used according to equation 5 to take time steps. Figure 2 shows comparable textures, in parameter space and on the surface, with and without the correction described in this section.

## 4.1 Sewing patches together

It is often difficult or impossible to describe a complex surface using a single parametric function. Even simple surfaces, such as the sphere, cannot be parameterized without introducing singularities. These problems cannot be solved using the correction described above. However, it should be possible to solve them using piecewise parameterizations, letting each patch provide boundary conditions for its neighbors. Differential geometry provides a formalism for piecewise parameterizations in the construct of *coordinate charts and atlases* [21]. Roughly speaking, a chart is a parameterization for a piece of the surface, and

Figure 2: Correcting parametric distortion. The object on the left has been mapped with an uncorrected texture, showing marked parametric distortion. The object on the right has been mapped with a corrected texture, synthesized to appear undistorted on the surface. The raw textures appear behind each object.

an atlas contains sufficient overlapping charts to cover the surface, together with functions that map among the charts where they overlap. For example, the faces of a cube can serve as an atlas for a sphere. Although we have not yet implemented this scheme for curved surfaces, we have tested the use of boundary conditions to join planar patches and to create seamless periodic texture using cyclic boundary conditions. Figure 3 includes such a periodic texture.

# 5 Efficient Solution Methods

The Euler simulation method of section 2 is adequate for low-resolution simulations, but its computational complexity is unfortunately at least $O(r^4)$ where $r = 1/h$ is the sampling rate or resolution of the pattern. In order to improve on this bound, we develop two alternative algorithms capable of achieving $O(r^2)$ performance. The first of these algorithms is based on Gaussian convolutions, while the second is a *multi-grid* algorthm.

While the full non-linear reaction-diffusion equation is very difficult to analyze, we can gain substantial insight into the complexity of the computation by considering the linear differential equation which arises when $R = 0$ in equation 1 and the matrix $A$ is constant. For this special case of pure diffusion and dissipation, there exists an analytic form for the solution [10]:

$$C_{t+\Delta t}(x, y) = C_{t_0}(x, y) * G_{\Delta t}$$

where

$$G_{\Delta t}(x, y) = -\frac{1}{4\pi \Delta t \sqrt{\det(A)}} \exp\left(\frac{-p^T A p}{4\Delta t \det(A)} - bt\right) \tag{9}$$

is known as the Green's function of the differential equation. The solution is the convolution of the initial conditions with a Gaussian that has been aligned with the principal axes of the matrix $A$ and scaled to take account of the dissipation rate. The size of the Gaussian is proportional to $\sqrt{\Delta t}$.

Consider trying to compute the above solution with the Euler method of section 2. Each iteration is a convolution of the initial conditions with a $3 \times 3$ kernel. Variances add under repeated convolution [4], so after $n$ iterations, the resulting standard deviation of the Gaussian will be proportional to $\sqrt{n}$. Achieving a fixed kernel size therefore takes $O(r^2)$ iterations. Since each iteration takes $O(r^2)$ work, the total computation is $O(r^4)$. Clearly this can be a serious obstacle to synthesizing high-resolution patterns.

## 5.1 Gaussian Convolution

Instead of simulating the large-kernel convolution with a series of small convolutions, we can simply convolve $G$ with $C$ and get the same result. Using a direct spatial convolution also results in $O(r^4)$ complexity, but there are several ways of doing the convolution more efficiently. Two-dimensional Gaussians are separable, so they can be factored into the product of one-dimensional Gaussians. This makes it possible to convert the two-dimensional convolution into two one-dimensional convolutions and thereby reduce the complexity to $O(r^3)$. If each of these one-dimensional convolutions is approximated with recursive filters[16], the complexity is further reduced to $O(r^2)$. Another alternative is to use hierarchic convolutions [5] which achieve $O(r^2)$ complexity by using image pyramids.

While the above techniques efficiently compute the effects of diffusion and dissipation alone, we still need to incorporate the effects of reaction in order to simulate the full differential equation. Using the Green's function again, we can write the solution to the full differential equation as follows:

$$C_{t_0+\Delta t} = C_{t_0} * G_{\Delta t} + \int_0^{\Delta t} (R * G_u)\, du. \tag{10}$$

We already know an efficient way to compute the first term on the right in equation 10. Now we seek a simple, efficient approximation to the second term in order to complete the solution method. One way to do this is to use a constant approximation $\hat{R}(x, y, t) = R(x, y, t_0)$ leading to the iterative formula

$$C_{t_0+\Delta t} = C_{t_0} * G_{\Delta t} + \hat{R} * \int_{t_0}^{t_0+\Delta t} G_u \, du, \qquad (11)$$

where it remains to evaluate the definite time integral of the Green's function.

Unfortunately, $G$ is not integrable, so even the piecewise constant approximation to $R$ is somewhat problematic. We have three natural choices. First, we can perform the integral numerically. Second, it *is* possible to obtain $\int_0^\infty G\,dt$ by means of *Hankel Functions* [10], allowing us to solve each constant approximation to equilibrium. Third, and by far the simplest, we can render the integral trivial by approximating $R$ as an *impulse* applied at $t = t_i$. This option leads directly to the algorithm

$$C_{t_0+\Delta t} = \left[C_{t_0} + \gamma R_{t_0}\right] * G_{\Delta t}, \qquad (12)$$

where $\gamma$ is a factor intended to correct for $R$'s application at the beginning of the step, rather than throughout. To make the space integral of $C$ after the step be the same as it would have been under a constant, rather than impulsive, approximation to $R$, this factor should be

$$\gamma = \frac{e^{b\,\Delta t} - 1}{b}.$$

The algorithm that results from this approximation allows for diffusion with $O(r^2)$ computation using hierarchic convolutions or separable recursive approximations to Gaussians. The chief limitation is that the technique only works when the matrix $A$ does not vary over space. Subject to this limitation, however, it offers a potentially dramatic performance advantage over the methods that have been used previously, particularly for large step sizes or high diffusion rates. Swindale [22] arrived at a similar algorithm by a different path in the course of modeling the formation of ocular dominance columns.

### 5.2 Multi Grid

Another approach to avoiding the $O(r^4)$ behavior of the Euler simulation is to use multi-grid techniques[8]. The basic idea of these techniques is to simulate the equations on a series of grids of different sizes. Iterations on the coarser grids allow the simulation to proceed very rapidly, while iterations on the finer grids provide the detail necessary in the final result. If the grid sizes differ by a factor of two in each dimension from one level to the next, then the total number of samples in the grids is approximately $4/3$ as many as in the finest grid. As a result, a constant number of iterations on each of the grids can be accomplished in $O(r^2)$ time.

In some contexts, effective multi-grid implementations require complex control strategies to switch from one grid level to another. In order to synthesize reaction-diffusion textures, however, we have found a simple strategy to be very effective. We begin with the coarsest grid able to resolve details at the intrinsic scale of the pattern being synthesized. We do a small fixed number of iterations on that grid and then interpolate the result onto the next finer grid. This is repeated for all the remaining grids. Iterations on the different grids make use of the same $3 \times 3$ matrix $M$ as the Euler method. The only change is that the grid-spacing $h$ changes as we move from one grid to another. The resulting multi-grid method can be as efficient as the Gaussian convolution method, but is not subject to the limitation that the matrix $A$ be constant.

### 5.3 Binary Convolution

Convolutions of binary data with an integer-valued mask can be performed efficiently by means of lookup tables: accessing eight consecutive binary data points as a byte, the sum of the eight corresponding convolution values can be obtained in a single table lookup. Although $O(r^4)$, binary convolution may nevertheless be the fastest option for convolution with small masks. For reaction functions that are expressible in binary form, the algorithm of equation 12 may be reduced to one of iterated binary convolution by allowing the diffusion constant, $b$ to grow very large, rendering the contribution of the old concentrations negligible. In the resulting simplified algorithm, the binary reaction function is applied to the concentrations, with binary convolution applied to the result. Binary convolution has been used previously to compute RD patterns by Young [25].

## 6 Results

Although we have described one basic pattern-forming mechanism, a wide variety of RD textures can be produced by varying the initial and boundary conditions, the number of morphogens involved, the rate constants for each, the reaction functions that govern their interactions and the manner in which concentrations are mapped into surface appearance. In this section we show the textures we have produced and describe the choices that led to their creation.

All of the images that accompany this paper were rendered using Photorealistic RenderMan. RD textures were used as displacement and texture maps. In most images, monochrome concentration maps were used to blend between pairs of colors or other parameters such as opacity and specularity.

### 6.1 Isotropic Patterns

To create a simple isotropic RD pattern, we can use two concentration arrays $C^+$ and $C^-$, with different diffusion rates $a^+$ and $a^-$, producing convolution masks $M^+$ and $M^-$ according to equation 4. A threshold on the difference $C^+ - C^-$ serves as the reaction function:

$$R^+ = R^- = \text{if}\,(C^+ > C^-)\,\text{then}\,k\,\text{otherwise}\,0 \quad (13)$$

where $k$ is a reaction constant. Starting this RD system from initial conditions which are zero except on a jittered diamond grid produces a roughly cellular pattern that strikingly resembles giraffe markings (figure 3-1b). A similar pattern (3-1a), finer in scale and rendered with displacement mapping, looks reptilian. Varying the reaction rate constant $k$ (from equation 13) over time as the pattern is formed produces very different results (3-4a, 3-4c).

## 6.2 Simple Anisotropy: Stripes

The simple two-morphogen system used to produce the giraffe markings involves two morphogens diffusing isotropically, but at different rates. Introducing anisotropy allows more freedom. If we describe anisotropic diffusion using triples $P = [\theta, a_1, a_2]$, for each concentration map $C$, then branching and merging stripe patterns are produced with $P^+ = [\theta, es, s]$, and $P^- = [\theta, es, ds]$, which makes both morphogens diffuse at the same rate in the $\theta$ direction, but different rates in the perpendicular direction. Satisfactory zebra-like stripes can be produced with $e = 2.0$, $d = 1.5$, $s = 1.0$, $b = 1.0$, $k = 1.0$, $h = 1.0$, $\Delta t = .02$, and $C^+$ and $C^-$ initialized to random noise in the interval $[-1, 1]$. A typical zebra pattern is shown in figure 3-4b. A very similar RD pattern, rendered as a displacement map with appropriate coloring, resembles rippled sand. The addition of a fine noise-based grain texture (figure 5) enhances the effect.

## 6.3 Competing Orientations: weaves, lattices, and mazes

The interesting behavior of the anisotropic system described above led us to consider more elaborate systems involving multiple orientations. The general idea we considered was to replace the single antagonistic pair of morphogens with a set of such pairs, each pair differently oriented. Thus, a two-direction system might involve an antagonistic pair of morphogens biased toward horizontal diffusion, as well as a vertically biased pair.

Within this framework we discovered two reaction functions that produce particularly interesting patterns. (We denote by $D_i$ the difference $C^+ - C^-$ for the $i$th pair of concentrations.) The first is a "max of differences" (M-D),

$$\begin{aligned} R &= k, \quad \text{if} \quad \max_j D_j > \rho, \\ &= 0, \quad \text{otherwise.} \end{aligned} \quad (14)$$

where $\rho$ is a threshold, and the second, a "difference of abs's" (D-A):

$$\begin{aligned} R &= k, \quad \text{if} \quad \text{abs}\max_j D_j > \text{abs}\min_j D_j \\ &= 0, \quad \text{otherwise.} \end{aligned} \quad (15)$$

Although the D-A and M-D reaction functions appear similar, the patterns they produce could hardly be more different. Figure 3-3b shows a two-direction D-A texture, which has a maze-like appearance. In contrast, a two-direction M-D texture (3-4e) appears woven, although such irregularities as splitting and merging of "threads" give it a distinctly organic appearance. Figures 3-2b and 3-1c show three- and five- direction M-D textures, while figure 3-2c shows a five-direction D-A texture. All of these derive from uniform random initial conditions.

## 6.4 Spatial Variation

Figures 3b, 4b, 4c, and 4d show RD patterns governed by diffusion maps. Figure 3-3d is a two-orientation M-D pattern grown on a radial/concentric orientation map. Figure 3-2a shows a similar pattern, but with rotation of the map orientations to produce a double spiral. Figure 3-2e shows two competing nearly-radial orientations. Figure 3-3c shows the merger, with smoothing, of three uniform orientation fields, resembling a zebra's haunch markings. Figures 3-1d and 3-4d show more complicated orientation patterns. All of these diffusion maps were generated using simple analytic forms.

## 6.5 Boundary Conditions

An unusual feature of RD textures is that texture patches that join seamlessly can be created by copying data across the boundaries at each iteration. This is illustrated in figure 3-2d: a texture was grown using doubly cyclic boundary conditions, giving it the topology of a torus. This was accomplished simply by wrapping the array references across both horizontal and vertical boundaries while calculating the convolution $C * M$. In the resulting pattern, the left edge joins smoothly to the right, and the upper edge to the lower. The figure shows how the replicated pattern tiles the image without seams. The replication itself is easily perceived, due to the repetition of gross features within the texture. However, the seams between the tiles are invisible.

# 7 Conclusion

Texture synthesis is a hard problem because the range of natural textures, and of texture-forming processes, is vast. Given this diversity, we cannot expect to find a single, universal texture generator. Nonetheless, by identifying

processes that are widespread in nature, we can develop models that are broadly useful for texture synthesis.

Although RD models have been applied to problems in a variety of fields, their use in computer graphics is in its infancy. Already, RD models significantly extend the range of textures that can be synthesized. Their characteristic organic appearance lends an interesting new element to synthetic imagery. In addition, RD textures have the potential to extend the range of surfaces to which textures can be applied because they can be grown to compensate for parametric distortion and joined smoothly patch to patch.

## Acknowledgements

The research reported in this paper was conducted at Carnegie Mellon University, and at Apple Computer. At Carnegie Mellon, work was supported in part by grants from Apple Computer and from the Siemens Corporation, and by an equipment grant from Silicon Graphics, Inc. Photorealistic RenderMan software, which was used to render all the images appearing in this paper, was provided to Carnegie Mellon through Pixar's RenderMan Education Program. The "Space Cookies" and "Fungi" images were created by Drew Olbrich of Carnegie Mellon. Drew Olbrich, Michael Gleicher, William Welch, and Wendy Plesniak provided valuable assistance.

## References

[1] Jonathan Bard and Ian Lauder. How well does turing's theory of morphogenesis work? *Journal of Theoretical Biology*, 45:501–531, 1974.

[2] Jonathan B.L. Bard. A model for generating aspects of zebra and other mammalian coat patterns. *Journal of Theoretical Biology*, 93:501–531, 1981.

[3] Michael Barnsley. *Fractals Everywhere*. Academic Press, San Diego, 1988.

[4] R. N. Bracewell. *The Fourier Transform and its Applications*. McGraw-Hill, New York, 1986.

[5] P. J. Burt. Fast hierarchical correlations with gaussian-like kernels. Technical Report TR 860, Dept. of Computer Science, U. of Maryland, 1980.

[6] S. Ei and M. Mimura. Pattern formation in heterogeneous reaction-diffusion-advection systems with an application to population dynamics. *SIAM J. on Mathematical Analysis*, 21(2):346–361, 1990.

[7] Andre Gagalowicz and Song De Ma. Sequential synthesis of natural textures. *CVGIP*, 30:289–315, 1985.

[8] W. Hackbusch. *Multi-Grid Methods and Applications*. Springer-Verlag, New York, 1985.

[9] Michael Kass and Andrew Witkin. Analyzing oriented patterns. *Computer Vision, Graphics and Image Processing*, 37:362–385, 1987.

[10] Granino Korn and Thresa Korn. *Mathematical Handbook for Scientists and Engineers*. McGraw Hill, New York, 1968.

[11] K. Kunish and H. Schelch. Parameter estimation in a special reaction-diffusion system modelling man-environment diseases. *Journal of Mathematical Biology*, 27(6):633–665, 1989.

[12] B. Mandelbrot. *Fractals: Form, Chance, and Dimension*. W.H. Freeman, San Fransico, 1977.

[13] Kazunori Miyata. A method of generating stone wall patterns. *Computer Graphics*, 24(4):387–394, 1990.

[14] J. D. Murray. On pattern formation mechanisms for lepidopteran wing patterns and mammalian coat markings. *Philosophical Transactions of the Royal Society (B)*, 295:473–496, 1981.

[15] J. D. Murray. A pre-pattern formation mechanism for animal coat markings. *Journal of Theoretical Biology*, 88:161–199, 1981.

[16] A. Openheim and R. Schafer. *Digital Signal Processing*. Prentice-Hall, Englewood Cliffs, New Jersey, 1975.

[17] Darwyn R. Peachey. Solid texturing of complex surfaces. *Computer Graphics*, 19:279–286, 1985.

[18] Ken Perlin. An image synthesizer. *Computer Graphics*, 19:287–296, 1985.

[19] C. Price, P. Wambacq, and A. Ooosterlinck. Applications of reaction-diffusion equations to image processing. In *Third Int. Conf. on Image Processing and its Applications*, pages 49–53, 1989.

[20] Karl Sims. Leonardo's deluge (video). *Siggraph '89 Computer Graphics Theater*, 1989.

[21] M. Spivak. *A Comprehensive Introduction to Differential Geometry (5 vols)*. Publish or Perish Press, 1975.

[22] N.V. Swindale. A model for the formation of ocular dominance stripes. *Philosophical Transactions of the Royal Society (B)*, 208:243–264, 1980.

[23] Alan Turing. The chemical basis of morphogenesis. *Philosophical Transactions of the Royal Society (B)*, 237:37–72, 1952.

[24] Greg Turk. Generating synthetic textures using reaction-diffusion. Technical Report TR-90-018, University of North Carolina, Chapel Hill, 1990.

[25] David Young. A local activator-inhibitor model of vertebrate skin patterns. *Mathematical Biosciences*, 72(1), 1984.

Figure 3: **Texture Buttons.** **Row 1:** (a) reptile, (b) giraffe, (c) coral, (d) scalloped. **Row 2:** (a) spiral, (b) triweave, (c) twisty maze, (d) replication, (e) purple thing. **Row 3:** (a) sand, (b) maze, (c) zebra haunch, (d) radial. **Row 4:** (a) space giraffe, (b) zebra, (c) stucco, (d) beats us, (e) weave.

**By type.** Isotropic: reptile, giraffe, space-giraffe, stucco. Multi-orientation: coral (5), spiral (2), triweave (3), twisty maze (5), replication (3), purple thing (2), maze (2), radial (2), beats us (2), weave (2). Diffusion mapped: scaloped, spiral, purple thing, zebra haunch, radial, beats us.

Figure 4: Space Cookies. All texture and displacement maps, except those on the bag and the plate, are RD patterns.

Figure 5: Fungi. All texture and displacement maps are RD patterns, except the sky, the fine grain pattern on the sand, and the fluting on the front right mushroom.

# Spot Noise
## *Texture Synthesis for Data Visualization*

Jarke J. van Wijk
*Netherlands Energy Research Foundation ECN*
*P.O. Box 1, 1755 ZG Petten, The Netherlands*

**ABSTRACT**

The use of stochastic textures for the visualization of scalar and vector fields over surfaces is discussed. Current techniques for texture synthesis are not suitable, because they do not provide local control, and are not suited for the design of textures. A new technique, *spot noise,* is presented that does provide these features. Spot noise is synthesized by addition of randomly weighted and positioned spots. Local control of the texture is realized by variation of the spot. The spot is a useful primitive for texture design, because, in general, the relations between features of the spot and features of the texture are straightforward. Various examples and applications are shown. Spot noise lends itself well for the synthesis of texture over curved surfaces, and is therefore an alternative to solid texturing. The relations of spot noise with a variety of other techniques, such as random faults, filtering, sparse convolution, and particle systems, are discussed. It appears that spot noise provides a new perspective on those techniques.

**CR categories and subject descriptors:** I.3.3 [**Computer Graphics**]: Picture/Image generation; I.3.7 [**Computer Graphics**]: Three Dimensional Graphics and Realism - color, shading, and texture.

**Keywords:** texture synthesis, scientific visualization, flow visualization, fractals, particle systems.

### 1 INTRODUCTION

Scalar and vector fields over surfaces have many applications, ranging from common scalar functions of two variables, used in many disciplines, to the distribution of pressure and velocity over a ship hull or the wings of an airplane. The topic of this paper is the use of texture, loosely defined as the local variation in visual properties, for the visualization of fields over surfaces. Tufte [33] has shown that the use of fixed patterns leads to poor results. A better result can be expected if the texture is based on a stochastic, rather than a deterministic model. Several terms are used for such textures: stochastic textures, random fields, and noises.



Applications of stochastic texture in scientific visualization are rare. Krueger [16] has used texture to show the differences between related data sets. In the context of flow visualization it has been noted [34, 35, 38] that the simulation of particle convection leads to texture. If many particles are used, the individual particles cannot be distinguished any more and clouds, smoke and other typical textures that are well known in experimental flow visualization are perceived. These applications show that texture is a useful concept for scientific visualization, but it is not clear how the proposed techniques should be used for other applications.

In this paper a more general approach to the design and synthesis of texture for scientific visualization is presented. In section 2 the requirements are drawn up, and current techniques for texture synthesis are discussed. It appears that the techniques used for the synthesis of realistic textures do not fulfill these requirements. In section 3 *spot noise* is introduced. Its synthesis is based on the principle that the random placement of a small pattern, the spot, over a surface leads to texture. In section 4 it is shown that this technique is very appropriate for the design of textures, because the relations between the features of the spot and those of the corresponding texture are straightforward. In section 5 various applications of spot noise are presented, for data visualization and for image synthesis. In section 6 spot noise is compared with existing techniques, and directions for further research are indicated. Finally, in section 7 conclusions are drawn.

### 2 TEXTURE FOR DATA VISUALIZATION

#### 2.1 Requirements

Figure 1 shows a data flow diagram of texture synthesis for data visualization. The parameter values for the texture synthesis process are determined in two steps. First, the data are retrieved that correspond to the texture coordinates; second, these data are converted into parameter values according to a data mapping specified by a designer. The term *designer* is used here functionally: it can be an expert in visual communication, but also a researcher that wants to visualize his data. With this diagram in mind, the requirements on texture synthesis can easily be derived. They fall into two categories: texture generation and design.

The synthesis technique has to allow for non-stationary textures to express the variation in the data. Further, the model has to allow for a wide range of textures. The aim of realism is replaced by the aim of expressiveness: it must be possible for the designer to choose a texture that matches with the nature of the data, and variations in the data must lead to clear variations

©1991 ACM-0-89791-436-8/91/007/0309 $00.75

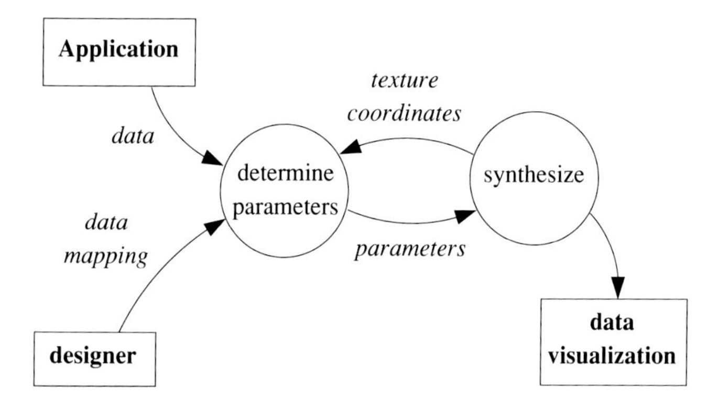


Fig. 1 Data flow diagram texture synthesis for data visualization

in the texture.

The selection of a suitable data mapping is an iterative design process. The efficiency of this process depends on several aspects. Obviously, the synthesis of the texture has to be efficient. Another way to improve efficiency is to use previews, simplified versions of the final result, during the design phase [13]. Finally, the number of iterations can be reduced if the relation between the specification and the resulting texture is clear to the designer [36]. The closest relation is one-to-one, but in order to limit the designer's work we further require that the specification should be of a suitable level: instead of drawing the texture himself, the designer must be enabled to specify the features of the texture and their relation with the data on a higher level.

Summarizing, a synthesis technique is required for non-stationary textures that can be specified in a simple, predictable way. In section 2.2 an overview is presented of the main current techniques for texture synthesis. In section 2.3 they are tested against our requirements.

## 2.2 Texture synthesis

Stochastic textures are realizations of a statistical model. There is a general consensus, supported by evidence from perception research [14], that second-order, or pairwise statistics suffice for the description of textures that can be discriminated by human observers. Techniques that use the full second-order statistics [23, 9] are very general and give impressive results [9]. However, they are also quite involved and have a brute-force character.

A convenient simplification is the restriction to so-called Gaussian textures. This simplification is similar to the common simplification for first-order statistics: if a normal or Gaussian distribution is assumed, the distribution can be fully described by its mean and variance. Gaussian textures are described by their autocorrelation function $C_f(\tau)$, which is the correlation of two random samples of $f$ at an interval $\tau$. For a one-dimensional stochastic function $f(t)$ with zero mean it is defined as

$$C_f(\tau) = \langle f(t) f(t+\tau) \rangle ,$$

where triangular brackets denote averages over many samples. $C_f(0)$ equals the variance $\sigma^2$ of $f$. If $C_f(\tau) = 0$, the function $f$ is completely uncorrelated for samples at distance $\tau$. For common stochastic functions, $C_f(\tau)$ approaches 0 with increasing $\tau$.

A strongly related technique is spectral modeling, which is based on the use of power spectra. The power spectrum $P_f(\omega)$ of a stochastic function $f(t)$ is

$$P_f(\omega) = \lim_{T\to\infty} \frac{1}{T} |F_T(\omega)|^2 ,$$

where $F_T(\omega)$ is the Fourier transform of a sample of $f(t)$ with length T. According to the Wiener-Khintchine relation [3], the autocorrelation function and the power spectrum provide equivalent information, because they are a Fourier transform pair:

$$P_f(\omega) = \int_{-\infty}^{\infty} C_f(\tau)\, e^{-i\omega\tau}\, d\tau .$$

The standard approach of spectral modeling is to filter white noise (with a constant power spectrum) with a transfer function $H(\omega)$. Voss [27] has used this technique to generate fractal textures and terrains: noises with power spectra $f^{-\beta}$. These noises are generalizations of Brownian motion ($\beta = 2$), and are called fractal Brownian motions (fBm) [21, 27]. The first simulations of fBm were based on considering Brownian motion as the cumulative displacement of a series of independent jumps or pulses [21]. This technique is generalized to surfaces by using random faults instead of random jumps.

Fournier, Fussel, and Carpenter [7] use stochastic subdivision to generate fractal terrains. Lewis [18] has generalized the stochastic subdivision technique for arbitrary power spectra and autocorrelation functions.

In [17] a technique is described for the synthesis of textures for digital painting. These textures are the result of weighted additions of a displaced, windowed texture sample, where the weights and displacements are chosen randomly. This process is equivalent to an out-of-order convolution of the sample with a sparse, white noise, hence it is named sparse convolution.

Perlin [28] generates solid textures through the composition of non-linear functions. For stochastic textures he defines the function $Noise(\mathbf{x})$ as a modeling primitive. This function is band-limited, statistically invariant under translations (stationary) and statistically invariant under rotations (isotropic). Fractal textures are modeled as linear combinations of the scaled noise function:

$$f(\mathbf{x}) = \sum_k \frac{Noise(2^k \mathbf{x})}{2^k} .$$

In a similar way turbulence, marble and a variety of other natural textures can be modeled.

## 2.3 Evaluation

The issue of local variation of texture is not mentioned in most of the literature. An exception is Lewis [18], who states that local variations of the texture may be effected by varying the model parameters or by simple postprocessing techniques, rather than by incorporating these variations in the original model. Both approaches are used by Musgrave et al. [24] for the synthesis of eroded terrain. His technique for the initial synthesis of the fractal terrain is based on Perlin's: the weights for the *Noise* function are functions of the altitude. This works well for isotropic textures, but the implementation of anisotropic textures with local variations is less straightforward. For instance, if we want to visualize a 2-D flow velocity field $\mathbf{v}(\mathbf{x})$ with an anisotropic texture, such that the dominant direction aligns with the direction of the flow, a natural solution would be:

$$f(\mathbf{x}) = Noise(\mathbf{x} - (\mathbf{x}\cdot\mathbf{v})\,\mathbf{v}) .$$

Here the primitive *Noise* texture is stretched according to the magnitude and direction of the velocity. If $\mathbf{v}(\mathbf{x})$ is constant, this gives the desired result, in most other cases, however, it does not. Other solutions in the same spirit could be devised, but they all share the same deficit: local deformations of texture cannot be modeled by global transformations (scaling etc.) of a texture.

The direct spectral approach and the random fault technique are not suitable for local, spatial control. With the other techniques it is indeed possible to vary the parameters as a function of space, but the literature does not make clear how this should be done to realize a desired effect.

This is related to the next point of our evaluation: the design of textures. As most authors aim at realism, again this issue is not mentioned often. The examples given in [28] for the construction of solid textures are based on more or less simplified models of physical processes. In [23, 9] the second-order statistics are derived by sampling real-world textures, for the generation of fractal terrains the power spectrum $f^{-\beta}$ is used as a starting point [21, 7, 27].

Let us therefore consider possible ways for a designer to specify a texture. For spectral modeling three options are available. First, a designer can enter a sample of the desired texture, from which the desired parameters are derived. However, it is not simple to render a suitable texture by hand. Further, the tautological character of this solution strongly suggests rejecting it. Second, the designer could enter an autocorrelation function. Advantages of the autocorrelation function are that the spatial domain is more familiar to most people than the spectral domain, and it directly reflects features such as the scale, period of oscillation, and directional tendencies. Although this is certainly true if a given autocorrelation function is analyzed, the design of an autocorrelation function, especially in two dimensions, is far less simple. Another severe problem is further that not every autocorrelation function leads to a realizable texture, because its Fourier transform, the power spectrum, must be non-negative. As a third approach, the designer could specify the power spectrum. In [17] it is stated that it is possible to acquire an intuitive feel for the relation between a painted spectrum and its corresponding texture. The author of that article could reliably paint spectra to simulate some textures, but this might be different for an arbitrary designer.

Besides the specification of a standard texture, the designer also has to specify how the texture has to be varied as a function of the data, which aggravates the problems of the three discussed options.

As a conclusion, we can state that no current technique for texture synthesis provides an easy solution that satisfies our requirements for data visualization. This can be explained from the difference between the applications. Traditionally, the focus is on the synthesis of realistic, stationary textures, whereas for the application discussed here clarity, ease of design, and local control are the main requirements. In the next sections, a texture synthesis technique is described that was developed with those requirements in mind.

## 3 SPOT NOISE

### 3.1 Definition

In this section a texture for data visualization is presented: *spot noise*. Spot noise has strong relations with the techniques discussed in the previous sections. The specific advantages of spot noise will emerge in practical applications, discussed in section 4 and 5.

Spot noise is the spatial analogue of shot noise. Shot noise [3] is a special kind of random function that has many applications in engineering. It is produced by the successive repetition at random intervals of independent pulses. If each pulse produces the profile $a_i h(t-t_i)$, the resultant function $f(t)$ is thus

$$f(t) = \sum_i a_i h(t-t_i) ,$$

where the values $t_i$ of the independent variable (e.g. time) form a random sequence. The power spectrum of $f(t)$ is directly related to the energy spectrum

$$S_h(\omega) = |H(\omega)|^2$$

of $h(t)$, where $H(\omega)$ is the Fourier transform of $h(t)$. If $a_i$ has zero mean, and if on average there are $\nu$ repetitions per unit time, then

$$P_f(\omega) = \nu < a_i^2 > S_h(\omega) .$$

The spatial analogue also has many applications, for instance in diffraction theory. For the application discussed here, the pulse $h(\mathbf{x})$ is considered as a spot that is dropped on the plane, hence we call the noise produced spot noise. The size of a spot is limited, and usually small compared to the size of the texture segment to be synthesized. In analogy with shot noise, spot noise is defined as

$$f(\mathbf{x}) = \sum_i a_i h(\mathbf{x}-\mathbf{x}_i)$$

where $\mathbf{x}_i$ are random positions on the plane. If on average there are $\nu$ repetitions per unit area then

$$P_f(\mathbf{k}) = \nu < a_i^2 > S_h(\mathbf{k}) ,$$

where $\mathbf{k}$ is the two-dimensional frequency vector.

### 3.2 Synthesis

The last relation of 3.1 is valuable for the synthesis of spot noise. It states that the power spectrum of the texture and the energy spectrum of the spot are the same, except for a scale factor. So, realizations of spot noise can be constructed in the frequency domain via the multiplication of the Fourier transform $H(\mathbf{k})$ with a scale factor and addition of a random phase shift $\alpha_\mathbf{k}$ to $H(\mathbf{k})$.

The addition of a random phase shift $\alpha_\mathbf{k}$ is equivalent to multiplication with $W(\mathbf{k}) = e^{i\alpha_\mathbf{k}}$. The power spectrum of $w(\mathbf{x})$ is evenly distributed over all frequencies, so $w(\mathbf{x})$ is white noise. According to the convolution theorem, multiplication in the frequency domain is equivalent to convolution in the spatial domain, hence spot noise can also be synthesized via convolution of $h(\mathbf{x})$ with white noise.

An example of white noise is a set of random values on a grid. Spot noise can therefore be synthesized through the convolution of a randomly filled grid with the spot. This method can be compared to the filtering of a very noisy image with the spot as the filter kernel, a standard technique in digital image processing [10]. In the natural texturing model [15] a similar technique is used to synthesize texture.

Another example of white noise is a Poisson point process: a set of randomly scaled delta functions $a_i \delta(\mathbf{x}_i)$, randomly distributed over the plane. Here we close the circle: the convolution of a Poisson point process with a spot boils down to dropping spots on the plane, which is the original definition of spot noise. Random faults [21] and sparse convolution [17] are based on the same principle.

Variation of the texture for data visualization can be realized via variation of the spot. This requires a variable spot $h(p, \mathbf{x})$, whose properties are controlled by a set of parameters $p$. These parameters are determined via a data mapping $m$ from the data $d(\mathbf{x})$ that belong to the texture coordinates $\mathbf{x}$. Spot noise for data visualization can thus be synthesized by using variable spots:

$$f(\mathbf{x}) = \sum_i a_i h(m(d(\mathbf{x}_i)), \mathbf{x}-\mathbf{x}_i) .$$

A drawback of this method is that the data to be visualized are smeared out. At each point several spots that correspond to different data values overlap. This is not a problem if the variation in the data is small relative to the size of the spot. Another solution is to use an alternative definition for variable spot noise:

$$f(\mathbf{x}) = \sum_i a_i h(m(d(\mathbf{x})), \mathbf{x} - \mathbf{x}_i),$$

i.e. the texture at a point $\mathbf{x}$ is considered as if it is part of a stationary texture constructed with identical spots that have the properties that correspond to the data at point $\mathbf{x}$. Another interpretation is that the spot is used as a (position dependent) filter-kernel for a Poisson point process. A possible implementation, though not very efficient for large spots, is via Perlin's approach. The preceding discussion reveals how this can be done: not via scaling, but via convolution of *Noise*:

$$f(x, y) = \sum_i \sum_j h(m(d(\mathbf{x})), x+i, y+j)\, Noise(x+i, y+j).$$

As a final remark, the variance of spot noise is given by

$$\sigma^2 = v < a_i^2 > \iint h^2(\mathbf{x})\, d\mathbf{x}.$$

Note that in general the variance of $a_i$ has to be adapted as a function of $\mathbf{x}_i$ if a constant variance of the texture is desired with a varying spot.

## 4 SPOT AND TEXTURE

In the preceding section we saw the strong relation between the energy spectrum of the spot and the power spectrum of the texture, and hence also between their autocorrelation functions. In this section the relation between a spot and the resulting texture is discussed from a designer's point of view. Given a simple spot, how are its features, such as size and shape, related to features of the texture, such as granularity and isotropy ? This will be shown with a number of examples, leading to rules of thumb that can be used for texture design. In this section all examples of textures are stationary, in the next section the use of space-variant spots will be discussed. The images in this section are made via addition of a random phase shift to the Fourier transform of the spot, followed by an inverse Fourier transform and normalization.

### 4.1 Size

A disk is the simplest spot that can be used. Figure 2 shows three disks with different radii and the corresponding textures. The differences in the textures can be explained from their power spectra. In figure 3 the power spectrum sinc$^2$ of the one-dimensional equivalent of a disk, the rectangular pulse, is shown. For the graphical display of a random function in the spatial domain, a finite band in the frequency domain has to be selected, because of limitations in resolution. The display of a large sample (narrow pulses) comes down to the selection of a band in the low frequencies, whereas the display of a small sample (wide pulses) is equivalent to selection of a band in the high frequencies. Thus, figure 3 shows that narrow pulses lead to white noise. For wide pulses, the right flank is dominant. This flank falls off with $f^{-2}$, which is the same as for Brownian motion. If the width of the pulse lies between those extrema, the corresponding random function is white noise that has been passed through a low-pass filter.

For two-dimensional signals, i.e. textures, a similar result can be derived in the frequency domain. However, a derivation in the spatial domain is instructive as well. If small spots are used, samples at different locations are uncorrelated, and hence the result is white noise. Large spots degenerate to random faults, so the result will be fractal. Here the texture is shown as a variation in the intensity, which gives a cloud-like result. For intermediate size spots these two effects occur simultaneously. At a large scale the result is white noise, while details have a fractal character.

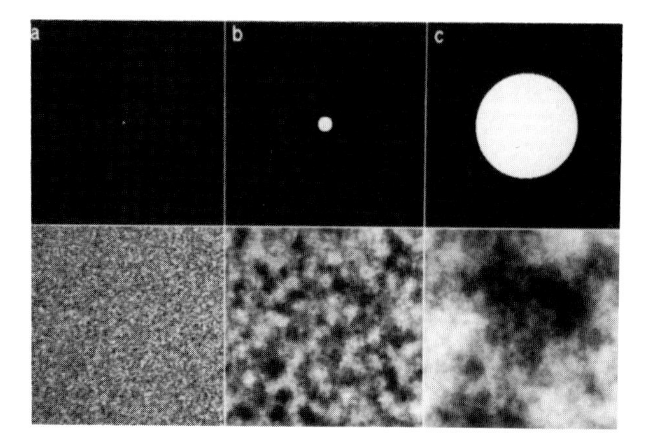

Fig. 2 Different sizes of spot

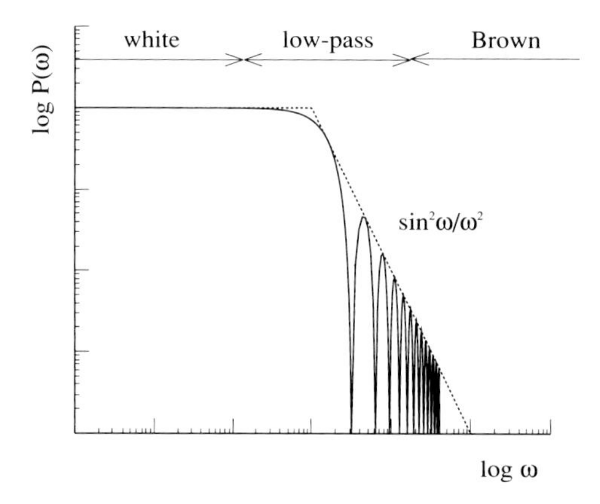

Fig. 3 Power spectrum rectangular pulse

For the autocorrelation function of two-level spots ($h(\mathbf{x}) = 1$ or 0), a simple geometric interpretation can be used: the normalized autocorrelation $K(\Delta)$ ($= C(\Delta)/\sigma^2$) is equal to the area of the overlap of a spot $h(\mathbf{x})$ and a displaced spot $h(\mathbf{x}-\Delta)$, divided by the area of the spot (fig. 4). In general, if two spots do not overlap for a displacement $\Delta$, then the texture is uncorrelated for samples at a distance $\Delta$. Therefore, the size of the spot determines the maximum correlation length or the granularity of the texture.

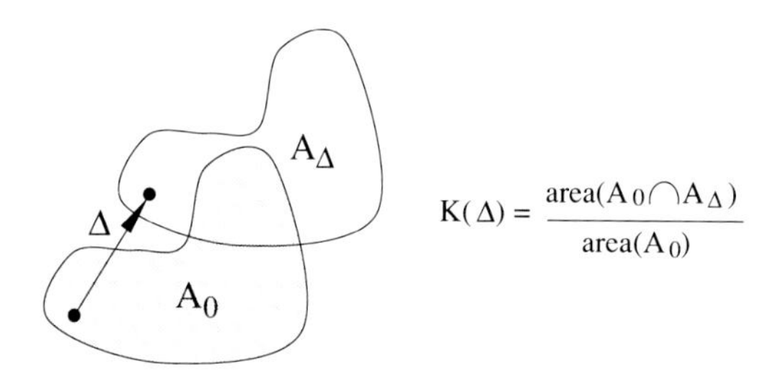

Fig. 4 Autocorrelation function for two-level spots

## 4.2 Edges

We saw that a sharp edge, i.e. a discontinuity at the transition from the interior to the exterior of the spot, leads to a fractal texture. Figure 5 shows the effect of the use of different types of transitions from the interior to the exterior of the spot. Besides a disk, a cone-shaped spot with a triangular cross-section and a spot with a Gaussian cross-section are used. The last two spots act as steep low-pass filters. The right flank of the power spectrum of a triangular filter falls off with $f^{-4}$, the power spectrum of a Gaussian filter falls off exponentially. The visual effect is that details below the scale of the spot are removed: a smooth texture is generated. Whereas in image processing usually such filters are preferred above the box or pulse filter, for texture synthesis this is a matter of taste. The smooth textures appear out of focus, whereas textures that result from spots with sharp edges affirm the theorem *fractal = natural*.

The difference between the use of a triangular and a Gaussian cross-section is small, whereas the difference between the smooth and the fractal texture is large. Textures between smooth and fractal can be synthesized via the use of spots with a trapezoidal cross-section.

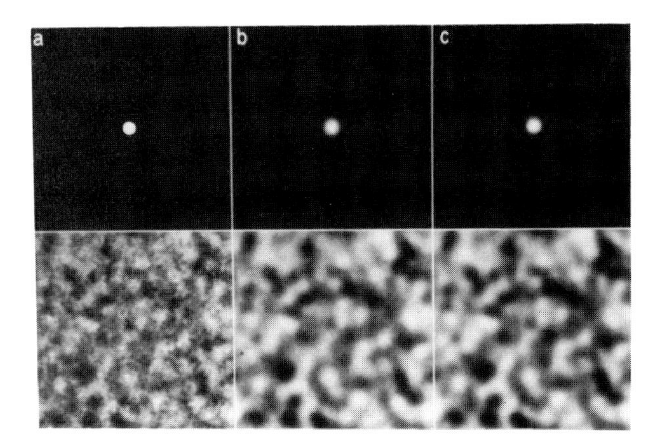


Fig. 5 (a) Disk, (b) cone, (c) Gaussian spot

## 4.3 Direction

The textures presented so far were invariant under rotation, i.e. isotropic. A texture will be isotropic if the spot is rotationally symmetric, or if each spot is, besides randomly positioned, also randomly rotated. The power spectrum $P_f(\mathbf{k})$ of the noise $f(\mathbf{x})$ that results from the use of a randomly rotated spot $h(x, y)$ with energy spectrum $S_h(k_1, k_2)$ is given by

$$P_f(\mathbf{k}) = v < a_i^2 > \frac{1}{2\pi|\mathbf{k}|} \int_0^{2\pi} S_h(|\mathbf{k}|\cos\alpha,\ |\mathbf{k}|\sin\alpha)\, d\alpha\ .$$

If no random rotation is used, the use of straight lines in a spot always leads to an anisotropic texture.

A simple way to generate an anisotropic texture is to scale a spot non-proportionally. Figure 6 shows the effect of the use of ellipses as opposed to disks. For elongated ellipses the texture has a fractal character in the direction of the longest axis, and a white noise character in the direction of the shortest axis. The effect of scaling the spot is not simply scaling the texture. Instead the texture is stretched locally, the large details in the texture remain at the same place.

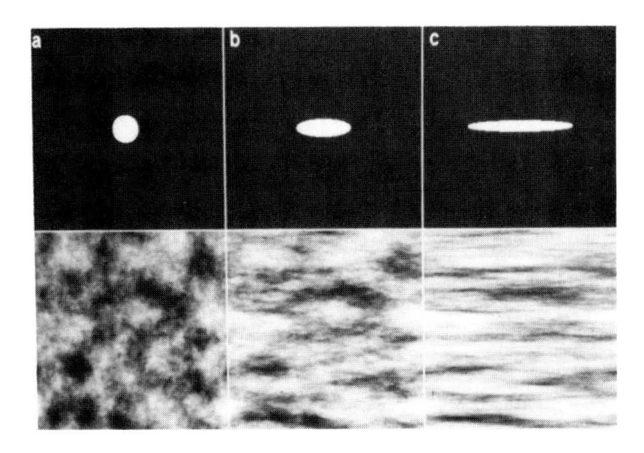


Fig. 6 Non-proportional scaling

## 4.4 Patterns

Many textures exhibit patterns, i.e. structures are repeated over some distance. Such patterns show up in the autocorrelation function as oscillations with a decreasing magnitude. Figure 7 shows that if the spot exhibits some regular pattern, the resulting texture also does. A spot composed of concentric circles leads to an isotropic, enamel-like texture, the use of a small sample of a grid as a spot leads to a textile-like texture. The corresponding autocorrelation functions are easily imaginable if the rule shown in fig. 4 is used.

Such spots have three levels of detail; each level corresponds to one feature of the corresponding texture. The global size of the spot determines the scale of the white noise component, the width and spacing of the lines determine the width and spacing of the pattern, and the sharp edges lead to fractal detail.

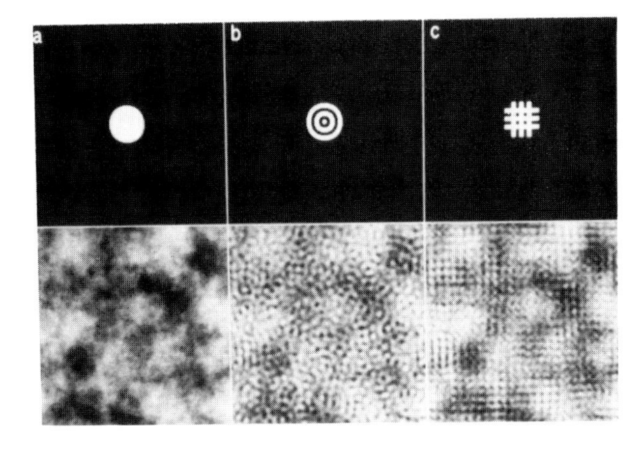


Fig. 7 Regular patterns

## 4.5 Shape

The preceding examples show that the shape of the spot strongly influences the texture. Some further examples are shown in fig. 8. The use of a square leads to a texture with strong horizontal and vertical patterns (fig. 8a). If the square is distorted into a diamond, the result is easily predictable (fig. 8b). The relation between the shape and the texture is not always so obvious. Fig. 8c shows a spot with the shape of a quarter circle. The resulting texture bears a strong resemblance with a top-view of a planet surface or lunar landscape (without craters).

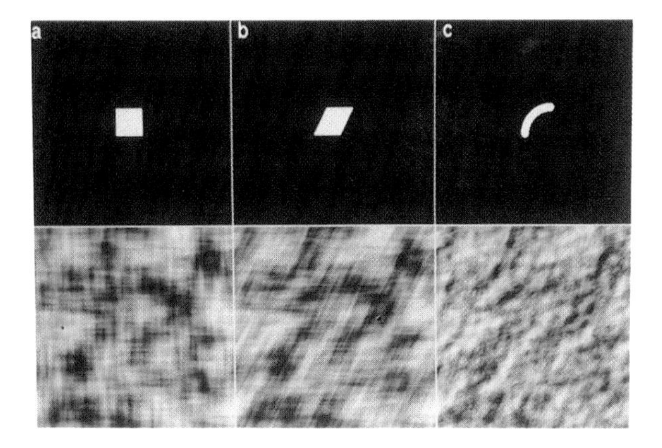


Fig. 8 Different shapes

### 4.6 Summary

In this section we have shown that the spot is a useful primitive for the design of stationary textures. In general, the relation between features of the spot and features of the texture is straightforward: size — granularity, edge — detail, rotational symmetry — isotropy, etc. Further, the spot is also of a suitable high level. Spots can, for example, be drawn with a simple drawing package. The amount of input is often minimal, because for practical applications often simple spots suffice.

## 5 APPLICATIONS

### 5.1 Scalar and vector fields

In this section various applications of variable spot noise are presented. For most images in this section, ellipses are used as spots. These ellipses are rendered via scan-conversion.

Figure 9 shows four examples of the use of texture for the visualization of scalar and vector fields. The colors indicate the value of a scalar field. A scale from saturated blue (negative) via grey to saturated red (positive) is used. The field was constructed by a B-spline approximation of randomly chosen values on a rectangular grid. In fig. 9a the variance of the texture indicates the absolute value. The type of texture indicates the sign: for negative values a $\times$-shaped spot was used, for positive values a +-shaped spot. In fig. 9b the gradients were emphasized by scaling the variance of the texture proportional to the norm of the gradient. For fig. 9c the scalar field was interpreted as a stream function $\psi(x, y)$, i.e.:

$$v_x = \frac{\partial \psi}{\partial y}, \text{ and } v_y = \frac{-\partial \psi}{\partial x}.$$

The flow velocity $\mathbf{v}$ was visualized by using an ellipse shaped spot with the long axis proportional to $|\mathbf{v}|$, the short axis proportional to $1/|\mathbf{v}|$, and the direction of the longest axis aligned with the direction of the flow. For fig. 9d the same principle was used, but here the scalar field was interpreted as a potential $p(x, y)$ that defines a vector field $\mathbf{v}(x, y)$, i.e.:

$$v_x = \frac{\partial p}{\partial x}, \text{ and } v_y = \frac{\partial p}{\partial y}.$$

In these examples texture was used to emphasize some aspect or interpretation of the field in addition to the information provided by the color. The power of the textures can be judged from figure 10, where color is used to visualize a different and unrelated scalar field. For this example the stream function texture (fig. 10c) is the strongest, the global structure of the texture can easily be discerned in spite of the unrelated colors. With the

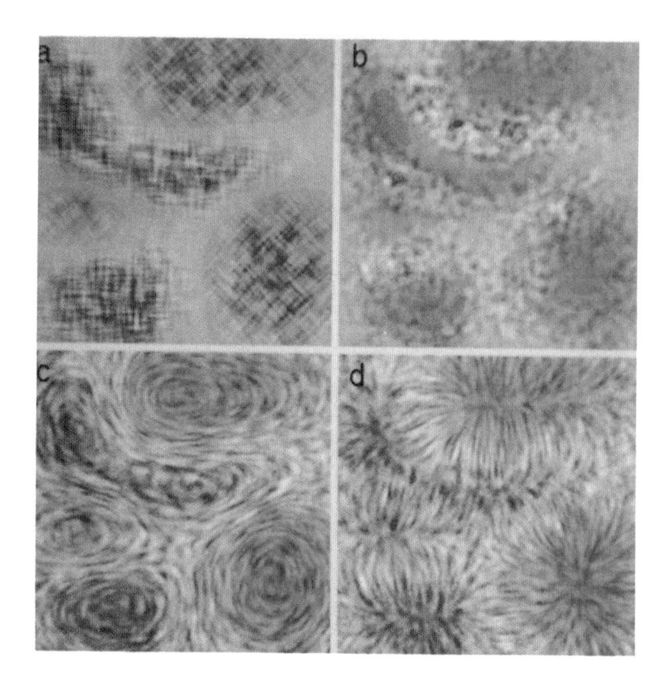


Fig. 9 Color denotes a scalar field. Texture is used to visualize attributes and interpretations of this field: (a) value, (b) gradients, (c) flow, (d) velocity potential.

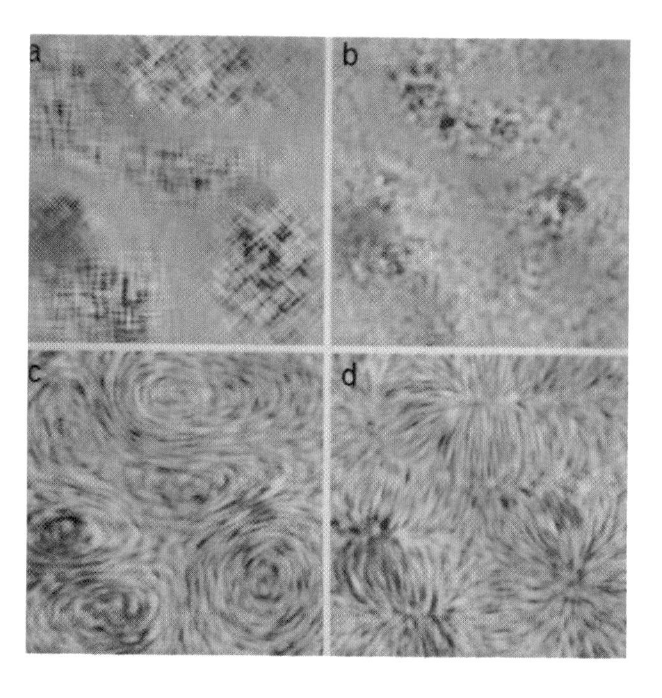


Fig. 10 Same texture as in fig. 9, color denotes an unrelated field.

other textures this is harder, but at least they still enable the observer to evaluate the value of the function depicted by the texture locally.

### 5.2 Flow visualization

The preceding example shows how spot noise can be used for capturing flow in still images. However, animations give a better impression of dynamic phenomena such as flow. In [38] a technique is presented for the animation of stationary two-

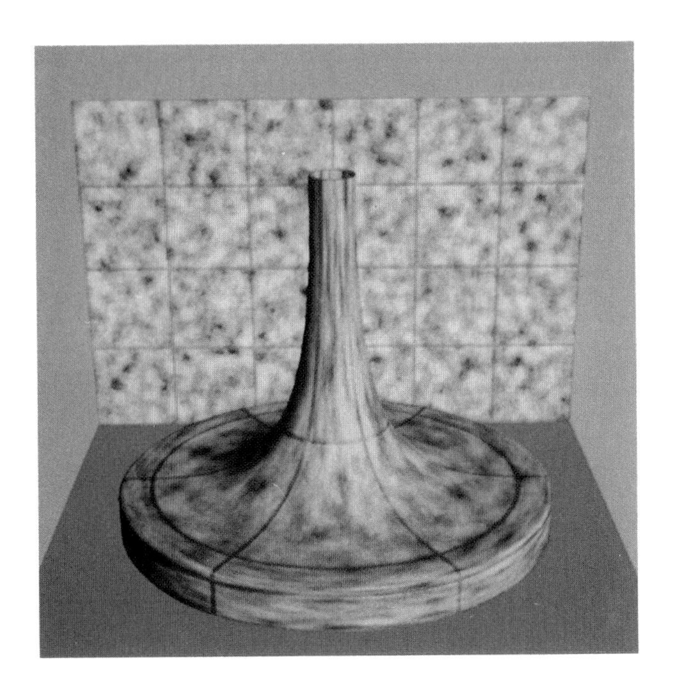

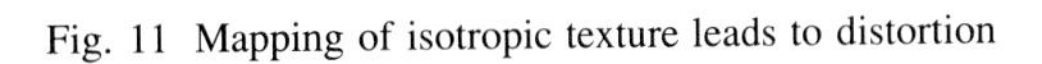

Fig. 11 Mapping of isotropic texture leads to distortion

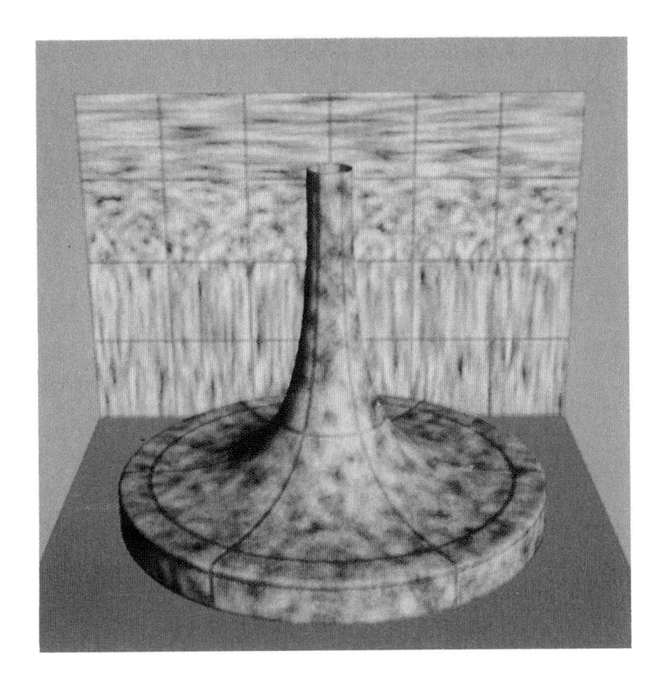

Fig. 12 Mapping of distorted texture

dimensional flow, based on particles and cyclic display. The particles used were point-shaped and no motion blur was applied, so that the flow was visualized as a noisy, moving texture. The same technique can easily be used with spot noise. Hereto we redefine the spots as moving particles. During a lifetime $T$, we let each spot glow up and decay, while it moves over a small distance. Besides a random position and a random maximal intensity, each spot also has a random time at which it starts its cycle.

Various shapes of spots can be used. The use of circles gives isotropic textures. If ellipses are used, two options are open. If the longest axis of the ellipse aligns with the direction of the flow, the visual effect is that of motion blurred particles. If the longest axis of the ellipse is perpendicular to the direction of the flow, the visual effect is that of short-crested waves, perpendicular to the flow direction.

### 5.3 Texture mapping on parametric surfaces

The preceding examples were two-dimensional. However, in many cases the data have to be visualized over curved surfaces in space. Typical applications are found in computational fluid dynamics. This requires the mapping of a texture on a surface. Texture mapping was introduced in 1974 by Catmull [2], and since then many techniques and refinements have been developed. For an overview see [12].
Figure 11 shows a problem of standard texture mapping techniques: the isotropic texture (yellow) is distorted when it is mapped onto a parametric surface (orange). The solid texturing technique [25, 28] does not suffer from these artifacts. In section 3.2 we have shown how spot noise can be generated with this method. This technique has some disadvantages however. The proposed convolution is not very efficient, and for animations the texture has to be calculated anew for each frame.

An alternative solution, similar to the one proposed in [20], is shown in figure 12. Here the texture is distorted in texture space $(u, v)$, so that when it is mapped onto the parametric surface, the resulting texture is stationary in object space $(x, y, z)$. Spot noise lends itself very well to this kind of local distortions.

Figure 13 shows a practical application of the techniques presented : the visualization of the flow around a ship calculated by the DAWSON package of MARIN [29]. The colors and the white contour lines indicate the hydrodynamic pressure on the ship hull: red denotes high, and blue denotes low pressure. The shape of the ship is visualized via shading and black equidistant cross-section lines. The technique used for rendering the lines with constant width in object space is described in [37]. The flow velocity on the hull is visualized via spot noise. Ellipses were used as spots, with the longest axis aligned with the flow direction. Texture distortion was used to compensate for the distortion due to the parametrization of the surface.

### 5.4 Image synthesis

Figure 14 shows an application that lies in between scientific visualization and realistic image synthesis. It is a frame of an animation of the dynamics of a ship in sea waves. For the modeling of the dynamics of large ships, only waves with a long wavelength (50 m and more) are of interest [4]. Further, the steepness of such waves is small, compared to shorter waves. The straightforward visualization of the results of those simulations with flat shading gives disappointing results. First, the shape of the sea surface is hard to grasp, and second, the sea surface does not look realistic, which is important when the results are presented to principals. Both problems could be solved with spot noise. Here bump mapping [1] was used for mapping the texture onto the surface. The amplitude of the spots was varied via a tent function of time to obtain a turbulent sea surface. A risk of polishing scientific results in this way, is that it can add false information. Therefore, the position of the spots was fixed, and the size of the spots was chosen such that the texture does not interfere with the results of the simulation.

For the rendering of waves, many techniques have been proposed that are more accurate and more elaborate [22, 8, 26]. The simple technique used here, however, serves its purpose in the sense that a fairly realistic result is achieved, and that the shape of the waves is presented more clearly.

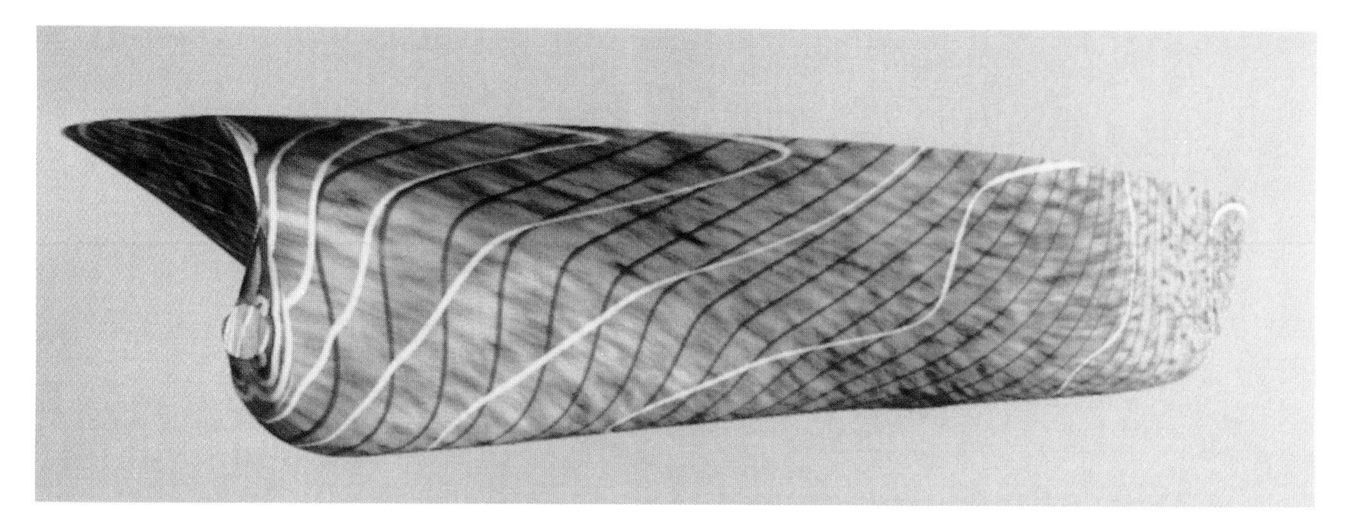

Fig. 13 Visualization of velocity and pressure on ship hull. Texture indicates flow velocity, white contour lines and color indicate pressure, black lines are cross-section lines. *Courtesy data: H.C. Raven, MARIN*

Figure 15 shows an application of space-variant spot noise that is not related to scientific visualization. First, a low-resolution letter was drawn with a painting package. Next, a height field was constructed by approximation of the values in the bitmap with a B-spline surface. Spot noise was used to give the impression of distorted material. The texture was generated with the same technique as used for fig. 9c, and bump mapping was used for mapping the texture onto the surface.

The use of texture in image synthesis leads to much more realistic images, compared to the use of uniform surfaces without detail. Images such as fig. 15 suggest that this statement can be transposed: local variation in texture, as opposed to uniform texture, can lead to even more realistic results.

## 6 DISCUSSION

### 6.1 Relations with other work

Throughout this paper, several relations of spot noise with other techniques were mentioned. Here they are discussed in order.

First, spots can be viewed as degenerated *random faults*. A disadvantage of the use of random faults is its poor efficiency. If smaller shapes are used, this disadvantage disappears, but also the fractal property at all scales disappears. However, textures do not necessarily have to be fractal to be useful and interesting.

Second, spots can be viewed as *filter kernels* that are applied to white noise. A good example is fig. 8 in [5], where the effect

Fig. 14 Visualization of ship dynamics
*Courtesy data: R. Dallinga, MARIN*

Fig. 15 P.

of an adaptive filter width on white noise is shown in the context of stochastic sampling. For such applications, the aim is removal of high frequency noise, so the filter kernels are chosen from a standard set of rotationally symmetric filter kernels like the tent, the Gaussian, and the squared cosine. The observation that the use of a banana-shaped filter leads to lunar landscapes has not yet been mentioned in image processing literature.

Third, spot noise synthesis can be considered as *sparse convolution*. In contrast to using a texture sample [17], however, a spot is used, i.e. a simple geometric pattern. The examples in section 4 show that such a simple pattern is easier to use for texture design than the autocorrelation function and the power spectrum.

Fourth, spots can be viewed as *particles*, or brush strokes, and spot noise as the result of particle systems [30, 31, 32], or abstract image representations [11]. Although it has been noted before that the use of many overlapping particles leads to texture, this has not yet been analyzed in the frequency domain.

Fifth, spot noise can be viewed as an application of Perlin's *solid texturing* technique [28]. Perlin typically uses scaling of *Noise* to achieve certain effects, here it has been shown that for controlled, local variations convolution has to be used. Another relation between the concepts discussed here and *Noise* can be found in [19]. Here sparse convolution is used, i.e. convolution of a filter kernel with a Poisson point process, for the implementation of *Noise* itself.

We conclude from the preceding discussion that spot noise can be considered as a new concept that provides a new perspective on a series of so far unrelated techniques, and that provides an elegant basis for their analysis.

### 6.2 Texture for data visualization

The application aimed at for spot noise was texture synthesis for data visualization. We therefore test spot noise here against the requirements of section 2. Spot noise does allow easy local control, and a wide variety of textures can be synthesized. The specification of a texture by the designer requires few inputs, and in most cases the relation between his input and the resulting texture is straightforward. The synthesis process is reasonably efficient. Previews can easily be generated by using few spots, so that the separate spots can be distinguished. For images such as fig. 13, the use of previews, where the object of interest is covered with iconic representations of the texture, is very useful to establish the data mapping from velocity to spot.

Another point is whether the use of texture for data visualization itself is a useful concept. The use of texture means that resolution is sacrificed, i.e. the largest scale of the texture has to be smaller than the scale of variation in the data. However, in contrast to the use of color alone, it does allow the display of vector fields, and has more degrees of freedom. Further, the examples for flow visualization show that the resulting images are suggestive, if not natural and realistic. Thus, texture is probably more suited for global and qualitative visualization of data than for detailed and quantitative analysis, and it is more suited for external presentations than for regular use by researchers.

Spot noise was used here in its simplest form: straightforward mapping of intensity values. Several techniques can be used to enhance the results. The mapping of the data to the parameters of the texture used here was continuous, an alternative is to use discrete bands or bins. Non-linear transformations of the intensity values of the texture can be applied to achieve special effects. Examples are squaring the value of texture, clamping, and the use of the value of the texture as an index in a color table. Finally, besides intensity, also the hue and saturation of the spots can be varied as a function of the data.

### 6.3 Further work

An approach to gain more insight in the relation between the shape of the spot and the resulting texture, is to attempt to derive spots from sampled real-world textures. This step is the inverse of that from spot to texture. A spot $h(\mathbf{x})$ has to be constructed such that its energy spectrum is the same as the power spectrum of the texture, and such that it corresponds to the notion of the spot used here, i.e. satisfies some criterion such as minimal size or minimal variance.

If such a technique can be developed, the application of the spot might expand from texture design to texture analysis. It is an open question whether such derived spots provide additional insight above the autocorrelation function and the power spectrum.

## 7 CONCLUSIONS

- — Texture is a useful visual primitive for data visualization;
- — Spot noise satisfies the requirements for texture for data visualization: efficient synthesis with local control, and ease of design;
- — Spot noise is an alternative to solid texturing for the synthesis of stochastic textures over curved surfaces;
- — Spot noise provides a new perspective on a series of techniques: random faults, filtering, sparse convolution, particle systems, and solid texturing;
- — Spot noise is a hot noise.

## ACKNOWLEDGEMENTS

The discussions with Teun Burgers, Wim Rijnsburger (ECN), and Pieter-Jan Stappers (Delft University of Technology — DUT) were very helpful during the development of the work described here. Valuable comments on earlier versions of this paper were given by Wim Bronsvoort (DUT), and Gonno Leendertse (ECN). I further thank Hoyte Raven, Reint Dallinga, René Huijsmans, and Hans van der Kam (Maritime Research Institute Netherlands — MARIN) for providing interesting data sets, for the pleasant cooperation, and for their support of the ECN Scientific Visualization Project.

## REFERENCES

1. BLINN, J.F. Simulation of wrinkled surfaces. *Computer graphics 12*, 3, (1978), 286-292.
2. CATMULL, E. *A subdivision algorithm for computer display of curved surfaces.* Ph.D. Thesis, Report UTEC-CSc-74-133, Computer Science Department, University of Utah, Salt Lake City, 1974.
3. CHAMPENEY, D.C. *Fourier transforms and their physical applications.* Academic Press, London, 1973.
4. DALLINGA, R. Seakeeping characteristics of SWATH vessels. In *Proceedings 13th WEGEMT Graduate school on design techniques for advanced marine vehicles and high speed displacement ships,* Delft University of Technology, 1989.
5. DIPPE, M.A.Z., AND WOLD, E.H. Anti-aliasing through stochastic sampling. *Computer Graphics 19*, 3 (1985), 69-78.
6. FOLEY, J.D., DAM, A. VAN, FEINER, S.K. AND HUGHES, J.F. *Computer graphics: principles and practice.* Second edition, Addison-Wesley, Reading, MA, 1990.

7. FOURNIER A., FUSSEL, D. AND CARPENTER, L. Computer rendering of stochastic models. *Communications ACM 25*, 6 (1982), 371-384.

8. FOURNIER, A., AND REEVES, W.T. A simple model of ocean waves. *Computer Graphics 20*, 4 (1986), 75-84.

9. GAGALOWICZ, A., AND MA, S.D. Sequential synthesis of natural textures. *Computer Graphics, Vision, and Image Processing 30* (1985), 289-315.

10. GONZALEZ, R., AND WINTZ P. *Digital image processing.* Second edition, Addison-Wesley, Reading, MA, 1987.

11. HAEBERLI, P. Paint by numbers: abstract image representations. *Computer Graphics 24*, 4 (1990), 207-214.

12. HECKBERT, P.S. Survey of texture mapping. *IEEE Computer Graphics and Applications 6*, 11 (1986), 56-67.

13. JANSEN, F.W., AND WIJK, J.J. VAN. Previewing techniques in raster graphics. *Computer & Graphics 8*, 2 (1984), 149-161.

14. JULESZ, B. Visual pattern discrimination. *IRE Trans. Inform. Theory,* IT-8 (1962), 84-92.

15. KRUEGER, W. Intensity fluctuations and natural texturing. *Computer Graphics 22*, 4 (1988), 213-220.

16. KRUEGER, W. Volume rendering and data feature enhancement. In Grave, M., and Y. le Lous (eds.), *Proceedings of the Eurographics Workshop on Visualization in Scientific Computing,* to be published by Springer-Verlag, Berlin.

17. LEWIS, J.P. Texture synthesis for digital painting. *Computer Graphics 18*, 3 (1984), 245-252.

18. LEWIS, J.P. Generalized stochastic subdivision. *ACM Transactions on Graphics 6*, 3 (1987), 167-190.

19. LEWIS, J.P. Algorithms for solid noise synthesis. *Computer Graphics 23*, 3 (1989), 263-270.

20. MA, S.D., AND GAGALOWICZ, A. Determination of local coordinate systems for texture synthesis for 3-D surfaces. In Vandoni, C.E. (ed.), *Proceedings Eurographics'85,* North-Holland, 1985, 109-118.

21. MANDELBROT, B.B. *The fractal geometry of nature.* W.H. Freeman and Co., New York, 1982.

22. MAX, N. Vectorized procedural models for natural terrains: waves and islands in the sunset. *Computer Graphics 15*, 3 (1981), 317-324.

23. MONNE, J., SCHMITT, F. AND MASSALOUX, D. Bidimensional texture synthesis by Markov chains. *Computer Graphics and Image Processing 17* (1981), 1-23.

24. MUSGRAVE, F.K., KOLB, C.E. AND MACE, R.S. The synthesis and rendering of eroded fractal terrains. *Computer Graphics 23*, 3 (1989), 41-50.

25. PEACHEY, D.R. Solid texturing of complex surfaces. *Computer Graphics 19*, 3 (1985), 279-286.

26. PEACHEY, D.R. Modeling waves and surf. *Computer Graphics 20*, 4 (1986), 65-74.

27. PEITGEN, H.-O., AND SAUPE, D. (eds.). *The science of fractal images.* Springer-Verlag, New York, 1988.

28. PERLIN, K. An image synthesizer. *Computer Graphics 19*, 3 (1985), 287-296.

29. RAVEN, H.C. Variations on a theme by Dawson. In *Proceedings of the 17th Symposium on Naval Hydrodynamics,* The Hague, 1988, 151-172.

30. REEVES, W.T. Particle systems - a technique for modeling a class of fuzzy objects. *Computer Graphics 17*, 3 (1983), 389-399.

31. REEVES, W.T., AND BLAU, R. Approximate and probabilistic algorithms for shading and rendering structured particle systems. *Computer Graphics 19*, 3 (1985), 313-322.

32. SIMS, K. Particle animation and rendering using data parallel computation. *Computer Graphics 24*, 4 (1990), 405-413.

33. TUFTE, E.R. *The visual display of quantitative information.* Graphics Press, Cheshire, Connecticut, 1983.

34. UPSON, C. The visual simulation of amorphous phenomena. *Visual Computer 1*, 2 (1986), 321-326.

35. UPSON, C. ET AL. The Application Visualization System: a computational environment for scientific visualization. *IEEE Computer Graphics and Applications 9*, 4 (1989), 30-42.

36. WIJK, J.J. VAN, BRONSVOORT, W.F., AND JANSEN, F.W. Some issues in designing user interfaces to 3D raster graphics. *Computer Graphics Forum 4* (1985), 5-10.

37. WIJK, J.J. VAN. Rendering lines on curved surfaces. In Grave, M., and Y. le Lous (eds.), *Proceedings of the Eurographics Workshop on Visualization in Scientific Computing,* to be published by Springer-Verlag, Berlin.

38. WIJK, J.J. VAN. A raster graphics approach to flow visualization. In Vandoni, C.E., and D.A. Duce (eds.), *Proceedings Eurographics'90,* North-Holland, Amsterdam, 1990, 251-259.

# Artificial Evolution for Computer Graphics

Karl Sims

Thinking Machines Corporation
245 First Street, Cambridge, MA 02142

## 1 ABSTRACT

This paper describes how evolutionary techniques of variation and selection can be used to create complex simulated structures, textures, and motions for use in computer graphics and animation. Interactive selection, based on visual perception of procedurally generated results, allows the user to direct simulated evolutions in preferred directions. Several examples using these methods have been implemented and are described. 3D plant structures are grown using fixed sets of genetic parameters. Images, solid textures, and animations are created using mutating symbolic lisp expressions. Genotypes consisting of symbolic expressions are presented as an attempt to surpass the limitations of fixed-length genotypes with predefined expression rules. It is proposed that artificial evolution has potential as a powerful tool for achieving flexible complexity with a minimum of user input and knowledge of details.

## 2 INTRODUCTION

Procedural models are increasingly employed in computer graphics to create scenes and animations having high degrees of complexity. A price paid for this complexity is that the user often loses the ability to maintain sufficient control over the results. Procedural models can also have limitations because the details of the procedure must be conceived, understood, and designed by a human. The techniques presented here contribute towards solutions to these problems by enabling "evolution" of procedural models using interactive "perceptual selection." Although they do not give complete control over every detail of the results, they do permit the creation of a large variety of complex entities which are still user directed, and the user is not required to understand the underlying creation process involved.

Many years ago Charles Darwin proposed the theory that all species came about via the process of evolution [2]. Evolution is now considered not only powerful enough to bring about biological entities as complex as humans and consciousness, but also useful in simulation to create algorithms and structures of higher levels of complexity than could easily be built by design. Genetic algorithms have shown to be a useful method of searching large spaces using simulated systems of variation and selection [5, 6, 7, 23]. In *The Blind Watchmaker*, Dawkins has demonstrated the power of Darwinism with a simulated evolution of 2D branching structures made from a set of genetic parameters. The user selects the "biomorphs" that survive and reproduce to create each new generation [3, 4]. Latham and Todd have applied these concepts to help generate computer sculptures made with constructive solid geometry techniques [9, 28].

Variations on these techniques are used here with the emphasis on the potential of creating forms, textures, and motions that are useful in the production of computer graphics and animation, and also on the potential of using representations that are not bounded by a fixed space of possible results.

### 2.1 Evolution

Both biological and simulated evolutions involve the basic concepts of genotype and phenotype, and the processes of expression, selection, and reproduction with variation.

The *genotype* is the genetic information that codes for the creation of an individual. In biological systems, genotypes are normally composed of DNA. In simulated evolutions there are many possible representations of genotypes, such as strings of binary digits, sets of procedural parameters, or symbolic expressions. The *phenotype* is the individual itself, or the form that results from the developmental rules and the genotype. *Expression* is the process by which the phenotype is generated from the genotype. For example, expression can be a biological developmental process that reads and executes the information from DNA strands, or a set of procedural rules that utilize a set of genetic parameters to create a simulated structure. Usually, there is a significant amplification of information between the genotype and phenotype.

*Selection* is the process by which the fitness of phenotypes is determined. The likelihood of survival and the number of new offspring an individual generates is proportional to its fitness measure. *Fitness* is simply the ability of an organism to survive and reproduce. In simulation, it can be calculated by an explicitly defined fitness evaluation function, or it can be provided by a human observer as it is in this work.

*Reproduction* is the process by which new genotypes are generated from an existing genotype or genotypes. For evolution to progress there must be *variation* or mutations in new genotypes with some frequency. Mutations are usually probabilistic as opposed to deterministic. Note that selection is, in general, non-random and is performed on phenotypes; variation is usually random and is performed on the corresponding genotypes [See figure 1].



©1991 ACM-0-89791-436-8/91/007/0319 $00.75

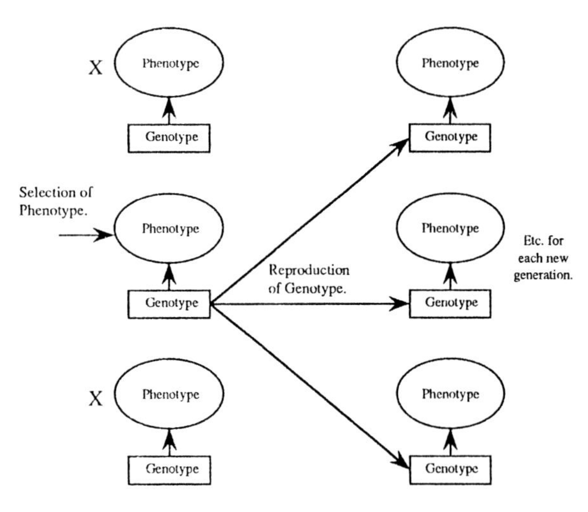


Figure 1: Phenotype selection, genotype reproduction.

The repeated cycle of reproduction with variation and selection of the most fit individuals drives the evolution of a population towards higher and higher levels of fitness.

*Sexual combination* can allow genetic material of more than one parent to be mixed together in some way to create new genotypes. This permits features to evolve independently and later be combined into a single individual. Although it is not necessary for evolution to occur, it is a valuable practice that can enhance progress in both biological and simulated evolutions.

### 2.2 Genetic Algorithms

Genetic algorithms were first developed by Holland [11] as robust searching techniques in which populations of test points are evolved by random variation and selection. They have become widely used in a number of applications to find optima in very large search spaces [6, 7, 23].

Genetic algorithms differ from the examples presented in this paper in that they usually utilize an explicit analytic function to measure the fitness of phenotypes. Since it is difficult to automatically measure the aesthetic visual success of simulated objects or images, here the fitness is provided by a human user based on visual perception. Some combinations of automatic selection and interactive selection are also utilized.

Population sizes used for genetic algorithms are usually fairly large (100 to 1000 or more) to allow searching of many test points and avoiding only local optima. At each generation, many individuals survive and reproduce to create the next generation. For the examples presented in this paper, the success of a solution is dependent on human opinion, therefore there is no single global optimum. Many local optima are potentially interesting solutions. For this reason, and also because of user interface practicality, a smaller population size has been used (20 - 40), and only one or two individuals are chosen to reproduce for each new generation.

Genotypes used in genetic algorithms traditionally consist of fixed-length character strings used by fixed expression rules. This is appropriate for searching predefined dimensional spaces for optimum solutions, but these restrictions are sometimes limiting. Koza [12, 13] has used hierarchical lisp expressions as genotypes such that the dimensionality of the search space itself can be extended to successfully solve problems such as artificial ant navigation and game strategies. Discovery systems, such as AM, Eurisko, and Cyrano, also utilize a form of mutating lisp programs [8, 14]. The examples of evolving images, volume textures, and animations presented here also use genotypic representations composed of lisp expressions, although the set of functions used includes various vector transformations, noise generators, and image processing operations, as well as standard numerical functions.

In the next section, techniques for using artificial evolution to explore samples in parameter spaces are discussed. In section 4, examples of evolving images, volume textures, and animations which utilize mutating symbolic expressions as genotypes are presented. Finally, results, suggestions for future work, and conclusions are given in the last three sections.

## 3 EXPLORING PARAMETER SPACES

Procedural models such as fractals, graftals, and procedural texturing allow a user to create a high degree of complexity with relatively simple input information [18, 19, 21, 25]. One method of procedural structure creation involves a set of $N$ input parameters each of which has an effect on a developmental process which assembles the structure. The set of possible structures corresponds to the $N$-dimensional space of possible parameter values. Consider an array of knobs, each controlling one parameter, that can be experimentally turned to adjust the results. As more options are added to the procedure for more variation of results, the number of input parameters grows and it can become increasingly difficult for a user to predict the effects of adjusting particular parameters and combinations of parameters, and to adjust the knobs effectively by hand.

An alternative approach is to sample randomly in the neighborhood of a currently existing parameter set by making random alterations to a parameter or several parameters, then inspect and select the best sample or samples of those presented. This allows exploration through the parameter space in incremental arbitrary directions without requiring knowledge of the specific effects of each parameter. This is artificial evolution in which the genotype is the parameter set, and the phenotype is the resulting structure. Selection is performed by the user picking preferred phenotypes from groups of samples, and as long as the samples can be generated and displayed quickly enough, it can be a useful technique.

### 3.1 Evolving 3D Plant Structures

The first example of artificial evolution involves 3D plant structures which can be grown using a set of "genetic" parameters. Plant generation algorithms of various types have been shown to be useful examples of procedurally generated structures [1, 16, 21, 22, 25, 29]. The model used in this work is described briefly below, but details have been omitted as the emphasis is on the evolutionary process.

Parameters describing fractal limits, branching factors, scaling, stochastic contributions, etc., are used to generate 3-dimensional tree structures consisting of connected segments. Growth rules use 21 genetic parameters and the hierarchy location of each segment in the tree to determine how fast that segment should grow, when it should generate new buds, and in which directions. The tree structures are grown in arbitrarily small increments for smooth simulation of development.

After a desirable tree structure has been evolved using interactive selection and the mutation methods described below, its phenotype can be saved for further manipulation. Solid polygonal branches can be generated with connected cylinders and cone shapes, and leaves can be generated by connecting sets of peripheral nodes with polygonal surfaces. Shading parameters, color, and bump textures can be assigned to make bark and leaf surfaces. These additional properties could also be selected and adjusted using artificial evolution, but due to the longer computation times involved to test samples, these parameters were adjusted by hand. In some cases, leaf shapes were evolved independently and then explicitly added to the tip segments of other evolved plant structures. A forest of plant structures created using these methods is shown in figure 3.

### 3.2 Mutating Parameter Sets

For artificial evolution of parameter sets to occur, they must be reproduced with some probability of mutation. There are many possible methods for mutating parameter sets. The technique used here involves normalizing each parameter for a genetic value between .0 and 1.0, and then copying each genetic value or gene, $g_i$, from the parent to the child with a certain probability of mutation, $m$. A mutation is achieved by adding a random amount, $\pm d$, to the gene. So, a new genotype, $G'$, is created using each gene, $g_i$, of a parent genotype, $G$, as follows:

For each $g_i$
  If $rand(.0, 1.0) < m$
    then $g'_i = g_i + rand(-d, d)$
      clamp or wrap $g'_i$ to legal bounds.
    else $g'_i = g_i$

The normalized values are scaled, offset, and optionally squared to give the parameter values actually used. This allows the mutation distances, $\pm d$, to be proportional to the scale of the range of valid parameter values. Squaring or raising some values to even higher powers can be useful because it causes more sensitivity in the lower region of the range of parameter values. The mutation rate and amount are easily adjusted, but are commonly useful at much higher values than in natural systems ($m = 0.2, d = 0.4$). The random value between $-d$ and $d$ might preferably be found using a Gaussian distribution instead of this simple linear distribution, giving smaller mutations more likelihood than larger ones.

### 3.3 Mating Parameter Sets

When two parameter sets are found that both create structures with different successful features, it is sometimes desirable to combine these features into a single structure. This can be accomplished by mating them. Reproducing two parameter sets with sexual combination can be performed in many ways. Four possible methods are listed below with some of their resulting effects:

1. *Crossovers* can be performed by sequentially copying genes from one parent, but with some frequency the source genotype is switched to the other parent. This causes adjacent genes to be more likely to stick together than genes at opposite ends of the sequence. Each pair of genes has a *linkage* probability depending on their distance from each other.

2. Each gene can be independently copied from one parent or the other with equal probability. If the parent genes each correspond to a point in $N$-dimensional genetic space, then the genes of the possible children using this method correspond to the $2^N$ corners of the $N$-dimensional rectangular solid connecting the two parent points. This method is the most commonly used in this work and is demonstrated in figure 2. Two parent plant structures are shown in the upper left boxes, and the remaining forms are their children.

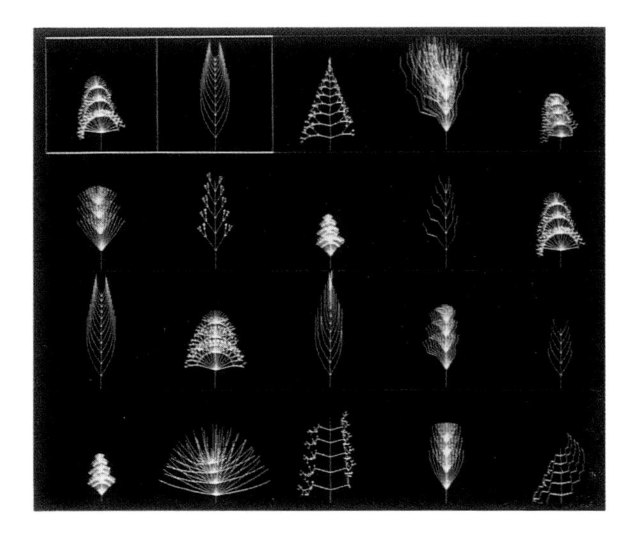

Figure 2: Mating plant structures.

Figure 3: Forest of "evolved" plants.

3. Each gene can receive a random percentage, $p$, of one parent's genes, and a $1 - p$ percentage of the other parent's genes. If the percentage is the same for each gene, linear *interpolation* between the parent genotypes results, and the children will fall randomly on the line between the $N$-dimensional points of the parents. If evenly spaced samples along this line were generated, a *genetic dissolve* could be made that would cause a smooth transition between the parent phenotypes if the changing parameters had continuous effects on the phenotypes. This is an example of utilizing the underlying genetic representation for specific manipulation of the results. Interpolation could also be performed with three parents to create children that fall on a triangular region of a plane in the $N$-dimensional genetic space.

4. Finally, each new gene can receive a random value between the two parent values of that gene. This is like the interpolation scheme above, except each gene is independently interpolated be-

tween the parent genes. This method results in possible children anywhere within the $N$-dimensional rectangular solid connecting the parent points.

Mutating and mating parameter sets allow a user to explore and combine samples in a given parameter space. In the next section, methods are presented that allow mutations to add new parameters and extend the space, instead of simply adjusting existing parameter values.

## 4 SYMBOLIC EXPRESSIONS AS GENOTYPES

A limitation of genotypes consisting of a fixed number of parameters and fixed expression rules as described above is that there are solid boundaries on the set of possible phenotypes. There is no possibility for the evolution of a new developmental rule or a new parameter. There is no way for the genetic space to be extended beyond its original definition – the $N$-dimensional genetic space will remain only $N$-dimensional.

To surpass this limitation, it is desirable to include procedural information in the genotype instead of just parameter data, and the procedural and data elements of the genotype should not be restricted to a specific structure or size.

Symbolic lisp expressions are used as genotypes in an attempt to meet these needs. A set of lisp functions and a set of argument generators are used to create arbitrary expressions which can be mutated, evolved, and evaluated to generate phenotypes. Some mutations can create larger expressions with new parameters and extend the space of possible phenotypes, while others just adjust existing parts of the expression. Details of this process are best described by the examples below.

Figure 4: Simple expression examples.

(reading left to right, top to bottom)
a. *X*
b. *Y*
c. *(abs X)*
d. *(mod X (abs Y))*
e. *(and X Y)*
f. *(bw-noise .2 2)*
g. *(color-noise .1 2)*
h. *(grad-direction (bw-noise .15 2) .0 .0)*
i. *(warped-color-noise (* X .2) Y .1 2)*

### 4.1 Evolving Images

The second example of artificial evolution involves the generation of textures by mutating symbolic expressions. Equations that calculate a color for each pixel coordinate $(x, y)$ are evolved using a *function set* containing some standard common lisp functions [26], vector transformations, procedural noise generators, and image processing operations:

> +, −, *, /, *mod, round, min, max, abs, expt, log, and, or, xor, sin, cos, atan, if, dissolve, hsv-to-rgb, vector, transform-vector, bw-noise, color-noise, warped-bw-noise, warped-color-noise, blur, band-pass, grad-mag, grad-dir, bump, ifs, warped-ifs, warp-abs, warp-rel, warp-by-grad.*

Each function takes a specified number of arguments and calculates and returns an image of scalar (b/w) or vector (color) values.

Noise generators can create solid 2D scalar and vector noise at various frequencies with random seeds passed as arguments so specific patterns can be preserved between generations [figure 4f, and 4i]. The warped versions of functions take $(U, V)$ coordinates as arguments instead of using global $(X, Y)$ pixel coordinates, allowing the result to be distorted by an arbitrary inverse mapping function [figure 4i]. Boolean operations (*and*, *or*, and *xor*) operate on each bit of floating-point numbers and can cause fractal-like grid patterns [figure 4e]. Versions of *sin* and *cos* which normalize their results between .0 and 1.0 instead of -1.0 and 1.0 can be useful. Some functions such as blurs, convolutions, and those that use gradients also use neighboring pixel values to calculate their result [figure 4h]. *Band-pass* convolutions can be performed using a difference of Gaussians filter which can enhance edges. Iterative function systems (*ifs*) can generate fractal patterns and shapes.

Details of the specific implementations of these functions are not given here because they are not as important as the methods used for combining them into longer expressions. Many other functions would be interesting to include in this *function set*, but these have provided for a fairly wide variety of resulting images.

Simple random expressions are generated by choosing a function at random from the *function set* above, and then generating as many random arguments as that function requires. Arguments to these functions can be either scalars or vectors, and either constant values or images of values. Random arguments can be generated from the following forms:

- A random scalar value such as *.4*
- A random 3-element vector such as *#(.42 .23 .69)*
- A variable such as the $X$ or $Y$ pixel coordinates.
- Another lisp expression which returns a b/w or color image.

Most of the functions have been adapted to either coerce the arguments into the required types, or perform differently according to the argument types given to them. Arguments to certain functions can optionally be restricted to some subset of the available types. For the most part these functions receive and return images, and can be considered as image processing operations. Expressions are simply evaluated to produce images. Figure 4 shows examples of some simple expressions and their resulting images.

Artificial evolution of these expressions is performed by first generating and displaying a population of simple random expressions in a grid for interactive selection. The expressions of images selected by the user are reproduced with mutations for each new generation such that more and more complex expressions and more perceptually successful images can evolve. Some images evolved with this process are shown in figures 9 to 13.

### 4.2 Mutating Symbolic Expressions

Symbolic expressions must be reproduced with mutations for evolution of them to occur. There are several properties of symbolic expression mutation that are desirable. Expressions should often be only slightly modified, but sometimes significantly adjusted in structure and size. Large random changes in genotype usually result in large jumps in phenotype which are less likely to be improvements, but are necessary for extending the expression to more complex forms.

A recursive mutation scheme is used to mutate expressions. Lisp expressions are traversed as tree structures and each node is in turn subject to possible mutations. Each type of mutation occurs at different frequencies depending on the type of node:

1. Any node can mutate into a new random expression. This allows for large changes, and usually results in a fairly significant alteration of the phenotype.

2. If the node is a scalar value, it can be adjusted by the addition of some random amount.

3. If the node is a vector, it can be adjusted by adding random amounts to each element.

4. If the node is a function, it can mutate into a different function. For example *(abs X)* might become *(cos X)*. If this mutation occurs, the arguments of the function are also adjusted if necessary to the correct number and types.

5. An expression can become the argument to a new random function. Other arguments are generated at random if necessary. For example $X$ might become *(* X .3)*.

6. An argument to a function can jump out and become the new value for that node. For example *(* X .3)* might become $X$. This is the inverse of the previous type of mutation.

7. Finally, a node can become a copy of another node from the parent expression. For example *(+ (abs X) (* Y .6))* might become *(+ (abs (* Y .6)) (* Y .6))*. This causes effects similar to those caused by mating an expression with itself. It allows for sub-expressions to duplicate themselves within the overall expression.

Other types of mutations could certainly be implemented, but these are sufficient for a reasonable balance of slight modifications and potential for changes in complexity.

It is preferable to adjust the mutation frequencies such that a decrease in complexity is slightly more probable than an increase. This prevents the expressions from drifting towards large and slow forms without necessarily improving the results. They should still easily evolve towards larger sizes, but a larger size should be due to selection of improvements instead of random mutations with no effect.

The relative frequencies for each type of mutation above can be adjusted and experimented with. The overall mutation frequency is scaled inversely in proportion to the length of the parent expression. This decreases the probability of mutation at each node when the parent expression is large so that some stability of the phenotypes is maintained.

The evaluation of expressions and display of the resulting images can require significant calculation times as expressions increase in complexity. To keep image evolution at interactive speeds, estimates of compute speeds are calculated for each expression by summing pre-computed runtime averages for each function. Slow expressions are eliminated before ever being displayed to the user. New offspring with random mutations are generated and tested until fast enough expressions result. In this way automatic selection is combined with interactive selection. If necessary, this technique could also be performed to keep memory usage to a minimum.

### 4.3 Mating Symbolic Expressions

Symbolic expressions can be reproduced with sexual combinations to allow sub-expressions from separately evolved individuals to be mixed into a single individual. Two methods for mating symbolic expressions are described.

The first method requires the two parents to be somewhat similar in structure. The nodes in the expression trees of both parents are simultaneously traversed and copied to make the new expression. When a difference is encountered between the parents, one of the two versions is copied with equal probability. For example, the following two parents can be mated to generate four different expressions, two of which are equal to the parents, and two of which have some portions from each parent:

parent1: *(* (abs X) (mod X Y))*
parent2: *(* (/ Y X) (* X -.7))*

child1: *(* (abs X) (mod X Y))*
child2: *(* (abs X) (* X -.7))*
child3: *(* (/ Y X) (mod X Y))*
child4: *(* (/ Y X) (* X -.7))*

This method is often useful for combining similar expressions that each have some desired property. It usually generates offspring without very large variations from the parents. Two expressions with different root nodes will not form any new combinations. This might be compared to the inability of two different species to mate and create viable offspring.

The second method for mating expressions combines the parents in a less constrained way. A node in the expression tree of one parent is chosen at random and replaced by a node chosen at random from the other parent. This *crossing over* technique allows any part of the structure of one parent to be inserted into any part of the other parent and permits parts of even dissimilar expressions to be combined. With this method, the parent expressions above can generate 61 different child expressions – many more than the 4 of the first method.

### 4.4 Evolving Volume Textures

A third variable, $Z$, is added to the list of available arguments to enable functions to be evolved that calculate colors for each point in $(X, Y, Z)$ space. The *function set* shown in section 4.1 is adjusted for better results: 2D functions that require neighboring pixel values such as convolutions and warps are removed, and 3D solid noise generating functions are added.

These expressions are more difficult to visualize because they encompass all of 3D space. They are evaluated on the surfaces

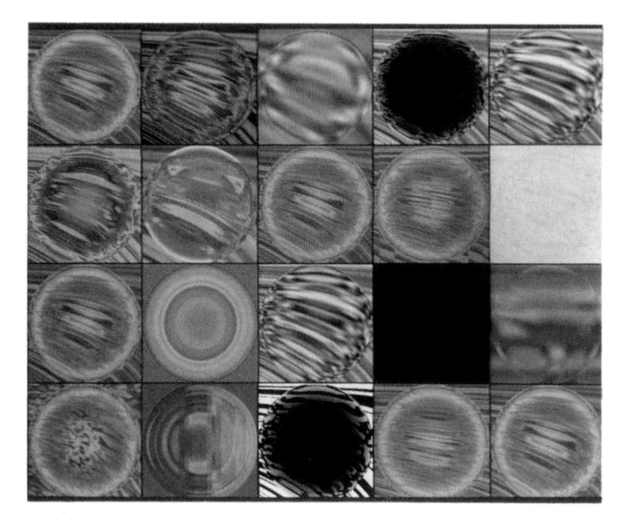

Figure 5: Parent with 19 random mutations.

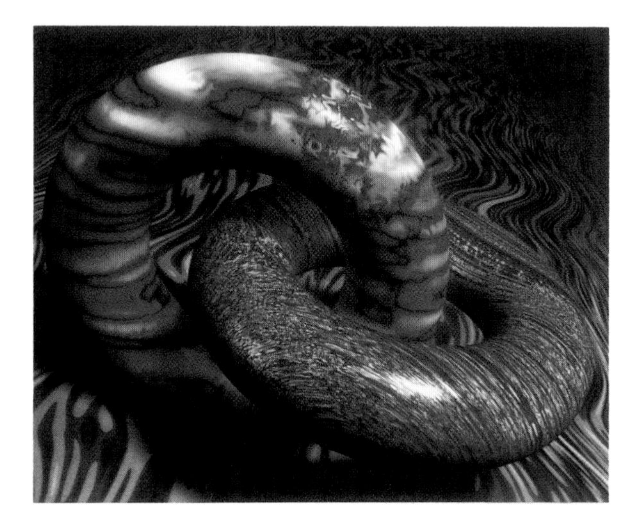

Figure 6: Marble and wooden tori.

of spheres and planes for fast previewing and selection as shown in figure 5. Evolved volume expressions can then be incorporated into procedural shading functions to texture arbitrary objects. This process allows complex volume textures such as those described in [18] and [19] to be evolved without requiring specific equations to be understood and carefully adjusted by hand. Figure 6 was generated by evolving three volume texture expressions and then evaluating them at the surfaces positions of three objects during the rendering process.

### 4.5 Evolving Animations

Several extensions to the image evolution system described above can be used to evolve moving images. Five methods for incorporating a temporal dimension in symbolic expressions are proposed:

1. Another input variable, $Time$, can be added to the list of available arguments. Expressions can be evolved that are functions of $X, Y$, and $Time$ such that different images are produced as the value of $Time$ is smoothly animated. More computation is required to generate, display and select samples because a sequence of images must be calculated. An alternate method of display involves displaying various slices of the $(X, Y, Time)$ space (although operations requiring neighboring pixel values might not receive the correct information if the values of $Time$ vary between them).

2. *Genetic cross dissolves* can be performed between two expressions of similar structure. Interpolation between two expressions is performed by matching the expressions where they are identical and interpolating between the results where they are different. Results of differing expression branches are first calculated and dissolved, and then used by the remaining parts of the expression. If the two expressions have different root nodes, a conventional image dissolve will result. If only parts within their structures are different, interesting motions can occur. This technique utilizes the existing genetic representation of evolved still images to generate in-betweens for a smooth transition from one to another. It is an example of the usefulness of the alternate level of control given by the underlying genetic information. A series of frames from a genetic cross dissolve are shown in figure 7.

3. An input image can be added to the list of available arguments to make functions of $X, Y$, and $Image$. The input image can then be animated and processed by evaluating the expression multiple times for values of $Image$ corresponding to frames of another source of animation such as hand drawn or traditional 3D computer graphics. This is effectively a technique for evolving complex image processing and warping functions that compute new images from given input images. Figure 8 was created in this way with an input image of a human face.

4. The images that use the pixel coordinates $(X, Y)$ to determine the colors at each pixel can be animated by altering the mappings of $X$ and $Y$ before the expression is evaluated. Simple zooming and panning can be performed as well as 3D perspective transformations and arbitrary patterns of distortion.

5. Evolved expressions can be adjusted and experimented with by hand. If parameters in expressions are smoothly interpolated to new values, the corresponding image will change in potentially interesting ways. For example, solid noise can be made to change frequency, colors can be dissolved into new shades, and angles can be rotated. This is another example of utilizing the underlying genetic information to manipulate images. A small change in the expression can result in a powerful alteration of the resulting image.

Finally, the techniques above can be used together in various combinations to make an even wider range of possibilities for evolving animations.

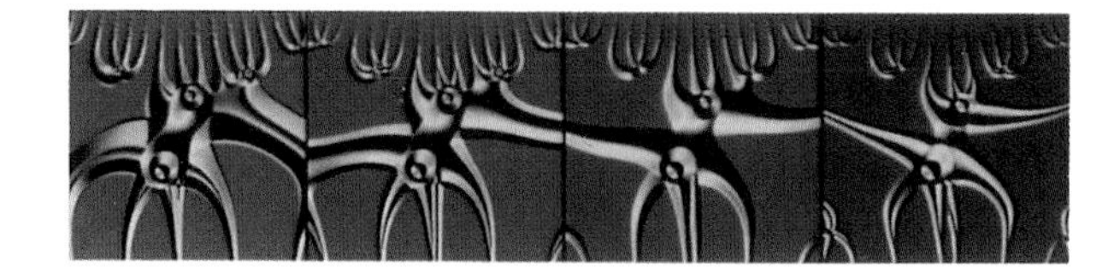

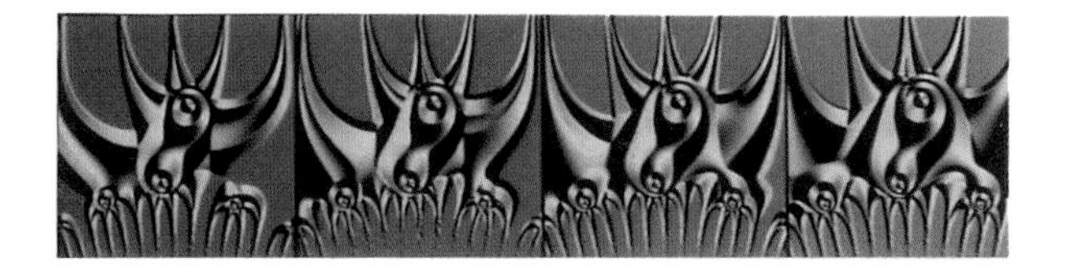

Figure 7: Frames from a "genetic cross dissolve."

Figure 8: Fire of Faces.

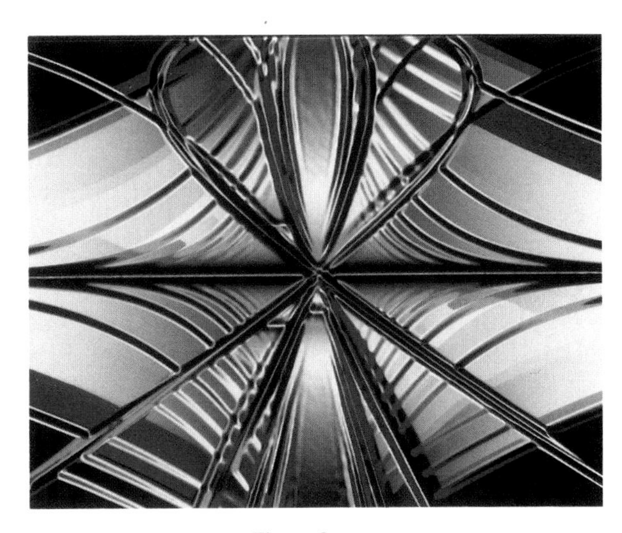

Figure 9.

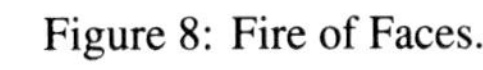

## 5 RESULTS

Evolution of 3D plant structures, images, solid textures, and animations have been implemented on the Connection Machine (R) system CM-2, a data parallel supercomputer [10, 27]. The parallel implementation details will not be discussed in this paper, but each application is reasonably suited for highly parallel representation and computation. Lisp expression mutations and combinations are performed on a *front-end* computer and the Connection Machine system is used to evaluate the expression for all pixels in parallel using *Starlisp* and display the resulting image.

3D Plant structures have been evolved and used in the animated short *Panspermia* [24]. A frame from this sequence is shown in figure 3 which contains a variety of species created using these techniques. An interactive system for quickly growing, displaying, and selecting sample structures allows a wide range of plant shapes to be efficiently created by artificial evolution. Populations of samples can be displayed for selection in wire frame in a grid format as shown in figure 2, or displayed as separate higher-resolution images which can be interactively flipped through by scrolling with a mouse. Typically between 5 and 20 generations are necessary for acceptable structures to emerge.

Images, volume textures, and various animations have been created using mutating symbolic expressions. These sometimes require more generations to evolve complex expressions that give interesting images - often at least 10 to 40 generations. Again, an interactive tool for quickly displaying grids of sample images to be selected amongst makes the evolution process reasonably efficient. [See figure 5.] The number of possible symbolic expressions of acceptable length is extremely large, and a wide variety of textures and patterns can occur. Completely unexpected kinds of images have emerged. Figure 9 was created from the following evolved expression:

*(round (log (+ y (color-grad (round (+ (abs (round (log (+ y (color-grad (round (+ y (log (invert y) 15.5)) x) 3.1 1.86 #(0.95 0.7 0.59) 1.35)) 0.19) x)) (log (invert y) 15.5)) x) 3.1 1.9 #(0.95 0.7 0.35) 1.35)) 0.19) x)*

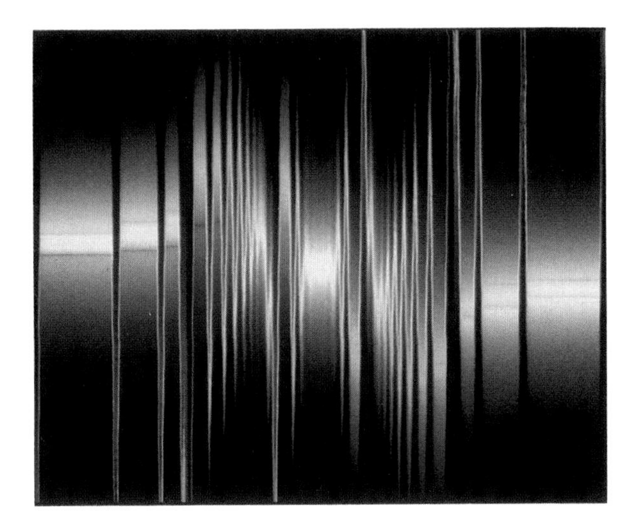

Figure 10.

Figure 11.

Figure 13 was created from this expression:

*(sin (+ (- (grad-direction (blur (if (hsv-to-rgb (warped-color-noise #(0.57 0.73 0.92) (/ 1.85 (warped-color-noise x y 0.02 3.08)) 0.11 2.4)) #(0.54 0.73 0.59) #(1.06 0.82 0.06)) 3.1) 1.46 5.9) (hsv-to-rgb (warped-color-noise y (/ 4.5 (warped-color-noise y (/ x y) 2.4 2.4)) 0.02 2.4))) x))*

Note that expressions only five or six lines long can generate images of fair complexity. Equations such as these can be evolved from scratch in timescales of only several minutes - probably much faster than they could be designed.

Figures 10, 11, and 12 were also created from expressions of similar lengths. Fortunately, analysis of expressions is not required when using these methods to create them. Users usually stop attempting to understand why each expression generates each image. However, for those interested, expressions for other figures are listed in the appendix.

Two different approaches of user selection behavior are possible. The user can have a goal in mind and select samples that are closer to that goal until it is hopefully reached. Alternatively, the user can follow the more interesting samples as they occur without attempting to reach any specific goal.

The results of these various types of evolved expressions can be saved in the very concise form of the final genotypic expression itself. This facilitates keeping large libraries of evolved forms which can then be used to contribute to further evolutions by mating them with other forms or further evolving them in new directions.

## 6 FUTURE WORK

Artificial evolution has many other possible applications for computer graphics and animation. Procedures that use various other forms of solid noise could be explored, such as those that create objects, create density functions, or warp objects [20, 15]. Procedures could be evolved that generate motion from a set of rules (possibly cellular automata, or particle systems), or that control distributions and characteristics of 2D objects such as lines, solid shapes, or brush strokes. Algorithms that use procedural construction rules to create 3D objects from polygons, or functions that generate, manipulate, and combine geometric primitives could also be explored.

These techniques might also make valuable tools in domains beyond computer simulations. New possibilities for shapes and textures could be explored for use in product design or the fashion industry.

Several variations on the methods for artificial evolution described above might make interesting experiments. Mutation frequencies could be included in the genotype itself so that they also can be mutated. This might allow for the evolution of evolvability [4]. Frequencies from the most successful evolutions could be kept as the defaults.

It might be interesting to attempt to automatically evolve a symbolic expression that could generate a simple specific goal image. An image differencing function could be used to calculate a *fitness* based on how close a test image was to the goal, and an expression could be searched for by automatic selection. Then, interactive selection could be used to evolve further images starting with that expression.

Large amounts of information of all the human selection choices of many evolutions could be saved and analyzed. A difficult challenge would be to create a system that could generalize and "understand" what makes an image visually successful, and even generate other images that meet these learned criteria.

Combinations of random variations and non-random variations using learned information might be helpful. If a user picks phenotypes in a certain direction from the parent, mutations for the next generation might have a tendency to continue in that same direction, causing evolution to have "momentum."

Also, combinations of evolution and the ability to apply specific adjustments to the genotype might allow more user control over evolved results. Automatic "genetic engineering" could permit a user to request an evolved image to be more blue, or a texture more grainy.

## 7 CONCLUSION

Artificial evolution has been demonstrated to be a potentially powerful tool for the creation of procedurally generated structures, textures, and motions. Reproduction with random variations and survival of the visually interesting can lead to useful results. Representations for genotypes which are not limited to fixed spaces and can grow in complexity have shown to be worthwhile.

Evolution is a method for creating and exploring complexity that does not require human understanding of the specific process involved. This process of artificial evolution could be considered as a system for helping the user with creative explorations, or it might be considered as a system which attempts to "learn" about human aesthetics from the user. In either case, it allows the user and computer to interactively work together in a new way to produce results that neither could easily produce alone.

An important limiting factor in the usefulness of artificial evolution is that samples need to be generated quickly enough such that it is advantageous for the user to choose from random samples instead of carefully adjusting new samples by hand. The computer needs to generate and display samples fast enough to keep the user interested while selecting amongst them. As computation becomes more powerful and available, artificial evolution will hopefully become advantageous in more and more domains.

## 8 Acknowledgments

Thanks to Lew Tucker, Jim Salem, Gary Oberbrunner, Matt Fitzgibbon, Dave Sheppard, and Zotje Maes for help and support. Thanks to Peter Schröder for being a helpful and successful user of these tools. Thanks to Luis Ortiz and Katy Smith for help with document preparation. And thanks to Danny Hillis, Larry Yaeger, and Richard Dawkins for discussions and inspiration.

## 9 APPENDIX

Figure 5, Parent expression:

(warped-color-noise (warped-bw-noise (dissolve x 2.53 y) z 0.09 12.0) (invert z) 0.05 -2.06)

Figure 6, Marble torus:

(dissolve (cos (and 0.25 #(0.43 0.73 0.74))) (log (+ (warped-bw-noise (min z 11.1) (log (rotate-vector (+ (warped-bw-noise (cos x) (dissolve (cos (and 0.25 #(0.43 0.73 0.74))) (log (+ (warped-bw-noise (max (min z 8.26) (/ -0.5 #(0.82 0.39 0.19))) (log (+ (warped-bw-noise (cos x) z -0.04 0.89) #(0.82 0.39 0.19)) #(0.15 0.34 0.50)) -0.04

Figure 12.

Figure 13.

-3.0) y) #(0.15 0.34 0.50)) y) -0.04 -3.0) x) z y) #(0.15 0.34 0.5)) -0.02 -1.79) -0.4) #(-0.09 0.34 0.55)) -0.7)

Figure 7, Cross dissolve:

(hsv-to-rgb (bump (hsv-to-rgb (ifs 2.29 0.003 (dissolve 1.77 3.67 time) 2.6 0.1 (dissolve 5.2 3.2 time) -31.0 (dissolve 23.9 -7.4 time) (dissolve 1.13 9.5 time) (dissolve 4.8 0.16 time) 20.7 4.05 (dissolve 0.48 0.46 time) (dissolve 2.94 -0.68 time) (dissolve 0.42 0.54 time) (dissolve 0.09 0.54 time))) (atan 2.25 (dissolve 0.1 0.11 time) 0.15) (dissolve 4.09 8.23 time) (dissolve #(0.41 0.36 0.08) #(0.68 0.22 0.31) time) #(0.36 0.31 0.91) (dissolve 6.2 4.3 time) (dissolve 0.16 0.40 time) (dissolve 2.08 0.23 time)))

Figure 8, Fire of Faces:

(+ (min 10.8 (warp-rel image image (bump image x 9.6 #(0.57 0.02 0.15) #(0.52 0.03 0.38) 3.21 2.49 10.8))) (dissolve #(0.81 0.4 0.16) x (dissolve y #(0.88 0.99 0.66) image)))

Figure 10:

(rotate-vector (log (+ y (color-grad (round (+ (abs (round (log #(0.01 0.67 0.86) 0.19) x)) (hsv-to-rgb (bump (if x 10.7 y) #(0.94 0.01 0.4) 0.78 #(0.18 0.28 0.58) #(0.4 0.92 0.58) 10.6 0.23 0.91))) x) 3.1 1.93 #(0.95 0.7 0.35) 3.03)) -0.03) x #(0.76 0.08 0.24))

Figure 11 is unfortunately "extinct" because it was created before the genome saving utility was complete.

Figure 12:

(cos (round (atan (log (invert y) (+ (bump (+ (round x y) y) #(0.46 0.82 0.65) 0.02 #(0.1 0.06 0.1) #(0.99 0.06 0.41) 1.47 8.7 3.7) (color-grad (round (+ y y) (log (invert x) (+ (invert y) (round (+ y x) (bump (warped-ifs (round y y) y 0.08 0.06 7.4 1.65 6.1 0.54 3.1 0.26 0.73 15.8 5.7 8.9 0.49 7.2 15.6 0.98) #(0.46 0.82 0.65) 0.02 #(0.1 0.06 0.1) #(0.99 0.06 0.41) 0.83 8.7 2.6))))) 3.1 6.8 #(0.95 0.7 0.59) 0.57))) #(0.17 0.08 0.75) 0.37) (vector y 0.09 (cos (round y y)))))

#### References


[1] Aono, M., and Kunii, T. L., "Botanical Tree Image Generation," *IEEE Computer Graphics and Applications*, Vol.4, No.5, May 1982.

[2] Darwin, Charles, *The Origin of Species*, New American Library, Mentor paperback, 1859.

[3] Dawkins, Richard, *The Blind Watchmaker*, Harlow Logman, 1986.

[4] Dawkins, Richard, "The Evolution of Evolvability," *Artificial Life Proceedings*, 1987, pp.201-220.

[5] Goldberg, D. E., *Genetic Algorithms in Search, Optimization, and Machine Learning*, 1989, Addison-Wesley Publishing Co.

[6] Grenfenstette, J. J., *Proceedings of the First International Conference on Genetic Algorithms and Their Applications*, Hillsdale, New Jersey, Lawrence Erlbaum Associates, 1985.

[7] Grenfenstette, J. J., *Genetic Algorithms and Their Applications: Proceedings of the Second International Conference on Genetic Algorithms*, 1987, (Hillsdale, New Jersey: Lawrence Erlbaum Associates.)

[8] Haase, K., "Automated Discovery," *Machine Learning: Principles and Techniques*, by Richard Forsyth, Chapman & Hall 1989, pp.127-155.

[9] Haggerty, M., "Evolution by Esthetics, an Interview with W. Latham and S. Todd," *IEEE Computer Graphics*, Vol.11, No.2, March 1991, pp.5-9.

[10] Hillis, W. D., "The Connection Machine," *Scientific American*, Vol. 255, No. 6, June 1987.

[11] Holland, J. H., *Adaptation in Natural and Artificial Systems*, Ann Arbor, MI: University of Michigan Press, 1975.

[12] Koza, J. R. "Genetic Programming: A Paradigm for Genetically Breeding Populations of Computer Programs to Solve Problems," Stanford University Computer Science Department Technical Report STAN-CS-90-1314, June 1990.

[13] Koza, J. R. "Evolution and Co-Evolution of Computer Programs to Control Independently Acting Agents," *Conference on Simulation of Adaptive Behavior* (SAB-90) Paris, Sept.24-28, 1990.

[14] Lenat, D. B. and Brown,J.S. "Why AM and EURISKO appear to work," *Artificial intelligence*, Vol.23, 1984, pp.269-294.

[15] Lewis, J. P., "Algorithms for Solid Noise Synthesis," *Computer Graphics*, Vol.23, No.3, July 1989, pp.263-270.

[16] Oppenheimer, P. "Real time design and animation of fractal plants and trees." *Computer Graphics*, Vol.20, No.4, 1986, pp.55-64.

[17] Oppenheimer, P. "The Artificial Menagerie" *Artificial Life Proceedings*, 1987, pp.251-274.

[18] Peachy, D., "Solid Texturing of Complex Surfaces," *Computer Graphics* Vol.19, No.3, July 1985, pp.279-286.

[19] Perlin, K., "An Image Synthesizer," *Computer Graphics*, Vol.19, No.3, July 1985, pp.287-296.

[20] Perlin, K., "Hypertexture," *Computer Graphics*, Vol.23, No.3, July 1989, pp.253-262.

[21] Prusinkiewicz, P., Lindenmayer, A., and Hanan, J., "Developmental Models of Herbaceous Plants for Computer Imagery Purposes," *Computer Graphics*, Vol.22 No.4, 1988, pp.141-150.

[22] Reffye, P., Edelin, C., Francon, J., Jaeger, M., Puech, C. "Plant Models Faithful to Botanical Structure and Development," *Computer Graphics* Vol.22, No.4, 1988, pp.151-158.

[23] Schaffer, J. D., "Proceedings of the Third international Conference on Genetic Algorithms," June 1989, Morgan Kaufmann Publishers, Inc.

[24] Sims, K., *Panspermia*, Siggraph Video Review 1990.

[25] Smith, A. R., "Plants, Fractals, and Formal Languages," *Computer Graphics*, Vol.18, No.3, July 1984, pp.1-10.

[26] Steele, G., *Common Lisp, The Language*, Digital Press, 1984.

[27] Thinking Machines Corporation, *Connection Machine Model CM-2 Technical Summary*, technical report, May 1989.

[28] Todd, S. J. P., and Latham, W., "Mutator, a Subjective Human Interface for Evolution of Computer Sculptures," IBM United Kingdom Scientific Centre Report 248, 1991.

[29] Viennot, X., Eyrolles, G., Janey, N., and Arques, D., "Combinatorial Analysis of Ramified Patterns and Computer Imagery of Trees," *Computer Graphics*, Vol.23, No.3, July 1989, pp.31-40.

# Specifying Gestures by Example

Dean Rubine
Information Technology Center
Carnegie Mellon University
Pittsburgh, PA
Dean.Rubine@cs.cmu.edu

## Abstract

Gesture-based interfaces offer an alternative to traditional keyboard, menu, and direct manipulation interfaces. The ability to specify objects, an operation, and additional parameters with a single intuitive gesture appeals to both novice and experienced users. Unfortunately, gesture-based interfaces have not been extensively researched, partly because they are difficult to create. This paper describes GRANDMA, a toolkit for rapidly adding gestures to direct manipulation interfaces. The trainable single-stroke gesture recognizer used by GRANDMA is also described.

**Keywords** — gesture, interaction techniques, user interface toolkits, statistical pattern recognition

## 1 Introduction

Gesture, as the term is used here, refers to hand markings, entered with a stylus or mouse, that indicate scope and commands [18]. Buxton gives the example of a proofreader's mark for moving text [1]. A single stroke indicates the operation (move text), the operand (the text to be moved), and additional parameters (the new location of the text). The intuitiveness and power of this gesture hints at the great potential of gestural interfaces for improving input from people to machines, historically the bottleneck in human-computer interaction. Additional motivation for gestural input is given by Rhyne [18] and Buxton [1].

A variety of gesture-based applications have been created. Coleman implemented a text editor based on proofreader's marks [3]. Minsky built a gestural interface to the LOGO programming language [13]. A group at IBM constructed a spreadsheet application that combines gesture and handwriting [18]. Buxton's group produced a musical score editor that uses gestures for entering notes [2] and more recently a graphical editor [9]. In these gesture-based applications (and many others) the module that distinguishes between the gestures expected by the system, known as the *gesture recognizer*, is hand coded. This code is usually complicated, making the systems (and the set of gestures accepted) difficult to create, maintain, and modify.

Creating hand-coded recognizers is difficult. This is one reason why gestural input has not received greater attention. This paper describes how gesture recognizers may be created automatically from example gestures, removing the need for hand coding. The recognition technology is incorporated into GRANDMA (Gesture Recognizers Automated in a Novel Direct Manipulation Architecture), a toolkit that enables an implementor to create gestural interfaces for applications with direct manipulation ("click-and-drag") interfaces. In the current work, such applications must themselves be built using GRANDMA. Hopefully, this paper will stimulate the integration of gesture recognition into other user interface construction tools.

Very few tools have been built to aid development of gesture-based applications. Artkit [7] provides architectural support for gestural interfaces, but no support for creating recognizers. Existing trainable character recognizers, such as those built from neural networks [6] or dictionary lookup [15], have significant shortcomings when applied to gestures, due to the different requirements gesture recognition places on a recognizer. In response, Lipscomb [11] has built a trainable recognizer specialized toward gestures, as has this author.

The recognition technology described here produces a small, fast, and accurate recognizers. Each recognizer is rapidly trained from a small number of examples of each gesture. Some gestures may vary in size and/or orientation while others depend on size and/or orientation for discrimination. Dynamic attributes (left-to-right or right-to-left, fast or slow) may be considered in classification. The gestural attributes used for classification are generally meaningful, and may be used as parameters to application routines.

The remainder of the paper describes various facets of GRANDMA. GDP, a gesture-based drawing program built using GRANDMA, is used as an example. First GDP's



©1991 ACM-0-89791-436-8/91/007/0329 $00.75

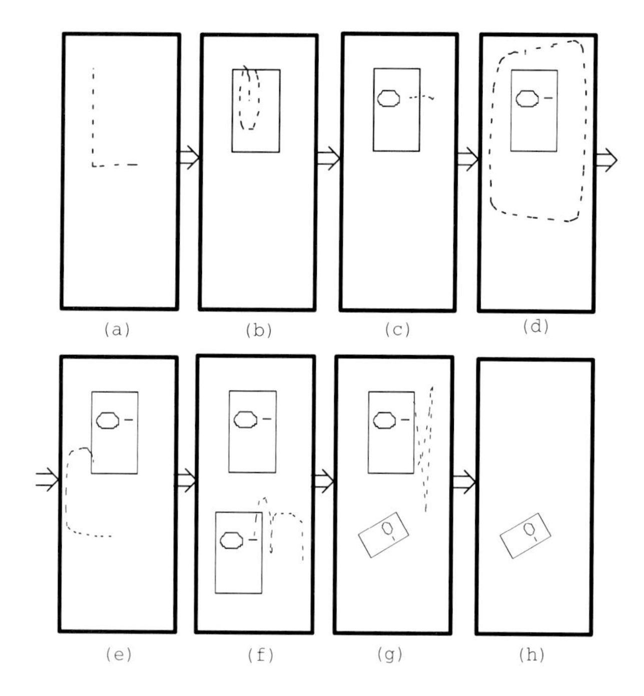


Figure 1: GDP, a gesture-based drawing program.
*The figure shows a sequence of windows in a GDP session. Gestures are illustrated with dotted lines, and the resulting graphics with solid lines. The effect of each gesture is shown in the panel which follows it; for example panel (a) shows a* rectangle *gesture, and panel (b) shows the created rectangle.*

operation is sketched from the user's point of view. Next, the gesture designer's use of GRANDMA to add gestures to a click-and-drag version of GDP is described. The details of the single-stroke gesture recognition and training algorithms are then covered. This is followed by a brief discussion of two extensions of the algorithms, eager recognition (in which a gesture is recognized as soon as enough of it has been seen to do so unambiguously) and multi-finger gesture recognition. The paper concludes with an eye toward future work. A more detailed treatment of the topics covered in this paper may be found in the author's dissertation [20].

## 2 GDP, an Example Gesture-based Application

Figure 1 shows some snapshots of GDP in action. When first started, GDP presents the user with a blank window. Panel **(a)** shows the screen as a rectangle gesture is being entered. The user begins the gesture by positioning the mouse cursor and pressing a mouse button. The user then draws the gesture by moving the mouse. The inking, shown with dotted lines in the figure, disappears as soon as the gesture is recognized.

The end of the gesture is indicated in one of two ways. If the user simply releases the mouse button immediately after drawing "L," a rectangle is created, one corner of which is at the start of the gesture (where the button was first pressed), and the opposite corner is at the end of the gesture (where the button was released). Another way to end the gesture is to stop moving the mouse for a given amount of time (0.2 seconds by default), while still pressing the mouse button. In this case, a rectangle is created with one corner at the start of the gesture, and the opposite corner at the mouse's location when the timeout occurs. As long as the button is held, that corner is dragged by the mouse, enabling the size and shape of the rectangle to be determined interactively.

Panel **(b)** of Figure 1 shows the created rectangle and an ellipse gesture, whose starting point is the center of the new ellipse. After recognition the ellipse's size and eccentricity may be interactively determined by dragging.

Panel **(c)** shows the created ellipse, and a line gesture. As expected, the start of the gesture determines one endpoint of the line, and the mouse position after the gesture has been recognized determines the other endpoint, allowing the line to be rubberbanded.

Panel **(d)** shows all three shapes being encircled by a pack gesture. This gesture groups all the objects that it encloses into a single composite object, which can then be manipulated as a unit.

Panel **(e)** shows a copy gesture: the composite object is copied and the copy is then dragged by the mouse.

Panel **(f)** shows the rotate-scale gesture. The object is made to rotate around the starting point of the gesture; a point on the object is dragged by the mouse allowing the user to interactively determine the size and orientation of the object.

Panel **(g)** shows the delete gesture, essentially an "X" drawn with a single stroke. In GDP, the start of the gesture (rather than its self-intersection point) determines the object to be deleted.

Each GDP gesture corresponds to a high-level operation. The class of the gesture determines the operation; attributes of the gesture determine the operands (scope) as well as any additional parameters. For example, the delete gesture specifies the object to be deleted, the pack gesture specifies the objects to be grouped, and the line gesture specifies the endpoints of the line. Note how gesturing and direct-manipulation are combined in a new two-phase interaction technique: when the gesture collection phase ends, gesture classification occurs, and the manipulation phase begins.

The gestures used in GDP are all single strokes. This is an intentional limitation of GRANDMA, and a marked departure from multi-stroke gesture-based systems. The single-stroke restriction avoids the segmentation problem of multi-stroke character recognition [21], allowing shorter timeouts to be used. Also, the emphasis on single strokes has led to the new two-phase interaction technique as well as to eager recognition (both of which are potentially applicable to multi-stroke gestures). Finally, with single-stroke gestures an entire command coincides with a single physical tensing and relaxing of the user, a property thought to contribute positively to the usability of user interfaces [1].

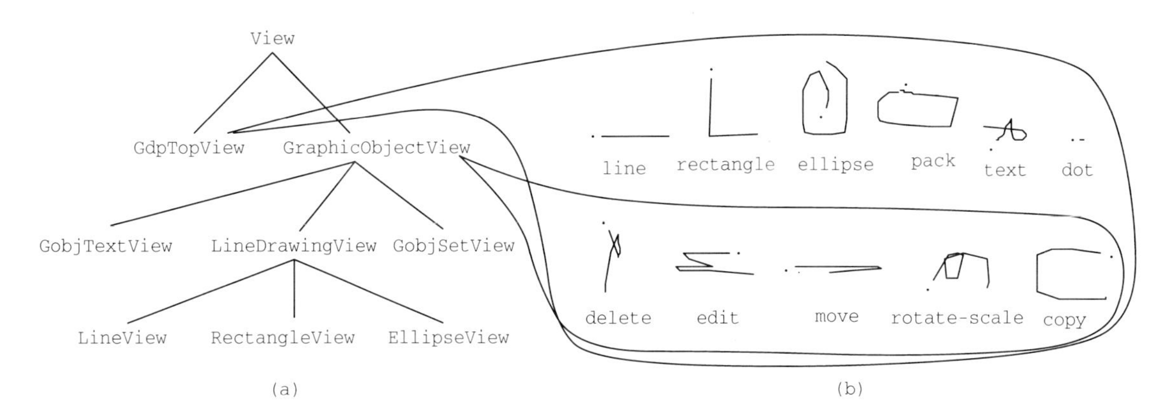


Figure 2: GDP view classes and associated gesture sets (a period marks the first point of each gesture).

One obvious disadvantage is that many intuitive symbols (e.g. "X" and "—>") are ruled out.

# 3 Design GDP's Gestures with GRANDMA

Given a click-and-drag interface to an application, the gesture designer modifies the way input is handled, leaving the output mechanisms untouched. Both the click-and-drag interface and the application must be built using the object-oriented toolkit GRANDMA. Figure 2a shows GDP's view class hierarchy, the heart of its output mechanism. The gesture designer must first determine which of the view classes are to have associated gestures, and then design a set of intuitive gestures for them. Figure 2b shows the sets of gestures associated with GDP's `GdpTopView` and `GraphicObjectView` classes. A `GdpTopView` object refers to the window in which GDP runs. A `GraphicObjectView` object is either a line, rectangle, ellipse, or text object, or a set of these.

GRANDMA is a Model/View/Controller-like system [8]. In GRANDMA, a single input event handler (a "controller" in MVC terms) may be associated with a view class, and thus shared between all instances of the class (including instances of subclasses). This adds flexibility while eliminating a major overhead of Smalltalk MVC, where one controller object is associated with each view object that expects input.

The gesture designer adds gestures to GDP's initial click-and-drag interface at runtime. First, a new gesture handler is created and associated with the `GraphicObjectView` class, easily done using GRANDMA. Figure 3 shows the gesture handler window after four gestures have been created (using the "new class" button), and Figure 4 shows the window in which seven examples of the delete gesture have been entered. Empirical evidence suggests that 15 training examples per gesture class is adequate (see Section 4.5). These 15 examples should reflect any desired variance in size and/or orientation of the gesture.

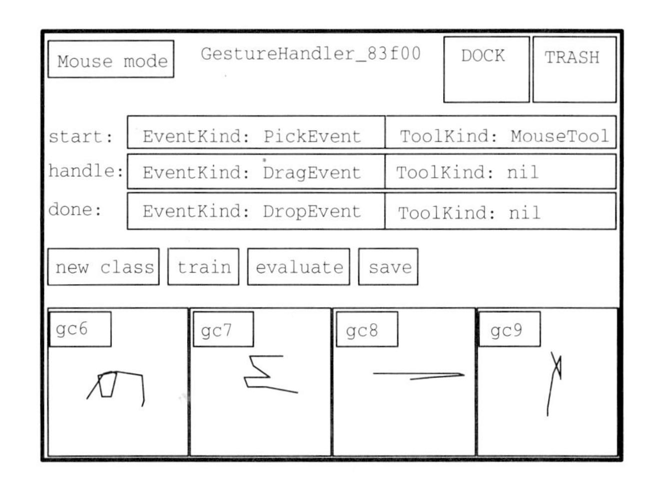


Figure 3: Manipulating gesture handlers at runtime. *This window allows gestures to be added to or deleted from the set of gestures recognized by a particular view class.*

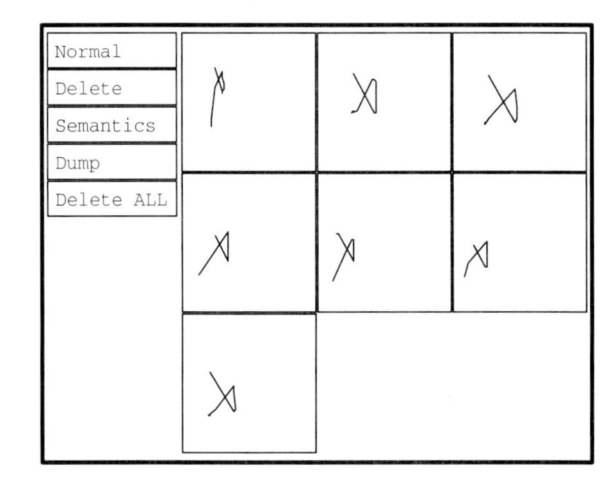


Figure 4: Entering examples of the delete gesture. *In this window, training examples of a gesture class may be added or deleted. The "Delete ALL" button deletes all the gesture's examples, making it easy to try out various forms of a gesture.*

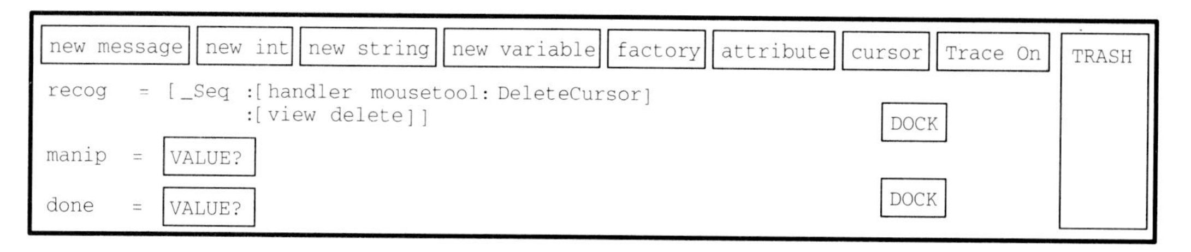


Figure 5: Editing the semantics of the delete gesture.

The "Semantics" button is used to initiate editing of the semantics of each gesture in the handler's set. Clicking on the button brings up a structured editing and browsing interface to a simple Objective-C [4] interpreter (Figure 5). The designer enters an expression for each of the three semantic components: `recog` is evaluated when the gesture is recognized (i.e. when the mouse stops moving), `manip` is evaluated on subsequent mouse points, and `done` is evaluated when the mouse button is released. The delete semantics shown in the figure simply change the mouse cursor to a delete cursor (providing feedback to the user), and then delete the view at which the gesture was aimed. The designer may now immediately try out the delete gesture, as in Figure 1g.

The designer repeats the process to create a gesture handler for the set of gestures associated with class `GdpTopView`, the view that refers to the window in which GDP runs. This handler recognizes the line, rectangle, and ellipse gestures (which create graphic objects), the pack gesture (which creates a set out of the enclosed graphic objects), the dot gesture (which repeats the last command), the text gesture (which allows text to be entered from the keyboard), and the delete, edit, move, rotate-scale, and copy gestures (which are also handled by `GraphicObjectView`'s gesture handler but when made at a `GdpTopView` simply change the cursor without operating directly on a graphic object).

The attributes of the gesture may be used in the gesture semantics. For example, the semantics of the line gesture are:

```
 recog =
    [Seq :[handler mousetool:LineCursor]
         :[[view createLine]
             setEndpoint:0
             x:<startX> y:<startY>]];
manip = [recog setEndpoint:1
          x:<currentX> y:<currentY>];
done = nil;
```

The semantic expressions execute in a rich environment. For example, `view` is bound to the view at which the gesture was directed (in this case a `GdpTopView`) and `handler` is bound to the current gesture handler. Note that `Seq` executes its arguments sequentially, returning the last value, in this case the newly created line. The last value is bound to `recog` for later use in the `manip` expression.

The example shows how the gesture attributes, shown in angle brackets, are useful in the semantic expressions. The attributes `<startX>` and `<startY>`, the coordinates of the first point in the gesture, determine one endpoint of the line, while `<currentX>` and `<currentY>`, the mouse coordinates, determine the other endpoint.

Other gestural attributes are useful in gesture semantics. For example, the length of the line gesture can be used to control the line thickness. The initial angle of the rectangle gesture can determine the orientation of the rectangle. The attribute `<enclosed>`, which contains the list of views enclosed by the gesture, is used, for example, by the pack gesture (Figure 1d).

When a gesture is made over multiple gesture-handling views, the union of the set of gestures recognized by each handler is used, with priority given to the topmost view. For example, any gesture made at a GDP `GraphicObjectView` is necessarily made over the `GdpTopView`. A delete gesture would be handled by the `GraphicObjectView` while a line gesture would be handled by the `GdpTopView`. Set union also occurs when gestures are (conceptually) inherited via the view class hierarchy. For example, the gesture designer might create a new gesture handler for the `GobjSetView` class containing an unpack gesture. The set of gestures recognized by `GobjSetViews` would then consist of the unpack gesture as well as the five gestures already handled by `GraphicObjectView`.

Space limitations preclude an explanation of how GRANDMA's object-oriented user interface toolkit is used to construct applications and their click-and-drag interfaces. Also omitted is a discussion of GRANDMA's internals. The interested reader is referred to the author's dissertation[20].

# 4 Statistical Single-Stroke Gesture Recognition

This section discusses the low-level recognition of two-dimensional, single-stroke gestures. Both the classification and the training algorithms are short and self-contained, making them useful for those wishing to include trainable gesture recognition in their interfaces.

For the present, it is assumed that the start and end of the input gesture are clearly delineated. As mentioned previously, the start of the gesture is typically indicated by the pressing of a mouse button, while the end is indicated by releasing the button or ceasing to move the mouse.

Each gesture is an array $g$ of $P$ time-stamped sample points:

$$g_p = (x_p, y_p, t_p) \qquad 0 \le p < P$$

Some simple preprocessing is done to eliminate jiggle: an input point within 3 pixels of the previous input point is discarded.

The gesture recognition problem is stated as follows: There is a set of $C$ gesture classes, numbered 0 through $C-1$. Each class is specified by example gestures. Given an input gesture $g$, determine the class to which $g$ belongs (*i.e.* the class whose members are most like $g$).

Statistical gesture recognition is done in two steps. First, a vector of features, $\mathbf{f} = [f_1, \ldots, f_F]$, is extracted from the input gesture. Then, the feature vector is classified as one of the $C$ possible gestures via a linear machine.

## 4.1 The Features

Features were chosen according to the following criteria. Each feature should be incrementally computable in constant time per input point, which allows arbitrarily large gestures to be handled as efficiently as small ones. Since the classification algorithm performs poorly when a class has a feature with a multimodal distribution, a small change in the input should result in a correspondingly small change in each feature. Each feature should be meaningful so that is can be used in gesture semantics as well as for recognition. Finally, there should be enough features to provide differentiation between all gestures that might reasonably be expected, but, for efficiency reasons, there should not be too many.

Figure 6 shows the actual features used, both geometrically and algebraically. The features are the cosine ($f_1$) and the sine ($f_2$) of the initial angle of the gesture, the length ($f_3$) and the angle ($f_4$) of the bounding box diagonal, the distance ($f_5$) between the first and the last point, the cosine ($f_6$) and the sine ($f_7$) of the angle between the first and last point, the total gesture length ($f_8$), the total angle traversed ($f_9$), the sum of the absolute value of the angle at each mouse point ($f_{10}$), the sum of the squared value of those angles ($f_{11}$), the maximum speed (squared) of the gesture ($f_{12}$), and the duration of the gesture ($f_{13}$).

An angle's cosine and sine are used as features rather than the angle itself to avoid a discontinuity as the angle passes through $2\pi$ and wraps to 0. The "sharpness" feature, $f_{11}$, is needed to distinguish between smooth gestures and those with sharp angles, e.g. "U" and "V." Features $f_{12}$ and $f_{13}$ add a dynamic component so that gestures are not simply static pictures. Some applications may wish to disable these two features. The initial angle features, $f_1$ and $f_2$, are computed from the first and third mouse point because the result is generally less noisy than when computed from the first two points.

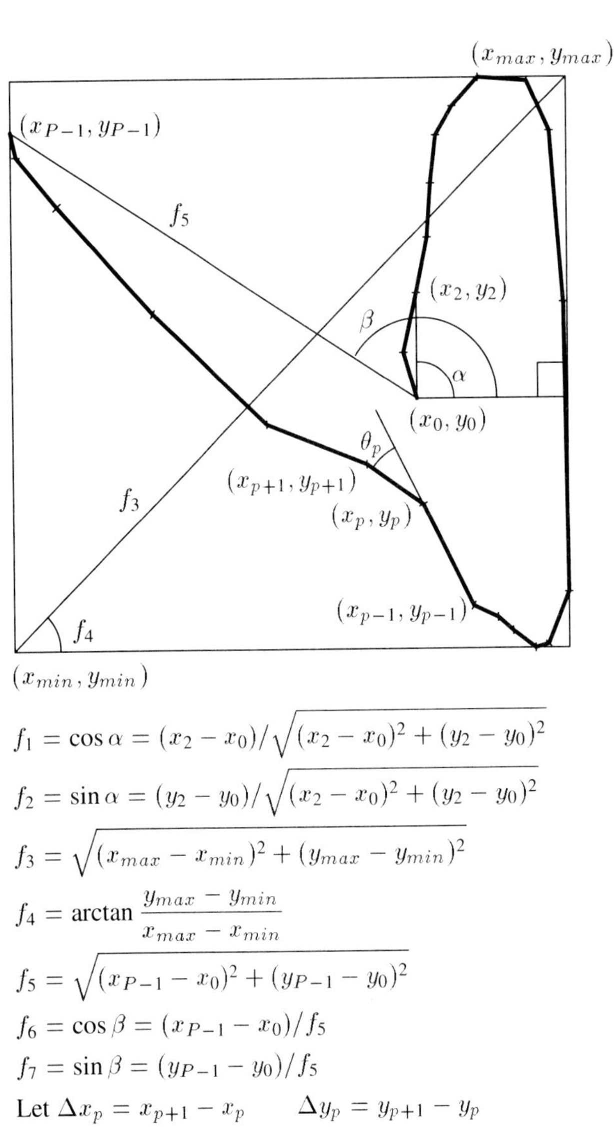


$$f_1 = \cos\alpha = (x_2 - x_0)/\sqrt{(x_2 - x_0)^2 + (y_2 - y_0)^2}$$

$$f_2 = \sin\alpha = (y_2 - y_0)/\sqrt{(x_2 - x_0)^2 + (y_2 - y_0)^2}$$

$$f_3 = \sqrt{(x_{max} - x_{min})^2 + (y_{max} - y_{min})^2}$$

$$f_4 = \arctan \frac{y_{max} - y_{min}}{x_{max} - x_{min}}$$

$$f_5 = \sqrt{(x_{P-1} - x_0)^2 + (y_{P-1} - y_0)^2}$$

$$f_6 = \cos\beta = (x_{P-1} - x_0)/f_5$$

$$f_7 = \sin\beta = (y_{P-1} - y_0)/f_5$$

Let $\Delta x_p = x_{p+1} - x_p \qquad \Delta y_p = y_{p+1} - y_p$

$$f_8 = \sum_{p=0}^{P-2} \sqrt{\Delta x_p^2 + \Delta y_p^2}$$

Let $\theta_p = \arctan \dfrac{\Delta x_p \Delta y_{p-1} - \Delta x_{p-1} \Delta y_p}{\Delta x_p \Delta x_{p-1} + \Delta y_p \Delta y_{p-1}}$

$$f_9 = \sum_{p=1}^{P-2} \theta_p$$

$$f_{10} = \sum_{p=1}^{P-2} |\theta_p|$$

$$f_{11} = \sum_{p=1}^{P-2} \theta_p^2$$

Let $\Delta t_p = t_{p+1} - t_p$

$$f_{12} = \max_{p=0}^{P-2} \frac{\Delta x_p^2 + \Delta y_p^2}{\Delta t_p^2}$$

$$f_{13} = t_{P-1} - t_0$$

Figure 6: Features used to identify strokes

The aforementioned feature set was empirically determined by the author to work well on a number of different gesture sets. Unfortunately, there are cases in which the features fail to distinguish between obviously different gestures (e.g. because the features take no account of the ordering of angles in a gesture). In such cases an additional feature may be added to discriminate between the thus far indistinguishable gestures. The extensibility of the feature set is a potential advantage that this statistical gesture recognition algorithm has over most known methods for online character recognition [21].

## 4.2 Gesture Classification

Given the feature vector $\mathbf{f}$ computed for an input gesture $g$, the classification algorithm is quite simple and efficient. Associated with each gesture class is a linear evaluation function over the features. Gesture class $c$ has weights $w_{\hat{c}i}$ for $0 \leq i \leq F$, where $F$ is the number of features, currently 13. (Per-gesture-class variables are written with hatted subscripts to indicate their class.) The evaluations, $v_{\hat{c}}$, are calculated as follows:

$$v_{\hat{c}} = w_{\hat{c}0} + \sum_{i=1}^{F} w_{\hat{c}i} f_i \qquad 0 \leq c < C \tag{1}$$

The classification of gesture $g$ is simply the $c$ which maximizes $v_{\hat{c}}$. The possibility of rejecting $g$ is discussed in section 4.4.

## 4.3 Training

Practitioners of pattern recognition will recognize this as the classic linear discriminator [5]. The training problem is to determine the weights $w_{\hat{c}i}$ from the example gestures. Iterative techniques were avoided to get efficient training. Instead, a well-known closed formula is used. The formula is known to produce optimal classifiers under certain rather strict normality assumptions on the per-class distributions of feature vectors. Even though these assumptions generally do not hold in practice, the formula still produces good classifiers.

Let $f_{\hat{c}ei}$ be the $i^{\text{th}}$ feature of the $e^{\text{th}}$ example of gesture class $c$, $0 \leq e < E_{\hat{c}}$, where $E_{\hat{c}}$ is the number of training examples of class $c$. The sample estimate of the mean feature vector per class, $\overline{\mathbf{f}}_{\hat{c}}$, is simply the average of the features in the class:

$$\overline{f}_{\hat{c}i} = \frac{1}{E_{\hat{c}}} \sum_{e=0}^{E_{\hat{c}}-1} f_{\hat{c}ei}$$

The sample estimate of the covariance matrix of class $c$, $\mathbf{\Sigma}_{\hat{c}ij}$, is computed as:

$$\mathbf{\Sigma}_{\hat{c}ij} = \sum_{e=0}^{E_{\hat{c}}-1} (f_{\hat{c}ei} - \overline{f}_{\hat{c}i})(f_{\hat{c}ej} - \overline{f}_{\hat{c}j})$$

(For convenience in the next step, the usual $1/(E_{\hat{c}} - 1)$ factor has not been included in $\mathbf{\Sigma}_{\hat{c}ij}$.) The $\mathbf{\Sigma}_{\hat{c}ij}$ are averaged to yield $\mathbf{\Sigma}_{ij}$, an estimate of the common covariance matrix.

$$\mathbf{\Sigma}_{ij} = \frac{\sum_{c=0}^{C-1} \mathbf{\Sigma}_{\hat{c}ij}}{-C + \sum_{c=0}^{C-1} E_{\hat{c}}} \tag{2}$$

The sample estimate of the common covariance matrix $\mathbf{\Sigma}_{ij}$ is then inverted. The result is denoted $(\mathbf{\Sigma}^{-1})_{ij}$. The weights $w_{\hat{c}j}$ are computed from the estimates as follows:

$$w_{\hat{c}j} = \sum_{i=1}^{F} (\mathbf{\Sigma}^{-1})_{ij} \overline{f}_{\hat{c}i} \qquad 1 \leq j \leq F$$

$$w_{\hat{c}0} = -\frac{1}{2} \sum_{i=1}^{F} w_{\hat{c}i} \overline{f}_{\hat{c}i}$$

A singular matrix can usually be handled by discarding a subset of the features.

## 4.4 Rejection

A linear classifier will always classify a gesture $g$ as one of the $C$ gesture classes. This section presents methods for rejecting ambiguous gestures and outliers.

Intuitively, if there is a near tie for the maximum per-class evaluation function $v_{\hat{i}}$ the gesture is ambiguous. Given a gesture $g$ with feature vector $\mathbf{f}$ classified as class $i$ (i.e. $v_{\hat{i}} > v_{\hat{j}}$ for all $j \neq i$)

$$\tilde{P}(\hat{i} \mid g) = \frac{1}{\sum_{j=0}^{C-1} e^{(v_{\hat{j}} - v_{\hat{i}})}}$$

is an estimate of the probability that $g$ was classified correctly. Rejecting gestures in which $\tilde{P}(\hat{i} \mid g) < 0.95$ works well in practice.

The Mahalanobis distance [5] can be used to determine number of standard deviations a gesture $g$ is away from the mean of its chosen class $i$.

$$\delta^2 = \sum_{j=1}^{F} \sum_{k=1}^{F} (\mathbf{\Sigma}^{-1})_{jk} (f_j - \overline{f}_{\hat{i}j})(f_k - \overline{f}_{\hat{i}k})$$

Rejecting gestures for which $\delta^2 > \frac{1}{2}F^2$ eliminates the obvious outliers. Unfortunately, this thresholding also tends to reject many seemingly good gestures, making it less than ideal.

Generally, a gesture-based system will ignore a rejected gesture, and the user can immediately try the gesture again. In contrast, the effect of a misclassified gesture will typically be undone before the gesture is retried. If undo is quick

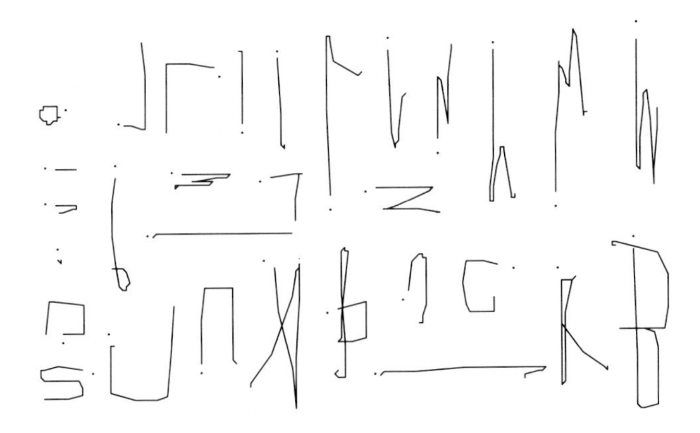

Figure 7: GSCORE gesture set used for evaluation (a period marks the start of each gesture).

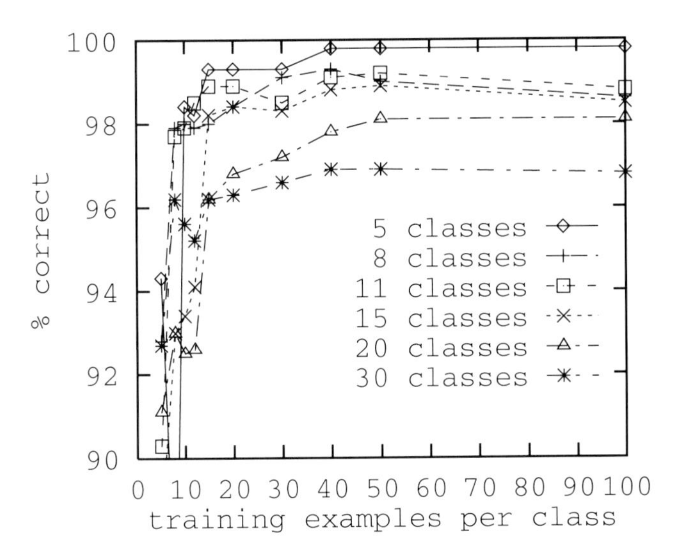


Figure 8: Recognition rate vs. training set size.

and easy, the time spent retrying the gesture will dominate. Since rejection increases the number of gestures that need to be redone (because inevitably some gestures that would have been classified correctly will be rejected), rejection should be disabled in applications with good undo facilities. Of course in applications without undo, rejection is preferable to misclassification and should be enabled.

## 4.5 Evaluation

Despite their simplicity, classifiers trained using this algorithm usually perform quite well in practice. Performance has been evaluated on 10 different gesture sets. Figure 8 shows some typical results for the gesture set shown in Figure 7. The gestures are from GSCORE, an editor for musical scores. The plot shows the recognition rate as a function of the number of training examples per class for various subsets of the GSCORE gestures. In the cases where 15 or fewer gesture classes are recognized by a classifier trained with 15 or more examples per class, at least 98% of the test gestures are classified correctly. The 30 class classifier trained with 40 examples per class has a 97% recognition rate. Recognition dropped to 96% when given only 15 training examples per class. Many of the misclassifications can be attributed to poor mouse tracking.

Figure 9 shows the recognition rate for five gesture sets. Each set was trained on fifteen examples per class and evaluated on 50 test gestures per class. In all cases the author was the gesturer; preliminary evaluations on other subjects show comparable performance.

On a DEC MicroVAX II, the classifier spends 0.2 milliseconds per mouse point calculating the feature vector, and then 0.3 msec per class to do the classification (8 msec to choose between 30 classes). Training time is 4 msec per training example, 80 msec to compute and invert the covariance matrix, and 5 msec per class to compute the weights. The per-mouse point and per-gesture calculations are done incrementally as the gesture is entered and thus never noticed by the user. Performance improves by a factor of 12 on a DEC PMAX-3100. In short, the classification time is negligible and the training is fast enough to be done in response to user input, such as the first time a gesture is made over a particular view class.

# 5 Extensions

Versions of GDP utilizing eager recognition and multi-finger recognition have been built by the author to demonstrate the feasibility of the concepts. Unfortunately, space limitations preclude a thorough discussion. For more details, the reader is again referred to [20].

## 5.1 Eager Recognition

Eager recognition refers to the recognition of gestures as soon as they are unambiguous. The author's approach [19, 20] uses the basic stroke recognition algorithm to classify subgestures (gestures in progress) as ambiguous or unambiguous. Note that classification occurs on every mouse point.

In GDP, a user presses a mouse button, enters the "L" gesture, stops and waits for a rectangle to appear (while still holding the button), and then manipulates one of the rectangle's corners. Eager recognition eliminates the stop: the system recognizes the rectangle gesture *while the user is making it*, and then creates the rectangle, allowing the user to drag the corner. What begins as a gesture changes into a rubberbanding interaction with no explicit indication from the user.

## 5.2 Multi-finger recognition

Recognizing gestures made with multiple fingers simultaneously has recently become of interest due to the availability of new input devices, including multi-finger touch pads [10],

| Set Name | Gesture Classes | Number of Classes | Recognition Rate |
|---|---|---|---|
| Coleman | 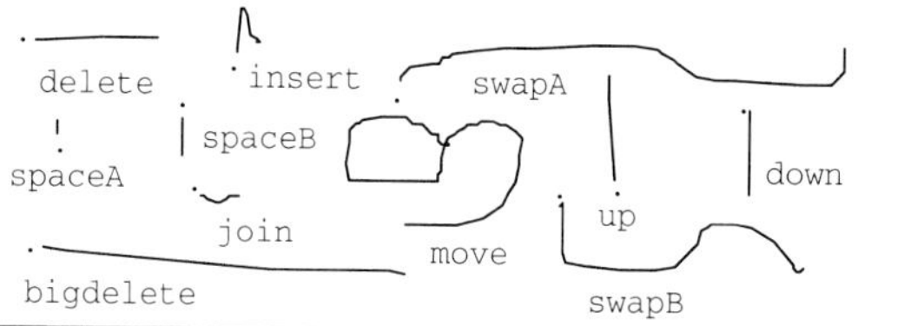 delete insert swapA spaceA spaceB down join up move bigdelete swapB | 11 | 100.0% |
| Digits | 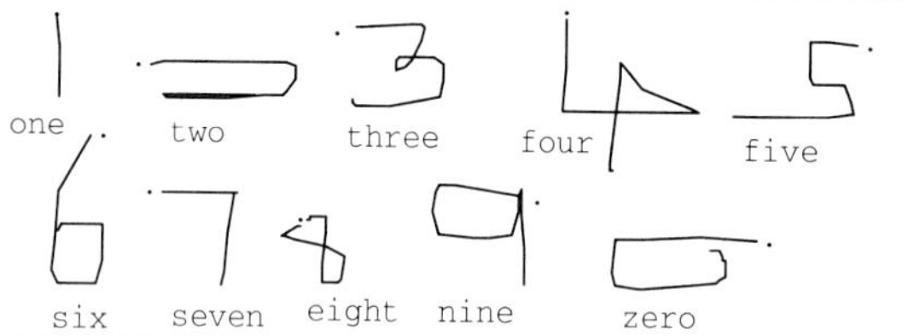 one two three four five six seven eight nine zero | 10 | 98.5% |
| Let:a-m | 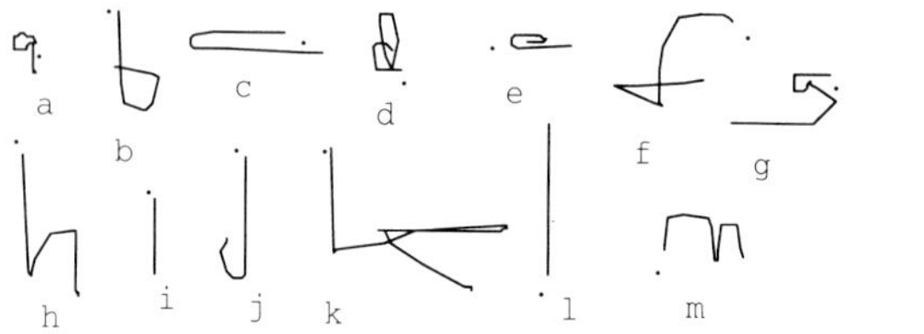 a b c d e f g h i j k l m | 13 | 99.2% |
| Let:n-z | 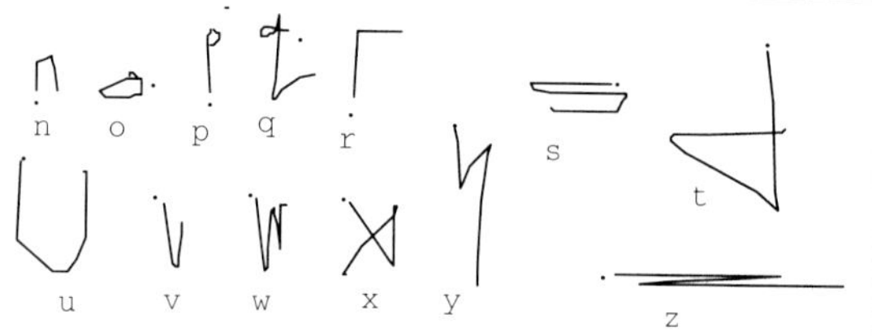 n o p q r s t u v w x y z | 13 | 98.4% |
| Letters | Union of Let:a-m and Let:n-z | 26 | 97.1% |

Figure 9: Recognition rates for various gesture sets.

the VPL DataGlove [22], and the Sensor Frame [12]. By treating the multi-finger input as multi-path data (e.g. the paths of the fingertips) the single-stroke recognition algorithm may be applied to each of the paths individually and the results combined to classify the multi-path gesture. A decision tree is used to combine the single-stroke classifications, and a set of global features is used to discriminate between different multi-path gestures whose corresponding paths are indistinguishable.

Note that the stroke recognition cannot immediately be applied to DataGlove finger paths, because the DataGlove has no way of indicating the start of a gesture, and also because the paths are three dimensional. This is one area for future work.

## 6 Conclusion and Future Directions

This paper described GRANDMA, a tool that dramatically reduces the effort involved in creating a gesture-based interface to an application. Starting with an application with a traditional direct manipulation interface, GRANDMA lets the designer specify gestures by example, associate those gestures with views in the interface, and specify the effect each gesture has on its associated views through a simple programming interface. Since the attributes of the gesture are available for use as parameters to application routines, a single gesture can be very powerful.

Some parameters of application commands are best determined at the time the gesture is recognized; others require subsequent manipulation and feedback to determine. This is the motivation behind the two-phase interaction technique that combines gesturing and direct manipulation. After recognition the user can manipulate additional parameters as long as the mouse button remains pressed. Eager recognition smooths the transition from gesturing to manipulation.

The foundation of this work is a new algorithm for recognizing single-stroke gestures specified by example. The combination of a meaningful, extensible feature set and well-understood statistical pattern recognition techniques appears to be flexible enough to evolve beyond two-dimensional single-stroke gesture recognition into the gesture recognizers of the future. The recognition technology is in no way dependent on the GRANDMA toolkit and its integration into other systems is strongly encouraged.

Based on the experience with GRANDMA, gestures are now being integrated into the NeXT Application Kit [16], the Andrew Toolkit [17], and Garnet [14]. This should allow gestural interfaces to be added to existing applications, enabling further use and study of this promising input technique.

## Acknowledgements

I wish to thank CMU's School of Computer Science and CMU's Information Technology Center for their support of this work. I am also grateful to Roger Dannenberg and some anonymous reviewers for their helpful criticism of an earlier draft of this paper. Special thanks goes to Klaus Gross, whose detailed comments greatly improved this paper.

## References

[1] BUXTON, W. Chunking and phrasing and the design of human-computer dialogues. In *Information Processing 86* (North Holland, 1986), Elsevier Science Publishers B.V.

[2] BUXTON, W., SNIDERMAN, R., REEVES, W., PATEL, S., AND BAECKER, R. The evolution of the SSSP score-editing tools. In *Foundations of Computer Music*, C. Roads and J. Strawn, Eds. MIT Press, Cambridge, Mass., 1985, ch. 22, pp. 387–392.

[3] COLEMAN, M. L. Text editing on a graphic display device using hand-drawn proofreader's symbols. In *Pertinent Concepts in Computer Graphics, Proceedings of the Second University of Illinois Conference on Computer Graphics*, M. Faiman and J. Nievergelt, Eds. University of Illinois Press, Urbana, Chicago, London, 1969, pp. 283–290.

[4] COX, B. J. *Object Oriented Programming: An Evolutionary Approach*. Addison-Wesley, 1986.

[5] DUDA, R., AND HART, P. *Pattern Classification and Scene Analysis*. Wiley Interscience, 1973.

[6] GUYON, I., ALBRECHT, P., CUN, Y. L., DENKER, J., AND HUBBARD, W. Design of a neural network character recognizer for a touch terminal. *Pattern Recognition* (forthcoming).

[7] HENRY, T., HUDSON, S., AND NEWELL, G. Integrating gesture and snapping into a user interface toolkit. In *UIST '90* (1990), ACM, pp. 112–122.

[8] KRASNER, G. E., AND POPE, S. T. A description of the Model-View-Controller user interface paradigm in the Smalltalk-80 system. *Journal of Object Oriented Programming 1*, 3 (Aug. 1988), 26–49.

[9] KURTENBACH, G., AND BUXTON, W. GEdit: A test bed for editing by contiguous gestures. To be published in SIGCHI Bulletin, 1991.

[10] LEE, S., BUXTON, W., AND SMITH, K. A multi-touch three dimensional touch tablet. In *Proceedings of CHI'85 Conference on Human Factors in Computing Systems* (1985), ACM, pp. 21–25.

[11] LIPSCOMB, J. S. A trainable gesture recognizer. *Pattern Recognition* (1991). Also available as IBM Tech Report RC 16448 (#73078).

[12] MCAVINNEY, P. Telltale gestures. *Byte 15*, 7 (July 1990), 237–240.

[13] MINSKY, M. R. Manipulating simulated objects with real-world gestures using a force and position sensitive screen. *Computer Graphics 18*, 3 (July 1984), 195–203.

[14] MYERS, B. A., GIUSE, D., DANNENBERG, R. B., ZANDEN, B. V., KOSBIE, D., PERVIN, E., MICKISH, A., AND MARCHAL, P. Comprehensive support for graphical, highly-interactive user interfaces: The Garnet user interface development environment. *IEEE Computer 23*, 11 (Nov 1990).

[15] NEWMAN, W., AND SPROULL, R. *Principles of Interactive Computer Graphics*. McGraw-Hill, 1979.

[16] NEXT. *The NeXT System Reference Manual*. NeXT, Inc., 1989.

[17] PALAY, A., HANSEN, W., KAZAR, M., SHERMAN, M., WADLOW, M., NEUENDORFFER, T., STERN, Z., BADER, M., AND PETERS, T. The Andrew toolkit: An overview. In *Proceedings of the USENIX Technical Conference* (Dallas, February 1988), pp. 11–23.

[18] RHYNE, J. R., AND WOLF, C. G. Gestural interfaces for information processing applications. Tech. Rep. RC12179, IBM T.J. Watson Research Center, IBM Corporation, P.O. Box 218, Yorktown Heights, NY 10598, Sept. 1986.

[19] RUBINE, D. Integrating gesture recognition and direct manipulation. In *Proceedings of the Summer '91 USENIX Technical Conference* (1991).

[20] RUBINE, D. *The Automatic Recognition of Gestures*. PhD thesis, School of Computer Science, Carnegie Mellon University, forthcoming, 1991.

[21] SUEN, C., BERTHOD, M., AND MORI, S. Automatic recognition of handprinted characters: The state of the art. *Proceedings of the IEEE 68*, 4 (April 1980), 469–487.

[22] ZIMMERMAN, T., LANIER, J., BLANCHARD, C., BRYSON, S., AND HARVILL, Y. A hand gesture interface device. *CHI+GI* (1987), 189–192.

# Computer Animation of Knowledge-Based Human Grasping

Hans Rijpkema and Michael Girard

SCAN (National Institute for Computer Animation)
Groningen, the Netherlands

## Abstract

The synthesis of human hand motion and grasping of arbitrary shaped objects is a very complex problem. Therefore high-level control is needed to perform these actions. In order to satisfy the kinematic and physical constraints associated with the human hand and to reduce the enormous search space associated with the problem of grasping objects, a knowledge based approach is used. A three-phased scheme is presented which incorporates the role of the hand, the object, the environment and the animator. The implementation of a hand simulation system HANDS is discussed.

**CR Categories:** I.3.5: computational geometry and object modeling; I.3.7: Three-Dimensional graphics and realism;
**Keywords:** Grasp Planning, Animation, Simulation, Robotics

## 1.Introduction

Although there has been some progress on simulating the geometric deformation of the hand during a grasping contact [Gourret 89], animating the grasping motion behavior of the hand remains a difficult task for the computer animator. Even the use of advanced inverse-kinematic and physically-based limb control techniques demand that the animator tediously position the palm, the thumb, and each finger of the hand until the grasped object appears to be trapped by the hand in a natural, physically credible way.

Special input devices that attempt to digitize hand motion, such as the *data-glove*, do not yet record precise individual finger and thumb joint motion or provide the feedback required for intuitive interactive grasping [Fisher 86] [Iwata 90]. Augmenting digitized motion with some grasping intelligence may help to reduce the need for such extensive feedback. However, the focus of this paper is on the problem of *synthesizing grasping motion*, rather than simply recording it.

Since the hand is a multi-limbed system, recent computer animation and robotics research directed at problems associated with modelling limb kinematics and dynamics [Armstrong 86] [Badler 87] [Girard 87] [Isaacs 87] [Korein 82] [Walker 82] [Barzel 88] [Wilhelms 87] [Schoner 90], collision detection [Gilbert 89] [Moore 88] [Baraff 89], motion planning [Lozano-Perez 82] [Brooks 83], and optimizing motion in the presence of kinematic and physically-based constraints [Girard 90] [Kirckanski 82] [Lin 83] [Sahar 85] [Tan 88] [Witkin 87] have helped to lay the basis for controlling individual fingers. However, the selection of grasping positions, the coordination of fingers, and the determination of the palm's motion trajectory during a grasping action requires a higher-level analysis and a control system that operates as a function of the hand's geometric, kinematic, and physical characterics taken as a whole.

Although we are able to easily pick up most objects with little effort, the human capability for manually grasping objects is a non-trivial task. Grasping strategies must take into account the geometry and dynamic characteristics of the object to be grasped, the selection of contact between the object and the fingers, thumb and palm of the hand, and the problems associated with finding collision-free paths in the context of the general environment.

Our approach begins with the realization that the ease with which a person is able to decide how and where to grasp an object depends on the person's familiarity with that object. We view this human capability as a multi-stage process, in an approach that is similar to that suggested by Tomovic [Tomovic 87] in the robotics literature.

First, the object is identified according to its similarity to a given class of shapes, such as a block, sphere, torus, cone, or cylinder. Then, in the second stage, a grasping strategy associated with the object's classification is chosen from a knowlege-base of class specific, parameterized techniques. In the third stage, the grasp is marginally adjusted to manage the object's deviation in shape from its classified shape. In this way, the astronomical search space of grasping techniques and grasping locations which are possible between the hand and an arbitrary three-dimensional object may be restricted to the much smaller set of frequently used human grasping methods.

In the next section, we begin with a kinematic description of the hand. In section 3 the high-level control of the hand is discussed. In section 4, we give an overview of the grasp planning problem and the knowledge-based approach toward its solution. Finally, in section 5, we give our conclusions with suggestions for future research.

## 2. Kinematics of the hand

### 2.1 Model of a human hand

The fingers have 4 DOF, two at the connection with the palm, one at the end of the first finger part and one at the end of the second finger part [See figure 1]. From this we can establish the link coordinate frames of the fingers and obtain the four Denavit-Hartenberg parameters [Denavit 55] for each link.



©1991 ACM-0-89791-436-8/91/007/0339 $00.75

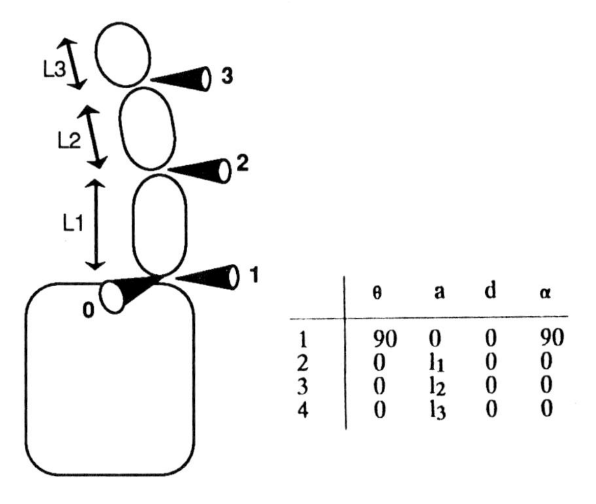


|   | θ | a | d | α |
|---|---|---|---|---|
| 1 | 90 | 0 | 0 | 90 |
| 2 | 0 | $l_1$ | 0 | 0 |
| 3 | 0 | $l_2$ | 0 | 0 |
| 4 | 0 | $l_3$ | 0 | 0 |

*fig. 1: model of a finger*

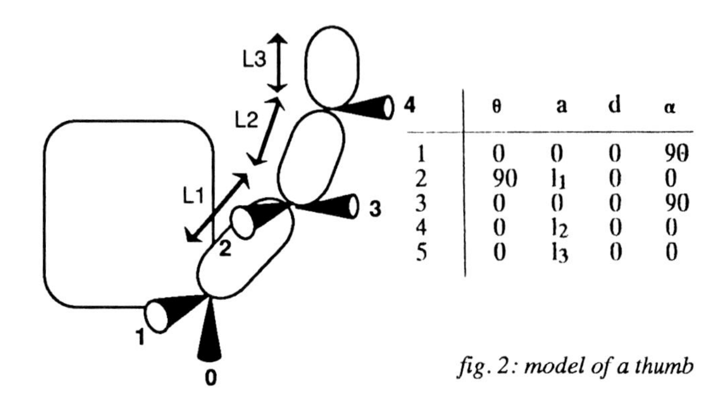


|   | θ | a | d | α |
|---|---|---|---|---|
| 1 | 0 | 0 | 0 | 90 |
| 2 | 90 | $l_1$ | 0 | 0 |
| 3 | 0 | 0 | 0 | 90 |
| 4 | 0 | $l_2$ | 0 | 0 |
| 5 | 0 | $l_3$ | 0 | 0 |

*fig. 2: model of a thumb*

The thumb is very dextrous and therefore a more complicated manipulator. Because a large part of the thumb seems to be part of the palm of the hand and the joints are moving along non-trivial axes, the motion of a thumb is not easily understood. A workable model of the thumb that approximates the motions of a real human thumb is a manipulator with 5 DOF [See figure 2]. From this we can establish the link coordinate frames of the thumb and obtain the four Denavit and Hartenberg parameters for each link.

**2.2 Basic motion control**

From the Denavit-Hartenberg parameters, it is possible to find the transformation matrices for adjacent coordinate systems. The forward kinematics problem is easily solved by using the product of these transformation matrices [Fu 87]. Forward kinematics is useful for bending fingers at the joints. However we are also interested in simulating the human ability to place the tip of the finger at a certain location. For this inverse kinematics is required.

***2.2.1. Inverse kinematics of the fingers***

A human finger has the property that it is (almost) impossible to move the joint of the last link (joint *4*) without moving the next to last joint (joint *3*) and vice-versa, without forcing one of the two not to move in some unnatural way. Therefore, there is a dependancy between these two joints that is caused by the tendon that runs through the finger. Careful observation reveals that there is an almost linear relationship between the joint angles q3 and q4. [See figure 3].

After measuring several human subjects, we found this could be reasonably approximated by:

$$q4 = 2/3 * q3$$

By making q4 fully dependent on q3 , the number of degrees of freedom is reduced. The solution of the inverse kinematics will now be of the form:

$$q = (q1, q2, q3, 2/3*q3)$$

Landsmeer's [Landsmeer 55, 58, 63] empirical studies of the physiology of the human hand addressed the relationship between the joint angles of the fingers and the activation of the tendons. Other studies support the finding that the relationship between the joint angles is not completely linear [Armstrong 78]. We are planning to incorporate this more accurate model in the near future.

A second way to simplify the problem is to note that the finger is a planar manipulator with the exception of the first joint. From this it follows that q1 can be calculated directly from the displacement of the fingertip in the x0 and y0 direction, and that it is completely independant of the other joint angles. [See figure 4a].

From the fact that q3 and q4 are fully dependent, it can be seen that in order to reach an arbitrary point at distance d from the origin of the 0th coordinate frame, there is a unique solution for q3, and therefore

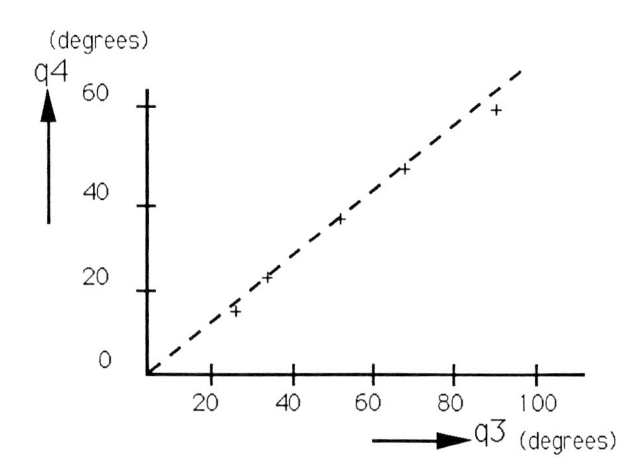


*fig. 3: dependancy of joint angles*

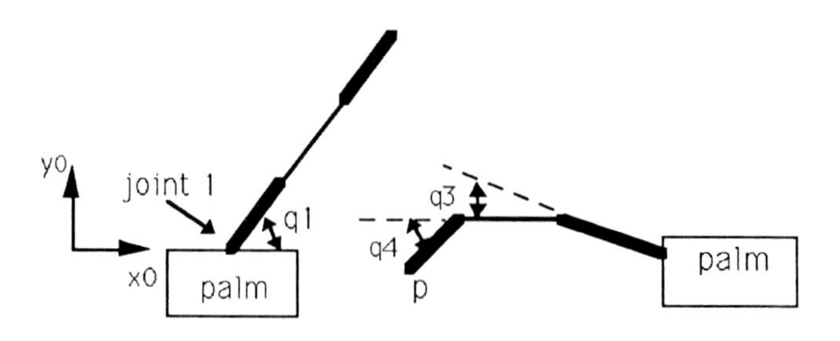


*fig. 4: inverse kinematics of the finger*

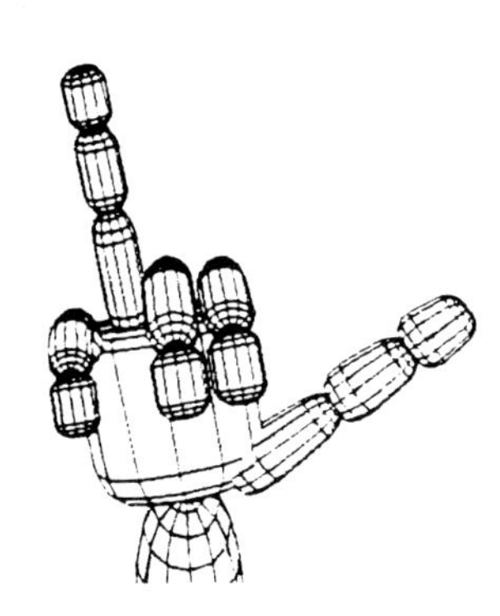

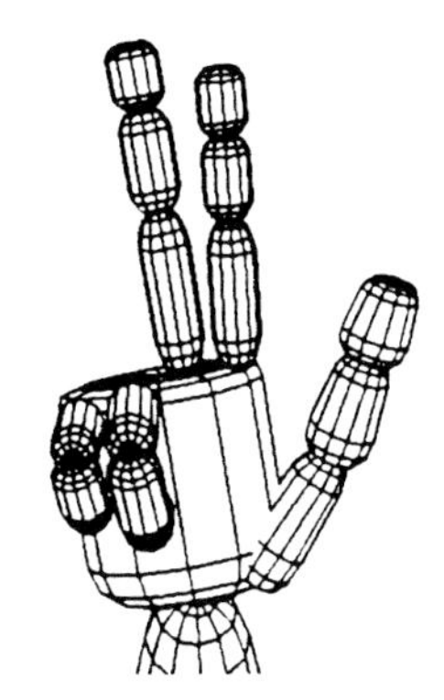

*fig. 5: single finger control* *fig. 6: group control* *fig. 7: hand control*

also for q4. [See figure 4b]. These angles can be calculated using a binary search on q3 that converges quickly. The remaining joint angle q2 can now be calculated such that the tip of the finger will be at the correct location.

***2.2.2. Inverse kinematics of the thumb***

Due to the greater kinematic complexity of the thumb, a closed-form solution was not found. Instead we employed the resolved motion rate control method, in which the desired joint-space solution of the thumb is satisfied as a secondary goal [Liegeois 77] [Klein 83]. An excellent review of this method, along with a means of solving difficulties with singularities of the pseudo-inverse jacobian, may be found in [Maciej 90]. The thumb's joint-space secondary goal, in context of our kinematic model, is recalculated at each position to minimize deviations from joint angles matching the following experimental observations:

$q3 = 2*(q2 - 1/6*\pi)$ and

$q5 = 7/5 * q4$.

## 3. High level control of the hand

Attaining a desired posture by moving all the different joints of the fingers separately is a very tedious and time consuming process. Higher level control has been incorporated in our system, called HANDS, to ease the burden of manipulating many degrees of freedom and to prevent unnatural hand postures from occuring.

The interactive positioning of a hand into a desired gesture in HANDS may be accomplished by using a set of functions that give the animator different levels of control over the hand.

### 3.1 Single-finger control

The lowest level of control involves direct independant control over each finger. [see figure 5]. This can be done using both forward and inverse kinematics of fingers, which satisfy the constraints of natural movement discussed in the previous section.

### 3.2 Group control

The second level of control is that of group control. [see figure 6]. The user can select which fingers belong to a group and then use a number of functions to change the hand posture:

- *Closing and opening of a group.*
  This function closes or opens all fingers that are part of the group at the same time, in the same way as this can be done for single fingers.
- *Spreading of a group*
  The fingers of the group are spread outward or inward by changing the joint angle of the first joint of all the fingers in the group, depending on their location on the hand and the joint angles of the two most outward fingers.

### 3.3 Hand control

The last level of control is complete hand control [see figure 7].

- *Hand posture library*
  The user can build up a hand posture library from which he can choose desired hand postures. These hand postures are made with the use of the above functions and can then be stored with an unique name in the library. Thus hand postures can be added to and deleted from the library. The advantage of this is clear: a posture can be constructed once and then easily be recalled from the library and then pasted in.

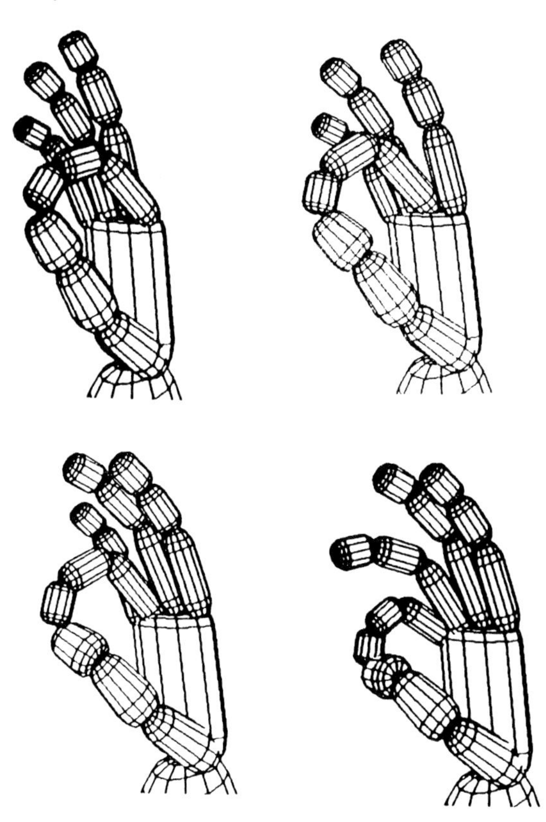

*fig. 8: the pinches of the hand*

*Precalculcated postures*
Besides the user-defined hand postures there are also system-defined hand postures. These are hand postures that might be difficult to achieve with the controls mentioned above or postures that are very often used. Examples of these hand postures are the hand at a rest position, a fist and some pinches. A pinch is the state in which the tip of the thumb is placed against the tip of a finger. These postures are calculated using collision detection [Gilbert 88] [Rypkema 90] so that the tips are exactly touching each other, and not intersecting. [see figure 8].

## 4. Grasp Planning

### 4.1 The elements involved in grasping

When grasping behavior is incorporated into an interactive computer animation system, four elements are of main importance:

- the object
- the hand
- the environment
- the user-interface

These elements have certain characteristics that influence the design of the grasping motion [see figure 9].

*Characteristics of the target object:*

Geometrical: What is the size and the shape of the object?
Physical: What are the mass, distribution of mass, and inertia of the object?
Mechanical: What is the rigidness (i.e. is it completely rigid, elastic or flexible) and the coefficient of friction of the object? [Wang 88].

*Characteristics of the hand.*

Geometrical: How large is the hand, what is the shape of the hand?
Physical: What is the strength of the hand?
Mechanical: Dexterity (how skilled is the hand?), grip (what is the friction coefficient of the hand?)
Naturalness: Human sensory motor control, muscular con straints.
Topological: What are the connections and degrees of free dom at each of the joints of the hand.

*Characteristics of the environment*

Information about the environment is required to determine potential obstacles and collisions.
Spatial complexity: Where are all other objects (location and orientation)?
Dynamical complexity: How do other objects, arms, etc. move in time?

*Characteristics of the user-interface*

Expression: How does a user want to express his ideas?
Automation: How much does the user want to be done automati cally?
Control: Under what circumstances does a user want to be able to take control?
Output: When there are multiple solutions, when should the system offer choices and when must it out put just one, working solution?

### 4.2 A Knowledge Based approach

Previous research on the analysis of human hand motion supports a knowledge-based approach to the synthesis of a grasping behavior [Tomovic 87] [Iberall 88].

Human beings perform grasping tasks by using *experience* that has been gathered over time. The approach followed here is to incorporate this experience into a knowledge base. The knowledge base can be seen as a collection of precalculated strategies for different categories of situations, thus partitioning the enormous search space of possible solutions into computationally managable subsets.

Each of the knowledge-based strategies assumes the form of a three-phased decomposition into the following subtasks [see figure 10]:

1. The task initialization phase
2. The target approach phase
3. The grasp execution phase

In the task initialization phase, the target object is classified as a primitive and the overall strategy for grasping the object is determined. During the target approach phase, all possible grasp positions are filtered to obtain the feasible ones from which the hand is preshaped to assume an optimal or user-selected grasp position. Once the hand is preshaped to the primitive, the grasp execution phase ensures that the fingers will close around the actual object.

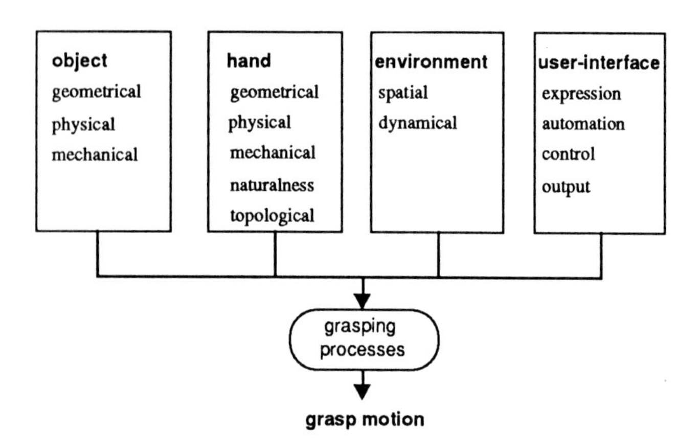


*fig. 9: elements involved in grasping*

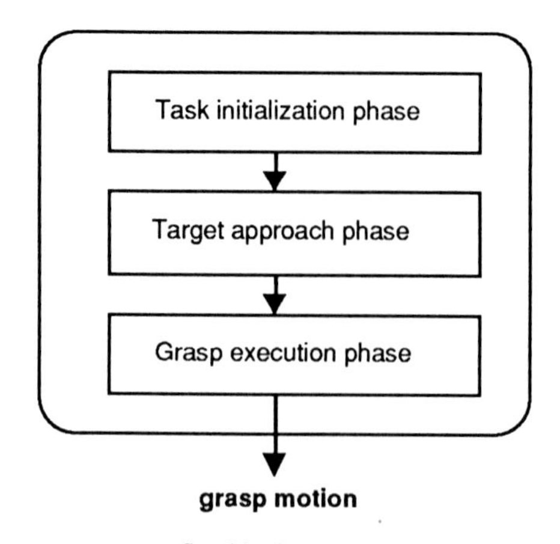


*fig. 10: decomposition of grasping task*

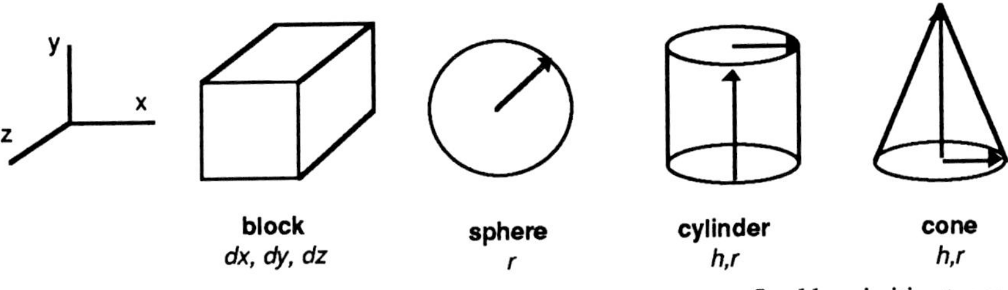


*fig. 11: primitive types*

### 4.3 The task initialization phase

When a specific grasping task is to be carried out, the motion is influenced by the *high-level goal* that leads to the grasping motion. For example a hammer should be grasped differently depending on whether one wishes to pound a nail in or pull a nail out. Therefore the *context* of the action should be made clear in the task initialization phase, in order to be able to exclude at this early stage all possible grasp configurations that do not satisfy some desired goal. The classification of grasps in terms of goals has not been implemented.

Thus far, our knowledge base consists of classifications based only on the shape of the object. During the object identification process [see figure13] the object is classified as one of the primitive object types (block, sphere, cylinder etc.) [see figure 11] and the values of the attributes are specified. Classification of complex 3D shapes as generic primitives is a difficult problem that has been addressed in the computer vision literature [Fu 87] [Marr 82]. Objects can be compared with the different primitive types by looking at volume, center of gravity, etc. The primitives must also be oriented in such a way that the best matching between the primitive and the target object is achieved by minimization of differences in their occupied volumes.

Human beings have a very good sense of classifying objects as primitives. Therefore in the current version of the grasping system, the classification of the object as a certain primitive is left to the user. This can be done in a simple interactive way by selecting a primitive from a pop-up menu and then visually positioning the primitive so that it circumscribes the object.

Once the primitive is known, the values for the attributes of the primitive can be computed automatically. These attributes are very simple. For a block they are the lengths along the three axes: dx, dy and dz. For a sphere they are the radius *r* and for a cylinder and a cone they are the radius *r* and the height *h* [see figure 11].

Finally, information about the environment should be gathered. The environment can put restrictions on the way an object is grasped. Objects other than the target object can block the path for the hand, so as to make it impossible to reach certain points or surfaces of the object.

### 4.4 The target approach phase

The position of the hand includes both the position of the palm and the positions of the fingers. As a convention, we will call a hand position that specifies a grasp a *grasp position.*

The search space of possible grasp positions for a given object is enormously large, so it would be very time consuming to find a correct and natural grasp by simply searching all these possibilities. This follows partially from the fact that the hand has a large number of degrees of freedom. In the model every finger has 4 DOF, the thumb has 5 DOF and the hand 3 DOF, so this gives (4x4)+5+3 = 24 DOF, which shows how dextrous a human hand is. Also, when only considering finger-object contact types the number of possible contacts is extremely large. Salisbury has shown that a hand with five three-linked fingers may touch a ball in 840 ways [Mason 85].

A grasp should be found from this large solution space that minimizes muscle tension and optimizes the stability of the grip on the object. The number of possibilities may be limited by enforcing a set of *constraints and properties* that can be derived from observing how human beings tend to grasp objects.

The first property that decreases the large number of possible grasps is the observation that humans tend to pick up objects with the fingers placed on *opposite faces*. This also makes sense physically, because in this way the forces that the fingers need to exert on the object in order to obtain a stable grasp is probably less than the forces needed when grasping the object in any other way.

A second property of human grasping is that *the thumb almost always takes part in the grasp*. Grasps without the thumb are very rare and they don't look natural. When picking up an object using opposite faces, the thumb is placed on one face of the object and the other fingers that take part in the grasp are placed on the opposite face.

These two constraints/properties mean in the case of grasping a block that the number of grasp types is limited to 24:

*#opp.faces . #thumb locations . #palm locations =*

3 . 2 . 4 = 24

[see figure 12]

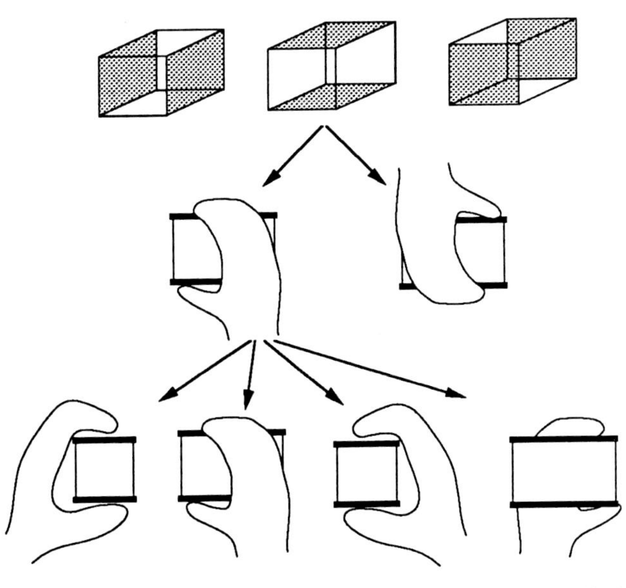

*fig. 12: grasp positions for a block*

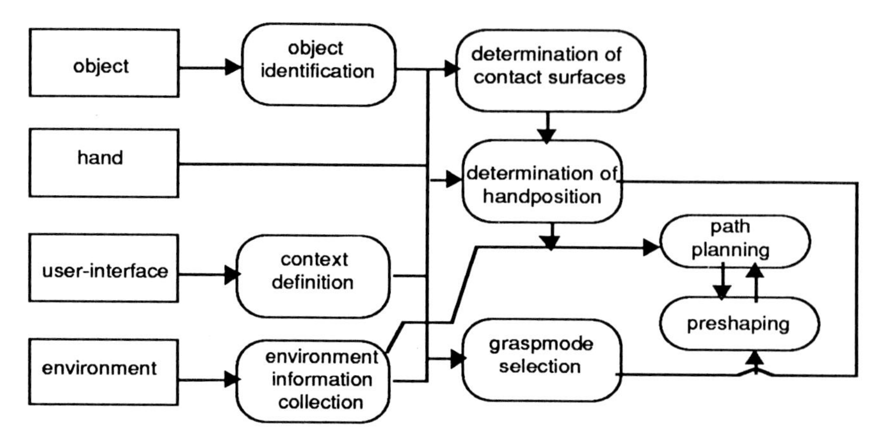


*fig. 13: task initialization and target approach*

In order to automate grasping we need to first determine which grasp positions are feasible. Then we wish to select the 'best' or optimal grasp out of this feasible set. Instead of computing every possible grasp position defined by the constraints and properties discussed in the previous section, a series of more computationally efficient tests may be applied to incrementally rule out infeasible grasps.

The target approach phase first applies these tests and then orders the feasible grasps in accordance with an optimization criterion. Then the hand is lead from an arbitrary position to the vicinity of the object, with the hand preshaped to grasp the target object's associated primitive. The target approach phase consists of the following subtasks [see fig. 13]:

1. determination of contact surfaces of the object's associated primitive
2. selecting the hand position with respect to the feasible contact surfaces
3. selecting the graspmode and hand structure for the chosen hand position
4. preshaping of all fingers to grasp the object's primitive
5. path generation of the palm towards the preshaped hand position

### *4.4.1 Contact surface determination*

The first phase in which infeasible grasp positions are eliminated is the determination of contact surfaces. To determine whether a certain contact surface combination will lead to incorrect grasps, four tests can be applied:

1. are the contact surfaces reachable?
2. is it possible to spread the hand enough so that the fingers can close around the object?
3. are both the contact surfaces free, i.e. are they not blocked by other objects?
4. does it make sense to grasp the object with these contact surfaces, i.e. does the contact surface combination conflict with the high level goal?

If any of the above tests is not satisfied, that contact surface combination should be deleted from the list of possibilities. In the current version of the grasping system only the first two tests are applied. (The other two tests need information that should be collected during the task initialization phase, outlined in section 4.3).

The first test, to determine if the contact surfaces are reachable, is done by calculating the distance from the base of the arm to each contact surface. If the distance for at least one of the two contact surfaces is larger than the length of the arm, it means that the contact surface combination is not reachable, and therefore it has failed the test.

The second test deals with the *spread of the hand* and the size of the primitive. The spread of the hand is a measure for the distance between the tip of the thumb and the the tip of another finger. When the hand is flat and the thumb is pointing outwards the maximum spread can be determined for each thumb-finger combination by calculating the distance between the two tips. The maximum spread of the hand is then the maximum of all these maximum spreads of the fingers. Objects can only be grasped with contact surfaces that are no further apart than the maximum spread of the hand.

### *4.4.2 Determination of the grasp position*

The second level of deleting infeasible grasps is the selection of the grasp position. To do this the following tests can be applied:

- is the hand position within the reach of the arm?
- will the grasp follow from an feasible (and optimal) arm motion?

The first test to determine whether the hand position is within reach of the arm is done by calculating the location of the wrist at the desired hand position. Then the distance from the base of the arm to the desired wrist location is calculated. If this distance is larger than the length of the arm minus the length of the hand then the desired hand position is not reachable and is therefore excluded from further consideration.

In the case of the second test a difficulty is that the selection of the best grasp must take into account the motion of the entire arm. For example, the best grasp may be the one which is reached by the minimum energy path. The constrained optimization of collision free limb trajectories requires numerical methods such as steepest descent gradient techniques [Witkin 87], or dynamic programming [Girard 90]. These techniques are extremely costly, requiring optimization of path and speed distribution in terms of cost criteria involving both kinematic and dynamics based quantities. A further complexity arises due to the need to calculate the actual tension in the tendons and muscles rather than the idealized rotational torques of inverse-dynamics formulations.

Therefore we use a heuristic approach that orders the feasible grasps, but leaves the final decision to the user. A heuristic that has proven effective is to minimize the weighted sum of the translational and rotational distance between the initial hand position and the final grasp position. The translational displacement is given by the distance from the initial wrist location to the final wrist location. The rotational displacement of the hand can be calculated by using the quaternion formulation [Shoemake 85] [Pletinckx 89].

#### *4.4.3 Grasp mode and hand structure selection*

With the contact surfaces for the thumb and the fingers known, we must still determine the grasp mode and hand structure for the grasp. The selection of the grasp mode depends mainly on the purpose of the action. The grasp mode may be a lateral or palmar grasp [see figure 14]. A glass is picked up most of the time with a lateral grasp when the goal is to put the glass on the shelf, but when the same glass is used for drinking it will probably be picked up with a palmar grasp (unless the contents of the glass are very hot). Sometimes the selection of the grasp mode can also depend on the characteristics of the object. If an object is very heavy, a power grasp is needed to be able to lift the object. So when restricting the grasp modes to lateral and palmar grasps the determination of which of the two should be applied depends on the high-level goal. In in our current implementation the selection of graspmode is left to the user.

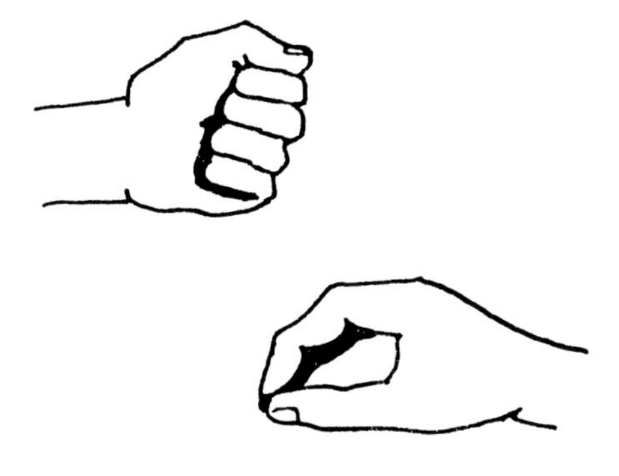

*fig. 14: palmar and lateral grasp*

Although there are a large number of hand structures that are possible to use when grasping objects, in practice, only a small number of them are used.

With the following notation: *T = thumb, I = index finger, M = middle finger, R = ring finger and L = little finger*, the most natural grasps can be defined as [Tomovic 87]:

***2-fingered structures (pinches)***
pinch-TI
pinch-TM
pinch-TR
pinch-TL

***3-fingered structures***
three-TIM
three-TMR
three-TRL

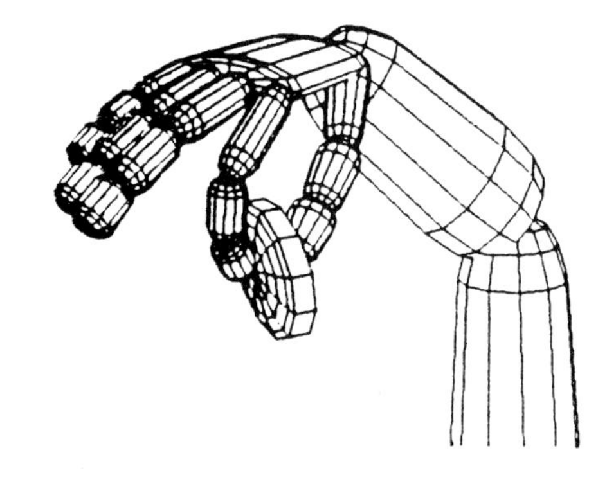

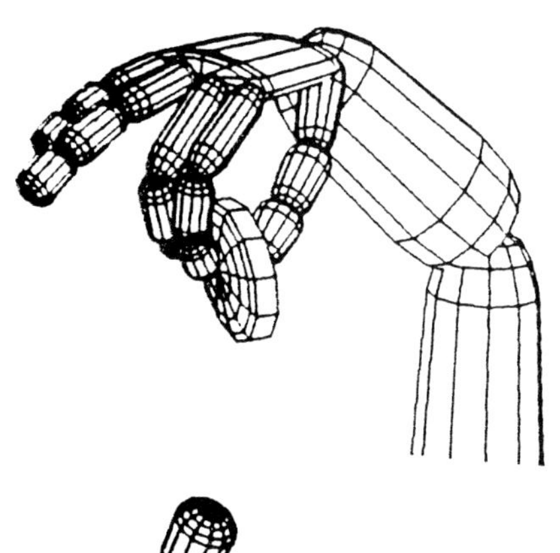

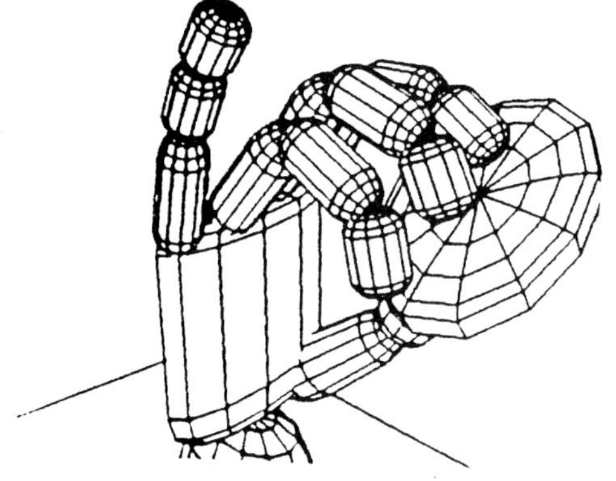

*fig. 15: hand structures*

***4-fingered structures***
four-TIMR
four-TMRL

***5-fingered structures***
five-TIMRL

The above add to a total of ten hand structures [see figure 15]. The selection of the hand structure can be subdivided into two different problems:
- How many fingers can be used?
- Which fingers can be used?

The maximum number of fingers that can be used in the grasp depends on the size of the object and the size of the hand. The available space on the object must be compared with the space occupied by a single finger to give an indication about the maximum number of fingers.

The determination of which fingers are valid for the desired grasp also depends on the relative size of the hand and object. The distance between the two contact surfaces determines how much the fingers must be spread to grasp the object. The selection of the contact surfaces computed at an earlier stage guarantees that there is at least one finger for which the maximum spread is larger than this distance. All fingers that have a maximum spread larger than this distance are valid grasp fingers.

After calculating the maximum number of grasp fingers and determining which fingers are valid we must still choose the best combination of fingers. Our observation of human grasping have lead us to formulate the following general rules to select a hand structure: **1)** maximize the number of fingers (since more contacts improve stability) and **2)** favour the use of fingers closer to the thumb (since they are stronger). Our implementation HANDS, picks a hand structure using the above rules [see figure 18] but allows the user to intervene and select another hand structure [see figure 19].

#### *4.4.4 Preshaping of the fingers*

Having established the contact surfaces, the approximate grasp position, hand structure and grasp mode, a more precise hand position must now be calculated. The palm position must allow the fingers to be placed on the object in such a way that the forces they exert on the object produce a stable grasp.

Using the notion of the *pinch-line*, the correct hand position can be calculated in a geometrical way. The pinch-line is the imaginary line between the thumb and a finger, called the *pinch finger* [see figure 16]. The forces that both fingers of the pinch exert on the object are directed along this pinch-line. In order to establish a stable grasp it makes sense that this pinch-line should go through the center of gravity of the object. Another assumption that can be made is that the thumb and pinch finger are placed on opposite contact surfaces in such a way that the forces exerted by the fingers are directed perpendicular to these contact surfaces.

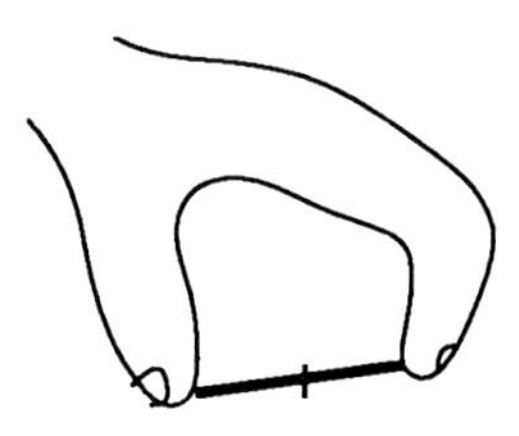

*fig. 16: the pinch-line*

The choice of which of the grasp fingers is the pinch finger can be based on the same observations made in selecting the hand structure: the grasp finger closest to the thumb is most likely to be the pinch finger.

The orientation of the pinch-line varies as a complex function of the natural kinematics of the pinch fingers. The configuration in which the pinch fingers are a certain distance apart may be found by interpolating the thumb and pinch finger between their rest position and their relaxed pinch positions. The relaxed pinches of the hand, as shown in [figure 8], are automatically precalculated to satisfy the joint angle constraints of the fingers and thumb using the inverse-kinematics procedures described in section 2. The desired distance between the fingertips may be quickly achieved by using a binary search. The pinch-line is now the line between the tip of the thumb and the tip of the pinch finger expressed with respect to the hand coordinate system.

The hand can now be placed so that the pinch-line is perpendicular to the contact surfaces. To complete the preshaping of the hand all the grasp fingers are moved from their rest position to their relaxed pinch position until they collide with the primitive associated with the object.

#### *4.4.5 Path generation*

Knowing the initial configuration of the hand and arm and the preshaped configuration of the hand, the approach path of the hand towards the object needs to be determined.

Experiments have shown that this approach path has a *predictable shape* [Paillard 82] [Tomovic 87]. Seen from one side the hand travels along a *straight line* and seen from another side it travels along a *curve* [see figure 17]. This property can be incorporated into the grasping system by adding another key position, called the approach position, along the desired path. Inverse-kinematics using pseudo-inverse control [Girard 90] [Liegeois 77] [Maciej 90] is used to move the hand along the designated path.

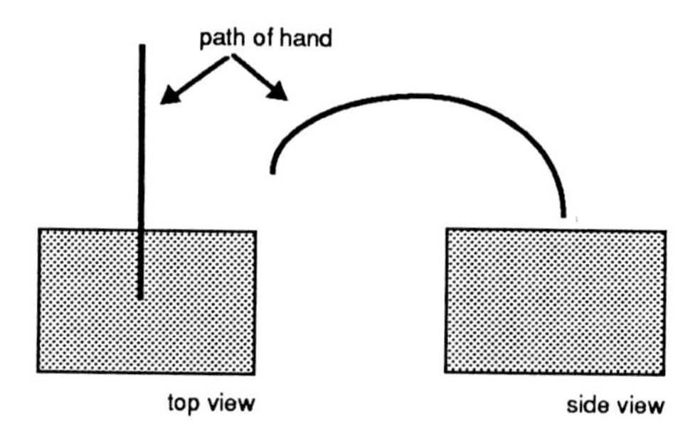


*fig. 17: approach path of the hand*

### 4.6 The grasp execution phase

To complete the grasp, the fingers need to move from their position on the primitive associated with the object so that they are touching the object itself. The thumb and pinch finger move towards each other by interpolating their current position and their completed pinch position. When one of the links of the finger collides with the object, that link cannot be moved anymore. This means that when link $i$ collides, joints $j$ with $j = 0,1,..i$ must be locked. The same procedure is used for the other fingers. Collisions between the fingers and the target object are calculated by using an octree spatial decomposition method for concave polygonal objects [Rijpkema 91] and a fast procedure for computing the distance between convex polygonal objects [Gilbert 88]. A discussion of our collision detection scheme is beyond the scope of this paper.

## 5. Conclusion

The development of knowledge-based hand behavior has made the task of computer animated grasping relatively simple, while still maintaining the creative role and guidance of the animator. We are currently extending our grasping knowledge-base to include more complex classification primitives, for example poking one's finger through the hole of a torus-like cup handle. The approach we have taken will allow us to add more complicated sequences of actions, such as shovelling a book up from a table by one's thumb before grasping it.

We think that the use of knowledge-based techniques will play an increasingly important role in the modeling of motions that involve complex physical and geometric constraints, particularly when optimal behaviors must be selected from a broad set of feasible actions.

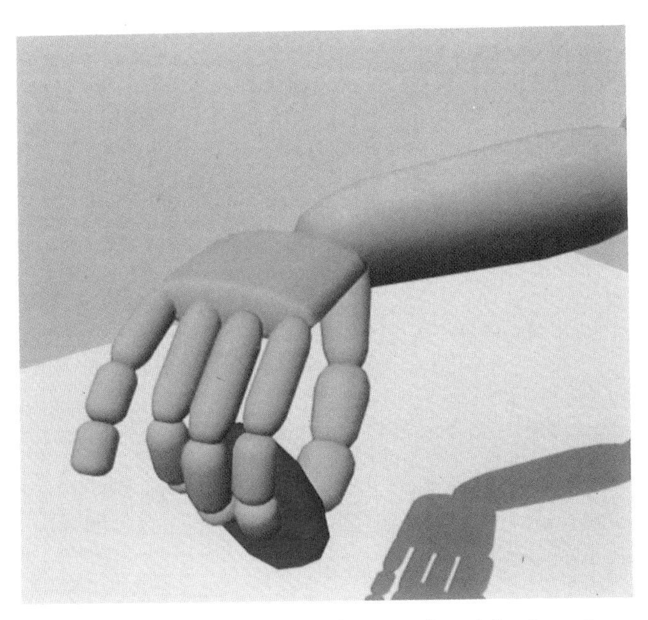

*fig. 18: example of grasp selected by the system*

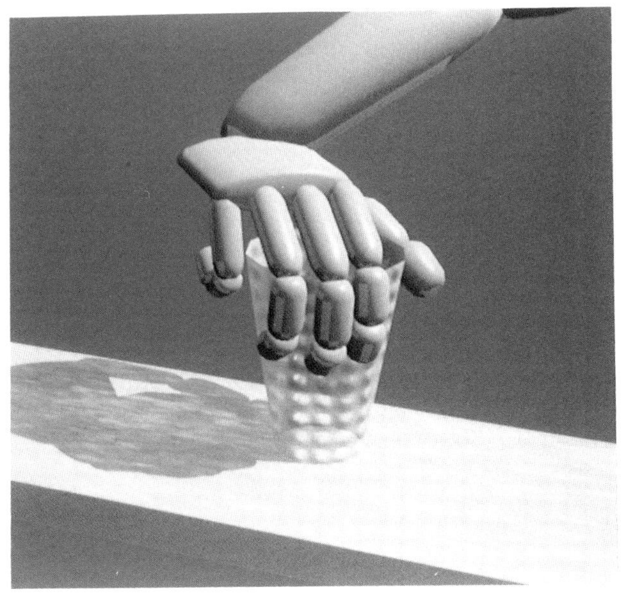

*fig. 19: example of grasp selected by the user*


## Acknowledgements

We would like to thank Rob v.d. Weg and Wiek Vervoort of the University of Twente (the Netherlands) for their advice and constructive remarks during this research. Special thanks to Susan Amkraut for creating and adapting software for our purposes. And all at SCAN, without whom......


## References


[Armstrong 86] W.W. Armstrong, M. Green and R. Lake, Near-real-time control of human figure models, Proceedings of Graphics Interface 1986

[Armstrong 78] T.J. Armstrong and D.B. Chaffin, An investigation of the relationship between displacements of the finger and wrist joints and the extrinsic finger flexor tendons, iomechanics, vol. 11, pp 119-128, Pergamon Press Ltd., 1978 (great-Britrain)

[Badler 87] N.I. Badler, K.H. Manoochehri and G. Walters, Articulated figure positioning by multiple constraints, IEEE Computer Graphics and Animation 7(6), 1987

[Baraff 89] D. Baraff, Analytical Methos for Dynamic Simulation of Non-penetrating Rigid Bodies, Computer Graphics, Vol. 23, No. 3, july 1989

[Barzell 88] R. Barzel and A.H. Barr, A Modeling system based on dynamic constraints, Proc. Siggraph, vol 22., No. 4, August 1988

[Brooks 83] R.A. Brooks, Planning Collision Free Motions for Pick-and-Place Operations, The international Journal of Robotics Research, Vol.2, No. 4, Winter 1983

[Denavit 55] J. Denavit and R. Hartenberg, A kinematic Notation for Lower Pair Mechanisms Based on Matrices, J. App. Mech., Vol. 77, pp 215-221, 1955

[Fisher 86] S.S. Fisher, M. McGreevy, J. Humphries and W. Robinett, Virtual environment display system, Proc 1986 ACM Workshop on Interactive Graphics, October 23-24, Chapel Hill, North Carolina.

[Fu 87] K.S. Fu, R.C. Gonzalez and C.S.G. Lee, Robotics: Control, Sensing, Vision and Intelligence, McGraw-Hill Book Company, 1987

[Gilbert 88] E. Gilbert, D.W. Johnson and S. Sathiya Keerthi, A fast Procedure fot Computing the Distance Between Complex Objects in Three-Dimensional Space, IEEE Journal of Robotics and Automation, Vol. 4, No. 2, april 1988

[Girard 87] M. Girard, Interactive design of 3D Computer Animated Legged Animal Motion. Computer Graphics and Applications june 1987.

[Girard 90] M. Girard, Constrained optimization of articulated animal movement in computer animation, Making them move (mechanics, control, and animation of articulated figures), Eds: Badler, Barsky and Zeltzer, Morgan Kaufmann Publishers, 1990

[Gourret 89] J.P. Gourret, N.M. Thalmann, D. Thalmann, Simulation of object and human skin deformations in a grasping task., ACM Siggraph Proceedings 1989.

[Iberall 88] T. Iberall, J. Jackson, L. Labbe and R. Zampang, Knowledge-based prehension: Capturing Human Dexterity, Proceedings of the IEEE on Robotics and Automation 1988. pp 82-87.

[Isaacs 87] P. Isaacs and R. Cohen, Controlling dynamic simulation with kinematic constraints, behavior functions and inverse dynamics, Computer Graphics, ACM Siggraph Proceedings 1987

[Iwata 90] H. Iwata, Artificial Reality with force-feedback: development of desktop virtual space with compact master manipulator, Computer Graphics, ACM Siggraph Proceedings 1990

[Kirckanski 82] M. Kirckanski and M. Vukobratovic, A method for optimal synthesis of manipulation robot trajectories, Trans. ASME, J. Dynamic Systems, Measurements and Control 104, 1982

[Klein 83] C.A. Klein and C.H. Huang, Review of pseudo-inverse control for use with kinematically redundant manipulators, IEEE Transactions on systems, Man and Cybernetics, SMC-13(2), march/april 1983

[Korein 82] J.U. Korein and N.I. Badler, Techniques for generating the goal-directed motion of articulated structures, IEEE Computer Graphics and applications, pp 71-81, 1982

[Landsmeer 55] J.M.F. Landsmeer, Anatomical and functional investigations on the articulations of the human fingers, Acta anatomica, suppl. 25, 1-69, 1955

[Landsmeer 58] J.M.F. Landsmeer, A report on the coordination of the interphalangeal joints of the human finger and it's disturbances, Acta Morphologica Neerlando-Scandinavica 2. 59-84, 1958

[Landsmeer 63] J.M.F. Landsmeer, The coordination of finger joint motions, J. Bone Jnt. Sur. 45, 1654-1662, 1963

[Liegeois 77] A. Liegeois, Automatic Supervisory control of the configuration and behavior of multibody mechanisms, IEEE Transactions on systems, Man and Cybernetics, SMC-7 (12), december 1977

[Lin 83] C. Lin, P. Chang and J. Luh, Formulation and optimization cubic polynomial joint trajectories for industrial robots, IEEE Trans. Automatic Control AC-28(12), 1983

[Lozano-Perez] T. Lozano-Perez, Spatial Planning: a Configuration Approach, IEEE Transactions on Computers, Vol C-32, No.2, feb 1982

[Maciej 90] A.A. Maciejewski, Dealing with the ill-conditioned equations of motion for articulated figures, IEEE Computer Graphics and Applications, May 1990

[Marr 82] Vision, Freeman Press, San Fransisco, California, 1982

[Moore 88] M. Moore and J. Wilhelms, Collision detection and response for computer animation, Proc. ACM Siggraph 1988, Computer Graphics 22(4)

[Paillard 82] J. Paillard, The contribution of perifpheral and central vision to visuallly guided reaching, Analysis of visual behavior, (eds: Ingle, Goodale, Mansfield) Cambridge, Mass. MIT Press, pp 367-385, 1982

[Pletinckx 89] D. Pletinckx, Quaternion calculus as a basic tool in computer graphics, The Visual Computer 1989

[Rijpkema 91] M. Girard and H. Rijpkema, efficient collision detection for convex and concave polyhedral objects, to be submitted.

[Sahar 85] G. Sahar and J. Hollerbach, Planning of minimum time trajectories for robot arms, IEEE International Conference on Robotics and Automation, march 1985

[Schoner 90] P. Schoner and D. Zeltzer, The virtual erector set: Dynamic simulation with linear recursive constraint propagation. Proc. 1990 Symposium on Interactive 3D Graphics March 25-28, Snowbird, Utah

[Shoemake 85] K. Shoemake, Animating Rotation with Quaternion Curves, ACM Siggraph Proceedings 1985

[Tan 88] H. Tan and R. Potts, Minimum time trajectory planner for discrete dynamic robot model with dynamic constraints, IEEE J. of Robotics and Automation 4(2), 1988

[Tomovic 87] R. Tomovic, G.A. Bekey and W.J. Karplus, A strategy for grasp synthesis with multifingered robot hands, Proceedings of the IEEE on Robotics and Automation 1987. pp 83-89.

[Walker 82] M. Walker and D. Orin, Efficient dynamic simulation of robot mechanisms, Trans. ASME, J. Dynamic Systems, Measurements and Control, 1982

[Wang 88] G. Wang and H.E. Stephanou, Chopstick manipulation with an articulated hand: a qualitative analysis, Proceedings of the IEEE on Robotics and Automation 1988. pp 94-99.

[Whitney 69] D.E. Whitney, Resolved motion rate control of manipulators and human protheses, IEEE Transactions on Man-Machine systemsm MMS-10(2) pp 47-53, june 1969

[Wilhelms 87] J. Wilhelms, Using dynamic analysis for realistic animation of articulated bodies, IEEE Computer Graphics and Applications 7(6), 1987

[Witkin 87] A. Witkin and M. Kass, Spacetime constraints, ACM Computer Graphics, Siggraph Proceedings 1987

# Animation of Dynamic Legged Locomotion

Marc H. Raibert
MIT Leg Laboratory

Jessica K. Hodgins
IBM Watson Research Center

## 1 Abstract

This paper is about the use of control algorithms to animate dynamic legged locomotion. Control could free the animator from specifying the details of joint and limb motion while producing both physically realistic and natural-looking results. We implemented computer animations of a biped robot, a quadruped robot, and a kangaroo. Each creature was modeled as a linked set of rigid bodies with compliant actuators at its joints. Control algorithms regulated the running speed, organized use of the legs, and maintained balance. All motions were generated by numerically integrating equations of motion derived from the physical models. The resulting behavior included running at various speeds, traveling with several gaits (run, trot, bound, gallop, and hop), jumping, and traversing simple paths. Whereas the use of control permitted a variety of physically realistic animated behavior to be generated with limited human intervention, the process of designing the control algorithms was not automated: the algorithms were "tweaked" and adjusted for each new creature.

**Key Words and Phrases:** computer animation, motion control, legged locomotion, robotics, dynamical simulation, physically realistic modeling.

## 2 Introduction

An important goal of computer graphics is to generate physically realistic animation of *actuated systems*. Actuated systems are those that use muscles, motors, or some other kind of actuator to convert stored energy into time-varying forces that act within the system's mechanical structure. Animals, robots, and vehicles are examples of actuated systems. Actuated systems can create their own motions when asked to perform a task, often without help from an outside agent. We distinguish actuated systems from passive physical objects; both can move with physical realism, but only actuated systems can power and regulate their own motions.

A key step in animating actuated systems is to formulate control algorithms that transform expressions of desired behavior into detailed actuator control signals that produce the necessary motion. This step can be quite challenging because the relationship between task and motion is usually indirect. Desired behavior is typically expressed at a time scale and in a coordinate system associated with the task, whereas actuator control signals operate in the coordinate system and at the time scale of the mechanical system. For example, the desired behavior "Run forward at 2 m/s using a trotting gait" does little to specify how the hip joint on leg 2 should move at various times throughout the locomotion cycle. In legged locomotion the transformation from task specification to actuator specification is central, in that motions of the legs and feet are only intermittently related to the basic functional goals of providing support, stability, and propulsion.

A second reason that control of actuated systems is challenging is the presence of significant system dynamics. In dynamic systems the forces and torques exerted by the actuators on the mechanism are just one of the factors that influence the movement. Energy stored, recovered, and exchanged among the various mechanical components of the system and external forces influence the present and future motion of the system. The control algorithms must anticipate the response to actuation in the context of the ongoing activity. In a fast-moving legged system, for example, kinetic energy stored in the rotation of the leg can be large compared to the energy immediately available from the hip actuators. If the control algorithms are to swing the leg forward soon enough to place the foot for the next step, they must begin reversing the leg's motion early in the cycle. Each mass, moment of inertia, and compliant element in the system stores energy that might influence behavior. In most cases it is not correct to think of the control as providing "commands" to the mechanism through the actuators. The control inputs are more like "suggestions" that must be reconciled with the dynamic state and structure of the system.

Whereas the difficulty of achieving control of dynamic systems poses certain problems, the system dynamics also present opportunities. For instance, the

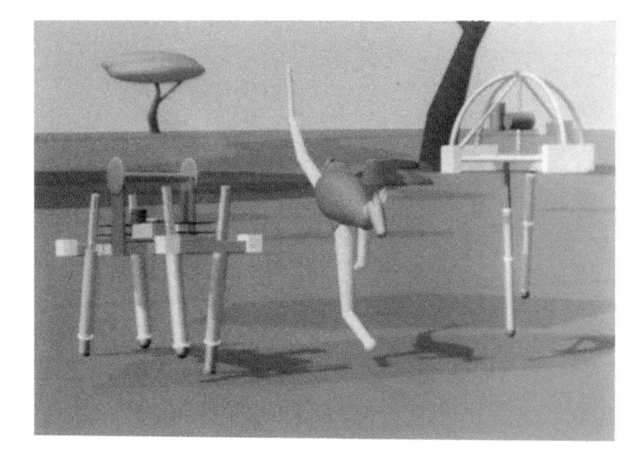

**Figure 1:** Biped, quadruped, and kangaroo models used to study control of running.

motions of dynamic systems are not limited by the instantaneous power available from the actuators. Stored energy can be used to generate motion. The difference achieved in the standing long jump vs. the running long jump is an example, (about 3.8 m vs. 8.5 m). The dynamics of a system can also contribute to energetic efficiency. Most running animals use some of the energy from one step to power the next, by temporarily storing it in stretched tendons and ligaments. The kangaroo achieves a significant energy savings with this trick [2].

This paper describes efforts to use control for animation of dynamic legged locomotion. We have restricted attention to fairly low-level desired behaviors, such as the speed and path of travel, posture, gait, and gait transitions. The starting point was our previous work on the control of one-, two-, and four-leg laboratory robots. Considered collectively, these robots ran at specified speeds, ran fast (13 mph), ran with several gaits, changed gait during running, jumped, climbed a flight of 3 stairs, and performed rudimentary gymnastic maneuvers [7, 8, 9, 12, 13]. We have adapted these robot control algorithms for animation of a biped that runs, gallops, and follows simple paths, a quadruped that trots, bounds, gallops, changes gait, and turns, and a planar one-legged kangaroo that hops and jumps. The creature models are shown in Figure 1.

Despite several variations, the control algorithms for the three models share a common set of basic elements. The common elements include a symmetry principle used for balance, decomposition of the control algorithms into separate parts for regulating hopping, speed, and posture, and the use of elastic energy storage in the legs. One might characterize these common elements of the control as a tool box for handcrafting control algorithms for new creatures with reasonable effort. At the moment, the control algorithms for each new creature or behavior require adjustment and tuning. For instance, the control algorithms that make the kangaroo run at a range of speeds had to be adjusted manually before they could maintain balance when the kangaroo took a big jump. We look forward to more automation of the control design process.

Once the control algorithms are implemented, behavior of each model is found by numerically integrating its equations of motion while the control algorithms monitor progress of the behavior and apply actuator forces. The animator specifies input to the control algorithms, but does not manipulate the model or its output directly. The resulting behavior was found to be qualitatively and quantitatively similar to that of the systems being modeled.

The next section describes previous work on the use of control in animation of legged locomotion. Then we describe the basic elements of the locomotion control algorithms and the models we used for testing. We close with results and a discussion.

## 3 Background

The opportunity to use control in computer animation has been recognized for about ten years. Progress has been slow because dynamical systems complex enough to be of interest are difficult to construct, computationally expensive to simulate, and difficult to stabilize and control. Researchers have taken a variety of approaches to simplifying the models. The trick is to simplify the model and the control problem sufficiently that animation is computationally and intellectually tractable, while retaining the underlying dynamics and realistic results.

Wilhelms and her colleagues implemented several systems that allowed the animator to explore various techniques for control of dynamic systems [16, 17]. The user selects which links are modeled kinematically and which have full dynamics. The system provides several low-level control options ranging from position control with springs and dampers to a mode which attempts to respond to gravitational forces with external forces to maintain balance. Joint limits and ground reaction forces are modeled with springs and dampers. One result of this work was the recognition that inverse dynamics is limited as a tool for computer graphics. Inverse dynamics is good for transforming detailed motion trajectories into force functions, once the detailed motions are known. However, the difficult part of the problem is finding the desired motions, and knowledge of the forces is not of vital interest in computer graphics, once the motion trajectories are known.

Bruderlin and Calvert used a dynamic model and control system to generate the leg motions for a human walking figure [3]. They used a telescoping leg with two degrees of freedom as the leg model for the stance phase and a compound pendulum model for the swing phase. They controlled walking using techniques adapted from biomechanics, which focused on synergy and a hierarchy of motor programs. Once the walking motion was calculated, a foot and upper body with arms were added to the model kinematically. These extra degrees of freedom were made to move in an oscillatory pattern similar to the pattern observed in humans. Bruderlin identified several key parameters of the walking motion and allowed the animator to change them. The details of the complete walking motion were generated automatically by the control system in concert with the dynamic model.

McKenna and Zeltzer's work on an animated cockroach fully embraced the idea that numerical integration of a dynamic model could be used to generate all motions of an animated creature, and that the control algorithms could influence behavior only through forces exerted by the actuators [10]. They implemented a dynamical model of the cockroach, and relied on a control system to pattern its motion. Their cockroach had springy legs, so the load of the body was distributed on the support legs. The walking algorithms they used were based on motion patterns that have been observed in insect locomotion. McKenna and Zeltzer's work is closely related to our own, in that we too rely on behavior of the dynamical model for all motion generation and restrict human intervention to specifying desired behavior to the control. Our work differs from theirs in the sort of locomotion studied and the nature of the control algorithms: they concentrated on statically stable multi-legged walking, while we focus on running and jumping with a ballistic flight phase, and on the role of the springy leg in generating the running cycle.

Optimization techniques and modern control theory offer the hope of automatically producing control systems by specifying task constraints or optimization functions. Witkin and Kass used their "spacetime" approach to produce a remarkable animation of a dynamic lamp [18]. Panne, Fiume, Vranesic used techniques from modern control theory to allow the lamp to perform a flip [15]. The potential generality of these approaches and their ability to deal with anticipation makes them among the most interesting new methods for animation of dynamic systems. The potential liability is the growth of the search spaces when applied to more complex systems.

Girard and Maciejewski do not use numerical integration of physical models, but rely instead on rules associated with dynamics [4, 5]. For instance, they programmed a sinusoidal vertical motion of the body to approximate the motion of a massful body bouncing on springy legs. They coordinated the joints of their human figures to keep the center of mass over the support feet, as required for balance. These techniques resulted in some of the best looking animation of legged locomotion that we have seen.

## 4 Animation, Control, and Modeling

Figure 2 shows the general process we use for animation. The user provides the control system with information about the desired animated behavior, such as speed, gait, path, etc. The user also initializes the legged model by placing it in a particular state. Once the animation is started, the control algorithms are responsible for stabilizing posture, maintaining the locomotion cycle, controlling speed and direction of travel, and regulating the behavior of the joints. Because the control is able to coordinate the lower levels of behavior for a task, the animator is free from direct involvement in specifying the joint torques or the details of the actual movements.

The three legged models are shown in Figure 1. Two of the models are patterned after physical robots that we built and use for laboratory experiments. One robot model is of a biped with telescoping legs and ball-joint hips. The other robot model is of a quadruped with telescoping legs and gimbal hips. The third model is a simplified version of a kangaroo. It is simplified in that it is planar, has one leg and arm instead of two, and it has fewer links in the tail than the animal. A total of six gaits were implemented and tested: biped running and galloping, quadruped trotting, bounding, and galloping, and kangaroo hopping. All of these gaits are technically classified as running, because they include at least one flight phase per cycle, a period when all feet leave the ground at the same time.

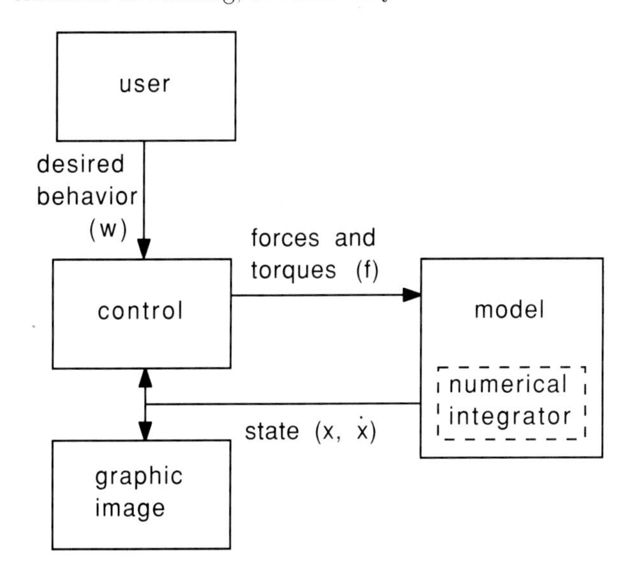


**Figure 2:** Block diagram of animation process. The model consists of equations of motion for the rigid bodies of the legged system, actuator and sensor models, force equations for ground-interaction, and a numerical integrator that produces motion as a function of time. The model calculates its behavior once every integration interval, 0.0004 s. The control calculates the force or torque to be exerted by each actuator based on the current state of the model, $\mathbf{X}, \dot{\mathbf{X}}$ and the user input $\mathbf{W}$. The control calculation is done every control interval, which is usually a few ms. The human animator specifies desired behavior $\mathbf{W}$, which consists of desired running speed, the path along which to travel, and any event information, such as when and how high to jump. The animator specifies his or her input before the animation process begins. In the current implementation, the animator must also initialize the state of the model.

### Control

In this section we describe the control algorithms used for animation of running. A control system for running must perform three primary functions

- cause the legs to step, exchanging support,
- provide balance to regulate the running speed, and
- maintain the body in an upright posture.

These three functions can be called *hopping*, *speed control*, and *posture control*.

### Hopping Control

An idea that developed in biomechanics over the last fifteen years is that animals use elastic structures in their limbs to improve the energetic efficiency of their locomotion. Tendons and ligaments in the legs and feet stretch during each collision with the ground, converting some the system's kinetic energy into elastic strain energy. The stored energy is returned during the next step, when the elastic structures rebound. A significant fraction of the total running energy, perhaps 20% to 40%, recirculates from one step to the next, without needing resupply from the muscles. Kangaroos use their substantial Achilles tendons to perform this energy recovery function whereas Alexander argues that humans store energy in their Achilles tendons and the ligaments that support the arch of the foot [1]. Compliant legs and feet also reduce peak loads that occur in running when the feet strike the ground at the end of each flight phase [11, 1].

We use compliance in the legs to produce the vertical oscillations needed in running. The control algorithms allow the mass of the body to rebound on the springy leg during ground collisions and to be drawn back to earth by gravity during the flight phase. The biped and quadruped legs were made springy with spring-damper actuator models for the telescoping joint. The kangaroo leg was made springy by modeling the ankle actuator as a torsional spring-damper with adjustable rest length. Both actuator models have the form

$$f = k(x - x_r) + b\dot{x} \qquad (1)$$

where $f$ is the actuator force, $k$ is the spring constant, $b$ the damping constant, $x$ the spring length, and $x_r$ the spring rest length.

Control of the spring rest length is used to inject or remove energy from the system in order to initiate the oscillation, modulate it, or stop it. For vertical hopping with a massless leg, the altitude of a particular hop is predicted by the sum of the potential strain energy in the leg spring, the potential energy of elevation of the system mass, and the kinetic energy due to motion of the body

$$h = (PE_{strain} + PE_{elevation} + KE)/Mg \qquad (2)$$

where h is the expected altitude of the hop, M is the system mass, and g is the acceleration of gravity. The control system can inject or remove energy to influence this outcome. This hopping control mechanism takes advantage of the dynamic interaction between the mechanical system and the control to generate the motion. No trajectory is specified.

### Speed Control

Legged systems are like inverted pendulums: they tip and accelerate whenever the point of support is

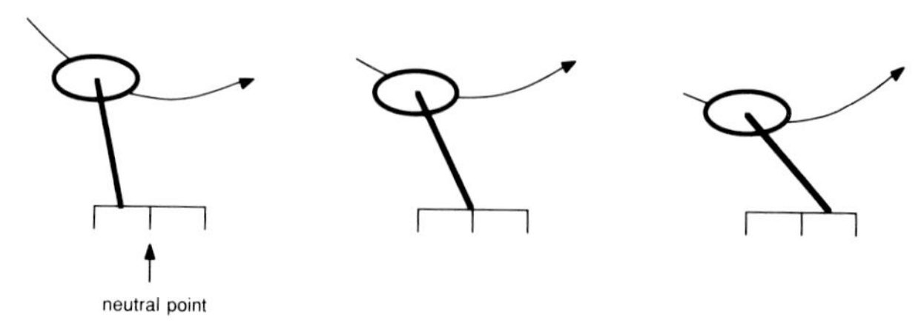


**Figure 3:** When the foot is positioned at the neutral point, the body travels along a symmetric path that leaves the system unaccelerated in the forward direction. Displacement of the foot from the neutral point accelerates the body by skewing the symmetry of the body's trajectory. When the foot is placed closer to the hip than the neutral point, the body accelerates forward during stance and the forward speed at liftoff is higher than the forward speed at touchdown (left). When the foot is placed further from the hip than the neutral point, the body decelerates during stance and the forward speed at liftoff is slower than the forward speed at touchdown (right). Horizontal lines under each figure indicate the distance the body travels during stance, and the curved lines indicate the path of the body.

displaced from the projection of the center of mass [6]. If the average point of support is kept under the average location of the center of mass, the system may tip for short periods, without tipping over entirely. One way to achieve such a balancing relationship between the feet and the center of mass is to move the body in a symmetric fashion over the supporting feet during each support period. When the control system places the foot to obtain a symmetric sweeping pattern, the forward speed will remain the same at liftoff as it was at touchdown. We call this position of the foot the *neutral point*. When the control system displaces the foot from the neutral point, the body accelerates, with the magnitude and direction of acceleration related to the magnitude and direction of the displacement, as shown in figure 3. The control system displaces the foot from the neutral point by a distance proportional to the difference between the actual speed and the desired speed. The control system computes the desired foot position as:

$$x_{fh,d} = \frac{\dot{x}T_s}{2} + k_{\dot{x}}(\dot{x} - \dot{x}_d) \qquad (3)$$

where $x_{fh,d}$ is the forward displacement of the foot from the projection of the center of gravity, $\dot{x}$ is the forward speed, $\dot{x}_d$ is the desired forward speed, $T_s$ is the predicted duration of the next support period, and $k_{\dot{x}}$ is a gain. The first term of equation 3 is an estimate of the neutral point and the second term is a correction for any error in forward speed or for a desired acceleration. The duration of the next support period is predicted to be the same as the measured duration of the previous support period. After the control system finds $x_{fh,d}$, a kinematic transformation determines the joint angles that will position the foot as specified.

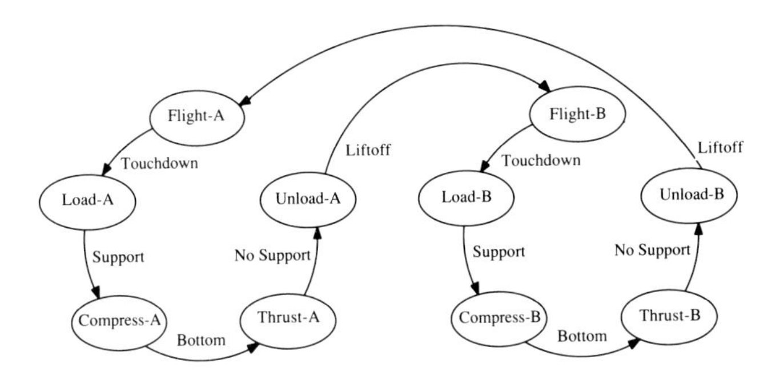


| State | Actions |
|---|---|
| FLIGHT | |
| Active leg leaves ground | Interchange active, idle legs<br>Lengthen active leg for landing<br>Position active leg for landing<br>Shorten idle leg |
| LOADING | |
| Active leg touches ground | Zero active hip torque<br>Keep idle leg short |
| COMPRESSION | |
| Active leg spring shortens | Servo pitch with active hip<br>Keep idle leg short |
| THRUST | |
| Active leg spring lengthens | Extend active leg<br>Servo pitch with active hip<br>Keep idle leg short |
| UNLOADING | |
| Active leg spring approaches full length | Shorten active leg<br>Zero hip torques active leg<br>Keep idle leg short |

**Figure 4:** Finite state machine that coordinates running. The state shown in the left column is entered when the sensory event, listed just below the state name, occurs. Actions are listed on the right. The controller advances through the states in sequence. The diagram is for a two-legged gait.

## Posture Control

Depending on the number of legs, the gait, and whether there is a tail, the trunk may pitch and roll during running. The long-term attitude of the trunk must be stabilized if the system is to remain upright. The control system we implemented regulates the orientation of the trunk by applying torques to the body during the support phase. In the biped and quadruped models, the hip actuators are used to apply the torques required for attitude control. In the kangaroo model, the knee is used to perform this function. Vertical loading on the feet keeps the leg from slipping when the torque is applied. The posture control torques are generated by a linear servo:

$$\tau = -k_p(\phi - \phi_d) - k_v(\dot{\phi}) \tag{4}$$

where $\tau$ is the leg torque, $\phi$ is the angle of the body, $\phi_d$ is the desired angle of the body, $\dot{\phi}$ is the angular rate of the body, and $k_p$, $k_v$ are gains.

The control systems for running use separate algorithms for stabilizing hopping, forward speed, and posture of the trunk. Each of these parts of the control acts independently, as though it influences just one component of the behavior. Interactions due to imperfect decoupling are treated as disturbances. This decoupling simplifies the control implementation.

In addition to the control algorithms described so far, each implementation uses a finite state machine to track the ongoing behavior of the model, to synchronize the control actions to the running behavior, and to do some bookkeeping. Figure 4 shows a state machine for the biped.

## Gaits

We implemented a total of six gaits: biped running and galloping; quadruped trotting, bounding, and galloping; and kangaroo hopping. The running algorithms for all six gaits are based on control originally developed for one-legged hopping. For each gait we tailored the state machine to cycle through the legs in the correct order and to invoke suitable versions of the algorithms that distribute the load among the support legs.

Bipedal running is like one-legged hopping, except there is an extra *idle* leg, in addition to the active leg. The idle leg is kept short and out of the way while the active leg performs the functions described earlier to control forward speed, hopping height, and balance. The state machine for bipedal running is shown in figure 4.

In quadruped trotting and bounding, the legs are coordinated to work together in pairs. The coordination we used makes each pair of legs act collectively like a single leg, called a *virtual leg*. The members of each pair strike the ground in unison and leave the ground in unison. Diagonal legs form pairs in trotting and front legs and rear legs form pairs in bounding. One can think of these quadruped gaits as *virtual biped gaits*, with the active pair of legs providing support while the idle pair swings forward in preparation for the next step. The higher levels of the control system ignore the individual physical legs, pretending to do biped control on the two virtual legs as described earlier.

Quadruped galloping is similar to bounding except that the legs of the front and rear pairs no longer strike and leave the ground in perfect unison. The stance phase is composed of a single support phase, a double support phase, and then a second single support phase. The legs are positioned on the ground with a separation both in time and space. The stance phase is extended and the legs of each pair share the work of rebounding the body. Biped galloping is similar to quadruped galloping in that the two stance legs share a single support phase. We implemented two styles of biped galloping. In one style the legs swing forward together during the flight phase. In the other style they swing forward independently during the other leg's single support phase. The first style produces a motion that is similar to the front half of a galloping horse while the second is closer to the pattern used by galloping humans. Pitching of the body in response to swinging of the legs is greatly reduced in the second form of galloping.

### Kangaroo control

Control algorithms for the kangaroo were essentially the same as for the robot models, with additional provisions for coordinating the joints of the articulated leg and for moving the tail. Kangaroos have legs with rotary joints. In the kangaroo model we eliminated the toe joint, leaving an ankle, a knee, and a hip, all of which have axes perpendicular to the sagittal plane. We made several decisions that constrained the behavior of the leg and allowed us to program it using methods originally developed for robot telescoping legs.

We decided to use the ankle joint as the primary energy storage element in the leg. We assumed that the ankle actuator consisted of a spring-damper mechanism with an adjustable zero spring length. This mechanism models a muscle acting in series with a springy Achilles tendon. We adjusted the spring and damper characteristics so that a significant fraction of the energy stored in the spring during leg compression was returned during leg extension.

We decided to configure the leg so the ground reaction force generated during hopping passes approximately through the knee. This configuration minimizes the moment required at the knee to resist support and thrust forces. In balanced running, the ground reaction forces act along a line passing from the toe through the system center of mass. The control system servoes the hip joint to keep the knee on this thrust line during stance.

Because torque about the knee is not needed to support the body, we use the knee to maintain the body in a level posture. The linear servo given in equation (4) operates at the knee during the stance phase to eliminate errors in body orientation and orientation rate.

The tail is made to counteroscillate with the leg, keeping the angular momentum of the entire system near zero throughout the running cycle. When the leg strokes backward during the stance phase, the tail strokes downward. The tail motion is produced by making a step change in the spring rest length for the actuator at the base joint of the tail. The spring damper characteristics of the joint is tuned to oscillate in period with the running motion. The two peripheral joints in the tail are actuated by a spring damper with fixed rest length. The head was servoed to stay level throughout the running motion.

### Modeling

Each of the legged systems was modeled as a tree of rigid bodies, each connected to its parent by rotary or sliding joints. The mass, mass center, and moment of inertia

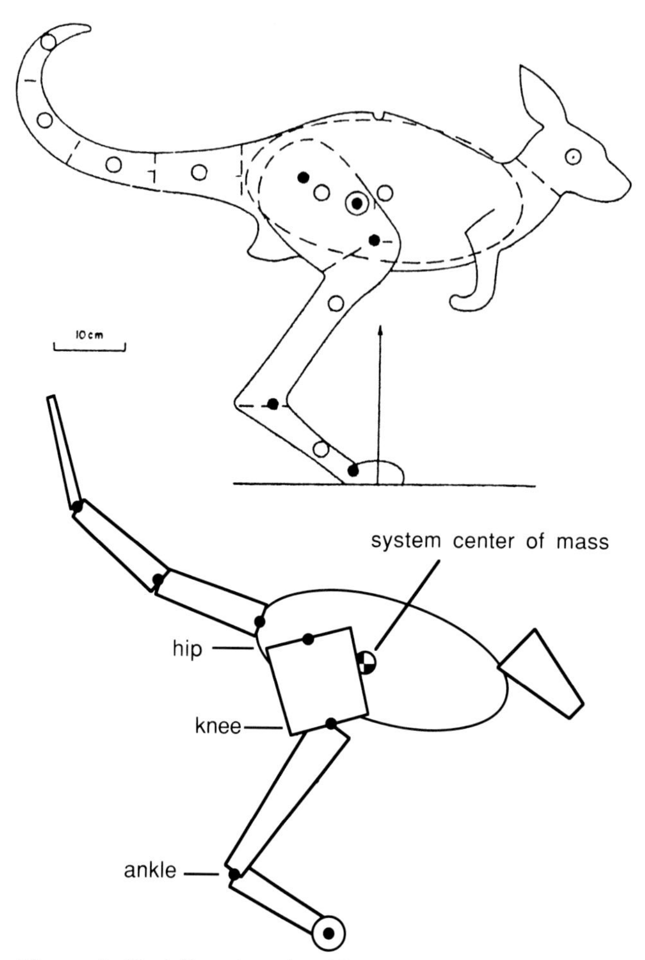


**Figure 5:** Top) Drawing of real kangaroo used as the basis of the kangaroo model. It was a juvenile red kangaroo weighing 6.6 kg. Drawing is from [2]. Bottom) Diagram of kangaroo model. Except for the trunk, each link was modeled as the frustum of a cone, with pivots at the base and tip. The two legs of the real kangaroo were combined into one model leg. All dimensions were chosen to match the real kangaroo in link length and link mass, assuming the kangaroo was the density of water. Mass centers and moments of inertia were calculated from the geometric model.

for each body were determined in one of two ways. For the robot models we used actual measurements of the mass properties. For the kangaroo model we used the link length, mass, and mass center data given in [2]. We calculated the moments of inertia of the links from the geometry used in the graphics, typically assuming the density of water.

An actuator capable of exerting forces or torques was located at each joint. The lowest level of control used linear servo mechanisms to specify actuator forces:

$$f = -k_p(\theta - \theta_d) - k_v\dot{\theta} \qquad (5)$$

where $f$ is the force or torque acting on the joint, $\theta$ is the joint angle or length, and $k_p$ and $k_v$ are position and velocity feedback gains. These joint servos have the same dynamical behavior as a spring-damper mechanism with programmable rest length. Depending on one's point of view and the design of the control system, these joint servos can be regarded as part of the control system or as part of the model.

Environmental interaction was restricted to gravitational forces and ground contact forces. A single point on each foot could make contact with the ground. The ground contact model for each foot consisted of four spring and damper sets: one vertical, two tangent to the surface, and one torsional about the ground surface normal. The rest length of each spring was reset when a foot first touched the ground during a support period. The ground contact compliance represents the compliance of the "paw pad", the elastic elements on the bottom of the feet, plus any compliance provided by the support surface. The kangaroo model used a non-linear paw pad spring in the vertical direction:

$$f_z = k_{gz} \frac{k_r}{k_r + z - 1} \qquad \text{for } z < 0 \qquad (6)$$

where $f_z$ is the vertical spring force, $k_{gz}$ is the paw pad stiffness, $k_r$ is the paw pad thickness, and $z$ is the altitude of the foot contact point above the ground. We chose a non-linear spring for this part of the model because it is consistent with compression of an elastic material between two surfaces, it reduced the maximum deflection during the support period, and it allowed vertical forces to develop more slowly at initial impact.

We assume that once ground contact is made, there is no slipping between the foot and the ground. This is equivalent to an infinite coefficient of friction. To test this assumption we used data from typical runs to calculate the coefficient of friction that would have prevented slipping. For the biped, this value was always less than 1. With the exception of the very beginning and end of the support period, a coefficient of friction of about 0.5 would have prevented slipping for the quadruped and kangaroo. At the very beginning of the support period, when the feet begin to make contact with the ground, however, there is a period of up to 10 ms during which the coefficient of friction would have had to be almost 2.0 to prevent slipping. A similar period occurred at the very end of the stance phase. On a day without oil leaks, the coefficient of friction between a robot foot and the floor of our laboratory is about 1.0.

Equations of motion were generated for the structure with a commercially available program [14]. The program generates efficient subroutines ($O(n)$ where $n$ is the number of links) that implement the equations of motion using a variant of Kane's method and a symbolic simplification phase. The equations of motion were numerically integrated using Euler's method, with time steps of about 0.0004 s. Simulations of a single creature ran between 7 and 10 times slower than real time on a SUN Sparc2.

### Dynamic Scaling

We used the basic principles of allometry to scale the size of a model, along with its control system and movements. Adult animals of a single species generally scale uniformly in all linear dimensions, and thereby maintain their proportions [11]. For a system scaled in this fashion, Table 1 gives rules for scaling the control system and the motions. Suppose we want to animate a kangaroo that is $L$ times bigger than normal. Using the table we see that it will hop $L$ times as high, travel $\sqrt{L}$ as fast, and have a cadence $1/\sqrt{L}$ of the original cadence.

| Quantity | Units | Scale Factor |
|---|---|---|
| Basic variables | | |
| length | $L$ | $L$ |
| time | $T$ | $L^{1/2}$ |
| force | $F$ | $L^3$ |
| torque | $FL$ | $L^4$ |
| Motion variables | | |
| displacement | $L$ | $L$ |
| velocity | $LT^{-1}$ | $L^{1/2}$ |
| acceleration | $LT^{-2}$ | 1 |
| angular displacement | – | 1 |
| angular velocity | $T^{-1}$ | $L^{-1/2}$ |
| angular acceleration | $T^{-2}$ | $L^{-1}$ |
| Mechanical parameters | | |
| mass | $FL^{-1}T^2$ | $L^3$ |
| stiffness | $FL^{-1}$ | $L^2$ |
| damping | $FL^{-1}T$ | $L^{5/2}$ |
| moment of inertia | $FLT^2$ | $L^5$ |
| torsional stiffness | $FL$ | $L^4$ |
| torsional damping | $FLT$ | $L^{9/2}$ |

**Table 1:** Scaling rules that preserve geometric similarity. If a system is scaled in size by a factor $L$ and its mechanical parameters are each scaled according to the table, then the motion of the scaled system can be found from the motion of the original unscaled system. The table is derived assuming uniform scaling in all dimensions (geometric similarity), and that the acceleration of gravity is invariant to scale.

There are two ways to use these scaling rules. One way is to generate a new model of the creature and a new control system, based on the scaled mechanical parameters available from the table. Behavior of the scaled model can be used directly. An alternative is to implement a single model and control system at scale 1, but to scale all input to the animation as a function of $1/L$, and all output as a function of $L$. For example, if $L = 2$, initial positions would be scaled by $L^{-1} = 1/2$, initial times and the integration time step would be scaled by $L^{-1/2} = 1/\sqrt{2}$, and desired running speed would be scaled by $L^{-1/2} = 1/\sqrt{2}$. The animation could then be run at scale 1. The outputs are scaled before displayed: positions and geometry by $L = 2$ and time by $L^{1/2} = \sqrt{2}$. We used the latter approach, but both give identical results.

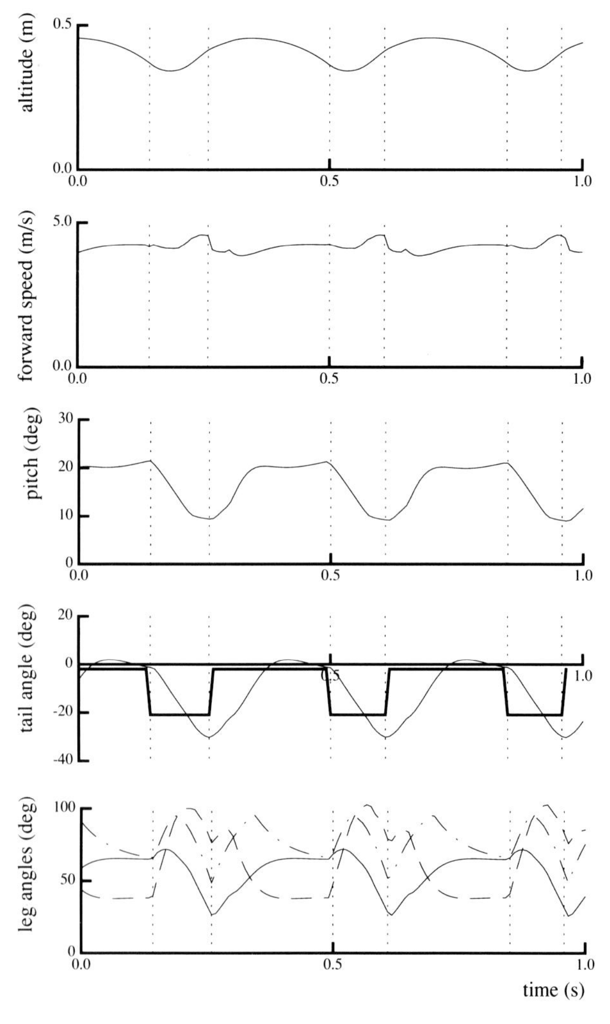


**Figure 6:** Data recorded from planar kangaroo model during three steps of running with a desired speed of 5 m/s. The vertical dashed lines bracket the stance phase. The leg joint angles are defined in Figure 5. Key to joints in leg angle plot: (solid) hip, (dashed) knee, (dot-dashed) ankle.

## 5 Results

Table 2 compares the behavior of each animated runner to the physical system it is designed to model. The data indicate that there are many similarities. For example, the extended flight phase is shorter than the gathered flight phase for both the physical and the animated quadruped during bounding. The kangaroo's body and tail oscillate as it runs and the magnitude of the oscillations are similar. The table also illustrates a number of differences. For instance, the gathered flight phase of the animated quadruped is twice that of the robot quadruped. The animated biped spent a great deal more time in flight than the robot.

Another difference between the animated and real kangaroo is in the behavior of the feet at impact. The real kangaroo accelerates its feet to the speed of the ground just before they touch, so they do not scuff or have a tangential impact. We call this *ground speed*

| Quantity | Robot/ Animal | Animation |
|---|---|---|
| **Quadruped Bound** | | |
| pitch magnitude (deg) | 26.4 | 25.8 |
| stride length (m) | 1.15 | 1.22 |
| stride duration (s) | 0.37 | 0.43 |
| gathered flight phase duration (s) | 0.11 | 0.22 |
| extended flight phase duration (s) | 0.04 | 0.03 |
| stance duration, front legs (s) | 0.10 | 0.10 |
| stance duration, rear legs (s) | 0.12 | 0.08 |
| change of leg length during support (m) | 0.085 | 0.092 |
| running speed (m/s) | 2.9 | 2.8 |
| error in running speed (m/s) | 1.25 | 1.2 |
| **Quadruped Trot** | | |
| pitch magnitude (deg) | 2.2 | 6.2 |
| stride length (m) | 1.84 | 1.49 |
| stride duration (s) | 0.80 | 0.54 |
| flight duration (s) | 0.27 | 0.18 |
| stance duration (s) | 0.12 | 0.09 |
| change of leg length during support (m) | 0.04 | 0.03 |
| desired running speed (m/s) | 2.3 | 2.3 |
| error in running speed (m/s) | 0.7 | 0.2 |
| **Biped Run** | | |
| pitch magnitude (deg) | 2.0 | 3.4 |
| roll magnitude (deg) | 6.7 | 11.5 |
| stride length (m) | 0.57 | 0.74 |
| stride duration (s) | 0.36 | 0.47 |
| flight duration (s) | 0.18 | 0.29 |
| stance duration (s) | 0.18 | 0.18 |
| change of leg length during support (m) | 0.01 | 0.04 |
| error in running speed (m/s) | -0.3 | 0.2 |
| **Kangaroo Hop** | | |
| peak vertical acceleration (g) | 5 | 4.6 |
| pitch magnitude (deg) | 10 | 12 |
| magnitude of tail wag relative to trunk (deg) | 30 | 31 |
| stride length (m) | 2.2 | 1.5 |
| stride duration (s) | 0.35 | 0.35 |
| flight duration (s) | 0.25 | 0.24 |
| stance duration (s) | 0.10 | 0.11 |
| desired running speed (m/s) | 6.2 | 5.0 |

**Table 2:** Comparison between behavior of physical robot and animation, and between real and animated kangaroo. The runs were selected to match running speed as closely as possible, so running speed should not be used for comparison. The kangaroo data are from [2], and the quadruped robot data are from [13].

*matching*. The animated kangaroo does not do ground speed matching.

The control algorithms were successful in providing balanced running, regulating the speed of travel to within about 10% of the desired value, and in steering the creatures along specified paths. To get each new creature or gait working required some adjustment of the control parameters. For example, to improve the appearance of the quadruped trotting and bounding motions, we reduced the standing length of the legs. To get the kangaroo tail to oscillate in rhythm with the running motion, we adjusted the spring and damping constants of the tail joint servo until the natural frequency was about equal to the hopping frequency. To make the kangaroo jump over an obstacle, a number of additional states were added to the state machine. These states allowed stiffer operation of the legs for the jump, more dissipation in the legs during landing after the jump, and a number of cosmetic changes. Once adjusted, the locomotion proceeded without adjustment.

## 6 Discussion

The motions described in this paper are physically realistic in that they were generated by applying forces and torques to physical models of a mechanical system. The degree of physical realism depends on the degree to which the system is accurately modeled. For instance the mass parameters of the links, structural strength of the links, torque available from the actuators, actuator bandwidth, stiffness of the feet, and external friction are parameters that help determine the overall appearance of a motion.

There is no guarantee, however, that physically realistic motion will be "natural looking motion". It seems that animals move with a smoothness and coordination that is not required by physical realism alone. Constraints on smoothness, compliance, or energetic efficiency could eventually lead to uniformly natural looking behavior. We found that increasing the compliance of the actuators generally improved the appearance of the animated motions. We expect that constraints that lower the overall energy expenditure will also contribute to more natural looking locomotion.

As mentioned earlier, the methods described in this paper might be thought of as a tool box for handcrafting control systems for new creatures and behaviors. We expect that further development of control systems for computer animation will proceed in two steps. First, we expect control algorithms for individual creatures to become capable of a wider variety of behavior with less manual adjustment. Eventually, it should be possible to design control algorithms that will make creatures autonomous enough to "do what they are told". The animator should be able to direct the behavior at a relatively high level, and let the control system propel the system from one place to another at the desired rate along the specified path, use specified gaits, change between gaits, and maintain balance, all while adhering to physical realism. For well defined sets of creatures and behaviors, this goal is within sight.

Second, we think it is possible to automate the process of generating control algorithms for new creatures. Given control algorithms that work correctly for the locomotion of a horse, for example, it should be possible to automatically generate control algorithms for an antelope, dog, cat, or elephant. Initially such automatically generated control might be restricted to a limited repertoire of behavior. A first cut might aim at balanced running at a range of speeds with several gaits and transitions between gaits. It is difficult to predict how long it will take to achieve this level of control automatically, or to go beyond it to automate more complicated creatures or higher-level function.

One might expect the various workers involved in the study of control algorithms for legged locomotion—animators, robot engineers, and biological scientists—to differ in their criteria for successful algorithms. Such criteria could include precision of control, generality of control algorithms with respect to diverse behaviors and diverse creatures, the aesthetic appearance of the resulting movement, the simplicity and elegance of the solution, or the degree to which an algorithm explains the workings of animals. We might find, however, that the solutions that best explain animal behavior will be similar to those that produce the best robot behavior, and that the easiest way to make an animation look animal-like is to use a control system like the animal's. It is also possible that techniques successful in producing animations that are visually pleasing and natural will lead to a better understanding of the control at work in animals and to the construction of more effective robots.

## 7 Acknowledgements

We thank Tom McMahon for helping us appreciate the beauty of dynamic scaling laws, and Takashi Aoki and Don Floyd for contributing to the software used in this project. This research was supported by contracts from the DARPA Information Sciences and Technology Office and the Charles Stark Draper Laboratory.

## 8 References

1. Alexander, R. McN. 1988. *Elastic Mechanisms in Animal Movement* (Cambridge University Press: New York).

2. Alexander, R. McN., Vernon, A. 1975. The mechanics of hopping by kangaroos (Macropodidas). *J. Zoology (London)* 177:265–303.

3. Bruderlin, A., Calvert, T. W. 1989. Goal-Directed, Dynamic Animation of Human Walking. *Computer Graphics* 23(3):233–242.

4. Girard, M. 1987. Interactive design of 3-D computer animated legged animal motion. *IEEE Computer Graphics and Animation* June: 39–51.

5. Girard, M. and Maciejewski, A. A, 1985. Computational Modeling for the Computer Animation of Legged Figures. *Siggraph* 19(3): 263–270.

6. Hemami, H., Weimer, F. C., Koozekanani, S. H. 1973. Some aspects of the inverted pendulum problem for modeling of locomotion systems. *IEEE Trans. Automatic Control* AC-18:658–661.

7. Hodgins, J., Raibert, M. H. 1990. Biped Gymnastics. *International Journal of Robotics Research*, 9(2):115–132.

8. Hodgins, J., Raibert, M. H., 1991, Adjusting step length for rough terrain locomotion, *IEEE J. Robotics and Automation*, Sacramento.

9. Hodgins, J., Koechling, J., Raibert, M. H. 1985. Running experiments with a planar biped. *Third International Symposium on Robotics Research*, Cambridge: MIT Press.

10. McKenna, M. and Zeltzer, D. 1990. Dynamic Simulation of Autonomous Legged Locomotion. *Computer Graphics* 24(4):29–38.

11. McMahon, T. A. 1984. *Muscles, Reflexes, and Locomotion*. Princeton: Princeton University Press.

12. Raibert, M. H. 1985. *Legged Robots That Balance*. Cambridge: MIT Press.

13. Raibert, M. H., 1990. Trotting, pacing, and bounding by a quadruped robot, *J. Biomechanics*, Vol.23, Suppl.1, 79–98.

14. Rosenthal, D. E., Sherman, M. A., 1986. High performance multibody simulations via symbolic equation manipulation and Kane's method. *J. Astronautical Sciences* 34:3, 223–239.

15. van de Panne M., Fiume, E., Vranesic, Z. 1990. Reusable Motion Synthesis Using State-Space Controllers *Computer Graphics* 24(4): 225–234.

16. Wilhelms, J. 1986. Virya–A motion control editor for kinematic and dynamic animation. *Graphics Interface '86* 141–146.

17. Wilhelms, J. 1987. Using Dynamic Analysis for Realistic Animation of Articulated Bodies. *IEEE Computer Graphics and Animation* June: 12–27.

18. Witkin, A., Kass, M., 1988. Spacetime Constraints. *Computer Graphics* 22(4):159–168.

## 9 Appendix: Physical Parameters of Models

| Link | Link length ($m$) | Mass center ($m$) | Mass ($kg$) | Moment of Inertia ($kg - m^2$) |
|---|---|---|---|---|
| Biped | | | | |
| trunk | | | 23.1 | [.17 .17 .30] |
| upper leg | .20 | .095 | 1.4 | [.018 .017 .0014] |
| lower leg | .63 | .22 | .64 | [.02 .02 .00018] |
| Hip location wrt trunk center of mass: $x = 0.0$, $y = \pm 0.072$, $z = 0.0$ | | | | |
| Quadruped | | | | |
| trunk | | | 10.0 | [.54 2.35 2.39] |
| upper leg | .41 | .2 | 1.5 | [.043 .043 0] |
| lower leg | .4 | .2 | 1.0 | [.0035 .0035 0] |
| Hip location wrt trunk center of mass: $x = \pm 0.39$, $y = \pm 0.12$, $z = 0.0$ | | | | |
| Kangaroo | | | | |
| trunk | | | 3.67 | .034 |
| thigh | .13 | .064 | 1.62 | .0039 |
| shin | .26 | .105 | .60 | .0033 |
| foot | .174 | .082 | .14 | .00038 |
| tail1 | .166 | .079 | .24 | .00058 |
| tail2 | .166 | .071 | .14 | .00033 |
| tail3 | .166 | .076 | .069 | .00016 |
| head | .13 | .04, .04 | .33 | .00046 |
| Hip location wrt trunk mass center: [-.11 0] | | | | |
| Head location wrt trunk mass center: [.21 0] | | | | |
| Tail location wrt trunk mass center: [.2 0] | | | | |

**Table 3:** Physical parameters of models used in animations. Link lengths are from proximal joint to distal joint. Mass centers are distances from the proximal joint of a link to the mass center. Moments of inertia are about the mass center of the link. The diagonal of the moment of inertia tensor is given.

# Interactive Behaviors for Bipedal Articulated Figures

Cary B. Phillips
Norman I. Badler

Computer Graphics Research Laboratory
Department of Computer and Information Science
University of Pennsylvania
Philadelphia, Pennsylvania 19104-6389

## Abstract

We describe techniques for interactively controlling bipedal articulated figures through kinematic constraints. These constraints model certain behavioral tendencies which capture some of the characteristics of human-like movement, and give us control over such elements as the figures' balance and stability. They operate in near real-time, so provide behavioral control for interactive manipulation. These constraints form the basis of an interactive motion-generation system that allows the active movement elements to be layered on top of the passive behavioral constraints.

**Keywords:** Interactive manipulation, inverse kinematics, articulated figures, balance, behavioral animation.

## 1. Introduction

In this paper, we describe techniques for interacting with two-footed articulated figures through kinematic constraints, concentrating on the movement of the feet and the center of mass. We particularly address the class of movements which are not bounded by dynamics. Such motions are typically executed at slow speed where inertial or frictional effects are minimal, and include standing, shifting the weight from one foot to the other, turning around, and taking small steps to the front, back, or to the side. In short, these motions encompass the types of movement which people act out while standing and moving but not actively locomoting from one place to another. We believe that this type of motion is of great importance to an animator, and we show how we describe these motions kinematically. We believe this approach provides superior control to dynamics techniques, particularly since these motions do not need the full complexity of a dynamic simulation.

Our movement primitives serve as the foundation for several higher level motion description mechanisms. Since they operate in near real time, they provide behavioral control for interactive manipulation. This allows the user to push, pull, and twist the figure interactively using our 3D direct manipulation interface, all while the figure maintains its balance. These primitives form the basis of an interactive animation system that allows the active movement elements to be layered on top of the passive behavioral constraints. Finally, these primitives provide the necessary interface to task level animation programs.

## 2. Background

Systems which provide goal directed motion have been used for the most part only on rather simple objects such as chains or mechanisms, and the available goals have been rather simplistic as well, such as point-to-nail or point-to-point constraints. Although such systems are very powerful for generating certain types of motion, they have not adequately addressed the problem of how an animator is to assemble a collection of goals which will accurately describe the intended motion [1]. Stating that such constraints will vary over time does not solve the fundamental problems of determining useful sets of constraints for human motion, negotiating their overlapping interactions, or organizing their timing for motion realism. In addition, they have not been successfully applied to highly articulated figures with expected behaviors. Flocking behavior-constraining functions have demonstrated particle motion within a global framework [5], but do not apply to articulated figures.

## 3. Articulated Figures and Inverse Kinematics

The techniques described in this paper are implemented as a part of *Jack*™, a multifaceted system for interactively modeling, manipulating, and animating articulated figures, principally human figures. *Jack* represents figures as collections of rigid segments connected by joints that may have arbitrary rotational or translational degrees of freedom. The model of the human figure that we use for the examples in this paper has 36 joints with a total of 88 degrees of freedom, excluding the hands and fingers. It has a torso consisting of 17 segments and 18 vertebral joints [2].

*Jack* uses an inverse kinematics algorithm that is based on a variable-metric optimization procedure, described in

† *Jack* is a trademark of the University of Pennsylvania. "Jack" is a nonsense name, not an acronym.



©1991 ACM-0-89791-436-8/91/007/0359 $00.75

detail in [6]. This method uses the gradient descent approach to minimize the potential energy described by a set of constraints. Each constraint describes a desired geometric relationship between an *end effector* and a *goal* position or orientation in space. The algorithm is an iterative numerical procedure. At each iteration it computes the Jacobian of the input joint set, which relates the change in each joint angle to the change in total potential energy, which is weighted sum of the energy from each constraint. This determines a joint-space trajectory to follow which minimizes the total energy. The algorithm handles arbitrary numbers of constraints and arbitrary numbers of degrees of freedom. The constraints may overlap in the sense that a single joint may affect several constraints.

### Generating Motion with Inverse Kinematics

Generating motion with inverse kinematics is somewhat different from constraint based systems that are based on dynamics. In particular, the only useful product of the inverse kinematics algorithm is the final position with the constraint energy minimized. The intermediate steps during the solution process should not be considered as "motion". To describe motion with inverse kinematics, we must select an appropriate set of end effectors and then describe the desired positions and/or orientations of these end effectors at each time increment. We then invoke the inverse kinematics algorithm at each time step to determine the set of joint angles that satisfies the desired relationships. The key to successfully describing motion through inverse kinematics is to choose properly the end effectors and then design sets of constraints that cause the figure to move in predictable patterns.

For the purposes of this paper, we consider the inverse kinematics algorithm as a black box that takes as input a set of constraints and a set of joints and returns with a set of joint angles that minimize the energy described by the constraints.

### Constraints as Handles

We use the constraints as handles by which to control parts of the figure. We can make a loose analogy between this and a marionette puppet controlled by strings, except that our strings need not hang vertically, and they can twist and push as well as pull. How do we pull on the strings to get the figure to move as we want? How many strings do we need? Where should we attach them? We choose not to shape the goal-control mechanism into highly specific motion control elements to perform tasks like walking or running, but to design general purpose motion building blocks that stand by themselves as useful mechanisms of control.

We are not overly concerned here with the physical laws of nature but in capturing some of the global characteristics of human-like movement. We are willing to sacrifice some degree of Newtonian realism in order to achieve greater interactive control. We believe that a large portion of these characteristics can be captured through some simple behavioral tendencies, the most important of which are balance and stability. By phrasing these tendencies as figure *behaviors*, we can view the effect of the constraints in a more intuitive light.

## 4. Behaviors for Articulated Figures

The basic architecture of our system lets us treat time in one of two ways. We can "freeze time" and make postural adjustments to the figure through the real-time interaction mechanism. In this case, we can think of each iteration of the interaction as a time step. Alternatively, we can set up a series of primitive *actions* and then start the system time running from a certain point. The primitive actions cause the motion to take place.

### The Feet

We begin by recognizing the importance of the support structure of the human body, i.e. its feet and legs and how they support the body's weight. As bipedal creatures, human beings have a built-in closed loop between the feet and legs that they are very good at manipulating. Unfortunately, because we model articulated figures as a hierarchy, we must take special care in modeling the connection between the feet and the ground. We do this by designating one foot or the other as dominant, and we the root the figure hierarchy through that foot. We hold the other foot in place by a constraint located at the ball of the foot. The orientation component of the foot constraint keeps the foot flat on the floor while allowing it to twist.

### The Center of Mass and Balance

The center of mass is of critical importance because so many aspects of the movement through space of a human figure are dictated by the need to maintain balance. In addition, many types of movement, such as stepping and walking, involve intentional shifts in the center of mass away from the support polygon, followed by actions of the feet and legs to restore the balance. We consider balance as one of the most significant behaviors to model in a human figure, both the ability to maintain it and the ability to deviate from it.

We model balance in the figure as a constraint on the center of mass to remain vertically above a point in the support polygon. We associate the center of mass logically with the lower torso region of the figure, and we use this as the end effector of the constraint, with the ankle, knee, and hip joints of the dominant leg as the constraint variables. During the constraint satisfaction process at each time step, the center of mass is not recomputed. Since the center of mass belongs logically to the lower torso, its position relative to the torso remains fixed as the inverse kinematics algorithm positions the ankle, knee, and hip so that the previously computed center of mass point lies above the balance point. There are generally other constraints active at the same time, along with other postural adjustments, so that several parts of the figure assume different postures during the process.

After we solve the constraints, we recompute the center of mass. It will generally lie in a different location because of the postural adjustments, indicating that the figure is not balanced as it should be. Therefore, we must solve the constraints again, and repeat the process until the balance condition is satisfied. In this case the structure of the human figure helps. Most of the postural adjustments take place on the first iteration, so on subsequent iterations the changes in the center of mass relative to the rest of the body are quite minor. We measure the distance that the center of mass changes from one iteration to the next, and we accept the posture when the change is below a certain threshold. Although it is difficult to guarantee the convergence theoretically, in practice it seldom takes more than two iterations to achieve balance.

### The Spine and Torso

Monheit [2] has developed a computational model for describing movements of the spine in terms of total bending angles in the forward, lateral, and axial directions. The technique uses weighting factors that distribute the total bending angle to the individual vertebrae in such as way that respects the proper coupling between the joints. Different weight distributions generate bends of different flavors, such as neck curls or motions confined to the lower back.

We have an optional behavior that holds constant the global orientation of the head. To model this type of behavior, we monitor the global orientation of the neck as the body posture changes at each time step. We measure the difference in euler angles between the current and desired neck orientation, and then apply these rotations to the spine.

### The Pelvis

The pelvis connects the lower part of the spine to the upper legs. This is the general area of the center mass, so its position is governed primarily by the center of mass constraint. Therefore, our constraints on the pelvis involve only its orientation. The passive behavior of the pelvis involves holding its current orientation. Because of its central location, manipulations of the pelvis provide a powerful control over the general posture of a figure, especially when combined with the balance and torso constraints.

## 5. Real-time Interaction

The real-time interaction mechanism is described in [3] and [4]. Using this facility, we can interactively move and rotate the goals of constraints around in space through a 3D direct manipulation technique which gets its input from a three button mouse. This mechanism provides a nice form of postural control, although it is not so good at choreographing complex *motions* interactively.

We provide the following types of interaction. Each of these corresponds to a *Jack* system command which allows the appropriate property to be manipulated interactively.

**bend torso** This follows the technique described in [2]. The center of mass constraint causes automatic postural adjustments in the legs. For example, if we bend the torso forward, the hips automatically shift backwards so that the center of mass remains over the same point. Figure 1 shows how the hips automatically shift backwards to maintain balance as we bend the figure forwards.

**rotate pelvis** This interactively changes the orientation of the constraint on the pelvis. We can rotate the pelvis forward and backward, side to side, or we can twist it vertically. The constraints on the feet keep them planted on the ground. For example, if we set up a constraint on the torso, and then rotate the pelvis forwards, the figure will automatically squat but keep its head up.

**move center of mass** To do this, we move the goal point for the center of mass constraint, which allows us to disturb the figure's balance. We can shift the center of forwards or backwards, side to side to concentrate the weight on one foot or the other, or up and down to make the figure squat or stand on its toes.

**move foot** One foot is always the dominant one, and it serves as the root of the figure hierarchy. The other foot is held in place by a constraint. We can interactively move either foot. The passive balance behavior can either hold the center of mass at a fixed point or allow it to float to a point between the feet. Figure 2 show the center of mass floating between the feet as we move the left foot backwards and to the side.

## 6. The Composition of Actions

The notion of *action* in *Jack* is a scripted change to a constraint controlling the body. An action has three distinct parts: its beginning, its application, and its termination. Each action has a distinct starting and ending time. Each action has its own set of constraints controlling part of the body. Its parameters control the velocity of the constraint's goal and the constraint's weight as a function of time. Through a windowed interface, we can create, modify, and delete actions and get a global picture of a movement sequence.

Our system has actions which correspond to each of the types of manipulation described in Section 5. Each action causes the appropriate body part to move to a specified position or assume a desired orientation. The user specifies the desired posture by moving the body part using the manipulation mechanisms. This may be changed interactively, so if an action does not have the desired affect it can be easily adjusted. The position and orientation of the goal of an action's constraint are interpolated between a starting and ending value. The starting value is the current position or orientation of the end effector when the constraint is activated.

Actions may overlap in time, even ones which control the same part of the body. Since each action has its own constraints, this simply means that during the period of overlap, there will be multiple constraints on that part of the body. This is handled automatically by the inverse kinematics algorithm. We must take special care to control the effect of constraints when this overlap occurs. If constraints die out abruptly, then their termination may cause discontinuities in the motion of the figure. This may happen if a constraint is pulling part of a figure in a certain direction opposed to another constraint. In this case, the constraint should be phased out gradually rather than terminated instantaneously.

We allow the weight factor of each constraint to be a function of time. The weighting function associated with a constraint may increase, decrease, ease in and then ease out, or remain constant over the lifetime of the action. In practice, constant weights suffices when there are not many active actions. However, actions controlling the same part of the

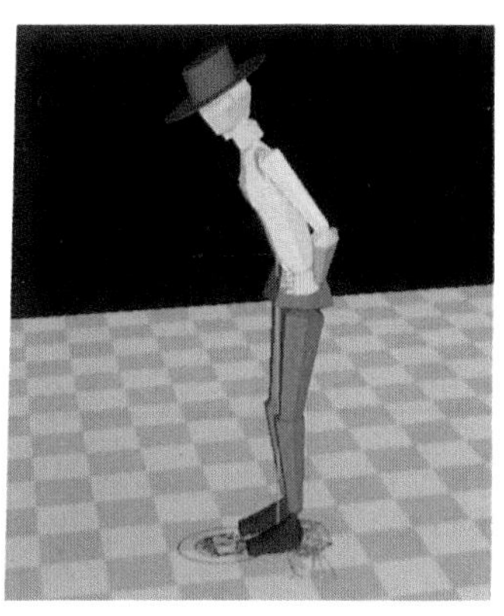
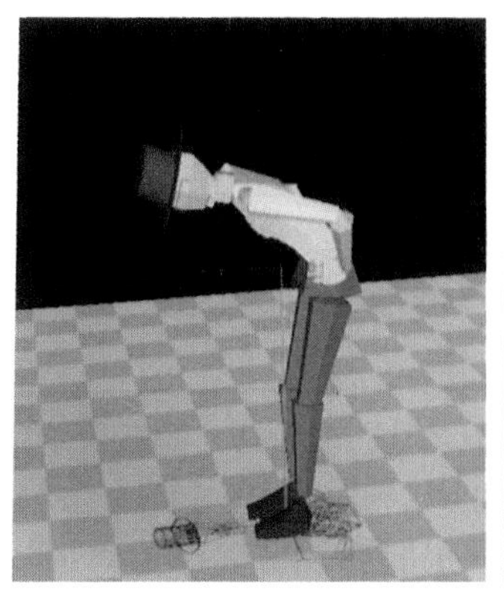
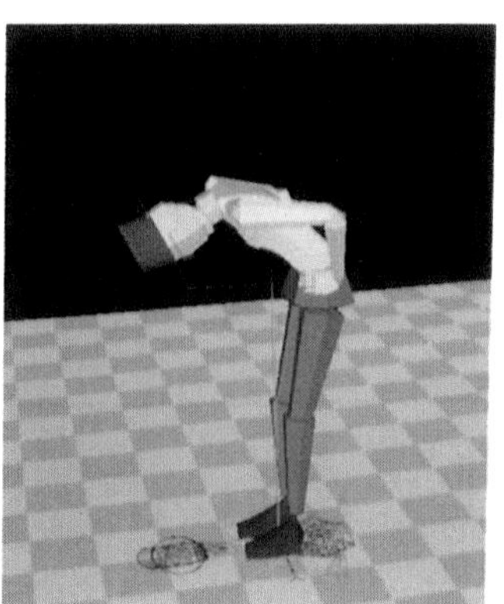

Figure 1: Interactively bending the spine

Figure 2: Interactively moving a foot

body that overlap in time should generally have the weight of the first action decay towards the end of its lifetime instead of remaining constant. It the current implementation of our system, it is up to the user to recognize this situation and set the weight functions accordingly.

## 7. Conclusions

We do not expect these elements alone to automatically generate realistic-looking human movement. Our approach has been to develop a general purpose set of movement elements which have specific effects. Some effects are local, such as moving a foot or raising a heel, while others are global, like maintaining balance or keeping the torso vertical. Taken together, these elements allow us to compose movement sequences of a quite general nature. In the future, we will consider how to automatically generate sequences of these actions to provide more "macro-like" control.

## Acknowledgments

This research is partially supported by Lockheed Engineering and Management Services (NASA Johnson Space Center), NASA Ames Grant NAG-2-426, NASA Goddard through University of Iowa UICR, FMC Corporation, Martin-Marietta Denver Aerospace, Deere and Company, Siemens Research, NSF CISE Grant CDA88-22719, and ARO Grant DAAL03-89-C-0031 including participation by the U.S. Army Human Engineering Laboratory and the U.S. Army Natick Laboratory.

## References


[1] Alan H. Barr, "Teleological Modeling," in *Making Them Move: Mechanics, Control, and Animation of Articulated Figures.* N. Badler, B. Barsky, and D. Zeltzer (eds.):315–321, Morgan-Kaufmann, 1990.

[2] Gary Monheit and Norman I. Badler, "A Kinematic Model of the Human Spine and Torso," *Computer Graphics and Applications*, Vol. 11, No. 2, March, 1991.

[3] Cary Phillips, Norman I. Badler, "Jack: A Toolkit for Manipulating Articulated Figures," *ACM/SIGGRAPH Symposium on User Interface Software*: 221–229, Banff, Canada, 1988.

[4] Cary Phillips, Jianmin Zhao and Norman I. Badler, "Interactive Real-time Articulated Figure Manipulation Using Multiple Kinematic Constraints," *Computer Graphics* 24(2):245–250, 1990.

[5] Craig W. Reynolds, "Flocks, Herds, and Schools: A Distributed Behavioral Model," *Computer Graphics*, 21(4):25–34, 1987.

[6] Jianmin Zhao and Norman I. Badler, "Real Time Inverse Kinematics with Joint Limits and Spatial Constraints," Technical Report MS-CIS-89-09, Department of Computer and Information Science, University of Pennsylvania, Philadelphia, PA, 1989.

# Panels

## Intellectual Property Rights

*Chair:* Michel Denber, Xerox Corporation

*Panelists:* John P. Barlow, Electronic Frontier Foundation
Issaac Victor Kerlow, Pratt Institute
Pamela Samuelson, University of Pittsburgh
Richard M. Stallman, League for Programming Freedom

The issues surrounding software patents and intellectual property rights are controversial and timely. They have a direct and important bearing on the computer graphics community (both technical and artistic) as well as the programming and end-user communities as a whole. The issues have been brought to the fore by a series of highly-publicized (and highly controversial) lawsuits in recent years involving major industry players including Xerox, Apple, Lotus, Microsoft, Hewlett-Packard, NEC, Intel, Fujitsu, and IBM over cases ranging from copyrights on microcode to the "look and feel" of graphical user interfaces. Equally important is the recent stream of patents on specific computer algorithms. Despite the publicity (or perhaps because of it), there seems to be much confusion among programmers regarding the basic principles of trade secret law, copyright, and patent law, not to mention the ultimate implications of these developments. Even within the legal community, there is considerable disagreement over specific interpretations of the law.

This panel examines software copyrights, patents, and intellectual property rights in a discussion between parties on both sides of the fence, hopefully leading to a greater understanding of the issues involved and how they will affect computer graphics practitioners.

## Computer Graphics: More Unsolved Problems

*Co-Chairs:* Franklin Crow, Apple Computer, Inc.
Steve Feiner, Columbia University

*Panelists:* Alan Barr, California Institute of Technology
Frederick P. Brooks, Jr., University of North Carolina at Chapel Hill
Stuart Card, Xerox PARC
James Clark, Silicon Graphics Computer Systems
A. Robin Forrest, University of East Anglia
Pat Hanrahan, Princeton University
Andries van Dam, Brown University

Where is computer graphics heading? Twenty-five years ago, Ivan Sutherland wrote a paper that sketched 10 unsolved problems in the emerging field of interactive computer graphics. This panel reviews our successes in addressing those problems and explores other current unsolved research problems, the impact of solving them, and some possible directions for solutions.

The problems include: managing complexity in rendering, modeling, and interaction; solving the rendering equation; interactively constructing constrained 3D models; achieving geometric robustness; designing a new graphics standard; developing efficient general-purpose graphics architectures; and automating the design of rich graphical environments.

## Graphic Design in the Nineties: New Roles, Options, and Definitions

*Chair:* Doug Hesseltine, Quorum Incorporated

*Panelists:* Michael Cronan, Cronan Design
Joel Katz, Katz/Wheeler Design
Clement Mok, Clement Mok Design
John Waters, Waters Design Associates, Inc.

What is the future of graphic design? While traditional roles will continue to exist for some time, computer technology is creating new demands, options, and definitions for the design professional. The technology is both marvelous and dangerous. Through it, designers can attain new levels of freedom with the possibility of significant breakthroughs in creative thinking and problem solving. They can also become mesmerized by the cosmetic wizardry displayed on their screens, which can seduce designers and their clients into believing that effective communication is nothing more than mere visual presentation.

In addition, computer technology raises questions about the role of design and designers. How will information design and esthetic design evolve? As the value of their expertise changes, must designers become generalists or will specialty areas of design grow and even proliferate? What will the new opportunities in multimedia and interface design create and how will the print medium be affected in the next 10 years?

This panel will explore and clarify these issues in an attempt to guide designers into the technological future of their rapidly changing profession.

**Making Virtual, Artificial, or Real Computer Art**

*Chair:* Gregory P. Garvey, The New England School of Art and Design

*Panelists:* Matt Elson, Symbolics, Inc.
Cynthia Goodman, Author and Independent Curator
Lauretta Jones, IBM T.J. Watson Research Center
Jane Veeder, San Francisco State University

This panel compares different viewpoints on the computer as a natural tool of choice for making art. It also explores how the very nature of the computer itself shapes the artistic esthetic, by changing the way in which art is both created and experienced. Whether the end result is graphic design, photo-realistic rendering, low-resolution paint system output, hypermedia user interfaces, interactive computer-controlled installations, scientific visualization, or virtual and artificial realities, more and more work is being done in the name of art. Panelists review these forms, compare their underlying similarities and differences, and discuss how artistic esthetics emerge with the use of the technology.

**Scientific Visualization on Advanced Architectures**

*Chair:* T. Todd Elvins, San Diego Supercomputer Center

*Panelists:* Thomas A. DeFanti, University of Illinois at Chicago
Henry Fuchs, University of North Carolina at Chapel Hill
John Fowler, Los Alamos National Laboratory
Lewis Tucker, Thinking Machines Corporation

This panel discusses the issues involved in performing scientific visualization on advanced architectures, the problems that need to be addressed when using an advanced architecture within a visualization environment, and the features that should be included in the next generation of advanced architectures. The focus is not "whiz-bang algorithms" that have been developed for a high-performance machine, but rather, the problems encountered, solutions found, and benefits realized when high-performance and/or programmable special purpose hardware is integrated into existing visualization environments.

The panel brings together researchers involved with several different visualization projects undertaken on unusual hardware architectures to enhance interaction, computation, and/or insight,

**The Third Dimension: It's Not a Virtual One**

*Chair:* Stewart Dickson, The Post Group Digital Center

*Panelists:* Bruce Beasley, Sculptor
Helaman Ferguson, Sculptor
Rob Fisher, Sculptor
Frank McGuire, Sculptor

Sculptors are sculptors because of a need to physicalize their work. Because their work ultimately exists as a physical entity in the real world, they envision their work in three dimensions and think deeply in 3D terms before ever considering computer-aided implementation of their designs. They find the experience of viewing 3D space through the glass front of a CRT fundamentally unsatisfying.

This session features a panel of professional sculptors, who critically discuss what has been perceived to be the SIGGRAPH philosophy of 3D modeled computer graphics and compare their design process with the approach of designers who use a 3D computer modeling system to compose pictures.

**Future Directions of Visualization Software Environment**

*Chair:* Craig Upson, Silicon Graphics Computer Systems

*Panelists:* Bob Brown, Silicon Graphics Computer Systems
Scott Dyer, The Ohio State University
Dave Kamins, Stardent Computer, Inc.
John Rasure, University of New Mexico

Several systems have been developed around the concepts of: applying visual languages to visualization application-building; decomposing a visualization application into separable processes (such as data analysis, geometric representation, and rendering); and finally, creating a realtime development environment where applications are created interactively. These systems have given rise to disposable applications by utilizing reusable repositories of visualization and graphics algorithms. These techniques can be connect in a visual manner to create problem-targeted applications with a short lifetime, which dramatically reduces the time devoted to problem solving.

Because of their focus, these systems blur the distinction between program visualization (the process of dynamically viewing the execution ordering of a program), visualization programming (creating visualization applications utilizing graphics libraries), and visualization prototyping (building visualization applications interactively). This panel focuses on the future directions of such systems and includes discussions on the systems-oriented components, new data analysis and visualization representation styles, and the user interface subsystem.

**Designing for New Media: Technologists and Visual Designers Working as a Team**

*Chair:* Kristee Rosendahl, Apple Multimedia Lab

*Panelists:* Alyce Kaprow, The New Studio
David Lawrence, Independent Designer/Producer
Harry Marks, Harry Marks Productions
Dick Phillips, Los Alamos National Laboratory

The increasing complexity and highly visual nature of new media require that all kinds of designers become involved in a collaborative effort from the beginning. This panel focuses specifically on the role of the visual designer who works in these new media as a graphical problem solver. For these designers, the communicative power and esthetic integrity of new media are of primary concern and can only be realized if they become part of the creative team early on in the design process. This panel has two goals: to expose the technology community to these concerns and considerations, and to help designers establish the common language they need for effective collaboration.

**HDTV: Technologies and Directions**

*Co-Chair:* Branko J. Gerovac, Digital Equipment Corporation/MIT Media Lab
John F. Mareda, Sandia National Laboratories

*Panelists:* Gary Demos, DemoGraFX
Hugo Gaggioni, Sony Advanced Systems
Charles A. Poynton, Sun Microsystems, Inc.

High definition television (HDTV) is coming, but why are we interested? Twenty years ago, the initial motivation for HDTV was to provide higher resolution, wider aspect ratio consumer television. Now graphical interaction and presentation are important components of day-to-day computing, and high resolution computer graphics techniques have become fundamental tools for entertainment, science, and engineering. As a result, there is growing interest in the interplay among HDTV, computer graphics, and computing technologies.

This panel presents the relationship of HDTV to computer graphics and computing, the interplay among underlying technologies, the potential for standards, and current and future directions for products and applications.

**Education Technology: Doing With Images Makes Symbols**

*Chair:* Coco Conn, Homer & Associates

*Panelists:* Jay Fenton, Farallon
Dave Master, Rowland High School
Warren Robinett, University of North Carolina
Larry Yaeger, Apple Computer, Inc.

Just as education has much to gain from the incorporation of computers into the learning process, so does the computer graphics community stand to profit from discoveries made in the course of educational research on the nature of the learning process, interactivity, interface design, and graphics. Thus, using computers to create environments for educating kids is an endeavor that will benefit both sides of the equation.

This panel reviews the opportunities for educators, students, and technology developers with illustrations of: virtual reality research for education; Rowland High School, which has one of the nation's most successful student animation programs; the Vivarium Project; and hacking for education.

Because of its significance, this session is being shared between panels and the educators' program.

**Applications of Virtual Reality: Reports From The Field**

*Co-Chair:* Jaron Lanier, VPL Research, Inc.
Linda Nonno, Los Alamos National Laboratory

*Panelists:* Joe Hale, NASA Marshall Space Flight Center
Wolfgang Krueger, Art+Com
Junji Nomura, Matsushita Electric Works
Alain Guiot, Videosystem
Joseph Rosen, Dartmouth/Stanford
Alex Singer, MCA/Universal Studios
Jim Fleming, Brooks Air Force Base

Over the past two years, the extraordinary publicity and speculation devoted to virtual reality has concealed a little-known fact: there are a number of people actually using VR in practical applications. In order to balance and focus the current enthusiasm, it is time to bring users into the VR discussion. This panel of first-generation VR users brings the dialogue about VR technology down to earth and helps prioritize the agenda for VR researchers.

**Semiconductor Requirements For Merging Imaging And Graphics**

*Chair:* Jack Bresenham, Winthrop College

*Panelists:* Karl Guttag, Texas Instruments
Jeff Teza, Brooktree Corporation
Joseph Krauskopf, Intel Corporation
Nick England, Sun Microsystems, Inc.

This panel discusses issues relating to future trends in semiconductors for merging computer imaging and graphics, including: hardwired versus programmable approaches, special imaging and graphics processors versus general purpose processors with hardware accelerators, the need for full-motion video versus document processing in the office, whether full-motion video will be a software application or hardwired solution, and how imaging and graphics can or cannot be served by the same products. Panelists represent a variety of viewpoints on these approaches.

This panel begins where the SIGGRAPH '87 panel "A Comparison of VLSI Graphic Solutions" ended.

**Desperately Seeking Standards**

*Chair:* M. W. Mantle, Pixar

*Panelists:* James C. King, Adobe Systems Inc.
Peter Bono, Fraunhofer Computer Graphics Research Group (USA)
Carl Bass, Ithaca Software
Eileen McGinnis, Sun Microsystems, Inc.

There is general agreement that industry standards are important, but one question remains: How should future standards be chosen? Should they be chosen by committee or should the market decide? Should committees standardize current practice or design tomorrows? How standards are formulated has great impact on their final form.

The panel consists of people who have been at the forefront of developing both committee and *de facto* standards. They assert and defend interesting propositions surrounding proprietary technology, committee standards, the open market, and prototypes.

**Managing Time in Multimedia**

*Chair:* Jonathan Rosenberg, Bellcore

*Panelists:* Thomas Little, Syracuse University
Roger Dannenberg, Carnegie Mellon University
Steven Newcomb, Florida State University
Bill Buxton, Xerox PARC/University of Toronto
Karon Weber, Xerox PARC

Much attention has been focused on techniques for dealing with static (non-temporal) multimedia presentations, but methodologies for temporal, full-motion video, audio, and animated multimedia presentations have been largely ad hoc. Recently, researchers have begun a series of careful investigations to determine appropriate representations for temporal information in multimedia presentations and techniques for delivering them.

This panel assembles prominent researchers active in the areas of multimedia documents and time-based media to discuss the management of temporal multimedia information. They address: what sort of temporal information should be represented and manipulated; why temporal information should be represented declaratively or procedurally; current formalisms and representations; and the latest research in these areas.

**Object-Oriented Graphics**

*Chair:* Nancy Knolle Craighill, Sony Corporation, AVTC

*Panelists:* Polly Baker, University of Illinois at Champaign-Urbana
Martin W. Fong, SRI International
Bob Howard, The Whitewater Group
William J. Kubitz, University of Illinois
Peter Wisskirchen, Gesellschaft für Mathematik und Daten Verarbeitung

Object-oriented programming is revolutionizing software production and marketing. Computer graphics "parts" are already appearing on the market in the form of class libraries, and developers are selecting reusable, interchangeable parts from those libraries to improve productivity. Technically, this approach shows great promise and is just beginning to be accepted by the industry.

This panel reviews applications that demonstrate the need for object-oriented graphics classes (beyond user interface toolkits). Panelists present several commercial graphics class libraries that meet these application needs and discuss graphics standardization efforts that are seriously considering the class library approach.

**Networked Digital Video**

*Chair:* David L. Nelson, Fluent Machines, Inc.

*Panelists:* Andrew Lippman, MIT Media Lab
Dan Heist, Protocom Corporation
Eric Hoffert, Apple Computer, Inc.

The analog video era is ending. Digitization and computerization of motion video will qualitatively transform both computer and video-based applications, but video networking presents a special set of challenges.

Motion video is necessarily a real-time process, and current approaches treat the transmission of digital video as an equivalent real-time problem. This has created an impasse, because personal computers, contention-based LANs, and packet-switched WANs are notoriously poor at delivering real-time data. One solution is to implement spatial and temporal scalability in the video compression technique, allowing for dynamic trade-offs among pixel resolution, frame rate, quality (bits/pixel), and therefore bit rate. End-to-end network protocols can take advantage of scalability to relax the real-time nature of video transmission, which in turn enables development of a new class of video applications using available network technologies.

In this panel, a taxonomy of current applications such as video mail, video-based training, and desktop video conferencing is presented according to whether the video is delivered in real time, stored and forwarded, or published, and whether the interaction is one-to-one, peer-to-peer, or one-to-many. Enabling technologies for these applications are identified with particular emphasis on the problems associated with networking video over LANs and WANs. The role of standards such as JPEG and MPEG is also considered.

# Electronic Theatre

**The Ancient World Revisited**

This animation was originally produced for the NHK documentary series "The Treasure of the British Museum". It aims to reproduce as accurately as possible the architecture and cityscapes of ancient civilizations such as Ur, Absimbel and Tinochtitlan, based on archaeology and architectural data. Produced in HDTV.

Makoto Majima
Taisei Corporation
Design & Proposal Division
25-1, Nishi-Shinjuku
1-Chome, Shinjuku-ku
Tokyo 163 Japan
81-3-3348-1111
81-3-3345-6256 (fax)

**Broadcast Designers Association Open**

Completely synthetic imagery is used to create a black and white animated woodblock effect.

Helene Plotkin
Xaos Inc.
350 Townsend Street, #101
San Francisco, CA 94107 USA
1-415-243-8467
1-415-243-9562 (fax)

**The Astronomers**

Cosmic phenomena are visualized by Kleiser-Walczak Construction Co., in association with Santa Barbara Studios for KCET's series "The Astronomers."

Jeff Kleiser
6105 Mulholland Highway
Hollywood, CA 90068 USA
1-213-467-3563
1-213-467-3583 (fax)

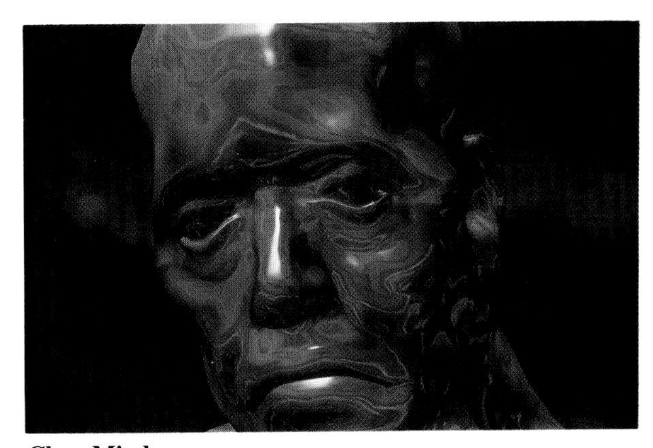

**Clear Mind**

Fluidity of head shape is achieved by moving various wave patterns through a geometric database. Particle system effects are used to create illusions including smoke, aerosol spray, and waterfalls.

Dobbie Schiff
MetroLight Studios, Inc.
5724 W. 3rd Street
Suite 400
Los Angeles, CA 90036 USA
1-213-932-0400
1-213-932-8440 (fax)

**Color Bars**

Michael Keeler
Kubota Pacific Computer
2630 Walsh Avenue
Santa Clara, CA 95051 USA
1-408-748-6314
1-408-748-6301 (fax)

**Digitaline**

Finger games - Naughty games.

Jean Francois Matteudi
Agave S.A.
67 Rue Robespierre
CAP 108
93558 Montreuil Cedex France
33-1-48-57-89-06
33-1-48-57-93-32 (fax)

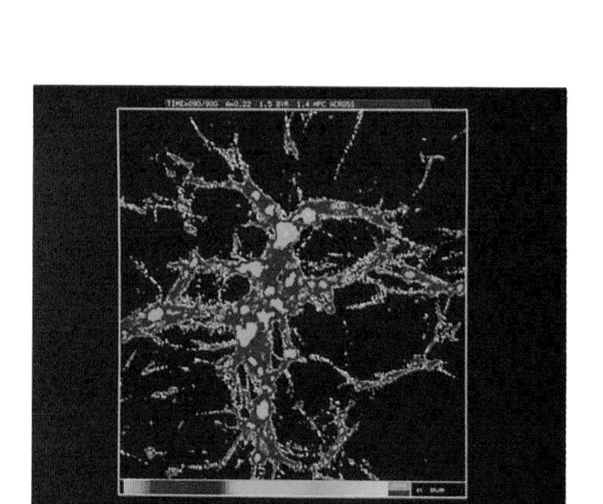

**Cosmological N-Body Simulations**

Cosmological N-Body Simulations model the formation and clustering of galaxies, using large numbers of particles representing clouds of dark matter, which move according to Newton's laws in an expanding universe.

Peter Richards
Massachusetts Institute of Technology
Technology Licensing Office
Building E 32-300
28 Carleton Street
Cambridge, MA 02139 USA
1-617-253-6966
1-617-258-6790 (fax)

**Don Quichotte**

In the famous episode of the battle against the windmills, Don Quichotte demonstrates the ability of computer graphics to animate a hero of mankind's collective imagination, linking a long-standing myth to state-of-the-art technology.

Alain J. Guiot
Videosystem
107 Rue du Fg. St. Honore
75008 Paris France
33-1-42-56-42-33
33-1-45-63-68-35 (fax)

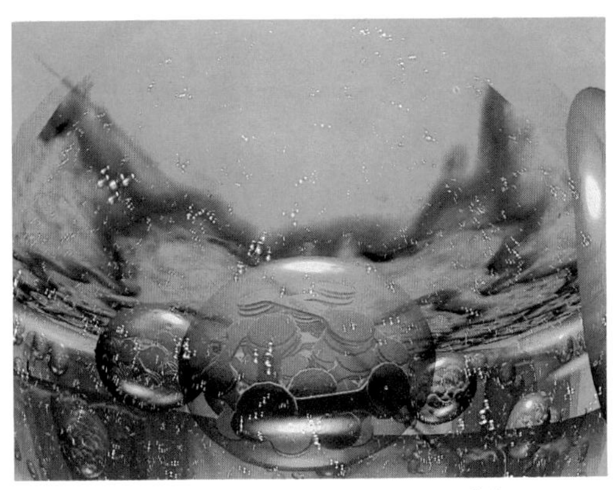

**Echoes of the Sun (excerpt, stereoscopic)**

The film shows the production of sugar in plants, using water from the roots, carbon dioxide from the air, and energy from the sun, and its use to make human muscles move. Originally produced in IMAX SOLIDO format for alternate-eye stereo dome projection.

Fumio Sumi
Fujitsu Limited
Computer Graphics Systems Dept.
1-17-25, Shinkamata, Ota-Ku
Tokyo 144 Japan
81-3-3730-3229
81-3-3734-4691 (fax)

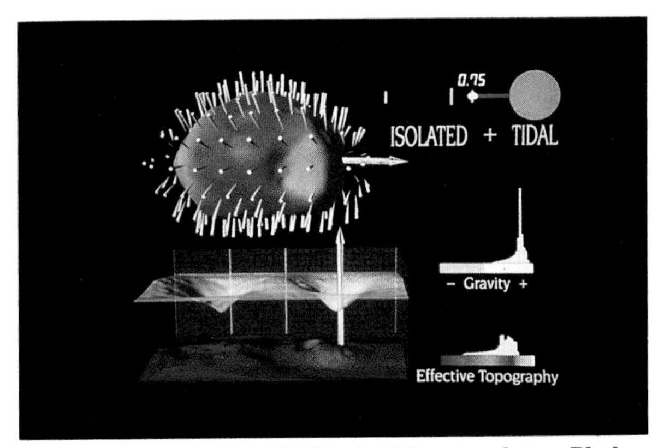


**Evolution of Gravity and Effective Topography on Phobos**

Using data collected by Viking spacecraft, this visualization depicts the effects of Martian tidal forces on Phobos, the larger of Mars' two moons. Phobos approximates the size of Manhattan.

Wayne Lytle
Cornell Natl. Supercomputer Facility
619 Theory Center Building
Cornell University
Ithaca, NY 14853 USA
1-607-254-8793
1-607-254-8888 (fax)

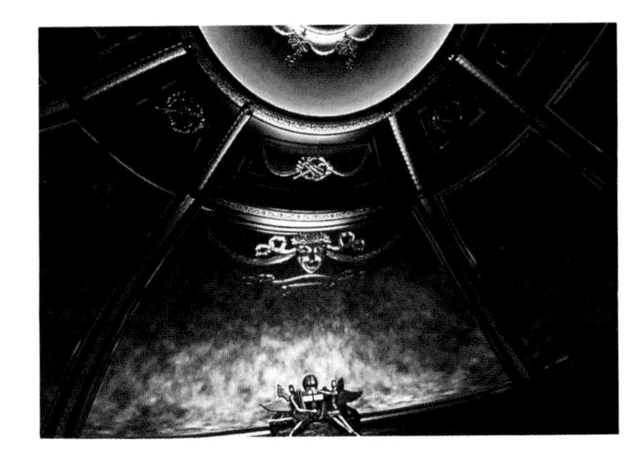

**Enter the Elgin**

An 80-second architectural fly-through of the Elgin Theatre was created for the galas of the 1990 Toronto International Film Festival.

Pat Hunter
ALIAS Research, Inc.
110 Richmond St. East
Toronto, Ontario
M5C 1P1 Canada
1-416-362-9181
1-416-362-0630 (fax)

**Festival (excerpt)**

The motion of the creatures in the brilliant world were generated for the future universe. These images were rendered for HDTV (1920 x1080 pixels).

Yoichiro Kawaguchi
Nippon Electronics College
1-25-4, Hyakunin cho.
Shinjuku-ku
Tokyo 169 Japan
81-3-3369-1995
81-3-3363-7685 (fax)

**Fire Beast**

Inspired by the Japanese tale "Kaguya-hime", this piece enhances the tale's fire beast with irridescent fur. The fur renderer is an application of Digital Differential Analyzer, (DDA).

Ryoichiro Debuchi
Court-Setagaya-101
1-15-11, Mishyuku
Setagaya-ku
Tokyo 154 Japan
81-3-3711-5111
81-3-3711-5110 (fax)

**The Invisible Man in Blind Love**

Georges Pansu
Eurocitel
1 Quai Gabriel Peri
94340 Joinville le Pont, France
33-1-4397-2525
33-1-4397-1923 (fax)

Pascal Vuong
10 Place du Theatre
92310 Sevres, France
33-1-4626-7606
33-1-4293-5344 (fax)

**IGT (Inter Galactic Travel)**

This film was produced for the people's motion simulator ride system "Conceptor", of Fujita Corporation in Tokyo.

Masaaki Taira
3-13-6 Higashi-Shinagawa
Shinagawa-Ku
Tokyo 140 Japan
81-3-3450-8181
81-3-3471-2607 (fax)

**Into the 4th Dimension (stereoscopic)**

Produced as a theme park attraction involving motion-based seats, 12-channel stereo sound, twin 70mm projection, and in-theater lasers. The SIGGRAPH presentation is a reduced film format (twin-35mm with 2-channel stereo sound).

Gary Goddard
Landmark Entertainment Group
5200 Lankershim Boulevard
N. Hollywood, CA 91601 USA
1-818-753-6700
1-818-753-6767 (fax)

Rick Harper
Harper Films Inc.
2027 Montrose Avenue
Montrose, CA 91020 USA
1-818-249-2630
1-818-790-3305 (fax)

**The Key is Light**

Le Corbusier's famous Chapel at Ronchamp is recreated using radiosity and ray tracing techniques. A slow walk from a side chapel, through the nave, and ending behind the main alter, reveals the forms of light used by Le Corbusier.

Becky K. Naqvi
Hewlett Packard Company MS 74
3404 East Harmony Road
Fort Collins, CO 80525 USA
1-303-229-4503
1-303-229-6649 (fax)

**Leaf Magic**

A group of wind blown leaves cavorts in a playground. Realistic leaf motion is generated using a physically-based aerodynamics model.

Alan Norton
IBM TJ Watson Research Center
P.O. Box 704
Yorktown Heights, NY 10598 USA
1-914-784-7195
1-914-784-6273 (fax)

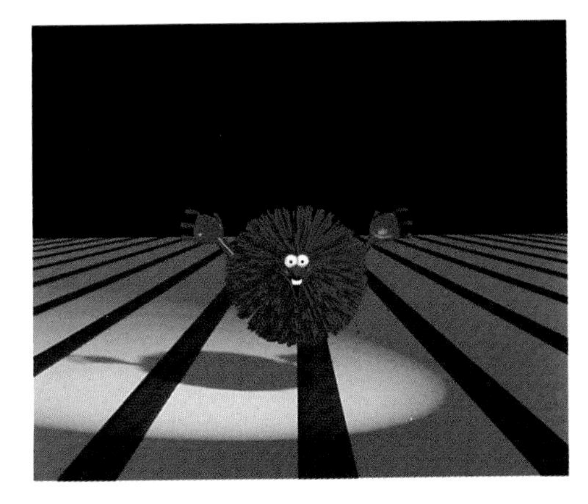

**Kooshball**

Kooshball was created as an experimental piece to demonstrate strand dynamic simulation.

Dobbie Schiff
MetroLight Studios, Inc.
5724 W. 3rd Street
Suite 400
Los Angeles, CA 90036 USA
1-213-932-0400
1-213-932-8440 (fax)

**Lifesavers: The Good Times Roll**

A Lifesavers roll proves its musicianship as it careens across a piano, guitar, and drums, to a "Jerry Lee Lewis meets Stevie Ray Vaughn" sound track. The right hand movements of the studio pianist were converted from MIDI to drive the animated piano keyboard.

Chris Wallace
Topix Computer Graphics and Animation Inc.
217 Richmond Street West, 2nd Floor
Toronto, Ontario M5V 1W2 Canada
1-416-971-7711
1-416-971-6188 (fax)

**The Listener**

Parameterized facial animation and sound mapping techniques are used to tell a fable of frustration, realization, and self discovery.

Christopher Landreth
c/o North Carolina
Supercomputing Center
P.O. Box 12889
Research Triangle Park, NC 27709 USA
1-919-248-1141
1-919-248-1101 (fax)

**Luxo Jr. in "Light & Heavy" and "Surprise"**

Luxo Jr. returns to help children understand the difference between "light" and "heavy", and the complex meaning of the word "surprise". Photo: (c) 1991 Childrens Television Workshop. Courtesy Sesame Street

Ralph Guggenheim
Pixar
1001 W. Cutting Boulevard
Richmond, CA 94804 USA
1-415-236-4000
1-415-236-0388 (fax)

**Lost Animals**

High definition computer graphics recreate animals that have become extinct through natural or human causes.

Jean Kim
NHK HD/CG New York
34-12 36th
Astoria, NY 11106 USA
1-718-361-1118
1-718-361-1758 (fax)

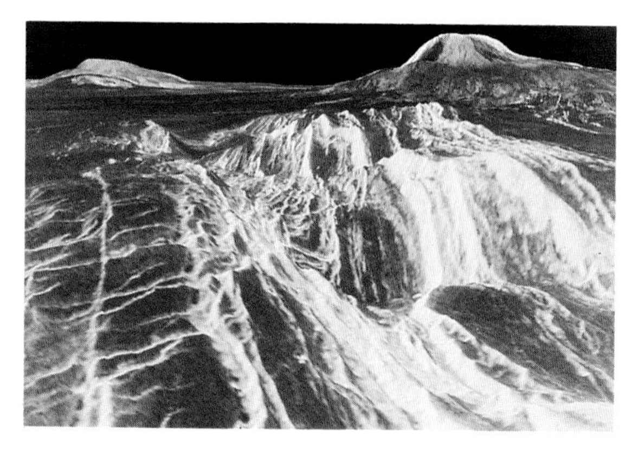

**Magellan at Venus**

Computer animation techniques create a simulated flight over the surface of Venus using radar mapping data recorded by the Magellan Spacecraft during September and October of 1990.

Betsy Hall
Jet Propulsion Laboratory
4800 Oak Grove Drive
M/S 168-522
Pasadena, CA 91109 USA
1-818-354-0225
1-818-393-6962 (fax)

**Match Light "One Match"**

An advertisement for Match Light charcoal. 100% hyper-realism.

Charles Gibson
Rhythm & Hues, Inc.
910 N. Sycamore Avenue
Hollywood, CA 90038 USA
1-213-851-6500
1-213-851-5505 (fax)

**Memory of Moholy-Nagy (excerpt)**

A journey through the animated colors, compositions, and constructions of the Hungarian artist Lazlo Maholy-Nagy.

Tamas Waliczky
H-1011 Budapest
Markovits Ivan Utca 4. V/21 Hungary
36-1-202-0061
36-1-131-5307 (fax)

**Maxwell's Demon**

When the world shifts to being information and service-based tourists visit polluted sites to reminisce about their heritage. This is the story of a fish suicide and a large-scale chemical fire.

James Duesing
ML #16
University of Cincinnati
Cincinnati, OH 45219 USA
1-513-556-0288
1-513-556-3288 (fax)

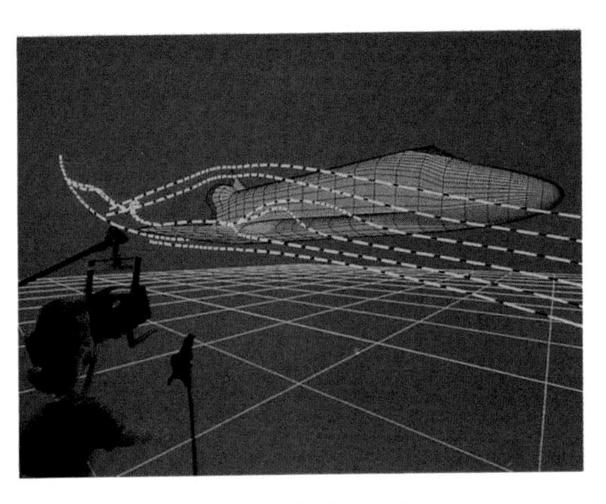

**NASA Ames Virtual Windtunnel**

Computational fluid dynamics techniques are used to simulate a virtual environment for the visualization of 3D fluid flow structures.

Steve Bryson
MSTO45-1
NASA Ames Research Center
Moffett Field, CA 94035 USA
1-415-604-4524
1-415-604-3957 (fax)

**Nintendo Dragon**

Using organic modeling features of SCENIX, Angel Studios created a fully-detailed organic model, intact with subtle surface qualities and body articulations, for unique movements.

Jill Hunt
Angel Studios
5677 Oberlin Drive, Suite 101
San Diego, CA 92121 USA
1-619-452-7775
1-619-452-8073 (fax)

**On The Run**

Control algorithms and physical models are used to create computer animations of legged locomotion.

Marc Raibert
545 Technology Sq.
Cambridge, MA 02139 USA
1-617-253-2478
1-617-258-8682 (fax)

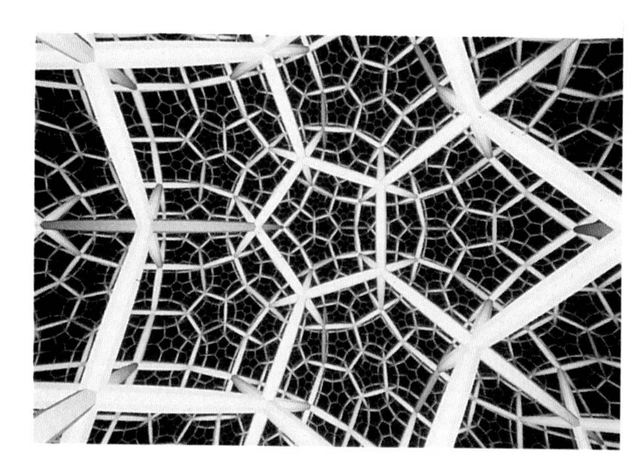

**Not Knot (excerpt)**

An introduction to the fascinating world of knots, as seen from a mathematician's perspective. Relying on visual imagery rather than technical language, it takes the viewer to the edge of current research, culminating in a pioneering fly-through of hyperbolic space.

Charlie Gunn
1300 S. 2nd Street
Minneapolis, MN 55454 USA
1-612-624-5058
1-612-626-7131 (fax)

**Operation C**

Action-packed, character-oriented work is developed for computer game manufacturers.

Larry Lamb
1010 South 7th Street, Suite 600
Minneapolis, MN 55415 USA
1-612-333-8666
1-612-333-9173 (fax)

**Opening Sequence (stereoscopic)**

Wild ideas are visualized using custom particle system software. The PartAnim system combines language and WYSIWYG interactive capabilities to provide artists with immediate feedback.

Alain Chesnais
Studio Base 2
121 Route de Bordeaux
16000 Angouleme, France
33-45-928-411
33-45-958-730 (fax)

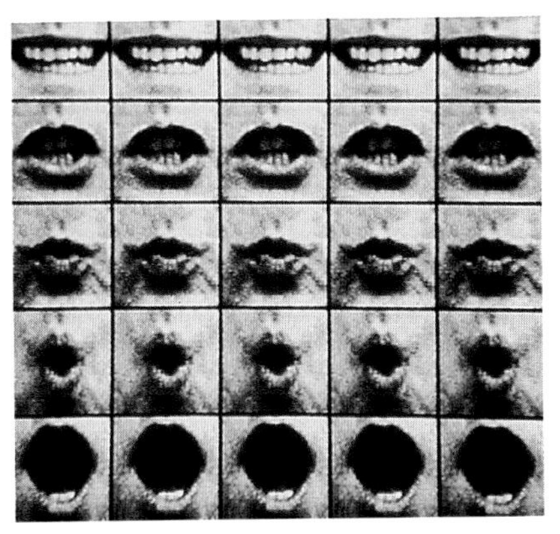

**Poems of Ernst Jandl (Gedichte V.E.)**

Poetic visions from the work of poet Ernst Jandl are transformed into computer images, creating a relationship between the computer and the human mind. The purely systematic and analytic nature of a computer is appropriate for this study, as these are the methods used by Ernst Jandl. A talking screen is created by applying Dadaist principles to Jandl's work.

Eku Wand
Essener Str. 20A
1000 Berlin 21 Germany
49-30-393-8438
49-30-862-1864 (fax)

**PDI Morph Reel**

A compilation of new pieces featuring PDI's morph technique.

Deborah Giarratana
Pacific Data Images
1111 Karlstad Drive
Sunnyvale, CA 94089 USA
1-408-745-6755
1-408-745-6746 (fax)

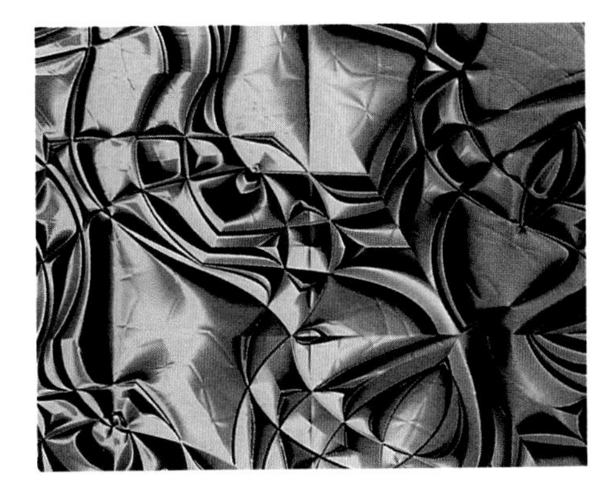

**Primordial Dance**

Images and animations are generated by sequences which emerge from interactively "evolving" equations.

Karl Sims
245 First Street
Cambridge, MA 02142 USA
1-617-234-1000
1-617-234-4444 (fax)

**Reaction-Diffusion Textures**

Reaction-diffusion equations are used to synthesize and animate textures.

Andrew Witkin
School of Computer Science
Carnegie Mellon University
Pittsburgh, PA 15213 USA
1-412-268-6244
1-412-681-5739 (fax)

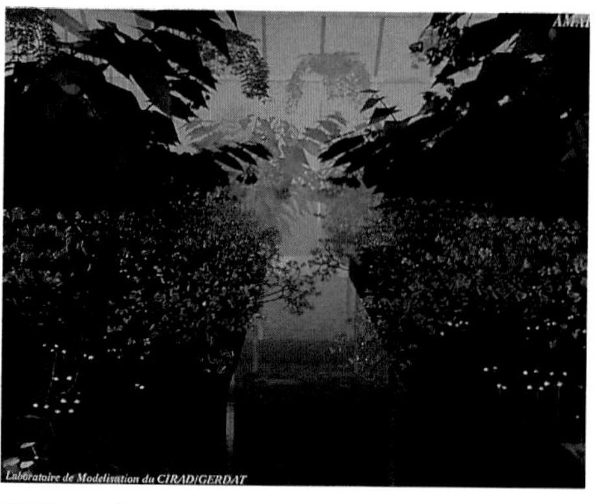


**20 Begonias**

Observations of begonias by botanists at the "Laboratoire de Modelisation du CIRAD" are converted into statistical laws to create 3D images of the measured plants.

Pierre Dinouard
Laboratoire de Modelisation du CIRAD
B.P. 5035
34032 Montpellier Cedex 1 France
33-67-615-995
33-67-615-820 (fax)

**"Terminator 2" Computer Graphics Effects**

Excerpts from the motion picture "Terminator 2" illlustrate computer graphics special effects .

Douglas Kay
Industrial Light and Magic
P.O. Box 2459
San Rafael, CA 94912 USA
1-415-258-2000
1-415-454-4768 (fax)

**un Natural Phenomena**

The parameter space of 3D linear fractals is explored via continuous interpolation, from a forest of elms, spruces, and twindragon grass, to massless fractal extensions of Pluto's solids, such as Menger's Sponge and Von Kosh's Snowflake-a-hedron.

John Hart
Electronic Visualization Laboratory
EECS Dept. M/C 154
University of Illinois at Chicago
Chicago, IL 60680-4348 USA
1-312-996-3002
1-312-413-7585 (fax)

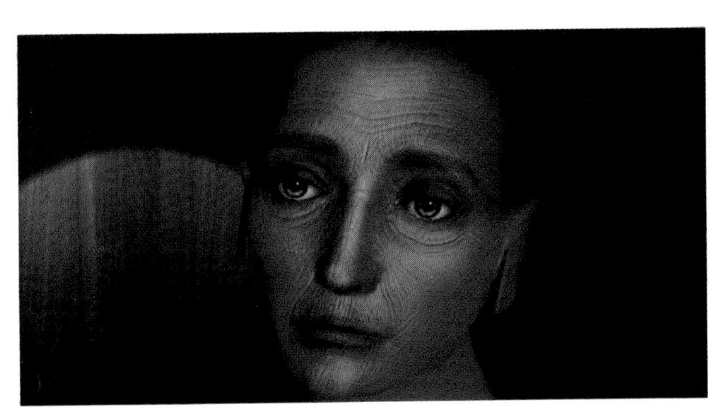

**Virtually Yours**

A slice of life in virtual reality.

Matt Elson
1401 Westwood Boulevard
Los Angeles, CA 90024 USA
1-213-478-0681
1-213-478-1346 (fax)

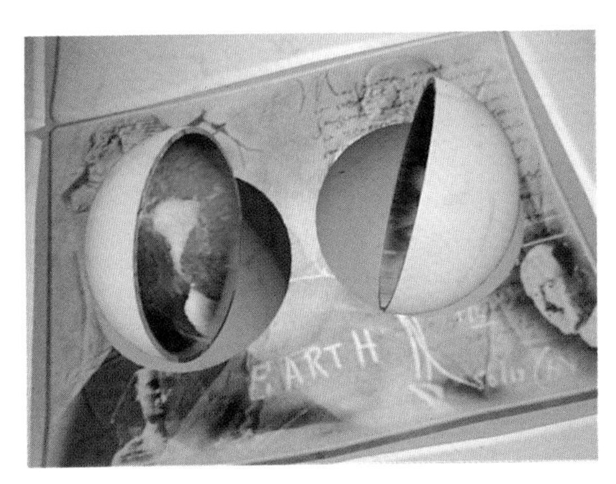

**Voyager**

Two parts of an antique map rise from a globe of the world and melt together into a ball, which rolls through a timeless museum-like space.

Anne Van Ogtrop
Valkieser Group B.V.
S'Gravelandseweg odo a
1217 EW Helversum Holland
31-35-234-858
31-35-232-711 (fax)

**Visualization of Battlefield Obscurants**

Textured ellipsoids are used to visualize time histories of a variety of battlefield obscurants, generated from a U.S. Army physical model.

Geoffrey Y. Gardner
Grumman Data Systems
MS D12-237
1000 Woodbury Road
Woodbury, NY 11797 USA
1-516-682-8417
1-516-682-8022 (fax)

**Wack**

Harold Buchman
Rhythm and Hues, Inc.
910 N. Sycamore Ave.
Hollywood, CA 90038 USA
1-213-851-6500
1-213-851-5505 (fax)

**Wanting for Bridge**

A requiem for those who have died at the hands of others.

Joan Staveley
OSC/ACCAD
1224 Kinnear Road
Columbus, OH 43212 USA
1-614-292-3274
1-614-292-7168 (fax)

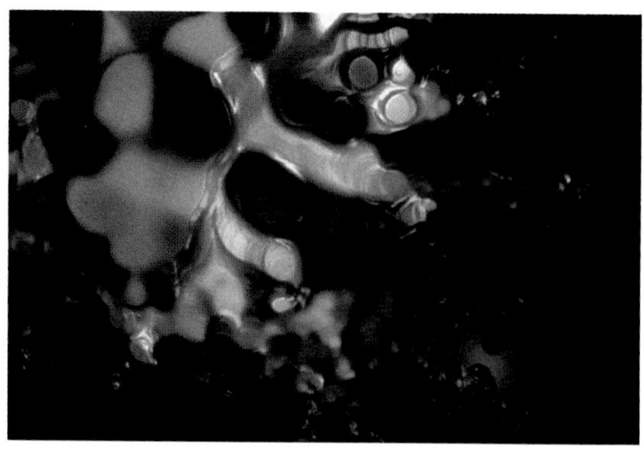

**Wet Science**

A moving collage of swirling color and animated organic surfaces demonstrates custom software techniques.

Helene Plotkin
Xaos Inc.
350 Townsend Street, Suite 101
San Francisco, CA 94107 USA
1-415-243-8467
1-415-243-9562 (fax)

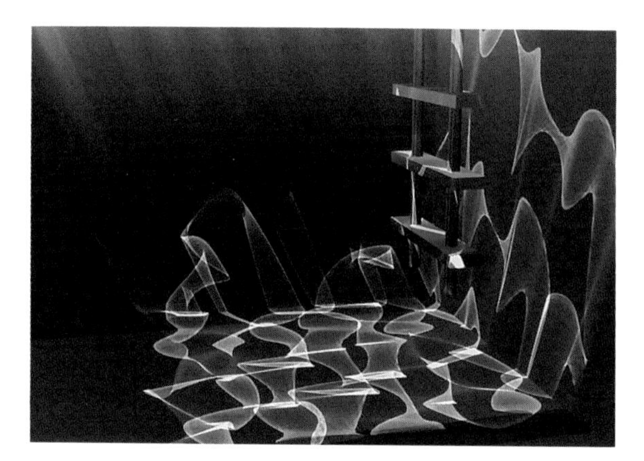

**Water Caustics**

Two short sequences which illustrate the pattern light makes when refracted through water.

Mark Watt
22 Rue Hegesippe-Moreau
75018 Paris France
33-1-4387-5858
33-1-4387-6111 (fax)

**The Works of a Landscape Painter**

Diffraction effects, atmospheric scattering models, solar penumbra, and water color simulation are used to render photorealistic landscape images.

EihachiroNakamae
Faculty of Engineering
Hiroshima University
4-1, Kagamiyama 1 Chome
Higashi-hiroshima 724 Japan
81-8-2422-7111 (ex. 3445)
81-8-2422-7195 (fax)

**Les Xons "Crac-Crac"**

Les Xons, the tribe of little monstrous skeletons, dance and play tricks on each other, on their hell planet.

Mac Guff Ligne
4 Passage de la Main d'Or
75011 Paris, France
33-1-4338-4455
33-1-4700-1014 (fax)

**Audience Participation**

Now's your chance to be a pixel in a crazy, first time anywhere experiment, consisting of you, reflectors, lights, video cameras, frame grabbers, computers, and lots o' software.

Loren Carpenter
Pixar
1001 W. Cutting Boulevard
Richmond, CA 94084 USA
1-415-236-1000
1-415-236-0388 (fax)

**"Invisible Site" George Coates Performance Works**

A multimedia production in which performers interact with projected stereoscopic and real-time computer animation.

Beau Takahara
George Coates Performance Works
110 McAllister Street
San Francisco, CA 94102 USA
1-415-863-8520
1-415-863-7939 (fax)

# Tomorrow's Realities

Tomorrow's Realities, a new venue at SIGGRAPH '91, is specially designed to introduce attendees to new interactive environments generated by dynamic interaction of advanced technologies. This juried exhibit of working virtual reality applications includes environment and experience simulation and hypermedia technologies. The focus of the gallery is functional applications, not glitzy technology.

The applications exhibited were selected for their overall design, the attention to detail in relation to human factors engineering concerns, and the overall experience for the user performing the applications. The jury and co-chairs attempted to establish some standards for workable applications of these technologies that act to codify and encourage the development of new, exciting applications.

The SIGGRAPH '91 virtual reality exhibits are distinguished by the following taxonomy: This year there are three basic categories—**player systems**, which are interactive single-user systems; **authoring systems**, or high productivity construction applications that are used for creation of 2D and 3D data and/or presentations; and **multi-user systems**, for player and authoring systems, that allow networked users which describe how the user relates to the experience—for workgroup, shared space, or collaborative vitual reality. There are three very different metaphors which describe how the user relates to the experience: immersive/inclusive, desktop/vehicle, and third-person.

Tomorrow's Realities also includes more than a dozen hypermedia displays which merge still and dynamic images, print, and audio to create interactive, educational environments. Hypermedia creates entertaining, engaging, interactive environments which encourage exploration. Their imaginative applications of computer graphics technologies allow observers to move seamlessly from general information to specific details, and back again.

## Virtual Reality

### The Assembly Modeler — A Manufacturing and Engineering Operations Simulator

*Contact:* Mike Fusco
SimGraphics Engineering Corporation
1137 Huntington Drive
Suite A-1
South Pasadena, CA 91030
213-255-0900

*Application:* Engineering design, industrial product design
*Metaphor:* Desktop/Vehicle
*Type of system:* Authoring and Player/Multi-user and Single-user

The AAAP Assembly Modeler allows multiple users to manipulate graphically rendered objects as they would maneuver real parts during manufacturing, maintenance or actual use operations. Users select parts or subassemblies that move according to kinematic constraints, allowing accurate depiction of part-to-part collisions and visualization of tooling needs. This is particularly suited for concurrent industrial design since it provides design and manufacturing engineers insight into problems which normally would not appear until late in a product's manufacturing cycle.

### Battletech Multi-Player Virtual World Simulator

*Contact:* Jordon Weisman
Virtual Worlds Entertainment, Inc.
1026 West Van Buren
Chicago, IL 60607
312-243-5660

*Application:* Entertainment
*Metaphor:* Desktop/Vehicle
*Type of system:* Player/Multi-user

Each player navigates a BattleMech, a 30-foot tall human-shaped fighting tank, over 100 miles of computer-generated terrain. The high-tech cockpits in which the players sit contain over 100 I/O devices including primary and secondary screen displays, foot pedals, joysticks, throttles, LED displays, and switches. The primary and secondary screens give each player a radar screen to track enemy movement and satellite view of the battlefield, while numerous LED displays represent the allocation of an arsenal of high-tech weapons. A multi-unit system was recently installed in Chicago at the North Pier where teams test their tactical skills and strategies by engaging in battles over alien terrain.

**Be Here Now**

*Contact:* Mark Bolas
Fake Space Labs
935 Hamilton Avenue
Menlo Park, CA 94025
415-688-1940

*Application:* Visualization/Entertainment
*Metaphor:* Immersive/Inclusive
*Type of system:* Authoring and Player/Single-user

This exhibit uses a Silicon Graphics VGX Graphics Workstation coupled with a Fake Space Labs' BOOM viewing device. The BOOM is an alternative to head-mounted displays. It uses Cathode Ray Tubes for the binocular display and optical encoders for head tracking—thus providing sharp images with very little tracing delay. The BOOM allows users to simply turn from a desk and enter virtual reality without the awkward process of suiting up. This type of immersive and inclusive application is ideally suited for near term design engineering and simulation applications.

At SIGGRAPH '91 users can turn from the conference and enter: **A Virtual Windtunnel**, where the user faces a full-size space shuttle inside a virtual windtunnel and interactively explores its aerodynamic properties; **Tape World**, where no two users will have the same experience, as each is generated by an algorithm; and **Flatland**, a place where users experience the strange illusions which perspective can play on the unsuspecting virtual participant.

Software and support for these worlds has come from Steve Bryson and Creon Levit of the NAS group at NASA Ames Research Center; Mark Bolas, Ian McDowall and Russell Mead of Fake Space Labs; and Joshua Mogal of Silicon Graphics Corporation.

**Boeing VSX: Operations with Virtual Aircraft in Virtual Space**

*Contact:* Chris Esposito, Meredith Bricken, and Keith Butler
Boeing Advanced Technology Center
P.O. Box 24346, Mail Stop 7L-64
Seattle, WA 98124-0346
206-865-3162

*Application:* Engineering designed aerospace
*Metaphor:* Immersive/Inclusive
*Type of system:* Authoring and Player/Single-user

The VSX is a conceptual demonstration of how virtual space would be applied to the design of aircraft and other complex systems that require intense human interaction. This system is ideal for engineers or pilots who seek to evaluate an aircraft's design for such qualities as operability, maintainability, and manufacturability. The user interacts with a 3D surface model of the tilt-rotor aircraft, using VPL Eyephones and the Dataglove for navigation and part or subassembly manipulation.

**Mandala System: Virtual Corridors, Authoring and Virtual Constructions, and Teleconferencing**

*Contact:* Vincent John Vincent
Vivid Effects Inc.
317 Adelaide Street W., #302
Toronto, Ontario, Canada
H5V 1P9
416-340-9290

*Application:* Entertainment, Education, and Communications
*Metaphor:* Third-person
*Type of system:* Authoring and Player/Single- and Multi-user

Users can access the Mandala System in three different ways. In Virtual Corridors, users navigate through 3D virtual corridors, both real-world and animated, to a number of rooms where they participate in interactive training simulations in areas of design engineering and visualization or machine models. The user's real video image with a laserdisc control matrix allows for 3D 360 laservideo world in real-time.

In the Authoring and Virtual Constructions system, a mouse-driven menu system allows users to quickly create and experiment with virtual worlds in minutes. The user is provided with a high-end workstation that has hundreds of objects that he or she can call up to implement through various event commands.

The Teleconferencing VR system allows multiple people in different cities to be viewed and have their live images projected into a mutual real-time virtual world—where they can interactively control aspects of their virtual world together.

**Naimark VR Application:
EAT - A Virtual Dining Environment**

*Contact:* Michael Naimark
Naimark & Company
216 Filbert Steps
San Francisco, CA 94133
415-391-4817

*Application:* Art
*Metaphor:* Immersive/Inclusive
*Type of system:* Player/Single-user

''EAT'' is an art installation about consumption.

It was produced as a class project for Michael Naimark's ''Virtual Environments'' class in 1989 at the San Francisco Art Institute where it received an SFAI Spring Show Gold Award.

''EAT'' is a short single-user experience, where the participant is seated alone at a formal dining arrangement and orders food from a live waiter with a menu. The waiter then lifts up the plate cover, revealing the requested ''food'' projected on the dinner plate. Also on the table, a large red button labelled ''EAT'' may be pressed.

"EAT" consists of a formally arranged dining table, video projector, videodisc and player, Mac II computer, hardcopy menu and guest checks, and live performer. The table, props, menu, guest checks, videodisc, and programming were all produced by the students from the "Virtual Environments" class.

**Naimark VR Application:**
**VBK - A Moviemap of Karlsruhe**

*Contact:* Michael Naimark
Naimark & Company
216 Filbert Steps
San Francisco, CA 94133
415-391-4817

*Application:* Surrogate Travel
*Metaphor:* "Desktop"/Vehicle
*Type of system:* Player/Single-user

VBK was commissioned by the Zentrum fur Kunst und Medientechnologie (ZKM), a state-funded arts and media lab under contruction in the town of Karlsruhe, Germany. Karlsruhe has a well-known tramway system, with over 100 km of track snaking from the downtown pedestrian area out to neighboring villages at the edge of the Black Forest.

The entire tram system was shot in both directions from a tramcar outfitted with a camera triggered by the tram's electronic odometer (at 2, 4, and 8 meters per frame depending on the location). The tracks assured unrivaled stability and seamless match-cuts. The delivery system consists of a Mac II computer, a Pioneer 8000 videodisc player, a video projector, and custom input.

The intention is to abstract rather than simulate reality, to provide an experience not possible in the real world: the system allows continuous speeds up to one kilometer per second.

**NPSNET: A 3D Visual Simulator for Virtual World Exploration and Experience**

*Contact:* Michael J. Zyda, David R. Pratt
Naval Postgraduate School
Code CS/ZK
Department of Computer Science
Monterey, CA 93943-5100
408-646-2305

*Application:* Engineering simulation: aerospace
*Metaphor:* Desktop/Vehicle
*Type of system:* Player/Multi-user

NPSNET is a real-time, 3D visual simulation system capable of displaying vehicle movement over the ground or in the air. Displays show on-ground cultural features such as roads, buildings, soil types, and elevations. The system is capable of environmental effects such as San Francisco-like fog or Los Angeles brown haze. NPSNET supports a full complement of vehicles, houses, trees, signs, watertowers, and cows. The user selects a vehicle to drive by means of a button box. A vehicle is controlled by a six degree of freedom Space Ball. Vehicles can interact with other vehicles. These vehicles can be controlled by a pre-written script or driven interactively from other workstations, with the communications medium being broadcast via Ethernet.

**Performance Cartoons**

*Contact:* Chris Walker
Mr. Film
228 Main Street
Venice, CA 90291
213-396-0146

*Application:* Entertainment
*Metaphor:* Desktop/Vehicle
*Type of system:* Authoring and Player/Single- or Multi-user

The user can access on-line, real-time animation of a sleek star, Silver Suzy, using Sim Graphics VR *Workbench*™, the Flying Mouse and the DataGlove (as motion inputs) and a VGX Silicon Graphics simulator. Like the Silver Surfer, Silver Suzy tilts in all directions and has a sense of balance which the user can maneuver to achieve speed in any direction on her surf board. This demonstration represents a technical milestone in computer animation and will be the first demonstration of a real-time cartoon animation at broadcast video display quality using an actor or actress performance metaphor.

**Plasm: Above the Drome**

*Contact:* Peter Broadwell, Rob Myers
Silicon Graphics Computer Systems, Inc.
2011 N. Shoreline Boulevard
Mountain View, CA 94043
415-960-1980

*Application:* Entertainment and Education
*Metaphor:* Desktop/Vehicle
*Type of system:* Player/Multi-user

In a cooperative virtual area, the user or users engage in a 3D dance with artificial life forms and with each other, shaping a consensual artscape for mutual exploration. Each remote site features a radical skim board, coupled to a personal viewpoint into a common virtual aerodrome. The board underfoot is instrumented as a full body input device, driving a rich, highly responsive synthetic graphics representation "out the front window" using wide-angle high-resolution to get each air-surfer and their local cheering section involved in the central networked action. A wide range of pursuits are possible: exploring, athletic styling, systematic treasure hunting, game creating and playing, and cooperative form making.

**Portrait One**

*Contact:* Luc Courchesne
School of Industrial Design
University of Montreal
P.O. Box 6128, Station A
Montreal, Quebec, Canada
H3C 3J7
514-343-7495

*Application:* Education and Entertainment
*Metaphor:* Desktop/Vehicle
*Type of system:* Single-user

A ghostlike image of a woman, Marie, a 34-year-old French-speaking Montrealer played by acress Paula Ducharme, appears to be floating in space. Breathing calmly, she seems lost in reverie. A visitor approaching her may try to get her attention: When clicking (using the mouse) ''Excuse me'' on the display, Marie suddenly stares at the visitor; then, clicking among a choice of questions like ''Do you have the time?'', ''Are you looking at me?'' or simply ''May I ask you something?'', Marie starts a conversation that will develop according to the visitor's curiosity and Marie's moods. The encounter may be cut short because of the visitor's lack of tact or it may develop into an intimate conversation about love in the context of a virtual realities.

The software for Portrait One consists of a 30-minute video disc (Laservision CAV/NTSC) and Hypercard stacks on a floppy disk. The installation requires any Macintosh, a videodisc player and a television monitor. In the current version of the installation, the ghostlike image of Marie is produced by the reflection of the videoscreen on a glass plate facing the visitor. To interact with the installation, the visitor activates a set of preestablished questions via Hypercard buttons using the mouse. The course of the conversation is determined by the visitor's choices among a set of approximately 300 options and a bank of 120 video segments. The initial question selected defines the language, either French or English, of the conversation. In the English version of Portrait One, Marie's answers are delivered in French with English subtitles.

Portrait One is the first of a series of six interactive video portraits using the same hardware configuration. This first generation of interactive portraits was developed in Montreal between 1989 and 1991 and was funded by the Canadian Arts Council.

**Throwing Real Objects in Virtual Spaces**

*Contact:* David Thiel, Tim Skelly
Incredible Technologies
709 W. Algonquin Road
Arlington Heights, IL 60625
708-437-2433

*Application:* Entertainment
*Metaphor:* Desktop/Vehicle
*Type of system:* Player/Single-user

The video game ''Match Five'' employes a natural, gestural interface — a device that reads the entry position, direction and speed of an ordinary cue ball. In other words, players use a real cue stick and ball to interact with the simulation. When this interface is positioned beneath a monitor displaying the ball's resulting translation into computer space, the illusion is created that the ball's motion from the real world into the video screen has been uninterrupted.

As our electronic environment becomes more multidimensional, more tangible, computer users will expect the ability to pass more dimensions of physical information into the electronic universe. With the cue ball, the translation of position, direction, and velocity is achieved. We could just as well (if not as easily) translate an object's mass, temperature, texture, and shape.

The wall dividing the two realities is a thin one.

**Five Applications using Head-Mounted Displays**

*Contact:* Fred Brooks, Henry Fuchs, and
Warren Robinett
Department of Computer Science
University of North Carolina at Chapel Hill
Chapel Hill, NC 27599-3175
919-962-1700

Five applications involve molecular modeling, medical imaging, architecture previewing, and general 3D modeling. Navigation methods include flying under 3D mouse control, walking on a treadmill, pedaling a bicycle, and walking naturally in a specially instrumented room

Custom equipment for these applications includes: a) Pixel-Planes 5 graphics engine with several dozen single-board 32-bit processors and over 300,000 one-bit pixel processors, and b) a 10 x 12-foot (but potentially much wider-working area) head-tracking system using ceiling-aimed helmet-mounted cameras and ceiling-mounted infra-red LEDs.

Major Support by DARPA, NSF, NIH, ONR, and Digital Equipment Corp.

**UNC Application 1:
A Two-Person 3D Modeling System**

*Contact:* Jeff Butterworth, Andrew Davidson,
Stephen Hench, and T. Marc Olano

*Application:* 3D CAD or geometry authoring and Education
*Metaphor:* Immersive/Inclusive
*Type of system:* Networked/Authoring

3dm is a geometric modeling tool that allows the users, with head-mounted displays, to enter into the space in which the models are created and modified. Although both users can explore the models, only the main user, the ''designer,'' can modify them. In addition to the models themselves, the distinguished objects are a 3D cursor (that changes shape according to mode), a Macdraw-like toolbox, a "magic carpet," and the checkerboard floor of the virtual world. The magic carpet represents the extent of the tracking range and is a handy way of indicating how far the user can walk around the physical room. The user can change his or her own size and the size of the models independently so that both building-sized objects and tiny details can be manipulated easily. The user navigates around the models by "flying" his magic carpet about the virtual world.

### UNC Application 2: Flying Through a Protein Molecule

*Contact:* Richard Holloway and Warren Robinett

*Application:* Molecular modeling
*Metaphor:* Immersive/Inclusive
*Type of system:* Player/Single-user

Using a head-mounted display and hand-held input device, the user flies through a virtual world containing several different giant molecules. Due to the molecules' large size, the user literally flies inside them and sees them from the perspective of an atom. The world contains several different representations for molecules, including simple sphere-only molecules, a ball-and-stick model, as well as a "ribbon" model which represents the backbone of a protein molecule. The user can control his or her own velocity so that it varies from rocketing between molecules to a slow fly-by of individual atoms.

### UNC Application 3: Building Walkthrough with a Treadmill or by Natural Walking

*Contact:* Software: J. Alspaugh, R. Brown, C. Hill, A. Varshney, Y. Wang, X. Yuan, F. Brooks;
Tracker: R. Azuma, B. Bennett, V. Chi, C. Clegg, J. Eyles, S. Gottschalk, J. Kite, J. Thomas, M. Ward, H. Fuchs

*Application:* Architectural engineering
*Metaphor:* Immersive/Inclusive
*Type of system:* Networked/Single-user

Walkthrough is a system to help architects and their clients to explore a building design prior to its construction. Two different navigation modes are demonstrated: a) walking on a treadmill with steerable handlebars that give roughly the impression of pushing a shopping cart through a store, and b) walking freely about a specially-prepared 10 x 12 foot room in which the user's helmet is optically tracked. The building models are created using AutoCAD. Realism is enhanced by calculating a radiosity solution for the lighting model.

### UNC Application 4: A Mountain Bike with Force Feedback Pedals

*Contact:* Erick Erikson, Ryutarou Ohbuchi, Russell Taylor, Andrei State

*Application:* Entertainment and Recreation
*Metaphor:* Immersive/Inclusive
*Type of system:* Player/Single-user

Using a mountain bike with force feedback added to pedaling, the user rides around mountainous terrain: The bike is mounted on a stand and its rear wheel is connected to a computer-controlled eddy current resistance device. The rider views a 3D shaded model on the screen and the pedaling resistance varies with grade and the weight of the rider. A rotary encoder connected to the handlebar of the bicycle measures the direction of steering and adjusts the bike's direction of movement over the terrain.

### UNC Application 5: Radiation Therapy Treatment Planning with a Head-Mounted Display

*Contact:* James C. Chung, Suresh Balu, Brad A. Crittendon, Terry Yoo

*Application:* Medical: treatment simulation
*Metaphor:* Immersive/Inclusive
*Type of system:* Player/Single-user

Wearing a head-mounted display, the user is presented with a polygonal surface model of a cancer patient's anatomy. Using a 6D mouse, the user grabs a treatment beam from its storage rack, drags it, and positions it to pass through the tumor — avoiding as much healthy tissue as possible. This process can be repeated with several beams to ensure complete tumor coverage while minimizing contact with the healthy tissue.

### VideoDesk TeleTutoring

*Contact:* Myron Krueger
Artificial Reality
Box 786
Vernon, CT 06066
203-871-1375

*Application:* Education
*Metaphor:* Third-person
*Type of system:* Author and Player/Multi-user

The VIDEODESK employs the video image of the user's hands as an input device. Several applications are demonsrated that allow the user to menu, draw, and point with his or her hands. One of the advantages of this approach is that the user can assert multi-point control by using the two hands independently. In addition, the user's hands are joined by the hands of an expert user sitting at another VIDEODESK. The expert explains the operation of the system both verbally and by demonstrating with her hands. The shared workspace created by this experience is exactly as if the user and the teletutor are sitting side by side at the same desk.

**Virtual Acoustic Environments: The Convolvotron**

*Contact:* Elizabeth M. Wenzel
NASA Ames Research Center
Mail Stop 262-2
Moffett Field, CA 94035
415-604-6290
beth@eos.arc.nasa.gov

Scott Foster
Crystal River Engineering
12350 Wards Ferry Road
Groveland, CA 95321

*Application:* Architectual Acoustics
*Metaphor:* Immersive/Inclusive
*Type of system:* Player/Single-user

The Convolvotron provides an artificially generated virtual reality with an inclusive dynamic viewing metaphor that allows the listener to navigate via a world-in-hand metaphor or by simply moving through an acoustic environment. Externalized 3D sound cues are synthesized over headphones in real-time using filters, based on measurements of the Head-Related Transfer Function (HRTF); the listener specific, direction-dependent acoustic effects imposed on an incoming signal by the outer ears. Up to four independent, simultaneous sources are generated with a computational speed sufficient for simulating relatively small reverberant environments. An interactive scenario will be demonstrated involving a virtual room simulation in which the user can manipulate the dimensions of the room in real time.

This demonstration illustrates an innovative application such as studio mixing of music signals.

**Vision — Virtual Environment Terminal — Tele-Presense, Tactile Feedback, Molecular Modeling and General VR Concepts**

*Contact:* Charles Grimsdale
Division Ltd.
Quarry Road, Chirping Sodbury
Bristol, Avon, United Kingdom
BS17 6AX
44-454-324527

*Application:* Engineering molecular modeling and Entertainment
*Metaphor:* Immersive/Inclusive
*Type of system:* Authoring and Player/Multi-user

Through three different systems, users are able to: control a remote camera platform by remote viewing and virtual controls; enter a demonstration platform for the prototype tactile feedback glove; and explore some of the basic metaphors — molecular modeling, model building, model interaction, and modeling real-world focuses.

# Hypermedia

**An Interactive Video News Magazine**

*Contact:* Randy Koons
The Interactive Media Project
IBM T.J. Watson Computer Science Research
Hawthorne, NY
914-784-7602 or 914-784-7966

*Credits:* The Interactive Media Project, IBM T.J. Watson CSR
Mark Laff, Project Manager
Nancy Frishberg, Moe Desrosiers, Randy Koons,
Paul Kosinski, Mary Van Deusen

One of the goals of the Interactive Media Project (IMP) is the development of an authoring system (IMP Builder) to produce high-quality, interactive productions incorporating video, audio, text, and graphics. Another goal is to produce multimedia applications. An Interactive Video News Magazine is the current multimedia application using the latest tool set, serving as a forum for current developments in the IBM Research Divisions worldwide, via stand-alone kiosk (IMP Player).

The IMP Builder is a robust authoring system under Smalltalk/V PM, running in OS/2. The user interface is designed for the non-programmer, enabling an author to assemble various source materials into hypermedia productions. The IMP Player is the delivery portion of this integrated system, allowing the user to interactively browse the production at a variety of interest levels. The current configuration uses an IBM PS/2 with a laserdisc player. Source video is displayed on a touchscreen using the M-Motion Video Adapter.

**Beethoven's Symphony No. 9**

*Contact:* Bob Stein
The Voyager Company
1351 Pacific Coast Highway
Santa Monica, CA 90401
213-451-1383
213-394-2156 (fax)

*Credits:* Program design: Robert Winter; publisher: The Voyager Company; producer: Peter Bogdanoff; editor, Jane Wheeler; programmer: Steve Riggins

In this exhilarating multimedia program, music historian and ULCA professor Robert Winter examines why Beethoven's *Ninth Symphony* continues as one of the world's most recognized and beloved classical works.

*The Beethoven CD Companion* includes an electrifying performance by Hans Schmidt-Isserstedt conducting the Vienna State Opera Chorus and the Vienna Philharmonic (on compact disk), accompanied by a five-part HyperCard program that features:

*The Pocket Guide* lets you select and immediately hear any section of the entire Ninth Symphony; *Beethoven's World* presents the composer's life and times; *The Art of Listening* gives an introduction to the symphony interesting to novice and sophisticated music lover alike; *A Close Reading* provides real-time commentary by author Robert Winter; and *The Ninth Game*, for one to four players, ingeniously tests your understanding of Beethoven with audio-based questions.

*Beethoven No. 9 is the winner of MacWorld's 1991 SuperStack Award.*

**ClickOn MSU**

*Contact:* Carrie Heeter
Hypermedia Coordinator
Michigan State University
400 Computer Center
Michigan State University
East Lansing, MI 48824
517-353-0722
517-336-1244 (fax)

*Credits:* Carrie Heeter (Comm Tech Lab Director)
Pericles Gomes, Sr. (Hypermedia designer)
Randy Russell, Sr. (Hypermedia Programmer)
Steve Sneed, Rachel Torgoff, Faran Thomason, Karen Harry,
Mark LaForest, Greg Gohl and Greg Newton (Hypermedia assistants).
Video and stills provided by Instructional Media Center,
Instructional Television, WKAR Television,
The Wharton Center for Performing Arts
The Public Relations Dept. of
Michigan State University
Funding and editorial assistance provided by the Vice President for Student Affairs and Services, the Assistant Provost for Computing and Technology and the Dean of the College of Communication Arts and Sciences.

ClickOn MSU stylistically portrays Michigan State University with a sense of whimsy and magic through animated interactivity, painting with video, and merging reality with fantasy.

The software authoring environment is Director on the Macintosh, an interactive computer animation package which allows experimentation with animated menus and animated icons. "ClickOns" in ClickOn MSU are animated, context appropriate, fuzzy beasts which direct the user through the program.

The hypermedia kiosk combines videodisc and interactive computer animation on a single monitor using a RasterOps 364 board. Still and motion video can thus be displayed in a rectangle of any size on the screen, and of any aspect ratio. "Hypermedia tools provide the wherewithal to create interesting worlds which merge fantasy and reality-like movies such as "Dick Tracy", "Batman", and "Roger Rabbit", but — at a much cheaper cost.

**Expo '92 Visitor Information System**

*Contact:* Lauretta Jones
IBM T. J. Watson Research Center
Box 704 J2-A31
Yorktown Heights, NY 10598-0704
914-784-7622
914-784-6324 (fax)

*Credits:* Lauretta Jones, Stephen J. Boies, Charles Wiecha, William E. Bennett, Sharon Greene, Susan Spraragen
This system was developed with the assistance of CTL, IBM Spain: Angel Llopis, Richard Mushlin, Paco Curbera, Javier Romero

Interactive Transaction Systems (ITS) a software tools project at IBM Research, is used in collaboration with IBM Spain to develop the visitor information system for EXPO '92, the universal exposition scheduled for Seville. This touch-screen system allows visitors to explore EXPO through image-based hyperstories. Network communications combined with magnetically-encoded tickets enable users of any of the 200-300 stations located throughout the site to make restaurant reservations, send messages, compete in games and art contests, and read regularly updated news, sports, and weather information. ITS enables the rapid development of applications such as EXPO by separating interface content from style. The content controls what is presented in an interface; style controls how it is presented. Style is automatically generated by executable rules which embody decisions of graphic designers and human factors engineers. ITS will result in better interface design and reduced development time.

**Interactive Color: A Guide for Color in Computer Graphics**

*Contact:* Holliday R. Horton, Senior Animator
Advanced Scientific Visualization Laboratory
San Diego Supercomputer Center
10100 Hopkins Drive
La Jolla, CA 92037
619-534-5000
619-534-5113 (fax)
HORTONH@SDS.SDSC.EDU

*Credits:* Holliday R. Horton & Gail Bamber - Design and Layout
John Moreland - Programming GURU -

''Interactive Color: A Guide for Color in Computer Graphics'' is an interactive tutorial designed as an aid for color instruction. The inspiration for the project came as a result of the confusion and frustration surrounding computer color interaction for artists and scientists. Generally, users have a difficult time dealing with the modern technology of color selection and mixing because the computer system uses color in an entirely different way from the traditional color systems. The hypertext program addresses these differences and illustrates with examples. It is filled with many interactive color demonstrations which help the user have a more intuitive and concrete understanding of color.

**Life on a Slice**

*Contact:* Beverly Reiser
Beverly Reiser Design
6979 Exeter Dr
Oakland, CA 94611
415-482-2483

*Credits:* Bill Fleming, Marjorie Franklin, Beverly Reiser, and Hans Reiser

Life on a Slice is an interactive video/computer installation that explores choice making and provides an environmental metaphor for decision-making based on information slices.

When the participant signals a choice, a change occurs. The effect of the choice remains and the participant is again offered more choices that stem from and augment the previous choice. The sequence of choices continue until the poem, sound image, or story is completed. In this way, a story or poem will have one beginning but many possible endings. In addition, the moment of choice is accentuated by digitized sound effects. The participant sees his or her live image merged wth the computer image on the screen throughout the interactive session.

The interaction takes place with an Amiga 2000 computer, an A-live Digitizer, a video camera, and a large monitor. Participants may choose from titles including: ''A Poem,'' ''The Phosphorescent Samarai,'' ''The Geisha/Snail,'' and ''Town.''

**Mars Navigator**

*Contact:* Karl W. Anderson
703 Dona Ave.
Sunnyvale, CA 94087
408-737-8374
kanderson@cdp.uucp

*Credits:* Karl W. Anderson
Volotta Interactive Video
Apple Computer, Inc.
Jet Propulsion Laboratory

Mars Navigator is an interactive videodisc-based system for exploring Mars. This database contains information about both the history and the future of Mars exploration and also detailed physical data on Mars. Users fly over computer-rendered terrain of the martian surface, switching between different paths. Computer overlays and alert text fields point out interesting features along the path, encouraging users to explore deeper into database of video clips, animations, and text.

Throughout the flight, users can switch the main viewport from actual color to an alternate view, such as a terraformed view or a geological representation of Mars. Mars Navigator will be installed in The Technology Center of Silicon Valley located in San Jose, Calif. which opened in the fall of 1990.

**Simulation of Myocardial Infarction**

*Contact:* Lee T. Andrews
Medical College of Ohio
3000 Arlington Avenue
Toledo, OH 43614
419-381-3653
419-385-3490 (fax)

*Credits:* Lee T.Andrews, Joseph W.Klinger, Michael S.Begeman, Richard F.Leighton, Jacob Zeiss, Konstantyn Y.Szwajkun, Carlos A.Baptista, Thomas G.Kubit, Bradley C Behrendt, John Sully, Jay Humphrey

Acute myocardial infarction (heart attack) represents one of the leading causes of death in the United States. This hypermedia presentation was created to help students at the Medical College of Ohio better understand the mechanisms leading to an acute myocardial infarction (MI) and the functional changes which occur during and after the event. A 3D computer model was created from Magnetic Resonance Images (MRI) of normal subjects and patients with an MI. The location of the coronary arteries was determined from MRI images and anatomical samples.

The presentation simulates normal cardiac performance, using opaque and transparent computer graphic models to allow viewing of internal structures (such as the left ventricular chamber). By selecting the left anterior descending coronary artery (LAD), the student can fly down the artery beginning in a normal region and then enter a branch with arterial sclerosis. This unstable region erupts, resulting in a closure of the artery when platelets adhere to this lesion. Simultaneous presentation of the surface electrocardiogram (ECG) and graphs of myocardial wall thickening demonstrates the dynamic changes during this acute MI. Each section of the presentation contains an audio track with comments from a physician explaining the pertinent information in the scene. Additional material describing the methods of measurement and diagnostic equipment used for evaluation of cardiac performance is also presented.

**Super Image**

*Contact:* Joseph W. Klingler
Medical College of Ohio
3000 Arlington Avenue
Toledo, OH 43614
419-381-4586
419-382-3465 (fax)

*Credits:* Joseph Klingler, Lee Andrews, Brad Behrendt (Image Analysis Research Center, The Medical College of Ohio)

Super Image familiarizes medical students and technical professionals with the basics of digital imagery. It was originally intended for medical personnel who work with images in digital form, (medical scanning devices such as digital X-ray, Ultrasound, CT and MR cross-sectional scanners) but has proven useful for desktop publishing personnel who work with scanners and resolution issues for general publishing applications.The introductory section, entitled "What's a Digital Image?," deals with the definition of pixels, resolution, and quantization through a tutorial that constructs a common image from gray scale blocks—the way a mosaic is constructed from stones. The stack goes on to discuss how changes in stone size and color (resolution and quantization) affect image quality, histograms, animation, and the basics of color. The goal is to provide the reader with a number of animated visual examples of common issues in digital imagery.

**Time Table of History: Science and Innovation**

*Contact:* Jerry Isdale
Xiphias
Helms Hall
8758 Venice Blvd.
Los Angeles, CA 90034
213-841-2790
213-841-2559 (fax)
isdale%aludra.usc.edu%usc.edu

*Credits:* Peter Black, Jerry Isdale, Gerry Jenkins, Michael Hadjioannou, Richard Addison, Jim Plack, Phillip M. Milburn, Sue Black, Hugh Esten, Holly Erickson, James Duffin, Steve Burr, Brad Smillie, Christelle Bella, and Kirk Scadden.

The Xiphias Time Table of History: Science and Innovation is a CD-ROM hypermedia document for the Commodore CDTV. It contains over 6,000 stories covering key events in the development of our understanding and exploitation of the world around us. The stories are linked to multimedia effects such as photographs, animations, a zoom-in atlas, powers-of-ten altitude animations, first-person quotations, an electromagnetic spectrum map, a full-featured periodic table, and graphic bibliography. The product has a "7:30 Interface," meaning it can be used at the end of a long day without major cognitive effort.

It was designed for use on a standard home television at a distance of 8 to 10 feet. Hypertext linkage between stories is accomplished by using a full text inversion method similar to classic text retrieval systems. Each word of the text is "hot" making for a very interesting exploritorium of history.

**Treasures of the Smithsonian**

*Contact:* Jim Hoekema
Hoekema Interactive
9411 Rosehill Drive
Bethesda, MD 20817-2045
301-909-2644
301-907-2645 (fax)
Compuserve: 76117, 1736

*Credits:* Designer/producer: Jim Hoekema; co-publishers: Smithsonian Institution, American Interactive Media; programmers: John Singer, John Hight; writers: Ted Park, Mike Nibley; production: Amy Hough; audio: Mark Phinney; graphics: Michael Gallelli, Shoshonah Dubiner; photo research: Juliana Montfort; model work: Taylor Made Images; and production facility: Capitol Video

Treasures of the Smithsonian is one of the first titles relesased for the Compact Disc Interactive (CD-I) consumer entertainment system. This interactive multimedia program allows home viewers to browse through a sampling of art works, airplanes, animals, and artifacts from 14 museums of the Smithsonian Institution in Washington, D.C. Choosing by museum, date, category, or theme, viewers play audio-visual commentaries, read text notes, and explore "links" between objects. Sometimes users zoom in for a close-up view, to walk around an object, or to click on the object to produce appropriate sounds. The program contains approximately 2½ hours of audio (A-level stereo) and about a thousand images, mostly in the high-quality DYUV format. Principal design and production work was completed in May 1989; release date is September 1991.

Treasures of the Smithsonian won a First Place "Muse Award" from the American Association of Museums in May 1991.

**Watch Yourself**

*Contact:* Timothy Binkley
Institute for Computers in the Arts
School of Visual Arts
209 East 23 Street
New York, NY 10010
212-679-7350
212-725-3587 (fax)

*Credits:* Timothy Binkley, Claire Boger, Chrissy Conant, John F. Simon Jr., and Trevor G. Thomson

Watch Yourself is an installation where participants interact with computer-processed video images of themselves integrated with well-known images from the history of art. It reverses the traditional stance viewers assume toward passive icons by allowing them to put themselves in the picture. One motivation of the installation is to play the active involvement of a computer in the gallery against the passive role assumed by traditional works of art. Another aim is to enhance personal involvement with impersonal cultural paradigms. It makes iconoclasm palpable by allowing users to "vandalize" these revered pictures with their own visages. Unlike iconoclasts of the past who were often merely lobbying for replacement icons, its purpose is rather to highlight the radically different cultural possibilities opened up by interactive computers.

# Index

(Pages marked with an * contain panel abstracts only.)

# Credits for Cover and Title Images

Front cover


**Artist: Dan Murphy**
Production: Debra Adams, Rick Beach, Maureen Stone, Ken Fishkin
**Reference:** *"Model-Based Matching and Hinting of Fonts,"* Roger Hersch and Claude Betrisey, p 80.

Title Image

Figure 11, a view of the Palazzo from "Les Contes de Hoffman"
**Reference:** *"Design and Simulation of Opera Lighting and Projection Effects,"* Julie O'Dorsey, Francois Sillion, Donald Greenberg, p 48.

Back cover, top left and right

A stereo pair from "Journey Into Nature," a twin-70 mm 3D film

Executive producer: Gary Goddard
Produced and directed by: Rick Harper
CGI Supervisors: Mark Wahrman and Brad deGraf
**Reference:** p 370.

Back cover, middle right

"Evolution of Gravity and Effective Topography on Phobos"

Contact: Wayne Lytle
**Reference:** p 369.

Back cover, middle left

Figure 11, from an extinct genome.
**Reference:** *"Artificial Evolution for Computer Graphics,"* Karl Sims, p 325.

Back cover, bottom left

Color plate 6 mesh for a proposed theater designed by Mark Mack Architects.
**References:** *"Making Radiosity Usable: Automatic Preprocessing and Meshing Techniques for the Generation of Accurate Radiosity Solutions,"* Daniel Baum, Stephen Mann, Kevin Smith, James Win, p 60.

Back cover, bottom right

"Space Cookies," Figure 4.
**Reference:** *"Reaction-Diffusion Textures,"* Andrew Witkin and Michael Kass, p 308.

# NOTES

# NOTES

# NOTES